THE CONCISE
OXFORD DICTIONARY OF
QUOTATIONS

The Concise
Oxford Dictionary of
Quotations

SECOND EDITION

Oxford   New York

OXFORD UNIVERSITY PRESS

Oxford University Press, Walton Street, Oxford OX2 6DP

London Glasgow New York Toronto
Delhi Bombay Calcutta Madras Karachi
Kuala Lumpur Singapore Hong Kong Tokyo
Nairobi Dar es Salaam Cape Town
Melbourne Auckland
and associates in
Beirut Berlin Ibadan Mexico City Nicosia

Oxford is a trade mark of Oxford University Press

Selection and arrangement
© Oxford University Press, 1981

First edition 1964, Second edition 1981
Paperback edition reprinted 1982, 1983
Hardback edition reprinted 1983

British Library Cataloguing in Publication Data
The concise Oxford dictionary of quotations.
–2nd ed.
1. Quotations
808.88'2   PN6081
ISBN 0-19-211588-X
ISBN 0-19-281324-2 Pbk

Set at the University Press, Oxford
Printed in the United States of America

CONTENTS

PUBLISHER'S FOREWORD

WHEN *The Oxford Dictionary of Quotations* first appeared in the difficult days of 1941, it was immediately taken to the hearts of the English-speaking world and it has remained a standard work of reference. From the second edition of 1953 was drawn *The Concise Oxford Dictionary of Quotations* in 1964, 'to meet the demand for a shorter dictionary containing such quotations as might be used daily by the man in the street'. The parent volume appeared in its third edition in 1979; this new edition of the *Concise O.D.Q.* is based on that, and the principles of selection are broadly similar.

Items from the first edition have been retained only if they continue to be widely familiar, and the consequent excisions have made room not only for quotations first uttered or written in the last twenty years but also for gems from earlier authors which have gained currency in that time. Even greater strictness has been exercised in removing proverbs (which are comprehensively dealt with in the *Oxford Dictionary of English Proverbs*); nursery rhymes, exhaustively collected by Peter and Iona Opie in the *Oxford Dictionary of Nursery Rhymes*, have been ousted; no attempt has been made to represent the multiplicity of catch-phrases from radio, films, and television, as much because of the impossibility of rational selection as of the obscurity of their true authorship; and, regretfully, phrases from popular songs from music-hall to the age of rock have been set aside where it was considered that these are recalled only with their tunes in mind.

The book owes its form and its very existence to the distinguished line of compilers and advisers who laboured on its predecessors, from Bernard Darwin, editor of the first edition of the *O.D.Q.*, to the intrepid team listed by name in its third edition. Mention should also be made of the numerous members of the public who have over the years showered the publishers with comments, suggestions, and advice; they have made a significant and welcome contribution.

B. J. PALMER

March, 1981

HOW TO USE THE DICTIONARY

THE arrangement is alphabetical by the names of authors; their surnames mostly, but sometimes their titles, and monarchs by their imperial or royal titles. In general the best-known names are given, and usually in the form most used. Sections such as the Anonymous one, Ballads, the Bible, the Mass in Latin, etc., are included in the alphabetical order.

Under each author, quotations are arranged by the alphabetical order of the titles of the works from which they come: books, plays, poems. These are printed in bold italic type. Titles of pieces (e.g., articles, essays, short stories) that constitute part of a published volume are in bold roman (the volume title having been given in bold italic). Quotations from diaries, letters, speeches, etc., however, are given in chronological order, and normally follow the literary works quoted. Poetry quotations precede prose ones for poets; and vice versa for writers most of whose work was in prose. Quotations cited from biographies or other writers' works are kept to the end under each author; sources are then given conventionally with titles of books or plays in italic (not bold) type. Books of the Bible are presented in canonical order, not alphabetically.

Numerical source references are given for the first line of each quotation, by, e.g., act, scene, and, if appropriate, line number; by chapter or by page or section or verse number. Each quotation without a full source given depends from its immediate predecessor. If no source reference is given at all, the quotation is from the same poem or chapter or whatever as the last preceding named or numbered one.

A date in brackets is of the first performance or publication of the work cited.

Italic has been used for all quotations in foreign languages and Latin. Throughout, spelling and capitalization have been modernized, except in English writers of the Middle Ages.

Running headlines give the names of the first and last authors *starting* a section on each page (not usually of the author of the first quotation on a page).

Quotations

ACCIUS 170–c.90 B.C.

1 *Oderint, dum metuant.*
Let them hate, so long as they fear.
Atreus. Seneca, *De Ira,* I, 20, 4

DEAN ACHESON 1893–1971

2 Great Britain has lost an Empire and has not yet found a role.
Speech at the Military Academy, West Point, 5 Dec. 1962

LORD ACTON 1834–1902

3 Power tends to corrupt and absolute power corrupts absolutely.
Letter to Bishop Mandell Creighton, 3 Apr. 1887. See *Life and Letters of Mandell Creighton* (1904), i.372. See 183:7

HENRY ADAMS 1838–1918

4 A friend in power is a friend lost.
The Education of Henry Adams, ch.7

SAMUEL ADAMS 1722–1803

5 A nation of shop-keepers are very seldom so disinterested.
Oration said to have been delivered at Philadelphia, 1 Aug. 1776. See 174:12, 242:1

SARAH F. ADAMS 1805–1848

6 Nearer, my God, to thee,
Nearer to thee!
Nearer My God to Thee

JOSEPH ADDISON 1672–1719

7 'Tis not in mortals to command success,
But we'll do more, Sempronius; we'll deserve it.
Cato, I.ii.43

8   What pity is it
That we can die but once to serve our country!
IV.iv 81

9 Eternity! thou pleasing, dreadful thought!
V.i.10

10 Thus I live in the world rather as a spectator of mankind than as one of the species.
The Spectator, 1

11 In all thy humours, whether grave or mellow,
Thou'rt such a touchy, testy, pleasant fellow;
Hast so much wit, and mirth, and spleen about thee,
There is no living with thee, nor without thee.
68. See 161:8

12 I have often thought, says Sir Roger, it happens very well that Christmas should fall out in the Middle of Winter.
269

13 I value my garden more for being full of blackbirds than of cherries, and very frankly give them fruit for their songs.
477

14 If we may believe our logicians, man is distinguished from all other creatures by the faculty of laughter.
494

15 'We are always doing', says he, 'something for Posterity, but I would fain see Posterity do something for us.'
583

AESCHYLUS 525/4–456 B.C.

16 ὤμοι, πέπληγμαι καιρίαν πληγὴν ἔσω.
Oh me, I have been struck a mortal blow right inside.
Agamemnon, 1343

17 ποντίων τε κυμάτων ἀνήριθμον γέλασμα.
Innumerable twinkling of the waves of the sea.
Prometheus Bound, 89

AGATHON 446?–c.401 B.C.

18 Even God cannot change the past.
Aristotle, *Nicomachean Ethics,* VI.2.1139b

ALCUIN c.735–804

1 *Nec audiendi qui solent dicere, Vox populi,*
vox Dei, quum tumultuositas vulgi semper
insaniae proxima sit.
And those people should not be listened to
who keep saying the voice of the people is
the voice of God, since the riotousness of
the crowd is always very close to madness.
Letter to Charlemagne, A.D.800. *Works,*
Epist.127

DEAN ALDRICH 1647–1710

2 If all be true that I do think,
There are five reasons we should drink;
Good wine—a friend—or being dry—
Or lest we should be by and by—
Or any other reason why.
Reasons for Drinking

MRS. ALEXANDER 1818–1895

3 All things bright and beautiful,
  All creatures great and small,
All things wise and wonderful,
  The Lord God made them all.
All Things Bright and Beautiful (1848)

4 The rich man in his castle,
  The poor man at his gate,
God made them, high or lowly,
  And order'd their estate.

ALFONSO THE WISE, KING OF CASTILE 1221–1284

5 Had I been present at the Creation, I
would have given some useful hints for the
better ordering of the universe.
Said after studying the Ptolemaic system. Attr.

ABBÉ D'ALLAINVAL 1700–1753

6 *L'embarras des richesses.*
The more alternatives, the more difficult
the choice.
Title of comedy, 1726

WILLIAM ALLINGHAM 1828–1889

7 Up the airy mountain,
Down the rushy glen,
We daren't go a-hunting,
For fear of little men.
The Fairies

ST. AMBROSE c.339–397

8 *Si fueris Romae, Romano vivito more;*
Si fueris alibi, vivito sicut ibi.
If you are at Rome live in the Roman style;
  if you are elsewhere live as they live
elsewhere.
Jeremy Taylor, *Ductor Dubitantium*, I.i.5. Usually quoted as 'When in Rome, do as the Romans
do.'

FISHER AMES 1758–1808

9 A monarchy is a merchantman which sails
well, but will sometimes strike on a rock,
and go to the bottom; a republic is a raft
which will never sink, but then your feet
are always in the water.
House of Representatives, 1795

KINGSLEY AMIS 1922–

10 More will mean worse.
Encounter, July 1960

BISHOP LANCELOT ANDREWES 1555–1626

11 It was no summer progress. A cold coming they had of it, at this time of the year;
just, the worst time of the year, to take a
journey, and specially a long journey, in.
The ways deep, the weather sharp, the
days short, the sun farthest off *in solstitio
brumali*, the very dead of Winter.
Sermon 15, Of the Nativity (1622)

ANONYMOUS

ENGLISH

12 Absence makes the heart grow fonder.
Davison, *Poetical Rhapsody*, 1602

13 A Company for carrying on an undertaking of Great Advantage, but no one to
know what it is.
The South Sea Company Prospectus, 1711.
Cowles, *The Great Swindle* (1963), ch.5

14 Adam
Had 'em.
On the antiquity of Microbes. (Claimed as the
shortest poem.)

15 A gentleman haranguing on the perfection
of our law, and that it was equally open to
the poor and the rich, was answered by
another, 'So is the London Tavern'.
Tom Paine's Jests... (1794), 23. Also attr. to
John Horne Tooke (1736–1812) in W. Hazlitt,
The Spirit of the Age (1825), 'Mr. Horne Tooke'.

16 All human beings are born free and equal
in dignity and rights.
Universal Declaration of Human Rights (1948),
Article 1

17 All present and correct.
King's Regulations (Army). Report of the Order-
ly Sergeant to the Officer of the Day

1 All this buttoning and unbuttoning.
18th Century suicide note

2 Along the electric wire the message came:
He is not better—he is much the same.
Said to be from a poem on the illness of the
Prince of Wales, afterwards Edward VII, often
attr. to Alfred Austin (1835–1913), Poet
Laureate. Gribble, *Romance of the Cambridge
Colleges* (1913) p 226

3 An abomination unto the Lord, but a very
present help in time of trouble. [A lie.]
(Cf. Proverbs 12:22; Psalms 46:1)

4 Appeal from Philip drunk to Philip sober.
Valerius Maximus, *Facta ac Dicta Memorabilia*
(c. A.D. 32), VI, ii

5 Are we downhearted? No!
Expression much used by British soldiers in
1914-18, probably based on 66:11

6 A sympathetic Scot summed it all up very
neatly in the remark, 'You should make a
point of trying every experience once, excepting incest and folk-dancing'.
Sir Arnold Bax (1883–1953), *Farewell My Youth*
(1943), 'Cecil Sharp'

7 Be happy while y'er leevin,
For y'er a lang time deid.
Scottish motto for a house. N. & Q. 7 Dec. 1901,
469

8 Conduct…to the prejudice of good order
and military discipline.
Army Act, 40

9 Dear Sir, Your astonishment's odd:
I am always about in the Quad.
And that's why the tree
Will continue to be,
Since observed by Yours faithfully, God.
Reply to limerick on idealism. See 147:5

10 *Knowledge:* Everyman, I will go with thee,
and be thy guide.
In thy most need to go by thy side.
Everyman (c.500), l.522

11 From ghoulies and ghosties and long-
leggety beasties
And things that go bump in the night,
Good Lord, deliver us!
Cornish

12 God be in my head,
And in my understanding;

God be in my eyes,
And in my looking;

God be in my mouth,
And in my speaking;

God be in my heart,
And in my thinking;

God be at my end,

And at my departing.
Sarum Missal

13 Happy is that city which in time of peace
thinks of war. (Inscription in the armoury
of Venice.)
Burton, *Anatomy of Melancholy*, pt.ii, 3,
memb.6. See 261:18

14 Here lies a poor woman who always was
tired,
For she lived in a place where help wasn't
hired.
Her last words on earth were, Dear friends
I am going
Where washing ain't done nor sweeping
nor sewing,
And everything there is exact to my
wishes,
For there they don't eat and there's no
washing of dishes…
Don't mourn for me now, don't mourn for
me never,
For I'm going to do nothing for ever and
ever.
Epitaph in Bushey churchyard, before 1860, destroyed by 1916. Quoted in a letter to the *Spectator*, 2 Sept. 1922

15 Here's tae us; wha's like us?
Gey few, and they're a' deid.
Scottish Toast, probably of nineteenth-century
origin. The first line appears in Crosland, *The
Unspeakable Scot* (1902), p.24n. Various ver-
sions of the second line are current.

16 Hierusalem, my happy home
When shall I come to thee?
When shall my sorrows have an end,
Thy joys when shall I see?
Hierusalem. See *Songs of Praise Discussed*

17 'How different, how very different from
the home life of our own dear Queen!'
Irvin S. Cobb, *A Laugh a Day*. Comment by a
middle-aged British matron at a performance of
Cleopatra by Sarah Bernhardt. The story is probably apocryphal.

18 I feel no pain dear mother now
But oh, I am so dry!
O take me to a brewery
And leave me there to die.
Parody of 97:12

19 If God were to take one or other of us, I
should go and live in Paris.
Reported in S. Butler, *Notebooks*, ed. G. Keynes
and B. Hill, 1951, p.193

20 I met wid Napper Tandy, and he took me
by the hand,
And he said, 'How's poor ould Ireland,
and how does she stand?'
She's the most disthressful country that
iver yet was seen,

For they're hangin' men an' women there
    for the wearin' o' the Green.
The Wearin' o' the Green. (Famous street ballad,
later added to by Boucicault.)

1   It is positively dangerous to sit to Sargent.
    It's taking your face in your hands.
    W. Graham Robertson, *Time Was* (1931), ch.21

2   Like a fine old English gentleman,
    All of the olden time.
    The Fine Old English Gentleman. *Oxford Song
    Book*

3   Lizzie Borden took an axe
    And gave her mother forty whacks;
    When she saw what she had done
    She gave her father forty-one!
    Lizzie Borden was acquitted of murdering her
    father and stepmother on 4 Aug. 1892 in Fall
    River, Massachusetts

4   Love me little, love me long,
    Is the burden of my song.
    Love me Little, Love me Long (1569-70)

5   *Child:* Mamma, are Tories born wicked,
    or do they grow wicked afterwards?
    Mother: They are born wicked, and grow
    worse.
    G.W.E. Russell, *Collections and Recollections*,
    ch.10

6   Matthew, Mark, Luke, and John,
    The Bed be blest that I lie on.
    Four angels to my bed,
    Four angels round my head,
    One to watch, and one to pray,
    And two to bear my soul away.
    Thomas Ady, *A Candle in the Dark* (1656)

7   Miss Buss and Miss Beale
    Cupid's darts do not feel.
    How different from us,
    Miss Beale and Miss Buss.
    Of the Headmistress of the North London Colle-
    giate School and the Principal of the Ladies'
    College, Cheltenham, c. 1884

8   Multiplication is vexation,
    Division is as bad;
    The Rule of three doth puzzle me,
    And Practice drives me mad.
    Elizabethan MS. dated 1570

9   My name is George Nathaniel Curzon,
    I am a most superior person.
    The Masque of Balliol, composed by and current
    among members of Balliol College in the late
    1870's. See 17:11, 245:5-6

10 My face is pink, my hair is sleek,
    I dine at Blenheim once a week.
    (A later addition.)

11 Now I lay me down to sleep;
    I pray the Lord my soul to keep.
    If I should die before I wake,

I pray the Lord my soul to take.
First printed in a late edition of the *New England
Primer*, 1781

12 O Death, where is thy sting-a-ling-a-ling,
    O Grave, thy victoree?
    The bells of Hell go ting-a-ling-a-ling
    For you but not for me.
    Song popular in the British Army, 1914-18

13 O God, if there be a God, save my soul, if
    I have a soul!
    Prayer of a common soldier before the battle of
    Blenheim (see N. & Q., clxxiii.264). Quoted in
    Newman's *Apologia*

14 Oh my dear fellow, the noise...and the
    people!
    Of the Battle of Bastogne. Attr. to a Captain
    Strahan. See Griffin, 'Dialogue with W.H.
    Auden', *Hudson Review* III, iv, Winter 51, p.583

15 One Cartwright brought a Slave from
    Russia, and would scourge him, for which
    he was questioned: and it was resólved,
    That England was too pure an Air for
    Slaves to breathe in.
    'In the 11th of Elizabeth' (17 Nov. 1568-16 Nov.
    1569). Rushworth, *Historical Collections*
    (1680-1722), II, p.468

16 Please do not shoot the pianist. He is do-
    ing his best.
    Oscar Wilde, *Impressions of America.* 'Leadville'

17 Please to remember the Fifth of Novem-
    ber,
    Gunpowder Treason and Plot.
    We know no reason why gunpowder
    treason
    Should ever be forgot.
    Traditional since 17th cent.

18 Since wars begin in the minds of men, it is
    in the minds of men that the defences of
    peace must be constructed.
    Constitution of the United Nations Educational,
    Scientific and Cultural Organisation (1946)

19 Sumer is icumen in,
        Lhude sing cuccu!
    Groweth sed, and bloweth med,
        And springth the wude nu.
    Cuckoo Song, c. 1250, sung annually at Reading
    Abbey gateway. First recorded by John Fornset,
    a monk of Reading Abbey

20 That this house will in no circumstances
    fight for its King and country.
    Motion passed at the Oxford Union, 9 Feb. 1933

21 The almighty dollar is the only object of
    worship.
    Philadelphia Public Ledger, 2 Dec. 1836

22 The eternal triangle.
    Book Review in the *Daily Chronicle*, 5 Dec. 1907

1 The ministry of all the talents.
A name given ironically to Grenville's Coalition
of 1806; also applied to later coalitions. See
G.W. Cooke, *History of Party* (1837), III, p.460

2 There is so much good in the worst of us,
And so much bad in the best of us,
That it hardly becomes any of us
To talk about the rest of us.
Good and Bad. Attr. to Edward Wallis Hoch
(1849–1925) but disclaimed by him; and to many
others.

3 There's nae luck about the house,
    There's nae luck at a',
There's nae luck about the house
    When our gudeman's awa'.
The Mariner's Wife

4 They come as a boon and a blessing to
    men,
The Pickwick, the Owl, and the Waverley
    pen.
Advertisement by MacNiven and Cameron Ltd,
Edinburgh and Birmingham

5 Thirty days hath September,
April, June, and November;
All the rest have thirty-one,
Excepting February alone,
And that has twenty-eight days clear
And twenty-nine in each leap year.
Stevins MS. (c.1555)

6 The singer not the song.
From a West Indian calypso and used as the title
of a novel (1959) by Audrey Erskine Lindop

7 Thought shall be the harder, heart the
keener, courage the greater, as our might
lessens.
The Battle of Maldon. Tr. R.K. Gordon (1926)
from Anglo-Saxon.

8 To many people Victorian wit and humour is summed up by *Punch*, when every
joke is supposed to end with 'Collapse of
Stout Party', though this phrase tends to
be as elusive as 'Elementary, my dear Watson' in the Sherlock Holmes sagas.
R. Pearsall, *Collapse of Stout Party* (1975),
Introduction

9 We hold these truths to be self-evident,
that all men are created equal, that they
are endowed by their Creator with certain
unalienable rights, that among these are
life, liberty and the pursuit of happiness.
The American Declaration of Independence, 4
July 1776. See 130:9

10 Western wind, when wilt thou blow,
    The small rain down can rain?
Christ, if my love were in my arms
    And I in my bed again!
Oxford Book of 16th Cent. Verse

11 When Israel was in Egypt land,
    Let my people go,
Oppressed so hard they could not stand,
    Let my people go.
        Go down, Moses,
        Way-down in Egypt land,
        Tell old Pharaoh
        To let my people go.
Negro Spiritual. See 23:13

12 Whose Finger do you want on the Trigger
When the World Situation Is So Delicate?
Headline in the *Daily Mirror*, see H. Cudlipp,
Publish and Be Damned (1953), p.263

13 Would you like to sin
With Elinor Glyn
On a tiger-skin?
Or would you prefer
to err
with her
on some other fur?
c. 1907. A. Glyn, *Elinor Glyn* (1955), pt.II.30

14 You pays your money and you takes your
choice.
From a peepshow rhyme. See V.S. Lean, *Collectanea* (1902-4)

FRENCH

15 *Cet animal est très méchant,*
    Quand on l'attaque il se défend.
This animal is very bad; when attacked it
    defends itself.
La Ménagerie, by Théodore P.K., 1828

16 *Chevalier sans peur et sans reproche.*
Knight without fear and without blemish.
Description in contemporary chronicles of Pierre
Bayard, 1476-1524

17 *Honi soit qui mal y pense.*
Evil be to him who evil thinks [of it].
Motto of the Order of the Garter, originated by
Edward III probably on 23 Apr. of 1348 or 1349.

18 *Je suis le capitaine de vingt-quatre soldats,*
et sans moi Paris serait pris? [Answer!] *A.*
Hugh Rowley, *Puniana: or thoughts wise and
otherwise a new collection of the best* (1867), p.42.
The saying 'With twenty-six lead soldiers [the
characters of the alphabet set up for printing] I
can conquer the world' may be derived from this
riddle, but probably arose independently.

19 *La grande phrase reçue, c'est* qu'il ne faut
pas être plus royaliste que le roi. *Cette
phrase n'est pas du moment; elle fut inven-
tée sous Louis XVI: elle enchaîna les mains
des fidèles, pour ne laisser libre que le bras
du bourreau.*
The big catch-phrase is *that you mustn't be
more of a royalist than His Royal Highness.*
This expression is not new; it was coined
under the reign of Louis XVI: it chained

up the hands of the loyal, leaving free only
the arm of the hangman.
Chateaubriand, *De La Monarchie selon la
Charte*, II, xli

1 *Laisser-nous-faire.*

M. Colbert assembla plusieurs Deputés de commerce chez lui pour leur demander ce qu'il pourroit
faire pour le commerce; le plus raisonnable et le
moins flatteur d'entre eux, lui dit ce seul mot:
'Laissez-nous-faire.' *Journal Oeconomique*, Paris,
Apr. 1751. See 7:19, 193:10

2 *Liberté! Égalité! Fraternité!*
Freedom! Equality! Brotherhood!
Motto of the French Revolution, but of earlier
origin. The Club des Cordeliers passed a motion,
30 June 1793, 'que les propriétaires seront in-
vités,...de faire peindre sur la façade de leurs mai-
sons, en gros caractères, ces mots: Unité, indivisi-
bilité de la République, Liberté, Égalité, Fraternité ou la mort': *Journal de Paris*, 182. From 1795
the words 'ou la mort' were dropped from this
prescription. See 67:3

3 *Nous n'irons plus aux bois, les lauriers sont
coupés.*
We'll to the woods no more,
The laurels all are cut.
Old nursery rhyme quoted by Banville in *Les
Cariatides, les stalactites*. Tr. Housman, *Last
Poems*, introductory

4 *Revenons à ces moutons.*
Let us return to our sheep. (Let us get back
to the subject.)
Maistre Pierre Pathelin (line 1191). Often quoted
as 'Retournons à nos moutons'

5 *Tout passe, tout casse, tout lasse.*
Everything passes, everything perishes,
everything palls.
Cahier, *Quelques six mille proverbes*

GREEK

6 γνῶθι σεαυτόν.
Know thyself.
Inscribed on the temple of Apollo at Delphi.
Plato, *Protagoras*, 343 b, ascribes the saying to
the Seven Wise Men.

7 μηδὲν ἄγαν.
Nothing in excess.

8 ὅταν δ' ὁ δαίμων ἀνδρὶ πορσύνῃ κακά,
τὸν νοῦν ἔβλαψε πρῶτον, ᾧ βουλεύ-
εται.
Whenever God prepares evil for a man, He
first damages his mind.
Scholiast on Sophocles, *Antigone*, 622 ff. See
R.C. Jebb's edn. (1906), Appendix, pp.255-6.
Perhaps best known in Latin translation. See
92:2

ITALIAN

9 *Se non è vero, è molto ben trovato.*
If it is not true, it is a happy invention.
Apparently a common saying in the sixteenth
century. Found in Giordano Bruno (1585) in the
above form, and in Antonio Doni (1552) as 'Se
non è vero, egli è stato un bel trovato.'

LATIN

10 *Adeste, fideles,
Laeti triumphantes;
Venite, venite in Bethlehem.*
O come, all ye faithful,
Joyful and triumphant,
O come, ye, O come ye to Bethlehem.
French or German hymn of 18th Cent. Trans. F.
Oakeley in *Murray's Hymnal*, 1852. See *Songs of
Praise Discussed*

11 *Venite adoremus, venite adoremus,
Venite adoremus Dominum.*
O come, let us adore him! O come, let us
adore him!
O come, let us adore him, Christ the Lord!

12 *Ad majorem Dei gloriam.*
To the greater glory of God.
Motto of the Society of Jesus

13 *Ave Caesar, morituri te salutant.*
Hail Caesar; those who are about to die
salute you.
Gladiators saluting the Roman Emperor. See
Suetonius, *Claudius*, 21

14 *Ave Maria, gratia plena, Dominus tecum:
Benedicta tu in mulieribus, et benedictus
fructus ventris tui, Jesus.*
Hail Mary, full of grace, the Lord is with
thee: Blessed art thou among women, and
blessed is the fruit of thy womb, Jesus.
Ave Maria, also known as *The Angelic Saluta-
tion*, dating from the 11th cent.

15 *Ave verum corpus,
Natum Ex Maria Virgine.*
Hail the true body, born of the Virgin
Mary.
Eucharistic hymn, dating probably from the
14th cent.

16 *Et in Arcadia ego.*
And I too in Arcadia.
Tomb inscription often depicted in classical
paintings. The meaning is disputed.

17 *Gaudeamus igitur,
Juvenes dum sumus,
Post jucundam juventutem,
Post molestam senectutem,
Nos habebit humus.*
Let us then rejoice,
While we are young.
After the pleasures of youth
And the tiresomeness of old age

Earth will hold us.
Medieval students' song, traced to 1267, but revised in the 18th cent.

1 *Nemo me impune lacessit.*
No one provokes me with impunity.
Motto of the Crown of Scotland and of all Scottish regiments

2 *Per ardua ad astra.*
Hard and high to the stars!
Motto of the Mulvany family, quoted in Rider Haggard, *The People of the Mist* (1894), ch.1, proposed by J.S. Yule in 1912, adopted as official motto of the Royal Flying Corps and approved by King George V in 1913, still in use as motto of the R.A.F. See P.G. Hering, *Customs and Traditions of the Royal Air Force* (1961) Rider Haggard's rendering was 'Through Struggle to the Stars'.

3 *Post coitum omne animal triste.*
After coition every animal is sad.
Post-classical

4 *Quidquid agas, prudenter agas, et respice finem.*
Whatever you do, do cautiously, and look to the end.
Gesta Romanorum, 103

5 *Sic transit gloria mundi.*
Thus passes the glory of the world.
Spoken during the coronation of a new Pope, while flax is burned to represent the transitoriness of earthly glory. Used at the coronation of Alexander V, Pisa, 7 July 1409, but earlier in origin. See 256:18

6 *Si monumentum requiris, circumspice.*
If you seek for a monument, gaze around.
Inscription in St. Paul's Cathedral, London, attr. to the son of the architect, Sir Christopher Wren.

7 *Te Deum laudamus: Te Dominum confitemur.*
We praise thee, God: we own thee Lord.
Te Deum. Hymn traditionally ascribed to St. Ambrose and St. Augustine in 387, but some modern scholars attribute it to St. Niceta (d.c.414)

8 *Tempora mutantur, et nos mutamur in illis.*
Times change, and we change with them.
Harrison, *Description of Britain* (1577), III, iii, 99. Attributed to the Emperor Lothar I (795-855) in the form *Omnia mutantur, nos et mutamur in illis*

9 *Vox et praeterea nihil.*
A voice and nothing more.
Of a nightingale. See also Plutarch, *Moralia*, 'Sayings of Spartans', 233a

F. ANSTEY 1856-1934

10 Drastic measures is Latin for a whopping.
Vice Versa, ch.7

THOMAS GOLD APPLETON
1812-1884

11 Good Americans, when they die, go to Paris.
O.W. Holmes, *Autocrat of the Breakfast Table*, 6

ARABIAN NIGHTS

12 Who will change old lamps for new ones? ...new lamps for old ones?
The History of Aladdin

13 Open Sesame!
The History of Ali Baba

WILLIAM ARABIN 1773-1841

14 If ever there was a case of clearer evidence than this of persons acting in concert together, this case is that case.
Sir R. Megarry, *Arabinesque at Law* (1969)

15 They will steal the very teeth out of your mouth as you walk through the streets. I know it from experience.
[The citizens of Uxbridge.]

16 Prisoner, God has given you good abilities, instead of which you go about the country stealing ducks.
See N. & Q., clxx.310

ARCHILOCHUS fl. c.650 B.C.

17 πολλ᾽ οἶδ᾽ ἀλώπηξ, ἀλλ᾽ ἐχῖνος ἓν μέγα.
The fox knows many things—the hedgehog one *big* one.
E. Diehl (ed.), *Anth. Lyr. Gr.*, I, p.241, no.103

ARCHIMEDES 287-212 B.C.

18 εὕρηκα.
Eureka! (I've got it!)
Vitruvius Pollio, *De Architectura*, ix.215

MARQUIS D'ARGENSON 1694-1757

19 *Laisser-faire.*
No interference.
Mémoires, vol.5, p.364. See 6:1

COMTE D'ARGENSON 1696-1764

20 Abbé Guyot Desfontaines: *Il faut que je vive.*
D'Argenson: *Je n'en vois pas la nécessité.*
Desfontaines: I must live.
D'Argenson: I do not see the necessity.
Voltaire, *Alzire, Discours Préliminaire*

LUDOVICO ARIOSTO 1474–1533

1 *Natura il fece, e poi roppe la stampa.*
Nature made him, and then broke the
mould.
Orlando Furioso, x.84

ARISTOPHANES c.444–c.380 B.C.

2 βούλει Νεφελοκοκκυγίαν;
How about 'Cloudcuckooland'?
Birds, 819. Naming the capital city of the Birds.

3 βρεκεκεκέξ κοὰξ κοάξ.
Brekekekex koax koax.
Frogs, 209 and elsewhere. Cry of the Frogs.

ARISTOTLE 384–322 B.C.

4 ἄνθρωπος φύσει πολιτικὸν ζῷον.
Man is by nature a political animal.
Politics, i.2.1253a

5 ἔστιν οὖν τραγῳδία μίμησις πράξεως
σπουδαίας καὶ τελείας μέγεθος ἐχούσης
... δι' ἐλέου καὶ φόβου περαίνουσα τὴν
τῶν τοιούτων παθημάτων κάθαρσιν.
Tragedy is thus a representation of an action that is worth serious attention, complete in itself and of some amplitude...by
means of pity and fear bringing about the
purgation of such emotions.
Poetics, 6.1449b

6 διὸ καὶ φιλοσοφώτερον καὶ σπουδαιό-
τερον ποίησις ἱστορίας ἐστίν.
For this reason poetry is something more
philosophical and more worthy of serious
attention than history.
9.1451b

7 προαιρεῖσθαί τε δεῖ ἀδύνατα εἰκότα
μᾶλλον ἢ δυνατὰ ἀπίθανα.
Probable impossibilities are to be
preferred to improbable possibilites.
24.1460a

8 *Amicus Plato, sed magis amica veritas.*
Plato is dear to me, but dearer still is truth.
Greek original ascribed to Aristotle

DR. JOHN ARMSTRONG 1709–1779

9 Of right and wrong he taught
Truths as refin'd as ever Athens heard;
And (strange to tell!) he practis'd what he
preach'd.
Art of Preserving Health (1744), bk.iv, l.303

NEIL A. ARMSTRONG 1930–

10 That's one small step for a man, one giant
leap for mankind.
On landing on the moon, 21 July 1969. First
reported without the word 'a'.

MATTHEW ARNOLD 1822–1888

11 And we forget because we must
And not because we will.
Absence

12 Ah, love, let us be true
To one another!
Dover Beach, l.29

13 And we are here as on a darkling plain
Swept with confused alarms of struggle
and flight,
Where ignorant armies clash by night.
l.35

14 Wandering between two worlds, one
dead,
The other powerless to be born.
The Grande Chartreuse, l.85

15 Yes! in the sea of life enisled,
With echoing straits between us thrown,
Dotting the shoreless watery wild,
We mortal millions live *alone*.
To Marguerite—Continued, l.1

16 Creep into thy narrow bed,
Creep, and let no more be said!
Vain thy onset! all stands fast.
Thou thyself must break at last.

Let the long contention cease!
Geese are swans, and swans are geese.
Let them have it how they will!
Thou art tired; best be still.
The Last Word

17 Strew on her roses, roses,
And never a spray of yew.
In quiet she reposes:
Ah! would that I did too.
Requiescat

18 Her cabin'd ample Spirit,
It flutter'd and fail'd for breath.
To-night it doth inherit
The vasty hall of death.

19 Go, for they call you, Shepherd, from the
hill.
The Scholar-Gipsy (1853), l.1

20 Crossing the stripling Thames at Bab-
lock-hithe,
Trailing in the cool stream thy fingers
wet,
As the slow punt swings round.
l.74

21 Thou waitest for the spark from heaven!
and we,
Light half-believers in our casual creeds...
Who hesitate and falter life away,
And lose to-morrow the ground won to-
day—

Ah, do not we, Wanderer, await it too?
l.171

1 Others abide our question. Thou art free.
We ask and ask: Thou smilest and art still,
Out-topping knowledge.
Shakespeare

2 Truth sits upon the lips of dying men.
Sohrab and Rustum (1853), l.656

3 And that sweet City with her dreaming
spires,
She needs not June for beauty's
heightening.
Thyrsis, l.19

4 Too quick despairer, wherefore wilt thou
go?
l.61

5 Who saw life steadily, and saw it whole:
The mellow glory of the Attic stage;
Singer of sweet Colonus, and its child.
[Sophocles.]
To a Friend

6 Our society distributes itself into Barbarians, Philistines, and Populace; and
America is just ourselves, with the Barbarians quite left out, and the Populace
nearly.
Culture and Anarchy (1869), preface

7 The pursuit of perfection, then, is the pursuit of sweetness and light...He who works
for sweetness and light united, works to
make reason and the will of God prevail.
i. See 248:17

8 Beautiful city! so venerable, so lovely, so
unravaged by the fierce intellectual life of
our century, so serene!...whispering from
her towers the last enchantments of the
Middle Age...Home of lost causes, and
forsaken beliefs, and unpopular names,
and impossible loyalties! [Oxford.]
Essays in Criticism, First Series (1865), preface

9 The theatre is irresistible; organise the
theatre!
*Irish Essays. **The French Play in London***

10 Miracles do not happen.
Literature and Dogma, preface to 1883 edition,
last words

11 The true meaning of religion is thus not
simply morality, but morality touched by
emotion.
i, 2

12 Conduct is three-fourths of our life and its
largest concern.
3

13 But there remains the question: what
righteousness really is. The method and
secret and sweet reasonableness of Jesus.
xii, 2

14 I am past thirty, and three parts iced over.
Letter to A.H. Clough, 12 Feb. 1853

15 People think that I can teach them style.
What stuff it all is! Have something to say,
and say it as clearly as you can. That is the
only secret of style.
G.W.E. Russell, *Collections and Recollections*,
ch.13

DR. THOMAS ARNOLD 1795-1842

16 My object will be, if possible, to form
Christian men, for Christian boys I can
scarcely hope to make.
Letter, in 1828, on appointment to Headmaster-
ship of Rugby

17 As for rioting, the old Roman way of
dealing with that is always the right one;
flog the rank and file, and fling the ringleaders from the Tarpeian rock.
From an unpublished letter written before 1828,
quoted by M. Arnold, *Cornhill Magazine,* Aug.
1868

ROGER ASCHAM 1515-1568

18 There is no such whetstone, to sharpen a
good wit and encourage a will to learning,
as is praise.
The Schoolmaster (1570), 1

19 *Inglese Italianato, è un diavolo incarnato,*
that is to say, you remain men in shape
and fashion, but become devils in life and
condition.
Of Englishmen travelling in Italy

DAISY ASHFORD 1881-1972

20 Bernard always had a few prayers in the
hall and some whiskey afterwards as he
was rarther pious but Mr Salteena was not
very addicted to prayers so he marched up
to bed.
The Young Visiters (1919) ch.3

21 My dear Clincham, The bearer of this
letter is an old friend of mine not quite the
right side of the blanket as they say in fact
he is the son of a first rate family but his
mother was a decent family called
Hyssopps of the Glen so you see he is not
so bad and is desireus of being the correct
article.
ch.5

H.H. ASQUITH 1852-1928

22 We had better wait and see.
Phrase used repeatedly in speeches in 1910, refer-

ring to the rumour that the House of Lords was to be flooded with new Liberal peers to ensure the passage of the Finance Bill. R.Jenkins, *Asquith*, ch.14

MARGOT ASQUITH 1865–1945

1 Ettie has told enough white lies to ice a cake.
Nicholas Mosley, *Julian Grenfell* (1976), ch.3. Of Lady Desborough (1867–1952)

SIR JACOB ASTLEY 1579–1652

2 O Lord! thou knowest how busy I must be this day: if I forget thee, do not thou forget me.
Prayer before the Battle of Edgehill. Sir Philip Warwick, *Memoires*, 1701, p.229

SURGEON-CAPTAIN E.L. ATKINSON 1882–1929
and   APSLEY   CHERRY-GARRARD 1882–1959

3 Hereabouts died a very gallant gentleman, Captain L.E.G. Oates of the Inniskilling Dragoons. In March 1912, returning from the Pole, he walked willingly to his death in a blizzard, to try and save his comrades, beset by hardships.
Epitaph on a cairn and cross erected in the Antarctic, November 1912

JOHN AUBREY 1626–1697

4 The parliament intended to have hanged him; and he expected no less, but resolved to be hanged with the Bible under one arm and Magna Carta under the other.
Brief Lives. **David Jenkins**

5 Sciatica: he cured it, by boiling his buttock.
Sir Jonas Moore

6 When he killed a calf he would do it in a high style, and make a speech.
William Shakespeare

7 Anno 1670, not far from Cirencester, was an apparition; being demanded whether a good spirit or a bad? returned no answer, but disappeared with a curious perfume and most melodious twang. Mr W. Lilly believes it was a fairy.
Miscellanies. **Apparitions** (1696)

W.H. AUDEN 1907–1973

8 I'll love you, dear, I'll love you
   Till China and Africa meet,
And the river jumps over the mountain
   And the salmon sing in the street.

I'll love you till the ocean
   Is folded and hung up to dry
And the seven stars go squawking
   Like geese about the sky.
As I Walked Out One Evening

9 O let not Time deceive you,
   You cannot conquer Time.

10 O plunge your hands in water,
   Plunge them in up to the wrist;
Stare, stare in the basin
   And wonder what you've missed.

The glacier knocks in the cupboard,
   The desert sighs in the bed,
And the crack in the tea-cup opens
   A lane to the land of the dead.

11 O stand, stand at the window
   As the tears scald and start;
You shall love your crooked neighbour
   With your crooked heart.

12 August for the people and their favourite islands.
Birthday Poem

13 Perfection, of a kind, was what he was after,
   And the poetry he invented was easy to understand;
He knew human folly like the back of his hand,
   And was greatly interested in armies and fleets;
When he laughed, respectable senators burst with laughter,
   And when he cried the little children died in the streets.
Epitaph on a Tyrant. See 174:4

14   Clutching a little case,
He walks out briskly to infect a city
Whose terrible future may have just arrived.
Gare du Midi

15 He disappeared in the dead of winter:
   The brooks were frozen, the airports almost deserted,
And snow disfigured the public statues.
In Memory of W.B. Yeats, I

16   Now Ireland has her madness and her weather still,
For poetry makes nothing happen.

17 Earth, receive an honoured guest:
William Yeats is laid to rest.
Let the Irish vessel lie
Emptied of its poetry.

Time that is intolerant
Of the brave and innocent,
And indifferent in a week
To a beautiful physique,

Worships language and forgives
Everyone by whom it lives.
III

1   In the deserts of the heart
Let the healing fountain start,
In the prison of his days
Teach the free man how to praise.

2   Put the car away; when life fails,
What's the good of going to Wales?
It's no use raising a Shout

3   Lay your sleeping head, my love,
Human on my faithless arm;
Time and fevers burn away
Individual beauty from
Thoughtful children, and the grave
Proves the child ephemeral:
But in my arms till break of day
Let the living creature lie,
Mortal, guilty, but to me
The entirely beautiful.
Lullaby

4   Look, stranger, on this island now.
On This Island

5   Harrow the house of the dead; look shining at
New styles of architecture, a change of heart.
Petition

6   Hunger allows no choice
To the citizen or the police;
We must love one another or die.
September 1, 1939

7   Private faces in public places
Are wiser and nicer
Than public faces in private places.
Collected Poems, 11 *1927-1932, Shorts*

8   To the man-in-the-street, who, I'm sorry to say,
Is a keen observer of life,
The word 'Intellectual' suggests straight away
A man who's untrue to his wife.
IV *1939-47, Shorts*

9   A poet's hope: to be,
like some valley cheese,
local, but prized elsewhere.
XII *1958-1971, Shorts II*

10 Tomorrow for the young the poets exploding like bombs.
Spain 1937

11   History to the defeated
May say Alas but cannot help nor pardon.

12 Thou shalt not live within thy means
Nor on plain water and raw greens.
If thou must choose
Between the chances, choose the odd:

Read *The New Yorker*, trust in God;
And take short views.
Under which Lyre. See 242:15

13 The sky is darkening like a stain;
Something is going to fall like rain,
And it won't be flowers.
The Witnesses (1932 poem)

ÉMILE AUGIER 1820-1889

14 *La nostalgie de la boue!*
Longing to be back in the mud!
Le Mariage d'Olympe, I.i

ST. AUGUSTINE 354-430

15 *Da mihi castitatem et continentiam, sed noli modo.*
Give me chastity and continency—but not yet!
Confessions, bk.viii, ch.7

16 *Tolle lege, tolle lege.*
Take up and read, take up and read.
ch.12

17 *Da quod iubes et iube quod vis. Imperas nobis continentiam.*
Give what you command, and command what you will. You impose continency upon us.
bk.x, ch.29

18 *Salus extra ecclesiam non est.*
There is no salvation outside the church.
De Bapt. IV, c.xvii.24. See 81:6

19 *Dilige et quod vis fac.*
Love and do what you will.
(Often quoted as *Ama et fac quod vis*.)
In Epist. Joann. Tractatus, vii, 8

20 *Cum dilectione hominum et odio vitiorum.*
With love for mankind and hatred of sins.
Often quoted in the form: Love the sinner but hate the sin. *Opera Omnia*, vol.II. col.962, letter 211. Migne's *Patrologiae* (1845), vol.XXXIII

21 *Roma locuta est; causa finita est.*
Rome has spoken; the case is concluded.
Sermons, bk.i

EMPEROR AUGUSTUS 63 B.C.–A.D. 14

22 I inherited it brick and left it marble.
Suetonius, *Divus Augustus*, 28. Of the city of Rome.

JANE AUSTEN 1775-1817

23 The sooner every party breaks up the better. [Mr. Woodhouse.]
Emma, ch.25

24 One has no great hopes from Birming-

ham. I always say there is something direful in the sound. [Mrs. Elton.]
ch.36

1 Nothing can be said in his vindication, but that his abolishing Religious Houses and leaving them to the ruinous depredations of time has been of infinite use to the landscape of England in general.
The History of England (1791)

2 There certainly are not so many men of large fortune in the world, as there are pretty women to deserve them.
Mansfield Park, ch.1

3 A large income is the best recipe for happiness I ever heard of. It certainly may secure all the myrtle and turkey part of it.
ch.22

4 Let other pens dwell on guilt and misery.
ch.48

5 Oh! who can ever be tired of Bath?
Northanger Abbey, ch.10

6 Where people wish to attach, they should always be ignorant. To come with a well-informed mind, is to come with an inability of administering to the vanity of others, which a sensible person would always wish to avoid. A woman especially, if she have the misfortune of knowing any thing, should conceal it as well as she can.
ch.14

7 From politics, it was an easy step to silence.

8 'My idea of good company, Mr Elliot, is the company of clever, well-informed people, who have a great deal of conversation; that is what I call good company.' 'You are mistaken,' said he gently, 'that is not good company, that is the best.'
Persuasion, ch.16

9 My sore throats are always worse than anyone's. [Mary Musgrove.]
ch.18

10 All the privilege I claim for my own sex …is that of loving longest, when existence or when hope is gone. [Anne.]
ch.23

11 It is a truth universally acknowledged, that a single man in possession of a good fortune, must be in want of a wife.
Pride and Prejudice, ch.1

12 May I ask whether these pleasing attentions proceed from the impulse of the moment, or are the result of previous study? [Mr. Bennet.]
ch.14

13 For what do we live, but to make sport for our neighbours, and laugh at them in our turn? [Mr. Bennet.]
ch.57

14 'I am afraid,' replied Elinor, 'that the pleasantness of an employment does not always evince its propriety.'
Sense and Sensibility, ch.13

15 Where so many hours have been spent in convincing myself that I am right, is there not some reason to fear I may be wrong?
ch.31

16 We met…Dr Hall in such very deep mourning that either his mother, his wife, or himself must be dead.
Letter to Cassandra Austen, 17 May 1799

17 The little bit (two inches wide) of ivory on which I work with so fine a brush as produces little effect after much labour.
Letter, 16 Dec. 1816

W.E. AYTOUN 1813–1865

18 Fhairshon had a son,
  Who married Noah's daughter,
And nearly spoiled ta Flood,
  By trinking up ta water:

Which he would have done,
  I at least pelieve it,
Had the mixture peen
  Only half Glenlivet.
The Massacre of the Macpherson, vii

CHARLES BABBAGE 1792–1871

19 Every moment dies a man,
Every moment $1\frac{1}{16}$ is born.
See *New Scientist*, 4 Dec. 1958, p.1428. Unpublished letter to Tennyson, whose *Vision of Sin* this parodies. See 255:18

FRANCIS BACON 1561–1626

20 All good moral philosophy is but an handmaid to religion.
Advancement of Learning, II.xxii.14

21 Wise nature did never put her precious jewels into a garret four stories high: and therefore…exceeding tall men had ever very empty heads.
Apophthegms, 17

22 Silence is the virtue of fools.
De Dignitate et Augmentis Scientiarum, I, vi, 31. Antitheta, 6 (ed. 1640, tr. Gilbert Watts)

23 A little philosophy inclineth man's mind to atheism, but depth in philosophy bringeth men's minds about to religion.
Essays. 16. **Atheism**

1 There is no excellent beauty that hath not some strangeness in the proportion.
43. **Of Beauty**

2 Mahomet made the people believe that he would call a hill to him, and from the top of it offer up his prayers for the observers of his law. The people assembled: Mahomet called the hill to come to him again and again; and when the hill stood still, he was never a whit abashed, but said, 'If the hill will not come to Mahomet, Mahomet will go to the hill.' (Proverbially, 'If the mountain will not...')
12. **Boldness**

3 A wise man will make more opportunities than he finds.
52. **Of Ceremonies and Respects**

4 In things that are tender and unpleasing, it is good to break the ice by some whose words are of less weight, and to reserve the more weighty voice to come in as by chance.
22. **Of Cunning**

5 Men fear death as children fear to go in the dark; and as that natural fear in children is increased with tales, so is the other.
2. **Of Death**

6 It is as natural to die as to be born; and to a little infant, perhaps, the one is as painful as the other.

7 If a man look sharply, and attentively, he shall see Fortune: for though she be blind, yet she is not invisible.
40. **Of Fortune**

8 Cure the disease and kill the patient.
27. **Of Friendship**

9 God Almighty first planted a garden; and, indeed, it is the purest of human pleasures.
46. **Of Gardens**

10 It is a strange desire to seek power and to lose liberty.
11. **Of Great Place**

11 He that hath wife and children hath given hostages to fortune; for they are impediments to great enterprises, either of virtue or mischief.
8. **Of Marriage and Single Life.** See 155:2

12 There are some other that account wife and children but as bills of charges.

13 Wives are young men's mistresses, companions for middle age, and old men's nurses.

14 He was reputed one of the wise men that made answer to the question when a man should marry? 'A young man not yet, an elder man not at all.'

15 Children sweeten labours, but they make misfortunes more bitter.
7. **Of Parents and Children**

16 Revenge is a kind of wild justice, which the more man's nature runs to, the more ought law to weed it out.
4. **Of Revenge**

17 Money is like muck, not good except it be spread.
15. **Of Seditions and Troubles**

18 The remedy is worse than the disease.

19 Studies serve for delight, for ornament, and for ability.
50. **Of Studies**

20 Some books are to be tasted, others to be swallowed, and some few to be chewed and digested; that is, some books are to be read only in parts; others to be read but not curiously; and some few to be read wholly, and with diligence and attention. Some books also may be read by deputy, and extracts made of them by others.

21 Reading maketh a full man; conference a ready man; and writing an exact man.

22 Histories make men wise; poets, witty; the mathematics, subtile; natural philosophy, deep; moral, grave; logic and rhetoric, able to contend.

23 There is a superstition in avoiding superstition.
17. **Of Superstition**

24 Travel, in the younger sort, is a part of education; in the elder, a part of experience. He that travelleth into a country before he hath some entrance into the language, goeth to school, and not to travel.
18. **Of Travel**

25 What is truth? said jesting Pilate; and would not stay for an answer.
1. **Of Truth.** See 37:4

26 It is the wisdom of the crocodiles, that shed tears when they would devour.
23. **Of Wisdom for a Man's Self**

27 Lucid intervals and happy pauses.
History of King Henry VII, par.3

28 I have taken all knowledge to be my province.
Letter to Lord Burleigh, 1592

29 Opportunity makes a thief.
Letter to the Earl of Essex, 1598

30 *Quod enim mavult homo verum esse, id potius credit.*
For what a man would like to be true, that

he more readily believes.
Novum Oganum, bk.I, Aphor.49. See 59:9

1 *Magna ista scientiarum mater.*
That great mother of sciences.
80. [Of natural philosophy]

2 *Nam et ipsa scientia potestas est.*
Knowledge itself is power.
Religious Meditations. Of Heresies

3 What then remains, but that we still
should cry,
Not to be born, or being born, to die?
The World

KARL BAEDEKER 1801–1859

4 Oxford is on the whole more attractive
than Cambridge to the ordinary visitor;
and the traveller is therefore recommended
to visit Cambridge first, or to omit it altogether if he cannot visit both.
Baedeker's Great Britain (1887), 30. **From London to Oxford**

WALTER BAGEHOT 1826–1877

5 There is a glare in some men's eyes which
seems to say, 'Beware, I am dangerous;
Noli me tangere.' Lord Brougham's face
has this. A mischievous excitability is the
most obvious expression of it. If he were a
horse, nobody would buy him; with that
eye no one could answer for his temper.
Biographical Studies. Essay II, **Lord Brougham**

6 It has been said that England invented the
phrase, 'Her Majesty's Opposition'; that it
was the first government which made a
criticism of administration as much a part
of the polity as administration itself. This
critical opposition is the consequence of
cabinet government.
The English Constitution (1867), 1. **The Cabinet**

7 The Sovereign has, under a constitutional
monarchy such as ours, three rights—the
right to be consulted, the right to encourage, the right to warn.
3. **The Monarchy** (continued)

8 A constitutional statesman is in general a
man of common opinion and uncommon
abilities.
**Historical Essays. The Character of Sir Robert
Peel**

9 One of the greatest pains to human nature
is the pain of a new idea.
Physics and Politics, No.v

BRUCE BAIRNSFATHER 1888–1959

10 Well, if you knows of a better 'ole, go to it.
Fragments from France, No.1 (1915)

MICHAEL BAKUNIN 1814–1876

11 *Die Lust der Zerstörung ist zugleich eine
schaffende Lust!*
The urge for destruction is also a creative
urge!
'Die Reaktion in Deutschland' in *Jahrbuch für
Wissenschaft und Kunst* (1842), under the pseu-
donym 'Jules Elysard'

12 We wish, in a word, equality—equality in
fact as corollary, or rather, as primordial
condition of liberty. From each according
to his faculties, to each according to his
needs; that is what we wish sincerely and
energetically.
Declaration signed by forty-seven anarchists on
trial after the failure of their uprising at Lyons in
1870. See J. Morrison Davidson, *The Old Order
and the New,* 1890. See 162:6

STANLEY BALDWIN 1867–1947

13 A lot of hard-faced men who look as if
they had done very well out of the war.
Of the House of Commons returned after the
election of 1918. J.M. Keynes, *Economic Consequences of the Peace,* ch.5; and see Middlemass
and Barnes, *Baldwin,* p.72n.

14 I shall be but a short time to-night. I have
seldom spoken with greater regret, for my
lips are not yet unsealed. Were these
troubles over I would make a case, and I
guarantee that not a man would go into
the Lobby against us.
10 Dec. 1935, speech on the Abyssinian crisis.
Usually quoted as 'My lips are sealed.'

A.J. BALFOUR 1848–1930

15 Frank Harris...said...: 'The fact is, Mr
Balfour, all the faults of the age come from
Christianity and journalism.' 'Christian-
ity, of course but why journalism?'
Margot Asquith, *Autobiography,* I, 10

BALLADS

16 Goodman, you've spoken the foremost
word!
Get up and bar the door.
Get Up and Bar the Door

17 'What gat ye to your dinner, Lord Randal, my Son?
What gat ye to your dinner, my handsome young man?'
'I gat eels boil'd in broo'; mother, make
my bed soon,
For I'm weary wi' hunting, and fain
wald lie down.'
Lord Randal

18 When captains couragious whom death

could not daunte,
Did march to the seige of the city of
    Gaunt,
They mustered their soldiers by two and
    by three,
And the foremost in battle was Mary Am-
    bree.
Mary Ambree

1 Yestreen the Queen had four Maries,
    The night she'll hae but three;
There was Marie Seaton, and Marie
    Beaton,
    And Marie Carmichael, and me.
The Queen's Maries

2 There are twelve months in all the year,
    As I hear many men say,
But the merriest month in all the year
    Is the merry month of May.
Robin Hood and the Widow's Three Sons

3 'I saw the new moon late yestreen
    Wi' the auld moon in her arm;
And if we gang to sea master,
    I fear we'll come to harm.'
Sir Patrick Spens

4 O waly, waly, up the bank,
    And waly, waly, doun the brae,
And waly, waly, yon burn-side,
    Where I and my Love wont to gae!
Waly, Waly

5 But had I wist, before I kist,
    That love had been sae ill to win,
I had lock'd my heart in a case o' gowd,
    And pinn'd it wi' a siller pin.

6 'Tom Pearse, Tom Pearse, lend me your
    grey mare,
All along, down along, out along, lee.
For I want for to go to Widdicombe Fair,
Wi' Bill Brewer, Jan Stewer, Peter Gurney,
    Peter Davey, Dan'l Whiddon, Harry
    Hawk,
    Old Uncle Tom Cobbleigh and all.
    Old Uncle Tom Cobbleigh and all.'
Widdicombe Fair

RICHARD BANCROFT 1544–1610

7 Where Christ erecteth his Church, the
devil in the same churchyard will have his
chapel.
Sermon at Paul's Cross, 9 Feb. 1588

EDWARD BANGS fl. 1775

8 Yankee Doodle came to town
    Riding on a pony;
Stuck a feather in his cap
    And called it Macaroni.
Yankee Doodle; or Father's Return to Camp. See
Nicholas Smith, *Stories of Great National Songs*

REVD. R.H. BARHAM 1788–1845

9 She help'd him to lean, and she help'd him
    to fat,
And it look'd like hare—but it might have
    been cat.
The Ingoldsby Legends. **The Bagman's Dog**

10 What Horace says is,
Eheu fugaces
Anni labuntur, Postume, Postume!
Years glide away, and are lost to me, lost
    to me!
Epigram: Eheu fugaces. See 124:4

11 And six little Singing-boys,—dear little
    souls!
In nice clean faces, and nice white stoles.
The Jackdaw of Rheims

12 Never was heard such a terrible curse!
    But what gave rise to no little surprise,
Nobody seem'd one penny the worse!

13 Heedless of grammar, they all cried,
    'That's him!'

14 But when the Crier cried, 'O Yes!' the
    people cried, 'O No!'
Misadventures at Margate

15 It's very odd that Sailor-men should talk
    so very queer—
And then he hitch'd his trousers up, as is,
    I'm told, their use,
It's very odd that Sailor-men should wear
    those things so loose.

16 He smiled and said, 'Sir, does your mother
    know that you are out?'

RICHARD BARNFIELD 1574–1627

17 As it fell upon a day
In the merry month of May,
Sitting in a pleasant shade,
Which a grove of myrtles made,
Beasts did leap and birds did sing,
Trees did grow and plants did spring,
Everything did banish moan,
Save the nightingale alone.
She, poor bird, as all forlorn,
Lean'd her breast up-till a thorn,
And there sung the dolefull'st ditty
That to hear it was great pity.
Fie, fie, fie, now would she cry;
Tereu, Tereu, by and by.
An Ode. Also attr. Shakespeare

PHINEAS T. BARNUM 1810–1891

18 There's a sucker born every minute.
Attr.

J.M. BARRIE 1860–1937

1 His Lordship may compel us to be equal upstairs, but there will never be equality in the servants' hall.
The Admirable Crichton, I

2 When the first baby laughed for the first time, the laugh broke into a thousand pieces and they all went skipping about, and that was the beginning of fairies.
Peter Pan, I

3 Every time a child says 'I don't believe in fairies' there is a little fairy somewhere that falls down dead.

4 To die will be an awfully big adventure.
III

5 Do you believe in fairies?…If you believe, clap your hands!
IV

6 It's a sort of bloom on a woman. If you have it [charm], you don't need to have anything else; and if you don't have it, it doesn't much matter what else you have.
What Every Woman Knows, I

7 There are few more impressive sights in the world than a Scotsman on the make.
II

CHARLES BARTLETT 1921–

8 The hawks favoured an air strike to eliminate the Cuban missile bases…. The doves opposed the air strike and favoured a blockade.
Saturday Evening Post, 8 Dec. 1962

BERNARD M. BARUCH 1870–1965

9 Let us not be deceived—we are today in the midst of a cold war.
Speech before South Carolina Legislature, 16 Apr. 1947. Mr. Baruch said the expression 'cold war' was suggested to him by H.B. Swope, former editor of the New York *World*.

THOMAS BASTARD 1566–1618

10 Age is deformed, youth unkind,
We scorn their bodies, they our mind.
Chrestoleros (1598), Bk.7, Epigram 9

CHARLES BAUDELAIRE 1821–1867

11 *Hypocrite lecteur,—mon semblable,—mon frère.*
Hypocrite reader—my likeness—my brother.
Les Fleurs du Mal, Préface

12 *Là, tout n'est qu'ordre et beauté,
Luxe, calme et volupté.*
Everything there is simply order and beauty, luxury, peace and sensual indulgence.
liii, **L'Invitation au Voyage**

13 *Quelle est cette île triste et noire? C'est Cythère,
Nous dit-on, un pays fameux dans les chansons,
Eldorado banal de tous les vieux garçons.
Regardez, après tout, c'est un pauvre terre.*
What sad, black isle is that? It's Cythera, so they say, a land celebrated in song, the banal Eldorado of all the old fools. Look, after all, it's a land of poverty.
cxvi, **Un Voyage à Cythère**

PIERRE-AUGUSTIN CARON DE BEAUMARCHAIS 1732–1799

14 *Aujourd'hui ce qui ne vaut pas la peine d'être dit, on le chante.*
Today if something is not worth saying, people sing it.
Le Barbier de Séville, I.ii

15 *Je me presse de rire de tout, de peur d'être obligé d'en pleurer.*
I make myself laugh at everything, for fear of having to weep.

16 *Boire sans soif et faire l'amour en tout temps, madame, il n'y a que ça qui nous distingue des autres bêtes.*
Drinking when we are not thirsty and making love all year round, madam; that is all there is to distinguish us from other animals.
Le Mariage de Figaro, II.xxi

17 *Parce que vous êtes un grand seigneur, vous vous croyez un grand génie!…Vous vous êtes donné la peine de naître, et rien de plus.*
Because you are a great lord, you believe yourself to be a great genius!…You took the trouble to be born, but no more.

FRANCIS BEAUMONT 1584–1616

18   What things have we seen,
Done at the Mermaid!
Letter to Ben Jonson

FRANCIS BEAUMONT 1584–1616
and
JOHN FLETCHER 1579–1625
(see also under FLETCHER)

19 You are no better than you should be.
The Coxcomb, IV.iii

20 I care not two-pence.

21 It is always good

When a man has two irons in the fire.
The Faithful Friends, I.ii (attr.)

1 Those have most power to hurt us, that we
love.
The Maid's Tragedy, V.iv

2 *Philaster:* Oh, but thou dost not know
What 'tis to die.
Bellario: Yes, I do know, my Lord:
'Tis less than to be born; a lasting sleep;
A quiet resting from all jealousy,
A thing we all pursue; I know besides,
It is but giving over of a game,
That must be lost.
Philaster, III.i

3 Kiss till the cow comes home.
The Scornful Lady, II.ii

LORD BEAVERBROOK 1879–1964

4 Our cock won't fight.
Said to W.S. Churchill during the abdication
crisis, 1936. Frances Donaldson, *Edward VIII*,
ch.22

SAMUEL BECKETT 1906–

5 *Estragon:* Let's go.
Vladimir: We can't.
Estragon: Why not?
Vladimir: We're waiting for Godot.
Waiting for Godot (1954), I

PETER BECKFORD 1740–1811

6 The colour I think of little moment; and
am of opinion with our friend Foote, re-
specting his negro friend, that a good dog,
like a good candidate, cannot be of a bad
colour.
Thoughts upon Hare and Fox Hunting (1781),
letter 3

THOMAS BECON 1512–1567

7 For when the wine is in, the wit is out.
Catechism, 375

SIR THOMAS BEECHAM 1879–1961

8 Too much counterpoint; what is worse,
Protestant counterpoint. [Of Bach.]
Neville Cardus, *Guardian*, 8 Mar. 1971

9 A musicologist is a man who can read
music but can't hear it.
H. Proctor-Gregg, *Beecham Remembered* (1976),
p.154

10 In the first movement alone, I took note of
six pregnancies and at least four miscarriages. [Of Bruckner's 7th Symphony.]
Oral trad.

REVD. H.C. BEECHING 1859–1919

11 First come I; my name is Jowett.
There's no knowledge but I know it.
I am Master of this college:
What I don't know isn't knowledge.
The Masque of Balliol, composed by and current
among members of Balliol College in the late
1870's. See 4:9, 245:5–6

MAX BEERBOHM 1872–1956

12 Most women are not so young as they are
painted.
A Defence of Cosmetics

13 To give an accurate and exhaustive account of that period would need a far less
brilliant pen than mine.
1880

14 The Nonconformist Conscience makes
cowards of us all.
King George the Fourth

15 Not that I had any special reason for hating school. Strange as it may seem to my
readers, I was not unpopular there. I was a
modest, good-humoured boy. It is Oxford
that has made me insufferable.
More. **Going back to School**

16 Undergraduates owe their happiness
chiefly to the fact that they are no longer at
school…The nonsense which was knocked
out of them at school is all put gently back
at Oxford or Cambridge.

17 The fading signals and grey eternal walls
of that antique station, which, familiar to
them and insignificant, does yet whisper to
the tourist the last enchantment of the
Middle Age.
Zuleika Dobson, ch.1

18 Zuleika, on a desert island, would have
spent most of her time in looking for a
man's foot-print.
ch.2

19 The dullard's envy of brilliant men is always assuaged by the suspicion that they
will come to a bad end.
ch.4

20 Only the insane take themselves quite seriously.
Lord David Cecil, *Max* (1964), ch.2

LUDWIG VAN BEETHOVEN
1770–1827

21 *Muss es sein? Es muss sein.*
Must it be? It must be.
Epigraph to String Quartet in F Major, Opus
135

MRS. APHRA BEHN 1640–1689

1 Faith, Sir, we are here to-day, and gone
to-morrow.
The Lucky Chance, IV

HILAIRE BELLOC 1870–1953

2 Child! do not throw this book about;
Refrain from the unholy pleasure
Of cutting all the pictures out!
Preserve it as your chiefest treasure.
Bad Child's Book of Beasts, dedication

3 Your little hands were made to take
The better things and leave the worse ones:
They also may be used to shake
The massive paws of elder persons.

4 The Dromedary is a cheerful bird:
I cannot say the same about the Kurd.
The Dromedary

5 When people call this beast to mind,
They marvel more and more
At such a little tail behind,
So large a trunk before.
The Elephant

6 I shoot the Hippopotamus
With bullets made of platinum,
Because if I use leaden ones
His hide is sure to flatten 'em.
The Hippopotamus

7 Mothers of large families (who claim to
common sense)
Will find a Tiger well repay the trouble
and expense.
The Tiger

8 Godolphin Horne was nobly born;
He held the human race in scorn.
Cautionary Tales. Godolphin Horne

9 The chief defect of Henry King
Was chewing little bits of string.
Henry King

10 Physicians of the utmost fame
Were called at once, but when they came
They answered, as they took their fees,
'There is no cure for this disease.'

11 'Oh, my friends, be warned by me,
That breakfast, dinner, lunch, and tea
Are all the human frame requires…'
With that the wretched child expires.

12 And always keep a hold of Nurse
For fear of finding something worse.
Jim

13 We had intended you to be
The next Prime Minister but three:
The stocks were sold; the Press was
squared;
The Middle Class was quite prepared.

But as it is!…My language fails!
Go out and govern New South Wales!
Lord Lundy

14 Matilda told such Dreadful Lies,
It made one Gasp and Stretch one's Eyes;
Her Aunt, who, from her Earliest Youth,
Had kept a Strict Regard for Truth,
Attempted to Believe Matilda:
The effort very nearly killed her.
Matilda

15 Summoned the Immediate Aid
Of London's Noble Fire Brigade.

16 For every time she shouted 'Fire!'
They only answered 'Little Liar!'

17 She was not really bad at heart,
But only rather rude and wild;
She was an aggravating child.
Rebecca

18 The moon on the one hand, the dawn on
the other:
The moon is my sister, the dawn is my
brother.
The moon on my left and the dawn on my
right.
My brother, good morning: my sister,
good night.
The Early Morning

19 I said to Heart, 'How goes it?' Heart re-
plied:
'Right as a Ribstone Pippin!' But it lied.
Epigrams. **The False Heart**

20 I'm tired of Love: I'm still more tired of
Rhyme.
But Money gives me pleasure all the time.
Fatigue

21 When I am dead, I hope it may be said:
'His sins were scarlet, but his books were
read.'
On his Books

22 The accursed power which stands on Pri-
vilege
(And goes with Women, and Champagne,
and Bridge)
Broke—and Democracy resumed her
reign:
(Which goes with Bridge, and Women and
Champagne).
On a Great Election

23 I am a sundial, and I make a botch
Of what is done far better by a watch.
On a Sundial

24 Pale Ebenezer thought it wrong to fight,
But Roaring Bill (who killed him) thought
it right.
The Pacifist

25 Remote and ineffectual Don

That dared attack my Chesterton.
Lines to a Don

1 Don different from those regal Dons!
With hearts of gold and lungs of bronze,
Who shout and bang and roar and bawl
The Absolute across the hall,
Or sail in amply billowing gown,
Enormous through the Sacred Town.

2 Lord Finchley tried to mend the Electric
    Light
Himself. It struck him dead: and serve him
    right!
It is the business of the wealthy man
To give employment to the artisan.
Lord Finchley

3 The nuisance of the tropics is
The sheer necessity of fizz.
The Modern Traveller (1898), iv

4 Whatever happens, we have got
The Maxim Gun, and they have not.
vi

5 Oh! let us never, never doubt
What nobody is sure about!
More Beasts for Worse Children. **The Microbe**

6 Like many of the upper class
He liked the sound of broken glass.
New Cautionary Tales. **About John**

7 When I am living in the Midlands
    That are sodden and unkind…
    The great hills of the South Country
Come back into my mind.
The South Country

8 Do you remember an Inn,
Miranda?
Tarantella

9 The fleas that tease in the high Pyrenees.

P.-L. B. DU BELLOY 1725–1775

10 *Plus je vis d'étrangers, plus j'aimai ma pat-*
    rie.
    The more foreigners I saw, the more I
        loved my homeland.
Le Siège de Calais (1765), II.iii

JULIEN BENDA 1868–1956

11 *La trahison des clercs.*
The intellectuals' betrayal.
Title of book (1927)

STEPHEN VINCENT BENÉT 1898–1943

12 I shall not rest quiet in Montparnasse.
I shall not lie easy at Winchelsea.
You may bury my body in Sussex grass,
You may bury my tongue at Champmédy.

I shall not be there, I shall rise and pass.
Bury my heart at Wounded Knee.
American Names

ARNOLD BENNETT 1867–1931

13 Journalists say a thing that they know
isn't true, in that hope that if they keep on
saying it long enough it will be true.
The Title, Act II

JEREMY BENTHAM 1748–1832

14 The greatest happiness of the greatest
number is the foundation of morals and
legislation.
The Commonplace Book (*Works*, x.142). See
128:11

15 Prose is when all the lines except the last
go on to the end. Poetry is when some of
them fall short of it.
M. St.J. Packe, *Life of John Stuart Mill*, bk.I,
ch.ii

EDMUND CLERIHEW BENTLEY 1875–1956

16 The art of Biography
Is different from Geography.
Geography is about maps,
But Biography is about chaps.
Biography for Beginners

17 What I like about Clive
Is that he is no longer alive.
There is a great deal to be said
For being dead.

18 Sir Humphrey Davy
Abominated gravy.
He lived in the odium
Of having discovered Sodium.

19 John Stuart Mill
By a mighty effort of will
Overcame his natural bonhomie
And wrote 'Principles of Political Eco-
nomy'.

20 Sir Christopher Wren
Said, 'I am going to dine with some men.
If anybody calls
Say I am designing St Paul's.'

21 George the Third
Ought never to have occurred.
One can only wonder
At so grotesque a blunder.
More Biography

LORD CHARLES BERESFORD 1846–1919

22 Very sorry can't come. Lie follows by
post.

Telegram to the Prince of Wales after an eleventh-hour summons to dine. R. Nevill, *The World of Fashion 1837–1922* (1923), ch 5. See 192:6

BISHOP BERKELEY 1685–1753

1 [Tar water] is of a nature so mild and benign and proportioned to the human constitution, as to warm without heating, to cheer but not inebriate.
Siris, par.217

BERNARD OF CHARTRES d. c.1130

2 We are like dwarfs on the shoulders of giants, so that we can see more than they, and things at a greater distance, not by virtue of any sharpness of sight on our part, or any physical distinction, but because we are carried high and raised up by their giant size.
John of Salisbury, *Metalogicon* (1159), bk.III. ch.iv. See also R.K. Merton, *On the Shoulders of Giants* (1965)

LORD BERNERS 1883–1950

3 He's always backing into the limelight.
Oral tradition, of T.E. Lawrence

THEOBALD VON BETHMANN HOLLWEG 1856–1921

4 Just for a word—'neutrality', a word which in wartime has so often been disregarded, just for a scrap of paper—Great Britain is going to make war.
To Sir Edward Goschen, 4 Aug. 1914

SIR JOHN BETJEMAN 1906–

5 He sipped at a weak hock and seltzer,
As he gazed at the London skies
Through the Nottingham lace of the curtains
Or was it his bees-winged eyes?
The Arrest of Oscar Wilde at the Cadogan Hotel

6 Rest you there, poor unbelov'd ones,
Lap your loneliness in heat.
All too soon the tiny breakfast,
Trolley-bus and windy street!
Business Girls

7 And girls in slacks remember Dad,
And oafish louts remember Mum,
And sleepless children's hearts are glad,
And Christmas morning bells say
'Come!'
Even to shining ones who dwell
Safe in the Dorchester Hotel.

And is it true? And is it true,
This most tremendous tale of all,
Seen in a stained-glass window's hue,
A Baby in an ox's stall?
Christmas

8 Oh! chintzy, chintzy cheeriness,
Half dead and half alive!
Death in Leamington

9 Spirits of well-shot woodcock, partridge, snipe
Flutter and bear him up the Norfolk sky.
Death of King George V

10 Old men in country houses hear clocks ticking
Over thick carpets with a deadened force;
Old men who never cheated, never doubted,
Communicated monthly, sit and stare
At the new suburb stretched beyond the run-way
Where a young man lands hatless from the air.

11 Rime Intrinsica, Fontmell Magna, Sturminster Newton and Melbury Bubb,
Whist upon whist upon whist upon whist drive, in Institute, Legion and Social Club.
Horny hands that hold the aces which this morning held the plough—
While Tranter Reuben, T.S. Eliot, H.G. Wells and Edith Sitwell lie in Mellstock churchyard now.
Dorset. See 114:9

12 You ask me what it is I do. Well actually, you know,
I'm partly a liaison man and partly P.R.O.
Essentially I integrate the current export drive
And basically I'm viable from ten o'clock till five.
Executive

13 Phone for the fish-knives, Norman,
As Cook is a little unnerved;
You kiddies have crumpled the serviettes
And I must have things daintily served.
How to Get On in Society

14 Milk and then just as it comes dear?
I'm afraid the preserve's full of stones;
Beg pardon, I'm soiling the doileys
With afternoon tea-cakes and scones.

15 It's awf'lly bad luck on Diana,
Her ponies have swallowed their bits;
She fished down their throats with a spanner

And frightened them all into fits.
Hunter Trials

1 Oh wasn't it naughty of Smudges?
    Oh, Mummy, I'm sick with disgust.
She threw me in front of the judges
    And my silly old collarbone's bust.

2 In the Garden City Café with its murals
        on the wall
Before a talk on 'Sex and Civics' I meditat
    ed on the Fall.
Huxley Hall

3 'Let us not speak, for the love we bear one
        another—
        Let us hold hands and look.'
She, such a very ordinary little woman;
    He, such a thumping crook;
But both, for a moment, little lower than
        the angels
    In the teashop's ingle-nook.
In a Bath Teashop. See 116:13

4 Gracious Lord, oh bomb the Germans.
    Spare their women for Thy Sake,
And if that is not too easy
    We will pardon Thy Mistake.
But, gracious Lord, whate'er shall be,
    Don't let anyone bomb me.
In Westminster Abbey

5 Think of what our Nation stands for,
    Books from Boots' and country lanes,
Free speech, free passes, class distinction,
    Democracy and proper drains.
Lord, put beneath Thy special care
    One-eighty-nine Cadogan Square.

6 Take me, Lieutenant, to that Surrey
        homestead!
Love in a Valley

7 Gaily into Ruislip Gardens
    Runs the red electric train,
With a thousand Ta's and Pardon's
    Daintily alights Elaine.
Middlesex

8 Well-cut Windsmoor flapping lightly,
    Jacqmar scarf of mauve and green
Hiding hair which, Friday nightly,
    Delicately drowns in Drene.

9 And my childish wave of pity, seeing chil-
        dren carrying down
Sheaves of drooping dandelions to the
        courts of Kentish Town.
Parliament Hill Fields

10 Pam, I adore you, Pam, you great big
        mountainous sports girl,
Whizzing them over the net, full of the
        strength of five.
Pot Pourri from a Surrey Garden

11 Come, friendly bombs, and fall on Slough

It isn't fit for humans now,
There isn't grass to graze a cow
    Swarm over, Death!
Slough

12 Come, friendly bombs, and fall on Slough
To get it ready for the plough.
The cabbages are coming now:
    The earth exhales.

13 Miss Joan Hunter Dunn, Miss Joan Hunt-
        er Dunn,
How mad I am, sad I am, glad that you
        won.
The warm-handled racket is back in its
        press,
But my shock-headed victor, she loves me
        no less.
A Subaltern's Love Song

14 Miss Joan Hunter Dunn, Miss Joan Hunt-
        er Dunn,
I can hear from the car-park the dance has
        begun.
Oh! full Surrey twilight! importunate
        band!
Oh! strongly adorable tennis-girl's hand!

15 *Ghastly Good Taste,* or *A Depressing Story
    of the Rise and Fall of English Architecture.*
Book title (1933)

ANEURIN BEVAN 1897–1960

16 No amount of cajolery, and no attempts
    at ethical and social seduction, can eradi-
    cate from my heart a deep burning hatred
    for the Tory Party...So far as I am con-
    cerned they are lower than vermin.
    Speech at Manchester, 4 July 1948

17 If you carry this resolution and follow out
    all its implications and do not run away
    from it you will send a Foreign Minister,
    whoever he may be, naked into the confer-
    ence chamber.
    M. Foot, *Aneurin Bevan,* vol. ii (1973), ch 15.
    Speech at Labour Party Conference, 3 Oct. 1957,
    against motion proposing unilateral nuclear dis-
    armament by the U.K.

ERNEST BEVIN 1881–1951

18 My [foreign] policy is to be able to take a
    ticket at Victoria Station and go anywhere
    I damn well please.
    Spectator, 20 Apr. 1951

19 If you open that Pandora's Box you never
    know what Trojan 'orses will jump out.
    On the Council of Europe. Sir Roderick Barclay,
    Ernest Bevin and the Foreign Office (1975), p.67

THE BIBLE

OLD TESTAMENT

1 In the beginning God created the heaven and the earth.
Genesis 1:1

2 And God said, Let there be light: and there was light.
3

3 And the evening and the morning were the first day.
5

4 And God saw that it was good.
10

5 Male and female created he them.
27

6 Be fruitful, and multiply, and replenish the earth, and subdue it.
28

7 But of the tree of the knowledge of good and evil, thou shalt not eat of it: for in the day that thou eatest thereof thou shalt surely die.
2:17

8 It is not good that the man should be alone; I will make him an help meet for him.
18

9 And the Lord God caused a deep sleep to fall upon Adam, and he slept: and he took one of his ribs, and closed up the flesh instead thereof;
And the rib, which the Lord God had taken from man, made he a woman.
21

10 Bone of my bones, and flesh of my flesh.
23

11 Therefore shall a man leave his father and his mother, and shall cleave unto his wife: and they shall be one flesh.
24

12 And they sewed fig leaves together, and made themselves aprons [breeches in Genevan Bible, 1560].
And they heard the voice of the Lord God walking in the garden in the cool of the day.
3:7

13 In sorrow thou shalt bring forth children.
16

14 In the sweat of thy face shalt thou eat bread.
19

15 For dust thou art, and unto dust shalt thou return.

16 Am I my brother's keeper?
4:9

17 And the Lord set a mark upon Cain.
15

18 And Cain went out from the presence of the Lord, and dwelt in the land of Nod, on the east of Eden.
16

19 There were giants in the earth in those days.
6:4

20 There went in two and two unto Noah into the Ark, the male and the female.
7:9

21 Whoso sheddeth man's blood, by man shall his blood be shed.
9:6

22 I do set my bow in the cloud, and it shall be for a token of a covenant between me and the earth.
13

23 Even as Nimrod the mighty hunter before the Lord.
10:9

24 His [Ishmael's] hand will be against every man, and every man's hand against him.
16:12

25 But his wife looked back from behind him, and she became a pillar of salt.
19:26

26 Behold behind him a ram caught in a thicket by his horns.
22:13

27 Esau selleth his birthright for a mess of potage.
Heading to chapter 25 in Genevan Bible

28 And he sold his birthright unto Jacob.
25:33

29 Behold, Esau my brother is a hairy man, and I am a smooth man.
27:11

30 The voice is Jacob's voice, but the hands are the hands of Esau.
22

31 Thy brother came with subtilty, and hath taken away thy blessing.
35

32 And he dreamed, and behold a ladder set up on the earth, and the top of it reached to heaven: and behold the angels of God ascending and descending on it.
28:12

1 And Jacob served seven years for Rachel; and they seemed unto him but a few days, for the love he had to her.
29:20

2 Mizpah; for he said, The Lord watch between me and thee, when we are absent one from another.
31:49

3 Now Israel loved Joseph more than all his children, because he was the son of his old age; and he made him a coat of many colours.
37:3

4 Behold, this dreamer cometh.
19

5 Jacob saw that there was corn in Egypt.
42:1

6 Bring down my gray hairs with sorrow to the grave.
38

7 Ye shall eat the fat of the land.
45:18

8 I have been a stranger in a strange land.
Exodus 2:22. See Exodus 18:3

9 Behold, the bush burned with fire, and the bush was not consumed.
3:2

10 Put off thy shoes from off thy feet, for the place whereon thou standest is holy ground.
5

11 A land flowing with milk and honey.
8

12 I AM THAT I AM.
14

13 Let my people go.
7:16

14 Darkness which may be felt.
10:21

15 With your loins girded, your shoes on your feet, and your staff in your hand; and ye shall eat it in haste; it is the Lord's passover.
12:11

16 There was a great cry in Egypt; for there was not a house where there was not one dead.
30

17 And the Lord went before them by day in a pillar of a cloud, to lead them the way; and by night in a pillar of fire, to give them light.
13:21

18 Life for life,

Eye for eye, tooth for tooth, hand for hand, foot for foot.
21:23

19 Thou shalt not suffer a witch to live.
22:18

20 Thou shalt not seethe a kid in his mother's milk.
23:19

21 A stiffnecked people.
33:3

22 There shall no man see me and live.
20

23 Let him go for a scapegoat into the wilderness.
Leviticus 16:10

24 Thou shalt love thy neighbour as thyself.
19:18. See Matt. 19:19

25 The Lord bless thee, and keep thee:
The Lord make his face shine upon thee, and be gracious unto thee:
The Lord lift up his countenance upon thee, and give thee peace.
Numbers 6:24

26 The men which Moses sent to spy out the land.
13:16

27 What hath God wrought!
23:23. Quoted by Samuel Morse in the first electric telegraph message, Washington, 24 May 1844

28 Be sure your sin will find you out.
32:23

29 I call heaven and earth to witness against you this day.
Deuteronomy 4:26

30 Hear, O Israel: The Lord our God is one Lord.
6:4

31 For the Lord thy God is a jealous God.
15

32 A dreamer of dreams.
13:1

33 The wife of thy bosom.
6

34 Thou shalt not muzzle the ox when he treadeth out the corn.
25:4

35 Cursed be he that removeth his neighbour's landmark.
27:17

36 I have set before you life and death, blessing and cursing: therefore choose life that

both thou and thy seed may live.
30:19

1 For they are a very froward generation,
children in whom is no faith.
32:20

2 The eternal God is thy refuge, and underneath are the everlasting arms.
33:27

3 Be strong and of a good courage; be not
afraid, neither be thou dismayed: for the
Lord thy God is with thee, whithersoever
thou goest.
Joshua 1:9

4 Let them live; but let them be hewers of
wood and drawers of water unto all the
congregation.
9:21

5 The stars in their courses fought against
Sisera.
Judges 5:20

6 She brought forth butter in a lordly dish.
[Jael.]
25

7 The Lord is with thee, thou mighty man of
valour.
6:12

8 Faint, yet pursuing.
8:4

9 Then said they unto him, Say now Shibboleth: and he said Sibboleth: for he could
not frame to pronounce it right. Then they
took him, and slew him.
12:6

10 Out of the eater came forth meat, and out
of the strong came forth sweetness.
14:14

11 He smote them hip and thigh.
15:8

12 With the jawbone of an ass, heaps upon
heaps, with the jaw of an ass have I slain a
thousand men.
16

13 The people arose as one man.
20:8

14 Intreat me not to leave thee, or to return
from following after thee: for whither thou
goest, I will go; and where thou lodgest, I
will lodge: thy people shall be my people,
and thy God my God.
Ruth 1:16

15 Speak, Lord; for thy servant heareth.
1 Samuel 3:9

16 Quit yourselves like men, and fight.
4:9

17 And she named the child I-chabod, saying, The glory is departed from Israel.
21

18 God save the king.
10:24

19 A man after his own heart.
13:14

20 I did but taste a little honey with the end
of the rod that was in mine hand, and, lo, I
must die.
14:43

21 Agag came unto him delicately.
15:32

22 Now he was ruddy, and withal of a beautiful countenance, and goodly to look to.
16:12

23 And Saul said, God hath delivered him
into mine hand.
23:7

24 Behold, I have played the fool, and have
erred exceedingly. [Saul.]
26:21

25 The beauty of Israel is slain upon thy high
places: how are the mighty fallen!
Tell it not in Gath, publish it not in the
streets of Askelon; lest the daughters of the
Philistines rejoice, lest the daughters of the
uncircumcised triumph.
2 Samuel 1:19

26 Saul and Jonathan were lovely and
pleasant in their lives, and in their death
they were not divided: they were swifter
than eagles, they were stronger than lions.
23

27 How are the mighty fallen in the midst of
the battle! O Jonathan, thou wast slain in
thine high places.
I am distressed for thee, my brother Jonathan: very pleasant hast thou been unto
me: thy love to me was wonderful, passing
the love of women.
25

28 The poor man had nothing, save one little
ewe lamb.
12:3

29 O my son Absalom, my son, my son Absalom! would God I had died for thee, O
Absalom, my son, my son!
18:33

30 By my God have I leaped over a wall.
22:30

31 And Zadok the priest took an horn of oil
out of the tabernacle, and anointed Solomon. And they blew the trumpet; and all

the people said, God save king Solomon.
1 Kings 1:39

1 A proverb and a byword among all people.
9:7

2 Behold, the half was not told me.
10:7

3 Once in three years came the navy of Tharshish, bringing gold, and silver, ivory, and apes, and peacocks.
22

4 My father hath chastised you with whips, but I will chastise you with scorpions.
12:11

5 There ariseth a little cloud out of the sea, like a man's hand.
18:44

6 A still small voice.
19:12

7 And Ahab spake unto Naboth, saying, Give me thy vineyard, that I may have it for a garden of herbs, because it is near unto my house.
21:2

8 Feed him with bread of affliction and with water of affliction, until I come in peace.
22:27

9 And a certain man drew a bow at a venture, and smote the king of Israel between the joints of the harness.
34

0 There is death in the pot.
2 Kings 4:40

1 Is thy servant a dog, that he should do this great thing?
8:13

2 The driving is like the driving of Jehu, the son of Nimshi; for he driveth furiously.
9:20

3 She painted her face, and tired her head, and looked out at a window.
30

4 Thou trustest upon the staff of this bruised reed, even upon Egypt, on which if a man lean, it will go into his hand, and pierce it.
18:21

15 He died in a good old age, full of days, riches, and honour.
1 Chronicles 29:28

16 The man whom the king delighteth to honour.
Esther 6:6

17 And the Lord said unto Satan, Whence comest thou? Then Satan answered the Lord, and said, From going to and fro in the earth, and from walking up and down in it.
Job 1:7

18 The Lord gave, and the Lord hath taken away; blessed be the name of the Lord.
21

10 Curse God, and die.
2:9

20 There the wicked cease from troubling, and there the weary be at rest.
3:17

21 Man is born unto trouble, as the sparks fly upward.
5:7

22 Canst thou by searching find out God?
11:7

23 No doubt but ye are the people, and wisdom shall die with you.
12:2

24 Man that is born of a woman is of few days, and full of trouble.
He cometh forth like a flower, and is cut down: he fleeth also as a shadow, and continueth not.
14:1

25 Miserable comforters are ye all.
16:2

26 I am escaped with the skin of my teeth.
19:20

27 Oh that my words were now written! oh that they were printed in a book!
23

28 I know that my redeemer liveth, and that he shall stand at the latter day upon the earth.
25

29 The price of wisdom is above rubies.
28:18

30 I am a brother to dragons, and a companion to owls.
30:29

31 My desire is...that mine adversary had written a book.
31:35

32 Gird up now thy loins like a man.
38:3

33 When the morning stars sang together, and all the sons of God shouted for joy.
7

34 He saith among the trumpets, Ha, ha; and he smelleth the battle afar off, the thunder

of the captains, and the shouting.
39:25

1 Behold now behemoth, which I made with thee; he eateth grass as an ox.
40:15

2 Canst thou draw out leviathan with an hook?
41:1

For psalms in the Book of Common Prayer see PRAYER BOOK.

3 Surely in vain the net is spread in the sight of any bird.
Proverbs 1:17

4 For whom the Lord loveth he correcteth.
3:12

5 Length of days is in her right hand; and in her left hand riches and honour.
16

6 Her ways are ways of pleasantness, and all her paths are peace.
17

7 Wisdom is the principal thing; therefore get wisdom: and with all thy getting get understanding.
4:7

8 Go to the ant thou sluggard; consider her ways, and be wise.
6:6

9 Yet a little sleep, a little slumber, a little folding of the hands to sleep.
10. See Prov. 24:33

10 He goeth after her straightway, as an ox goeth to the slaughter.
7:22

11 Stolen waters are sweet, and bread eaten in secret is pleasant.
9:17

12 A wise son maketh a glad father: but a foolish son is the heaviness of his mother.
10:1

13 The destruction of the poor is their poverty.
15

14 A virtuous woman is a crown to her husband.
12:4

15 A righteous man regardeth the life of his beast: but the tender mercies of the wicked are cruel.
10

16 Hope deferred maketh the heart sick.
13:12

17 The way of transgressors is hard.
15

18 He that spareth his rod hateth his son.
24

19 A soft answer turneth away wrath.
15:1

20 A merry heart maketh a cheerful counte nance.
13

21 Better is a dinner of herbs where love is than a stalled ox and hatred therewith.
17. Better is a mess of pottage with love, than fat ox with evil will. (Matthew's Bible, 1535)

22 Pride goeth before destruction, and a haughty spirit before a fall.
16:18

23 There is a friend that sticketh closer than brother.
18:24

24 Wine is a mocker, strong drink is raging.
20:1

25 Train up a child in the way he should go and when he is old, he will not depart from it.
22:6

26 Look not thou upon the wine when it i red, when it giveth his colour in the cup,... At the last it biteth like a serpent, an stingeth like an adder.
23:31

27 Heap coals of fire upon his head.
25:21

28 As cold waters to a thirsty soul, so is goo news from a far country.
25

29 Answer a fool according to his folly, les he be wise in his own conceit.
26:5

30 As a dog returneth to his vomit, so a foo returneth to his folly.
11

31 The slothful man saith, There is a lion in the way: a lion is in the streets.
13

32 The wicked flee when no man pursueth but the righteous are bold as a lion.
28:1

33 The way of an eagle in the air; the way of serpent upon a rock; the way of a ship in the midst of the sea; and the way of a man with a maid.
30:19

34 Who can find a virtuous woman? for her

price is far above rubies.
31:10

1 Her children arise up, and call her blessed.
28

2 Vanity of vanities, saith the Preacher, vanity of vanities; all is vanity.
Ecclesiastes 1:2

3 The thing that hath been, it is that which shall be; and that which is done is that which shall be done: and there is no new thing under the sun.
9

4 All is vanity and vexation of spirit.
14

5 He that increaseth knowledge increaseth sorrow.
18

6 To every thing there is a season, and a time to every purpose under the heaven:
A time to be born, and a time to die; a time to plant, and a time to pluck up that which is planted.
3:1

7 A time to love, and a time to hate; a time of war, and a time of peace.
8

8 The sleep of a labouring man is sweet.
5:12

9 As the crackling of thorns under a pot, so is the laughter of a fool.
7:6

10 One man among a thousand have I found; but a woman among all those have I not found.
28

11 There is no discharge in that war.
8:8

12 A man hath no better thing under the sun, than to eat, and to drink, and to be merry.
15. See 28:25 and Luke 12:19

13 A living dog is better than a dead lion.
9:4

14 Go thy way, eat thy bread with joy, and drink thy wine with a merry heart; for God now accepteth thy works.
7

15 Whatsoever thy hand findeth to do, do it with thy might; for there is no work, nor device, nor knowledge, nor wisdom, in the grave, whither thou goest.
10

16 The race is not to the swift, nor the battle to the strong.
11

17 He that diggeth a pit shall fall into it.
10:8

18 Woe to thee, O land, when thy king is a child, and thy princes eat in the morning!
16

19 Wine maketh merry: but money answereth all things.
19

20 Cast thy bread upon the waters: for thou shalt find it after many days.
11:1

21 Remember now thy Creator in the days of thy youth, while the evil days come not, nor the years draw nigh, when thou shalt say, I have no pleasure in them.
12:1

22 And desire shall fail: because man goeth to his long home, and the mourners go about the streets:
Or ever the silver cord be loosed, or the golden bowl be broken, or the pitcher be broken at the fountain, or the wheel broken at the cistern.
Then shall the dust return to the earth as it was: and the spirit shall return unto God who gave it.
5

23 Of making many books there is no end; and much study is a weariness of the flesh.
12

24 Fear God, and keep his commandments: for this is the whole duty of man.
13

25 A bundle of myrrh is my wellbeloved unto me; he shall lie all night betwixt my breasts.
Song of Solomon 1:13

26 I am the rose of Sharon, and the lily of the valleys.
2:1

27 His banner over me was love.
4

28 Stay me with flagons, comfort me with apples: for I am sick of love.
His left hand is under my head, and his right hand doth embrace me.
5

29 Rise up, my love, my fair one, and come away.
For, lo, the winter is past, the rain is over and gone;
The flowers appear on the earth; the time of the singing of birds is come, and the voice of the turtle is heard in our land.
2:10

1 Take us the foxes, the little foxes, that spoil the vines.
15

2 My beloved is mine, and I am his: he feedeth among the lilies.
Until the day break, and the shadows flee away.
16

3 Behold, thou art fair, my love; behold, thou art fair; thou hast doves' eyes within thy locks: thy hair is as a flock of goats, that appear from mount Gilead.
Thy teeth are like a flock of sheep that are even shorn, which came up from the washing; whereof every one bear twins, and none is barren among them.
Thy lips are like a thread of scarlet, and thy speech is comely: thy temples are like a piece of a pomegranate within thy locks.
4:1

4 Thy two breasts are like two young roes that are twins, which feed among the lilies.
5

5 Many waters cannot quench love, neither can the floods drown it: if a man would give all the substance of his house for love, it would utterly be contemned.
8:7

6 Though your sins be as scarlet, they shall be as white as snow.
Isaiah 1:18

7 They shall beat their swords into plowshares, and their spears into pruninghooks: nation shall not lift up sword against nation, neither shall they learn war any more.
2:4

8 What mean ye that ye beat my people to pieces, and grind the faces of the poor?
3:15

9 Woe unto them that join house to house, that lay field to field, till there be no place.
5:8

10 Woe unto them that rise up early in the morning, that they may follow strong drink.
11

11 Woe unto them that call evil good, and good evil.
20

12 In the year that king Uzziah died I saw also the Lord sitting upon a throne, high and lifted up, and his train filled the temple.

Above it stood the seraphims: each one had six wings; with twain he covered his face, and with twain he covered his feet and with twain he did fly.
And one cried unto another, and said, Holy, holy, holy, is the Lord of hosts: the whole earth is full of his glory.
6:1

13 Then said I, Woe is me! for I am undone; because I am a man of unclean lips, and I dwell in the midst of a people of unclean lips.
5

14 Whom shall I send, and who will go for us? Then said I, Here am I; send me.
8

15 Then said I, Lord, how long?
11

16 Behold, a virgin shall conceive, and bear a son, and shall call his name Immanuel.
7:14

17 Wizards that peep and that mutter.
8:19

18 The people that walked in darkness have seen a great light.
9:2

19 For unto us a child is born, unto us a son is given: and the government shall be upon his shoulder: and his name shall be called Wonderful, Counsellor, The mighty God, The everlasting Father, The Prince of Peace.
6

20 And there shall come forth a rod out of the stem of Jesse, and a Branch shall grow out of his roots.
11:1

21 The wolf also shall dwell with the lamb, and the leopard shall lie down with the kid; and the calf and the young lion and the fatling together; and a little child shall lead them.
6

22 Dragons in their pleasant palaces.
13:22

23 How art thou fallen from heaven, O Lucifer, son of the morning!
14:12

24 Watchman, what of the night? Watchman, what of the night?
The watchman said, The morning cometh, and also the night.
21:11

25 Let us eat and drink; for to morrow we

shall die.
22:13. See 27:12 and 1 Cor. 15:32

For precept must be upon precept, precept upon precept; line upon line, line upon line; here a little, and there a little.
28:10

2 We have made a covenant with death, and with hell are we at agreement.
1f

3 The bread of adversity, and the waters of affliction.
30:20

4 This is the way, walk ye in it.
21

5 The desert shall rejoice, and blossom as the rose.
35:1

6 Sorrow and sighing shall flee away.
10

7 Set thine house in order: for thou shalt die, and not live.
38:1

8 Comfort ye, comfort ye my people, saith your God.
Speak ye comfortably to Jerusalem, and cry unto her, that her warfare is accomplished.
40:1

9 Every valley shall be exalted, and every mountain and hill shall be made low: and the crooked shall be made straight, and the rough places plain:
And the glory of the Lord shall be revealed, and all flesh shall see it together: for the mouth of the Lord hath spoken it.
4

10 He shall feed his flock like a shepherd: he shall gather the lambs with his arm, and carry them in his bosom, and shall gently lead those that are with young.
11

11 There is no peace, saith the Lord, unto the wicked.
48:22

12 How beautiful upon the mountains are the feet of him that bringeth good tidings, that publisheth peace; that bringeth good tidings of good, that publisheth salvation; that saith unto Zion, Thy God reigneth!
52:7

13 For they shall see eye to eye, when the Lord shall bring again Zion.
8

14 He is despised and rejected of men; a man of sorrows, and acquainted with grief: and we hid as it were our faces from him; he was despised, and we esteemed him not.
Surely he hath borne our griefs, and carried our sorrows.
53:3

15 But he was wounded for our transgressions, he was bruised for our iniquities: the chastisement of our peace was upon him; and with his stripes we are healed.
All we like sheep have gone astray; we have turned every one to his own way; and the Lord hath laid on him the iniquity of us all.
5

16 He is brought as a lamb to the slaughter.
7

17 Seek ye the Lord while he may be found, call ye upon him while he is near.
55:6

18 For my thoughts are not your thoughts, neither are your ways my ways, saith the Lord.
8

19 Peace to him that is far off, and to him that is near.
57:19

20 To bind up the brokenhearted, to proclaim liberty to the captives, and the opening of the prison to them that are bound.
61:1

21 Who is this that cometh from Edom, with dyed garments from Bozrah?
63:1

22 Stand by thyself, come not near to me; for I am holier than thou.
65:5

23 For, behold, I create new heavens and a new earth.
17

24 Saying, Peace, peace; when there is no peace.
Jeremiah 6:14

25 Is there no balm in Gilead?
8:22

26 Can the Ethiopian change his skin, or the leopard his spots?
13:23

27 The heart is deceitful above all things, and desperately wicked.
17:9

28 Is it nothing to you, all ye that pass by? behold, and see if there be any sorrow like

unto my sorrow.
Lamentations 1:12

1 The wormwood and the gall.
3:19

2 It is good for a man that he bear the yoke in his youth.
27

3 As is the mother, so is her daughter.
Ezekiel 16:44

4 The fathers have eaten sour grapes, and the children's teeth are set on edge.
18:2

5 When the wicked man turneth away from his wickedness that he hath committed, and doeth that which is lawful and right, he shall save his soul alive.
27

6 The valley which was full of bones.
37:1

7 Can these bones live?
3

8 Cast into the midst of a burning fiery furnace.
Daniel 3:6

9 And this is the writing that was written, MENE, MENE, TEKEL, UPHARSIN. This is the interpretation of the thing: MENE; God hath numbered thy kingdom, and finished it.
TEKEL; Thou art weighed in the balances and art found wanting.
PERES; Thy kingdom is divided, and given to the Medes and Persians.
5:25

10 Now, O king, establish the decree, and sign the writing, that it be not changed, according to the law of the Medes and Persians, which altereth not.
6:8

11 The Ancient of days did sit, whose garment was white as snow, and the hair of his head like the pure wool.
7:9

12 They have sown the wind, and they shall reap the whirlwind.
Hosea 8:7

13 I will restore to you the years that the locust hath eaten, the cankerworm, and the caterpillar, and the palmerworm.
Joel 2:25

14 Your sons and your daughters shall prophesy, your old men shall dream dreams, your young men shall see visions.
28

15 Beat your plowshares into swords, an your pruninghooks into spears.
3:10

16 Multitudes, multitudes in the valley of d cision.
14

17 They shall sit every man under his vin and under his fig tree.
Micah 4:4

18 But thou, Beth-lehem Ephratah, thoug thou be little among the thousands of Ju dah, yet out of thee shall he come fort unto me that is to be ruler in Israel.
5:2

19 What doth the Lord require of thee, but t do justly, and to love mercy, and to wal humbly with thy God?
6:8

APOCRYPHA

20 I shall light a candle of understanding i thine heart, which shall not be put out.
2 Esdras 14:25

21 We will fall into the hands of the Lor and not into the hands of men: for as h majesty is, so is his mercy.
Ecclesiasticus 2:18

22 Judge none blessed before his death.
11:28

23 He that toucheth pitch shall be defile therewith.
13:1

24 Leave off first for manners' sake.
31:17

25 Wine is as good as life to a man, if it b drunk moderately: what life is then to man that is without wine? for it was mad to make men glad.
27

26 He that sinneth before his Maker, Let hir fall into the hand of the physician.
38:15

27 Let us now praise famous men, and ou fathers that begat us.
44:1

28 And some there be, which have no me morial.
9

29 Their name liveth for evermore.
14

30 When he was at the last gasp.
2 Maccabees 7:9

NEW TESTAMENT

1 There came wise men from the east to
Jerusalem,
Saying, Where is he that is born King of
the Jews? for we have seen his star in the
east, and are come to worship him.
St. Matthew 2:1

2 They presented unto him gifts; gold, and
frankincense, and myrrh.
11

3 Repent ye: for the kingdom of heaven is at
hand.
3:2

4 The voice of one crying in the wilderness,
Prepare ye the way of the Lord, make his
paths straight.
3. See Isaiah 40:3

5 O generation of vipers, who hath warned
you to flee from the wrath to come?
7

6 And now also the axe is laid unto the root
of the trees.
10

7 This is my beloved Son, in whom I am well
pleased.
17

8 Man shall not live by bread alone, but by
every word that proceedeth out of the
mouth of God.
4:4. See Deut. 8:3

9 Thou shalt not tempt the Lord thy God.
7 and Deut. 6:16

10 [Jesus] saith unto them, Follow me, and I
will make you fishers of men.
19

11 Blessed are the poor in spirit: for theirs is
the kingdom of heaven.
Blessed are they that mourn: for they shall
be comforted.
Blessed are the meek: for they shall inherit
the earth.
Blessed are they which do hunger and
thirst after righteousness: for they shall be
filled.
Blessed are the merciful: for they shall obtain mercy.
Blessed are the pure in heart: for they shall
see God.
Blessed are the peacemakers: for they shall
be called the children of God.
5:3

12 Ye are the salt of the earth: but if the salt
have lost his savour, wherewith shall it be
salted?
13

13 Ye are the light of the world. A city that is
set on an hill cannot be hid.
14

14 Let your light so shine before men, that
they may see your good works.
16

15 Think not that I am come to destroy the
law, or the prophets: I am come not to
destroy, but to fulfil.
17

16 Let your communication be Yea, yea;
Nay, nay.
37

17 Resist not evil: but whosoever shall smite
thee on thy right cheek, turn to him the
other also.
39

18 He maketh his sun to rise on the evil and
on the good, and sendeth rain on the just
and on the unjust.
45

19 Be ye therefore perfect, even as your
Father which is in heaven is perfect.
48

20 When thou doest alms, let not thy left
hand know what thy right hand doeth.
6:3

21 After this manner therefore pray ye: Our
Father which art in heaven, Hallowed be
thy name.
Thy kingdom come. Thy will be done in
earth, as it is in heaven.
Give us this day our daily bread.
And forgive us our debts, as we forgive our
debtors.
And lead us not into temptation, but deliver us from evil: For thine is the kingdom,
and the power, and the glory, for ever.
Amen.
9 and Luke 11:2

22 Lay not up for yourselves treasures upon
earth, where moth and rust doth corrupt,
and where thieves break through and steal:
But lay up for yourselves treasures in
heaven.
19

23 Where your treasure is, there will your
heart be also.
21

24 No man can serve two masters...Ye cannot serve God and mammon.
24

25 Consider the lilies of the field, how they
grow; they toil not, neither do they spin:
And yet I say unto you, That even Solomon in all his glory was not arrayed like

one of these.
28

1 Take therefore no thought for the morrow: for the morrow shall take thought for the things of itself. Sufficient unto the day is the evil thereof.
34

2 Judge not, that ye be not judged.
7:1. See Luke 6:37

3 Why beholdest thou the mote that is in thy brother's eye, but considerest not the beam that is in thine own eye?
3

4 Neither cast ye your pearls before swine.
6

5 Ask, and it shall be given you; seek, and ye shall find; knock, and it shall be opened unto you.
7

6 Or what man is there of you, whom if his son ask bread, will he give him a stone?
9

7 Therefore all things whatsoever ye would that men should do to you, do ye even so to them: for this is the law and the prophets.
12

8 Wide is the gate, and broad is the way, that leadeth to destruction, and many there be that go in thereat.
13

9 Strait is the gate, and narrow is the way, which leadeth unto life, and few there be that find it.
14

10 Beware of false prophets, which come to you in sheep's clothing, but inwardly they are ravening wolves.
15

11 Do men gather grapes of thorns, or figs of thistles?
16

12 By their fruits ye shall know them.
20

13 Every one that heareth these sayings of mine, and doeth them not, shall be likened unto a foolish man, which built his house upon the sand:
And the rain descended, and the floods came, and the winds blew, and beat upon that house; and it fell: and great was the fall of it.
27

14 I am a man under authority, having soldiers under me: and I say to this man, Go,
and he goeth; and to another, Come, and he cometh; and to my servant, Do this and he doeth it.
8:9

15 But the children of the kingdom shall be cast out into outer darkness: there shall be weeping and gnashing of teeth.
12

16 The foxes have holes, and the birds of the air have nests; but the Son of man hath not where to lay his head.
20

17 Let the dead bury their dead.
22

18 Why eateth your Master with publicans and sinners?
9:11

19 I am not come to call the righteous, but sinners to repentance.
13

20 Neither do men put new wine into old bottles.
17

21 Thy faith hath made thee whole.
22

22 The maid is not dead, but sleepeth.
24

23 When ye depart out of that house or city, shake off the dust of your feet.
10:14

24 Be ye therefore wise as serpents, and harmless as doves.
16

25 Are not two sparrows sold for a farthing? and one of them shall not fall on the ground without your Father.
29. See 35:19

26 The very hairs of your head are all numbered.
30

27 I came not to send peace, but a sword.
34

28 He that findeth his life shall lose it: and he that loseth his life for my sake shall find it.
39

29 Whosoever shall give to drink unto one of these little ones a cup of cold water only in the name of a disciple, verily I say unto you, he shall in no wise lose his reward.
42

30 What went ye out into the wilderness to see? A reed shaken with the wind?
11:7

31 Come unto me, all ye that labour and are

heavy laden, and I will give you rest.
28

1 For my yoke is easy, and my burden is light.
30

2 He that is not with me is against me.
12:30 and Luke 11:23

3 He findeth it empty, swept, and garnished.
44

4 Some seeds fell by the wayside.
13:4

5 An enemy hath done this.
28

6 The kingdom of heaven is like to a grain of mustard seed.
31

7 One pearl of great price.
46

8 A prophet is not without honour, save in his own country, and in his own house.
57

9 They be blind leaders of the blind. And if the blind lead the blind, both shall fall into the ditch.
15:14

10 The dogs eat of the crumbs which fall from their masters' table.
27

11 The signs of the times.
16:3

12 Thou art Peter, and upon this rock I will build my church; and the gates of hell shall not prevail against it.
18

13 Get thee behind me, Satan.
23

14 What is a man profited, if he shall gain the whole world, and lose his own soul?
26 and Mark 8:36

15 Except ye be converted, and become as little children, ye shall not enter into the kingdom of heaven.
18:3

16 Whoso shall offend one of these little ones which believe in me, it were better for him that a millstone were hanged abut his neck, and that he were drowned in the depth of the sea.
6

17 If thine eye offend thee, pluck it out, and cast it from thee.
9

18 For where two or three are gathered together in my name, there am I in the midst of them.
20

19 Lord, how oft shall my brother sin against me, and I forgive him? till seven times?
Jesus saith unto him I say not unto thee, Until seven times: but Until seventy times seven. [To Peter.]
21

20 What therefore God hath joined together, let not man put asunder.
19:6

21 If thou wilt be perfect, go and sell that thou hast, and give to the poor, and thou shalt have treasure in heaven.
21

22 It is easier for a camel to go through the eye of a needle, than for a rich man to enter into the kingdom of God.
24

23 With men this is impossible; but with God all things are possible.
26

24 But many that are first shall be last; and the last shall be first.
30

25 Which have borne the burden and heat of the day.
20:12

26 It is written, My house shall be called the house of prayer; but ye have made it a den of thieves.
21:13 and Is. 56:7

27 For many are called, but few are chosen.
22:14

28 Render therefore unto Caesar the things which are Caesar's; and unto God the things that are God's.
21

29 For in the resurrection they neither marry, nor are given in marriage.
30

30 Blind guides, which strain at a gnat, and swallow a camel.
23:24

31 Ye are like unto whited sepulchres, which indeed appear beautiful outward, but are within full of dead men's bones, and of all uncleanness.
27

32 Ye shall hear of wars and rumours of wars.
24:6

33 For nation shall rise against nation, and

kingdom against kingdom.
7

1 The abomination of desolation.
15 and Dan. 12:11

2 Wheresoever the carcase is, there will the eagles be gathered together.
28

3 Heaven and earth shall pass away, but my words shall not pass away.
35

4 Watch therefore: for ye know not what hour your Lord doth come.
42

5 Well done, thou good and faithful servant.
25:21

6 Unto every one that hath shall be given, and he shall have abundance: but from him that hath not shall be taken away even that which he hath.
29

7 And he shall set the sheep on his right hand, but the goats on the left.
33

8 For I was an hungred, and ye gave me meat: I was thirsty and ye gave me drink: I was a stranger, and ye took me in:
Naked, and ye clothed me: I was sick, and ye visited me: I was in prison, and ye came unto me.
35

9 Inasmuch as ye have done it unto one of the least of these my brethren, ye have done it unto me.
40

10 What will ye give me, and I will deliver him unto you? And they covenanted with him for thirty pieces of silver.
26:15

11 Jesus took bread, and blessed it, and brake it, and gave it to the disciples, and said, Take, eat; this is my body.
26

12 This night, before the cock crow, thou shalt deny me thrice.
34

13 If it be possible, let this cup pass from me.
39

14 What, could ye not watch with me one hour?
40

15 Watch and pray, that ye enter not into temptation: the spirit indeed is willing but

the flesh is weak.
41

16 All they that take the sword shall perish with the sword.
52

17 He saved others; himself he cannot save.
27:42

18 Eli, Eli, lama sabachthani?...My God, my God, why hast thou forsaken me?
46. See Psalms 22:1

19 And, lo, I am with you alway, even unto the end of the world.
28:20

20 The sabbath was made for man, and not man for the sabbath.
St. Mark 2:27

21 If a house be divided against itself, that house cannot stand.
3:25

22 He that hath ears to hear, let him hear.
4:9

23 My name is Legion: for we are many.
5:9

24 Clothed, and in his right mind.
15

25 Lord, I believe; help thou mine unbelief.
9:24

26 Suffer the little children to come unto me, and forbid them not: for of such is the kingdom of God.
10:14

27 Hail, thou art highly favoured, the Lord is with thee: blessed art thou among women.
St. Luke 1:28

28 My soul doth magnify the Lord,
And my spirit hath rejoiced in God my Saviour.
For he hath regarded the low estate of his handmaiden: for, behold, from henceforth all generations shall call me blessed.
46

29 He hath shewed strength with his arm; he hath scattered the proud in the imagination of their hearts.
He hath put down the mighty from their seats, and exalted them of low degree.
He hath filled the hungry with good things; and the rich he hath sent empty away.
51

30 To give light to them that sit in darkness and in the shadow of death, to guide our feet into the way of peace.
79

1 She brought forth her firstborn son, and wrapped him in swaddling clothes, and laid him in a manger; because there was no room for them in the inn.
And there were in the same country shepherds abiding in the field, keeping watch over their flock by night.
And, lo, the angel of the Lord came upon them, and the glory of the Lord shone round about them: and they were sore afraid.
2:7

2 Behold, I bring you good tidings of great joy.
10

3 Glory to God in the highest, and on earth peace, good will toward men.
14

4 Lord, now lettest thou thy servant depart in peace, according to thy word.
29

5 Wist ye not that I must be about my Father's business?
49

6 Physician, heal thyself.
4:23

7 Love your enemies, do good to them which hate you.
6:27

8 Give, and it shall be given unto you; good measure, pressed down, and shaken together, and running over, shall men give into your bosom.
38

9 Her sins, which are many, are forgiven; for she loved much.
7:47

10 No man, having put his hand to the plough, and looking back, is fit for the kingdom of God.
9:62

11 For the labourer is worthy of his hire.
10:7

12 A certain man went down from Jerusalem to Jericho, and fell among thieves.
30

13 He passed by on the other side.
31

14 Go, and do thou likewise.
37

15 But Martha was cumbered about much serving.
40

16 He taketh from him all his armour where-in he trusted, and divideth his spoils.
11:22

17 No man, when he hath lighted a candle, putteth it in a secret place, neither under a bushel.
33

18 Woe unto you, lawyers! for ye have taken away the key of knowledge.
52

19 Are not five sparrows sold for two farthings, and not one of them is forgotten before God?
12:6. See 32:25

20 Thou fool, this night thy soul shall be required of thee.
20

21 Friend, go up higher.
14:10

22 For whosoever exalteth himself shall be abased; and he that humbleth himself shall be exalted.
11 and Matt. 23:12

23 Bring in hither the poor, and the maimed, and the halt, and the blind.
21

24 Rejoice with me; for I have found my sheep which was lost.
15:6

25 Joy shall be in heaven over one sinner that repenteth, more than over ninety and nine just persons, which need no repentance.
7

26 Wasted his substance with riotous living.
13

27 I will arise and go to my father, and will say unto him, Father, I have sinned against heaven, and before thee,
And am no more worthy to be called thy son.
18

28 Bring hither the fatted calf, and kill it.
23

29 This my son was dead, and is alive again; he was lost, and is found.
24

30 I cannot dig; to beg I am ashamed.
16:3

31 The crumbs which fell from the rich man's table.
21

32 And it came to pass that the beggar died, and was carried by the angels into Abraham's bosom.
22

1 Between us and you there is a great gulf fixed.
26

2 It were better for him that a millstone were hanged about his neck, and he cast into the sea.
17:2

3 The kingdom of God is within you.
21

4 God, I thank thee, that I am not as other men are.
18:11

5 God be merciful to me a sinner.
13

6 In your patience possess ye your souls.
21:19

7 Nevertheless, not my will, but thine, be done.
22:42

8 Father, forgive them: for they know not what they do.
23:34

9 Lord, remember me when thou comest into thy kingdom.
42

10 To day shalt thou be with me in paradise.
43

11 Father, into thy hands I commend my spirit.
46. See Psalms 31:6

12 In the beginning was the Word, and the Word was with God, and the Word was God.
St. John 1:1

13 And the light shineth in darkness; and the darkness comprehended it not.
5

14 That was the true Light, which lighteth every man that cometh into the world.
9

15 He came unto his own, and his own received him not.
11

16 And the Word was made flesh, and dwelt among us.
14

17 He it is, who coming after me is preferred before me, whose shoe's latchet I am not worthy to unloose.
27

18 Behold the Lamb of God, which taketh away the sin of the world.
29

19 Woman, what have I to do with thee? mine hour is not yet come.
2:4

20 The wind bloweth where it listeth, and thou hearest the sound thereof, but canst not tell whence it cometh, and whither it goeth.
3:8

21 God so loved the world, that he gave his only begotten Son, that whosoever believeth in him should not perish, but have everlasting life.
16

22 Rise, take up thy bed, and walk.
5:8

23 Him that cometh to me I will in no wise cast out.
6:37

24 Verily, verily, I say unto you, He that believeth on me hath everlasting life.
47

25 And the scribes and the Pharisees brought unto him a woman taken in adultery.
8:3

26 He that is without sin among you, let him first cast a stone at her.
7

27 Neither do I condemn thee: go, and sin no more.
11

28 And ye shall know the truth, and the truth shall make you free.
32

29 There is no truth in him. When he speaketh a lie, he speaketh of his own: for he is a liar, and the father of it.
44

30 The night cometh, when no man can work.
9:4

31 I am the good shepherd: the good shepherd giveth his life for the sheep.
10:11

32 I am the resurrection, and the life.
11:25

33 Jesus wept.
35

34 It is expedient for us, that one man should die for the people, and that the whole nation perish not.
50

35 The poor always ye have with you.
12:8

36 Let not your heart be troubled: ye believe

in God, believe also in me.
14:1

1 In my Father's house are many mansions...I go to prepare a place for you.
2

2 I am the way, the truth, and the life: no man cometh unto the Father, but by me.
6

3 Greater love hath no man than this, that a man lay down his life for his friends.
15:13

4 Pilate saith unto him, What is truth?
18:38

5 Now Barabbas was a robber.
40

6 What I have written I have written.
19:22

7 Woman, behold thy son!...
Behold thy mother!
26

8 It is finished.
30

9 They have taken away my Lord, and I know not where they have laid him.
20:13

10 Touch me not.
17. See 41:24

11 Blessed are they that have not seen, and yet have believed.
29

12 And suddenly there came a sound from heaven as of a rushing mighty wind.
Acts of the Apostles 2:2

13 Silver and gold have I none; but such as I have give I thee.
3:6

14 Walking, and leaping, and praising God.
8

15 Breathing out threatenings and slaughter.
9:1

16 Saul, Saul, why persecutest thou me?
4

17 It is hard for thee to kick against the pricks.
5

18 God is no respecter of persons.
10:34. See Romans 2:11

19 Come over into Macedonia, and help us.
16:9

20 What must I do to be saved?
30

21 Certain lewd fellows of the baser sort.
17:5

22 Those that have turned the world upside down.
6

23 I found an altar with this inscription, TO THE UNKNOWN GOD.
23

24 For in him we live, and move, and have our being.
28

25 All with one voice about the space of two hours cried out, Great is Diana of the Ephesians.
19:34

26 It is more blessed to give than to receive.
20:35

27 But Paul said, I am a man which am a Jew of Tarsus, a city in Cilicia, a citizen of no mean city.
21:39

28 Hast thou appealed unto Caesar? unto Caesar shalt thou go.
25:12

29 Paul, thou art beside thyself; much learning doth make thee mad.
26:24

30 Almost thou persuadest me to be a Christian.
28

31 The just shall live by faith.
Romans 1:17

32 Let us do evil, that good may come.
3:8

33 Who against hope believed in hope.
4:18

34 Shall we continue in sin, that grace may abound?
6:1

35 Christ being raised from the dead dieth no more; death hath no more dominion over him.
9

36 The wages of sin is death.
23

37 For the good that I would I do not: but the evil which I would not, that I do.
7:19. See 178:22

38 All things work for good to them that love God.
8:28

39 For I am persuaded, that neither death, nor life, nor angels, nor principalities, nor

powers, nor things present, nor things to come,

Nor height, nor depth, nor any other creature, shall be able to separate us from the love of God, which is in Christ Jesus our Lord.
38

1 I beseech you therefore, brethren, by the mercies of God, that ye present your bodies a living sacrifice, holy, acceptable unto God.
12:1

2 Vengeance is mine; I will repay, saith the Lord.
19

3 Be not overcome of evil, but overcome evil with good.
21

4 Let every soul be subject unto the higher powers...the powers that be are ordained of God.
13:1

5 Let us therefore cast off the works of darkness, and let us put on the armour of light.
12

6 Doubtful disputations.
14:1

7 Salute one another with an holy kiss.
16:16

8 Your body is the temple of the Holy Ghost.
1 Corinthians 6:19

9 It is better to marry than to burn.
7:9

10 I am made all things to all men.
9:22

11 All things are lawful for me, but all things are not expedient.
10:23

12 For the earth is the Lord's, and the fulness thereof.
26. See Psalms 24:1

13 Doth not even nature itself teach you, that, if a man have long hair, it is a shame unto him?
But if a woman have long hair, it is a glory to her.
11:14

14 Though I speak with the tongues of men and of angels, and have not charity, I am become as sounding brass, or a tinkling cymbal.
And though I have the gift of prophecy, and understand all mysteries, and all knowledge; and though I have all faith, so that I could remove mountains, and have not charity, I am nothing.
13:1

15 Charity suffereth long, and is kind; charity envieth not; charity vaunteth not itself, is not puffed up,
Doth not behave itself unseemly, seeketh not her own, is not easily provoked, thinketh no evil;
Rejoiceth not in iniquity, but rejoiceth in the truth;
Beareth all things, believeth all things, hopeth all things, endureth all things.
Charity never faileth: but whether there be prophecies, they shall fail; whether there be tongues, they shall cease; whether there be knowledge, it shall vanish away.
For we know in part, and we prophesy in part.
4

16 When I was a child, I spake as a child, I understood as a child, I thought as a child: but when I became a man, I put away childish things.
For now we see through a glass, darkly; but then face to face: now I know in part; but then shall I know even as also I am known.
And now abideth faith, hope, charity, these three; but the greatest of these is charity.
11

17 Let all things be done decently and in order.
14:40

18 But now is Christ risen from the dead, and become the firstfruits of them that slept.
15:20

19 The last enemy that shall be destroyed is death.
26

20 Evil communications corrupt good manners.
33

21 The first man is of the earth, earthy.
47

22 Behold, I shew you a mystery; We shall not all sleep, but we shall all be changed,
In a moment, in the twinkling of an eye, at the last trump: for the trumpet shall sound, and the dead shall be raised incorruptible, and we shall be changed.
51

23 O death, where is thy sting? O grave,

where is thy victory?
55

1 Quit you like men, be strong.
16:13

2 The letter killeth, but the spirit giveth life.
2 Corinthians 3:6

3 We have a building of God, a house not made with hands, eternal in the heavens.
5:1

4 God loveth a cheerful giver.
9:7

5 For ye suffer fools gladly, seeing ye yourselves are wise.
19

6 There was given to me a thorn in the flesh, the messenger of Satan to buffet me.
12:7

7 The right hands of fellowship.
Galatians 2:9

8 Ye are fallen from grace.
5:4

9 Be not deceived; God is not mocked: for whatsoever a man soweth, that shall he also reap.
6:7

10 Ye see how large a letter I have written unto you with mine own hand.
11

11 That we henceforth be no more carried about with every wind of doctrine.
Ephesians 4:14

12 We are members one of another.
25

13 Be ye angry and sin not: let not the sun go down upon your wrath.
26

14 Put on the whole armour of God.
6:11

15 For we wrestle not against flesh and blood, but against principalities, against powers, against the rulers of the darkness of this world, against spiritual wickedness in high places.
Wherefore take unto you the whole armour of God, that ye may be able to withstand in the evil day, and having done all, to stand.
Stand therefore, having your loins girt about with truth, and having on the breastplate of righteousness.
12

16 God hath also highly exalted him, and given him a name which is above every name:

That at the name of Jesus every knee should bow.
Philippians 2:9

17 Work out your own salvation with fear and trembling.
12

18 Rejoice in the Lord alway: and again I say, Rejoice.
1:1

19 The peace of God, which passeth all understanding, shall keep your hearts and minds through Christ Jesus.
7

20 Whatsoever things are true, whatsoever things are honest, whatsoever things are just, whatsoever things are pure, whatsoever things are lovely, whatsoever things are of good report; if there be any virtue and if there be any praise, think on these things.
8

21 I can do all things through Christ which strengtheneth me.
13

22 Luke, the beloved physician, and Demas, greet you.
Colossians 4:14

23 Remembering without ceasing your work of faith and labour of love.
1 Thessalonians 1:3

24 Prove all things; hold fast that which is good.
5:21

25 If any would not work, neither should he eat.
2 Thessalonians 3:10

26 Let the woman learn in silence with all subjection.
But I suffer not a woman to teach, nor to usurp authority over the man, but to be in silence.
1 Timothy 2:11

27 Not given to wine, no striker, not greedy of filthy lucre; but patient, not a brawler, not covetous.
3:3

28 Refuse profane and old wives' fables.
4:7

29 Drink no longer water, but use a little wine for thy stomach's sake and thine often infirmities.
5:23

30 For we brought nothing into this world,

and it is certain we can carry nothing out.
6:7

1 The love of money is the root of all evil.
10

2 Fight the good fight of faith, lay hold on eternal life.
12

3 Rich in good works.
18

4 I have fought a good fight, I have finished my course, I have kept the faith.
2 Timothy 4:7

5 Unto the pure all things are pure.
Titus 1:15

6 Without shedding of blood is no remission.
Hebrews 9:22

7 It is a fearful thing to fall into the hands of the living God.
10:31

8 Faith is the substance of things hoped for, the evidence of things not seen.
11:1

9 Wherefore seeing we also are compassed about with so great a cloud of witnesses, let us lay aside every weight, and the sin which doth so easily beset us, and let us run with patience the race that is set before us,
Looking unto Jesus the author and finisher of our faith.
12:1

10 Whom the Lord loveth he chasteneth.
6

11 Be not forgetful to entertain strangers: for thereby some have entertained angels unawares.
13:2

12 Jesus Christ the same yesterday, and to day, and for ever.
8

13 For here have we no continuing city, but we seek one to come.
14

14 Faith without works is dead.
James 2:20

15 Ye have heard of the patience of Job.
5:11

16 Let your yea be yea; and your nay, nay.
12

17 All flesh is as grass, and all the glory of man as the flower of grass. The grass withereth, and the flower thereof falleth away.
1 Peter 1:24. See Isaiah 40:6

18 But ye are a chosen generation, a royal priesthood, an holy nation, a peculiar people.
2:9

19 Honour all men. Love the brotherhood. Fear God. Honour the king.
17

20 Giving honour unto the wife, as unto the weaker vessel.
3:7

21 Charity shall cover the multitude of sins.
4:8

22 Be sober, be vigilant; because your adversary the devil, as a roaring lion, walketh about, seeking whom he may devour.
5:8

23 The dog is turned to his own vomit again.
2 Peter 2:22

24 If we say that we have no sin, we deceive ourselves, and the truth is not in us.
1 John 1:8

25 He that loveth not knoweth not God; for God is love.
4:8

26 There is no fear in love; but perfect love casteth out fear.
18

27 If a man say, I love God, and hateth his brother, he is a liar: for he that loveth not his brother whom he hath seen, how can he love God whom he hath not seen?
20

28 I am Alpha and Omega, the beginning and the ending, saith the Lord.
Revelation 1:8

29 Be thou faithful unto death, and I will give thee a crown of life.
2:10

30 Behold, I stand at the door, and knock.
3:20

31 Holy, holy, holy, Lord God Almighty which was, and is, and is to come.
4:8

32 And I looked, and behold a pale horse: and his name that sat on him was Death.
6:8

33 God shall wipe away all tears from their eyes.
7:17

34 And when he had opened the seventh seal, there was silence in heaven about the space

of half an hour.
8:1

1 And there were stings in their tails.
9:10

2 And that no man might buy or sell, save he that had the mark, or the name of the beast, or the number of his name.
13:17

3 Let him that hath understanding count the number of the beast: for it is the number of a man; and his number is Six hundred threescore and six.
18

4 Babylon is fallen, is fallen, that great city.
14:8

5 MYSTERY, BABYLON THE GREAT, THE MOTHER OF HARLOTS AND ABOMINATIONS OF THE EARTH.
17:5

6 And the sea gave up the dead which were in it.
20:13

7 And I saw a new heaven and a new earth: for the first heaven and the first earth were passed away; and there was no more sea.
21:1

8 And God shall wipe away all tears from their eyes; and there shall be no more death, neither sorrow, nor crying, neither shall there be any more pain: for the former things are passed away.
4

9 I will give unto him that is athirst of the fountain of the water of life freely.
6

10 Amen. Even so, come, Lord Jesus.
22:20

VULGATE

11 *Dominus illuminatio mea, et salus mea, quem timebo?*
The Lord is the source of my light and my safety, so whom shall I fear?
Psalm 26:1 (A.V. Psalm 27:1)

12 *Asperges me hyssopo, et mundabor; lavabis me, et super nivem dealbabor.*
You will sprinkle me with hyssop, and I shall be made clean; you will wash me and I shall be made whiter than snow.
50:9 (A.V. Psalm 51:7)

13 *Beatus vir qui timet Dominum, in mandatis ejus volet nimis!*
Happy is the man who fears the Lord, who is only too willing to follow his orders.
111:1 (A.V. Psalm 112:1)

14 *Non nobis, Domine, non nobis; sed nomini tuo da gloriam.*
Not unto us, Lord, not unto us; but to thy name give glory.
113:(9) (A.V. Psalm 115:1)

15 *Nisi Dominus aedificaverit domum, in vanum laboraverunt qui aedificant eam.*
Nisi Dominus custodierit civitatem, frustra vigilat qui custodit eam.
Unless the Lord has built the house, its builders have laboured in vain. Unless the Lord guards the city, it's no use its guard staying awake.
126:1 (A.V. Psalm 127:1) [Shortened to *Nisi Dominus frustra* as the motto of the city of Edinburgh.]

16 *De profundis clamavi ad te, Domine; Domine, exaudi vocem meam.*
Up from the depths I have cried to thee, Lord; Lord, hear my voice.
129:1 (A.V. Psalm 130:1)

17 *Vanitas vanitatum, dixit Ecclesiastes; vanitas vanitatum, et omnia vanitas.*
Vanity of vanities, said the preacher; vanity of vanities, and everything is vanity.
Ecclesiastes 1:2

18 *Magnificat anima mea Dominum; Et exsultavit spiritus meus in Deo salutari meo.*
My soul doth magnify the Lord: and my spirit hath rejoiced in God my Saviour. [Tr. Book of Common Prayer]
Ev. S. Luc. 1:46

19 *Nunc dimittis servum tuum, Domine, secundum verbum tuum in pace.*
Lord, now lettest thou thy servant depart in peace: according to thy word. [Tr. Book of Common Prayer]
2:29

20 *Pax Vobis.*
Peace be unto you.
24:36

21 *Quo vadis?*
Where are you going?
Ev. S. Joann. 16:5

22 *Ecce homo.*
Behold the man.
19:5

23 *Consummatum est.*
It is achieved.
30

24 *Noli me tangere.*
Do not touch me.
20:17

25 *Magna est veritas, et praevalet.*

Great is truth, and it prevails.
3 Esdr. 4:41

ISAAC BICKERSTAFFE 1735?-1812?

1 There was a jolly miller once,
    Lived on the river Dee;
  He worked and sang from morn till night;
    No lark more blithe than he.
  Love in a Village (1762), I.v

2 And this the burthen of his song,
    For ever us'd to be,
  I care for nobody, not I,
    If no one cares for me.

3 In every port he finds a wife.
  Thomas and Sally (1761), ii

REVD. E.H. BICKERSTETH 1825-1906

4 Peace, perfect peace, in this dark world of sin?
  The Blood of Jesus whispers peace within.
  Songs in the House of Pilgrimage (1875)

JOSH BILLINGS (HENRY WHEELER SHAW) 1818-1885

5 Thrice is he armed that hath his quarrel just,
  But four times he who gets his blow in fust.
  Josh Billings, his Sayings (1865). See 214:12

LAURENCE BINYON 1869-1943

6 They shall grow not old, as we that are left grow old:
  Age shall not weary them, nor the years condemn.
  At the going down of the sun and in the morning
  We will remember them.
  Poems For the Fallen

EARL OF BIRKENHEAD (F.E. SMITH) 1872-1930

7 We have the highest authority for believing that the meek shall inherit the Earth; though I have never found any particular corroboration of this aphorism in the records of Somerset House.
  Contemporary Personalities (1924). **Marquess Curzon**

8 Nature has no cure for this sort of madness [Bolshevism], though I have known a legacy from a rich relative work wonders.
  Law, Life and Letters (1927), ii. ch.19

9 The world continues to offer glittering prizes to those who have stout hearts and sharp swords.
  Rectorial Address, Glasgow University, 7 Nov. 1923

10 *Judge Willis:* What do you suppose I am on the Bench for, Mr Smith?
  Smith: It is not for me to attempt to fathom the inscrutable workings of Providence.
  Birkenhead, *Frederick Elwin, Earl of Birkenhead* (1933), vol.I, ch.9

PRINCE BISMARCK 1815-1898

11 *Die Politik ist die Lehre von Möglichen.*
  Politics is the art of the possible.
  In conversation with Meyer von Waldeck, 11 Aug. 1867

12 *Die Politik ist keine Wissenschaft...sondern eine Kunst.*
  Politics is not a science...but an art.
  Reichstag, 15 Mar. 1884

13 If there is ever another war in Europe, it will come out of some damned silly thing in the Balkans.
  Said to Herr Ballen 'towards the end of [Bismarck's] life', and related by Ballen to Winston S. Churchill a fortnight before World War I. See *Hansard*, Vol.413, col.84

SIR WILLIAM BLACKSTONE 1723-1780

14 The king never dies.
  Commentaries on the Laws of England, bk.i.7

15 That the king can do no wrong, is a necessary and fundamental principle of the English constitution.
  iii.17

16 It is better that ten guilty persons escape than one innocent suffer.
  iv.27

WILLIAM BLAKE 1757-1827

17 To see a World in a Grain of Sand,
    And a Heaven in a Wild Flower,
  Hold Infinity in the palm of your hand,
    And Eternity in an hour.
  Auguries of Innocence, 1

18 A Robin Redbreast in a Cage
  Puts all Heaven in a Rage.
  5

19 The harlot's cry from street to street
  Shall weave old England's winding sheet.
  115

20 The Vision of Christ that thou dost see
  Is my vision's greatest enemy.
  Thine has a great hook nose like thine,

Mine has a snub nose like to mine.
The Everlasting Gospel, a, l.1

1 I am sure this Jesus will not do,
Either for Englishman or Jew.
f

2 And did those feet in ancient time
Walk upon England's mountains green?
And was the holy Lamb of God
On England's pleasant pastures seen?

And did the Countenance Divine
Shine forth upon our clouded hills?
And was Jerusalem builded here
Among these dark Satanic mills?

Bring me my bow of burning gold!
Bring me my arrows of desire!
Bring me my spear! O clouds, unfold!
Bring me my chariot of fire!

I will not cease from Mental Fight,
Nor shall my Sword sleep in my hand,
Till we have built Jerusalem,
In England's green & pleasant Land.
Milton, preface

3 Mock on, mock on, Voltaire, Rousseau;
Mock on, mock on, 'tis all in vain!
You throw the sand against the wind,
And the wind blows it back again.
MS. Notebooks, 1800-03, p.7

4 [On Cromek]
A petty sneaking knave I knew—
O! Mr Cr—, how do ye do?
1808-11, p.29

5 Great things are done when men and
mountains meet;
This is not done by jostling in the street.
p.43

6 Hear the voice of the Bard!
Who present, past, and future sees.
Songs of Experience, introduction

7 Tyger! Tyger! burning bright
In the forests of the night,
What immortal hand or eye
Could frame thy fearful symmetry?
The Tyger

8 And what shoulder, and what art,
Could twist the sinews of thy heart?
And when thy heart began to beat,
What dread hand? and what dread feet?

9 Did he who made the Lamb make thee?

10 Love seeketh not itself to please,
Nor for itself hath any care,
But for another gives its ease,
And builds a Heaven in Hell's despair.
The Clod and the Pebble

11 Love seeketh only Self to please,
To bind another to its delight,

Joys in another's loss of ease,
And builds a Hell in Heaven's despite.

12 Piping down the valleys wild,
Piping songs of pleasant glee,
On a cloud I saw a child,
And he laughing said to me:

'Pipe a song about a Lamb!'
So I piped with merry cheer.
'Piper, pipe that song again;'
So I piped: he wept to hear.

'Drop thy pipe, thy happy pipe;
Sing thy songs of happy cheer:'
So I sang the same again,
While he wept with joy to hear.
Songs of Innocence, introduction

13 And I wrote my happy songs
Every child may joy to hear.

14 Little Lamb, who made thee?
Dost thou know who made thee?
The Lamb

15 My mother bore me in the southern wild,
And I am black, but O! my soul is white;
White as an angel is the English child,
But I am black, as if bereav'd of light.
The Little Black Boy

16 When the voices of children are heard on
the green,
And laughing is heard on the hill.
Nurse's Song

17 When my mother died I was very young,
And my father sold me while yet my
tongue
Could scarcely cry, "weep! 'weep! 'weep!
'weep!'
So your chimneys I sweep, and in soot I
sleep.
The Chimney Sweeper

18 To Mercy, Pity, Peace, and Love
All pray in their distress.
The Divine Image

19 For Mercy has a human heart,
Pity a human face,
And Love, the human form divine,
And Peace, the human dress.

20 Can I see another's woe,
And not be in sorrow too?
Can I see another's grief,
And not seek for kind relief?
On Another's Sorrow

21 Energy is Eternal Delight.
The Marriage of Heaven and Hell: **The Voice of
the Devil**

22 The reason Milton wrote in fetters when
he wrote of Angels and God, and at liberty
when of Devils and Hell, is because he was

a true Poet, and of the Devil's party without knowing it.
(note)

1 The road of excess leads to the palace of wisdom.
Proverbs of Hell

2 A fool sees not the same tree that a wise man sees.

3 Eternity is in love with the productions of time.

4 If the fool would persist in his folly he would become wise.

5 The tigers of wrath are wiser than the horses of instruction.

6 Damn braces. Bless relaxes.

7 Sooner murder an infant in its cradle than nurse unacted desires.

8 I was in a printing house in Hell, and saw the method in which knowledge is transmitted from generation to generation.
A Memorable Fancy, pl.12-13

9 If the doors of perception were cleansed everthing would appear as it is, infinite.
pl.14

LESLEY BLANCH 1907–

10 She was an Amazon. Her whole life was spent riding at breakneck speed along the wilder shores of love.
The Wilder Shores of Love, 2. **Jane Digby El Mezrab**

PHILIP PAUL BLISS 1838–1876

11 Hold the fort, for I am coming.
The Charm. Ho, My Comrades, See the Signal!

EDMUND BLUNDEN 1896–1974

12 I have been young, and now am not too old;
And I have seen the righteous forsaken,
His health, his honour and his quality taken.
    This is not what we formerly were told.
Report on Experience. See 188:23

BOETHIUS c.480–c.524

13 *Nam in omni adversitate fortunae infelicissimum genus est infortunii, fuisse felicem.*
For in every ill-turn of fortune the most unhappy sort of misfortune is to have been happy.
Consolation of Philosophy, bk.ii, prose 4

HUMPHREY BOGART 1899–1957

14 If she can stand it I can. Play it!
Casablanca (1942), script by Julius J. Epstein, Philip G. Epstein, Howard Koch. Often quoted as 'Play it again, Sam.'

JOHN B. BOGART 1845–1921

15 When a dog bites a man that is not news, but when a man bites a dog that is news.
Oral tradition: also attr. Charles Dana and Amos Cummings

HENRY ST. JOHN, VISCOUNT BOLINGBROKE 1678–1751

16 They make truth serve as a stalking-horse to error.
On the Study of History, letter 1

SIR DAVID BONE 1874–1959

17 It's 'Damn you, Jack—I'm all right!' with you chaps.
The Brassbounder (1910), ch.3

DANIEL J. BOORSTIN 1914–

18 The celebrity is a person who is known for his well-knownness.
The Image (1961), ch.2, **From Hero to Celebrity: The Human Pseudo-event**, pt.iii

19 A best-seller was a book which somehow sold well simply because it was selling well.
ch.4, **From Shapes to Shadows: Dissolving Forms**, pt.viii

JORGE LUIS BORGES 1899–

20 *El original es infiel a la traducción.*
The original is unfaithful to the translation (Henley's translation of Beckford's *Vathek*).
Sobre el 'Vathek' de William Beckford

CESARE BORGIA 1476–1507

21 *Aut Caesar, aut nihil.*
Caesar or nothing.
Motto

GEORGE BORROW 1803–1881

22 There's night and day, brother, both sweet things; sun, moon, and stars, brother, all sweet things; there's likewise a wind on the heath. Life is very sweet, brother; who would wish to die?
Lavengro, ch.25

23 Youth will be served, every dog has his

day, and mine has been a fine one.
ch.92

MARÉCHAL BOSQUET 1810–1861

1 *C'est magnifique, mais ce n'est pas la
guerre.*
It is magnificent, but it is not war.
Remark on the charge of the Light Brigade, 1854

JOHN COLLINS BOSSIDY 1860–1928

2 And this is good old Boston,
    The home of the bean and the cod,
Where the Lowells talk only to Cabots,
    And the Cabots talk only to God.
Toast at Holy Cross Alumni dinner, 1910

JACQUES-BÉNIGNE BOSSUET
1627–1704

3 *L'Angleterre, ah, la perfide Angleterre, que
le rempart de ses mers rendoit inaccessible
aux Romains, la foi du Sauveur y est abor-
dée.*
England, ah, faithless England, which the
protection afforded by its seas rendered
inaccessible to the Romans, the faith of the
Saviour spread even there.
*Premier Sermon pour La Fête de la Circoncision
de Notre Seigneur*

JAMES BOSWELL 1740–1795

4 Most vices may be committed very genteelly: a man may debauch his friend's wife
genteelly: he may cheat at cards genteelly.
Life of Johnson, vol.ii, p.340. 6 Apr. 1775

DION BOUCICAULT 1820?–1890

5 Men talk of killing time, while time quietly
kills them.
London Assurance (1841), II.i

**ANTOINE BOULAY
DE LA MEURTHE** 1761–1840

6 *C'est pire qu'un crime, c'est une faute.*
It is worse than a crime, it is a blunder.
On hearing of the execution of the Duc d'En-
ghien, 1804

MATTHEW BOULTON 1728–1809

7 I sell here, Sir, what all the world desires
to have—POWER.
[To Boswell, of his engineering works.]
Boswell, *Life of Johnson*, vol.ii, p.459. 22 Mar.
1776

F.W. BOURDILLON 1852–1921

8 The night has a thousand eyes,
    And the day but one;
Yet the light of the bright world dies,
    With the dying sun.

The mind has a thousand eyes,
    And the heart but one;
Yet the light of a whole life dies,
    When love is done.
Light. See 155:16

LORD BOWEN 1835–1894

9 The rain it raineth on the just
    And also on the unjust fella:
But chiefly on the just, because
    The unjust steals the just's umbrella.
Walter Sichel, *Sands of Time*

10 On a metaphysician: A blind man in a
dark room—looking for a black hat
—which isn't there.
Attr. See N. & Q., clxxxii.153

E.E. BOWEN 1836–1901

11 Forty years on, when afar and asunder
Parted are those who are singing to-day.
Forty Years On. Harrow School Song

12 Follow up! Follow up! Follow up! Follow
up! Follow up!

ELIZABETH BOWEN 1899–1973

13 Art is the only thing that can go on mattering once it has stopped hurting.
The Heat of the Day (1949), ch.16

14 There is no end to the violations committed by children on children, quietly talking
alone.
The House in Paris (1935), pt.I, ch.2

15 Nobody speaks the truth when there's
something they must have.
ch.5

JOHN BRADFORD 1510?–1555

16 But for the grace of God there goes John
Bradford.
D.N.B. Exclamation on seeing some criminals
taken to execution.

F.H. BRADLEY 1846–1924

17 The secret of happiness is to admire without desiring. And that is not happiness.
Aphorisms (1930), 33

ANNE BRADSTREET 1612–1672

1 I am obnoxious to each carping tongue,
Who sayes my hand a needle better fits.
The Prologue

JOHN BRAHAM 1774?–1856

2 England, home and beauty.
The Americans (1811). Song, **The Death of Nelson**

HARRY BRAISTED nineteenth century

3 If you want to win her hand,
Let the maiden understand
That she's not the only pebble on the beach.
You're Not the Only Pebble on the Beach

ERNEST BRAMAH 1868–1942

4 It is a mark of insincerity of purpose to spend one's time in looking for the sacred Emperor in the low-class tea-shops.
The Wallet of Kai Lung. **Transmutation of Ling**

5 However entrancing it is to wander unchecked through a garden of bright images, are we not enticing your mind from another subject of almost equal importance?
Kai Lung's Golden Hours. **Story of Hien**

REVD. JAMES BRAMSTON 1694?–1744

6 What's not destroy'd by Time's devouring hand?
Where's Troy, and where's the Maypole in the Strand?
The Art of Politicks (1729), l.71

RICHARD BRATHWAITE 1588?–1673

7 To Banbury came I, O profane one!
Where I saw a Puritane-one
Hanging of his cat on Monday
For killing of a mouse on Sunday.
Barnabee's Journal (1638), pt.i

BERTOLT BRECHT 1898–1956

8 *Erst kommt das Fressen, dann kommt die Moral.*
First comes fodder, then comes morality.
Die Dreigroschenoper, II, finale

9 Andrea: *Unglücklich das Land, das keine Helden hat!...*
Galileo: *Nein, unglücklich das Land, das Helden nötig hat.*
Andrea: Unhappy the land that has no heroes.

Galileo: No, unhappy the land that needs heroes.
Leben des Galilei, sc.13

NICHOLAS BRETON 1545?–1626?

10 We rise with the lark and go to bed with the lamb.
The Court and Country, par.8

ROBERT BRIDGES 1844–1930

11 I love all beauteous things,
I seek and adore them;
God hath no better praise,
And man in his hasty days
Is honoured for them.
I Love All Beauteous Things

12 When men were all asleep the snow came flying,
In large white flakes falling on the city brown,
Stealthily and perpetually settling and loosely lying,
Hushing the latest traffic of the drowsy town.
London Snow

13 Whither, O splendid ship, thy white sails crowding,
Leaning across the bosom of the urgent West,
That fearest nor sea rising, nor sky clouding,
Whither away, fair rover, and what thy quest?
A Passer-By

JOHN BRIGHT 1811–1889

14 The angel of death has been abroad throughout the land; you may almost hear the beating of his wings.
House of Commons, 23 Feb. 1855

15 I am for 'Peace, retrenchment, and reform', the watchword of the great Liberal party 30 years ago.
Birmingham, 28 Apr. 1859

16 My opinion is that the Northern States will manage somehow to muddle through.
During the American Civil War. Justin McCarthy, *Reminiscences* (1899)

17 England is the mother of Parliaments.
Birmingham, 18 Jan. 1865

ANTHELME BRILLAT-SAVARIN 1755–1826

18 *Dis-moi ce que tu manges, je te dirai ce que tu es.*
Tell me what you eat and I will tell you

what you are.
Physiologie du Goût (1825), **Aphorismes…pour**
servir de prolégomènes… iv. See 98:1

CHARLOTTE BRONTË 1816–1855

1 Reader, I married him.
Jane Eyre, ch.38

EMILY BRONTË 1818–1848

2 No coward soul is mine,
No trembler in the world's storm-troubled
sphere:
I see Heaven's glories shine,
And faith shines equal, arming me from
fear.
Last Lines

3 Cold in the earth—and fifteen wild De-
cembers,
From those brown hills, have melted into
spring.
Remembrance

REVD. PATRICK BRONTË 1777–1861

4 No quailing, Mrs Gaskell! no drawing
back!
About her undertaking to write the life of Charlotte Brontë. Elizabeth Gaskell, letter to Ellen
Nussey, 24 July 1855

RUPERT BROOKE 1887–1915

5 Blow out, you bugles, over the rich Dead!
There's none of these so lonely and poor
of old,
But, dying, has made us rarer gifts than
gold.
These laid the world away; poured out the
red
Sweet wine of youth; gave up the years to
be
Of work and joy, and that unhoped
serene,
That men call age; and those who would
have been,
Their sons, they gave, their immortality.
The Dead

6 The cool kindliness of sheets, that soon
Smooth away trouble; and the rough male
kiss of blankets.
The Great Lover

7 The benison of hot water.

8 One may not doubt that, somehow, good
Shall come of water and of mud;
And, sure, the reverent eye must see
A purpose in liquidity.
Heaven

9 But somewhere, beyond space and time,

Is wetter water, slimier slime!

10 Here tulips bloom as they are told;
Unkempt about those hedges blows
An English unofficial rose.
The Old Vicarage, Grantchester

11 Curates, long dust, will come and go
On lissom, clerical, printless toe;
And oft between the boughs is seen
The sly shade of a Rural Dean.

12 God! I will pack, and take a train,
And get me to England once again!

13 For Cambridge people rarely smile,
Being urban, squat, and packed with guile.

14 Stands the Church clock at ten to three?
And is there honey still for tea?

15 Now, God be thanked Who has matched
us with His hour,
And caught our youth, and wakened us
from sleeping.
Peace

16 If I should die, think only this of me:
That there's some corner of a foreign field
That is for ever England. There shall be
In that rich earth a richer dust concealed;
A dust whom England bore, shaped, made
aware,
Gave, once, her flowers to love, her ways
to roam,
A body of England's, breathing English
air,
Washed by the rivers, blest by suns of
home.
And think, this heart, all evil shed away,
A pulse in the eternal mind, no less
Gives somewhere back the thoughts by
England given.
Her sights and sounds; dreams happy as
her day;
And laughter, learnt of friends; and gentle-
ness,
In hearts at peace, under an English
heaven.
The Soldier

THOMAS BROOKS 1608–1680

17 For *(magna est veritas et praevalebit)*
great is truth, and shall prevail.
The Crown and Glory of Christianity (1662),
p.407. See 41:25

JOHN BROWN 1715–1766

18 Altogether upon the high horse.
Letter to Garrick, 27 Oct. 1765

THOMAS BROWN 1663–1704

1 A little before you made a leap into the dark.
Letters from the Dead. See 120:2

2 I do not love you, Dr Fell,
But why I cannot tell;
But this I know full well,
I do not love you, Dr Fell.
Works (1719), vol.IV, p.113. See 161:8

T.E. BROWN 1830–1897

3 A garden is a lovesome thing, God wot!
My Garden

CECIL BROWNE

4 But not so odd
As those who choose
A Jewish God,
But spurn the Jews.
Reply to 97:9

SIR THOMAS BROWNE 1605–1682

5 Dreams out of the ivory gate, and visions before midnight.
On Dreams

6 There is another man within me, that's angry with me, rebukes, commands, and dastards me.
Religio Medici (1643), pt.i, 7

7 I love to lose myself in a mystery; to pursue my reason to an *O altitudo!*
10

8 We all labour against our own cure, for death is the cure of all diseases.
pt.ii, 9

9 For the world, I count it not an inn, but an hospital, and a place, not to live, but to die in.
11

10 There is surely a piece of divinity in us, something that was before the elements, and owes no homage unto the sun.

11 Old mortality, the ruins of forgotten times.
Urn Burial (1658), Epistle Dedicatory

12 What song the Syrens sang, or what name Achilles assumed when he hid himself among women, though puzzling questions, are not beyond all conjecture.
ch. 5

13 Man is a noble animal, splendid in ashes, and pompous in the grave.

WILLIAM BROWNE 1591–1643

14 Underneath this sable hearse
Lies the subject of all verse,
Sidney's sister, Pembroke's mother;
Death! ere thou hast slain another,
Fair and learn'd, and good as she,
Time shall throw a dart at thee.
Epitaph. On the Countess of Pembroke

SIR WILLIAM BROWNE 1692–1774

15 The King to Oxford sent a troop of horse,
For Tories own no argument but force:
With equal skill to Cambridge books he sent,
For Whigs admit no force but argument.
Reply to Trapp's epigram. See 259:22. Nichols' *Literary Anecdotes*, vol.III, p.330

ELIZABETH BARRETT BROWNING 1806–1861

16 What was he doing, the great god Pan,
Down in the reeds by the river?
Spreading ruin and scattering ban,
Splashing and paddling with hoofs of a goat,
And breaking the golden lilies afloat
With the dragon-fly on the river.
A Musical Instrument

17 How do I love thee? Let me count the ways.
Sonnets from the Portugese, 43

ROBERT BROWNING 1812–1889

18 On the earth the broken arcs; in the heaven, a perfect round.
Abt Vogler, ix

19 The high that proved too high, the heroic for earth too hard,
The passion that left the ground to lose itself in the sky,
Are music sent up to God by the lover and the bard;
Enough that he heard it once: we shall hear it by and by.
x

20   I feel for the common chord again...
The C Major of this life.
xii

21 Ah, but a man's reach should exceed his grasp,
Or what's a heaven for?
Andrea del Sarto, l.97

22 One who never turned his back but marched breast forward,
Never doubted clouds would break,

Never dreamed, though right were worst-
    ed, wrong would triumph,
    Held we fall to rise, are baffled to fight
      better,
    Sleep to wake.
***Asolando*, Epilogue**

1 And then how I shall lie through cen-
    turies,
  And hear the blessed mutter of the mass,
  And see God made and eaten all day long,
  And feel the steady candle-flame, and taste
  Good strong thick stupefying incense-
    smoke!
  ***The Bishop Orders His Tomb at Saint Praxed's
  Church*, l.80**

2 I was so young, I loved him so, I had
  No mother, God forgot me, and I fell.
  ***A Blot in the 'Scutcheon* (1843), I.iii.l.508**

3 I shall be found by the fire, suppose,
    O'er a great wise book as beseemeth age,
    While the shutters flap as the cross-wind
      blows
    And I turn the page, and I turn the page,
    Not verse now, only prose!
  ***By the Fireside*, ii**

4 When earth breaks up and heaven ex-
    pands,
  How will the change strike me and you
  In the house not made with hands?
  xxvii. See 39:3

5 Oh, the little more, and how much it is!
    And the little less, and what worlds
      away!
  xxxix

6 Kentish Sir Byng stood for his King,
  Bidding the crop-headed Parliament
    swing:
  And, pressing a troop unable to stoop
  And see the rogues flourish and honest
    folk droop,
  Marched them along, fifty-score strong,
  Great-hearted gentlemen, singing this
    song.
  ***Cavalier Tunes*, 1. Marching Along**

7 Boot, saddle, to horse, and away!
  3. Boot and Saddle

8 Dauntless the slug-horn to my lips I set,
  And blew. '*Childe Roland to the Dark
    Tower came.*'
  ***Childe Roland to the Dark Tower Came*, xxxiv.**
  See 218:15

9 We loved, sir—used to meet:
  How sad and bad and mad it was—
  But then, how it was sweet!
  Confessions

0 He said, 'What's time? Leave Now for
    dogs and apes!

  Man has Forever.'
  ***A Grammarian's Funeral*, l.83**

11 That low man seeks a little thing to do,
    Sees it and does it:
  This high man, with a great thing to pur-
    sue,
    Dies ere he knows it:
  That low man goes on adding one to one,
    His hundred's soon hit:
  This high man, aiming at a million,
    Misses an unit.
  That, has the world here—should he need
    the next,
    Let the world mind him!
  This, throws himself on God, and unper-
    plext
    Seeking shall find Him.
  l.113

12 Oh, to be in England
  Now that April's there,
  And whoever wakes in England
  Sees, some morning, unaware,
  That the lowest boughs and the brush-
    wood sheaf
  Round the elm-tree bole are in tiny leaf,
  While the chaffinch sings on the orchard
    bough
  In England—now!
  Home-Thoughts, from Abroad

13 That's the wise thrush; he sings each song
    twice over,
  Lest you should think he never could re-
    capture
  The first fine careless rapture!

14   'With this same key
  Shakespeare unlocked his heart' once
    more!
  Did Shakespeare? If so, the less Shake-
    speare he!
  ***House*, x. See 277:3**

15 I sprang to the stirrup, and Joris, and he;
  I galloped, Dirck galloped, we galloped all
    three.
  ***How they brought the Good News from Ghent to
  Aix***

16 'You're wounded!' 'Nay,' the soldier's
    pride
    Touched to the quick, he said:
  'I'm killed, Sire!' And his chief beside
    Smiling the boy fell dead.
  Incident of the French Camp

17 Escape me?
  Never—
  Beloved!
  Life in a Love

18 Just for a handful of silver he left us,

Just for a riband to stick in his coat.
The Lost Leader

1 We that had loved him so, followed him,
    honoured him,
    Lived in his mild and magnificent eye,
    Learned his great language, caught his
      clear accents,
    Made him our pattern to live and to die!
  Shakespeare was of us, Milton was for us,
  Burns, Shelley, were with us—they watch
      from their graves!

2 Never glad confident morning again!

3 Ah, did you once see Shelley plain,
    And did he stop and speak to you
  And did you speak to him again?
    How strange it seems, and new!
  Memorabilia

4 That's my last Duchess painted on the
    wall,
  Looking as if she were alive.
  My Last Duchess, l.1

5   She had
  A heart—how shall I say?—too soon made
    glad,
  Too easily impressed; she liked whate'er
  She looked on, and her looks went every-
    where.
    l.21

6 Never the time and the place
    And the loved one all together!
  Never the Time and the Place

7 Round the cape of a sudden came the sea,
  And the sun looked over the mountain's
    rim;
  And straight was a path of gold for him,
  And the need of a world of men for me.
  Parting at Morning

8 It was roses, roses, all the way.
  The Patriot

9 Hamelin Town's in Brunswick,
    By famous Hanover city;
  The river Weser, deep and wide,
    Washes its walls on the southern side.
  The Pied Piper of Hamelin, st.i

10 Anything like the sound of a rat
   Makes my heart go pit-a-pat!
   iv

11 'Come in!'—the Mayor cried, looking big-
     ger;
   And in did come the strangest figure!
   v

12 The year's at the spring
   And day's at the morn;
   Morning's at seven;
   The hill-side's dew-pearled;
   The lark's on the wing;

The snail's on the thorn:
God's in his heaven,
All's right with the world!
Pippa Passes, pt.I, l.222

13   Who fished the murex up?
What porridge had John Keats?
Popularity

14 The rain set early in to-night.
   Porphyria's Lover

15   All her hair
   In one long yellow string I wound
   Three times her little throat around,
   And strangled her. No pain felt she;
   I am quite sure she felt no pain.

16 And all night long we have not stirred,
   And yet God has not said a word!

17 Fear death?—to feel the fog in my throat,
     The mist in my face.
   Prospice

18   Grow old along with me!
      The best is yet to be.
   Rabbi ben Ezra, i

19 O lyric Love, half-angel and half-bird
   And all a wonder and a wild desire.
   The Ring and the Book, bk.i, l.1391

20 Gr-r-r- there go, my heart's abhorrence!
   Water your damned flower-pots, do!
   Soliloquy of the Spanish Cloister

21 What of soul was left, I wonder, when the
     kissing had to stop?
   A Toccata of Galuppi's, xiv

22 Dear dead women, with such hair
     too—what's become of all the gold
   Used to hang and brush their bosoms?
     feel chilly and grown old.
   xv

23   I pluck the rose
   And love it more than tongue can speak—
   Then the good minute goes.
   Two in the Campagna, 10

24 What's become of Waring
   Since he gave us all the slip?
   Waring, I.i

BEAU BRUMMELL 1778–1840

25 Who's your fat friend? (Of the Prince o
   Wales.)
   Gronow, *Reminiscences* (1862), p.63

26 I always like to have the morning well
   aired before I get up.
   Charles Macfarlane, *Reminiscences of a Literar
   Life*, 27

27 No perfumes, but very fine linen, plenty o

it, and country washing.
Harriette Wilson, *Memoirs*, ch.2

WILLIAM CULLEN BRYANT
1794–1878

1   They seemed
    Like old companions in adversity.
    A Winter Piece, l.26

GEORGE VILLIERS, SECOND DUKE OF BUCKINGHAM 1628–1687

2   The world is made up for the most part of
    fools and knaves.
    To Mr. Clifford, on his Humane Reason

3   Ay, now the plot thickens very much upon
    us.
    The Rehearsal (1671), III.ii

H. J. BUCKOLL 1803–1871

4   Lord, behold us with Thy blessing
    Once again assembled here.
    *Psalms and Hymns for the Use of Rugby School
    Chapel*. **Lord, Behold us with Thy Blessing**

5   Lord, dismiss us with Thy blessing,
    Thanks for mercies past receive.
    Lord, Dismiss us with Thy Blessing

COMTE DE BUFFON 1707–1788

6   *Ces choses sont hors de l'homme, le style
    est l'homme même.*
    These things [subject matter] are external
    to the man; style is the man.
    Discours sur le Style, address given to the Acadé-
    mie française, 25 Aug. 1753

7   *Le génie n'est qu'une plus grande aptitude à
    la patience.*
    Genius is only a greater aptitude for pat-
    ience.
    Hérault de Séchelles, *Voyage à Montbar* (1803),
    p.15

PROF. ARTHUR BULLER 1874–1944

8   There was a young lady named Bright,
    Whose speed was far faster than light;
        She set out one day
        In a relative way,
    And returned home the previous night.
    Punch, 19 Dec. 1923

COUNT VON BÜLOW 1849–1929

9   *Mit einem Worte: wir wollen niemand in
    den Schatten stellen aber wir verlangen
    auch unseren Platz an der Sonne.*
    In a word, we desire to throw no one into
    the shade [in East Asia], but we also de-
    mand our own place in the sun.
    Reichstag, 6 Dec. 1897

EDWARD GEORGE BULWER-LYTTON, BARON LYTTON 1803–1873

10 Here Stanley meets,—how Stanley scorns,
        the glance!
    The brilliant chief, irregularly great,
    Frank, haughty, rash, the Rupert of De
        bate.
    Of Edward Stanley, 14th Earl of Derby. *The
    New Timon* (1845-7), pt.I.vi. Quoting Disraeli's
    speech in the House of Commons, 24 Apr. 1844.

11 Beneath the rule of men entirely great
    The pen is mightier than the sword.
    Richelieu (1838), II.ii

12 Poverty has strange bedfellows.
    The Caxtons (1850), pt.iv, ch.4

13 There is no man so friendless but what he
    can find a friend sincere enough to tell him
    disagreeable truths.
    What Will He Do With It? (1858), bk.iii, ch.15
    (heading)

ALFRED BUNN 1796?–1860

14 Alice, where art thou?
    Song

15 I dreamt that I dwelt in marble halls,
    With vassals and serfs at my side.
    The Bohemian Girl, Act II

JOHN BUNYAN 1628–1688

16 As I walk'd through the wilderness of this
    world.
    The Pilgrim's Progress (1678), pt.i

17 The name of the slough was Despond.

18 The valley of Humiliation.

19 It beareth the name of Vanity-Fair, be-
    cause the town where 'tis kept, is lighter
    than vanity.
    See Psalms 62:9

20 Hanging is too good for him, said Mr
    Cruelty.

21 A castle, called Doubting-Castle, the own-
    er whereof was Giant Despair.

22 They came to the Delectable Mountains.

23 Sleep is sweet to the labouring man.
    See 27:8

24 So I awoke, and behold it was a dream.

25 A man that could look no way but down-
    wards, with a muckrake in his hand.
    pt.ii

26 He that is down needs fear no fall,

He that is low no pride.
He that is humble ever shall
   Have God to be his guide.
Shepherd Boy's Song

1 An ornament to her profession.

2 Who would true valour see,
      Let him come hither;
   One here will constant be,
      Come wind, come weather.
   There's no discouragement
   Shall make him once relent
   His first avow'd intent
      To be a pilgrim.

3 My sword, I give to him that shall succeed me in my pilgrimage, and my courage and skill to him that can get it.

4 So he passed over, and the trumpets sounded for him on the other side. [Mr. Valiant-for-Truth.]

GELETT BURGESS 1866–1951

5 I never saw a Purple Cow,
   I never hope to see one;
   But I can tell you, anyhow,
   I'd rather see than be one!
Burgess Nonsense Book. The Purple Cow

6 Ah, yes! I wrote the 'Purple Cow' —
   I'm sorry, now, I wrote it!
   But I can tell you anyhow,
   I'll kill you if you quote it!

DEAN BURGON 1813–1888

7 Match me such marvel save in Eastern clime,
   A rose-red city 'half as old as Time'!
Petra (1845). See 196:1

EDMUND BURKE 1729–1797

8 Well stored with pious frauds, and, like most discourses of the sort, much better calculated for the private advantage of the preacher than the edification of the hearers.
Observations on a Publication, 'The present state of the nation' (1769)

9 I am not one of those who think that the people are never in the wrong. They have been so, frequently and outrageously, both in other countries and in this. But I do say, that in all disputes between them and their rulers, the presumption is at least upon a par in favour of the people.
Thoughts on the Cause of the Present Discontents (1770)

10 We must soften into a credulity below the milkiness of infancy to think all men virtuous. We must be tainted with a malignity truly diabolical, to believe all the world to be equally wicked and corrupt.

11 So to be patriots, as not to forget we are gentlemen.

12 Would twenty shillings have ruined Mr Hampden's fortune? No! but the payment of half twenty shillings, on the principle it was demanded, would have made him a slave.
Speech on American Taxation (1774)

13 To tax and to please, no more than to love and to be wise, is not given to men.

14 Your representative owes you, not his industry only, but his judgement; and he betrays, instead of serving you, if he sacrifices it to your opinion.
Speech to the Electors of Bristol, 3 Nov. 1774

15 Parliament is not a *congress* of ambassadors from different and hostile interests; which interests each must maintain, as an agent and advocate, against other agents and advocates; but parliament is a *deliberative* assembly of *one* nation, with *one* interest, that of the whole; where, not local purposes, not local prejudices ought to guide, but the general good, resulting from the general reason of the whole. You choose a member indeed; but when you have chosen him, he is not member of Bristol, but he is a member of *parliament*.

16 The use of force alone is but *temporary*. It may subdue for a moment; but it does not remove the necessity of subduing again; and a nation is not governed, which is perpetually to be conquered.
Speech on Conciliation with America, (22 Mar. 1775)

17 I do not know the method of drawing up an indictment against an whole people.

18 By adverting to the dignity of this high calling, our ancestors have turned a savage wilderness into a glorious empire: and have made the most extensive, and the only honourable conquests, not by destroying, but by promoting the wealth, the number, the happiness of the human race.

19 I know many have been taught to think that moderation, in a case like this, is a sort of treason.
Letter to the Sheriffs of Bristol (1777)

20 Corrupt influence, which is itself the perennial spring of all prodigality, and of all disorder; which loads us, more than millions of debt; which takes away vigour from our arms, wisdom from our councils,

and every shadow of authority and credit from the most venerable parts of our constitution.
Speech on the Economical Reform, 11 Feb. 1780

1 The people are the masters.

2 Applaud us when we run; console us when we fall; cheer us when we recover; but let us pass on—for God's sake, let us pass on!
Speech at Bristol previous to the Election, 1780

3 Not merely a chip of the old 'block', but the old block itself.
On Pitt's First Speech, 1781

4 Your governor stimulates a rapacious and licentious soldiery to the personal search of women, lest these unhappy creatures should avail themselves of the protection of their sex to secure any supply for their necessities.
Speech on Fox's East India Bill, 1 Dec. 1783 (Of Warren Hastings in India).

5 The people never give up their liberties but under some delusion.
Speech at County Meeting of Buckinghamshire, 1784

6 An event has happened, upon which it is difficult to speak, and impossible to be silent.
Impeachment of Warren Hastings, 5 May 1789

7 I impeach him in the name of the people of India, whose rights he has trodden under foot, and whose country he has turned into a desert. Lastly, in the name of human nature itself, in the name of both sexes, in the name of every age, in the name of every rank, I impeach the common enemy and oppressor of all!
Impeachment of Warren Hastings, as recorded by Macaulay in his essay on Warren Hastings

8 People will not look forward to posterity, who never look backward to their ancestors.
Reflections on the Revolution in France (1790)

9 I thought ten thousand swords must have leaped from their scabbards to avenge even a look that threatened her with insult. But the age of chivalry is gone. That of sophisters, economists, and calculators, has succeeded; and the glory of Europe is extinguished for ever.
Of Queen Marie Antoinette

10 Vice itself lost half its evil, by losing all its grossness.

11 Superstition is the religion of feeble minds.

12 Somebody had said, that a king may make a nobleman, but he cannot make a gentleman.
Letter to Wm. Smith, 29 Jan. 1795

13 The storm has gone over me; and I lie like one of those old oaks which the late hurricane has scattered about me. I am stripped of all my honours; I am torn up by the roots, and lie prostrate on the earth!
A Letter to a Noble Lord (1796)

14 And having looked to government for bread, on the very first scarcity they will turn and bite the hand that fed them.
Thoughts and Details on Scarcity (1797)

FANNY BURNEY 1752–1840

15 'The whole of this unfortunate business,' said Dr Lyster, 'has been the result of PRIDE AND PREJUDICE.'
Cecilia (1782), bk.x, ch.10

JOHN BURNS 1858–1943

16 I have seen the Mississippi. That is muddy water. I have seen the St Lawrence. That is crystal water. But the Thames is liquid history.
Oral trad.

ROBERT BURNS 1759–1796

17 Then gently scan your brother man,
    Still gentler sister woman;
Tho' they may gang a kennin wrang,
    To step aside is human.
Address to the Unco Guid

18 Ae fond kiss, and then we sever;
Ae fareweel, and then for ever!
Ae Fond Kiss

19 But to see her was to love her,
Love but her, and love for ever.

20 Had we never lov'd sae kindly,
Had we never lov'd sae blindly,
Never met—or never parted,
We had ne'er been broken-hearted.

21 Should auld acquaintance be forgot,
    And never brought to mind?
Auld Lang Syne

22 We'll tak a cup o' kindness yet,
    For auld lang syne.

23 And there's a hand, my trusty fiere,
    And gie's a hand o'thine.

24 Freedom and Whisky gang thegither!
The Author's Earnest Cry and Prayer, xxxi

25 Bonnie wee thing, cannie wee thing,
    Lovely wee thing, wert thou mine,
I wad wear thee in my bosom,

Lest my jewel I should tine.
The Bonnie Wee Thing

1 Gin a body meet a body
   Coming through the rye;
   Gin a body kiss a body,
   Need a body cry?
Coming Through the Rye (taken from an old song, *The Bob-tailed Lass*).

2 They never sought in vain that sought the Lord aright!
The Cotter's Saturday Night, vi

3 Is there, in human-form, that bears a heart—
      A wretch! a villain! lost to love and truth!
   That can, with studied, sly, ensnaring art,
      Betray sweet Jenny's unsuspecting youth?
                    x

4 I wasna fou, but just had plenty.
Death and Dr. Hornbook, iii

5 On ev'ry hand it will allow'd be,
   He's just—nae better than he should be.
A Dedication to Gavin Hamilton, l.25

6 A Workhouse! ah, that sound awakes my woes,
   And pillows on the thorn my racked repose!
   In durance vile here must I wake and weep,
   And all my frowzy couch in sorrow steep.
Epistle from Esopus to Maria, l.57

7 Flow gently, sweet Afton, among thy green braes,
   Flow gently, I'll sing thee a song in thy praise.
   My Mary's asleep by thy murmuring stream,
   Flow gently, sweet Afton, disturb not her dream.
Flow gently, sweet Afton

8 The rank is but the guinea's stamp,
   The man's the gowd for a' that!
For a' that and a' that

9 A man's a man for a' that.

10 Go fetch to me a pint o' wine,
   An' fill it in a silver tassie.
Go Fetch to Me a Pint

11 The soger frae the wars returns,
      The sailor frae the main,
   But I hae parted frae my Love,
      Never to meet again, my dear,
      Never to meet again.
It was a' for our Rightfu' King

12 John Anderson my jo, John,
      When we were first acquent,

Your locks were like the raven,
   Your bonny brow was brent.
John Anderson My Jo

13 Some have meat and cannot eat,
      Some cannot eat that want it:
   But we have meat and we can eat,
      Sae let the Lord be thankit.
The Kirkudbright Grace. (Also known as the Selkirk Grace.)

14 I once was a maid, tho' I cannot tell when
   And still my delight is in proper young men.
Love and Liberty—A Cantata, l.57

15 Man's inhumanity to man
   Makes countless thousands mourn!
Man was made to Mourn

16 My heart's in the Highlands, my heart not here;
   My heart's in the Highlands a-chasing the deer;
   Chasing the wild deer, and following the roe,
   My heart's in the Highlands, wherever go.
My Heart's in the Highlands

17 O, my Luve's like a red red rose
      That's newly sprung in June:
   O my Luve's like the melodie
      That's sweetly play'd in tune.
My Love is like a Red Red Rose

18 The wan moon sets behind the white wave,
   And time is setting with me, Oh.
Open the door to me, Oh

19 The mair they talk I'm kent the better.
The Poet's Welcome (to his bastard child)

20 Scots, wha hae wi' Wallace bled,
   Scots, wham Bruce has aften led,
   Welcome to your gory bed,
      Or to victorie.
   Now's the day, and now's the hour;
   See the front o' battle lour!
   See approach proud Edward's power—
      Chains and slaverie!
Scots, Wha Hae (Robert Bruce's March to Bannockburn)

21 Liberty's in every blow!
      Let us do or die!

22 While we sit bousing at the nappy,
   And getting fou and unco happy,
   We think na on the lang Scots miles,
   The mosses, waters, staps, and styles,
   That lie between us and our hame,
   Whare sits our sulky sullen dame,
   Gathering her brows like gathering storm

Nursing her wrath to keep it warm.
Tam o' Shanter, l.10

1 As Tammie glowr'd, amaz'd, and curious,
The mirth and fun grew fast and furious.
l.143

2 Tam tint his reason a' thegither,
And roars out, 'Weel done, Cutty-sark!'
l.188

3 To make a happy fire-side clime
To weans and wife,
That's the true pathos and sublime
Of human life.
To Dr. Blacklock

4 O wad some Pow'r the giftie gie us
To see oursels as others see us!
It wad frae mony a blunder free us,
And foolish notion.
To a Louse

5 Wee, sleekit, cow'rin', tim'rous beastie,
O what a panic's in thy breastie!
Thou need na start awa sae hasty,
Wi' bickering brattle!
I wad be laith to rin an' chase thee,
Wi' murd'ring pattle!
To a Mouse

6 The best laid schemes o' mice an' men
Gang aft a-gley.

7 O whistle, and I'll come to you, my lad:
O whistle, and I'll come to you, my lad:
Tho' father and mither and a' should gae
mad,
O whistle, and I'll come to you, my lad.
Whistle, and I'll come to you, my Lad

8 Ye banks and braes o' bonny Doon,
How can ye bloom sae fresh and fair?
How can ye chant, ye little birds,
And I sae weary fu' o' care?
Ye Banks and Braes o' Bonny Doon

9 Thou minds me o' departed joys,
Departed never to return.

0 Don't let the awkward squad fire over me.
A. Cunningham, *Works of Burns; with his Life*,
1834, vol.i, p.344

SIR FRED BURROWS 1887–1973

1 Unlike my predecessors, I have devoted
more of my life to shunting and hooting
than to hunting and shooting.
Speech as last Governor of undivided Bengal
(1946-7), having been President of the National
Union of Railwaymen. Obituary, *Daily Telegraph*, 24 Apr. 1973

SIR RICHARD BURTON 1821–1890

2 Don't be frightened; I am recalled. Pay,
pack, and follow at convenience.

Note to Isabel Burton, 19 August 1871 on being
replaced as Consul to Damascus. Isabel Burton,
Life of Sir Richard Burton, ch.21

ROBERT BURTON 1577–1640

13 I had no time to lick it into form, as she [a
bear] doth her young ones.
Anatomy of Melancholy. **Democritus to the
Reader**

14 Like watermen, that row one way and
look another.

15 *Hinc quam sit calamus saevior ense patet.*
From this it is clear how much the pen is
worse than the sword.
pt.i, 2, memb.4, subsect.4

16 Every thing, saith Epictetus, hath two
handles, the one to be held by, the other
not.
pt.ii, 3, memb.3

17 What is a ship but a prison?
memb.4

18 To these crocodile's tears, they will add
sobs, fiery sighs, and sorrowful countenance.
pt.iii, 2, memb.2, subsect.4

19 England is a paradise for women, and hell
for horses: Italy a paradise for horses, hell
for women, as the diverb goes.
3, memb.1, subsect.2

20 One religion is as true as another.
4, memb.2, subsect.1

21 Be not solitary, be not idle.
final words

HERMANN BUSENBAUM 1600–1668

22 *Cum finis est licitus, etiam media sunt lici-
ta.*
The end justifies the means.
Medulla Theologiae Moralis (1650)

COMTE DE BUSSY-RABUTIN
1618–1693

23 *L'amour vient de l'aveuglement,
L'amitié de la connaissance.*
Love comes from blindness, friendship
from knowledge.
Histoire Amoureuse des Gaules. **Maximes d'Am-
our,** pt.I

24 *L'absence est à l'amour ce qu'est au feu le
vent;
Il éteint le petit, il allume le grand.*
Absence is to love what wind is to fire; it
extinguishes the small, it enkindles the
great.
pt.II. See 102:7, 149:11

1 *Comme vous savez, Dieu est d'ordinaire pour les gros escadrons contre les petits.*
As you know, God is usually on the side of the big squadrons against the small.
Letter to the Comte de Limoges, 18 Oct. 1677.
Cf. Tacitus, *Histories,* iv. 17

NICHOLAS MURRAY BUTLER
1862–1947

2 An expert is one who knows more and more about less and less.
attr. to a Commencement Address. Columbia University

SAMUEL BUTLER 1612–1680

3 What ever sceptic could inquire for;
For every why he had a wherefore.
Hudibras, pt.I, c.1, l.131

4 He knew what's what, and that's as high
As metaphysic wit can fly.
l.149

5 Compound for sins, they are inclin'd to
By damning those they have no mind to.
l.213

6 He ne'er consider'd it, as loth
To look a gift-horse in the mouth.
l.483

7   I'll make the fur
Fly 'bout the ears of the old cur.
c.3, l.277

8 Doubtless the pleasure is as great
Of being cheated, as to cheat.
As lookers-on feel most delight,
That least perceive a juggler's sleight,
And still the less they understand,
The more th' admire his sleight of hand.
pt.II, c.3, l.1

9 For in what stupid age or nation
Was marriage ever out of fashion?
pt.III, c.1, l.817

10 What makes all doctrines plain and clear?
About two hundred pounds a year.
And that which was prov'd true before,
Prove false again? Two hundred more.
l.1277

11 He that complies against his will,
Is of his own opinion still.
c.3, l.547

12 The best of all our actions tend
To the preposterousest end.
Genuine Remains: **Satire upon the Weakness and Misery of Man,** l.41

13 All love at first, like generous wine,
Ferments and frets until 'tis fine;
But when 'tis settled on the lee,
And from th' impurer matter free,

Becomes the richer still the older,
And proves the pleasanter the colder.
Miscellaneous Thoughts

SAMUEL BUTLER 1835–1902

14 It has, I believe, been often remarked, that a hen is only an egg's way of making another egg.
Life and Habit, ch.8

15 Genius...has been defined as a supreme capacity for taking trouble...It might be more fitly described as a supreme capacity for getting its possessors into pains of all kinds, and keeping them therein so long as the genius remains.
Note Books, selected and edited by H. Festing Jones (1912), ch.XI

16 An honest God's the noblest work of man.
Further extracts from the Note Books, selected and edited by A. Bartholomew (1934), p.26. See 129:13, 185:18

17 'Man wants but little here below' but likes that little good—and not too long in coming.
p.61. See 110:12, 280:10

18 My Lord, I do not believe. Help thou mine unbelief.
Note Books, selected and edited by G. Keynes and B. Hill (1951), p.284

19 They would have been equally horrified at hearing the Christian religion doubted and at seeing it practised.
The Way of All Flesh, ch.15

20 The advantage of doing one's praising for oneself is that one can lay it on so thick and exactly in the right places.
ch.34

21 There's many a good tune played on an old fiddle.
ch.61

22 'Tis better to have loved and lost, than never to have lost at all.
ch.77. See 252:13

23 O God! Oh Montreal!
Psalm of Montreal

24 It was very good of God to let Carlyle and Mrs Carlyle marry one another and so make only two people miserable instead of four, besides being very amusing.
Letter to Miss Savage, 21 Nov. 1884

WILLIAM BUTLER 1535–1618

25 Doubtless God could have made a better berry [strawberry], but doubtless God never did.
Walton, *Compleat Angler,* pt.i, ch.5

JOHN BYROM 1692–1763

1 Some say, that Signor Bononcini,
Compar'd to Handel's a mere ninny;
Others aver, to him, that Handel
Is scarcely fit to hold a candle.
Strange! that such high dispute shou'd be
'Twixt Tweedledum and Tweedledee.
Epigram on the Feuds between Handel and
Bononcini

2 God bless the King, I mean the Faith's
Defender;
God bless—no harm in blessing—the
Pretender;
But who Pretender is, or who is King,
God bless us all—that's quite another
thing.
To an Officer in the Army

LORD BYRON 1788–1824

3 In short, he was a perfect cavaliero,
And to his very valet seem'd a hero.
Beppo, st.33. See 78:9

4 His heart was one of those which most
enamour us,
Wax to receive, and marble to retain.
st.34

5 The nursery still leaps out in all they utter—
Besides, they always smell of bread and
butter.
st.39

6 Mark! where his carnage and his con-
quests cease!
He makes a solitude, and calls it—peace!
The Bride of Abydos, c.II.st.20. See 250:8

7 War, war is still the cry, 'War even to the
knife!'
Childe Harold's Pilgrimage, c.I.st.86. See 179:17

8 Hereditary bondsmen! know ye not
Who would be free themselves must strike
the blow?
c.II.st.76

9 There was a sound of revelry by night,
And Belgium's capital had gather'd then
Her beauty and her chivalry, and bright
The lamps shone o'er fair women and
brave men;
A thousand hearts beat happily; and when
Music arose with its voluptuous swell,
Soft eyes look'd love to eyes which spake
again,
And all went merry as a marriage bell;
But hush! hark! a deep sound strikes like a
rising knell!
c.III.st.11

10 Did ye not hear it?—No; 'twas but the
wind,
Or the car rattling o'er the stony street;
On with the dance! let joy be unconfined;
No sleep till morn, when Youth and
Pleasure meet
To chase the glowing Hours with flying
feet.
st.12

11 The earth is cover'd thick with other
clay,
Which her own clay shall cover, heap'd
and pent,
Rider and horse,—friend, foe,—in one red
burial blent!
st.28

12 Yet, Freedom! yet thy banner, torn, but
flying,
Streams like the thunder-storm *against* the
wind.
c.IV.st.98

13 *There* were his young barbarians all at
play,
There was their Dacian mother— he, their
sire,
Butcher'd to make a Roman holiday.
st.141

14 While stands the Coliseum, Rome shall
stand;
When falls the Coliseum, Rome shall fall;
And when Rome falls—the World.
st.145

15 Roll on, thou deep and dark blue Ocean—
roll!
Ten thousand fleets sweep over thee in
vain;
Man marks the earth with ruin—his con-
trol
Stops with the shore.
st.179

16 The Assyrian came down like the wolf on
the fold,
And his cohorts were gleaming in purple
and gold;
And the sheen of their spears was like stars
on the sea,
When the blue wave rolls nightly on deep
Galilee.
Destruction of Sennacherib

17 For the Angel of Death spread his wings
on the blast,
And breathed in the face of the foe as he
pass'd.

18 What men call gallantry, and gods adultery,

Is much more common where the climate's sultry.
Don Juan, c.I.st.63

1 A little still she strove, and much repented,
And whispering 'I will ne'er consent'—consented.
st.117

2 Man's love is of man's life a thing apart,
'Tis woman's whole existence.
st.194

3 Let us have wine and women, mirth and laughter,
Sermons and soda-water the day after.
c.II.st.178

4 'Tis melancholy, and a fearful sign
Of human frailty, folly, also crime,
That love and marriage rarely can combine,
Although they both are born in the same clime;
Marriage from love, like vinegar from wine—
A sad, sour, sober beverage—by time
Is sharpen'd from its high celestial flavour,
Down to a very homely household savour.
c.III.st.5

5 All tragedies are finish'd by a death,
All comedies are ended by a marriage.
st.9

6 The isles of Greece, the isles of Greece!
Where burning Sappho loved and sung,
Where grew the arts of war and peace,
Where Delos rose, and Phoebus sprung!
Eternal summer gilds them yet,
But all, except their sun, is set.
st.86, 1

7 The mountains look on Marathon—
And Marathon looks on the sea;
And musing there an hour alone,
I dream'd that Greece might still be free.
3

8 A king sate on the rocky brow
Which looks o'er sea-born Salamis;
And ships, by thousands, lay below,
And men in nations;—all were his!
He counted them at break of day—
And when the sun set where were they?
4

9 For what is left the poet here?
For Greeks a blush—for Greece a tear.
6

10 Earth! render back from out thy breast
A remnant of our Spartan dead!
Of the three hundred grant but three,

To make a new Thermopylae!
7

11 And if I laugh at any mortal thing,
'Tis that I may not weep.
c.IV.st.4

12 John Keats, who was kill'd off by one critique,
Just as he really promised something great,
If not intelligible, without Greek
Contrived to talk about the Gods of late,
Much as they might have been supposed to speak.
Poor fellow! His was an untoward fate;
'Tis strange the mind, that very fiery particle,
Should let itself be snuff'd out by an article.
c.XI.st.60

13 Merely innocent flirtation,
Not quite adultery, but adulteration.
c.XII.st.63

14 The English winter—ending in July,
To recommence in August.
c.XIII.st.42

15 'Tis strange—but true; for truth is always strange;
Stranger than fiction.
c.XIV.st.101

16 With just enough of learning to misquote.
English Bards and Scotch Reviewers, l.66

17 Though women are angels, yet wedlock's the devil.
Hours of Idleness. **To Eliza**

18 Who killed John Keats?
'I,' says the Quarterly,
So savage and Tartarly;
''Twas one of my feats.'
John Keats

19 Maid of Athens, ere we part,
Give, oh give me back my heart!
Or, since that has left my breast,
Keep it now, and take the rest!
Maid of Athens

20 I am the very slave of circumstance
And impulse—borne away with every breath!
Sardanapalus, IV.i

21 She walks in beauty, like the night
Of cloudless climes and starry skies;
And all that's best of dark and bright
Meet in her aspect and her eyes.
She Walks in Beauty

22 So, we'll go no more a roving
So late into the night,
Though the heart be still as loving,

And the moon be still as bright.
So, We'll Go No More a Roving

1 Though the night was made for loving,
    And the day returns too soon,
Yet we'll go no more a-roving
    By the light of the moon.

2 Oh, talk not to me of a name great in
    story;
The days of our youth are the days of our
    glory;
And the myrtle and ivy of sweet two-and-
    twenty
Are worth all your laurels, though ever so
    plenty.
*Stanzas Written on the Road between Florence
and Pisa*

3 When we two parted
    In silence and tears,
Half broken-hearted
    To sever for years,
Pale grew thy cheek and cold,
    Colder thy kiss.
When We Two Parted

4 You should have a softer pillow than my
heart.
To his wife. E.C. Mayne, ed., *The Life and Letters of Anne Isabella, Lady Noel Byron*, ch.11

5 Love in this part of the world is no sine-
cure.
Letter to John Murray from Venice, 27 Dec.
1816

6 I awoke one morning and found myself
famous.
(Referring to the instantaneous success of *Childe
Harold*). Moore, *Life of Byron*, I, 347

JAMES BRANCH CABELL 1879–1958

7 The optimist proclaims that we live in the
best of all possible worlds; and the pessimist fears this is true.
The Silver Stallion, bk.iv, ch.26

AUGUSTUS CAESAR
see AUGUSTUS

JULIUS CAESAR 102?–44 B.C.

8 *Gallia est omnis divisa in partes tres.*
Gaul as a whole is divided into three parts.
De Bello Gallico, I.i

9 *Fere libenter homines id quod volunt credunt.*
Men willingly believe what they wish.
iii.18

10 *Et tu, Brute?*

You too Brutus?
Oral trad. See 216:9 and Philemon Holland,
trans., Suetonius, *Historie of Twelve Caesars*
(1606), 'Some have written that as M. Brutus
came running upon him, he said
"καὶ σύ, τέκνον", "And you, my son."'

11 *Veni, vidi, vici.*
I came, I saw, I conquered.
Suetonius, *Divus Julius*, xxxvii.2. (Inscription
displayed in Caesar's Pontic triumph, or, according to Plutarch, 1.2, written in a letter by
Caesar, announcing the victory of Zela which
concluded the Pontic campaign)

12 The die is cast.
xxxii. At the crossing of the Rubicon. Often
quoted in Latin, *'Iacta alea est,'* but originally
spoken in Greek: Plutarch, *Pompey*, 60.2

13 Caesar's wife must be above suspicion.
Oral trad. See Plutarch, *Lives*, Julius Caesar, x.6

CALLIMACHUS c.305–c.240 B.C.

14 μέγα βιβλίον ἴσον τῷ μεγάλῳ κακῷ.
A great book is like great evil.
Fragments, ed. R. Pfeiffer, 465. Proverbially reduced to μέγα βιβλίον μέγα· κακόν. 'Great
book, great evil'

**CHARLES ALEXANDRE DE
CALONNE** 1734–1802

15 *Madame, si c'est possible, c'est fait; impossible? cela se fera.*
Madam, if a thing is possible, consider it
done; the impossible? that will be done.
J. Michelet, *Histoire de la Révolution Française*
(1847), vol.I, pt.ii, sect 8. Better known as the
U.S. Armed Forces slogan, 'The difficult we do
immediately; the impossible takes a little longer.'

C.S. CALVERLEY 1831–1884

16 The farmer's daughter hath soft brown
    hair;
    (Butter and eggs and a pound of cheese)
And I met with a ballad, I can't say where,
    Which wholly consisted of lines like
    these.
Ballad

17 O Beer! O Hodgson, Guinness, Allsopp,
    Bass!
Names that should be on every infant's
    tongue!
Beer

18 I cannot sing the old songs now!
    It is not that I deem them low;
'Tis that I can't remember how
    They go.
Changed. See 73:1

1 A bare-legg'd beggarly son of a gun.
The Cock and the Bull

2 Life is with such all beer and skittles;
They are not difficult to please
About their victuals.
Contentment

3 Sweet, when the morn is grey;
Sweet, when they've cleared away
Lunch; and at close of day
Possibly sweetest.
Ode to Tobacco

4 I have a liking old
For thee, though manifold
Stories, I know, are told
Not to thy credit.

GENERAL CAMBRONNE 1770–1842

5 *La Garde meurt, mais ne se rend pas.*
The Guards die but do not surrender.
Attr. to Cambronne when called upon to surrender at Waterloo. Cambronne denied the saying at a banquet at Nantes, 19 Sept. 1830

6 *Merde!*
Said to be Cambronne's actual reply to the call to surrender: euphemistically known as '*Le mot de Cambronne*'.

CHARLES PRATT, LORD CAMDEN 1714–1794

7 Taxation and representation are inseparable…whatever is a man's own, is absolutely his own; no man hath a right to take it from him without his consent either expressed by himself or representative.
House of Lords, 7 Mar. 1766. See 178:17

WILLIAM CAMDEN 1551–1623

8 My friend, judge not me,
Thou seest I judge not thee.
Betwixt the stirrup and the ground
Mercy I asked, mercy I found.
Remains. Epitaph for a Man Killed by Falling from His Horse

BARON CAMPBELL 1779–1861

9 So essential did I consider an Index to be to every book, that I proposed to bring a Bill into parliament to deprive an author who publishes a book without an Index of the privilege of copyright; and, moreover, to subject him, for his offence, to a pecuniary penalty.
Lives of the Chief Justices, preface to vol.iii, which included an index to the previously published vols.

MRS. PATRICK CAMPBELL 1865–1940

10 Some day you'll eat a pork chop, Joey, and then God help all women.
To George Bernard Shaw, a vegetarian. Alexander Woollcott, *While Rome Burns,* Some Neighbours, 3

11 I don't mind where people make love, so long as they don't do it in the street and frighten the horses.
Oral tradition

12 Marriage is the result of the longing for the deep, deep peace of the double bed after the hurly-burly of the chaise-longue.
Oral tradition

ROY CAMPBELL 1901–1957

13 You praise the firm restraint with which
they write—
I'm with you there, of course:
They use the snaffle and the curb all right,
But where's the bloody horse?
On Some South African Novelists

14 South Africa, renowned both far and wide
For politics and little else beside.
The Wayzgoose (1928)

THOMAS CAMPBELL 1777–1844

15 O leave this barren spot to me!
Spare, woodman, spare the beechen tree.
The Beech-Tree's Petition

16 'Tis the sunset of life gives me mystical
lore,
And coming events cast their shadows before.
Lochiel's Warning

17 A chieftain to the Highlands bound
Cries, 'Boatman, do not tarry!
And I'll give thee a silver pound
To row us o'er the ferry.'
Lord Ullin's Daughter

18 'Tis distance lends enchantment to the
view,
And robes the mountain in its azure hue.
Pleasures of Hope, pt.i, l.7

19 Now Barabbas was a publisher.
Often attributed to Byron

THOMAS CAMPION 1567–1620

20 There is a garden in her face,
Where roses and white lilies grow;
A heav'nly paradise is that place,
Wherein all pleasant fruits do flow.
There cherries grow, which none may buy

Till 'Cherry ripe' themselves do cry.
Fourth Book of Airs, vii. Also attr. Richard Alison.

GEORGE CANNING 1770–1827

1 A steady patriot of the world alone,
The friend of every country but his own.
[The Jacobin.]
New Morality, l.113. See 178:18

2 Give me the avowed, erect and manly foe,
Firm I can meet, perhaps return the blow;
But of all plagues, good Heaven, thy wrath
    can send,
Save me, oh, save me, from the candid
    friend.
l.207

DOMENICO CARACCIOLO 1715–1789

3 *Il y a en Angleterre soixante sectes religieuses différentes, et une seule sauce.*
In England there are sixty different religions, and only one sauce.
Attr. N. & Q., Dec. 1968

HENRY CAREY 1693?–1743

4 Of all the girls that are so smart
    There's none like pretty Sally,
She is the darling of my heart,
    And she lives in our alley.
Sally in our Alley

5 Of all the days that's in the week
    I dearly love but one day—
And that's the day that comes betwixt
    A Saturday and Monday.

JANE WELSH CARLYLE 1801–1866

6 I am not at all the sort of person you and I
took me for.
Letter to Thomas Carlyle, 7 May 1822

THOMAS CARLYLE 1795–1881

7 A well-written Life is almost as rare as a
well-spent one.
Critical and Miscellaneous Essays, vol.i. Richter

8 The three great elements of modern civilization, Gunpowder, Printing, and the
Protestant Religion.
State of German Literature. See Bacon, *Novum Organum, bk.I, aphor. 129.*

9 In epochs when cash payment has become
the sole nexus of man to man.
vol.iv. **Chartism,** ch.6

0 'Genius' (which means transcendent capacity of taking trouble, first of all).
Frederick the Great, bk.iv, ch.3. See 51:7

11 Happy the people whose annals are blank
in history-books!
bk.xvi, ch.1

12 A whiff of grapeshot.
History of the French Revolution, pt.I, bk.v, ch.3

13 The seagreen Incorruptible. [Robespierre.]
pt.II, bk.iv, ch.4

14 No great man lives in vain. The history of
the world is but the biography of great
men.
Heroes and Hero-Worship, i. **The Hero as Divinity**

15 The true University of these days is a collection of books.
v. **The Hero as Man of Letters**

16 Respectable Professors of the Dismal
Science. [Political Economy.]
Latter-Day Pamphlets, No.1. **The Present Time**

17 A Parliament speaking through reporters
to Buncombe and the twenty-seven millions mostly fools.
No.6. **Parliaments**

18 The unspeakable Turk should be immediately struck out of the question.
Letter to G. Howard, 24 Nov. 1876

19 Transcendental moonshine.
Life of John Sterling, pt.i, ch.15

20 Man is a tool-using animal...Without
tools he is nothing, with tools he is all.
Sartor Resartus, bk.i, ch.5

21 The folly of that impossible precept,
'Know thyself'; till it be translated into this
partially possible one, 'Know what thou
canst work at'.
bk.ii.ch.7. See 6:6

22 I don't pretend to understand the Universe — it's a great deal bigger than I am
...People ought to be modester.
To Wm. Allingham. D.A. Wilson and D. Wilson
MacArthur, *Carlyle in Old Age*

23 If Jesus Christ were to come to-day,
people would not even crucify him. They
would ask him to dinner, and hear what he
had to say, and make fun of it.
D.A. Wilson, *Carlyle at his Zenith*

24 Macaulay is well for a while, but one
wouldn't *live* under Niagara.
R.M. Milnes, *Notebook,* 1838

25 *Margaret Fuller:* I accept the universe.
Carlyle: Gad! she'd better!
Attr. William James, *Varieties of Religious Experience,* II, p.41

ANDREW CARNEGIE 1835–1919

1 The man who dies…rich dies disgraced.
North American Review, June 1889, **'The Gospel of Wealth',** pt.I

JULIA A. CARNEY 1823–1908

2 Little drops of water,
    Little grains of sand,
Make the mighty ocean
    And the beauteous land.

And the little moments,
    Humble though they be,
Make the mighty ages
    Of eternity.
Little Things (1845). Reprinted in *Juvenile Missionary Magazine,* 10, Apr. 1853

JOSEPH EDWARDS CARPENTER 1813–1885

3 What are the wild waves saying
    Sister, the whole day long.
What are the Wild Waves Saying?

LEWIS CARROLL 1832–1898

4 What I tell you three times is true.
The Hunting of the Snark, Fit 1. **The Landing**

5 He would answer to 'Hi!' or to any loud
        cry,
    Such as 'Fry me!' or 'Fritter-my-wig!'

6 His intimate friends called him 'Candle-
        ends',
    And his enemies, 'Toasted-cheese'.

7 But oh, beamish nephew, beware of the
        day,
    If your Snark be a Boojum! For then
You will softly and suddenly vanish away,
    And never be met with again!
Fit 3. **The Baker's Tale**

8 They sought it with thimbles, they sought
        it with care;
    They pursued it with forks and hope;
They threatened its life with a railway-
        share;
    They charmed it with smiles and soap.
Fit 5. **The Beaver's Lesson**

9 For the Snark *was* a Boojum, you see.
Fit 8. **The Vanishing**

10 He thought he saw an Elephant,
        That practised on a fife:
He looked again, and found it was
        A letter from his wife.
'At length I realize,' he said,
        'The bitterness of life!'
Sylvie and Bruno, ch.5

11 He thought he saw a Rattlesnake
        That questioned him in Greek,

He looked again and found it was
    The Middle of Next Week.
'The one thing I regret,' he said,
    'Is that it cannot speak!'
ch.6

12 He thought he saw a Banker's Clerk
        Descending from the bus:
He looked again, and found it was
        A Hippopotamus:
'If this should stay to dine,' he said,
        'There won't be much for us.'
ch.7

13 'What is the use of a book', thought Alice
    'without pictures or conversations?'
Alice's Adventures in Wonderland, ch.1

14 Do cats eat bats?…Do bats eat cats?

15 'Curiouser and curiouser!' cried Alice.
ch.2

16 How doth the little crocodile
        Improve his shining tail,
And pour the waters of the Nile
        On every golden scale!
See 266:16

17 The Duchess! The Duchess! Oh my dear
paws! Oh my fur and whiskers!
ch.4

18 'You are old, Father William,' the young
        man said,
    'And your hair has become very white;
And yet you incessantly stand on your
        head—
    Do you think, at your age, it is right?'

'In my youth,' Father William replied to
        his son,
    'I feared it might injure the brain;
But now that I'm perfectly sure I have
        none,
    Why, I do it again and again.'
ch.5. See 243:21

19 'I have answered three questions, and that
        is enough,'
    Said his father; 'don't give yourself airs!
Do you think I can listen all day to such
        stuff?
    Be off, or I'll kick you downstairs!'

20 'I shall sit here,' he said, 'on and off, for
days and days.'
ch.6

21 'If everybody minded their own business,'
said the Duchess in a hoarse growl, 'the
world would go round a deal faster than it
does.'

22 Speak roughly to your little boy,
        And beat him when he sneezes;
He only does it to annoy,
        Because he knows it teases.

1 This time it vanished quite slowly, beginning with the end of the tail, and ending with the grin, which remained some time after the rest of it had gone. [The Cheshire Cat.]

2 'Then you should say what you mean,' the March Hare went on. 'I do,' Alice hastily replied; 'at least—at least I mean what I say—that's the same thing, you know.'
'Not the same thing a bit!' said the Hatter. 'Why, you might just as well say that "I see what I eat" is the same thing as "I eat what I see!"'
ch.7

3 'It was the *best* butter,' the March Hare meekly replied.

4 Twinkle, twinkle, little bat!
How I wonder what you're at!
Up above the world you fly!
Like a teatray in the sky.
See 250:18

5 'Take some more tea,' the March Hare said to Alice, very earnestly.
'I've had nothing yet,' Alice replied in an offended tone, 'so I can't take more.'
'You mean you can't take *less*,' said the Hatter: 'it's very easy to take *more* than nothing.'

6 The Queen was in a furious passion, and went stamping about, and shouting, 'Off with his head!' or 'Off with her head!' about once in a minute.
ch.8

7 Take care of the sense, and the sounds will take care of themselves.
ch.9

8 I only took the regular course...the different branches of Arithmetic—Ambition, Distraction, Uglification and Derision.

9 'That's the reason they're called lessons,' the Gryphon remarked: 'because they lessen from day to day.'

0 'Will you walk a little faster?' said a whiting to a snail,
'There's a porpoise close behind us, and he's treading on my tail.'
ch.10

1 Will you, won't you, will you, won't you, will you join the dance?

2 The further off from England the nearer is to France—
Then turn not pale, beloved snail, but come and join the dance.

3 'Tis the voice of the lobster; I heard him declare,

'You have baked me too brown, I must sugar my hair.'
See 266:18

14 Soup of the evening, beautiful Soup!

15 'Where shall I begin, please your Majesty?' he asked.
'Begin at the beginning,' the King said, gravely, 'and go on till you come to the end: then stop.
ch.11

16 'Twas brillig, and the slithy toves
Did gyre and gimble in the wabe;
All mimsy were the borogoves,
And the mome raths outgrabe.

'Beware the Jabberwock, my son!
The jaws that bite, the claws that catch!'
Through the Looking-Glass, ch.1

17 And as in uffish thought he stood,
The Jabberwock, with eyes of flame,
Came whiffling through the tulgey wood,
And burbled as it came!

One, two! One, two! And through and through
The vorpal blade went snicker-snack!
He left it dead, and with its head
He went galumphing back.

'And hast thou slain the Jabberwock?
Come to my arms, my beamish boy!
O frabjous day! Callooh! Callay!'
He chortled in his joy.

18 Curtsey while you're thinking what to say. It saves time.
ch.2

19 Speak in French when you can't think of the English for a thing.

20 Now, *here,* you see, it takes all the running *you* can do, to keep in the same place. If you want to get somewhere else, you must run at least twice as fast as that!

21 Tweedledum and Tweedledee
Agreed to have a battle;
For Tweedledum said Tweedledee
Had spoilt his nice new rattle.

Just then flew down a monstrous crow,
As black as a tar-barrel;
Which frightened both the heroes so,
They quite forgot their quarrel.
ch.4

22 'Contrariwise,' continued Tweedledee, 'if it was so, it might be; and if it were so, it would be: but as it isn't, it ain't. That's logic.'

23 The sun was shining on the sea,
Shining with all his might:

He did his very best to make
    The billows smooth and bright—
And this was odd, because it was
    The middle of the night.

1 The Walrus and the Carpenter
        Were walking close at hand;
They wept like anything to see
        Such quantities of sand:
'If this were only cleared away,'
        They said, 'it would be grand!'

'If seven maids with seven mops
        Swept it for half a year,
Do you suppose,' the Walrus said,
        'That they could get it clear?'
'I doubt it,' said the Carpenter,
        And shed a bitter tear.

2 'The time has come,' the Walrus said,
    'To talk of many things:
Of shoes—and ships—and sealing wax—
    Of cabbages—and kings—
And why the sea is boiling hot—
    And whether pigs have wings.'

3   But answer came there none—
    And this was scarcely odd because
    They'd eaten every one.
    See 201:12

4 'Let's fight till six, and then have dinner,'
    said Tweedledum.

5 The rule is, jam to-morrow and jam yes-
    terday—but never jam to-day.
    ch.5

6 Why, sometimes I've believed as many as
    six impossible things before breakfast.

7 They gave it me,—for an un-birthday
    present.
    ch.6

8 'There's glory for you!' 'I don't know
    what you mean by "glory",' Alice said. 'I
    meant, "there's a nice knock-down argu-
    ment for you!"' 'But "glory" doesn't mean
    "a nice knock-down argument",' Alice ob-
    jected. 'When *I* use a word,' Humpty
    Dumpty said in a rather scornful tone, 'it
    means just what I choose it to mean
    —neither more nor less.'

9 'The question is,' said Humpty Dumpty,
    'which is to be master—that's all.'

10 You see it's like a portmanteau—there are
    two meanings packed up into one word.

11 He's an Anglo-Saxon Messenger—and
    those are Anglo-Saxon attitudes.
    ch.7

12 It's as large as life, and twice as natural!

13 The [White] Knight said…'It's my own

invention.'
    ch.8

14 I'll tell thee everything I can:
        There's little to relate.
    I saw an aged, aged man,
        A-sitting on a gate.

15 Or madly squeeze a right-hand foot
    Into a left-hand shoe.

16 'Speak when you're spoken to!' the Re‹
    Queen sharply interrupted her.
    ch.9

17 It isn't etiquette to cut any one you'v‹
    been introduced to. Remove the joint.

18 I am fond of children (except boys).
    Letter to Kathleen Eschwege. S.D. Collingwoo‹
    The Life and Letters of Lewis Carroll (1898‹
    p.416

HENRY CARTER d. 1806

19 From distant climes, o'er widespread sea‹
        we come,
    Though not with much *éclat* or beat o‹
        drum;
    True patriots we; for be it understood,
    We left our country for our country'‹
        good.
    No private views disgraced our generou‹
        zeal,
    What urged our travels was our country'‹
        weal;
    And none will doubt but that our emigra‹
        tion
    Has proved most useful to the British na‹
        tion.
    Prologue for the opening of the Playhouse‹
    Sydney, New South Wales, 16 Jan. 1796, whe‹
    the actors were principally convicts. See *Austra‹*
    ian Encyclopedia, 1958. See 98:13

JOHN CARTWRIGHT 1740–1824

20 One man shall have one vote.
    People's Barrier Against Undue Influence (1780)‹
    p.5

PHOEBE CARY 1824–1871

21 And though hard be the task,
    'Keep a stiff upper lip'.
    Keep a Stiff Upper Lip

L. CASSIUS LONGINUS RAVILLA late‹
2nd cent. B.C.

22 *Cui bono?*
    To whose profit?
    Cicero, *pro Rosc. Am.* XXX.84 and *Pro Milone*
    XII.32

REVD. EDWARD CASWALL
1814–1878

1 Jesu, the very thought of Thee
With sweetness fills the breast.
Jesu, The Very Thought of Thee (tr. from Latin)

EMPRESS CATHERINE THE GREAT
1729–1796

2 *Moi, je serai autocrate; c'est mon métier.*
Et le bon Dieu me pardonnera: c'est son
métier.
I shall be an autocrat: that's my trade. And
the good Lord will forgive me: that's his.
Attr. See also 116:15

THE ELDER CATO, THE CENSOR
234–149 B.C

3 *Delenda est Carthago.*
Carthage must be destroyed.
Pliny the Elder, *Naturalis Historia*, xv.18.74

CATULLUS 87–54? B.C.

4 *Lugete, O Veneres Cupidinesque,*
Et quantum est hominum venustiorum.
Passer mortuus est meae puellae,
Passer, deliciae meae puellae.
Mourn, you powers of Charm and Desire,
and all you who are endowed with
charm. My lady's sparrow is dead, the
sparrow which was my lady's darling.
Carmina, iii

5 *Vivamus, mea Lesbia, atque amemus,*
Rumoresque senum severiorum
Omnes unius aestimemus assis.
Soles occidere et redire possunt:
Nobis cum semel occidit brevis lux
Nox est perpetua una dormienda.
My sweetest Lesbia let us live and love,
And though the sager sort our deeds re-
prove,
Let us not weigh them: Heav'n's great
lamps do dive
Into their west, and straight again revive,
But soon as once set is our little light,
Then must we sleep one ever-during night.
v. Tr. Campion, *A Book of Airs*, i.

6 *Da mi basia mille, deinde centum,*
Dein mille altera, dein secunda centum,
Deinde usque altera mille, deinde centum.
Give me a thousand kisses, then a hundred, then another thousand, then a
second hundred, then yet another
thousand, then a hundred.

7 *Paene insularum, Sirmio, insularumque*
Ocelle.
Sirmio, bright eye of peninsulas and
islands.
xxxi

8 *Nam risu inepto res ineptior nulla est.*
For there is nothing sillier than a silly
laugh.
xxxix

9 *Ille mi par esse deo videtur,*
Ille, si fas est, superare divos,
Qui sedens adversus identidem te
*   Spectat et audit*
Dulce ridentem, misero quod omnis
Eripit sensus mihi.
Like to a god he seems to me,
Above the gods, if so may be,
Who sitting often close to thee
May see and hear
Thy lovely laugh: ah, luckless man!
li, tr. Sir William Marris. Itself a translation of
199:12

10 *Chommoda dicebat, si quando commoda*
vellet
Dicere.
'Hamenities' he used to say, meaning
'amenities'. (Of Arrius.)
lxxxiv

11 *Odi et amo: quare id faciam, fortasse re-*
quiris.
Nescio, sed fieri sentio et excrucior.
I hate and I love: why I do so you may well
ask. I do not know, but I feel it happen
and am in agony.
lxxxv

CONSTANTINE CAVAFY 1863–1933

12 What shall become of us without any bar-
barians?
Those people were a kind of solution.
Expecting the Barbarians

EDITH CAVELL 1865–1915

13 Standing, as I do, in the view of God and
eternity I realize that patriotism is not
enough. I must have no hatred or bitter-
ness towards anyone.
Spoken to the chaplain who attended her before
her execution by firing squad, 12 Oct. 1915. *The*
Times, 23 Oct. 1915

ROBERT CECIL
see SALISBURY

THOMAS OF CELANO c.1190–1260

14 *Dies irae, dies illa,*
Solvet saeclum in favilla,
Teste David cum Sibylla.
That day, the day of wrath, will turn the
universe to ashes, as David foretells

(and the Sibyl too).
Dies irae, l. Attr. Printed in Missal, Mass for the Dead

1 *Tuba mirum sparget sonum*
Per sepulchra regionum,
Coget omnes ante thronum.

Mors stupebit et natura,
Cum resurget creatura
Iudicanti responsura.

Liber scriptus proferetur,
In quo totum continetur
Unde mundus iudicetur.

The trumpet will fling out a wonderful sound through the tombs of all regions, it will drive everyone before the throne. Death will be aghast and so will nature, when creation rises again to make answer to the judge. The written book will be brought forth, in which everything is included whereby the world will be judged.
7

2 *Rex tremendae maiestatis,*
Qui salvandos salvas gratis,
Salva me, fons pietatis!
O King of tremendous majesty, who freely saves those who should be saved, save me, O source of pity!
22

3 *Inter oves locum praesta*
Et ab haedis me sequestra
Statuens in parte dextra.
Among the sheep set me a place and separate me from the goats, standing me on the right-hand side.
43

MRS. CENTLIVRE 1667?–1723

4 The real Simon Pure.
A Bold Stroke for a Wife, V.i

MIGUEL DE CERVANTES 1547–1616

5 *El Caballero de la Triste Figura.*
The Knight of the Doleful Countenance.
Don Quixote, pt.i, ch.19

6 *La mejor salsa del mundo es el hambre.*
Hunger is the best sauce in the world.
pt.ii, ch.5

7 *Dos linages sólos hay en el mundo, como decia una abuela mia, que son el tenir y el no tenir.*
There are only two families in the world, as a grandmother of mine used to say: the haves and the have-nots.
ch.20

8 *Digo, paciencia y barajar.*

What I say is, patience, and shuffle the cards.
ch.23

PATRICK REGINALD CHALMERS
1872–1942

9 What's lost upon the roundabouts we pulls up on the swings!
Green Days and Blue Days: Roundabouts and Swings

JOSEPH CHAMBERLAIN 1836–1914

10 Provided that the City of London remains as it is at present, the clearing-house of the world.
Guildhall, London, 19 Jan. 1904

11 We are not downhearted. The only trouble is, we cannot understand what is happening to our neighbours.
Smethwick, 18 Jan. 1906

NEVILLE CHAMBERLAIN 1869–1940

12 In war, whichever side may call itself the victor, there are no winners, but all are losers.
Kettering, 3 July 1938

13 How horrible, fantastic, incredible, it is that we should be digging trenches and trying on gas-masks here because of a quarrel in a far-away country between people of whom we know nothing.
(Of Germany's annexation of the Sudetenland.) Radio broadcast, 27 Sept. 1938. K.Feiling, *Life of Neville Chamberlain,* bk.iv, ch.28

14 I believe it is peace for our time…peace with honour.
After Munich Agreement. 30 Sept. 1938. See 87:2

HADDON CHAMBERS 1860–1921

15 The long arm of coincidence.
Captain Swift (1888), Act II

NICOLAS-SÉBASTIEN CHAMFORT
1741–1794

16 *Des qualités trop supérieures rendent souvent un homme moins propre à la société. On ne va pas au marché avec des lingots; on y va avec de l'argent ou de la petite monnaie.*
Qualities too elevated often unfit a man for society. We don't take ingots with us to market; we take silver or small change.
Maximes et Pensées (1796), ch.3

17 *L'amour, tel qu'il existe dans la société, n'est que l'échange de deux fantaisies et le*

contact de deux épidermes.
Love, in the form in which it exists in society, is nothing but the exchange of two fantasies and the superficial contact of two bodies.
ch.6

1 *Je dirais volontiers des métaphysiciens ce que Scalinger disait des Basques, on dit qu'ils s'entendent, mais je n'en crois rien.*
I am tempted to say of metaphysicians what Scalinger used to say of the Basques: they are said to understand one another, but I don't believe a word of it.
ch.7

2 *Les pauvres sont les nègres de l'Europe.*
The poor are Europe's blacks.
ch.8

3 *Sois mon frère, ou je te tue.*
Be my brother, or I kill you.
Oeuvres, I, 'Notice sur la vie de Chamfort'. Interpretation of *'Fraternité ou la mort'.* See 6:2

JOHN CHANDLER 1806-1876

4 Conquering kings their titles take
From the foes they captive make:
Jesu, by a nobler deed,
From the thousands He hath freed.
Hymns Ancient and Modern. (Tr. from Latin)

RAYMOND CHANDLER 1888-1959

5 The demand was for constant action; if you stopped to think you were lost. When in doubt have a man come through a door with a gun in his hand. This could get to be pretty silly but somehow it didn't seem to matter.
The Simple Art of Murder (1950), preface, referring to the policy of light crime fiction magazines

6 Down these mean streets a man must go who is not himself mean; who is neither tarnished nor afraid.
The Simple Art of Murder

GEORGE CHAPMAN 1559?-1634?

7 Speed his plough.
Bussy D'Ambois, I.i

8 I am ashamed the law is such an ass.
Revenge for Honour, III.ii

KING CHARLES I 1600-1649

9 I see all the birds are flown.
Said in the House of Commons, 4 Jan. 1642, after attempting to arrest the Five Members. *Parliamentary History,* vol.II (1807), col.1010

KING CHARLES II 1630-1685

10 It is upon the navy under the Providence of God that the safety, honour, and welfare of this realm do chiefly attend.
Articles of War (1652), Preamble

11 Better than a play.
(On the Debates in the House of Lords on Lord Ross's Divorce Bill, 1670.) A. Bryant, *King Charles II*

12 This is very true: for my words are my own, and my actions are my ministers'.
Reply to Lord Rochester's Epitaph on him. See 195:15

13 Let not poor Nelly starve.
Burnet, *History of My Own Time,* vol.II, bk.iii, ch.17

14 He had been, he said, an unconscionable time dying; but he hoped that they would excuse it.
Macaulay, *Hist. England,* 1849, vol.i, ch.4, p.437

EMPEROR CHARLES V 1500-1558

15 *Je parle espagnol à Dieu, italien aux femmes, français aux hommes et allemand à mon cheval.*
To God I speak Spanish, to women Italian, to men French, and to my horse —German.
Attr.

PIERRE CHARRON 1541-1603

16 *La vraye science et le vray étude de l'homme, c'est l'homme.*
The true science and study of man is man.
De la Sagesse (1601), bk.I, ch.i

EARL OF CHATHAM
see WILLIAM PITT

GEOFFREY CHAUCER 1340?-1400
All line references are to the various fragments as collected in *The Works of Geoffrey Chaucer,* ed. F.N. Robinson, 2nd edition (1957)

17 Whan that Aprill with his shoures soote
The droghte of March hath perced to the roote.
The Canterbury Tales, General Prologue, l.1

18 And smale foweles maken melodye,
That slepen al the nyght with open ye
(So priketh hem nature in hir corages);
Thanne longen folk to goon on pilgrimages.
l.9

19 He was a verray, parfit gentil knyght.
l.72

1 He was as fressh as is the month of May.
  1.92

2 Ful weel she soong the service dyvyne,
  Entuned in hir nose ful semely,
  And Frenssh she spak ful faire and fetisly,
  After the scole of Stratford atte Bowe,
  For Frenssh of Parys was to hire un-
  knowe.
  1.122

3 Of smal coral aboute hire arm she bar
  A peire of bedes, gauded al with grene,
  And theron heng a brooch of gold ful
  sheene,
  On which ther was first write a crowned A,
  And after *Amor vincit omnia.*
  1.158

4 A Clerk ther was of Oxenford also,
  That unto logyk hadde longe ygo.
  As leene was his hors as is a rake,
  And he nas nat right fat, I undertake,
  But looked holwe, and therto sobrely.
  1.285

5 And gladly wolde he lerne and gladly
  teche.
  1.308

6 Nowher so bisy a man as he ther nas,
  And yet he semed bisier than he was.
  1.321

7 She was a worthy womman al hir lyve:
  Housbondes at chirche dore she hadde
  fyve.
  1.459

8 If gold ruste, what shall iren do?
  1.500

9 The smylere with the knyf under the cloke.
  The Knight's Tale, 1.1999

10 And what is bettre than wisedoom? Womman. And what is bettre than a good womman? Nothyng.
  The Tale of Melibee, 1.1107

11 'Tehee!' quod she, and clapte the wyndow
  to.
  The Miller's Tale, 1.3740

12 Whan that the month in which the world
  bigan,
  That highte March, whan God first maked
  man.
  The Nun's Priest's Tale, 1.3187

13 Mordre wol out, that se we day by day.
  1.4241

14 So was hir joly whistle wel ywet.
  The Reeve's Tale, 1.4155

15 'By God,' quod he, 'for pleynly, at a word,

Thy drasty rymyng is nat worth a toord!'
  Sir Thopas, 1.929

16 Yblessed be god that I have wedded fyve!
  Welcome the sixte, whan that evere he
  shal.
  For sothe, I wol nat kepe me chaast in al.
  Whan myn housbonde is fro the worlde
  ygon,
  Som Cristen man shall wedde me anon.
  The Wife of Bath's Prologue, 1.44

17 The bacon was nat fet for hem, I trowe,
  That som men han in Essex at Dunmowe.
  1.217

18 But, Lord Crist! whan that it remembreth
  me
  Upon my yowthe, and on my jolitee,
  It tikleth me aboute myn herte roote.
  Unto this day it dooth myn herte boote
  That I have had my world as in my tyme.
  1.469

19 And she was fayr as is the rose in May.
  The Legend of Cleopatra, 1.613

20 Farewel my bok, and my devocioun!
  The Legend of Good Women, The Prologue, 1.39

21 Thou shalt make castels thanne in Spayne,
  And dreme of joye, all but in vayne.
  The Romaunt of the Rose, 1.2573

22 So longe mote ye lyve, and alle proude,
  Til crowes feet be growen under youre yë.
  Troilus and Criseyde, ii, 1.402

23 It is nought good a slepyng hound to
  wake.
  iii, 1.764

24 Oon ere it herde, at tothir out it wente.
  iv, 1.434

25 But manly sette the world on six and
  sevene;
  And if thow deye a martyr, go to hevene!
  1.622

26 For tyme ylost may nought recovered be.
  1.1283

27 Go, litel bok, go, litel myn tragedye.
  v, 1.1786

28 O yonge, fresshe folkes, he or she.
  1.1835

29 Flee fro the prees, and dwelle with sothfastnesse.
  Truth: Balade de Bon Conseyle, 1.1

ANTON CHEKHOV 1860–1904

30 *Medvedenko:* Why do you wear black all
  the time?
  Masha: I'm in mourning for my life, I'm

unhappy.
The Seagull (1896), I

1 Women can't forgive failure.
II

2 People don't notice whether it's winter or summer when they're happy. If I lived in Moscow I don't think I'd care what the weather was like.
Three Sisters (1900 1), II

3 *Sonya:* I'm not beautiful.
Helen: You have lovely hair.
Sonya: No, when a woman isn't beautiful, people always say, 'You have lovely eyes, you have lovely hair.'
Uncle Vanya, III

EARL OF CHESTERFIELD 1694–1773

4 In my mind, there is nothing so illiberal and so ill-bred, as audible laughter.
Advice to his Son. **Graces, Laughter.** See 65:8

5 There is a Spanish proverb, which says very justly, Tell me whom you live with, and I will tell you who you are.
Letter to his son, 9 Oct. 1747

6 Take the tone of the company that you are in.

7 Do as you would be done by is the surest method that I know of pleasing.
16 Oct. 1747

8 I recommend you to take care of the minutes: for hours will take care of themselves.
6 Nov. 1747

9 Wear your learning, like your watch in a private pocket: and do not merely pull it out and strike it; merely to show that you have one.
22 Feb. 1748

10 If you happen to have an Elzevir classic in your pocket, neither show it nor mention it.

11 It must be owned, that the Graces do not seem to be natives of Great Britain; and I doubt, the best of us here have more of rough than polished diamond.
18 Nov. 1748

12 Idleness is only the refuge of weak minds.
20 July 1749

13 Putting moral virtues at the highest, and religion at the lowest, religion must still be allowed to be a collateral security, at least, to virtue; and every prudent man will sooner trust to two securities than to one.
8 Jan. 1750

14 Is it possible to love such a man? No. The utmost I can do for him is to consider him as a respectable Hottentot. [Lord Lyttelton.]
28 Feb. 1751

15 A chapter of accidents.
16 Feb. 1753

16 Religion is by no means a proper subject of conversation in a mixed company.
Undated Letter to his Godson, No.112

17 Cunning is the dark sanctuary of incapacity.
Letters from a Celebrated Nobleman to his Heir (1783), **Letter to his godson and heir, to be delivered after his own death**

G.K. CHESTERTON 1874–1936

18 Talk about the pews and steeples
And the cash that goes therewith!
But the souls of Christian peoples...
Chuck it, Smith!
Antichrist, or the Reunion of Christendom

19 I tell you naught for your comfort,
Yea, naught for your desire,
Save that the sky grows darker yet
And the sea rises higher.
Ballad of the White Horse, bk.i

20 For the great Gaels of Ireland
Are the men that God made mad,
For all their wars are merry,
And all their songs are sad.
bk.ii

21 Because it is only Christian men
Guard even heathen things.
bk.iii

22 'The high tide!' King Alfred cried.
'The high tide and the turn!'
bk.vii

23 When fishes flew and forests walked
And figs grew upon thorn,
Some moment when the moon was blood
Then surely I was born.

With monstrous head and sickening cry
And ears like errant wings,
The devil's walking parody
On all four-footed things.
The Donkey

24 Fools! For I also had my hour;
One far fierce hour and sweet:
There was a shout about my ears,
And palms before my feet.

25 They died to save their country and they
only saved the world.
The English Graves

26 White founts falling in the courts of the sun,

And the Soldan of Byzantium is smiling as
they run.
Lepanto

1 Strong gongs groaning as the guns boom
far,
Don John of Austria is going to the war.

2 Before the Roman came to Rye or out to
Severn strode,
The rolling English drunkard made the
rolling English road.
The Rolling English Road

3 The night we went to Birmingham by way
of Beachy Head.

4 For there is good news yet to hear and fine
things to be seen,
Before we go to Paradise by way of Kensal
Green.

5 For there is good news yet to hear and fine
things to be seen,
Before we go to Paradise by way of Kensal
Green.

6 Smile at us, pay us, pass us; but do not
quite forget.
For we are the people of England, that
never have spoken yet.
The Secret People

7 God made the wicked Grocer
For a mystery and a sign.
That men might shun the awful shops
And go to inns to dine.
Song Against Grocers

8 And Noah he often said to his wife when
he sat down to dine,
'I don't care where the water goes if it
doesn't get into the wine.'
Wine and Water

9 One sees great things from the valley; only
small things from the peak.
The Hammer of God

10 The artistic temperament is a disease that
afflicts amateurs.
Heretics (1905), ch.17

11 The human race, to which so many of my
readers belong.
The Napoleon of Notting Hill, ch.1

12 The Christian ideal has not been tried and
found wanting. It has been found difficult;
and left untried.
What's Wrong with the World (1910), i.5. **The
Unfinished Temple**

13 If a thing is worth doing, it is worth doing
badly.
iv.14. **Folly and Female Education**

14 Chesterton taught me this: the only way to
be sure of catching a train is to miss the
one before it.
P. Daninos, *Vacances à tous prix* (1958), 'Le
supplice de l'heure'

WILLIAM CHILLINGWORTH
1602–1644

15 I once knew a man out of courtesy help a
lame dog over a stile, and he for requital
bit his fingers.
The Religion of Protestants (1637)

PROFESSOR NOAM CHOMSKY
1928–

16 Colourless green ideas sleep furiously.
An example of a sentence which, though gram-
matically acceptable, is without meaning.
Syntactic Structures (1957), 2.3

CHUANG TSE 4th–3rd cent. B.C.

17 I do not know whether I was then a man
dreaming I was a butterfly, or whether I
am now a butterfly dreaming I am a man.
H.A. Giles, *Chuang Tse*, ch.2

CHARLES CHURCHILL 1731–1764

18 By different methods different men excel;
But where is he who can do all things well?
An Epistle to William Hogarth, l.573

19 Be England what she will,
With all her faults, she is my country still.
The Farewell, l.27. See 79:20

20 Just to the windward of the law.
The Ghost, bk.iii, l.56

21 Keep up appearances; there lies the test;
The world will give thee credit for the rest.
Outward be fair, however foul within;
Sin if thou wilt, but then in secret sin.
Night, l.311

22 Who often, but without success, have
pray'd
For apt Alliteration's artful aid.
The Prophecy of Famine, l.85

LORD RANDOLPH CHURCHILL
1849–1894

23 Ulster will fight; Ulster will be right.
Letter, 7 May 1886

24 An old man in a hurry. [Gladstone.]
To the Electors of South Paddington, June 1886

25 I never could make out what those damned dots meant. (Decimal points.)
W.S.Churchill, *Lord Randolph Churchill*, vol.ii,
p.184

WINSTON CHURCHILL 1874–1965

1 It cannot in the opinion of His Majesty's Government be classified as slavery in the extreme acceptance of the word without some risk of terminological inexactitude.
House of Commons, 22 Feb. 1906. See R.S. Churchill, *Winston S. Churchill* (1967), II.167: 'This celebrated example of polysyllabic humour was always to be misunderstood and to be regarded as a nice substitute for "lie" which it plainly was not intended to be.'

2 The maxim of the British people is 'Business as usual'.
Guildhall, 9 Nov. 1914

3 I cannot forecast to you the action of Russia. It is a riddle wrapped in a mystery inside an enigma.
Broadcast talk, 1 Oct. 1939

4 I would say to the House, as I said to those who have joined this Government, 'I have nothing to offer but blood, toil, tears and sweat'.
House of Commons, 13 May 1940

5 We shall go on to the end, we shall fight in France, we shall fight on the seas and oceans, we shall fight with growing confidence and growing strength in the air, we shall defend our island, whatever the cost may be, we shall fight on the beaches, we shall fight on the landing grounds, we shall fight in the fields and in the streets, we shall fight in the hills; we shall never surrender.
4 June 1940

6 Let us therefore brace ourselves to our duties and so bear ourselves that if the British Empire and its Commonwealth last for a thousand years men will still say, 'This was their finest hour'.
18 June 1940

7 Never in the field of human conflict was so much owed by so many to so few.
20 Aug. 1940

8 Give us the tools, and we will finish the job.
Radio Broadcast, 9 Feb. 1941. (Addressing President Roosevelt.)

9 What kind of people do they [the Japanese] think we are?
To U.S. Congress, 24 Dec. 1941

10 When I warned them [the French Government] that Britain would fight on alone whatever they did, their Generals told their Prime Minister and his divided Cabinet: 'In three weeks England will have her neck wrung like a chicken.'

Some chicken! Some neck!
To the Canadian Parliament, 30 Dec. 1941

11 This is not the end. It is not even the beginning of the end. But it is, perhaps, the end of the beginning.
Mansion House, 10 Nov. 1942. (Of the Battle of Egypt.)

12 An iron curtain has descended across the Continent.
Address at Westminster College, Fulton, U.S.A., 5 Mar. 1946. The expression 'iron curtain' had been previously applied by others to the Soviet Union or its sphere of influence, e.g., Ethel Snowden, *Through Bolshevik Russia* (1920); Dr. Goebbels, *Das Reich* (25 Feb. 1945); and by Churchill himself in a cable to President Truman (4 June 1945).

13 Many forms of government have been tried, and will be tried in this world of sin and woe. No one pretends that democracy is perfect or all-wise. Indeed, it has been said that democracy is the worst form of Government except all those other forms that have been tried from time to time.
House of Commons, 11 Nov. 1947

14 To jaw-jaw is better than to war-war.
Washington, 26 June 1954

15 It was the nation and the race dwelling all round the globe that had the lion's heart. I had the luck to be called upon to give the roar.
Speech at Palace of Westminster on his 80th birthday, 30 Nov. 1954

16 It is a good thing for an uneducated man to read books of quotations.
My Early Life (1930), ch.9

17 In war, resolution; in defeat, defiance; in victory, magnanimity; in peace, goodwill.
Epigram after the Great War, 1914–18. Sir Edward Marsh, *A Number of People* (1939), p.152. Later used as the 'Moral of the Work' in each volume of *The Second World War.*

18 When you have to kill a man it costs nothing to be polite.
(On the ceremonial form of the declaration of war against Japan, 8 Dec. 1941.) vol.iii, *The Grand Alliance* (1950), p.543

19 In defeat, unbeatable; in victory, unbearable.
(Of Viscount Montgomery.) Edward Marsh, *Ambrosia and Small Beer*, ch.5

20 This is the sort of English up with which I will not put.
Attr. comment against clumsy avoidance of a preposition at the end of a sentence. E. Gowers, *Plain Words*, ch.9, 'Troubles with Prepositions', i

21 Don't talk to me about naval tradition.

It's nothing but rum, sodomy and the lash.
Sir Peter Gretton, *Former Naval Person,* ch.1.
Sometimes quoted as 'Rum, buggery and the
lash'; compare 'Rum, bum, and bacca' and
'Ashore it's wine women and song, aboard it's
rum, bum and concertina', naval catch-phrases
dating from the nineteenth century.

COLLEY CIBBER 1671–1757

1 What! now your fire's gone, you would
knock me down with the butt-end, would
you?
The Refusal, Act I

2 Off with his head—so much for Buckingham.
Richard III, (adapted from Shakespeare) IV.iii

3 Perish the thought!
V.v

4 Stolen sweets are best.
The Rival Fools, Act I

CICERO 106–43 B.C.

5 There is nothing so absurd but some philosopher has said it.
De Divinatione, ii.58

6 *Salus populi suprema est lex.*
The good of the people is the chief law.
De Legibus, III.iii.8

7 *'Ipse dixit.' 'Ipse' autem erat Xytjcwozas.*
'He himself said it', and this 'himself' was
Pythagoras.
De Natura Deorum, I.v.10

8 *Cedant arma togae, concedant lqwrea lau-
di.*
Let war yield to peace, laurels to paeans.
De Officiis, I.xxii.82

9 *Numquam se minus otiosum esse quam cum
otiosus, nec minus solum quam cum solus
esset.*
Never less idle than when wholly idle, nor
less alone than when wholly alone.
III.i.1

10 *Quousque tandem abutere, Catilina, pat-
ientia nostra?*
How long will you abuse our patience,
Catiline?
In Catilinam, I.i.1

11 *O tempora, O mores!*
Oh, the times! Oh, the manners!

12 *Civis Romanus sum.*
I am a Roman citizen.
In Verrem, V.lvii.147

13 *Nervos belli, pecuniam infinitam.*
The sinews of war, unlimited money.
Philippic, V.ii.5

14 *Id quod est praestantissimum maximeque
optabile omnibus sanis et bonis et beatis,
cum dignitate otium.*
The thing which is the most outstanding
and chiefly to be desired by all healthy and
good and well-off persons, is leisure with
honour.
Pro Sestio, xlv.98

15 *O fortunatam natam me consule Romam!*
O happy Rome, born when I was consul!
Juvenal, x.122

JOHN CLARE 1793–1864

16 When badgers fight then everyone's a foe.
Badger

17 He could not die when the trees were
green,
For he loved the time too well.
The Dying Child

18 My life hath been one chain of contrad-
ictions,
Madhouses, prisons, whore-shops.
The Exile

19 They took me from my wife, and to save
trouble
I wed again, and made the error double.

20 A quiet, pilfering, unprotected race.
Gypsies

21 I am—yet what I am, none cares or
knows;
My friends forsake me like a memory
lost:
I am the self-consumer of my woes.
I Am

22 When fishes leap in silver stream…
And forest bees are humming near,
And cowslips in boys' hats appear…
We then may say that May is come.
May. See N. Ault, *A Treasury of Unfamiliar
Lyrics* (1938), p.473

23 Dear Sir,—I am in a Madhouse and quite
forget your name or who you are.
Letter, 1860

EARL OF CLARENDON 1609–1674

24 Without question, when he [Hampden]
first drew the sword, he threw away the
scabbard.
History of the Rebellion, ed. Macray (1888),
III.vii.84

25 So enamoured on peace that he would
have been glad the King should have
bought it at any price.
233

CLARIBEL (MRS. C.A. BARNARD) 1840–1869

1 I cannot sing the old songs
I sang long years ago,
For heart and voice would fail me,
And foolish tears would flow.
Fireside Thoughts

JOHN CLARKE fl. 1639

2 Home is home, though it be never so
homely.
Paraemiologia Anglo-Latina (1639)

KARL VON CLAUSEWITZ 1780–1831

3 *Der Krieg ist nichts als eine Fortsetzung der
politischen Verkehrs mit Einmischung anderer Mittel.*
War is nothing but the continuation of
politics with the admixture of other means.
Vom Kriege, (memorial ed. 1952) p.888, commonly rendered in the form 'War is the continuation of politics by other means'.

GEORGES CLEMENCEAU 1841–1929

4 *Quatorze? Le bon Dieu n'a que dix.*
Fourteen? The good Lord has only ten.
Attr. comment on hearing of Woodrow Wilson's
Fourteen Points (1918)

5 War is much too serious a thing to be left
to the military.
Attr. Also attr. Talleyrand and Briand. See, e.g.,
John Bailey, *Letters and Diaries* (1935), p.176

POPE CLEMENT XIII 1693–1769

6 *Sint ut sunt aut non sint.*
Let them be as they are or not be at all.
Reply to request for changes in the constitutions
of the Society of Jesus, 27 Jan. 1762. See J.A.M.
Crétineau-Joly, *Clément XIV et les Jésuites*
(1847), p.370n.

LORD CLIVE 1725–1774

7 By God, Mr Chairman, at this moment I
stand astonished at my own moderation!
Reply during Parliamentary cross-examination,
1773

ARTHUR HUGH CLOUGH 1819–1861

8 Am I prepared to lay down my life for the
British female?
Really, who knows?...
Ah, for a child in the street I could strike;
for the full-blown lady—
Somehow, Eustace, alas! I have not felt the
vocation.
Amours de Voyage, c.II.iv

9 But for his funeral train which the bridegroom sees in the distance,
Would he so joyfully, think you, fall in
with the marriage-procession?
c.III.vi

10 Good, too, Logic, of course; in itself, but
not in fine weather.
The Bothie of Tober-na-Vuolich, ii

11 How pleasant it is to have money, heigh
ho!
How pleasant it is to have money.
Dipsychus, sc.v

12 Thou shalt have one God only; who
Would be at the expense of two?
The Latest Decalogue

13 Thou shalt not kill; but need'st not strive
Officiously to keep alive.

14 Do not adultery commit;
Advantage rarely comes of it.

15 Thou shalt not steal; an empty feat,
When it's so lucrative to cheat.

16 Thou shalt not covet; but tradition
Approves all forms of competition.

17 Say not the struggle naught availeth,
The labour and the wounds are vain,
The enemy faints not, nor faileth,
And as things have been, things remain.

If hopes were dupes, fears may be liars;
It may be, in yon smoke concealed,
Your comrades chase e'en now the fliers,
And, but for you, possess the field.

For while the tired waves, vainly breaking,
Seem here no painful inch to gain,
Far back through creeks and inlets making
Comes silent, flooding in, the main.

And not by eastern windows only,
When daylight comes, comes in the
light,
In front the sun climbs slow, how slowly,
But westward, look, the land is bright.
Say Not the Struggle Naught Availeth

18 That out of sight is out of mind
Is true of most we leave behind.
Songs in Absence, **That Out of Sight**

19 What shall we do without you? Think
where we are. Carlyle has led us all out
into the desert, and he has left us there.
Parting words to Emerson, 15 July 1848. See
E.E. Hale, *James Russell Lowell and his Friends*
(1889), ch.19

WILLIAM COBBETT 1762–1835

20 But what is to be the fate of the great wen
[London] of all? The monster, called...'the

metropolis of the empire'?
Rural Rides

JEAN COCTEAU 1889-1963

1 *Victor Hugo...un fou qui se croyait Victor Hugo.*
Victor Hugo...A madman who thought he was Victor Hugo.
See **Opium,** 1930 ed., p.77

DESMOND COKE 1879-1931

2 His blade struck the water a full second before any other...until...as the boats began to near the winning-post, his own was dipping into the water *twice* as often as any other.
Sandford of Merton (1903), ch.xii. Often quoted as 'All rowed fast but none so fast as stroke', and attr. to Ouida.

SIR EDWARD COKE 1552-1634

3 For a man's house is his castle, *et domus sua cuique est tutissimum refugium.*
Institutes: Commentary upon Littleton. Third Institute, cap.73

4 They [corporations] cannot commit treason, nor be outlawed, nor excommunicate, for they have no souls.
Sutton's Hospital Case, 10 Rep.32b

SAMUEL TAYLOR COLERIDGE 1772-1834

5 It is an ancient Mariner,
And he stoppeth one of three.
'By thy long grey beard and glittering eye,
Now wherefore stopp'st thou me?'
The Ancient Mariner, pt.i

6 He holds him with his skinny hand,
'There was a ship,' quoth he.
'Hold off! unhand me, grey-beard loon!'
Eftsoons his hand dropt he.

He holds him with his glittering eye...
He cannot choose but hear;
And thus spake on that ancient man,
The bright-eyed Mariner.

7 The Wedding-Guest here beat his breast,
For he heard the loud bassoon.

8 'God save thee, ancient Mariner!
From the fiends that plague thee thus!—
Why look'st thou so?'—With my cross-bow
I shot the Albatross.

9 As idle as a painted ship
Upon a painted ocean.
pt.ii

10 Water, water, every where,
And all the boards did shrink;
Water, water, every where,
Nor any drop to drink.

The very deep did rot: O Christ!
That ever this should be!
Yea, slimy things did crawl with legs
Upon the slimy sea.

11 The Sun's rim dips; the stars rush out:
At one stride comes the dark.

12 The hornèd Moon, with one bright star
Within the nether tip.

13 'I fear thee, ancient Mariner!
I fear thy skinny hand!
And thou art long, and lank, and brown,
As is the ribbed sea-sand.'
pt.iv

14 Alone, alone, all, all alone,
Alone on a wide wide sea!
And never a saint took pity on
My soul in agony.

15 And a thousand thousand slimy things
Lived on; and so did I.

16 Oh Sleep! it is a gentle thing,
Beloved from pole to pole,
To Mary Queen the praise be given!
She sent the gentle sleep from Heaven,
That slid into my soul.
pt.v

17 We were a ghastly crew.

18 Like one, that on a lonesome road
Doth walk in fear and dread,
And having once turned round walks on,
And turns no more his head;
Because he knows, a frightful fiend
Doth close behind him tread.
pt.vi

19 I pass, like night, from land to land;
I have strange power of speech.
pt.vii

20 He prayeth well, who loveth well
Both man and bird and beast.

He prayeth best, who loveth best
All things both great and small;
For the dear God who loveth us,
He made and loveth all.

21 A sadder and a wiser man,
He rose the morrow morn.

22 A sight to dream of, not to tell!
Christabel, pt.i

23 What is an Epigram? a dwarfish whole,
Its body brevity, and wit its soul.
Epigram

24 Swans sing before they die—'twere no bad

thing,
Did certain persons die before they sing.
Epigram on a Volunteer Singer

1 At this moment he was unfortunately
called out by a person on business from
Porlock.
Kubla Khan, Preliminary note

2 In Xanadu did Kubla Khan
A stately pleasure-dome decree:
Where Alph, the sacred river, ran
Through caverns measureless to man
   Down to a sunless sea.
So twice five miles of fertile ground
With walls and towers were girdled round.

3 But oh! that deep romantic chasm which
      slanted
Down the green hill athwart a cedarn cov-
      er!
A savage place! as holy and enchanted
As e'er beneath a waning moon was
      haunted
By woman wailing for her demon-lover!
And from this chasm, with ceaseless tur-
      moil seething,
As if this earth in fast thick pants were
      breathing,
A mighty fountain momently was forced.

4 Five miles meandering with a mazy mo-
      tion
Through wood and dale the sacred river
      ran.

5 And 'mid this tumult Kubla heard from
      far
Ancestral voices prophesying war!

6 A damsel with a dulcimer
In a vision once I saw:
It was an Abyssinian maid,
And on her dulcimer she played,
Singing of Mount Abora.

7 Weave a circle round him thrice,
And close your eyes with holy dread,
For he on honey-dew hath fed,
And drunk the milk of Paradise.

8 With Donne, whose muse on dromedary
      trots,
Wreathe iron pokers into true-love knots.
On Donne's Poetry

9 He who begins by loving Christianity better than Truth will proceed by loving his
own sect or church better than Christianity, and end by loving himself better than
all.
*Aids to Reflection: Moral and Religious Aphor-
isms,* XXV

10 That willing suspension of disbelief for the

moment, which constitutes poetic faith.
Biographia Literaria, ch.14

11 Summer has set in with its usual severity.
Quoted in Lamb's letter to V. Novello, 9 May
1826

12 To see him [Kean] act, is like reading
Shakespeare by flashes of lightning.
Table Talk, 27 Apr. 1823

13 I wish our clever young poets would
remember my homely definitions of prose
and poetry; that is prose ; words in their
best order;—poetry ; the *best* words in the
best order.
12 July 1827

14 The man's desire is for the woman; but the
woman's desire is rarely other than for the
desire of the man.
23 July 1827

15 In politics, what begins in fear usually
ends in folly.
5 Oct. 1830·

WILLIAM COLLINGBOURNE d. 1484

16 The Cat, the Rat, and Lovell our dog
Rule all England under a hog.
R. Holinshed, *Chronicles* (1586), iii.746. Of Sir
William Catesby (d.1485), Sir Richard Ratcliffe
(d.1485), Lord Lovell (1454–?1487) (whose crest
was a dog), and King Richard III (whose emblem was a wild boar). Collingbourne was executed on Tower Hill.

JESSE COLLINGS 1831–1920

17 Three acres and a cow.
Phrase used in his land-reform propaganda of
1885. See 165:19

ADMIRAL COLLINGWOOD
1750–1810

18 Now, gentlemen, let us do something to-
day which the world may talk of hereafter.
Said before the Battle of Trafalgar, 21 Oct. 1805.
G.L. Newnham Collingwood, ed., *Correspondence and Memoir of Lord Collingwood*

R.G. COLLINGWOOD 1889–1943

19 Perfect freedom is reserved for the man
who lives by his own work, and in that
work does what he wants to do.
Speculum Mentis, Prologue

MORTIMER COLLINS 1827–1876

20 A man is as old as he's feeling,
A woman as old as she looks.
The Unknown Quantity

WILLIAM COLLINS 1721–1759

1 To fair Fidele's grassy tomb
 Soft maids and village hinds shall bring
Each opening sweet of earliest bloom,
 And rifle all the breathing spring.
Dirge in Cymbeline

GEORGE COLMAN 1732–1794

2 Love and a cottage! Eh, Fanny! Ah, give
me indifference and a coach and six!
The Clandestine Marriage, I.ii

GEORGE COLMAN THE YOUNGER
1762–1836

3 Oh, London is a fine town,
 A very famous city,
Where all the streets are paved with gold,
 And all the maidens pretty.
The Heir at Law (1797), I.ii

4 Not to be sneezed at.
II.i

5 Says he, 'I am a handsome man, but I'm a
gay deceiver.'
Love Laughs at Locksmiths (1808), Act II

CHARLES CALEB COLTON 1780?–
1832

6 When you have nothing to say, say
nothing.
Lacon (1820), vol.i, No.183

7 Man is an embodied paradox, a bundle of
contradictions.
No.408

IVY COMPTON-BURNETT 1892–1969

8 'Time has too much credit,' said Bridget.
'I never agree with the compliments paid
to it. It is not a great healer. It is an indifferent and perfunctory one. Sometimes it
does not heal at all. And sometimes when
it seems to, no healing has been necessary.'
Darkness and Day (1951), ch.7

9 'We may as well imagine the scene.'
'No, my mind baulks at it.'
'Mine does worse. It constructs it.'
A Family and a Fortune (1939), ch.9

10 'She still seems to me in her own way a
person born to command,' said Luce...
'I wonder if anyone is born to obey,' said
Isabel. 'That may be why people command
rather badly, that they have no suitable
material to work on.'
Parents and Children (1941), ch.3

AUGUSTE COMTE 1798–1857

11 M. Comte used to reproach his early English admirers with maintaining the 'conspiracy of silence' concerning his later per-
formances.
J.S. Mill, *Auguste Comte and Positivism* (1865),
p.199

WILLIAM CONGREVE 1670–1729

12 She lays it on with a trowel.
The Double Dealer (1694), III.x

13 See how love and murder will out.
IV.vi

14 Has he not a rogue's face?...a hanging-
look to me...has a damn'd Tyburn-face,
without the benefit o' the Clergy...
Love for Love (1695), II.vii

15 I know that's a secret, for it's whispered
every where.
III.iii

16 Aye, 'tis well enough for a servant to be
bred at an University. But the education is
a little too pedantic for a gentleman.
V.iii

17 Nay, for my part I always despised Mr
Tattle of all things; nothing but his being
my husband could have made me like him
less.
xi

18 Music has charms to sooth a savage
breast.
The Mourning Bride (1697), I.i

19 Heav'n has no rage, like love to hatred
turn'd,
Nor Hell a fury, like a woman scorn'd.
III.viii

20 *Sharper:* Thus grief still treads upon the
heels of pleasure:
Marry'd in haste, we may repent at leisure.
Setter: Some by experience find those
 words mis-plac'd:
At leisure marry'd, they repent in haste.
The Old Bachelor (1693), V.viii and ix

21 I always take blushing either for a sign of
guilt, or of ill breeding.
The Way of the World (1700), I.ix

22 Say what you will, 'tis better to be left
than never to have been loved.
II.i

23 Here she comes i' faith full sail, with her
fan spread and streamers out, and a shoal
of fools for tenders.
iv

24 A little disdain is not amiss; a little scorn is

alluring.
III.v

1 I nauseate walking; 'tis a country diversion, I loathe the country.
IV.iv

2 Let us be very strange and well-bred: Let us be as strange as if we had been married a great while, and as well-bred as if we were not married at all.
v

3 These articles subscrib'd, if I continue to endure you a little longer, I may by degrees dwindle into a wife.

JAMES M. CONNELL 1852–1929

4 The people's flag is deepest red;
It shrouded oft our martyred dead,
And ere their limbs grew stiff and cold,
Their heart's blood dyed its every fold.
    Then raise the scarlet standard high!
    Within its shade we'll live or die.
    Tho' cowards flinch and traitors sneer,
    We'll keep the red flag flying here.
The Red Flag (1889), in H.E. Piggot, *Songs that made History*, ch.6

CYRIL CONNOLLY 1903–1974

5 The Mandarin style...is beloved by literary pundits, by those who would make the written word as unlike as possible to the spoken one. It is the title of those writers whose tendency is to make their language convey more than they mean or more than they feel.
Enemies of Promise (1938), pt.I. **Predicament,** ch.ii

6 She [the artist's wife] will know that there is no more sombre enemy of good art than the pram in the hall.
pt.II. **The Charlock's Shade,** ch.xiv

7 There is no fury like an ex-wife searching for a new lover.
The Unquiet Grave (1944), Part I. **Ecce Gubernator**

8 Arrival-Angst is closely connected with guilt, with the dread of something terrible having happened during our absence. Death of parents. Entry of bailiffs. Flight of loved one. Sensations worse at arriving in the evening than in the morning, and much worse at Victoria and Waterloo, than at Paddington.

9 Imprisoned in every fat man a thin one is wildly signalling to be let out.
Part II. **Te Palinure Petens.** See 178:9

10 It is closing time in the gardens of the West and from now on an artist will be judged only by the resonance of his solitude or the quality of his despair.
'Comment', *Horizon,* Nos. 120-121, Dec. 1949 –Jan. 1950. (Final Issue)

JOSEPH CONRAD 1857–1924

11 The conquest of the earth, which mostly means the taking it away from those who have a different complexion or slightly flatter noses than ourselves, is not a pretty thing when you look into it too much.
The Heart of Darkness (1902), ch.1

12 Mistah Kurtz—he dead.
ch.3

13 The terrorist and the policeman both come from the same basket.
The Secret Agent (1907), ch.4

JOHN CONSTABLE 1776–1837

14 The amiable but eccentric Blake...said of a beautiful drawing of an avenue of fir trees...'Why, this is not drawing, but *inspiration.*'...[Constable] replied, 'I never knew it before; I meant it for drawing.'
Leslie, *Life of John Constable* (1843), ch.17

15 In Claude's landscape all is lovely—all amiable—all is amenity and repose;—the calm sunshine of the heart.
ch.18. A Course of Lectures to the Royal Institution. Lecture II, 2 June 1836.

BENJAMIN CONSTANT 1767–1834

16 *Dîner avec Robinson, écolier de Schelling. Son travail sur l'esthétique du Kant. Idées très ingénieuses. L'art pour l'art et sans but; tout but dénature l'art. Mais l'art atteint au but qu'il n'a pas.*
Dinner with [Crabb] Robinson, a pupil of Schelling. His work on Kant's aesthetics. Very clever notions. Art for art's sake and with no purpose; any purpose perverts art. But art achieves a purpose which is not its own.
Journal intime, 11 février 1804

EMPEROR CONSTANTINE 288?–337

17 *In hoc signo vinces.*
In this sign shalt thou conquer.
Traditional form of words of Constantine's vision (312). Reported in Greek, τούτῳ νίκα, 'By this, conquer', Eusebius, *Life of Constantine,* i.28

ELIZA COOK 1818–1889

1 I love it, I love it; and who shall dare
To chide me for loving that old arm-chair?
The Old Arm-chair

CALVIN COOLIDGE 1872–1933

2 He said he was against it.
On being asked what had been said by a clergy-
man who preached on sin.

BISHOP RICHARD CORBET 1582–1635

3 Farewell, rewards and Fairies,
Good housewives now may say,
For now foul sluts in dairies
Do fare as well as they.
The Fairies' Farewell

PIERRE CORNEILLE 1606–1684

4 *Un premier mouvement ne fut jamais un
crime.*
A first impulse was never a crime.
Horace (1640), V.iii. See 172:9

FRANCES CORNFORD 1886–1960

5 Whoso maintains that I am humbled now
(Who wait the Awful Day) is still a liar;
I hope to meet my Maker brow to brow
And find my own the higher.
Epitaph for a Reviewer

6 How long ago Hector took off his plume,
Not wanting that his little son should cry,
Then kissed his sad Andromache good-
bye—
And now we three in Euston waiting-
room.
Parting in Wartime

7 O fat white woman whom nobody loves,
Why do you walk through the fields in
gloves...
Missing so much and so much?
To a Fat Lady Seen from a Train

F.M. CORNFORD 1874–1943

8 Every public action which is not customary, either is wrong or, if it is right, is a
dangerous precedent. It follows that
nothing should ever be done for the first
time.
Microcosmographia Academica, vii

MME CORNUEL 1605–1694

9 *Il n'y a point de héros pour son valet de
chambre.*

No man is a hero to his valet.
Lettres de Mlle Aïssé, xii, 13 août, 1728

WILLIAM CORY 1823–1892

10 Jolly boating weather,
And a hay harvest breeze,
Blade on the feather,
Shade off the trees
Swing, swing together
With your body between your knees.
Eton Boating Song, see E. Parker, *Floreat* (1923),
p.109. First published in *Eton Scrap Book,* 1865

11 Nothing in life shall sever
The chain that is round us now.

12 They told me, Heraclitus, they told me
you were dead,
They brought me bitter news to hear and
bitter tears to shed.
I wept as I remembered how often you and
I
Had tired the sun with talking and sent
him down the sky.
Heraclitus. Translation of Callimachus, *Epi-
grams,* 2

13 You promise heavens free from strife,
Pure truth, and perfect change of will;
But sweet, sweet is this human life,
So sweet, I fain would breathe it still;
Your chilly stars I can forgo,
This warm kind world is all I know.
Mimnermus in Church

CHARLES COTTON 1630–1687

14 The shadows now so long do grow,
That brambles like tall cedars show,
Molehills seem mountains, and the ant
Appears a monstrous elephant.
Evening Quatrains, iii

ÉMILE COUÉ 1857–1926

15 *Tous les jours, à tous points de vue, je vais
de mieux en mieux.*
Every day, in every way, I am getting better and better.
Formula in his clinic at Nancy

VICTOR COUSIN 1792–1867

16 *Il faut de la religion pour la religion, de la
morale pour la morale, comme de l'art pour
l'art...le beau ne peut être la voie ni de
l'utile, ni du bien, ni du saint; il ne conduit
qu'à lui-même.*
We must have religion for religion's sake,
morality for morality's sake, as with art
for art's sake...the beautiful cannot be the
way to what is useful, or to what is good,

or to what is holy; it leads only to itself.
Du vrai, du beau, et du bien (Sorbonne lecture, 1818). See 77:16

THOMAS COVENTRY, BARON COVENTRY 1578–1640

1 The dominion of the sea, as it is an ancient and undoubted right of the crown of England, so it is the best security of the land. The wooden walls are the best walls of this kingdom.
Speech to the Judges, 17 June 1635. See Rushworth, *Hist. Coll.* (1680), vol.ii, p.297. Cf. Herodotus, VII. 141-3

NOËL COWARD 1899–1973

2 Very flat, Norfolk.
Private Lives, I

3 Extraordinary how potent cheap music is.

4 Certain women should be struck regularly, like gongs.
III

5 Mad dogs and Englishmen go out in the mid-day sun;
The Japanese don't care to, the Chinese wouldn't dare to;
Hindus and Argentines sleep firmly from twelve to one,
But Englishmen detest a
Siesta.
Mad Dogs and Englishmen

6 Don't put your daughter on the stage, Missis Worthington
Don't put your daughter on the stage.
Mrs. Worthington

7 Poor little rich girl
You're a bewitched girl,
Better beware!
Poor Little Rich Girl from *Charlot's Revue* of 1926

8 The Stately Homes of England
How beautiful they stand,
To prove the upper classes
Have still the upper hand.
The Stately Homes of England from *Operette* (1938) See 117:2

9 Tho' the pipes that supply the bathroom burst
And the lavat'ry makes you fear the worst
It was used by Charles the First
Quite informally
And later by George the Fourth
On a journey North.

ABRAHAM COWLEY 1618–1667

10 Love in her sunny eyes does basking play;
Love walks the pleasant mazes of her hair;
Love does on both her lips for ever stray;
And sows and reaps a thousand kisses there.
In all her outward parts Love's always seen;
But, oh, he never went within.
The Change

11 God the first garden made, and the first city Cain.
The Garden

WILLIAM COWPER 1731–1800

12 John Gilpin was a citizen
Of credit and renown,
A train-band captain eke was he
Of famous London town.
John Gilpin

13 Beware of desp'rate steps. The darkest day
(Live till tomorrow) will have pass'd away.
The Needless Alarm, l.132

14 God moves in a mysterious way
His wonders to perform;
He plants his footsteps in the sea,
And rides upon the storm.
Olney Hymns, 35

15 Toll for the brave—
The brave! that are no more:
All sunk beneath the wave,
Fast by their native shore.
On the Loss of the Royal George

16 His sword was in the sheath,
His fingers held the pen,
When Kempenfelt went down
With twice four hundred men.

17 Winks hard, and talks of darkness at noon-day.
The Progress of Error, l.451

18 Thou god of our idolatry, the press...
Thou fountain, at which drink the good and wise;
Thou ever-bubbling spring of endless lies;
Like Eden's dread probationary tree,
Knowledge of good and evil is from thee.
l.461

19 God made the country, and man made the town.
The Task, bk.i, **The Sofa,** l.749

20 England, with all thy faults, I love thee still—
My country!
bk.ii, **The Timepiece,** l.206. See 70:19

1 Variety's the very spice of life,
That gives it all its flavour.
l.606

2 I was a stricken deer, that left the herd
Long since.
bk.iii, **The Garden**, l.108. See 210:6

3 How various his employments, whom the
world
Calls idle.
l.352

4 Now stir the fire, and close the shutters
fast,
Let fall the curtains, wheel the sofa round,
And, while the bubbling and loud-hissing
urn
Throws up a steamy column, and the cups,
That cheer but not inebriate, wait on each,
So let us welcome peaceful ev'ning in.
bk.iv, **The Winter Evening**, l.34. See 20:1

5 I am monarch of all I survey,
My right there is none to dispute.
*Verses Supposed to be Written by Alexander Sel-
kirk*

ARCHBISHOP CRANMER 1489–1556

6 This was the hand that wrote it, therefore
it shall suffer first punishment.
At the stake, 21 March 1556. Green, *Short History of The English People*, p.367

RICHARD CRASHAW 1612?–1649

7 By all the eagle in thee, all the dove.
*The Flaming Heart upon the Book of Saint Tere-
sa*, l.95

8 Love, thou art absolute sole Lord
Of life and death.
*Hymn to the Name & Honour of the Admirable
Saint Teresa*, l.1

9 Lo here a little volume, but large book.
Prayer…prefixed to a little Prayer-book

10 It is love's great artillery
Which here contracts itself and comes to
lie
Close couch'd in your white bosom.

11 Whoe'er she be,
That not impossible she
That shall command my heart and me.
Wishes to his supposed Mistress

BISHOP MANDELL CREIGHTON 1843–1901

12 No people do so much harm as those who
go about doing good.
Life (1904), vol.ii, p.503

SIR RANULPHE CREWE 1558–1646

13 And yet time hath his revolution; there
must be a period and an end to all temporal things, *finis rerum*, an end of names and
dignities and whatsoever is terrene; and
why not of De Vere? Where is Bohun,
where's Mowbray, where's Mortimer?
Nay, which is more and most of all, where
is Plantagenet? They are entombed in the
urns and sepulchres of mortality. And yet
let the name and dignity of De Vere stand
so long as it pleaseth God.
Oxford Peerage Case, 1625. See D.N.B.

OLIVER CROMWELL 1599–1658

14 Such men as had the fear of God before
them and as made some conscience of
what they did…the plain russet-coated
captain that knows what he fights for and
loves what he knows.
Letter of Sept. 1643. Carlyle, *Letters and
Speeches of Oliver Cromwell*

15 I beseech you, in the bowels of Christ,
think it possible you may be mistaken.
Letter to the General Assembly of the Church of
Scotland, 3 Aug. 1650

16 Mr Lely, I desire you would use all your
skill to paint my picture truly like me, and
not flatter me at all; but remark all these
roughnesses, pimples, warts, and everything as you see me, otherwise I will never
pay a farthing for it.
Walpole, *Anecdotes of Painting*, ch.12

17 Take away that fool's bauble, the mace.
At the dismissal of the Rump Parliament, 20
Apr. 1653. Bulstrode Whitelock, *Memorials*
(1682), p.554. Often quoted as 'Take away these
baubles'.

18 You have sat too long here for any good
you have been doing. Depart, I say, and let
us have done with you. In the name of
God, go!
Addressing the Rump Parliament, 20 Apr. 1653.
See Bulstrode Whitelock, *Memorials* (1682),
p.554. Quoted by L.S. Amery from the back
benches of Neville Chamberlain's Government,
House of Commons, 7 May 1940.

19 Necessity hath no law. Feigned necessities, imaginary necessities,…are the
greatest cozenage that men can put upon
the Providence of God, and make
pretences to break known rules by.
Speech to Parliament, 12 Sept. 1654

20 My design is to make what haste I can to
be gone.
Last words. Morley, *Life*. v, ch.10

BISHOP RICHARD CUMBERLAND
1631–1718

1 It is better to wear out than to rust out.
G. Horne, *The Duty of Contending for the Faith*

E.E. CUMMINGS 1894–1962

2 who knows if the moon's
a balloon, coming out of a keen city
in the sky—filled with pretty people?
& [AND] (1925), N&:VII

3   listen: there's a hell
of a good universe next door; let's go.
pity this busy monster, manunkind

ALLAN CUNNINGHAM 1784–1842

4 A wet sheet and a flowing sea,
A wind that follows fast
And fills the white and rustling sail
And bends the gallant mast.
A Wet Sheet and a Flowing Sea

JOHN PHILPOT CURRAN 1750–1817

5 The condition upon which God hath
given liberty to man is eternal vigilance;
which condition if he break, servitude is at
once the consequence of his crime, and the
punishment of his guilt.
Speech on the Right of Election of Lord Mayor
of Dublin, 10 July 1790

ST. CYPRIAN d. 258

6 *Habere non potest Deum patrem qui ecclesiam non habet matrem.*
He cannot have God for his father who
has not the church for his mother.
De Cath. Eccl. Unitate, vi. See 11:18

DANTE 1265–1321

7 *Nel mezzo del cammin di nostra vita.*
In the middle of the road of our life.
Divina Commedia (ed. Sinclair, 1971). **Inferno,** i.1

8 *LASCIATE OGNI SPERANZA VOI CH'ENTRATE!*
Abandon all hope, you who enter!
iii.1. Inscription at the entrance to Hell

9 *Il gran rifiuto.*
The great refusal.
60

10 *Nessun maggior dolore,
Che ricordarsi del tempo felice
Nella miseria.*
There is no greater sorrow than to recall a
time of happiness in misery.
v.121. See 44:13

DANTON 1759–1794

11 *De l'audace, et encore de l'audace, et toujours de l'audace!*
Boldness, and again boldness, and always
boldness!
Speech to the Legislative Committee of General
Defence, 2 Sept. 1792. *Le Moniteur,* 4 Sept. 1792

12 Thou wilt show my head to the people: it
is worth showing.
5 Apr. 1794. Carlyle, *French Revolution,* bk.VI,
ch.2

GEORGE DARLEY 1795–1846

13   O blest unfabled Incense Tree,
That burns in glorious Araby.
Nepenthe, l.147

CHARLES DARWIN 1809–1882

14 A hairy quadruped, furnished with a tail
and pointed ears, probably arboreal in its
habits.
Descent of Man (1871), ch.21

15 I have called this principle, by which each
slight variation, if useful, is preserved, by
the term of Natural Selection.
On the Origin of Species (1859), ch.3

16 What a book a devil's chaplain might
write on the clumsy, wasteful, blundering,
low, and horribly cruel works of nature!
Letter to J.D. Hooker, 13 July 1856

CHARLES DAVENANT 1656–1714

17 Custom, that unwritten law,
By which the people keep even kings in
awe.
Circe, II.iii

SIR WILLIAM DAVENANT 1606–1668

18 In ev'ry grave make room, make room!
The world's at an end, and we come, we
come.
The Law against Lovers, III.i

JOHN DAVIDSON 1857–1909

19 A runnable stag, a kingly crop.
A Runnable Stag

SIR JOHN DAVIES 1569–1626

20 Wedlock, indeed, hath oft compared been
To public feasts where meet a public rout,
Where they that are without would fain go
in

And they that are within would fain go out.
A Contention Betwixt a Wife, a Widow, and a Maid for Precedence, l.193

1 I know my life's a pain and but a span,
I know my sense is mock'd in every thing;
And to conclude, I know myself a man,
Which is a proud and yet a wretched thing.
Nosce Teipsum, xlv

W.H. DAVIES 1870–1940

2 It was the Rainbow gave thee birth,
And left thee all her lovely hues.
The Kingfisher

3 What is this life if, full of care,
We have no time to stand and stare?
Leisure

BETTE DAVIS 1908–

4 Fasten your seatbelts. It's going to be a bumpy night.
All About Eve (1950), script by Joseph Mankiewicz

STEPHEN DECATUR 1779–1820

5 Our country! In her intercourse with foreign nations, may she always be in the right; but our country, right or wrong.
Decatur's Toast (1816), see A.S. Mackenzie, *Life of Decatur,* ch.xiv

CHARLES DE GAULLE 1890–1970

6 *On ne peut rassembler les Français que sous le coup de la peur. On ne peut pas rassembler à froid un pays qui compte 265 spécialités de fromages.*
The French will only be united under the threat of danger. Nobody can simply bring together a country that has 265 kinds of cheese.
Speech after the *recul* of the R.P.P. at the elections of 1951

THOMAS DEKKER 1570?–1641?

7 Golden slumbers kiss your eyes,
Smiles awake you when you rise:
Sleep, pretty wantons, do not cry,
And I will sing a lullaby:
Rock them, rock them, lullaby.
Patient Grissil, Act IV.ii

WALTER DE LA MARE 1873–1956

8 Oh, no man knows
Through what wild centuries
Roves back the rose.
All That's Past

9 He is crazed with the spell of far Arabia,

They have stolen his wits away.
Arabia

10 When I lie where shades of darkness
Shall no more assail mine eyes.
Fare Well, i

11 Look thy last on all things lovely,
Every hour—let no night
Seal thy sense in deathly slumber
Till to delight
Thou have paid thy utmost blessing;
Since that all things thou wouldst praise
Beauty took from those who loved them
In other days.
iii

12 Nought but vast sorrow was there—
The sweet cheat gone.
The Ghost

13 'Is there anybody there?' said the traveller,
Knocking on the moonlit door.
The Listeners

14 'Tell them I came, and no one answered,
That I kept my word,' he said.

15 Ay, they heard his foot upon the stirrup,
And the sound of iron on stone,
And how the silence surged softly backward,
When the plunging hoofs were gone.

16 Three jolly Farmers
Once bet a pound
Each dance the others would
Off the ground.
Off the Ground

17 Slowly, silently, now the moon
Walks the night in her silver shoon.
Silver

LORD DENMAN 1779–1854

18 Trial by jury itself, instead of being a security to persons who are accused, will be a delusion, a mockery, and a snare.
Judgement in O'Connell v. the Queen, 4 Sept. 1844

C.J. DENNIS 1876–1938

19 Me name is Mud.
The Sentimental Bloke: **A Spring Song,** st.2 (1916)

JOHN DENNIS 1657–1734

20 A man who could make so vile a pun would not scruple to pick a pocket.
The Gentleman's Magazine (1781), p.324 (Edit. note)

21 Damn them! They will not let my play

run, but they steal my thunder!
W.S. Walsh, *Handy-book of Literary Curiosities*

THOMAS DE QUINCEY 1785-1859

1 It was a Sunday afternoon, wet and cheer-
less: and a duller spectacle this earth of
ours has not to show than a rainy Sunday
in London.
Confessions of an English Opium Eater, pt.ii,
The Pleasures of Opium

2 Murder Considered as One of the Fine
Arts.
Essay

EDWARD STANLEY, EARL OF DERBY 1799-1869

3 When I first came into Parliament, Mr
Tierney, a great Whig authority, used always to say that the duty of an Opposition
was very simple—it was, to oppose everything, and propose nothing.
House of Commons, 4 June 1841

4 The foreign policy of the noble Earl [Rus-
sell]...may be summed up in two short
homely but expressive words:—'meddle
and muddle'.
Speech on the Address, House of Lords, 4 Feb.
1864

DESCARTES 1596-1650

5 *Cogito, ergo sum.*
I think, therefore I am.
Le Discours de la Méthode

PHILIPPE NÉRICAULT called DESTOUCHES 1680-1754

6 *Les absents ont toujours tort.*
The absent are always in the wrong.
L'Obstacle imprévu, I.vi

SERGE DIAGHILEV 1872-1929

7 *Étonne-moi.*
Said to Jean Cocteau who was questioning
his lack of praise and encouragement in
1912. Cocteau continues, 'In 1917, the
evening of the première of *Parade*, I surprised him'.
The Journals of Jean Cocteau, 1

CHARLES DIBDIN 1745-1814

8 In every mess I finds a friend,
In every port a wife.
Jack in his Element

9 Here, a sheer hulk, lies poor Tom Bowling,

The darling of our crew.
Tom Bowling

10 Faithful, below, he did his duty;
But now he's gone aloft.

THOMAS DIBDIN 1771-1841

11 Oh! what a snug little Island,
A right little, tight little Island!
The Snug Little Island

CHARLES DICKENS 1812-1870

12 Jarndyce and Jarndyce still drags its
dreary length before the Court, perennially hopeless.
Bleak House, ch.1

13 This is a London particular...A fog, miss.
ch.3

14 Educating the natives of Borrioboola-
Gha, on the left bank of the Niger. [Mrs.
Jellyby.]
ch.4

15 'Not to put too fine a point upon it'—a
favourite apology for plain-speaking with
Mr Snagsby.
ch.11

16 He wos wery good to me, he wos! [Jo.]

17 'It is,' says Chadband, 'the ray of rays, the
sun of suns, the moon of moons, the star
of stars. It is the light of Terewth.'
ch.25

18 O let us love our occupations,
Bless the squire and his relations,
Live upon our daily rations,
And always know our proper stations.
The Chimes, **2nd Quarter**

19 'God bless us every one!' said Tiny Tim,
the last of all.
A Christmas Carol, stave 3

20 It *was* a turkey! He could never have stood
upon his legs, that bird. He would have
snapped 'em off short in a minute, like
sticks of sealing-wax.
stave 5

21 'I am a lone lorn creetur',' were Mrs Gum-
midge's words,...'and everythink goes
contrary with me.'
David Copperfield, ch.3

22 Barkis is willin'.
ch.5

23 I have known him [Micawber] come home
to supper with a flood of tears, and a
declaration that nothing was now left but
a jail; and go to bed making a calculation
of the expense of putting bow-windows to

the house, 'in case anything turned up,' which was his favourite expression.
ch. 11

1 Annual income twenty pounds, annual expenditure nineteen nineteen six, result happiness. Annual income twenty pounds, annual expenditure twenty pounds ought and six, result misery. [Mr. Micawber.]
ch. 12

2 I am well aware that I am the 'umblest person going....My mother is likewise a very 'umble person. We live in a numble abode. [Uriah Heep.]
ch.16

3 The mistake was made of putting some of the trouble out of King Charles's head into my head. [Mr. Dick.]
ch.17

4 I only ask for information. [Miss Rosa Dartle.]
ch.20

5 'People can't die, along the coast,' said Mr Peggotty, 'except when the tide's pretty nigh out. They can't be born, unless it's pretty nigh in—not properly born, till flood. He's a going out with the tide.'
ch.30

6 It's only my child-wife. [Dora.]
ch.44

7 'Wal'r, my boy,' replied the Captain, 'in the Proverbs of Solomon you will find the following words, "May we never want a friend in need, nor a bottle to give him!" 'When found, make a note of.' [Captain Cuttle.]
Dombey and Son, ch.15

8 You don't object to an aged parent, I hope? [Wemmick.]
Great Expectations, ch.25

9 Whatever was required to be done, the Circumlocution Office was beforehand with all the public departments in the art of perceiving—HOW NOT TO DO IT.
Little Dorrit, bk.i, ch.10

10 Father is rather vulgar, my dear. The word Papa, besides, gives a pretty form to the lips. Papa, potatoes, poultry, prunes, and prism, are all very good words for the lips: especially prunes and prism. [Mrs. General.]
bk.ii, ch.5

11 With affection beaming in one eye, and calculation shining out of the other. [Mrs. Todgers.]
Martin Chuzzlewit, ch.8

12 'Mrs Harris,' I says, 'leave the bottle on the chimley-piece, and don't ask me to take none, but let me put my lips to it when I am so dispoged.' [Mrs. Gamp.]
ch.19

13 Therefore I *do* require it, which I makes confession, to be brought reg'lar and draw'd mild. [Mrs. Gamp.]
ch.25

14 He'd make a lovely corpse. [Mrs. Gamp.]

15 We never knows wot's hidden in each other's hearts; and if we had glass winders there, we'd need keep the shutters up, some on us, I do assure you! [Mrs Gamp.]
ch.29

16 A lane was made; and Mrs Hominy, with the aristocratic stalk, the pocket handkerchief, the clasped hands, and the classical cap, came slowly up it, in a procession of one.
ch.34

17 'Bother Mrs Harris!' said Betsey Prig....'I don't believe there's no sich a person!'
ch.49

18 The words she spoke of Mrs Harris, lambs could not forgive...nor worms forget. [Mrs. Gamp.]

19 EDUCATION.—At Mr Wackford Squeers's Academy, Dotheboys Hall, at the delightful village of Dotheboys, near Greta Bridge in Yorkshire, Youth are boarded, clothed, booked, furnished with pocket-money, provided with all necessaries, instructed in all languages living and dead, mathematics, orthography, geometry, astronomy, trigonometry, the use of the globes, algebra, single stick (if required), writing, arithmetic, fortification, and every other branch of classical literature. Terms, twenty guineas per annum. No extras, no vacations, and diet unparalleled.
Nicholas Nickleby, ch.3

20 Here's richness! [Mr. Squeers.]
ch.5

21 C-l-e-a-n, clean, verb active, to make bright, to scour. W-i-n, win, d-e-r, der, winder, a casement. When the boy knows this out of the book, he goes and does it. [Mr. Squeers.]
ch.8

22 As she frequently remarked when she made any such mistake, it would be all the same a hundred years hence. [Mrs. Squeers.]
ch.9

1 What's the demd total? [Mr Mantalini.]
ch.21

2 Language was not powerful enough to describe the infant phenomenon.
ch.23

3 All is gas and gaiters. [The Gentleman in the Small-clothes.]
ch.49

4 He has gone to the demnition bow-wows. [Mr. Mantalini.]
ch.64

5 Oliver Twist has asked for more! [Bumble.]
Oliver Twist, ch.2

6 Known by the *sobriquet* of 'The artful Dodger.'
ch.8

7 'Hard,' replied the Dodger. 'As nails,' added Charley Bates.
ch.9

8 'If the law supposes that,' said Mr Bumble…'the law is a ass—a idiot.'
ch.51. See 67:8

9 The question [with Mr. Podsnap] about everything was, would it bring a blush into the cheek of the young person?
Our Mutual Friend, bk.1, ch.11

0 I think…that it is the best club in London. [Mr. Twemlow, on the House of Commons.]
bk.ii, ch.3

1 He'd be sharper than a serpent's tooth, if he wasn't as dull as ditch water. [Fanny Cleaver.]
bk.iii, ch.10

2 I want to be something so much worthier than the doll in the doll's house. [Bella.]
bk.iv, ch.5

3 Kent, sir—everybody knows Kent—apples, cherries, hops, and women. [Jingle.]
Pickwick Papers, ch.2

4 I wants to make your flesh creep. [The Fat Boy.]
ch.8

5 'It's always best on these occasions to do what the mob do.' 'But suppose there are two mobs?' suggested Mr Snodgrass. 'Shout with the largest,' replied Mr Pickwick.
ch.13

6 Battledore and shuttlecock's a wery good game, vhen you an't the shuttlecock and two lawyers the battledores, in which case

it gets too excitin' to be pleasant.
ch.20

17 Mr Weller's knowledge of London was extensive and peculiar.

18 Be wery careful o' vidders all your life. [Mr. Weller.]

19 Keep yourself *to* yourself. [Mr. Raddle.]
ch.32

20 Put it down a we, my Lord, put it down a we. [Mr. Weller.]
ch.34

21 'You must not tell us what the soldier, or any other man, said, sir,' interposed the judge; 'it's not evidence.'

22 'Yes, I have a pair of eyes,' replied Sam, 'and that's just it. If they wos a pair o' patent double million magnifyin' gas microscopes of hextra power, p'raps I might be able to see through a flight o' stairs and a deal door; but bein' only eyes, you see my wision's limited.'

23 Oh Sammy, Sammy, vy worn't there a alleybi! [Mr. Weller.]

24 Miss Bolo rose from the table considerably agitated, and went straight home, in a flood of tears and a Sedan chair.
ch.35

25 A friendly swarry, consisting of a boiled leg of mutton with the usual trimmings.
ch.37

26 The have-his-carcase, next to the perpetual motion, is vun of the blessedest things as wos ever made. [Sam Weller.]
ch.43

27 Anythin' for a quiet life, as the man said wen he took the sitivation at the lighthouse. [Sam Weller.]

28 A smattering of everything, and a knowledge of nothing. [Minerva House.]
Sketches by Boz, Tales, ch.3. **Sentiment**

29 It was the best of times, it was the worst of times, it was the age of wisdom, it was the age of foolishness, it was the epoch of belief, it was the epoch of incredulity, it was the season of Light, it was the season of Darkness, it was the spring of hope, it was the winter of despair, we had everything before us, we had nothing before us, we were all going direct to Heaven, we were all going direct the other way.
A Tale of Two Cities, bk.i, ch.1

30 It is a far, far better thing that I do, than I have ever done; it is a far, far better rest that I go to, than I have ever known.

[Sydney Carton's thoughts on the scaffold.]
bk.iii, ch.15

EMILY DICKINSON 1830–1886

1 Because I could not stop for Death—
He kindly stopped for me—
The Carriage held but just Ourselves—
And Immortality.
Because I could not stop for Death

2 The Bustle in a House
The Morning after Death
Is solemnest of industries
Enacted upon Earth—

The Sweeping up the Heart
And putting love away
We shall not want to use again
Until Eternity.
The Bustle in a House

3 My life closed twice before its close;
It yet remains to see
If Immortality unveil
A third event to me,

So huge, so hopeless to conceive
As these that twice befel.
Parting is all we know of heaven
And all we need of hell.
My life closed twice before its close

4 Success is counted sweetest
By those who ne'er succeed.
To comprehend a nectar
Requires sorest need.
Success is counted sweetest

5 This quiet Dust was Gentlemen and Ladies
And Lads and Girls—
Was laughter and ability and Sighing,
And Frocks and Curls.
This quiet Dust was Gentlemen and Ladies

6 What Soft—Cherubic Creatures—
These Gentlewomen are—
One would as soon assault a Plush—
Or violate a Star—

Such Dimity Convictions—
A Horror so refined
Of freckled Human Nature—
Of Deity—ashamed.
What Soft—Cherubic Creatures

JOHN DICKINSON 1732–1808

7 Then join hand in hand, brave Americans all,—
By uniting we stand, by dividing we fall.
The Liberty Song (1768). *Memoirs of the Historical Soc. of Pennsylvania*, vol.xiv

DENIS DIDEROT 1713–1784

8 *L'esprit de l'escalier.*
Staircase wit.
An untranslatable phrase, the meaning of which is that one only thinks on one's way downstairs of the smart retort one might have made in the drawing-room. *Paradoxe sur le Comédien*

9 *Voyez-vous cet oeuf. C'est avec cela qu'or renverse toutes les écoles de théologie, e tous les temples de la terre.*
See this egg. It is with this that all the schools of theology and all the temples o the earth are to be overturned.
Le Rêve de d'Alembert, pt.i

DIOGENES c.400–c.325 B.C.

10 ``μικρόν``, εἶπεν, ``ἀπὸ τοῦ ἡλίου μετά στῆθι.``
Alexander...asked him if he lacked any thing. 'Yea,' said he, 'that I do: that you stand out of my sun a little.'
Plutarch, *Life of Alexander,* 14 (North's translation)

DIONYSIUS OF HALICARNASSUS fl. 30–7 B.C.

11 History is philosophy from examples.
Ars Rhetorica, xi.2

BENJAMIN DISRAELI 1804–1881

12 Though I sit down now, the time wil come when you will hear me.
Maiden speech, 7 Dec. 1837. Meynell, *Disrael* i.43

13 The Continent will not suffer England to be the workshop of the world.
House of Commons, 15 Mar. 1838

14 Thus you have a starving population, ar absentee aristocracy, and an alien Church and in addition the weakest executive in the world. That is the Irish Question.
16 Feb. 1844

15 The right hon Gentleman [Sir Rober Peel] caught the Whigs bathing, and walked away with their clothes.
28 Feb. 1845

16 He [Sir C. Wood] has to learn that petu lance is not sarcasm, and that insolence i not invective.
16 Dec. 1852

17 England does not love coalitions.

18 Is man an ape or an angel? Now I am or the side of the angels.
Meeting of Society for Increasing Endowment of Small Livings in the Diocese of Oxford, 2. Nov. 1864

You behold a range of exhausted volcanoes. (Of the Treasury Bench.)
Manchester, 3 Apr. 1872

Lord Salisbury and myself have brought you back peace—but a peace I hope with honour.
House of Commons, 16 July 1878. The phrase 'peace with honour' had been used by Lord John Russell in a speech at Greenock, 19 Sept, 1853.

A sophistical rhetorician, inebriated with the exuberance of his own verbosity. (Gladstone.)
At Banquet in Riding School, Knightsbridge, 17 July 1878

Damn your principles! Stick to your party.
Attr. (To Bulwer Lytton.) Latham, *Famous Sayings*

We authors, Ma'am. (To Queen Victoria.)
Monypenny and Buckle, *Life of Disraeli*, v.49

Everyone likes flattery; and when you come to Royalty you should lay it on with a trowel.
G.W.E. Russell, *Collections and Recollections*, ch.23 (To Matthew Arnold)

His Christianity was muscular.
Endymion (1880), ch.14

The blue ribbon of the turf. [The Derby.]
Life of Lord George Bentinck (1854), ch.26

Every woman should marry—and no man.
Lothair (1870), ch.30

'I rather like bad wine,' said Mr Mountchesney; 'one gets so bored with good wine.'
Sybil (1845), bk.i, ch.1

Little things affect little minds.
bk.iii, ch.2

I was told that the Privileged and the People formed Two Nations.
bk.iv, ch.8

A *dark* horse, which had never been thought of, and which the careless St James had never even observed in the list, rushed past the grand stand in sweeping triumph.
The Young Duke (1831), bk.ii, ch.5

I will not go down to posterity talking bad grammar.
Said while correcting proofs of his last Parliamentary speech, 31 March 1881. Blake, *Disraeli, ch.32*

There are three kinds of lies: lies, damned lies and statistics.
Attr. Mark Twain, *Autobiography*, I.246

AELIUS DONATUS fl. 4th cent. A.D.

16 *Pereant, inquit, qui ante nos nostra dixerunt.*
Confound those who have said our remarks before us.
St Jerome, *Commentary on Ecclesiastes*, 1. Migne, *Patrologiae Lat. Cursus*, 23.390

JOHN DONNE 1571?–1631

17 All other things, to their destruction draw,
   Only our love hath no decay;
This, no to morrow hath, nor yesterday,
Running it never runs from us away,
But truly keeps his first, last, everlasting
   day.
The Anniversary

18 Come live with me, and be my love,
And we will some new pleasures prove
Of golden sands, and crystal brooks,
With silken lines, and silver hooks.
The Bait. See also 160:14

19 The day breaks not, it is my heart.
Break of Day (Attr. also to John Dowland)

20 For God's sake hold your tongue, and let
   me love.
The Canonization

21 No Spring, nor Summer beauty hath such
   grace,
As I have seen in one Autumnal face.
Elegies, No.9. **The Autumnal**

22 By our first strange and fatal interview
By all desires which thereof did ensue.
No.16. **On His Mistress**

23 Nurse, O! my love is slain; I saw him go
O'er the white Alps alone.

24   We easily know
By this these angels from an evil sprite,
Those set our hairs, but these our flesh
   upright.
No.19. **Going to Bed**

25 Licence my roving hands, and let them go,
Before, behind, between, above, below.
O my America! my new-found-land,
My kingdom, safliest when with one man
   mann'd.

26 Where, like a pillow on a bed,
A pregnant bank swelled up, to rest
The violet's reclining head,
Sat we two, one another's best.
The Extasy

27 So must pure lovers' souls descend
T'affections, and to faculties,

Which sense may reach and apprehend,
Else a great Prince in prison lies.

1 I wonder by my troth, what thou, and I
Did, till we lov'd? were we not wean'd till
then?
But suck'd on country pleasures, childish-
ly?
Or snorted we in the Seven Sleepers den?
The Good-Morrow

2 At the round earth's imagined corners,
blow
Your trumpets, Angels, and arise, arise.
Holy Sonnets (2), vii

3 Death be not proud, though some have
called thee
Mighty and dreadful, for thou art not so,
For those whom thou think'st thou dost
overthrow,
Die not, poor death, nor yet canst thou kill
me.
From rest and sleep, which but thy pic-
tures be,
Much pleasure, then from thee much more
must flow,
And soonest our best men with thee do go,
Rest of their bones and soul's delivery.
x

4 One short sleep past, we wake eternally,
And death shall be no more; death, thou
shalt die.

5 What if this present were the world's last
night?
xiii

6 Batter my heart, three person'd God; for,
you
As yet but knock, breathe, shine, and seek
to mend.
xiv

7 Take me to you, imprison me, for I
Except you enthrall me, never shall be free,
Nor ever chaste, except you ravish me.

8 Seal then this bill of my Divorce to all.
*Hymn to Christ, at the author's last going into
Germany*

9 Sir, more than kisses, letters mingle souls.
Letters to Severall Personages, **To Sir Henry
Wotton**

10 And seeing the snail, which everywhere
doth roam,
Carrying his own house still, still is at
home,
Follow (for he is easy paced) this snail,
Be thine own palace, or the world's thy
gaol.

11 I long to talk with some old lover's ghost,

Who died before the god of love was born
Love's Deity

12 Nature's great masterpiece, an Elephant,
The only harmless great thing.
Progress of the Soul, xxxix

13 When my grave is broke up again
Some second guest to entertain,
(For graves have learnt that woman-head
To be to more than one a bed)
And he that digs it spies
A bracelet of bright hair about the bone,
Will he not let us alone?
The Relic

14 Sweetest love, I do not go,
For weariness of thee,
Nor in hope the world can show
A fitter Love for me;
But since that I
Must die at last, 'tis best,
To use my self in jest
Thus by feigned deaths to die.
Song

15 Go, and catch a falling star,
Get with child a mandrake root,
Tell me, where all past years are,
Or who cleft the Devil's foot.
Song, Go and Catch a Falling Star

16 And swear
No where
Lives a woman true and fair.

17 Though she were true, when you met her,
And last, till you write your letter,
Yet she
Will be
False, ere I come, to two, or three.

18 Busy old fool, unruly Sun,
Why dost thou thus,
Through windows, and through curtain
call on us?
Must to thy motions lovers' seasons run?
The Sun Rising

19 This bed thy centre is, these walls th
sphere.

20 Send me not this, nor that, t'increase m
store,
But swear thou think'st I love thee, and n
more.
The Token

21 I am two fools, I know,
For loving, and for saying so
In whining Poetry.
The Triple Fool

22 I have done one braver thing
Than all the Worthies did,
And yet a braver thence doth spring,

Which is, to keep that hid.
The Undertaking

1 But I do nothing upon my self, and yet I am mine own *Executioner*.
Devotions upon Emergent Occasions. Meditation XII

2 No man is an *Island*, entire of it self.
Meditation XVII

3 Any man's *death* diminishes *me*, because I am involved in *Mankind*; And therefore never send to know for whom the *bell* tolls; It tolls for *thee*.

4 Poor intricated soul! Riddling, perplexed, labyrinthical soul!
LXXX Sermons (1640), xlviii, 25 Jan. 1628/9

LORD ALFRED DOUGLAS 1870–1945

5 I am the Love that dare not speak its name.
Two Loves

JAMES DOUGLAS, EARL OF MORTON d. 1581

6 Here lies he who neither feared nor flattered any flesh.
Of John Knox, said as he was buried, 26 Nov. 1572. G.R. Preedy, *Life of John Knox*, VII

ERNEST DOWSON 1867–1900

7 I have forgot much, Cynara! gone with the wind,
Flung roses, roses, riotously, with the throng,
Dancing, to put thy pale, lost lilies out of mind.
Non Sum Qualis Eram

8 I have been faithful to thee, Cynara! in my fashion.

9 They are not long, the days of wine and roses.
Vitae Summa Brevis

SIR ARTHUR CONAN DOYLE 1859–1930

10 Singularity is almost invariably a clue. The more featureless and commonplace a crime is, the more difficult is it to bring it home.
The Adventures of Sherlock Holmes. **The Boscombe Valley Mystery**

11 A little monograph on the ashes of one hundred and forty different varieties of pipe, cigar, and cigarette tobacco.

12 It is quite a three-pipe problem.
The Red-Headed League

13 I have nothing to do to-day. My practice is never very absorbing.

14 You see, but you do not observe.
Scandal in Bohemia

15 It is a capital mistake to theorize before one has data.

16 You know my methods, Watson.
The Memoirs of Sherlock Holmes. The Crooked Man

17 'Excellent!' I [Dr. Watson] cried. 'Elementary,' said he [Holmes].

18 He [Professor Moriarty] is the Napoleon of crime.
The Final Problem

19 'The dog did nothing in the night-time.'
'That was the curious incident,' remarked Sherlock Holmes.
Silver Blaze

20 There is a spirituality about the face, however…which the typewriter does not generate. The lady is a musician.
The Return of Sherlock Holmes. **The Solitary Cyclist**

21 But here, unless I am mistaken, is our client.
His Last Bow. **Wisteria Lodge**

22 There is but one step from the grotesque to the horrible.

23 An experience of women which extends over many nations and three separate continents.
The Sign of Four

24 How often have I said to you that when you have eliminated the impossible, whatever remains, *however improbable*, must be the truth?

25 You know my methods. Apply them.

26 'Wonderful!' I [Dr. Watson] ejaculated. 'Commonplace,' said Holmes.
A Study in Scarlet

27 The vocabulary of 'Bradshaw' is nervous and terse, but limited.
The Valley of Fear

28 Mediocrity knows nothing higher than itself, but talent instantly recognizes genius.

SIR FRANCIS DOYLE 1810–1888

29 Last night, among his fellow roughs, He jested, quaff'd, and swore.
The Private of the Buffs

SIR FRANCIS DRAKE 1540?–1596

1 There must be a beginning of any great matter, but the continuing unto the end until it be thoroughly finished yields the true glory.
Dispatch to Sir Francis Walsingham, 17 May 1587. Navy Records Society, vol. XI (1898), p.134

2 There is plenty of time to win this game, and to thrash the Spaniards too.
Attr. D.N.B.

3 I remember Drake, in the vaunting style of a soldier, would call the Enterprise the singeing of the King of Spain's Beard. (Of the expedition to Cadiz, 1587.)
Bacon, *Considerations touching a War with Spain* (*Harleian Misc.* 1745, vol.v, p.85, col.1)

4 I must have the gentleman to haul and draw with the mariner, and the mariner with the gentleman...I would know him, that would refuse to set his hand to a rope, but I know there is not any such here.
Corbett, *Drake and the Tudor Navy*, i.249

MICHAEL DRAYTON 1562–1631

5 Fair stood the wind for France
When we our sails advance,
Nor now to prove our chance
    Longer will tarry.
To the Cambro-Britons. **Agincourt**

6 Since there's no help, come let us kiss and part,
Nay, I have done: you get no more of me.
Sonnets, lxi

WILLIAM DRENNAN 1754–1820

7 The men of the Emerald Isle.
Erin

THOMAS DRUMMOND 1797–1840

8 Property has its duties as well as its rights.
Letter to the Earl of Donoughmore, 22 May 1838

JOHN DRYDEN 1631–1700

9 In pious times, ere priestcraft did begin,
Before polygamy was made a sin.
Absalom and Achitophel, pt.i, l.1

10 Then Israel's monarch, after Heaven's own heart,
His vigorous warmth did, variously, impart
To wives and slaves: and, wide as his command,

Scatter'd his Maker's image through the land.
l.7

11 The Jews, a headstrong, moody, murmuring race
As ever tried the extent and stretch of grace,
God's pampered people, whom debauched with ease,
No king could govern nor no God could please.
l.45

12 A fiery soul, which working out its way,
Fretted the pigmy body to decay:
And o'er informed the tenement of clay.
l.156

13 Great wits are sure to madness near alli'd.
And thin partitions do their bounds divide.
l.163

14 And all to leave what with his toil he won
To that unfeather'd two-legged thing, a son.
l.169

15 But far more numerous was the herd of such
Who think too little and who talk too much.
l.533

16 A man so various that he seem'd to be
Not one, but all mankind's epitome.
Stiff in opinions, always in the wrong;
Was everything by starts, and nothing long:
But, in the course of one revolving moon,
Was chemist, fiddler, statesman, and buffoon.
l.545

17 Railing and praising were his usual themes;
And both (to show his judgement) in extremes.
l.555

18 During his office treason was no crime,
The sons of Belial had a glorious time.
l.597

19 None but the brave deserves the fair.
Alexander's Feast, l.15

20 Errors, like straws, upon the surface flow;
He who would search for pearls must dive below.
All for Love, Prologue

21 Whistling to keep myself from being afraid.
Amphitryon, III.i

22 I am as free as nature first made man,
Ere the base laws of servitude began,

When wild in woods the noble savage ran.
The Conquest of Granada, pt.i, I.i

1 Thou strong seducer, opportunity!
pt.ii, IV.iii

2 Bold knaves thrive without one grain of
sense,
But good men starve for want of impudence.
Epilogue to Constantine the Great

3 Here lies my wife: here let her lie!
Now she's at rest, and so am I.
Epitaph Intended for Dryden's Wife

4 Either be wholly slaves or wholly free.
The Hind and the Panther, pt.ii, 1.285

5 Fairest Isle, all isles excelling,
Seat of pleasures, and of loves;
Venus here will choose her dwelling,
And forsake her Cyprian groves.
King Arthur, V. **Song of Venus**

6 I am to be married within these three days;
married past redemption.
Marriage à la Mode, I.i

7 But treason is not own'd when 'tis des-
cried;
Successful crimes alone are justified.
The Medal, 1.207

8 Like pilgrims to th' appointed place we
tend;
The world's an inn, and death the journey's end.
Palamon and Arcite, bk.iii, 1.887

9 From harmony, from heavenly harmony
This universal frame began:
From harmony to harmony
Through all the compass of the notes it
ran,
The diapason closing full in Man.
A Song for St. Cecilia's Day, i

10 The trumpet shall be heard on high,
The dead shall live, the living die,
And Music shall untune the sky.
Grand Chorus

11 There is a pleasure sure,
In being mad, which none but madmen
know!
The Spanish Friar, I.i

12 We must beat the iron while it is hot, but
we may polish it at leisure.
Aeneis, Dedication

13 'Tis sufficient to say [of Chaucer], according to the proverb, that here is God's
plenty.
Fables, Preface

ALEXANDER DUBCEK 1921–

14 Communism with a human face.
Attr. A resolution by the party group in the
Ministry of Foreign Affairs, in 1968, referred to
Czechoslovak foreign policy acquiring 'its own
defined face'. *Rudé právo*, 14 Mar. 1968

JOACHIM DU BELLAY 1522–1560

15 *Heureux qui comme Ulysse a fait un beau
voyage.*
Happy he who like Ulysses has made a
great journey.
Sonnets

MME DU DEFFAND 1697–1780

16 *La distance n'y fait rien; il n'y a que le
premier pas qui coûte.*
The distance is nothing; it is only the first
step that is difficult.
Commenting on the legend that St. Denis, carrying his head in his hands, walked two leagues.
Letter to d'Alembert, 7 July 1763

GEORGE DUFFIELD 1818–1888

17 Stand up!—stand up for Jesus!
The Psalmist, **Stand Up, Stand Up for Jesus**

ALEXANDRE DUMAS 1802–1870

18 *Cherchons la femme.*
Let us look for the woman.
*Les Mohicans de Paris, passim (Cherchez la
femme.* Attributed to Joseph Fouche.)

19 *Tous pour un, un pour tous.*
All for one, one for all.
Les Trois Mousquetiers, passim

GENERAL DUMOURIEZ 1739–1823

20 *Les courtisans qui l'entourent n'ont rien
oublié et n'ont rien appris.*
The courtiers who surround him have forgotten nothing and learnt nothing.
Of Louis XVIII, at the time of the Declaration of
Verona, Sept. 1795. *Examen*. Later used by Napoleon in his Declaration to the French on his
return from Elba. See 250:14

WILLIAM DUNBAR 1465?–1530?

21 *Timor mortis conturbat me.*
Lament for the Makaris

22 London, thou art of townes *A per se.*
London, 1.1

23 London, thou art the flower of cities all!
Gemme of all joy, jasper of jocunditie.
1.16

JOHN DUNNING, BARON ASHBURTON 1731–1783

1 The influence of the Crown has increased, is increasing, and ought to be diminished.
Motion passed in the House of Commons, 1780

JAMES DUPORT 1606–1679

2 *Quem Jupiter vult perdere, dementat prius.*
Whom God would destroy He first sends mad.
Homeri Gnomologia (1660), p.282. See 6:8

RICHARD DUPPA 1770–1831

3 In language, the ignorant have prescribed laws to the learned.
Maxims (1830), 252

SIR EDWARD DYER c.1540–1607

4 My mind to me a kingdom is,
    Such present joys therein I find,
That it excels all other bliss
    That earth affords or grows by kind.
Though much I want which most would have,
Yet still my mind forbids to crave.
My Mind to Me a Kingdom Is

JOHN DYER fl. 1714

5 And he that will this health deny,
Down among the dead men let him lie.
Toast: Here's a Health to the King

MARIA EDGEWORTH 1767–1849

6 Well! some people talk of morality, and some of religion, but give me a little snug property.
The Absentee, ch.2

THOMAS ALVA EDISON 1847–1931

7 Genius is one per cent inspiration and ninety-nine per cent perspiration.
Life (1932), ch.24

JAMES EDMESTON 1791–1867

8 Lead us, Heavenly Father, lead us
    O'er the world's tempestuous sea;
Guard us, guide us, keep us, feed us,
    For we have no help but Thee.
Sacred Lyrics, Set 2. **Lead Us, Heavenly Father**

KING EDWARD III 1312–1377

9 Also say to them, that they suffre hym this day to wynne his spurres, for if god be pleased, I woll this journey be his, and the honoure therof.
(Of the Black Prince at Crécy, 1345. Commonly quoted as 'Let the boy win his spurs.') Berners' *Froissart's Chronicle*, 1812, I, cxxx, 158

KING EDWARD VIII 1894–1972

10 These works [derelict steel-works] brought all these people here. Something must be done to find them work.
Speaking in S. Wales during the Depression. In Donaldson, *Edward VIII* (1974), ch.19

11 I have found it impossible to carry the heavy burden of responsibility and to discharge my duties as King as I would wish to do without the help and support of the woman I love.
Broadcast, 11 Dec. 1936

JONATHAN EDWARDS 1629–1712

12 The bodies of those that made such a noise and tumult when alive, when dead lie as quietly among the graves of their neighbours as any others.
Procrastination

OLIVER EDWARDS 1711–1791

13 I have tried too in my time to be a philosopher; but, I don't know how, cheerfulness was always breaking in.
Boswell's *Johnson*, 17 Apr. 1778

ALBERT EINSTEIN 1879–1955

14 *Gott würfelt nicht.*
God does not play dice. [Einstein's habitually expressed reaction to the quantum theory.]
B. Hoffman, *Albert Einstein, Creator and Rebel*, ch.10

GEORGE ELIOT 1819–1880

15 I'm not denyin' the women are foolish: God Almighty made 'em to match the men.
Adam Bede (1859), ch. 53

16 Gossip is a sort of smoke that comes from the dirty tobacco-pipes of those who diffuse it: it proves nothing but the bad taste of the smoker.
Daniel Deronda (1874–6), bk.ii, ch.13

17 There is a great deal of unmapped country within us which would have to be taken into account in an explanation of our gusts and storms.
bk.iii, ch.24

18 Half the sorrows of women would be averted if they could repress the speech

they know to be useless; nay, the speech they have resolved not to make.
Felix Holt (1866), ch.2

1 An election is coming. Universal peace is declared, and the foxes have a sincere interest in prolonging the lives of the poultry.
ch.5

2 A woman can hardly ever choose...she is dependent on what happens to her. She must take meaner things, because only meaner things are within her reach.
ch.27

3 A woman, let her be as good as she may, has got to put up with the life her husband makes for her.
Middlemarch (1871–2), ch. 25

4 A man is seldom ashamed of feeling that he cannot love a woman so well when he sees a certain greatness in her: nature having intended greatness for men.
ch.39

5 It was a room where you had no reason for sitting in one place rather than in another.
ch.54

6 The happiest women, like the happiest nations, have no history.
The Mill on the Floss (1860), bk.vi, ch.3

7 By the time you receive this letter I shall have been married to Mr J.W. Cross who now that I am alone sees his happiness in the dedication of his life to me.
Letter to Barbara Bodichon, 5 May 1880

8 I am not an optimist but a meliorist.
Laurence Housman, *A.E.H.* (1937), p.72

T.S. ELIOT 1888–1965

9 Because I do not hope to know again
The infirm glory of the positive hour.
Ash Wednesday, 1

0 Teach us to care and not to care
Teach us to sit still.

1 Round and round the circle
Completing the charm
So the knot be unknotted
The crossed be uncrossed
The crooked be made straight
And the curse be ended.
The Family Reunion, II.iii

2 Sometimes these cogitations still amaze
The troubled midnight and the noon's repose.
La Figlia Che Piange

3 Time present and time past

Are both perhaps present in time future,
And time future contained in time past.
Four Quartets. **Burnt Norton,** 1

14 Human kind
Cannot bear very much reality.

15 In my beginning is my end.
East Coker, 1

16 A way of putting it—not very satisfactory:
A periphrastic study in a worn-out poetical fashion,
Leaving one still with the intolerable wrestle
With words and meanings.
2

17 The wounded surgeon plies the steel
That questions the distempered part;
Beneath the bleeding hands we feel
The sharp compassion of the healer's art
Resolving the enigma of the fever chart.
4

18 Each venture
Is a new beginning, a raid on the inarticulate
With shabby equipment always deteriorating
In the general mess of imprecision of feeling.
5

19 What we call the beginning is often the end
And to make an end is to make a beginning.
The end is where we start from.
Little Gidding, 5

20 We shall not cease from exploration
And the end of all our exploring
Will be to arrive where we started
And know the place for the first time.

21 An old man in a dry month.
Gerontion

22 We are the hollow men
We are the stuffed men
Leaning together
Headpiece filled with straw. Alas!
The Hollow Men, 1

23 *Here we go round the prickly pear
Prickly pear prickly pear.*
5

24 This is the way the world ends
Not with a bang but a whimper.

25 A cold coming we had of it,
Just the worst time of the year
For a journey, and such a long journey:
The ways deep and the weather sharp,

The very dead of winter.
Journey of the Magi. See 2:11

1 And the cities hostile and the towns unfriendly
   And the villages dirty and charging high
   prices.

2   But set down
   This set down
   This: were we led all that way for
   Birth or Death? There was a Birth, certain-
   ly,
   We had evidence and no doubt. I had seen
   birth and death,
   But had thought they were different; this
   Birth was
   Hard and bitter agony for us, like Death,
   our death.
   We returned to our places, these King-
   doms,
   But no longer at ease here, in the old dis-
   pensation,
   With an alien people clutching their gods.
   I should be glad of another death.

3   Let us go then, you and I,
   When the evening is spread out against the
   sky
   Like a patient etherized upon a table.
   The Love Song of J. Alfred Prufrock

4 In the room the women come and go
   Talking of Michelangelo.
      The yellow fog that rubs its back upon
      the window-panes.

5 I have measured out my life with coffee
   spoons.

6 I should have been a pair of ragged claws
   Scuttling across the floors of silent seas.

7 No! I am not Prince Hamlet, nor was
   meant to be;
   Am an attendant lord, one that will do
   To swell a progress, start a scene or two.

8   I grow old...I grow old...
   I shall wear the bottoms of my trousers
   rolled.
      Shall I part my hair behind? Do I dare
      to eat a peach?
   I shall wear white flannel trousers, and
   walk upon the beach.
   I have heard the mermaids singing, each to
   each;
   I do not think that they will sing to me.

9 Macavity, Macavity, there's no one like
   Macavity,
   There never was a Cat of such deceitful-
   ness and suavity.
   He always has an alibi, and one or two to
   spare:

At whatever time the deed took place—
MACAVITY WASN'T THERE!
Macavity: The Mystery Cat

10 I am aware of the damp souls of house
   maids
   Sprouting despondently at area gates.
   Morning at the Window

11 Yet we have gone on living,
   Living and partly living.
   Murder in the Cathedral, pt.I

12 Friendship should be more than biting
   Time can sever.

13 The last temptation is the greatest treason:
   To do the right deed for the wrong reason.

14 The Naming of Cats is a difficult matter,
      It isn't just one of your holiday games;
   At first you may think I'm as mad as a
   hatter
   When I tell you a cat must have THREE
      DIFFERENT NAMES.
   The Naming of Cats

15 The winter evening settles down
   With smell of steaks in passageways.
   Six o'clock.
   The burnt-out ends of smoky days.
   Preludes, I

16   You'd be bored.
   Birth, and copulation, and death.
   That's all the facts when you come to brass
   tacks:
   Birth, and copulation and death.
   I've been born, and once is enough.
   Sweeney Agonistes, **Fragment of an Agon**

17 The nightingales are singing near
   The convent of the Sacred Heart,
      And sang within the bloody wood
   When Agamemnon cried aloud
   And let their liquid siftings fall
   To stain the stiff dishonoured shroud.
   Sweeney Among the Nightingales

18 April is the cruellest month, breeding
   Lilacs out of the dead land, mixing
   Memory and desire, stirring
   Dull roots with spring rain.
   The Waste Land. 1. **The Burial of the Dead**

19 And I will show you something different
      from either
   Your shadow at morning striding behind
      you,
   Or your shadow at evening rising to meet
      you
   I will show you fear in a handful of dust.

20 A crowd flowed over London Bridge, so
      many,
   I had not thought death had undone so
   many.

1 'O keep the Dog far hence, that's friend to
men,
'Or with his nails he'll dig it up again!
'You! hypocrite lecteur!—mon semblable,
—mon frère!'
See 16:11, 267:16

2 The Chair she sat in, like a burnished
throne,
Glowed on the marble.
2. A Game of Chess. See 203:22

3 But at my back from time to time I hear
The sound of horns and motors, which
shall bring
Sweeney to Mrs Porter in the spring.
O the moon shone bright on Mrs Porter
And on her daughter
They wash their feet in soda water.
3. The Fire Sermon. See 161:21

4 When lovely woman stoops to folly and
Paces about her room again, alone,
She smoothes her hair with automatic
hand,
And puts a record on the gramophone.
See 110:18

5 Where the walls
Of Magnus Martyr hold
Inexplicable splendour of Ionian white
and gold.

6 A woman drew her long black hair out
tight
And fiddled whisper music on those
strings.
5. What the Thunder Said

7 These fragments have I shored against my
ruins.

8 Webster was much possessed by death
And saw the skull beneath the skin.
Whispers of Immortality

9 Grishkin is nice: her Russian eye
Is underlined for emphasis;
Uncorseted, her friendly bust
Gives promise of pneumatic bliss.

10 The critic, one would suppose, if he is to
justify his existence, should endeavour to
discipline his personal prejudices and
cranks—tares to which we are all subject
—and compose his differences with as
many of his fellows as possible, in the common pursuit of true judgement.
The Function of Criticism (1923), i

11 The only way of expressing emotion in the
form of art is by finding an 'objective correlative'; in other words, a set of objects, a
situation, a chain of events which shall be
the formula of that *particular* emotion;
such that when the external facts, which

must terminate in sensory experience, are
given, the emotion is immediately evoked.
Hamlet (1919)

12 In the seventeenth century a dissociation
of sensibility set in from which we have
never recovered.
The Metaphysical Poets

QUEEN ELIZABETH I 1533–1603

13 'Twas God the word that spake it,
He took the Bread and brake it;
And what the word did make it;
That I believe, and take it.
Answer on being asked her opinion of Christ's
presence in the Sacrament. S. Clarke, *Marrow of
Ecclesiastical History*, pt.ii, Life of Queen Eli-
zabeth, ed. 1675

14 The queen of Scots is this day leichter of a
fair son, and I am but a barren stock.
Memoirs of Sir James Melville (1549–93)

15 Anger makes dull men witty, but it keeps
them poor.
Bacon, *Apophthegms*, 5

16 God may pardon you, but I never can. [To
the Countess of Nottingham.]
See Hume, *History of England under the House of
Tudor*, vol.ii, ch.7

17 If thy heart fails thee, climb not at all.
Lines written on a window after 194:5 Fuller,
Worthies of England, vol.i, p.419

18 *Semper eadem.* (Ever the same.)
Motto

19 I know I have the body of a weak and
feeble woman, but I have the heart and
stomach of a king, and of a king of England too; and think foul scorn that Parma
or Spain, or any prince of Europe, should
dare to invade the borders of my realm.
Speech to the Troops at Tilbury on the Approach of the Armada, 1588

20 Must! Is *must* a word to be addressed to
princes? Little man, little man! thy father,
if he had been alive, durst not have used
that word.
To Robert Cecil, on her death-bed. J.R. Green,
A Short History of the English People, ch.vii

JOHN ELLERTON 1826–1893

21 The day Thou gavest, Lord, is ended,
The darkness falls at Thy behest.
A Liturgy for Missionary Meetings

JANE ELLIOT 1727–1805

22 I've heard them lilting, at the ewe milking.
Lasses a' lilting, before dawn of day;
But now they are moaning, on ilka green
loaning;

The flowers of the forest are a' wede
away.
The Flowers of the Forest (1756) (Popular version
of the traditional lament for Flodden.)

GEORGE ELLIS 1753–1815

1 Snowy, Flowy, Blowy,
Showery, Flowery, Bowery,
Hoppy, Croppy, Droppy,
Breezy, Sneezy, Freezy.
The Twelve Months

PAUL ELUARD 1895–1952

2 *Adieu tristesse*
Bonjour tristesse
Tu es inscrite dans les lignes du plafond.
Farewell sadness
Good day sadness
You are inscribed in the lines of the ceiling.
A peine défigurée

RALPH WALDO EMERSON
1803–1882

3 If the red slayer think he slays,
   Or if the slain think he is slain,
They know not well the subtle ways
   I keep, and pass, and turn again.
Brahma

4 By the rude bridge that arched the flood,
   Their flag to April's breeze unfurl'd,
Here once the embattled farmers stood,
   And fired the shot heard round the
   world.
*Hymn Sung at the Completion of the Concord
Monument*

5 Things are in the saddle,
   And ride mankind.
Ode, Inscribed to W.H. Channing

6 Make yourself necessary to someone.
Conduct of Life. **Considerations by the way**

7 All sensible people are selfish, and nature
is tugging at every contract to make the
terms of it fair.

8 A person seldom falls sick, but the
bystanders are animated with a faint hope
that he will die.

9 Art is a jealous mistress.
Wealth

10 The louder he talked of his honour, the
faster we counted our spoons.
Worship. See 131:21

11 The only reward of virtue is virtue; the
only way to have a friend is to be one.
Essays, vi. **Friendship**

12 Tart, cathartic virtue.
viii. **Heroism**

13 There is properly no history; only bio
graphy.
i. **History**

14 In skating over thin ice, our safety is i
our speed.
vii. **Prudence**

15 A foolish consistency is the hobgoblin o
little minds.
ii. **Self-Reliance**

16 Is it so bad, then, to be misunderstood
Pythagoras was misunderstood, and Soc
rates, and Jesus, and Luther, and Coperni
cus, and Galileo, and Newton, and ever
pure and wise spirit that ever took flesh
To be great is to be misunderstood.

17 What is a weed? A plant whose virtue
have not been discovered.
Fortune of the Republic

18 Hitch your wagon to a star.
Society and Solitude. **Civilization**

19 If a man write a better book, preach a
better sermon, or make a better mouse
trap than his neighbour, tho' he build hi
house in the woods, the world will make a
beaten path to his door.
Mrs. Sarah S.B. Yule (1856–1916) credits th
quotation to Emerson in her *Borrowings* (1889)
stating in *The Docket*, Feb. 1912, that she copied
this in her handbook from a lecture delivered by
Emerson. The quotation was the occasion of a
long controversy, owing to Elbert Hubbard's
claim to its authorship.

WILLIAM EMPSON 1906–

20 Waiting for the end, boys, waiting for the
end.
What is there to be or do?
What's become of me or you?
Are we kind or are we true?
Sitting two and two, boys, waiting for the
end.
Just a Smack at Auden

21 Slowly the poison the whole blood stream
fills.
It is not the effort nor the failure tires.
The waste remains, the waste remains and
kills.
Missing Dates

FRIEDRICH ENGELS 1820–1895

22 *Der Staat wird nicht 'abgeschaft', er stirbt
ab.*
The State is not 'abolished', *it withers
away.*
Anti-Dühring, III.ii

ENNIUS 239–169 B.C.

1 *Unus homo nobis cunctando restituit rem.*
One man by delaying put the state to rights
for us.
Annals 12. Cicero, *De Off.*, I, 24, 84

2 *Moribus antiquis res stat Romana virisque.*
The Roman state survives by its ancient
customs and its manhood.
Annals. St. Augustine, *De Civ. Dei, 2, 21*

HENRI ESTIENNE 1531–1598

3 *Si jeunesse savoit; si vieillesse pouvoit.*
If youth knew; if age could.
Les Prémices, Épigramme cxei

EUCLID fl. c.300 B.C.

4 *Quod erat demonstrandum.* (trans. from
the Greek).
Which was to be proved.

EURIPIDES 480–406 B.C.

5 ἡ γλῶσσ᾽ ὀμώμοχ᾽, ἡ δὲ φρὴν ἀνώμοτος.
My tongue swore, but my mind's unsworn.
Hippolytus, 612

ABEL EVANS 1679–1737

6 Under this stone, Reader, survey
Dead Sir John Vanbrugh's house of clay.
Lie heavy on him, Earth! for he
Laid many heavy loads on thee!
Epitaph on Sir John Vanbrugh, Architect of Blenheim Palace

GAVIN EWART 1916–

7 Miss Twye was soaping her breasts in the
bath
When she heard behind her a meaning
laugh
And to her amazement she discovered
A wicked man in the bathroom cupboard.
Miss Twye

WILLIAM NORMAN EWER 1885–1976

8 I gave my life for freedom—This I know:
For those who bade me fight had told me
so.
Five Souls, 1917

9 How odd
Of God
To choose
The Jews.
How Odd. See 48:4

ROBERT FABYAN d. 1513

10 Finally he paid the debt of nature.
New Chronicles, pt.i, xli

LUCIUS CARY, VISCOUNT FALKLAND 1610?–1643

11 When it is not necessary to change, it is
necessary not to change.
A Speech concerning Episcopacy [delivered
1641]. *A Discourse of Infallibility*, 1660

EDWARD FARMER 1809?–1876

12 I have no pain, dear mother, now;
But oh! I am so dry:
Just moisten poor Jim's lips once more;
And, mother, do not cry!
The Collier's Dying Child. See 3:18

GEORGE FARQUHAR 1678–1707

13 My Lady Bountiful.
The Beaux' Stratagem, I.i

14 I believe they talked of me, for they laughed consumedly.
III.i

15 *Aimwell:* Then you understand Latin, Mr
Bonniface?
Bonniface: Not I, Sir, as the saying is, but
he talks it so very fast that I'm sure it must
be good.
ii

16 He answered the description the page gave
to a T, Sir.
Love and a Bottle, IV.iii

GUY FAWKES 1570–1606

17 A desperate disease requires a dangerous
remedy.
6 Nov. 1605. See D.N.B.

GEOFFREY FEARON

18 The 'angry young men' of England (who
refuse to write grammatically and syntactically in order to flaunt their proletarian
artistry).
Times Literary Supplement, 4 Oct. 1957 but see
also R. West, *Black Lamb and Grey Falcon*
(1941), 'Dalmatia'

EMPEROR FERDINAND I 1503–1564

19 *Fiat justitia et pereat mundus.*
Let justice be done, though the world perish.
Motto. Johannes Manlius, *Locorum Communium Collectanea* (Basle, 1563), II, 290. See
266:14

LUDWIG FEUERBACH 1804–1872

1 *Der Mensch ist, was er isst.*
Man is what he eats.
Advertisement to Moleschott, *Lehre der Nah-rungsmittel: Für das Volk* (1850). See 46:18

EUGENE FIELD 1850–1895

2 Wynken, Blynken, and Nod one night
    Sailed off in a wooden shoe—
Sailed on a river of crystal light,
    Into a sea of dew.
Wynken, Blynken, and Nod

3 He played the King as though under
momentary apprehension that someone
else was about to play the ace.
Of Creston Clarke as King Lear. Attr. to a re-view in the *Denver Tribune*, c.1880

HENRY FIELDING 1707–1754

4 Oh! The roast beef of England,
And old England's roast beef.
The Grub Street Opera, III.iii

5 He in a few minutes ravished this fair
creature, or at least would have ravished
her, if she had not, by a timely compliance,
prevented him.
Jonathan Wild, bk.iii, ch.7

6 Public schools are the nurseries of all vice
and immorality.
Joseph Andrews, bk, iii, ch.5

7 Some folks rail against other folks, be-cause other folks have what some folks
would be glad of.
bk.iv, ch.6

8 When I mention religion, I mean the
Christian religion; and not only the Chris-tian religion, but the Protestant religion;
and not only the Protestant religion but
the Church of England.
Tom Jones, bk.iii, ch.3

9 What is commonly called love, namely the
desire of satisfying a voracious appetite
with a certain quantity of delicate white
human flesh.
bk.vi, ch.1

10 An amiable weakness.
bk.x, ch.8

11 The dusky night rides down the sky,
    And ushers in the morn;
The hounds all join in glorious cry,
    The huntsman winds his horn:
        And a-hunting we will go.
A-Hunting We Will Go

LORD FISHER 1841–1920

12 Sack the lot!
The Times, 2 Sept. 1919

CHARLES FITZGEFFREY 1575?–1638

13 And bold and hard adventures t' under
    take,
Leaving his country for his country's sake
Sir Francis Drake (1596), st.213

EDWARD FITZGERALD 1809–1883

14 Awake! for Morning in the Bowl of Night
Has flung the Stone that puts the Stars to
    Flight:
    And Lo! the Hunter of the East ha
      caught
The Sultan's Turret in a Noose of Light.
The Rubáiyát of Omar Khayyám (1859), 1

15 Here with a Loaf of Bread beneath th
    bough,
A Flask of Wine, a Book of Verse—an
    Thou
    Beside me singing in the Wilderness—
And Wilderness is Paradise enow.
11
A Book of Verses underneath the Bough,
A Jug of Wine, a Loaf of Bread—and Thou
  Beside me singing in the Wilderness—
Oh, Wilderness were Paradise enow! 12 (ed.4)

16   Ah, take the Cash in hand and waiv
    the Rest;
Oh, the brave Music of a *distant* Drum!
12
  Ah, take the Cash, and let the Credit go,
Nor heed the rumble of a distant Drum! 13 (ed.4)

17 Think, in this batter'd Caravanserai
Whose Doorways are alternate Night and
    Day,
    How Sultan after Sultan with his Pomp
Abode his Hour or two, and went his way.
15
Think, in this batter'd Caravanserai
Whose Portals are alternate Night and Day,
  How Sultan after Sultan with his Pomp
Abode his destin'd Hour, and went his way. 17
(ed.4)

18 They say the Lion and the Lizard keep
The Courts where Jamshyd gloried and
    drank deep:
    And Bahram, that great Hunter—the
      Wild Ass
Stamps o'er his Head, and he lies fast
    asleep.
17
...but cannot break his Sleep. 18 (ed.4)

1 I sometimes think that never blows so red
   The Rose as where some buried Caesar
      bled;
      That every Hyacinth the Garden wears
   Dropt in her Lap from some once lovely
      Head.
   18

2 Lo! some we loved, the loveliest and best
   That Time and Fate of all their Vintage
      prest,
      Have drunk their Cup a Round or two
         before,
   And one by one crept silently to Rest.
   21
   For some we loved, the loveliest and the best
   That from his Vintage rolling Time hath prest.
   22 (ed.4)

3 Ah, make the most of what we yet may
      spend,
   Before we too into the Dust descend;
      Dust into Dust, and under Dust, to lie,
   Sans Wine, sans Song, sans Singer, and—
      sans End!
   23

4 Oh, come with old Khayyám, and leave
      the Wise
   To talk; one thing is certain, that Life flies;
      One thing is certain, and the Rest is
         Lies;
   The Flower that once hath blown for ever
      dies.
   26
   Oh threats of Hell and Hopes of Paradise!
   One thing at least is certain—*This* Life flies;
      One thing is certain and the rest is Lies;
   The Flower that once has blown for ever dies. 63
   (ed.4)

5 Myself when young did eagerly frequent
   Doctor and Saint, and heard great argu-
      ment
      About it and about: but evermore
   Came out by the same Door as I went.
   27
   Came out by the same Door wherein I went.
   (ed.4)

6 Ah, fill the Cup:—what boots it to repeat
   How Time is slipping underneath our
      Feet:
      Unborn **TO-MORROW**, and dead
         YESTERDAY,
   Why fret about them if **TO-DAY** be sweet!
   37

7 'Tis all a Chequer-board of Nights and
      Days
      Where Destiny with Men for Pieces plays:
         Hither and thither moves, and mates,
            and slays,

And one by one back in the Closet lays.
49
But helpless Pieces of the Game He plays
Upon this Chequer-board of Nights and Days;
   Hither and thither moves, and checks, and
      slays,
And one by one back in the Closet lays. 69 (ed.4)

8 The Ball no question makes of Ayes and
      Noes,
      But Here or There as strikes the Player
         goes;
         And He that toss'd you down into the
            Field,
   He knows about it all—HE knows—HE
      knows!
   70 (ed.4)

9 The Moving Finger writes; and, having
      writ,
      Moves on: nor all thy Piety nor Wit
         Shall lure it back to cancel half a Line,
   Nor all thy Tears wash out a Word of it.
   51 ...your Tears... 71 (ed.4)

10 And that inverted Bowl we call The Sky,
      Whereunder crawling coop't we live and
         die,
         Lift not thy hands to *It* for help—for It
   Rolls impotently on as Thou or I.
   52
   ...they call the Sky...
   As impotently moves as you or I. 72 (ed.4)

11 Indeed the Idols I have loved so long
      Have done my credit in this World much
         wrong:
         Have drown'd my Glory in a Shallow
            Cup
   And sold my Reputation for a Song.
   93 (ed.4)

12 And much as Wine has play'd the Infidel,
      And robb'd me of my Robe of Honour—
         Well,
         I often wonder what the Vintners buy
   One half so precious as the Goods they
      sell.
   71 ...the stuff they sell. 95 (ed.4)

13 Ah Love! could thou and I with Fate con-
      spire
      To grasp this sorry Scheme of Things en-
         tire,
         Would not we shatter it to bits—and
            then
   Re-mould it nearer to the Heart's Desire!
   73
   Ah Love! could you and I with Him conspire. 94
   (ed.4)

14 Ah, Moon of my Delight who know'st no
      wane,
      The Moon of Heav'n is rising once again:
         How oft hereafter rising shall she look

Through this same Garden after me—in
vain!

74

Yon rising Moon that looks for us again.
How oft hereafter will she wax and wane;
   How oft hereafter rising look for us
Through this same Garden—and for *one* in vain!
100 (ed.4)

1 And when Thyself with shining Foot shall
  pass
  Among the Guests Star-scattered on the
  Grass,
    And in thy joyous Errand reach the
    Spot
  Where I made one—turn down an empty
  Glass!

75

And when like her, O Saki, you shall pass...
And in your joyous errand reach the spot. 101
(ed.4)

F. SCOTT FITZGERALD 1896–1940

2 In the real dark night of the soul it is
  always three o'clock in the morning.
  The Crack-Up, ed. E. Wilson (1945), John Peale
  Bishop, *The Hours.* The phrase 'dark night of the
  soul' was used as the Spanish title of a work by
  St. John of the Cross known in English as *The
  Ascent of Mount Carmel* (1578–80)

3 Her voice is full of money.
  The Great Gatsby, ch.7

4 Let me tell you about the very rich. They
  are different from you and me.
  The Rich Boy. 'Notebooks E' in *The Crack-Up*
  records Ernest Hemingway's rejoinder: 'Yes,
  they have more money.'

ROBERT FITZSIMMONS 1862–1917

5 The bigger they come, the harder they fall.
  Said before his fight with Jefferies in San Francisco, 9 June 1899

GUSTAVE FLAUBERT 1821–1880

6 *Nous ferons tout ce qui nous plaira! nous
  laisserons pousser notre barbe!*
  We'll do just as we like! We'll grow beards!
  Bouvard et Pécuchet, ch.1

JAMES ELROY FLECKER 1884–1915

7 The dragon-green, the luminous, the dark,
  the serpent-haunted sea.
  The Gates of Damascus. West Gate

8 For lust of knowing what should not be
  known,
  We take the Golden Road to Samarkand.
  Hassan (1922), V. ii

9 I have seen old ships sail like swans asleep
  Beyond that village which men still call
  Tyre,

With leaden age o'ercargoed, dipping dee[p]
For Famagusta and the hidden sun
That rings black Cyprus with a lake of fire
The Old Ships (1915)

10 But now through friendly seas they softl[y]
  run,
  Painted the mid-sea blue or the shore-se[a]
  green,
  Still patterned with the vine and grapes i[n]
  gold.

11 It was so old a ship—who knows, wh[o]
  knows?
  And yet so beautiful, I watched in vain
  To see the mast burst open with a rose,
  And the whole deck put on its leave[s]
  again.

12 A ship, an isle, a sickle moon—
  With few but with how splendid stars
  The mirrors of the sea are strewn
  Between their silver bars.
  A Ship, an Isle, and a Sickle Moon

13 O friend unseen, unborn, unknown,
  Student of our sweet English tongue,
  Read out my words at night, alone:
  I was a poet, I was young.
  To a Poet a Thousand Years Hence

MARJORY FLEMING 1803–1811

14 The most devilish thing is 8 times 8 and [7]
  times 7 it is what nature itselfe cant en[-]
  dure.
  Journal, p.47

ANDREW FLETCHER OF SALTOUN 1655–1716

15 I knew a very wise man so much of Si[r]
  Chr—'s sentiment, that he believed if [a]
  man were permitted to make all the bal[-]
  lads, he need not care who should mak[e]
  the laws of a nation.
  Political Works. **Letter to the Marquis of Mon[-]
  trose, and Others** (1703)

JOHN FLETCHER 1579–1625
See also under BEAUMONT

16 Death hath so many doors to let out life.
  The Custom of the Country (with Massinger)
  II.ii. See 164:6, 203:6, 267:11

17 'Tis virtue, and not birth that makes u[s]
  noble:
  Great actions speak great minds, and suc[h]
  should govern.
  The Prophetess (with Massinger), II.iii

18 I'll have a fling.
  Rule a Wife and Have a Wife, III.v

19 Daisies smell-less, yet most quaint,

And sweet thyme true.
Two Noble Kinsmen (with Shakespeare). I.ii.

1 Whistle and she'll come to you.
Wit Without Money, IV.iv

2 Charity and beating begins at home.
V.ii

JEAN-PIERRE CLARIS DE FLORIAN 1755–1794

3 *Plaisir d'amour ne dure qu'un moment,*
Chagrin d'amour dure toute la vie.
Love's pleasure lasts but a moment; love's
sorrow lasts all through life.
Celestine

JOHN FLORIO 1553?–1625

4 England is the paradise of women, the
purgatory of men, and the hell of horses.
Second Frutes (1591)

DR F.J. FOAKES JACKSON 1855–1941

5 It's no use trying to be *clever*—we are all
clever here; just try to be *kind*—a little
kind.
Said to a recently elected young don at Jesus
College, Cambridge. Oral tradition. Noted in
A.C. Benson's Commonplace Book

MARSHAL FOCH 1851–1929

6 *Mon centre cède, ma droite recule, situa-*
tion excellente. J'attaque!
My centre is giving way, my right is in
retreat; situation excellent. I shall attack.
Aston, *Biography of Foch* (1929), ch.13

SAMUEL FOOTE 1720–1777

7 So she went into the garden to cut a
cabbage-leaf, to make an apple-pie; and at
the same time a great she-bear, coming up
the street, pops its head into the shop.
'What! no soap?' So he died, and she very
imprudently married the barber; and there
were present the Picninnies, and the Joblil-
lies, and the Garyalies, and the grand Panjandrum himself, with the little round button at top, and they all fell to playing the
game of catch as catch can, till the gun
powder ran out at the heels of their boots.
Farrago composed by Foote to test the vaunted
memory of the actor Charles Macklin. See *Quar-*
terly Review (1854), 95.516

8 He is not only dull in himself, but the
cause of dullness in others.
Boswell, *Life of Johnson,* ed. Powell, IV, p.178.
Parody of 212:19

MISS C.F. FORBES 1817–1911

9 The sense of being well-dressed gives a
feeling of inward tranquillity which religion is powerless to bestow.
Emerson, *Social Aims*

HENRY FORD 1863–1947

10 History is more or less bunk.
Chicago Tribune, 25 May 1916

HOWELL FORGY 1908–

11 Praise the Lord, and pass the ammunition.
Attr. when a Naval Lt., at Pearl Harbor, 7 Dec.
1941

E.M. FORSTER 1879–1970

12 Everything must be like something, so
what is this like?
Abinger Harvest (1936), **Our Diversions,** 3 'The
Doll Souse', first published 1924

13 Yes—oh dear yes—the novel tells a story.
Aspects of the Novel, ch.2

14 I felt for a moment that the whole Wilcox
family was a fraud, just a wall of news-
papers and motor-cars and golf-clubs, and
that if it fell I should find nothing behind it
but panic and emptiness.
Howards End, ch.4

15 All men are equal—all men, that is to say,
who possess umbrellas.
ch.6

16 Personal relations are the important thing
for ever and ever, and not this outer life of
telegrams and anger.
ch.19

17 Only connect! That was the whole of her
sermon. Only connect the prose and the
passion, and both will be exalted, and
human love will be seen at its highest.
ch.22

18 The so-called white races are really
pinko-gray.
A Passage to India, ch.7

19 God si Love. Is this the final message of
India?
ch.33

20 I do not believe in Belief...Lord I disbe-
lieve—help thou my unbelief.
Two Cheers for Democracy, pt.2. **What I Believe.**
See 56:18

21 I hate the idea of causes, and if I had to
choose between betraying my country and
betraying my friend, I hope I should have
the guts to betray my country.

1 So Two cheers for Democracy: one because it admits variety and two because it permits criticism. Two cheers are quite enough: there is no occasion to give three. Only Love the Beloved Republic deserves that.

CHARLES FOURIER 1772–1837

2 *L'extension des privilèges des femmes est le principe général de tous progrès sociaux.*
The extension of women's rights is the basic principle of all social progress.
Théorie des Quatre Mouvements (1808), II.iv

CHARLES JAMES FOX 1749–1806

3 How much the greatest event it is that ever happened in the world! and how much the best!
On the Fall of the Bastille. Letter to Fitzpatrick, 30 July 1789. Russell, *Life and Times of C.J. Fox,* vol.ii, p.361

HENRY STEPHEN FOX 1791–1846

4 I am so changed that my oldest creditors would hardly know me.
After an illness. Quoted by Byron in a letter to John Murray, 8 May 1817

ANATOLE FRANCE 1844–1924

5 *La majestueuse égalité des lois, qui interdit au riche comme au pauvre de coucher sous les ponts, de mendier dans les rues et de voler du pain.*
The majestic egalitarianism of the law, which forbids rich and poor alike to sleep under bridges, to beg in the streets, and to steal bread.
Le Lys Rouge (1894), ch.7

FRANCIS I 1494–1547

6 *De toutes choses ne m'est demeuré que l'honneur et la vie qui est saulve.*
Of all I had, only honour and life have been spared.
Letter to his mother after his defeat at Pavia, 1525. *Collection des Documents Inédits sur l'Histoire de France* (1847), I, 129. Usually cited as *'Tout est perdu fors l'honneur'* (All is lost save honour).

ST. FRANCIS DE SALES 1567–1622

7 *Ce sont les grans feux qui s'enflamment au vent, mays les petitz s'esteignent si on ne les y porte a couvert.*
Big fires flare up in a wind, but little ones are blown out unless they are carried in under cover.
Introduction à la vie dévote (1609), pt.III, ch.34

BENJAMIN FRANKLIN 1706–1790

8 Remember, that time is money.
Advice to Young Tradesman (1748)

9 No nation was ever ruined by trade.
Essays. Thoughts on Commercial Subjects

10 The having made a young girl miserabl may give you frequent bitter reflection none of which can attend the making of a old woman happy.
On the Choice of a Mistress (i.e. wife)

11 A little neglect may breed mischief,…fo want of a nail, the shoe was lost; for wan of a shoe the horse was lost; and for wan of a horse the rider was lost.
Maxims…Prefixed to *Poor Richard's Almanac* (1758)

12 We must indeed all hang together, or most assuredly, we shall all hang separate ly.
Remark to John Hancock, at the Signing of th Declaration of Independence, 4 July 1776

13 Man is a tool-making animal.
Boswell, *Life of Johnson,* 7 Apr. 1778

14 Here Skugg
Lies snug
As a bug
In a rug.
Letter to Georgiana Shipley on the death of he squirrel, 26 Sept. 1772. 'Skug' was a dialect word meaning 'squirrel'.

15 There never was a good war, or a bad peace.
Letter to Quincy, 11 Sept. 1783

16 But in this world nothing can be said to be certain, except death and taxes.
Letter to Jean Baptiste Le Roy, 13 Nov. 1789

17 What is the use of a new-born child?
When asked what was the use of a new invention. J. Parton, *Life and Times of Benjamin Franklin* (1864), pt.IV, ch.17

18 *Ça ira.*
That will go its way.
Oral trad. Remark made in Paris, 1776-7, on the American War of Independence. Taken up in the French Revolution and used as the refrain of the song to the tune *'Carillon national'* by 1790. Ladré later claimed to have written the words.

E.A. FREEMAN 1823–1892

19 History is past politics, and politics is present history.
Methods of Historical Study (1886), p.44

JOHN HOOKHAM FRERE 1769–1846

1 The feather'd race with pinions skim the
air—
Not so the mackerel, and still less the bear!
Progress of Man, l.34

ROBERT FROST 1874–1963

2 I have been one acquainted with the night.
I have walked out in rain—and back in
rain.
I have outwalked the furthest city light.

I have looked down the saddest city lane.
I have passed by the watchman on his beat
And dropped my eyes, unwilling to ex-
plain.
Acquainted with the Night

3 'Home is the place where, when you have
to go there,
They have to take you in'.

'I should have called it
Something you somehow haven't to de-
serve.'
The Death of the Hired Man

4 Spades take up leaves
No better than spoons,
And bags full of leaves
Are light as balloons.
Gathering Leaves

5 The land was ours before we were the
land's.
The Gift Outright

6 Forgive, O Lord, my little jokes on Thee
And I'll forgive Thy great big one on me.
In the clearing, **Cluster of Faith**

7 My apple trees will never get across
And eat the cones under his pines, I tell
him.
He only says, 'Good fences make good
neighbours.'
North of Boston (1914). **Mending Wall**

8 Two roads diverged in a wood, and I—
I took the one less traveled by,
And that has made all the difference.
The Road Not Taken

9 Whoever it is that leaves him out so late,
When other creatures have gone to stall
and bin,
Ought to be told to come and take him in.
The Runaway

10 The woods are lovely, dark, and deep,
But I have promises to keep,
And miles to go before I sleep,
And miles to go before I sleep.
Stopping by Woods on a Snowy Evening

11 To err is human, not to, animal.
The White-tailed Hornet

12 The ruling passion in man is not as Vien-
nese as is claimed. It is rather a gregarious
instinct to keep together by minding each
other's business. Grex rather than sex.
The Constant Symbol

13 Writing free verse is like playing tennis
with the net down.
Address at Milton Academy, Milton, Mass., 17
May 1935

14 Poetry is what gets lost in translation.
Attr.

J.A. FROUDE 1818–1894

15 Wild animals never kill for sport. Man is
the only one to whom the torture and
death of his fellow-creatures is amusing in
itself.
Oceana (1886), ch.5

CHRISTOPHER FRY 1907–

16 I sometimes think
His critical judgement is so exquisite
It leaves us nothing to admire except his
opinion.
The Dark is Light Enough (1954), Act II

17 Out there, in the sparkling air, the sun and
the rain
Clash together like the cymbals clashing
When David did his dance. I've an April
blindness.
You're hidden in a cloud of crimson
catherine-wheels.
The Lady's Not For Burning (1948), Act I

18 What, after all,
Is a halo? It's only one more thing to keep
clean.

19 Using words
That are only fit for the Bible.
Act II

20 The moon is nothing
But a circumambulating aphrodisiac
Divinely subsidized to provoke the world
Into a rising birth-rate.
Act III

21 A spade is never so merely a spade as the
word
Spade would imply.
Venus Observed (1950), II.i

RICHARD BUCKMINSTER FULLER
1895–

22 God, to me, it seems,
is a verb

not a noun,
proper or improper.
No More Secondhand God. See 127:15

THOMAS FULLER 1608–1661

1 Worldly wealth he cared not for, desiring
only to make both ends meet. [Of Edmund
Grindall.]
The History of the Worthies of England (1662),
Worthies of Cumberland

2 Light (God's eldest daughter) is a principal beauty in building.
The Holy State and the Profane State (1642),
bk.iii, ch.7. **Of Building**

3 Anger is one of the sinews of the soul.
ch.8. **Of Anger**

ROSE FYLEMAN 1877–1957

4 There are fairies at the bottom of our
garden.
Fairies and Chimneys

THOMAS GAINSBOROUGH
1727–1788

5 We are all going to Heaven, and Vandyke
is of the company.
Attr. last words. Boulton, *Thomas Gainsbor-
ough*, ch.9

REVD. THOMAS GAISFORD
1779–1855

6 Nor can I do better, in conclusion, than
impress upon you the study of Greek literature, which not only elevates above the
vulgar herd, but leads not infrequently to
positions of considerable emolument.
Christmas Day Sermon in the Cathedral, Oxford. Revd. W. Tuckwell, *Reminiscences of
Oxford* (2nd ed., 1907), p.124

HUGH GAITSKELL 1906–1963

7 There are some of us who will fight and
fight and fight again to save the party we
love.
Speech, Labour Party Conference, Scarborough,
5 Oct. 1960

GAIUS 2nd cent. A.D.

8 *Damnosa hereditas.*
Ruinous inheritance.
Institutes, ii.163

J.K. GALBRAITH 1908–

9 In the affluent society no useful distinction can be made between luxuries and
necessaries.
The Affluent Society, ch.21.iv

GALILEO GALILEI 1564–1642

10 *Eppur si muove.*
But it does move.
Attr. to Galileo after his recantation in 1632.
The earliest apppearance of the phrase is per-
haps in Baretti, *Italian Library* (1757), p.52

JOHN GALT 1779–1839

11 From the lone shieling of the misty island
Mountains divide us, and the waste of
seas —
Yet still the blood is strong, the heart is
Highland,
And we in dreams behold the Hebrides!
Fair these broad meads, these hoary
woods are grand;
But we are exiles from our fathers' land.
Attr. *Canadian Boat Song ('The Lone Shieling').*
'Noctes Ambrosianae', XLVI, *Blackwoods Ma-
gazine*, Sept. 1829

GRETA GARBO 1905–

12 I want to be alone.
Grand Hotel (1932), script by William A. Drake.
The phrase had frequently been attributed to
Garbo before being used in the film; she seems in
fact to have said on various occasions (off
screen) 'I want to be left alone' and 'Why don't
they leave me alone.'

FEDERICO GARCÍA LORCA
1899–1936

13 *Verde que te quiero verde,
Verde viento. Verde ramas.*
Green I love you green. Green wind.
Green branches.
Romance sonámbulo

DAVID GARRICK 1717–1779

14 Here lies Nolly Goldsmith, for shortness
call'd Noll,
Who wrote like an angel, but talk'd like
poor Poll.
Impromptu Epitaph

15 Kitty, a fair, but frozen maid,
Kindled a flame I still deplore;
The hood-wink'd boy I call'd in aid,
Much of his near approach afraid.
So fatal to my suit before.
A Riddle. *Lady's Magazine*, June 1762

WILLIAM LLOYD GARRISON
1805–1879

16 I am in earnest—I will not equivocate—I

will not excuse—I will not retreat a single inch—and I will be heard!
Salutatory Address of *The Liberator*, 1 Jan. 1831

SIR SAMUEL GARTH 1661–1719

1 A barren superfluity of words.
The Dispensary (1699), c.2, l.95

MRS GASKELL 1810–1865

2 A man…is *so* in the way in the house!
Cranford (1851-3), ch.1

3 [The Cranford ladies'] dress is very independent of fashion; as they observe, 'What does it signify how we dress here at Cranford, where everybody knows us?' And if they go from home, their reason is equally cogent: 'What does it signify how we dress here, where nobody knows us?'

4 'It is very pleasant dining with a bachelor,' said Miss Matty, softly, as we settled ourselves in the counting-house. 'I only hope it is not improper; so many pleasant things are!'
ch.4

GAVARNI 1804–1866

5 *Les enfants terribles.*
The embarrassing young.
Title of a series of prints

JOHN GAY 1685–1732

6 O ruddier than the cherry,
O sweeter than the berry.
Acis and Galatea (c.1720), ii

7 Do you think your mother and I should have liv'd comfortably so long together, if ever we had been married?
The Beggar's Opera (1728), Act I, sc. viii, air vii

8 Well, Polly; as far as one woman can forgive another, I forgive thee.
air ix

9 The comfortable estate of widowhood, is the only hope that keeps up a wife's spirits.
sc.x

10 Away, hussy. Hang your husband and be dutiful.

11 If with me you'd fondly stray.
Over the hills and far away.
sc.xiii, air xvi

12 If the heart of a man is deprest with cares,
The mist is dispell'd when a woman appears.
Act II, sc.iii, air xxi

13 Youth's the season made for joys,

Love is then our duty.
sc.iv, air xxii

14 How happy could I be with either,
Were t'other dear charmer away!
But while ye thus tease me together,
To neither a word will I say.
sc.xiii, air xxxv

15 She who has never lov'd, has never liv'd.
The Captives (1724), II.i

16 If e'er your heart has felt the tender passion
You will forgive this just, this pious fraud.
IV.x

17 Whence is thy learning? Hath thy toil
O'er books consum'd the midnight oil?
Fables (1727), introduction, l.15

18 And when a lady's in the case,
You know, all other things give place.
l. **The Hare and Many Friends**, l.41

19 Behold the bright original appear.
A Letter to a Lady, l.85

20 Life is a jest; and all things show it.
I thought so once; but now I know it.
My Own Epitaph

21 Variety's the source of joy below,
From whence still fresh revolving pleasures flow.
In books and love, the mind one end pursues,
And only change th'expiring flame renews.
On a Miscellany of Poems

22 No retreat.
No retreat.
They must conquer or die who've no retreat.
Polly (1729), II.x

23 All in the Downs the fleet was moor'd,
The streamers waving in the wind,
When black-ey'd Susan came aboard.
Sweet William's Farewell to Black-Eyed Susan

SIR ERIC GEDDES 1875–1937

24 The Germans, if this Government is returned, are going to pay every penny; they are going to be squeezed, as a lemon is squeezed— until the pips squeak. My only doubt is not whether we can squeeze hard enough, but whether there is enough juice.
Speech, Cambridge, 10 Dec. 1918. *Cambridge Daily News*, 3/2

LLOYD GEORGE 1863–1945

25 What is our task? To make Britain a fit country for heroes to live in.
Speech, Wolverhampton, 24 Nov. 1918

KING GEORGE I 1660-1727

1 I hate all Boets and Bainters.
Campbell, *Lives of the Chief Justices*, ch.30, Lord Mansfield

KING GEORGE II 1683-1760

2 *Non, j'aurai des maîtresses.*
No, I shall have mistresses.
Reply to Queen Caroline when, as she lay dying, she urged him to marry again. Her reply to this was '*Ah! mon dieu! cela n'empêche pas*'. Hervey, *Memoirs of George the Second* (1848), vol.ii

3 Mad, is he? Then I hope he will *bite* some of my other generals.
Reply to the Duke of Newcastle who complained that General Wolfe was a madman. Willson, *The life and letters of James Wolfe*, ch.17

KING GEORGE III 1738-1820

4 Born and educated in this country I glory in the name of Briton.
Speech from the Throne, 1760

5 'Was there ever,' cried he, 'such stuff as great part of Shakespeare? Only one must not say so! But what think you?—what? —Is there not sad stuff? what?— what?'
To Fanny Burney (in her *Diary*, 19 Dec. 1785)

EDWARD GIBBON 1737-1794

6 I sighed as a lover, I obeyed as a son.
Autobiography (World's Classics ed.), p.83

7 Crowds without company, and dissipation without pleasure. [Of London.]
p.90

8 It was at Rome, on the 15th of October, 1764, as I sat musing amidst the ruins of the Capitol, while the barefoot friars were singing vespers in the Temple of Jupiter, that the idea of writing the decline and fall of the city first started to my mind.
p.160

9 My English text is chaste, and all licentious passages are left in the decent obscurity of a learned language.
p.212

10 I must reluctantly observe that two causes, the abbreviation of time, and the failure of hope, will always tinge with a browner shade the evening of life.
p.221

11 His reign is marked by the rare advantage of furnishing very few materials for history; which is, indeed, little more than the register of the crimes, follies, and misfortunes of mankind.
The Decline and Fall of the Roman Empire (1776-88), ch.3 (Of Antoninus Pius, Roman Emperor, 137-161 A.D.) See 265:1

12 Twenty-two acknowledged concubines, and a library of sixty-two thousand volumes attested the variety of his inclinations; and from the productions which he left behind him, it appears that both the one and the other were designed for use rather than for ostentation. [Emperor Gordian the Younger.]
ch.7

ORLANDO GIBBONS 1583-1625

13 The silver swan, who, living had no note, When death approached unlocked her silent throat.
from *The First Set of Madrigals and Motets of Five Parts* (1612)

STELLA GIBBONS 1902-

14 Something nasty in the woodshed.
Cold Comfort Farm (1932), *passim*

WILFRED GIBSON 1878-1962

15 The heart-break in the heart of things.
Lament (1926). See 263:2

ANDRÉ GIDE 1869-1951

16 *Hugo—hélas!*
When asked to name the greatest poet of the nineteenth century. *André Gide-Paul Valéry Correspondance 1890-1942*, p.494

SIR HUMPHREY GILBERT 1539?-1583

17 We are as near to heaven by sea as by land!
Richard Hakluyt, *Voyages* (1600), iii, p.159

W.S. GILBERT 1836-1911

18 He had often eaten oysters, but had never had enough.
The 'Bab' Ballads (1866-71), **Etiquette**

19 The padre said, 'Whatever have you been and gone and done?'
Gentle Alice Brown

20 Which is pretty, but I don't know what it means.
Story of Prince Agib

21 Oh, I am a cook and a captain bold,
And the mate of the *Nancy* brig,
And a bo'sun tight, and a midshipmite,

And the crew of the captain's gig.
The Yarn of the 'Nancy Bell'

1 He led his regiment from behind—
He found it less exciting.
The Gondoliers (1899), I

2 That celebrated,
Cultivated,
Underrated
Nobleman
The Duke of Plaza Toro!

3 Of that there is no manner of doubt—
No probable, possible shadow of doubt—
No possible doubt whatever.

4 Oh, 'tis a glorious thing, I ween,
To be a regular Royal Queen!
No half-and-half affair, I mean,
But a right-down regular Royal Queen!

5 All shall equal be.
The Earl, the Marquis, and the Dook,
The Groom, the Butler, and the Cook,
The Aristocrat who banks with Coutts,
The Aristocrat who cleans the boots.

6 But the privilege and pleasure
That we treasure beyond measure
Is to run on little errands for the Ministers
of State.
II

7 With the gratifying feeling that our duty
has been done!

8 Take a pair of sparkling eyes,
Hidden, ever and anon,
In a merciful eclipse.

9 When every one is somebodee,
Then no one's anybody.

10 I see no objection to stoutness, in moderation.
Iolanthe (1882), I

11 Thou the singer; I the song!

12 The Law is the true embodiment
Of everything that's excellent.
It has no kind of fault or flaw,
And I, my Lords, embody the Law.

13 The constitutional guardian I
Of pretty young wards in Chancery,
All very agreeable girls—and none
Are over the age of twenty-one.
A pleasant occupation for
A rather susceptible Chancellor!

14 Hearts just as pure and fair
May beat in Belgrave Square
As in the lowly air
Of Seven Dials.

15 When I went to the Bar as a very young
man,

(Said I to myself—said I),
I'll work on a new and original plan,
(Said I to myself—said I).

16 I am an intellectual chap,
And think of things that would astonish
you.
I often think it's comical
How Nature always does contrive
That every boy and every gal,
That's born into the world alive,
Is either a little Liberal,
Or else a little Conservative!
II

17 When in that House MPs divide,
If they've a brain and cerebellum too,
They have to leave that brain outside,
And vote just as their leaders tell 'em to.

18 The prospect of a lot
Of dull MPs in close proximity,
All thinking for themselves is what
No man can face with equanimity.

19 The House of Peers, throughout the war,
Did nothing in particular,
And did it very well:
Yet Britain set the world ablaze
In good King George's glorious days!

20 When you're lying awake with a dismal
headache, and repose is taboo'd by
anxiety,
I conceive you may use any language you
choose to indulge in, without impropriety.

21 For you dream you are crossing the Channel, and tossing about in a steamer
from Harwich—
Which is something between a large bathing machine and a very small second
class carriage.

22 And you're giving a treat (penny ice and
cold meat) to a party of friends and
relations—
They're a ravenous horde—and they all
came on board at Sloane Square and
South Kensington Stations.
And bound on that journey you find your
attorney (who started that morning
from Devon);
He's a bit undersized, and you don't feel
surprised when he tells you he's only
eleven.

23 In your shirt and your socks (the black
silk with gold clocks), crossing Salisbury Plain on a bicycle.

24 A wandering minstrel I—
A thing of shreds and patches,
Of ballads, songs and snatches,

And dreamy lullaby!
The Mikado (1885), I

1 I can trace my ancestry back to a proto-plasmal primordial atomic globule. Conse-quently, my family pride is something in-conceivable. I can't help it. I was born sneering.

2 It revolts me, but I do it!

3 I accept refreshment at any hands, how-ever lowly.

4 As some day it may happen that a victim must be found,
I've got a little list—I've got a little list
Of society offenders who might well be under ground
And who never would be missed—who never would be missed!

5 The idiot who praises, with enthusiastic tone,
All centuries but this, and every country but his own.
See 61:1, 178:18

6 Three little maids from school are we,
Pert as a schoolgirl well can be,
Filled to the brim with girlish glee.

7 Three little maids who, all unwary,
Come from a ladies' seminary.

8 Modified rapture!

9 Awaiting the sensation of a short, sharp shock,
From a cheap and chippy chopper on a big black block.

10 Here's a how-de-doo!
II

11 My object all sublime
I shall achieve in time—
To let the punishment fit the crime—
The punishment fit the crime.

12 I have a left shoulder-blade that is a mi-racle of loveliness. People come miles to see it. My right elbow has a fascination that few can resist.

13 Something lingering, with boiling oil in it, I fancy.

14 Merely corroborative detail, intended to give artistic verisimilitude to an otherwise bald and unconvincing narrative.

15 The flowers that bloom in the spring,
Tra la,
Have nothing to do with the case.

16 I've got to take under my wing,
Tra la,
A most unattractive old thing,
Tra la,

With a caricature of a face.

17 On a tree by a river a little tom-tit
Sang 'Willow, titwillow, titwillow!'
And I said to him, 'Dicky-bird, why do you sit
Singing Willow, titwillow, titwillow?'

18 'Is it weakness of intellect, birdie?' I cried,
'Or a rather tough worm in your little inside?'
With a shake of his poor little head he replied,
'Oh, willow, titwillow, titwillow!'

19 If you're anxious for to shine in the high aesthetic line as a man of culture rare.
Patience (1881), I

20 The meaning doesn't matter if it's only idle chatter of a transcendental kind.

21 Though the Philistines may jostle, you will rank as an apostle in the high aesthetic band,
If you walk down Piccadilly with a poppy or a lily in your medieval hand.

22 Francesca di Rimini, miminy, piminy,
Je-ne-sais-quoi young man!

23 A greenery-yallery, Grosvenor Galley,
Foot-in-the-grave young man!

24 I'm called Little Buttercup—dear Little Buttercup,
Though I could never tell why.
H.M.S. Pinafore (1878), I

25 I am the Captain of the *Pinafore*;
And a right good captain too!

26 And I'm never, never sick at sea!
What, never?
No, never!
What, *never*?
Hardly ever!
He's hardly ever sick at sea!

27 Though 'Bother it' I may
Occasionally say,
I never use a big, big D—

28 When I was a lad I served a term
As office boy to an Attorney's firm.
I cleaned the windows and I swept the floor,
And I polished up the handle of the big front door.
I polished up that handle so carefullee
That now I am the Ruler of the Queen's Navee!

29 Stick close to your desks and never go to sea,
And you all may be Rulers of the Queen's Navee!

30 Poor wandering one!

Though thou hast surely strayed,
Take heart of grace,
Thy steps retrace,
Poor wandering one!
The Pirates of Penzance (1879), I

1 I'm very good at integral and differential
  calculus,
  I know the scientific names of beings ani-
  malculous·
  In short, in matters vegetable, animal, and
  mineral,
  I am the very model of a modern Major-
  General.

2 When constabulary duty's to be done,
  A policeman's lot is not a happy one.
  II

3 With all our faults, we love our Queen.

4 You must stir it and stump it,
    And blow your own trumpet,
  Or trust me, you haven't a chance.
  Ruddigore (1887), I

5 He combines the manners of a Marquis
  with the morals of a Methodist.

6 When he's excited he uses language that
  would make your hair curl.

7 Some word that teems with hidden
  meaning —like Basingstoke.
  II

8 This particularly rapid, unintelligible patter
  Isn't generally heard, and if it is it doesn't
  matter.

9 So I fell in love with a rich attorney's
  Elderly ugly daughter.
  Trial by Jury (1875)

10 She may very well pass for forty-three
   In the dusk with a light behind her!

11 For now I am a Judge,
   And a good Judge too.

12 'Tis ever thus with simple folk—an accept-
   ed wit has but to say 'Pass the mustard',
   and they roar their ribs out!
   The Yeoman of the Guard (1888), II

ERIC GILL 1882–1940

13 That state is a state of Slavery in which a
   man does what he likes to do in his spare
   time and in his working time that which is
   required of him.
   Slavery and Freedom (1918)

W.E. GLADSTONE 1809–1898

14 You cannot fight against the future. Time
   is on our side.
   Speech on the Reform Bill, 1866

15 [The Turks] one and all, bag and baggage,
   shall, I hope, clear out from the province
   they have desolated and profaned.
   House of Commons, 7 May 1877

16 We are part of the community of Europe,
   and we must do our duty as such.
   Carnarvon, 10 Apr. 1888

MRS. HANNAH GLASSE fl. 1747

17 Take your hare when it is cased...
   The Art of Cookery Made Plain and Easy (1747),
   ch.1. Cased ; skinned. The proverbial 'First catch
   your hare', recorded since c. 1300, has frequently been misattributed to Mrs. Glasse.

DUKE OF GLOUCESTER 1743–1805

18 Another damned, thick, square book! Always scribble, scribble, scribble! Eh! Mr
   Gibbon?
   Best's *Literary Memorials.* (Boswell's *Johnson,*
   vol.ii, p.2n)

A.D. GODLEY 1856–1925

19 What is this that roareth thus?
   Can it be a Motor Bus?
   Yes, the smell and hideous hum
   Indicat Motorem Bum...
   How shall wretches live like us
   Cincti Bis Motoribus?
   Domine, defende nos
   Contra hos Motores Bos!
   The Motor Bus. Letter to C.R.L.F., 10 Jan. 1914

HERMANN GOERING 1893–1946

20 Guns will make us powerful; butter will
   only make us fat.
   Radio Broadcast, summer of 1936, often mis-
   quoted as 'Guns before butter'.

**JOHANN WOLFGANG VON
GOETHE** 1749–1832

21 *Ich kenne mich auch nicht und Gott soll
   mich auch davor behüten.*
   I do not know myself, and God forbid that
   I should.
   Conversations with Eckermann, 10 Apr. 1829.
   See 6:6

22 *Entbehren sollst Du! sollst entbehren!
   Das ist der ewige Gesang.*
   Deny yourself! You must deny yourself!
   That is the song that never ends.
   Faust, pt.1 (1808). **Studierzimmer**

23 *Meine Ruh' ist hin,
   Mein Herz ist schwer.*
   My peace is gone,
   My heart is heavy.
   Gretchen am Spinnrad

1 *Die Tat ist alles, nichts der Ruhm.*
The deed is all, and not the glory.
pt.ii (1832). **Hochgebirg**

2 *Über allen Gipfeln*
Ist Ruh'.
Over all the mountain tops is peace.
Wanderers Nachtlied

3 *Kennst du das Land, wo die Zitronen blühn?*
Im dunkeln Laub die Gold-Orangen glühn,
Ein sanfter Wind vom blauen Himmel weht,
Die Myrte still und hoch der Lorbeer
steht—
Kennst du es wohl?
Dahin! Dahin!
Möcht ich mit dir, o mein Geliebter, ziehn!
Know you the land where the lemon-trees
bloom? In the dark foliage the gold
oranges glow; a soft wind hovers from
the sky, the myrtle is still and the laurel
stands tall—do you know it well?
There, there, I would go, O my be-
loved, with thee!
Wilhelm Meisters Lehrjahre (1795–6), III.i.

4 *Mehr Licht!*
More light!
Attr. dying words. (Actually: *'Macht doch den
zweiten Fensterladen auch auf, damit mehr Licht
hereinkomme'*: 'Open the second shutter, so that
more light can come in.')

OLIVER GOLDSMITH 1730–1774

5 Sweet Auburn, loveliest village of the
plain.
The Deserted Village (1770), l.1

6 Ill fares the land, to hast'ning ills a prey,
Where wealth accumulates, and men decay;
Princes and lords may flourish, or may
fade;
A breath can make them, as a breath has
made;
But a bold peasantry, their country's
pride,
When once destroy'd, can never be sup-
plied.
l.51

7 The watchdog's voice that bay'd the whis-
p'ring wind,
And the loud laugh that spoke the vacant
mind.
l.121. See 65:8

8 A man he was to all the country dear,
And passing rich with forty pounds a year.
l.141

9 Truth from his lips prevail'd with double
sway,

And fools, who came to scoff, remain'd to
pray.
l.179

10 In arguing too, the parson own'd his skill,
For e'en though vanquish'd, he could
argue still.
l.211

11 And still they gaz'd, and still the wonder
grew,
That one small head could carry all he
knew.
l.215

12 Man wants but little here below,
Nor wants that little long.
Edwin and Angelina, or the Hermit (1766). See
280:10

13 Good people all, of every sort,
Give ear unto my song;
And if you find it wond'rous short,
It cannot hold you long.
Elegy on the Death of a Mad Dog

14 The dog, to gain some private ends,
Went mad and bit the man.

15 The man recover'd of the bite,
The dog it was that died.

16 Who, too deep for his hearers, still went
on refining,
And thought of convincing, while they
thought of dining. [Edmund Burke].
Retaliation (1774), l.29

17 Let schoolmasters puzzle their brain,
With grammar, and nonsense, and
learning,
Good liquor, I stoutly maintain,
Gives genius a better discerning.
She Stoops to Conquer, I.i, song

18 When lovely woman stoops to folly
And finds too late that men betray,
What charm can soothe her melancholy,
What art can wash her guilt away?
The only art her guilt to cover,
To hide her shame from every eye,
To give repentance to her lover
And wring his bosom—is to die.
Song from **The Vicar of Wakefield**, ch.29

19 I'm now no more than a mere lodger in
my own house.
The Good-Natured Man (1768), I

20 The very pink of perfection.
She Stoops to Conquer (1773), I

21 This is Liberty-Hall, gentlemen.
II

22 As for murmurs, mother, we grumble a
little now and then, to be sure. But there's

no love lost between us.
IV

1 There is no arguing with Johnson; for when his pistol misses fire, he knocks you down with the butt end of it.
Boswell, *Life of Johnson,* 26 Oct. 1769. See 72:1

SAMUEL GOLDWYN 1882–1974

2 In two words: im possible.
Alva Johnson, *The Great Goldwyn*

3 You can include me out.
See Zierold, *The Hollywood Tycoons* (1969), ch.3

EDMUND GOSSE 1849–1928

4 A sheep in sheep's clothing.
Of T. Sturge Moore, c.1906. Ferris Greenslet, *Under the Bridge,* ch.12. Also attr. Winston Churchill of Clement Attlee.

SIR ERNEST GOWERS 1880–1966

5 It is not easy nowadays to remember anything so contrary to all appearances as that officials are the servants of the public; and the official must try not to foster the illusion that it is the other way round.
Plain Words, ch. 3, **The Elements**

CLEMENTINA STIRLING GRAHAM 1782–1877

6 The best way to get the better of temptation is just to yield to it.
Mystifications (1859), **Soirée at Mrs Russel's**

HARRY GRAHAM 1874–1936

7 Weep not for little Léonie
Abducted by a French *Marquis!*
Though loss of honour was a wrench
Just think how it's improved her French.
More Ruthless Rhymes for Heartless Homes.
Compensation

8 O'er the rugged mountain's brow
     Clara threw the twins she nursed,
And remarked, 'I wonder now
     Which will reach the bottom first?'
Ruthless Rhymes for Heartless Homes.
Calculating Clara

9 'There's been an accident!' they said,
'Your servant's cut in half; he's dead!'
'Indeed!' said Mr Jones, 'and please
Send me the half that's got my keys.'
Mr. Jones

0 Billy, in one of his nice new sashes,
Fell in the fire and was burnt to ashes;
Now, although the room grows chilly,
I haven't the heart to poke poor Billy.
Tender-Heartedness

KENNETH GRAHAME 1859–1932

11 Believe me, my young friend, there is *nothing*—absolutely nothing—half so much worth doing as simply messing about in boats.
The Wind in the Willows (1908), ch.1

12 The clever men at Oxford
     Know all that there is to be knowed.
But they none of them know one half as much
     As intelligent Mr Toad.
ch.10

GEORGE GRANVILLE, BARON LANSDOWNE 1666–1735

13 Bright as the day, and like the morning, fair,
Such Cloe is…and common as the air.
Cloe

ROBERT GRAVES 1895–

14 His eyes are quickened so with grief,
He can watch a grass or leaf
Every instant grow.
Lost Love

PATRICK, 6TH LORD GRAY d.1612

15 A dead woman bites not.
Oral tradition. Gray advocated the execution of Mary, Queen of Scots, 1587. See J.B. Black, *The Reign of Elizabeth (1558–1603),* 2nd edn. (1959), ch.10: The Master of Gray whispered…'Mortui non mordent'.

THOMAS GRAY 1716–1771

16 Ruin seize thee, ruthless King!
     Confusion on thy banners wait,
Tho' fann'd by Conquest's crimson wing
     They mock the air with idle state.
The Bard (1757), I.i

17 Youth on the prow, and Pleasure at the helm.
II.ii

18 The curfew tolls the knell of parting day,
     The lowing herd wind slowly o'er the lea,
The ploughman homeward plods his weary way,
     And leaves the world to darkness and to me.

Now fades the glimmering landscape on the sight,
     And all the air a solemn stillness holds,

Save where the beetle wheels his droning
    flight,
And drowsy tinklings lull the distant
    folds.
Elegy in a Country Churchyard (1742–50), 1

1 Save that from yonder ivy-mantled tow'r,
    The moping owl does to the moon com-
        plain.
  3

2 Beneath those rugged elms, that yew-
    tree's shade,
  Where heaves the turf in many a moul-
    dering heap,
Each in his narrow cell for ever laid,
  The rude forefathers of the hamlet sleep.

3 Let not ambition mock their useful toil,
  Their homely joys, and destiny obscure;
Nor grandeur hear with a disdainful smile,
  The short and simple annals of the poor.

The boast of heraldry, the pomp of pow'r,
  And all that beauty, all that wealth e'er
    gave,
Awaits alike th' inevitable hour,
  The paths of glory lead but to the grave.
  8

4 Can storied urn or animated bust
  Back to its mansion call the fleeting
    breath?
Can honour's voice provoke the silent
    dust,
  Or flatt'ry soothe the dull cold ear of
    death?
  11

5 Full many a gem of purest ray serene,
  The dark unfathom'd caves of ocean
    bear:
Full many a flower is born to blush un-
    seen,
  And waste its sweetness on the desert
    air.

Some village-Hampden, that with daunt-
    less breast
  The little tyrant of his fields withstood;
Some mute inglorious Milton here may
    rest,
  Some Cromwell guiltless of his
    country's blood.
  14

6 Far from the madding crowd's ignoble
    strife,
  Their sober wishes never learn'd to
    stray;
Along the cool sequester'd vale of life
  They kept the noiseless tenor of their
    way.
  19

7 Not all that tempts your wand'ring eyes

And heedless hearts, is lawful prize;
Nor all, that glisters, gold.
Ode on the Death of a Favourite Cat (1747)

8 Ye distant spires, ye antique towers,
  That crown the wat'ry glade.
Ode on a Distant Prospect of Eton College (1747)
l.1

9 Still as they run they look behind,
They hear a voice in every wind,
  And snatch a fearful joy.
l.38

10 Alas, regardless of their doom,
  The little victims play!
No sense have they of ills to come,
  Nor care beyond to-day.
l.51

11 To each his suff'rings, all are men,
  Condemn'd alike to groan;
The tender for another's pain,
  Th' unfeeling for his own.
l.91

12 No more; where ignorance is bliss,
  'Tis folly to be wise.
l.99

13 He saw; but blasted with excess of light,
Closed his eyes in endless night.
The Progress of Poesy (1757), iii.2 (Milton.)

HORACE GREELY 1811–1872

14 Go West, young man, and grow up with
the country.
Hints toward Reform. See 243:15

GRAHAM GREENE 1904–

15 Against the beautiful and the clever and
the successful, one can wage a pitiless war,
but not against the unattractive.
The Heart of the Matter (1948), bk.1, pt.1, ch.2

16 Any victim demands allegiance.
bk.3, pt.1, ch.1

17 Perhaps if I wanted to be understood or to
understand I would bamboozle myself
into belief, but I am a reporter; God exists
only for leader-writers.
The Quiet American (1955), pt.I, ch.iv.2

ROBERT GREENE 1560?–1592

18 For there is an upstart crow, beautified
with our feathers, that with his tiger's
heart wrapped in a player's hide, supposes
he is as well able to bumbast out a blank
verse as the best of you; and being an
absolute *Iohannes fac totum*, is in his own

conceit the only Shake-scene in a country.
Groatsworth of Wit Bought with a Million of Repentance (1592)

POPE GREGORY THE GREAT
c.540-604

1 *Non Angli sed Angeli.*
Not Angles but Angels.
Bede, *Historia Ecclesiastica*, II.i, recorded: *Responsum est, quod Angli vocarentur. At ille: 'Bene,' inquit; 'nam et angelicam habent faciem, et tales angelorum in caelis decet esse coheredes.'*
They answered that they were called Angles. 'It is well,' he said, 'for they have the faces of angels, and such should be the co-heirs of the angels of heaven.'

STEPHEN GRELLET 1773-1855

2 I expect to pass through this world but once; any good thing therefore that I can do, or any kindness that I can show to any fellow-creature, let me do it now; let me not defer or neglect it, for I shall not pass this way again.
Attr. See John o' London's *Treasure Trove* (1925). Many other claimants to authorship

JULIAN GRENFELL 1888-1915

3 The naked earth is warm with Spring,
    And with green grass and bursting trees
Leans to the sun's kiss glorying,
    And quivers in the sunny breeze;

And life is colour and warmth and light
    And a striving evermore for these;
And he is deaf, who will not fight
And who dies fighting has increase.
Into Battle, published in *The Times,* 27 May 1915

LORD GREY OF FALLODON
1862-1933

4 The lamps are going out all over Europe; we shall not see them lit again in our lifetime.
3 Aug. 1914. *Twenty-Five Years, 1892-1916* (1925), vol.ii, ch.18

GEORGE GROSSMITH 1847-1912
and WEEDON GROSSMITH 1854-1919

5 I left the room with silent dignity, but caught my foot in the mat.
The Diary of a Nobody (1894), ch.12

PHILIP GUEDALLA 1889-1944

6 The work of Henry James has always seemed divisible by a simple dynastic arrangement into three reigns: James I,

James II, and the Old Pretender.
Collected Essays, vol.iv. **Men of Letters: Mr. Henry James**

NELL GWYN 1650-1687

7 Pray, good people, be civil. I am the Protestant whore.
In Oxford, during the Popish Terror, 1681. Bevan, *Nell Gwyn,* ch.iii

EMPEROR HADRIAN A..76-138

8 *Animula vagula blandula,*
  Hospes comesque corporis,
  Quae nunc abibis in loca
  Pallidula rigida nudula,
  Nec ut soles dabis iocos!
Ah! gentle, fleeting, wav'ring sprite,
Friend and associate of this clay!
    To what unknown region borne,
Wilt thou now wing thy distant flight?
No more with wonted humour gay,
    But pallid, cheerless, and forlorn.
J.W. Duff (ed.). *Minor Latin Poets* (1934) 445.
Trans. Byron, *Adrian's Adress to His Soul When Dying*

EARL HAIG 1861-1928

9 Every position must be held to the last man: there must be no retirement. With our backs to the wall, and believing in the justice of our cause, each one of us must fight on to the end.
Order to the British Troops, 12 Apr. 1918

EDWARD EVERETT HALE 1822-1909

10 'Do you pray for the senators, Dr Hale?'
'No, I look at the senators and I pray for the country.'
Van Wyck Brooks, *New England Indian Summer* (1940), p.418n.

NATHAN HALE 1755-1776

11 I only regret that I have but one life to lose for my country.
Speech before being executed as a spy by the British, 22 Sept. 1776. See 1:8

MRS. SARAH JOSEPHA HALE
1788-1879

12 Mary had a little lamb,
    Its fleece was white as snow,
And everywhere that Mary went
    The lamb was sure to go.
Poems for Our Children (1830). **Mary's Little Lamb**

GEORGE SAVILE, MARQUIS OF HALIFAX 1633–1695

1 When the People contend for their Liberty, they seldom get anything by their Victory but new masters.
Political, Moral, and Miscellaneous Thoughts and Reflections (1750). **Of Prerogative, Power and Liberty**

2 Power is so apt to be insolent and Liberty to be saucy, that they are very seldom upon good Terms.

3 Men are not hanged for stealing horses, but that horses may not be stolen.
Of Punishment

4 He [Halifax] had said he had known many kicked down stairs, but he never knew any kicked up stairs before.
Burnet, *Original Memoirs* (c.1697)

FRIEDRICH HALM 1806–1871

5 *Mein Herz ich will dich fragen:*
Was ist denn Liebe? Sag'!—
'Zwei Seelen und ein Gedanke,
Zwei Herzen und ein Schlag!'
What love is, if thou wouldst be taught,
  Thy heart must teach alone—
Two souls with but a single thought,
  Two hearts that beat as one.
Der Sohn der Wildnis (1842), Act II *ad fin*. Trans. by Maria Lovell in *Ingomar the Barbarian*

MINNY MAUD HANFF 1880–1942

6 Since then they called him Sunny Jim.
Advertisement for Force, a breakfast food, c.1902

EDMOND HARAUCOURT 1856–1941

7 *Partir c'est mourir un peu,*
C'est mourir à ce qu'on aime:
On laisse un peu de soi-même
En toute heure et dans tout lieu.
To go away is to die a little, it is to die to that which one loves: everywhere and always, one leaves behind a part of oneself.
Seul (1891), **Rondel de l'Adieu**

THOMAS HARDY 1840–1928

8 When the Present has latched its postern behind my tremulous stay,
  And the May month flaps its glad green leaves like wings,
Delicate-filmed as new-spun silk, will the neighbours say,
  'He was a man who used to notice such things'?
Afterwards

9 William Dewy, Tranter Reuben, Farmer Ledlow late at plough,
    Robert's kin, and John's, and Ned's,
And the Squire, and Lady Susan, lie in Mellstock churchyard now!
Friends Beyond

10 I am the family face;
Flesh perishes, I live on.
Heredity

11 Only a man harrowing clods
  In a slow silent walk
With an old horse that stumbles and nods
  Half asleep as they stalk.

Only thin smoke without flame
  From the heaps of couch grass;
Yet this will go onward the same
  Though Dynasties pass.

Yonder a maid and her wight
  Come whispering by:
War's annals will cloud into night
  Ere their story die.
In Time of 'The Breaking of Nations'

12 In the third-class seat sat the journeying boy
And the roof-lamp's oily flame
Played on his listless form and face,
Bewrapt past knowing to what he was going,
Or whence he came.
Midnight on the Great Western

13 —'You left us in tatters, without shoes or socks,
Tired of digging potatoes, and spudding up docks;
And now you've gay bracelets and bright feathers three!'—
'Yes: that's how we dress when we're ruined,' said she.
The Ruined Maid

14   Every branch big with it,
       Bent every twig with it;
     Every fork like a white web-foot;
     Every street and pavement mute:
Some flakes have lost their way, and grope back upward, when
Meeting those meandering down they turn and descend again.
Snow in the Suburbs

15 This is the weather the cuckoo likes,
  And so do I;
When showers betumble the chestnut spikes,
  And nestlings fly:
And the little brown nightingale bills his best,

And they sit outside at 'The Travellers'
   Rest'.
Weathers

1 This is the weather the shepherd shuns,
   And so do I.

2 And drops on gate-bars hang in a row,
   And rooks in families homeward go,
   And so do I.

3 When I set out for Lyonnesse,
      A hundred miles away,
      The rime was on the spray,
   And starlight lit my lonesomeness
   When I set out for Lyonnesse
      A hundred miles away.
   When I Set Out for Lyonnesse

4 When I came back from Lyonnesse
      With magic in my eyes,
      All marked with mute surmise
   My radiance rare and fathomless,
   When I came back from Lyonnesse
      With magic in my eyes!

5 'Justice' was done, and the President of
   the Immortals (in Aeschylean phrase) had
   ended his sport with Tess.
   Tess of the D'Urbervilles (1891), ch.59

MAURICE EVAN HARE 1886–1967

6 Alfred de Musset
   Used to call his cat Pusset.
   His accent was affected.
   That was only to be expected.
   Byway in Biography

7 There once was a man who said, 'Damn!
   It is borne in upon me I am
      An engine that moves
      In predestinate grooves,
   I'm not even a bus, I'm a tram.'
   Written, as above, at St. John's College, Oxford,
   in 1905

SIR JOHN HARINGTON 1561–1612

8 Treason doth never prosper, what's the
   reason?
   For if it prosper, none dare call it treason.
   Epigrams (1618), bk.iv, No.5. **Of Treason**

JOEL CHANDLER HARRIS 1848–1908

9 Tar-baby ain't sayin' nuthin', en Brer
   Fox, he lay low.
   Uncle Remus. Legends of the Old Plantation
   (1881), ch.2. **Tar-Baby Story**

0 Bred en bawn in a brier-patch!
   ch.4

BRET HARTE 1836–1902

11 If, of all words of tongue and pen,
   The saddest are, 'It might have been,'
   More sad are these we daily see:
   'It is, but hadn't ought to be!'
   Mrs. Judge Jenkins. See 270:10

12 Which I wish to remark,
      And my language is plain,
   That for ways that are dark
   And for tricks that are vain,
   The heathen Chinee is peculiar,
   Which the same I would rise to explain.
   Plain Language from Truthful James (1870)

13 We are ruined by Chinese cheap labour.

14 And he smiled a kind of sickly smile, and
      curled up on the floor,
   And the subsequent proceedings interested
      him no more.
   The Society upon the Stanislaus

L.P. HARTLEY 1895–1972

15 The past is a foreign country: they do
   things differently there.
   The Go-Between, Prologue

M. LOUISE HASKINS 1875–1957

16 And I said to the man who stood at the
   gate of the year: 'Give me a light that I
   may tread safely into the unknown'. And
   he replied: 'Go out into the darkness and
   put your hand into the hand of God. That
   shall be to you better than light and safer
   than a known way.'
   The Desert (c.1908), Introduction. Quoted by
   King George VI in a Christmas Broadcast, 25
   Dec. 1939, after the lines had been quoted in
   'Points from Letters' in *The Times* a few months
   earlier

REVD. R.S. HAWKER 1803–1875

17 And have they fixed the where and when?
      And shall Trelawny die?
   Here's twenty thousand Cornish men
      Will know the reason why!
   Song of the Western Men. The last three lines
   have existed since the imprisonment by James II,
   1688, of the seven Bishops, including Trelawny,
   Bishop of Bristol.

IAN HAY 1876–1952

18 What do you mean, funny? Funny-
   peculiar or funny-ha-ha?
   The Housemaster (1936), Act III

J. MILTON HAYES 1884-1940

1 There's a one-eyed yellow idol to the
north of Khatmandu,
There's a little marble cross below the
town;
There's a broken-hearted woman tends the
grave of Mad Carew
And the Yellow God forever gazes down.
The Green Eye of the Yellow God (1911)

WILLIAM HAZLITT 1778-1830

2 His worst is better than any other person's
best.
English Literature, ch.xiv. **Sir Walter Scott**

3 He [Coleridge] talked on for ever; and you
wished him to talk on for ever.
Lectures on the English Poets. Lecture viii, **On
the Living Poets**

4 One of the pleasantest things in the world
is going on a journey; but I like to go by
myself.
Table Talk, xix. **On Going a Journey**

5 Give me the clear blue sky over my head,
and the green turf beneath my feet, a winding road before me, and a three hours'
march to dinner—and then to thinking! It
is hard if I cannot start some game on
these lone heaths.

6 The English (it must be owned) are rather
a foul-mouthed nation.
xxii. **On Criticism**

7 We can scarcely hate any one that we
know.

8 No young man believes he shall ever die.
Uncollected Essays, xviii. **On the Feeling of Immortality in Youth**

EDWARD HEATH 1916-

9 It is the unpleasant and unacceptable face
of capitalism but one should not suggest
that the whole of British industry consists
of practices of this kind.
House of Commons, 15 May 1973

BISHOP REGINALD HEBER
1783-1826

10 What though the spicy breezes
Blow soft o'er Ceylon's isle;
Though every prospect pleases,
And only man is vile:

In vain with lavish kindness
The gifts of God are strown;
The heathen in his blindness
Bows down to wood and stone.
From Greenland's Icy Mountains. This is the
most familiar version. Bishop Heber originally

wrote 'The savage in his blindness'. He altered
this, and also altered 'Ceylon's' to 'Java's'.

G.W.F. HEGEL 1770-1831

11 What experience and history teach is this
—that people and governments never have
learned anything from history, or acted on
principles deduced from it.
Philosophy of History. Introduction

HEINRICH HEINE 1797-1856

12   *Dort,wo man Bücher
Verbrennt, verbrennt man auch am End
Menschen.*
Wherever books are burned, men also, in
the end, are burned.
Almansor (1820-1), l.245

13 *Sie hatten sich beide so herzlich lieb,
Spitzbübin war sie, er war ein Dieb.*
They loved each other beyond belief—
She was a strumpet, he was a thief.
Neue Gedichte (1844), **Romanzen**, I. 'Ein Weib'
Trans. Louis Untermeyer (1938)

14 *Dieses merkt Euch, Ihr stolzen Männer de
Tat. Ihr seid nichts als unbewusste Hand
langer der Gedankenmänner...Maximilian
Robespierre war nichts als die Hand von
Jean Jacques Rousseau, die blutige Hand
die aus dem Schosse der Zeit den Leib her
vorzog, dessen Seele Rousseau geschaffen.*
Note this, you proud men of action. You
are nothing but the unconscious hodmen
of the men of ideas...Maximilien Robespierre was nothing but the hand of Jean
Jacques Rousseau, the bloody hand tha
drew from the womb of time the body
whose soul Rousseau had created.
*Zur Geschichte der Religion und Philosophie in
Deutschland* (1834), bk.3

15 *Dieu me pardonnera. C'est son métier.*
God will pardon me. It is His trade.
On his deathbed. Attr. Edmond and Charle
Goncourt, *Journal,* 23 Feb. 1863

LILLIAN HELLMAN 1905-

16 I cannot and will not cut my conscience to
fit this year's fashions.
Letter to the Honourable John S. Wood, Chair
man of the House Committee on un-American
Activities, 19 May 1952

C.-A. HELVÉTIUS 1715-1771

17 *L'éducation nous faisait ce que nou
sommes.*
Education made us what we are.
Discours XXX, ch.30

MRS. HEMANS 1793–1835

1 The boy stood on the burning deck
  Whence all but he had fled;
  The flame that lit the battle's wreck
  Shone round him o'er the dead.
  Casabianca

2 The stately homes of England,
  How beautiful they stand!
  Amidst their tall ancestral trees,
  O'er all the pleasant land.
  The Homes of England

JOHN HEMING d.1630
and **HENRY CONDELL** d.1627

3 Well! it is now public, and you will stand
for your privileges we know: to read, and
censure. Do so, but buy it first. That doth
best commend a book, the stationer says.
  Preface to the First Folio Shakespeare, 1623

4 Who, as he was a happy imitator of Nature, was a most gentle expresser of it. His
mind and hand went together: And what
he thought, he uttered with that easiness,
that we have scarce received from him a
blot.

ERNEST HEMINGWAY 1898–1961

5 But did thee feel the earth move?
  For Whom the Bell Tolls (1940), ch.13

W.E. HENLEY 1849–1903

6 Out of the night that covers me,
  Black as the Pit from pole to pole,
  I thank whatever gods may be
  For my unconquerable soul.

  In the fell clutch of circumstance,
  I have not winced nor cried aloud:
  Under the bludgeonings of chance
  My head is bloody, but unbowed.
  Echoes (1888), iv. **Invictus. In Mem. R.T.H.B.**

7 It matters not how strait the gate,
  How charged with punishments the scroll,
  I am the master of my fate:
  I am the captain of my soul.

8 Madam Life's a piece in bloom
  Death goes dogging everywhere;
  She's the tenant of the room,
  He's the ruffian on the stair.
  ix. **To W.R.**

9 Or ever the Knightly years were gone
  With the old world to the grave,
  I was a King in Babylon
  And you were a Christian Slave.
  xxxvii. **To W.A.**

10 What have I done for you,

England, my England?
  What is there I would not do,
  England, my own?
  For England's Sake (1900), iii. **Pro Rege Nostro**

HENRI IV 1553–1610

11 *Je veux qu'il n'y ait si pauvre paysan en
mon royaume qu'il n'ait tous les dimanches
sa poule au pot.*
I want there to be no peasant in my kingdom so poor that he is unable to have a
chicken in his pot every Sunday.
  Hardouin de Péréfixe, *Hist. de Henry le Grand*,
1681

12 *Pends toi, brave Crillon; nous avons com
battu à Arques et tu n'y étais pas.*
Hang yourself, brave Crillon; we fought at
Arques and you were not there.
  Traditional form given by Voltaire to a letter of
Henri to Crillon. *Lettres missives de Henri IV,
Collection des documents inédits de l'histoire de
France,* vol.iv, 1847, p.848. Henri's actual words,
in a letter to Crillon of 20 Sept. 1597, were *Brave
Crillon, pendez-vous de n'avoir été ici près de moi
lundi dernier à la plus belle occasion qui se soit
jamais vue et qui peut-être se verra jamais.*

13 *Paris vaut bien une messe.*
Paris is well worth a mass.
  Attr. either to Henri IV or to his minister Sully,
in conversation with Henri. *Caquets de l'Accou-
chée,* 1622

14 The wisest fool in Christendom.
  Of James I of England. Remark attr. to Henri IV
and Sully. The French is not known

PATRICK HENRY 1736–1799

15 Caesar had his Brutus—Charles the First,
his Cromwell—and George the Third
—('Treason,' cried the Speaker)...*may
profit by their example.* If *this* be treason,
make the most of it.
  Speech in the Virginia Convention, May 1765.
Wirt, *Patrick Henry* (1818), p.65

16 I know not what course others may take;
but as for me, give me liberty, or give me
death!
  20 Mar. 1775. Wirt, *Patrick Henry* (1818), p.123

KING HENRY II 1133–1189

17 Will no one revenge me of the injuries I
have sustained from one turbulent priest?
  Of St. Thomas Becket (Dec. 1170). Oral trad.
See G. Lyttelton, *History of the Life of King
Henry the Second* (1769), IV, p.353; also Herbert
of Bosham, *Vita S. Thomae* in *Materials for the
History of Archbishop Thomas Becket* (Rolls
Series), III (1887), p.487

HERACLITUS fl. 513 B.C.

1 παντα χωρει, ουδεν μενει.
Everything flows and nothing stays.
Plato, *Cratylus,* 402a

2 δις ες τον αυτον ποταμον ουκ αν εμβαιης.
You can't step twice into the same river.

A.P. HERBERT 1890-1971

3 Let's find out what everyone is doing,
    And then stop everyone from doing it.
Let's Stop Somebody

GEORGE HERBERT 1593-1633

4 He that makes a good war makes a good
peace.
Outlandish Proverbs, 420

5 He that lives in hope danceth without
musick.
1006

6 Let all the world in ev'ry corner sing
        My God and King.
The Temple (1633). **Antiphon**

7 I struck the board, and cried, 'No more;
    I will abroad.'
The Collar

8 But as I rav'd and grew more fierce and
wild
            At every word,
Methought I heard one calling, 'Child';
            And I replied, 'My Lord.'

9 A servant with this clause
Makes drudgery divine;
Who sweeps a room as for Thy laws
Makes that and th' action fine.
The Elixir

10 Who would have thought my shrivel'd
heart
Could have recovered greenness?
The Flower

11 Love bade me welcome; yet my soul drew
back,
            Guilty of dust and sin.
But quick-ey'd Love, observing me grow
slack
            From my first entrance in,
Drew nearer to me, sweetly questioning
            If I lack'd any thing.
Love

12   When boyes go first to bed,
They step into their voluntarie graves.
Mortification

13 Prayer the Church's banquet…
Exalted manna, gladness of the best,
Heaven in ordinary, man well drest,
The Milkie Way, the bird of Paradise…

The land of spices; something understood.
Prayer

14 When God at first made man,
Having a glass of blessings standing by;
Let us (said he) pour on him all we can:
Let the world's riches, which dispersed lie,
Contract into a span.
The Pulley

15 The God of love my Shepherd is,
And He that doth me feed,
While He is mine, and I am His,
What can I want or need?
23rd Psalm

16 I would not use a friend as I use Thee.
Unkindness

ROBERT HERRICK 1591-1674

17 Cherry-ripe, ripe, ripe, I cry,
Full and fair ones; come and buy:
If so be, you ask me where
They do grow? I answer, there,
Where my Julia's lips do smile;
There's the land, or cherry-isle.
Hesperides (1648). **Cherry-Ripe**

18 A sweet disorder in the dress
Kindles in clothes a wantonness:
A lawn about the shoulders thrown
Into a fine distraction…
A careless shoe-string, in whose tie
I see a wild civility:
Do more bewitch me, than when Art
Is too precise in every part.
Delight in Disorder

19 More discontents I never had
Since I was born, than here;
Where I have been, and still am sad,
    In this dull Devonshire.
Discontents in Devon

20 Night makes no difference 'twixt the
        Priest and Clerk;
Joan as my Lady is as good i' th' dark.
No Difference i' th' Dark

21 Fain would I kiss my Julia's dainty leg,
Which is as white and hairless as an egg.
On Julia's Legs

22 Fair daffodils, we weep to see
You haste away so soon.
To Daffodils

23 Gather ye rosebuds while ye may,
Old Time is still a-flying:
And this same flower that smiles to-day,
To-morrow will be dying.
To the Virgins, to Make Much of Time

24 Her pretty feet
Like snails did creep
A little out, and then,

As if they started at bo-peep,
Did soon draw in agen.
Upon her Feet

1 Whenas in silks my Julia goes,
Then, then (methinks) how sweetly flows
That liquefaction of her clothes.

Next, when I cast mine eyes and see
That brave vibration each way free;
O how that glittering taketh me!
Upon Julia's Clothes

2 Here a little child I stand,
Heaving up my either hand;
Cold as paddocks though they be,
Here I lift them up to Thee,
For a benison to fall
On our meat, and on us all. Amen.
Noble Numbers. **Another Grace for a Child**

JAMES HERVEY 1714-1758

3 E'en crosses from his sov'reign hand
Are blessings in disguise.
Reflections on a Flower-Garden

LORD HERVEY 1696-1743

4 Whoever would lie usefully should lie seldom.
Memoirs of the Reign of George II, vol.I, ch.19

LORD HEWART 1870-1943

5 It is not merely of some importance but is of fundamental importance that justice should not only be done, but should manifestly and undoubtedly be seen to be done.
Rex v. Sussex Justices, 9 Nov. 1923 (King's Bench Reports, 1924, vol.i, p.259)

SIR SEYMOUR HICKS 1871-1949

6 You will recognize, my boy, the first sign of old age: it is when you go out into the streets of London and realize for the first time how young the policemen look.
Attr. C. Pulling, *They Were Singing,* 7

W.E. HICKSON 1803-1870

7 'Tis a lesson you should heed,
Try, try again.
If at first you don't succeed,
Try, try again.
Try and Try Again

JOE HILL 1879-1914

8 You will eat (You will eat)
Bye and bye (Bye and bye)
In that glorious land above the sky (Way
up high)
Work and pray (Work and pray)
Live on hay (Live on hay)
You'll get pie in the sky when you die
(That's a lie.)
The Preacher and the Slave

REVD. ROWLAND HILL 1744-1833

9 He did not see any reason why the devil should have all the good tunes.
E.W.Broome, *Rev. Rowland Hill,* vii

HILLEL 'THE ELDER'
?70 B.C.–A.D. 10?

10 If I am not for myself who is for me; and being for my own self what am I? If not now when?
Pirque Aboth. See *Sayings of the Jewish Fathers,* ed. C. Taylor (1877), i. 15.

HIPPOCLEIDES 6th cent. B.C.

11 οὐ φροντὶς Ἱπποκλείδῃ.
Hippocleides doesn't care.
Herodotus, *Histories,* vi.129.4

HIPPOCRATES 5th cent. B.C.

12 ὁ βίος βραχύς, ἡ δὲ τέχνη μακρή.
The life so short, the craft so long to learn.
Aphorisms, I.i. Trans. Chaucer, *Parliament of Fowls,* l.1. Often quoted in Latin as *Ars longa, vita brevis.* See Seneca, *De Brevitate Vitae,* 1

ADOLF HITLER 1889-1945

13 *Die breite Masse eines Volkes...einer grossen Lüge leichter zum Opfer fällt als einer kleinen.*
The broad mass of a nation...will more easily fall victim to a big lie than to a small one.
Mein Kampf, I.x

14 I go the way that Providence dictates with the assurance of a sleepwalker.
Speech in Munich, 15 Mar. 1936, after the successful re-occupation of the Rhineland, against the experts' advice. See Alan Bullock, *Hitler, A Study in Tyranny* (1952), ch.7, pt.i

15 My patience is now at an end.
Speech, 26 Sept. 1938

16 It is the last territorial claim which I have to make in Europe. [The Sudetenland.]

THOMAS HOBBES 1588-1679

17 During the time men live without a common power to keep them all in awe, they are in that condition which is called war; and such a war as is of every man against

every man...the nature of war consisteth not in actual fighting, but in the known disposition thereto during all the time there is no assurance to the contrary.
Leviathan (1651), pt.i, ch.13

1 No arts; no letters; no society; and which is worst of all, continual fear and danger of violent death; and the life of man, solitary, poor, nasty, brutish, and short.

2 I am about to take my last voyage, a great leap in the dark.
Last words. Watkins, *Anecdotes of Men of Learning*

JOHN CAM HOBHOUSE, BARON BROUGHTON 1786–1869

3 When I invented the phrase 'His Majesty's Opposition' [Canning] paid me a compliment on the fortunate hit.
Recollections of a Long Life (1865), ii, ch.12

RALPH HODGSON 1871–1962

4 'Twould ring the bells of Heaven
The wildest peal for years,
If Parson lost his senses
And people came to theirs,
And he and they together
Knelt down with angry prayers
For tamed and shabby tigers
And dancing dogs and bears,
And wretched, blind, pit ponies,
And little hunted hares.
The Bells of Heaven

5 Time, you old gypsy man,
   Will you not stay,
Put up your caravan
   Just for one day?
Time, You Old Gypsy Man

6 Last week in Babylon,
   Last night in Rome,
Morning, and in the crush
   Under Paul's dome.

HEINRICH HOFFMANN 1809–1894

7 Augustus was a chubby lad;
Fat ruddy cheeks Augustus had:
And everybody saw with joy
The plump and hearty, healthy boy.
He ate and drank as he was told,
And never let his soup get cold.
But one day, one cold winter's day,
He screamed out, 'Take the soup away!
O take the nasty soup away!
I won't have any soup today.'
Struwwelpeter (1845, translated 1848). **Augustus**

8 Let me see if Philip can

Be a little gentleman;
Let me see, if he is able
To sit still for once at table.
Fidgety Philip

9 Look at little Johnny there,
Little Johnny Head-In-Air!
Johnny Head-In-Air

10 The door flew open, in he ran,
The great, long, red-legged scissor-man.
The Little Suck-a-Thumb

11 'Ah!' said Mamma, 'I knew he'd come
To naughty little Suck-a-Thumb.'

12 Anything to me is sweeter
Than to see Shock-headed Peter.
Shock-Headed Peter

JAMES HOGG 1770–1835

13 Where the pools are bright and deep
Where the gray trout lies asleep,
Up the river and o'er the lea
That's the way for Billy and me.
A Boy's Song

14 We'll o'er the water, we'll o'er the sea,
We'll o'er the water to Charlie;
Come weel, come wo, we'll gather and go,
And live or die wi' Charlie.
Jacobite Relics of Scotland (1819-20), ii.76. **O'er the Water to Charlie**

REVD. JOHN H. HOLMES 1879–1964

15 The universe is not hostile, nor yet is it friendly. It is simply indifferent.
A Sensible Man's View of Religion (1933)

OLIVER WENDELL HOLMES 1809–1894

16 Man wants but little drink below,
But wants that little strong.
A Song of other Days. See 110:12, 280:10

17 Man has his will,—but woman has her way.
The Autocrat of the Breakfast-Table (1858), ch.1

JOHN HOME 1722–1808

18 My name is Norval; on the Grampian hills
My father feeds his flocks; a frugal swain,
Whose constant cares were to increase his store.
Douglas (1756), II.1

HOMER 8th cent. B.C.

19 μῆνιν ἄειδε, θεά, Πηληϊάδεω ᾽Αχιλῆος
οὐλομένην, ἥ μυρί᾽ ᾽Αχαιοῖς ἄλγε᾽ ἔθηκε
Achilles' cursed anger sing, O goddess,
that son of Peleus, which started a myriad

sufferings for the Achaeans.
Achilles' wrath, to Greece the direful
spring
Of woes unnumbered, heavenly goddess,
sing.
(Alexander Pope's translation.)
Iliad, i.1

1 ἄνδρα μοι ἔννεπε, Μοῦσα, πολύτροπον,
ὃς μάλα πολλὰ
πλάγχθη, ἐπεὶ Τροίηι ἱερὸν πτολίεθ-
ρον ἔπερσε,
πολλῶν δ᾽ ἀνθρώπων ἴδεν ἄστεα καὶ
νόον ἔγνω.
Tell me, Muse, of the man of many tricks,
who wandered far and wide after he had
sacked Troy's sacred city, and saw the
towns of many men and knew their mind.
Odyssey, i.1. Of Odysseus

2 ῥοδοδάκτυλος Ἠώς.
Rosy-fingered dawn.
ii.1, and elsewhere

WILLIAM HONE 1780–1842

3 John Jones may be described as 'one of
the *has* beens.'
Every-Day Book (1826-7), vol.ii, 820

THOMAS HOOD 1799–1845

4 It was not in the winter
   Our loving lot was cast!
It was the time of roses,
   We plucked them as we passed!
Ballad: It Was Not in the Winter

5 Ben Battle was a soldier bold,
   And used to war's alarms:
But a cannon-ball took off his legs,
   So he laid down his arms!
Faithless Nelly Gray

6 His death, which happen'd in his berth,
   At forty-odd befell:
They went and told the sexton, and
   The sexton toll'd the bell.
Faithless Sally Brown

7 I remember, I remember,
   The house where I was born,
The little window where the sun
   Came peeping in at morn;
He never came a wink too soon,
   Nor brought too long a day,
But now, I often wish the night
   Had borne my breath away!
I Remember

8 He never spoils the child and spares the
   rod,
   But spoils the rod and never spares the
   child.
The Irish Schoolmaster, xii

9 No sun—no moon!
No morn—no noon
No dawn—no dusk—no proper time of
   day.
No!

10 No warmth, no cheerfulness, no healthful
   ease,
No comfortable feel in any member—
No shade, no shine, no butterflies, no bees,
No fruits, no flowers, no leaves, no
   birds,—
November!

11 She stood breast high amid the corn,
Clasp'd by the golden light of morn,
Like the sweetheart of the sun,
Who many a glowing kiss had won.
Ruth

12 With fingers weary and worn,
   With eyelids heavy and red,
A woman sat, in unwomanly rags,
   Plying her needle and thread—
   Stitch! stitch! stitch!
In poverty, hunger, and dirt.
The Song of the Shirt (1843)

13 Oh! God! that bread should be so dear,
   And flesh and blood so cheap!

ELLEN STURGIS HOOPER 1816–1841

14 I slept, and dreamed that life was Beauty;
I woke, and found that life was Duty.
Beauty and Duty (1840)

ANTHONY HOPE 1863–1933

15 His foe was folly and his weapon wit.
Inscription on the tablet to W.S. Gilbert, Victoria Embankment, London (1915)

LAURENCE HOPE
(MRS. M.H. NICOLSON) 1865–1904

16 Pale hands I loved beside the Shalimar,
Where are you now? Who lies beneath
   your spell?
*The Garden of Kama and other Love Lyrics from
India* (1901). **Pale Hands I Loved**

GERARD MANLEY HOPKINS
1844–1889

17 Towery city and branchy between towers.
Duns Scotus' Oxford

18 The world is charged with the grandeur of
   God.
   It will flame out like shining from shook
   foil.
God's Grandeur

19 Elected Silence, sing to me
And beat upon my whorlèd ear,
Pipe me to pastures still and be

The music that I care to hear.
The Habit of Perfection

1 No worst, there is none. Pitched past pitch
    of grief,
More pangs will, schooled at forepangs,
    wilder wring.
Comforter, where, where is your comfort-
    ing?
No Worst, there is None

2 O the mind, mind has mountains; cliffs of
    fall
Frightful, sheer, no-man-fathomed. Hold
    them cheap
May who ne'er hung there.

3 Glory be to God for dappled things.
Pied Beauty

4 All things counter, original, spare,
    strange;
    Whatever is fickle, freckled (who knows
    how?)
        With swift, slow; sweet, sour; adazzle,
        dim;
    He fathers-forth whose beauty is past
    change:
        Praise him.

5 Margaret, are you grieving
Over Goldengrove unleaving?
Spring and Fall. To a young child

6 It is the blight man was born for,
It is Margaret you mourn for.

7 Look at the stars! look, look up at the
    skies!
O look at all the fire-folk sitting in the air!
The bright boroughs, the circle-citadels
    there!
The Starlight Night

8 Thou art indeed just, Lord, if I contend
With thee; but, sir, so what I plead is just.
Why do sinners' ways prosper? and why
    must
Disappointment all I endeavour end?
Thou Art Indeed Just, Lord

9 I caught this morning morning's minion,
    kingdom of daylight's dauphin,
    dapple-dawn-drawn Falcon.
The Windhover

10   My heart in hiding
Stirred for a bird,—the achieve of, the
    mastery of the thing!

11   I did say yes
O at lightning and lashed rod;
Thou heardst me truer than tongue con-
    fess
    Thy terror, O Christ, O God.
The Wreck of the Deutschland, I.2

HORACE 65–8 B.C.

12 *Inceptis gravibus plerumque et magne*
        professis
    Purpureus, late qui splendeat, unus et alter
    Adsuitur pannus.
    Frequently with serious works and ones of
        great import, some purple patch or
        other is stitched on, to show up far and
        wide.
Ars Poetica, 14

13 *Grammatici certant et adhuc sub iudice lis*
        est.
    Scholars dispute, and the case is still be-
        fore the courts.
    78

14 *Proicit ampullas et sesquipedalia verba.*
    Throws aside his paint-pots and his words
        a foot and a half long.
    97

15 *Parturient montes, nascetur ridiculus mus.*
    Mountains will heave in childbirth, and a
        silly little mouse will be born.
    139

16 *Non fumum ex fulgore, sed ex fumo dare*
        lucem
    Cogitat.
    His thinking does not result in smoke after
        the flashing fire, but in light emerging
        from the smoke.
    143

17 *Semper ad eventum festinat et in medias res*
    Non secus ac notas auditorem rapit.
    He always hurries to the main event and
        whisks his audience into the middle of
        things as though they knew already.
    148

18 *Difficilis, querulus, laudator temporis acti*
    Se puero.
    Tiresome, complaining, a praiser of the
        times that were when he was a boy.
    173

19   *Vos exemplaria Graeca*
    Nocturna versate manu, versate diurna.
    For your own good, turn the pages of your
        Greek exemplars by night and by day.
    268

20 *Indignor quandoque bonus dormitat*
        Homerus.
    I'm aggrieved when sometimes even excel-
        lent Homer nods.
    359

21   *Nonumque prematur in an-*
        num,
    Membranis intus positis: delere licebit
    Quod non edideris; nescit vox missa reverti.
    Let it be kept till the ninth year, th

manuscript put away at home: you
may destroy whatever you haven't
published; once out, what you've said
can't be stopped.

388. See 123:5

1   *Nullius addictus iurare in verba magistri,*
    Quo me cumque rapit tempestas, deferor
    hospes.

Not bound to swear allegiance to any master, wherever the wind takes me I travel
as a visitor.

Epistles, I.i.14. *Nullius in verba* is the motto of
the Royal Society.

2   *Si possis recte, si non, quocumque modo*
    rem.

If possible honestly, if not, somehow,
make money.

66. Alexander Pope's translation:
Get place and wealth, if possible, with grace;
If not, by any means get wealth and place.

3   *Dimidium facti qui coepit habet: sapere*
    aude.

To have begun is half the job: be bold and
be sensible.

ii.40

4   *Naturam expellas furca, tamen usque re-*
    curret.

You may drive out nature with a pitchfork, yet she'll be constantly running
back.

x.24

5   *Et semel emissum volat irrevocabile ver-*
    bum.

And once sent out a word takes wing irrevocably.

xviii.71. See 122:21

6   *Nam tua res agitur, paries cum proximus*
    ardet.

For it is your business, when the wall next
door catches fire.

84

7   *Atque inter silvas Academi quaerere verum.*

And seek for truth in the groves of
Academe.

II.ii.45

8   *Quid te exempta iuvat spinis de pluribus*
    una?
    Vivere si recte nescis, decede peritis.
    Lusisti satis, edisti satis atque bibisti:
    Tempus abire tibi est.

What pleasure does it give to be rid of one
thorn out of many? If you don't know
how to live right, give way to those
who are expert at it. You have had
enough fun, eaten and drunk enough:
time you were off.

212

9   *Beatus ille, qui procul negotiis,*
    Ut prisca gens mortalium,
    Paterna rura bubus exercet suis,
    Solutus omni faenore.

He's happy who, far away from business,
like the race of men of old, tills his
ancestral fields with his own oxen, unbound by any interest to pay.

Epodes, ii.1

10   *Illi robur et aes triplex*
    Circa pectus erat, qui fragilem truci
    Commisit pelago ratem
    Primus.

His breast must have been protected all
round with oak and three-ply bronze,
who first launched his frail boat on the
rough sea.

Odes, I.iii.9

11 *Nil desperandum Teucro duce et auspice.*

Teucer shall lead and his star shall preside.
No cause for despair, then.

vii.27. Tr. James Michie

12 *Cras ingens iterabimus aequor.*

Tomorrow we'll be back on the vast ocean.

32

13 *Tu ne quaesieris, scire nefas, quem mihi,*
    quem tibi
    Finem di dederint.

Do not try to find out—we're forbidden to
know—what end the gods have in store
for me, or for you.

xi.1

14   *Dum loquimur, fugerit invida*
    Aetas: carpe diem, quam minimum credula
    postero.

While we're talking, time will have meanly
run on: pick today's fruits, not relying
on the future in the slightest.

7

15 *O matre pulchra filia pulchrior.*

What a beautiful mother, and yet more
beautiful daughter!

xvi.1

16 *Integer vitae scelerisque purus.*

Of unblemished life and spotless record.

xxii.1

17 *Dulce ridentem Lalagen amabo,*
    Dulce loquentem.

I will go on loving Lalage, who laughs so
sweetly and talks so sweetly.

23

18 *Nunc est bibendum, nunc pede libero*
    Pulsanda tellus.

Now for drinks, now for some dancing
with a good beat.

xxxvii.1

1 *Persicos odi, puer, apparatus.*
I hate all that Persian gear, boy.
xxxviii.1

2 *Ille terrarum mihi praeter omnis*
Angulus ridet.
That corner of the world smiles for me
more than anywhere else.
II.vi.13

3 *Auream quisquis mediocritatem*
Diligit.
Someone who loves the golden mean.
x.5

4 *Eheu fugaces, Postume, Postume,*
Labuntur anni.
Ah me, Postumus, Postumus, the fleeting
years are slipping by.
xiv.1

5 *Odi profanum vulgus et arceo;*
Favete linguis; carmina non prius
Audita Musarum sacerdos
Virginibus puerisque canto.
I hate the unholy masses and I keep away
from them. Hush your tongues; as a
priest of the Muses, I sing songs never
heard before to virgin girls and boys.
III.i.1

6 *Post equitem sedet atra Cura.*
At the rider's back sits dark Anxiety.
40

7 *Dulce et decorum est pro patria mori.*
Lovely and honourable it is to die for one's
country.
ii.13

8 *Vis consili expers mole ruit sua.*
Force, if unassisted by judgement, col-
lapses through its own mass.
iv.65

9 *Splendide mendax et in omne virgo*
Nobilis aevum.
Gloriously deceitful and a virgin renowned
for ever.
xi.35. Of the Danaid Hypermestra.

10 *O fons Bandusiae splendidior vitro.*
O spring of Bandusia, glinting more than
glass.
xiii.1

11 *Vixi puellis nuper idoneus*
Et militavi non sine gloria;
Nunc arma defunctumque bello
Barbiton hic paries habebit.
My life with girls has ended, though till
lately I was up to it and soldiered on
not ingloriously; now on this wall will
hang my weapons and my lyre, discharged from the war.
xxvi.1

12 *Exegi monumentum aere perennius.*
I have executed a memorial longer lasting
than bronze.
xxx.1

13 *Non omnis moriar.*
I shall not altogether die.
6

14 *Non sum qualis eram bonae*
Sub regno Cinarae. Desine, dulcium
Mater saeva Cupidinum.
I am not as I was when dear Cinara was
my queen. Don't force me, cruel
mother of the lovely Cupids.
IV.i.3

15 *Diffugere nives, redeunt iam gramina cam-*
pis
Arboribusque comae.
The snows have dispersed, now grass returns to the fields and leaves to the
trees.
vii.1

16 *Dignum laude virum Musa vetat mori.*
The man worthy of praise the Muse forbids to die.
viii.28

17 *Vixere fortes ante Agamemnona*
Multi.
Many brave men lived before Agamemnon's time.
ix.25

18 *Misce stultitiam consiliis brevem:*
Dulce est desipere in loco.
Mix a little foolishness with your serious
plans: it's lovely to be silly at the right
moment.
xii.27

19 *Mutato nomine de te*
Fabula narratur.
Change the name and it's about you, that
story.
Satires, I.i.69

20 *Hoc genus omne.*
All that tribe.
ii.2

21 *Ab ovo*
Usque ad mala.
From the egg right through to the apples.
iii.6. Meaning, from the start to the finish (of a
meal).

22 *Etiam disiecti membra poetae.*
Even though broken up, the limbs of a
poet.
iv.62. Of Ennius.

23 *Credat Iudaeus Apella,*
Non ego.

Let Apella the Jew believe it; I shan't.
v.100

1 *Hoc erat in votis: modus agri non ita mag-*
nus,
Hortus ubi et tecto vicinus iugis aquae fons
Et paulum silvae super his foret.
This was one of my prayers: for a parcel of
land not so very large, which should
have a garden and a spring of ever-
flowing water near the house, and a bit
of woodland as well as these.
II.vi.1

BISHOP SAMUEL HORSLEY
1733–1806

2 In *this* country, my Lords,...the individual
subject...'has nothing to do with the laws
but to obey them.'
House of Lords, 13 Nov. 1795. Bishop Horsley
was defending a maxim which he had earlier
used in committee.

A.E. HOUSMAN 1859–1936

3 From Clee to heaven the beacon burns,
    The shires have seen it plain,
From north and south the sign returns
    And beacons burn again.
A Shropshire Lad (1896), 1. **1887**

4 Loveliest of trees, the cherry now
Is hung with bloom along the bough,
And stands about the woodland ride
Wearing white for Eastertide.

Now of my threescore years and ten,
Twenty will not come again,
And take from seventy springs a score,
It only leaves me fifty more.

And since to look at things in bloom
Fifty springs are little room,
About the woodlands I will go
To see the cherry hung with snow.
2

5 Up, lad: when the journey's over
    There'll be time enough to sleep.
4. **Reveillé**

6 And naked to the hangman's noose
    The morning clocks will ring
A neck God made for other use
    Than strangling in a string.
9

7 When I was one-and-twenty
    I heard a wise man say,
'Give crowns and pounds and guineas
    But not your heart away;
Give pearls away and rubies,
    But keep your fancy free.'
But I was one-and-twenty,
    No use to talk to me.
13

8 Look not in my eyes, for fear
    They mirror true the sight I see,
And there you find your face too clear
    And love it and be lost like me.
One the long night through must lie
    Spent in star-defeated sighs,
But why should you as well as I
    Perish? gaze not in my eyes.
15

9 Twice a week the winter thorough
    Here stood I to keep the goal:
Football then was fighting sorrow
    For the young man's soul.

Now in Maytime to the wicket
    Out I march with bat and pad:
See the son of grief at cricket
    Trying to be glad.
17

10 Oh, when I was in love with you,
    Then I was clean and brave,
And miles around the wonder grew
    How well did I behave.

And now the fancy passes by,
    And nothing will remain,
And miles around they'll say that I
    Am quite myself again.
18

11 And round that early-laurelled head
Will flock to gaze the strengthless dead,
And find unwithered on its curls
The garland briefer than a girl's.
19. **To an Athlete Dying Young**

12 In summertime on Bredon
    The bells they sound so clear;
Round both the shires they ring them
    In steeples far and near,
    A happy noise to hear.

Here of a Sunday morning
    My love and I would lie,
And see the coloured counties,
    And hear the larks so high
    About us in the sky.
21. **Bredon Hill**

13 'Come all to church, good people,'—
    Oh, noisy bells, be dumb;
I hear you, I will come.

14 The lads in their hundreds to Ludlow
    come in for the fair,
    There's men from the barn and the forge
        and the mill and the fold,
    The lads for the girls and the lads for the
        liquor are there,
    And there with the rest are the lads that
        will never be old.
23

1 They carry back bright to the coiner the mintage of man,
    The lads that will die in their glory and never be old.

2 'Is my team ploughing,
    That I was used to drive
And hear the harness jingle
    When I was man alive?'
27

3 The goal stands up, the keeper
    Stands up to keep the goal.

4 On Wenlock Edge the wood's in trouble;
    His forest fleece the Wrekin heaves;
The gale, it plies the saplings double,
    And thick on Severn snow the leaves.
31

5 The gale, it plies the saplings double,
    It blows so hard, 'twill soon be gone:
Today the Roman and his trouble
    Are ashes under Uricon.

6 You and I must keep from shame
    In London streets the Shropshire name;
On banks of Thames they must not say
    Severn breeds worse men than they.
37

7 Into my heart an air that kills
    From yon far country blows:
What are those blue remembered hills,
    What spires, what farms are those?

That is the land of lost content,
    I see it shining plain,
The happy highways where I went
    And cannot come again.
40

8 Shot? so quick, so clean an ending?
    Oh that was right, lad, that was brave.
44

9 Be still, be still, my soul; it is but for a season:
    Let us endure an hour and see injustice done.
48

10 Think no more; 'tis only thinking
    Lays lads underground.
49

11 With rue my heart is laden
    For golden friends I had,
For many a rose-lipt maiden
    And many a lightfoot lad.
54

12 Malt does more than Milton can
    To justify God's ways to man.
62

13 And down in lovely muck I've lain,
    Happy till I woke again.

14 —I tell the tale that I heard told.
    Mithridates, he died old.

15 I 'listed at home for a lancer,
    Oh who would not sleep with the brave?
Last Poems (1922), 6. **Lancer**

16 The troubles of our proud and angry dust
    Are from eternity, and shall not fail.
Bear them we can, and if we can we must.
    Shoulder the sky, my lad, and drink your ale.
9

17 I, a stranger and afraid
    In a world I never made.
12

18 He stood, and heard the steeple
    Sprinkle the quarters on the morning town.
15. **Eight O'Clock**

19 The Spartans on the sea-wet rock sat down and combed their hair.
25. **The Oracles**

20 Their shoulders held the sky suspended;
    They stood, and earth's foundations stay;
What God abandoned, these defended,
    And saved the sum of things for pay.
37. **Epitaph on an Army of Mercenaries**

21 Tell me not here, it needs not saying,
    What tune the enchantress plays.
40

22 The cuckoo shouts all day at nothing
    In leafy dells alone;
And traveller's joy beguiles in autumn
    Hearts that have lost their own.

23 They say my verse is sad: no wonder;
    Its narrow measure spans
Tears of eternity, and sorrow,
    Not mine, but man's.
More Poems (1936), epigraph

24 Crossing alone the nighted ferry
    With the one coin for fee,
Whom, on the wharf of Lethe waiting,
    Count you to find? Not me.
23

25 Because I liked you better
    Than suits a man to say,
It irked you, and I promised
    To throw the thought away.
31

26 Here dead lie we because we did not choose
    To live and shame the land from which we sprung.

Life, to be sure, is nothing much to lose;
But young men think it is, and we were
young.
36

1 The stars have not dealt me the worst they
could do:
My pleasures are plenty, my troubles are
two.
But oh, my two troubles they reave me of
rest,
The brains in my head and the heart in my
breast.
Collected Poems (1939), **Additional Poems,** 17

2 Oh they're taking him to prison for the
colour of his hair.
18

3 O suitably attired in leather boots
Head of a traveller, wherefore seeking
whom
Whence by what way how purposed art
thou come
To this well-nightingaled vicinity?
My object in enquiring is to know.
But if you happen to be deaf and dumb
And do not understand a word I say,
Nod with your hand to signify as much.
Fragment of a Greek Tragedy, Trinity Magazine,
Feb. 1921; first published in *The Bromsgrovian,*
1883

4 Mud's sister, not himself, adorns my
shoes.

5 Reader, behold! this monster wild
Has gobbled up the infant child.
The infant child is not aware
It has been eaten by the bear.
Infant Innocence. Laurence Housman, *A.E.H.*
(1937), p.256

6 Three minutes' thought would suffice to
find this out, but thought is irksome and
three minutes is a long time.
Juvenalis Saturae (ed.) (1905), Preface

7 Gentlemen who use MSS as drunkards
use lamp-posts—not to light them on their
way but to dissimulate their instability.
M. Manilii Astronomicon Liber Primus (ed.)
(1903), introduction, I

8 The University which once saw Wordsworth drunk and once saw Porson sober
will see a better scholar than Wordsworth,
and a better poet than Porson, betwixt and
between.
Speech at farewell dinner, University College,
London, before going to Cambridge as Kennedy
Professor of Latin, 1911. Laurence Housman,
A.E.H. (1937), p.101

JULIA WARD HOWE 1819–1910

9 Mine eyes have seen the glory of the coming of the Lord:
He is trampling out the vintage where the
grapes of wrath are stored.
Battle Hymn of the American Republic (Dec.
1861)

MARY HOWITT 1799–1888

10 Buttercups and daisies,
Oh, the pretty flowers;
Coming ere the Springtime,
To tell of sunny hours.
Buttercups and Daisies

11 'Will you walk into my parlour?' said a
spider to a fly:
"Tis the prettiest little parlour that ever
you did spy.'
The Spider and the Fly

EDMOND HOYLE 1672–1769

12 When in doubt, win the trick.
Hoyle's Games (c. 1756). **Whist, Twenty-four
Short Rules for Learners**

FRIEDRICH VON HÜGEL 1852–1926

13 The golden rule is, to help those we love to
escape from us; and never try to begin to
help people, or influence them till they ask,
but wait for them. (To his niece, in conversation.)
Letters…to a Niece (1928), introduction

THOMAS HUGHES 1822–1896

14 It's more than a game. It's an institution.
[Cricket.]
Tom Brown's Schooldays, pt.ii, ch.7

VICTOR HUGO 1802–1885

15 *Le mot, c'est le Verbe, et le Verbe, c'est
Dieu.*
The word is the Verb, and the Verb is God.
Contemplations (1856), I.viii

16 *On résiste à l'invasion des armées; on ne
résiste pas à l'invasion des idées.*
A stand can be made against invasion by
an army; no stand can be made against
invasion by an idea.
Histoire d'un Crime, La Chute, X

DAVID HUME 1711–1776

17 If we take in our hand any volume; of
divinity or school metaphysics, for in-
stance; let us ask, *Does it contain any ab-
stract reasoning concerning quantity or*

number? No. *Does it contain any experimental reasoning, concerning matter of fact and existence?* No. Commit it then to the flames: for it can contain nothing but sophistry and illusion.
An Enquiry Concerning Human Understanding (1748), sec.12, pt.III

1 It cannot reasonably be doubted, but a little miss, dressed in a new gown for a dancing-school ball, receives as complete enjoyment as the greatest orator, who triumphs in the splendour of his eloquence, while he governs the passions and resolutions of a numerous assembly.
Essays (1741–2). **The Sceptic**

G.W. HUNT 1829?–1904

2 We don't want to fight, but, by jingo if we do,
We've got the ships, we've got the men, we've got the money too.
We've fought the Bear before, and while Britons shall be true,
The Russians shall not have Constantinople.
We Don't Want to Fight. Music hall song, 1878

LEIGH HUNT 1784–1859

3 Abou Ben Adhem (may his tribe increase!)
Awoke one night from a deep dream of peace.
Abou Ben Adhem and the Angel

4   'I pray thee then,
Write me as one that loves his fellow-men.'

5 Jenny kissed me when we met,
Jumping from the chair she sat in;
Time, you thief, who love to get
Sweets into your list, put that in:
Say I'm weary, say I'm sad,
Say that health and wealth have missed me,
Say I'm growing old, but add,
Jenny kissed me.
Rondeau

6 Stolen sweets are always sweeter,
Stolen kisses much completer,
Stolen looks are nice in chapels,
Stolen, stolen, be your apples.
Song of Fairies Robbing an Orchard

7 The two divinest things this world has got,
A lovely woman in a rural spot!
The Story of Rimini, iii, l.257

ANNE HUNTER 1742–1821

8 My mother bids me bind my hair
With bands of rosy hue,
Tie up my sleeves with ribbons rare,
And lace my bodice blue.
My Mother Bids Me Bind My Hair

SIR GERALD HURST 1877–1957

9 One of the mysteries of human conduct is why adult men and women all over England are ready to sign documents which they do not read, at the behest of canvassers whom they do not know, binding them to pay for articles which they do not want, with money which they have not got.
Closed Chapters (1942), p.141

JOHN HUSS c.1372–1415

10 *O sancta simplicitas!*
O holy simplicity!
At the stake, seeing an old peasant bringing a faggot to throw on the pile. Zincgreff-Weidner, *Apophthegmata.* (Amsterdam, 1653), pt.iii, p.383. See 130:15

FRANCIS HUTCHESON 1694–1746

11 That action is best, which procures the greatest happiness for the greatest numbers.
Inquiry into the Original of our Ideas of Beauty and Virtue (1725). Treatise II. **Concerning Moral Good and Evil**, sec.3, 8

T.H. HUXLEY 1825–1895

12 I took thought, and invented what I conceived to be the appropriate title of 'agnostic'.
Collected Essays, v. **Agnosticism**

13 It is the customary fate of new truths to begin as heresies and to end as superstitions.
Science and Culture, xii. **The Coming of Age of the Origin of Species**

14 I asserted—and I repeat—that a man has no reason to be ashamed of having an ape for his grandfather. If there were an ancestor whom I should feel shame in recalling it would rather be a *man*—a man of restless and versatile intellect—who, not content with an equivocal success in his own sphere of activity, plunges into scientific questions with which he has no real acquaintance, only to obscure them by an aimless rhetoric, and distract the attention of his hearers from the real point at issue by eloquent digressions and skilled appeals to religious prejudice.
Replying to Bishop Samuel Wilberforce in the debate on Darwin's theory of evolution during the meeting of the British Association at Oxford, 30 June 1860. See *Life and Letters of Thomas*

Henry Huxley (1900), vol.i, p.185, letter from J.R. Green to Professor Boyd Dawkins. Huxley, in a letter to Francis Darwin, agreed that this account was fair if not wholly accurate: there is no reliable verbatim transcript.

1 I am too much of a sceptic to deny the possibility of anything.
Letter to Herbert Spencer, 22 March 1886

EDWARD HYDE
see EARL OF CLARENDON

DOLORES IBÁRRURI 'LA PASIONARIA' 1895–

2 *No pasarán!*
They shall not pass.
H. Thomas, *The Spanish Civil War* (1961), ch.16. See 177:5

3 It is better to die on your feet than to live on your knees.
Speech in Paris, 3 Sept. 1936

HENRIK IBSEN 1828–1906

4 The majority has the might—more's the pity—but it hasn't right…The minority is always right.
An Enemy of the People (1882), Act 4

5 You should never have your best trousers on when you turn out to fight for freedom and truth.
Act 5

6 It's not just what we inherit from our mothers and fathers that haunts us. It's all kinds of old defunct theories, all sorts of old defunct beliefs, and things like that. It's not that they actually *live* on in us; they are simply lodged there, and we cannot get rid of them. I've only to pick up a newspaper and I seem to see ghosts gliding between the lines.
Ghosts (1881), Act 2

7 Mother, give me the sun.
Act 3

8 Ten o'clock…and back he'll come. I can just see him. With vine leaves in his hair. Flushed and confident.
Hedda Gabler (1890), Act 2

9 Youth will come here and beat on my door, and force its way in.
The Master Builder (1892), Act 1

10 Take the life-lie away from the average man and straight away you take away his happiness.
The Wild Duck (1884), Act 5

IVAN ILLICH 1926–

11 In a consumer society there are inevitably two kinds of slaves: the prisoners of addiction and the prisoners of envy.
Tools for Conviviality (1973)

DEAN INGE 1860–1954

12 *Nisi monumentum requiris, circumspice.*
(Of the traffic outside St. Paul's.)
Attr. see 7:6

ROBERT G. INGERSOLL 1833–1899

13 An honest God is the noblest work of man.
Gods, pt.1, p.2. See 185:18

J.A.D. INGRES 1780–1867

14 *Le dessin est la probité de l'art.*
Drawing is the true test of art.
Pensées d'Ingres, 1922, p.70

WASHINGTON IRVING 1783–1859

15 A tart temper never mellows with age, and a sharp tongue is the only edged tool that grows keener with constant use.
The Sketch Book (1819–20). **Rip Van Winkle**

CHRISTOPHER ISHERWOOD 1904–

16 The common cormorant or shag
Lays eggs inside a paper bag
The reason you will see no doubt
It is to keep the lightning out.
But what these unobservant birds
Have never noticed is that herds
Of wandering bears may come with buns
And steal the bags to hold the crumbs.
The Common Cormorant

17 I am a camera with its shutter open, quite passive, recording, not thinking.
Goodbye to Berlin, **A Berlin Diary,** Autumn 1930

JACOPONE DA TODI c.1230–1306

18 *Stabat Mater dolorosa,*
Iuxta crucem lacrimosa
Dum pendebat Filius.
There was standing the sorrowing Mother, beside the cross weeping while her Son hung upon it.
Stabat Mater dolorosa. Hymn also ascribed to Pope Innocent III and St. Bonaventure

REVD. RICHARD JAGO 1715–1781

19 With leaden foot time creeps along
While Delia is away.
Absence

KING JAMES I OF ENGLAND AND VI OF SCOTLAND 1566–1625

1 Dr Donne's verses are like the peace of God; they pass all understanding.
Saying recorded by Archdeacon Plume (1630–1704)

HENRY JAMES 1843–1916

2 Live all you can; it's a mistake not to. It doesn't so much matter what you do in particular, so long as you have your life. If you haven't had that what *have* you had?
The Ambassadors (1903), bk.5, ch.2

3 The black and merciless things that are behind the great possessions.
The Ivory Tower (1917), Notes, p.287

4 Cats and monkeys, monkeys and cats— all human life is there.
The Madonna of the Future (1879)

5 The perfect presence of mind, unconfused, unhurried by emotion, that any artistic performance requires and that all, whatever the instrument, require in exactly the same degree.
The Tragic Muse (1890), ch.19

6 So here it is at last, the distinguished thing. [Of his own death.]
Edith Wharton, *A Backward Glance,* ch.14

7 I can stand a great deal of gold. [On seeing a partularly grand drawing room.]
Attr. by D. McCarthy, *The Legend of the Master* (compiled by S. Nowell-Smith, 1947) 'Social Occasions'.

WILLIAM JAMES 1842–1910

8 The moral flabbiness born of the bitchgoddess SUCCESS. That—with the squalid cash interpretation put on the word success—is our national disease.
Letter to H.G. Wells, 11 Sept. 1906

PRESIDENT THOMAS JEFFERSON 1743–1826

9 We hold these truths to be sacred and undeniable; that all men are created equal and independent, that from that equal creation they derive rights inherent and inalienable, among which are the preservation of life, and liberty, and the pursuit of happiness.
Original draft for the Declaration of Independence. See 5:9

10 The tree of liberty must be refreshed from time to time with the blood of patriots and tyrants. It is its natural manure.
Letter to W.S. Smith, 13 Nov. 1787

11 To attain all this [universal republicanism], however, rivers of blood must ye flow, and years of desolation pass over; ye the object is worth rivers of blood, an years of desolation.
To John Adams, 4 Sept. 1823

12 When a man assumes a public trust, h should consider himself as publi property.
Remark to Baron von Humboldt, 1807. Rayne *Life of Jefferson* (1834), p.356

13 No duty the Executive had to perform wa so trying as to put the right man in th right place.
J.B. MacMaster, *History of the People of th U.S.,* vol.ii, ch.13, p.586

FRANCIS, LORD JEFFREY 1773–1850

14 This will never do.
On Wordsworth's 'Excursion'. *Edinburgh Re view,* Nov. 1814, p.1

ST. JEROME c.342–420

15 *Venerationi mihi semper fuit non verbos rusticitas, sed sancta simplicitas.*
I have revered always not crude verbosity but holy simplicity.
Letters, 57, xii (*Patrologia Latina* xxii, 579)

JEROME K. JEROME 1859–1927

16 Love is like the measles; we all have to g through it.
The Idle Thoughts of an Idle Fellow (1889). O Being in Love

17 George goes to sleep at a bank from ten t four each day, except Saturdays, when they wake him up and put him outside a two.
Three Men in a Boat (1889), ch.2

18 I like work: it fascinates me. I can sit anc look at it for hours. I love to keep it by me the idea of getting rid of it nearly break my heart.
ch.15

DOUGLAS JERROLD 1803–1857

19 Love's like the measles—all the worse when it comes late in life.
Wit and Opinions of Douglas Jerrold (1859), A Philanthropist

20 We love peace, as we abhor pusillanimity. but not peace at any price. There is a peace more destructive of the manhood of living man than war is destructive of his materia

body. Chains are worse than bayonets.
Peace

HIRAM JOHNSON 1866–1945

1 The first casualty when war comes is truth.
Speech, U.S. Senate, 1917

PHILANDER CHASE JOHNSON 1866–1939

2 Cheer up, the worst is yet to come.
Shooting Stars. See *Everybody's Magazine,* May 1920

SAMUEL JOHNSON 1709–1784

3 Sir, we are a nest of singing birds.
Of Pembroke College, Oxford. Boswell, *Life of Johnson* (L.F. Powell's revision of G.B. Hill's edition), vol.i, p.75. 1730

4 It is incident to physicians, I am afraid, beyond all other men, to mistake subsequence for consequence.
Review of Dr. Lucas's *Essay on Waters.* p.91n. 25 Nov. 1734

5 I'll come no more behind your scenes, David; for the silk stockings and white bosoms of your actresses excite my amorous propensities.
To Garrick; p.201. 1750

6 A man may write at any time, if he will set himself doggedly to it.
p.203. Mar. 1750

7 I had done all I could; and no man is well pleased to have his all neglected, be it ever so little.
p.261. Letter to Lord Chesterfield, 7 Feb. 1755

8 The shepherd in Virgil grew at last acquainted with Love, and found him a native of the rocks.
p.261. Letter to Lord Chesterfield, 7 Feb. 1755

9 Is not a Patron, my Lord, one who looks with unconcern on a man struggling for life in the water, and, when he has reached ground, encumbers him with help? The notice which you have been pleased to take of my labours, had it been early, had been kind; but it has been delayed till I am indifferent, and cannot enjoy it; till I am solitary, and cannot impart it; till I am known, and do not want it.

10 This man I thought had been a Lord among wits; but, I find, he is only a wit among Lords.
Of Lord Chesterfield. p.266. 1754

11 They teach the morals of a whore, and the manners of a dancing master.
Of Lord Chesterfield's *Letters.* p.266. 1754

12 Ignorance, madam, pure ignorance.
When asked by a lady why he defined 'pastern' as the 'knee' of a horse, in his Dictionary. p.293. 1755

13 Lexicographer: a writer of dictionaries, a harmless drudge.
p.296. 1755

14 If a man does not make new acquaintance as he advances through life, he will soon find himself left alone. A man, Sir, should keep his friendship in constant repair.
p.300. 1755

15 No man will be a sailor who has contrivance enough to get himself into a jail; for being in a ship is being in a jail, with the chance of being drowned…A man in a jail has more room, better food, and commonly better company.
p.348. 16 Mar. 1759

16 *Boswell*: I do indeed come from Scotland, but I cannot help it…
Johnson: That, Sir, I find, is what a very great many of your countrymen cannot help.
p.392. 16 May 1763

17 You *may* abuse a tragedy, though you cannot write one. You may scold a carpenter who has made you a bad table, though you cannot make a table. It is not your trade to make tables.
Of literary criticism. p.409. 25 June 1763

18 Great abilities are not requisite for an Historian…Imagination is not required in any high degree.
p.424. 6 July 1763

19 Norway, too, has noble wild prospects; and Lapland is remarkable for prodigious noble wild prospects. But, Sir, let me tell you, the noblest prospect which a Scotchman ever sees, is the high road that leads him to England!
p.425. 6 July 1763

20 A man ought to read just as inclination leads him; for what he reads as a task will do him little good.
p.428. 14 July 1763

21 But if he does really think that there is no distinction between virtue and vice, why, Sir, when he leaves our houses let us count our spoons.
p.432. 14 July 1763

22 You never find people labouring to convince you that you may live very happily

upon a plentiful fortune.
p.441. 20 July 1763

1 Truth, Sir, is a cow, which will yield such people [sceptics] no more milk, and so they are gone to milk the bull.
p.444. 21 July 1763

2 Young men have more virtue than old men; they have more generous sentiments in every respect.
p.445. 22 July 1763

3 It is no matter what you teach them [children] first, any more than what leg you shall put into your breeches first.
p.452. 26 July 1763

4 Why, Sir, Sherry [Thomas Sheridan] is dull, naturally dull; but it must have taken him a great deal of pains to become what we now see him. Such an excess of stupidity, Sir, is not in Nature.
p.453. 28 July 1763

5 A woman's preaching is like a dog's walking on his hinder legs. It is not done well; but you are surprised to find it done at all.
p.463. 31 July 1763

6 I look upon it, that he who does not mind his belly will hardly mind anything else.
p.467. 5 Aug. 1763

7 [Of Bishop Berkeley's theory of the non-existence of matter, Boswell observed that though they were satisfied it was not true, they were unable to refute it. Johnson struck his foot against a large stone, till he rebounded from it, saying]
I refute it *thus*.
p.471. 6 Aug. 1763

8 A very unclubable man.
Sir John Hawkins. p.480n. 1764

9 That all who are happy, are equally happy, is not true. A peasant and a philosopher may be equally *satisfied*, but not equally *happy*. Happiness consists in the multiplicity of agreeable consciousness.
vol.ii, p.9. Feb. 1766

10 It is our first duty to serve society, and, after we have done that, we may attend wholly to the salvation of our own souls. A youthful passion for abstracted devotion should not be encouraged.
p.10. Feb. 1766

11 Sir, if a man has a mind to *prance*, he must study at Christ-Church and All-Souls.
p.68n. Autumn, 1769

12 Let me smile with the wise, and feed with the rich.
p.79. 6 Oct. 1769

13 We *know* our will is free, and *there's* an end on't.
p.82. 16 Oct. 1769

14 I would not *coddle* the child.
p.101. 26 Oct. 1769

15 The triumph of hope over experience.
Of a man who remarried immediately after the death of a wife with whom he had been very unhappy. p.128. 1770

16 He has, indeed, done it very well; but it is a foolish thing well done.
On Goldsmith's apology in the *London Chronicle* for beating Evans the bookseller. p.210. 3 Apr. 1773

17 All intellectual improvement arises from leisure.
p.219. 13 Apr. 1773

18 Read over your compositions, and where ever you meet with a passage which you think is particularly fine, strike it out.
Quoting a college tutor. p.237. 30 Apr. 1773

19 I think the full tide of human existence is at Charing-Cross.
p.337. 2 Apr. 1775

20 It is wonderful, when a calculation is made, how little the mind is actually employed in the discharge of any profession.
p.344. 6 Apr. 1775

21 Patriotism is the last refuge of a scoundrel.
p.348. 7 Apr. 1775

22 That is the happiest conversation where there is no competition, no vanity, but a calm quiet interchange of sentiments.
p.359. 14 Apr. 1775

23 In lapidary inscriptions a man is not upon oath.
p.407. 1775

24 Nothing odd will do long. *Tristram Shandy* did not last.
p.449. 20 Mar. 1776

25 There is nothing which has yet been contrived by man, by which so much happiness is produced as by a good tavern or inn.
p.452. 21 Mar. 1776

26 No man but a blockhead ever wrote, except for money.
vol.iii, p.19. 5 Apr. 1776

27 The grand object of travelling is to see the shores of the Mediterranean.
p.36. 11 Apr. 1776

28 'Sir, what is poetry?'
'Why Sir, it is much easier to say what it is not. We all *know* what light is; but it is not

easy to *tell* what it is.'
p.38. 10 Apr. 1776

1 Dine with Jack Wilkes, Sir! I'd as soon dine with Jack Ketch.
p.66. 'This has been circulated as if actually said by Johnson; when the truth is, it was only *supposed* by me.' (Boswell's note.)

2 *Olivarii Goldsmith, Poetae, Physici, Historici, Qui nullum fere scribendi genus non tetigit, Nullum quod tetigit non ornavit.*
To Oliver Goldsmith, A Poet, Naturalist, and Historian, who left scarcely any style of writing untouched, and touched none that he did not adorn.
p.82. 22 June 1776. Epitaph on Goldsmith

3 If I had no duties, and no reference to futurity, I would spend my life in driving briskly in a post-chaise with a pretty woman.
p.162. 19 Sept. 1777

4 Depend upon it, Sir, when a man knows he is to be hanged in a fortnight, it concentrates his mind wonderfully.
p.167. 19 Sept. 1777

5 When a man is tired of London, he is tired of life; for there is in London all that life can afford.
p.178. 20 Sept. 1777

6 John Wesley's conversation is good, but he is never at leisure. He is always obliged to go at a certain hour. This is very disagreeable to a man who loves to fold his legs and have out his talk, as I do.
p.230. 31 Mar. 1778

7 Johnson had said that he could repeat a complete chapter of 'The Natural History of Iceland', from the Danish of Horrebow, the whole of which was exactly thus:—'CHAP. LXXII. *Concerning snakes.* There are no snakes to be met with throughout the whole island.'
p.279. 13 Apr. 1778

8 As the Spanish proverb says, 'He, who would bring home the wealth of the Indies, must carry the wealth of the Indies with him.' So it is in travelling; a man must carry knowledge with him, if he would bring home knowledge.
p.302. 17 Apr. 1778

9 Sir, the insolence of wealth will creep out.
p.316. 18 Apr. 1778

10 There are innumerable questions to which the inquisitive mind can in this state receive no answer: Why do you and I exist? Why was this world created? Since it was to be created, why was it not created sooner?
p.341. 9 May 1778

11 Claret is the liquor for boys; port for men; but he who aspires to be a hero must drink brandy.
p.381. 7 Apr. 1779

12 Worth seeing? yes; but not worth going to see.
Of the Giant's Causeway. p.410. 12 Oct. 1779

13 If you are idle, be not solitary; if you are solitary, be not idle.
p.415. Letter to Boswell, 27 Oct. 1779. See 55:21

14 I have got no further than this: Every man has a right to utter what he thinks truth, and every other man has a right to knock him down for it. Martyrdom is the test.
vol.iv, p.12. 1780

15 They are forced plants, raised in a hotbed; and they are poor plants; they are but cucumbers after all.
Of Gray's *Odes.* p.13. 1780

16 This merriment of parsons is mighty offensive.
p.76. Mar. 1781

17 We are not here to sell a parcel of boilers and vats, but the potentiality of growing rich, beyond the dreams of avarice.
At the sale of Thrale's brewery. p.87. 6 Apr. 1781. See 172:11

18 'The woman had a bottom of good sense.' The word '*bottom*' thus introduced, was so ludicrous,...that most of us could not forbear tittering...
'Where's the merriment?...I say the *woman* was *fundamentally* sensible.'
p.99. 20 Apr. 1781

19 Always, Sir, set a high value on spontaneous kindness. He whose inclination prompts him to cultivate your friendship of his own accord, will love you more than one whom you have been at pains to attach to you.
p.115. May 1781

20 Resolve not to be poor: whatever you have, spend less. Poverty is a great enemy to human happiness; it certainly destroys liberty, and it makes some virtues impracticable and others extremely difficult.
p.157. 7 Dec. 1782

21 I hate a fellow whom pride, or cowardice, or laziness drives into a corner, and who does nothing when he is there but sit and *growl*; let him come out as I do, and *bark*.
p.161, n.3. 14 Nov. 1782

22 There is a wicked inclination in most

people to suppose an old man decayed in his intellects. If a young or middle-aged man, when leaving a company, does not recollect where he laid his hat, it is nothing; but if the same inattention is discovered in an old man, people will shrug up their shoulders, and say, 'His memory is going.'
p.181. 1783

1 Sir, there is no settling the point of precedency between a louse and a flea.
To Maurice Morgann who asked him whether he reckoned Derrick or Smart the better poet. p.192. 1783

2 My dear friend, clear your *mind* of cant... You may *talk* in this manner; it is a mode of talking in Society: but don't *think* foolishly.
p.221. 15 May 1783

3 Boswell is a very clubable man.
p.254n. 1783

4 Milton, Madam, was a genius that could cut a Colossus from a rock; but could not carve heads upon cherry-stones.
To Miss Hannah More, who had expressed a wonder that the poet who had written *Paradise Lost* should write such poor Sonnets. p.305. 13 June 1784

5 No man is a hypocrite in his pleasures.
p.316. June 1784

6 Dublin, though a place much worse than London, is not so bad as Iceland.
Letter to Mrs. Christopher Smart. p.359n. 1791

7 Sir, I look upon every day to be lost, in which I do not make a new acquaintance.
p.374. Nov. 1784

8 An odd thought strikes me:—we shall receive no letters in the grave.
p.413. Dec. 1784

9 A cucumber should be well sliced, and dressed with pepper and vinegar, and then thrown out, as good for nothing.
5 Oct., p.354

10 What is written without effort is in general read without pleasure.
Johnsonian Miscellanies (1897), vol.ii, p.309

11 Fly fishing may be a very pleasant amusement; but angling or float fishing I can only compare to a stick and a string, with a worm at one end and a fool at the other.
Attrib. Johnson by Hawker in *Instructions to Young Sportsmen* (1859), p.197. Not found in his works. See N. & Q., 11 Dec. 1915

12 A general anarchy prevails in my kitchen.
Mme D'Arblay, *Diary and Letters* (1891 edn.), vol.i, ch.iii, p.63 (Sept. 1778)

13 Every other author may aspire to praise the lexicographer can only hope to escape reproach.
Dictionary of the English Language (1775), Preface

14 Change is not made without inconvenience, even from worse to better.
Quoting Richard Hooker, *Of the Laws of Ecclesiastical Polity*, IV.xiv

15 I am not yet so lost in lexicography, as to forget that words are the daughters of earth, and that things are the sons of heaven.

16 *Dull.* 8. To make dictionaries is dull work.

17 *Excise.* A hateful tax levied upon commodities.

18 *Net.* Anything reticulated or decussated at equal distances, with interstices between the intersections.

19 *Oats.* A grain, which in England is generally given to horses, but in Scotland supports the people.

20 *Patron.* Commonly a wretch who supports with insolence, and is paid with flattery.

21 When two Englishmen meet, their first talk is of the weather.
The Idler (1758-60), No.11

22 Nothing is more hopeless than a scheme of merriment.
No.58

23 I do not much wish well to discoveries, for I am always afraid they will end in conquest and robbery.
Letter to W.S. Johnson, 4 Mar. 1773

24 The reciprocal civility of authors is one of the most risible scenes in the farce of life.
Life of Sir Thomas Browne, first published as preface to his 1756 edition of *Christian Morals*

25 I am disappointed by that stroke of death which has eclipsed the gaiety of nations and impoverished the public stock of harmless pleasure. [Garrick's death.]
Lives of the English Poets (1779-81). **Edmund Smith**

26 In the character of his Elegy I rejoice to concur with the common reader.
Gray

27 A man, doubtful of his dinner, or trembling at a creditor, is not much disposed to abstracted meditation, or remote enquiries.
Collins

28 He [the poet] must write as the interpreter of nature, and the legislator of mankind.

and consider himself as presiding over the thoughts and manners of future generations; as a being superior to time and place.
Rasselas (1759), ch.10

1 Human life is everwhere a state in which much is to be endured, and little to be enjoyed.
ch.11

2 Marriage has many pains, but celibacy has no pleasures.
ch.26

3 Example is always more efficacious than precept.
ch.29

4 Notes are often necessary, but they are necessary evils.
Plays of William Shakespeare, with Notes (1765), preface

5 Here falling houses thunder on your head, And here a female atheist talks you dead.
London (1738), l.17

6 This mournful truth is ev'rywhere confess'd,
Slow rises worth by poverty depress'd.
l.176

7 The stage but echoes back the public voice.
The drama's laws the drama's patrons give,
For we that live to please, must please to live.
Prologue at the Opening of the Theatre in Drury Lane, 1747

8 Let observation with extensive view, Survey mankind, from China to Peru;
Remark each anxious toil, each eager strife,
And watch the busy scenes of crowded life.
The Vanity of Human Wishes (1749), l.1

9 Deign on the passing world to turn thine eyes,
And pause awhile from letters to be wise;
There mark what ills the scholar's life assail,
Toil, envy, want, the patron, and the jail.
See nations slowly wise, and meanly just,
To buried merit raise the tardy bust.
l.157

10 His fall was destined to a barren strand, A petty fortress, and a dubious hand;
He left the name, at which the world grew pale,

To point a moral, or adorn a tale. [Charles XII of Sweden.]
l.219

JOHN BENN JOHNSTONE 1803–1891

11 I want you to assist me in forcing her on board the lugger; once there, I'll frighten her into marriage.
Since quoted as: Once aboard the lugger and the maid is mine. *The Gipsy Farmer*

HANNS JOHST 1890–

12 *Wenn ich Kultur höre...entsichere ich meinen Browning!*
Whenever I hear the word 'culture'...I release the safety-catch on my pistol.
Schlageter (1934), I.i. Often attrib. Goering

AL JOLSON 1886–1950

13 You ain't heard nothin' yet, folks.
In the first talking film, *The Jazz Singer,* July 1927

HENRY ARTHUR JONES 1851–1929
and **HENRY HERMAN** 1832–1894

14 O God! Put back Thy universe and give me yesterday.
The Silver King

JOHN PAUL JONES 1747–1792

15 I have not yet begun to fight.
On being hailed to know whether he had struck his flag, as his ship was sinking, 23 Sept. 1779. De Koven, *Life and Letters of J.P. Jones*, vol.i

BEN JONSON 1573?–1637

16 Fortune, that favours fools.
The Alchemist (1610), prologue

17 Thou look'st like Antichrist in that lewd hat.
IV.vii

18 Slow, slow, fresh fount, keep time with my salt tears.
Cynthia's Revels (1600), I.i

19 Queen and huntress, chaste and fair, Now the sun is laid to sleep,
Seated in thy silver chair,
State in wonted manner keep:
Hesperus entreats thy light,
Goddess, excellently bright.
V.iii

20 Alas, all the castles I have, are built with air, thou know'st.
Eastward Ho (1604), II.ii.226

21 Rest in soft peace, and, ask'd say here doth lye

Ben Jonson his best piece of poetrie.
Epigrams (1672), xlv. **On My First Son**

1 I have it here in black and white.
Every Man in his Humour (1598), IV.ii

2 It must be done like lightning.
v

3 Drink to me only with thine eyes,
    And I will pledge with mine;
Or leave a kiss but in the cup,
    And I'll not look for wine.
The thirst that from the soul doth rise
    Doth ask a drink divine;
But might I of Jove's nectar sup,
    I would not change for thine.

I sent thee late a rosy wreath,
    Not so much honouring thee,
As giving it a hope that there
    It could not wither'd be.
The Forest (1616), ix. **To Celia**

4 Ramp up my genius, be not retrograde;
But boldly nominate a spade a spade.
The Poetaster (1601), v.i

5 This figure that thou here seest put,
It was for gentle Shakespeare cut,
Wherein the graver had a strife
With Nature, to out-do the life:
O could he but have drawn his wit
As well in brass, as he has hit
His face; the print would then surpass
All that was ever writ in brass:
But since he cannot, reader, look
Not on his picture, but his book.
On the Portrait of Shakespeare, To the Reader

6 And though thou hadst small Latin, and
less Greek.
To the Memory of My Beloved, the Author, Mr.
William Shakespeare

7 He was not of an age, but for all time!

8 I remember the players have often men-
tioned it as an honour to Shakespeare that
in his writing (whatsoever he penned) he
never blotted out a line. My answer hath
been 'Would he had blotted a thousand'.
Which they thought a malevolent speech. I
had not told posterity this, but for their
ignorance, who chose that circumstance to
commend their friend by wherein he most
faulted; and to justify mine own candour:
for I loved the man, and do honour his
memory, on this side idolatry, as much as
any.
Timber, or Discoveries made upon Men and Mat-
ter (1641). **De Shakespeare Nostrati. Augustus in**
Haterium. See 117:4

9 Have you seen but a bright lily grow,
    Before rude hands have touch'd it?
Have you mark'd but the fall o' the snow

Before the soil hath smutch'd it?...
O so white! O so soft! O so sweet is she!
The Underwood (1640). **Celebration of Charis, iv**
Her Triumph

10 Come, my Celia, let us prove,
While we can, the sports of love.
Volpone (1605), III.v. See 65:5

11 Suns, that set, may rise again;
But if once we lose this light,
'Tis with us perpetual night.

12 His censure of the English poets wa
this...
That Donne...deserved hanging.
That Shakespeare wanted Art.
Conversations with William Drummond o
Hawthornden (1619), III

JOHN JORTIN 1698–1770

13 *Palmam qui meruit, ferat.*
Let him who has won it bear the palm.
Lusus Poetici (1722): **Ad Ventos.** Adopted a
motto by Lord Nelson.

BENJAMIN JOWETT 1817–1893

14 At Oxford, as you know, we follow the
Cambridge lead, sometimes with uncertain
steps.
Letter to Professor Marshall, 5 Jan. 1886

15 My dear child, you must believe in God in
spite of what the clergy tell you.
Private conversation with Margot Asquith
shortly after the near-fatal illness a year before
his death. Asquith, *Autobiography*, ch.8

JAMES JOYCE 1882–1941

16 riverrun, past Eve and Adam's, from
swerve of shore to bend of bay, brings us
by a commodius vicus of recirculation
back to Howth Castle and Environs.
Finnegans Wake (1939), standard edition. Opening words.

17 If you don't like my story get out of the
punt.
p.206

18 All moanday, tearsday, wailsday, thumpsday, frightday, shatterday.
p.301

19 Three quarks for Muster Mark!
p.383

20 Soft morning, city!
p.619

21 Poor Parnell! he cried loudly. My dead
King!
A Portrait of the Artist as a Young Man (1916),
ch.1

1 Ireland is the old sow that eats her farrow.
ch.5

2 April 27. Old father, old artificer, stand
me now and ever in good stead.
closing words

3 The snotgreen sea. The scrotumtightening
sea.
Ulysses (1922). **Telemachus**

4 It is a symbol of Irish art. The cracked
lookingglass of a servant.

5 I fear those big words, Stephen said,
which make us so unhappy.
Nestor

6 History is a nightmare from which I am
trying to awake.

7 A base barreltone voice.
Lestrygonians

8 Greater love than this, he said, no man
hath that a man lay down his wife for a
friend. Go thou and do likewise. Thus, or
words to that effect, saith Zarathustra,
sometime regius professor of French letters to the University of Oxtail.
Oxen of the Sun

9 And I thought well as well him as another
and then I asked him with my eyes to ask
again yes and then he asked me would I
yes to say yes my mountain flower and
first I put my arms around him yes and
drew him down to me so he could feel my
breasts all perfume yes and his heart was
going like mad and yes I said yes I will Yes.
Penelope, closing words

EMPEROR JULIAN THE APOSTATE
c.332–363

0 *Vicisti, Galilaee.*
You have won, Galilean.
Supposed dying words; but a late embellishment
of Theodoret, *Hist. Eccles.*, iii.25

DAME JULIAN OF NORWICH
1343–1443

1 Sin is behovely, but all shall be well and all
shall be well and all manner of thing shall
be well.
Revelations of Divine Love, ch.27

2 Wouldest thou wit thy Lord's meaning in
this thing? Wit it well: Love was his meaning. Who shewed it thee? Love. What
shewed He thee? Love. Wherefore shewed
it He? for Love…Thus was I learned that
Love is our Lord's meaning.
ch.86

JUVENAL A.D. c.60–c.130

13 *Difficile est saturam non scribere.*
It's hard not to write satire.
Satires, i.30

14 *Si natura negat, facit indignatio versum.*
Even if nature says no, indignation makes
me write verse.
79

15 *Quidquid agunt homines, votum timor ira
voluptas
Gaudia discursus nostri farrago libelli est.*
Everything mankind does, their hope,
fear, rage, pleasure, joys, business, are
the hotch-potch of my little book.
85

16 *Nemo repente fuit turpissimus.*
No one ever suddenly became depraved.
ii.83

17 *Iam pridem Syrus in Tiberim defluxit
Orontes
Et linguam et mores.*
The Syrian Orontes has now for long been
pouring into the Tiber, with its own
language and ways of behaving.

18 *Grammaticus, rhetor, geometres, pictor,
aliptes,
Augur, schoenobates, medicus, magus, omnia novit
Graeculus esuriens: in caelum iusseris ibit.*
Scholar, public speaker, geometrician,
painter, physical training instructor,
diviner of the future, rope-dancer, doctor, magician, the hungry little Greek
can do everything: send him
to—Heaven (and he'll go there).
iii.76

19 *Haud facile emergunt quorum virtutibus
obstat
Res angusta domi.*
It's not easy for people to rise out of obscurity when they have to face
straitened circumstances at home.
164

20 *Rara avis in terris nigroque simillima
cycno.*
A rare bird on this earth, like nothing so
much as a black swan.
vi.165

21 *'Pone seram, cohibe.' Sed quis custodiet ipsos
Custodes? Cauta est et ab illis incipit uxor.*
'Bolt her in, keep her indoors.' But who is
to guard the guards themselves? Your
wife arranges accordingly and begins
with them.
347

1   *Tenet insanabile multos*
Scribendi cacoethes et aegro in corde sen-
    escit.
Many suffer from the incurable disease of
writing, and it becomes chronic in their
sick minds.
vii.51

2 *Occidit miseros crambe repetita magistros.*
That cabbage hashed up again and again
proves the death of the wretched teach-
ers.
154

3   *Verbosa et grandis epistula venit*
A Capreis.
A huge wordy letter came from Capri.
x.71. The Emperor Tiberius's letter to the Senate
that caused the downfall of Sejanus, A.D. 31.

4   *Duas tantum res anxius optat,*
Panem et circenses.
Only two things does he worry about or
long for—bread and the big match.
80. Of the citizen these days.

5 *Orandum est ut sit mens sana in corpore*
    sano.
You should pray to have a sound mind in
a sound body.
356

IMMANUEL KANT 1724–1804

6 Two things fill the mind with ever new and
increasing wonder and awe, the more often
and the more seriously reflection concentrates upon them: the starry heaven above
me and the moral law within me.
Critique of Practical Reason, conclusion

7 *Dieser Imperativ ist kategorisch...Dieser*
Imperativ mag der der Sittlichkeit heissen.
This imperative is Categorical...This im-
perative may be called that of Morality.
Grundlegung zur Metaphysik der Sitten, trans.
T.K. Abbot, Section II

8 *Wer den Zweck will, will (so fern die Ver-*
nunft auf seine Handlungen entscheidenden
Einfluss hat) auch das dazu unentbehrlich
notwendige Mittel, das in seiner Gewalt ist.
Whoever wills the end, wills also (so far as
reason decides his conduct) the means in
his power which are indispensably necessary thereto.

9 *Handle so, dass du die Menschheit, sowohl*
in deiner Person, als in der Person eines
jeden andern, jederzeit zugleich als Zweck,
niemals bloss als Mittel brauchest.
So act as to treat humanity, whether in
thine own person or in that of any other, in
every case as an end withal, never as means
only.

10 *Aus so krummem Holze, als woraus de*
Mensch gemacht ist, kann nichts ganz ge
rades gezimmert werden.
Out of the crooked timber of humanity n
straight thing can ever be made.
Idee zu einer allgemeinen Geschichte in weltbür
gerlicher Absicht

ALPHONSE KARR 1808–1890

11 *Plus ça change, plus c'est la même chose.*
The more things change, the more they ar
the same.
Les Guêpes, Jan. 1849. vi

12 *Si l'on veut abolir la peine de mort en c*
cas, que MM les assassins commencent.
If we are to abolish the death penalty,
should like to see the first step taken b
our friends the murderers.

CHRISTOPH KAUFMANN 1753–1795

13 *Sturm und Drang.*
Storm and stress.
Phrase suggested to F.M. Klinger (1752–1831
as a better title for his play originally called *De*
Wirrwarr; the suggestion was adopted, the pla
produced in 1777, and a literary period was thu
named.

DENIS KEARNEY 1847–1907

14 Horny-handed sons of toil.
Speech, San Francisco, c.1878

JOHN KEATS 1795–1821

15 A thing of beauty is a joy for ever:
Its loveliness increases; it will never
Pass into nothingness.
Endymion (1818), bk.i, l.1

16 St Agnes' Eve—Ah, bitter chill it was!
The owl, for all his feathers, was a-cold;
The hare limp'd trembling through the
    frozen grass,
And silent was the flock in woolly fold.
The Eve of Saint Agnes, 1

17 The silver, snarling trumpets 'gan to
chide.
4

18 A casement high and triple-arch'd there
    was,
All garlanded with carven imag'ries
Of fruits, and flowers, and bunches o
    knot-grass,
And diamonded with panes of quaint de-
    vice,
Innumerable of stains and splendid dyes,
As are the tiger-moth's deep-damask'd
    wings.
24

1 And they are gone: aye, ages long ago
  These lovers fled away into the storm.
  42

2 Ever let the fancy roam,
  Pleasure never is at home.
  Fancy, l.1

3 Oh, what can ail thee, Knight at arms
    Alone and palely loitering;
  The sedge is wither'd from the lake,
    And no birds sing.
  La Belle Dame Sans Merci

4 I see a lily on thy brow,
    With anguish moist and fever dew;
  And on thy cheek a fading rose
    Fast withereth too.

  I met a lady in the meads
    Full beautiful, a faery's child;
  Her hair was long, her foot was light,
    And her eyes were wild.

5 She look'd at me as she did love,
    And made sweet moan.

6 And there I shut her wild, wild eyes
    With kisses four.

7   'La belle Dame sans Merci
      Hath thee in thrall!'

8 Love in a hut, with water and a crust,
  Is—Love, forgive us!—cinders, ashes,
    dust;
  Love in a palace is perhaps at last
  More grievous torment than a hermit's
    fast.
  Lamia, pt.ii, l.1

9 Philosophy will clip an Angel's wings.
  l.234

10 Souls of poets dead and gone,
   What Elysium have ye known,
   Happy field or mossy cavern,
   Choicer than the Mermaid Tavern?
   Have ye tippled drink more fine
   Than mine host's Canary wine?
   Lines on the Mermaid Tavern

11 Bards of Passion and of Mirth,
   Ye have left your souls on earth!
   Have ye souls in heaven too?
   Ode. Written on the blank page before Beau-
   mont and Fletcher's *Fair Maid of the Inn.*

12 Thou still unravish'd bride of quietness,
    Thou foster-child of silence and slow
      time.
   Ode on a Grecian Urn

13 Heard melodies are sweet, but those un-
     heard
     Are sweeter; therefore, ye soft pipes,
       play on;

Not to the sensual ear, but, more endear'd,
  Pipe to the spirit ditties of no tone.

14 For ever wilt thou love, and she be fair!

15 O Attic shape! Fair attitude!

16 'Beauty is truth, truth beauty,'—that is all
    Ye know on earth, and all ye need to
      know.

17 Or if thy mistress some rich anger shows,
    Emprison her soft hand and let her rave,
    And feed deep, deep upon her peerless
      eyes.

  She dwells with Beauty—Beauty that must
    die;
  And Joy, whose hand is ever at his lips
  Bidding adieu; and aching Pleasure nigh,
    Turning to Poison while the bee-mouth
      sips.
  Ode on Melancholy

18 My heart aches, and a drowsy numbness
     pains
     My sense, as though of hemlock I had
       drunk.
   Ode to a Nightingale

19 O for a beaker full of the warm South,
    Full of the true, the blushful Hippo-
      crene,
      With beaded bubbles winking at the
        brim,
        And purple-stained mouth;
    That I might drink, and leave the world
      unseen,
      And with thee fade away into the
        forest dim.

  Fade far away, dissolve, and quite forget
    What thou among the leaves hast never
      known,
  The weariness, the fever, and the fret,
    Here, where men sit and hear each other
      groan.

20 Already with thee! tender is the night,
    And haply the Queen-Moon is on her
      throne,
      Clustered around by all her starry
        Fays.

21 The coming musk-rose, full of dewy wine,
   The murmurous haunt of flies on sum-
     mer eves.

22 Darkling I listen; and, for many a time
    I have been half in love with easeful
      Death,
    Call'd him soft names in many a mused
      rhyme,
    To take into the air my quiet breath;
    Now more than ever seems it rich to die,
      To cease upon the midnight with no
        pain,

While thou art pouring forth thy soul
abroad
In such an ecstasy!
Still wouldst thou sing, and I have ears
in vain—
To thy high requiem become a sod.

1 Thou wast not born for death, immortal
Bird!
No hungry generations tread thee down;
The voice I hear this passing night was
heard
In ancient days by emperor and clown:
Perhaps the self-same song that found a
path
Through the sad heart of Ruth, when
sick for home,
She stood in tears amid the alien corn;
The same that oft-times hath
Charm'd magic casements, opening on
the foam
Of perilous seas, in faery lands for-
lorn.

Forlorn! the very word is like a bell
To toll me back from thee to my sole
self!
Adieu! the fancy cannot cheat so well
As she is fam'd to do, deceiving elf.
Adieu! adieu! thy plaintive anthem fades
Past the near meadows, over the still
stream,
Up the hill-side; and now 'tis buried
deep
In the next valley-glades:
Was it a vision, or a waking dream?
Fled is that music:—Do I wake or
sleep?

2 I had a dove and the sweet dove died;
And I have thought it died of grieving:
O, what could it grieve for? Its feet were
tied,
With a silken thread of my own hand's
weaving.
Song

3 Much have I travell'd in the realms of
gold,
And many goodly states and kingdoms
seen.
**Sonnets. On First Looking into Chapman's
Homer**

4 Then felt I like some watcher of the skies
When a new planet swims into his ken;
Or like stout Cortez when with eagle eyes
He star'd at the Pacific—and all his men
Look'd at each other with a wild sur-
mise—
Silent, upon a peak in Darien.

5 Aye on the shores of darkness there is
light,

And precipices show untrodden green,
There is a budding morrow in midnight,
There is a triple sight in blindness keen.
To Homer

6 Glory and loveliness have pass'd away.
To Leigh Hunt. Dedication of *Poems*, 1817

7 To one who has been long in city pent;
'Tis very sweet to look into the fair
And open face of heaven.
To One Who Has Been Long

8 Turn the key deftly in the oiled wards,
And seal the hushed Casket of my Soul.
To Sleep

9 When I have fears that I may cease to be
Before my pen has glean'd my teeming
brain.
When I Have Fears

10 Then on the shore
Of the wide world I stand alone, and think
Till love and fame to nothingness do sink.

11 In a drear-nighted December,
Too happy tree,
Thy branches ne'er remember
Their green felicity.
Stanzas

12 Season of mists and mellow fruitfulness,
Close bosom-friend of the maturing
sun;
Conspiring with him how to load and bless
With fruit the vines that round the
thatch-eaves run.
To Autumn

13 Who hath not seen thee oft amid thy
store?
Sometimes whoever seeks abroad may
find
Thee sitting careless on a granary floor,
Thy hair soft-lifted by the winnowing
wind;
Or on a half-reap'd furrow sound asleep,
Drows'd with the fume of poppies, while
thy hook
Spares the next swath and all its
twined flowers.

14 Where are the songs of Spring? Ay, where
are they?
Think not of them, thou hast thy music
too.

15 I am certain of nothing but the holiness of
the heart's affections and the truth of
imagination—what the imagination seizes
as beauty must be truth—whether it existed before or not.
Letters. To Benjamin Bailey, 22 Nov. 1817

16 Negative Capability, that is, when a man

is capable of being in uncertainties, mysteries, doubts, without any irritable reaching after fact and reason.
To G. and T. Keats, 21 Dec. 1817

1 There is nothing stable in the world; uproar's your only music.
To G. and T. Keats, 13 Jan. 1818

2 It is impossible to live in a country which is continually under hatches...Rain! Rain! Rain!
To J.H. Reynolds, 10 Apr. 1818 (from Devon)

3 I wish I could say Tom was any better. His identity presses upon me so all day that I am obliged to go out.
Of his youngest brother. To C.W. Dilke, 21 Sept. 1818

4 There is an awful warmth about my heart like a load of immortality.
To J.H. Reynolds, 22 Sept. 1818

5 I think I shall be among the English Poets after my death.
To George and Georgiana Keats, 14 Oct. 1818

6 My friends should drink a dozen of Claret on my Tomb.
To Benjamin Bailey, 14 Aug. 1819

7 You, I am sure, will forgive me for sincerely remarking that you might curb your magnanimity, and be more of an artist, and load every rift of your subject with ore.
To Shelley, Aug. 1820

8 Here lies one whose name was writ in water.
Epitaph. Lord Houghton, *Life of Keats*, ii.91

JOHN KEBLE 1792-1866

9 The trivial round, the common task,
Would furnish all we ought to ask;
Room to deny ourselves; a road
To bring us, daily, nearer God.
The Christian Year (1827). **Morning**

10 There is a book, who runs may read,
Which heavenly truth imparts,
And all the lore its scholars need,
Pure eyes and Christian hearts.
Septuagesima

11 The voice that breathed o'er Eden.
Holy Matrimony

GEORGE KEITH, 5th EARL MARISCHAL 1553-1623

12 They haif said: Quhat say they? Lat thame say.
Motto of the Earls Marischal of Scotland, inscribed at Marischal College, founded by the

fifth Earl at Aberdeen in 1593. A similarly defiant motto in Greek has been found engraved in remains from classical antiquity.

THOMAS À KEMPIS
See THOMAS

JOHN FITZGERALD KENNEDY 1917-1963

13 And so, my fellow Americans: ask not what your country can do for you—ask what you can do for your country. My fellow citizens of the world: ask not what America will do for you, but what together we can do for the freedom of man.
Inaugural address, 20 Jan. 1961. Not the first use of this form of words: a similiar exhortation may be found in the funeral oration for John Greenleaf Whittier.

14 All free men, wherever they may live, are citizens of Berlin. And therefore, as a free man, I take pride in the words *Ich bin ein Berliner*.
Speech at City Hall, West Berlin, 26 June 1963

FRANCIS SCOTT KEY 1779-1843

15 'Tis the star-spangled banner; O long may it wave
O'er the land of the free, and the home of the brave!
The Star-Spangled Banner (1814)

J.M. KEYNES 1883-1946

16 The important thing for Government is not to do things which individuals are doing already, and to do them a little better or a little worse; but to do those things which at present are not done at all.
The End of Laisser-Faire (1926), IV. See 178:15

17 I think that Capitalism, wisely managed, can probably be made more efficient for attaining economic ends than any alternative system yet in sight, but that in itself it is in many ways extremely objectionable.
V

18 This goat-footed bard, this half-human visitor to our age from the hag-ridden magic and enchanted woods of Celtic antiquity. [Lloyd George.]
Essays and Sketches in Biography (1933)

19 There are the *Trade-Unionists*, once the oppressed, now the tyrants, whose selfish and sectional pretensions need to be bravely opposed.
Liberalism and Labour (1926)

20 For him [Keynes] the short run was much more significant than the long run—that

long run in which, as he used to say, 'we are all dead'.
A.C. Pigou, *Proceedings of the British Academy*, v.32, p.13

[ALFRED] JOYCE KILMER 1886–1918

1 I think that I shall never see
A poem lovely as a tree.
Trees (1914)

2 Poems are made by fools like me,
But only God can make a tree.

REVD. FRANCIS KILVERT 1840–1879

3 Of all noxious animals, too, the most noxious is a tourist. And of all tourists the most vulgar, ill-bred, offensive and loathsome is the British tourist.
Diary, 5 Apr. 1870

4 The Vicar of St Ives says the smell of fish there is sometimes so terrific as to stop the church clock.
21 July 1870

BENJAMIN FRANKLIN KING 1857–1894

5 Nothing to do but work,
Nothing to eat but food,
Nothing to wear but clothes
To keep one from going nude.
The Pessimist

BISHOP HENRY KING 1592–1669

6 But hark! My pulse like a soft drum
Beats my approach, tells thee I come.
The Exequy

REVD. MARTIN LUTHER KING 1929–1968

7 A riot is at bottom the language of the unheard.
Chaos or Community (1967), ch.4

8 I have a dream that one day this nation will rise up, live out the true meaning of its creed: we hold these truths to be self-evident, that all men are created equal.
Washington, 27 Aug. 1963. The phrase 'I have a dream' was used by him in other speeches during the summer of that year.

CHARLES KINGSLEY 1819–1875

9 Be good, sweet maid, and let who can be clever;
Do lovely things, not dream them, all day long;
And so make Life, and Death, and that For Ever,

One grand sweet song.
A Farewell. To C.E.G.

10 What we can we will be,
Honest Englishmen.
Do the work that's nearest,
Though it's dull at whiles,
Helping, when we meet them,
Lame dogs over stiles.
Letter to Thomas Hughes

11 Welcome, wild North-easter!
Shame it is to see
Odes to every zephyr;
Ne'er a verse to thee.
Ode to the North-East Wind

12 'O Mary, go and call the cattle home,
And call the cattle home,
And call the cattle home,
Across the sands of Dee.'
The western wind was wild and dank with foam,
And all alone went she.
The Sands of Dee

13 Three fishers went sailing away to the west,
Away to the west as the sun went down;
Each thought on the woman who loved him best,
And the children stood watching them out of the town.
The Three Fishers

14 For men must work, and women must weep.

15 I once had a sweet little doll, dears
The prettiest doll in the world;
Her cheeks were so red and so white dears,
And her hair was so charmingly curled.
Songs from *The Water Babies* (1863). **My Little Doll**

16 When all the world is young, lad,
And all the trees are green;
And every goose a swan, lad,
And every lass a queen;
Then hey for boot and horse, lad,
And round the world away:
Young blood must have its course, lad,
And every dog his day.
Young and Old

17 We have used the Bible as if it was a constable's handbook—an opium-dose for keeping beasts of burden patient while they are being overloaded.
Letters to the Chartists, no.2. See 162:7

18 Mrs Bedonebyasyoudid is coming.
The Water Babies (1863), ch.5

19 The loveliest fairy in the world; and he

name is Mrs Doasyouwouldbedoneby.

1 More ways of killing a cat than choking her with cream.
Westward Ho! (1855), ch.20

2 Some say that the age of chivalry is past, that the spirit of romance is dead. The age of chivalry is never past, so long as there is a wrong left unredressed on earth.
Mrs C. Kingsley, *Life* (1079), vol.ii, ch.28

HUGH KINGSMILL 1889–1949

3 What, still alive at twenty-two,
A clean upstanding chap like you?
Sure, if your throat 'tis hard to slit,
Slit your girl's, and swing for it.
Two Poems after A.E. Housman, 1

4 But bacon's not the only thing
That's cured by hanging from a string.

5 'Tis Summer Time on Bredon,
And now the farmers swear;
The cattle rise and listen
In valleys far and near,
And blush at what they hear.

But when the mists in autumn
On Bredon top are thick,
The happy hymns of farmers
Go up from fold and rick,
The cattle then are sick.
2

RUDYARD KIPLING 1865–1936

6 When you've shouted 'Rule Britannia', when you've sung 'God save the Queen',
When you've finished killing Kruger with your mouth.
The Absent-Minded Beggar

7 He's an absent-minded beggar, and his weaknesses are great.

8 Duke's son—cook's son—son of a hundred Kings—
(Fifty thousand horse and foot going to Table Bay!)

9 Oh, East is East, and West is West, and never the twain shall meet,
Till Earth and Sky stand presently at God's great Judgment Seat;
But there is neither East nor West, Border, nor Breed, nor Birth,
When two strong men stand face to face, though they come from the ends of earth!
The Ballad of East and West

0 Ah! What avails the classic bent
And what the cultured word,

Against the undoctored incident
That actually occurred?
The Benefactors. See 148:12

11 And a woman is only a woman, but a good cigar is a Smoke.
The Betrothed

12 'Oh, where are you going to, all you Big Steamers,
With England's own coal, up and down the salt seas?'
'We are going to fetch you your bread and your butter,
Your beef, pork, and mutton, eggs, apples, and cheese.'
Big Steamers

13 We're   foot—slog—slog—slog—sloggin' over Africa—
Foot—foot—foot—foot—sloggin' over Africa—
(Boots—boots—boots—boots—movin' up an' down again!)
There's no discharge in the war!
Boots. See 27:11

14 These were our children who died for our lands...
    But who shall return us the children?
The Children

15 Land of our birth, we pledge to thee
Our love and toil in the years to be;
When we are grown and take our place,
As men and women with our race.
The Children's Song

16 Gold is for the mistress—silver for the maid—
Copper for the craftsman cunning at his trade.
'Good!' said the Baron, sitting in his hall,
'But Iron—Cold Iron—is master of them all.'
Cold Iron

17 They've taken of 'is buttons off an' cut 'is stripes away,
An' they're hangin' Danny Deever in the mornin'.'
Danny Deever

18 Winds of the World, give answer! They are whimpering to and fro—
And what should they know of England who only England know?
The English Flag

19 I could not look on Death, which being known,
Men led me to him, blindfold and alone.
Epitaphs of the War. The Coward

20 When the Himalayan peasant meets the he-bear in his pride,

He shouts to scare the monster, who will
   often turn aside.
But the she-bear thus accosted rends the
   peasant tooth and nail
For the female of the species is more deadly than the male.
The Female of the Species

1 Gentleman-rankers out on the spree,
   Damned from here to Eternity,
   God ha' mercy on such as we,
      Baa! Yah! Bah!
Gentleman-Rankers

2 Our England is a garden that is full of
      stately views,
   Of borders, beds and shrubberies and
      lawns and avenues,
   With statues on the terraces and peacocks
      strutting by;
   But the Glory of the Garden lies in more
      than meets the eye.
The Glory of the Garden

3 Our England is a garden, and such gar-
      dens are not made
   By singing:—'Oh, how beautiful!' and sit-
      ting in the shade,
   While better men than we go out and start
      their working lives
   At grubbing weeds from gravel paths with
      broken dinner-knives.

4 Oh, Adam was a gardener, and God who
      made him sees
   That half a proper gardener's work is done
      upon his knees.

5 Though I've belted you an' flayed you,
   By the livin' Gawd that made you,
   You're a better man than I am, Gunga
      Din!
Gunga Din

6 What is a woman that you forsake her,
   And the hearth-fire and the home-acre,
   To go with the old grey Widow-maker?
Harp Song of the Dane Women

7 If you can keep your head when all about
      you
      Are losing theirs and blaming it on you,
   If you can trust yourself when all men
      doubt you,
      But make allowance for their doubting
      too;
   If you can wait and not be tired by waiting,
      Or being lied about, don't deal in lies,
   Or being hated, don't give way to hating,
      And yet don't look too good, nor talk
      too wise:

   If you can dream—and not make dreams
      your master;
      If you can think—and not make

thoughts your aim;
If you can meet with Triumph and Disas
   ter
   And treat those two impostors just the
   same.
If—

8 If you can make one heap of all you
      winnings
   And risk it on one turn of pitch-and-
      toss,
   And lose, and start again at your begin
      nings
   And never breathe a word about you
      loss.

9 If you can talk with crowds and keep you
      virtue,
   Or walk with Kings—nor lose the com
      mon touch,
   If neither foes nor loving friends can hur
      you,
   If all men count with you, but none too
      much;
   If you can fill the unforgiving minute
      With sixty seconds' worth of distance
      run,
   Yours is the Earth and everything that's i
      it,
   And—which is more—you'll be a Man
      my son!

10 There are nine and sixty ways of con
      structing tribal lays,
   And—every—single—one—of—them—is
      —right!
In the Neolithic Age

11 Then ye returned to your trinkets; then ye
      contented your souls
   With the flannelled fools at the wicket o
      the muddied oafs at the goals.
The Islanders

12 The Camel's hump is an ugly lump
   Which well you may see at the Zoo;
   But uglier yet is the Hump we get
   From having too little to do.
Just-So Stories (1902). **How the Camel Got Hi
Hump**

13 The cure for this ill is not to sit still,
   Or frowst with a book by the fire;
   But to take a large hoe and a shovel also,
   And dig till you gently perspire.

14 I keep six honest serving-men
      (They taught me all I knew);
   Their names are What and Why and When
      And How and Where and Who.
I keep six honest serving-men

15 I've taken my fun where I've found it,
   An' now I must pay for my fun,
   For the more you 'ave known o' the others

The less will you settle to one;
An' the end of it's sittin' and thinkin',
An' dreamin' Hell-fires to see.
So be warned by my lot (which I know you
   will not),
An' learn about women from me!
The Ladies

1 For the Colonel's Lady an' Judy O'Grady
   Are sisters under their skins!

2 Now this is the Law of the Jungle—as old
   and as true as the sky;
   And the Wolf that shall keep it may
   prosper, but the Wolf that shall break
   it must die.
   The Law of the Jungle

3 Come you back to Mandalay,
   Where the old Flotilla lay:
   Can't you 'ear their paddles chunkin' from
   Rangoon to Mandalay?
   On the road to Mandalay,
   Where the flyin'-fishes play,
   An' the dawn comes up like thunder outer
   China 'crost the Bay!
   Mandalay

4 Ship me somewheres east of Suez, where
   the best is like the worst,
   Where there aren't no Ten Commandments, an' a man can raise a thirst:
   For the temple-bells are callin', an' it's
   there that I would be—
   By the old Moulmein Pagoda, looking lazy
   at the sea.

5 If I were hanged on the highest hill,
   Mother o' mine, O mother o' mine!
   I know whose love would follow me still,
   Mother o' mine, O mother o' mine!
   Mother O' Mine

6 And the epitaph drear: 'A Fool lies here
   who tried to hustle the East.'
   The Naulahka (1892), heading of ch.5

7 A Nation spoke to a Nation,
   A Throne sent word to a Throne:
   'Daughter am I in my mother's house,
   But mistress in my own.
   Our Lady of the Snows

8 The toad beneath the harrow knows
   Exactly where each tooth-point goes;
   The butterfly upon the road
   Preaches contentment to that toad.
   Pagett M.P.

9 Brothers and Sisters, I bid you beware
   Of giving your heart to a dog to tear.
   The Power of the Dog

10 God of our fathers, known of old,
   Lord of our far-flung battle-line,
   Beneath whose awful Hand we hold

Dominion over palm and pine—
Lord God of Hosts, be with us yet,
Lest we forget—lest we forget!

The tumult and the shouting dies;
The Captains and the Kings depart:
Still stands Thine ancient sacrifice,
An humble and a contrite heart.
Lord God of Hosts, be with us yet,
Lest we forget—lest we forget!
Recessional (1897)

11 Lo, all our pomp of yesterday
   Is one with Nineveh and Tyre!

12 If, drunk with sight of power, we loose
   Wild tongues that have not Thee in awe,
   Such boastings as the Gentiles use,
   Or lesser breeds without the Law.

13 And I've lost Britain, and I've lost Gaul,
   And I've lost Rome and, worst of all,
   I've lost Lalage!
   Rimini

14 Shillin' a day,
   Bloomin' good pay—
   Lucky to touch it, a shillin' a day!
   Shillin' a Day

15 Them that asks no questions isn't told a
   lie.
   Watch the wall, my darling, while the Gen-
   tlemen go by!
       Five and twenty ponies,
       Trotting through the dark—
       Brandy for the Parson,
       'Baccy for the Clerk;
   Laces for a lady, letters for a spy,
   Watch the wall, my darling, while the Gen-
   tlemen go by!
   A Smuggler's Song

16 Through the Jungle very softly flits a
   shadow and a sigh—
   He is Fear, O Little Hunter, he is Fear!
   The Song of the Little Hunter

17 Mithras, God of the Morning, our trumpets waken the Wall!
   'Rome is above the Nations, but Thou art
   over all!'
   A Song to Mithras

18 God gives all men all earth to love,
   But, since man's heart is small,
   Ordains for each one spot shall prove
   Belovèd over all.
   Each to his choice, and I rejoice
   The lot has fallen to me
   In a fair ground—in a fair ground—
   Yea, Sussex by the sea!
   Sussex. See 188:11

19 Oh, it's Tommy this, an' Tommy that, an'
   'Tommy, go away';

But it's 'Thank you, Mister Atkins,' when
the band begins to play.
Tommy

1 Then it's Tommy this, an' Tommy that,
an' 'Tommy 'ow's yer soul?'
But it's 'Thin red line of 'eroes' when the
drums begin to roll.

2 Of all the trees that grow so fair,
Old England to adorn,
Greater are none beneath the Sun,
Than Oak, and Ash, and Thorn.
A Tree Song. The association of these trees is
traditional

3 Ellum she hateth mankind and waiteth
Till every gust be laid
To drop a limb on the head of him
That anyway trusts her shade.

4 A fool there was and he made his prayer
(Even as you and I!)
To a rag and a bone and a hank of hair
(We called her the woman who did not
care)
But the fool he called her his lady fair—
(Even as you and I!)
The Vampire

5 They shut the road through the woods
Seventy years ago.
The Way Through the Woods

6 When 'Omer smote 'is bloomin' lyre,
'E'd 'eard men sing by land an' sea;
An' what 'e thought 'e might require,
'E went an' took—the same as me!
When 'Omer Smote. (Barrack-Room Ballads
(1892): Introduction)

7 Take up the White Man's burden—
Send forth the best ye breed—
Go, bind your sons to exile
To serve your captives' need;
To wait in heavy harness
On fluttered folk and wild—
Your new-caught, sullen peoples,
Half-devil and half-child.
The White Man's Burden

8 'Ave you 'eard o' the Widow at Windsor
With a hairy gold crown on 'er 'ead?
She 'as ships on the foam—she 'as millions
at 'ome,
An' she pays us poor beggars in red.
The Widow at Windsor

9 Down to Gehenna or up to the Throne,
He travels the fastest who travels alone.
The Winners

10 Good hunting!
The Jungle Book (1894). **Kaa's Hunting**

11 We be of one blood, thou and I.

12 He was a man of infinite-resource-and-
sagacity.
Just So Stories (1902). **How the Whale Got His
Throat**

13 Most 'scruciating idle.
How the Camel Got His Hump

14 There lived a Parsee from whose hat the
rays of the sun were reflected in more-
than-oriental-splendour.
How the Rhinoceros Got His Skin

15 An Elephant's Child—who was full of
'satiable curtiosity.
The Elephant's Child

16 The great grey-green, greasy Limpopo
River, all set about with fever-trees.

17 He walked by himself, and all places were
alike to him.
The Cat That Walked by Himself

18 He went back through the Wet Wild
Woods, waving his wild tail, and walking
by his wild lone. But he never told anybody.

19 The mad all are in God's keeping.
Kim (1901), ch.2

20 She was as immutable as the Hills. But not
quite so green.
Plain Tales from the Hills (1888). **Venus Anno-
domini**

21 Lalun is a member of the most ancient
profession in the world.
Soldiers Three (1888). **On the City Wall**

22 Being kissed by a man who didn't wax his
moustache was—like eating an egg without salt.
The Gadsbys. Poor Dear Mamma

23 Steady the Buffs.

24 I gloat! Hear me gloat!
Stalky & Co. (1899). **The Ambush**

25 A Jelly-bellied Flag-flapper.
The Flag of Their Country

26 'Tisn't beauty, so to speak, nor good talk
necessarily. It's just IT. Some women'll
stay in a man's memory if they once walked down a street.
Traffics and Discoveries (1904). **Mrs. Bathurst**

27 Gawd knows, an' 'E won't split on a pal.
Wee Willie Winkie (1888). **Drums of the Fore and
Aft**

28 A Soldier of the Great War Known unto
God.
Inscription on gravestones above unidentified
bodies, chosen by Kipling as literary adviser for
the Imperial War Graves Commission, 1919.
Gavin Stamp (ed.), *Silent Cities* (1977), p.13

29 Power without responsibility—the prero-

gative of the harlot throughout the ages.
In conversation with Max Aitken (Lord Beaver-brook); later used by Stanley Baldwin. See Lord Baldwin, *Address to the Kipling Society*, Oct. 1971

PAUL KLEE 1879–1940

1 An *active* line on a walk moving freely, without goal. A walk for a walk's sake.
Pedagogical Sketchbook (1925), 1.1

FRIEDRICH KLOPSTOCK 1724–1803

2 God and I both knew what it meant once; now God alone knows.
C. Lombroso, *The Man of Genius* (1891), pt.I, ch.2. Also attr. to Browning in the form 'When [*Sordello*] was written, God and Robert Browning knew what it meant; now only God knows.'

MARY KNOWLES 1733–1807

3 He [Dr. Johnson] gets at the substance of a book directly; he tears out the heart of it.
Boswell's *Johnson* (ed. 1934), vol.iii, p.284. 15 Apr. 1778

JOHN KNOX 1505–1572

4 The First Blast of the Trumpet Against the Monstrous Regiment of Women.
Title of Pamphlet, 1558

MGR. RONALD KNOX 1888–1957

5 There once was a man who said 'God
Must think it exceedingly odd
    If he finds that this tree
    Continues to be
When there's no one about in the Quad.'
Attr. Langford Reed, *The Limerick Book*. For the answer see 3:9

6 Evangelical vicar, in want of a portable, second-hand font, would dispose, for the same, of a portrait, in frame, of the bishop, elect, of Vermont.
Advertisement placed in a newspaper. See W.S. Baring-Gould, *The Lure of the Limerick*, pt.I.ch.1.n.5

VICESIMUS KNOX 1752–1821

7 That learning belongs not to the female character, and that the female mind is not capable of a degree of improvement equal to that of the other sex, are narrow and unphilosophical prejudices.
Essays, vol.3, 142. (*The British Essayists* (1823), vol.37)

8 Can anything be more absurd than keeping women in a state of ignorance, and yet so vehemently to insist on their resisting

temptation?
See Mary Wollstonecraft, *A Vindication of the Rights of Woman* (1792)

THOMAS KYD 1558?–1594?

9 What outcries pluck me from my naked bed?
The Spanish Tragedy (1592), II.v.1

10 Why then I'll fit you,
IV.i.69

JEAN DE LA FONTAINE 1621–1695

11 *Aide-toi, le ciel t'aidera.*
Help yourself, and heaven will help you.
Fables (1668), vi.18. **Le Chartier Embourbé**

12 *Je plie et ne romps pas.*
I bend and I break not.
i.22. **Le Chêne et le Roseau**

13 *Il connaît l'univers et ne se connaît pas.*
He knows the world and does not know himself.
(1678–9), viii.26. **Démocrite et les Abdéritains**

14 *La raison du plus fort est toujours la meilleure.*
The reason of the strongest is always the best.
i.10. **Le Loup et l'Agneau**

JULES LAFORGUE 1860–1887

15 *Ah! que la vie est quotidienne.*
Oh, what a day-to-day business life is.
Complainte sur certains ennuis (1885)

ALPHONSE DE LAMARTINE 1790–1869

16 *Un seul être vous manque, et tout est dépeuplé.*
Only one being is wanting, and your whole world is bereft of people.
Premières Méditations poétiques (1820), **L'Isolement**

LADY CAROLINE LAMB 1785–1828

17 Mad, bad, and dangerous to know.
Of Byron, in her journal after their first meeting at a ball in March 1812. See Jenkins, *Lady Caroline Lamb* (1932), ch.6

CHARLES LAMB 1775–1834

18 The man must have a rare recipe for melancholy, who can be dull in Fleet Street.
The Londoner, in letter to Thomas Manning, 15 Feb. 1802

19 His face when he repeats his verses hath its ancient glory, an Archangel a little damaged. [Coleridge.]
Letter to Wordsworth, 26 Apr. 1816

1 When my sonnet was rejected, I ex-
claimed, 'Damn the age; I will write for
Antiquity!'
Letter to B.W. Procter, 22 Jan. 1829

2 Books of the true sort, not those things in
boards that moderns mistake for books—
what they club for at book clubs.
Letter to J. Gillman, 30 Nov. 1829

3 The greatest pleasure I know, is to do a
good action by stealth, and to have it
found out by accident.
Table Talk by the late Elia. *The Athenaeum,* 4
Jan. 1834

4 I have had playmates, I have had compan-
ions,
In my days of childhood, in my joyful
school-days,—
All, all are gone, the old familiar faces.
The Old Familiar Faces

5 I do not [know the lady]; but damn her at
a venture.
E.V. Lucas, *Charles Lamb* (1905), vol.i, p.320,
note

6 I noted one odd saying of Lamb's that 'the
last breath he drew in he wished might be
through a pipe and exhaled in a pun'.
Macready, *Journal,* 9 Jan. 1834

**JOHN GEORGE LAMBTON, FIRST
EARL OF DURHAM** 1792–1840

7 £40,000 a year a moderate income — such
a one as a man *might jog on with.*
The Creevey Papers (13 Sept. 1821), ii.32

WALTER SAVAGE LANDOR
1775–1864

8 I strove with none; for none was worth my
strife;
Nature I loved, and, next to Nature,
Art;
I warmed both hands before the fire of life;
It sinks, and I am ready to depart.
Finis

9 He says, *my reign is peace,* so slays
A thousand in the dead of night.
Are you all happy now? he says,
And those he leaves behind cry *quite.*
He swears he will have no contention,
And sets all nations by the ears;
He shouts aloud, *No intervention!*
Invades, and drowns them all in tears.
A Foreign Ruler (1863)

10 Past ruin'd Ilion Helen lives,
Alcestis rises from the shades;

Verse calls them forth; 'tis verse that gives
Immortal youth to mortal maids.
Ianthe

11 Ireland never was contented...
Say you so? You are demented.
Ireland was contented when
All could use the sword and pen,
And when Tara rose so high
That her turrets split the sky,
And about her courts were seen
Liveried Angels robed in green,
Wearing, by St Patrick's bounty,
Emeralds big as half a county.
The Last Fruit Off an Old Tree (1853), **Epigram**
LXXXIV

12 Ah, what avails the sceptred race!
Ah, what the form divine!
What every virtue, every grace!
Rose Aylmer, all were thine.
Rose Aylmer

13 How many verses have I thrown
Into the fire because the one
Peculiar word, the wanted most,
Was irrecoverably lost.
Verses Why Burnt

14 Clear writers, like fountains, do not seem
so deep as they are; the turbid look the
most profound.
Imaginary Conversations (1823). **Southey and
Porson**

15 Fleas know not whether they are upon the
body of a giant or upon one of ordinary
stature.

ANDREW LANG 1844–1912

16   And through the music of the languid
hours
They hear like Ocean on a western beach
The surge and thunder of the Odyssey.
As One That for a Weary Space has Lain

17 If the wild bowler thinks he bowls,
Or if the batsman thinks he's bowled,
They know not, poor misguided souls,
They too shall perish unconsoled.
I am the batsman and the bat,
I am the bowler and the ball,
The umpire, the pavilion cat,
The roller, pitch, and stumps, and all.
Brahma. See 96:3

JULIA S. LANG 1921–

18 Are you sitting comfortably? Then I'll be-
gin.
Preamble to children's story in *Listen With
Mother,* B.B.C. radio programme, from 1950

FREDERICK LANGBRIDGE 1849–1923

1 Two men look out through the same bars:
  One sees the mud, and one the stars.
  A Cluster of Quiet Thoughts (1896) (Religious
  Tract Society Publication)

WILLIAM LANGLAND 1330?–1400?

2 In a somer seson whan soft was the sonne.
  The Vision of William concerning Piers the Plow-
  man (ed. Skeat), B Text, Prologue, l.1

ARCHBISHOP STEPHEN LANGTON
d. 1228

3 *Veni, Sancte Spiritus,*
  Et emitte coelitus
  Lucis tuae radium.
  Come, Holy Spirit, and send out from
    heaven the beam of your light.
  The 'Golden Sequence' for Whitsunday. Attr.

LÂO TSE ?6th cent. B.C.

4 Heaven and Earth are not ruthful;
  To them the Ten Thousand Things are but
    as straw dogs.
  Tao-te-ching, 5. Tr. Arthur Waley. (The Ten
  Thousand Things: all life forms. Straw dogs:
  sacrificial tokens.)

PHILIP LARKIN 1922–

5 Nothing, like something, happens any-
    where.
  I Remember, I Remember

6 Perhaps being old is having lighted rooms
  Inside your head, and people in them, act-
    ing.
  People you know, yet can't quite name.
  The Old Fools

7 Why should I let the toad *work*
    Squat on my life?
  Can't I use my wit as a pitchfork
    And drive the brute off?
  Toads

DUC DE LA ROCHEFOUCAULD
1613–1680

8 *Dans l'adversité de nos meilleurs amis, nous*
  trouvons toujours quelque chose qui ne nous
  déplaît pas.
  In the misfortune of our best friends, we
  always find something which is not displeasing to us.
  Réflexions ou Maximes Morales (1665), 99

9 *Il y a de bons mariages, mais il n'y en a*
  point de délicieux.
  There are good marriages, but no delightful ones.
  Réflexions ou Sentences et Maximes Morales
  (1678), 113

10 *L'hypocrisie est un hommage que le vice*
   rend à la vertu.
   Hypocrisy is a tribute which vice pays to
   virtue.
   218

11 *L'absence diminue les médiocres passions,*
   et augmente les grandes, comme le vent
   éteint les bougies, et allume le feu.
   Absence diminishes commonplace passions and increases great ones, as the wind
   extinguishes candles and kindles fire.
   276. See 55:24. 102:7

12 *L'accent du pays où l'on est né demeure*
   dans l'esprit et dans le coeur comme dans le
   langage.
   The accent of one's birthplace lingers in
   the mind and in the heart as it does in one's
   speech.
   342

BISHOP HUGH LATIMER c.1485–1555

13 *Gutta cavat lapidem, non vi sed saepe*
   cadendo.
   The drop of rain maketh a hole in the
   stone, not by violence, but by oft falling.
   7th Sermon preached before Edward VI (1549).
   See Ovid, *Epistulae Ex Ponto,* IV.x.5

14 Be of good comfort Master Ridley, and
   play the man. We shall this day light such
   a candle by God's grace in England, as (I
   trust) shall never be put out.
   16 Oct. 1555. Foxe, *Actes and Monuments*
   (1562–3), 1570 edn., p.1937

D.H. LAWRENCE 1885–1930

15 To the Puritan all things are impure, as
   somebody says.
   Etruscan Places (1932). Cerveteri

16 How beastly the bourgeois is
   especially the male of the species.
   How beastly the bourgeois is

17 Not I, not I, but the wind that blows
     through me!
   Song of a man who has come through

18 Never trust the artist. Trust the tale. The
   proper function of a critic is to save the
   tale from the artist who created it.
   Studies in Classic American Literature (1924),
   ch.1

EMMA LAZARUS 1849–1887

19   Give me your tired, your
     poor,

Your huddled masses yearning to breathe free.
The New Colossus

STEPHEN LEACOCK 1869–1944

1 Lord Ronald...flung himself upon his horse and rode madly off in all directions.
Nonsense Novels (1911). **Gertrude the Governess**

EDWARD LEAR 1812–1888

2 There was an Old Man with a beard,
Who said, 'It is just as I feared!—
Two Owls and a Hen,
Four Larks and a Wren,
Have all built their nests in my beard!'
Book of Nonsense (1846)

3 There was an old man who said, 'Hush!
I perceive a young bird in this bush!'
When they said, 'Is it small?'
He replied, 'Not at all!
It is four times as big as the bush!'

4 'How pleasant to know Mr Lear!'
Who has written such volumes of stuff!
Some think him ill-tempered and queer,
But a few think him pleasant enough.
Nonsense Songs (1871), preface

5 He has ears, and two eyes, and ten fingers,
Leastways if you reckon two thumbs;
Long ago he was one of the singers,
But now he is one of the dumbs.

6 His body is perfectly spherical,
He weareth a runcible hat.

7 On the coast of Coromandel
Where the early pumpkins blow,
In the middle of the woods,
Lived the Yonghy-Bonghy-Bó.
Two old chairs, and half a candle;—
One old jug without a handle,—
These were all his worldly goods.
The Courtship of the Yonghy-Bonghy-Bó

8 I can merely be your friend.

9 And who so happy,—O who,
As the Duck and the Kangaroo?
The Duck and the Kangaroo

10 O My agéd Uncle Arly!
Sitting on a heap of Barley
Thro' the silent hours of night,—
Close beside a leafy thicket:—
On his nose there was a Cricket,—
In his hat a Railway-Ticket;—
(But his shoes were far too tight.)
Incidents in the Life of my Uncle Arly

11 Far and few, far and few,
Are the lands where the Jumblies live;
Their heads are green, and their hands are blue,

And they went to sea in a Sieve.
The Jumblies

12 In spite of all their friends could say,
On a winter's morn, on a stormy day,
In a Sieve they went to sea!

13 The Owl and the Pussy-Cat went to sea
In a beautiful pea-green boat.
They took some honey, and plenty money,
Wrapped up in a five-pound note.
The Owl looked up to the Stars above
And sang to a small guitar,
'Oh lovely Pussy! O Pussy, my love,
What a beautiful Pussy you are.'
The Owl and the Pussy-Cat

14 Pussy said to the Owl, 'You elegant fowl!
How charmingly sweet you sing!
O let us be married! too long we ha' tarried:
But what shall we do for a ring?'
They sailed away for a year and a day,
To the land where the Bong-tree grows
And there in a wood a Piggy-wig stood
With a ring at the end of his nose.

15 'Dear Pig, are you willing to sell for a shilling
Your ring?' Said the Piggy, 'I will.'

16 They dined on mince, and slices of quince
Which they ate with a runcible spoon;
And hand in hand, on the edge of the sand
They danced by the light of the moon.

17 Plumpskin, Plashkin, Pelican jill!
We think so then, and we thought so still!
The Pelican Chorus

18 The Pobble who has no toes
Had once as many as we;
When they said, 'Some day you may lose them all';—
He replied,—'Fish fiddle de-dee!'
The Pobble Who Has No Toes

19 He has gone to fish, for his Aunt Jobiska
Runcible Cat with crimson whiskers!

20 And she said, 'It's a fact the whole world knows,
That Pobbles are happier without their toes.'

21 Who, or why, or which, or what,
Is the Akond of Swat?
1888 edn. **The Akond of Swat**

22 There was an old man of Thermopylae,
Who never did anything properly;
But they said, 'If you choose
To boil eggs in your shoes,

You shall never remain in Thermopylae.'
One Hundred Nonsense Pictures and Rhymes

LE CORBUSIER 1887–1965

1 *La maison est une machine à habiter.*
A house is a living-machine.
Vers une architecture (1923), p.ix

ALEXANDRE AUGUSTE LEDRU-ROLLIN 1807–1874

2 *Eh! je suis leur chef, il fallait bien les suivre.*
Ah well! I am their leader, I really ought to follow them!
E. de Mirecourt, *Histoire Contemporaine* no.79, 'Ledru-Rollin' (1857)

HENRY LEE 1756–1818

3 A citizen, first in war, first in peace, and first in the hearts of his countrymen.
Resolutions Adopted by the Congress on the Death of Washington, 19 Dec. 1799; moved by John Marshall and misquoted in his *Life of Washington* as '...first in the hearts of his fellow citizens.'

NATHANIEL LEE 1653?–1692

4 When Greeks joined Greeks, then was the tug of war!
The Rival Queens (1677), IV.ii

V.I. LENIN 1870–1924

5 We shall now proceed to construct the socialist order.
Opening words of congress after the capture of the Winter Palace, 26 Oct. 1917, Trotsky, *History of the Russian Revolution,* ch.10

6 The substitution of the proletarian for the bourgeois state is impossible without a violent revolution.
State and Revolution, (1917), ch.1.4

7 Communism is Soviet power plus the electrification of the whole country.
Report at the eighth All-Russia Congress of Soviets on the work of the Council of People's Commissars, 22 Dec. 1920

SPEAKER WILLIAM LENTHALL 1591–1662

8 I have neither eye to see, nor tongue to speak here, but as the House is pleased to direct me.
4 Jan. 1642. Said to Charles I, who had asked if he saw any of the five M.P.s whom the King had ordered to be arrested. Rushworth, *Historical Collections* (1703–08), iv.238

G.E. LESSING 1729–1781

9 *Gestern liebt' ich,*
Heute leid' ich,
Morgen sterb' ich:
Dennoch denk' ich
Heut und morgen
Gern an gestern.
Yesterday I loved, today I suffer, tomorrow I die: but I still think fondly, today and tomorrow, of yesterday.
Lied aus dem Spanischen

ADA LEVERSON 1865–1936

10 The last gentleman in Europe.
Of Oscar Wilde. Wilde, *Letters to the Sphinx.* 'Reminiscences', 2

DUC DE LÉVIS 1764–1830

11 *Noblesse oblige.*
Nobility has its obligations.
Maximes et Réflexions, 1812 ed., Morale, 'Maximes et Préceptes', lxxiii

12 *Gouverner, c'est choisir.*
To govern is to make choices.
Politique, 'Maximes de Politique', xix

C.S. LEWIS 1898–1963

13 A sensible human once said...'She's the sort of woman who lives for others—you can tell the others by their hunted expression.'
The Screwtape Letters (1942), XXVI

LIBERACE 1920–

14 I cried all the way to the bank.
Liberace: An Autobiography, ch.2. After hostile criticism

CHARLES-JOSEPH, PRINCE DE LIGNE 1735–1814

15 *Le congrès ne marche pas, il danse.*
The Congress makes no progress; it dances.
La Garde-Chambonas, *Souvenirs du Congrès de Vienne, 1814–1815,* c.I

ABRAHAM LINCOLN 1809–1865

16 The ballot is stronger than the bullet.
Speech, 19 May 1856

17 'A house divided against itself cannot stand.' I believe this government cannot endure permanently, half slave and half free.
Speech, 16 June 1858. See 34:21

18 You can fool all the people some of the

time, and some of the people all the time, but you can not fool all the people all of the time.
Attr. words in a speech at Clinton, 8 Sept. 1858. N.W. Stephenson, *Autobiography of A. Lincoln* (1927). Attr. also to Phineas Barnum

1 This country, with its institutions, belongs to the people who inhabit it. Whenever they shall grow weary of the existing government, they can exercise their constitutional right of amending it, or their revolutionary right to dismember or overthrow it.
First Inaugural Address, 4 Mar. 1861

2 My paramount object in this struggle is to save the Union...If I could save the Union without freeing any slave, I would do it; and if I could save it by freeing all the slaves, I would do it; and if I could save it by freeing some and leaving others alone, I would also do that.
Letter to Horace Greeley, 22 Aug. 1862

3 With malice toward none; with charity for all; with firmness in the right, as God gives us to see the right, let us strive on to finish the work we are in: to bind up the nation's wounds; to care for him who shall have borne the battle, and for his widow and his orphan, to do all which may achieve and cherish a just and lasting peace among ourselves, and with all nations.
Second Inaugural Address, 4 Mar. 1865

4 People who like this sort of thing will find this the sort of thing they like.
Judgement on a book. G.W.E. Russell, *Collections and Recollections*, ch.30

5 The Lord prefers common-looking people. That is why he makes so many of them.
James Morgan, *Our President*, ch.6

6 So you're the little woman who wrote the book that made this great war!
On meeting Harriet Beecher Stowe. Carl Sandburg, *Abraham Lincoln: The War Years*, vol.II, ch.39

GEORGE LINLEY 1798–1865

7 Among our ancient mountains,
And from our lovely vales,
Oh, let the prayer re-echo:
'God bless the Prince of Wales!'
God Bless the Prince of Wales

MAXIM LITVINOFF 1876–1951

8 Peace is indivisible.
First used publicly 25 Feb. 1920. A.U. Pope, *Maxim Litvinoff*, p.234. Also used in a speech to the 16th Plenum of the League of Nations on July 1936. See *Against Aggression* (1939), p.45

LIVY
59 B.C.–A.D. 17 or 64 B.C.–A.D. 12

9 *Vae victis.*
Down with the defeated.
Ab Urbe Condita, 5.48.9. Shouted by Brennu the Gallic King, who had captured Rome (3⁹ B.C.), but a proverbial cry.

JOHN LOCKE 1632–1704

10 New opinions are always suspected, an usually opposed, without any other reaso but because they are not already common
An Essay concerning Human Understandi (1690), dedicatory epistle

11 It is one thing to show a man that he is i an error, and another to put him in posse sion of truth.
bk.iv, ch.7, sec.11

12 All men are liable to error; and most me are, in many points, by passion or interes under temptation to it.
ch.20, sec.17

FREDERICK LOCKER-LAMPSON
1821–1895

13 If you lift a guinea-pig up by the tail
His eyes drop out!
A Garden Lyric

JOHN GIBSON LOCKHART
1794–1854

14 It is a better and a wiser thing to be starved apothecary than a starved poet; s back to the shop Mr John, back to 'pla ters, pills, and ointment boxes.'
Review of Keats's *Endymion* in *Blackwood Magazine*, 1818; authorship attr. to Lockhart.

FRIEDRICH VON LOGAU 1604–1655

15 *Gottesmühlen mahlen langsam, mahle aber trefflich klein;*
Ob aus Langmut Er sich säumet, bringt m Schärf' Er alles ein.
Though the mills of God grind slowly, y they grind exceeding small;
Though with patience He stands waitin with exactness grinds He all.
Sinngedichte (1653), III.ii.24 (tr. H.W. Longfe low). The first line is a translation of a Gree hexameter by an unnamed poet quoted in Sextu Empiricus *adversus Mathematicos*, I.287.

HENRY WADSWORTH
LONGFELLOW 1807-1882

I shot an arrow into the air,
It fell to earth, I knew not where.
The Arrow and the Song

Thou, too, sail on, O Ship of State!
Sail on, O Union, strong and great!
The Building of the Ship

The cares that infest the day
Shall fold their tents, like the Arabs,
    And as silently steal away.
The Day is Done

The shades of night were falling fast,
As through an Alpine village passed
A youth, who bore, 'mid snow and ice,
A banner with the strange device,
                    Excelsior!
Excelsior

A traveller, by the faithful hound,
Half-buried in the snow was found.

The heights by great men reached and
    kept
Were not attained by sudden flight,
But they, while their companions slept,
Were toiling upward in the night.
The Ladder of Saint Augustine

A boy's will is the wind's will
And the thoughts of youth are long, long
    thoughts.
My Lost Youth

Listen, my children, and you shall hear
Of the midnight ride of Paul Revere,
On the eighteenth of April in Seventy-five.
Paul Revere's Ride (1861)

Tell me not, in mournful numbers,
    Life is but an empty dream!
For the soul is dead that slumbers,
    And things are not what they seem.

Life is real! Life is earnest!
    And the grave is not its goal;
Dust thou art, to dust returnest,
    Was not spoken of the soul.
A Psalm of Life

Lives of great men all remind us
    We can make our lives sublime,
And, departing, leave behind us
    Footprints on the sands of time.

Let us, then, be up and doing,
    With a heart for any fate;
Still achieving, still pursuing,
    Learn to labour and to wait.

By the shore of Gitche Gumee,
By the shining Big-Sea-Water,
Stood the wigwam of Nokomis,

Daughter of the Moon, Nokomis.
The Song of Hiawatha (1855), iii. **Hiawatha's Childhood**

13 From the waterfall he named her,
    Minnehaha, Laughing Water.
    iv. **Hiawatha and Mudjekeewis**

14 As unto the bow the cord is,
    So unto the man is woman;
    Though she bends him, she obeys him,
    Though she draws him, yet she follows;
    Useless each without the other!
    x. **Hiawatha's Wooing**

15 Onaway! Awake, beloved!
    xi. **Hiawatha's Wedding-feast**

16 Ships that pass in the night, and speak
        each other in passing.
    Tales of a Wayside Inn, pt.III (1874), **The Theologian's Tale. Elizabeth, iv**

17 Under the spreading chestnut tree
        The village smithy stands;
    The smith, a mighty man is he,
        With large and sinewy hands;
    And the muscles of his brawny arms
        Are strong as iron bands.
    The Village Blacksmith

18 Something attempted, something done,
        Has earned a night's repose.

19 It was the schooner Hesperus,
        That sailed the wintry sea;
    And the skipper had taken his little daughter,
        To bear him company.
    The Wreck of the Hesperus

20 There was a little girl
    Who had a little curl
    Right in the middle of her forehead,
    When she was good
    She was very, very good,
    But when she was bad she was horrid.
    B.R.T. Machetta, *Home Life of Longfellow*

FREDERICK LONSDALE 1881-1934

21 Don't keep finishing your sentences. I am
    not a bloody fool.
    Frances Donaldson, *Child of the Twenties*
    (1959), p.11

ANITA LOOS 1893-

22 A girl like I.
    Gentlemen Prefer Blondes (1925), *passim*

23 Fate keeps on happening.
    ch.2 (heading)

24 Kissing your hand may make you feel very
    very good but a diamond and safire

bracelet lasts forever.
ch.4

1 You have got to be a Queen to get away with a hat like that.

2 Fun is fun but no girl wants to laugh all of the time.

3 So then Dr Froyd said that all I needed was to cultivate a few inhibitions and get some sleep.
ch.5

FEDERICO GARCÍA LORCA
see GARCIA LORCA

LOUIS XIV 1638-1715

4 *Il n'y a plus de Pyrénées.*
The Pyrenees have ceased to exist.
At the accession of his grandson to the throne of Spain, 1700. Attr. Voltaire, *Siècle de Louis XIV,* ch.28

5 *L'État c'est moi.*
I am the State.'
Attr. remark before the Parlement de Paris, 13 Apr. 1655. Dulaure, *Histoire de Paris* (1834), vol.6, p.298. Probably apocryphal.

6 *J'ai failli attendre.*
I almost had to wait.
Attrib. expression of impatience. Attribution doubted by e.g. E. Fournier, *L'Esprit dans l'Histoire* (4th edition, 1884), ch.xlviii

LOUIS XVIII 1755-1824

7 *Il n'est aucun de vous qui n'ait dans sa giberne le baton du duc de Reggio; c'est à vous à l'en faire sortir.*
There is not one of you who has not in his knapsack the field marshal's baton; it is up to you to bring it out.
Speech to the Saint-Cyr cadets, 9 Aug 1819. *Moniteur,* 10 Aug. 1819

8 *L'exactitude est la politesse des rois.*
Punctuality is the politeness of kings.
Attr. *Souvenirs de J. Lafitte* (1844), bk.1, ch.3

RICHARD LOVELACE 1618-1658

9 Stone walls do not a prison make
Nor iron bars a cage;
Minds innocent and quiet take
That for an hermitage;
If I have freedom in my love,
And in my soul am free;
Angels alone, that soar above,
Enjoy such liberty.
To Althea, From Prison

10 Tell me not (Sweet) I am unkind,
That from the nunnery

Of thy chaste breast, and quiet mind,
To war and arms I fly.
To Lucasta, Going to the Wars

11 I could not love thee (Dear) so much,
Lov'd I not honour more.

ROBERT LOWE, VISCOUNT SHERBROOKE 1811-1892

12 I believe it will be absolutely necessar that you should prevail on our future ma ters to learn their letters.
House of Commons, 15 July 1867, on the pas ing of the Reform Bill. Popularized as 'We mu educate our masters.'

13 The Chancellor of the Exchequer is a ma whose duties make him more or less of taxing machine. He is intrusted with a ce tain amount of misery which it is his dut to distribute as fairly as he can.
House of Commons, 11 Apr. 1870

AMY LOWELL 1856-1943

14 And the softness of my body will b guarded from embrace
By each button, hook, and lace.
For the man who should loose me is dead.
Fighting with the Duke in Flanders,
In a pattern called a war.
Christ! What are patterns for?
Patterns

JAMES RUSSELL LOWELL 1819-189

15 You've a darned long row to hoe.
The Biglow Papers, First Series (1848), No.1

16 I *don't* believe in princerple,
But O, I *du* in interest.
No.6. **The Pious Editor's Creed**

17 Once to every man and nation comes th moment to decide,
In the strife of Truth with Falsehood, fo the good or evil side.
The Present Crisis

18 Truth forever on the scaffold, Wron forever on the throne, —
Yet that scaffold sways the future, and behind the dim unknown,
Standeth God within the shadow, keepin watch above his own.

19 New occasions teach new duties: Tim makes ancient good uncouth;
They must upward still, and onward, wh would keep abreast of Truth.

WILLIAM LOWNDES 1652-1724

20 Take care of the pence, and the pound will take care of themselves.

Lord Chesterfield, letter to his son, 5 Feb. 1750. In an earlier letter (6 Nov. 1747) the formula is given as '...for the pounds...'

LUCAN A.D. 39–65

1 *Victrix causa deis placuit, sed victa Catoni.*
The winning cause pleased the gods, but the losing one pleased Cato.
Bellum Civile, I.128

2 *Conlunx*
Est mihi, sunt nati: dedimus tot pignora fatis.
I have a wife, I have sons: all of them hostages given to fate.
Works, VII.661

LUCILIUS d.102/1 B.C.

3 *Maior erat natu; non omnia possumus omnes.*
He was older; there are some things we cannot all do.
See Macrobius, *Saturnalia*, VI.i.35

LUCRETIUS 94?–55 B.C.

4 *Tantum religio potuit suadere malorum.*
So much wrong could religion induce.
De Rerum Natura, i.101

5 *Nil posse creari*
De nilo.
Nothing can be created out of nothing.
155

6 *Suave, mari magno turbantibus aequora ventis,*
E terra magnum alterius spectare laborem.
Lovely it is, when the winds are churning up the waves on the great sea, to gaze out from the land on the great efforts of someone else.
ii.1

7 *Augescunt aliae gentes, aliae minuuntur,*
Inque brevi spatio mutantur saecla animantum
Et quasi cursores vitai lampada tradunt.
Some races increase, others are reduced, and in a short while the generations of living creatures are changed and like runners relay the torch of life.
7

8 *Scire licet nobis nil esse in morte timendum*
Nec miserum fieri qui non est posse neque hilum
Differre an nullo fuerit iam tempore natus,
Mortalem vitam mors cum immortalis ademit.
We can know there is nothing to be feared in death, that one who is not cannot be made unhappy, and that it matters not

a scrap whether one might ever have been born at all, when death that is immortal has taken over one's mortal life.
iii.866

9 *Medio de fonte leporum*
Surgit amari aliquid quod in ipsis floribus angat.
From the midst of the fountain of delights rises something bitter that chokes them all amongst the flowers.
iv.1133

MARTIN LUTHER 1483–1546

10 *Darum gibt unser Herr Gott gemeiniglich Reichtum den grossen Eseln, denen er sonst nichts gönnt.*
So our Lord God commonly gives riches to those gross asses to whom He vouchsafes nothing else.
Colloquia (collected 1566, J. Aurifaber), ch.XX

11 *Esto peccator et pecca fortiter, sed fortius fide et gaude in Christo.*
Be a sinner and sin strongly, but more strongly have faith and rejoice in Christ.
Letter to Melanchthon. *Epistolae*, Jena (1556), i.345

12 *Hier stehe ich. Ich kann nicht anders. Gott helfe mir. Amen.*
Here stand I. I can do no other. God help me. Amen.
Speech at the Diet of Worms, 18 Apr. 1521

13 *Wer nicht liebt Wein, Weib und Gesang,*
Der bleibt ein Narr sein Leben lang.
Who loves not woman, wine, and song Remains a fool his whole life long.
Attr. Written in the Luther room in the Wartburg, but no proof exists of its authorship

14 *Ein' feste Burg ist unser Gott,*
Ein' gute Wehr und Waffen.
A safe stronghold our God is still, A trusty shield and weapon.
Klug'sche Gesangbuch (1529). Tr. Carlyle

JOHN LYLY 1554?–1606

15 Cupid and my Campaspe play'd At cards for kisses, Cupid paid.
Campaspe (1584), III.v

16 Night hath a thousand eyes.
Maides Metamorphose (1600), III.i

BARON LYNDHURST 1772–1863

17 Campbell has added another terror to death.
On being assured that he had not yet been included in Lord Campbell's *Lives of the Lord*

Chancellors; attr. by Sir H. Poland. See E. Bowen-Rowlands, *Seventy-Two Years At the Bar*, ch.10. See 269:6

LYSANDER d. 395 B.C.

1 Deceive boys with toys, but men with oaths.
Plutarch, *Lives, Lysander,* 8

H.F. LYTE 1793–1847

2 Abide with me; fast falls the eventide;
The darkness deepens; Lord, with me abide;
When other helpers fail, and comforts flee,
Help of the helpless, O, abide with me.

Swift to its close ebbs out life's little day;
Earth's joys grow dim, its glories pass away;
Change and decay in all around I see;
O Thou, who changest not, abide with me.
Abide with Me

LORD MACAULAY 1800–1859

3 Lars Porsena of Clusium
By the nine gods he swore
That the great house of Tarquin
Should suffer wrong no more.
By the Nine Gods he swore it,
And named a trysting day,
And bade his messengers ride forth,
East and west and south and north,
To summon his array.
Lays of Ancient Rome (1842). **Horatius,** 1

4 Then out spake brave Horatius,
The Captain of the Gate:
'To every man upon this earth
Death cometh soon or late.
And how can man die better
Than facing fearful odds,
For the ashes of his fathers,
And the temples of his Gods?'
27

5 To save them from false Sextus
That wrought the deed of shame.
28

6 'Now who will stand on either hand,
And keep the bridge with me?'
29

7 Then none was for a party;
Then all were for the state;
Then the great man helped the poor,
And the poor man loved the great:
Then lands were fairly portioned;
Then spoils were fairly sold:
The Romans were like brothers

In the brave days of old.
31

8 Was none who would be foremost
To lead such dire attack;
But those behind cried 'Forward!'
And those before cried 'Back!'
50

9 'Oh, Tiber! father Tiber
To whom the Romans pray,
A Roman's life, a Roman's arms,
Take thou in charge this day!'
59

10 And even the ranks of Tuscany
Could scarce forbear to cheer.
60

11 When the oldest cask is opened,
And the largest lamp is lit;…
With weeping and with laughter
Still is the story told,
How well Horatius kept the bridge
In the brave days of old.
69-70

12 Those trees in whose dim shadow
The ghastly priest doth reign,
The priest who slew the slayer,
And shall himself be slain.
The Battle of Lake Regillus, 10

13 His imagination resembled the wings of an ostrich. It enabled him to run, though not to soar.
Essays and Biographies. **John Dryden** (*Edinburgh Review,* Jan, 1828)

14 The business of everybody is the business of nobody.
Historical Essays Contributed to the 'Edinburgh Review'. **Hallam's 'Constitutional History'** (Sept 1828)

15 The gallery in which the reporters sit has become a fourth estate of the realm.

16 Every schoolboy knows who imprisoned Montezuma, and who strangled Atahualpa.
Lord Clive (Jan. 1840)

17 She [the Roman Catholic Church] may still exist in undiminished vigour when some traveller from New Zealand shall, in the midst of a vast solitude, take his stand on a broken arch of London Bridge to sketch the ruins of St Paul's.
Von Ranke (Oct. 1840)

18 She [the Church of Rome] thoroughly understands what no other church has ever understood, how to deal with enthusiasts.

19 There is only one cure for the evils which newly acquired freedom produces; and

that is freedom.
Literary Essays Contributed to the 'Edinburgh Review'. **Milton** (Aug. 1825)

1 Many politicians of our time are in the habit of laying it down as a self-evident proposition, that no people ought to be free till they are fit to use their freedom. The maxim is worthy of the fool in the old story, who resolved not to go into the water till he had learnt to swim. If men are to wait for liberty till they become wise and good in slavery, they may indeed wait for ever.

2 We know no spectacle so ridiculous as the British public in one of its periodical fits of morality.
Moore's 'Life Of Lord Byron' (June 1830)

3 The Puritan hated bear-baiting, not because it gave pain to the bear, but because it gave pleasure to the spectators.
History of England, vol.i (1849), ch.2

4 Thank you, madam, the agony is abated. [Reply, aged four.]
Trevelyan, *Life and Letters of Macaulay,* ch.1

5 We were regaled by a dogfight...How odd that people of sense should find any pleasure in being accompanied by a beast who is always spoiling conversation.
ch.14

ROSE MACAULAY 1889–1958

6 'Take my camel, dear,' said my aunt Dot as she climbed down from this animal on her return from High Mass.
The Towers of Trebizond (1956), p.1

GENERAL GEORGE B. McCLELLAN 1826–1885

7 All quiet along the Potomac.
Attr. in the American Civil War

DR. JOHN McCRAE 1872–1918

8 In Flanders fields the poppies blow Between the crosses, row on row,
    That mark our place.
In Flanders Fields. Ypres Salient, 3 May 1915

9   If ye break faith with us who die We shall not sleep, though poppies grow In Flanders fields.

WILLIAM McGONAGALL 1825–1902

10 Alas! Lord and Lady Dalhousie are dead, and buried at last,
    Which causes many people to feel a little

downcast.
The Death of Lord and Lady Dalhousie

11 Beautiful Railway Bridge of the Silv'ry Tay!
Alas, I am very sorry to say
That ninety lives have been taken away
On the last Sabbath day of 1879,
Which will be remember'd for a very long time.
The Tay Bridge Disaster

CHARLES MACKAY 1814–1889

12 There's a good time coming, boys,
    A good time coming.
The Good Time Coming

SIR COMPTON MACKENZIE 1883–1972

13 You are offered a piece of bread and butter that feels like a damp handkerchief and sometimes, when cucumber is added to it, like a wet one. [An English tea party.]
Vestal Fire (1927), ch.3

SIR JAMES MACKINTOSH 1765–1832

14 The Commons, faithful to their system, remained in a wise and masterly inactivity.
Vindiciae Gallicae (1791), 1

ARCHIBALD MACLEISH 1892–

15 A poem should not mean
But be.
Ars poetica

MARSHALL McLUHAN 1911–

16 The medium is the message.
Understanding Media (1964), pt.i, ch.1

MARSHAL MACMAHON 1808–1893

17 *J'y suis, j'y reste.*
Here I am, and here I stay.
At the taking of the Malakoff, 8 Sept. 1855. MacMahon later cast doubt on the attribution: *'Je ne crois pas...avoir donné à ma pensée cette forme lapidaire.'* See Hanoteaux, *Histoire de la France Contemporaine,* vol.II, ch.1, sect.i

HAROLD MACMILLAN 1894–

18 Let's be frank about it; most of our people have never had it so good.
Speech at Bedford, 20 July 1957. 'You Never Had It So Good' was the Democratic Party slogan in the U.S. election campaign of 1952.

19 On 7 January [1958]...I made a short and carefully prepared statement...I referred to 'some recent difficulties' in our affairs at

home which had 'caused me a little anxiety'. However, 'I thought the best thing to do was to settle up these little local difficulties and then to turn to the wider vision of the Commonwealth.'
Referring to the sterling crisis and to Thorneycroft's resignation. *Riding The Storm, 1956–1959* (1971), ch.11, **Money and Men**

1 The most striking of all the impressions I have formed since I left London a month ago is of the strength of this African national consciousness…The wind of change is blowing through this continent.
Speech to the South African Houses of Parliament, Cape Town, 3 Feb. 1960. The speech was drafted by Sir David Hunt as described by him in *On the Spot: An Ambassador Remembers* (1975)

LEONARD MACNALLY 1752–1820

2 This lass so neat, with smiles so sweet,
Has won my right good-will,
I'd crowns resign to call thee mine,
Sweet lass of Richmond Hill.
The Lass of Richmond Hill. E. Duncan, *Minstrelsy of England* (1905), i.254. Attr. also to W. Upton in *Oxford Song Book,* and to W. Hudson in Baring-Gould, *English Minstrelsie* (1895), iii.54

LOUIS MACNEICE 1907–1963

3 All of London littered with remembered kisses.
Autumn Journal, iv

4 There will be time to audit
The accounts later, there will be sunlight later
And the equation will come out at last.
xxiv

5 It's no go the merrygoround, it's no go the rickshaw,
All we want is a limousine and a ticket for the peepshow.
Bagpipe Music

6 It's no go the picture palace, it's no go the stadium,
It's no go the country cot with a pot of pink geraniums,
It's no go the Government grants, it's no go the elections,
Sit on your arse for fifty years and hang your hat on a pension.

7 The glass is falling hour by hour, the glass will fall for ever,
But if you break the bloody glass, you won't hold up the weather.

8 Time was away and somewhere else,
There were two glasses and two chairs
And two people with the one pulse

(Somebody stopped the moving stairs):
Time was away and somewhere else.
Meeting Point

9 I am not yet born; O fill me
With strength against those who woulc
freeze my
humanity, would dragoon me into a letha
automaton,
would make me a cog in a machine, a thing
with
one face, a thing, and against all those
who would dissipate my entirety, would
blow me like thistledown hither and
thither or hither and thither
like water held in the
hands would spill me.
Prayer before Birth

10 The sunlight on the garden
Hardens and grows cold,
We cannot cage the minute
Within its nets of gold,
When all is told
We cannot beg for pardon.
The Sunlight on the Garden

GEOFFREY MADAN 1895–1947

11 The devil finds some mischief still for hands that have not learnt how to be idle.
L.S.N., *Twelve Reflections* (privately printed, 1934)

12 The dust of exploded beliefs may make a fine sunset.

SAMUEL MADDEN 1686–1765

13 Words are men's daughters, but God's sons are things.
Boulter's Monument (1745), l.377

MAURICE MAETERLINCK 1862–1949

14 *Il n'y a pas de morts.*
There are no dead.
L'Oiseau bleu (1909), IV.ii

MAGNA CARTA 1215

15 *Quod Anglicana ecclesia libera sit.*
That the English Church shall be free.
1

16 *Nullus liber homo capiatur, vel imprisonetur, aut dissaisiatur, aut utlagetur, aut exuletur, aut aliquo modo destruatur, nec super eum ibimus, nec super eum mittemus, nisi per legale judicium parium suorum vel per legem terrae.*
No free man shall be taken or imprisoned or dispossessed, or outlawed or exiled, or in any way destroyed, nor will we go upon

him, nor will we send against him except by the lawful judgement of his peers or by the law of the land.
39

1 *Nulli vendemus, nulli negabimus aut differemus, rectum aut justitiam.*
To no man will we sell, or deny, or delay, right or justice.
40

ALFRED T. MAHAN 1840-1914

2 Those far distant, storm-beaten ships, upon which the Grand Army never looked, stood between it and the dominion of the world.
The Influence of Sea Power upon the French Revolution and Empire, 1793-1812 (1892), ii.118

JOSEPH DE MAISTRE 1753-1821

3 *Toute nation a le gouvernement qu'elle mérite.*
Every country has the government it deserves.
Lettres et Opuscules Inédits, i. p.215, 15 Aug. 1811

STÉPHANE MALLARMÉ 1842-1898

4 *La chair est triste, hélas! et j'ai lu tous les livres.*
The flesh, alas, is wearied; and I have read all the books there are.
Brise Marin

GEORGE LEIGH MALLORY 1886-1924

5 Because it is there.
Answer to the question repeatedly asked him on his American lecture tour of 1923, 'Why do you want to climb Mt. Everest?' D. Robertson, *George Mallory* (1969), p.215

SIR THOMAS MALORY d. 1471

6 Whoso pulleth out this sword of this stone and anvil is rightwise King born of all England.
Le Morte D'Arthur (finished 1469-70, printed 1485), bk.i, ch.4

THOMAS ROBERT MALTHUS 1766-1834

7 Population, when unchecked, increases in a geometrical ratio. Subsistence only increases in an arithmetical ratio.
The Principle of Population (1798), 1

W.R. MANDALE nineteenth century

8 Up and down the City Road,
In and out the Eagle,
That's the way the money goes—
Pop goes the weasel!
Pop Goes the Weasel

MANILIUS 1st cent. A.D.

9 *Eripuitque Jovi fulmen viresque tonandi*
And snatched from Jove the lightning shaft and power to thunder.
Astronomica, i.104. Of human intelligence

MRS. MANLEY 1663-1724

10 No time like the present.
The Lost Lover (1696), IV.i

LORD MANSFIELD 1705-1793

11 The constitution does not allow reasons of state to influence our judgments: God forbid it should! We must not regard political consequences; however formidable soever they might be: if rebellion was the certain consequence, we are bound to say '*fiat justitia, ruat caelum*'.
Rex v. Wilkes, 8 June 1768

12 Consider what you think justice requires, and decide accordingly. But never give your reasons; for your judgement will probably be right, but your reasons will certainly be wrong.
Advice to a newly appointed colonial governor ignorant in the law. Campbell, *Lives of the Chief Justices,* ch.40

MAO TSE-TUNG 1893-1976

13 Letting a hundred flowers blossom and a hundred schools of thought contend is the policy.
Speech, 2 May 1956. See Roderick MacFarquhar, *Origins of the Cultural Revolution* (1974), vol.1, p.51

14 Every Communist must grasp the truth, 'Political power grows out of the barrel of a gun.'
Selected Works (Peking, 1961), vol.II. **Problems of War and Strategy,** ii, 6 Nov. 1938

15 The atomic bomb is a paper tiger which the US reactionaries use to scare people. It looks terrible, but in fact it isn't...All reactionaries are paper tigers.
vol.IV. **Talk with Anna Louise Strong,** Aug. 1946

WILLIAM LEARNED MARCY 1786-1857

16 To the victor belong the spoils of the

enemy.
Parton, *Life of Jackson* (1860), vol.iii, p.378

QUEEN MARIE-ANTOINETTE
1755–1793

1 *Qu'ils mangent de la brioche.*
Let them eat cake.
On being told that her people had no bread.
Attributed to Marie-Antoinette, but much older.
Rousseau refers in his *Confessions*, 1740, to a
similar remark, as a well known saying. Louis
XVIII in his *Relation d'un Voyage à Bruxelles et
à Coblentz en 1791* (1823, p.59) attributes to
Marie-Thérèse (1638–83), wife of Louis XIV,
'Que ne mangent-ils de la croûte de pâté?' ('Why
don't they eat pastry?')

SARAH, 1ST DUCHESS OF
MARLBOROUGH 1660–1744

2 The Duke returned from the wars today
and did pleasure me in his top-boots.
Oral trad. Attr. in various forms

CHRISTOPHER MARLOWE
1564–1593

3 Why this is hell, nor am I out of it:
Thinkst thou that I who saw the face of
God,
And tasted the eternal joys of heaven,
Am not tormented with ten thousand hells
In being deprived of everlasting bliss!
Doctor Faustus (1604), I.iii.76

4 Hell hath no limits nor is circumscrib'd
In one self place, where we are is Hell,
And where Hell is, there must we ever be.
And to be short, when all the world dis-
solves,
And every creature shall be purified,
All places shall be hell that are not heaven.
II.i.120

5 Was this the face that launch'd a thousand
ships,
And burnt the topless towers of Ilium?
Sweet Helen, make me immortal with a
kiss!
V.i.97

6 Now hast thou but one bare hour to live,
And then thou must be damned perpetu-
ally;
Stand still you ever-moving spheres of
heaven,
That time may cease, and midnight never
come.
Fair nature's eye, rise, rise again and make
Perpetual day, or let this hour be but
A year, a month, a week, a natural day,
That Faustus may repent and save his
soul.

O lente, lente currite noctis equi:
The stars move still, time runs, the clock
will strike,
The devil will come, and Faustus must be
damn'd.
O I'll leap up to my God: who pulls me
down?
See see where Christ's blood streams in the
firmament.
One drop would save my soul, half a drop,
ah my Christ.
ii.127

7 O soul, be changed into little water drops,
And fall into the ocean, ne'er be found:
My God, my God, look not so fierce on
me.
179

8 Cut is the branch that might have grown
full straight,
And burnèd is Apollo's laurel bough,
That sometime grew within this learned
man.
epilogue

9 My men, like satyrs grazing on the lawns,
Shall with their goat feet dance an antic
hay.
Edward II (1593), I.i.59

10 I count religion but a childish toy,
And hold there is no sin but ignorance.
The Jew of Malta (c.1592), prologue

11 And, as their wealth increaseth, so enclose
Infinite riches in a little room.
I.i.36

12 As for myself, I walk abroad o' nights
And kill sick people groaning under walls:
Sometimes I go about and poison wells.
II.iii.172

13 *Barnadine:* Thou hast committed—
Barabas: Fornication? But that was in another country: and besides, the wench is
dead.
IV.i.40

14 Come live with me, and be my love,
And we will all the pleasures prove,
That valleys, groves, hills and fields,
Woods or steepy mountain yields.
The Passionate Shepherd to his Love. See
87:18

15 From jigging veins of rhyming mother-
wits.
Tamburlaine the Great (1590), prologue

16 Is it not passing brave to be a King,
And ride in triumph through Persepolis?
pt.I, l.758

17 Now walk the angels on the walls of
heaven,

As sentinels to warn th' immortal souls,
To entertain divine Zenocrate.
pt.II, l.2983

1 Holla, ye pampered Jades of Asia:
What, can ye draw but twenty miles a day?
l.3980. See 212:25

DON MARQUIS 1878–1937

2 but wotthehell archy wotthehell
jamais triste archy jamais triste
that is my motto.
archy and mehitabel, xlvi. **mehitabel sees paris**

3 toujours gai, archy, toujours gai.
archys life of mehitabel, i. **the life of mehitabel the
cat**

4 now and then
there is a person born
who is so unlucky
that he runs into accidents
which started out to happen
to somebody else.
xli. **archy says**

CAPTAIN MARRYAT 1792–1848

5 As savage as a bear with a sore head.
The King's Own (1830), ch.26

6 If you please, ma'am, it was a very little
one. [The nurse excusing her illegitimate
baby.]
Mr. Midshipman Easy (1836), ch.3

7 I never knows the children. It's just six of
one and half-a-dozen of the other.
The Pirate (1836), ch.4

MARTIAL b. A.D. 43

8 *Non amo te, Sabidi, nec possum dicere
quare:
Hoc tantum possum dicere, non amo te.*
I don't love you, Sabidius, and I can't tell
you why; all I can tell you is this, that I
don't love you.
Epigrammata, I.xxxii

9 *Difficilis facilis, iucundus acerbus es idem:
Nec tecum possum vivere nec sine te.*
Difficult or easy, pleasant or bitter, you
are the same you: I cannot live with
you—nor without you.
XII.xlvi (xlvii)

10 *Rus in urbe.*
Country in the town.
lvii

ANDREW MARVELL 1621–1678

11 Where the remote Bermudas ride
In th' ocean's bosom unespied.
Bermudas

12 Echo beyond the Mexique Bay.

13 My love is of a birth as rare
As 'tis for object strange and high:
It was begotten by despair
Upon impossibility.
The Definition of Love

14 As lines so loves oblique may well
Themselves in every angle greet
But ours so truly parallel,
Though infinite can never meet.

15 What wond'rous life is this I lead!
Ripe apples drop about my head;
The luscious clusters of the vine
Upon my mouth do crush their wine;
The nectarine and curious peach,
Into my hands themselves do reach;
Stumbling on melons, as I pass,
Insnar'd with flow'rs, I fall on grass.
The Garden, 5

16 Annihilating all that's made
To a green thought in a green shade.
6

17 He nothing common did or mean
Upon that memorable scene:
But with his keener eye
The axe's edge did try. [Charles I.]
*An Horatian Ode upon Cromwell's Return from
Ireland* (1650), l.57

18 But bowed his comely head,
Down as upon a bed.
l.63

19 Ye country comets, that portend
No war, nor prince's funeral,
Shining unto no higher end
Then to presage the grasses' fall.
The Mower to the Glow-worms

20 Had we but world enough, and time,
This coyness, Lady, were no crime.
We would sit down, and think which way
To walk, and pass our long love's day.
Thou by the Indian Ganges' side
Shouldst rubies find: I by the tide
Of Humber would complain. I would
Love you ten years before the Flood:
And you should if you please refuse
Till the conversion of the Jews.
My vegetable love should grow
Vaster than empires, and more slow.
To His Coy Mistress

21 But at my back I always hear
Time's wingèd chariot hurrying near.
And yonder all before us lie
Deserts of vast eternity.
Thy beauty shall no more be found;
Nor, in thy marble vault, shall sound

My echoing song: then worms shall try
That long preserved virginity:
And your quaint honour turn to dust;
And into ashes all my lust.
The grave's a fine and private place,
But none I think do there embrace.

1 Let us roll all our strength and all
Our sweetness up into one ball,
And tear our pleasures with rough strife
Thorough the iron gates of life:
Thus, though we cannot make our sun
Stand still, yet we will make him run.

2 Thrice happy he who, not mistook,
Hath read in Nature's mystic book.
Upon Appleton House, to my Lord Fairfax, lxxiii

KARL MARX 1818–1883

3 A spectre is haunting Europe—The spectre of Communism.
The Communist Manifesto (1848), opening
words

4 The history of all hitherto existing society
is the history of class struggle.

5 The workers have nothing to lose in this
[revolution] but their chains. They have a
world to gain. Workers of the world, unite!
closing words

6 From each according to his abilities, to
each according to his needs.
Criticism of the Gotha Programme (1875). See
14:12

7 Religion…is the opium of the people.
Critique of Hegel's Philosophy of Right (1843–4),
Introduction. See 142:17

8 Hegel says somewhere that all great events
and personalities in world history reap-
pear in one fashion or another. He forgot
to add: the first time as tragedy, the second
as farce.
The Eighteenth Brumaire of Louis Napoleon
(1852), 1

9 The philosophers have only interpreted
the world in various ways; the point is to
change it.
Theses on Feuerbach (1888), xi

10 What I did that was new to prove…
that the class struggle necessarily leads to
the dictatorship of the proletariat.
Letter to Weydemeyer 5 Mar. 1852. The phrase
'dictatorship of the proletariat' had earlier been
used in the Constitution of the World Society of
Revolutionary Communists (1850), signed by
Marx, Engels, Adam and J. Vidil, G. Julian Har-
ney, and August Willich. Marx claimed that the
phrase had been coined by Auguste Blanqui
(1805–1881), but it has not been found in this
form in Blanqui's work. See Marx, *Political
Writings* (ed. Fernbach, 1973), vol.1, p.24.

11 All I know is that I am not a Marxist.
Attr. in Engels, letter to C. Schmidt, 5 Aug. 1890

MARY TUDOR 1516–1558

12 When I am dead and opened, you shall
find 'Calais' lying in my heart.
Holinshed, *Chronicles,* iii.1160

QUEEN MARY 1867–1953

13 Really! this might be Roumania!
(The abdication crisis, 1936.) James Pope-
Hennessy, *Life of Queen Mary* (1959), ch.7.ii

JOHN MASEFIELD 1878–1967

14 Quinquireme of Nineveh from distant
Ophir
Rowing home to haven in sunny Palestine,
With a cargo of ivory,
And apes and peacocks,
Sandalwood, cedarwood, and sweet white
wine.
Cargoes. See 25:3

15 Dirty British coaster with a salt-caked
smoke stack,
Butting through the Channel in the mad
March days,
With a cargo of Tyne coal,
Road-rail, pig-lead,
Firewood, iron-ware, and cheap tin trays

16 Oh some are fond of Spanish wine, and
some are fond of French,
And some'll swallow tay and stuff fit only
for a wench.
Captain Stratton's Fancy

17 Oh some are fond of fiddles, and a song
well sung,
And some are all for music for to lilt upon
the tongue;
But mouths were made for tankards, and
for sucking at the bung,
Says the old bold mate of Henry Morgan.

18 In the dark womb where I began
My mother's life made me a man.
Through all the months of human birth
Her beauty fed my common earth.
I cannot see, nor breathe, nor stir,
But through the death of some of her.
C.L.M.

19 I must down to the seas again, to the
lonely sea and the sky,
And all I ask is a tall ship and a star to
steer her by,
And the wheel's kick and the wind's song
and the white sail's shaking,
And a grey mist on the sea's face and a

grey dawn breaking.
Sea Fever

1 I must down to the seas again, for the call
of the running tide
Is a wild call and a clear call that may not
be denied.

2 I must down to the seas again, to the
vagrant gypsy life,
To the gull's way and the whale's way
where the wind's like a whetted knife;
And all I ask is a merry yarn from a laughing fellow-rover,
And quiet sleep and a sweet dream when
the long trick's over.

3 Friends and loves we have none, nor
wealth, nor blessed abode,
But the hope of the City of God at the
other end of the road.
The Seekers

4 It is good to be out on the road, and going
one knows not where,
Going through meadow and village, one
knows not whither nor why.
Tewkesbury Road

5 It's a warm wind, the west wind, full of
birds' cries;
I never hear the west wind but tears are in
my eyes.
For it comes from the west lands, the old
brown hills,
And April's in the west wind, and daffodils.
The West Wind

THE MASS IN LATIN

6 *Dominus vobiscum.*
    Et cum spiritu tuo.
The Lord be with you.
    And with thy spirit.

7 *In Nomine Patris, et Filii, et Spiritus Sanc-
ti.*
In the Name of the Father, and of the Son,
and of the Holy Ghost.
The Ordinary of the Mass

8 *Gloria Patri, et Filio, et Spiritui Sancto.*
    *Sicut erat in principio, et nunc, et semper,
    et in saecula saeculorum.*
Glory be to the Father, and to the Son,
and to the Holy Ghost.
As it was in the beginning, is now, and
ever shall be, world without end.

9 *Quia peccavi nimis cogitatione, verbo, et
opere, mea culpa, mea culpa, mea maxima
culpa.*
That I have sinned exceedingly in thought,
word, and deed, through my fault,

through my fault, through my most grievous fault.

10 *Kyrie eleison, Kyrie eleison, Kyrie eleison.*
    *Christe eleison, Christe eleison, Christe
    eleison.*
Lord, have mercy upon us.
    Christ, have mercy upon us.

11 *Requiem aeternam dona eis, Domine: et lux
perpetua luceat eis*
Grant them eternal rest, O Lord; and let
perpetual light shine on them.
[To be said only at Masses for the dead.]

12 *Gloria in excelsis Deo, et in terra pax
hominibus bonae voluntatis. Laudamus te,
benedicimus te, adoramus te, glorificamus
te.*
Glory be to God on high, and on earth
peace to men of good will. We praise thee,
we bless thee, we adore thee, we glorify
thee.

13 *Credo in unum Deum, Patrem
omnipotentem, factorem coeli et terrae, visibilium omnium et invisibilium.*
I believe in one God, the Father almighty,
maker of heaven and earth, and of all
things visible and invisible.
See 187:12

14 *Oremus.*
Let us pray.

15 *Sursum corda.*
Lift up your hearts.

16 *Sanctus, sanctus, sanctus, Dominus Deus
Sabaoth. Pleni sunt coeli et terra gloria tua.
Hosanna in excelsis. Benedictus qui venit in
nomine Domini.*
Holy, holy, holy, Lord God of Hosts.
Heaven and earth are full of thy glory.
Hosanna in the highest. Blessed is he that
cometh in the name of the Lord.

17 *Pax Domini sit semper vobiscum.*
The peace of the Lord be always with you.

18 *Agnus Dei, qui tollis peccata mundi,
miserere nobis.*
    *Agnus Dei, qui tollis peccata mundi, dona
    nobis pacem.*
Lamb of God, who takest away the sins of
the world, have mercy on us.
Lamb of God, who takest away the sins of
the world, give us peace.

19 *Ite missa est.*
Go, you are dismissed.

20 *Requiescant in pace.*
May they rest in peace.
[In Masses for the dead.]

21 VERBUM CARO FACTUM EST.

THE WORD WAS MADE FLESH.
See 36:12

PHILIP MASSINGER 1583–1640

1 He that would govern others, first should
   be
   The master of himself.
   The Bondman (1624), I.iii

2 Pray enter
   You are learned Europeans and we worse
   Than ignorant Americans.
   The City Madam (1658), III.iii

3   I am driven
   Into a desperate strait and cannot steer
   A middle course.
   The Great Duke of Florence (1635), III.i

4 What pity 'tis, one that can speak so well,
   Should in his actions be so ill!
   The Parliament of Love (1624), III.iii

5   Serves and fears
   The fury of the many-headed monster,
   The giddy multitude.
   The Unnatural Combat (1639), III.ii

6 Death has a thousand doors to let out life:
   I shall find one.
   A Very Woman, V.iv. See 100:16, 203:6, 267:11

LORD JUSTICE SIR JAMES MATHEW 1830–1908

7 In England, Justice is open to all, like the
   Ritz hotel.
   R.E. Megarry, *Miscellany-at-Law* (1955), p.254.
   See 2:15

SOMERSET MAUGHAM 1874–1965

8 Dying is a very dull, dreary affair. And my
   advice to you is to have nothing whatever
   to do with it.
   Robin Maugham, *Escape from the Shadows*, 5

BILL MAULDIN 1921–

9 I feel like a fugitive from th' law of averages.
   Up Front (1946), p.39

JONATHAN MAYHEW 1720–1766

10 Rulers have no authority from God to do
   mischief.
   **A Discourse Concerning Unlimited Submission
   and Non-Resistance to the Higher Powers**, 30 Jan.
   1750

HUGHES MEARNS 1875–1965

11 As I was going up the stair
   I met a man who wasn't there.

He wasn't there again to-day.
I wish, I wish he'd stay away.
The Psychoed

COSIMO DE MEDICI 1389–1464

12 We read that we ought to forgive ou
   enemies; but we do not read that we ough
   to forgive our friends.
   Bacon, *Apophthegms*, 206

LORD MELBOURNE 1779–1848

13 I like the Garter; there is no damned mer
   in it.
   On the Order of the Garter. H.Dunckley, *Lo
   Melbourne* (1890)

14 Things have come to a pretty pass whe
   religion is allowed to invade the sphere c
   private life.
   Remark on hearing an evangelical sermo
   G.W.E. Russell, *Collections and Recollection
   ch.6

15 Now, is it to lower the price of corn, c
   isn't it? It is not much matter which w
   say, but mind, we must all say *the same*.
   (At a Cabinet meeting.) Attr. See Bagehot, *Th
   English Constitution*, ch.1

16 God help the Minister that meddles wit
   art!
   Lord David Cecil, *Lord M*, ch.3

17 What I want is men who will support m
   when I am in the wrong.
   ch.4. 'Reply to a politician' who said 'I will sup
   port you as long as you are in the right.'

18 I have always thought complaints of ill
   usage contemptible, whether from a se
   duced disappointed girl or a turned ou
   Prime Minister.
   After his dismissal by William IV. See letter fror
   Emily Eden to Mrs. Lister, 23 Nov. 1834, in *Mis
   Eden's Letters*, ed. V. Dickinson (1919)

HERMAN MELVILLE 1819–1891

19 Call me Ishmael.
   Moby Dick, ch.1, opening words

GILLES MÉNAGE 1613–1692

20 *Comme nous nous entretenions de ce qu
   pouvait rendre heureux, je lui dis;* Sanita
   sanitatum, et omnia sanitas.
   While we were discussing what could mak
   one happy, I said to him: *Sanitas sanitat
   um et omnia sanitas.*
   Ménagiana (1693), p.166. Part of a conversatio
   with Jean-Louis Guez de Balzac (1594–1654)
   See 27:2

MENANDER 342/1–293/89 B.C.

1 ὃν οἱ θεοὶ φιλοῦσιν ἀποθνῄσκει νέος.
Whom the gods love dies young.
Dis Exapaton, fr.4

GEORGE MEREDITH 1828–1909

2 But, as you will! we'll sit contentedly,
And eat our pot of honey on the grave.
Modern Love (1862), xxix

3   In tragic life, God wot,
No villain need be! Passions spin the plot:
We are betrayed by what is false within.
xliii

4 Love, that had robbed us of immortal
    things,
This little moment mercifully gave,
Where I have seen across the twilight wave
The swan sail with her young beneath her
    wings.
xlvii

5 Ah, what a dusty answer gets the soul
When hot for certainties in this our life!
l

6 Enter these enchanted woods,
          You who dare.
The Woods of Westermain

7 I expect that Woman will be the last thing
civilized by Man.
The Ordeal of Richard Feverel (1859), ch.1

8 Kissing don't last: cookery do!
ch.28

DIXON LANIER MERRITT 1879–1954

9 A wonderful bird is the pelican,
His bill will hold more than his belican.
    He can take in his beak
    Food enough for a week,
But I'm damned if I see how the helican.
The Pelican

LE CURÉ MESLIER 1664?–1733

10 *Il me souvient à ce sujet d'un souhait que
faisait autrefois un homme, qui n'avait ni
science ni étude...Il souhaitait, disait-il
...que tous les grands de la terre et que tous
les nobles fussent pendus et étranglés avec
les boyaux des prêtres.*
I remember, on this matter, the wish made
once by an ignorant, uneducated man
...He said he wished...that all the great
men in the world and all the nobility could
be hanged, and strangled in the guts of
priests.
Testament (ed. R. Charles, 1864), I.ch.2. Often
quoted as *'Je voudrais... que le dernier des rois fût
étranglé avec les boyaux du dernier prêtre'* or in

Diderot's version:
*Et des boyaux du dernier prêtre
Serrons le cou du dernier roi.*

PRINCE METTERNICH 1773–1859

11 *L'erreur n'a jamais approché de mon esprit.*
Error has never approached my spirit.
(Spoken to Guizot in 1848.) Guizot, *Mémoires*
(1858–1867), vol.IV, p.21

12 *Italien ist ein geographischer Begriff.*
Italy is a geographical expression.
Letter, 19 Nov. 1849

CHARLOTTE MEW 1869–1928

13   She sleeps up in the attic there
          Alone, poor maid. 'Tis but a stair
Betwixt us. Oh! my God! the down,
    The soft young down of her, the
        brown,
The brown of her—her eyes, her hair, her
    hair!
The Farmer's Bride

JOHN STUART MILL 1806–1873

14 Unearned increment.
Dissertations and Discussions, vol.iv (1876),
p.299

15 The only purpose for which power can be
rightfully exercised over any member of a
civilized community, against his will, is to
prevent harm to others. His own good,
either physical or moral, is not a sufficient
warrant.
On Liberty (1859), ch.1

16 We can never be sure that the opinion we
are endeavouring to stifle is a false opinion; and if we were sure, stifling it would
be an evil still.
ch.2

17 The liberty of the individual must be thus
far limited; he must not make himself a
nuisance to other people.
ch.3

18 The worth of a State, in the long run, is
the worth of the individuals composing it.
ch.5

19 When the land is cultivated entirely by the
spade and no horses are kept, a cow is kept
for every three acres of land.
Principles of Political Economy (1848).
A Treatise on Flemish Husbandry

20 The principle which regulates the existing
social relations between the two sexes—t-
he legal subordination of one sex to the
other—is wrong in itself, and now one of
the chief hindrances to human improve-

ment; and…it ought to be replaced by a principle of perfect equality, admitting no power or privilege on the one side, nor disability on the other.
The Subjection of Women (1869), ch.1

1 The most important thing women have to do is to stir up the zeal of women themselves.
Letter to Alexander Bain, 14 July 1869

2 Were there but a few hearts and intellects like hers this earth would already become the hoped-for heaven.
Epitaph (1858-9) for his wife Harriet, cemetery of St. Véran, near Avignon. See M. St.J. Packe, *Life of John Stuart Mill* (1954), bk.VII, ch. iii

EDNA ST. VINCENT MILLAY
1892-1950

3 Gently they go, the beautiful, the tender, the kind;
Quietly they go, the intelligent, the witty, the brave.
I know. But I do not approve. And I am not resigned.
The Buck in the Snow, III, **Dirge without Music**

4 Childhood is the kingdom where nobody dies.

Nobody that matters, that is.
Childhood is the Kingdom where Nobody dies

5 Man has never been the same since God died.
He has taken it very hard. Why, you'd think it was only yesterday,
The way he takes it.
Not that he says much, but he laughs much louder than he used to,
And he can't bear to be left alone even for a minute, and he can't
Sit still.
Conversation at Midnight, IV

6 My candle burns at both ends;
It will not last the night;
But ah, my foes, and oh my friends—
It gives a lovely light!
A Few Figs from Thistles (1920). **First Fig**

7 Was it for this I uttered prayers,
And sobbed and cursed and kicked the stairs,
That now, domestic as a plate,
I should retire at half-past eight?
Grown-up

8 Death devours all lovely things:
Lesbia with her sparrow
Shares the darkness,—presently
Every bed is narrow.
Passer Mortuus Est. See 65:4

9 After all, my erstwhile dear,
My no longer cherished,
Need we say it was not love,
Just because it perished?

WILLIAM MILLER 1810-1872

10 Wee Willie Winkie rins through the town,
Up stairs and down stairs in his nicht gown,
Tirling at the window, crying at the lock,
Are the weans in their bed, for it's now ten o'clock?
Willie Winkie (1841)

A.A. MILNE 1882-1956

11 They're changing guard at Buckingham Palace—
Christopher Robin went down with Alice.
Alice is marrying one of the guard.
'A soldier's life is terrible hard,'
Says Alice.
When We Were Very Young (1924). **Buckingham Palace**

12 James James
Morrison Morrison
Weatherby George Dupree
Took great
Care of his Mother
Though he was only three.
Disobedience

13 You must never go down to the end of the town if you don't go down with me.

14 The King asked
The Queen, and
The Queen asked
The Dairymaid:
'Could we have some butter for
The Royal slice of bread?'
The King's Breakfast

15 I do like a little bit of butter to my bread!

16 *What* is the matter with Mary Jane?
She's perfectly well and she hasn't a pain,
And it's lovely rice pudding for dinner again,—
What *is* the matter with Mary Jane?
Rice Pudding

17 Little Boy kneels at the foot of the bed,
Droops on the little hands, little gold head;
Hush! Hush! Whisper who dares!
Christopher Robin is saying his prayers.
Vespers

18 Isn't it funny
How a bear likes honey?
Buzz! Buzz! Buzz!
I wonder why he does?
Winnie-the-Pooh (1926), ch.1

1 I am a Bear of Very Little Brain, and long words Bother me.
ch.4

2 Time for a little something.
ch.6

3 When I was young, we *always* had mornings like this.
Toad of Toad Hall (1929), II.3. Milne's dramatization of Kenneth Grahame's *The Wind in the Willows.*

LORD MILNER 1854–1925

4 If we believe a thing to be bad, and if we have a right to prevent it, it is our duty to try to prevent it and to damn the consequences. [The Peers and the Budget.]
Speech at Glasgow, 26 Nov. 1909

JOHN MILTON 1608–1674

5 Blest pair of Sirens, pledges of Heaven's joy,
Sphere-born harmonious sisters, Voice and Verse.
At a Solemn Music

6 Come, knit hands, and beat the ground,
In a light fantastic round.
Comus (1634), l.143

7 Where an equal poise of hope and fear
Does arbitrate th' event, my nature is
That I incline to hope rather than fear,
And gladly banish squint suspicion.
l.410

8 How charming is divine philosophy!
Not harsh, and crabbed as dull fools suppose,
But musical as is Apollo's lute,
And a perpetual feast of nectared sweets,
Where no crude surfeit reigns.
l.476

9 Sabrina fair,
  Listen where thou art sitting
Under the glassy, cool, translucent wave,
  In twisted braids of lilies knitting
The loose train of thy amber-dropping hair.
l.859

10 Hence, vain deluding joys,
The brood of Folly without father bred.
Il Penseroso (1632), l.1

11 Hail divinest Melancholy.
l.12

12 Come, pensive Nun, devout and pure,
Sober, steadfast, and demure.
l.31

13 Where glowing embers through the room

Teach light to counterfeit a gloom,
Far from all resort of mirth,
Save the cricket on the hearth.
l.79

14 Hence, loathed Melancholy,
  Of Cerberus, and blackest Midnight born,
In Stygian cave forlorn,
  'Mongst horrid shapes, and shrieks, and sights unholy.
L'Allegro (1632), l.1

15 So buxom, blithe, and debonair.
l.24

16 Haste thee Nymph, and bring with thee
Jest and youthful jollity,
Quips and cranks, and wanton wiles,
Nods, and becks, and wreathed smiles.
l.25

17 Sport that wrinkled Care derides,
And Laughter holding both his sides.
Come, and trip it as ye go
On the light fantastic toe,
And in thy right hand lead with thee
The mountain nymph, sweet Liberty.
l.31

18 Of herbs, and other country messes,
Which the neat-handed Phyllis dresses.
l.85

19 Or sweetest Shakespeare, Fancy's child,
Warble his native wood-notes wild.
l.133

20 Alas! what boots it with uncessant care
  To tend the homely, slighted, shepherd's trade,
And strictly meditate the thankless Muse?
Were it not better done, as others use,
To sport with Amaryllis in the shade,
Or with the tangles of Neaera's hair.
Fame is the spur that the clear spirit doth raise
(That last infirmity of noble mind)
To scorn delights, and live laborious days;
But the fair guerdon when we hope to find,
And think to burst out into sudden blaze,
Comes the blind Fury with th' abhorred shears
And slits the thin-spun life.
Lycidas (1637), l.64

21   Their lean and flashy songs
Grate on their scrannel pipes of wretched straw,
The hungry sheep look up, and are not fed,
But, swoln with wind and the rank mist they draw,
Rot inwardly and foul contagion spread;
Besides what the grim wolf with privy paw
Daily devours apace, and nothing said.

But that two-handed engine at the door
Stands ready to smite once, and smite no
more.
l.123

1 Look homeward, Angel, now, and melt
with ruth.
l.163

2 For Lycidas your sorrow is not dead,
Sunk though he be beneath the watery
floor;
So sinks the day-star in the ocean bed,
And yet anon repairs his drooping head,
And tricks his beams, and with new
spangled ore,
Flames in the forehead of the morning sky:
So Lycidas sunk low, but mounted high,
Through the dear might of Him that walk-
ed the waves.
l.166

3 There entertain him all the saints above,
In solemn troops and sweet societies
That sing, and singing in their glory move,
And wipe the tears for ever from his eyes.
l.178

4 Thus sang the uncouth swain to th' oaks
and rills,
While the still morn went out with sandals
gray;
He touch'd the tender stops of various
quills,
With eager thought warbling his Doric lay.
l.186

5 At last he rose, and twitch'd his mantle
blue;
To-morrow to fresh woods, and pastures
new.
l.192

6 What needs my Shakespeare for his
honour'd bones,
The labour of an age in piled stones,
Or that his hallow'd relics should be hid
Under a star-y-pointing pyramid?
On Shakespeare (1630)

7 It was the winter wild
While the Heav'n-born child
All meanly wrapt in the rude manger
lies,
Nature in awe to him
Had doff't her gawdy trim
With her great Master so to sympathize.
On the Morning of Christ's Nativity (1629), l.29

8 Ring out ye crystal spheres,
Once bless our human ears
(If ye have power to touch our senses so)
And let your silver chime
Move in melodious time;
And let the base of heav'n's deep organ
blow,
And with your ninefold harmony
Make up full consort to th' angelic
symphony.
l.125

9 For if such holy song
Enwrap our fancy long,
Time will run back, and fetch the age of
gold
And speckled Vanity
Will sicken soon and die.
l.133

10 Showed him his room where he must
lodge that night,
Pulled off his boots, and took away the
light.
If any ask for him, it shall be said,
'Hobson has supped, and's newly gone to
bed.'
On the University Carrier

11 Fly, envious Time, till thou run out thy
race:
Call on the lazy leaden-stepping hours.
On Time, l.1

12 Of Man's first disobedience, and the fruit
Of that forbidden tree, whose mortal taste
Brought death into the world, and all our
woe,
With loss of Eden.
Paradise Lost (1667), 1668 ed. bk.i, l.1

13 Things unattempted yet in prose or
rhyme.
l.16

14   What in me is dark
Illumine, what is low raise and support;
That to the highth of this great argument
I may assert eternal Providence,
And justify the ways of God to Men.
l.22

15 Here we may reign secure, and in my
choice
To reign is worth ambition though in hell:
Better to reign in hell, than serve in heav'n.
l.261

16   And when night
Darkens the streets, then wander forth the
sons
Of Belial, flown with insolence and wine.
l.500

17   Who overcomes
By force, hath overcome but half his foe.
l.648

18   Let none admire
That riches grow in hell; that soil may best
Deserve the precious bane.
l.690

1   From morn
To noon he fell, from noon to dewy eve,
A summer's day; and with the setting sun
Dropt from the zenith like a falling star.
l.742

2   Pandoemonium, the high capitol
Of Satan and his peers.
l.756

3   Who shall tempt with wand'ring feet
The dark unbottom'd infinite abyss
And through the palpable obscure find out
His uncouth way.
bk.ii, l.404

4 With ruin upon ruin, rout on rout,
Confusion worse confounded.
l.995

5 So on this windy sea of land, the Fiend
Walked up and down alone bent on his
    prey.
bk.iii, l.440

6 So farewell hope, and with hope farewell
    fear,
Farewell remorse: all good to me is lost;
Evil be thou my Good.
bk.iv, l.108

7 For contemplation he and valour formed;
For softness she and sweet attractive
    grace,
He for God only, she for God in him:
His fair large front and eye sublime de-
    clared
Absolute rule.
l.297

8 Adam, the goodliest man of men since
    born
His sons; the fairest of her daughters Eve.
l.323

9   These two
Imparadised in one another's arms,
The happier Eden, shall enjoy their fill
Of bliss on bliss.
l.505

10 God is thy law, thou mine: to know no
    more
Is woman's happiest knowledge and her
    praise.
With thee conversing I forget all time.
l.637

11 But wherefore thou alone? Wherefore
    with thee
Came not all hell broke loose?
l.917

12 Best image of myself and dearer half.
bk.v, l.95

13 Standing on earth, not rapt above the
    Pole,

More safe I sing with mortal voice, un-
    chang'd
To hoarse or mute, though fall'n on evil
    days,
On evil days though fall'n, and evil
    tongues.
bk.vii, l.23

14   Drive far off the barb'rous disso-
    nance
Of Bacchus and his revellers.
l.32

15   Necessity and chance
Approach not me, and what I will is fate.
l.172

16 Tell me, how may I know him, how adore,
From whom I have that thus I move and
    live,
And feel that I am happier than I know?
bk.viii, l.280

17 As one who long in populous city pent,
Where houses thick and sewers annoy the
    air,
Forth issuing on a summer's morn to
    breathe
Among the pleasant villages and farms
Adjoin'd, from each thing met conceives
    delight.
bk.ix, l.445

18 She fair, divinely fair, fit love for Gods.
l.489

19   Flesh of flesh,
Bone of my bone thou art, and from thy
    state
Mine never shall be parted, weal or woe.
l.915

20   Yet I shall temper so
Justice with mercy.
bk.x, l.77

21 Demoniac frenzy, moping melancholy,
And moon-struck madness.
bk.xi, l.485

22 The world was all before them, where to
    choose
Their place of rest, and Providence their
    guide:
They hand in hand with wandering steps
    and slow
Through Eden took their solitary way.
bk.xii, l.646

23 Of whom to be dispraised were no small
    praise.
Paradise Regained (1671), bk.iii, l.56

24 A little onward lend thy guiding hand
To these dark steps, a little further on.
Samson Agonistes (1671), l.1

1 Eyeless in Gaza, at the mill with slaves.
l.41

2 O dark, dark, dark, amid the blaze of noon,
Irrecoverably dark, total eclipse
Without all hope of day!
l.80

3 To live a life half dead, a living death.
l.100

4 For evil news rides post, while good news baits.
l.1538

5   Samson hath quit himself
Like Samson, and heroically hath finish'd
A life heroic.
l.1709

6 Nothing is here for tears, nothing to wail
Or knock the breast; no weakness, no contempt,
Dispraise or blame; nothing but well and fair,
And what may quiet us in a death so noble.
l.1721

7 His servants he with new acquist
Of true experience from this great event
With peace and consolation hath dismiss'd,
And calm of mind all passion spent.
l.1752

8 How soon hath Time, the subtle thief of youth
Stoln on its wing my three and twentieth year.
Sonnet ii. **On his having arrived at the age of twenty-three**

9 Avenge, O Lord, thy slaughtered saints, whose bones
Lie scattered on the Alpine mountains cold;
Ev'n them who kept thy truth so pure of old,
When all our fathers worshipped stocks and stones,
Forget not.
xv. **On the late Massacre in Piedmont**

10 When I consider how my light is spent,
E're half my days, in this dark world and wide,
And that one Talent which is death to hide,
Lodg'd with me useless.
xvi. **On His Blindness**

11   Thousands at his bidding speed
And post o'er Land and Ocean without rest:

They also serve who only stand and wait.

12 Methought I saw my late espousèd Saint
Brought to me like Alcestis from the grave.
xix. **On His Deceased Wife**

13 For what can war but endless war still breed?
On the Lord General Fairfax

14   Peace hath her victories
No less renowned than war.
To the Lord General Cromwell, May 1652

15 As good almost kill a man as kill a good book: who kills a man kills a reasonable creature, God's image; but he who destroys a good book, kills reason itself, kills the image of God, as it were in the eye.
Areopagitica (1644)

16 A good book is the precious life-blood of a master spirit, embalmed and treasured up on purpose to a life beyond life.

17 I cannot praise a fugitive and cloistered virtue, unexercised and unbreathed, that never sallies out and sees her adversary, but slinks out of the race, where that immortal garland is to be run for, not without dust and heat. Assuredly we bring not innocence into the world, we bring impurity much rather: that which purifies us is trial, and trial is by what is contrary.

18 If we think to regulate printing thereby to rectify manners, we must regulate all recreations and pastimes, all that is delightful to man.

19 Let not England forget her precedence of teaching nations how to live.
The Doctrine and Discipline of Divorce (1643)

20 I owe no light or leading received from any man in the discovery of this truth.
The Judgement of Martin Bucer Concerning Divorce

21 What I have spoken, is the language of that which is not called amiss *The good old Cause*.
The Ready and Easy Way to Establish a Free Commonwealth (1660)

MISSAL

22 *O felix culpa, quae talem ac tantum meruit habere Redemptorem.*
O happy fault, which has deserved to have such and so mighty a Redeemer.
'Exsultet' on Holy Saturday

MARGARET MITCHELL 1900–1949

23 After all, tomorrow is another day.
Gone with the Wind (1936), closing words.

NANCY MITFORD 1904–1973

1 'Twenty-three and a quarter minutes past', Uncle Matthew was saying furiously, 'in precisely six and three-quarter minutes the damned fella will be late.'
Love in a Cold Climate, pt.1, ch.13

2 When the loo paper gets thicker and the writing paper thinner it's always a bad sign, at home.
pt.2, ch.2

3 Abroad is unutterably bloody and foreigners are fiends.
The Pursuit of Love, ch.15

EMILIO MOLA d. 1937

4 *La quinta columna.*
The fifth column.
A reference to Mola's expectation of help from civilians in Madrid, reported in *Mundo Obrero* in the first week of Oct. 1936; but the phrase may not have been coined with direct reference to the Madrid offensive, since there is doubt over the number of columns deployed in his march on the city. See, e.g., G. Hills, *The Battle for Madrid* (1976), p.85n, and *Madrid: Servicio Histórico Militar*, La Marcha sobre Madrid (1968), p.88 n.70

MOLIÈRE (J.-B. POQUELIN) 1622–1673

5 *Il faut manger pour vivre et non pas vivre pour manger.*
One should eat to live, and not live to eat.
L'Avare (1668), III.v

6 *Par ma foi! il y a plus de quarante ans que je dis de la prose sans que j'en susse rien.*
Good heavens! For more than forty years I have been speaking prose without knowing it.
Le Bourgeois Gentilhomme (1670), II.iv

7 *Tout ce qui n'est point prose est vers; et tout ce qui n'est point vers est prose.*
All that is not prose is verse; and all that is not verse is prose.

8 *On ne meurt qu'une fois, et c'est pour si longtemps!*
One dies only once, and it's for such a long time!
Le Dépit Amoureux (1656), V.iii

9 *Que diable allait-il faire dans cette galère?*
What the devil would he be doing in this gang?
Les Fourberies de Scapin (1671), II.vii

0 *Vous l'avez voulu, Georges Dandin, vous l'avez voulu.*
You asked for it, George Dandin, you

asked for it.
Georges Dandin (1668), I.ix

11 *Oui, cela était autrefois ainsi, mais nous avons changé tout cela.*
Yes, in the old days that was so, but we have changed all that.
Le Médecin malgré lui (1666), II.iv

12 *Ils commencent ici par faire pendre un homme et puis ils lui font son procès.*
Here [in Paris] they hang a man first, and try him afterwards.
Monsieur de Pourceaugnac (1669), III.ii

13 *Assassiner c'est le plus court chemin.*
Assassination is the quickest way.
Le Sicilien (1668), XIII

14 *Le scandale du monde est ce qui fait l'offense, Et ce n'est pas pécher que pécher en silence.*
It is public scandal that constitutes offence, and to sin in secret is not to sin at all.
Le Tartuffe (1664), IV.v

HELMUTH VON MOLTKE 1800–1891

15 *Der Krieg ein Glied in Gottes Weltordnung ...Ohne den Krieg würde die Welt in Materialismus versumpfen.*
War is a necessary part of God's arrangement of the world...Without war, the world would slide dissolutely into materialism.
Letter to Dr. J.K. Bluntschli, 11 Dec. 1880

LADY MARY WORTLEY MONTAGU 1689–1762

16 People wish their enemies dead—but I do not; I say give them the gout, give them the stone!
Letter from Horace Walpole to the Earl of Harcourt, 17 Sept. 1778

MONTAIGNE 1533–1592

17 *Je veux...que la mort me trouve plantant mes choux, mais nonchalant d'elle, et encore plus de mon jardin imparfait.*
I want death to find me planting my cabbages, but caring little for it, and even less for the imperfections of my garden.
Essais, I.xx. [References are to M. Rat's edition of the *Essais* (1958) which, in accordance with the Strowski and Gebelin text (1906-1933), conflates the 1580 edition of books I and II, the revised and enlarged 1588 edition of all three books, and later manuscript additions published posthumously.]

18 *Il faut noter, que les jeux d'enfants ne sont pas jeux: et les faut juger en eux, comme*

leurs plus sérieuses actions.
It should be noted that children at play are not playing about; their games should be seen as their most serious-minded activity.
xxiii

1 *Si on me presse de dire pourquoi je l'aimais, je sens que cela ne se peut s'exprimer, qu'en répondant: 'Parce que c'était lui; parce que c'était moi.'*
If I am pressed to say why I loved him, I feel it can only be explained by replying: 'Because it was he; because it was me.'
[Of his friend Étienne de la Boétie.] xxviii

2 *Il n'y a guère moins de tourment au gouvernement d'une famille que d'un état entier …et, pour être les occupations domestiques moins importantes, elles n'en sont pas moins importunes.*
There is scarcely any less bother in the running of a family than in that of an entire state. And domestic business is no less importunate for being less important.
xxxix

3 *La plus grande chose du monde, c'est de savoir être à soi.*
The greatest thing in the world is to know how to be one's own.

4 *Notre religion est faite pour extirper les vices; elle les couvre, les nourrit, les incite.*
Our religion is made so as to wipe out vices; it covers them up, nourishes them, incites them.
II.xii

5 *'Que sais-je?'*
What do I know?

6 *L'homme est bien insensé. Il ne saurait forger un ciron, et forge des Dieux à douzaines.*
Man is quite insane. He wouldn't know how to create a maggot, and he creates Gods by the dozen.

7 *Quelqu'un pourrait dire de moi que j'ai seulement fait ici un amas de fleurs étrangères, m'y ayant fourni du mien que le filet à les lier.*
It could be said of me that in this book I have only made up a bunch of other men's flowers, providing of my own only the string that ties them together.
III.xii

FIELD-MARSHAL MONTGOMERY
1887-1976

8 The U.S. has broken the second rule of war. That is, don't go fighting with your land army on the mainland of Asia. Rule One is don't march on Moscow. I devel-

oped these two rules myself.
Of American policy in Vietnam. Chalfon
Montgomery of Alamein (1976), p.318

CASIMIR, COMTE DE MONTRONI
1768-1843

9 *Défiez-vous des premiers mouvement parce qu'ils sont bons.*
Have no truck with first impulses as the are always generous ones.
Attr., Comte J. d'Estournel, *Derniers Souvenir.*
Also attr. Talleyrand. See 78:4

EDWARD MOORE 1712-1757

10 This is adding insult to injuries.
The Foundling (1747-8), V.ii

11 I am rich beyond the dreams of avarice.
The Gamester (1753), II.ii

MARIANNE MOORE 1887-1972

12 My father used to say
'Superior people never make long visits.'
Silence

THOMAS MOORE 1779-1852

13 Believe me, if all those endearing youn, charms,
Which I gaze on so fondly today,
Were to change by tomorrow, and fleet i my arms,
Like fairy gifts fading away!
Thou wouldst still be ador'd as this mo ment thou art,
Let thy loveliness fade as it will,
And, around the dear ruin, each wish o my heart
Would entwine itself verdantly still.
Irish Melodies (1807). **Believe Me, if all thos Endearing Young Charms**

14 The harp that once through Tara's halls
The soul of music shed,
Now hangs as mute on Tara's walls
As if that soul were fled. —
So sleeps the pride of former days,
So glory's thrill is o'er;
And hearts, that once beat high for praise,
Now feel that pulse no more.
The Harp that Once

15 No, there's nothing half so sweet in life
As love's young dream.
Love's Young Dream

16 The Minstrel Boy to the war is gone,
In the ranks of death you'll find him;
His father's sword he has girded on,
And his wild harp slung behind him.
The Minstrel Boy

1 She is far from the land where her young
　　hero sleeps,
　And lovers are round her, sighing:
　But coldly she turns from their gaze, and
　　weeps,
　　For her heart in his grave is lying.
She is Far

2 'Tis the last rose of summer
　　Left blooming alone;
　All her lovely companions
　　Are faded and gone.
'Tis the Last Rose

3 I never nurs'd a dear gazelle,
　　To glad me with its soft black eye,
　But when it came to know me well,
　　And love me, it was sure to die!
Lalla Rookh (1817). **The Fire-Worshippers,** i.
l.283

4 Oft, in the stilly night,
　　Ere Slumber's chain has bound me,
　Fond Memory brings the light
　　Of other days around me.
National Airs (1815). **Oft in the Stilly Night**

THOMAS OSBERT MORDAUNT
1730-1809

5 Sound, sound the clarion, fill the fife,
　　Throughout the sensual world proclaim,
　One crowded hour of glorious life
　　Is worth an age without a name.
Verses Written During the War, 1756-1763. *The
Bee,* 12 Oct. 1791

SIR THOMAS MORE 1478-1535

6 I pray you, master Lieutenant, see me safe
up, and my coming down let me shift for
my self. [On mounting the scaffold.]
Roper, *Life of Sir Thomas More* (1935), p.103

7 This hath not offended the king. [As he
drew his beard aside on placing his head
on the block.]
Bacon, *Apophthegms,* 22

THOMAS MORELL 1703-1784

8 See, the conquering hero comes!
Sound the trumpets, beat the drums!
Joshua (1748), pt.iii (Libretto for Handel's ora-
torio)

LORD MORLEY (3rd EARL OF
MORLEY) 1843-1905

9 I am always very glad when Lord Salisbury makes a great speech,...It is sure to
contain at least one blazing indiscretion
which it is a delight to remember.
Speech, Hull, 25 Nov. 1887

'COUNTESS MORPHY' (MARCELLE
AZRA FORBES) fl. 1930-50

10 The tragedy of English cooking is that
'plain' cooking cannot be entrusted to
'plain' cooks.
English Recipes (1935), p.17

DESMOND MORRIS 1928-

11 There are one hundred and ninety-three
living species of monkeys and apes. One
hundred and ninety-two of them are
covered with hair. The exception is a
naked ape self-named *Homo sapiens.*
The Naked Ape (1967), Introduction

GENERAL GEORGE POPE MORRIS
1802-1864

12 Woodman, spare that tree!
　　Touch not a single bough!
In youth it sheltered me,
　　And I'll protect it now.
Woodman, Spare That Tree (1830)

WILLIAM MORRIS 1834-1896

13 What is this, the sound and rumour? What
　　is this that all men hear,
Like the wind in hollow valleys when the
　　storm is drawing near,
Like the rolling on of ocean in the eventide
　　of fear?
　　'Tis the people marching on.
Chants for Socialists (1885), **The March of the
Workers**

14 Forget six counties overhung with smoke,
Forget the snorting steam and piston
　　stroke,
Forget the spreading of the hideous town;
Think rather of the pack-horse on the
　　down,
And dream of London, small and white
　　and clean,
The clear Thames bordered by its gardens
　　green.
The Earthly Paradise (1868-70). Prologue. **The
Wanderers,** l.1

15 And ever she sung from noon to noon,
'Two red roses across the moon.'
Two Red Roses Across the Moon

16 Have nothing in your houses that you do
not know to be useful, or believe to be
beautiful.
Hopes and Fears for Art (1882), p.108

J.B. MORTON ('BEACHCOMBER')
1893–1979

1 Hush, hush,
Nobody cares!
Christopher Robin
Has
Fallen
Down-
Stairs.
By the Way (1931), 18 Dec. **Now We are Sick.**
See 166:17

THOMAS MORTON 1764?–1838

2 Approbation from Sir Hubert Stanley is
praise indeed.
A Cure for the Heartache (1797), V.ii

3 Always ding, dinging Dame Grundy into
my ears—what will Mrs Grundy zay?
What will Mrs Grundy think?
Speed the Plough (1798), I.i

JOHN LOTHROP MOTLEY 1814–1877

4 As long as he lived, he was the guiding-
star of a whole brave nation, and when he
died the little children cried in the streets.
[William of Orange.]
Rise of the Dutch Republic (1856), pt.vi, ch.vii

5 Give us the luxuries of life, and we will
dispense with its necessities.
O.W. Holmes, *Autocrat of the Breakfast-Table*,
ch.6

WILHELM MÜLLER 1794–1827

6 *Vom Abendrot zum Morgenlicht*
Ward mancher Kopf zum Greise.
Wer glaubt's? Und meiner ward es nicht
Auf dieser ganzen Reise.
Between dusk and dawn many a head has
turned white. Who can believe it? And
mine has not changed on all this long
journey.
Die Winterreise, 14. **Der greise Kopf**

ALFRED DE MUSSET 1810–1857

7 *Le seul bien qui me rest au monde*
Est d'avoir quelquefois pleuré.
The only good thing left to me is that I
have sometimes wept.
Poèmes

8 *Malgré moi l'infini me tourmente.*
I can't help it, the idea of the infinite tor-
ments me.
Premières Poésies. L'Espoir en Dieu

NAPOLEON I 1769–1821

9 *Du sublime au ridicule il n'y a qu'un pas.*
There is only one step from the sublime t
the ridiculous.
To De Pradt, Polish ambassador, after the re
treat from Moscow in 1812. De Pradt, *Histoir
de l'Ambassade dans le grand-duché de Varsovi
en 1812*, ed.1815, p.215. See 179:13

10 *Quant au courage moral, il avait trouvé for
rare, disait-il, celui de deux heures aprè
minuit; c'est-à-dire le courage de l'impro
viste.*
As to moral courage, I have very rarel
met with two o'clock in the morning cour
age: I mean instantaneous courage.
Las Cases, Mémorial de Ste-Hélène, Dec. 4-5
1815

11 *La carrière ouverte aux talents.*
The career open to talents.
O'Meara, *Napoleon in Exile* (1822), vol.i, p.103

12 *L'Angleterre est une nation de boutiquiers.*
England is a nation of shopkeepers.
Attr. by B.E. O'Meara, *Napoleon at St. Helena*
vol.ii. See 1:5, 242:1

13 Has he luck?
Attr. Habitually asked, to assess a man's prob
able practical value. See A.J.P. Taylor, *Politics i
Wartime* (1964), ch.16

14 An army marches on its stomach.
Attr. See, e.g., *Windsor Magazine*, 1904, p.268
Probably condensed from a long passage in La
Cases, *Mémorial de Ste-Hélène* (Nov. 1816)
Also attr. to Frederick the Great.

OGDEN NASH 1902–1971

15 One would be in less danger
From the wiles of a stranger
If one's own kin and kith
Were more fun to be with.
Family Court

16 Candy
Is dandy
But liquor
Is quicker.
Reflections on Ice-Breaking

17 When I consider how my life is spent,
I hardly ever repent.
Reminiscent Reflection. See 170:10

18 I think that I shall never see
A billboard lovely as a tree
Indeed, unless the billboards fall
I'll never see a tree at all.
Song of the Open Road. See 142:1

19 The turtle lives 'twixt plated decks
Which practically conceal its sex.
I think it clever of the turtle

In such a fix to be so fertile.
The Turtle

1 Sure, deck your lower limbs in pants;
Yours are the limbs, my sweeting.
You look divine as you advance—
Have you seen yourself retreating?
What's the Use?

THOMAS NASHE 1567–1601

2 Brightness falls from the air;
Queens have died young and fair;
Dust hath closed Helen's eye.
I am sick, I must die.
    Lord have mercy on us.
In Time of Pestilence

3 Spring, the sweet spring, is the year's
        pleasant king;
Then blooms each thing, then maids dance
        in a ring,
Cold doth not sting, the pretty birds do
        sing:
    Cuckoo, jug-jug, pu-we, to-witta-woo.
Songs from *Summer's Last will and Testament*
(1600)

HORATIO, LORD NELSON 1758–1805

4 I have only one eye,—I have a right to be
blind sometimes:...I really do not see the
signal!
At the battle of Copenhagen. Southey, *Life of
Nelson*, ch. 7

5 I believe my arrival was most welcome,
not only to the Commander of the Fleet
but almost to every individual in it; and
when I came to explain to them the *'Nelson
touch'*, it was like an electric shock. Some
shed tears, all approved—'It was new—it
was singular—it was simple!'...Some may
be Judas's; but the majority are much
pleased with my commanding them.
Letter to Lady Hamilton, 1 Oct. 1805

6 England expects that every man will do his
duty.
At the battle of Trafalgar

7 This is too warm work, Hardy, to last
long.

8 Thank God, I have done my duty.

9 Kiss me, Hardy.

EMPEROR NERO A.D. 37–68

10 *Qualis artifex pereo!*
What an artist dies with me!
Suetonius, *Life of Nero*, xlix.1

GÉRARD DE NERVAL 1808–1855

11 *Je suis le ténébreux,—le veuf,—l'inconsolé,*
Le prince d'Aquitaine à la tour abolie:
Ma seule étoile *est morte, et mon luth con-*
stellé
Porte le soleil *noir de la* mélancolie.
I am the darkly shaded, the bereaved, the
inconsolate, the prince of Aquitaine,
with the blasted tower. My only *star* is
dead, and my star-strewn lute carries
on it the black *sun* of *melancholy*.
El Desdichado

SIR HENRY NEWBOLT 1862–1938

12 Admirals all, for England's sake,
    Honour be yours, and fame!
And honour, as long as waves shall break,
    To Nelson's peerless name!
Admirals All, i

13 He clapped the glass to his sightless eye,
    And 'I'm damned if I see it', he said.
See 175:4

14 Drake he's in his hammock till the great
        Armadas come.
    (Capten, art tha sleepin' there below?)
The Island Race. Drake's Drum (1896)

15 There's a breathless hush in the Close to-
        night—
    Ten to make and the match to win—
A bumping pitch and a blinding light,
    An hour to play and the last man in.
And it's not for the sake of a ribboned
        coat,
    Or the selfish hope of a season's fame,
But his Captain's hand on his shoulder
        smote—
    'Play up! play up! and play the game!'
Vitaï Lampada

16 Now the sunset breezes shiver,
And she's fading down the river,
But in England's song for ever
    She's the Fighting Téméraire.
The Fighting Téméraire

17 'Ye have robb'd,' said he, 'ye have slaugh-
        ter'd and made an end,
Take your ill-got plunder, and bury the
        dead.'
He Fell Among Thieves

CARDINAL NEWMAN 1801–1890

18 It is very difficult to get up resentment
towards persons whom one has never seen.
Apologia pro Vita Sua (1864). **Mr. Kingsley's
Method of Disputation**

19 There is such a thing as legitimate warfare:
war has its laws; there are things which

may fairly be done, and things which may not be done...He has attempted (as I may call it) to *poison the wells.*

1 It is almost a definition of a gentleman to say that he is one who never inflicts pain.
The Idea of a University (1852). **Knowledge and Religious Duty**

2 It is as absurd to argue men, as to torture them, into believing.
Sermon at Oxford, 11 Dec. 1831

3 Praise to the Holiest in the height,
And in the depth be praise;
In all his words most wonderful,
Most sure in all His ways.
The Dream of Gerontius (1865)

4 Lead, kindly Light, amid the encircling gloom,
Lead thou me on.
The Pillar of Cloud. **Lead Kindly Light** (1833)

5 *We can believe what we choose.* We are answerable for what we choose to believe.
Letter to Mrs. William Froude, 27 June 1848

6 Though you can believe what you choose, you must believe what you ought.
3 July 1848

SIR ISAAC NEWTON 1642–1727

7 If I have seen further it is by standing on the shoulders of giants.
Letter to Robert Hooke, 5 Feb. 1675/6. See 20:2

8 I do not know what I may appear to the world, but to myself I seem to have been only like a boy playing on the sea-shore, and diverting myself in now and then finding a smoother pebble or a prettier shell than ordinary, whilst the great ocean of truth lay all undiscovered before me.
L.T. More, *Isaac Newton* (1934), p.664

EMPEROR NICHOLAS I OF RUSSIA 1796–1855

9 *Nous avons sur les bras un homme malade — un homme gravement malade.*
We have on our hands a sick man—a very sick man.
[The sick man of Europe, the Turk.]
Parliamentary Papers. Accounts and Papers, vol.lxxi, pt.5. Eastern Papers, p.2. Sir G.H. Seymour to Lord John Russell, 11 Jan. 1853

10 Russia has two generals in whom she can confide—Generals Janvier and Février.
Attr. See *Punch*, 10 Mar. 1853

ROBERT NICHOLS 1893–1944

11 Was there love once? I have forgotten her
Was there grief once? grief yet is mine.
Fulfilment

REINHOLD NIEBUHR 1892–1971

12 Man's capacity for justice makes democracy possible; but man's inclination injustice makes democracy necessary.
The Children of Light and the Children of Darness (1944), foreword

FRIEDRICH NIETZSCHE 1844–1900

13 *Ich lehre euch den Übermenschen. Der Mensch ist Etwas, das überwunden werden soll.*
I teach you the superman. Man is something to be surpassed.
Also Sprach Zarathustra. Prologue (1883)

14 *Lachende Löwen müssen kommen.*
Laughing lions must come.
IV, **Die Begrüssung**

15 *Wie ich den Philosophen verstehe, als eine furchtbaren Explosionsstoff, vor dem Alle in Gefahr ist.*
What I understand by 'philosopher': terrible explosive in the presence of which everything is in danger.
Ecce Homo, **Die Unzeitgemässen**

16 *Gott ist tot: aber so wie die Art der Menschen ist, wird es vielleicht noch jartausendlang Höhlen geben, in denen man seinen Schatten zeigt.*
God is dead: but considering the state the species Man is in, there will perhaps be caves, for ages yet, in which his shadow will be shown.
Die fröhliche Wissenschaft, III.108

17 *Moralität ist Herden-Instinkt in Einzelnen*
Morality is the herd-instinct in the individual.
116

18 *Der christliche Entschluss, die Welt hässlich und schlecht zu finden, hat die Welt hässlich und schlecht gemacht.*
The Christian resolution to find the world ugly and bad has made the world ugly and bad.
130

19 *Glaubt es mir!—das Geheimniss, um die grösste Fruchtbarkeit und den grössten Genuss vom Dasein einzuernten, heisst gefährlich leben!*
Believe me! The secret of reaping the greatest fruitfulness and the greatest en

joyment from life is to *live dangerously!*
IV.283

1 *Wer mit Ungeheuern kämpft, mag zusehn,
dass er nicht dabei zum Ungeheuer wird.
Und wenn du lange in einen Abgrund
blickst, blickt der Abgrund auch in dich
hinein.*
He who fights with monsters might take
care lest he thereby become a monster.
And if you gaze for long into an abyss, the
abyss gazes also into you.
Jenseits von Gut und Böse, IV.146

2 *Herren-Moral und Sklaven-Moral.*
Master-morality and slave-morality.
IX.260

3 *Auf dem Grunde aller dieser vornehmen
Rassen ist das Raubtier, die prachtvolle
nach Beute und Sieg lüstern schweifende
blonde Bestie nicht zu verkennen.*
At the base of all these aristocratic races
the predator is not to be mistaken, the
splendorous *blond beast,* avidly rampant
for plunder and victory.
Zur Genealogie der Moral, I.11

FLORENCE NIGHTINGALE
1820–1910

4 To understand God's thoughts we must
study statistics, for these are the measure
of his purpose.
Attr. See K. Pearson, *Life...of Francis Galton,*
vol.II, ch.xiii, sect.i

GENERAL R.-G. NIVELLE 1856–1924

5 *Ils ne passeront pas.*
They shall not pass.
Used as a slogan throughout the defence of Ver-
dun and often attributed to Marshal Pétain.
Nivelle's Order of the Day dated 26 Feb. 1916
read *'Vous ne les laisserez pas passer.'* Taken up
by the Republicans in the Spanish Civil War as
'No pasarán!'

CHARLES HOWARD, DUKE OF
NORFOLK 1746–1815

6 I cannot be a good Catholic; I cannot go
to heaven; and if a man is to go to the
devil, he may as well go thither from the
House of Lords as from any other place on
earth.
Henry Best, *Personal and Literary Memorials*
(1829), ch.18

ALFRED NOYES 1880–1958

7 Go down to Kew in lilac-time, in lilac-
time, in lilac-time;

Go down to Kew in lilac-time (it isn't
far from London!)
Barrel Organ

8 The wind was a torrent of darkness
among the gusty trees,
The moon was a ghostly galleon tossed
upon cloudy seas,
The road was a ribbon of moonlight over
the purple moor,
And the highwayman came riding—
Riding—riding—
The highwayman came riding, up to the
old inn-door.
The Highwayman

SEAN O'CASEY 1884–1964

9 The whole counthry's in a state of chassis.
[Boyle.]
Juno and the Paycock (1924), II. Meaning 'a
state of chaos'. In Act I and Act III (last line)
used of the whole world.

WILLIAM OCCAM c.1280–1349

10 *Entia non sunt multiplicanda praeter neces-
sitatem.*
No more things should be presumed to
exist than are absolutely necessary.
'Occams's Razor'. Ancient philosophical principle, often attributed to Occam, but used by
many earlier thinkers. Not found in this form in
his writings, though he frequently used similar
expressions, e.g. *Pluralitas non est ponenda sine
necessitate* (*Quodlibeta,* c.1324, V, Q.i).

ADOLPH S. OCHS 1858–1935

11 All the news that's fit to print.
Motto of the *New York Times*

JAMES OGILVY, FIRST EARL OF
SEAFIELD 1664–1730

12 Now there's ane end of ane old song.
As he signed the engrossed exemplification of the
Act of Union, 1706. *Lockhart Papers* (1817),
i.223

DANIEL O'CONNELL 1775–1847

13 [Sir Robert] Peel's smile: like the silver
plate on a coffin.
Quoting J.P. Curran (1750–1817), Irish politician and lawyer. See *Hansard,* 26 Feb. 1835

JOHN O'KEEFFE 1747–1833

14 Amo, amas, I love a lass,
As a cedar tall and slender;
Sweet cowslip's grace
Is her nom'native case,
And she's of the feminine gender.
The Agreeable Surprise (1781), II.ii

1 Fat, fair and forty were all the toasts of the young men.
Irish Mimic (1795), ii

2 You should always except the present company.
London Hermit (1793), I.ii

DENNIS O'KELLY 1720?–1787

3 Eclipse first, the rest nowhere.
Epsom, 3 May 1769. *Annals of Sporting,* vol.ii, p.271. D.N.B. gives the occasion as the Queen's Plate at Winchester, 1769.

FRANK WARD O'MALLEY 1875–1932

4 Life is just one damned thing after another.
Attr. See *Literary Digest,* 5 Nov. 1932. Also attr. Elbert Hubbard

BARONESS ORCZY 1865–1947

5 We seek him here, we seek him there,
  Those Frenchies seek him everywhere.
  Is he in heaven?—Is he in hell?
  That demmed, elusive Pimpernel?
The Scarlet Pimpernel (1905), ch.12

GEORGE ORWELL 1903–1950

6 Four legs good, two legs bad.
Animal Farm (1945), ch.3

7 All animals are equal but some animals are more equal than others.
ch.10

8 Whatever is funny is subversive, every joke is ultimately a custard pie... A dirty joke is...a sort of mental revolution.
The Art of Donald McGill (1945)

9 I'm fat, but I'm thin inside. Has it ever struck you that there's a thin man inside every fat man, just as they say there's a statue inside every block of stone?
Coming Up For Air (1939), Part I, ch.3. See 77:9

10 Big Brother is watching you.
1984 (1949), p.1

11 *Doublethink* means the power of holding two contradictory beliefs in one's mind simultaneously, and accepting both of them.
pt.II, ch.9

12 If you want a picture of the future, imagine a boot stamping on a human face—for ever.
pt.III, ch.3

13 At 50, everyone has the face he deserves.
Closing words, MS Notebook, 17 Apr. 1949

ARTHUR O'SHAUGHNESSY
1844–1881

14 We are the music makers,
  We are the dreamers of dreams.
Ode

JOHN L. O'SULLIVAN 1813–1895

15 All government is evil, and the parent c evil...The best government is that whic governs least.
Introduction to *The United States Magazine an Democratic Review* (1837)

16 Our manifest destiny to overspread th continent allotted by Providence for th free development of our yearly multiplyin millions.
vol.xvii, July-Aug. 1845, p.5

JAMES OTIS 1725–1783

17 Taxation without representation tyranny.
Watchword (coined 1761?) of the American Re volution. See Samuel Eliot Morison, 'Jame Otis', *Dict. Am. Biog.,* xiv.102

SIR THOMAS OVERBURY 1581–1613

18 He disdains all things above his reach, an preferreth all countries before his own.
Miscellaneous Works. **An Affectate Traveller**

OVID 43 B.C–A.D. 17

19 *Procul hinc, procul este, severae!*
  Far hence, keep far from me, you grir women!
Amores, II.i.3

20 *Iuppiter ex alto periuria ridet amantum.*
  Jupiter from on high laughs at lovers' pe juries.
Ars Amatoria, i.633

21 *Medio tutissimus ibis.*
  A middle course is the safest for you t take.
Metamorphoses, ii.137

22   *Video meliora, proboque;*
  Deteriora sequor.
  I see the better way, and approve it; follow the worse.
vii.20

23 *Principiis obsta; sero medicina paratur*
    Cum mala per longas convaluere moras.
  Stop it at the start, it's late for medicine t be prepared when disease has grow

strong through long delays.
Remedia Amoris, 91

1 *Sponte sua carmen numeros veniebat ad aptos,*
   Et quod temptabam dicere versus erat.
   Of its own accord my song would come in the right rhythms, and what I was try-ing to say was poetry.
   Tristia, IV.x.25

WILFRED OWEN 1893-1918

2 Above all, this book is not concerned with Poetry.
   The subject of it is War, and the Pity of War.
   The Poetry is in the pity.
   Poems (1920), Preface

3 All the poet can do today is to warn.
   That is why the true Poets must be truth-ful.

4 What passing-bells for these who die as cattle?
   Only the monstrous anger of the guns.
   Only the stuttering rifles' rapid rattle
   Can patter out their hasty orisons.
   Anthem for Doomed Youth

5 The pallor of girls' brows shall be their pall;
   Their flowers the tenderness of patient minds,
   And each slow dusk a drawing-down of blinds.

6 Was it for this the clay grew tall?
   —O what made fatuous sunbeams toil
   To break earth's sleep at all?
   Futility

7 Red lips are not so red
   As the stained stones kissed by the English dead.
   Greater Love

8 Hour after hour they ponder the warm field,—
   And the far valley behind, where the but-tercup
   Had blessed with gold their slow boots coming up.
   Spring Offensive

9 It seemed that out of battle I escaped
   Down some profound dull tunnel, long since scooped
   Through granites which titanic wars had groined.
   Strange Meeting

10 'Strange friend,' I said, 'here is no cause to mourn.'
   'None,' said the other, 'save the undone years,
   The hopelessness. Whatever hope is yours
   Was my life also; I went hunting wild
   After the wildest beauty in the world.'

11 I am the enemy you killed, my friend.

TOM PAINE 1737-1809

12 It is necessary to the happiness of man that he be mentally faithful to himself. Infidelity does not consist in believing, or in disbelieving, it consists in professing to believe what one does not believe.
   The Age of Reason (1794), pt.i

13 The sublime and the ridiculous are often so nearly related, that it is difficult to class them separately. One step above the sub-lime, makes the ridiculous; and one step above the ridiculous, makes the sublime again.
   pt.ii (1795), p.20

14 As to religion, I hold it to be the indispens-able duty of government to protect all con-scientious professors thereof, and I know of no other business which government hath to do therewith.
   Common Sense (1776), ch.4

15 These are the times that try men's souls. The summer soldier and the sunshine pat-riot will, in this crisis, shrink from the service of their country; but he that stands it *now*, deserves the love and thanks of men and women.
   The Crisis, Intro. (Dec. 1776)

16 A share in two revolutions is living to some purpose.
   See Eric Foner, *Tom Paine and Revolutionary America* (1976), ch.7

JOSÉ DE PALAFOX 1780-1847

17 War to the knife.
   On 4 Aug. 1808, at the siege of Saragossa, the French general Verdier sent a one-word sugges-tion: 'Capitulation'. Palafox replied '*Guerra y cuchillo*' (War and the knife), later reported as '*Guerra a cuchillo*' and commonly rendered as above. The correctness of the former is confirm-ed by its appearance, at the behest of Palafox himself, on survivors' medals. Gómez de Ar-teche, *Guerra de la Independencia* (1868-1903), II, iv

REVD. WILLIAM PALEY 1743-1805

18 Who can refute a sneer?
   Principles of Moral and Political Philosophy (1785), bk.v, ch.9

LORD PALMERSTON 1784–1865

1 You may call it coalition, you may call it the accidental and fortuitous concurrence of atoms.
Of a projected Palmerston-Disraeli coalition. House of Commons, 5 Mar. 1857

2 Die, my dear Doctor, that's the last thing I shall do!
Attr. last words

DOROTHY PARKER 1893–1967

3 Oh, life is a glorious cycle of song,
A medley of extemporanea;
And love is a thing that can never go wrong,
And I am Marie of Roumania.
Comment

4 Four be the things I'd been better without:
Love, curiosity, freckles, and doubt.
Inventory

5 Men seldom make passes
At girls who wear glasses.
News Item

6 Razors pain you;
Rivers are damp;
Acids stain you;
And drugs cause cramp.
Guns aren't lawful;
Nooses give;
Gas smells awful;
You might as well live.
Résumé

7 By the time you swear you're his,
Shivering and sighing,
And he vows his passion is
Infinite, undying—
Lady, make a note of this:
One of you is lying.
Unfortunate Coincidence

8 She ran the whole gamut of the emotions from A to B.
Of Katharine Hepburn in a Broadway play

9 How could they tell?
[On being told of the death of President Coolidge.]
John Keats, *You might as well live* (1971), Foreword

10 If all the girls attending it [the Yale Prom] were laid end to end, I wouldn't be at all surprised.
A. Woollcott, *While Rome Burns*, 'Some Neighbours', IV: Our Mrs. Parker

MARTIN PARKER d. 1656?

11 You gentlemen of England
Who live at home at ease,

How little do you think
On the dangers of the seas.
The Valiant Sailors. See *Early Naval Ballads* (Percy Society, 1841), p.34

THEODORE PARKER 1810–1860

12 There is what I call the American idea... This idea demands...a democracy, that is, a government of all the people, by all the people, for all the people; of course, a government after the principles of eternal justice, the unchanging law of God; for shortness' sake, I will call it the idea of freedom.
Speech at N.E. Anti-Slavery Convention, Boston, 29 May 1850. *Discourses of Slavery* (1863), i

C. NORTHCOTE PARKINSON 1909–

13 Work expands so as to fill the time available for its completion.
Parkinson's Law (1958), I, opening words

CHARLES STEWART PARNELL 1846–1891

14 No man has a right to fix the boundary of the march of a nation; no man has a right to say to his country—thus far shalt thou go and no further.
Speech at Cork, 21 Jan. 1885

BLAISE PASCAL 1623–1662

15 *Quand on voit le style naturel, on est tout étonné et ravi, car on s'attendait de voir un auteur, et on trouve un homme.*
When we see a natural style, we are quite surprised and delighted, for we expected to see an author and we find a man.
Pensées, ed. L. Brunschvicg (5th edn. 1909), i.29

16 *Tout le malheur des hommes vient d'une seule chose, qui est de ne savoir pas demeurer en repos dans une chambre.*
All the misfortunes of men derive from one single thing, which is their inability to be at ease in a room [at home].
ii.139

17 *Le nez de Cléopâtre: s'il eût été plus court, toute la face de la terre aurait changé.*
Had Cleopatra's nose been shorter, the whole face of the world would have changed.
162

18 *Le silence éternel de ces espaces infinis m'effraie.*
The eternal silence of these infinite spaces [the heavens] terrifies me.
iii.206

1   *On mourra seul.*
    We shall die alone.
    211

2   *Le coeur a ses raisons que la raison ne*
    connaît point.
    The heart has its reasons which reason
    knows nothing of.
    iv.277

3   *L'homme n'est qu'un roseau, le plus faible*
    de la nature; mais c'est un roseau pensant.
    Man is only a reed, the weakest thing in
    nature; but he is a thinking reed.
    vi.347

4   *Je n'ai fait celle ci plus longue que parce*
    que je n'ai pas eu le loisir de la faire plus
    courte.
    I have made this letter longer than usual,
    only because I have not had the time to
    make it shorter.
    Lettres Provinciales (1657), xvi

5   *FEU. Dieu d'Abraham, Dieu d'Isaac, Dieu*
    de Jacob, non des philosophes et savants.
    Certitude. Certitude. Sentiment. Joie. Paix.
    FIRE. God of Abraham, God of Isaac,
    God of Jacob, not of the philosophers and
    scholars. Certainty. Certainty. Feeling.
    Joy. Peace.
    On a paper dated 23 Nov. 1654, stitched into the
    lining of his coat and found after his death.

LOUIS PASTEUR 1822-1895

6   *Dans les champs de l'observation le hasard*
    ne favorise que les esprits préparés.
    Where observation is concerned, chance
    favours only the prepared mind.
    Address given on the inauguration of the Fac-
    ulty of Science, University of Lille, 7 Dec. 1854.
    De nos jours, le hasard ne favorise l'invention que
    pour des esprits préparés aux découvertes par de
    patientes études et de persévérants efforts. 'Pour-
    quoi la France n'a pas trouvé d'hommes supérieurs
    au moment du péril,' La Salut public, Lyons,
    Mar. 1871

7   *Il n'existe pas de sciences appliquées, mais*
    seulement des applications de la science.
    There are no such things as applied
    sciences, only applications of science.
    Address, 11 Sept. 1872, *Comptes rendus des trav-*
    aux du Congrès viticole et séricicole de Lyon,
    9–14 septembre 1872, p.49

WALTER PATER 1839-1894

8   She is older than the rocks among which
    she sits; like the vampire, she has been
    dead many times, and learned the secrets
    of the grave; and has been a diver in deep

seas, and keeps their fallen day about her.
    Studies in the History of the Renaissance (1873)
    Leonardo da Vinci (1869)

9   All art constantly aspires towards the con-
    dition of music.
    The School of Giorgione

10 To burn always with this hard, gemlike
    flame, to maintain this ecstasy, is success
    in life.
    Conclusion

MARK PATTISON 1813-1884

11 In research the horizon recedes as we ad-
    vance, and is no nearer at sixty than it was
    at twenty. As the power of endurance
    weakens with age, the urgency of the pur-
    suit grows more intense...And research is
    always incomplete.
    Isaac Casaubon (1875), ch.10

JAMES PAYN 1830-1898

12 I had never had a piece of toast
    Particularly long and wide,
    But fell upon the sanded floor,
    And always on the buttered side.
    Chambers's Journal, 2 Feb. 1884. See 173:3

J.H. PAYNE 1791-1852

13 Mid pleasures and palaces though we may
        roam,
    Be it ever so humble, there's no place like
        home.
    Clari, the Maid of Milan (1823), **Home, Sweet**
    Home

14 Home, home, sweet, sweet home!
    There's no place like home! there's no
        place like home!

THOMAS LOVE PEACOCK 1785-1866

15 'I distinguish the picturesque and the
    beautiful, and I add to them, in the laying
    out of grounds, a third and distinct cha-
    racter, which I call *unexpectedness.*'
    'Pray, sir,' said Mr Milestone, 'by what
    name do you distinguish this character,
    when a person walks round the grounds
    for the second time?'
    Headlong Hall (1816), ch.4

16 The mountain sheep are sweeter,
        But the valley sheep are fatter;
    We therefore deemed it meeter
        To carry off the latter.
    The Misfortunes of Elphin (1823), ch.11. **The**
    War-Song of Dinas Vawr

17 In a bowl to sea went wise men three,
        On a brilliant night in June:

They carried a net, and their hearts were
set
On fishing up the moon.
The Wise Men of Gotham

SIR ROBERT PEEL 1788-1850

1 I may be a Tory. I may be an illiberal—
but...Tory as I am, I have the further
satisfaction of knowing that there is not a
single law connected with my name which
has not had as its object some mitigation
of the criminal law; some prevention of
abuse in the exercise of it; or some security
for its impartial administration.
House of Commons, 1 May 1827

GEORGE PEELE 1558?-1597?

2 When as the rye reach to the chin,
And chopcherry, chopcherry ripe within,
Strawberries swimming in the cream,
And schoolboys playing in the stream,
Then O, then O, then O, my true love said,
Till that time come again,
She could not live a maid.
The Old Wives' Tale, l.81

1ST EARL OF PEMBROKE 1501?-1570

3 Out ye whores, to work, to work, ye
whores, go spin.
Aubrey, *Brief Lives*. Commonly quoted as 'Go
spin, you jades, go spin.' See Sir W. Scott, *Journal*, 9 Feb. 1826

2ND EARL OF PEMBROKE
c.1534-1601

4 A parliament can do any thing but make a
man a woman, and a woman a man.
Quoted in Speech made by his son, the 4th Earl
on 11 Apr. 1648, proving himself Chancellor of
Oxford. *Harleian Miscellany* (1810), Vol.5, p.113

VLADIMIR PENIAKOFF 1897-1951

5 A message came on the wireless for me. It
said 'SPREAD ALARM and DESPONDENCY'...The date was, I think, May
18th, 1942.
Private Army, II, v.128. See also Army Act 42 &
43 Vict.33 sect.5 (1879): 'Every person subject to
military law who...spreads reports calculated to
create unnecessary alarm or despondency...shall
...be liable to suffer penal servitude.'

WILLIAM PENN 1644-1718

6 The taking of a Bribe or Gratuity, should
be punished with as severe Penalties as the
defrauding of the State.
Some Fruits of Solitude, in Reflections and Maxims relating to the conduct of Humane Life
(1693), pt.i, No.384

SAMUEL PEPYS 1633-1703

7 And so to bed.
Diary, 20 Apr. 1660

8 I went out to Charing Cross, to see
Major-general Harrison hanged, drawn
and quartered; which was done there, he
looking as cheerful as any man could do in
that condition.
13 Oct. 1660

9 A woman sober, and no high flyer, as he
calls it.
27 May 1663

10 Pretty witty Nell. [Nell Gwynne.]
3 Apr. 1665

11 Music and women I cannot but give way
to, whatever my business is.
9 Mar. 1665-6

12 And mighty proud I am (and ought to be
thankful to God Almighty) that I am able
to have a spare bed for my friends.
8 Aug. 1666

13 This day my wife made it appear to me
that my late entertainment this week cost
me above £12, an expense which I am
almost ashamed of, though it is but once in
a great while, and is the end for which, in
the most part, we live, to have such a
merry day once or twice in a man's life.
6 Mar. 1669

14 And so I betake myself to that course
which is almost as much as to see myself
go into my grave—for which, and all the
discomforts that will accompany my being
blind, the good God prepare me!
Closing words, 31 May 1669

PERICLES c.495-429 B.C.

15 ἀνδρῶν γὰρ ἐπιφανῶν πᾶσα γῆ τάφος
For famous men have the whole earth as
their memorial.
Funeral Oration, Athens, 430 B.C., as reported
by Thucydides, *Histories* ii.43, 3. Trans. Rex
Warner

CHARLES PERRAULT 1628-1703

16 *'Anne, ma soeur Anne, ne vois-tu rien venir?' Et la soeur Anne lui répondit, 'Je ne vois
rien que le soleil qui poudroye, et l'herbe qui
verdoye.'*
'Anne, sister Anne, do you see nothing
coming?' And her sister Anne replied, '

see nothing but the sun making a dust, and the grass looking green.'
Histoires et Contes du Temps Passé (1697)

PETRONIUS A.D. 1st cent.

1 *Canis ingens, catena vinctus, in pariete erat pictus superque quadrata littera scriptum 'Cave canem.'*
A huge dog, tied by a chain, was painted on the wall and over it was written in capital letters 'Beware of the dog.'
Satyricon: Cena Trimalchionis, 29.1

2 *Abiit ad plures.*
He's gone to join the majority.
42.5. Meaning the dead.

3 *Foeda est in coitu et brevis voluptas Et taedet Veneris statim peractae.*
Delight of lust is gross and brief And weariness treads on desire.
A. Baehrens, *Poetae Latinae Minores,* vol.IV, no.101. Tr. Helen Waddell.

EDWARD JOHN PHELPS 1822–1900

4 The man who makes no mistakes does not usually make anything.
Speech at Mansion House, 24 Jan. 1899.

WENDELL PHILLIPS 1811–1884

5 Every man meets his Waterloo at last.
Speeches (1880), Lecture at Brooklyn, N.Y., 1 Nov. 1859

WILLIAM PITT, EARL OF CHATHAM 1708–1778

6 The atrocious crime of being a young man...I shall neither attempt to palliate nor deny.
House of Commons, 27 Jan. 1741

7 Unlimited power is apt to corrupt the minds of those who possess it.
House of Lords, 9 Jan. 1770. See 1:3

8 You cannot conquer America.
18 Nov. 1777

9 I invoke the genius of the Constitution!

0 The lungs of London. [The parks.]
William Windham, in a Speech in House of Commons, 30 June 1808

WILLIAM PITT 1759–1806

1 England has saved herself by her exertions, and will, as I trust, save Europe by her example.
Guildhall, 1805

2 Roll up that map; it will not be wanted these ten years.
On a map of Europe, after hearing the news of the Battle of Austerlitz Dec. 1805. Lord Stanhope, *Life of the Rt. Hon. William Pitt* (1862), vol.iv, p.369

13 Oh, my country! how I leave my country!
Last words. Stanhope (1879), iii. p.397; in the 1st edn. (1862), iv, p.369, the words were given as 'How I love my country' and in G. Rose, *Diaries and Correspondence,* 23 Jan. 1806, as simply 'My country! oh, my country!' Oral tradition reports the alternative, 'I think I could eat one of Bellamy's veal pies.'

PLATO c.429–347 B.C.

14 Σωκράτη φησὶν ἀδικεῖν τούς τε νέους διαφθείροντα καὶ θεοὺς οὓς ἡ πόλις νομίζει οὐ νομίζοντα, ἕτερα δὲ δαιμόνια καινά.
It is said that Socrates commits a crime by corrupting the young men and not recognizing the gods that the city recognizes, but some other new religion.
Apologia, 24b

15 οὐ μὲν οὖν τῇ ἀληθείᾳ, φάναι, ὦ φιλούμενε Ἀγάθων, δύνασαι ἀντιλέγειν, ἐπεὶ Σωκράτει γε οὐδὲν χαλεπόν.
But, my dearest Agathon, it is truth which you cannot contradict; you can without any difficulty contradict Socrates.
Symposium, 201

PLAUTUS d. c.184 B.C.

16 *Lupus est homo homini, non homo, quom qualis sit non novit.*
A man is a wolf rather than a man to another man, when he hasn't yet found out what he's like.
Asinaria, 495. Often cited simply as *Homo homini lupus* (A man is a wolf to another man.)

17 *Dictum sapienti sat est.*
What's been said is enough for anyone with sense.
Persa, 729. Proverbially later, *Verbum sapienti sat est,* A word is enough for the wise.

PLUTARCH A.D.c.50–c. 120

18 He who cheats with an oath acknowledges that he is afraid of his enemy, but that he thinks little of God.
Lives: Lysander, 8. See 156:1

EDGAR ALLAN POE 1809–1849

19 I was a child and she was a child,
In this kingdom by the sea;
But we loved with a love which was more than love—

I and my Annabel Lee.
Annabel Lee (1849)

1 The fever call'd 'Living'
  Is conquer'd at last.
  For Annie

2 Take thy beak from out my heart, and
  take thy form from off my door!
      Quoth the Raven, 'Nevermore'.
  The Raven (1845), xvii

3 Helen, thy beauty is to me
  Like those Nicean barks of yore,
  That gently, o'er a perfumed sea,
  The weary, wayworn wanderer bore
  To his own native shore.

  On desperate seas long wont to roam,
  Thy hyacinth hair, thy classic face,
  Thy Naiad airs have brought me home,
  To the glory that was Greece
  And the grandeur that was Rome.
  To Helen, l.1

JOHN POMFRET 1667–1702

4 We live and learn, but not the wiser grow.
  Reason (1700), l.112

MADAME DE POMPADOUR
1721–1764

5 *Après nous le déluge.*
  After us the deluge.
  Madame de Hausset, *Mémoires*, p.19

JOHN POOLE 1786?–1872

6 I hope I don't intrude?
  Paul Pry (1825), I.ii

ALEXANDER POPE 1688–1744

7 A brain of feathers, and a heart of lead.
  The Dunciad (1728), bk.ii, l.44

8 A wit with dunces, and a dunce with wits.
  bk.iv (1742), l.90

9 May you, may Cam, and Isis, preach it
  long,
  The Right Divine of Kings to govern
  wrong.
  l.187

10 Stretch'd on the rack of a too easy chair.
   l.342

11 Is there no bright reversion in the sky,
   For those who greatly think, or bravely
   die?
   Elegy to the Memory of an Unfortunate Lady
   (1717), l.9

12 On all the line a sudden vengeance waits,
   And frequent hearses shall besiege your
   gates.
   l.37

13 How shall I lose the sin, yet keep the sense
   And love the offender, yet detest th
   offence?
   How the dear object from the crime re
   move,
   Or how distinguish penitence from love?
   Eloisa to Abelard (1717), l.191. See 11:20

14 How happy is the blameless Vestal's lot?
   The world forgetting, by the world forgot.
   l.207

15 You beat your pate, and fancy wit wil
   come;
   Knock as you please, there's nobody a
   home.
   Epigram

16 I am his Highness' dog at Kew;
   Pray, tell me sir, whose dog are you?
   *Epigram Engraved on the Collar of a Dog which
   gave to his Royal Highness*

17 Sir, I admit your gen'ral rule
   That every poet is a fool;
   But you yourself may serve to show it,
   That every fool is not a poet.
   Epigram from the French

18 Shut, shut the door, good John! fatigu'd
   said,
   Tie up the knocker; say I'm sick, I'm dead.
   The Dog-star rages!
   Epistle to Dr. Arbuthnot (1735), l.1 (Imitation o
   Horace)

19 As yet a child, nor yet a fool to fame,
   I lisp'd in numbers, for the numbers came.
   l.127. See 179:1

20 Damn with faint praise, assent with civi
   leer,
   And, without sneering, teach the rest to
   sneer. [Addison.]
   l.201. See 278:6

21 Satire or sense, alas! can Sporus feel?
   Who breaks a butterfly upon a wheel'
   [Lord Hervey.]
   l.307

22 Yet let me flap this bug with gilded wings,
   This painted child of dirt, that stinks and
   stings. [Lord Hervey.]
   l.309

23 'Tis Education forms the common mind,
   Just as the twig is bent, the tree's inclin'd.
   Epistles to Several Persons Ep.i. **To Lord Cob-
   ham** (1734), l.149

24 You purchase pain with all that joy can
   give,
   And die of nothing but a rage to live.
   Ep.ii. **To a Lady** (1735), l.99

Still round and round the ghosts of beauty
glide,
And haunt the places where their honour
died.
l.241

The ruling passion, be it what it will,
The ruling passion conquers reason still.
Ep.iii. **To Lord Bathurst** (1733), l.153

Consult the genius of the place in all.
Ep.iv. **To Lord Burlington** (1731), l.57

Another age shall see the golden ear
Imbrown the slope, and nod on the par-
terre,
Deep harvests bury all his pride has
plann'd,
And laughing Ceres re-assume the land.
l.173

Statesman, yet friend to truth! of soul sin-
cere,
In action faithful, and in honour clear;
Who broke no promise, serv'd no private
end,
Who gain'd no title, and who lost no
friend.
Ep.v. **To Mr. Addison** (1721), l.67

Nature, and Nature's laws lay hid in
night:
God said, *Let Newton be!* and all was light.
Epitaphs. **Intended for Sir Isaac Newton.** See
245:8

Some have at first for wits, then poets
pass'd,
Turn'd critics next, and prov'd plain fools
at last.
An Essay on Criticism (1711), l.36

A little learning is a dang'rous thing;
Drink deep, or taste not the Pierian spring:
There shallow draughts intoxicate the
brain,
And drinking largely sobers us again.
l.215

True wit is nature to advantage dress'd,
What oft was thought, but ne'er so well
express'd.
l.297

A needless Alexandrine ends the song,
That, like a wounded snake, drags its slow
length along.
l.356

To err is human, to forgive, divine.
l.525

All seems infected that th'infected spy,
As all looks yellow to the jaundic'd eye.
l.558

The bookful blockhead, ignorantly read,

With loads of learned lumber in his head.
l.612

14 For fools rush in where angels fear to
tread.
l.625

15 Hope springs eternal in the human breast;
Man never Is, but always To be blest.
An Essay on Man. Epistle i (1733), l.95

10 And, spite of pride, in erring reason's
spite,
One truth is clear, 'Whatever IS, is
RIGHT.'
l.293

17 Know then thyself, presume not God to
scan,
The proper study of mankind is man.
Ep.ii (1733), l.1. See 67:16

18 A wit's a feather, and a chief a rod;
An honest man's the noblest work of God.
Ep.iv (1734), l.247

19 Thou wert my guide, philosopher, and
friend.
l.390

20 There St John mingles with my friendly
bowl
The feast of reason and the flow of soul.
Imitations of Horace. Hor.II, Sat.1 (1733). **To
Mr. Fortescue,** l.127

21 For I, who hold sage Homer's rule the
best,
Welcome the coming, speed the going
guest.
Hor.II, Sat.2 (1734). **To Mr. Bethel,** l.159

22 Welcome the coming, speed the parting
guest.
Odyssey (1725–6), xv.83

23 Where'er you walk, cool gales shall
fan the glade,
Trees, where you sit, shall crowd into a
shade:
Where'er you tread, the blushing flow'rs
shall rise,
And all things flourish where you turn
your eyes.
Pastorals (1709), **Summer,** l.73

24 They shift the moving Toyshop of their
heart.
The Rape of the Lock (1714), c.i, l.100

25 Fair tresses man's imperial race insnare,
And beauty draws us with a single hair.
l.27

26 At ev'ry word a reputation dies.
c.iii, l.16

27 This is the Jew

That Shakespeare drew.
Of Macklin's performance of Shylock, 14 Feb. 1741. Baker, Reed & Jones, *Biographia Dramatica* (1812), vol.I, pt.ii, p.469

1 A man should never be ashamed to own he has been in the wrong, which is but saying, in other words, that he is wiser to-day than he was yesterday.
Thoughts on Various Subjects (1706)

2 Here am I, dying of a hundred good symptoms.
15 May 1744. Joseph Spence, *Anecdotes by and about Alexander Pope*, p.637

BEILBY PORTEUS 1731–1808

3 War its thousands slays, Peace its ten thousands.
Death (1759), l.179

4   Teach him how to live,
And, oh! still harder lesson! how to die.
l.319

BEATRIX POTTER 1866–1943

5 Don't go into Mr McGregor's garden: your Father had an accident there; he was put in a pie by Mrs McGregor.
The Tale of Peter Rabbit (1902)

EZRA POUND 1885–1972

6 Winter is icummen in,
Lhude sing Goddamm,
Raineth drop and staineth slop,
And how the wind doth ramm!
Sing: Goddamm.
Ancient Music. See 4:19

7 Hang it all, Robert Browning,
there can but be the one 'Sordello'.
Cantos, 2

8 His true Penelope was Flaubert.
Hugh Selwyn Mauberley, I

9 All things are a flowing,
Sage Heracleitus says;
But a tawdry cheapness
Shall outlast our days.
III. See 118:1

10 There died a myriad,
And of the best, among them,
For an old bitch gone in the teeth,
For a botched civilization.
V

11 I make a pact with you, Walt Whitman—
I have detested you long enough…
It was you that broke the new wood,
Now is a time for carving.
We have one sap and one root—

Let there be commerce between us.
Lustra (1915), **A Pact**

12 O woe, woe,
People are born and die,
We also shall be dead pretty soon
Therefore let us act as if we were dead already.
Mr. Housman's Message

13 I had over-prepared the event,
   that much was ominous.
With middle-ageing care
   I had laid out just the right books.
I had almost turned down the pages.
Villanelle: the psychological hour

14 Literature is news that STAYS news.
ABC of Reading (1934), ch.2

JOHN O'CONNOR POWER

15 The mules of politics: without pride of ancestry, or hope of posterity.
Quoted in H.H. Asquith, *Memories and Reflections*, i.123

WINTHROP MACKWORTH PRAED 1802–1839

16 My own Araminta, say 'No!'
A Letter of Advice

PRAYER BOOK 1662

17 Dearly beloved brethren, the Scripture moveth us in sundry places to acknowledge and confess our manifold sins and wickedness.
Morning Prayer. After the beginning Sentences

18 We have erred, and strayed from thy ways like lost sheep. We have followed too much the devices and desires of our own hearts.
General Confession

19 We have left undone those things which we ought to have done; And we have done those things which we ought not to have done; And there is no health in us.

20 And grant, O most merciful Father, for his sake; That we may hereafter live a godly, righteous, and sober life.

21 And forgive us our trespasses, As we forgive them that trespass against us.
The Lord's Prayer. See 31:21

22 Give peace in our time, O Lord.
Versicle

23 In Quires and Places where they sing, here followeth the Anthem.
Rubric after Third Collect

24 When two or three are gathered together

in thy Name thou wilt grant their requests.
Prayer of St. Chrysostom

1 Lighten our darkness, we beseech thee, O Lord; and by thy great mercy defend us from all perils and dangers of this night.
Evening Prayer. Third Collect

2 Have mercy upon us miserable sinners.
The Litany

3 From all blindness of heart; from pride, vain-glory, and hypocrisy; from envy, hatred, and malice, and from all uncharitableness,
   Good Lord, deliver us.

4 O God, the Creator and Preserver of all mankind, we humbly beseech thee for all sorts and conditions of men.
Collect or Prayer for all Conditions of Men

5 We commend to thy fatherly goodness all those, who are any ways afflicted, or distressed, in mind, body, or estate; that it may please thee to comfort and relieve them, according to their several necessities, giving them patience under their sufferings, and a happy issue out of all their afflictions.

6 Almighty God, give us grace that we may cast away the works of darkness, and put upon us the armour of light, now in the time of this mortal life.
Collects. 1st Sunday in Advent

7 Blessed Lord, who hast caused all holy Scriptures to be written for our learning; Grant that we may in such wise hear them read, mark, learn, and inwardly digest them.
2nd Sunday in Advent

8 Lord of all power and might, who art the author and giver of all good things.
7th Sunday after Trinity

9 An open and notorious evil liver.
Holy Communion. Introductory rubric

10 Incline our hearts to keep this law.
Response to Commandments

11 Thou shalt do no murder.
6th Commandment

12 I believe in one God the Father Almighty, Maker of heaven and earth, And of all things visible and invisible.
Nicene Creed. See also Apostles' Creed. See 163:13

13 And he shall come again with glory to judge both the quick and the dead.

14 And I believe one Catholick and Apostolick Church.

15 Let us pray for the whole state of Christ's Church militant here in earth.
Prayer for the Church Militant

16 It is meet and right so to do.
Versicles and Responses

17 O merciful God, grant that the old Adam in this Child may be so buried, that the new man may be raised up in him.
Publick Baptism of Infants. Invocation of blessing on the child

18 *Question.* What is your Name?
Answer. N or M.
Question. Who gave you this Name?
Answer. My Godfathers and Godmothers in my Baptism; wherein I was made a member of Christ, the child of God, and an inheritor of the kingdom of heaven.
Catechism

19 I should renounce the devil and all his works, the pomps and vanity of this wicked world, and all the sinful lusts of the flesh.

20 To keep my hands from picking and stealing, and my tongue from evil-speaking, lying, and slandering.

21 Not to covet nor desire other men's goods; but to learn and labour truly to get mine own living, and to do my duty in that state of life, unto which it shall please God to call me.

22 *Question.* What meanest thou by this word *Sacrament?*
Answer. I mean an outward and visible sign of an inward and spiritual grace.

23 If any of you know cause, or just impediment, why these two persons should not be joined together in holy Matrimony, ye are to declare it. This is the first [*second,* or *third*] time of asking.
Solemnization of Matrimony. The Banns

24 Not by any to be enterprised, nor taken in hand, unadvisedly, lightly, or wantonly, to satisfy men's carnal lusts and appetites, like brute beasts that have no understanding.
Exhortation

25 First, It was ordained for the procreation of children.

26 If any man can shew any just cause, why they may not lawfully be joined together, let him now speak, or else hereafter for ever hold his peace.

27 Forsaking all other, keep thee only unto her, so long as ye both shall live?
Betrothal

28 I *N* take thee *N* to my wedded husband, to

have and to hold from this day forward, for better for worse, for richer for poorer, in sickness and in health, to love, cherish, and to obey, till death us do part, according to God's holy ordinance; and thereto I give thee my troth.
The Man will have used the words 'I plight thee my troth' and not 'to obey'.

1 With this Ring I thee wed, with my body I thee worship, and with all my worldly goods I thee endow.
Wedding

2 Those whom God hath joined together let no man put asunder.

3 The Office ensuing is not to be used for any that die unbaptized, or excommunicate, or have laid violent hands upon themselves.
Burial of the Dead. Introductory rubric

4 In the midst of life we are in death.
First anthem

5 Forasmuch as it hath pleased Almighty God of his great mercy to take unto himself the soul of our dear brother here departed, we therefore commit his body to the ground; earth to earth, ashes to ashes, dust to dust; in sure and certain hope of the Resurrection to eternal life.
Interment

6 Why do the heathen so furiously rage together: and why do the people imagine a vain thing?
Psalms 2:1

7 Out of the mouth of very babes and sucklings hast thou ordained strength, because of thine enemies.
8:2

8 Up, Lord, and let not man have the upper hand.
9:19

9 The fool hath said in his heart: There is no God.
14:1

10 Lord, who shall dwell in thy tabernacle: or who shall rest upon thy holy hill?
15:1

11 The lot is fallen unto me in a fair ground: yea, I have a goodly heritage.
16:7. The Authorized Version of the Bible (Psalms 16:6) has 'The lines are fallen unto me in pleasant places'.

12 The heavens declare the glory of God: and the firmament sheweth his handy-work.
19:1

13 Some put their trust in chariots, and some

in horses: but we will remember the Name of the Lord our God.
20:7

14 Many oxen are come about me: fat bulls of Basan close me in on every side.
22:12

15 The Lord is my shepherd: therefore can I lack nothing.
He shall feed me in a green pasture: and lead me forth beside the waters of comfort.
23:1

16 Yea, though I walk through the valley of the shadow of death, I will fear no evil: for thou art with me; thy rod and thy staff comfort me.
Thou shalt prepare a table before me against them that trouble me: thou hast anointed my head with oil, and my cup shall be full.
But thy loving-kindness and mercy shall follow me all the days of my life: and I will dwell in the house of the Lord for ever.
4

17 The earth is the Lord's, and all that therein is: the compass of the world, and they that dwell therein.
24:1

18 Lift up your heads, O ye gates, and be ye lift up, ye everlasting doors: and the King of glory shall come in.
7

19 Even the Lord of hosts, he is the King of glory.
10

20 O remember not the sins and offences of my youth.
25:6

21 In his pleasure is life: heaviness may endure for a night, but joy cometh in the morning.
30:5

22 Sing unto the Lord a new song: sing praises lustily unto him with a good courage.
33:3

23 I have been young, and now am old: and yet saw I never the righteous forsaken, nor his seed begging their bread.
37:25

24 I myself have seen the ungodly in great power: and flourishing like a green bay-tree.
36

25 Lord, let me know mine end, and the number of my days: that I may be certified

how long I have to live.
39:5

1 Like as the hart desireth the water-brooks:
so longeth my soul after thee, O God.
42:1

2 The King's daughter is all glorious within:
her clothing is of wrought gold.
45:14

3 God is our hope and strength: a very
present help in trouble.
Therefore will we not fear, though the
earth be moved: and though the hills be
carried into the midst of the sea.
46:1

4 God is gone up with a merry noise: and
the Lord with the sound of the trump.
47:5

5 Behold, I was shapen in wickedness: and
in sin hath my mother conceived me.
51:5

6 Thou shalt purge me with hyssop, and I
shall be clean: thou shalt wash me, and I
shall be whiter than snow.
7

7 For thou desirest no sacrifice, else would I
give it thee: but thou delightest not in
burnt-offerings.
The sacrifice of God is a troubled spirit: a
broken and contrite heart, O God, shalt
thou not despise.
16

8 O that I had wings like a dove: for then
would I flee away, and be at rest.
55:6

9 They are as venomous as the poison of a
serpent: even like the deaf adder that stoppeth her ears;
Which refuseth to hear the voice of the
charmer: charm he never so wisely.
58:4

10 Moab is my wash-pot; over Edom will I
cast out my shoe.
60:8

11 Let them fall upon the edge of the sword:
that they may be a portion for foxes.
63:11

12 God be merciful unto us, and bless us: and
shew us the light of his countenance, and
be merciful unto us;
That thy way may be known upon earth:
thy saving health among all nations.
67:1

13 The zeal of thine house hath even eaten
me.
69:9

14 Thy rebuke hath broken my heart; I am
full of heaviness.
21

15 For promotion cometh neither from the
east, nor from the west: nor yet from the
south.
75:7

16 So the Lord awaked as one out of sleep:
and like a giant refreshed with wine.
78:66

17 O how amiable are thy dwellings: thou
Lord of hosts!
My soul hath a desire and longing to enter
into the courts of the Lord: my heart and
my flesh rejoice in the living God.
Yea, the sparrow hath found her an house,
and the swallow a nest where she may lay
her young: even thy altars, O Lord of
hosts, my King and my God.
84:1

18 Blessed is the man whose strength is in
thee: in whose heart are thy ways.
Who going through the vale of misery use
it for a well: and the pools are filled with
water.
They will go from strength to strength.
5

19 For one day in thy courts: is better than a
thousand.
I had rather be a door-keeper in the house
of my God: than to dwell in the tents of
ungodliness.
10

20 Lord, thou hast been our refuge: from one
generation to another.
90:1

21 For a thousand years in thy sight are but
as yesterday: seeing that is past as a watch
in the night.
As soon as thou scatterest them they are
even as a sleep: and fade away suddenly
like the grass.
In the morning it is green, and groweth up:
but in the evening it is cut down, dried up,
and withered.
4

22 The days of our age are threescore years
and ten; and though men be so strong that
they come to fourscore years: yet is their
strength then but labour and sorrow; so
soon passeth it away, and we are gone.
10

23 So teach us to number our days: that we
may apply our hearts unto wisdom.
12

24 He shall defend thee under his wings, and

thou shalt be safe under his feathers: his faithfulness and truth shall be thy shield and buckler.

Thou shalt not be afraid for any terror by night: nor for the arrow that flieth by day;

For the pestilence that walketh in darkness: nor for the sickness that destroyeth in the noon-day.
91:4

1 For he shall give his angels charge over thee: to keep thee in all thy ways.

They shall bear thee in their hands: that thou hurt not thy foot against a stone.
11

2 O come, let us sing unto the Lord: let us heartily rejoice in the strength of our salvation.

Let us come before his presence with thanksgiving: and shew ourselves glad in him with psalms.
95:1

3 O sing unto the Lord a new song: for he hath done marvellous things.
98:1

4 O be joyful in the Lord, all ye lands: serve the Lord with gladness, and come before his presence with a song.
100:1

5 Man goeth forth to his work, and to his labour: until the evening.
104:23

6 The iron entered into his soul.
105:18

7 Their soul abhorred all manner of meat: and they were even hard at death's door.
107:18

8 They that go down to the sea in ships: and occupy their business in great waters;

These men see the works of the Lord: and his wonders in the deep.
23

9 They reel to and fro, and stagger like a drunken man: and are at their wit's end.

So when they cry unto the Lord in their trouble: he delivereth them out of their distress.
27

10 The Lord said unto my Lord: Sit thou on my right hand, until I make thine enemies thy footstool.
110:1

11 The fear of the Lord is the beginning of wisdom.
111:10

12 The mountains skipped like rams: and the

little hills like young sheep.
114:4

13 They have mouths, and speak not: eye have they, and see not.

They have ears, and hear not: noses hav they, and smell not.

They have hands, and handle not: fee have they, and walk not: neither spea they through their throat.
115:5

14 I said in my haste, All men are liars.
116:10

15 The same stone which the builders re fused: is become the head-stone in th corner.
118:22

16 I will lift up mine eyes unto the hills: from whence cometh my help.

My help cometh even from the Lord: wh hath made heaven and earth.

He will not suffer thy foot to be moved and he that keepeth thee will not sleep.

Behold, he that keepeth Israel: shal neither slumber not sleep.

The Lord himself is thy keeper: the Lord i thy defence upon thy right hand;

So that the sun shall not burn thee by day neither the moon by night.
121:1

17 The Lord shall preserve thy going out and thy coming in: from this time forth fo evermore.
8

18 I was glad when they said unto me: W will go into the house of the Lord.
122:1

19 Except the Lord build the house: thei labour is but lost that build it.

Except the Lord keep the city: the watch man waketh but in vain.
127:1

20 Like as the arrows in the hand of the giant: even so are the young children.

Happy is the man that hath his quiver ful of them: they shall not be ashamed when they speak with their enemies in the gate.
5

21 Thy wife shall be as the fruitful vine: upor the walls of thine house.

Thy children like the olive-branches round about thy table.
128:3

22 Out of the deep have I called unto thee, C Lord: Lord, hear my voice.
130:1

23 O give thanks unto the Lord, for he is

gracious: and his mercy endureth for ever.
136:1

1 By the waters of Babylon we sat down and
wept: when we remembered thee, O Sion.
As for our harps, we hanged them up:
upon the trees that are therein.
For they that led us away captive required
of us then a song, and melody, in our
heaviness: Sing us one of the songs of Sion.
How shall we sing the Lord's song in a
strange land?
If I forget thee, O Jerusalem: let my right
hand forget her cunning.
If I do not remember thee, let my tongue
cleave to the roof of my mouth: yea, if I
prefer not Jerusalem in my mirth.
137:1

2 Such knowledge is too wonderful and excellent for me: I cannot attain unto it.
139:5

3 If I take the wings of the morning: and
remain in the uttermost parts of the sea;
Even there also shall thy hand lead me:
and thy right hand shall hold me.

4 I will give thanks unto thee, for I am
fearfully and wonderfully made.
13

5 O put not your trust in princes, nor in any
child of man: for there is no help in them.
146:2

6 The Lord careth for the strangers; he defendeth the fatherless and widow: as for
the way of the ungodly, he turneth it upside down.
9

7 To bind their kings in chains: and their
nobles with links of iron.
149:8

8 Praise him upon the well-tuned cymbals:
praise him upon the loud cymbals.
Let every thing that hath breath: praise the
Lord.
150:5

9 Be pleased to receive into thy Almighty
and most gracious protection the persons
of us thy servants, and the Fleet in which
we serve.
Forms of Prayer to be Used at Sea. 1st prayer

0 That we may be...a security for such as
pass on the seas upon their lawful occasions.

1 We therefore commit his body to the deep,
to be turned into corruption, looking for
the resurrection of the body (when the Sea
shall give up her dead).
At the Burial of their Dead at Sea

12 Come, Holy Ghost, our souls inspire,
And lighten with celestial fire.
Thou the anointing Spirit art,
Who dost thy seven-fold gifts impart.
Ordering of Priests. Veni, Creator Spiritus

13 Holy Scripture containeth all things necessary to salvation.
Articles of Religion (1562). 6

14 It is lawful for Christian men at the commandment of the Magistrate, to wear
weapons, and serve in the wars.
37

KEITH PRESTON 1884–1927

15 Of all the literary scenes
Saddest this sight to me:
The graves of little magazines
Who died to make verse free.
The Liberators

MATTHEW PRIOR 1664–1721

16 Be to her virtues very kind;
Be to her faults a little blind;
Let all her ways be unconfin'd;
And clap your padlock — on her mind.
An English Padlock, l.79

17 For as our diff'rent ages move,
    'Tis so ordained, would Fate but mend
    it,
That I shall be past making love,
    When she begins to comprehend it.
To a Child of Quality of Five Years Old

18 No, no; for my virginity,
When I lose that, says Rose, I'll die:
Behind the elms last night, cried Dick,
Rose, were you not extremely sick?
A True Mind

ALEXANDRE PRIVAT
D'ANGLEMONT 1820?–1859

19 *Je les ai épatés, les bourgeois.*
I flabbergasted them, the *bourgeois.*
Attr. Also attr. to Baudelaire, in the form *Il faut
épater le bourgeois.*

ADELAIDE ANN PROCTER 1825–1864

20 Seated one day at the organ,
    I was weary and ill at ease,
And my fingers wandered idly
    Over the noisy keys.
Legends and Lyrics (1858). **A Lost Chord**

21 But I struck one chord of music,
    Like the sound of a great Amen.

PROPERTIUS b. c.51 B.C.

1 *Quod si deficiant vires, audacia certe*
   Laus erit: in magnis et voluisse sat est.
   Even if strength fail, boldness at least will
   deserve praise: in great endeavours
   even to have had the will is enough.
   Elegies, II.x.5

PROTAGORAS c.481–411 B.C.

2 Man is the measure of all things.
   Plato, *Theaetetus*, 160d

PIERRE-JOSEPH PROUDHON
1809–1865

3 *La propriété c'est le vol.*
   Property is theft.
   Qu'est-ce que la Propriété? (1840), ch.1

MARCEL PROUST 1871–1922

4 *Longtemps je me suis couché de bonne*
   heure.
   For a long time I used to go to bed early.
   A la Recherche du Temps Perdu, tr. C.K. Scott-
   Moncrieff and S. Hudson (1922–1931), **Du côté
   de chez Swann**, opening sentence

5 *On l'enterra, mais toute la nuit funèbre,*
   aux vitrines éclairées, ses livres disposés
   trois par trois veillaient commes des anges
   aux ailes éployées et semblaient, pour celui
   qui n'était plus, le symbole de sa résurrec-
   tion.
   They buried him, but all through the night
   of mourning, in the lighted windows, his
   books arranged three by three kept watch
   like angels with outspread wings and
   seemed, for him who was no more, the
   symbol of his resurrection.
   La Prisonnière, vol.I, ch.1

6 *Ces dépêches dont M. de Guermantes avait*
   spirituellement fixé le modèle: 'Impossible
   venir, mensonge suit.'
   One of those telegrams of which M. de
   Guermantes had wittily fixed the formula:
   'Cannot come, lie follows'.
   Le Temps Retrouvé, vol.I, ch.1. See 19:22

7 *Les vrais paradis sont les paradis qu'on a*
   perdus.
   The true paradises are paradises we have
   lost.
   vol.II, ch.3

PUBLILIUS SYRUS 1st cent. B.C.

8 *Inopi beneficium bis dat qui dat celeriter.*
   He gives the poor man twice as much good

who gives quickly.
   Sententiae, 274. J.W. and A.M. Duff, *Mino[
   Latin Poets,* Loeb edn. (1934). Proverbially *B[
   dat qui cito dat* (He gives twice who gives soon.)

9 *Necessitas dat legem non ipsa accipit.*
   Necessity gives the law without itse[
   acknowledging one.
   444. Proverbially *Necessitas non habet lege[*
   (Necessity has no law.)

JOHN PUDNEY 1909–1977

10 Do not despair
    For Johnny head-in-air;
    He sleeps as sound
    As Johnny underground.
    For Johnny

PUNCH

11 Advice to persons about to marry.–
    'Don't.'
    vol.viii, p.1. 1845

12 Never do to-day what you can put off ti[
    to-morrow.
    vol.xvii, p.241. 1849

13 Who's 'im, Bill?
    A stranger!
    'Eave 'arf a brick at 'im.
    vol.xxvi, p.82. 1854

14 *'Peccavi*—I've Scinde' wrote Lord Elle[
    so proud.
    More briefly Dalhousie wrote—'*Vovi*—
    I've Oude'.
    vol.xxx, p.118. 1856. See 273:4

15 It ain't the 'unting as 'urts 'im, it's th
    'ammer, 'ammer, 'ammer along the 'ar[
    'igh road.
    p.218. 1856

16 Go directly—see what she's doing, and te[
    her she mustn't.
    vol.lxiii, p.202. 1872

17 There was one poor tiger that hadn't *got [*
    Christian.
    vol.lxviii, p.143. 1875

18 It's worse than wicked, my dear, it'
    vulgar.
    Almanac. 1876

19 What sort of a doctor is he?
    Oh, well, I don't know very much abou[
    his ability; but he's got a very good bedsid[
    manner!
    vol.lxxxvi, p.121. 1884

20 I used your soap two years ago; since the[
    I have used no other.
    p.197. 1884

21 Don't look at me, Sir, with—ah—in tha[

tone of voice.
vol.lxxxvii, p.38. 1884

1 Oh yes! I'm sure he's not so fond of me as
at first. He's away so much, neglects me
dreadfully, and he's so cross when he
comes home. What *shall* I do?
Feed the brute!
vol.lxxxix, p.206. 1885

2 I'm afraid you've got a bad egg, Mr Jones.
Oh no, my Lord, I assure you! Parts of it
are excellent!
vol.cix, p.222. 1895

ISRAEL PUTNAM 1718–1790

3 Men, you are all marksmen—don't one ol
you fire until you see the whites of their
eyes.
Bunker Hill, 1775. Frothingham, *History of the
Siege of Boston* (1873), ch.5, note. Also attributed to William Prescott (1726-95)

PYRRHUS 319–272 B.C

4 One more such victory and we are lost.
Plutarch, *Pyrrhus*. After defeating the Romans
at Asculum, 279 B.C.

FRANCIS QUARLES 1592–1644

5 Be wisely worldly, be not worldly wise.
Emblems (1643), bk.ii, No.2, l.46

6 Man is Heaven's masterpiece.
No.6, Epig.6

7 Thou art my way; I wander, if thou fly;
Thou art my light; if hid, how blind am I!
Thou art my life; if thou withdraw, I die.
bk.iii, No.7

8 Our God and soldiers we alike adore
Ev'n at the brink of danger; not before:
After deliverance, both alike requited,
Our God's forgotten, and our soldiers
slighted.
Epigram

9 My soul, sit thou a patient looker-on;
Judge not the play before the play is done:
Her plot hath many changes; every day
Speaks a new scene; the last act crowns the
play.
Epigram. Respice Finem

FRANÇOIS QUESNAY 1694–1774

10 *Vous ne connaissez qu'une seule règle du
commerce; c'est (pour me servir de vos
propres termes) de laisser passer et de laisser faire tous les acheteurs et tous les vend-
eurs quelconques.*
You recognize but one rule of commerce;
that is (to avail myself of your own terms)

to allow free passage and freedom of action to all buyers and sellers whoever they
may be.
Letter from M. Alpha: see Salleron, *François
Quesnay et la Physiocratie* (1958), II.940. Also
attr. Marquis d'Argenson, *Mémoires* (1736). See
6:1, 7:19

SIR ARTHUR QUILLER-COUCH 1863–1944

11 The best is the best, though a hundred
judges have declared it so.
Oxford Book of English Verse (1900), Preface

FRANÇOIS RABELAIS 1494?–c.1553

12 *L'appétit vient en mangeant.*
The appetite grows with eating.
Gargantua (1534), I.v

13 *Natura vacuum abhorret.*
Nature abhors a vacuum.
Quoting, in Latin, article of ancient wisdom.
Compare Plutarch, *Moralia*, 'De placitis philo-
sophorum', I.xviii

14 *Fay ce que vouldras.*
Do what you like.
lvii

15 *Il aurait répondu à un page…'Je vais quérir
un grand peut-être…' Puis il avait expiré en
disant 'Tirez le rideau, la farce est jouée'.*
He answered a page…'I am going to seek a
great perhaps…' Then he died, saying
'Bring down the curtain, the farce is played
out.'
Attr. last words. See Jean Fleury, *Rabelais et ses
oeuvres* (1877), vol.I, ch.3, pt.15, p.130. Fleury
adds, '*Rien, dans les contemporains, m'autorise
ces récits…Tout cela fait partie de la légende
rabelaisienne.*'

JEAN RACINE 1639–1699

16 *Elle flotte, elle hésite; en un mot, elle est
femme.*
She floats, she hesitates; in a word, she's a
woman.
Athalie (1691), iii.3

17 *Ce n'est plus une ardeur dans mes veines
cachée:
C'est Vénus tout entière à sa proie attachée.*
It's no longer a warmth hidden in my
veins: it's Venus entire and whole fastening on her prey.
Phèdre (1677), I.iii

18 *Point d'argent, point de Suisse, et ma porte
était close.*

No money, no service, and my door stayed shut.
Les Plaideurs (1668), I.i

THOMAS RAINBOROWE d. 1648

1 The poorest he that is in England hath a life to live as the greatest he.
In the Army debates at Putney, 29 Oct. 1647. Peacock, *Life of Rainborowe*.

SIR WALTER RALEGH 1552?–1618

2 If all the world and love were young,
And truth in every shepherd's tongue,
These pretty pleasures might me move
To live with thee, and be thy love.
Answer to Marlow. See 160:14

3 Only we die in earnest, that's no jest.
On the Life of Man

4 Give me my scallop-shell of quiet,
My staff of faith to walk upon,
My scrip of joy, immortal diet,
My bottle of salvation,
My gown of glory, hope's true gage,
And thus I'll take my pilgrimage.
The Passionate Man's Pilgrimage

5 Fain would I climb, yet fear I to fall.
Line written on a Window-Pane. Fuller, *Worthies of England*, vol.i, p.419. See 95:17

6 O eloquent, just, and mighty Death!
...thou hast drawn together all the far-stretched greatness, all the pride, cruelty, and ambition of man, and covered it all over with these two narrow words, *Hic jacet.*
A History of the World (1614), bk.v, ch.vi, 12

7 [Feeling the edge of the axe before his execution:]
'Tis a sharp remedy, but a sure one for all ills.
David Hume, *History of Great Britain* (1754), vol.i, ch.iv, p.72

8 [When asked which way he preferred to lay his head on the block:]
So the heart be right, it is no matter which way the head lies.
W. Stebbing, *Sir Walter Raleigh*, ch.xxx

9 I have a long journey to take, and must bid the company farewell.
Edward Thompson, *Sir Walter Raleigh*, ch.26

SIR WALTER RALEIGH 1861–1922

10 I wish I loved the Human Race;
I wish I loved its silly face;
I wish I liked the way it walks;
I wish I liked the way it talks;
And when I'm introduced to one

I wish I thought *What Jolly Fun!*
Laughter from a Cloud (1923), p.228. **Wishes o** an Elderly Man

JULIAN RALPH 1853–1903

11 News value.
Lecture to Brander Matthews's English Class Columbia, 1892. Thomas Beer, *Mauve Decade*

TERENCE RATTIGAN 1911–1977

12 *Brian:* Elle a des idées au-dessus de sa gare.
Kenneth: You can't do it like that. You can't say au-dessus de sa gare. It isn't that sort of station.
French Without Tears (1937), Act I

CHARLES READE 1814–1884

13 Sow an act, and you reap a habit. Sow a habit, and you reap a character. Sow a character, and you reap a destiny.
Attr. See N. & Q., 9th series, vol.12, p.377

HENRY REED 1914–

14 To-day we have naming of parts. Yesterday
We had daily cleaning. And tomorrow morning,
We shall have what to do after firing. But to-day,
To-day we have naming of parts.
Naming of Parts (1946)

JOHN REED 1887–1920

15 Ten Days that Shook the World.
Book title, 1919

GENERAL JOSEPH REED 1741–1785

16 I am not worth purchasing, but such as I am, the King of Great Britain is not rich enough to do it.
U.S. Congress, 11 Aug. 1878. Reed understood himself to have been offered a bribe on behalf of the British Crown.

JULES RENARD 1864–1910

17 *Les bourgeois, ce sont les autres.*
The bourgeois are other people.
Journal, 28 Jan. 1890

DR. MONTAGUE JOHN RENDALL 1862–1950

18 Nation shall speak peace unto nation.
Written as the motto of the BBC in 1927 by Dr Rendall, one of the first Governors of the Corporation

FREDERIC REYNOLDS 1764–1841

1 How goes the enemy? [Said by Mr. Ennui,
'the timekiller'.]
The Dramatist (1789), I.i

GRANTLAND RICE 1880–1954

2 For when the One Great Scorer comes
　To write against your name,
He marks—not that you won or lost—
But how you played the game.
Alumnus Football

SIR STEPHEN RICE 1637–1715

3 I will drive a coach and six horses through
the Act of Settlement.
W. King, *State of the Protestants of Ireland*
(1672), ch.3, sect.8, p.6

MANDY RICE-DAVIES 1944–

4 He would, wouldn't he?
When told that Lord Astor had denied her alleg-
ations. Trial of Stephen Ward, 29 June, 1963

RAINER MARIA RILKE 1875–1926

5 *So leben wir und nehmen immer Abschied.*
Thus we live, forever taking leave.
Duineser Elegien, VIII

6 The love which consists in this, that two
solitudes protect and limit and greet each
other.
Briefe an einem jungen Dichter (1929), 14 May
1904

MARTIN RINKART 1586–1649

7 *Nun danket alle Gott.*
Now thank you all your God.
Das Danklied (1636). Sung as a hymn to the tune
by Johann Crüger (1598–1662) composed in
1649

ARTHUR RIMBAUD 1854–1891

8 *Ô saisons, ô châteaux!*
Quelle âme est sans défauts?
O seasons, O castles! What soul is without
fault?
Ô saisons, ô châteaux

ANTOINE DE RIVAROL 1753–1801

9 *Ce qui n'est pas clair n'est pas français.*
What is not clear is not French.
Discours sur l'Universalité de la Langue Française
(1784)

MAXIMILIEN ROBESPIERRE
1758–1794

10 *Toute loi qui viole les droits imprescript-*
ibles de l'homme, est essentiellement injuste
et tyrannique; elle n'est point une loi.
Any law which violates the indefeasible
rights of man is essentially unjust and
tyrannical; it is not a law at all.
Déclaration des Droits de l'homme, 24 Apr. 1793,
XVIII. This article, in slightly different form, is
recorded as having figured in Robespierre's
Projet of 21 Apr. 1793.

SIR BOYLE ROCHE 1743–1807

11 He regretted that he was not a bird, and
could not be in two places at once.
Attr.

12 Mr Speaker, I smell a rat; I see him form-
ing in the air and darkening the sky; but
I'll nip him in the bud.
Attr.

**JOHN WILMOT, EARL OF
ROCHESTER** 1647–1680

13 What vain, unnecessary things are men!
How well we do without 'em!
Fragment

14 　　'Is there then no more?'
She cries. 'All this to love and rapture's
due;
Must we not pay a debt to pleasure too?'
The Imperfect Enjoyment

15 Here lies a great and mighty king
　　Whose promise none relies on;
He never said a foolish thing,
　　Nor ever did a wise one.
The King's Epitaph. An alternative version of the
first line is: 'Here lies our sovereign lord the
King.' For Charles II's answer see 67:12

16 A merry monarch, scandalous and poor.
*A Satire on King Charles II for which he was
banished from the Court,* l.19

17 Ancient person, for whom I
All the flattering youth defy,
Long be it ere thou grow old,
Aching, shaking, crazy, cold;
　　But still continue as thou art,
　　Ancient person of my heart.
A Song of a Young Lady to her Ancient Lover

SAMUEL ROGERS 1763–1855

18 Think nothing done while aught remains
to do.
Human Life (1819), l.49. See Lucan, *Works,*
II.657

19 But there are moments which he calls his
own,

Then, never less alone than when alone,
Those whom he loved so long and sees no
more,
Loved and still loves—not dead—but gone
before,
He gathers round him.
l.755

1 By many a temple half as old as Time.
Italy. A Farewell (1828), ii.5

2 It doesn't much signify whom one mar-
ries, for one is sure to find next morning
that it was someone else.
Table Talk (ed. Alexander Dyce, 1860)

MME ROLAND 1754–1793

3 *O liberté! O liberté! que de crimes on com-
met en ton nom!*
O liberty! O liberty! what crimes are committed in thy name!
Lamartine, *Histoire des Girondins* (1847), livre li,
ch.8

4 The more I see of men, the better I like
dogs.
Attr.

FR. ROLFE, BARON CORVO
1860–1913

5 Pray for the repose of His soul. He was so
tired.
Hadrian VII (1904), last words

PIERRE DE RONSARD 1524–1585

6 *Quand vous serez bien vieille, au soir, à la
chandelle,
Assise auprès du feu, dévidant et filant,
Direz, chantant mes vers, en vous émerveil-
lant,
Ronsard me célébrait du temps que j'étais
belle.*
When you are very old, and sit in the
candle-light at evening spinning by the
fire, you will say, as you murmur my
verses, a wonder in your eyes, 'Ronsard sang of me in the days when I was
fair.'
Sonnets pour Hélène (1578), ii.43

PRESIDENT FRANKLIN D.
ROOSEVELT 1882–1945

7 I pledge you—I pledge myself—to a new
deal for the American people.
Chicago Convention, 2 July 1932. (See also N. &
Q., cxciv, p.529.)

8 Let me assert my firm belief that the only

thing we have to fear is fear itself.
First Inaugural Address, 4 Mar. 1933

9 In the field of world policy; I would ded
cate this nation to the policy of the goo
neighbour.

10 A radical is a man with both feet firml
planted in the air.
Broadcast address to Forum on Current Prob
lems, 26 Oct. 1939

11 We must be the great arsenal of democ
racy.
29 Dec. 1940

12 In the future days, which we seek to mak
secure, we look forward to a world found
ed upon four essential human freedoms.
The first is freedom of speech and expres
sion—everywhere in the world.
The second is freedom of every person t
worship God in his own way—everywher
in the world.
The third is freedom from want...
The fourth is freedom from fear.
Address to Congress, 6 Jan. 1941

PRESIDENT THEODORE
ROOSEVELT 1858–1919

13 There is a homely adage which run
'Speak softly and carry a big stick; you wi
go far.'
Minnesota State Fair, 2 Sept. 1901

14 The men with the muck-rakes are ofte
indispensable to the well-being of society
but only if they know when to stop rakin
the muck.
At the laying of the corner-stone of the Offic
Building of House of Representatives, 14 Ap
1906

15 Every reform movement has a lunati
fringe.
Speaking of the Progressive Party, in 1913

LORD ROSEBERY 1847–1929

16 Imperialism, sane Imperialism, as distin
guished from what I may call wild-ca
Imperialism, is nothing but this—a large
patriotism.
Speech at a City Liberal Club dinner, 5 Ma
1899

PILOT OFFICER V.A. ROSEWARN
1916–1940

17 The universe is so vast and so ageless tha
the life of one man can only be justified b
the measure of his sacrifice.
Last letter to his mother, published in *The Time*
18 June 1940, and inscribed on the portrait of th
'Young Airman' by Frank Salisbury in th
R.A.F. Museum, Hendon

ALAN C. ROSS 1907–

1 'U' and 'Non-U'.
*Upper Class English Usage, Bulletin de la Société
Neo-Philologique de Helsinki* 1954. Reprinted in
Noblesse Oblige (1956), ed. Nancy Mitford

SIR RONALD ROSS 1857–1932

2 This day relenting God
  Hath placed within my hand
A wondrous thing; and God
  Be praised. At His command,

Seeking His secret deeds
  With tears and toiling breath,
I find thy cunning seeds,
  O million-murdering Death.

I know this little thing
  A myriad men may save.
O Death, where is thy sting?
  Thy victory, O Grave?
In Exile, VI. **Reply,** i. See 38:23. Of his part in
the discovery of the life-cycle of the malaria
parasite.

CHRISTINA ROSSETTI 1830–1894

3 My heart is like a singing bird
Whose nest is in a watered shoot;
My heart is like an apple-tree
Whose boughs are bent with thickset fruit;
My heart is like a rainbow shell
That paddles in a halcyon sea;
My heart is gladder than all these
Because my love is come to me.
A Birthday

4 Come to me in the silence of the night;
  Come in the speaking silence of a
    dream;
Come with soft rounded cheeks and eyes
  as bright
As sunlight on a stream;
  Come back in tears,
O memory, hope, love of finished years.
Echo

5 In the bleak mid-winter
  Frosty wind made moan,
Earth stood hard as iron,
  Water like a stone;
Snow had fallen, snow on snow,
  Snow on snow,
In the bleak mid-winter,
  Long ago.
Mid-Winter

6 Better by far you should forget and smile
Than that you should remember and be
  sad.
Remember

7 When I am dead, my dearest,
  Sing no sad songs for me;
Plant thou no roses at my head,
  Nor shady cypress tree:
Be the green grass above me
  With showers and dewdrops wet;
And if thou wilt, remember,
  And if thou wilt, forget.
Song: 'When I am Dead'

DANTE GABRIEL ROSSETTI
1828–1882

8 The blessed damozel leaned out
  From the gold bar of Heaven;
Her eyes were deeper than the depth
  Of waters stilled at even,
She had three lilies in her hand,
  And the stars in her hair were seven.
The Blessed Damozel (1850), i

9 I have been here before,
  But when or how I cannot tell:
I know the grass beyond the door,
  The sweet keen smell,
The sighing sound, the lights around the
  shore.
Sudden Light, i

GIOACCHINO ROSSINI 1792–1868

10 *Monsieur Wagner a de beaux moments,
mais de mauvais quart d'heures.*
Wagner has lovely moments but awful
quarters of an hour.
Said to Emile Naumann, April 1867. Naumann,
Italienische Tondichter (1883), IV, 541

EDMOND ROSTAND 1868–1918

11 *Le seul rêve intéresse,
Vivre sans rêve, qu'est-ce?
Et j'aime la Princesse
  Lointaine.*
The dream, alone, is of interest. What is
  life, without a dream? And I love the
  Distant Princess.
La Princesse Lointaine, I.iv

LEO C. ROSTEN 1908–

12 Any man who hates dogs and babies can't
be all bad.
Of W.C. Fields, and often attributed to him.
Speech at Masquers' Club dinner, 16 Feb. 1939.
See letter, *T.L.S.* 24 Jan. 1975

NORMAN ROSTEN

13 And there's the outhouse poet, anonymous:
    Soldiers who wish to be a hero
    Are practically zero

But those who wish to be civilians
        Jesus they run into millions.
The Big Road (1946), pt.V

C.-J. ROUGET DE LISLE 1760–1836

1 *Allons, enfants de la patrie,*
Le jour de gloire est arrivé.
Come, children of our country, the day of glory has arrived.
La Marseillaise (25 Apr. 1792)

JEAN-JACQUES ROUSSEAU 1712–1778

2 *L'homme est né libre, et partout il est dans les fers.*
Man was born free, and everywhere he is in chains.
Du Contrat Social, ch.1

DR. ROUTH 1755–1854

3 You will find it a very good practice always to verify your references, sir!
Burgon, *Quarterly Review*, July 1878, vol.cxlvi, p.30, and *Lives of Twelve Good Men* (1888 edn.), vol I, p.73

NICHOLAS ROWE 1674–1718

4 Is this that haughty, gallant, gay Lothario?
The Fair Penitent (1703), V.i

DAMON RUNYON 1884–1946

5 More than somewhat.
Phrase used frequently in Runyon's work, and adopted as book-title in 1937.

JOHN RUSKIN 1819–1900

6 I have seen, and heard, much of Cockney impudence before now; but never expected to hear a coxcomb ask two hundred guineas for flinging a pot of paint in the public's face.
[On Whistler's 'Nocturne in Black and Gold'] *Fors Clavigera* letter lxxix, 18 June 1877. See 269:13

7 Life without industry is guilt, and industry without art is brutality.
Lectures on Art, 3. **The Relation of Art to Morals,** 23 Feb. 1870

8 All violent feelings...produce in us a falseness in all our impressions of external things, which I would generally characterize as the 'Pathetic Fallacy'.
Modern Painters (1888), vol.iii

9 Which of us...is to do the hard and dirty work for the rest—and for what pay? Who is to do the pleasant and clean work, and for what pay?
Sesame and Lilies (1865), Lecture i. **Of King's Treasuries,** 30, note

10 There is really no such thing as bad weather, only different kinds of good weather.
Quoted by Lord Avebury

BERTRAND RUSSELL 1872–1970

11 Mathematics, rightly viewed, possesses not only truth, but supreme beauty—a beauty cold and austere, like that of sculpture.
Mysticism and Logic (1918), ch.4

LORD JOHN RUSSELL 1792–1878

12 It is impossible that the whisper of a faction should prevail against the voice of a nation.
Letter to T. Attwood, Oct. 1831, after the rejection in the House of Lords of the Reform Bill (7 Oct. 1831)

13 Among the defects of the Bill, which were numerous, one provision was conspicuous by its presence and another by its absence.
Speech to the electors of the City of London, Apr. 1859

JOHN RUSSELL 1919–

14 Certain phrases stick in the throat, even if they offer nothing that is analytically improbable. 'A dashing Swiss officer' is one such.
Paris (1960), ch.11

SIR WILLIAM HOWARD RUSSELL 1820–1907

15 They dashed on towards that *thin red line tipped with steel.*
The British Expedition to the Crimea (1877), p.156. Of the Russians charging the British. Russell's original dispatch to *The Times*, 25 Oct. 1854, read 'This thin red streak tipped with a line of steel', *The War* (1855)

LORD RUTHERFORD 1871–1937

16 We haven't the money, so we've got to think.
Attr. in Prof. R.V. Jones, 1962 Brunel Lecture, 14 Feb. 1962

GILBERT RYLE 1900–1976

17 The dogma of the Ghost in the machine.
The Concept of Mind (1949), passim

VICTORIA SACKVILLE-WEST
1892–1962

1 The greater cats with golden eyes
Stare out between the bars.
King's Daughter, II.i

CHARLES-AUGUSTIN SAINTE-BEUVE 1804–1869

2   *Et Vigny plus secret,*
Comme en sa tour d'ivoire, avant midi rentrait.
And Vigny more reserved,
Returned ere noon, within his ivory tower.
Les Pensées d'Août, à M. Villemain, p.152

'SAKI' (H.H. MUNRO) 1870–1916

3 Romance at short notice was her speciality.
Beasts and Super-Beasts (1914). **The Open Window**

4 There are so many things to complain of in this household that it would never have occurred to me to complain of rheumatism.
The Chronicles of Clovis (1911). **The Quest**

5 Never be a pioneer. It's the Early Christian that gets the fattest lion.
Reginald (1904), **Reginald's Choir Treat**

6 The cook was a good cook, as cooks go; and as cooks go she went.
Reginald on Besetting Sins

LORD SALISBURY 1830–1903

7 No lesson seems to be so deeply inculcated by the experience of life as that you never should trust experts. If you believe the doctors, nothing is wholesome: if you believe the theologians, nothing is innocent: if you believe the soldiers, nothing is safe.
Letter to Lord Lytton, 15 June 1877. Lady Gwendolen Cecil, *Life of Robert, Marquis of Salisbury*, vol.II, ch.4

8 We are part of the community of Europe and we must do our duty as such.
Speech at Caernarvon, 11 Apr. 1888. Lady Gwendolen Cecil, *Life of Robert, Marquis of Salisbury*, vol.IV, ch.4

9 By office boys for office boys.
Of the Daily Mail. See H. Hamilton Fyfe, *Northcliffe, an Intimate Biography*, ch.4

SALLUST c.86–c.35 B.C.

10 *Esse quam videri bonus malebat.*
He preferred to be rather than to seem good.
Catiline, 54. Of Cato

CARL SANDBURG 1878–1967

11 Pile the bodies high at Austerlitz and Waterloo.
Shovel them under and let me work—
        I am the grass; I cover all.
Grass

SAPPHO b. c.612 B.C.

12 φαίνεταί μοι κῆνος ἴσος θέοισιν
    ἔμμεν' ὤνηρ, ὄττις ἐνάντιός τοι
    ἰσδάνει καὶ πλάσιον ἆδυ φωνεί-
        σας ὑπακούει
    καὶ γελαίσας ἰμέροεν, τό μ' ἦ μὰν
    καρδίαν ἐν στήθεσιν ἐπτόαισεν,
    ὡς γὰρ ἔς σ' ἴδω βρόχε', ὥς με φώναι-
        σ' οὐδ' ἐν ἔτ' εἴκει,
    ἀλλ' ἄκαν μεν γλῶσσα πεπαγε, λέπτον
    δ' αὔτικα χρῶι πῦρ ὑπαδεδρόμηκεν,
    ὀππάτεσσι δ' οὐδ' ἐν ὄρημμ', ἐπιρρόμ-
        βεισι δ' ἄκουαι,
    κὰδ δέ μ' ἴδρως κακχέεται, τρόμος δὲ
    παῖσαν ἄγρει, χλωροτέρα δὲ ποίας
    ἔμμι, τεθνάκην δ' ὀλίγω 'πιδεύης
        φαίνομ' ἔμ' αὔται.

That man seems to me on a par with the gods who sits in your company and listens to you so close to him speaking sweetly and laughing sexily, such a thing makes my heart flutter in my breast, for when I see you even for a moment, then power to speak another word fails me, instead my tongue freezes into silence, and at once a gentle fire has caught throughout my flesh, and I see nothing with my eyes, and there's a drumming in my ears, and sweat pours down me, and trembling seizes all of me, and I become paler than grass, and I seem to fail almost to the point of death in my very self.
D.L. Page, *Lyrica Selecta Graeca* (1968)

1 οἶον τὸ γλυκύμαλον ἐρεύθεται ἄκρῳ ἐπ'
  ὔσδῳ,
  ἄκρον ἐπ' ἀκροτάτῳ, λελάθοντο δὲ
  μαλοδρόπηες,
  οὐ μὰν ἐκλελάθοντ', ἀλλ' οὐκ ἐδύναντ'
  ἐπίκεσθαι.

Just as the sweet-apple reddens on the high
  branch, high on the highest, and the
  apple-pickers missed it, or rather did
  not miss it out, but dared not reach it.
105(a). Of a girl before her marriage

JEAN-PAUL SARTRE 1905–1980

2 *Pas besoin de gril, l'Enfer, c'est les Autres.*
No need of a gridiron, [when it come to]
Hell, it's other people.
Huis Clos, sc.v

3 *Trois heures, c'est toujours trop tard ou
trop tôt pour tout ce qu'on veut faire.*
Three o'clock is always too late or too
early for anything you want to do.
La Nausée, Vendredi

SIEGFRIED SASSOON 1886–1967

4 If I were fierce and bald and short of
  breath,
   I'd live with scarlet Majors at the Base,
And speed glum heroes up the line to
  death.
Base Details

5 And when the war is done and youth stone
  dead
I'd toddle safely home and die—in bed.

6 I'd like to see a Tank come down the
  stalls,
   Lurching to rag-time tunes, or 'Home,
   sweet Home,'—
And there'd be no more jokes in Music-
  halls
To mock the riddled corpses round Ba-
  paume.
'Blighters'

7 Does it matter?—losing your legs?…
For people will always be kind,
And you need not show that you mind
When others come in after hunting
To gobble their muffins and eggs.

Does it matter?—losing your sight?…
There's such splendid work for the blind;
And people will always be kind,
As you sit on the terrace remembering
And turning your face to the light.
Does it Matter?

8 Why do you lie with your legs ungainly
  huddled,
And one arm bent across your sullen, cold
Exhausted face?
The Dug-Out

9 You are too young to fall asleep for ever;
And when you sleep your remind me of th
  dead.

10 Everyone suddenly burst out singing.
Everyone Sang

11   The song was wordless;
The singing will never be done.

12 'Good morning; good morning!' th
  general said
When we met him last week on our way t
  the line.
Now the soldiers he smiled at are most o
  'em dead,
And we're cursing his staff for incom
  petent swine.
'He's a cheery old card,' grunted Harry t
  Jack
As they slogged up to Arras with rifle an
  pack…
But he did for them both with his plan o
  attack.
The General

13 Quoting, for shallow conversational ends.
What Shelley shrilled, what Blake onc
  wildly muttered…

How can they use such names and not b
  humble?
I have sat silent; angry at what they ut
  tered.
The Grandeur of Ghosts

14 In me the tiger sniffs the rose.
The Heart's Journey, VIII

15 A sallow waiter brings me beans an
  pork…
Outside there's fury in the firmament.
Ice-cream, of course, will follow; and I'r
  content.
O Babylon! O Carthage! O New York!
Storm on Fifth Avenue

GEORGE SAVILE, MARQUIS OF
HALIFAX
see HALIFAX

DOROTHY L. SAYERS 1893–1957

16 I admit it is more fun to punt than to b
punted, and that a desire to have all th
fun is nine-tenths of the law of chivalry.
Gaudy Night, ch.14

17 As I grow older and older,
And totter towards the tomb,
I find that I care less and less
Who goes to bed with whom.
That's why I never read modern novels

FRIEDRICH VON SCHELLING
1775–1854

1 Architecture in general is frozen music.
Philosophie der Kunst (1809)

FRIEDRICH VON SCHILLER
1759–1805

2 *Freude, schöner Götterfunken,*
Tochter aus Elysium,
Wir betreten feuertrunken,
Himmlische, dein Heiligtum.
Deine Zauber binden wieder,
Was die Mode streng geteilt,
Alle Menschen werden Brüder
Wo dein sanfter Flügel weilt.
Joy, beautiful radiance of the gods, daughter of Elysium, we set foot in your heavenly shrine dazzled by your brilliance. Your charms re-unite what common use has harshly divided: all men become brothers under your tender wing.
An die Freude (1786)

3 *Mit der Dummheit kämpfen Götter selbst vergebens.*
With stupidity the gods themselves struggle in vain.
Die Jungfrau von Orleans (1801), III.vi

4 *Die Weltgeschichte ist das Weltgericht.*
The world's history is the world's judgement.
First lecture as Prof. of History, Jena. 26 May 1789

PROFESSOR E.F. SCHUMACHER
1911–1977

5 Small is beautiful.
Title of book (1973)

CARL SCHURZ 1829–1906

6 Our country, right or wrong! When right, to be kept right; when wrong, to be put right!
Speech, U.S. Senate, 1872. See 82:5

C.P. SCOTT 1846–1932

7 Comment is free but facts are sacred.
Manchester Guardian, 6 May 1926

8 Television? The word is half Latin and half Greek. No good can come of it.
Attr.

CAPTAIN ROBERT FALCON SCOTT
1868–1912

9 For God's sake look after our people.
Journal, 25 Mar. 1912

10 Had we lived, I should have had a tale to tell of the hardihood, endurance, and courage of my companions which would have stirred the heart of every Englishman. These rough notes and our dead bodies must tell the tale.
Message to the Public

SIR WALTER SCOTT 1771–1832

11 Come fill up my cup, come fill up my can,
Come saddle your horses, and call up your men;
Come open the West Port, and let me gang free,
And it's room for the bonnets of Bonny Dundee!
Bonny Dundee. (The Doom of Devorgoil, 1830, Act II, sc.ii, also Rob Roy, 1817, ch.23)

12 But answer came there none.
The Bridal of Triermain (1813), c.III.x

13 Huntsman, rest! thy chase is done.
The Lady of the Lake (1810), c.I. xxxii

14 Hail to the Chief who in triumph advances!
c.II.xix

15 The way was long, the wind was cold,
The Minstrel was infirm and old;
His wither'd cheek and tresses grey,
Seem'd to have known a better day.
The Lay of the Last Minstrel (1805), introd. l.1

16 Breathes there the man, with soul so dead,
Who never to himself hath said,
This is my own, my native land!
c.VI.i

17 To the vile dust, from whence he sprung,
Unwept, unhonour'd, and unsung.

O Caledonia! stern and wild,
Meet nurse for a poetic child!

18 O, young Lochinvar is come out of the west,
Through all the wide Border his steed was the best.
Marmion (1808), c.V.xii

19 So faithful in love, and so dauntless in war,
There never was knight like the young Lochinvar.

20 For a laggard in love, and a dastard in war,
Was to wed the fair Ellen of brave Lochinvar.

21 'O come ye in peace here, or come ye in war,
Or to dance at our bridal, young Lord Lochinvar?'

1 O what a tangled web we weave,
   When first we practise to deceive!
   c.VI.xvii

2 O Woman! in our hours of ease,
   Uncertain, coy, and hard to please,
   And variable as the shade
   By the light quivering aspen made;
   When pain and anguish wring the brow,
   A ministering angel thou!
   xxx

3 'Charge, Chester, charge! On, Stanley,
      on!'
   Were the last words of Marmion.
   xxxii

4 You...whirl'd them to the back o' beyont.
   The Antiquary (1816), ch.2

5 Look not thou on beauty's charming,—
   Sit thou still when kings are arming,—
   Taste not when the wine-cup glistens,—
   Speak not when the people listens,—
   Stop thine ear against the singer,—
   From the red gold keep thy finger;—
   Vacant heart and hand, and eye,—
   Easy live and quiet die.
   The Bride of Lammermoor (1819), ch.3

6 Touch not the cat but a glove.
   The Fair Maid of Perth (1828), ch.34. but ; without.

7 *Mrs. Bertram:* That sounds like nonsense,
   my dear.
   Mr. Bertram: May be so, my dear; but it
   may be very good law for all that.
   Guy Mannering (1815), ch.9

8 Fair, fat, and forty.
   St. Ronan's Well (1823), ch.7

9 The play-bill, which is said to have an-
   nounced the tragedy of Hamlet, the character of the Prince of Denmark being left
   out.
   The Talisman (1825), introd. For an earlier report of this anecdote see *T.L.S.* 3 June 1939

10 The Big Bow-Wow strain I can do myself
   like any now going; but the exquisite
   touch, which renders ordinary commonplace things and characters interesting,
   from the truth of the description and the
   sentiment, is denied to me. [On Jane Austen.]
   Journal, 14 Mar. 1826

11 I would like to be there, were it but to see
   how the cat jumps.
   7 Oct. 1826

12 I never saw a richer country or to speak
   my mind a finer people. The worst of them
   is the bitter and envenomed dislike which
   they have to each other their factions have
   been so long envenomed and having so
   little ground to fight their battle in that
   they are like people fighting with daggers
   in a hogshead.
   Letter to Joanna Baillie, 12 Oct. 1825

13 All men who have turned out worth anything have had the chief hand in their own
   education.
   Letter to J.G. Lockhart, c.16 June 1830

14 We shall never learn to feel and respect
   our real calling and destiny, unless we have
   taught ourselves to consider every thing as
   moonshine, compared with the education
   of the heart.
   To J.G. Lockhart (Aug. 1825), quoted in Lockhart's *Life of Sir Walter Scott*, vol. 6 (1837), ch.2

SCOTTISH METRICAL PSALMS 1650

15 The Lord's my shepherd, I'll not want.
      He makes me down to lie
   In pastures green: he leadeth me
      the quiet waters by.
   My soul he doth restore again;
      and me to walk doth make
   Within the paths of righteousness,
      ev'n for his own name's sake.
   Psalm xxiii.1

SIR CHARLES SEDLEY 1639?–1701

16 Love still has something of the sea
      From whence his mother rose.
   Love still has Something

ALAN SEEGER 1888–1916

17 I have a rendezvous with Death
   At some disputed barricade.
   I Have a Rendezvous with Death (*North American
   Review*, Oct. 1916)

JOHN SELDEN 1584–1654

18 Ignorance of the law excuses no man; not
   that all men know the law, but because 'tis
   an excuse every man will plead, and no
   man can tell how to confute him.
   Table Talk (1689), 1892 edn. p.99. **Law**

19 Take a straw and throw it up into the air,
   you shall see by that which way the wind
   is.
   p.105. **Libels**

20 Pleasure is nothing else but the intermis-
   sion of pain, the enjoying of something I
   am in great trouble for till I have it.
   p.132. **Pleasure**

W.C. SELLAR 1898–1951
and **R.J. YEATMAN** 1898?–1968

1 The Roman Conquest was, however, a
Good Thing.
1066, And All That (1930), ch.1

2 The Cavaliers (Wrong but Wromantic)
and the Roundheads (Right but Repul-
sive).
ch.35

3 The National Debt is a very Good Thing
and it would be dangerous to pay it off for
fear of Political Economy.
ch.38

4 A Bad Thing: America was thus clearly
top nation, and History came to a
ch.62

SENECA 4 B.C./A.D. 1–65

5 *Homines dum docent discunt.*
Even while they teach, men learn.
Letters, 7.8

6 Anyone can stop a man's life, but no one
his death; a thousand doors open on to it.
Phoenissae, 152

ROBERT W. SERVICE 1874–1958

7 Ah! the clock is always slow;
It is later than you think.
Ballads of a Bohemian. **Spring,** ii

8 And watching his luck was his light-o'-
love, the lady that's known as Lou.
Songs of a Sourdough (1907). **The Shooting of
Dan McGrew**

EDWARD SEXBY d. 1658

9 Killing no Murder Briefly Discourst in
Three Questions.
Title of Pamphlet, 1657

ANNE SEXTON 1928–1974

0 In a dream you are never eighty.
Old

WILLIAM SHAKESPEARE 1564–1616

The line number is given without brackets where
the scene is all verse up to the quotation and the
line number is certain, and in square brackets
where prose makes it variable. All references are
to the Oxford Standard Authors Shakespeare in
one volume.

1 It were all one
That I should love a bright particular star
And think to wed it, he is so above me.
All's Well That Ends Well, I.i.[97]

2 Your virginity, your old virginity, is like

one of our French withered pears; it looks
ill, it eats drily.
[176]

13 It is like a barber's chair that fits all but-
tocks.
II.ii.[18]

14 A young man married is a man that's
marred.
iii.[315]

15 I know a man that had this trick of melancholy sold a goodly manor for a song.
III.ii.[8]

16 The triple pillar of the world transform'd
Into a strumpet's fool.
Antony and Cleopatra, I.i.12

17 Cleopatra: I'll set a bourn how far to be
belov'd.
Antony: Then must thou needs find out
new heaven, new earth.
16

18 There's a great spirit gone!
ii.[131]

19 Where's my serpent of old Nile?
v.25

20 My salad days,
When I was green in judgment.
73

21 I do not much dislike the matter, but
The manner of his speech.
II.ii.117

22 The barge she sat in, like a burnish'd
throne,
Burn'd on the water; the poop was beaten
gold,
Purple the sails, and so perfumed, that
The winds were love-sick with them, the
oars were silver,
Which to the tune of flutes kept stroke,
and made
The water which they beat to follow faster,
As amorous of their strokes. For her own
person,
It beggar'd all description.
[199]

23 I saw her once
Hop forty paces through the public street;
And having lost her breath, she spoke, and
panted
That she did make defect perfection,
And, breathless, power breathe forth.
[236]

24 Age cannot wither her, nor custom stale
Her infinite variety; other women cloy
The appetites they feed, but she makes
hungry
Where most she satisfies; for vilest things

Become themselves in her, that the holy priests
Bless her when she is riggish.
[243]

1 The music, ho!
v.2

2 Let's have one other gaudy night: call to me
All my sad captains; fill our bowls once more;
Let's mock the midnight bell.
III.xi.182

3 To business that we love we rise betime,
And go to 't with delight.
IV.iv.20

4 Unarm, Eros; the long day's task is done,
And we must sleep.
IV.xii.35

5 I am dying, Egypt, dying; only
I here importune death awhile, until
Of many thousand kisses the poor last
I lay upon thy lips.
xiii.18

6 O! wither'd is the garland of the war,
The soldier's pole is fall'n; young boys and girls
Are level now with men; the odds is gone,
And there is nothing left remarkable
Beneath the visiting moon.
64

7 What's brave, what's noble,
Let's do it after the high Roman fashion,
And make death proud to take us.
86

8 Finish, good lady; the bright day is done,
And we are for the dark.
V.ii.192

9 I know that a woman is a dish for the gods, if the devil dress her not.
[274]

10 Give me my robe, put on my crown; I have
Immortal longings in me.
[282]

11 Peace! peace!
Dost thou not see my baby at my breast,
That sucks the nurse asleep?
[310]

12 Now boast thee, death, in thy possession lies
A lass unparallel'd.
[317]

13 Fleet the time carelessly, as they did in the golden world.
As You Like It, I.i.[126]

14 Thus men may grow wiser every day: it i
the first time that I ever heard breaking c
ribs was sport for ladies.
ii.[146]

15 Hereafter, in a better world than this,
I shall desire more love and knowledge c
you.
[301]

16 Sweet are the uses of adversity,
Which like the toad, ugly and venomous,
Wears yet a precious jewel in his head;
And this our life, exempt from publi
haunt,
Finds tongues in trees, books in the rur
ning brooks,
Sermons in stones, and good in everything
II.i.12

17 Though I look old, yet I am stron
and lusty;
For in my youth I never did apply
Hot and rebellious liquors in my blood.
iii.47

18 As true a lover
As ever sigh'd upon a midnight pillow.
iv.[26]

19 Under the greenwood tree
Who loves to lie with me,
And turn his merry note
Unto the sweet bird's throat,
Come hither, come hither, come hither:
Here shall he see
No enemy
But winter and rough weather.
v.1

20 I can suck melancholy out of a song as
weasel sucks eggs.
[12]

21 Call me not fool till heaven hath sent m
fortune.
vii.19

22 And so, from hour to hour, we ripe an
ripe,
And then from hour to hour, we rot an
rot:
And thereby hangs a tale.
26

23 A worthy fool! Motley's the only wear.
34

24 If ever you have look'd on better days,
If ever been where bells have knoll'd t
church,
If ever sat at any good man's feast,
If ever from your eyelids wip'd a tear,
And know what 'tis to pity, and be pitied,
Let gentleness my strong enforcement be.
113

1   All the world's a stage,
And all the men and women merely play-
   ers:
They have their exits and their entrances;
And one man in his time plays many parts,
His acts being seven ages. At first the in-
   fant,
Mewling and puking in the nurse's arms.
And then the whining schoolboy, with his
   satchel,
And shining morning face, creeping like
   snail
Unwillingly to school. And then the lover,
Sighing like furnace, with a woful ballad
Made to his mistress' eyebrow. Then a
   soldier,
Full of strange oaths, and bearded like the
   pard,
Jealous in honour, sudden and quick in
   quarrel,
Seeking the bubble reputation
Even in the cannon's mouth. And then the
   justice,
In fair round belly with good capon lin'd,
With eyes severe, and beard of formal cut,
Full of wise saws and modern instances;
And so he plays his part. The sixth age
   shifts
Into the lean and slipper'd pantaloon,
With spectacles on nose and pouch on
   side,
His youthful hose well sav'd a world too
   wide
For his shrunk shank; and his big manly
   voice,
Turning again towards childish treble,
   pipes
And whistles in his sound. Last scene of
   all,
That ends this strange eventful history,
Is second childishness, and mere oblivion,
Sans teeth, sans eyes, sans taste, sans
   everything.
   139

2 Blow, blow, thou winter wind,
Thou art not so unkind
     As man's ingratitude.
   174

3 Run, run, Orlando: carve on every tree
The fair, the chaste, and unexpressive she.
III.ii.9

4 Let us make an honourable retreat;
though not with bag and baggage, yet with
scrip and scrippage.
[170]

5 O wonderful, wonderful, and most wonderful wonderful! and yet again wonderful, and after that, out of all whooping!
[202]

6   Down on your knees,
And thank heaven, fasting, for a good
   man's love.
v.57

7 I pray you, do not fall in love with me,
For I am falser than vows made in wine.
[72]

8 Dead shepherd, now I find thy saw of
   might:
'Who ever lov'd that lov'd not at first
   sight?'
[81]. Quoting Marlowe, *Hero and Leander,* First
Sestiad, l.176

9 Come, woo me, woo me; for now I am in a
holiday humour, and like enough to consent.
IV.i.[70]

10 Men are April when they woo, December
when they wed: maids are May when they
are maids, but the sky changes when they
are wives.
[153]

11 O coz, coz, coz, my pretty little coz, that
thou didst know how many fathom deep I
am in love!
[217]

12 It was a lover and his lass,
   With a hey, and a ho, and a hey nonino,
That o'er the green cornfield did pass,
   In the spring time, the only pretty ring
    time,
When birds do sing, hey ding a ding, ding;
Sweet lovers love the spring.
V.iii.[18]

13 A poor virgin, sir, an ill-favoured thing,
sir, but mine own.
iv.[60]

14 I am known to be...one that loves a cup of
hot wine with not a drop of allaying Tiber
in't.
Coriolanus, II.i.[52]

15   Bid them wash their faces,
And keep their teeth clean.
[65]

16 My gracious silence, hail!
[194]

17 Hear you this Triton of the minnows?
   mark you
His absolute 'shall'?
III.i.88

18   Despising,
For you, the city, thus I turn my back:

There is a world elsewhere.
iii.131

1   Like an eagle in a dove-cote, I
Flutter'd your Volscians in Corioli:
Alone I did it.
V.v.115

2 If she be furnish'd with a mind so rare,
She is alone the Arabian bird, and I
Have lost the wager. Boldness be my
    friend!
Arm me, audacity.
Cymbeline, I.vi.16

3 Hark! hark! the lark at heaven's gate
    sings,
    And Phoebus 'gins arise…
With everything that pretty is,
    My lady sweet, arise!
II.iii.[22]

4 Fear no more the heat o' the sun,
    Nor the furious winter's rages;
Thou thy worldly task hast done,
    Home art gone and ta'en thy wages:
Golden lads and girls all must,
As chimney-sweepers, come to dust.

Fear no more the frown o' the great,
    Thou art past the tyrant's stroke:
Care no more to clothe and eat;
    To thee the reed is as the oak:
The sceptre, learning, physic, must
All follow this, and come to dust.

Fear no more the lightning flash,
    Nor the all-dreaded thunder-stone;
Fear not slander, censure rash;
    Thou hast finish'd joy and moan:
All lovers young, all lovers must
Consign to thee, and come to dust.

No exorciser harm thee!
    Nor no witchcraft charm thee!
Ghost unlaid forbear thee!
    Nothing ill come near thee!
Quiet consummation have;
And renowned be thy grave!
IV.ii.258

5 You come most carefully upon your hour.
Hamlet, I.i.6

6 For this relief much thanks; 'tis bitter cold
And I am sick at heart.
8

7 In the most high and palmy state of
    Rome,
A little ere the mightiest Julius fell,
The graves stood tenantless and the sheet-
    ed dead
Did squeak and gibber in the Roman
    streets.
113

8 And then it started like a guilty thing
Upon a fearful summons.
148

9 It faded on the crowing of the cock.
Some say that ever 'gainst that season
    comes
Wherein our Saviour's birth is celebrated,
The bird of dawning singeth all night long;
And then, they say, no spirit can walk
    abroad;
The nights are wholesome; then no planets
    strike,
No fairy takes, nor witch hath power to
    charm,
So hallow'd and so gracious is the time.
157

10 But, look, the morn, in russet mantle clad,
Walks o'er the dew of yon high eastern
    hill.
166

11 A little more than kin, and less than kind.
ii.65

12 Not so, my lord; I am too much i' the sun.
67

13 Seems, madam! Nay, it is; I know not
    'seems'.
76

14 But I have that within which passeth
    show;
These but the trappings and the suits of
    woe.
85

15 O! that this too too solid flesh would melt,
Thaw, and resolve itself into a dew;
Or that the Everlasting had not fix'd
His canon 'gainst self-slaughter! O God! O
    God!
How weary, stale, flat, and unprofitable
Seem to me all the uses of this world.
Fie on't! O fie! 'tis an unweeded garden,
That grows to seed; things rank and gross
    in nature
Possess it merely. That it should come to
    this!
But two months dead: nay, not so much,
    not two:
So excellent a king; that was, to this,
Hyperion to a satyr: so loving to my
    mother,
That he might not beteem the winds of
    heaven
Visit her face too roughly. Heaven and
    earth!
Must I remember? Why, she would hang
    on him,
As if increase of appetite had grown
By what it fed on; and yet, within a month,

Let me not think on't: Frailty, thy name is
    woman!
A little month; or ere those shoes were old
With which she follow'd my poor father's
    body,
Like Niobe, all tears; why she, even she,—
O God! a beast, that wants discourse of
    reason,
Would have mourn'd longer,—married
    with mine uncle,
My father's brother, but no more like my
    father
Than I to Hercules.
129

1 We'll teach you to drink deep ere you
    depart.
175

2 Thrift, thrift, Horatio! the funeral bak'd
    meats
Did coldly furnish forth the marriage
    tables.
Would I had met my dearest foe in heaven
Ere I had ever seen that day, Horatio!
180

3 He was a man, take him for all in all,
I shall not look upon his like again.
187

4 A countenance more in sorrow than in
    anger.
231

5 Do not, as some ungracious pastors do,
Show me the steep and thorny way to
    heaven,
Whiles, like a puff'd and reckless libertine,
Himself the primrose path of dalliance
    treads,
And recks not his own rede.
iii.47

6 And these few precepts in thy memory
Look thou character. Give thy thoughts
    no tongue,
Nor any unproportion'd thought his act.
Be thou familiar, but by no means vulgar;
The friends thou hast, and their adoption
    tried,
Grapple them to thy soul with hoops of
    steel;
But do not dull thy palm with entertain-
    ment
Of each new-hatch'd, unfledg'd comrade. Beware
Of entrance to a quarrel; but, being in,
Bear't that th' opposed may beware of
    thee.
Give every man thine ear, but few thy
    voice;
Take each man's censure, but reserve thy
    judgment.

Costly thy habit as thy purse can buy,
But not express'd in fancy; rich, not gaudy;
For the apparel oft proclaims the man,
And they in France of the best rank and
    station
Are most select and generous, chief in that.
Neither a borrower, nor a lender be;
For loan oft loses both itself and friend,
And borrowing dulls the edge of hus-
    bandry,
This above all: to thine own self be true,
And it must follow, as the night the day,
Thou canst not then be false to any man.
58

7 *Hamlet:* The air bites shrewdly; it is very
    cold.
Horatio: It is a nipping and an eager air.
iv.1

8 But to my mind,—though I am native
    here,
And to the manner born,—it is a custom
More honour'd in the breach than the ob-
    servance.
14

9 Angels and ministers of grace defend us!
39

10   Unhand me, gentlemen,
By heaven! I'll make a ghost of him that
    lets me.
84

11 Something is rotten in the state of Den-
    mark.
90

12 Murder most foul, as in the best it is;
But this most foul, strange, and unnatural.
v.27

13   O my prophetic soul!
My uncle!
40

14 But, soft! methinks I scent the morning
    air.
58

15 O, horrible! O, horrible! most horrible!
80

16   Leave her to heaven,
And to those thorns that in her bosom
    lodge,
To prick and sting her.
86

17 O most pernicious woman!
O villain, villain, smiling, damned villain!
My tables,—meet it is I set it down,
That one may smile, and smile, and be a
    villain;
At least I'm sure it may be so in Denmark.
105

1 There are more things in heaven and earth, Horatio,
Than are dreamt of in your philosophy.
166

2 Rest, rest, perturbed spirit.
182

3 The time is out of joint; O cursed spite,
That ever I was born to set it right!
188

4 By indirections find directions out.
II.i.66

5 Brevity is the soul of wit.
ii.90

6   To define true madness,
What is't but to be nothing else but mad?
93

7 More matter with less art.
95

8 That he is mad, 'tis true; 'tis true 'tis pity;
And pity 'tis 'tis true: a foolish figure;
But farewell it, for I will use no art.
97

9 *Polonius:* What do you read, my lord?
Hamlet: Words, words, words.
[195]

10 Though this be madness, yet there is method in't.
[211]

11 Faith, her privates, we.
[242]

12 There is nothing either good or bad, but thinking makes it so.
[259]

13 O God! I could be bounded in a nut-shell, and count myself a king of infinite space, were it not that I have bad dreams.
[264]

14 What a piece of work is a man! How noble in reason! how infinite in faculty! in form, in moving, how express and admirable! in action how like an angel! in apprehension how like a god! the beauty of the world! the paragon of animals! And yet, to me, what is this quintessence of dust? man delights not me; no, nor woman neither, though, by your smiling, you seem to say so.
[323]

15 He that plays the king shall be welcome; his majesty shall have tribute of me.
[341]

16 .I am but mad north-north-west; when the wind is southerly, I know a hawk from a handsaw.
[405]

17 The play, I remember, pleased not the million; 'twas caviare to the general.
[465]

18 Good my lord, will you see the players well bestowed? Do you hear, let them be well used; for they are the abstracts and brief chronicles of the time: after your death you were better have a bad epitaph than their ill report while you live.
[553]

19 Use every man after his desert, and who should 'scape whipping?
[561]

20 O, what a rogue and peasant slave am I:
Is it not monstrous that this player here,
But in a fiction, in a dream of passion,
Could force his soul so to his own conceit
That from her working all his visage wann'd,
Tears in his eyes, distraction in 's aspect,
A broken voice, and his whole function suiting
With forms to his conceit? and all for nothing!
For Hecuba!
What's Hecuba to him or he to Hecuba
That he should weep for her?
[584]

21   He would drown the stage with tears,
And cleave the general ear with horrid speech,
Make mad the guilty, and appal the free,
Confound the ignorant, and amaze, indeed,
The very faculties of eyes and ears.
[596]

22   Bloody, bawdy villain!
Remorseless, treacherous, lecherous, kindless villain!
[616]

23   The play's the thing
Wherein I'll catch the conscience of the king.
[641]

24 To be, or not to be: that is the question:
Whether 'tis nobler in the mind to suffer
The slings and arrows of outrageous fortune,
Or to take arms against a sea of troubles,
And by opposing end them? To die: to sleep;
No more; and, by a sleep to say we end
The heart-ache and the thousand natural shocks

That flesh is heir to, 'tis a consummation
Devoutly to be wish'd. To die, to sleep;
To sleep: perchance to dream: ay, there's
    the rub;
For in that sleep of death what dreams
    may come
When we have shuffled off this mortal coil,
Must give us pause. There's the respect
That makes calamity of so long life;
For who would bear the whips and scorns
    of time,
The oppressor's wrong, the proud man's
    contumely,
The pangs of dispriz'd love, the law's de-
    lay,
The insolence of office, and the spurns
That patient merit of the unworthy takes,
When he himself might his quietus make
With a bare bodkin? Who would fardels
    bear,
To grunt and sweat under a weary life,
But that the dread of something after
    death,
The undiscover'd country from whose
    bourn
No traveller returns, puzzles the will,
And makes us rather bear those ills we
    have,
Than fly to others that we know not of?
Thus conscience doth make cowards of us
    all;
And thus the native hue of resolution
Is sicklied o'er with the pale cast of
    thought,
And enterprises of great pith and moment
With this regard their currents turn awry,
And lose the name of action.
III.i.56

            For, to the noble mind,
Rich gifts wax poor when givers prove
    unkind.
100

2 Get thee to a nunnery: why wouldst thou
be a breeder of sinners?
[124]

3 What should such fellows as I do crawling
between heaven and earth? We are arrant
knaves, all; believe none of us.
[132]

4 I have heard of your paintings too, well
enough. God hath given you one face and
you make yourselves another.
[150]

5 I say, we will have no more marriages.
[156]

6 O! what a noble mind is here o'erthrown:
The courtier's, soldier's, scholar's, eye,
    tongue, sword;

The expectancy and rose of the fair state,
The glass of fashion, and the mould of
    form,
The observed of all observers, quite, quite,
    down!
And I, of ladies most deject and wretched,
That suck'd the honey of his music vows,
Now see that noble and most sovereign
    reason,
Like sweet bells jangled, out of tune and
    harsh;
That unmatch'd form and figure of blown
    youth,
Blasted with ecstasy: O! woe is me,
To have seen what I have seen, see what I
    see!
[159]

7 Speak the speech, I pray you, as I pro-
nounced it to you, trippingly on the
tongue; but if you mouth it, as many of
your players do, I had as lief the town-crier
spoke my lines. Nor do not saw the air too
much with your hand, thus; but use all
gently: for in the very torrent, tempest, and
—as I may say—whirlwind of passion, you
must acquire and beget a temperance, that
may give it smoothness. O! it offends me to
the soul to hear a robustious periwig-pated
fellow tear a passion to tatters, to very
rags, to split the ears of the groundlings,
who for the most part are capable of
nothing but inexplicable dumb-shows and
noise: I would have such a fellow whipped
for o'erdoing Termagant; it out-herods
Herod: pray you, avoid it.
ii.1

8 Be not too tame neither, but let your own
discretion be your tutor: suit the action to
the word, the word to the action; with this
special observance, that you o'erstep not
the modesty of nature; for anything so
overdone is from the purpose of playing,
whose end, both at the first and now, was
and is, to hold, as 'twere, the mirror up to
nature.
[19]

9   Give me that man
That is not passion's slave, and I will wear
    him
In my heart's core, ay, in my heart of
    heart,
As I do thee.
[76]

10 The chameleon's dish: I eat the air,
promise-crammed; you cannot feed cap-
ons so.
[98]

1 Here's metal more attractive.
[117]

2 The lady doth protest too much, methinks.
[242]

3 *Hamlet:* No, no, they do but jest, poison
in jest; no offence i' the world.
King: What do you call the play?
Hamlet: The Mouse-trap.
[247]

4 We that have free souls, it touches us not:
let the galled jade wince, our withers are
unwrung.
[255]

5 What! frighted with false fire?
[282]

6 Why, let the stricken deer go weep,
  The hart ungalled play;
For some must watch, while some must
   sleep:
  So runs the world away.
[287]

7 You would play upon me; you would
seem to know my stops; you would pluck
out the heart of my mystery; you would
sound me from my lowest note to the top
of my compass.
[387]

8 *Hamlet:* Do you see yonder cloud that's
almost in shape of a camel?
Polonius: By the mass, and 'tis like a
camel, indeed.
Hamlet: Methinks it is like a weasel.
Polonius: It is backed like a weasel.
Hamlet: Or like a whale?
Polonius: Very like a whale.
[400]

9 'Tis now the very witching time of night,
  When churchyards yawn and hell itself
   breathes out
  Contagion to this world: now could I
   drink hot blood,
  And do such bitter business as the day
  Would quake to look on.
[413]

10 Let me be cruel, not unnatural;
I will speak daggers to her, but use none.
[420]

11 O! my offence is rank, it smells to heaven.
iii.36

12 My words fly up, my thoughts remain
  below:
  Words without thoughts never to heaven
  go.
97

13 How now! a rat? Dead, for a ducat, dead!
iv.23

14 Thou wretched, rash, intruding foo
  farewell!
I took thee for thy better.
31

15 Look here, upon this picture, and on this.
53

16 You cannot call it love, for at your age
The hey-day in the blood is tame, it's hum
  ble,
And waits upon the judgment.
68

17   Nay, but to live
In the rank sweat of an enseamed bed,
Stew'd in corruption, honeying and ma
  ing love
Over the nasty sty.
91

18 A king of shreds and patches.
102

19 Assume a virtue, if you have it not.
160

20 I must be cruel only to be kind.
178

21 For 'tis the sport to have the enginer
Hoist with his own petar.
206

22   Diseases desperate grown,
By desperate appliances are reliev'd,
Or not at all.
IV.iii.9

23 How all occasions do inform against me,
And spur my dull revenge!
iv.32

24   Rightly to be great
Is not to stir without great argument,
But greatly to find quarrel in a straw
When honour's at the stake.
53

25 How should I your true love know
     From another one?
By his cockle hat and staff,
     And his sandal shoon.
v.[23]

26 He is dead and gone, lady,
     He is dead and gone,
At his head a grass-green turf;
     At his heels a stone.
[29]

27 White his shroud as the mountain snow..
     Larded with sweet flowers;
Which bewept to the grave did go

With true-love showers.
[36]

1 Lord! we know what we are, but know not what we may be.
[43]

2 Then up he rose, and donn'd his clothes.
[53]

3 Come, my coach! Good-night, ladies; good-night, sweet ladies; good night, good-night.
[72]

4 When sorrows come, they come not single spies,
But in battalions.
[78]

5 There's such divinity doth hedge a king,
That treason can but peep to what it would.
[123]

6 There's rosemary, that's for remembrance; pray, love, remember: and there is pansies, that's for thoughts.
[174]

7 There's fennel for you, and columbines; there's rue for you; and here's some for me; we may call it herb of grace o' Sundays. O! you must wear your rue with a difference.
[179]

8 And where the offence is let the great axe fall.
[218]

9 There is a willow grows aslant a brook,
That shows his hoar leaves in the glassy stream;
There with fantastic garlands did she come,
Of crow-flowers, nettles, daisies, and long purples,
That liberal shepherds give a grosser name,
But our cold maids do dead men's fingers call them.
vii.167

0 Cudgel thy brains no more about it, for your dull ass will not mend his pace with beating.
V.i.[61]

1 Alas, poor Yorick. I knew him, Horatio; a fellow of infinite jest, of most excellent fancy; he hath borne me on his back a thousand times; and now, how abhorred in my imagination it is! my gorge rises at it. Here hung those lips that I have kissed I know not how oft. Where be your gibes now? your gambols? your songs? your

flashes of merriment, that were wont to set the table on a roar? Not one now, to mock your own grinning? quite chap-fallen? Now get you to my lady's chamber, and tell her, let her paint an inch thick, to this favour she must come; make her laugh at that.
[201]

12 Imperious Caesar, dead, and turn'd to clay,
Might stop a hole to keep the wind away.
[235]

13   Lay her i' the earth;
And from her fair and unpolluted flesh
May violets spring! I tell thee, churlish priest,
A ministering angel shall my sister be,
When thou liest howling.
[260]

14 Sweets to the sweet: farewell!
[265]

15 There's a divinity that shapes our ends,
Rough-hew them how we will.
ii.10

16 I once did hold it, as our statists do,
A baseness to write fair, and labour'd much
How to forget that learning; but, sir, now
It did me yeoman's service.
33

17 Not a whit, we defy augury; there's a special providence in the fall of a sparrow. If it be now, 'tis not to come; if it be not to come, it will be now; if it be not now, yet it will come: the readiness is all.
[232]

18 I have shot mine arrow o'er the house,
And hurt my brother.
[257]

19 A hit, a very palpable hit.
[295]

20   This fell sergeant, death,
Is swift in his arrest.
[350]

21   Report me and my cause aright
To the unsatisfied.
[353]

22 If thou didst ever hold me in thy heart,
Absent thee from felicity awhile,
And in this harsh world draw thy breath in pain,
To tell my story.
[360]

23 The rest is silence.
[372]

1 Now cracks a noble heart. Good-night,
   sweet prince,
And flights of angels sing thee to thy rest!
   [373]

2 Rosencrantz and Guildenstern are dead.
   [385]

3   Let four captains
Bear Hamlet, like a soldier, to the stage;
For he was likely, had he been put on,
To have prov'd most royally.
   [409]

4 Let us be Diana's foresters, gentlemen of
the shade, minions of the moon.
   Henry IV, Part 1, I.ii.[28]

5 If all the year were playing holidays,
To sport would be as tedious as to work;
But when they seldom come, they wish'd
   for come.
   [226]

6   O! the blood more stirs
To rouse a lion than to start a hare.
   iii.197

7 I know a trick worth two of that.
   II.i.[40]

8 Go hang thyself in thine own heir-
apparent garters!
   ii.[49]

9   Falstaff sweats to death
And lards the lean earth as he walks along.
   [119]

10 Out of this nettle, danger, we pluck this
flower, safety.
   iii.[11]

11 Nay that's past praying for.
   iv.[214]

12 A plague of sighing and grief! it blows a
man up like a bladder.
   [370]

13 *Glendower:* I can call spirits from the vasty
   deep.
   Hotspur: Why, so can I, or so can any
   man;
But will they come when you do call for
   them?
   III.i.[53]

14 Now I perceive the devil understands
Welsh.
   [233]

15 My near'st and dearest enemy.
   ii.123

16 Shall I not take mine ease in mine inn but I
shall have my pocket picked?
   iii.[91]

17 Thou seest I have more flesh than another

man, and therefore more frailty.
   [187]

18 What is honour? A word. What is that
word, honour? Air. A trim reckoning
Who hath it? He that died o' Wednesday.
   V.i.[137]

19 I am not only witty in myself, but the
cause that wit is in other men.
   Henry IV, Part 2, I.ii.[10]

20 It is the disease of not listening, the ma-
lady of not marking, that I am troubled
withal.
   [139]

21 I am as poor as Job, my lord, but not so
patient.
   [145]

22 Well, I am loath to gall a new-healed
wound.
   [169]

23   When we mean to build,
We first survey the plot, then draw the
   model;
And when we see the figure of the house,
Then we must rate the cost of the erection;
Which if we find outweighs ability,
What do we then but draw anew the model
In fewer offices, or at last desist
To build at all?
   iii.[41]

24 A hundred mark is a long one for a poor
lone woman to bear; and I have borne, and
borne, and borne; and have been fubbed
off, and fubbed off, and fubbed off, from
this day to that day, that it is a shame to be
thought on.
   II.i.[36]

25   Shall pack-horses,
And hollow pamper'd jades of Asia,
Which cannot go but thirty miles a day,
Compare with Caesars, and with Canni-
   bals,
And Trojan Greeks? nay, rather damn
   them with
King Cerberus; and let the welkin roar.
   iv.[176]. See 161:1

26 Is it not strange that desire should so
many years outlive performance?
   [283]

27   Then, happy low, lie down!
Uneasy lies the head that wears a crown.
   III.i.30

28 We have heard the chimes at midnight.
   ii.[231]

29 I care not; a man can die but once; we owe

God a death.
[253]

Thy wish was father, Harry, to that
thought.
IV.v.91

Commit
The oldest sins the newest kind of ways.
124

This is the English, not the Turkish court;
Not Amurath an Amurath succeeds,
But Harry, Harry.
V.ii.47

My father is gone wild into his grave.
123

Under which king, Bezonian? speak, or
die!
iii.[116]

I know thee not, old man: fall to thy prayers;
How ill white hairs become a fool and
jester!
v.[52]

O! for a Muse of fire, that would ascend
The brightest heaven of invention.
Henry V, Chorus, 1

Can this cockpit hold
The vasty fields of France? or may we
cram
Within this wooden O the very casques
That did affright the air at Agincourt?
11

Consideration like an angel came,
And whipp'd the offending Adam out of
him.
I.i.28

His present and your pains we thank you
for:
When we have match'd our rackets to
these balls,
We will in France, by God's grace, play a
set
Shall strike his father's crown into the ha-
zard.
ii.260

Now all the youth of England are on fire,
And silken dalliance in the wardrobe lies.
II. Chorus, 1

He's in Arthur's bosom, if ever man went
to Arthur's bosom. A' made a finer end,
and went away an it had been any christom child; a' parted even just between
twelve and one, even at the turning o' the
tide: for after I saw him fumble with the
sheets and play with flowers and smile
upon his fingers' ends, I knew there was
but one way; for his nose was as sharp as a

pen, and a' babbled of green fields.
iii.[9]

13 So a' bade me lay more clothes on his feet:
I put my hand into the bed and felt them,
and they were as cold as any stone; then I
felt to his knees, and so upward, and upward, and all was as cold as any stone.
[23]

14 Once more unto the breach, dear friends,
once more;
Or close the wall up with our English dead!
In peace there's nothing so becomes a man
As modest stillness and humility:
But when the blast of war blows in our
ears,
Then imitate the action of the tiger;
Stiffen the sinews, summon up the blood,
Disguise fair nature with hard-favour'd
rage.
III.i.1

15 I see you stand like greyhounds in the
slips,
Straining upon the start. The game's
afoot:
Follow your spirit; and, upon this charge
Cry 'God for Harry! England and Saint
George!'
31

16 A' never broke any man's head but his
own, and that was against a post when he
was drunk.
ii.[43]

17 A little touch of Harry in the night.
IV. Chorus, 47

18 Discuss unto me; art thou officer?
Or art thou base, common and popular?
i.37

19 The king's a bawcock, and a heart of gold,
A lad of life, an imp of fame,
Of parents good, of fist most valiant:
I kiss his dirty shoe, and from my heart-
string
I love the lovely bully.
44

20 Though it appear a little out of fashion,
There is much care and valour in this
Welshman.
[86]

21 I think the king is but a man, as I am: the
violet smells to him as it doth to me.
[106]

22 Every subject's duty is the king's; but
every subject's soul is his own.
[189]

23 'Tis not the balm, the sceptre and the ball,
The sword, the mace, the crown imperial,

The intertissued robe of gold and pearl,
The farced title running 'fore the king,
The throne he sits on, nor the tide of pomp
That beats upon the high shore of this
world,
No, not all these, thrice-gorgeous cere-
mony,
Not all these, laid in bed majestical,
Can sleep so soundly as the wretched
slave,
Who with a body fill'd and vacant mind
Gets him to rest, cramm'd with distressful
bread.
[280]

1 O God of battles! steel my soldiers' hearts.
[309]

2   O! that we now had here
But one ten thousand of those men in
England
That do no work to-day.
iii.16

3 If we are mark'd to die, we are enow
To do our country loss; and if to live,
The fewer men, the greater share of honour.
20

4 He which hath no stomach to this fight,
Let him depart; his passport shall be made,
And crowns for convoy put into his purse:
We would not die in that man's company
That fears his fellowship to die with us.
This day is called the feast of Crispian:
He that outlives this day and comes safe
home,
Will stand a tip-toe when this day is
nam'd,
And rouse him at the name of Crispian.
He that shall live this day, and see old age,
Will yearly on the vigil feast his neigh-
bours,
And say, 'To-morrow is Saint Crispian:'
Then will he strip his sleeve and show his
scars,
And say, 'These wounds I had on Crispin's
day.'
Old men forget: yet all shall be forgot,
But he'll remember with advantages
What feats he did that day. Then shall our
names,
Familiar in his mouth as household words,
Harry the King, Bedford and Exeter,
Warwick and Talbot, Salisbury and
Gloucester,
Be in their flowing cups freshly remem-
ber'd.
This story shall the good man teach his
son;
And Crispin Crispian shall ne'er go by,
From this day to the ending of the world,

But we in it shall be remembered;
We few, we happy few, we band (
brothers;
For he to-day that sheds his blood with m
Shall be my brother; be he ne'er so vile
This day shall gentle his condition:
And gentlemen in England, now a-bed
Shall think themselves accurs'd they we
not here,
And hold their manhoods cheap while
any speaks
That fought with us upon Saint Crispin
day.
35

5   Let it not disgrace me
If I demand before this royal view,
What rub or what impediment there is,
Why that the naked, poor, and mangle
Peace,
Dear nurse of arts, plenties, and joyf
births,
Should not in this best garden of th
world,
Our fertile France, put up her lovely v
sage?
V.ii.31

6 Expect Saint Martin's summer, halcyo
days.
Henry VI, Part 1, I.ii.131

7   Unbidden guests
Are often welcomest when they are gone.
II.ii.55

8 I owe him little duty and less love.
IV.iv.34

9 She's beautiful and therefore to be woo'd
She is a woman, therefore to be won.
V.iii.78. See also *Titus Andronicus*, II.1.82

10 Is this the fashion of the court of England
Is this the government of Britain's isle,
And this the royalty of Albion's king?
Henry VI, Part 2, I.iii.[46]

11 She bears a duke's revenues on her back,
And in her heart she scorns our poverty.
[83]

12 Thrice is he arm'd that hath his quarre
just.
III.ii.233

13 Forbear to judge, for we are sinners all.
Close up his eyes, and draw the curtai
close;
And let us all to meditation.
iii.31

14 The first thing we do, let's kill all th
lawyers.
IV.ii.[86]

1 And Adam was a gardener.
[146]

2 Away with him! away with him! he speaks
Latin.
vii.[62]

3 O tiger's heart wrapp'd in a woman's hide!
Henry VI, Part 3, I.iv.137

4 If I chance to talk a little wild, forgive me;
I had it from my father.
Henry VIII, I.iv.26

5 Go with me, like good angels, to my end;
And, as the long divorce of steel falls on
me,
Make of your prayers one sweet sacrifice,
And lift my soul to heaven.
II.i.75

6 Heaven will one day open
The king's eyes, that so long have slept
upon
This bold bad man.
ii.[42]

7 Orpheus with his lute made trees,
And the mountain-tops that freeze,
Bow themselves when he did sing.
III.i.3

8 I shall fall
Like a bright exhalation in the evening,
And no man see me more.
ii.226

9 Farewell! a long farewell, to all my great-
ness!
This is the state of man: to-day he puts
forth
The tender leaves of hope; to-morrow
blossoms,
And bears his blushing honours thick
upon him;
The third day comes a frost, a killing frost;
And, when he thinks, good easy man, full
surely
His greatness is a-ripening, nips his root,
And then he falls, as I do. I have ventur'd,
Like little wanton boys that swim on blad-
ders,
This many summers in a sea of glory,
But far beyond my depth: my high-blown
pride
At length broke under me, and now has
left me
Weary and old with service, to the mercy
Of a rude stream that must for ever hide
me.
Vain pomp and glory of this world, I hate
ye:
I feel my heart new open'd. O how wret-
ched
Is that poor man that hangs on princes'
favours!
There is, betwixt that smile we would as-
pire to,
That sweet aspect of princes, and their
ruin,
More pangs and fears than wars or women
have;
And when he falls, he falls like Lucifer,
Never to hope again.
352

10 Cromwell, I charge thee, fling away ambition:
By that sin fell the angels; how can man
then,
The image of his Maker, hope to win by't?
Love thyself last: cherish those hearts that
hate thee;
Corruption wins not more than honesty.
441

11 Had I but serv'd my God with half the
zeal
I serv'd my king, he would not in mine age
Have left me naked to mine enemies.
456

12 Men's evil manners live in brass; their
virtues
We write in water.
IV.ii.45

13 Hence! home, you idle creatures, get you
home:
Is this a holiday?
Julius Caesar, I.i.1

14 Beware the ides of March.
ii.18

15 Well, honour is the subject of my story.
I cannot tell what you and other men
Think of this life: but, for my single self,
I had as lief not be as live to be
In awe of such a thing as I myself.
92

16 Why, man, he doth bestride the narrow
world
Like a Colossus; and we petty men
Walk under his huge legs, and peep about
To find ourselves dishonourable graves.
Men at some time are masters of their
fates:
The fault, dear Brutus, is not in our stars,
But in ourselves, that we are underlings.
134

17 Let me have men about me that are fat;
Sleek-headed men and such as sleep o'
nights;
Yond' Cassius has a lean and hungry look;
He thinks too much: such men are dangerous.
191

1 Seldom he smiles, and smiles in such a sort
  As if he mock'd himself, and scorn'd his
    spirit,
  That could be mov'd to smile at anything.
  204

2 *Cassius:* Did Cicero say any thing?
  Casca: Ay, he spoke Greek.
  Cassius: To what effect?
  Casca: Nay, an I tell you that, I'll ne'er
  look you i' the face again; but those that
  understood him smiled at one another and
  shook their heads; but, for mine own part,
  it was Greek to me.
  [282]

3 Between the acting of a dreadful thing
  And the first motion, all the interim is
  Like a phantasma, or a hideous dream.
  II.i.63

4 Let's carve him as a dish fit for the gods,
  Not hew him as a carcass fit for hounds.
  173

5 But when I tell him he hates flatterers,
  He says he does, being then most flattered.
  207

6 Cowards die many times before their
    deaths;
  The valiant never taste of death but once.
  Of all the wonders that I yet have heard,
  It seems to me most strange that men
    should fear;
  Seeing that death, a necessary end,
  Will come when it will come.
  ii.32

7 *Caesar:* The ides of March are come.
  Soothsayer: Ay, Caesar; but not gone.
  III.i.1

8 If I could pray to move, prayers would
    move me;
  But I am constant as the northern star,
  Of whose true-fix'd and resting quality
  There is no fellow in the firmament.
  59

9 *Et tu, Brute?*
  77. See 59:10

10   Live a thousand years,
  I shall not find myself so apt to die:
  No place will please me so, no mean of
    death,
  As here by Caesar, and by you cut off,
  The choice and master spirits of this age.
  159

11 O! pardon me, thou bleeding piece of
    earth,
  That I am meek and gentle with these
    butchers;
  Thou art the ruins of the noblest man

That ever lived in the tide of times.
254

12   Caesar's spirit, ranging for revenge,
  With Ate by his side, come hot from hell,
  Shall in these confines, with a monarch'
    voice
  Cry, 'Havoc!' and let slip the dogs of war.
  270

13 Not that I loved Caesar less, but that
  loved Rome more.
  ii.[22]

14 As he was valiant, I honour him: but, a
  he was ambitious, I slew him.
  [27]

15 Who is here so base that would be a bond
  man? If any, speak; for him have I offend
  ed. Who is here so rude that would not b
  a Roman? If any, speak; for him have
  offended. Who is here so vile that will no
  love his country? If any, speak; for hin
  have I offended.
  [31]

16 Friends, Romans, countrymen, lend m
    your ears;
  I come to bury Caesar, not to praise him.
  The evil that men do lives after them,
  The good is oft interred with their bones;
  So let it be with Caesar. The noble Brutus
  Hath told you Caesar was ambitious;
  If it were so, it was a grievous fault;
  And grievously hath Caesar answer'd it.
  Here, under leave of Brutus and the rest,—
  For Brutus is an honourable man;
  So are they all, all honourable men,—
  Come I to speak in Caesar's funeral.
  [79]

17 He was my friend, faithful and just to me:
  But Brutus says he was ambitious;
  And Brutus is an honourable man.
  [91]

18 But yesterday the word of Caesar might
  Have stood against the world; now lies h
    there,
  And none so poor to do him reverence.
  [124]

19 If you have tears, prepare to shed then
    now.
  [174]

20 This was the most unkindest cut of all;
  For when the noble Caesar saw him stab,
  Ingratitude, more strong than traitors
    arms,
  Quite vanquish'd him: then burst hi
    mighty heart;
  And, in his mantle muffling up his face,
  Even at the base of Pompey's statua,
  Which all the while ran blood, great Cae
    sar fell.

O! what a fall was there, my countrymen;
Then I, and you, and all of us fell down,
Whilst bloody treason flourish'd over us.
[188]

He shall not live; look, with a spot I damn
him.
IV.i.6

2 Let me tell you, Cassius, you yourself
Are much condemn'd to have an itching
palm.
iii.7

3 There is a tide in the affairs of men,
Which, taken at the flood, leads on to
fortune;
Omitted, all the voyage of their life
Is bound in shallows and in miseries.
On such a full sea are we now afloat,
And we must take the current when it
serves,
Or lose our ventures.
217

4 *Brutus:* Then I shall see thee again?
Ghost: Ay, at Philippi.
Brutus: Why, I will see thee at Philippi,
then.
283

5 If we do meet again, why, we shall smile!
If not, why then, this parting was well
made.
V.i.118

6 This was the noblest Roman of them all;
All the conspirators save only he
Did that they did in envy of great Caesar;
He, only, in a general honest thought
And common good to all, made one of
them.
His life was gentle, and the elements
So mix'd in him that Nature might stand
up
And say to all the world, 'This was a man!'
v.68

7 Mad world! mad kings! mad composition!
King John, II.i.561

8 Well, whiles I am a beggar, I will rail,
And say there is no sin, but to be rich;
And, being rich, my virtue then shall be,
To say there is no vice, but beggary.
593

9 Bell, book, and candle shall not drive me
back,
When gold and silver becks me to come
on.
III.iii.12

10 Grief fills the room up of my absent child,
Lies in his bed, walks up and down with
me,

Puts on his pretty looks, repeats his words,
Remembers me of all his gracious parts,
Stuffs out his vacant garments with his
form:
Then have I reason to be fond of grief.
iv.93

11 Life is as tedious as a twice-told tale,
Vexing the dull ear of a drowsy man.
108

12 To gild refined gold, to paint the lily,
To throw a perfume on the violet,
To smooth the ice, or add another hue
Unto the rainbow, or with taper light
To seek the beauteous eye of heaven to
garnish,
Is wasteful and ridiculous excess.
IV.ii.11

13 Another lean unwash'd artificer
Cuts off his tale and talks of Arthur's
death.
201

14 Heaven take my soul, and England keep
my bones!
iii.10

15   I do not ask you much:
I beg cold comfort.
V.vii.41

16 This England never did, nor never shall,
Lie at the proud foot of a conqueror,
But when it first did help to wound itself.
Now these her princes are come home
again,
Come the three corners of the world in
arms,
And we shall shock them: nought shall
make us rue,
If England to itself do rest but true.
112

17 Nothing will come of nothing: speak
again.
King Lear, I.i.[92]

18 *Lear:* So young, and so untender?
Cordelia: So young, my lord, and true.
[108]

19   Why bastard? wherefore base?
When my dimensions are as well compact,
My mind as generous, and my shape as
true,
As honest madam's issue? Why brand they
us
With base? with baseness? bastardy? base,
base?
Who in the lusty stealth of nature take
More composition and fierce quality
Than doth, within a dull, stale, tired bed,
Go to creating a whole tribe of fops,

Got 'tween asleep and wake?
ii.6

1   I grow, I prosper;
Now, gods, stand up for bastards!
21

2 *Lear:* Dost thou call me fool, boy?
Fool: All thy other titles thou hast given
away; that thou wast born with.
iv.[163]

3 How sharper than a serpent's tooth it is
To have a thankless child!
[312]

4 O! let me not be mad, not mad, sweet
heaven;
Keep me in temper; I would not be mad!
v.[51]

5   I will do such things,—
What they are yet I know not,—but they
shall be
The terrors of the earth.
II.iv.[283]

6 Blow, winds, and crack your cheeks! rage!
blow!
You cataracts and hurricanoes, spout
Till you have drench'd our steeples,
drown'd the cocks!
III.ii.1

7 Rumble thy bellyful! Spit, fire! Spout,
rain!
Nor rain, wind, thunder, fire, are my
daughters:
I tax not you, you elements, with unkindness.
14

8 No, I will be the pattern of all patience; I
will say nothing.
[37]

9   I am a man
More sinned against than sinning.
[59]

10 O! that way madness lies; let me shun that.
iv.21

11   Take physic, pomp;
Expose thyself to feel what wretches feel.
33

12 Keep thy foot out of brothels, thy hand
out of plackets, thy pen from lenders'
books, and defy the foul fiend.
[96]

13 The prince of darkness is a gentleman.
[148]

14 Poor Tom's a-cold.
[151]

15 Child Roland to the dark tower came,

His word was still, Fie, foh, and fum,
I smell the blood of a British man.
[185].

16   Out, vile jelly!
Where is thy lustre now?
vii.[83]

17   The worst is not,
So long as we can say, 'This is the worst.'
IV.i.27

18 As flies to wanton boys, are we to th
gods;
They kill us for their sport.
36

19 *Gloucester:* Is't not the king?
Lear: Ay, every inch a king.
vi.[110]

20 The wren goes to't, and the small gilde
fly
Does lecher in my sight.
Let copulation thrive.
[116]

21 Give me an ounce of civet, good apothe
cary, to sweeten my imagination; there
money for thee.
Gloucester: O! let me kiss that hand!
Lear: Let me wipe it first; it smells of mo
tality.
[133]

22 Why dost thou lash that whore? Stri
thine own back;
Thou hotly lust'st to use her in that kind
For which thou whipp'st her.
[166]

23 Thou must be patient; we came cryin
hither:
Thou know'st the first time that we sme
the air
We waul and cry.
[183]

24   Mine enemy's dog,
Though he had bit me, should have stoo
that night
Against my fire.
vii.36

25 I am a very foolish, fond old man,
Fourscore and upward, not an hour mor
or less;
And, to deal plainly,
I fear I am not in my perfect mind.
60

26   Men must endure
Their going hence, even as their comin
hither:
Ripeness is all.
V.ii.9

27   Come, let's away to prison;

We two alone will sing like birds i' the
    cage:
When thou dost ask me blessing, I'll kneel
    down,
And ask of thee forgiveness.
iii.8

1 The wheel is come full circle.
[176]

2 Howl, howl, howl, howl! O! you are men
    of stones:
Had I your tongue and eyes, I'd use them
    so
That heaven's vaults should crack. She's
    gone for ever!
[259]

3   Her voice was ever soft,
Gentle and low, an excellent thing in
    woman.
[274]

4 And my poor fool is hang'd! No, no, no
    life!
Why should a dog, a horse, a rat, have life,
And thou no breath at all? Thou'lt come
    no more,
Never, never, never, never, never!
Pray you, undo this button.
[307]

5 Vex not his ghost: O! let him pass; he hates
    him
That would upon the rack of this tough
    world
Stretch him out longer.
[314]

6 Cormorant devouring Time.
Love's Labour's Lost, I.i.4

7 Study is like the heaven's glorious sun,
    That will not be deep-search'd with
        saucy looks.
84

8   At Christmas I no more desire a rose
Than wish a snow in May's new-fangled
    mirth;
    But like of each thing that in season
        grows.
105

9 A wightly wanton with a velvet brow,
With two pitch balls stuck in her face for
    eyes;
Ay, and, by heaven, one that will do the
    deed
Though Argus were her eunuch and her
    guard.
III.i.[206]

0 They have been at a great feast of languages, and stolen the scraps.
V.i.[39]

11 Henceforth my wooing mind shall be ex-
    press'd
In russet yeas and honest kersey noes:
And, to begin, wench,—so God help me,
    la!—
My love to thee is sound, sans crack or
    flaw.
ii.413

12 A jest's prosperity lies in the ear
Of him that hears it, never in the tongue
Of him that makes it.
[869]

13 When daisies pied and violets blue
    And lady-smocks all silver-white
And cuckoo-buds of yellow hue
    Do paint the meadows with delight,
The cuckoo then, on every tree,
Mocks married men; for thus sings he,
        Cuckoo;
Cuckoo, cuckoo; O, word of fear,
Unpleasing to a married ear!
[902]

14 When icicles hang by the wall,
    And Dick the shepherd, blows his nail,
And Tom bears logs into the hall,
    And milk comes frozen home in pail,
When blood is nipp'd and ways be foul,
Then nightly sings the staring owl,
        Tu-who;
Tu-whit, tu-who—a merry note,
While greasy Joan doth keel the pot.

When all aloud the wind doth blow,
And coughing drowns the parson's saw;
And birds sit brooding in the snow,
And Marion's nose looks red and raw,
When roasted crabs hiss in the bowl.
[920]

15 The words of Mercury are harsh after the
songs of Apollo. You, that way: we, this
way.
[938]

16 *First Witch:* When shall we three meet
    again
In thunder, lightning, or in rain?
Second Witch: When the hurly-burly's
    done,
When the battle's lost and won.
Third Witch: That will be ere the set of
    sun.
First Witch: Where the place?
Second Witch: Upon the heath.
Third Witch: There to meet with Macbeth.
First Witch: I come, Graymalkin!
Second Witch: Paddock calls.
Third Witch: Anon!
All: Fair is foul, and foul is fair:

Hover through the fog and filthy air.
Macbeth, I.i.1

1 What bloody man is that?
ii.1

2 A sailor's wife had chestnuts in her lap,
   And munch'd, and munch'd, and
       munch'd: 'Give me,' quoth I:
   'Aroint thee, witch!' the rump-fed ronyon
       cries.
   Her husband's to Aleppo gone, master o'
       the Tiger:
   But in a sieve I'll thither sail,
   And, like a rat without a tail,
   I'll do, I'll do, and I'll do.
   iii.4

3 Sleep shall neither night nor day
   Hang upon his pent-house lid.
   He shall live a man forbid.
   Weary se'nnights nine times nine
   Shall he dwindle, peak, and pine:
   Though his bark cannot be lost,
   Yet it shall be tempest-tost.
   19

4 So foul and fair a day I have not seen.
   38

5   Say, from whence
   You owe this strange intelligence? or why
   Upon this blasted heath you stop our way
   With such prophetic greeting?
   72

6   Two truths are told,
   As happy prologues to the swelling act
   Of the imperial theme.
   127

7 This supernatural soliciting
   Cannot be ill, cannot be good.
   130

8   Come what come may,
   Time and the hour runs through the
       roughest day.
   146

9 *Malcolm:* Nothing in his life
   Became him like the leaving it: he died
   As one that had been studied in his death
   To throw away the dearest thing he owed
   As 'twere a careless trifle.
   Duncan: There's no art
   To find the mind's construction in the
       face;
   He was a gentleman on whom I built
   An absolute trust.
   iv.7

10 Glamis thou art, and Cawdor; and shalt
       be
   What thou art promis'd. Yet I do fear thy
       nature;

It is too full o' the milk of human kindness
To catch the nearest way; thou wouldst b
    great,
Art not without ambition; but without
The illness should attend it; what tho
    wouldst highly,
That thou wouldst holily.
v.[16]

11   The raven himself is hoarse
That croaks the fatal entrance of Duncan
Under my battlements. Come, you spirits
That tend on mortal thoughts! unsex m
    here,
And fill me from the crown to the toe to
    full
Of direst cruélty; make thick my blood,
Stop up the access and passage to remorse
That no compunctious visitings of nature
Shake my fell purpose, nor keep peac
    between
The effect and it! Come to my woman'
    breasts,
And take my milk for gall, you murderin
    ministers,
Wherever in your sightless substances
You wait on nature's mischief! Come
    thick night,
And pall thee in the dunnest smoke of hell
That my keen knife see not the wound i
    makes,
Nor heaven peep through the blanket c
    the dark,
To cry 'Hold, hold!'
[38]

12 Your face, my thane, is as a book wher
    men
May read strange matters. To beguile th
    time,
Look like the time; bear welcome in you
    eye,
Your hand, your tongue: look like the in
    nocent flower,
But be the serpent under't.
[63]

13 If it were done when 'tis done, then 'twer
    well
It were done quickly: if the assassination
Could trammel up the consequence, an
    catch
With his surcease success; that but thi
    blow
Might be the be-all and the end-all here,
But here, upon this bank and shoal c
    time,
We'd jump the life to come. But in thes
    cases
We still have judgment here; that we bu
    teach

Bloody instructions.
vii.1

1   Besides, this Duncan
Hath borne his faculties so meek, hath
    been
So clear in his great office, that his virtues
Will plead like angels trumpet-tongu'd,
    against
The deep damnation of his taking off;
And pity, like a naked new-born babe,
Striding the blast, or heaven's cherubim,
    hors'd
Upon the sightless couriers of the air,
Shall blow the horrid deed in every eye,
That tears shall drown the wind. I have no
    spur
To prick the sides of my intent, but only
Vaulting ambition, which o'erleaps itself,
And falls on the other.
16

2 We will proceed no further in this busi-
    ness:
He hath honour'd me of late; and I have
    bought
Golden opinions from all sorts of people.
31

3   Was the hope drunk,
Wherein you dress'd yourself?
35

4 Letting 'I dare not' wait upon 'I would,'
Like the poor cat i' the adage?
44

5 I dare do all that may become a man;
Who dares do more is none.
46

6 *Lady Macbeth:* I have given suck, and
    know
How tender 'tis to love the babe that milks
    me:
I would, while it was smiling in my face,
Have pluck'd my nipple from his boneless
    gums,
And dash'd the brains out, had I so sworn
    as you
Have done to this.
Macbeth: If we should fail,—
Lady Macbeth: We fail!
But screw your courage to the sticking-
    place,
And we'll not fail.
54

7   Bring forth men-children only;
For thy undaunted mettle should compose
Nothing but males.
72

8 False face must hide what the false heart

doth know.
82

9   There's husbandry in heaven;
Their candles are all out.
II.i.4

10 Is this a dagger which I see before me,
The handle toward my hand? Come, let me
    clutch thee:
I have thee not, and yet I see thee still.
33

11   The bell invites me.
Hear it not, Duncan; for it is a knell
That summons thee to heaven or to hell.
62

12 That which hath made them drunk hath
    made me bold,
What hath quench'd them hath given me
    fire.
ii.1

13   The attempt and not the deed,
Confounds us.
12

14   Had he not resembled
My father as he slept I had done't.
14

15   Wherefore could not I pronounce
    'Amen'?
I had most need of blessing, and 'Amen'
Stuck in my throat.
32

16 Methought I heard a voice cry, 'Sleep no
    more!
Macbeth does murder sleep,' the innocent
    sleep,
Sleep that knits up the ravell'd sleave of
    care,
The death of each day's life, sore labour's
    bath,
Balm of hurt minds, great nature's second
    course,
Chief nourisher in life's feast.
36

17 Glamis hath murder'd sleep, and therefore
    Cawdor
Shall sleep no more, Macbeth shall sleep
    no more!
43

18   Infirm of purpose!
Give me the daggers. The sleeping and the
    dead
Are but as pictures; 'tis the eye of child-
    hood
That fears a painted devil. If he do bleed
I'll gild the faces of the grooms withal;
For it must seem their guilt.
54

1 Will all great Neptune's ocean wash this blood
Clean from my hand? No, this my hand will rather
The multitudinous seas incarnadine,
Making the green one red.
61

2 A little water clears us of this deed.
68

3 *Macduff:* What three things does drink especially provoke?
Porter: Marry, sir, nose-painting, sleep, and urine. Lechery, sir, it provokes, and unprovokes; it provokes the desire, but it takes away the performance.
iii.[28]

4 The labour we delight in physics pain.
[56]

5 The night has been unruly: where we lay
Our chimneys were blown down; and, as they say,
Lamentings heard i' the air; strange screams of death,
And prophesying with accents terrible
Of dire combustion and confus'd events
New-hatch'd to the woeful time.
[60]

6 *Macduff:* Our royal master's murder'd!
Lady Macbeth: Woe, alas!
What! in our house?
[95]

7 All is but toys; renown and grace is dead,
The wine of life is drawn, and the mere lees
Is left this vault to brag of.
[101]

8 Who can be wise, amazed, temperate, and furious,
Loyal and neutral, in a moment? No man.
[115]

9 *Lady Macbeth:* Help me hence, ho!
Macduff: Look to the lady.
[125]

10 There's daggers in men's smiles: the near in blood,
The nearer bloody.
[147]

11 A falcon, towering in her pride of place,
Was by a mousing owl hawk'd at and kill'd.
iv.12

12 *Lady Macbeth:* Things without all remedy
Should be without regard: what's done is done.
Macbeth: We have scotch'd the snake, not killed it.
III.ii.11

13 Duncan is in his grave;
After life's fitful fever he sleeps well.
22

14 There shall be done
A deed of dreadful note.
43

15 Come, seeling night,
Scarf up the tender eye of pitiful day,
And with thy bloody and invisible hand,
Cancel and tear to pieces that great bond
Which keeps me pale! Light thickens, an
the crow
Makes wing to the rooky wood;
Good things of day begin to droop an
drowse,
Whiles night's black agents to their prey
do rouse.
46

16 Now I am cabin'd, cribb'd, confin'd
bound in
To saucy doubts and fears.
iv.24

17 Now good digestion wait on appetite,
And health on both!
38

18 Thou canst not say I did it: never shake
Thy gory locks at me.
50

19 Stand not upon the order of your going,
But go at once.
119

20 It will have blood, they say; blood wi
have blood.
122

21 I am in blood
Stepp'd in so far that, should I wade n
more,
Returning were as tedious as go o'er.
136

22 Double, double toil and trouble;
Fire burn and cauldron bubble.
IV.i.10

23 Finger of birth-strangled babe
Ditch-deliver'd by a drab,
Make the gruel thick and slab.
30

24 By the pricking of my thumbs,
Something wicked this way comes.
44

25 *Macbeth:* How now, you secret, black
and midnight hags!
What is't you do?
Witches: A deed without a name.
48

26 Be bloody, bold, and resolute; laugh t

scorn
The power of man, for none of woman
  born
Shall harm Macbeth.
79

1 But yet, I'll make assurance double sure,
And take a bond of fate.
83

2 What! will the line stretch out to the crack
of doom?
117

3 His flight was madness: when our actions
  do not,
Our fears do make us traitors.
ii.3

4 Stands Scotland where it did?
iii.164

5 What! all my pretty chickens and their
  dam,
At one fell swoop?
220

6 Out, damned spot! out, I say! One; two:
why then, 'tis time to do't. Hell is murky!
Fie, my lord, fie! a soldier, and afeard!
What need we fear who knows it, when
none can call our power to account? Yet
who would have thought the old man to
have had so much blood in him?
V.i.[38]

7 What! will these hands ne'er be clean? No
more o' that, my lord, no more o' that: you
mar all with this starting.
[47]

8 Here's the smell of the blood still: all the
perfumes of Arabia will not sweeten this
little hand. Oh! oh! oh!
[55]

9 Wash your hands, put on your night-
gown; look not so pale.
[67]

10 What's done cannot be undone. To bed,
to bed, to bed.
[74]

11 The devil damn thee black, thou cream-
faced loon!
Where gott'st thou that goose look?
iii.11

12 I have lived long enough: my way of life
Is fall'n into the sear, the yellow leaf.
22

13 *Macbeth:* Canst thou not minister to a
  mind diseas'd,
Pluck from the memory a rooted sorrow,
Raze out the written troubles of the brain,
And with some sweet oblivious antidote

Cleanse the stuff'd bosom of that perilous
  stuff
Which weighs upon the heart?
Doctor: Therein the patient
Must minister to himself.
Macbeth: Throw physic to the dogs; I'll
  none of it.
37

14 I have supp'd full with horrors.
v.13

15 She should have died hereafter;
There would have been a time for such a
  word,
To-morrow, and to-morrow, and to-
  morrow,
Creeps in this petty pace from day to day,
To the last syllable of recorded time;
And all our yesterdays have lighted fools
The way to dusty death. Out, out, brief
  candle!
Life's but a walking shadow, a poor play-
  er,
That struts and frets his hour upon the
  stage,
And then is heard no more; it is a tale
Told by an idiot, full of sound and fury,
Signifying nothing.
16

16   Lay on, Macduff;
And damn'd be him that first cries, 'Hold,
  enough!'
vii.62

17   O! it is excellent
To have a giant's strength, but it is tyran-
  nous
To use it like a giant.
Measure for Measure, II.ii.107

18   Man, proud man,
Drest in a little brief authority.
117

19 That in the captain's but a choleric word,
Which in the soldier is flat blasphemy.
130

20   Ever till now
When men were fond, I smil'd and wonder'd how.
186

21 Be absolute for death; either death or life
Shall thereby be the sweeter. Reason thus
  with life:
If I do lose thee, I do lose a thing
That none but fools would keep: a breath
  thou art
Servile to all the skyey influences,
That dost this habitation, where thou
  keep'st,
Hourly afflict. Merely, thou art death's

fool;
For him thou labour'st by thy flight to shun,
And yet run'st toward him still.
III.i.5

1 The sense of death is most in apprehen-
sion,
And the poor beetle, that we tread upon,
In corporal sufferance finds a pang as great
As when a giant dies.
76

2   If I must die,
I will encounter darkness as a bride,
And hug it in mine arms.
81

3   Sure, it is no sin;
Or of the deadly seven it is the least.
108

4 Ay, but to die, and go we know not where;
To lie in cold obstruction and to rot;
This sensible warm motion to become
A kneaded clod; and the delighted spirit
To bathe in fiery floods or to reside
In thrilling region of thick-ribbed ice;
To be imprisoned in the viewless winds,
And blown with restless violence round about
The pendant world; or to be worse than worst
Of those that lawless and incertain thoughts
Imagine howling: 'tis too horrible!
The weariest and most loathed worldly life
That age, ache, penury, and imprisonment
Can lay on nature, is a paradise
To what we fear of death.
116

5 There, at the moated grange, resides this dejected Mariana.
[279]

6 Some report a sea-maid spawn'd him; some that he was begot between two stock-fishes. But it is certain that when he makes water his urine is congealed ice.
ii.[117]

7 Take, O take those lips away,
   That so sweetly were forsworn;
And those eyes, the break of day,
   Lights that do mislead the morn:

But my kisses bring again, bring again;
Seals of love, but seal'd in vain, seal'd in vain.
IV.i.1

8 I am a kind of burr; I shall stick.
iii.[193]

9 They say best men are moulded out of faults,
And, for the most, become much more the better
For being a little bad: so may my husband
V.i.[440]

10 In sooth I know not why I am so sad:
It wearies me; you say it wearies you;
But how I caught it, found it, or came by it,
What stuff 'tis made of, whereof it is born,
I am to learn;
And such a want-wit sadness makes of me
That I have much ado to know myself.
The Merchant of Venice, I.i.1

11   Now, by two-headed Janus,
Nature hath fram'd strange fellows in her time.
50

12 By my troth, Nerissa, my little body is aweary of this great world.
ii.1

13 They are as sick that surfeit with too much, as they that starve with nothing.
[5]

14 If to do were as easy as to know what were good to do, chapels had been churches and poor men's cottages princes' palaces. It is a good divine that follows his own instructions; I can easier teach twenty what were good to be done, than be one of the twenty to follow mine own teaching.
[13]

15 He doth nothing but talk of his horse.
[43]

16 God made him, and therefore let him pass for a man.
[59]

17 I will buy with you, sell with you, talk with you, walk with you, and so following; but I will not eat with you, drink with you, nor pray with you. What news on the Rialto?
iii.[36]

18 How like a fawning publican he looks!
I hate him for he is a Christian.
[42]

19 If I can catch him once upon the hip,
I will feed fat the ancient grudge I bear him.
[47]

20 The devil can cite Scripture for his purpose.
[99]

21 Signior Antonio, many a time and oft
In the Rialto you have rated me
About my moneys and my usances:

Still have I borne it with a patient shrug,
For sufferance is the badge of all our tribe.
You call me misbeliever, cut-throat dog,
And spet upon my Jewish gabardine,
And all for use of that which is mine own.
[107]

1 You that did void your rheum upon my
   beard,
And foot me as you spurn a stranger cur
Over your threshold: moneys is your suit.
What should I say to you? Should I not
   say,
'Hath a dog money? Is it possible
A cur can lend three thousand ducats?' or
Shall I bend low, and in a bondman's key,
With bated breath, and whispering hum-
   bleness,
Say this:—
'Fair sir, you spat on me Wednesday last;
You spurn'd me such a day; another time
You call'd me dog; and for these courtesies
I'll lend you thus much moneys?'
[118]

2 Mislike me not for my complexion,
The shadow'd livery of the burnish'd sun,
To whom I am a neighbour and near bred.
II.i.1

3 It is a wise father that knows his own
   child.
ii.[83]

4 Truth will come to light; murder cannot
be hid long.
[86]

5 There is some ill a-brewing towards my
   rest.
For I did dream of money-bags to-night.
v.17

6 Love is blind, and lovers cannot see
The pretty follies that themselves commit.
vi.36

7 What! must I hold a candle to my shames?
41

8 The portrait of a blinking idiot.
ix.54

9 Let him look to his bond.
III.i.[51, 52, 54]

0 Hath not a Jew eyes? hath not a Jew
hands, organs, dimensions, senses, affections, passions? fed with the same food,
hurt with the same weapons, subject to the
same diseases, healed by the same means,
warmed and cooled by the same winter
and summer, as a Christian is? If you prick
us, do we not bleed? if you tickle us, do we
not laugh? if you poison us, do we not die?
and if you wrong us, shall we not revenge?

If we are like you in the rest, we will resemble you in that.
63

11 I would not have given it for a wilderness
of monkeys.
[130]

12 Tell me where is fancy bred.
   Or in the heart or in the head?
How begot, how nourished?
   Reply, reply.

It is engender'd in the eyes,
With gazing fed; and fancy dies
In the cradle where it lies.
   Let us all ring fancy's knell:
   I'll begin it,—Ding, dong, bell.
ii.63

13 So may the outward shows be least themselves:
The world is still deceived with ornament.
73

14 Some men there are love not a gaping pig;
Some, that are mad if they behold a cat;
And others, when the bagpipe sings i' the
   nose,
Cannot contain their urine.
IV.i.47

15 A harmless necessary cat.
55

16 I am a tainted wether of the flock,
Meetest for death: the weakest kind of
   fruit
Drops earliest to the ground.
114

17 The quality of mercy is not strain'd,
It droppeth as the gentle rain from heaven
Upon the place beneath: it is twice bless'd;
It blesseth him that gives and him that
   takes:
'Tis mightiest in the mightiest: it becomes
The throned monarch better than his
   crown;
His sceptre shows the force of temporal
   power,
The attribute to awe and majesty,
Wherein doth sit the dread and fear of
   kings;
But mercy is above this sceptred sway,
It is enthroned in the hearts of kings,
It is an attribute to God himself,
And earthly power doth then show likest
   God's
When mercy seasons justice. Therefore,
   Jew,
Though justice be thy plea, consider this,
That in the course of justice none of us
Should see salvation: we do pray for
   mercy,

And that same prayer doth teach us all to render
The deeds of mercy.
[184]

1 A Daniel come to judgment! yea, a Daniel!
O wise young judge, how I do honour thee!
[223]

2 A second Daniel, a Daniel, Jew!
Now, infidel, I have thee on the hip.
[334]

3 He is well paid that is well satisfied.
[416]

4 The moon shines bright: in such a night as this,
When the sweet wind did gently kiss the trees
And they did make no noise, in such a night
Troilus methinks mounted the Troyan walls,
And sigh'd his soul toward the Grecian tents,
Where Cressid lay that night.
V.i.1

5 How sweet the moonlight sleeps upon this bank!
Here will we sit, and let the sounds of music
Creep in our ears; soft stillness and the night
Become the touches of sweet harmony.
Sit, Jessica: look, how the floor of heaven
Is thick inlaid with patines of bright gold:
There's not the smallest orb which thou behold'st
But in his motion like an angel sings
Still quiring to the young-eyed cherubins;
Such harmony is in immortal souls;
But, whilst this muddy vesture of decay
Doth grossly close it in, we cannot hear it.
54

6 I am never merry when I hear sweet music.
69

7 The man that hath no music in himself,
Nor is not mov'd with concord of sweet sounds,
Is fit for treasons, stratagems, and spoils;
The motions of his spirit are dull as night,
And his affections dark as Erebus:
Let no such man be trusted.
79

8 How far that little candle throws his beams!
So shines a good deed in a naughty world.
90

9 How many things by season season'd are

To their right praise and true perfection!
Peace, ho! the moon sleeps with Endymion,
And would not be awak'd!
107

10 Here will be an old abusing of God's patience, and the king's English.
The Merry Wives of Windsor, I.iv.[5]

11 Why, then the world's mine oyster,
Which I with sword will open.
II.ii.2

12 To live a barren sister all your life,
Chanting faint hymns to the cold fruitless moon.
Thrice blessed they that master so their blood,
To undergo such maiden pilgrimage;
But earthlier happy is the rose distill'd,
Than that which withering on the virgin thorn
Grows, lives, and dies, in single blessedness.
A Midsummer Night's Dream, I.i.72

13 Ay me! for aught that ever I could read,
Could ever hear by tale or history,
The course of true love never did run smooth.
132

14 Things base and vile, holding no quantity,
Love can transpose to form and dignity.
Love looks not with the eyes, but with the mind,
And therefore is wing'd Cupid painted blind.
232

15 I could play Ercles rarely, or a part to tear a cat in, to make all split.
ii.[31]

16 I will roar you as gently as any sucking dove; I will roar you as 'twere any nightingale.
[85]

17 Over hill, over dale,
Thorough bush, thorough brier,
Over park, over pale,
Thorough flood, thorough fire,
I do wander everywhere,
Swifter than the moone's sphere;
And I serve the fairy queen,
To dew her orbs upon the green:
The cowslips tall her pensioners be;
In their gold coats spots you see;
Those be rubies, fairy favours,
In those freckles live their savours:
I must go seek some dew-drops here,
And hang a pearl in every cowslip's ear.
II.i.2

1 Ill met by moonlight, proud Titania.
60

2 The fold stands empty in the drowned
field,
And crows are fatted with the murrion
flock;
The nine men's morris is filled up with
mud.
96

3 In maiden meditation, fancy-free.
164

4 I'll put a girdle round about the earth
In forty minutes.
175

5 I know a bank whereon the wild thyme
blows,
Where oxlips and the nodding violet grows
Quite over-canopied with luscious woodbine,
With sweet musk-roses, and with eglan-
tine:
There sleeps Titania some time of the
night,
Lull'd in these flowers with dances and
delight;
And there the snake throws her enamell'd
skin,
Weed wide enough to wrap a fairy in.
249

6 You spotted snakes with double tongue,
Thorny hedge-hogs, be not seen;
Newts, and blind-worms, do no wrong;
Come not near our fairy queen.
ii.9

7 Weaving spiders come not here;
Hence you long-legg'd spinners, hence!
Beetles black, approach not near;
Worm nor snail, do no offence.
20

8 What angel wakes me from my flowery
bed?
[135]

9 Out of this wood do not desire to go.
[159]

0 Lord, what fools these mortals be!
ii.115

1   So we grew together,
Like to a double cherry, seeming parted,
But yet an union in partition;
Two lovely berries moulded on one stem;
So, with two seeming bodies, but one
heart.
208

2 Ay, do, persever, counterfeit sad looks,
Make mouths upon me when I turn my
back.
237

13 O! when she's angry she is keen and
shrewd.
She was a vixen when she went to school:
And though she be but little, she is fierce.
323

14   Jack shall have Jill;
        Nought shall go ill;
The man shall have his mare again,
And all shall be well.
461

15 So musical a discord, such sweet thunder.
IV.i.[121]

16 The eye of man hath not heard, the ear of
man hath not seen, man's hand is not able
to taste, his tongue to conceive, nor his
heart to report, what my dream was.
[218]

17 The lunatic, the lover, and the poet,
Are of imagination all compact.
V.i.7

18 The poet's eye, in a fine frenzy rolling,
Doth glance from heaven to earth, from
earth to heaven;
And, as imagination bodies forth
The forms of things unknown, the poet's
pen
Turns them to shapes, and gives to airy
nothing
A local habitation and a name.
12

19 That is, hot ice and wondrous strange
snow.
59

20 If we offend, it is with our good will.
That you should think, we come not to
offend,
But with good will. To show our simple
skill,
That is the true beginning of our end.
Consider then we come but in despite.
We do not come as minding to content
you,
Our true intent is. All for your delight,
We are not here.
[108]

21 Whereat, with blade, with bloody blame-
ful blade,
He bravely broach'd his boiling bloody
breast.
[148]

22 I see a voice: now will I to the chink,
To spy an I can hear my Thisby's face.
[195]

23 The best in this kind are but shadows, and

the worst are no worse, if imagination amend them.
[215]

1 Now the hungry lion roars,
    And the wolf behowls the moon;
  Whilst the heavy ploughman snores,
    All with weary task fordone.
  ii.1

2   Not a mouse
  Shall disturb this hallow'd house:
  I am sent with broom before,
  To sweep the dust behind the door.
  17

3 If we shadows have offended,
  Think but this, and all is mended,
  That you have but slumber'd here
  While these visions did appear.
  54

4 *Beatrice:* I wonder that you will still be talking, Signior Benedick: nobody marks you.
  Benedick: What! my dear Lady Disdain, are you yet living?
  Much Ado About Nothing, I.i.[121]

5 Speak low, if you speak love.
  II.i.[104]

6 No, sure, my lord, my mother cried; but then there was a star danced, and under that was I born.
  [350]

7 Sigh no more, ladies, sigh no more,
    Men were deceivers ever;
  One foot in sea, and one on shore,
  To one thing constant never.
        Then sigh not so,
        But let them go,
    And be you blithe and bonny,
  Converting all your sounds of woe
    Into Hey nonny, nonny.
  iii.[65]

8 For look where Beatrice, like a lapwing, runs
  Close by the ground, to hear our counsel.
  III.1.24

9 Benedick, love on; I will requite thee,
    Taming my wild heart to thy loving hand.
  111

10 He hath a heart as sound as a bell, and his tongue is the clapper; for what his heart thinks his tongue speaks.
  ii.[12]

11 Comparisons are odorous.
  v.[18]

12 I do love nothing in the world so well as you: is not that strange?
  IV.i.[271]

13 There was never yet philosopher
  That could endure the toothache patiently
  V.i.35

14 But I will wear my heart upon my sleeve
  For daws to peck at: I am not what I am.
  Othello, I.i.64

15 Your daughter and the Moor are now making the beast with two backs.
  [117]

16 Keep up your bright swords, for the dew will rust them.
  ii.59

17 Most potent, grave, and reverend signiors,
  My very noble and approv'd good masters.
  iii.76

18   Yet, by your gracious patience,
  I will a round unvarnish'd tale deliver.
  89

19 I do perceive here a divided duty.
  181

20 Put money in thy purse.
  [345]

21   If it were now to die,
  'Twere now to be most happy.
  II.i.[192]

22 I have very poor and unhappy brains for drinking: I could well wish courtesy would invent some other custom of entertainment.
  iii.[34]

23 Silence that dreadful bell! it frights the isle From her propriety.
  [177]

24 Reputation, reputation, reputation! O! I have lost my reputation. I have lost the immortal part of myself, and what remains is bestial. My reputation, Iago, my reputation!
  [264]

25 O God! that men should put an enemy in their mouths to steal away their brains.
  [293]

26 Excellent wretch! Perdition catch my soul
  But I do love thee! and when I love thee not,
  Chaos is come again.
  III.iii.90

27 Good name in man and woman, dear my lord,
  Is the immediate jewel of their souls;
  Who steals my purse steals trash; 'tis

something, nothing;
'Twas mine, 'tis his, and has been slave to
    thousands;
But he that filches from me my good name
Robs me of that which not enriches him,
And makes me poor indeed.
155

1 O! beware, my lord, of jealousy;
It is the green-ey'd monster which doth
    mock
The meat it feeds on.
165

2 I humbly do beseech you of your pardon
For too much loving you.
212

3   Trifles light as air
Are to the jealous confirmations strong
As proofs of holy writ.
323

4   O! now, for ever
Farewell the tranquil mind; farewell con-
    tent!
Farewell the plumed troop and the big
    wars
That make ambition virtue! O, farewell!
348

5 Othello's occupation's gone!
358

6 This denoted a foregone conclusion.
429

7 But yet the pity of it, Iago! O! Iago, the
pity of it, Iago!
IV.i.[205]

8   But, alas! to make me
The fixed figure for the time of scorn
To point his slow and moving finger at.
ii.52

9 The poor soul sat sighing by a sycamore
    tree,
Sing all a green willow;
Her hand on her bosom, her head on her
    knee,
Sing willow, willow, willow:
The fresh streams ran by her, and mur-
    mur'd her moans;
Sing willow, willow, willow:
Her salt tears fell from her, and soften'd
    the stones;
Sing willow, willow, willow:
Sing all a green willow must be my gar-
    land.
iii.[41]

10 *Desdemona:* Mine eyes do itch;
Doth that bode weeping?
Emilia: 'Tis neither here nor there.
[59]

11   This is the night
That either makes me or fordoes me quite.
V.i.128

12 It is the cause, it is the cause, my soul;
Let me not name it to you, you chaste
    stars!
It is the cause.
ii.1

13 Put out the light, and then put out the
    light:
If I quench thee, thou flaming minister,
I can again thy former light restore,
Should I repent me; but once put out thy
    light,
Thou cunning'st pattern of excelling na-
    ture,
I know not where is that Promethean heat
That can thy light relume.
7

14   May his pernicious soul
Rot half a grain a day!
153

15 I have done the state some service, and
    they know 't;
No more of that. I pray you, in your let-
    ters,
When you shall these unlucky deeds relate,
Speak of me as I am; nothing extenuate,
Nor set down aught in malice: then, must
    you speak
Of one that lov'd not wisely but too well;
Of one not easily jealous, but, being
    wrought,
Perplex'd in the extreme; of one whose
    hand,
Like the base Indian, threw a pearl away
Richer than all his tribe.
338

16 I kiss'd thee ere I kill'd thee, no way but
    this,
Killing myself to die upon a kiss.
356

17 Mine honour is my life; both grow in one;
Take honour from me, and my life is done.
Richard II, I.i.182

18 We were not born to sue, but to com-
    mand.
196

19 Teach thy necessity to reason thus;
There is no virtue like necessity.
iii.277

20   The apprehension of the good
Gives but the greater feeling to the worse.
300

21 More are men's ends mark'd than their
    lives before:

The setting sun, and music at the close,
As the last taste of sweets, is sweetest last,
Writ in remembrance more than things
    long past.
II.i.11

1 Methinks I am a prophet new inspir'd,
And thus expiring do foretell of him:
His rash fierce blaze of riot cannot last,
For violent fires soon burn out themselves;
Small showers last long, but sudden
    storms are short;
He tires betimes that spurs too fast be-
    times.
31

2 This royal throne of kings, this scepter'd
    isle,
This earth of majesty, this seat of Mars,
This other Eden, demi-paradise,
This fortress built by Nature for herself
Against infection and the hand of war,
This happy breed of men, this little world,
This precious stone set in the silver sea,
Which serves it in the office of a wall,
Or as a moat defensive to a house,
Against the envy of less happier lands,
This blessed plot, this earth, this realm,
    this England,
This nurse, this teeming womb of royal
    kings,
Fear'd by their breed and famous by their
    birth,
Renowned for their deeds as far from
    home,—
For Christian service and true chivalry,—
As is the sepulchre in stubborn Jewry
Of the world's ransom, blessed Mary's
    Son:
This land of such dear souls, this dear,
    dear land,
Dear for her reputation through the
    world,
Is now leas'd out,—I die pronouncing it,—
Like to a tenement or pelting farm:
England, bound in with the triumphant
    sea,
Whose rocky shore beats back the envious
    siege
Of watery Neptune, is now bound in with
    shame,   .
With inky blots, and rotten parchment
    bonds:
That England, that was wont to conquer
    others,
Hath made a shameful conquest of itself.
40

3 I count myself in nothing else so happy
As in a soul remembering my good friends.
iii.46

4 Grace me no grace, nor uncle me no uncle.
87

5 Not all the water in the rough rude sea
Can wash the balm from an anointed king.
III.ii.54

6 O! call back yesterday, bid time return.
69

7 Let's talk of graves, of worms, and epi-
    taphs;
Make dust our paper, and with rainy eyes
Write sorrow on the bosom of the earth.
Let's choose executors, and talk of wills.
145

8 For God's sake, let us sit upon the ground
And tell sad stories of the death of kings.
155

9 What must the king do now? Must he
    submit?
The king shall do it: must he be depos'd?
The king shall be contented: must he lose
The name of king? o' God's name, let it go.
I'll give my jewels for a set of beads,
My gorgeous palace for a hermitage,
My gay apparel for an almsman's gown,
My figur'd goblets for a dish of wood,
My sceptre for a palmer's walking staff,
My subjects for a pair of carved saints,
And my large kingdom for a little grave,
A little little grave, an obscure grave.
iii.143

10 Shall we play the wantons with our woes,
And make some pretty match with shed-
    ding tears?
164

11 Give me the crown. Here, cousin, seize the
    crown;
Here cousin,
On this side my hand and on that side
    thine.
IV.i.181

12 God pardon all oaths that are broke to
    me!
God keep all vows unbroke are made to
    thee!
214

13 Mine eyes are full of tears, I cannot see:
And yet salt water blinds them not so
    much
But they can see a sort of traitors here.
244

14 A brittle glory shineth in this face:
As brittle as the glory is the face.
287

15 I have been studying how I may compare
This prison where I live unto the world.
V.v.1

1 I wasted time, and now doth time waste
  me.
  49

2 Now is the winter of our discontent
  Made glorious summer by this sun of
  York.
  Richard III, I.i.1

3 And therefore, since I cannot prove a lov-
  er,
  To entertain these fair well-spoken days,
  I am determined to prove a villain,
  And hate the idle pleasures of these days.
  28

4 Teach not thy lip such scorn, for it was
  made
  For kissing, lady, not for such contempt.
  ii.172

5 Was ever woman in this humour woo'd?
  Was ever woman in this humour won?
  229

6 I am not in the giving vein to-day.
  IV.ii.115

7 Harp not on that string.
  iv.365

8 The king's name is a tower of strength.
  V.iii.12

9 A horse! a horse! my kingdom for a horse!
  iv.7

10 From forth the fatal loins of these two
  foes
      A pair of star-cross'd lovers take their
      life.
  Romeo and Juliet, Prologue

11 The fearful passage of their death-mark'd
  love,
      And the continuance of their parents'
      rage,
  Which, but their children's end, nought
      could remove,
      Is now the two hours' traffick of our
      stage.

12 Do you bite your thumb at us, sir?
  I.i.[50]

13 You and I are past our dancing days.
  v.[35]

14 O! she doth teach the torches to burn
  bright.
  It seems she hangs upon the cheek of night
  Like a rich jewel in an Ethiop's ear;
  Beauty too rich for use, for earth too dear.
  [48]

15 My only love sprung from my only hate!
  [142]

16 He jests at scars, that never felt a wound.

But, soft! what light through yonder win-
  dow breaks?
It is the east, and Juliet is the sun.
  II.ii.1

17 See! how she leans her cheek upon her
  hand:
  O! that I were a glove upon that hand,
  That I might touch that cheek.
  23

18 O Romeo, Romeo! wherefore art thou
  Romeo?
  Deny thy father, and refuse thy name;
  Or, if thou wilt not, be but sworn my love,
  And I'll no longer be a Capulet.
  33

19 What's in a name? that which we call a
  rose
  By any other name would smell as sweet.
  43

20 *Romeo:* Lady, by yonder blessed moon I
  swear
  That tips with silver all these fruit-tree
  tops,—
  Juliet: O! swear not by the moon, the in-
  constant moon,
  That monthly changes in her circled orb,
  Lest that thy love prove likewise variable.
  107

21 How silver-sweet sound lovers' tongues by
  night,
  Like softest music to attending ears!
  165

22 Good-night, good-night! parting is such
  sweet sorrow
  That I shall say good-night till it be morrow.
  185

23 One, two, and the third in your bosom.
  iv.[24]

24 O flesh, flesh, how art thou fishified!
  [41]

25 I am the very pink of courtesy.
  [63]

26 Thy head is as full of quarrels as an egg is
  full of meat.
  III.i.[23]

27 No, 'tis not so deep as a well, nor so wide
  as a church door; but 'tis enough, 'twill
  serve.
  [100]

28   A plague o' both your houses!
  They have made worms' meat of me.
  [112]

29 O! I am Fortune's fool.
  [142]

1 Gallop apace, you fiery-footed steeds,
   Towards Phoebus' lodging.
   ii.1

2 Night's candles are burnt out, and jocund
      day
   Stands tiptoe on the misty mountain tops.
   v.9

3 Farewell! God knows when we shall meet
      again.
   I have a faint cold fear thrills through my
      veins,
   That almost freezes up the heat of life.
   IV.iii.14

4 Being holiday, the beggar's shop is shut.
   V.i.56

5 Tempt not a desperate man.
   iii.59

6   Eyes, look your last!
   Arms, take your last embrace! and, lips, O
      you
   The doors of breath, seal with a righteous
      kiss
   A dateless bargain to engrossing death!
   112

7 Seal up the mouth of outrage for a while,
   Till we can clear these ambiguities.
   216

8 Kiss me Kate, we will be married o' Sun-
      day.
   The Taming of The Shrew, II.i.318

9   She shall watch all night:
   And if she chance to nod I'll rail and
      brawl,
   And with the clamour keep her still awake.
   This is the way to kill a wife with kindness.
   IV.i.[208]

10 Thy husband is thy lord, thy life, thy keep-
      er,
   Thy head, thy sovereign; one that cares for
      thee,
   And for thy maintenance commits his
      body
   To painful labour both by sea and land.
   V.ii.147

11   What seest thou else
   In the dark backward and abysm of time?
   The Tempest, I.ii.49

12 You taught me language; and my profit
      on't
   Is, I know how to curse.
   363

13 Come unto these yellow sands,
      And then take hands:
   Curtsied when you have, and kiss'd,—
      The wild waves whist,—
   Foot it featly here and there;

And, sweet sprites, the burden bear.
375

14 This music crept by me upon the waters,
   Allaying both their fury, and my passion,
   With its sweet air.
   389

15 Full fathom five thy father lies;
      Of his bones are coral made:
   Those are pearls that were his eyes:
      Nothing of him that doth fade,
   But doth suffer a sea-change
   Into something rich and strange.
   Sea-nymphs hourly ring his knell:
                Ding-dong.
   Hark! now I hear them,—ding-dong, bell.
   394

16 A very ancient and fish-like smell.
   II.ii.[27]

17 When they will not give a doit to relieve a
   lame beggar, they will lay out ten to see a
   dead Indian.
   [33]

18 Misery acquaints a man with strange bed
   fellows.
   [42]

19 Thou deboshed fish thou.
   III.ii.[30]

20 Flout 'em, and scout 'em; and scout 'em
      and flout 'em;
   Thought is free.
   [133]

21 He that dies pays all debts.
   [143]

22 Be not afeard: the isle is full of noises,
   Sounds and sweet airs, that give delight
      and hurt not.
   [147]

23   In dreaming,
   The clouds methought would open and
      show riches
   Ready to drop upon me; that, when
      wak'd
   I cried to dream again.
   [152]

24 Our revels now are ended. These our ac
      tors,
   As I foretold you, were all spirits and
   Are melted into air, into thin air:
   And, like the baseless fabric of this vision,
   The cloud-capp'd towers, the gorgeous pa
      laces,
   The solemn temples, the great globe itself,
   Yea, all which it inherit, shall dissolve
   And, like this insubstantial pageant faded,
   Leave not a rack behind. We are such stuff
   As dreams are made on, and our little life

Is rounded with a sleep.
IV.i.148

1   This rough magic
I here abjure...
      I'll break my staff,
Bury it certain fathoms in the earth,
And, deeper than did ever plummet sound,
I'll drown my book.
V.i.50

2 Where the bee sucks, there suck I
In a cowslip's bell I lie;
There I couch when owls do cry.
On the bat's back I do fly
After summer merrily:
Merrily, merrily shall I live now
Under the blossom that hangs on the
   bough.
88

3 How many goodly creatures are there
here!
How beauteous mankind is! O brave new
   world,
That has such people in't.
182

4   The strain of man's bred
   out
Into baboon and monkey.
Timon of Athens, I.i.[260]

5 We have seen better days.
IV.ii.27

6 This is the monstruosity in love, lady, that
the will is infinite, and the execution confined; that the desire is boundless, and the
act a slave to limit.
Troilus and Cressida, III.ii.[85]

7   To be wise, and love,
Exceeds man's might.
[163]

8 Time hath, my lord, a wallet at his back,
Wherein he puts alms for oblivion.
iii.145

9 One touch of nature makes the whole
   world kin.
175

10 We two, that with so many thousand sighs
Did buy each other, must poorly sell our-
   selves
With the rude brevity and discharge of
   one.
IV.iv.[39]

11   Fie, fie upon her!
There's language in her eye, her cheek, her
   lip,
Nay, her foot speaks; her wanton spirits
   look out

At every joint and motive of her body.
v.54

12 What's past, and what's to come is strew'd
   with husks
And formless ruin of oblivion.
165

13   The end crowns all,
And that old common arbitrator, Time,
Will one day end it
223

14 If music be the food of love, play on;
Give me excess of it, that, surfeiting,
The appetite may sicken, and so die.
That strain again! it had a dying fall:
O! it came o'er my ear like the sweet sound
That breathes upon a bank of violets,
Stealing and giving odour! Enough! no
   more:
'Tis not so sweet now as it was before.
Twelfth Night, I.i.1

15 He's as tall a man as any's in Illyria.
iii.[21]

16 He plays o' the viol-de-gamboys, and
speaks three or four languages word for
word without book, and hath all the good
gifts of nature.
[27]

17 Is it a world to hide virtues in?
[142]

18 Many a good hanging prevents a bad marriage.
v.[20]

19 A plague o' these pickle herring!
[127]

20 Make me a willow cabin at your gate,
And call upon my soul within the house.
[289]

21 Not to be a-bed after midnight is to be up
betimes.
II.iii.1

22 O mistress mine! where are you roaming?
O! stay and hear; your true love's coming,
   That can sing both high and low.
Trip no further, pretty sweeting;
Journeys end in lovers meeting,
   Every wise man's son doth know...

What is love? 'tis not hereafter;
Present mirth hath present laughter;
   What's to come is still unsure:
In delay there lies no plenty;
Then come kiss me, sweet and twenty,
   Youth's a stuff will not endure.
[42]

23 Dost thou think, because thou art virtu-

ous, there shall be no more cakes and ale?
[124]

1 My purpose is, indeed, a horse of that colour.
[184]

2   Let still the woman take
An elder than herself.
iv.29

3 Come away, come away, death,
  And in sad cypress let me be laid;
Fly away, fly away, breath:
I am slain by a fair cruel maid.
My shroud of white, stuck all with yew,
  O! prepare it.
My part of death no one so true
  Did share it.
51

4   She never told her love,
But let concealment, like a worm i' the bud,
Feed on her damask cheek: she pin'd in thought;
And with a green and yellow melancholy,
She sat like patience on a monument,
Smiling at grief.
[111]

5 I am all the daughters of my father's house,
And all the brothers too.
[122]

6 But be not afraid of greatness: some men are born great, some achieve greatness, and some have greatness thrust upon them.
v.[158]

7 O! what a deal of scorn looks beautiful
In the contempt and anger of his lip.
III.i.[159]

8 In the south suburbs, at the Elephant,
Is best to lodge.
iii.39

9 Why, this is very midsummer madness.
iv.[62]

10 More matter for a May morning.
[158]

11 Still you keep o' the windy side of the law.
[183]

12 He is knight dubbed with unhatched rapier, and on carpet consideration.
[260]

13 Thus the whirligig of time brings in his revenges.
V.i.[388]

14 When that I was and a little tiny boy,
  With hey, ho, the wind and the rain;

A foolish thing was but a toy,
  For the rain it raineth every day.
[401]

15 A great while ago the world begun,
  With hey, ho, the wind and the rain;
But that's all one, our play is done,
  And we'll strive to please you every day.
[417]

16 Home-keeping youth have ever homely wits.
The Two Gentlemen of Verona, I.i.2

17 O! how this spring of love resembleth
  The uncertain glory of an April day,
Which now shows all the beauty of the sun,
  And by and by a cloud takes all away!
iii.84

18 Who is Sylvia? what is she,
  That all our swains commend her?
Holy, fair, and wise is she;
  The heaven such grace did lend her,
That she might admired be.

Is she kind as she is fair?
  For beauty lives with kindness:
Love doth to her eyes repair,
  To help him of his blindness;
And, being help'd, inhabits there.

Then to Silvia let us sing,
  That Silvia is excelling;
She excels each mortal thing
  Upon the dull earth dwelling;
To her let us garlands bring.
IV.ii.40

19   We were, fair queen,
Two lads that thought there was no more behind
But such a day to-morrow as to-day,
And to be boy eternal.
The Winter's Tale, I.ii.62

20   A sad tale's best for winter.
I have one of sprites and goblins.
II.i.24

21 *Exit, pursued by a bear.*
III.iii. Stage Direction.

22 My father named me Autolycus; who being, as I am, littered under Mercury, was likewise a snapper-up of unconsidered trifles.
IV.ii.[24]

23 Jog on, jog on the foot-path way,
  And merrily hent the stile-a:
A merry heart goes all the day,
  Your sad tires in a mile-a.
[133]

24 For you there's rosemary and rue; these keep

Seeming and savour all the winter long.
iii.74

1   Daffodils,
That come before the swallow dares, and
    take
The winds of March with beauty; violets
    dim,
But sweeter than the lids of Juno's eyes
Or Cytherea's breath; pale prime-roses,
That die unmarried, ere they can behold
Bright Phoebus in his strength.
118

2 Though I am not naturally honest, I am so
  sometimes by chance.
  [734]

3   O! she's warm.
If this be magic, let it be an art
Lawful as eating.
V.iii.109

4 Crabbed age and youth cannot live
    together:
  Youth is full of pleasance, age is full of
    care.
  The Passionate Pilgrim, xii

5 Age, I do abhor thee, youth, I do adore
    thee.

6 Who buys a minute's mirth to wail a
    week?
  Or sells eternity to get a toy?
  For one sweet grape who will the vine
    destroy?
  The Rape of Lucrece, l.213

7 And now this pale swan in her watery nest
  Begins the sad dirge of her certain ending.
  l.1611

8 To the onlie begetter of these insuing son-
    nets, Mr. W.H.
  Sonnets, Dedication (also attr. Thomas Thorpe)

9 Shall I compare thee to a summer's day?
  Thou art more lovely and more temperate:
  Rough winds do shake the darling buds of
    May,
  And summer's lease hath all too short a
    date:
  Sometimes too hot the eye of heaven
    shines,
  And often is his gold complexion dimm'd;
  And every fair from fair sometime de-
    clines,
  By chance, or nature's changing course
    untrimm'd;
  But thy eternal summer shall not fade,
  Nor lose possession of that fair thou ow'st,
  Nor shall death brag thou wander'st in his
    shade,
  When in eternal lines to time thou grow'st;
    So long as men can breathe, or eyes can
      see,

So long lives this, and this gives life to
    thee.
18

10 Weary with toil, I haste me to my bed,
   The dear repose for limbs with travel tired;
   But then begins a journey in my head
   To work my mind, when body's work's
     expired.
   27

11 When in disgrace with fortune and men's
     eyes
   I all alone beweep my outcast state,
   And trouble deaf heaven with my bootless
     cries,
   And look upon myself and curse my fate,
   Wishing me like to one more rich in hope,
   Featur'd like him, like him with friends
     possess'd,
   Desiring this man's art, and that man's
     scope,
   With what I most enjoy contented least;
   Yet in these thoughts myself almost de-
     spising,
   Haply I think on thee, — and then my state,
   Like to the lark at break of day arising
   From sullen earth, sings hymns at heaven's
     gate;
     For thy sweet love remember'd such
       wealth brings
       That then I scorn to change my state
         with kings.
   29

12 When to the sessions of sweet silent
     thought
   I summon up remembrance of things past,
   I sigh the lack of many a thing I sought,
   And with old woes new wail my dear
     times' waste.
   30

13 But if the while I think on thee, dear
     friend,
   All losses are restor'd and sorrows end.

14 Full many a glorious morning have I seen
   Flatter the mountain-tops with sovereign
     eye,
   Kissing with golden face the meadows
     green,
   Gilding pale streams with heavenly al-
     chemy.
   33

15 Why didst thou promise such a beauteous
     day,
   And make me travel forth without my
     cloak
   To let base clouds o'ertake me in my way,

Hiding thy bravery in their rotten smoke?
34

1 What is your substance, whereof are you
made,
That millions of strange shadows on you
tend?
53

2 Not marble, nor the gilded monuments
Of princes, shall outlive this powerful
rime.
55

3 Being your slave, what should I do but
tend
Upon the hours and times of your desire?
57

4 No longer mourn for me when I am dead
Than you shall hear the surly sullen bell
Give warning to the world that I am fled
From this vile world, with vilest worms to
dwell.
71

5 That time of year thou mayst in me behold
When yellow leaves, or none, or few, do
hang
Upon those boughs which shake against
the cold,
Bare ruin'd choirs, where late the sweet
birds sang.
73

6 Farewell! thou art too dear for my pos-
sessing,
And like enough thou know'st thy esti-
mate:
The charter of thy worth gives thee releas-
ing;
My bonds in thee are all determinate.
For how do I hold thee but by thy grant-
ing?
And for that riches where is my deserving?
The cause of this fair gift in me is wanting,
And so my patent back again is swerving.
Thyself thou gav'st, thy own worth then
not knowing,
Or me, to whom thou gav'st it, else mistak-
ing;
So thy great gift, upon misprision grow-
ing,
Comes home again, on better judgment
making.
Thus have I had thee, as a dream doth
flatter,
In sleep a king, but, waking, no such
matter.
87

7 For sweetest things turn sourest by their
deeds;
Lilies that fester smell far worse than
weeds.
94

8 How like a winter hath my absence been
From thee, the pleasure of the fleeting
year!
What freezings have I felt, what dark days
seen!
What old December's bareness every
where!
97

9 From you have I been absent in the
spring,
When proud-pied April, dress'd in all his
trim,
Hath put a spirit of youth in everything.
98

10 When in the chronicle of wasted time
I see descriptions of the fairest wights,
And beauty making beautiful old rime,
In praise of ladies dead and lovely knights.
106

11 Alas! 'tis true I have gone here and there,
And made myself a motley to the view.
110

12 Let me not to the marriage of true minds
Admit impediments. Love is not love
Which alters when it alteration finds,
Or bends with the remover to remove:
O, no! it is an ever-fixed mark,
That looks on tempests and is never
shaken;
It is the star to every wandering bark,
Whose worth's unknown, although his
height be taken.
Love's not Time's fool, though rosy lips
and cheeks
Within his bending sickle's compass come;
Love alters not with his brief hours and
weeks,
But bears it out even to the edge of doom.
If this be error, and upon me prov'd,
I never writ, nor no man ever lov'd.
116

13 The expense of spirit in a waste of shame
Is lust in action.
129

14 My mistress' eyes are nothing like the sun;
Coral is far more red than her lips' red:
If snow be white, why then her breasts are
dun;
If hairs be wires, black wires grow on her
head.
130

15 Whoever hath her wish, thou hast thy
Will,
And Will to boot, and Will in over-plus.
135

1 When my love swears that she is made of truth,
I do believe her, though I know she lies.
138

2 Two loves I have of comfort and despair,
Which like two spirits do suggest me still:
The better angel is a man right fair,
The worser spirit a woman colour'd ill.
144

3 So shalt thou feed on Death, that feeds on men,
And Death once dead, there's no more dying then.
146

4 For I have sworn thee fair, and thought thee bright,
Who art as black as hell, as dark as night.
147

5 Good friend, for Jesu's sake forbear
To dig the dust enclosed here.
Blest be the man that spares these stones,
And curst be he that moves my bones.
Epitaph on his tomb at Stratford-on-Avon, supposed to have been chosen by himself.

6 Item, I give unto my wife my second best bed, with the furniture.
Will, 1616

GEORGE BERNARD SHAW 1856–1950

7 I never resist temptation, because I have found that things that are bad for me do not tempt me.
The Apple Cart (1929), Act II

8 You can always tell an old soldier by the inside of his holsters and cartridge boxes. The young ones carry pistols and cartridges: the old ones, grub.
Arms and the Man (1898), Act I

9 I never apologise.
Act III

10 Do you think that the things people make fools of themselves about are any less real and true than the things they behave sensibly about?
Candida (1898), Act I

11 I'm only a beer teetotaller, not a champagne teetoller.
Act III

12 The British soldier can stand up to anything except the British War Office.
The Devil's Disciple, (1897), Act III

13 Stimulate the phagocytes.
The Doctor's Dilemma (1906), Act I

14 All professions are conspiracies against the laity.

15 With the single exception of Homer, there is no eminent writer, not even Sir Walter Scott, whom I can despise so entirely as I despise Shakespeare when I measure my mind against his...It would positively be a relief to me to dig him up and throw stones at him.
Dramatic Opinions and Essays (1907), vol.II, p.52

16 You don't expect me to know what to say about a play when I don't know who the author is, do you?...If it's by a good author, it's a good play, naturally. That stands to reason.
Fanny's First Play (1911), Epilogue

17 The one point on which all women are in furious secret rebellion against the existing law is the saddling of the right to a child with the obligation to become the servant of a man.
Getting Married (1908), Preface

18 The captain is in his bunk, drinking bottled ditchwater; and the crew is gambling in the forecastle. She will strike and sink and split. Do you think the laws of God will be suspended in favour of England because you were born in it?
Heartbreak House (1917), Act III

19 The greatest of evils and the worst of crimes is poverty.
Major Barbara (1907), Preface

20 The universal regard for money is the one hopeful fact in our civilization, the one sound spot in our social conscience. Money is the most important thing in the world. It represents health, strength, honour, generosity, and beauty as conspicuously as the want of it represents illness, weakness, disgrace, meanness, and ugliness.

21 Cusins is a very nice fellow, certainly: nobody would ever guess that he was born in Australia.
Act I

22 You darent handle high explosives; but youre all ready to handle honesty and truth and justice and the whole duty of man, and kill one another at that game. What a country! What a world!
Act III

23 Nothing is ever done in this world until men are prepared to kill one another if it is not done.

24 A lifetime of happiness! No man alive could bear it: it would be hell on earth.
Man and Superman (1903), Act I

1 We are ashamed of everything that is real about us; ashamed of ourselves, of our relatives, of our incomes, of our accents, of our opinions, of our experience, just as we are ashamed of our naked skins.

2 Vitality in a woman is a blind fury of creation.

3 The true artist will let his wife starve, his children go barefoot, his mother drudge for his living at seventy, sooner than work at anything but his art.

4 Very nice sort of place, Oxford, I should think, for people that like that sort of place.
Act II

5 It is a woman's business to get married as soon as possible, and a man's to keep un-married as long as he can.

6 You can be as romantic as you please about love, Hector; but you mustnt be romantic about money.

7 Hell is full of musical amateurs: music is the brandy of the damned.
Act III

8 An Englishman thinks he is moral when he is only uncomfortable.

9 There are two tragedies in life. One is not to get your heart's desire. The other is to get it.
Act IV

10 The Golden Rule is that there are no gol-den rules.
Maxims for Revolutionists (by 'John Tanner'): **'The Golden Rule'**

11 He who can, does. He who cannot teaches.
'Education'

12 Marriage is popular because it combines the maximum of temptation with the max-imum of opportunity.
'Marriage'

13 Home is the girl's prison and the woman's workhouse.
'Women in the Home'

14 Every man over forty is a scoundrel.
'Stray Sayings'

15 Youth, which is forgiven everything, for-gives itself nothing: age, which forgives itself anything, is forgiven nothing.

16 The English have no respect for their lan-guage, and will not teach their children to speak it...It is impossible for an English-man to open his mouth, without making

some other Englishman despise him.
Pygmalion (1912), Preface

17 Gin was mother's milk to her.
Act III

18 Walk! Not bloody likely. I am going in a taxi.

19 If you are going to have doctors you had better have doctors well off; just as if you are going to have a landlord you had bet-ter have a rich landlord. Taking all the round of professions and occupations, you will find that every man is the worse for being poor; and the doctor is a specially dangerous man when poor.
The Socialist Criticism of the Medical Profession
Paper read to the Medico-Legal Society, 16 Feb 1909

THOMAS SHAW 1694-1751

20 I hate a *cui bono* man.
Attr. Boswell's *Life of Johnson*, IV, 112. May 1781

LORD SHAWCROSS 1902-

21 'The question is,' said Humpty Dumpty 'which is to be master—that's all.'
We are the masters at the moment, and not only at the moment, but for a very long time to come.
House of Commons, 2 Apr. 1946. Often mis-quoted as 'We are the masters now.' See **64:9**

PATRICK SHAW STEWART 1888-1917

22 I saw a man this morning
Who did not wish to die;
I ask, and cannot answer
If otherwise wish I.
Written during the Gallipoli expedition, 1915. N Mosley, *Julian Grenfell* (1976), ch.31

23 I will go back this morning
From Imbros over the sea;
Stand in the trench, Achilles,
Flame-capped, and shout for me.

PERCY BYSSHE SHELLEY 1792-1822

24 I weep for Adonais—he is dead!
O, weep for Adonais! though our tears
Thaw not the frost which binds so dear a head!
Adonais (1821), I

25 A pard-like Spirit, beautiful and swift.
XXXII

26 He has out-soared the shadow of our night;
Envy and calumny and hate and pain,

And that unrest which men miscall delight,
Can touch him not and torture not again;
From the contagion of the world's slow
     stain
He is secure, and now can never mourn
A heart grown cold, a head grown grey in
     vain.
XL

1   The One remains, the many change and
         pass;
    Heaven's light forever shines, Earth's
         shadows fly;
    Life, like a dome of many-coloured glass,
    Stains the white radiance of Eternity,
    Until Death tramples it to fragments.
    LII

2   A widow bird sate mourning for her love
         Upon a wintry bough;
    The frozen wind crept on above,
         The freezing stream below.
    Charles the First (1822), sc.v, l.10

3   I never was attached to that great sect,
    Whose doctrine is that each one should
         select
    Out of the crowd a mistress or a friend,
    And all the rest, though fair and wise,
         commend
    To cold oblivion.
    Epipsychidion (1821), l.149

4   The world's great age begins anew,
    The golden years return,
    The earth doth like a snake renew
    Her winter weeds outworn;
    Heaven smiles, and faiths and empires
         gleam,
    Like wrecks of a dissolving dream.
    Hellas (1822), l.1060

5   Although a subtler Sphinx renew
    Riddles of death Thebes never knew.
    l.1082

6   I arise from dreams of thee
    In the first sweet sleep of night.
    When the winds are breathing low,
    And the stars are shining bright.
    The Indian Serenade

7   We watched the ocean and the sky to-
         gether,
    Under the roof of blue Italian weather.
    Letter to Maria Gisborne (1820), l.146

8   When the lamp is shattered
         The light in the dust lies dead—
    When the cloud is scattered
         The rainbow's glory is shed.
    When the lute is broken,
         Sweet tones are remembered not;
    When the lips have spoken,

Loved accents are soon forgot.
Lines: When the Lamp

9   I met Murder in the way—
    He had a mask like Castlereagh.
    The Mask of Anarchy (1819), II

10 His big tears, for he wept full well,
    Turned to mill-stones as they fell.

    And the little children, who
    Round his feet played to and fro,
    Thinking every tear a gem,
    Had their brains knocked out by them.
    IV. Of 'Fraud' (Lord Eldon)

11 Rise like Lions after slumber
    In unvanquishable number
    Shake your chains to earth like dew
    Which in sleep had fallen on you—
    Ye are many—they are few.
    XXXVIII and XCI

12 O wild West Wind, thou breath of
         Autumn's being,
    Thou, from whose unseen presence the
         leaves dead
    Are driven, like ghosts from an enchanter
         fleeing,

    Yellow, and black, and pale, and hectic
         red,
    Pestilence-stricken multitudes.
    Ode to the West Wind (1819), l.1

13 If I were a dead leaf thou mightest bear;
    If I were a swift cloud to fly with thee;
    A wave to pant beneath thy power, and
         share

    The impulse of thy strength, only less free
    Than thou, O uncontrollable!
    l.43

14 Oh, lift me as a wave, a leaf, a cloud!
    I fall upon the thorns of life! I bleed!
    l.53

15 Be through my lips to unawakened earth

    The trumpet of a prophecy! O, Wind,
    If Winter comes, can Spring be far behind?
    l.68

16 I met a traveller from an antique land
    Who said: Two vast and trunkless legs of
         stone
    Stand in the desert.
    Ozymandias

17 'My name is Ozymandias, king of kings:
    Look on my works, ye Mighty, and des-
         pair!'
    Nothing beside remains. Round the decay
    Of that colossal wreck, boundless and bare
    The lone and level sands stretch far away.

18 Rarely, rarely, comest thou,

Spirit of Delight!
Song

1 Men of England, wherefore plough
For the lords who lay you low?
Song to the Men of England

2 The seed ye sow, another reaps;
The wealth ye find, another keeps;
The robes ye weave, another wears;
The arms ye forge, another bears.

3 Lift not the painted veil which those who
live
Call Life.
Sonnet

4 Hail to thee, blithe Spirit!
Bird thou never wert,
That from Heaven, or near it,
Pourest thy full heart
In profuse strains of unpremeditated art.
To a Skylark (1819)

5 Teach me half the gladness
That thy brain must know,
Such harmonious madness
From my lips would flow
The world should listen then—as I am
listening now.

6 Swiftly walk over the western wave,
Spirit of Night!
Out of the misty eastern cave,
Where, all the long and lone daylight,
Thou wovest dreams of joy and fear,
Which make thee terrible and dear,—
Swift be thy flight!
To Night

7 Death will come when thou art dead,
Soon, too soon—
Sleep will come when thou art fled;
Of neither would I ask the boon
I ask of thee, beloved Night—
Swift be thine approaching flight,
Come soon, soon!

8 And like a dying lady, lean and pale,
Who totters forth, wrapped in a gauzy veil.
The Waning Moon

9 A single word even may be a spark of
inextinguishable thought.
A Defence of Poetry (1821)

10 The rich have become richer, and the poor
have become poorer; and the vessel of the
state is driven between the Scylla and
Charybdis of anarchy and despotism.

11 Poetry is the record of the best and happiest moments of the happiest and best
minds.

12 Poets are...the trumpets which sing to
battle and feel not what they inspire—
...Poets are the unacknowledged legisla-

tors of the world.
See 134:28

PHILIP HENRY SHERIDAN 1831–188?

13 The only good Indian is a dead Indian.
Attr., at Fort Cobb, Jan. 1869

RICHARD BRINSLEY SHERIDAN
1751–1816

14 Not a translation—only *taken from the*
French.
The Critic (1779), I.i

15 No scandal about Queen Elizabeth, I
hope?
II.i

16 O Lord, sir, when a heroine goes mad she
always goes into white satin.
III.i

17 I was struck all of a heap.
The Duenna (1775), II.ii

18 An aspersion upon my parts of speech!
The Rivals (1775), III.iii

19 If I reprehend any thing in this world, it is
the use of my oracular tongue, and a nice
derangement of epitaphs!

20 She's as headstrong as an allegory on the
banks of the Nile.

21 Too civil by half.
iv

22 I own the soft impeachment.
V.iii

23 *Mrs Candour:* I'll swear her colour is natural: I have seen it come and go.
Lady Teazle: I dare swear you have,
ma'am; it goes off at night, and comes
again in the morning.
The School for Scandal (1777), II.ii

24 I'm called away by particular business.
But I leave my character behind me.

25 Here's to the maiden of bashful fifteen;
Here's to the widow of fifty;
Here's to the flaunting, extravagant
quean;
And here's to the housewife that's
thrifty.
Let the toast pass,—
Drink to the lass,
I'll warrant she'll prove an excuse for the
glass.
III.iii. Song

26 An unforgiving eye, and a damned disinheriting countenance.
IV.i

27 The Right Honourable gentleman is in-

debted to his memory for his jests, and to his imagination for his facts.
Speech in Reply to Mr. Dundas. T. Moore, *Life of Sheridan* (1825), II.471

1 A man may surely be allowed to take a glass of wine by his own fireside.
On being encountered drinking a glass of wine in the street, while watching his theatre, the Drury Lane, burn down. II.20

JAMES SHIRLEY 1596–1666

2 The glories of our blood and state
Are shadows, not substantial things.
The Contention of Ajax and Ulysses (1659), I.iii

3 Only the actions of the just
Smell sweet, and blossom in their dust.

SIR PHILIP SIDNEY 1554–1586

4 My true love hath my heart and I have his,
By just exchange one for the other giv'n;
I hold his dear, and mine he cannot miss,
There never was a better bargain driv'n.
The Arcadia (1590), bk.iii

5 Biting my truant pen, beating myself for spite,
'Fool,' said my Muse to me, 'look in thy heart and write'.
Astrophel and Stella (1591), Sonnet 1

6 With a tale forsooth he cometh unto you, with a tale which holdeth children from play, and old men from the chimney corner. [The poet.]
Defence of Poesie (1579-80, pub. 1595)

7 Thy necessity is yet greater than mine.
On giving his water-bottle to a dying soldier on the battle-field of Zutphen, 1586. Sir Fulke Greville, *Life* (1652). The word 'necessity' is more often quoted as 'need'

ABBÉ EMMANUEL JOSEPH SIEYÈS 1748–1836

8 *J'ai vécu.*
I survived.
When asked what he had done during the French Revolution. V. Mignet, 'Notice Historique sur la Vie et les Travaux de M. le Comte de Sieyès'. *Recueil des Lectures…28 Déc. 1836.* He afterwards stated he could not recall having said it.

SIMONIDES c.556–468 B.C.

9 ὦ ξεῖν', ἀγγέλλειν Λακεδαιμονίοις ὅτι τῇδε
κείμεθα τοῖς κείνων ῥήμασι πειθόμενοι.
Go, tell the Spartans, thou who passest by,

That here obedient to their laws we lie.
Herodotus, *Histories*, vii, 228.

GEORGE R. SIMS 1847–1922

10 It is Christmas Day in the Workhouse.
The Dagonet and Other Poems (1903)

EDITH SITWELL 1887–1964

11 Daisy and Lily
Lazy and silly
Walk by the shore of the wan grassy sea
Talking once more 'neath a swan-bosomed tree.
Façade. **Waltz**

12 Still falls the Rain—
Dark as the world of man, black as our loss—
Blind as the nineteen hundred and forty nails
Upon the Cross.
The Raids 1940. **Still falls the Rain**

SIR OSBERT SITWELL 1892–1969

13 *Educ:* during the holidays from Eton.
Who's Who

B.F. SKINNER 1904–

14 Education is what survives when what has been learnt has been forgotten.
Education in 1984. *New Scientist,* 21 May 1964, p.484

CHRISTOPHER SMART 1722–1771

15 For I will consider my Cat Jeoffry.
For he is the servant of the Living God, duly and daily serving Him.
Jubilate Agno, XIX.51

16 For he counteracts the powers of darkness by his electrical skin and glaring eyes,
For he counteracts the Devil, who is death, by brisking about the Life.
XX.15

SAMUEL SMILES 1812–1904

17 A place for everything, and everything in its place.
Thrift (1875), ch.5

ADAM SMITH 1723–1790

18 People of the same trade seldom meet together, even for merriment and diversion, but the conversation ends in a conspiracy against the public, or in some contrivance to raise prices.
Wealth of Nations (ed. Todd, 1976), I.x.c.27

1 To found a great empire for the sole purpose of raising up a people of customers, may at first sight appear a project fit only for a nation of shopkeepers. It is, however, a project altogether unfit for a nation of shopkeepers; but extremely fit for a nation whose government is influenced by shopkeepers.
IV.vii.c.63. See 1:5, 174:12

2 The discipline of colleges and universities is in general contrived, not for the benefit of the students, but for the interest, or more properly speaking, for the ease of the masters.
V.i.f.15

3 There is no art which one government sooner learns of another than that of draining money from the pockets of the people.
ii.h.12

4 Be assured, my young friend, that there is a great deal of *ruin* in a nation.
Correspondence of Sir John Sinclair (1831), i.390-91

ALFRED EMANUEL SMITH
1873 1944

5 No matter how thin you slice it, it's still baloney.
Speech, 1936

6 The kiss of death.
Speech, 1926, referring to William Randolph Hearst's support of Ogden Mills

F.E. SMITH
see BIRKENHEAD

LOGAN PEARSALL SMITH 1865-1946

7 There is more felicity on the far side of baldness than young men can possibly imagine.
Afterthoughts (1931), ch.2. **Age and Death**

8 Married women are kept women, and they are beginning to find it out.
ch.3. **Other People**

9 To suppose, as we all suppose, that we could be rich and not behave as the rich behave, is like supposing that we could drink all day and keep absolutely sober.
ch.4. **In the World**

10 Thank heavens, the sun has gone in, and I don't have to go out and enjoy it.
Last Words (1933)

SAMUEL FRANCIS SMITH 1808-1895

11 My country, 'tis of thee,
Sweet land of liberty,
   Of thee I sing:
Land where my fathers died,
Land of the pilgrims' pride,
From every mountain-side
   Let freedom ring.
America (1831)

STEVIE SMITH 1902-1971

12 Oh I am a cat that likes to
Gallop about doing good.
The Galloping Cat

13 Nobody heard him, the dead man,
But still he lay moaning:
I was much further out than you thought
And not waving but drowning.
Not Waving But Drowning

14 This Englishwoman is so refined
She has no bosom and no behind.
This Englishwoman

REVD. SYDNEY SMITH 1771-1845

15 Take short views, hope for the best, an trust in God.
Lady Holland, *Memoir* (1st ed. 1855), vol.I, ch. p.48

16 Looked as if she had walked straight ou of the Ark.
ch.7, p.157

17 Madam, I have been looking for a perso who disliked gravy all my life; let us swea eternal friendship.
ch.9, p.257

18 As the French say, there are three sexe —men, women, and clergymen.
p.262

19 My definition of marriage:...it resembles pair of shears, so joined that they canno be separated; often moving in opposit directions, yet always punishing anyon who comes between them.
ch.11, p.363

20 He [Macaulay] has occasional flashes o silence, that make his conversation per fectly delightful.

21 Serenely full, the epicure would say,
Fate cannot harm me, I have dined to-day
Recipe for Salad, p.373

22 I never read a book before reviewing it; i prejudices a man so.
H. Pearson, *The Smith of Smiths* (1934), ch.i p.54

23 —'s idea of heaven is, eating *pâtés de foi*

gras to the sound of trumpets.
ch.10, p.236

1 The only way to deal with such a man as
O'Connell is to hang him up and erect a
statue to him under the gallows.
ch.11, p.272

2 I am just going to pray for you at St
Paul's, but with no very lively hope of
success.
ch.13, p.308

3 Where etiquette prevents me from doing
things disagreeable to myself, I am a perfect martinet.
Letters. To Lady Holland, 6 Nov. 1842

4 I have no relish for the country; it is a kind
of healthy grave.
To Miss G. Harcourt, 1838

C.P. SNOW 1905-1980

5 The official world, the corridors of power,
the dilemmas of conscience and egotism
— she disliked them all.
Homecomings (1956), ch.22. See also ch.14 'those
powerful anonymous *couloirs*'. Snow used the
phrase as the title of a subsequent novel: *Corridors of Power* (1964).

6 A good many times I have been present at
gatherings of people who, by the standards
of the traditional culture, are thought
highly educated and who have with considerable gusto been expressing their incredulity at the illiteracy of scientists. Once or
twice I have been provoked and have asked the company how many of them could
describe the Second Law of Thermodynamics. The response was cold: it was also
negative.
The Two Cultures, Rede Lecture, 1959, ch.1

SOCRATES 469-399 B.C.

7 ὁ δὲ ἀνεξέταστος βίος οὐ βιωτὸς ἀνθρώπῳ.
The unexamined life is not worth living.
Plato, *Apology*, 38a

8 ὦ Κρίτων, τῷ Ἀσκληπιῷ ὀφείλομεν
ἀλεκτρυόνα. ἀλλὰ ἀπόδοτε καὶ μὴ ἀμε-
λήσητε.
Crito, we owe a cock to Aesculapius;
please pay it and don't let it pass.
Plato, *Phaedo*, 118. Last words

9 πόσων ἐγὼ χρείαν οὐκ ἔχω.
How many things I can do without!
On looking at a multitude of wares exposed for
sale. Diogenes Laertius, *Lives of the Eminent
Philosophers*, II.25

SOLON c.630-c.555 B.C.

10 Laws are like spider's webs: if some poor
weak creature come up against them, it is
caught; but a bigger one can break
through and get away.
Diogenes Laertius, *Lives of the Eminent Philosophers*, I.58

11 γηράσκω δ' αἰεὶ πολλὰ διδασκόμενος.
I grow old ever learning many things.
Poetae Lyrici Graeci (ed. Bergk), Solon, 18

12 πρὶν δ' ἂν τελευτήσῃ, ἐπισχεῖν μηδὲ
καλέειν κω ὄλβιον, ἀλλ' εὐτυχέα.
Call no man happy till he dies, he is at best
but fortunate.
Herodotus, *Histories*, 1.32

SOPHOCLES 496-406 B.C.

13 πολλὰ τὰ δεινὰ κοὐδὲν ἀν-
θρώπου δεινότερον πέλει.
There are many wonderful things, and
nothing is more wonderful than man.
Antigone, 332

14 μὴ φῦναι τὸν ἅπαντα νι-
κᾷ λόγον.
Not to be born is, past all prizing, best.
Oedipus Coloneus, 1224. Tr. R.W. Jebb

JOHN L.B. SOULE 1815-1891

15 Go West, young man, go West!
Editorial, *Terre Haute* (Indiana) *Express* (1851)

ROBERT SOUTHEY 1774-1843

16 It was a summer evening,
Old Kaspar's work was done,
And he before his cottage door
Was sitting in the sun,
And by him sported on the green
His little grandchild Wilhelmine.
The Battle of Blenheim

17 But what they fought each other for,
I could not well make out.

18 'And everybody praised the Duke,
Who this great fight did win.'
'But what good came of it at last?'
Quoth little Peterkin.
'Why that I cannot tell,' said he,
'But 'twas a famous victory.'

19 No stir in the air, no stir in the sea,
The ship was still as she could be.
The Inchcape Rock

20 O Christ! It is the Inchcape Rock!

21 You are old, Father William, the young
man cried,
The few locks which are left you are
grey;

You are hale, Father William, a hearty old man,
Now tell me the reason, I pray.
The Old Man's Comforts, and how he Gained them

1 You are old, Father William, the young man cried
And pleasures with youth pass away,
And yet you lament not the days that are gone,
Now tell me the reason, I pray.

2 She has made me half in love with a cold climate.
Letter to his brother Thomas, 28 Apr. 1797

ROBERT SOUTHWELL 1561?–1595

3 Times go by turns, and chances change by course,
From foul to fair, from better hap to worse.
Times go by Turns. See 7:8

JOHN SPARROW 1906–

4 That indefatigable and unsavoury engine of pollution, the dog.
Letter to *The Times*, 30 Sept. 1975

HERBERT SPENCER 1820–1903

5 People are beginning to see that the first requisite to success in life is to be a good animal.
Education (1861), ch.2

6 This survival of the fittest implies multiplication of the fittest.
Principles of Biology (1865), pt.iii, ch.12, **Indirect Equilibration,** 164

7 How often misused words generate misleading thoughts.
Principles of Ethics, bk.I, pt.ii, ch.8, 152

8 A clever theft was praiseworthy amongst the Spartans; and it is equally so amongst Christians, provided it be on a sufficiently large scale.
Social Statics (1850), pt.ii, ch.16, 3

9 It was remarked to me by the late Mr Charles Roupell...that to play billards well was a sign of an ill-spent youth.
Duncan, *Life and Letters of Spencer* (1908), ch.20, p.298

STEPHEN SPENDER 1909–

10 I think continually of those who were truly great—
The names of those who in their lives fought for life,
Who wore at their hearts the fire's centre.
I Think Continually of Those

11 My parents kept me from children who were rough
Who threw words like stones and who wore torn clothes.
Preludes, 11. (*Collected Poems*, 1955)

12 What I had not foreseen
Was the gradual day
Weakening the will
Leaking the brightness away.
12

EDMUND SPENSER 1552?–1599

13 Triton blowing loud his wreathed horn.
Colin Clout's Come Home Again (1595), l.245

14 Ah! when will this long weary day have end,
And lend me leave to come unto my love?
Epithalamion (1595), l.278

15 A gentle knight was pricking on the plain.
The Faerie Queen (1596), bk.I, c.I.i

16 Sleep after toil, port after stormy seas,
Ease after war, death after life does greatl please.
c.IX.xl

17 And all for love, and nothing for reward.
bk,II, c.VIII.ii

18 And as she look'd about, she did behold,
How over that same door was likewis writ,
Be bold, be bold, and everywhere B bold...
At last she spied at that room's upper end
Another iron door, on which was writ
Be not too bold.
bk.III, c.XI.liv

19 Sweet Thames, run softly, till I end m Song.
Prothalamion (1596), l.54

20 At length they all to merry London came,
To merry London, my most kindly nurse,
That to me gave this life's first nativ source.
l.127

21 To be wise and eke to love,
Is granted scarce to God above.
The Shepherd's Calendar (1579), **March. Willy Emblem**

22 So now they have made our Englis tongue a gallimaufry or hodgepodge of a other speeches.
The Shepard's Calendar. **Letter to Gabriel Ha vey**

BARUCH SPINOZA 1632–1677

Sedula curavi, humanas actiones non ridere, non lugere, neque detestare, sed intelligere.
I have striven not to laugh at human actions, not to weep at them, nor to hate them, but to understand them.
Tractatus Politicus, 1, iv

REVD. WILLIAM ARCHIBALD SPOONER 1844–1930

2 You will find as you grow older that the weight of rages will press harder and harder on the employer.
Sir W. Hayter, *Spooner* (1977), ch.6. Many other Spoonerisms, such as those given in the previous editions of O.D.Q., are now known to be apocryphal.

3 Poor soul, very sad; her late husband, you know, a very sad death—eaten by missionaries—poor soul!

SIR CECIL ARTHUR SPRING-RICE 1858–1918

4 I vow to thee, my country—all earthly things above—
Entire and whole and perfect, the service of my love.
Last Poem

5 I am the Dean of Christ Church, Sir:
There's my wife; look well at her.
She's the Broad and I'm the High;
We are the University.
The Masque of Balliol, composed by and current among members of Balliol College, Oxford, in the late 1870s. This first couplet (identified as by C.A. Spring-Rice) was unofficially altered to:

6 I am the Dean, and this is Mrs Liddell;
She is the first and I the second fiddle.
See also 4:9–10, 17:11

J.C. (SIR JOHN) SQUIRE 1884–1958

7 God heard the embattled nations sing and shout
'Gott strafe England!' and 'God save the King!'
God this, God that, and God the other thing—
'Good God', said God, 'I've got my work cut out.'
Epigrams, no.1, **'The Dilemma'**

8 It did not last: the Devil howling 'Ho!
Let Einstein be!' restored the status quo.
Answer to 185:6

MME DE STAËL 1766–1817

9 *Tout comprendre rend très indulgent.*
To be totally understanding makes one very indulgent.
Corinne (1807), lib.iv, ch.2

JOSEPH STALIN 1879–1953

10 The Pope! How many divisions has *he* got?
When asked by Laval to encourage Catholicism in Russia to conciliate the Pope, 13 May 1935. Churchill, *The Second World War,* vol.i, 'The Gathering Storm', ch.8

SIR HENRY MORTON STANLEY 1841–1904

11 Dr Livingstone, I presume?
How I found Livingstone (1872), ch.11

COLONEL C.E. STANTON 1859–1933

12 Lafayette, we are here!
Address delivered at the grave of Lafayette, Paris, 4 July 1917. Often attr. to General John J. Pershing, but disclaimed by him

SIR RICHARD STEELE 1672–1729

13 There are so few who can grow old with a good grace.
The Spectator, No.263

14 Reading is to the mind what exercise is to the body.
The Tatler, No.147

15 It was very prettily said, that we may learn the little value of fortune by the persons on whom heaven is pleased to bestow it.
No.203. See 155:10

LINCOLN STEFFENS 1866–1936

16 I have seen the future, and it works.
After visiting Moscow in 1919, Steffens said to Bernard Baruch 'I have been over into the future, and it works.' He later improved the expression, and used it frequently in the shorter form. William C. Bullitt, the U.S. diplomat with whom Steffens was travelling, claimed he was rehearsing this formula long before seeing Lenin's Russia. J. Kaplan, *Lincoln Steffens* (1975), ch.13, ii

GERTRUDE STEIN 1874–1946

17 Rose is a rose is a rose is a rose.
Sacred Emily

18 You're all a lost generation.
Quoting (in translation), in a particular reference to 'all of you young people who served in the war', a mechanic's rebuke (in French) to his apprentice, who had made a shoddy repair to her

car. E. Hemingway, *A Moveable Feast*, ch.3.
Used as the epigraph to Hemingway's *The Sun
Also Rises* (1926).

1 What *is* the answer?...In that case, what is
the question?
Last words. Donald Sutherland, *Gertrude Stein,
A Biography of her Work* (1951), ch.6

J.K. STEPHEN 1859–1892

2 Two voices are there: one is of the deep;
It learns the storm-cloud's thunderous me-
lody,
Now roars, now murmurs with the chang-
ing sea,
Now bird-like pipes, now closes soft in
sleep:
And one is of an old half-witted sheep
Which bleats articulate monotony,
And indicates that two and one are three,
That grass is green, lakes damp, and
mountains steep
And, Wordsworth, both are thine.
Lapsus Calami (1896). **A Sonnet**

3 When the Rudyards cease from kipling
And the Haggards Ride no more.
To R.K.

LAURENCE STERNE 1713–1768

4 They order, said I, this matter better in
France.
A Sentimental Journey (1768), l.1

5 'I can't get out,—I can't get out,' said the
starling.
The Passport. The Hotel at Paris

6 God tempers the wind, said Maria, to the
shorn lamb.
Maria. From a French proverb, but familiar in
Sterne's form of words

7 I wish either my father or my mother, or
indeed both of them, as they were in duty
both equally bound to it, had minded what
they were about when they begot me.
Tristram Shandy (1760–67), bk.I, ch.1, opening
words

8 'Pray, my dear,' quoth my mother, 'have
you not forgot to wind up the clock?'—
'Good G—!' cried my father, making an
exclamation, but taking care to moderate
his voice at the same time,—'Did ever
woman, since the creation of the world,
interrupt a man with such a silly question?'

9 I should have no objection to this method,
but that I think it must smell too strong of
the lamp.
ch.23

10 The nonsense of the old women (of both
sexes) throughout the kingdom.
bk.v, ch.16

11 My brother Toby, quoth she, is going
be married to Mrs Wadman.
Then he will never, quoth my father,
diagonally in his bed again as long as l
lives.
bk.vi, ch.39

12 'A soldier,' cried my Uncle Toby, inte
rupting the corporal, 'is no more exem
from saying a foolish thing, Trim, than
man of letters.'—'But not so often, a
please your honour,' replied the corporal
bk.viii, ch.19

13 Said my mother, 'what is all this sto
about?'—
'A Cock and a Bull,' said Yorick.
bk.ix, ch.33

WALLACE STEVENS 1879–1955

14 The only emperor is the emperor of ic
cream.
The Emperor of Ice-Cream

15 Complacencies of the peignoir, and late
Coffee and oranges in a sunny chair.
And the green freedom of a cockatoo
Upon a rug mingle to dissipate
The holy hush of ancient sacrifice.
Sunday Morning, I

ADLAI STEVENSON 1900–1965

16 Someone asked me...how I felt, and I wa
reminded of a story that a fellow
townsman of ours used to tell—Abraha
Lincoln...He [a boy in Mr. Lincoln
story] said that he was too old to cry, but
hurt too much to laugh.
Speech, after electoral defeat, 5 Nov. 1952

17 He [Mr. Stevenson], derided the Secretar
[of State] for boasting of his brinkmanshi
—the art of bringing up to the edge of th
nuclear abyss.
New York Times, 26 Feb. 1956

ROBERT LOUIS STEVENSON
1850–1894

18 I regard you with an indifference close
bordering on aversion.
The New Arabian Nights (1882). **The Rajah
Diamond. Story of the Bandbox**

19 Fifteen men on the dead man's chest
Yo-ho-ho, and a bottle of rum!
Drink and the devil had done for th
rest—
Yo-ho-ho, and a bottle of rum!
Treasure Island (1883), ch.1

1 Tip me the black spot.
   ch.3

2 Many's the long night I've dreamed of
   cheese—toasted, mostly. [Ben Gunn.]
   ch.15

3 Marriage is like life in this—that it is a
   field of battle, and not a bed of roses.
   Virginibus Puerisque (1881), I.i

4 To travel hopefully is a better thing than
   to arrive, and the true success is to labour.
   VI. El Dorado

5 What hangs people...is the unfortunate
   circumstance of guilt.
   The Wrong Box (with Lloyd Osbourne, 1889),
   ch.7

6 Nothing like a little judicious levity.

7 A child should always say what's true,
   And speak when he is spoken to,
   And behave mannerly at table:
   At least as far as he is able.
   A Child's Garden of Verses (1885). V. **Whole
   Duty of Children**

8 Whenever the moon and stars are set,
   Whenever the wind is high,
   All night long in the dark and wet,
   A man goes riding by.
   Late in the night when the fires are out,
   Why does he gallop and gallop about?
   IX. **Windy Nights**

9 The world is so full of a number of things,
   I'm sure we should all be as happy as
   kings.
   XXIV. **Happy Thought**

10 But all that I could think of, in the darkness and the cold,
   Was that I was leaving home and my folks
   were growing old.
   Christmas at Sea

11 Give me the life I love,
   Let the lave go by me,
   Give the jolly heaven above
   And the byway nigh me.
   Bed in the bush with stars to see,
   Bread I dip in the river—
   There's the life for a man like me,
   There's the life for ever.
   Songs of Travel (1896). I. **The Vagabond**

12 I will make you brooches and toys for
   your delight
   Of bird-song at morning and star-shine at
   night.
   I will make a palace fit for you and me
   Of green days in forests and blue days at
   sea.
   XI

13 Bright is the ring of words

When the right man rings them,
Fair the fall of songs
   When the singer sings them.
XIV

14 Trusty, dusky, vivid, true,
   With eyes of gold and bramble-dew,
   Steel-true and blade-straight,
   The great artificer
   Made my mate.
   XXV. My Wife

15 Go, little book, and wish to all
   Flowers in the garden, meat in the hall,
   A bin of wine, a spice of wit,
   A house with lawns enclosing it,
   A living river by the door,
   A nightingale in the sycamore!
   Underwoods (1887), bk.I.i. **Envoy**. See 68:27

16 Under the wide and starry sky
   Dig the grave and let me lie.
   Glad did I live and gladly die,
      And I laid me down with a will.
   This be the verse you grave for me:
   'Here he lies where he longed to be;
   Home is the sailor, home from sea,
      And the hunter home from the hill.'
   xxi. **Requiem**

17 If I have faltered more or less
   In my great task of happiness;
   If I have moved among my race
   And shown no glorious morning face;
   If beams from happy human eyes
   Have moved me not; if morning skies,
   Books, and my food, and summer rain
   Knocked on my sullen heart in vain:—
   Lord, thy most pointed pleasure take
   And stab my spirit broad awake.
   xxii. **The Celestial Surgeon**

EDWARD STILLINGFLEET 1635-1699

18 'My Lord,' a certain nobleman is said to
   have observed, after sitting next to
   [Richard] Bentley at dinner, 'that chaplain
   of yours is a very extraordinary man.' Stillingfleet agreed, adding, 'Had he but the
   gift of humility, he would be the most
   extraordinary man in Europe.'
   R.J. White, *Dr. Bentley* (1965), ch.4

HARRIET BEECHER STOWE
1811-1896

19 'Do you know who made you?' 'Nobody,
   as I knows on,' said the child, with a short
   laugh...'I 'spect I grow'd.'
   Uncle Tom's Cabin (1852), ch.20

LORD STOWELL 1745–1836

1 The elegant simplicity of the three per cents.
Lord Campbell, *Lives of the Lord Chancellors* (1857), vol.x, ch.212, p.218

2 A precedent embalms a principle.
An Opinion, while Advocate-General, 1788. Attr.

SIR JOHN SUCKLING 1609–1642

3 Why so pale and wan, fond lover?
    Prithee, why so pale?
Will, when looking well can't move her,
    Looking ill prevail?
    Prithee, why so pale?
Aglaura (1637), IV.i. Song

4 Her feet beneath her petticoat,
Like little mice, stole in and out,
    As if they fear'd the light.
A Ballad upon a Wedding (1646), viii

5 At length the candle's out, and now
All that they had not done they do:
    What that is, who can tell?
But I believe it was no more
Than thou and I have done before
    With Bridget, and with Nell.
xi

6 Out upon it, I have loved
    Three whole days together;
And am like to love three more,
    If it prove fair weather.
A Poem with the Answer

SUETONIUS C.A.D. 69–c. 130

7 *Festina lente.* [σπεῦδε βραδέως.]
Make haste slowly.
Augustus, 25

MAXIMILIEN DE BÉTHUNE, DUC DE SULLY 1559–1641

8 *Les Anglais s'amusent tristement selon l'usage de leur pays.*
The English take their pleasures sadly after the fashion of their country.
Memoirs, c.1630

SU TUNG-P'O 1036–1101

9 Families, when a child is born
Want it to be intelligent.
I, through intelligence,
Having wrecked my whole life,
Only hope the baby will prove
Ignorant and stupid.
Then he will crown a tranquil life

By becoming a Cabinet Minister.
On the Birth of his Son, tr. Arthur Waley, *17 Chinese Poems* (1918), p.98

R.S. SURTEES 1803–1864

10 'Unting is all that's worth living for—a time is lost wot is not spent in 'unting— is like the hair we breathe—if we have not we die—it's the sport of kings, th image of war without its guilt, and on five-and-twenty per cent of its danger.
Handley Cross (1843), ch.7

11 He will bring his nightcap with him, fo where the M.F.H. dines he sleeps, an where the M.F.H. sleeps he breakfasts.
ch.15

12 It ar'n't that I loves the fox less, but that loves the 'ound more.
ch.16

13 Hellish dark, and smells of cheese!
ch.50

14 No one knows how ungentlemanly he ca look, until he has seen himself in a shock ing bad hat.
Mr. Facey Romford's Hounds (1865), ch.9

15 He was a gentleman who was general spoken of as having nothing a-year, pai quarterly.
Mr. Sponge's Sporting Tour (1853), ch.24

HANNEN SWAFFER 1879–1962

16 Freedom of the press in Britain is freedo to print such of the proprietor's prejudic as the advertisers don't object to.
In conversation with Tom Driberg, c.1928

JONATHAN SWIFT 1667–1745

17 Instead of dirt and poison we have rathe chosen to fill our hives with honey an wax; thus furnishing mankind with th two noblest of things, which are sweetnes and light.
The Battle of the Books (1704), preface

18 And he gave it for his opinion, tha whoever could make two ears of corn o two blades of grass to grow upon a spot o ground where only one grew before, woul deserve better of mankind, and do mor essential service to his country than th whole race of politicians put together.
Gulliver's Travels (1726). **Voyage to Brobding nag,** ch.7

19 He had been eight years upon a project fo extracting sun-beams out of cucumber which were to be put into vials hermetica ly sealed, and let out to warm the air i

raw inclement summers.
Voyage to Laputa, etc., ch.5

These unhappy people were proposing schemes for persuading monarchs to choose favourites upon the score of their wisdom, capacity and virtue; of teaching ministers to consult the public good; of rewarding merit, great abilities and eminent services; of instructing princes to know their true interest by placing it on the same foundation with that of their people: of choosing for employment persons qualified to exercise them; with many other wild impossible chimeras, that never entered before into the heart of man to conceive, and confirmed in me the old observation, that there is nothing so extravagant and irrational which some philosophers have not maintained for truth.
ch.6

I told him...that we ate when we were not hungry, and drank without the provocation of thirst.
A Voyage to the Houyhnhnms, ch.6

Will she pass in a crowd? Will she make a figure in a country church?
Journal to Stella, 9 Feb. 1711

I have ever hated all nations, professions and communities, and all my love is towards individuals...But principally I hate and detest that animal called man; although I heartily love John, Peter, Thomas, and so forth.
Letter to Pope, 29 Sept. 1725

Not die here in a rage, like a poisoned rat in a hole.
Letter to Bolingbroke, 21 Mar. 1729

I have been assured by a very knowing American of my acquaintance in London, that a young healthy child well nursed is at a year old a most delicious, nourishing, and wholesome food, whether stewed, roasted, baked, or boiled, and I make no doubt that it will equally serve in a fricassee, or a ragout.
A Modest Proposal for Preventing the Children of Ireland from being a Burden to their Parents or Country (1729)

Last week I saw a woman flayed, and you will hardly believe, how much it altered her person for the worse.
A Tale of a Tub (1704), ch.IX

When a true genius appears in the world, you may know him by this sign, that the dunces are all in confederacy against him.
Thoughts on Various Subjects (1706)

They never would hear,

But turn the deaf ear,
As a matter they had no concern in.
Dingley and Brent (1724), ii

10 Hail, fellow, well met,
All dirty and wet:
Find out, if you can,
Who's master, who's man.
My Lady's Lamentation (1728), l.171

11 Philosophy! the lumber of the schools.
Ode to Sir W. Temple (1692), ii

12 So, naturalists observe, a flea
Hath smaller fleas that on him prey;
And these have smaller fleas to bite 'em,
And so proceed *ad infinitum.*
Thus every poet, in his kind,
Is bit by him that comes behind.
On Poetry (1733), l.337

13 In Church your grandsire cut his throat;
    To do the job too long he tarry'd,
He should have had my hearty vote,
    To cut his throat before he marry'd.
Verses on the Upright Judge

14 *Ubi saeva indignatio ulterius cor lacerare nequit.*
Where fierce indignation can no longer tear his heart.
Swift's Epitaph

ALGERNON CHARLES SWINBURNE 1837–1909

15 When the hounds of spring are on winter's
        traces,
    The mother of months in meadow or
        plain
Fills the shadows and windy places
    With lisp of leaves and ripple of rain;
And the brown bright nightingale
        amorous
Is half assuaged for Itylus,
For the Thracian ships and the foreign
        faces,
    The tongueless vigil and all the pain.
Atalanta in Calydon (1865). Chorus

16 For winter's rains and ruins are over,
    And all the season of snows and sins;
The days dividing lover and lover,
    The light that loses, the night that wins;
And time remembered is grief forgotten,
And frosts are slain and flowers begotten,
And in green underwood and cover
    Blossom by blossom the spring begins.

17 We shift and bedeck and bedrape us,
    Thou art noble and nude and antique.
Dolores (1866), vii

18   Change in a trice
    The lilies and languors of virtue

For the raptures and roses of vice.
ix

1 From too much love of living,
  From hope and fear set free,
We thank with brief thanksgiving
  Whatever gods may be
That no man lives forever,
That dead men rise up never;
That even the weariest river
  Winds somewhere safe to sea.
The Garden of Proserpine

2 Glory to Man in the highest! for Man is
  the master of things.
Hymn of Man

3 Thou hast conquered, O pale Galilean; the
  world has grown grey from Thy
  breath;
We have drunken of things Lethean, and
  fed on the fullness of death.
Laurel is green for a season, and love is
  sweet for a day;
But love grows bitter with treason, and
  laurel outlives not May.
Hymn to Proserpine. See 137:10

4 And the best and the worst of this is
  That neither is most to blame,
If you have forgotten my kisses
  And I have forgotten your name.
An Interlude

5 Swallow, my sister, O sister swallow,
  How can thine heart be full of the
    spring?
Itylus (1864)

JOHN MILLINGTON SYNGE
1871–1909

6 I've lost the only playboy of the western
world.
The Playboy of the Western World, III, closing
words

TACITUS A.D. 55 or 56–c.120

7 *Nunc terminus Britanniae patet, atque
omne ignotum pro magnifico est.*
Now the boundary of Britain is revealed,
and everything unknown is held to be
glorious.
Agricola, 30. Allegedly reporting a British leader, 'Calgacus'.

8 *Solitudinem faciunt pacem appellant.*
They make a wilderness and call it peace.

9 *Sine ira et studio.*
Without either anger or zealousness.
Annals, i.1

10 *Elegantiae arbiter.*

The authority on taste.
xvi.18. Of Petronius

11 *Maior privato visus dum privatus fuit,
omnium consensu capax imperii nisi impe
asset.*
He seemed much greater than a priva
citizen while he still was a private citize
and had he never become emperor ever
one would have agreed that he had t
capacity to reign.
Histories, i.49. Of the Emperor Galba

**CHARLES-MAURICE DE
TALLEYRAND** 1754–1838

12 *Surtout, Messieurs, point de zèle.*
Above all, gentlemen, not the slighte
zeal.
P. Chasles, *Voyages d'un critique à travers la
et les livres* (1868), vol.2, p.407

13 *Qui n'a pas vécu dans les années voisines
1789 ne sait pas ce que c'est que le plaisir
vivre.*
He who has not lived during the yea
around 1789 can not know what is mea
by the pleasure of life.
M. Guizot, *Mémoires pour servir à l'histoire
mon temps* (1858), I, 6

14 *Ils n'ont rien appris, ni rien oublié.*
They have learnt nothing, and forgotte
nothing.
Attributed to Talleyrand by the Chevalier
Panat in a letter to Mallet du Pan, Jan. 179
'Personne n'est corrigé, personne n'a su ni ri
oublier ni rien apprendre.' *Mémoires et corr
spondance de Mallet du Pan* (1851), II.196. S
91:20

NAHUM TATE 1652–1715
and **NICHOLAS BRADY** 1659–1726

15 As pants the hart for cooling streams
  When heated in the chase.
New Version of the Psalms (1696). **As Pants t
Hart**

16 Through all the changing scenes of life.
Through all the Changing

17 While shepherds watch'd their flocks b
  night,
All seated on the ground,
The Angel of the Lord came down,
And glory shone around.
*Supplement to the New Version of the Psalm
(1700).* **While Shepherds Watched**

JANE TAYLOR 1783–1824

18 Twinkle, twinkle, little star,
How I wonder what you are!
Up above the world so high,

Like a diamond in the sky!
The Star

ARCHBISHOP WILLIAM TEMPLE
1881–1944

1 In place of the conception of the Power-State we are led to that of the Welfare-State.
Citizen and Churchman (1941), ch.II

SIR JOHN TENNIEL 1820–1914

2 Dropping the pilot.
Caption of a cartoon and title of a poem in *Punch,* 29 March 1890, referring to the departure from office of Bismark

ALFRED, LORD TENNYSON
1809–1892

3 As shines the moon in clouded skies,
  She in her poor attire was seen:
One praised her ankles, one her eyes,
  One her dark hair and lovesome mien.
So sweet a face, such angel grace,
  In all that land had never been:
Cophetua sware a royal oath:
  'This beggar maid shall be my queen!'
The Beggar Maid (1842)

4 Break, break, break,
  On thy cold gray stones, O Sea!
And I would that my tongue could utter
  The thoughts that arise in me.
Break, Break, Break (1842)

5 And the stately ships go on
  To their haven under the hill;
But O for the touch of a vanish'd hand,
  And the sound of a voice that is still!

6 I come from haunts of coot and hern,
I make a sudden sally
And sparkle out among the fern,
To bicker down a valley.
The Brook (1864), l.23

7 For men may come and men may go,
  But I go on for ever.
l.33

8 Half a league, half a league,
  Half a league onward,
All in the valley of Death
  Rode the six hundred.
The Charge of the Light Brigade (1854)

9 'Forward the Light Brigade!'
Was there a man dismay'd?
Not tho' the soldier knew
  Some one had blunder'd:
Their's not to make reply,
Their's not to reason why,
Their's but to do and die:

Into the valley of Death
  Rode the six hundred.

Cannon to right of them
Cannon to left of them,
Cannon in front of them
  Volley'd and thunder'd.

10 Into the jaws of Death,
Into the mouth of Hell.

11 Sunset and evening star,
  And one clear call for me!
And may there be no moaning of the bar
  When I put out to sea.
Crossing the Bar (1889)

12 A daughter of the gods, divinely tall
  And most divinely fair. [Iphigenia.]
A Dream of Fair Women (1833), l.87

13 He clasps the crag with crooked hands;
Close to the sun in lonely lands,
Ring'd with the azure world, he stands.
The wrinkled sea beneath him crawls;
He watches from his mountain walls,
And like a thunderbolt he falls.
The Eagle (1842)

14 More black than ashbuds in the front of March.
The Gardener's Daughter (1842), l.28

15 Wearing the white flower of a blameless life,
Before a thousand peering littlenesses,
In that fierce light which beats upon a throne,
And blackens every blot.
The Idylls of the King (1842–1885), Dedication, l.24

16 Clothed in white samite, mystic, wonderful.
The Coming of Arthur, l.284, and *The Passing of Arthur,* l.199

17 It was my duty to have loved the highest:
It surely was my profit had I known:
It would have been my pleasure had I seen.
We needs must love the highest when we see it,
Not Lancelot, nor another.
Guinevere, l.652

18 God make thee good as thou art beautiful.
The Holy Grail, l.136

19 Elaine the fair, Elaine the loveable,
Elaine, the lily maid of Astolat.
Lancelot and Elaine, l.1

20 The shackles of an old love straiten'd him,
His honour rooted in dishonour stood,
And faith unfaithful kept him falsely true.
l.870

1 Unfaith in aught is want of faith in all.
Merlin and Vivien, l.387

2 It is the little rift within the lute,
That by and by will make the music mute,
And ever widening slowly silence all.
l.388

3 Man dreams of fame while woman wakes
to love.
l.458

4 So all day long the noise of battle roll'd
Among the mountains by the winter sea.
The Passing of Arthur, l.170

5 The days darken round me, and the years,
Among new men, strange faces, other
minds.
l.405

6 And slowly answer'd Arthur from the
barge:
'The old order changeth, yielding place to
new,
And God fulfils himself in many ways,
Lest one good custom should corrupt the
world.'
l.407

7 If thou shouldst never see my face again,
Pray for my soul. More things are wrought
by prayer
Than this world dreams of.
l.414

8   I am going a long way
With these thou seest—if indeed I go
(For all my mind is clouded with a
doubt)—
To the island-valley of Avilion;
Where falls not hail, or rain, or any snow,
Nor ever wind blows loudly; but it lies
Deep-meadow'd, happy, fair with orchard
lawns
And bowery hollows crown'd with sum-
mer sea,
Where I will heal me of my grievous
wound.
l.424

9 Our little systems have their day;
    They have their day and cease to be:
    They are but broken lights of thee,
And thou, O Lord, art more than they.
In Memoriam A.H.H. (1850), prologue. (The
numbering of the Cantos includes the additional
Canto No. xxxix, first published in 1869)

10   Never morning wore
To evening, but some heart did break.
vi

11 And ghastly thro' the drizzling rain
    On the bald street breaks the blank day.
vii

12   The last red leaf is whirl'd away,
The rooks are blown about the skies.
xv

13   'Tis better to have loved and lost
Than never to have loved at all.
xxvii

14 Be near me when my light is low,
    When the blood creeps, and the nerve
      prick
    And tingle; and the heart is sick,
And all the wheels of Being slow.

Be near me when the sensuous frame
    Is rack'd with pains that conquer trust;
    And Time, a maniac scattering dust,
And Life, a Fury slinging flame.
l

15 Oh yet we trust that somehow good
    Will be the final goal of ill.
liv

16 So runs my dream: but what am I?
    An infant crying in the night:
    An infant crying for the light:
And with no language but a cry.

17   So careful of the type she seems,
So careless of the single life.
lv

18 Nature, red in tooth and claw.
lvi

19 So many worlds, so much to do,
    So little done, such things to be.
lxxiii

20   Fresh from brawling courts
And dusty purlieus of the law.
lxxxix

21   There lives more faith in honest doubt,
Believe me, than in half the creeds.
xcvi

22 He seems so near and yet so far.
xcvii

23 Ring out, wild bells, to the wild sky,
    The flying cloud, the frosty light:
    The year is dying in the night;
Ring out, wild bells, and let him die.
cvi

24 Ring out a slowly dying cause,
    And ancient forms of party strife.

25 Ring in the Christ that is to be.

26   Wearing all that weight
Of learning lightly like a flower.
cxxxi, st.13

27 Below the thunders of the upper deep;
Far, far beneath in the abysmal sea,
His ancient, dreamless, uninvaded sleep

The Kraken sleepeth.
The Kraken

1 There hath he lain for ages and will lie
Battening upon huge seaworms in his
   sleep,
Until the latter fire shall heat the deep.

2 Kind hearts are more than coronets,
And simple faith than Norman blood.
Lady Clara Vere de Vere, vi

3 On either side the river lie
Long fields of barley and of rye,
That clothe the wold and meet the sky.
The Lady of Shalott (1833), pt.i

4 She left the web, she left the loom,
She made three paces thro' the room
She saw the water-lily bloom,
She saw the helmet and the plume,
     She look'd down to Camelot.
Out flew the web and floated wide;
The mirror crack'd from side to side;
'The curse is come upon me,' cried
     The Lady of Shalott.
pt.iii

5 Comrades, leave me here a little, while as
   yet 'tis early morn:
Leave me here, and when you want me,
   sound upon the bugle-horn.
Locksley Hall (1842), l.1

6 Here about the beach I wander'd, nourishing a youth sublime
With the fairy tales of science, and the long
   result of Time.
l.11

7 In the Spring a livelier iris changes on the
   burnish'd dove;
In the Spring a young man's fancy lightly
   turns to thoughts of love.
l.19

8 As the husband is, the wife is: thou art
   mated with a clown,
And the grossness of his nature will have
   weight to drag thee down.

He will hold thee, when his passion shall
   have spent its novel force,
Something better than his dog, a little
   dearer than his horse.
l.47

9 This is truth the poet sings,
That a sorrow's crown of sorrow is
   remembering happier things.
l.75. See 44:13

10 For I dipt into the future, far as human
   eye could see,
Saw the Vision of the world, and all the
   wonder that would be;

Saw the heavens fill with commerce, argosies of magic sails,
Pilots of the purple twilight, dropping
   down with costly bales;

Heard the heavens fill with shouting, and
   there rain'd a ghastly dew
From the nations' airy navies grappling in
   the central blue;

Far along the world-wide whisper of the
   south-wind rushing warm,
With the standards of the peoples plunging thro' the thunder-storm;

Till the war-drum throbb'd no longer, and
   the battle-flags were furl'd
In the Parliament of man, the Federation
   of the world.
l.119

11 Knowledge comes, but wisdom lingers.
l.143

12 I will take some savage woman, she shall
   rear my dusky race.
l.168

13 Forward, forward let us range,
Let the great world spin for ever down the
   ringing grooves of change.
l.181

14 Better fifty years of Europe than a cycle of
   Cathay.
l.184

15 'Courage!' he said, and pointed toward
   the land,
'This mounting wave will roll us shore-
ward soon.'
In the afternoon they came unto a land
In which it seemed always afternoon.
The Lotos-Eaters (1833)

16 Music that gentlier on the spirit lies,
Than tir'd eyelids upon tir'd eyes.
Choric Song, i

17 I saw the flaring atom-streams
And torrents of her myriad universe,
Ruining along the illimitable inane.
Lucretius (1868), l.38

18 Weeded and worn the ancient thatch
Upon the lonely moated grange.

She only said, 'My life is dreary,
   He cometh not,' she said;
She said, 'I am aweary, aweary.
   I would that I were dead!'
Mariana (1830). See 224:5

19 Faultily faultless, icily regular, splendidly
null,
Dead perfection, no more.
Maud, (1855), Pt.I.ii

20 And ah for a man to arise in me,

That the man I am may cease to be!
x.6

1 Come into the garden, Maud,
  For the black bat, night, has flown
Come into the garden, Maud,
  I am here at the gate alone.
xxii.1

2 She is coming, my dove, my dear;
  She is coming, my life, my fate;
The red rose cries, 'She is near, she is near;'
  And the white rose weeps, 'She is late;'
The larkspur listens, 'I hear, I hear;'
  And the lily whispers, 'I wait.'

She is coming, my own, my sweet;
  Were it ever so airy a tread,
My heart would hear her and beat,
  Were it earth in an earthy bed;
My dust would hear her and beat,
  Had I lain for a century dead;
Would start and tremble under her feet,
  And blossom in purple and red.
10

3 You must wake and call me early, call me
    early, mother dear;
To-morrow 'ill be the happiest time of all
    the glad New-year;
Of all the glad New-year, mother, the
    maddest merriest day;
For I'm to be Queen o' the May, mother,
    I'm to be Queen o' the May.
The May Queen (1833)

4 But I knaw'd a Quaäker feller as often 'as
    towd me this:
'Doänt thou marry for munny, but goä
    wheer munny is!'
Northern Farmer. New Style (1847)

5 With prudes for proctors, dowagers for
    deans,
And sweet girl-graduates in their golden
    hair.
The Princess (1847), prologue, l.141

6 As thro' the land at eve we went,
    And pluck'd the ripen'd ears,
We fell out, my wife and I,
    O we fell out I know not why,
And kiss'd again with tears.
And blessings on the falling out
    That all the more endears,
When we fall out with those we love
    And kiss again with tears!
ii. Song

7 O hard, when love and duty clash!
ii, l.273

8 Sweet and low, sweet and low,
    Wind of the western sea,
Low, low, breathe and blow,
    Wind of the western sea!

Over the rolling waters go,
Come from the dying moon, and blow,
    Blow him again to me;
While my little one, while my pretty one
    sleeps.
iii. Song

9 The splendour falls on castle walls
    And snowy summits old in story:
The long light shakes across the lakes,
    And the wild cataract leaps in glory.
Blow, bugle, blow, set the wild echoes fly-
    ing,
Blow, bugle; answer, echoes, dying, dying,
    dying.

O hark, O hear! how thin and clear,
    And thinner, clearer, farther going!
O sweet and far from cliff and scar
    The horns of Elfland faintly blowing!
iv. Song (1)

10 Tears, idle tears, I know not what the
    mean,
Tears from the depth of some divine des-
    pair
Rise in the heart, and gather to the eyes,
In looking on the happy Autumn-fields,
And thinking of the days that are no more
Song (2)

11 O tell her, Swallow, thou that knowes
    each,
That bright and fierce and fickle is th
    South,
And dark and true and tender is th
    North.
Song (3)

12 Man is the hunter; woman is his game:
The sleek and shining creatures of th
    chase,
We hunt them for the beauty of their skins
They love us for it, and we ride ther
    down.
v, l.147

13 Home they brought her warrior dead.
She nor swoon'd, nor utter'd cry:
All her maidens, watching said,
'She must weep or she will die.'
vi. Song

14 Now sleeps the crimson petal, now th
    white.
vii. Song (2)

15 Now droops the milk-white peacock like
    ghost,
And like a ghost she glimmers on to me.

Now lies the Earth all Danaë to the stars,
And all thy heart lies open unto me.

16 Now folds the lily all her sweetness up,
And slips into the bosom of the lake:

So fold thyself, my dearest, thou, and slip
Into my bosom and be lost in me.

1   Come down, O maid, from yonder moun-
        tain height:
    What pleasure lives in height?
    Song (3)

2   The moan of doves in immemorial elms,
    And murmuring of innumerable bees.

3   At Flores in the Azores Sir Richard
            Grenville lay,
    And a pinnace, like a fluttered bird, came
        flying from far away:
    'Spanish ships of war at sea! we have sight-
        ed fifty-three!'
    Then sware Lord Thomas Howard: ''Fore
        God I am no coward;
    But I cannot meet them here, for my ships
        are out of gear,
    And the half my men are sick. I must fly,
        but follow quick.
    We are six ships of the line; can we fight
        with fifty-three?'
    The Revenge (1880), i

4   Let us bang these dogs of Seville, the chil-
        dren of the devil,
    For I never turn'd my back upon Don or
        devil yet.'
    iv

5   Sink me the ship, Master Gunner—sink
        her, split her in twain!
    Fall into the hands of God, not into the
        hands of Spain.
    xi

6   And they praised him to his face with their
        courtly foreign grace;
    But he rose upon their decks, and he cried:
    'I have fought for Queen and Faith like a
        valiant man and true;
    I have only done my duty as a man is
        bound to do:
    With a joyful spirit I Sir Richard Grenville
        die!'
    And he fell upon their decks, and he died.
    xiii

7   My strength is as the strength of ten,
        Because my heart is pure.
    Sir Galahad (1842)

8   Alone and warming his five wits,
    The white owl in the belfry sits.
    Song. The Owl (1830)

9   The woods decay, the woods decay and
        fall,
    The vapours weep their burthen to the
        ground,
    Man comes and tills the field and lies
        beneath,

And after many a summer dies the swan.
Tithonus (c.1833, pub.1860), l.1

10 It little profits that an idle king,
    By this still hearth, among these barren
        crags,
    Match'd with an aged wife, I mete and
        dole
    Unequal laws unto a savage race.
    Ulysses (1842), l.1

11   I will drink
    Life to the lees: all times I have enjoy'd
    Greatly, have suffer'd greatly, both with
        those
    That loved me, and alone.
    l.6

12 Much have I seen and known; cities of
        men
    And manners, climates, councils, govern-
        ments,
    Myself not least, but honour'd of them all;
    And drunk delight of battle with my peers,
    Far on the ringing plains of windy Troy.
    l.13

13 How dull it is to pause, to make an end,
    To rust unburnish'd, not to shine in use!
    As tho' to breathe were life.
    l.22

14 Death closes all: but something ere the
        end,
    Some work of noble note, may yet be
        done,
    Not unbecoming men that strove with
        gods.
    l.51

15 It may be we shall touch the Happy Isles,
    And see the great Achilles, whom we
        knew.
    l.63

16 Made weak by time and fate, but strong in
        will
    To strive, to seek, to find, and not to yield.
    l.69

17 Fur hoffens we talkt o' my darter es died
        o' the fever at fall:
    An' I thowt 'twur the will o' the Lord, but
        Miss Annie she said it wur drääins.
    The Village Wife (1880), ii

18 Every moment dies a man,
        Every moment one is born.
    The Vision of Sin (1842), IV.ix

19 O plump head-waiter at the Cock,
        To which I must resort,
    How goes the time? 'Tis five o'clock.
        Go fetch a pint of port.
    Will Waterproof's Lyrical Monologue (1842), i

1 A louse in the locks of literature.
Said of Churton Collins to Edmund Gosse. Evan
Charteris, *Life and Letters of Sir Edmund Gosse*
(1931), ch.xiv

TERENCE c.190–159 B.C.

2 *Hinc illae lacrimae.*
Hence all those tears shed.
Andria, 126

3 *Homo sum; humani nil a me alienum puto.*
I am a man, I count nothing human
foreign to me.
Heauton Timorumenos, 77

4 *Quot homines tot sententiae: suo' quoique mos.*
There are as many opinions as there are
people: each has his own correct way.
Phormio, 454

ST. TERESA OF AVILA 1512–1582

5 *Oh, válame Dios, Señor cómo apretáis a
vestros amadores!*
Alas, O Lord, to what a state dost Thou
bring those who love Thee!
Interior Castles (Mansions), trans. by the Bene-
dictines of Stanbrook, 1921, VI, xi, 6

TERTULLIAN A.D. c.160–c.225

6 *O testimonium animae naturaliter Christ-
ianae.*
O evidence of a naturally Christian soul!
Apologeticus, 17

7 *Plures efficimus quoties metimur a vobis,
semen est sanguis Christianorum.*
As often as we are mown down by you, the
more we grow in numbers; the blood of
Christians is the seed.
50,13. Traditionally cited as, The blood of the
martyrs is the seed of the Church.

8 *Certum est quia impossibile est.*
It is certain because it is impossible.
De Carne Christi, 5. Often quoted as, *Credo quia
impossibile.*

WILLIAM MAKEPEACE THACKERAY 1811–1863

9 Kind, cheerful, merry Dr Brighton.
The Newcomes (1853-5), bk.i, ch.9

10 If a man's character is to be abused, say
what you will, there's nobody like a relation to do the business.
Vanity Fair (1847-8), ch.19

11 How to live well on nothing a year.
Title of ch.36

12 There's no sweeter tobacco comes from
Virginia, and no better brand than the

Three Castles.
The Virginians (1857-59), ch.1

13 Says gorging Jim to guzzling Jacky,
We have no wittles, so we must eat *we*.
Little Billee

14 There's little Bill as is young and tender,
We're old and tough—so let's eat *he*.

15 Werther had a love for Charlotte
Such as words could never utter;
Would you know how first he met her?
She was cutting bread and butter.
Sorrows of Werther

16 Charlotte, having seen his body
Borne before her on a shutter,
Like a well-conducted person,
Went on cutting bread and butter.

LOUIS ADOLPHE THIERS 1797–1877

17 *[Le roi] règne et le peuple se gouverne.*
The king reigns, and the people govern
themselves.
Le National, 20 Jan. 1830. The article in which
this appears was unsigned. In *Le National*,
Feb. 1830, a signed article by Thiers states *'Le roi
n'administre pas, ne gouverne pas, il règne.'*

THOMAS A KEMPIS c.1380–1471

18 *O quam cito transit gloria mundi.*
Oh how quickly the world's glory passes
away!
Of the Imitation of Christ, I.iii.6. See 7:5

19 *Nam homo proponit, sed Deus disponit.*
For man plans, but God arranges.
xix.2

ST. THOMAS AQUINAS c.1225–1274

20 *Pange, lingua, gloriosi
    Corporis mysterium.*
Sing, my tongue, of the mystery of the
glorious Body.
Pange Lingua Gloriosi. Corpus Christi hymn

BRANDON THOMAS 1856–1914

21 I'm Charley's aunt from Brazil—where
the nuts come from.
Charley's Aunt (1892), Act 1

DYLAN THOMAS 1914–1953

22 Though they go mad they shall be sane,
Though they sink through the sea they
shall rise again;
Though lovers be lost love shall not;
And death shall have no dominion.
And death shall have no dominion. See 37:35

23 Do not go gentle into that good night,

Old age should burn and rave at close of
    day;
Rage, rage against the dying of the light.
Do not go gentle into that good night

1 And you, my father, there on that sad
    height,
  Curse, bless, me now with your fierce tears
    I pray.

2 Now as I was young and easy under the
    apple boughs
  About the lilting house and happy as the
    grass was green.
Fern Hill

3 Oh as I was young and easy in the mercy
    of his means,
     Time held me green and dying
    Though I sang in my chains like the sea.

4 The force that through the green fuse
    drives the flower
  Drives my green age; that blasts the roots
    of trees
  Is my destroyer.
  And I am dumb to tell the crooked rose
  My youth is bent by the same wintry fever.
*The force that through the green fuse drives the
flower*

5 The hand that signed the paper felled a
    city;
  Five sovereign fingers taxed the breath,
  Doubled the globe of death and halved a
    country;
  These five kings did a king to death.
The hand that signed the paper

6   It was my thirtieth year to heaven
  Woke to my hearing from harbour and
    neighbour wood
    And the mussel pooled and the heron
     Priested shore.
Poem in October

7   There could I marvel
    My birthday
  Away but the weather turned around.

8 After the first death, there is no other.
*A refusal to mourn the death, by fire, of a child in
London*

9 It is spring, moonless night in the small
  town, starless and bible-black, the
  cobblestreets silent and the hunched,
  courters'-and-rabbits' wood limping invisible down to the sloeblack, slow, black,
  crowblack, fishingboat-bobbing sea.
Under Milk Wood (1954)

10 *Mr Pritchard:* I must dust the blinds and
  then I must raise them.
  Mrs Ogmore-Pritchard: And before you
  let the sun in, mind it wipes its shoes.

11 Gomer Owen who kissed her once by the
  pig-sty when she wasn't looking and never
  kissed her again although she was looking
  all the time.

12 Nothing grows in our garden, only washing. And babies.

13 Oh, what can I do? I'll *never* be refined if I
  twitch.

14 You just wait. I'll sin till I blow up!

15 Dylan talked copiously, then stopped.
  'Somebody's boring me,' he said, 'I think
  it's me.'
  Rayner Heppenstall, *Four Absentees* (1960), xvi

EDWARD THOMAS 1878–1917

16 Yes. I remember Adlestrop—
  The name, because one afternoon
  Of heat the express train drew up there
  Unwontedly. It was late June.
Adlestrop

17 The past is the only dead thing that smells
    sweet.
Early One Morning

18 If I should ever by chance grow rich
  I'll buy Codham, Cockridden, and Chil-
    derditch,
  Roses, Pyrgo, and Lapwater,
  And let them all to my elder daughter.
If I should ever by chance

19 I have come to the borders of sleep,
  The unfathomable deep
  Forest where all must lose
  Their way, however straight,
  Or winding, soon or late;
  They cannot choose.
Lights Out

20 Out in the dark over the snow
  The fallow fawns invisible go
  With the fallow doe;
  And the winds blow
  Fast as the stars are slow.
Out in the Dark

21 As well as any bloom upon a flower
  I like the dust on the nettles, never lost
  Except to prove the sweetness of a shower.
Tall Nettles

FRANCIS THOMPSON 1859–1907

22 It is little I repair to the matches of the
    Southron folk,
  Though my own red roses there may blow;
  It is little I repair to the matches of the
    Southron folk,
    Though the red roses crest the caps I
    know.

For the field is full of shades as I near the
shadowy coast,
And a ghostly batsman plays to the bowl-
ing of a ghost,
And I look through my tears on a
soundless-clapping host
As the run-stealers flicker to and fro,
    To and fro:—
O my Hornby and my Barlow long ago!
At Lord's

1 I fled Him, down the nights and down the
    days;
    I fled Him, down the arches of the years;
I fled Him, down the labyrinthine ways
    Of my own mind; and in the mist of
    tears
I hid from Him, and under running laugh-
    ter.
The Hound of Heaven

2 But with unhurrying chase,
And unperturbèd pace,
Deliberate speed, majestic instancy,
They beat—and a Voice beat
More instant than the Feet—
'All things betray thee, who betrayest Me.'

3 Yea, faileth now even dream
The dreamer, and the lute the lutanist.

4   Ah! must—
    Designer infinite!—
Ah! must Thou char the wood ere Thou
canst limn with it?

5 And is thy earth so marred,
Shattered in shard on shard?
Lo, all things fly thee, for thou fliest Me!

6 O world invisible, we view thee,
O world intangible, we touch thee,
O world unknowable, we know thee,
Inapprehensible, we clutch thee!
In No Strange Land

7 'Tis ye, 'tis your estrangèd faces,
That miss the many-splendoured thing.

But (when so sad thou canst not sadder)
Cry;—and upon thy so sore loss
Shall shine the traffic of Jacob's ladder
Pitched betwixt Heaven and Charing
Cross.

8 Wake! for the Ruddy Ball has taken flight
That scatters the slow Wicket of the Night;
    And the swift Batsman of the Dawn has
    driven
Against the Star-spiked Rails a fiery
    Smite.
Wake! for the Ruddy Ball has Taken Flight. J.C.
Squire, *Apes and Parrots*. See 98:14

WILLIAM HEPWORTH
THOMPSON 1810–1886

9 I never could have supposed that w
should have had *so soon* to regret the de
parture of our dear friend the late Profes
sor.
On Seeley's inaugural lecture as Professor o
History at Cambridge, following Charles King
sley. A.J. Balfour, *Chapters of Autobiograph*
(1930), ch.4

10 We are none of us infallible—not even th
youngest of us.
Remark referring to G.W. Balfour, then Junio
Fellow of Trinity. G.W.E. Russell, *Collection*
and Recollections, ch.18

11 What time he can spare from the adorn
ment of his person he devotes to the neg
lect of his duties.
Of Sir Richard Jebb, afterwards Professor o
Greek at Cambridge. M.R. Bobbit, *Wit*
Dearest Love to All, ch.7

JAMES THOMSON 1700–1748

12 When Britain first, at heaven's command,
Arose from out the azure main,
This was the charter of the land,
And guardian angels sung this strain:
    'Rule, Britannia, rule the waves;
    Britons never will be slaves.'
Alfred: a Masque (1740), Act II, Scene the last

13 Delightful task! to rear the tende
    thought,
To teach the young idea how to shoot.
The Seasons (1728), **Spring**, l.1152

JAMES THOMSON 1834–1882

14 The City is of Night; perchance of Death,
But certainly of Night.
The City of Dreadful Night

LORD THOMSON OF FLEET
1894–1977

15 It's just like having a licence to print you
own money.
(After the opening of Scottish commercial televi
sion.) Braddon, *Roy Thomson of Fleet Street*
p.240

HENRY DAVID THOREAU 1817–1862

16 I heartily accept the motto, 'That government is best which governs least'; and I
should like to see it acted up to more rap-
idly and systematically. Carried out, it finally amounts to this, which I also believe,— 'That government is best which
governs not at all.'
Civil Disobedience (1849). See 178:15

1 Under a government which imprisons any unjustly, the true place for a just man is also a prison.

2 As if you could kill time without injuring eternity.
Walden (1854). **Economy**

3 The mass of men lead lives of quiet desperation.

4 There are now-a-days professors of philosophy but not philosophers.

5 As for Doing-good, that is one of the professions which are full. Moreover, I have tried it fairly, and, strange as it may seem, am satisfied that it does not agree with my constitution.

6 Our life is frittered away by detail…Simplify, simplify.
Where I lived, and what I lived for

7 It takes two to speak the truth,—one to speak, and another to hear.
A Week on the Concord and Merrimack Rivers (1849). **Wednesday**

8 Some circumstantial evidence is very strong, as when you find a trout in the milk.
Journal, 11 Nov. 1850 (pub. 1903)

9 Not that the story need be long, but it will take a long while to make it short.
Letter to Mr. B., 16 Nov. 1857. See 181:4

10 *Emerson:* Why are you here?
Thoreau: Why are you not here?
Thoreau was in prison for failure to pay taxes. Oral tradition in Emerson family, discounted for lack of documentary evidence. Harding, *A Thoreau Handbook* (1959), p.8

11 It were treason to our love
And a sin to God above
One iota to abate
Of a pure impartial hate.
Indeed, Indeed I Cannot Tell (1852)

JAMES THURBER 1894–1961

12 It's a Naïve Domestic Burgundy, Without Any Breeding, But I Think You'll be Amused by its Presumption.
Men, Women and Dogs. Cartoon caption

13 Well, if I Called the Wrong Number, Why Did You Answer the Phone?

14 All Right, Have It Your Way—You Heard a Seal Bark.
The Seal in the Bedroom. Cartoon caption

EDWARD, FIRST BARON THURLOW 1731–1806

15 Corporations have neither bodies to be punished, nor souls to be condemned, they therefore do as they like.
Poynder, *Literary Extracts* (1844), vol.I. Usually quoted as 'Did you ever expect a corporation to have a conscience, when it has no soul to be damned, and no body to be kicked?'

EMPEROR TITUS A.D. 39–81

16 *Amici, diem perdidi.*
Friends, I have lost a day.
Suetonius, *Titus,* 8, i

LEO TOLSTOY 1828–1910

17 All happy families resemble one another, but each unhappy family is unhappy in its own way.
Anna Karenina (1875-7), pt.i, ch.1. Tr. Maude

18 It is amazing how complete is the delusion that beauty is goodness.
The Kreutzer Sonata, 5. Tr. Maude

19 I sit on a man's back, choking him and making him carry me, and yet assure myself and others that I am very sorry for him and wish to ease his lot by all possible means—except by getting off his back.
What Then Must We Do? (1886), ch.16. Tr. Maude

CYRIL TOURNEUR c.1575–1626

20 Does the silk-worm expend her yellow labours
For thee? for thee does she undo herself?
The Revenger's Tragedy (1607), III.v.71

THOMAS TRAHERNE 1637?–1674

21 The corn was orient and immortal wheat, which never should be reaped, nor was ever sown.
Centuries of Meditations. Cent.iii, 3

JOSEPH TRAPP 1679–1747

22 The King, observing with judicious eyes
The state of both his universities,
To Oxford sent a troop of horse, and why?
That learned body wanted loyalty;
To Cambridge books, as very well discerning
How much that loyal body wanted learning.
On George I's Donation of the Bishop of Ely's Library to Cambridge University. Nichols, *Literary Anecdotes,* vol.iii, p.330. For the reply see 48:15

ANTHONY TROLLOPE 1815–1882

1 Of all the needs a book has the chief need is that it be readable.
Autobiography (1883), ch.19

2 No man thinks there is much ado about nothing when the ado is about himself.
The Bertrams (1859), ch.27

3 How I did respect you when you dared to speak the truth to me! Men don't know women, or they would be harder to them.
The Claverings (1867), ch.15

4 Let no man boast himself that he has got through the perils of winter till at least the seventh of May.
Doctor Thorne (1858), ch.47

5 I cannot hold with those who wish to put down the insignificant chatter of the world.
Framley Parsonage (1860), ch.10

6 It's dogged as does it. It ain't thinking about it.
The Last Chronicle of Barset (1867), ch.61

7 It is because we put up with bad things that hotel-keepers continue to give them to us.
Orley Farm (1862), ch.18

8 As for conceit, what man will do any good who is not conceited? Nobody holds a good opinion of a man who has a low opinion of himself.
ch.22

9 A fainéant government is not the worst government that England can have. It has been the great fault of our politicians that they have all wanted to do something.
Phineas Finn (1869), ch.13

10 Mr Turnbull had predicted evil consequences...and was now doing the best in his power to bring about the verification of his own prophecies.
ch.25

11 It is the necessary nature of a political party in this country to avoid, as long as it can be avoided, the consideration of any question which involves a great change...The best carriage horses are those which can most steadily hold back against the coach as it trundles down the hill.
Phineas Redux (1874), ch.4

12 It may almost be a question whether such wisdom as many of us have in our mature years has not come from the dying out of the power of temptation, rather than as the results of thought and resolution.
The Small House at Allington (1864), ch.14

13 And, above all things, never think tha you're not good enough yourself. A ma should never think that. My belief is tha in life people will take you very much ε your own reckoning.
ch.32

14 Love is like any other luxury. You have r right to it unless you can afford it.
The Way We Live Now (1875), ch.84

LEV TROTSKY 1879–1940

15 Old age is the most unexpected of all th things that happen to a man.
Diary in Exile, 8 May 1935

16 In a serious struggle there is no wors cruelty than to be magnanimous at a inopportune time.
The History of the Russian Revolution, tr. N Eastman (1933), vol.IV, ch.7

17 Where force is necessary, one shoul make use of it boldly, resolutely, and righ to the end. But it is as well to know th limitations of force; to know where t blend force with manoeuvre, assault wit conciliation.
Was nun? (1932), p.106

HARRY S. TRUMAN 1884–1972

18 The buck stops here.
Hand-lettered sign on President Truman's des Phillips, *The Truman Presidency,* ch.12

19 If you can't stand the heat, get out of th kitchen.
Mr. Citizen, ch.15. Perhaps proverbial in origi possibly echoing the expression 'kitchen ca inet'.

WALTER JAMES REDFERN TURNER 1889–1946

20 Chimborazo, Cotopaxi,
They had stolen my soul away!
Romance, vii

MARK TWAIN 1835–1910

21 There was things which he stretched, bu mainly he told the truth.
The Adventures of Huckleberry Finn (1884), ch.

22 There was some books...One was *Pi grim's Progress*, about a man that left h family, it didn't say why. I read conside able in it now and then. The statemen was interesting, but tough.
ch.17

1 Hain't we got all the fools in town on our side? and ain't that a big enough majority in any town?
ch.26

2 It is by the goodness of God that in our country we have those three unspeakably precious things: freedom of speech, freedom of conscience, and the prudence never to practise either of them.
Following the Equator (1897), heading of ch.20

3 Man is the only animal that blushes. Or needs to.
heading of ch.27

4 They spell it Vinci and pronounce it Vinchy; foreigners always spell better than they pronounce.
The Innocents Abroad (1869), ch.19

5 When angry, count a hundred; when very angry, swear.
Pudd'nhead Wilson's Calendar, March

6 The report of my death was an exaggeration.
Cable from Europe to the Associated Press

7 A verb has a hard time enough of it in this world when its all together. It's downright inhuman to split it up. But that's just what those Germans do. They take part of a verb and put it down here, like a stake, and they take the other part of it and put it away over yonder like another stake, and between these two limits they just shovel in German.
Address at dinner of the Nineteenth Century Club, New York, 20 Nov. 1900, to the toast, 'The Disappearance of Literature'

8 Something that everybody wants to have read and nobody wants to read. [A classic.]

DOMITIUS ULPIAN d. 228

9 *Nulla iniuria est, quae in volentem fiat.*
No injustice is done to someone who wants that thing done.
Corpus Iuris Civilis, Digests 47, X.i.5. Usually cited in the form *Volenti non fit iniuria,* To someone who wants it no injustice occurs.

SIR JOHN VANBRUGH 1664–1726

10 The want of a thing is perplexing enough, but the possession of it is intolerable.
The Confederacy (1705), I.ii

11 Much of a muchness.
The Provok'd Husband (1728), I.i

12 *Belinda:* Ay, but you know we must return good for evil.
Lady Brute: That may be a mistake in the translation.
The Provok'd Wife (1697), I.i

HENRY VAUGHAN 1622–1695

13 Man is the shuttle, to whose winding quest
And passage through these looms
God order'd motion, but ordain'd no rest.
Silex Scintillans (1650-55), **Man**

14 Happy those early days, when I
Shin'd in my angel-infancy.
Before I understood this place
Appointed for my second race,
Or taught my soul to fancy aught
But a white, celestial thought.
The Retreat, l.1

15 They are all gone into the world of light,
And I alone sit lingering here.
They Are All Gone

16 I saw Eternity the other night,
Like a great ring of pure and endless light,
All calm, as it was bright;
And round beneath it, Time in hours, days, years,
Driv'n by the spheres
Like a vast shadow mov'd; in which the world
And all her train were hurl'd.
The World

THORSTEIN VEBLEN 1857–1929

17 Conspicuous consumption of valuable goods is a means of reputability to the gentleman of leisure.
The Theory of the Leisure Class (1899), ch.iv

VEGETIUS 4th–5th cent. A.D.

18 *Qui desiderat pacem, praeparet bellum.*
Let him who desires peace, prepare for war.
De Re Mil. 3, prol. Usually cited in the form *Si vis pacem, para bellum* (If you want peace, prepare for war.)

VENANTIUS FORTUNATUS c.530–c.610

19 *Pange, lingua, gloriosi*
Proelium certaminis.
Sing, my tongue, of the battle in the glorious struggle.
Pange lingua gloriosi. Passiontide hymn, see J.P. Migne, *Patrologia Latina,* 88

20 *Vexilla regis prodeunt,*
Fulget crucis mysterium;
Qua vita mortem pertulit,
Et morte vitam protulit.
The banners of the king advance, the

mystery of the cross shines bright;
where his life went through with death,
and from death brought forth life.
Vexilla Regis. Analecta Hymnica, 50, No.67,
p.74

PIERRE VERGNIAUD 1753–1793

1 *Il a été permis de craindre que la Révolution, comme Saturne, dévorât successive-
ment tous ses enfants.*
There was reason to fear that the Revolution, like Saturn, might devour in turn
each one of her children.
Lamartine, *Histoire des Girondins* (1847),
bk.xxxviii, ch.20

PAUL VERLAINE 1844–1896

2 *Les sanglots longs
Des violons
De l'automne
Blessent mon coeur
D'une langueur
Monotone.*
The drawn-out sobs of the violins of
autumn wound my heart with a mono-
tonous languor.
Chanson de l'automne

3 *Et tout le reste est littérature.*
All the rest is mere fine writing.
Jadis et Naguère (1885). **L'art poétique**

4 *Et, Ô ces voix d'enfants chantants dans la
coupole!*
And oh those children's voices, singing
beneath the dome!
Parsifal, A Jules Tellier

EMPEROR VESPASIAN A.D. 9–79

5 *Pecunia non olet.*
Money has no smell.
Traditional summary of Suetonius, *Vespasian*,
23,3. Vespasian was answering Titus's objection
to his tax on public lavatories; holding a coin to
Titus's nose and being told it didn't smell, he
replied:
Atqui e lotio est.
Yet that's made from urine.

6 *Vae, puto deus fio.*
Woe is me, I think I am becoming a god.
Suetonius, *Vespasian*, 23,4. Said when fatally ill

QUEEN VICTORIA 1819–1901

7 I will be good.
To Baroness Lehzen, 11 Mar. 1830. Martin, *The
Prince Consort* (1875), vol.i, p.13

8 The Queen is most anxious to enlist every
one who can speak or write to join in
checking this mad, wicked folly of
'Woman's Rights', with all its attendant
horrors, on which her poor feeble sex i
bent, forgetting every sense of womanly
feeling and propriety. Lady— ought to ge
a *good whipping*.
It is a subject which makes the Queen so
furious that she cannot contain herself
God created men and women differen
—then let them remain each in their own
position.
Letter to Sir Theodore Martin, 29 May 1870

9 We are not amused.
Attr. *Notebooks of a Spinster Lady*, 2 Jan. 1900

10 We are not interested in the possibilities o
defeat; they do not exist.
To A.J. Balfour, in 'Black Week', Dec. 1899

11 He [Mr Gladstone] speaks to Me as if
was a public meeting.
G.W.E. Russell, *Collections and Recollections*
ch.14

PHILIPPE-AUGUSTE VILLIERS DE L'ISLE-ADAM 1838–1889

12 *Vivre? les serviteurs feront cela pour nous.*
Living? The servants will do that for us.
Axël (1890), IV, sect 2

FRANÇOIS VILLON b. 1431

13 *Mais où sont les neiges d'antan?*
But where are the snows of yesteryear?
Le Grand Testament (1461). **Ballade des Dames
du Temps Jadis.** Tr. D.G. Rossetti

14 *En ceste foy je veuil vivre et mourir.*
In this faith I wish to live and to die.
Ballade pour prier Nostre Dame

VIRGIL 70–19 B.C.

15 *Arma virumque cano, Troiae qui primus ab
oris
Italiam fato profugus Laviniaque venit
Litora, multum ille et terris iactatus et alto
Vi superum, saevae memorem Iunonis ob
iram.*
I sing of arms and the man who first from
the shores of Troy came destined an
exile to Italy and the Lavinian beaches,
much buffeted he on land and on the
deep by force of the gods because of
fierce Juno's never-forgetting anger.
Aeneid, i.1

16 *Tantae molis erat Romanam condere gen-
tem.*
So massive was the effort to found the
Roman nation.
33

17 *Forsan et haec olim meminisse iuvabit.*

Maybe one day we shall be glad to remember even these things.
203

1 *Et vera incessu patuit dea.*
And in her walk it showed, she was in truth a goddess.
405

2 *En Priamus. Sunt hic etiam sua praemia laudi,*
Sunt lacrimae rerum et mentem mortalia tangunt.
Look, there's Priam! Even here prowess has its due rewards, there are tears shed for things even here and mortality touches the heart.
461

3 *Equo ne credite, Teucri.*
Quidquid id est, timeo Danaos et dona ferentis.
Do not trust the horse, Trojans. Whatever it is, I fear the Greeks even when they bring gifts.
ii.48

4 *Quantum mutatus ab illo*
Hectore qui redit exuvias indutus Achilli.
How greatly changed from that Hector who comes home wearing the armour stripped from Achilles!
274

Moriamur et in media arma ruamus.
Una salus victis nullam sperare salutem.
Let us die even as we rush into the midst of the battle. The only safe course for the defeated is to expect no safety.
353

5 *Dis aliter visum.*
The gods thought otherwise.
428

6 *Non tali auxilio nec defensoribus istis*
Tempus eget.
Now is not the hour that requires such help, nor those defenders.
521

7 *Varium et mutabile semper*
Femina.
Fickle and changeable always is woman.
iv.569. Richard Stanyhurst's translation (1582):
    A windfane changabil huf puffe
    Always is a woomman.

8 *Hos successus alit: possunt, quia posse videntur.*
These success encourages: they can because they think they can.
v.231

9 *Bella, horrida bella,*
Et Thybrim multo spumantem sanguine cerno.
I see wars, horrible wars, and the Tiber foaming with much blood.
vi.86

10 *Facilis descensus Averno:*
Noctes atque dies patet atri ianua Ditis;
Sed revocare gradum superasque evadere ad auras,
Hoc opus, hic labor est.
Easy is the way down to the Underworld: by night and by day dark Dis's door stands open; but to withdraw one's steps and to make a way out to the upper air, that's the task, that is the labour.
126

11 *Procul, o procul este, profani.*
Far off, Oh keep far off, you uninitiated ones.
258

12 *Ibant obscuri sola sub nocte per umbram*
Perque domos Ditis vacuas et inania regna.
Darkling they went under the lonely night through the shadow and through the empty dwellings and unsubstantial realms of Dis.
268

13 *Stabant orantes primi transmittere cursum*
Tendebantque manus ripae ulterioris amore.
They stood begging to be the first to make the voyage over and they reached out their hands in longing for the further shore.
313

14 *Tu regere imperio populos, Romane, memento*
(Hae tibi erunt artes), pacique imponere morem,
Parcere subiectis et debellare superbos.
You, Roman, make your task to rule nations by your government (these shall be your skills), to impose ordered ways upon a state of peace, to spare those who have submitted and to subdue the arrogant.
851

15 *Heu, miserande puer, si qua fata aspera rumpas,*
Tu Marcellus eris. Manibus date lilia plenis.
Alas, pitiable boy—if only you might break your cruel fate!—you are to be Marcellus. Give me lilies in armfuls.
882

16 *Geniumque loci primamque deorum*
Tellurem Nymphasque et adhuc ignota precatur
Flumina.
He prays to the spirit of the place and to Earth the first of the gods and to the

Nymphs and as yet unknown rivers.
vii.136

1 *Quadripedante putrem sonitu quatit ungula campum.*
Hooves with a galloping sound are shaking the powdery plain.
viii.596

2 *Macte nova virtute, puer, sic itur ad astra.*
Blessings on your young courage, boy; that's the way to the stars.
ix.641

3 *Experto credite.*
Trust one who has gone through it.
xi.283

4 *Trahit sua quemque voluptas.*
Everyone is dragged on by their favourite pleasure.
Eclogue, ii.65

5 *Latet anguis in herba.*
There's a snake hidden in the grass.
iii.93

6 *Ultima Cumaei venit iam carminis aetas;*
Magnus ab integro saeclorum nascitur ordo.
Iam redit et virgo, redeunt Saturnia regna,
Iam nova progenies caelo demittitur alto.
Now has come the last age according to the oracle at Cumae; the great series of lifetimes starts anew. Now too the virgin goddess returns, the golden days of Saturn's reign return, now a new race descends from high heaven.
iv.4

7 *Ambo florentes aetatibus, Arcades ambo.*
Both in the flower of their youth, Arcadians both.
vii.4

8 *Omnia vincit Amor: et nos cedamus Amori.*
Love conquers all things: let us too give in to Love.
x.69

9 *Ultima Thule.*
Farthest Thule.
Georgics, i.30

10 *Ter sunt conati imponere Pelio Ossam*
Scilicet atque Ossae frondosum involvere Olympum;
Ter pater exstructos disiecit fulmine montis.
Three times they endeavoured to pile Ossa on Pelion, no less, and to roll leafy Olympus on top of Ossa; three times our Father scattered the heaped-up mountains with a thunderbolt.
281

11 *O fortunatos nimium, sua si bona norint, Agricolas!*
O farmers excessively fortunate if only

they recognized their blessings!
ii.458

12 *Felix qui potuit rerum cognoscere causas.*
Lucky is he who has been able to understand the causes of things.
490

13 *Sed fugit interea, fugit inreparabile tempus*
But meanwhile it is flying, irretrievabl time is flying.
iii.284

VOLTAIRE 1694–1778

14 *Si nous ne trouvons pas des choses agré ables, nous trouverons du moins des chose nouvelles.*
If we do not find anything pleasant, a least we shall find something new.
Candide (1759), ch.17

15 *Dans ce pays-ci il est bon de tuer de temp en temps un amiral pour encourager le autres.*
In this country [England] it is thought we to kill an admiral from time to time t encourage the others.
ch.23

16 *Tout est pour le mieux dans le meilleur de mondes possibles.*
All is for the best in the best of possibl worlds.
ch.30

17 *Cela est bien dit, répondit Candide, mais faut cultiver notre jardin.*
'That is well said,' replied Candide, 'bu we must cultivate our garden.' (We mus attend to our own affairs.)

18 *Le mieux est l'ennemi du bien.*
The best is the enemy of the good.
Dict. Philosophique (1764). **Art Dramatique**

19 *La superstition met le monde entier e flammes; la philosophie les éteint.*
Superstition sets the whole world i flames; philosophy quenches them.
Superstition

20 *Si Dieu n'existait pas, il faudrait l'inventer.*
If God did not exist, it would be necessar to invent him.
Épîtres, xcvi. **A l'Auteur du Livre des Trois In posteurs**

21 *Ce corps qui s'appelait et qui s'appelle er core le saint empire romain n'était en au cune manière ni saint, ni romain, ni empire.*
This agglomeration which was called an which still calls itself the Holy Roman Em pire was neither holy, nor Roman, nor a

empire.
Essai sur les Moeurs et l'Esprit des Nations
(1769), lxx

1 *En effet, l'histoire n'est que le tableau des crimes et des malheurs.*
Indeed, history is nothing more than a tableau of crimes and misfortunes.
L'Ingénu (1767), ch.10

2 *Quoi que vous fassiez, écrasez l'infâme, et aimez qui vous aime.*
Whatever you do, stamp out abuses, and love those who love you.
Letter to M. d'Alembert, 28 Nov. 1762

3 *Je ne suis pas comme une dame de la cour de Versailles, qui disait: c'est bien dommage que l'aventure de la tour de Babel ait produit la confusion des langues; sans cela tout le monde aurait toujours parlé français.*
I am not like a lady at the court of Versailles, who said: 'What a dreadful pity that the bother at the tower of Babel should have got language all mixed up; but for that, everyone would always have spoken French.'
Letter to Catherine the Great, 26 May 1767

4 *C'est une des superstitions de l'esprit humain d'avoir imaginé que la virginité pouvait être une vertu.*
It is one of the superstitions of the human mind to have imagined that virginity could be a virtue.
Notebooks, ed. T. Besterman, 2nd edn. (1968), vol.II, **The Leningrad Notebooks** (c.1735–c.1750), p.455

5 *Il faut qu'il y ait des moments tranquilles dans les grands ouvrages, comme dans la vie après les instants de passions, mais non pas des moments de dégoût.*
There ought to be moments of tranquillity in great works, as in life after the experience of passions, but not moments of disgust.
The Piccini Notebooks, p.500

6 *Il faut, dans le gouvernement, des bergers et des bouchers.*
Governments need to have both shepherds and butchers.
p.517

7 *Dieu n'est pas pour les gros bataillons, mais pour ceux qui tirent le mieux.*
God is on the side not of the heavy battalions, but of the best shots.
p.547. See 56:1

8 *On doit des égards aux vivants; on ne doit aux morts que la vérité.*
We owe respect to the living; to the dead

we owe only truth.
Oeuvres (1785), vol.I, p.15n. (**Première Lettre sur Oedipe**)

9 *Le secret d'ennuyer est…de tout dire.*
The way to be a bore is to say everything.
Sept Discours en vers sur l'Homme, VI. **Sur la Nature de l'Homme.** v.174-5

10 I disapprove of what you say, but I will defend to the death your right to say it.
Attr. in S.G. Tallentyre, *The Friends of Voltaire* (1907), p.199

WILLIAM ROSS WALLACE d. 1881

11 The hand that rocks the cradle
Is the hand that rules the world.
J.K. Hoyt, *Cyclopedia of Practical Quotations* (1896), 402

GRAHAM WALLAS 1858-1932

12 The little girl had the making of a poet in her who, being told to be sure of her meaning before she spoke, said: 'How can I know what I think till I see what I say?'
The Art of Thought

EDMUND WALLER 1606-1687

13   Go, lovely Rose!
Tell her, that wastes her time and me,
    That now she knows,
When I resemble her to thee,
How sweet and fair she seems to be.
Song: 'Go Lovely Rose!'

14 Small is the worth
    Of beauty from the light retir'd;
Bid her come forth,
    Suffer herself to be desir'd,
And not blush so to be admir'd.

HORACE WALPOLE, FOURTH EARL OF ORFORD 1717-1797

15 [Lovat] was beheaded yesterday, and died extremely well, without passion, affectation, buffoonery or timidity: his behaviour was natural and intrepid.
Letters. To Mann, 10 Apr. 1747

16 [Strawberry Hill] is a little plaything-house that I got out of Mrs Chenevix's shop, and is the prettiest bauble you ever saw. It is set in enamelled meadows, with filigree hedges.
To Conway, 8 June 1747

17 Every drop of ink in my pen ran cold.
To Montagu, 3 July 1752

18 What has one to do, when one grows tired of the world, as we both do, but to draw nearer and nearer, and gently waste the

remains of life with friends with whom one began it?
To Montagu, 21 Nov. 1765

1 The way to ensure summer in England is to have it framed and glazed in a comfortable room.
To Cole, 28 May 1774

2 This world is a comedy to those that think, a tragedy to those that feel.
To the Countess of Upper Ossory, 16 Aug. 1776

3 Tell me, ye divines, which is the most virtuous man, he who begets twenty bastards, or he who sacrifices an hundred thousand lives?
To Mann, 7 July 1778

4 When will the world know that peace and propagation are the two most delightful things in it?

5 All his [Sir Joshua Reynolds's] own geese are swans, as the swans of others are geese.
To the Countess of Upper Ossory, 1 Dec. 1786

6 I do not dislike the French from the vulgar antipathy between neighbouring nations, but for their insolent and unfounded airs of superiority.
To Hannah More, 14 Oct. 1787

7 Virtue knows to a farthing what it has lost by not having been vice.
L. Kronenberger, *The extraordinary Mr. Wilkes* (1974), Part 3, ch.2, 'The Ruling Class'

SIR ROBERT WALPOLE, FIRST EARL OF ORFORD 1676–1745

8 They now *ring* the bells, but they will soon *wring* their hands.
On the declaration of war with Spain, 1739. W. Coxe, *Memoirs of Sir Robert Walpole* (1798), vol.i, p.618

9 The balance of power.
House of Commons, 13 Feb. 1741

IZAAK WALTON 1593–1683

10 Look to your health; and if you have it, praise God, and value it next to a good conscience; for health is the second blessing that we mortals are capable of; a blessing that money cannot buy.
The Compleat Angler (1653), pt.i, ch.21

BISHOP WILLIAM WARBURTON 1698–1779

11 Orthodoxy is my doxy; heterodoxy is another man's doxy.
To Lord Sandwich. Priestley, *Memoirs* (1807), vol.i, p.372

MRS. HUMPHRY WARD 1851–1920

12 'Propinquity does it'—as Mrs Thornburgh is always reminding us.
Robert Elsmere (1888), bk.i, ch.2

GEORGE WASHINGTON 1732–1799

13 Father, I cannot tell a lie, I did it with my little hatchet.
Attr. Mark Twain, *Mark Twain as George Washington.* Another version is: I can't tell a lie, Pa you know I can't tell a lie. I did cut it with my hatchet. Weems, *Washington,* (Fifth edition 1806)

WILLIAM WATSON 1559?–1603

14 *Fiat justitia et ruant coeli.*
Let justice be done though the heavens fall.
A Decacordon of Ten Quodlibeticall Questions Concerning Religion and State (1602). First citation in an English work of a famous maxim. See 97:19

ISAAC WATTS 1674–1748

15 Birds in their little nests agree
And 'tis a shameful sight,
When children of one family
Fall out, and chide, and fight.
Divine Songs for Children, xvii. **Love between Brothers and Sisters**

16 How doth the little busy bee
Improve each shining hour,
And gather honey all the day
From every opening flower!
xx. **Against Idleness and Mischief**

17 In works of labour, or of skill,
I would be busy too;
For Satan finds some mischief still
For idle hands to do.

18 'Tis the voice of the sluggard; I heard him complain,
'You have wak'd me too soon, I must slumber again'.
As the door on its hinges, so he on his bed,
Turns his sides and his shoulders and his heavy head.
Moral Songs, i. **The Sluggard**

EVELYN WAUGH 1903–1966

19 The sound of the English county families baying for broken glass.
Decline and Fall (1928), Prelude

20 Feather-footed through the plashy fen passes the questing vole.
Scoop (1938), bk.I, ch.1

1 Up to a point, Lord Copper.
Meaning 'No'. *passim*

BEATRICE WEBB 1848–1943

2 If I ever felt inclined to be timid as I was
going into a room full of people, I would
say to myself, 'You're the cleverest member of one of the cleverest families in the
cleverest class of the cleverest nation in the
world, why should you be frightened?'
Bertrand Russell, *Portraits from Memory* (1956),
VIII. Sidney and Beatrice Webb

SIDNEY WEBB 1859 1947

3 The inevitability of gradualness.
Presidential address to the annual conference of
the Labour Party, 1920

4 Marriage is the waste-paper basket of the
emotions.
Attr. by Beatrice Webb. Bertrand Russell, *Portraits from Memory* (1956), VIII. Sidney and
Beatrice Webb

DANIEL WEBSTER 1782–1852

5 There is always room at the top.
When advised not to become a lawyer as the
profession was overcrowded

JOHN WEBSTER 1580?–1625?

6 Vain the ambition of kings
Who seek by trophies and dead things,
To leave a living name behind,
And weave but nets to catch the wind.
The Devil's Law-Case, V.iv

7 *Ferdinand:* And women like that part
which, like the lamprey,
Hath never a bone in't.
Duchess: Fie, sir!
Ferdinand: Nay,
I mean the tongue; variety of courtship:
What cannot a neat knave with a smooth
tale
Make a woman believe?
The Duchess of Malfi (1623), ed. C.B. Wheeler
(1915), I.ii.43

8 Why should only I…
Be cas'd up, like a holy relic? I have youth
And a little beauty.
III.ii.135

9 O, that it were possible,
We might but hold some two days' confer-
ence
With the dead!
IV.ii.18

0 I am Duchess of Malfi still.
146

11 I know death hath ten thousand several
doors
For men to take their exits.
222. See 100:16, 164:6, 203:6

12 *Ferdinand:* Cover her face; mine eyes dazzle: she died young.
Bosola: I think not so; her infelicity
Seem'd to have years too many.
267

13 A mere tale of a tub, my words are idle.
The White Devil (1612), II.i.92

14 Only the deep sense of some deathless
shame.
ii.67

15 A rape! a rape!…
Yes, you have ravish'd justice;
Forced her to do your pleasure.
III.i.271

16 But keep the wolf far thence that's foe to
men,
For with his nails he'll dig them up again.
V.iv.108

17 We think caged birds sing, when indeed
they cry.
128

18 I have caught
An everlasting cold; I have lost my voice
Most irrecoverably.
vi.270

JOSIAH WEDGWOOD 1730–1795

19 Am I not a man and a brother.
Legend on Wedgwood cameo depicting a kneel-
ing negro slave in chains, reproduced in facsimile
in E. Darwin, *The Botanic Garden* pt.1 (1791),
facing p.87

THOMAS EARLE WELBY 1881–1933

20 'Turbot, Sir,' said the waiter, placing before me two fishbones, two eyeballs, and a
bit of black mackintosh.
The Dinner Knell

DUKE OF WELLINGTON 1769–1852

21 It has been a damned serious business
—Blücher and I have lost 30,000 men. It
has been a damned nice thing—the nearest
run thing you ever saw in your life…By
God! I don't think it would have done if I
had not been there.
Creevey Papers, ch.x, p.236

22 All the business of war, and indeed all the
business of life, is to endeavour to find out
what you don't know by what you do;
that's what I called 'guessing what was at

the other side of the hill'.
Croker Papers (1885), vol.iii, p.276

1 I believe I forgot to tell you I was made a Duke.
Postscript to a letter to his nephew Henry Wellesley, 22 May 1814

2 I never saw so many shocking bad hats in my life.
On seeing the first Reformed Parliament. Sir William Fraser, *Words on Wellington* (1889), p.12

3 You must build your House of Parliament upon the river: so...that the populace cannot exact their demands by sitting down round you.
p.163

4 The battle of Waterloo was won on the playing fields of Eton.
See Montalembert, *De l'Avenir Politique de l'Angleterre* (1856). The attribution was refuted by the 7th Duke.

5 I always say that, next to a battle lost, the greatest misery is a battle gained.
Frances, Lady Shelley, *Diary*, p.102

6 In my situation as Chancellor of the University of Oxford, I have been much exposed to authors.
G.W.E. Russell, *Collections and Recollections*, ch.2.

7 Hard pounding this, gentlemen; let's see who will pound longest.
At Waterloo. Sir W. Scott, *Paul's Letters* (1815)

8 I used to say of him [Napoleon] that his presence on the field made the difference of forty thousand men.
Stanhope, *Notes of Conversations with the Duke of Wellington*, 2 Nov. 1831

9 Ours [our army] is composed of the scum of the earth—the mere scum of the earth.
4 Nov. 1831

10 What is the best to be done for the country? How can the Government be carried on?
18 May 1839

11 When I reflect upon the characters and attainments of some of the general officers of this army, and consider that these are the persons on whom I am to rely to lead columns against the French, I tremble; and as Lord Chesterfield said of the generals of his day, 'I only hope that when the enemy reads the list of their names, he trembles as I do.'
Dispatch to Torrens, 29 Aug. 1810. Usually quoted as 'I don't know what effect these men will have upon the enemy, but, by God, they frighten me.' Also attributed to George III.

12 [To a gentleman who accosted him in the street saying, 'Mr. Jones, I believe?']
If you believe that you will believe anything.
Attr.

13 Up Guards and at them again!
Letter from Captain Batty 22 June 1815. Booth *Battle of Waterloo*. See also Croker, *Correspondence and Diaries* (1884), III, 280

14 Publish and be damned.
Attr. According to legend, Wellington wrote these words across a blackmailing letter from Stockdale, publisher of Harriette Wilson's *Memoirs*, and posted it back to him. See Elizabeth Pakenham, *Wellington: The Years of the Sword* (1969), ch.10

H.G. WELLS 1866–1946

15 'I expect,' he said, 'I was thinking jest what a Rum Go everything is. I expect it was something like that.'
Kipps, bk.iii, ch.3, 8

16 The Social Contract is nothing more or less than a vast conspiracy of human beings to lie to and humbug themselves and one another for the general Good. Lies are the mortar that bind the savage individual man into the social masonry.
Love and Mr. Lewisham, ch.23

17 Human history becomes more and more a race between education and catastrophe.
The Outline of History, ch.40 of the 1951 edn.

CHARLES WESLEY 1707–1788

18 Gentle Jesus, meek and mild,
Look upon a little child;
Pity my simplicity,
Suffer me to come to thee.
Hymns and Sacred Poems (1742), **Gentle Jesus Meek and Mild**

JOHN WESLEY 1703–1791

19 Let it be observed, that slovenliness is no part of religion; that neither this, nor any text of Scripture, condemns neatness of apparel. Certainly this is a duty, not a sin. 'Cleanliness is, indeed, next to godliness.'
Sermons, No. xciii. **On Dress**

20 We should constantly use the most common, little, easy words (so they are pure and proper) which our language affords.
Of preaching to 'plain people'. R. Southey, *Life of Wesley* (1820), ch.16

REVD. SAMUEL WESLEY 1662–1735

21 Style is the dress of thought; a modest dress,

Neat, but not gaudy, will true critics
please.
An Epistle to a Friend concerning Poetry (1700)

MAE WEST 1892?–1980

1 'Goodness, what beautiful diamonds.'
'Goodness had nothing to do with it,
dearie,'
Night After Night (1932), script by Vincent Lawrence

2 Why don't you come up sometime, see
me?
She Done Him Wrong (1933). Commonly mis-
quoted as 'Come up and see me sometime'.

DAME REBECCA WEST 1892–

3 God forbid that any book should be
banned. The practice is as indefensible as
infanticide.
The Strange Necessity (1928). **The Tosh Horse**

RICHARD BETHELL, LORD
WESTBURY 1800–1873

4 Then, sir, you will turn it over once more
in what you are pleased to call your mind.
Related by Jowett and denied, not very convinc-
ingly, by Westbury. T.A. Nash, *Life of Lord
Westbury* (1888), bk.2, ch.12

JOHN FANE, LORD
WESTMORLAND 1759–1841

5 *Merit,* indeed!…We are come to a pretty
pass if they talk of *merit* for a bishopric.
Noted in Lady Salisbury's diary, 9 Dec. 1835. C.
Oman, *The Gascoyne Heiress* (1968), V

SIR CHARLES WETHERELL
1770–1846

6 Then there is my noble and biographical
friend who has added a new terror to
death.
Of Lord Campbell. Lord St. Leonards, *Misrep-
resentations in Campbell's Lives of Lyndhurst and
Brougham* (1869), p.3. See 155:17

ROBERT WEVER fl. 1550

7 In a harbour grene aslepe whereas I lay,
The byrdes sang swete in the middes of the
day,
I dreamèd fast of mirth and play:
    In youth is pleasure, in youth is
    pleasure.
Lusty Juventus

EDITH WHARTON 1862–1937

8 Mrs Ballinger is one of the ladies who
pursue Culture in bands, as though it were
dangerous to meet it alone.
Xingu (1916), ch.1

9 Another unsettling element in modern art
is that common symptom of immaturity,
the dread of doing what has been done
before.
The Writing of Fiction, ch.1, pt.iii

WILLIAM WHEWELL 1794–1866

10 Hence no force however great can stretch
a cord however fine into an horizontal line
which is accurately straight: there will always be a bending downwards.
Elementary Treatise on Mechanics, (1819), ch.IV,
prob.ii. Often cited as an example of accidental
metre and rhyme, and changed in later editions.

JAMES McNEILL WHISTLER
1834–1903

11 I am not arguing with you—I am telling
you.
The Gentle Art of Making Enemies (1890)

12 'I only know of two painters in the world,'
said a newly introduced feminine enthu-
siast to Whistler, 'yourself and Velasquez.'
'Why,' answered Whistler in dulcet tones,
'why drag in Velasquez?'
D.C. Seitz, *Whistler Stories* (1913), p.27

13 [In answer to the question 'For two days'
labour, you ask two hundred guineas?']
No, I ask it for the knowledge of a lifetime.
p.40

14 [Answering Oscar Wilde's 'I wish I had
said that']
You will, Oscar, you will.
L.C. Ingleby, *Oscar Wilde*, p.67

WILLIAM WHITING 1825–1878

15 O hear us when we cry to Thee
For those in peril on the sea.
Eternal Father Strong to Save

WALT WHITMAN 1819–1892

16 Silent and amazed even when a little boy,
I remember I heard the preacher every
        Sunday put God in his statements,
As contending against some being or influ-
ence.
A Child's Amaze

17 Full of life now, compact, visible,
I, forty year old the eighty-third year of the
States,
To one a century hence or any number of

centuries hence,
To you yet unborn these, seeking you.
Full of life now

1 O Captain! my Captain! our fearful trip is
    done,
  The ship has weather'd every rack, the
    prize we sought is won.
  O Captain! My Captain! (1865-6), i

2 Out of the cradle endlessly rocking,
  Out of the mocking-bird's throat, the mus-
    ical shuttle...
  A reminiscence sing.
  Out of the Cradle endlessly Rocking (1860)

3 Camerado, this is no book,
  Who touches this touches a man,
  (Is it night? Are we here together alone?)
  So Long!

4 I celebrate myself, and sing myself.
  Song of Myself (1855), 1

5 A child said *What is the grass?* fetching it
    to one with full hands
  How could I answer the child? I do not
    know what it is any more than he.
  6

6 I think I could turn and live with animals,
    they are so placid and self-contain'd,
  I stand and look at them long and long.
  They do not sweat and whine about their
    condition,
  They do not lie awake in the dark and
    weep for their sins,
  They do not make me sick discussing their
    duty to God,
  Not one is dissatisfied, not one is dement-
    ed with the mania of owning things,
  Not one kneels to another, nor to his kind
    that lived thousands of years ago,
  Not one is respectable or unhappy over the
    whole earth.
  32

7 Do I contradict myself?
  Very well then I contradict myself,
  (I am large, I contain multitudes.)
  51

8 The earth does not argue,
  Is not pathetic, has no arrangements,
  Does not scream, haste, persuade,
    threaten, promise,
  Makes no discriminations, has no conceiv-
    able failures,
  Closes nothing, refuses nothing, shuts
    none out.
  To the sayers of words, 2

JOHN GREENLEAF WHITTIER
1807-1892

9 'Shoot, if you must, this old gray head,
  But spare your country's flag,' she said.

  A shade of sadness, a blush of shame,
  Over the face of the leader came.
  Barbara Frietchie, l.35

10 For all sad words of tongue or pen,
  The saddest are these: 'It might have been!
  Maud Muller, l.105

ROBERT WHITTINGTON fl.1520

11 As time requireth, a man of marvellous
  mirth and pastimes, and sometime of a
  sad gravity, as who say: a man for all
  seasons.
  [Of Sir Thomas More.] *Vulgaria* (1521). pt.II, **De
  constructione nominum.** Erasmus famously applied the idea to More, writing in his prefatory
  letter to *In Praise of Folly* (1509), in Latin, that
  he played *'omnium horarum hominem.'*

BENJAMIN WHORF 1897-1941

12 We dissect nature along lines laid down by
  our native language...Language is no
  simply a reporting device for experience
  but a defining framework for it.
  Thinking in Primitive Communities, in Hoye
  (ed.), *New Directions in the Study of Language*
  1964

CORNELIUS WHURR c.1845

13 What lasting joys the man attend
  Who has a polished female friend.
  The Accomplished Female Friend

GEORGE JOHN WHYTE-MELVILLE
1821-1878

14 Then drink, puppy, drink, and let ev'ry
    puppy drink,
  That is old enough to lap and to swallow;
  For he'll grow into a hound, so we'll pass
    the bottle round,
  And merrily we'll whoop and we'll holloa.
  Drink, Puppy, Drink, chorus

BISHOP SAMUEL WILBERFORCE
1805-1873

15 If I were a cassowary
  On the plains of Timbuctoo,
  I would eat a missionary,
  Cassock, band, and hymn-book too.
  Impromptu verse, ascribed also to W.M. Thack-
  eray

RICHARD WILBUR 1921–

1 We milk the cow of the world, and as we do
   We whisper in her ear, 'You are not true.'
Epistemology, ii

ELLA WHEELER WILCOX 1855–1919

2 Laugh and the world laughs with you;
   Weep, and you weep alone;
For the sad old earth must borrow its mirth,
   But has trouble enough of its own.
Solitude

OSCAR WILDE 1854–1900

3 Yet each man kills the thing he loves,
   By each let this be heard,
Some do it with a bitter look,
   Some with a flattering word.
The coward does it with a kiss,
   The brave man with a sword!
The Ballad of Reading Gaol, (1898), I.vii

4 And the wild regrets, and the bloody sweats,
   None knew so well as I:
For he who lives more lives than one
   More deaths than one must die.
III.xxxvii

5 As long as war is regarded as wicked, it will always have its fascination. When it is looked upon as vulgar, it will cease to be popular.
The Critic as Artist, Part 2

6 The truth is rarely pure, and never simple.
The Importance of Being Earnest (1895), Act 1

7 In married life three is company and two none.

8 To lose one parent, Mr Worthing, may be regarded as a misfortune; to lose both looks like carelessness.

9 All women become like their mothers. That is their tragedy. No man does. That's his.

0 The good ended happily, and the bad unhappily. That is what Fiction means. [Miss Prism on her novel.]
Act II

1 The chapter on the Fall of the Rupee you may omit. It is somewhat too sensational.

2 I hope you have not been leading a double life, pretending to be wicked and being really good all the time. That would be hypocrisy.

3 On an occasion of this kind it becomes more than a moral duty to speak one's mind. It becomes a pleasure.

14 I couldn't help it. I can resist everything except temptation.
Lady Windermere's Fan (1891), Act I

15 Do you know, Mr Hopper, dear Agatha and I are so much interested in Australia. It must be so pretty with all the dear little kangaroos flying about. [Duchess of Berwick.]
Act II

16 We are all in the gutter, but some of us are looking at the stars.
Act III

17 A man who knows the price of everything and the value of nothing.
Definition of a cynic

18 There is no such thing as a moral or an immoral book. Books are well written, or badly written.
The Picture of Dorian Gray (1891), preface

19 The nineteenth century dislike of Realism is the rage of Caliban seeing his own face in the glass.

20 There is only one thing in the world worse than being talked about, and that is not being talked about.
ch.1

21 A cigarette is the perfect type of a perfect pleasure. It is exquisite, and it leaves one unsatisfied. What more can one want?
ch.6

22 Anybody can be good in the country.
ch.19

23 *Mrs Allonby:* They say, Lady Hunstanton, that when good Americans die they go to Paris.
Lady Hunstanton: Indeed? And when bad Americans die, where do they go to?
Lord Illingworth: Oh, they go to America.
A Woman of No Importance (1893), Act I. See 7:11

24 The English country gentleman galloping after a fox—the unspeakable in full pursuit of the uneatable.

25 One should never trust a woman who tells one her real age. A woman who would tell one that, would tell one anything.

26 *Lord Illingworth:* The Book of Life begins with a man and a woman in a garden.
Mrs Allonby: It ends with Revelations.

27 Children begin by loving their parents; after a time they judge them; rarely, if ever, do they forgive them.

28 No publisher should ever express an opinion of the value of what he publishes. That

is a matter entirely for the literary critic to decide.
Letter in *St. James's Gazette*, 28 June 1890

1 *Voulez-vous savoir le grand drame de ma vie? C'est que j'ai mis mon génie dans ma vie; je n'ai mis que mon talent dans mes oeuvres.*
Do you want to know the great drama of my life? It's that I have put my genius into my life; all I've put into my works is my talent.
Spoken to André Gide. Gide, *Oscar Wilde: In Memoriam*

2 [At the New York Custom House]
I have nothing to declare except my genius.
F. Harris, *Oscar Wilde* (1918), p.75

3 'Will you very kindly tell me, Mr Wilde, in your own words, your viewpoint of George Meredith?'
'George Meredith is a prose Browning, and so is Browning.'
'Thank you. His style?'
'Chaos, illumined by flashes of lightning.'
Ada Leverson, *Letters to the Sphinx* (1930), 'Reminiscences', 1

4 Work is the curse of the drinking classes.
H. Pearson, *Life of Oscar Wilde* (1946), ch.12

5 He has fought a good fight and has had to face every difficulty except popularity.
Unpublished character sketch of W.E. Henley written for Rothenstein's *English Portraits*. See W. Rothenstein, *Men and Memories*, vol. I, ch.25

6 [A huge fee for an operation was mentioned]
'Ah, well, then, I suppose that I shall have to die beyond my means.'
R.H. Sherard, *Life of Oscar Wilde* (1906), p.421

KAISER WILHELM II 1859–1941

7 It is my Royal and Imperial Command that you concentrate your energies, for the immediate present, upon one single purpose, and that is that you address all your skill and all the valour of my soldiers to exterminate first the treacherous English, and to walk over General French's contemptible little Army.
Of the British Expeditionary Force. Order dated Headquarters, Aix-la-Chapelle, 19 Aug. 1914, as reported in *The Times*, 1 Oct. 1914

JOHN WILKES 1727–1797

8 The chapter of accidents is the longest chapter in the book.
Attr. by Southey in *The Doctor* (1837), vol.iv, p.166

9 'Wilkes,' said Lord Sandwich, 'you will die either on the gallows, or of the pox.'
'That,' replied Wilkes blandly, 'must depend on whether I embrace your lordship's principles or your mistress.'
Charles Chenevix-Trench, *Portrait of a Patriot* (1962), ch.3. But see H. Brougham, *Statesmen of George III*, third series (1843), p.189. Also attr. Samuel Foote.

EMMA HART WILLARD 1787–1870

10 Rocked in the cradle of the deep.
Song

KING WILLIAM III 1650–1702

11 'Do you not see your country is lost?' asked the Duke of Buckingham. 'There is one way never to see it lost' replied William, 'and that is to die in the last ditch.'
Burnet, *History of his own Times* (1715), i.457

12 Every bullet has its billet.
John Wesley, *Journal*, 6 June 1765

WENDELL WILLKIE 1892–1944

13 The Constitution does not provide for first and second class citizens.
New York Herald Tribune, 13 June 1944

CHARLES ERWIN WILSON 1890–1961

14 For many years I thought what was good for our country was good for General Motors, and vice versa.
Testimony before the Senate Armed Services Committee, Jan. 1953

SIR HAROLD WILSON 1916–

15 That doesn't mean, of course, that the pound here in Britain—in your pocket or purse or in your bank—has been devalued.
Ministerial Broadcast, 19 Nov. 1967

16 The Britain that is going to be forged in the white heat of this revolution.
Speech at the Labour Party conference, Scarborough, 1 Oct. 1963. Usually quoted as 'the white heat of the technological revolution.'

17 A week is a long time in politics.
Phrase used a number of times in 1965-6

HARRIETTE WILSON 1789–1846

18 I shall not say why and how I became, at the age of fifteen, the mistress of the Earl of Craven.
Memoirs, First sentence

PRESIDENT WOODROW WILSON
1856–1924

1 There is such a thing as a man being too proud to fight.
Address at Philadelphia, 10 May 1915

2 The world must be made safe for democracy.
Address to Congress, 2 Apr. 1917

3 Open covenants of peace openly arrived at.
Address to Congress, 8 Jan. 1918. First of *Fourteen Points*.

CATHERINE WINKWORTH
1827–1878

4 *Peccavi*—I have Sindh.
Of Sir Charles Napier's conquest of Sind (1843). Pun sent to *Punch*, 13 May 1844, and printed as 'the most laconic despatch ever issued', supposedly sent by Napier to Lord Ellenborough, *Punch*, vi, p.209, 18 May 1844. See N.M. Billimoria, *Proceedings of the Sind Historical Society*, II (1938) and N. & Q., cxcix (1954), p.219.

OWEN WISTER 1860–1938

5 When you call me that, *smile*.
The Virginian (1902), ch.2

GEORGE WITHER 1588–1667

6 Shall I, wasting in despair,
    Die because a woman's fair?
Sonnet

LUDWIG WITTGENSTEIN 1889–1951

7 *Die Welt ist alles, was der Fall ist.*
The world is everything that is the case.
Tractatus Logico-Philosophicus (1922), 1

8 *Die Logik muss für sich selber sorgen.*
Logic must take care of itself.
5.473

9 *Die Welt des Glücklichen ist eine andere als die des Unglücklichen.*
The world of the happy is quite another than the world of the unhappy.
6.43

10 *Wovon man nicht sprechen kann, darüber muss man schweigen.*
Whereof one cannot speak, thereon one must remain silent.
7

P.G. WODEHOUSE 1881–1975

11 There was another ring at the front door. Jeeves shimmered out and came back with a telegram.
Carry on Jeeves (1925). **Jeeves Takes Charge**

12 He spoke with a certain what-is-it in his voice, and I could see that, if not actually disgruntled, he was far from being gruntled.
The Code of the Woosters (1938)

13 To my daughter Leonora without whose never-failing sympathy and encouragement this book would have been finished in half the time.
The Heart of a Goof (1926), dedication

14 The lunches of fifty-seven years had caused his chest to slip down to the mezzanine floor.
Chester Forgets Himself

15 She fitted into my biggest arm-chair as if it had been built round her by someone who knew they were wearing arm-chairs tight about the hips that season.
My Man Jeeves (1919). **Jeeves and the Unbidden Guest**

16 What with excellent browsing and sluicing and cheery conversation and what-not the afternoon passed quite happily.

17 Ice formed on the butler's upper slopes.
Pigs Have Wings (1952), ch.5. pt.i

18 The Right Hon was a tubby little chap who looked as if he had been poured into his clothes and had forgotten to say 'When!'
Very Good Jeeves (1930). **Jeeves and the Impending Doom**

CHARLES WOLFE 1791–1823

19 Not a drum was heard, not a funeral note,
    As his corse to the rampart we hurried.
The Burial of Sir John Moore at Corunna, i

20 We buried him darkly at dead of night,
    The sods with our bayonets turning.
ii

21 But he lay like a warrior taking his rest,
    With his martial cloak around him.
iii

22 We carved not a line, and we raised not a stone—
    But we left him alone with his glory.
viii

HUMBERT WOLFE 1886–1940

23 You cannot hope
    to bribe or twist,
thank God! the
    British journalist.

But, seeing what

the man will do
unbribed, there's
no occasion to.
The Uncelestial City, Bk.I. ii.2. **Over the Fire**

MARY WOLLSTONECRAFT
1759–1797

1 The *divine right* of husbands, like the divine right of kings, may, it is hoped, in this
enlightened age, be contested without
danger.
A Vindication of the Rights of Woman (1792),
ch.3

2 A king is always a king—and a woman
always a woman: his authority and her sex
ever stand between them and rational converse.
ch.4

3 I do not wish them [women] to have power
over men; but over themselves.

CARDINAL WOLSEY 1475?–1530

4 Father Abbot, I am come to lay my bones
amongst you.
Cavendish, *Negotiations of Thomas Woolsey*
(1641), p.108

5 Had I but served God as diligently as I
have served the King, he would not have
given me over in my gray hairs.
p.113

MRS. HENRY WOOD 1814–1887

6 Dead! and...never called me mother.
East Lynne (dramatized version by T.A. Palmer,
1874). These words do not occur in the novel

LIEUT.-COMMANDER THOMAS
WOODROOFE 1899–1978

7 The Fleet is all lit up.
First live outside broadcast, Coronation Spit-
head review, May 1937. See A. Briggs, *A History
of Broadcasting in the United Kingdom,* vol.II
(1965), pt.ii, 2

VIRGINIA WOOLF 1882–1941

8 So that is marriage, Lily thought, a man
and a woman looking at a girl throwing a
ball.
To the Lighthouse (1927), I.13

9 I have lost friends, some by death...others
through sheer inability to cross the street.
The Waves (1931), p.202

ELIZABETH WORDSWORTH
1840–1932

10 If all the good people were clever,

And all clever people were good,
The world would be nicer than ever
We thought that it possibly could.

But somehow, 'tis seldom or never
The two hit it off as they should;
The good are so harsh to the clever,
The clever so rude to the good!
St. Christopher and Other Poems: **Good an**
Clever

WILLIAM WORDSWORTH 1770–185C

11 And three times to the child I said,
'Why, Edward, tell me why?'
Anecdote for Fathers (1798)

12 The light that never was, on sea or land,
The consecration, and the Poet's dream.
Elegiac Stanzas (on a picture of Peele Castle in
storm, 1807)

13 Not in the lucid intervals of life
That come but as a curse to party strife...
Is Nature felt, or can be.
Evening Voluntaries (1835), iv

14 This dull product of a scoffer's pen.
The Excursion, (1814), bk.ii, 1.484. Of *Candide*

15   I have seen
A curious child, who dwelt upon a tract
Of inland ground applying to his ear
The convolutions of a smooth-lipped shel**l**
To which, in silence hushed, his very soul
Listened intensely; and his countenanc
soon
Brightened with joy; for from within wer
heard
Murmurings,   whereby   the   monito
expressed
Mysterious union with its native sea.
bk.iv, 1.1132

16 'To every Form of being is assigned',
Thus calmly spoke the venerable Sage,
'An *active* Principle.'
bk.ix, 1.1

17 Bliss was it in that dawn to be alive,
But to be young was very heaven!
French Revolution, as it Appeared to Enthusias
(1809), and *The Prelude,* bk.xi, 1.108

18 The moving accident is not my trade;
To freeze the blood I have no ready arts:
'Tis my delight, alone in summer shade,
To pipe a simple song for thinking hearts.
Hart-leap Well (1800), pt.2, 1.1

19 He whom you love, your Idiot Boy.
The Idiot Boy (1798), 1.371

20   All shod with steel
We hissed along the polished ice, in games

Confederate.
Influence of Natural Objects (1809) and *The Pre-lude*, bk.i, l.414

1   Yet still the solitary cliffs
Wheeled by me—even as if the earth had rolled
With visible motion her diurnal round!
(also *The Prelude*, bk.i, l.458)

2 I travelled among unknown men
    In lands beyond the sea;
Nor, England! did I know till then
    What love I bore to thee.
I Travelled among Unknown Men (1807)

3 I wandered lonely as a cloud
That floats on high o'er vales and hills,
When all at once I saw a crowd,
A host, of golden daffodils;
Beside the lake, beneath the trees,
Fluttering and dancing in the breeze.
I Wandered Lonely as a Cloud (1807)

4 For oft, when on my couch I lie
In vacant or in pensive mood,
They flash upon that inward eye
Which is the bliss of solitude;
And then my heart with pleasure fills,
And dances with the daffodils.

5 His little, nameless, unremembered, acts
Of kindness and of love.
Lines composed a few miles above Tintern Abbey
(1798), l.34

6 The still, sad music of humanity,
Nor harsh nor grating, though of ample power
To chasten and subdue.
l.91

7 What, you are stepping westward?
Memorials of a Tour in Scotland, 1803. viii. **Stepping Westward**

8 Behold her, single in the field,
    Yon solitary Highland lass!
ix. **The Solitary Reaper**

9 Will no one tell me what she sings?—
Perhaps the plaintive numbers flow
For old, unhappy, far-off things,
And battles long ago.

10   The good old rule
Sufficeth them, the simple plan,
That they should take, who have the power,
    And they should keep who can.
xi. **Rob Roy's Grave**

11 My heart leaps up when I behold
    A rainbow in the sky:
So was it when my life began;
So is it now I am a man;
So be it when I shall grow old,

Or let me die!
The Child is father of the Man.
My Heart Leaps Up (1807)

12   Move along these shades
In gentleness of heart; with gentle hand
Touch—for there is a spirit in the woods.
Nutting (1800)

13 There was a time when meadow, grove, and stream,
The earth, and every common sight,
    To me did seem
    Apparelled in celestial light,
The glory and the freshness of a dream.
It is not now as it hath been of yore;—
    Turn wheresoe'er I may,
    By night or day,
The things which I have seen I now can see no more.

        The rainbow comes and goes,
        And lovely is the rose,
        The moon doth with delight
Look round her when the heavens are bare,
        Waters on a starry night
        Are beautiful and fair;
    The sunshine is a glorious birth:
    But yet I know, where'er I go,
That there hath passed away a glory from the earth.
Ode. Intimations of Immortality (1807), i

14   The sun shines warm,
And the Babe leaps up on his Mother's arm.
iv

15 Whither is fled the visionary gleam?
Where is it now, the glory and the dream?

Our birth is but a sleep and a forgetting:
    The Soul that rises with us, our life's Star,
Hath had elsewhere its setting,
    And cometh from afar;
Not in entire forgetfulness,
And not in utter nakedness,
But trailing clouds of glory do we come
    From God, who is our home:
Heaven lies about us in our infancy!
Shades of the prison-house begin to close
Upon the growing boy.

16 Though nothing can bring back the hour
Of splendour in the grass, of glory in the flower;
We will grieve not, rather find
Strength in what remains behind.
ix

17 To me the meanest flower that blows can give
    Thoughts that do often lie too deep for tears.

1 Stern daughter of the voice of God!
  O Duty! if that name thou love
  Who art a light to guide, a rod
  To check the erring and reprove.
  Ode to Duty (1807)

2   Sweetest melodies
  Are those by distance made more sweet.
  Personal Talk (1807), ii

3 A primrose by a river's brim
  A yellow primrose was to him,
  And it was nothing more.
  Peter Bell (1819), pt.i, l.249

4 Is it a party in a parlour?
    Cramm'd just as they on earth were
      cramm'd—
  Some sipping punch, some sipping tea,
  But, as you by their faces see,
  All silent and all damn'd!
  (pt.i, st.66 in MS of 1819, later omitted)

5 Physician art thou?—one, all eyes,
  Philosopher!—a fingering slave,
  One that would peep and botanize
  Upon his mother's grave?
  A Poet's Epitaph (1800)

6 In common things that round us lie
  Some random truths he can impart,—
  The harvest of a quiet eye,
  That broods and sleeps on his own heart.

7   Where the statue stood
  Of Newton, with his prism and silent face,
  The marble index of a mind for ever
  Voyaging through strange seas of
    Thought, alone.
  The Prelude, (1850), bk.iii, l.61

8   Spirits overwrought
  Were making night do penance for a day
  Spent in a round of strenuous idleness.
  bk.iv, l.376

9   All things have second birth;
  The earthquake is not satisfied at once.
  bk.x, l.83

10 There was a roaring in the wind all night;
  The rain came heavily and fell in floods;
  But now the sun is rising, calm and bright.
  Resolution and Independence (1807), i

11 We poets in our youth begin in gladness;
  But thereof comes in the end despondency
    and madness.
  vii

12 Still glides the Stream, and shall for ever
    glide;
  The Form remains, the Function never
    dies.
  The River Duddon (1820), xxxiv. **After-Thought**

13 We feel that we are greater than we know.

14 She dwelt among the untrodden ways
    Beside the springs of Dove,
  A maid whom there were none to praise
    And very few to love:

  A violet by a mossy stone
    Half hidden from the eye!
  Fair as a star, when only one
    Is shining in the sky.

  She lived unknown, and few could know
    When Lucy ceased to be;
  But she is in her grave, and, oh,
    The difference to me!
  She Dwelt Among the Untrodden Ways (1800)

15 She was a phantom of delight
  When first she gleamed upon my sight.
  She was a Phantom of Delight (1807)

16 A perfect woman, nobly planned,
  To warn, to comfort, and command;
  And yet a spirit still, and bright
  With something of angelic light.

17 A slumber did my spirit seal;
    I had no human fears:
  She seemed a thing that could not feel
    The touch of earthly years.

  No motion has she now, no force;
    She neither hears nor sees;
  Rolled round in earth's diurnal course,
    With rocks, and stones, and trees.
  A Slumber did My Spirit Seal (1800)

18 Earth has not anything to show more fair;
  Dull would he be of soul who could pass
    by
  A sight so touching in its majesty:
  This City now doth, like a garment, wear
  The beauty of the morning; silent, bare,
  Ships, towers, domes, theatres, and tem-
    ples lie
  Open unto the fields, and to the sky;
  All bright and glittering in the smokeless
    air.
  Sonnets. **Composed upon Westminster Bridge**
  (1807)

19 Dear God! the very houses seem asleep;
  And all that mighty heart is lying still!

20 It is a beauteous evening, calm and free,
  The holy time is quiet as a nun,
  Breathless with adoration.
  It is a beauteous evening (1807)

21 We must be free or die, who speak the
    tongue
  That Shakespeare spake; the faith and
    morals hold
  Which Milton held.
  It is not to be thought of (1807)

22 Milton! thou shouldst be living at this
  hour:

England hath need of thee; she is a fen
Of stagnant waters.
Milton! thou shouldst (1807)

1 Plain living and high thinking are no
    more:
    The homely beauty of the good old cause
    Is gone.
    O friend! I know not (1807)

2 Once did she hold the gorgeous East in
    fee,
    And was the safeguard of the West.
    Once did she hold

3 Scorn not the Sonnet; Critic, you have
    frowned,
    Mindless of its just honours; with this key
    Shakespeare unlocked his heart.
    Scorn not the Sonnet (1827)

4 Surprised by joy—impatient as the Wind
    I turned to share the transport—Oh! with
    whom
    But Thee, deep buried in the silent tomb.
    Surprised by joy (1815)

5 Give all thou canst; high Heaven rejects
    the lore
    Of nicely-calculated less or more.
    Tax not the royal Saint (1822)

6 Two Voices are there; one is of the sea,
    One of the mountains; each a mighty
    Voice,
    In both from age to age thou didst rejoice,
    They were thy chosen music, Liberty!
    Two Voices are there (1807)

7 The world is too much with us; late and
    soon,
    Getting and spending, we lay waste our
    powers:
    Little we see in Nature that is ours.
    The world is too much with us (1807)

8   Great God! I'd rather be
    A Pagan suckled in a creed outworn,
    So might I, standing on this pleasant lea,
    Have glimpses that would make me less
    forlorn;
    Have sight of Proteus rising from the sea,
    Or hear old Triton blow his wreathed
    horn.
    See 244:13

9   Our meddling intellect
    Misshapes   the   beauteous   forms   of
    things:—
       We murder to dissect.

    Enough of science and of art;
       Close up these barren leaves.
    Come forth, and bring with you a heart

That watches and receives.
The Tables Turned (1798)

10 I've measured it from side to side:
    'Tis three feet long and two feet wide.
    The Thorn (1798), iii [early reading]

11 O blithe new-comer! I have heard,
    I hear thee and rejoice.
    O Cuckoo! Shall I call thee bird,
    Or but a wandering voice?
    To the Cuckoo (O blithe new-comer!, 1807)

12 Spade! with which Wilkinson hath tilled
    his lands.
    To the Spade of a Friend (1807)

13 Poetry is the spontaneous overflow of
    powerful feelings: it takes its origin from
    emotion recollected in tranquillity.
    Lyrical Ballads, preface to 2nd edn. (1802)

14 Every great and original writer, in propor-
    tion as he is great and original, must him-
    self create the taste by which he is to be
    relished.
    Letter to Lady Beaumont, 21 May 1807

SIR HENRY WOTTON 1568–1639

15 How happy is he born and taught
       That serveth not another's will;
    Whose armour is his honest thought,
       And simple truth his utmost skill!
    The Character of a Happy Life, i

16 This man is freed from servile bands,
       Of hope to rise, or fear to fall:—
    Lord of himself, though not of lands,
       And having nothing, yet hath all.
    vi

17 He first deceas'd; she for a little tri'd
    To live without him: lik'd it not, and di'd.
    Death of Sir Albertus Moreton's Wife

18 You meaner beauties of the night,
       That poorly satisfy our eyes,
    More by your number, than your light;
       You common people of the skies,
    What are you when the moon shall rise?
    On His Mistress, the Queen of Bohemia

19 In *Architecture* as in all other *Operative*
    Arts, the *end* must direct the *Operation*.
    The *end* is to build well. Well building hath
    three Conditions. *Commodity, Firmness,*
    and *Delight*.
    Elements of Architecture (1624), pt.I

20 Take heed of thinking, *The farther you go
    from the church of Rome, the nearer you are
    to God.*
    Izaak Walton, *Sir Henry Wotton,* in Christopher
    Wordsworth, *Ecclesiastical Biography* (1810),
    vol.V, p.44; first published in Walton's first edi-
    tion of *Reliquiae Wottonianae* (1651)

1 An ambassador is an honest man sent to lie abroad for the good of his country.
Written in the Album of Christopher Fleckmore (1604). Izaak Walton, *Life*

SIR THOMAS WYATT 1503?–1542

2 And wilt thou leave me thus?
    Say nay, say nay, for shame.
An Appeal

3 They flee from me, that sometime did me seek
    With naked foot, stalking in my chamber.
I have seen them gentle, tame, and meek,
    That now are wild, and do not remember
    That sometime they put themselves in danger
    To take bread at my hand.
Remembrance

4 When her loose gown from her shoulders did fall,
And she me caught in her arms long and small,
    Therewith all sweetly did me kiss
And softly said, 'Dear heart how like you this?'

WILLIAM WYCHERLEY 1640?–1716

5 A mistress should be like a little country retreat near the town, not to dwell in constantly, but only for a night and away.
The Country Wife (1672–3), Act I.i

6 You [drama critics] who scribble, yet hate all who write…
And with faint praises one another damn.
The Plain Dealer (1677), prologue

XENOPHON c.428/7–c.354 B.C.

7 θάλαττα θάλαττα.
The sea! the sea!
Anabasis, IV.vii.24

AUGUSTIN, MARQUIS DE XIMÉNÈZ 1726–1817

8 *Attaquons dans ses eaux*
La perfide Albion!
Let us attack in her own waters perfidious Albion!
L'Ère des Français (Oct. 1793). *Poésies Révolutionnaires et contre-révolutionnaires* (Paris, 1821), I, p.160. See 45:3

THOMAS RUSSELL YBARRA b. 1880

9 A Christian is a man who feels Repentance on a Sunday

For what he did on Saturday
And is going to do on Monday.
The Christian (1909)

W.F. YEAMES R.A. 1835–1918

10 And when did you last see your father?
Title of painting (1878) now in the Walker Ar Gallery, Liverpool

W.B. YEATS 1865–1939

11 O body swayed to music, O brightening glance,
How can we know the dancer from th dance?
Among School Children, VIII

12 That dolphin-torn, that gong-tormented sea.
Byzantium

13 The intellect of man is forced to choose Perfection of the life, or of the work.
The Choice

14   Now that my ladder's gone,
I must lie down where all the ladders start,
In the foul rag-and-bone shop of the heart
The Circus Animals' Desertion, III

15 A woman can be proud and stiff
When on love intent;
But Love has pitched his mansion in
The place of excrement;
For nothing can be sole or whole
That has not been rent.
Crazy Jane talks to the Bishop

16 Nor dread nor hope attend
A dying animal;
A man awaits his end
Dreading and hoping all.
Death

17 He knows death to the bone—
Man has created death.

18 Down by the salley gardens my love and I did meet;
She passed the salley gardens with little snow-white feet.
She bid me take love easy, as the leaves grow on the tree;
But I, being young and foolish, with her would not agree.
Down by the Salley Gardens

19 All changed, changed utterly:
A terrible beauty is born.
Easter 1916

20 Too long a sacrifice
Can make a stone of the heart.

21 Only God, my dear,
Could love you for yourself alone

And not your yellow hair.
For Anne Gregory

1 Never to have lived is best, ancient writers
   say;
   Never to have drawn the breath of life,
   never to have looked into the eye of
   day;
   The second best's a gay goodnight and
   quickly turn away.
From 'Oedipus at Colonus'

2 The ghost of Roger Casement
  Is beating on the door.
The Ghost of Roger Casement

3 I have spread my dreams under your feet;
  Tread softly because you tread on my
  dreams.
He wishes for the Cloths of Heaven

4 The innocent and the beautiful
  Have no enemy but time.
*In memory of Eva Gore-Booth and Con
Markiewicz*

5 I balanced all, brought all to mind,
  The years to come seemed waste of breath,
  A waste of breath the years behind
  In balance with this life, this death.
An Irish Airman Forsees his Death

6 None other knows what pleasures man
     At table or in bed.
*What shall I do for pretty girls
  Now my old bawd is dead?*
John Kinsella's Lament for Mrs. Mary Moore

7 I will arise and go now, and go to Innis-
   free,
   And a small cabin build there, of clay and
   wattles made:
   Nine bean-rows will I have there, a hive
   for the honey-bee,
   And live alone in the bee-loud glade.
The Lake Isle of Innisfree

8 I will arise and go now, for always night
  and day
  I hear lake water lapping with low sounds
  by the shore;
  While I stand on the roadway, or on the
  pavements gray,
  I hear it in the deep heart's core.

9 A shudder in the loins engenders there
  The broken wall, the burning roof and
  tower
  And Agamemnon dead.
Leda and the Swan

10 Think where man's glory most begins and
   ends,
   And say my glory was I had such friends.
The Municipal Gallery Revisited, VII

11 Where, where but here have Pride and
   Truth,
   That long to give themselves for wage,
   To shake their wicked sides at youth
   Restraining reckless middle age?
*On hearing that the Students of our New Univer-
sity have joined the Agitation against Immoral
Literature*

12 That is no country for old men. The young
   In one another's arms, birds in the trees
   —Those dying generations—at their song,
   The salmon-falls, the mackerel-crowded
   seas,
   Fish, flesh, or fowl, commend all summer
   long
   Whatever is begotten, born, and dies.
Sailing to Byzantium, I

13 An aged man is but a paltry thing,
   A tattered coat upon a stick, unless
   Soul clap its hands and sing, and louder
   sing
   For every tatter in its mortal dress.
   II

14 And therefore I have sailed the seas and
   come
   To the holy city of Byzantium.

15 Turning and turning in the widening gyre
   The falcon cannot hear the falconer;
   Things fall apart; the centre cannot hold;
   Mere anarchy is loosed upon the world,
   The blood-dimmed tide is loosed, and
   everywhere
   The ceremony of innocence is drowned;
   The best lack all conviction, while the
   worst
   Are full of passionate intensity.
The Second Coming

16 And what rough beast, its hour come
   round at last,
   Slouches towards Bethlehem to be born?

17 I thought no more was needed
   Youth to prolong
   Than dumb-bell and foil
   To keep the body young.
   *O who could have foretold
   That the heart grows old?*
A Song

18 And pluck till time and times are done
   The silver apples of the moon
   The golden apples of the sun.
The Song of Wandering Aengus

19 You think it horrible that lust and rage
   Should dance attention upon my old age;
   They were not such a plague when I was
   young;
   What else have I to spur me into song?
The Spur

20 When Pearse summoned Cuchulain to his
   side,

What stalked through the Post Office?
The Statues

1 Irish poets, learn your trade,
Sing whatever is well made,
Scorn the sort now growing up
All out of shape from toe to top.
Under Ben Bulben, V

2 Cast your mind on other days
That we in coming days may be
Still the indomitable Irishry.

3 Under bare Ben Bulben's head
In Drumcliff churchyard Yeats is laid…
On limestone quarried near the spot
By his command these words are cut:

> Cast a cold eye
> On life, on death.
> Horseman, pass by!

VI

4 While on the shop and street I gazed
My body of a sudden blazed;
And twenty minutes more or less
It seemed, so great my happiness,
That I was blessèd and could bless.
Vacillation

5 When you are old and gray and full of
sleep,
And nodding by the fire, take down this
book,
And slowly read, and dream of the soft
look
Your eyes had once, and of their shadows
deep;

How many loved your moments of glad
grace,
And loved your beauty with love false or
true,
But one man loved the pilgrim soul in you,
And loved the sorrows of your changing
face.
When you are Old

EDWARD YOUNG 1683–1765

6   Be wise with speed;
A fool at forty is a fool indeed.
Love of Fame: The Universal Passion (1725–8)
Sat.ii, l.281

7 With skill she vibrates her eternal tongue,
For ever most divinely in the wrong.
Sat.vi, l.106

8 Procrastination is the thief of time.
The Complaint: Night Thoughts (1742–5), Night
l.393

9   Beautiful as sweet!
And young as beautiful! and soft as young,
And gay as soft! and innocent as gay.
Night iii, l.81

10 Man wants but little; nor that little, long.
Night iv, l.122

11 By night an atheist half believes a God.
Night v, l.176

GEORGE W. YOUNG 1846–1919

12 Your lips, on my own, when they printed
'Farewell',
Had never been soiled by the 'beverage of
hell';
But they come to me now with the bacchanal sign,
And the lips that touch liquor must never
touch mine.
*The Lips That Touch Liquor Must Never Touch
Mine;* also attr., in a different form, to Harriet A.
Glazebrook

ÉMILE ZOLA 1840–1902

13 *J'accuse.*
I accuse.
Title of an open letter to the President of the
French Republic, in connection with the Dreyfus
case, published in *L'Aurore,* 13 Jan. 1898

Index

NOTE. The order of the index both in the keywords and in the entries following each keyword is strictly alphabetical. Singular and plural nouns (including their possessive forms) are grouped separately: for 'with some old lover's ghost' see 'lover'; for 'at lovers' perjuries' see 'lovers'. All spellings and word forms appear in the index precisely as they do in the main text.

Foreign words are included in the general alphabetical scheme. A separate Greek index follows the main index.

The references show the author's name, usually in an abbreviated form, followed by the page and item numbers: 163:15 = quotation 15 on page 163.

To save space, the definite and indefinite articles, and the words Oh, O, but, and, for, as, have been dropped from the beginning of most entries, and the alphabetical order is thus decided by more significant words: 'And is it true' is shown as 'is it true'.

Aesculapius: we owe a cock to A.	SOCR 243:8	**aggravating:** She was an a. child	BELL 18:17
aesthetic: high a. line	GILB 108:19	**Agincourt:** affright the air at A.	SHAK 213:8
high a. band	GILB 108:21	**a-gley:** Gang aft a.	BURNS 55:6
aestimemus: Omnes unius a. assis	CAT 65:5	**Agnes:** St A.' Eve	KEATS 138:16
Aetas: fugerit invida A.	HOR 123:14	**agnostic:** appropriate title of 'a.'	HUXL 128:12
afeard: Be not a.	SHAK 232:22	*Agnus: A. Dei*	MASS 163:18
soldier, and a.	SHAK 223:6	**agony:** a. is abated	MAC 157:4
affairs: tide in the a. of men	SHAK 217:3	Hard and bitter a. for us	ELIOT 94:2
affected: His accent was a.	HARE 115:6	it happen and am in a.	CAT 65:1
affection: With a. beaming in one	DICK 84:11	**agree:** does not a. with my constitution	
affections: his a. dark as Erebus	SHAK 226:7		THOR 259:5
holiness of the heart's a. and the truth		**agreement:** with hell are we at a.	BIBLE 30:2
	KEATS 140:15	*agri: modus a. non ita magnus*	HOR 125:1
souls descend T'a.	DONNE 87:27	**a-hunting:** a. we will go	FIEL 98:11
affliction: bread of a. and with water	BIBLE 25:8	We daren't go a.	ALL 2:7
waters of a.	BIBLE 29:3	**aid:** Alliteration's artful a.	CHUR 70:22
affluent: a. society no useful distinction		Summoned the Immediate A.	BELL 18:15
	GALB 104:9	*Aide-toi: A., le ciel t'aidera*	LA F 147:11
afford: unless you can a. it	TROL 260:14	**ail:** what can a. thee	KEATS 139:3
afloat: full sea are we now a.	SHAK 217:3	*aimai: plus j'a. ma patrie*	BELL 19:10
afraid: keep myself from being a.	DRYD 90:21	*aime: C'est mourir à ce qu'on a.*	HAR 114:7
neither tarnished nor a.	CHAN 67:6	*j'a. la Princesse Lointaine*	ROST 197:11
of his near approach a.	GARR 104:15	*aimez: et a. qui vous aime*	VOLT 265:2
stranger and a.	HOUS 126:17	**aiming:** a. at a million	BROW 49:11
that he is a. of his enemy	PLUT 183:18	**aimless:** obscure them by an a. rhetoric	
they were some a.	BIBLE 35:1		HUXL 128:14
Africa: Till China and A. meet	AUDEN 10:8	**ain't:** You a. heard nothin' yet	JOLS 135:13
African: strength of this A. national	MACM 158:1	**air:** a. a solemn stillness holds	GRAY 111:18
after: a. many a summer dies	TENN 255:9	are built with a.	JONS 135:20
A. the first death	THOM 257:8	breathing English a.	BROO 47:16
afternoon: which it seemed always a.	TENN 253:15	fire-folk sitting in the a.	HOPK 122:7
Afton: sweet A.	BURNS 54:7	firmly planted in the a.	RONS 196:10
Agag: A. came unto him delicately	BIBLE 24:21	into thin a.	SHAK 232:24
again: I do it again and a.	CARR 62:18	let out to warm the a.	SWIFT 248:19
Against: A. my fire	SHAK 218:24	my heart an a. that kills	HOUS 126:7
hand will be a. every man	BIBLE 22:24	nipping and an eager a.	SHAK 207:7
He said he was a. it	COOL 78:2	with pinions skim the a.	FRERE 103:1
is not with me is a. me	BIBLE 33:2	**airports:** a. almost deserted	AUDEN 10:15
Agamemnon: A. dead	YEATS 279:9	**airs:** 'don't give yourself a.	CARR 62:19
When A. cried aloud	ELIOT 94:17	Sounds and sweet a.	SHAK 232:22
Agamemnona: Vixere fortes ante A.	HOR 124:17	**Akond:** Is the A. of Swat	LEAR 150:21
age: a. are threescore years	PRAY 189:22	**al:** nat kepe me chaast in a.	CHAU 68:16
A. cannot wither her	SHAK 203:24	**ALARM:** It said 'SPREAD A.	PEN 182:5
A., I do abhor thee	SHAK 235:5	**alarms:** Swept with confused a. of struggle	
A. is deformed	BAST 16:10		ARN 8:13
a. of chivalry is gone	BURKE 53:9	**Alas:** A. but cannot help nor	AUDEN 11:11
a. of chivalry is never	KING 143:2	**Albatross:** I shot the A.	COL 74:8
A. shall not weary them	BINY 42:6	*Albion: La perfide A.*	XIM 278:8
a., which forgives itself	SHAW 238:15	**Alcestis:** me like A. from the grave	MILT 170:12
all the faults of the a.	BALF 14:15	**ale:** be no more cakes and a.	SHAK 233:23
companions for middle a.	BACON 13:13	drink your a.	HOUS 126:16
Crabbed a. and youth	SHAK 235:4	**Aleppo:** Her husband's to A. gone	SHAK 220:2
fetch the a. of gold	MILT 168:9	**Alexandrine:** needless A. ends the song	
He died in a good old a.	BIBLE 25:15		POPE 185:10
He was not of an a.	JONS 136:7	**Alfred:** high tide!' King A.	CHES 69:22
if a. could	EST 97:3	**alibi:** He always has an a.	ELIOT 94:9
Now has come the last a.	VIRG 264:6	**Alice:** A. is marrying one	MILNE 166:11
Old a. is the most unexpected	TROT 260:15	A., where art thou	BUNN 51:14
That men call a.	BROO 47:5	**alien:** a. Church	DISR 86:14
tiresomeness of old a.	ANON 6:17	tears amid the a. corn	KEATS 140:1
who tells one her real a.	WILDE 271:25	With an a. people clutching	ELIOT 94:2
With leaden a. o'ercargoed	FLEC 100:9	*alienum: humani nil a me a. puto*	TER 256:3
worth an a. without a name	MORD 173:5	**alights:** Daintily a. Elaine	BETJ 21:7
aged: a. man is but a paltry	YEATS 279:13	*aliquo: aut a. modo destruator*	MAGN 158:16
don't object to an a. parent	DICK 84:8	*aliter: Dis a. visum*	VIRG 263:5
I saw an a., aged man	CARR 64:14	**alive:** is a. again	BIBLE 35:29
agents: night's black a.	SHAK 222:15	it in that dawn to be a.	WORD 274:17
ages: acts being seven a.	SHAK 205:1	Looking as if she were a.	BROW 50:4
our diff'rent a. move	PRIOR 191:17	noise and tumult when a.	EDW 92:12

Officiously to keep a. CLOU 73:13
still a. at twenty-two KING 143:3
that he is no longer a. BENT 19:17
When I was man a. HOUS 126:2
all: a. for love SPEN 244:17
A. for one DUMAS 91:19
A. for your delight SHAK 227:20
a. hell broke loose MILT 169:11
A. is for the best VOLT 264:16
a. our yesterdays have SHAK 223:15
A. places shall be hell MARL 160:4
A.'s right with the world BROW 50:12
a. that's best of dark BYRON 58:21
A. things are lawful BIBLE 38:11
A. things bright and beautiful ALEX 2:3
a. things to all men BIBLE 38:10
Let a. the world in ev'ry HERB 118:6
man for a. seasons WHIT 270:11
Then a. were for the state MAC 156:7
to have his a. neglected JOHN 131:7
When a. the world is young KING 142:16
Allaying: A. both their fury SHAK 232:14
drop of a. Tiber SHAK 205:14
allegiance: Any victim demands a. GREE 112:16
to swear a. to any master HOR 123:1
allegory: headstrong as an a. SHER 240:20
allemand: hommes et a. à mon cheval CHAR 67:15
alles: Die Welt ist a. WITT 273:7
alley: she lives in our a. CAREY 61:4
alleybi: vy won't there a a. DICK 85:23
Alliteration: apt A.'s artful aid CHUR 70:22
Allons: A., enfants de la patrie ROUG 198:1
Allsopp: Guinness, A., Bass CALV 59:17
All-Souls: at Christ-Church and A. JOHN 132:11
alluring: little scorn is a. CONG 76:24
alms: he puts a. for oblivion SHAK 233:8
When thou doest a. BIBLE 31:20
aloft: now he's gone a. DIBD 83:10
alone: all a. went she KING 142:12
A. I did it SHAK 206:1
A. on a wide wide sea COL 74:14
A., poor maid MEW 165:13
alone than when wholly a. CIC 72:9
Are we here together a. WHIT 270:3
down a. bent on his prey MILT 169:5
In leafy dells a. HOUS 126:22
I want to be a. GARBO 104:12
left him a. with his glory WOLFE 273:22
mortal millions live *a.* ARN 8:15
never less a. than when ROG 195:19
that the man should be a. BIBLE 22:8
Will he not let us a. DONNE 88:13
Alph: A., the sacred river COL 75:2
Alpha: I am A. and Omega BIBLE 40:28
Alpine: on the A. mountains cold MILT 170:9
Alps: O'er the white A. alone DONNE 87:23
altar: a. with this inscription BIBLE 37:23
altars: even thy a., O Lord PRAY 189:17
alteration: alters when it a. finds SHAK 236:12
altered: a. her person for the worse SWIFT 249:7
alternatives: more a., the more difficult ALL 2:6
altogether: I shall not a. die HOR 124:13
alway: I am with you a. BIBLE 34:19
always: a. to verify your references ROUTH 198:3
research is a. incomplete PATT 181:11
am: Here I a., and here I stay MACM 157:17
I AM THAT I A. BIBLE 23:12
therefore I a. DESC 83:5
what I a., none cares CLARE 72:21

amantum: *alto periuria ridet a.* OVID 178:20
amari: *Surgit a. aliquid quod* LUCR 155:9
Amaryllis: To sport with A. MILT 167:20
amateurs: disease that afflicts a. CHES 70:10
amaz'd: a., and curious BURNS 55:1
amaze: these cogitations still a. ELIOT 93:13
amazed: a., temperate, and furious SHAK 222:8
Silent and a. even when WHIT 269:16
ambassador: a. is an honest man sent WOTT 278:1
ambiguities: Till we can clear these a. SHAK 232:7
Ambition: A., Distraction CARR 63:8
a. mock their useful toil GRAY 112:3
Art not without a. SHAK 220:10
fling away a. SHAK 215:10
That make a. virtue SHAK 229:4
Vaulting a. SHAK 221:1
ambitious: Brutus says he was a. SHAK 216:17
he was a.. SHAK 216:14
told you Caesar was a. SHAK 216:16
ambo: *Arcades a.* VIRG 264:7
âme: *Quelle â. est sans défauts* RIMB 195:8
amemus: *atque a.* CAT 65:5
Amen: A.' Stuck in my throat SHAK 221:15
sound of a great A. PROC 191:21
amenities: meaning 'a.' CAT 65:10
America: A. is just ourselves ARN 9:6
A. was thus clearly top SELL 203:4
ask not what A. will do KENN 141:13
O my A. DONNE 87:25
You cannot conquer A. PITT 183:8
American: new deal for the A. RONS 196:7
Americans: brave A. all DICK 86:7
Good A. APPL 7:11
when bad A. die WILDE 271:23
worse Than ignorant A. MASS 164:2
amiable: a. weakness FIEL 98:10
how a. are thy dwellings PRAY 189:17
Amicus: A. Plato ARIS 8:8
amidst: I sat musing a. the ruins GIBB 106:8
amiral: a. pour encourager les VOLT 264:15
amitié: L'a. de la connaissance BUSS 55:23
ammer: 'a. along the 'ard 'igh PUNCH 192:15
ammunition: pass the a. FORGY 101:11
Amo: A., amas OKEE 177:14
Non a. te, Sabidi MART 161:8
Odi et a. CAT 65:11
among: a. the English Poets KEATS 141:5
Amor: A. vincit omnia CHAU 68:3
Omnia vincit A. VIRG 264:8
amorous: a. of their strokes SHAK 203:22
excite my a. propensities JOHN 131:5
amour: *faire l'a. en tout temps* BEAU 16:16
L'a., tel qu'il existe CHAM 66:17
L'a. vient de l'aveuglement BUSS 55:23
ample: cabin'd a. Spirit ARN 8:18
ampullas: *a. et sesquipedalia verba* HOR 122:14
Amurath: Not A. an Amurath succeeds SHAK 213:3
Amused: be A. by its Presumption THUR 259:12
We are not a. VICT 262:9
amusent: *Anglais s'a. tristement* SULL 248:8
anarchy: a. and despotism SHEL 240:10
a. prevails in my kitchen JOHN 134:12
Mere a. is loosed upon YEATS 279:15
ancestors: look backward to their a. BURKE 53:8
ancestral: a. fields with his own HOR 123:9
ancestry: I can trace my a. back GILB 108:1
without pride of a. POWER 186:15
ancient: a. grudge I bear him SHAK 224:19

A. of days did sit	BIBLE 30:11
A. person of my heart	ROCH 195:17
a. profession in the world	KIPL 146:21
It is an a. Mariner	COL 74:5
Time makes a. good uncouth	LOW 154:19
very a. and fish-like smell	SHAK 232:16
anders: Ich kann nicht a.	LUTH 155:12
Anderson: John A. my jo	BURNS 54:12
angat: quod in ipsis floribus a.	LUCR 155:9
angel: a. of the Lord came upon	BIBLE 35:1
A. of the Lord came down	TATE 250:17
better a. is a man right fair	SHAK 231:2
in action how like an a.	SHAK 208:14
Is man an ape or an a.	DISR 86:18
ministering a. thou	SCOTT 202:2
ministering a. shall my	SHAK 211:13
What a. wakes me from my	SHAK 227:8
White as an a. is the English	BLAKE 43:15
Who wrote like an a.	GARR 104:14
Angeli: Non Angli sed A.	GREG 113:1
angelic: With something of a. light	WORD 276:16
angel-infancy: Shin'd in my a.	VAUG 261:14
angel of death: a. has been abroad throughout	BRIG 46:14
A. spread his wings	BYRON 57:17
Angels: A. alone, that soar above	LOV 154:9
A. and ministers of grace	SHAK 207:9
a. of God ascending	BIBLE 22:32
a. with outspread wings	PROU 192:5
By that sin fell the a.	SHAK 215:10
entertained a. unawares	BIBLE 40:11
flights of a. sing thee	SHAK 212:1
fools rush in where a.	POPE 185:14
Four a. to my bed	ANON 4:6
his a. charge over thee	PRAY 190:1
little lower than the a.	BETJ 21:3
nor life, nor a.	BIBLE 37:39
Now walk the a.	MARL 160:17
tongues of men and of a.	BIBLE 38:14
anger: Achilles' cursed a. sing	HOMER 120:19
A. is one of the sinews	FULL 104:3
A. makes dull men witty	ELIZ 95:15
either a. or zealousness	TAC 250:9
in sorrow than in a.	SHAK 207:4
In the contempt and a.	SHAK 234:7
Juno's never-forgetting a.	VIRG 262:15
life of telegrams and a.	FORS 101:16
thy mistress some rich a.	KEATS 139:17
anges: a. aux ailes éployées	PROU 192:5
Anglais: A. s'amusent tristement	SULL 248:8
angle: Themselves in every a. greet	MARV 161:14
Angles: Not A. but Angels	GREG 113:1
Angleterre: L'A. est une nation de boutiquiers	NAP 174:12
la perfide A.	BOSS 45:3
Anglicana: A. ecclesia libera	MAGN 158:15
angling: a. or float fishing I can	JOHN 134:11
Anglo-Saxon: those are A. attitudes	CARR 64:11
angry: 'a. young men' of England	FEAR 97:18
Be ye a. and sin not	BIBLE 39:13
proud and a. dust	HOUS 126:16
that's a. with me	BROW 48:6
when she's a. she is keen	SHAK 227:13
when very a., swear	TWAIN 261:5
anguis: Latet a. in herba	VIRG 264:5
anguish: When pain and a. wring	SCOTT 202:2
With a. moist and fever	KEATS 139:4
Angulus: A. ridet	HOR 124:2
angusta: Res a. domi	JUV 137:19

animae: a. naturaliter Christianae	TERT 256:6
animal: a., and mineral	GILB 109:1
by nature a political a.	ARIS 8:4
Cet a. est très méchant	ANON 5:15
coitum omne a. triste	ANON 7:3
err is human, not to, a.	FROST 103:11
life is to be a good a.	SPEN 244.5
Man is a noble a.	BROW 48:13
Man is a tool-making a.	FRAN 102:13
only a. that blushes	TWAIN 261:3
This a. is very bad	ANON 5:15
animalculous: scientific names of beings a.	GILB 109:1
animals: could turn and live with a.	WHIT 270:6
Animula: A. vagula blandula	HAER 113:8
ankles: One praised her a.	TENN 251:3
Annabel Lee: I and my A.	POE 183:19
annals: a. are blank in history-books	CARL 61:11
simple a. of the poor	GRAY 112:3
Anne: ma soeur A.	PERR 182:16
Annihilating: A. all that's made	MARV 161:16
annoy: He only does it to a.	CARR 62:22
anointed: a. Solomon	BIBLE 24:31
hast a. my head with oil	PRAY 188:16
wash the balm from an a.	SHAK 230:5
anointing: Thou the a. Spirit art	PRAY 191:12
another: love one a. or die	AUDEN 11:6
members one of a.	BIBLE 39:12
woman can forgive a.	GAY 105:8
Answer: A. a fool according	BIBLE 26:29
a. came there none	CARR 64:3
a. came there none	SCOTT 201:12
He would a. to 'Hi	CARR 62:5
soft a. turneth away wrath	BIBLE 26:19
what a dusty a. gets	MER 165:5
What *is* the a.	STEIN 246:1
Why Did You A. the Phone	THUR 259:13
answer'd: grievously hath Caesar. it	SHAK 216:16
answered: have a. three questions	CARR 62:19
He a. the description	FARQ 97:16
no one a.	DE L 82:14
ant: Go to the a. thou sluggard	BIBLE 26:8
antan: où sont les neiges d'a.	VILL 262:13
anthem: thy plaintive a. fades	KEATS 140:1
antic: dance an a. hay	MARL 160:9
Antichrist: like A. in that lewd hat	JONS 135:17
antidote: some sweet oblivious a.	SHAK 223:13
antique: noble and nude and a.	SWIN 249:17
traveller from an a. land	SHEL 239:16
Antiquity: I will write for A.	LAMB 148:1
anvil: sword of this stone and a.	MAL 159:6
anxiety: 'caused me a little a.'	MACM 157:19
repose is taboo'd by a.	GILB 107:20
rider's back sits dark A.	HOR 124:6
anxious: you're a. for to shine	GILB 108:19
any: If a. of you know cause	PRAY 187:23
anybody: 'Is there a. there	DE L 82:13
Then no one's a.	GILB 107:9
apart: of man's life a thing a.	BYRON 58:2
Things fall a.	YEATS 279:15
ape: a. for his grandfather	HUXL 128:14
exception is a naked a.	MORR 173:11
Is man an a. or an angel	DISR 86:18
apes: a., and peacocks	BIBLE 25:3
a. and peacocks	MAS 162:14
Now for dogs and a.	BROW 49:10
aphorism: corroboration of this a.	BIRK 42:7
aphrodisiac: circumambulating a.	FRY 103:20

Apollo: burnèd is A.'s laurel | MARL 160:8
harsh after the songs of A. | SHAK 219:15
apologise: I never a. | SHAW 237:9
apology: a. for plain-speaking with | DICK 83:15
apostle: rank as an a. in the high | GILB 108:21
Apostolick: Catholick and A. Church | PRAY 187:14
apothecary: starved a. than a starved poet | LOCK 152:14
apparel: a. oft proclaims the man | SHAK 207:6
apparition: was an a. | AUBR 10:7
Appeal: A. from Philip drunk | ANON 3:4
appearances: Keep up a. | CHUR 70:21
appétit: L'a. vient en mangeant | RAB 193:12
appetite: a. may sicken | SHAK 233:14
good digestion wait on a. | SHAK 222:17
increase of a. had grown | SHAK 206:15
satisfying a voracious a. | FIEL 98:9
appetites: men's carnal lusts and a. | PRAY 187:24
Applaud: A. us when we run | BURKE 53:2
apple: a. trees will never get | FROST 103:7
Just as the sweet-a. reddens | SAPP 200:1
young and easy under the a. | THOM 257:2
apple-pie: to make an a. | FOOTE 101:7
apples: a., cherries | DICK 85:13
comfort me with a. | BIBLE 27:28
Ripe a. drop about my head | MARV 161:15
silver a. of the moon | YEATS 279:18
stolen, be your a. | HUNT 128:6
apple-tree: My heart is like an a. | ROSS 197:3
applications: seulement des a. de la science | PAST 181:7
applied: such things as a. sciences | PAST 181:7
apply: a. our hearts unto wisdom | PRAY 189:23
apprehension: a. of the good | SHAK 229:20
of death is most in a. | SHAK 224:1
appris: Ils n'ont rien a. | TALL 250:14
oublié et n'ont rien a. | DUM 91:20
approach: Much of his near a. afraid | GARR 104:15
Approbation: A. from Sir Hubert Stanley | MORT 174:2
approve: I do not a. | MILL 166:3
April: A. is the cruellest month | ELIOT 94:18
A.'s in the west wind | MAS 163:5
I've an A. blindness | FRY 103:17
Men are A. when they woo | SHAK 205:10
Now that A.'s there | BROW 49:12
uncertain glory of an A. day | SHAK 234:17
When proud-pied A. | SHAK 236:9
Aprill: Whan that A. with his shoures | CHAU 67:17
aprons: made themselves a. | BIBLE 22:12
apt: a. Alliteration's artful | CHUR 70:22
find myself so a. to die | SHAK 216:10
aptitude: grande a. à la patience | BUFF 51:7
greater a. for patience | BUFF 51:7
Aquitaine: prince d'A. à la tour | NERV 175:11
Arabia: all the perfumes of A. | SHAK 223:8
with the spell of far A. | DE L 82:9
Arabian: She is alone the A. bird | SHAK 206:2
Arabs: like the A. | LONG 153:3
Araby: That burns in glorious A. | DARL 81:13
Araminta: A., say 'No | PRAED 186:16
arbiter: Elegantiae a. | TAC 250:10
arbitrate: Does a. th' event | MILT 167:7
arbitrator: that old common a. | SHAK 233:13
arboreal: probably a. in its habits | DARW 81:14
Arcades: A. ambo | VIRG 264:7
Arcadia: Et in A. ego | ANON 6:16
Arcadians: A. both | VIRG 264:7

arceo: Odi profanum vulgus et a. | HOR 124:5
Archangel: A. a little damaged | LAMB 147:19
arches: down the a. of the years | THOM 258:1
Architecture: A. in general is frozen | SCH 201:1
New styles of a. | AUDEN 11:5
archy: jamais triste a. | MARQ 161:2
arcs: earth the broken a. | BROW 48:15
ardet: paries cum proximus a. | HOR 123:6
ardeur: a. dans mes veines cachée | RAC 193:17
ardua: Per a. ad astra | ANON 7:2
are: Let them be as they a. | CLEM 73:6
we know what we a. | SHAK 211:1
will tell you what you a. | BRIL 46:18
argent: l'a. ou de la petite monnaie | CHAM 66:16
argosies: a. of magic sails | TENN 253:10
argue: earth does not a. | WHIT 270:8
he could a. still | GOLD 110:10
It is as absurd to a. men | NEWM 176:2
arguing: I am not a. with you | WHIS 269:11
There is no a. with Johnson | GOLD 111:1
argument: heard great a. | FITZ 99:5
highth of this great a. | MILT 168:14
nice knock-down a. for you | CARR 64:8
Tories own no a. but force | BROW 48:15
to stir without great a. | SHAK 210:24
Whigs admit no force but a. | BROW 48:15
Argus: Though A. were her eunuch | SHAK 219:9
aright: sought the Lord a. | BURNS 54:2
arise: ah for a man to a. in me | TENN 253:20
I will a. and go now | YEATS 279:7
My lady sweet, a. | SHAK 206:3
Aristocrat: A. who banks with Coutts | GILB 107:5
aristocratic: with the a. stalk | DICK 84:16
Arithmetic: different branches of A. | CARR 63:8
arithmetical: increases in an a. ratio | MALT 159:7
Ark: straight out of the A. | SMITH 242:16
two unto Noah into the A. | BIBLE 22:20
arm: gather the lambs with his a. | BIBLE 29:10
Human on my faithless a. | AUDEN 11:3
one a. bent across your | SASS 200:8
shewed strength with his a. | BIBLE 34:29
smal coral aboute hire a. | CHAU 68:3
Arma: A. virumque cano | VIRG 262:15
Cedant a. togae | CIC 72:8
Nunc a. defunctumque bello | HOR 124:11
Armadas: hammock till the great A. | NEWB 175:14
arm-chair: loving that old a. | ELIZ 78:1
arm-chairs: wearing a. tight | WOD 273:15
armies: ignorant a. clash by night | ARN 8:13
interested in a. and fleets | AUDEN 10:13
armour: a. stripped from Achilles | VIRG 263:4
his a. wherein he trusted | BIBLE 35:16
Put on the whole a. of God | BIBLE 39:14
put upon us the a. of light | PRAY 187:6
us put on the a. of light | BIBLE 38:5
Whose a. is his honest | WOTT 277:15
you the whole a. of God | BIBLE 39:15
arms: are the everlasting a. | BIBLE 24:2
a. against a sea of troubles | SHAK 208:24
a. and the man who first | VIRG 262:15
a. long and small | WYATT 278:4
A., take your last embrace | SHAK 232:6
a. ye forge, another bears | SHEL 240:2
corners of the world in a. | SHAK 217:16
if my love were in my a. | ANON 5:10
Imparadised in one another's a. | MILT 169:9
in my a. till break | AUDEN 11:3
So he laid down his a. | HOOD 121:5
To war and a. I fly | LOV 154:10

army: a. marches on its stomach | NAP 174:14
contemptible little A. | WILH 272:7
fighting with your land a. | MONT 172:8
Grand A. never looked | MAHAN 159:2
Aroint: A. thee, witch | SHAK 220:2
Arques: we fought at A. and you | HENR 117:12
arrangements: has no a. | WHIT 270:8
array: To summon his a. | MAC 156:3
arrayed: all his glory was not a. | BIBLE 31:25
arrest: Is swift in his a. | SHAK 211:20
Arrival Angots A. is closely connected | CONN 77:9
arrive: be to a. where we started | ELIOT 93:20
better thing than to a. | STEV 247:4
arriving: a. in the evening than | CONN 77:8
arrogant: submitted and to subdue the a. | VIRG 263:14
arrow: a. that flieth by day | PRAY 189:24
I have shot mine a. o'er | SHAK 211:18
I shot an a. into the air | LONG 153:1
arrows: a. in the hand of the giant | PRAY 190:20
Bring me my a. of desire | BLAKE 43:2
slings and a. of outrageous | SHAK 208:24
arse: Sit on your a. for fifty | MACN 158:6
arsenal: great a. of democracy | RONS 196:11
art: a. can wash her guilt | GOLD 110:18
a. constantly aspires towards | PATER 181:9
A. for art's sake and with | CONS 77:16
a. for art's sake…the beautiful | COUS 78:16
A. is a jealous mistress | EMER 96:9
A. is the only thing that | BOWEN 45:13
Desiring this man's a. | SHAK 235:11
emotion in the form of a. | ELIOT 95:11
ensnaring a. | BURNS 54:3
est la probité de l'a. | INGR 129:14
is the a. of the possible | BISM 42:11
is the true test of a. | INGR 129:14
l'a. beau ne peut être la | COUS 78:16
L'a. pour l'art et sans | CONS 77:16
Minister that meddles with a. | MELB 164:16
More matter with less a. | SHAK 208:7
next to Nature, A. | LAND 148:8
strains of unpremeditated a. | SHEL 240:4
symbol of Irish a. | JOYCE 137:4
That Shakespeare wanted A. | JONS 136:12
unsettling element in modern a. | WHAR 269:9
when A. Is too precise | HERR 118:18
without a. is brutality | RUSK 198:7
artes: (Hae tibi erunt a.) | VIRG 263:14
Arthur: He's in A.'s bosom | SHAK 213:12
talks of A.'s death | SHAK 217:13
article: be snuff'd out by an a. | BYRON 58:12
of being the correct a. | ASHF 9:21
artifex: Qualis a. pereo | NERO 175:10
artificer: Another lean unwash'd a. | SHAK 217:13
great a. Made my mate | STEV 247:14
Old father, old a. | JOYCE 137:2
artillery: It is love's great a. | CRAS 80:10
artisan: give employment to the a. | BELL 19:2
artist: Never trust the a. | LAWR 149:18
true a. will let his wife | SHAW 238:3
West and from now on an a. | CONN 77:10
What an a. dies with me | NERO 175:10
artistic: a. performance requires | JAMES 130:5
a. temperament is a disease | CHES 70:10
give a. verisimilitude | GILB 108:14
arts: Dear nurse of a. | SHAK 214:5
No a.; no letters | HOBB 120:1
Where grew the a. of war | BYRON 58:6

ascending: angels of God a. and descending | BIBLE 22:32
Ash: Oak, and A., and Thorn | KIPL 146:2
ashamed: are a. of our naked skins | SHAW 238:1
be a. to own he has been | POPE 186:1
to beg I am a. | BIBLE 35:30
ashbuds: More black than a. | TENN 251:14
ashes: Are a. under Uricon | HOUS 126:5
a. of his fathers | MAC 156:4
a. to ashes | PRAY 188:5
fire and was burnt to a. | GRAH 111:10
into a. all my lust | MARV 161:21
little monograph on the a. | DOYLE 89:11
splendid in a. | BROW 48:13
turn the universe to a. | CEL 65:14
Asia: army on the mainland of A. | MONT 172:8
ye pampered Jades of A. | MARL 161:1
Ask: A., and it shall be given | BIBLE 32:5
a. not what your country | KENN 141:13
asked: Oliver Twist has a. for more | DICK 85:5
You a. for it | MOL 171:10
Askelon: not in the streets of A. | BIBLE 24:25
asking: is the first time of a. | PRAY 187:23
asks: a. no questions isn't told | KIPL 145:15
asleep: are too young to fall a. | SASS 200:9
Got 'tween a. and wake | SHAK 217:19
he lies fast a. | FITZ 98:18
men were all a. the snow | BRID 46:12
sucks the nurse a. | SHAK 204:11
very houses seem a. | WORD 276:19
Asperges: A. me hyssopo | BIBLE 41:12
aspersion: a. upon my parts of speech | SHER 240:18
aspires: All art constantly a. towards | PATER 181:9
ass: ashamed the law is such an a. | CHAP 67:8
a. will not mend his pace | SHAK 211:10
Bumble…'the law is a a. | DICK 85:8
jaw of an a. have I slain | BIBLE 24:12
Wild A. | FITZ 98:18
Assassination: A. is the quickest way | MOL 171:13
if the a. Could trammel | SHAK 220:13
Assassiner: A. c'est le plus court | MOL 171:13
assassins: que MM les a. commencent | KARR 138:12
assembled: Once again a. here | BUCK 51:4
assembly: parliament is a *deliberative* a. | BURKE 52:15
assent: a. with civil leer | POPE 184:20
asses: riches to those gross a. | LUTH 155:10
assis: Omnes unius aestimemus a. | CAT 65:5
Assume: A. a virtue | SHAK 210:19
assumed: name Achilles a. | BROW 48:12
assurance: a. of a sleepwalker | HITL 119:14
I'll make a. double sure | SHAK 223:1
Assyrian: A. came down like the wolf | BYRON 57:16
Astolat: lily maid of A. | TENN 251:19
astonish: of things that would a. | GILB 107:16
astonished: a. at my own moderation | CLIVE 73:7
astonishment: Your a.'s odd | ANON 3:9
astra: Per ardua ad a. | ANON 7:2
sic itur ad a. | VIRG 264:2
astray: like sheep have gone a. | BIBLE 29:15
asunder: let not man put a. | BIBLE 33:20
together let no man put a. | PRAY 188:2
Atahualpa: who strangled A. | MAC 156:16
ate: a. when we were not hungry | SWIFT 249:2
He a. and drank as he was | HOFF 120:7
With A. by his side | SHAK 216:13
atheism: inclineth man's mind to a. | BACON 12:23

atheist: By night an a. half believes YOUNG 280:11
here a female a. talks JOHN 135:5
Athens: Truths as refin'd as ever A. ARMS 8:9
athirst: that is a. of the fountain BIBLE 41:9
Atkins: Thank you, Mister A. KIPL 145:19
atomic: a. bomb is a paper tiger MAO 159:15
primordial a. globule GILB 108:1
atoms: fortuitous concurrence of a. PALM 180:1
atom-streams: I saw the flaring a. TENN 253:17
attach: Where people wish to a. AUST 12:6
attack: both with his plan of a. SASS 200:12
dared a. my Chesterton BELL 18:25
I shall a. FOCH 101:6
attacked: when a. it defends itself ANON 5:15
attain: I cannot a. unto it PRAY 191:2
attained: Were not a. by sudden flight LONG 153:6
attaque: *Quand on l'a. il se défend* ANON 5:15
attempt: a. and not the deed SHAK 221:13
attempted: Something a., something done
LONG 153:18
attendant: Am an a. lord ELIOT 94:7
attendre: *J'ai failli a.* LOUI 154:6
attention: serious a. than history ARIS 8:6
attentions: a. proceed from the impulse
AUST 12:12
Attic: A. shape KEATS 139:15
glory of the A. stage ARN 9:5
She sleeps up in the a. MEW 165:13
attired: suitably a. in leather HOUS 127:3
attitudes: those are Anglo-Saxon a. CARR 64:11
attorney: in love with a rich a.'s GILB 109:9
office boy to an A.'s GILB 108:28
attribute: is an a. to God himself SHAK 225:17
Auburn: Sweet A. GOLD 110:5
audace: *et toujours de l'a.* DANT 81:11
audacia: *a. certe Laus erit* PROP 192:1
audacity: Arm me, a. SHAK 206:2
aude: *sapere a.* HOR 123:3
au-dessus: can't say a. de sa gare RATT 194:12
audience: a. into the middle HOR 122:17
audit: a. The accounts later MACN 158:4
auditorem: *secus ac notas a. rapit* HOR 122:17
Augescunt: *A. aliae gentes* LUCR 155:7
augury: we defy a. SHAK 211:17
August: A. for the people and their AUDEN 10:12
To recommence in A. BYRON 58:14
Augustus: A. was a chubby lad HOFF 120:7
Aureaṇ: *A. quisquis mediocritatem* HOR 124:3
austere: beauty cold and a. RUSS 198:11
Australia: so much interested in A. WILDE 271:15
that he was born in A. SHAW 237:21
Austria: Don John of A. is going CHES 70:1
auteur: *s'attendait de voir un a.* PASC 180:15
author: a. and giver of all good PRAY 187:8
If it's by a good a. SHAW 237:16
Jesus the a. and finisher BIBLE 40:9
authority: Dress'd in a little brief a. SHAK 223:18
I am a man under a. BIBLE 32:14
nor to usurp a. over BIBLE 39:26
Rulers have no a. from MAYH 164:10
authors: been much exposed to a. WELL 268:6
reciprocal civility of a. JOHN 134:24
We a. DISR 87:5
autocrate: *je serai a.* CATH 65:2
Autolycus: My father named me A. SHAK 234:22
automne: *violons De l'a.* VERL 262:2
autres: *ce sont les a.* REN 194:15
l'Enfer, c'est les A. SART 200:2
pour encourager les a. VOLT 264:15

Autumn: thou breath of A.'s being SHEL 239:12
traveller's joy beguiles in a. HOUS 126:22
when the mists in a. KING 143:5
Autumnal: have seen in one A. face DONNE 87:21
Autumn-fields: looking on the happy A.
TENN 254:10
availeth: struggle naught a. CLOU 73:17
avails: a. the sceptred race LAND 148:12
avarice: beyond the dreams of a. JOHN 133:17
beyond the dreams of a. MOORE 172:11
Ave: *A. Caesar* ANON 6:13
A. Maria ANON 6:14
A. verum corpus ANON 6:15
Avenge: A., O Lord MILT 170:9
averages: fugitive from th' law of a. MAUL 164:9
Averno: *Facilis descensus A.* VIRG 263:10
aversion: closely bordering on a. STEV 246:18
aveuglement: *L'amour vient de l'a.* BUSS 55:23
Avilion: island-valley of A. TENN 252:8
avis: *Rara a. in terris nigroque* JUV 137:20
avoiding: superstition in a. superstition
BACON 13:23
Awaiting: A. the sensation of a short GILB 108:9
Awake: A., beloved LONG 153:18
clamour keep her still a. SHAK 232:9
use its guard staying a. BIBLE 41:15
which I am trying to a. JOYCE 137:6
awaked: So the Lord a. as one out PRAY 189:16
aware: infant child is not a. HOUS 127:5
made a. BROO 47:16
away: I wish he'd stay a. MEAR 164:11
suddenly vanish a. CARR 62:7
awe: In a. of such a thing SHAK 215:15
increasing wonder and a. KANT 138:6
aweary: my little body is a. SHAK 224:12
awf'lly: It's a. bad luck on Diana BETJ 20:15
awkward: a. squad fire over me BURNS 55:10
awoke: a. one morning and found BYRON 59:6
axe: is laid unto the root BIBLE 31:6
a.'s edge did try MARV 161:17
Lizzie Borden took an a. ANON 4:3
offence is let the great a. SHAK 211:8
Azores: At Flores in the A. Sir TENN 255:3
babbled: a' b. of green fields SHAK 213:12
Babe: B. leaps up on his Mother's WORD 275:14
Finger of birth-strangled b. SHAK 222:23
like a naked new-born b. SHAK 221:1
love the b. that milks SHAK 221:6
Babel: bother at the tower of B. VOLT 265:3
babes: mouth of very b. and sucklings PRAY 188:7
babies: hates dogs and b. ROST 197:12
Bab-lock-hithe: stripling Thames at B. ARN 8:20
baboon: Into b. and monkey SHAK 233:4
Baby: B. in an ox's stall BETJ 20:7
first b. laughed BARR 16:2
not see my b. at my breast SHAK 204:11
Babylon: B. is fallen BIBLE 41:4
B.! O Carthage SASS 200:15
B. THE GREAT BIBLE 41:5
I was a King in B. HENL 117:9
waters of B. we sat PRAY 191:1
bacchanal: me now with the b. sign YOUNG 280:12
Bacchus: Of B. and his revellers MILT 169:14
Baccy: 'B. for the Clerk KIPL 145:15
bachelor: pleasant dining with a b. GASK 105:4
back: at my b. from time to time ELIOT 95:3
at my b. I always hear MARV 161:21
b. to the shop Mr John LOCK 152:14
borne me on his b. SHAK 211:11

I sit on a man's b. — TOLS 259:19
looking b. — BIBLE 35:10
never turned his b. — BROW 48:22
one by one b. in the Closet — FITZ 99:7
them to the b. o' beyont — SCOTT 202:4
wife looked b. — BIBLE 22:25
backing: always b. into the limelight — BERN 20:3
backs: making the beast with two b. — SHAK 228:15
With our b. to the wall — HAIG 113:9
backward: look b. to their ancestors — BURKE 53:8
bacon. b.'s not the only thing — KING 143:4
b. was nat fet for hem — CHAU 68:17
bad: b., and dangerous to know — LAMB 147:1
B. Thing — SELL 203:4
because we put up with b. — TROL 260:7
being a little b. — SHAK 224:9
bold b. man — SHAK 215:6
cannot be of a b. colour — BECK 17:6
find the world ugly and b. — NIET 176:18
it's always a b. sign — MITF 171:2
nothing either good or b. — SHAK 208:12
sad and b. and mad — BROW 49:9
shocking b. hats in my life — WELL 268:2
so much b. in the best — ANON 5:2
such thing as b. weather — RUSK 198:10
This animal is very b. — ANON 5:15
was not really b. at heart — BELL 18:17
badge: sufferance is the b. — SHAK 224:21
badgers: When b. fight then everyone's — CLARE 72:16
badly: it is worth doing b. — CHES 70:13
bag: b. and baggage — GLAD 109:15
eggs inside a paper b. — ISH 129:16
not with b. and baggage — SHAK 205:4
bagpipe: when the b. sings i' — SHAK 225:14
Bainters: hate all Boets and B. — GEOR 106:1
baits: while good news b. — MILT 170:4
baked: 'You have b. me too brown — CARR 63:13
balance: b. of power — WALP 266:9
In b. with this life — YEATS 279:5
balanced: I b. all — YEATS 279:5
balances: Thou art weighed in the b. — BIBLE 30:9
bald: b. and unconvincing narrative — GILB 108:14
If I were fierce and b. — SASS 200:4
baldness: felicity on the far side of b. — SMITH 242:7
bales: dropping down with costly b. — TENN 253:10
Balkans: damned silly thing in the B. — BISM 42:13
ball: at a girl throwing a b. — WOOLF 274:8
B. no question makes — FITZ 99:8
Ruddy B. has taken flight — THOM 258:8
ballad: I met with a b. — CALV 59:16
ballads: b., songs and snatches — GILB 107:24
permitted to make all the b. — FLET 100:15
balloon: moon's a b. — CUMM 81:2
balloons: Are light as b. — FROST 103:4
ballot: b. is stronger than — LINC 151:16
balls: our rackets to these b. — SHAK 213:10
two pitch b. — SHAK 219:9
Balm: B. of hurt minds — SHAK 221:16
Can wash the b. from — SHAK 230:5
Is there no b. in Gilead — BIBLE 29:25
baloney: it's still b. — SMITH 242:5
bamboozle: to understand I would b. — GREE 112:17
banal: *Eldorado b. de tous les vieux* — BAUD 16:13
Banbury: To B. came — BRAT 46:7
band: b., and hymn-book too — WILB 270:15
high aesthetic b. — GILB 108:21
we b. of brothers — SHAK 214:4
Bandusiae: *fons B. splendidior vitro* — HOR 124:10

bane: Deserve the precious b. — MILT 168:18
bang: b. these dogs of Seville — TENN 255:4
with a b. but a whimper — ELIOT 93:24
banish: Everything did b. moan — BARN 15:17
bank: b. and shoal of time — SHAK 220:13
b. whereon the wild thyme — SHAK 227:5
cried all the way to the b. — LIB 151:14
George goes to sleep at a b. — JER 130:17
moonlight sleeps upon this b. — SHAK 226:5
pregnant b. swelled up — DONNE 87:26
Bankers thought he saw a B.'s Clerk — CARR 62:12
banks: b. and braes o' bonny Doon — BURNS 55:8
banned: that any book should be b. — WEST 269:3
banner: b. with the strange device — LONG 153:4
His b. over me was love — BIBLE 27:27
'Tis the star-spangled b. — KEY 141:15
yet thy b. — BYRON 57:12
banners: b. of the king advance — VEN 261:20
Confusion on thy b. wait — GRAY 111:16
banquet: Prayer the Church's b. — HERB 118:13
Baptism: Godmothers in my B. — PRAY 187:18
bar: be no moaning of the b. — TENN 251:11
Get up and b. the door — BALL 14:16
When I went to the B. — GILB 107:15
Barabbas: Now B. was a robber — BIBLE 37:5
Now B. was a publisher — CAMP 60:19
barajar: *paciencia y b.* — CERV 66:8
barbarians: become of us without any b. — CAV 65:12
his young b. all at play — BYRON 57:13
with the B. quite left — ARN 9:6
barbe: *laisserons pousser notre b.* — FLAU 100:6
barber: b.'s chair that fits all — SHAK 203:13
Barbiton: *B. hic paries habebit* — HOR 124:11
Bard: Hear the voice of the B. — BLAKE 43:6
This goat-footed b. — KEYN 141:18
Bards: B. of Passion and of Mirth — KEATS 139:11
Bare: B. ruin'd choirs — SHAK 236:5
barefoot: b. friars were singing — GIBB 106:8
bare-legg'd: b. beggarly son of a gun — CALV 60:1
bareness: old December's b. — SHAK 236:8
bargain: dateless b. to engrossing death — SHAK 232:6
never was a better b. driv'n — SIDN 241:4
barge: b. she sat — SHAK 203:22
bark: come out as I do, and *b.* — JOHN 133:21
star to every wandering b. — SHAK 236:12
Though his b. cannot be — SHAK 220:3
You Heard a Seal B. — THUR 259:14
Barkis: B. is willin' — DICK 83:22
barley: fields of b. and of rye — TENN 253:9
Sitting on a heap of B. — LEAR 150:10
Barlow: my Hornby and my B. — THOM 257:22
barn: from the b. and the forge — HOUS 125:14
barreltone: base b. voice — JOYCE 137:7
barren: b. sister all your life — SHAK 226:12
b. superfluity of words — GARTH 105:1
Close up these b. leaves — WORD 277:9
I am but a b. stock — ELIZ 95:14
none is b. among them — BIBLE 28:3
barricade: At some disputed b. — SEEG 202:17
bars: Between their silver b. — FLEC 100:12
out through the same b. — LANG 149:1
Basan: fat bulls of B. — PRAY 188:14
base: b. barreltone voice — JOYCE 137:7
b., common and popular — SHAK 213:18
scarlet Majors at the B. — SASS 200:4
Things b. and vile — SHAK 226:14
wherefore b. — SHAK 217:19

baseless: b. fabric of this vision — SHAK 232:24
baser: lewd fellows of the b. — BIBLE 37:21
basia: Da mi b. mille — CAT 65:6
basically: b. I'm viable from ten — BETJ 20:12
basin: stare in the b. — AUDEN 10:10
Basingstoke: hidden meaning —like B. — GILB 109:7
Basques: Scalinger used to say of the B. — CHAM 67:1
Bass: Guinness, Allsopp, B. — CALV 59:17
bassoon: he heard the loud b. — COL 74:7
bastard: Why b. — SHAK 217:19
bastards: he who begets twenty b. — WALP 266:3
stand up for b. — SHAK 218:1
bat: black b., night — TENN 254:1
I march with b. and pad — HOUS 125:9
On the b.'s back I do — SHAK 233:2
bataillons: n'est pas pour les gros b. — VOLT 265:7
batallions: side not of the heavy b. — VOLT 265:7
bated: With b. breath — SHAK 225:1
Bath: can ever be tired of B. — AUST 12:5
soaping her breasts in the b. — EWART 97:7
sore labour's b. — SHAK 221:16
bathing: b. machine and a very small — GILB 107:21
Gentleman caught the Whigs b. — DISR 86:15
baton: field marshal's b. — LOUI 154:7
bats: ...Do b. eat cats — CARR 62:14
batsman: b. plays to the bowling — THOM 257:22
I am the b. and the bat — LANG 148:17
if the b. thinks he's bowled — LANG 148:17
swift B. of the Dawn has — THOM 258:8
Battening: B. upon huge seaworms — TENN 253:1
Batter: B. my heart — DONNE 88:6
battle: Agreed to have a b. — CARR 63:21
day long the noise of b. — TENN 252:4
drunk delight of b. with — TENN 255:12
foremost in b. was Mary Ambree — BALL 14:18
he smelleth the b. afar — BIBLE 25:34
next to a b. lost — WELL 268:5
nor the b. to the strong — BIBLE 27:16
of the b. in the glorious — VEN 261:19
See the front o' b. lour — BURNS 54:20
that it is a field of b. — STEV 247:3
trumpets which sing to b. — SHEL 240:12
When the b.'s lost — SHAK 219:16
Battledore: B. and shuttlecock's — DICK 85:16
battle-flags: b. were furl'd — TENN 253:10
battles: b. long ago — WORD 275:9
God of b. — SHAK 214:1
bauble: Take away that fool's b. — CROM 80:17
bawcock: king's a b. — SHAK 213:19
bawd: Now my old b. is dead — YEATS 279:6
bawdy: Bloody, b. villain — SHAK 208:22
bawl: bang and roar and b. — BELL 19:1
baying: families b. for broken — WAUGH 266:19
bayonets: Chains are worse than b. — JERR 130:20
sods with our b. turning — WOLFE 273:20
bay-tree: flourishing like a green b. — PRAY 188:24
be: b. rather than to seem — SALL 199:10
is that which shall b. — BIBLE 27:3
Let them b. as they are — CLEM 73:6
not mean But b. — MACL 157:15
To b., or not to be — SHAK 208:24
beach: about the b. I wander'd — TENN 253:6
only pebble on the b. — BRAI 46:3
walk upon the b. — ELIOT 94:8
Beachy Head: Birmingham by way of B. — CHES 70:3
beacon: From Clee to heaven the b. — HOUS 125:3
beaded: With b. bubbles winking — KEATS 139:19

beak: He can take in his b. — MERR 165:9
thy b. from out my heart — POE 184:2
beaker: b. full of the warm South — KEATS 139:19
Beale: Miss Buss and Miss B. — ANON 4:7
be-all: b. and the end-all here — SHAK 220:13
beam: b. that is in thine own — BIBLE 32:3
beamish: b. nephew — CARR 62:7
my b. boy — CARR 63:17
beams: tricks his b. — MILT 168:2
bean: home of the b. and the cod — BOSS 45:2
bean-rows: Nine b. will I have there — YEATS 279:7
Bear: B. of Very Little Brain — MILNE 167:1
B. them we can — HOUS 126:16
b. the yoke in his youth — BIBLE 30:2
b. with a sore head — MARR 161:5
has been eaten by the b. — HOUS 127:5
How a b. likes honey — MILNE 166:18
makes us rather b. those — SHAK 208:24
pursued by a b. — SHAK 234:21
still less the b. — FRERE 103:1
They shall b. thee in their — PRAY 190:1
We've fought the B. before — HUNT 128:2
bear-baiting: Puritan hated the b. — MAC 157:3
beard: b. of formal cut — SHAK 205:1
grey b. and glittering eye — COL 74:5
King of Spain's B. — DRAKE 90:3
void your rheum upon my b. — SHAK 225:1
was an Old Man with a b. — LEAR 150:2
bearded: b. like the pard — SHAK 205:1
beards: We'll grow b. — FLAU 100:6
Beareth: B. all things — BIBLE 38:15
bears: dancing dogs and b. — HODG 120:4
wandering b. may come with buns — ISH 129:16
beast: b. who is always spoiling — MAC 157:5
count the number of the b. — BIBLE 41:3
making the b. with two backs — SHAK 228:15
name of the b. — BIBLE 41:2
regardeth the life of his b. — BIBLE 26:15
splendorous *blond b.* — NIET 177:3
what rough b. — YEATS 279:16
beastie: tim'rous b. — BURNS 55:5
beasties: ghosties and long-leggety b. — ANON 3:11
Beasts: B. did leap and birds did — BARN 15:17
b. that have no understanding — PRAY 187:24
beat: b. him when he sneezes — CARR 62:22
b. the ground — MILT 167:6
b. their swords into plowshares — BIBLE 28:7
b. upon my whorlèd ear — HOPK 121:19
b. upon that house — BIBLE 32:13
watchman on his b. — FROST 103:2
when thy heart began to b. — BLAKE 43:8
ye b. my people to pieces — BIBLE 28:8
beating: b. myself for spite — SIDN 241:5
Charity and b. begins at home — FLET 101:2
hear the b. of his wings — BRIG 46:14
Is b. on the door — YEATS 279:2
not mend his pace with b. — SHAK 211:10
beats: light which b. upon a throne — TENN 251:15
Beatus: B. ille — HOR 123:9
B. vir qui timet Dominum — BIBLE 41:13
beau: l'art pour l'art...le b. — COUS 78:16
beauté: tout n'est qu'ordre et b. — BAUD 16:12
beauteous: How b. mankind is — SHAK 233:3
love all b. things — BRID 46:11
beauties: You meaner b. of the night — WOTT 277:18
beautified: b. with our feathers — GREE 112:18
beautiful: Against the b. — GREE 112:15
All things bright and b. — ALEX 2:3
art for art's sake...the b. — COUS 78:16

B. as sweet — YOUNG 280:9
B. Railway Bridge — MCG 157:11
b., the tender, the kind — MILL 166:3
believe to be b. — MORR 173:16
deal of scorn looks b. — SHAK 234:7
entirely b. — AUDEN 11:3
How b. upon the mountains — BIBLE 29:12
how b. — KIPL 144:3
indeed appear b. outward — BIBLE 33:31
innocent and the b. — YEATS 279:4
She's b. and therefore — SHAK 214:9
small is b. — SCH 201:5
thee good as thou art b. — TENN 251:18
when a woman isn't b. — CHEK 69:3
yet more b. daughter — HOR 123:15
beauty: After the wildest b. — OWEN 179:10
b. cold and austere — RUSS 198:11
b. draws us with a single — POPE 185:25
b. from the light retir'd — WALL 265:14
'B. is truth — KEATS 139:16
b. lives with kindness — SHAK 234:18
b. making beautiful old — SHAK 236:10
b. of Israel is slain — BIBLE 24:25
b. of the good old cause — WORD 277:1
b. that hath not some strangeness — BACON 13:1
B. that must die — KEATS 139:17
B. took from those who — DE L 82:11
B. too rich for use — SHAK 231:14
delusion that b. is goodness — TOLS 259:18
dreamed that life was B. — HOOP 121:14
Her b. fed my common earth — MAS 162:18
home and his — BRAH 46:2
is simply order and b. — BAUD 16:12
June for b.'s heightening — ARN 9:3
principal b. in building — FULL 104:2
round the ghosts of b. glide — POPE 185:1
seizes as b. must be truth — KEATS 140:15
She walks in b. — BYRON 58:21
terrible b. is born — YEATS 278:19
thing of b. is a joy — KEATS 138:15
thy b. is to me — POE 184:3
Thy b. shall no more be — MARV 161:21
whose b. is past change — HOPK 122:4
winds of March with b. — SHAK 235:1
youth And a little b. — WEBS 267:8
Because: B. it is there — MALL 159:5
'B. it was he — MONT 172:1
becks: b., and wreathed smiles — MILT 167:16
become: b. of us without any barbarians — CAV 65:12
do all that may b. a man — SHAK 221:5
becomes: peace there's nothing so b. — SHAK 213:14
bed: able to have a spare b. — PEPYS 182:12
Are the weans in their b. — MILL 166:10
b. after the hurly-burly — CAMP 60:12
B. be blest that I lie — ANON 4:6
B. in the bush with stars — STEV 247:11
die—in b. — SASS 200:5
Down as upon a b. — MARV 161:18
dull, stale, tired b. — SHAK 217:19
earth in an earthy b. — TENN 254:2
Every b. is narrow — MILL 166:8
I haste me to my b. — SHAK 235:10
I in my b. again — ANON 5:10
I put my hand into the b. — SHAK 213:13
I used to go to b. early — PROU 192:4
lie *diagonally* in his b. — STER 246:11
make my b. soon — BALL 14:17
newly gone to b. — MILT 168:10

not a b. of roses — STEV 247:3
pluck me from my naked b. — KYD 147:9
so to b. — PEPYS 182:7
sweat of an enseamed b. — SHAK 210:17
take up thy b. — BIBLE 36:22
This b. thy centre is — DONNE 88:19
To b., to bed, to bed — SHAK 223:10
When boyes go first to b. — HERB 118:12
Who goes to b. with whom — SAY 200:17
wife my second best b. — SHAK 237:6
bedes: peire of b. — CHAU 68:3
bedfellows: acquaints a man with strange b. — SHAK 232:18
Poverty has strange b. — BULW 51:12
Bedonebyasyoudid: Mrs B. is coming — KING 142:18
bedside: got a very good b. manner — PUNCH 192:19
bee: doth the little busy b. — WATTS 266:16
Where the b. sucks — SHAK 233:2
beef: roast b. of England — FIEL 98:4
bee-loud: live alone in the b. glade — YEATS 279:7
bee-mouth: to Poison while the b. — KEATS 139:17
been: b. and gone and done — GILB 106:19
Beer: B.! O Hodgson — CALV 59:17
I'm only a b. teetotaller — SHAW 237:11
such all b. and skittles — CALV 60:2
bees: forest b. are humming near — CLARE 72:22
murmuring of innumerable b. — TENN 255:2
bees-winged: was it his b. eyes — BETJ 20:5
beetle: poor b. — SHAK 224:1
Save where the b. wheels — GRAY 111:18
Beetles: B. black — SHAK 227:7
befell: At forty-odd b. — HOOD 121:6
Before: B., behind — DONNE 87:25
doing what has been done b. — WHAR 269:9
I have been here b. — ROSS 197:9
large a trunk b. — BELL 18:5
said our remarks b. — DON 87:16
those b. cried 'Back — MAC 156:8
beg: to b. I am ashamed — BIBLE 35:30
to b. in the streets — FRAN 102:5
We cannot b. for pardon — MACN 158:10
began: dark womb where I b. — MAS 162:18
was it when my life b. — WORD 275:11
begetter: To the onlie b. of these — SHAK 235:8
beggar: He's an absent-minded b. — KIPL 143:7
whiles I am a b. — SHAK 217:8
beggar'd: It b. all description — SHAK 203:22
beggary: no vice, but b. — SHAK 217:8
begging: his seed b. their bread — PRAY 188:23
Begin: 'B. at the beginning — CARR 63:15
Then I'll b. — LANG 148:18
truths to b. as heresies — HUXL 128:13
beginning: b. and the ending — BIBLE 40:28
b. God created the heaven — BIBLE 22:1
b. is often the end — ELIOT 93:19
b. of any great matter — DRAKE 90:1
Each venture Is a new b. — ELIOT 93:18
end of the b. — CHUR 71:11
In my b. is my end — ELIOT 93:15
In the b. was the Word — BIBLE 36:12
Lord is the b. of wisdom — PRAY 190:11
That is the true b. — SHAK 227:20
that was the b. of fairies — BARR 16:2
begins: she b. to comprehend it — PRIOR 191:17
world's great age b. anew — SHEL 239:4
begot: some that he was b. between — SHAK 224:6
were about when they b. me — STER 246:7
begotten: Whatever is b. — YEATS 279:12
beguile: To b. the time — SHAK 220:12

beguiles: traveller's joy b. in autumn HOUS 126:22
begun: have not yet b. to fight JONES 135:15
To have b. is half HOR 123:3
behave: b. as the rich behave SMITH 242:9
How well did I b. HOUS 125:10
behaving: language and ways of b. JUV 137:17
beheaded: was b. yesterday WALP 265:15
behemoth: Behold now b. BIBLE 26:1
behind: At such a little tail b. BELL 18:5
b., between DONNE 87:25
come no more b. your scenes JOHN 131:5
dusk with a light b. GILB 109:10
has no bosom and no b. SMITH 242:14
those b. cried 'Forward MAC 156:8
behold: b. a pale horse BIBLE 40:32
B. the man BIBLE 41:22
b. us with Thy blessing BUCK 51:4
being: have our b. BIBLE 37:24
beings: human b. are born free ANON 2:16
Belgrave Square: May beat in B. GILB 107:14
Belial: wander forth the sons Of B. MILT 168:16
belief: bamboozle myself into b. GREE 112:17
believe in B. I disbelieve FORS 101:20
loved each other beyond b. HEINE 116:13
beliefs: dust of exploded b. MADAN 158:12
sorts of old defunct b. IBSEN 129:6
two contradictory b. ORW 178:11
believe: b. also in me BIBLE 36:36
b. in God in spite of what JOW 136:15
b. to be beautiful MORR 173:16
b. what one does not believe PAINE 179:12
Do you b. in fairies BARR 16:5
I b. it was no more SUCK 248:5
I do b. her SHAK 237:1
I do not b. BUTL 56:18
I don't b. a word of it CHAM 67:1
If you b. the doctors SAL 199:7
If you b. that you will WELL 268:12
Let Apella the Jew b. it HOR 124:23
little ones which b. in me BIBLE 33:16
Lord, I b. BIBLE 34:25
We can b. what we choose NEWM 176:5
willingly b. what they wish CAES 59:9
you must b. what you ought NEWM 176:6
believed: against hope b. in hope BIBLE 37:33
seen, and yet have b. BIBLE 37:11
believes: that he more readily b. BACON 13:30
believeth: b. all things BIBLE 38:15
b. in him should not perish BIBLE 36:21
b. on me hath everlasting BIBLE 36:24
believing: torture them, into b. NEWM 176:2
Bell: b., book, and candle SHAK 217:9
b. invites me SHAK 221:11
heart as sound as a b. SHAK 228:10
hear the surly sullen b. SHAK 236:4
mock the midnight b. SHAK 204:2
sexton toll'd the b. HOOD 121:6
Silence that dreadful b. SHAK 228:23
to know for whom the *b.* DONNE 89:3
very word is like a b. KEATS 140:1
Bella: B., horrida bella VIRG 263:9
belle: du temps que j'étais b. RONS 196:6
belli: Nervos b. CIC 72:13
bells: b. have knoll'd to church SHAK 204:24
b. of Hell go ting-a-ling-a-ling ANON 4:12
b. they sound so clear HOUS 125:12
Like sweet b. jangled SHAK 209:6
noisy b., be dumb HOUS 125:13
'Twould ring the b. of Heaven HODG 120:4

bellum: *praeparet b.* VEG 261:18
belly: b. will mainly mind anything JOHN 132:6
bellyful: Rumble thy b. SHAK 218:7
belov'd: bourn how far to be b. SHAK 203:17
Beloved: B. from pole to pole COL 74:16
My b. is mine BIBLE 28:2
This is my b. Son BIBLE 31:7
below: above, b. DONNE 87:25
belted: Though I've b. you an' KIPL 144:5
Bench: suppose I am on the B. BIRK 42:10
bend: I b. and I break not LA F 147:12
bends: Though she b. him LONG 153:16
Benedictus: B. qui venit in nomine MASS 163:16
benefit: b. of the students SMITH 242:2
without the b. o' the Clergy CONG 76:14
benison: b. of hot water BROO 47:7
b. to fall On our meat HERR 119:2
bent: Just as the twig is b. POPE 184:23
My youth is b. by the same THOM 257:4
bereav'd: if b. of light BLAKE 43:15
bergers: des b. et des bouchers VOLT 265:6
Berliner: words *Ich bin ein B.* KENN 141:14
Bermudas: Where the remote B. ride MARV 161:11
berries: Two lovely b. moulded SHAK 227:11
berry: could have made a better b. BUTL 56:25
sweeter than the b. GAY 105:6
berth: which happen'd in his b. HOOD 121:6
beside: thou art b. thyself BIBLE 37:29
best: All is for the b. VOLT 264:6
b. and happiest moments SHEL 240:11
b. and the worst of this SWIN 250:11
b. be still ARN 8:16
b. government is that which OSUL 178:15
b. in this kind are SHAK 227:23
b. is like the worst KIPL 145:4
b. is the best QUIL 193:11
b. is the enemy VOLT 264:18
b. is yet to be BROW 50:18
b. lack all conviction YEATS 279:15
b. of all our actions tend BUTL 56:12
b. of all possible worlds CAB 59:7
b. trousers on when you IBSEN 129:5
b. words in the best order COL 75:13
It was the b. of times DICK 85:29
loveliest and b. FITZ 99:2
one another's b. DONNE 87:26
past all prizing, b. SOPH 243:14
Send forth the b. ye breed KIPL 146:7
strongest is always the b. LA F 147:14
than any other person's b. HAZL 116:2
Bestie: *lüstern schweifende* blonde B. NIET 177:3
bestow: religion is powerless to b. FORB 101:9
bestride: doth b. the narrow world SHAK 215:16
best-seller: b. was a book which somehow BOOR 44:19

betake: b. myself to that course PEPYS 182:14
Bethlehem: come ye to B. ANON 6:10
Slouches towards B. YEATS 279:16
venite in B. ANON 6:10
betimes: that spurs too fast b. SHAK 230:1
betray: 'All things b. thee THOM 258:2
B. sweet Jenny's unsuspecting BURNS 54:3
finds too late that men b. GOLD 110:18
guts to b. my country FORS 101:21
betrayed: b. by what is false within MER 165:3
better: am getting better and b. COUE 78:15
B. by far you should forget ROSS 197:6
b. for worse PRAY 187:28
b. than light and safer HASK 115:16

biting: more than b. Time can sever	ELIOT 94:12
bitter: do such b. business	SHAK 210:9
love grows b. with treason	SWIN 250:3
make misfortunes more b.	BACON 13:15
Some do it with a b. look	WILDE 271:3
something b. that chokes	LUCR 155:9
you frequent b. reflection	FRAN 102:10
bitterness: must have no hatred or b.	CAV 65:13
black: b. and merciless things	JAMES 130:3
B. as the Pit from pole	HENL 117:6
b. *sun* of *melancholy*	NERV 175:11
devil damn thee b.	SHAK 223:11
I am b.	BLAKE 43:15
it here in b. and white	JONS 136:1
looking for a b. hat	BOWEN 45:10
More b. than ashbuds	TENN 251:14
night's b. agents	SHAK 222:15
shirt and your socks (the b.	GILB 107:23
sloeblack, slow, b., crowblack	THOM 257:9
Tip me the b. spot	STEV 247:1
Who art as b. as hell	SHAK 237:4
you wear b. all the time	CHEK 68:30
blackbirds: full of b. than of cherries	ADD 1:13
blackens: b. every blot	TENN 251:15
blacks: poor are Europe's b.	CHAM 67:2
bladder: blows a man up like a b.	SHAK 212:12
bladders: boys that swim on b.	SHAK 215:9
Blade: B. on the feather	CORY 78:10
His b. struck the water	COKE 74:2
vorpal b. went snicker-snack	CARR 63:17
with bloody blameful b.	SHAK 227:21
blade-straight: Steel-true and b.	STEV 247:14
Blake: what B. once wildly muttered...	
	SASS 200:13
blame: That neither is most to b.	SWIN 250:4
blameless: white flower of a b. life	TENN 251:15
blandula: Animula vagula b.	HAER 113:8
blanket: right side of the b.	ASHF 9:21
through the b. of the dark	SHAK 220:11
blankets: rough male kiss of b.	BROO 47:6
blasphemy: soldier is flat b.	SHAK 223:19
blast: b. of war blows in our	SHAK 213:14
blasted: b. heath you stop our way	SHAK 220:5
b. with excess of light	GRAY 112:13
B. with ecstasy	SHAK 209:6
blazed: My body of a sudden b.	YEATS 280:4
bleak: In the b. mid-winter	ROSS 197:5
bleed: do we not b.	SHAK 225:10
I b.	SHEL 239:14
If he do b.	SHAK 221:18
bleeding: thou b. piece of earth	SHAK 216:11
blemish: without fear and without b.	ANON 5:16
Bless: B. her when she is riggish	SHAK 203:24
B. the squire and his relations	DICK 83:18
Curse, b., me now	THOM 257:1
'God b. us every one	DICK 83:19
him how to load and b.	KEATS 140:12
was blessèd and could b.	YEATS 280:4
Blessed: B. are the poor in spirit	BIBLE 31:11
B. art thou among women	ANON 6:14
b. art thou among women	BIBLE 34:27
b. be the name of the Lord	BIBLE 25:18
b. damozel leaned out	ROSS 197:8
B. is the man whose strength	PRAY 189:18
b. mutter of the mass	BROW 49:1
b. they that master so	SHAK 226:12
b. to give than to receive	BIBLE 37:26
buttercup Had b. with gold	OWEN 179:8
call her b.	BIBLE 27:1

generations shall call me b.	BIBLE 34:28
I was b. and could bless	YEATS 280:4
Judge none b. before his	BIBLE 30:22
This b. plot	SHAK 230:2
blessedness: in single b.	SHAK 226:12
blesseth: It b. him that gives	SHAK 225:17
blessing: behold us with Thy b.	BUCK 51:4
b. that money cannot buy	WALT 266:10
come as a boon and a b.	ANON 5:4
hath taken away thy b.	BIBLE 22:31
have paid thy utmost b.	DE L 82:11
When thou dost ask me b.	SHAK 218:27
blessings: Are b. in disguise	HERV 119:3
b. on the falling out	TENN 254:6
Having a glass of b. standing	HERB 118:14
they recognized their b.	VIRG 264:11
blest: always To be b.	POPE 185:15
Bed be b. that I lie	ANON 4:6
B. pair of Sirens	MILT 167:5
blight: is the b. man was born	HOPK 122:6
Blind: B. guides	BIBLE 33:30
b. man in a dark room	BOWEN 45:10
halt, and the b.	BIBLE 35:23
her faults a little b.	PRIOR 191:16
if the blind lead the b.	BIBLE 33:9
splendid work for the b.	SASS 200:7
though she be b.	BACON 13:7
will accompany my being b.	PEPYS 182:14
wing'd Cupid painted b.	SHAK 226:14
blindfold: b. and alone	KIPL 143:19
blindness: From all b. of heart	PRAY 187:3
is a triple sight in b.	KEATS 140:5
I've an April b.	FRY 103:17
To help him of his b.	SHAK 234:18
blinds: dusk a drawing-down of b.	OWEN 179:5
blind-worms: b., do no wrong	SHAK 227:6
blinking: portrait of a b. idiot	SHAK 225:8
Bliss: B. was it in that dawn	WORD 274:17
deprived of everlasting b.	MARL 160:3
Of bliss on b.	MILT 169:9
promise of pneumatic b.	ELIOT 95:9
where ignorance is b.	GRAY 112:12
Which is the b. of solitude	WORD 275:4
blithe: be you b. and bonny	SHAK 228:7
buxom, b., and debonair	MILT 167:15
Hail to thee, b. Spirit	SHEL 240:4
No lark more b. than he	BICK 42:1
block: chopper on a big black b.	GILB 108:9
old b. itself	BURKE 53:3
blockhead: bookful b.	POPE 185:13
man but a b. ever wrote	JOHN 132:26
blonde: b. Bestie *nicht zu verkennen*	NIET 177:3
blood: b. more stirs	SHAK 212:6
B. of Jesus whispers	BICK 42:4
b. of patriots and tyrants	JEFF 130:10
b. will have blood	SHAK 222:20
flesh and b. so cheap	HOOD 121:13
guiltless of his country's b.	GRAY 112:5
have had so much b. in him	SHAK 223:6
Here's the smell of the b.	SHAK 223:8
in b. Stepp'd in so far	SHAK 222:21
make thick my b.	SHAK 220:11
man shall his b. be shed	BIBLE 22:21
moment when the moon was b.	CHES 66:3
near in b.	SHAK 222:10
Neptune's ocean wash this b.	SHAK 222:1
not against flesh and b.	BIBLE 39:15
nothing to offer but b.	CHUR 71:4
now could I drink hot b.	SHAK 210:9

Let him look to his b.   SHAK 225:9
take a b. of fate   SHAK 223:1
bondman: base that would be a b.   SHAK 216:15
bonds: My b. in thee are all determinate
                                          SHAK 236:6
bondsmen: Hereditary b.   BYRON 57:8
Bone: B. of my bones   BIBLE 22:10
  B. of my bone thou art   MILT 169:19
  bright hair about the b.   DONNE 88:13
  Hath never a b. in't   WEBS 267:7
  He knows death to the b.   YEATS 278:17
  rag and a b. and a hank   KIPL 146:4
bones: be he that moves my b.   SHAK 237:5
  Can these b. live   BIBLE 30:7
  England keep my b.   SHAK 217:14
  I am come to lay my b.   WOLS 274:4
  Of his b. are coral made   SHAK 232:15
  their b. and soul's delivery   DONNE 88:3
  valley which was full of b.   BIBLE 30:6
  whose b. Lie scattered   MILT 170:9
  within full of dead men's b.   BIBLE 33:31
Bong-tree: To the land where the B.   LEAR 150:14
bonhomie: Overcame his natural b.   BENT 19:19
Bonnie: B. wee thing   BURNS 53:25
bonny: be you blithe and b.   SHAK 228:7
bono: Cui b.   CASS 64:22
Boojum: If your Snark be a B.   CARR 62:7
book: adversary had written a b.   BIBLE 25:31
  all the needs a b. has   TROL 260:1
  any b. should be banned   WEST 269:3
  Bell, b., and candle   SHAK 217:9
  b. a devil's chaplain   DARW 81:16
  b. is the precious life-blood   MILT 170:16
  B. of Life begins with   WILDE 271:26
  B. of Verse   FITZ 98:15
  Go, little b.   STEV 247:15
  his picture, but his b.   JONS 136:5
  hotch-potch of my little b.   JUV 137:15
  I'll drown my b.   SHAK 233:1
  is as a b. where men   SHAK 220:12
  knows this out of the b.   DICK 84:21
  moral or an immoral b.   WILDE 271:18
  not throw this b. about   BELL 18:2
  publishes a b. without an Index   CAMP 60:9
  read a b. before reviewing   SMITH 242:22
  square b.   GLOU 109:18
  substance of a b. directly   KNOW 147:3
  take down this b.   YEATS 280:5
  There is a b.   KEBLE 141:10
  they were printed in a b.   BIBLE 25:27
  this is no b.   WHIT 270:3
  'What is the use of a b.   CARR 62:13
  who destroys a good b.   MILT 170:15
  woman who wrote the b.   LINC 152:6
  written b. will be brought   CEL 66:1
book clubs: what they club for at b. LAMB 148:2
bookful: b. blockhead   POPE 185:13
Books: B., and my food   STEV 247:17
  b. consum'd the midnight   GAY 105:17
  b. in the running brooks   SHAK 204:16
  B. of the true sort   LAMB 148:2
  days is a collection of b.   CARL 61:15
  equal skill to Cambridge b.   BROW 48:15
  his b. arranged three   PROU 192:5
  his b. were read   BELL 18:21
  In b. and love   GAY 105:21
  laid out just the right b.   POUND 186:13
  many b. there is no end   BIBLE 27:23
  read all the b. there are   MALL 159:4

Some b. are to be tasted   BACON 13:20
Wherever b. are burned   HEINE 116:12
boon: b. and a blessing to men   ANON 5:4
Boot: B., saddle   BROW 49:7
  b. stamping on a human   ORW 178:12
boote: day it dooth myn herte b.   CHAU 68:18
boots: Aristocrat who cleans the b.   GILB 107:5
  attired in leather b.   HOUS 127:3
  Books from B.'   BETJ 21:5
  B.—boots—boots   KIPL 143:13
  pleasure me in his top-b.   MARL 160:2
bo-peep: if they started at b.   HERR 118:24
bore: b. me in the southern wild   BLAKE 43:15
  way to be a b. is to say   VOLT 265:9
bored: 'one gets so b. with good   DISR 87:10
boring: 'Somebody's b. me   THOM 257:15
born: b. King of the Jews   BIBLE 31:1
  b. when I was consul   CIC 72:15
  ever have been b. at all   LUCR 155:8
  Every moment one is b.   TENN 255:18
  Godolphin Horne was nobly b.   BELL 18:8
  house where I was b.   HOOD 121:7
  human beings are b. free   ANON 2:16
  I am not yet b.   MACN 158:9
  if anyone is b. to obey   COMP 76:10
  is the blight man was b.   HOPK 122:6
  I was b. sneering   GILB 108:1
  I was b. to set it right   SHAK 208:3
  Man is b. unto trouble   BIBLE 25:21
  Man that is b. of a woman   BIBLE 25:24
  Man was b. free   ROUS 198:2
  natural to die as to be b.   BACON 13:16
  not properly b.   DICK 84:5
  Not to be b.   BACON 14:3
  Not to be b. is   SOPH 243:14
  other powerless to be b.   ARN 8:14
  sucker b. every minute   BARN 15:18
  terrible beauty is b.   YEATS 278:19
  That's b. into this world   GILB 107:16
  that thou wast b. with   SHAK 218:2
  Then surely I was b.   CHES 69:23
  time to be b.   BIBLE 27:6
  'Tis less than to be b.   BEAU 17:2
  took the trouble to be b.   BEAU 16:17
  to the manner b.   SHAK 207:8
  unto us a child is b.   BIBLE 28:19
  We were not b. to sue   SHAK 229:18
  when a child is b.   SU T 248:9
borne: b. away with every breath   BYRON 58:20
  b. it with a patient shrug   SHAK 224:21
  Had b. my breath away   HOOD 121:7
  I have b., and borne   SHAK 212:24
borogoves: All mimsy were the b.   CARR 63:16
boroughs: bright b.   HOPK 122:7
borrow: earth must b. its mirth   WILC 271:9
borrower: b., nor a lender be   SHAK 207:6
bosom: angels into Abraham's b.   BIBLE 35:32
  b. of the urgent West   BRID 46:13
  carry them in his b.   BIBLE 29:10
  Cleanse the stuff'd b.   SHAK 223:13
  has no b. and no behind   SMITH 242:14
  third in your b.   SHAK 231:23
  those thorns that in her b.   SHAK 207:16
  wife of thy b.   BIBLE 23:33
  wring his b.   GOLD 110:18
bosoms: b. of your actresses excite   JOHN 131:5
  hang and brush their b.   BROW 50:22
Boston: this is good old B.   BOSS 45:2

bo'sun: b. tight   GILB 106:21
botanize: that would peep and b.   WORD 276:5
botched: b. civilization   POUND 186:10
both: long as ye b. shall live   PRAY 187:27
Bother: Though 'B. it' I may   GILB 108:27
bottle: 'leave the b. on the chimley-piece
    DICK 84:12
   My b. of salvation   RAL 194:4
   nor a b. to give him   DICK 84:7
   we'll pass the b. round   WHYT 270:14
bottles: new wine into old b.   BIBLE 32:20
bottom: Which will reach the b.   GRAH 111:8
   woman had a b. of good sense   JOHN 133:18
bouchers: des bergers et des b.   VOLT 265:6
boue: La nostalgie de la b.   AUG 11:14
bough: blossom that hangs on the b.   SHAK 233:2
   of Bread beneath the b.   FITZ 98:15
   Touch not a single b.   MORR 173:12
   with bloom along the b.   HOUS 125:4
boughs: b. and the brushwood sheaf   BROW 49:12
   b. which shake against   SHAK 236:5
bought: have b. it at any price   CLAR 72:25
bougies: le vent éteint les b.   LA R 149:11
bound: my duty as a man is b.   TENN 255:6
boundary: has a right to fix the b.   PARN 180:14
bounded: could be b. in a nut-shell   SHAK 208:13
boundless: that the desire is b.   SHAK 233:6
bourgeois: b. are other people   REN 194:17
   How beastly the b. is   LAWR 149:16
   proletarian for the b.   LEE 151:6
bourn: b. how far to be belov'd   SHAK 203:17
bousing: While we sit b. at the nappy BURNS 54:22
boutiquiers: L'Angleterre est une nation de b.
    NAP 174:12
bow: b. of burning gold   BLAKE 43:2
   B. themselves when he did   SHAK 215:7
   certain man drew a b.   BIBLE 25:9
   do set my b. in the cloud   BIBLE 22:22
   Jesus every knee should b.   BIBLE 39:16
   unto the b. the cord is   LONG 153:14
bowed: b. his comely head   MARV 161:18
bowels: in the b. of Christ   CROM 80:15
bowery: b. hollows crown'd with   TENN 252:8
Bowing: lies poor Tom B.   DIBD 83:9
bowl: b. to sea went wise men   PEAC 181:17
   golden b. be broken   BIBLE 27:22
   inverted B. we call The Sky   FITZ 99:10
   Morning in the B. of Night   FITZ 98:14
bowler: I am the b. and the ball   LANG 148:17
   If the wild b. thinks he   LANG 148:17
bowling: plays to the b. of a ghost   THOM 257:22
Bows: B. down to wood and stone   HEBER 116:10
Bow-windows: putting b. to the house   DICK 83:23
Bow-Wow: Big B. strain I can do   SCOTT 202:10
bow-wows: gone to the demnition b.   DICK 85:4
boxes: holsters and cartridge b.   SHAW 237:8
boy: Alas, pitiable b.   VIRG 263:15
   b. stood on the burning   HEM 117:1
   b.'s will is the wind's   LONG 153:7
   good-humoured b.   BEER 17:15
   hood-wink'd b. I call'd   GARR 104:15
   roughly to your little b.   CARR 62:22
   seat sat the journeying b.   HARDY 114:12
   Smiling the b. fell dead   BROW 49:16
   that were when he was a b.   HOR 122:18
   to be b. eternal   SHAK 234:19
   Upon the growing b.   WORD 275:15
   was and a little tiny b.   SHAK 234:14
boyaux: étranglés avec les b.   MESL 165:10

boyes: When b. go first to bed   HERB 118:12
boys: b. that swim on bladders   SHAK 215:9
   Christian b. I can scarcely   ARN 9:16
   Deceive b. with toys   LYS 156:1
   flies to wanton b.   SHAK 218:18
   of children (except b.   CARR 64:18
   office boys for office b.   SAL 199:9
   to virgin girls and b.   HOR 124:5
Bozrah: dyed garments from B.   BIBLE 29:21
brace: b. ourselves to our duties   CHUR 71:6
bracelet. b. of bright hair about   DONNE 88:13
bracelets: b. and bright feathers   HARDY 114:13
braces: Damn b.   BLAKE 44:6
Bradshaw: vocabulary of 'B.' is   DOYLE 89:27
braes: among thy green b.   BURNS 54:7
   banks and b. o' bonny Doon   BURNS 55:8
brag: Is left this vault to b.   SHAK 222:7
   Nor shall death b. thou   SHAK 235:9
braids: twisted b. of lilies knitting   MILT 167:9
Brain: Bear of Very Little B.   MILNE 167:1
   b. of feathers   POPE 184:7
   draughts intoxicate the b.   POPE 185:8
   glean'd my teeming b.   KEATS 140:9
   it might injure the b.   CARR 62:18
   schoolmasters puzzle their b.   GOLD 110:17
   to leave that b. outside   GILB 107:17
brains: b. in my head and the heart   HOUS 127:1
   Cudgel thy b. no more about   SHAK 211:10
   dash'd the b. out   SHAK 221:6
   Had their b. knocked out   SHEL 239:10
   to steal away their b.   SHAK 228:25
bramble-dew: With eyes of gold and b.
    STEV 247:14
Branch: B. shall grow out of his   BIBLE 28:20
   Cut is the b. that might   MARL 160:8
   Every b. big with it   HARDY 114:14
   reddens the b.   SAPP 200:1
branches: Thy b. ne'er remember   KEATS 140:11
branchy: city and b. between towers   HOPK 121:17
brandy: be a hero must drink b.   JOHN 133:11
   B. for the Parson   KIPL 145:15
   is the b. of the damned   SHAW 238:7
brass: am become as sounding b.   BIBLE 38:14
   evil manners live in b.   SHAK 215:12
   that was ever writ in b.   JONS 136:5
brave: b. man with a sword   WILDE 271:3
   b. men lived before Agamemnon's   HOR 124:17
   b. Music of a distant   FITZ 98:16
   b. new world   SHAK 233:3
   home of the b.   KEY 141:15
   intelligent, the witty, the b.   MILL 166:3
   In the b. days of old   MAC 156:7
   Of the b. and innocent   AUDEN 10:17
   passing b. to be a King   MARL 160:16
   that was b.   HOUS 126:8
   Then I was clean and b.   HOUS 125:10
   Toll for the b.   COWP 79:15
   What's b., what's noble   SHAK 204:7
   would not sleep with the b.   HOUS 126:15
braver: I have done one b. thing   DONNE 88:22
bravery: Hiding thy b. in their   SHAK 235:15
brawler: not a b., not covetous   BIBLE 39:27
Brazil: B.—where the nuts   THOM 256:21
breach: More honour'd in the b.   SHAK 207:8
   Once more unto the b.   SHAK 213:14
bread: bit of butter to my b.   MILNE 166:15
   b. and butter that feels   MACK 157:13
   b. and the big match   JUV 138:4
   b. eaten in secret is pleasant   BIBLE 26:11

B. I dip in the river · STEV 247:11
b. of adversity · BIBLE 29:3
b. of affliction and with · BIBLE 25:8
Cast thy b. upon the waters · BIBLE 27:20
cramm'd with distressful b. · SHAK 213:23
eat thy b. with joy · BIBLE 27:14
face shalt thou eat b. · BIBLE 22:14
Here with a Loaf of B. · FITZ 98:15
Jesus took b. · BIBLE 34:11
Man shall not live by b. · BIBLE 31:8
Royal slice of b. · MILNE 166:14
smell of b. and butter · BYRON 57:5
that b. should be so dear · HOOD 121:13
took the B. and brake it · ELIZ 95:13
to steal b. · FRAN 102:5
To take b. at my hand · WYATT 278:3
us this day our daily b. · BIBLE 31:21
was cutting b. and butter · THAC 256:15
whom if his son ask b. · BIBLE 32:6
Break: B., break, break · TENN 251:4
b. faith with us who die · MCCR 157:9
b. the ice by some whose · BACON 13:4
I bend and I b. not · LA F 147:12
I'll b. my staff · SHAK 233:1
lark at b. of day · SHAK 235:11
thyself must b. at last · ARN 8:16
you b. the bloody glass · MACN 158:7
breakfast: All too soon the tiny b. · BETJ 20:6
impossible things before b. · CARR 64:6
That b. · BELL 18:11
breakfasts: sleeps he b. · SURT 248:11
breaking: b. of ribs was sport · SHAK 204:14
cheerfulness was always b. · EDW 92:13
vainly b. · CLOU 73:17
breaks: b. a butterfly upon a wheel · POPE 184:21
day b. not · DONNE 87:19
breast: broach'd his boiling bloody b. · SHAK 227:21
charms to sooth a savage b. · CONG 76:18
eternal in the human b. · POPE 185:15
render back from out thy b. · BYRON 58:10
stood b. high amid the corn · HOOD 121:11
breastie: what a panic's in thy b. · BURNS 55:5
breastplate: b. of righteousness · BIBLE 39:15
breasts: all night betwixt my b. · BIBLE 27:25
b. are like two young roes · BIBLE 28:4
feel my b. all perfume · JOYCE 137:9
soaping her b. in the bath · EWART 97:7
why then her b. are dun · SHAK 236:14
breath: bald and short of b. · SASS 200:4
b. can make them · GOLD 110:6
b. thou art · SHAK 223:21
every thing that hath b. · PRAY 191:8
flutter'd and fail'd for b. · ARN 8:18
fly away, b. · SHAK 234:3
Had borne my b. away · HOOD 121:7
having lost her b. · SHAK 203:23
last b. he drew in · LAMB 148:6
mansion call the fleeting b. · GRAY 112:4
tears and toiling b. · ROSS 197:2
thou no b. at all · SHAK 219:4
waste of b. the years behind · YEATS 279:5
world draw thy b. in pain · SHAK 211:22
breathe: like the hair we b. · SURT 248:10
So long as men can b. · SHAK 235:9
tho' to b. were life · TENN 255:13
Breathes: B. there the man · SCOTT 201:16
breathing: b. English air · BROO 47:16
B. out threatenings · BIBLE 37:15

rifle all the b. spring · COLL 76:1
breathless: b. hush in the Close to-night · NEWB 175:15
B. with adoration · WORD 276:10
bred: strain of man's b. · SHAK 233:4
Bredon: In summertime on B. · HOUS 125:12
breed: endless war still b. · MILT 170:13
Fear'd by their b. · SHAK 230:2
This happy b. · SHAK 230:2
breeder: thou be a b. of sinners · SHAK 209:2
breeds: lesser b. without the Law · KIPL 145:12
Breezy: B., Sneezy · ELLIS 96:1
breite: b. Masse eines Volkes · HITL 119:13
Brekekekex: B. koax koax · ARIS 8:3
brent: Your bonny brow was b. · BURNS 54:12
brethren: Dearly beloved b. · PRAY 186:17
least of these my b. · BIBLE 34:9
Brevity: B. is the soul of wit · SHAK 208:5
Its body b. · COL 74:23
brewery: take me to a b. · ANON 3:18
Bribe: taking of a B. or Gratuity · PENN 182:6
to b. or twist · WOLFE 273:20
brick: I inherited it b. and left · AUG 11:22
stranger! 'Eave 'arf a b. · PUNCH 192:13
bridal: to dance at our b. · SCOTT 201:21
bride: encounter darkness as a b. · SHAK 224:2
unravish'd b. of quietness · KEATS 139:12
bridegroom: funeral train which the b. · CLOU 73:9
Bridge: Beautiful Railway B. · MCG 157:1|
keep the b. with me · MAC 156:6
well Horatius kept the b. · MAC 156:11
(Which goes with B. · BELL 18:22
bridges: alike to sleep under b. · FRAN 102:5
brief: Drest in a little b. authority · SHAK 223:18
lust is gross and b. · PETR 183:3
briefer: garland b. than a girl's · HOUS 125:11
brier: thorough b. · SHAK 226:17
brier-patch: Bred en bawn in a b. · HARR 115:10
bright: All things b. and beautiful · ALEX 2:3
Behold the b. original appear · GAY 105:9
b. and fierce and fickle · TENN 254:11
B. as the day · GRAN 111:13
b. day is done · SHAK 204:8
B. is the ring of words · STEV 247:13
b. to the coiner · HOUS 126:1
burning b. · BLAKE 43:9
garden of b. images · BRAM 46:5
Keep up your b. swords · SHAK 228:16
thought thee b. · SHAK 237:4
was a young lady named B. · BULL 51:8
Brightness: B. falls from the air · NASHE 175:2
Leaking the b. away · SPEN 244:12
Brighton: cheerful, merry Dr B. · THAC 256:9
brilliant: envy of b. men · BEER 17:19
less b. pen · BEER 17:13
brillig: 'Twas b. · CARR 63:16
brim: bubbles winking at the b. · KEATS 139:19
Bring: B. me my arrows of desire · BLAKE 43:2
would b. home knowledge · JOHN 133:3
bringeth: him that b. good tidings · BIBLE 29:12
brinkmanship: boasting of his b. · STEV 246:17
brioche: Qu'ils mangent de la b. · MAR 160:1
brisking: by b. about the Life · SMART 241:16
briskly: driving b. in a post-chaise · JOHN 133:3
Bristol: he is not member of B. · BURKE 52:15
Britain: boundary of B. is revealed · TAC 250:7
B. has lost an Empire · ACH 1:2
I've lost B. · KIPL 145:13
When B. first · THOM 258:12

Yet B. set the world ablaze	GILB 107:19
Britannia: Rule, B.	THOM 258:12
British: B. journalist	WOLFE 273:23
B. soldier can stand up	SHAW 237:12
loathsome is the B. tourist	KILV 142:3
smell the blood of a B.	SHAK 218:15
so ridiculous as the B.	MAC 157:2
Briton: glory in the name of B.	GEOR 106:4
Britons: B. never will be slaves	THOM 258:12
brittle: b. glory shineth in this	SHAK 230:14
Broad: B. and I'm the High	SPR 243.3
b. is the way	BIBLE 32:8
broke: b. any man's head but his	SHAK 213:16
then b. the mould	ARIO 8:1
you that b. the new wood	POUND 186:11
broken: baying for b. glass	WAUGH 266:19
b. and contrite heart	PRAY 189:7
earth the b. arcs	BROW 48:18
pitcher be b. at the fountain	BIBLE 27:22
sound of b. glass	BELL 19:6
When the lute is b.	SHEL 239:8
broken-hearted: Half b.	BYRON 59:3
To bind up the b.	BIBLE 29:20
We had ne'er been b.	BURNS 53:20
bronze: gold and lungs of b.	BELL 19:1
longer lasting than b.	HOR 124:12
with oak and three-ply b.	HOR 123:10
broo: eels boil'd in b.'	BALL 14:17
brooch: theron heng a b. of gold	CHAU 68:3
brooches: b. and toys for your delight	STEV 247:12
broods: b. and sleeps on his own	WORD 276:6
broom: I am sent with b. before	SHAK 228:2
brothels: Keep thy foot out of b.	SHAK 218:12
brother: Am I my b.'s keeper	BIBLE 22:16
Am I not a man and a b.	WEDG 267:19
Be my b.	CHAM 67:3
dawn is my b.	BELL 18:18
Esau my b. is a hairy	BIBLE 22:29
hateth his b.	BIBLE 40:27
hurt my b.	SHAK 211:18
I am a b. to dragons	BIBLE 25:30
our dear b. here departed	PRAY 188:5
Thy b. came with subtilty	BIBLE 22:31
brotherhood: Love the b.	BIBLE 40:19
brothers: all men become b. under	SCH 201:2
all the b. too	SHAK 234:5
Romans were like b.	MAC 156:7
we band of b.	SHAK 214:4
brought: Nor b. too long a day	HOOD 121:7
brow: meet my Maker brow to b.	CORN 78:5
wanton with a velvet b.	SHAK 219:9
Your bonny b. was brent	BURNS 54:12
brown: b. of her—her eyes	MEW 165:13
browner: always tinge with a b.	GIBB 106:10
Browning: *entsichere ich meinen B.*	JOHST 135:12
Hang it all, Robert B.	POUND 186:7
Meredith is a prose B.	WILDE 272:3
brows: Gathering her b. like gathering	BURNS 54:22
girls' b. shall be their pall	OWEN 179:5
browsing: b. and sluicing and cheery	WOD 273:16
bruised: staff of this b. reed	BIBLE 25:14
was b. for our iniquities	BIBLE 29:15
brush: hang and b. their bosoms	BROW 50:22
work with so fine a b.	AUST 12:17
brushwood: lowest boughs and the b.	BROW 49:12
brutality: industry without art is b.	RUSK 198:7
brute: b. beasts that have no	PRAY 187:24
Et tu, B.	CAES 59:10

Et tu, B.	SHAK 216:9
Feed the b.	PUNCH 193:1
brutish: nasty, b., and short	HOBB 120:1
Brutus: B. is an honourable man	SHAK 216:16
You too B.	CAES 59:10
bubbles: beaded b. winking at the brim	KEATS 139:19
bubus: *Paterna rura b.*	HOR 123:9
Bücher: *wo man B. Verbrennt*	HEINE 116:12
buck: b. stops here	TRUM 260:18
Buckingham: so much for B.	CIBB 72:2
buckler: shall be thy shield and b.	PRAY 189:24
bud: I'll nip him in the b.	ROCHE 195:12
budding: b. morrow in midnight	KEATS 140:5
buds: darling b. of May	SHAK 235:9
buffoon: statesman, and b.	DRYD 90:16
Buffs: Steady the B.	KIPL 146:23
bug: b. with gilded wings	POPE 184:22
bugle: b., blow	TENN 254:9
bugle-horn: sound upon the b.	TENN 253:5
build: b. your House of Parliament	WELL 268:3
end is to b. well	WOTT 277:19
Except the Lord b. the house	PRAY 190:19
When we mean to b.	SHAK 212:23
builders: b. have laboured in vain	BIBLE 41:15
stone which the b. refused	PRAY 190:15
building: principal beauty in b.	FULL 104:2
built: b. his house upon the sand	BIBLE 32:13
Lord has b. the house	BIBLE 41:15
bull: are gone to milk the b.	JOHN 132:1
Cock and a B.	STER 246:13
bullet: Every b. has its billet	WILL 272:12
is stronger than the b.	LINC 151:16
bullets: With b. made of platinum	BELL 18:6
bulls: fat b. of Basan	PRAY 188:14
bully: I love the lovely b.	SHAK 213:19
bumbast: to b. out a blank verse	GREE 112:18
bump: that go b. in the night	ANON 3:11
bumping: b. pitch and a blinding	NEWB 175:15
bunch: b. of other men's flowers	MONT 172:7
Buncombe: through reporters to B.	CARL 61:17
bundle: b. of contradictions	COLT 76:7
buns: bears may come with b.	ISH 129:16
burden: b. and heat of the day	BIBLE 33:25
carry the heavy b. of responsibility	EDW 92:11
Is the b. of my song	ANON 4:4
my b. is light	BIBLE 33:1
Take up the White Man's b.	KIPL 146:7
Burg: *Ein' feste B. ist unser*	LUTH 155:14
Burgundy: It's a Naïve Domestic B.	THUR 259:12
burial: in one red b. blent	BYRON 57:11
buried: Half-b. in the snow was	LONG 153:5
Rose as where some b. Caesar	FITZ 99:1
They b. him	PROU 192:5
We b. him darkly at dead	WOLFE 273:20
burn: beacons b. again	HOUS 125:3
better to marry than to b.	BIBLE 38:9
Old age should b. and rave	THOM 256:23
shall not b. thee by day	PRAY 190:16
To b. always	PATER 181:10
violent fires soon b. out	SHAK 230:1
Burn'd: B. on the water	SHAK 203:22
burnèd: b. is Apollo's laurel	MARL 160:8
bush b. with fire	BIBLE 23:9
Wherever books are b.	HEINE 116:12
burning: bow of b. gold	BLAKE 43:2
b. bright	BLAKE 43:7
b. fiery furnace	BIBLE 30:8

b. Sappho loved and sung | BYRON 58:6
Burns: B., Shelley, were with us | BROW 50:1
burnt-offerings: thou delightest not in b. |
| PRAY 189:7
burnt-out: b. ends of smoky days | ELIOT 94:15
burr: I am a kind of b. | SHAK 224:8
burst: mast b. open with a rose | FLEC 100:11
suddenly b. out singing | SASS 200:10
then b. his mighty heart | SHAK 216:20
bursting: green grass and b. trees | GREN 113:3
burthen: vapours weep their b. | TENN 255:9
Bury: B. it certain fathoms | SHAK 233:1
B. my heart at Wounded Knee | BENET 19:12
I come to b. Caesar | SHAK 216:16
Let the dead b. their dead | BIBLE 32:17
bus: Descending from the b. | CARR 62:12
I'm not even a b. | HARE 115:7
bush: Bed in the b. with stars | STEV 247:11
b. burned with fire | BIBLE 23:9
Thorough b. | SHAK 226:17
young bird in this b. | LEAR 150:3
bushel: neither under a b. | BIBLE 35:17
business: be about my Father's b. | BIBLE 35:5
British people is 'B. as usual' | CHUR 71:2
b. of everybody is | MAC 156:14
b. of the wealthy man | BELL 19:2
b. that we love we rise | SHAK 204:3
everybody minded their own b. | CARR 62:21
far away from b. | HOR 123:9
it is your b. | HOR 123:6
occupy their b. in great | PRAY 190:8
person on b. from Porlock | COL 75:1
proceed no further in this b. | SHAK 221:2
woman's b. to get married | SHAW 238:5
Buss: Miss B. and Miss Beale | ANON 4:7
bust: her friendly b. | ELIOT 95:9
merit raise the tardy b. | JOHN 135:9
storied urn or animated b. | GRAY 112:4
Bustle: B. in a House | DICK 86:2
Busy: B. old fool, unruly Sun | DONNE 88:18
thou knowest how b. I must | ASTL 10:2
but: tout b. dénature l'art | CONS 77:16
butcher: son of a first rate b. | ASHF 9:21
Butcher'd: B. to make a Roman holiday |
| BYRON 57:13
butchers: gentle with these b. | SHAK 216:11
have both shepherds and b. | VOLT 265:6
butler: on the b.'s upper slopes | WOD 273:17
butt: knocks you down with the b. | GOLD 111:1
butt-end: knock me down with the b. | CIBB 72:1
Butter: (B. and eggs and a pound | CALV 59:16
b. will only make us fat | GOER 109:20
'Could we have some b. | MILNE 166:14
forth b. in a lordly dish | BIBLE 24:6
'It was the *best* b. | CARR 63:3
little bit of b. to my bread | MILNE 166:15
piece of bread and b. | MACK 157:13
smell of bread and b. | BYRON 57:5
was cutting bread and b. | THAC 256:15
buttercup: b. Had blessed with gold | OWEN 179:8
I'm called Little B. | GILB 108:24
Buttercups: B. and daisies | HOW 127:10
buttered: always on the b. side | PAYN 181:12
butterfly: b. dreaming I am a man | CHUA 70:17
b. upon the road | KIPL 145:8
Who breaks a b. upon | POPE 184:21
buttock: by boiling his b. | AUBR 10:5
buttocks: chair that fits all b. | SHAK 203:13
button: little round b. at top | FOOTE 101:7

undo this b. | SHAK 219:4
buttoning: All this b. and unbuttoning | ANON 3:1
buxom: b., blithe, and debonair | MILT 167:15
buy: b. it first | HEM 117:3
Did b. each other | SHAK 233:10
I will b. with you | SHAK 224:17
no man might b. or sell | BIBLE 41:2
wonder what the Vintners b. | FITZ 99:12
buys: Who b. a minute's mirth | SHAK 235:6
by: shall hear it by and b. | BROW 48:19
byrdes: b. sang swete in the middes | WEVER 269:7
bystanders: b. are animated with | EMER 96:8
byword: proverb and a b. among | BIBLE 25:1
Byzantium: Soldan of B. is smiling | CHES 69:26
To the holy city of B. | YEATS 279:14
Caballero: C. de la Triste Figura | CERV 66:5
cabbage: That c. hashed up again | JUV 138:2
cabbage-leaf: garden to cut a c. | FOOTE 101:7
cabbages: c.—and kings | CARR 64:2
c. are coming now | BETJ 21:12
find me planting my c. | MONT 171:17
cabin: small c. build there | YEATS 279:9
willow c. at your gate | SHAK 233:20
cabin'd: c. ample Spirit | ARN 8:18
c., cribb'd, confin'd | SHAK 222:16
cabinet: consequence of c. government | BAG 14:6
Cabinet Minister: By becoming a C. | SU T 248:9
Cabots: Lowells talk only to C. | BOSS 45:2
cachée: ardeur dans mes veines c. | RAC 193:17
cacoethes: Scribendi c. et aegro | JUV 138:1
cadendo: non vi sed saepe c. | LAT 149:13
Cadogan: One-eighty-nine C. Square | BETJ 21:5
caelum: ruat c. | MANS 159:11
Caesar: Aut C., aut nihil | BORG 44:21
Ave C. | ANON 6:13
C. had his Brutus | HENRY 117:13
C.'s wife must be above | CAES 59:13
did in envy of great C. | SHAK 217:6
Hail C. | ANON 6:13
Imperious C., dead | SHAK 211:12
Not that I loved C. less | SHAK 216:13
Render therefore unto C. | BIBLE 33:28
speak in C.'s funeral | SHAK 216:16
unto C. shalt thou go | BIBLE 37:28
where some buried C. bled | FITZ 99:1
yesterday the word of C. | SHAK 216:16
Caesars: with C., and with Cannibals | SHAK 212:25
cage: Nor iron bars a c. | LOV 154:9
Robin Redbreast in a C. | BLAKE 42:18
sing like birds i' the c. | SHAK 218:27
We cannot c. the minute | MACN 158:10
caged: We think c. birds sing | WEBS 267:17
Cain: C. went out from the presence | BIBLE 22:18
first city C. | COWL 79:11
Lord set a mark upon C. | BIBLE 22:17
cake: Let them eat c. | MAR 160:1
cakes: shall be no more c. and ale | SHAK 233:23
Calais: 'C.' lying in my heart | MARY 162:13
calamity: That makes c. of so long | SHAK 208:24
calamus: sit c. saevior ense patet | BURT 55:15
calculated: Of nicely-c. less or more | WORD 277:5
calculation: c. shining out of the other | DICK 84:11
go to bed making a c. | DICK 83:23
calculus: integral and differential c. | GILB 109:1
Caledonia: O C.! stern and wild | SCOTT 201:17
calf: Bring hither the fatted c. | BIBLE 35:28
c. and the young lion | BIBLE 28:21
When he killed a c. he | AUBR 10:6
Caliban: rage of C. | WILDE 271:19

call: c. back yesterday	SHAK 230:6
C. me Ishmael	MELV 164:19
c. of the running tide	MAS 163:1
c. you, Shepherd	ARN 8:19
go and c. the cattle home	KING 142:12
one clear c. for me	TENN 251:11
shall please God to c. me	PRAY 187:21
they come when you do c.	SHAK 212:13
wake and c. me early	TENN 254:3
When you c. me that	WIST 273:5
called: many are c.	BIBLE 33:27
Out of the deep have I c.	PRAY 190:22
calling: dignity of this high c.	BURKE 52:18
calm: c. of mind all passion	MILT 170:7
calme: Luxe, c. et volupté	BAUD 16:12
Cambridge: C. people rarely smile	BROO 47:13
gently back at Oxford or C.	BEER 17:16
more attractive than C.	BAED 14:4
skill to C. books he sent	BROW 48:15
To C. books	TRAPP 259:22
we follow the C. lead	JOW 136:14
came: angel of the Lord c. upon	BIBLE 35:1
C. out by the same Door	FITZ 99:5
He c. unto his own	BIBLE 36:15
I c., I saw, I conquered	CAES 59:11
camel: almost in shape of a c.	SHAK 210:8
C.'s hump is an ugly lump	KIPL 144:12
It is easier for a c.	BIBLE 33:22
swallow a c.	BIBLE 33:30
Take my c., dear	MAC 157:6
camera: I am a c. with its shutter	ISH 129:17
Camerado: C., this is no book	WHIT 270:3
cammin: mezzo del c. di nostra vita	DANTE 81:7
can: because they think they c.	VIRG 263:8
He who c., does	SHAW 238:11
if we c. we must	HOUS 126:16
Cancel: C. and tear to pieces that	SHAK 222:15
it back to c. half a Line	FITZ 99:9
candid: from the c. friend	CANN 61:2
candidate: good dog, like a good c.	BECK 17:6
candle: Bell, book, and c.	SHAK 217:9
brief c.	SHAK 223:15
friends called him 'C.-ends'	CARR 62:6
hold a c. to my shames	SHAK 225:7
light a c. of understanding	BIBLE 30:20
little c. throws his beams	SHAK 226:8
My c. burns at both ends	MILL 166:6
this day light such a c.	LAT 149:14
when the hath lighted a c.	BIBLE 35:17
candle-light: c. at evening spinning	RONS 196:6
candles: Night's c. are burnt out	SHAK 232:2
Their c. are all out	SHAK 221:9
wind extinguishes c.	LA R 149:11
Candy: C. Is dandy	NASH 174:16
canem: littera scriptum 'Cave c.	PETR 183:1
cankerworm: c., and the caterpillar	BIBLE 30:13
Cannibals: with Caesars, and with C.	SHAK 212:25
cannie: c. wee thing	BURNS 53:25
Cannon: C. to right of them	TENN 251:9
Even in the c.'s mouth	SHAK 205:1
cannon-ball: c. took off his legs	HOOD 121:5
cannot: I c. sing the old songs	CLAR 73:1
some things we c. all do	LUC 155:3
cano: Arma virumque c.	VIRG 262:15
cant: clear your *mind* of c. You	JOHN 134:2
canvassers: c. whom they do not know	
	HURST 128:9
cap: Stuck a feather in his c.	BANGS 15:8
Capability: Negative C.	KEATS 140:16

capacity: described as a supreme c.	BUTL 56:15
that he had the c. to reign	TAC 250:11
transcendent c. of taking trouble	CARL 61:10
wisdom, c. and virtue	SWIFT 249:1
capax: c. imperii nisi imperasset	TAC 250:11
cape: Round the c. of a sudden	BROW 50:7
capiatur: Nullus liber homo c.	MAGN 158:16
capitaine: c. de vingt-quatre soldats	ANON 5:18
Capitalism: C., wisely managed	KEYN 141:17
unacceptable face of c.	HEATH 116:9
canons: you cannot feed c. so	SHAK 209:10
Capri: wordy letter came from C.	JUV 138:3
caps: roses crest the c. I know	THOM 257:22
captain: c. is in his bunk	SHAW 237:18
c.'s but a choleric word	SHAK 223:19
crew of the c.'s gig	GILB 106:21
I am a cook and a c. bold	GILB 106:21
I am the C. of the *Pinafore*	GILB 108:25
I am the c. of my soul	HENL 117:7
O Captain! my C.	WHIT 270:1
plain russet-coated c.	CROM 80:14
captains: All my sad c.	SHAK 204:2
C. and the Kings depart	KIPL 145:10
c. courageous whom death	BALL 14:18
thunder of the c.	BIBLE 25:34
captive: From the foes they c. make	CHAN 67:4
they that led us away c.	PRAY 191:1
captives: proclaim liberty to the c.	BIBLE 29:20
To serve your c.' need	KIPL 146:7
car: Put the c. away	AUDEN 11:2
caravan: Put up your c.	HODG 120:5
Caravanserai: in this batter'd C.	FITZ 98:17
carcase: Wheresoever the c. is	BIBLE 34:2
carcass: him as a c. fit for hounds	SHAK 216:4
card: 'He's a cheery old c.	SASS 200:12
cards: play'd At c. for kisses	LYLY 155:15
shuffle the c.	CERV 66:8
care: age is full of c.	SHAK 235:4
beneath Thy special c.	BETJ 21:5
c. and valour in this Welshman	SHAK 213:20
c. where the water goes	CHES 70:8
Hippocleides doesn't c.	HIPP 119:11
I c. for nobody	BICK 42:2
I c. not two-pence	BEAU 16:20
Nor c. beyond to-day	GRAY 112:10
ravell'd sleave of c.	SHAK 221:16
Sport that wrinkled C.	MILT 167:17
Take c. of the pence	LOWN 154:20
to take c. of the minutes	CHES 69:8
us to care and not to c.	ELIOT 93:10
With middle-ageing c.	POUND 186:13
career: c. open to talents	NAP 174:11
careful: c. of the type she seems	TENN 252:17
c. o' vidders all your	DICK 85:18
carefully: come most c. upon your hour	
	SHAK 206:5
careless: first fine c. rapture	BROW 49:13
So c. of the single life	TENN 252:17
'twere a c. trifle	SHAK 220:9
carelessness: lose both looks like c.	WILDE 271:8
cares: c. that infest the day	LONG 153:3
c. were to increase his	HOME 120:18
Hush, hush, Nobody c.	MORT 174:1
man is deprest with c.	GAY 105:12
Carew: tends the grave of Mad C.	HAYES 116:1
cargo: With a c. of ivory	MAS 162:14
caricature: With a c. of a face	GILB 108:16
Carlyle: C. and Mrs Carlyle marry	BUTL 56:24
C. has led us all out into	CLOU 73:19

carnage: c. and his conquests cease BYRON 57:6
carnal: men's c. lusts and appetites PRAY 187:24
CARO: VERBUM C. FACTUM EST
                                        MASS 163:21
carpe: c. diem HOR 123:14
Carpenter: Walrus and the C. CARR 64:1
  You may scold a c. who JOHN 131:17
carpet: on c. consideration SHAK 234:12
carpets: Over thick c. with a deadened BETJ 20:10
carping: obnoxious to each c. tongue BRAD 46:1
Carriage: C. held but just Ourselves DICK 86:1
  very small second class c. GILB 107:21
carry: c. them in his bosom BIBLE 29:10
  certain we can c. nothing out BIBLE 39:30
  choking him and making him c. TOLS 259:19
  man must c. knowledge with JOHN 133:8
  softly and c. a big stick RONS 196:13
  to c. the heavy burden EDW 92:11
Carthage: C. must be destroyed CATO 65:3
  O C.! O New York SASS 200:15
Carthago: Delenda est C. CATO 65:3
cartridge: holsters and c. boxes SHAW 237:8
carve: c. heads upon cherry-stones JOHN 134:4
  c. on every tree SHAK 205:3
  Let's c. him as a dish fit SHAK 216:4
carving: Now is a time for c. POUND 186:11
cas'd: c. up, like a holy relic WEBS 267:8
case: c. is concluded AUG 11:21
  Clutching a little c. AUDEN 10:14
  everything that is the c. WITT 273:7
  nothing to do with the c. GILB 108:15
  this c. is that case ARAB 7:14
  when a lady's in the c. GAY 105:18
casement: c. high and triple-arch'd KEATS 138:18
  ghost of Roger C. YEATS 279:2
casements: Charm'd magic c. KEATS 140:1
cash: c. that goes therewith CHES 69:18
  In epochs when c. payment CARL 61:9
  squalid c. interpretation put JAMES 130:8
  take the C. in hand FITZ 98:16
Casket: hushed C. of my Soul KEATS 140:8
casse: tout c. ANON 6:5
Cassock: C., band WILB 270:15
cassowary: If I were a c. WILB 270:15
Cast: C. a cold eye YEATS 280:3
  c. away the works of darkness PRAY 187:6
  c. off the works of darkness BIBLE 38:5
  C. thy bread upon the waters BIBLE 27:20
  c. ye your pearls before BIBLE 32:4
  first c. a stone at her BIBLE 36:26
  he c. into the sea BIBLE 36:2
  I will in no wise c. out BIBLE 36:23
  over Edom will I c. PRAY 189:10
  when I c. mine eyes HERR 119:1
castels: make c. thanne in Spayne CHAU 68:21
castitatem: Da mihi c. et continentiam AUG 11:15
castle: c., called Doubting-Castle BUNY 51:21
  man's house is his c. COKE 74:3
  rich man in his c. ALEX 2:4
  splendour falls on c. walls TENN 254:9
Castlereagh: He had a mask like C. SHEL 239:9
castles: all the c. I have JONS 135:20
casual: half-believers in our c. creeds ARN 8:21
casualty: first c. when war JOHN 131:1
Cat: C., the Rat, and Lovell COLL 75:16
  Hanging of his c. on Monday BRAT 46:7
  harmless necessary c. SHAK 225:15
  I am a c. that likes SMITH 242:12
  it might have been c. BARH 15:9

I will consider my C. Jeoffry SMART 241:15
  killing a c. than choking KING 143:1
  part to tear a c. SHAK 226:15
  pavilion c. LANG 148:17
  poor c. i' the adage SHAK 221:4
  Runcible C. with crimson LEAR 150:19
  to see how the c. jumps SCOTT 202:11
  Touch not the c. SCOTT 202:6
cataract: wild c. leaps in glory TENN 254:9
cataracts: You c. and hurricanoes SHAK 218:6
catastrophe: between education and c.
                                        WELLS 268:17
catch: c. a falling star DONNE 88:15
  game of catch as c. can FOOTE 101:7
  Perdition c. my soul SHAK 228:26
catching: c. a train is to miss CHES 70:14
Categorical: This imperative is C. imperative
                                        KANT 138:7
caterpillar: c., and the palmerworm BIBLE 30:13
Cathay: Europe than a cycle of C. TENN 253:14
catherine-wheels: in a cloud of crimson c.
                                        FRY 103:17
Catholic: I cannot be a good C. NORF 177:6
Catholick: C. and Apostolick Church
                                        PRAY 187:14
Catiline: abuse our patience, C. CIC 72:10
Cato: losing one pleased C. LUCAN 155:1
cats: Do c. eat bats CARR 62:14
  greater c. with golden eyes SACK 199:1
  monkeys and c. JAMES 130:4
  Naming of C. is a difficult ELIOT 94:14
cattle: c. rise and listen KING 143:5
  go and call the c. home KING 142:12
  these who die as c. OWEN 179:4
caught: c. his clear accents BROW 50:1
  c. in her arms long WYATT 278:4
  c. my foot in the mat GROS 113:3
  ram c. in a thicket BIBLE 22:26
cauldron: Fire burn and c. bubble SHAK 222:22
causa: c. finita est AUG 11:21
  Victrix c. deis placuit LUCAN 155:1
cause: beauty of the good old c. WORD 277:1
  called amiss *The good old C.* MILT 170:21
  c. of dullness in others FOOTE 101:8
  c., or just impediment PRAY 187:23
  c. that wit is in other SHAK 212:19
  in the justice of our c. HAIG 113:9
  it is the c., my soul SHAK 229:12
  man can shew any just c. PRAY 187:23
  Report me and my c. aright SHAK 211:21
  Ring out a slowly dying c. TENN 252:24
causes: I hate the idea of c. FORS 101:11
  understand the c. of things VIRG 264:12
cautiously: do c. ANON 7:4
cavaliero: he was a perfect c. BYRON 57:3
Cavaliers: C. (Wrong but Wromantic) SELL 203:2
Cave: littera scriptum 'C. canem PETR 183:1
caves: unfathom'd c. of ocean bear GRAY 112:5
caviare: 'twas c. to the general SHAK 208:17
Cawdor: Glamis thou art, and C. SHAK 220:10
cease: c. upon the midnight with KEATS 139:22
  have fears that I may c. KEATS 140:9
  not c. from Mental Fight BLAKE 43:2
ceasing: Remembering without c. BIBLE 39:23
cedars: brambles like tall c. show COTT 78:14
cedarwood: c., and sweet white wine MAS 162:14
ceiling: in the lines of the c. ELUA 96:2
celebrated: Saviour's birth is c. SHAK 206:9
celebrity: c. is a person who is known BOOR 44:18

celestial: Apparelled in c. light	WORD 275:13
lighten with c. fire	PRAY 191:12
celibacy: c. has no pleasures	JOHN 135:2
cell: Each in his narrow c.	GRAY 112:2
Celtic: enchanted woods of C. antiquity	
	KEYN 141:18
censure: Take each man's c.	SHAK 207:6
to read, and c.	HEM 117:3
centre: c. cannot hold	YEATS 279:15
Mon c. cède	FOCH 101:6
My c. is giving way	FOCH 101:6
centum: *deinde c.*	CAT 65:6
centuries: All c. but this	GILB 108:5
I shall lie through c.	BROW 49:1
Through what wild c.	DE L 82:8
century: intellectual life of our c.	ARN 9:8
seventeenth c. a dissociation	ELIOT 95:12
To one a c. hence or any	WHIT 269:17
Cerberus: damn them with King C.	SHAK 212:25
loathed Melancholy, Of C.	MILT 167:14
ceremony: c. of innocence is drowned	
	YEATS 279:15
thrice-gorgeous c.	SHAK 213:23
Ceres: laughing C. re-assume the land	POPE 185:4
certain: c. because it is impossible	TERT 256:8
c. hope of the Resurrection	PRAY 188:5
dirge of her c. ending	SHAK 235:7
one thing is c.	FITZ 99:4
certainties: When hot for c. in this	MER 165:5
certified: c. how long I have to live	PRAY 188:25
Ceylon: Blow soft o'er C.'s isle	HEBER 116:10
chaast: wol nat kepe me c. in al	CHAU 68:16
chaffinch: c. sings on the orchard	BROW 49:12
Chagrin: C. d'amour dure toute la	FLOR 101:3
chain: c. that is round us now	CORY 78:11
chains: bind their kings in c.	PRAY 191:7
C. and slaverie	BURNS 54:20
C. are worse than bayonets	JERR 130:20
everywhere he is in c.	ROUS 198:2
sang in my c. like the sea	THOM 257:3
Shake your c. to earth	SHEL 239:11
Chair: C. she sat	ELIOT 95:2
It is like a barber's c.	SHAK 203:13
La c. est triste	MALL 159:4
Seated in thy silver c.	JONS 135:19
chairs: two glasses and two c.	MACN 158:8
chaise-longue: hurly-burly of the c.	CAMP 60:12
chamber: into the conference c.	BEVAN 21:17
stalking in my c.	WYATT 278:3
chambre: demeurer en repos dans une c.	
	PASC 180:16
chameleon: c.'s dish	SHAK 209:10
champagne: not a c. teetoller	SHAW 237:11
Women and C.	BELL 18:22
chance: bludgeonings of c.	HENL 117:6
c. favours only the prepared	PAST 181:6
voice to come in as by c.	BACON 13:4
Chancellor: C. of the Exchequer is	LOWE 154:13
C. of the University	WELL 268:6
rather susceptible C.	GILB 107:13
Chancery: pretty young wards in C.	GILB 107:13
chances: c. change by course	SOUT 244:3
choose Between the c.	AUDEN 11:12
Change: C. and decay in all around	LYTE 156:2
C. is not made without	JOHN 134:14
c. of heart	AUDEN 11:5
c. best carriage horses	TROL 260:11
c. the name and it's about	HOR 124:19

c. th'expiring flame renews	GAY 105:21
God cannot c. the past	AGAT 1:18
How will the c. strike	BROW 49:4
is necessary not to c.	FALK 97:11
I would not c. for thine	JONS 136:3
more things c.	KARR 138:11
nous avons c. tout cela	MOL 171:11
point is to c.	MARX 162:9
ringing grooves of c.	TENN 253:13
scorn to c. my state	SHAK 235:11
take silver or small c.	CHAM 66:16
we c. with them	ANON 7:8
whose beauty is past c.	HOPK 122:4
wind of c. is blowing	MACM 158:1
changed: c. from that Hector who	VIRG 263:4
c. into little water drops	MARL 160:7
c. that my oldest creditors	FOX 102:4
c. utterly	YEATS 278:19
that it be not c.	BIBLE 30:10
we shall all be c.	BIBLE 38:22
changes: Her plot hath many c.	QUAR 193:9
changest: who c. not	LYTE 156:2
changing: c. guard at Buckingham Palace	
	MILNE 166:11
c. scenes of life	TATE 250:16
Channel: Butting through the C.	MAS 162:15
you are crossing the C.	GILB 107:21
chantants: Ô ces voix d'enfants c.	VERL 262:4
chante: on le c.	BEAU 16:14
Chanting: C. faint hymns to the cold	SHAK 226:12
Chaos: C., illumined	WILDE 272:3
C. is come again	SHAK 228:26
chapels: Stolen looks are nice in c.	HUNT 128:6
Chaplain: book a devil's c.	DARW 81:16
chaps: Biography is about c.	BENT 19:16
chapter: c. of accidents	CHES 69:15
c. of accidents is	WILK 272:8
c. of 'The Natural History	JOHN 133:7
char: c. the wood ere Thou canst	THOM 258:4
character: belongs not to the female c.	
	KNOX 147:7
I leave my c. behind me	SHER 240:24
man's c. is to be abused	THAC 256:10
Sow a c.	READE 194:13
Charge: 'C., Chester, charge!	SCOTT 202:3
shall give his angels c.	PRAY 190:1
charged: is c. with the grandeur	HOPK 121:18
charges: children but as bills of c.	BACON 13:12
Charing-Cross: human existence is at C.	
	JOHN 132:19
Pitched betwixt Heaven and C.	THOM 258:7
chariot: Bring me my c. of fire	BLAKE 43:2
chariots: c., and some in horses	PRAY 188:13
Charity: C. and beating begins	FLET 101:2
c. envieth not	BIBLE 38:15
C. never faileth	BIBLE 38:15
C. shall cover the multitude	BIBLE 40:21
C. suffereth long	BIBLE 38:15
c. vaunteth not itself	BIBLE 38:15
faith, hope, c.	BIBLE 38:16
greatest of these is c.	BIBLE 38:16
have not c.	BIBLE 38:14
with c. for all	LINC 152:3
Charles: used by C. the First	COW 79:9
Charlie: We'll o'er the water to C.	HOGG 120:14
Charlotte: Werther had a love for C.	THAC 256:15
charm: c. can soothe her melancholy	GOLD 110:18
c. he never so wisely	PRAY 189:9
Completing the c.	ELIOT 93:11

powers of C. and Desire — CAT 65:4
charmed: c. it with smiles and soap — CARR 62:8
charmer: hear the voice of the c. — PRAY 189:9
Were t'other dear c. away — GAY 105:14
charming: c. is divine philosophy — MILT 167:8
charmingly: How c. sweet you sing — LEAR 150:14
charms: Music has c. to sooth — CONG 76:18
those endearing young c. — MOORE 172:13
charter: c. of thy worth gives thee — SHAK 236:6
This was the c. of the land — THOM 258:12
Charybdis: Scylla and C. — SHEL 240:10
chase: c. the glowing Hours with — BYRON 57:10
shining creatures of the c. — TENN 254:12
thy c. is done — SCOTT 201:13
When heated in the c. — TATE 250:15
with unhurrying c. — THOM 258:2
chasm: romantic c. which slanted — COL 75:3
chassis: country's in a state of c. — OCAS 177:9
chaste: My English text is c. — GIBB 106:9
Nor ever c. — DONNE 88:7
nunnery Of thy c. breast — LOV 154:10
chasten: power To c. and subdue — WORD 275:6
chasteneth: Lord loveth he c. — BIBLE 40:10
chastised: father hath c. you with whips — BIBLE 25:4
chastisement: c. of our peace was upon — BIBLE 29:15
chastity: Give me c. and continency — AUG 11:15
châteaux: Ô saisons, ô c. — RIMB 195:8
chatter: insignificant c. of the world — TROL 260:5
matter if it's only idle c. — GILB 108:20
cheap: c. and chippy chopper — GILB 108:9
flesh and blood so c. — HOOD 121:13
hold their manhoods c. — SHAK 214:4
cheapness: tawdry c. Shall outlast — POUND 186:9
cheat: it's so lucrative to c. — CLOU 73:15
may c. at cards genteelly — BOSW 45:4
sweet c. gone — DE L 82:12
cheated: Of being c. — BUTL 56:8
Old men who never c. — BETJ 20:10
cheats: c. with an oath acknowledges — PLUT 183:18
check: To c. the erring and reprove — WORD 276:1
cheek: bring a blush into the c. — DICK 85:9
Feed on her damask c. — SHAK 234:4
hangs upon the c. of night — SHAK 231:14
leans her c. upon her hand — SHAK 231:17
on thy c. a fading rose — KEATS 139:4
Pale grew thy c. and cold — BYRON 59:3
smite thee on thy right c. — BIBLE 31:17
cheeks: crack your c. — SHAK 218:6
Fat ruddy c. Augustus had — HOFF 120:7
Her c. were so red — KING 142:15
cheer: c. us when we recover — BURKE 53:2
Could scarce forbear to c. — MAC 156:10
That c. but not inebriate — COWP 80:4
to c. but not inebriate — BERK 20:1
cheerful: c., merry Dr Brighton — THAC 256:9
Dromedary is a c. bird — BELL 18:4
heart maketh a c. countenance — BIBLE 26:20
he looking as c. as any — PEPYS 182:8
loveth a c. giver — BIBLE 39:4
cheerfulness: c. was always breaking — EDW 92:13
cheese: dreamed of c.—toasted — STEV 247:2
eggs and a pound of c. — CALV 59:16
like some valley c. — AUDEN 11:9
smells of c. — SURT 248:13
that has 265 kinds of c. — DE G 82:6
chef: je suis leur c. — LEDR 151:2
chemin: c'est le plus court c. — MOL 171:13

chemist: c., fiddler, statesman — DRYD 90:16
Chequer-board: C. of Nights and Days — FITZ 99:7
cherish: c. those hearts that hate — SHAK 215:10
love, c., and to obey — PRAY 187:28
cherries: c., hops — DICK 85:13
There c. grow — CAMP 60:20
cherry: c. now — HOUS 125:4
C.-ripe — HERR 118:17
Like to a double c. — SHAK 220:17
ruddier than the c. — GAY 105:6
see the c. hung with snow — HOUS 125:4
cherry-isle: There's the land, or c. — HERR 118:17
cherry-stones: not carve heads upon c. — JOHN 134:4
Cherubic: C. Creatures— These Gentlewomen — DICK 86:6
cherubim: heaven's c. — SHAK 221:1
cherubins: quiring to the young-eyed c. — SHAK 226:5
chest: caused his c. to slip down — WOD 273:14
men on the dead man's c. — STEV 246:13
Chester: 'Charge, C., charge! — SCOTT 202:3
Chesterton: dared attack my C. — BELL 18:25
chestnut: showers betumble the c. — HARDY 114:15
Under the spreading c. tree — LONG 153:17
chestnuts: sailor's wife had c. — SHAK 220:2
cheval: hommes et allemand à mon c. — CHAR 67:15
Chevalier: C. sans peur et sans reproche — ANON 5:16
chewed: few to be c. and digested — BACON 13:20
chewing: c. little bits of string — BELL 18:9
chicken: c. in his pot every Sunday — HENR 117:11
Some c. — CHUR 71:10
chickens: pretty c. and their dam — SHAK 223:5
Chief: Hail to the C. who in triumph — SCOTT 201:14
chiefly: c. on the just — BOWEN 45:9
chieftain: c. to the Highlands bound — CAMP 60:17
child: angel is the English c. — BLAKE 43:15
C.! do not throw this — BELL 18:2
c. in the street I could — CLOU 73:19
C. is father of the Man — WORD 275:11
c. may joy to hear — BLAKE 43:13
c. of God — PRAY 187:18
c. should always say what's — STEV 247:7
father that knows his own c. — SHAK 225:3
had been any christom c. — SHAK 223:13
healthy c. well nursed is — SWIFT 249:6
heard one calling, 'C.' — HERB 118:8
He never spoils the c. — HOOD 121:8
Here a little c. I stand — HERR 119:2
I was a c. and she was — POE 183:19
little c. shall lead them — BIBLE 28:21
named the c. I-chabod — BIBLE 24:17
On a cloud I saw a c. — BLAKE 43:12
room up of my absent c. — SHAK 217:10
saddling of the right to a c. — SHAW 237:17
seen A curious c. — WORD 274:15
She was an aggravating c. — BELL 18:11
This painted c. of dirt — POPE 184:22
To have a thankless c. — SHAK 218:3
Train up a c. in the way — BIBLE 26:25
unto us a c. is born — BIBLE 28:19
use of a new-born c. — FRAN 102:17
when a c. is born — SU T 248:9
When I was a c. — BIBLE 38:16
when thy king is a c. — BIBLE 27:18
would not *coddle* the c. — JOHN 132:14
wretched c. expires — BELL 18:11
yet a c. — POPE 184:19
childbirth: Mountains will heave in c. — HOR 122:15

Childe Roland: 'C. to the Dark Tower came
BROW 49:8

Childhood: C. is the kingdom where   MILL 166:4
'tis the eye of c.   SHAK 221:18
childish: again towards c. treble   SHAK 205:1
I put away c. things   BIBLE 38:16
my c. wave of pity   BETJ 21:9
childishness: Is second c.   SHAK 205:1
children: be called the c. of God   BIBLE 31:11
become as little c.   BIBLE 33:15
c. at play are not playing   MONT 171:18
C. begin by loving their   WILDE 271:17
c. cried in the streets   MOTL 174:4
c. in whom is no faith   BIBLE 24:1
c. like the olive-branches   PRAY 190:21
c., quietly talking alone   BOWEN 45:14
c.'s teeth are set   BIBLE 30:4
c. stood watching them   KING 142:13
C. sweeten labours   BACON 13:15
committed by c. on children   BOWEN 45:14
even so are the young c.   PRAY 190:20
fear death as c.   BACON 13:5
fond of c. (except boys)   CARR 64:18
Her c. arise up   BIBLE 27:1
I never knows the c.   MARR 161:7
me from c. who were rough   SPEN 244:11
procreation of c.   PRAY 187:25
shall return us the c.   KIPL 143:14
Suffer the little c.   BIBLE 34:26
those c.'s voices   VERL 262:4
thou shalt bring forth c.   BIBLE 22:13
When c. of one family   WATTS 266:15
when he cried the little c.   AUDEN 10:13
When the voices of c. are   BLAKE 43:16
which holdeth c. from play   SIDN 241:6
wife and c. hath given hostages   BACON 13:11
wife and c. but as bills   BACON 13:12
child-wife: It's only my c.   DICK 84:6
chill: bitter c. it was   KEATS 138:16
chilly: although the room grows c.   GRAH 111:10
c. stars I can forgo   CORY 78:13
I feel c. and grown old   BROW 50:22
Chimborazo: C., Cotopaxi   TURN 260:20
chime: let your silver c.   MILT 168:8
chimeras: other wild impossible c.   SWIFT 249:1
chimes: heard the c. at midnight   SHAK 212:28
chimneys: Our c. were blown down   SHAK 222:5
So your c. I sweep   BLAKE 43:17
chimney-sweepers: c., come to dust   SHAK 206:4
chin: rye reach to the c.   PEELE 182:2
China: from C. to Peru   JOHN 135:8
Till C. and Africa meet   AUDEN 10:8
Chinee: heathen C. is peculiar   HARTE 115:12
Chinese: ruined by C. cheap labour   HARTE 115:13
chintzy: c. cheeriness   BETJ 20:8
chip: Not merely a c.   BURKE 53:3
chippy: cheap and c. chopper   GILB 108:9
chirche: Housbondes at c. dore she   CHAU 68:7
chivalry: age of c. is gone   BURKE 53:9
age of c. is never past   KING 143:2
Christian service and true c.   SHAK 230:2
nine-tenths of the law of c.   SAY 200:16
choice: c. and master spirits   SHAK 216:10
Each to his c.   KIPL 145:18
money and you takes your c.   ANON 5:14
more difficult the c.   ALL 2:6
choirs: Bare ruin'd c.   SHAK 236:5
choisir: *c'est c.*   LEVIS 151:12
chokes: something bitter that c.   LUCR 155:9

choking: cat than c. her with cream   KING 143:1
c. him and making him carry   TOLS 259:19
choleric: captain's but a c. word   SHAK 223:19
Chommoda: *C. dicebat*   CAT 65:10
choose: *can believe what we c.*   NEWM 176:5
can believe what you c.   NEWM 176:6
c. A Jewish God   BROW 48:4
c. life that both thou   BIBLE 23:36
c. Their place of rest   MILT 169:22
Let's c. executors   SHAK 230:7
of man is forced to c.   YEATS 278:13
They cannot c.   THOM 257:19
To c. The Jews   EWER 97:9
chop: day you'll eat a pork c.   CAMP 60:10
chopcherry: c. ripe within   PEELE 182:2
chopper: cheap and chippy c.   GILB 108:9
chord: feel for the common c.   BROW 48:20
I struck one c. of music   PROC 191:21
chortled: He c. in his joy   CARR 63:17
chosen: few are c.   BIBLE 33:27
ye are a c. generation   BIBLE 40:18
choux: *trouve plantant mes c.*   MONT 171:17
Christ: C. being raised from   BIBLE 37:35
C. erecteth his Church   BANC 15:7
C. which strengtheneth   BIBLE 39:21
in the bowels of C.   CROM 80:15
is C. risen from the dead   BIBLE 38:18
Ring in the C. that is   TENN 252:25
Vision of C. that thou   BLAKE 42:20
where C.'s blood streams   MARL 160:6
Christ Church: I am the Dean of C.   SPR 245:5
study at C. and All-Souls   JOHN 132:11
Christe: *C. eleison*   MASS 163:10
Christian: Because it is only C. men   CHES 69:21
C. boys I can scarcely   ARN 9:16
C. ideal has not been tried   CHES 70:12
C. is a man who feels   YBAR 278:9
C. religion doubted   BUTL 56:19
C. resolution to find   NIET 176:18
C. service and true chivalry   SHAK 230:2
evidence of a naturally C. soul   TERT 256:6
hate him for he is a C.   SHAK 224:18
I mean the C. religion   FIEL 98:8
It's the Early C. that   SAKI 199:5
persuadest me to be a C.   BIBLE 37:30
souls of C. peoples...   CHES 69:18
tiger that hadn't *got* a C.   PUNCH 192:17
to form C. men   ARN 9:16
you were a C. Slave   HENL 117:9
Christianity: age come from C. and journalism
BALF 14:15
C. better than Truth will   COL 75:9
His C. was muscular   DISR 87:7
Christians: blood of C. is the seed   TERT 256:7
Christmas: C. I no more desire a rose   SHAK 219:8
C. morning bells say 'Come   BETJ 20:7
that C. should fall out   ADD 1:12
Christmas Day: It is C. in the Workhouse
SIMS 241:10
Christopher Robin: C. went down with Alice
MILNE 166:11
C. is saying his prayers   MILNE 166:17
chronicle: in the c. of wasted time   SHAK 236:10
chronicles: abstracts and brief c.   SHAK 208:18
Chuck: C. it, Smith   CHES 69:18
church: bells have knoll'd to c.   SHAK 204:24
Catholick and Apostolick C.   PRAY 187:14
Christ erecteth his C.   BANC 15:7
C. militant here in earth   PRAY 187:15

'Come all to c.   HOUS 125:13
English C. shall be free   MAGN 158:15
not the c. for his mother   CYPR 81:6
other c. has ever understood   MAC 156:18
rock I will build my c.   BIBLE 33:12
salvation outside the c.   AUG 11:18
Church of England: Protestant religion but the C.
                                             FIEL 98:8
churchyard: devil in the same c. will   BANC 15:7
lie in Mellstock c. now   HARDY 114:9
churchyards: When c. yawn and hell itself
                                             SHAK 210:9
cigar: c., and cigarette tobacco   DOYLE 89:11
good c. is a Smoke   KIPL 143:11
cigarette: c. is the perfect type   WILDE 271:21
Cilicia: city in C.   BIBLE 37:27
Cinara: when dear C. was my queen   HOR 124:14
Cinarae: Sub regno C.   HOR 124:14
circenses: Panem et c.   JUV 138:4
circle: Round and round the c.   ELIOT 93:11
Weave a c. round him thrice   COL 75:7
wheel is come full c.   SHAK 219:1
Circumlocution: C. Office was beforehand
                                             DICK 84:9
circumspice: monumentum requiris, c.   ANON 7:6
Nisi monumentum requiris, c.   INGE 129:12
circumstance: am the very slave of c.   BYRON 58:20
In the fell clutch of c.   HENL 117:6
circumstantial: c. evidence is very strong
                                             THOR 259:8
citadels: circle-c. there   HOPK 122:7
cities: c. hostile and the towns   ELIOT 94:1
thou art the flower of c.   DUNB 91:23
citizen: c. Of credit and renown   COWP 79:12
c. of no mean city   BIBLE 37:27
greater than a private c.   TAC 250:11
citizens: first and second class c.   WILL 272:13
city: briskly to infect a c.   AUDEN 10:14
citizen of no mean c.   BIBLE 37:27
C. is of Night   THOM 258:14
c. that is set on an hill   BIBLE 31:13
C. with her dreaming spires   ARN 9:3
Despising, For you, the c.   SHAK 205:18
Except the Lord keep the c.   PRAY 190:19
first c. Cain   COWL 79:11
Happy is that c. which   ANON 3:13
have we no continuing c.   BIBLE 40:13
long in populous c. pent   MILT 169:17
Lord guards the c.   BIBLE 41:15
rose-red c. 'half as old   BURG 52:7
Soft morning, c.   JOYCE 136:20
that great c.   BIBLE 41:4
This C. now doth   WORD 276:18
who has been long in c.   KEATS 140:7
City of London: C. remains as it is   CHAM 66:10
civet: Give me an ounce of c.   SHAK 218:21
Civics: talk on 'Sex and C.   BETJ 21:2
civil: good people, be c.   GWYN 113:7
Too c. by half   SHER 240:21
civilians: those who wish to be c.   ROST 197:13
civility: I see a wild c.   HERR 118:18
reciprocal c. of authors   JOHN 134:24
civilization: botched c.   POUND 186:10
great elements of modern c.   CARL 61:8
civilized: last thing c. by Man   MER 165:7
Civis: C. Romanus sum   CIC 72:12
claim: last territorial c. which   HITL 119:16
clair: pas c. n'est pas français   RIV 195:9
clamavi: De profundis c. ad te   BIBLE 41:16

clap: c. your hands   BARR 16:5
Soul c. its hands and sing   YEATS 279:13
clapping: tears on a soundless-c.   THOM 257:22
clapte: c. the wyndow   CHAU 68:11
Claret: C. is the liquor for boys   JOHN 133:11
dozen of C. on my Tomb   KEATS 141:6
Clash: sun and the rain C.   FRY 103:17
clasps: c. the crag with crooked   TENN 251:13
class: c. distinction   BETJ 21:5
c. struggle necessarily leads   MARX 162:10
history of c. struggle   MARX 162:4
Like many of the upper c.   BELL 19:6
classes: To prove the upper c.   COW 79:8
classic: happen to have an Elzevir c.   CHES 69:10
What avails the c. bent   KIPL 143:10
claw: Nature, red in tooth and c.   TENN 252:18
claws: been a pair of ragged c.   ELIOT 94:6
c. that catch   CARR 63:16
clay: associate of this c.   HAER 113:8
cover'd thick with other c.   BYRON 57:11
of c. and wattles made   YEATS 279:7
this the c. grew tall   OWEN 179:6
clean: c., verb active   DICK 84:21
I shall be c.   PRAY 189:6
keep their teeth c.   SHAK 205:15
one more thing to keep c.   FRY 103:18
small and white and c.   MORR 173:14
so c. an ending   HOUS 126:8
Then I was c. and brave   HOUS 125:10
these hands ne'er be c.   SHAK 223:7
cleaned: c. the windows and I swept   GILB 108:28
cleaning: We had daily c.   REED 194:11
Cleanliness: C. is, indeed   WESL 268:19
Cleanse: C. the stuff'd bosom   SHAK 223:13
cleansed: doors of perception were c.   BLAKE 44:9
clear: c. out from the province   GLAD 109:15
c. your *mind* of cant… You   JOHN 134:2
is not c. is not French   RIV 195:9
So c. in his great office   SHAK 221:1
cleared: c. away Lunch   CALV 60:3
clearer: case of c. evidence   ARAB 7:14
clearing-house: c. of the world   CHAM 66:10
clears: little water c. us of this   SHAK 222:2
cleave: the general ear with   SHAK 208:21
shall c. unto his wife   BIBLE 22:11
tongue c. to the roof   PRAY 191:1
Clee: C. to heaven the beacon   HOUS 125:3
Cleopatra: C.'s nose been shorter   PASC 180:17
clercs: La trahison des c.   BENDA 19:11
clergy: of what the c. tell you   JOW 136:15
without the benefit o' the C.   CONG 76:14
clergymen: men, women, and c.   SMITH 242:18
Clerk: C. ther was of Oxenford   CHAU 68:4
thought he saw a Banker's C.   CARR 62:12
clever: c. men at Oxford   GRAH 111:12
c. so rude to the good   WORD 274:10
c. theft was praiseworthy   SPEN 244:8
good people were c.   WORD 274:10
let who can be c.   KING 142:9
think it c. of the turtle   NASH 174:19
we are all c. here   FOAK 101:5
cleverest: 'You're the c. member   WEBB 267:2
cliffs: c. of fall   HOPK 122:2
Yet still the solitary c.   WORD 275:1
climate: love with a cold c.   SOUT 244:2
climb: c. not at all   ELIZ 95:11
Fain would I c.   RAL 194:5
clime: marvel save in Eastern c.   BURG 52:7
climes: Of cloudless c. and starry   BYRON 58:21

combustion: Of dire c. and confus'd ... SHAK 222:5
come: Cannot c., lie follows ... PROU 192:6
'C. all to church ... HOUS 125:13
c. and buy ... HERR 118:17
C., and he cometh ... BIBLE 32:14
C., friendly bombs ... BETJ 21:11
C., Holy Spirit ... LANG 149:3
C. in the speaking silence ... ROSS 197:4
C. into the garden ... TENN 254:1
c. is strew'd with husks ... SHAK 233:12
c., let us sing ... PRAY 190:2
C., my Celia ... JONS 136:10
C. over into Macedonia ... BIBLE 37:19
C. unto me ... BIBLE 32:31
C. unto these yellow sands ... SHAK 232:13
c. up sometime, see me ... WEST 269:2
C. what come may ... SHAK 220:8
c. with old Khayyám ... FITZ 99:4
Even so, c., Lord Jesus ... BIBLE 41:10
hour your Lord doth c. ... BIBLE 34:4
I will c. ... HOUS 125:13
jump the life to c. ... SHAK 220:13
King of glory shall c. ... PRAY 188:18
leave to c. unto my love ... SPEN 244:14
men may c. and men may ... TENN 251:7
mine hour is not yet c. ... BIBLE 36:19
O c., all ye faithful ... ANON 6:10
'O c. ye in peace here ... SCOTT 201:21
Suffer me to c. to thee ... WESL 268:18
tells thee I c. ... KING 142:6
That it should c. to this ... SHAK 206:15
they c. when you do call ... SHAK 212:13
'tis not to c. ... SHAK 211:17
Very sorry can't c. ... BER 19:22
we come, we c. ... DAV 81:18
What's to c. is still unsure ... SHAK 233:22
wheel is c. full circle ... SHAK 219:1
whistle, and I'll c. to you ... BURNS 55:7
Will come when it will c. ... SHAK 216:6
comedies: c. are ended by a marriage ... BYRON 58:5
comedy: This world is a c. to those ... WALP 266:2
comely: thy speech is c. ... BIBLE 28:3
comes: c. again in the morning ... SHER 240:23
comest: thou c. into thy kingdom ... BIBLE 36:9
cometh: canst not tell whence it c. ... BIBLE 36:20
He c. not ... TENN 253:18
Him that c. to me I will ... BIBLE 36:23
no man c. unto the Father ... BIBLE 37:2
comets: Ye country c. ... MARV 161:19
comfort: beside the waters of c. ... PRAY 188:15
c. ye my people ... BIBLE 29:8
I beg cold c. ... SHAK 217:15
I have of c. and despair ... SHAK 237:2
you naught for your c. ... CHES 69:19
comfortable: c. estate of widowhood ... GAY 105:9
comfortably: liv'd c. so long together ... GAY 105:7
Speak ye c. to Jerusalem ... BIBLE 29:8
comforted: they shall be c. ... BIBLE 31:11
comforters: Miserable c. are ye all ... BIBLE 25:25
comforting: where is your c. ... HOPK 122:1
comical: I often think it's c. ... GILB 107:16
coming: cold c. we had of it ... ELIOT 93:25
c. after me is preferred ... BIBLE 36:17
c. events cast their shadows ... CAMP 60:16
do you see nothing c. ... PERR 182:16
even as their c. hither ... SHAK 218:26
She is c., my dove ... TENN 254:2
command: c. what you will ... AUG 11:17
mortals to c. success ... ADD 1:7

That shall c. my heart ... CRAS 80:11
to c. ... SHAK 229:18
why people c. rather badly ... COMP 76:10
wide as his c. ... DRYD 90:10
commandments: Fear God, and keep his c. ... BIBLE 27:24
there aren't no Ten C. ... KIPL 145:4
commend: hands I c. my spirit ... BIBLE 36:11
That doth best c. a book ... HEM 117:3
Comment: C. is free but facts are ... SCOTT 201:7
commerce: heavens fill with c. ... TENN 253:10
Let there be c. between us ... POUND 186:11
recognize but one rule of c. ... QUES 193:10
commit: c. his body to the ground ... PRAY 188:5
c. his body to the deep ... PRAY 191:11
Do not adultery c. ... CLOU 73:14
Commodity: C., Firmness, and *Delight* ... WOTT 277:19
common: base, c. and popular ... SHAK 213:18
Cloe is…and c. as the air ... GRAN 111:13
c. enemy and oppressor ... BURKE 53:7
c. opinion and uncommon ... BAG 14:8
c. power to keep them all ... HOBB 119:17
c. pursuit of true judgement ... ELIOT 95:10
c. task ... KEBLE 141:9
concur with the c. reader ... JOHN 134:25
feel for the c. chord ... BROW 48:20
He nothing c. did or mean ... MARV 161:17
In c. things that round ... WORD 276:6
Is much more c. where ... BYRON 57:18
nor lose the c. touch ... KIPL 144:9
they are not already c. ... LOCKE 152:10
You c. people of the skies ... WOTT 277:18
common-looking: Lord prefers c. people ... LINC 152:5
Commonplace: 'C.,' said Holmes ... DOYLE 89:26
c. things and characters ... SCOTT 202:10
Commons: C., faithful to their ... MACK 157:14
communication: Let your c. be Yea ... BIBLE 31:16
communications: Evil c. corrupt good manners ... BIBLE 38:20
Communism: C. is Soviet power plus ... LEE 151:3
C. with a human face ... DUBC 91:14
spectre of C. ... MARX 162:3
Communist: C. must grasp the truth ... MAO 159:14
community: c. of Europe and we must ... SAL 199:8
part of the c. of Europe ... GLAD 109:16
compact: Are of imagination all c. ... SHAK 227:17
life now, c., visible ... WHIT 269:17
companion: c. to owls ... BIBLE 25:30
companions: c. for middle age ... BACON 13:13
I have had c. ... LAMB 148:4
Like old c. in adversity ... BRY 51:1
Company: C. for carrying on an undertaking ... ANON 2:13
except the present c. ... OKEE 178:2
is what I call good c. ... AUST 12:8
married life three is c. ... WILDE 271:7
Take the tone of the c. ... CHES 69:6
compare: been studying how I may c. ... SHAK 230:15
c. thee to a summer's day ... SHAK 235:9
Comparisons: C. are odorous ... SHAK 228:11
compass: c. of the notes it ran ... DRYD 91:9
c. of the world ... PRAY 188:17
note to the top of my c. ... SHAK 210:7
compassion: sharp c. of the healer's art ... ELIOT 93:17
compel: c. us to be equal upstairs ... BARR 16:1
competition: Approves all forms of c. ... CLOU 73:16

Complacencies: C. of the peignoir STEV 246:15
complain: Of Humber would c. MARV 161:20
  to me to c. of rheumatism SAKI 199:4
complaints: c. of ill-usage contemptible
  MELB 164:18
complexion: Mislike me not for my c. SHAK 225:2
  often is his gold c. dimm'd SHAK 235:9
compliance: by a timely c. FIEL 98:5
complies: that c. against his will BUTL 56:11
composition: mad c. SHAK 217:7
comprehend: When she begins to c. it
  PRIOR 191.17
comprehended: darkness c. it not BIBLE 36:13
comprendre: c. rend très indulgent STAEL 245:9
compunctious: That no c. visitings SHAK 220:11
Comrades: C., leave me here a little TENN 253:5
  Your c. chase e'en now CLOU 73:17
conati: Ter sunt c. imponere VIRG 264:10
conceal. should c. it as well AUST 12:6
concealment: c., like a worm SHAK 234:4
conceit: c., what man will do any TROL 260:8
  he be wise in his own c. BIBLE 26:29
  suiting With forms to his c. SHAK 208:20
conceive: c. you may use any language GILB 107:20
  so hopeless to c. DICK 86:3
  virgin shall c. BIBLE 28:16
conceived: sin hath my mother c. me PRAY 189:5
concentrates: it c. his mind wonderfully
  JOHN 133:4
concern: life and its largest c. ARN 9:12
  matter they had no c. SWIFT 249:9
concert: persons acting in c. together ARAB 7:14
concluded: case is c. AUG 11:21
concord: with c. of sweet sounds SHAK 226:7
concubines: Twenty-two acknowledged c.
  GIBB 106:12
concurrence: fortuitous c. of atoms PALM 180:1
condemn: Neither do I c. thee BIBLE 36:27
  nor the years c. BINY 42:6
Condemn'd: C. alike to groan GRAY 112:11
  c. to have an itching palm SHAK 217:2
condere: Tantae molis erat Romanam c.
  VIRG 262:16
condition: devils in life and c. ASCH 9:19
  man could do in that c. PEPYS 182:8
  primordial c. of liberty BAK 14:12
  that c. which is called war HOBB 119:17
conditions: sorts and c. of men PRAY 187:4
Conduct: C. is three-fourths ARN 9:12
  C. the prejudice of good ANON 3:8
cones: eat the c. under his pines FROST 103:7
confederacy: dunces are all in c. against
  SWIFT 249:8
Confederate: in games C. WORD 274:20
conference: c. a ready man BACON 13:21
  c. With the dead WEBS 267:9
  naked into the c. chamber BEVAN 21:17
confident: Flushed and c. IBSEN 129:8
  Never glad c. morning again BROW 50:2
confined: execution c. SHAK 233:6
conflict: in the field of human c. CHUR 71:7
confounded: Confusion worse c. MILT 169:4
Confusion: C. on thy banners wait GRAY 111:16
  C. worse confounded MILT 169:4
confute: man can tell how to c. him SELD 202:18
congrès: Le c. ne marche pas LIG 151:15
conjecture: are not beyond all c. BROW 48:12
connaissance: L'amitié de la c. BUSS 55:23
connaît: l'univers et ne se c. pas LA F 147:13

connect: Only c. the prose FORS 101:17
conquer: c. or die who've no retreat GAY 105:22
  that was wont to c. others SHAK 230:2
  this sign shalt thou c. CONS 77:17
  You cannot c. Time AUDEN 10:9
conquered: c., O pale Galilean SWIN 250:3
  I came, I saw, I c. CAES 59.11
  is perpetually to be c. BURKE 52:16
conquering: c. hero comes MOR 173:8
  C. kings their titles CHAN 67:4
conqueror: proud foot of a c. SHAK 217:16
conquest: c. of the earth CONR 77.11
  fann'd by C.'s crimson wing GRAY 111:16
  Hath made a shameful c. SHAK 230:2
  Roman C. was SELL 203:1
  will end in c. and robbery JOHN 134:23
conquests: his carnage and his c. BYRON 57:6
  only honourable c. BURKE 52:18
conscience: catch the c. of the king SHAK 208:23
  cut my c. to fit this year's HELL 116:16
  freedom of c. TWAIN 261:2
  Nonconformist C. makes cowards BEER 17:14
  some c. of what they did CROM 80:14
  Thus c. doth make cowards SHAK 208:24
consciousness: multiplicity of agreeable c.
  JOHN 132:9
consecration: c., and the Poet's dream
  WORD 274:12
consent: his c. either expressed CAMD 60:7
  like enough to c. SHAK 205:9
  whispering 'I will ne'er c.' BYRON 58:1
consented: will ne'er consent'— c. BYRON 58:1
consequence: c. of cabinet government BAG 14:6
  mistake subsequence for c. JOHN 131:4
consequences: prevent it and to damn the c.
  MILN 167:4
Conservative: else a little C. GILB 107:16
consider: c. her ways BIBLE 26:8
  c. how my light is spent MILT 170:10
  c. how my life is spent NASH 174:17
  C. the lilies of the field BIBLE 31:25
  I will c. my Cat Jeoffry SMART 241:15
Consideration: C. like an angel came SHAK 213:9
  on carpet c. SHAK 234:2
consiliis: Misce stultitiam c. HOR 124:18
consistency: foolish c. is the hobgoblin
  EMER 96:15
console: c. us when we fall BURKE 53:2
Conspicuous: C. consumption of valuable
  VEBL 261:17
  was c. by its presence RUSS 198:13
conspiracies: All professions are c. SHAW 237:14
conspiracy: c. against the public SMITH 241:18
  'c. of silence' concerning COMTE 76:11
  less than a vast c. WELLS 268:16
conspirators: All the c. SHAK 217:6
conspire: thou and I with Fate c. FITZ 99:13
Conspiring: C. with him how to load
  KEATS 140:12
constable: it was a c.'s handbook KING 142:17
constabulary: When c. duty's to be done
  GILB 109:2
constant: c. as the northern star SHAK 216:8
  One here will c. be BUNY 52:2
  To one thing c. never SHAK 228:7
Constantinople: Russians shall not have C.
  HUNT 128:2
Constitution: invoke the genius of the C.
  PITT 183:9

principle of the English c. BLAC 42:15
proportioned to the human c. BERK 20:1
constitutional: c. guardian GILB 107:13
c. right of amending it LINC 152:1
construct: to c. the socialist order LEE 151:5
constructed: defences of peace must be c.
ANON 4:18
construction: mind's c. in the face SHAK 220:9
constructs: worse. It c. it COMP 76:9
consul: born when I was c. CIC 72:15
consule: natam me c. Romam CIC 72:15
consulted: right to be c. BAG 14:7
consumed: bush was not c. BIBLE 23:9
consumer: In a c. society there are ILL 129:11
consummation: c. Devoutly to be wish'd
SHAK 208:24
Quiet c. have SHAK 206:4
Consummatum: C. est BIBLE 41:23
consumption: Conspicuous c. of valuable
VEBL 261:17
contact: deux fantaisies et le c. CHAM 66:17
contagion: c. of the world's slow SHEL 238:26
C. to this world SHAK 210:9
Rot inwardly and foul c. MILT 167:21
contemned: it would utterly be c. BIBLE 28:5
contemplation: c. he and valour formed
MILT 169:7
contempt: c. and anger of his lip SHAK 234:7
contemptible: complaints of ill-usage c.
MELB 164:18
c. little Army WILH 272:7
contend: schools of thought c. MAO 159:13
contending: c. against some being WHIT 269:16
content: land of lost c. HOUS 126:7
contented: king shall be c. SHAK 230:9
With what I most enjoy c. SHAK 235:11
contention: Let the long c. cease ARN 8:16
swears he will have no c. LAND 148:9
contentment: Preaches c. to that toad KIPL 145:8
continency: c.—but not yet AUG 11:15
You impose c. upon us AUG 11:17
Continent: C. will not suffer England DISR 86:13
destiny to overspread the c. OSUL 178:16
continentiam: Imperas nobis c. AUG 11:17
continents: nations and three separate c.
DOYLE 89:23
continual: c. fear and danger of violent
HOBB 120:1
continuing: c. unto the end until it DRAKE 90:1
here have we no c. city BIBLE 40:13
contract: every c. to make the terms EMER 96:7
Social C. is nothing more WELLS 268:16
contradict: Do I c. myself WHIT 270:7
truth which you cannot c. PLATO 183:15
contradictions: bundle of c. COLT 76:7
hath been one chain of c. CLARE 72:18
contrariy: everythink goes c. with me DICK 83:21
Contrariwise: C.,' continued Tweedledee
CARR 63:22
contrary: trial is by what is c. MILT 170:17
contrite: broken and c. heart PRAY 189:7
contrive: How Nature always does c. GILB 107:16
contumely: proud man's c. SHAK 208:24
convent: c. of the Sacred Heart ELIOT 94:17
conversation: c. perfectly delightful SMITH 242:20
have a great deal of c. AUST 12:8
proper subject of c. CHES 69:16
That is the happiest c. JOHN 132:22
who is always spoiling c. MAC 157:5

conversations: 'without pictures or c. CARR 62:13
converse: between them and rational c.
WOLL 274:2
conversion: Till the c. of the Jews MARV 161:20
converted: Except ye be c. BIBLE 33:15
conviction: best lack all c. YEATS 279:15
Convictions: Such Dimity C. DICK 86:6
convince: people labouring to c. JOHN 131:22
convincing: c. myself that I am right AUST 12:15
thought of c. GOLD 110:16
convoy: crowns for c. put into SHAK 214:4
cook: c. and a captain bold GILB 106:21
C. is a little unnerved BETJ 20:13
cook was a good c. SAKI 199:6
cookery: Kissing don't last: c. do MER 165:8
cooking: tragedy of English c. MORP 173:10
cooks: as c. go she went SAKI 199:6
entrusted to 'plain' c. MORP 173:10
cool: garden in the c. of the day BIBLE 22:12
coot: haunts of c. and hern TENN 251:6
Copper: C. for the craftsman cunning KIPL 143:16
copulation: c. and death ELIOT 94:16
Let c. thrive SHAK 218:20
corages: priketh hem nature in hir c.) CHAU 67:18
coral: c. aboute hire arm she CHAU 68:3
C. is far more red than SHAK 236:14
Of his bones are c. made SHAK 232:15
cord: c. however fine into WHEW 269:10
ever the silver c. be loosed BIBLE 27:22
unto the bow the c. is LONG 153:14
corda: Sursum c. MASS 163:15
cormorant: common c. or shag ISH 129:16
C. devouring Time SHAK 219:6
corn: breast high amid the c. HOOD 121:11
c. was orient and immortal TRAH 259:21
he treadeth out the c. BIBLE 23:34
tears amid the alien c. KEATS 140:1
that there was c. in Egypt BIBLE 23:5
two ears of c. SWIFT 248:18
corner: c. of a foreign field BROO 47:16
c. of the world smiles HOR 124:2
head-stone in the c. PRAY 190:15
corners: round earth's imagined c. DONNE 88:2
three c. of the world SHAK 217:16
cornfield: o'er the green c. did pass SHAK 205:12
Cornish: Here's twenty thousand C. men
HAWK 115:13
Coromandel: On the coast of C. LEAR 150:7
coronets: hearts are more than c. TENN 253:2
Corporations: C. have neither bodies THUR 259:15
corpore: mens sana in c. sano JUV 138:5
Corporis: C. mysterium THOM 256:20
corpse: He'd make a lovely c. DICK 84:14
corpses: To mock the riddled c. SASS 200:6
corpus: Ave verum c. ANON 6:15
correct: All present and c. ANON 2:17
each has his own c. way TER 256:4
correcteth: whom the Lord loveth he c. BIBLE 26:4
correlative: finding an 'objective c. ELIOT 95:11
corridors: c. of power SNOW 243:5
corroboration: particular c. of this aphorism
BIRK 42:7
corroborative: Merely c. detail GILB 108:14
corrupt: be equally wicked and c. BURKE 52:10
C. influence BURKE 52:20
moth and rust doth c. BIBLE 31:22
one good custom should c. TENN 252:6
Unlimited power is apt to c. PITT 183:7

cowslips: c. in boys' hats appear…	CLARE 72:22
c. tall her pensioners	SHAK 226:17
coy: c., and hard to please	SCOTT 202:2
coyness: c., Lady, were no crime	MARV 161:20
coz: my pretty little c.	SHAK 205:11
Crabbed: C. age and youth	SHAK 235:4
crabs: When roasted c. hiss	SHAK 219:14
crack: c. in the tea-cup opens	AUDEN 10:10
heaven's vaults should c.	SHAK 219:2
sans c. or flaw	SHAK 219:11
cracked: c. lookingglass of a servant	JOYCE 137:4
crackling: c. of thorns under a pot	BIBLE 27:9
cracks: Now c. a noble heart	SHAK 212:1
cradle: hand that rocks the c.	WALL 265:11
Out of the c. endlessly	WHIT 270:2
Rocked in the c. of the deep	WILL 272:10
craft: c. so long to learn	HIPP 119:12
craftsman: Copper for the c. cunning	KIPL 143:16
crag: He clasps the c. with crooked	TENN 251:13
crags: among these barren c.	TENN 255:10
crambe: miseros c. repetita magistros	JUV 138:2
cramm'd: they on earth were c.	WORD 276:4
cranks: personal prejudices and c.	ELIOT 95:10
Quips and c.	MILT 167:16
Cras: C. ingens iterabimus aequor	HOR 123:12
crawl: slimy things did c. with	COL 74:10
crawling: such fellows as I do c.	SHAK 209:3
crazed: c. with the spell of far	DE L 82:9
crazy: c., cold	ROCH 195:17
cream: than choking her with c.	KING 143:1
cream-faced: thou c. loon	SHAK 223:11
create: c. new heavens and a new	BIBLE 29:23
must himself c. the taste	WORD 277:14
created: beginning God c. the heaven	BIBLE 22:1
Male and female c.	BIBLE 22:5
Man has c. death	YEATS 278:17
men are c. equal	JEFF 130:9
that all men are c. equal	ANON 5:9
why was it not c. sooner	JOHN 133:10
creating: c. a whole tribe of fops	SHAK 217:19
Creation: been present at the C.	ALF 2:5
when c. rises again	CEL 66:1
woman is a blind fury of c.	SHAW 238:2
creative: destruction is also a c.	BAK 14:11
Creator: C. and Preserver of all	PRAY 187:4
Remember now thy C.	BIBLE 27:21
creatura: Cum resurget c.	CEL 66:1
creature: Let the living c. lie	AUDEN 11:3
creatures: c. great and small	ALEX 2:3
generations of living c.	LUCR 155:7
goodly c. are there here	SHAK 233:3
other c. have gone to stall	FROST 103:9
Credat: C. Iudaeus Apella	HOR 124:23
credit: citizen Of c. and renown	COWP 79:12
c. in this World much wrong	FITZ 99:11
give thee c. for the rest	CHUR 70:21
Not to thy c.	CALV 60:4
'Time has too much c.	COMP 76:8
credite: Experto c.	VIRG 264:3
creditor: trembling at a c.	JOHN 134:27
creditors: c. would hardly know me	FOX 102:4
Credo: C. in unum Deum	MASS 163:13
credulity: c. below the milkiness	BURKE 52:10
credunt: homines id quod volunt c.	CAES 59:9
creed: Pagan suckled in a c. outworn	WORD 277:8
creeds: half-believers in our casual c.	ARN 8:21
Creep: C. in our ears	SHAK 226:5
C. into thy narrow bed	ARN 8:16
Like snails did c.	HERR 118:24

Creeps: C. in this petty pace	SHAK 223:1
creetur: 'I am a lone lorn c.	DICK 83:2
crept: one c. silently to Rest	FITZ 99:
crew: c. is gambling in the forecastle	SHAW 237:1
c. of the captain's gig	GILB 106:2
darling of our c.	DIBD 83:
We were a ghastly c.	COL 74:1
Cricket: his nose there was a C.	LEAR 150:1
Save the c. on the hearth	MILT 167:1
son of grief at c.	HOUS 125:
cried: children c. in the streets	MOTL 174:
c. all the way to the bank	LIB 151:1
from the depths I have c.	BIBLE 41:1
I c. to dream again	SHAK 232:2
not winced nor c. aloud	HENL 117:
when he c.	AUDEN 10:1
Crier: when the C. cried	BARH 15:1
cries: heaven with my bootless c.	SHAK 235:
Crillon: brave C.	HENR 117:1
crime: C'est pire qu'un c.	BOUL 45:
commonplace a c. is	DOYLE 89:1
c. of being a young man…I	PITT 183:
He is the Napoleon of c.	DOYLE 89:1
impulse was never a c.	CORN 78:
It is worse than a c.	BOUL 45:
crimes: register of the c.	GIBB 106:1
Successful c. alone are	DRYD 91:
tableau des c. et des malheurs	VOLT 265:
what c. are committed	ROL 196:
worst of c. is poverty	SHAW 237:1
crisis: in this c.	PAINE 179:1
Crispian: called the feast of C.	SHAK 214:
Crispin: C. Crispian shall ne'er	SHAK 214:
Crist: C.! whan that it remembreth	CHAU 68:1
Cristen: C. man shall wedde	CHAU 68:1
critic: c., one would suppose	ELIOT 95:1
literary c. to decide	WILDE 271:2
critical: c. judgement is so exquisite	FRY 103:1
criticism: c. of administration	BAG 14:
two because it permits c.	FORS 102:
critics: Turn'd c. next	POPE 185:
croaks: That c. the fatal entrance	SHAK 200:1
crocodile: How doth the little c.	CARR 62:1
To these c.'s tears	BURT 55:1
crocodiles: is the wisdom of the c.	BACON 13:2
crois: mais je n'en c. rien	CHAM 67:
Cromwell: C. guiltless of his country's	GRAY 112:
crook: such a thumping c.	BETJ 21:
crooked: c. be made straight	ELIOT 93:1
c. shall be made straight	BIBLE 29:
c. timber of humanity	KANT 138:1
dumb to tell the c. rose	THOM 257:
With your c. heart	AUDEN 10:1
crop-headed: c. Parliament swing	BROW 49:
Croppy: C., Droppy	ELLIS 96:
cross: beside the c. weeping while	JAC 129:1
inability to c. the street	WOOLF 274:9
marble c. below the town	HAYES 116:
mystery of the c. shines	VEN 261:2
cross-bow: With my c.	COL 74:
crossed: c. be uncrossed	ELIOT 93:1
crosses: c., row on row	MCCR 157:8
E'en c. from his sov'reign	HERV 119:
Crossing: C. alone the nighted ferry	HOUS 126:2
C. the stripling Thames	ARN 8:2
crow: before the cock c.	BIBLE 34:1
c. Makes wing	SHAK 222:1
flew down a monstrous c.	CARR 63:2
there is an upstart c.	GREE 112:1

rowd: c. flowed over London Bridge	ELIOT 94:20
madding c.'s ignoble strife	GRAY 112:6
riotousness of the c. is	ALC 2:1
Will she pass in a c.	SWIFT 249:3
'rowds: C. without company	GIBB 106:7
If you can talk with c.	KIPL 144:9
rowes feet: Til c. be growen under	CHAU 68:22
rown: Give me the c.	SHAK 230:11
hairy gold c. on 'er 'ead	KIPL 146:8
head that wears a c.	SHAK 212:27
influence of the C. has	DUNN 92:1
place, the c. imperial	SHAK 213:25
put on my c.	SHAK 204:10
strike his father's c.	SHAK 213:10
That c. the wat'ry glade	GRAY 112:8
will give thee a c. of life	BIBLE 40:29
rowns: c. for convoy put into	SHAK 214:4
'Give c. and pounds	HOUS 125:7
I'd c. resign to call thee	MACN 158:2
last act c.	QUAR 193:9
royait: c. Victor Hugo	COCT 74:1
rucify: people would not even c. him	CARL 61:23
ruel: c., not unnatural	SHAK 210:10
c. works of nature	DARW 81:16
mercies of the wicked are c.	BIBLE 26:15
must be c. only to be kind	SHAK 210:20
ruellest: April is the c. month	ELIOT 94:18
ruelty: full Of direst c.	SHAK 220:11
rumbs: bags to hold the c.	ISH 129:16
c. which fell from	BIBLE 35:31
dogs eat of the c. which	BIBLE 33:10
rush: c. Under Paul's dome	HODG 120:6
'ry: C.;—and upon thy so sore	THOM 258:7
harlot's c. from street	BLAKE 42:19
monstrous head and sickening c.	CHES 69:23
that he was too old to c.	STEV 246:16
that we still should c.	BACON 14:3
was a great c. in Egypt	BIBLE 23:16
We waul and c.	SHAK 218:23
when indeed they c.	WEBS 267:17
rying: infant c. for the light	TENN 252:16
one c. in the wilderness	BIBLE 31:4
we came c. hither	SHAK 218:23
uccu: Lhude sing c.	ANON 4:19
uchulain: Pearse summoned C.	YEATS 279:20
uckoo: C., jug-jug	NASHE 175:3
C.! Shall I call thee	WORD 277:11
c. shouts all day at nothing	HOUS 126:22
c. then, on every tree	SHAK 219:13
This is the weather the c.	HARDY 114:15
uckoo-buds: c. of yellow hue	SHAK 219:13
ucumber: c. should be well sliced	JOHN 134:9
when c. is added to it	MACK 157:13
ucumbers: extracting sun-beams out of c.	
	SWIFT 248:19
they are but c. after all	JOHN 133:15
ui bono: I hate a c. man	SHAW 238:20
ulpa: felix c.	MISS 170:22
mea c.	MASS 163:9
ultivate: 'but we must c. our garden	VOLT 264:17
c. your friendship of his	JOHN 133:19
to c. a few inhibitions	LOOS 154:3
ultiver: il faut c. notre jardin	VOLT 264:17
ulture: hear the word 'c.'	JOHST 135:12
ladies who pursue C.	WHAR 269:8
man of c. rare	GILB 108:19
ultured: what the c. word	KIPL 143:10
'umaei: Ultima C. venit iam carminis	VIRG 264:6
umbered: Martha was c. about much	BIBLE 35:15

cunctando: homo nobis c. restituit rem	ENN 97:1
Cunning: C. is the dark sanctuary	CHES 69:17
I find thy c. seeds	ROSS 197:2
right hand forget her c.	PRAY 191:1
cup: c. of hot wine with not	SHAK 205:14
fill the C.	FITZ 99:6
giveth his colour in the c.	BIBLE 26:26
Have drunk their C. a Round	FITZ 99:2
let this c. pass from me	BIBLE 34:13
my c. shall be full	PRAY 188:16
my Glory in a Shallow C.	FITZ 99:11
tak a c. o' kindness yet	BURNS 53:22
cupboard: glacier knocks in the c.	AUDEN 10:10
man in the bathroom c.	EWART 97:7
Cupid: C.'s darts do not feel	ANON 4:7
wing'd C. painted blind	SHAK 226:14
Cupidinesque: Veneres C.	CAT 65:4
Cupidinum: Mater saeva C.	HOR 124:14
Cupids: mother of the lovely C.	HOR 124:14
cur: you spurn a stranger c.	SHAK 225:1
Cura: Post equitem sedet atra C.	HOR 124:6
curb: might c. your magnanimity	KEATS 141:7
use the snaffle and the c.	CAMP 60:13
cure: c. for the evils which	MAC 156:19
c. for this ill is not	KIPL 144:13
C. the disease and kill	BACON 13:8
is no c. for this disease	BELL 18:10
is the c. of all diseases	BROW 48:8
labour against our own c.	BROW 48:8
cured: c. by hanging from a string	KING 143:4
curfew: c. tolls the knell of parting	GRAY 111:18
curiosity: c., freckles	PARK 180:4
curious: amaz'd, and c.	BURNS 55:1
'That was the c. incident	DOYLE 89:19
Curiouser: 'C. and curiouser	CARR 62:15
curiously: others to be read but not c.	
	BACON 13:20
curl: Who had a little c.	LONG 153:20
would make your hair c.	GILB 109:6
curled: c. up on the floor	HARTE 115:14
curls: find unwithered on its c.	HOUS 125:11
Frocks and C.	DICK 86:5
current: take the c. when it serves	SHAK 217:3
currents: regard their c. turn awry	SHAK 208:24
curse: c. be ended	ELIOT 93:11
C., bless, me now	THOM 257:1
C. God	BIBLE 25:19
c. to party strife	WORD 274:13
heard such a terrible c.	BARH 15:12
I know how to c.	SHAK 232:12
look upon myself and c.	SHAK 235:11
'The c. is come upon me	TENN 253:4
Work is the c. of the drinking	WILDE 272:4
cursed: sobbed and c. and kicked	MILL 166:7
curst: c. be he that moves my	SHAK 237:5
curtain: draw the c. close	SHAK 214:13
iron c. has descended across	CHUR 71:12
saying 'Bring down the c.	RAB 193:15
curtains: Let fall the c.	COWP 80:4
curtiosity: full of 'satiable c.	KIPL 146:15
Curtsey: C. while you're thinking	CARR 63:18
Curzon: is George Nathaniel C.	ANON 4:9
custard pie: joke is ultimately a c.	ORW 178:8
Custodes: custodiet ipsos C.	JUV 137:21
custodierit: Nisi Dominus c. civitatem	BIBLE 41:15
custodiet: c. ipsos Custodes	JUV 137:21
custom: c. should corrupt the world	TENN 252:6
C., that unwritten law	DAV 81:17
nor c. stale	SHAK 203:24

customers: raising up a people of c.   SMITH 242:1
customs: ancient c. and its manhood   ENN 97:2
cut: an' c. 'is stripes away   KIPL 143:17
   c. his throat before he   SWIFT 249:13
   C. is the branch that might   MARL 160:8
   c. my conscience to fit   HELL 116:16
   in the evening it is c.   PRAY 189:21
   unkindest c. of all   SHAK 216:20
cutting: c. all the pictures out   BELL 18:2
   Went on c. bread and butter   THAC 256:16
Cutty-sark: Weel done, C.   BURNS 55:2
cymbal: tinkling c.   BIBLE 38:14
cymbals: upon the well-tuned c.   PRAY 191:8
Cynara: faithful to thee, C.   DOWS 89:8
cypress: in sad c. let me be laid   SHAK 234:3
Cyprus: black C. with a lake of fire   FLEC 100:9
Cythera: It's C.   BAUD 16:13
D: big D.   GILB 108:27
Da: D. mi basia mille   CAT 65:6
   D. mihi castitatem et continentiam   AUG 11:15
   D. quod iubes et iube quod   AUG 11:17
Daffodils: D., That come before   SHAK 235:1
   dances with the d.   WORD 275:4
   Fair d.   HERR 118:22
   host, of golden d.   WORD 275:3
   in the west wind, and d.   MAS 163:5
dagger: Is this a d. which I see   SHAK 221:10
daggers: fighting with d. in a hogshead
     SCOTT 202:12
   Give me the d.   SHAK 221:18
   I will speak d. to her   SHAK 210:10
   There's d. in men's smiles   SHAK 222:10
Dahin: D.! Dahin   GOE 110:3
daily: Give us this day our d. bread   BIBLE 31:21
daintily: have things d. served   BETJ 20:13
dairies: foul sluts in d.   CORB 78:3
daisies: Buttercups and d.   HOW 127:10
   d. pied and violets blue   SHAK 219:13
   D. smell-less   FLET 100:19
Daisy: D. and Lily   SITW 241:11
Dalhousie: Lady D. are dead   MCG 157:10
dalliance: d. in the wardrobe lies   SHAK 213:11
   primrose path of d. treads   SHAK 207:5
dam: pretty chickens and their d.   SHAK 223:5
damaged: Archangel a little d.   LAMB 147:19
damages: He first d. his mind   ANON 6:8
Dame: 'La belle D. sans Merci   KEATS 139:7
   sits our sulky sullen d.   BURNS 54:22
damn: d. her at a venture   LAMB 148:5
   'D. the age   LAMB 148:1
   D. with faint praise   POPE 184:20
   D. you, Jack   BONE 44:17
   praises one another d.   WYCH 278:6
   to d. the consequences   MILN 167:4
   with a spot I d. him   SHAK 217:1
damnation: deep d. of his taking-off   SHAK 221:1
damn'd: All silent and all d.   WORD 276:4
Damned: D. from here to Eternity   KIPL 144:1
   d. lies and statistics   DISR 87:15
   has been a d. nice thing   WELL 267:21
   'I'm d. if I see it'   NEWB 175:13
   is the brandy of the d.   SHAW 238:7
   must be d. perpetually   MARL 160:8
   one d. thing   OMAL 178:4
   Publish and be d.   WELL 268:14
   Water your d. flower-pots   BROW 50:20
   what those d. dots meant   CHUR 70:25
damning: By d. those they have no   BUTL 56:5
Damnosa: D. hereditas   GAIUS 104:8

damozel: blessed d. leaned out   ROSS 197:3
damp: d. souls of housemaids   ELIOT 94:16
damsel: d. with a dulcimer   COL 75:8
Danaë: Now lies the Earth all D.   TENN 254:1
Danaos: timeo D. et dona   VIRG 263:8
dance: d. an antic hay   MARL 160:5
   dancer from the d.   YEATS 278:1
   On with the d.   BYRON 57:16
   to d. at our bridal   SCOTT 201:2
   will you join the d.   CARR 63:1
danced: They d. by the light   LEAR 150:16
dancer: know the d. from the dance   YEATS 278:1
dances: makes no progress; it d.   LIG 151:5
danceth: in hope d. without musick   HERB 118:5
dancing: Fluttering and d.   WORD 275:3
   manners of a d. master   JOHN 131:1
   now for some d. with   HOR 123:18
   You and I are past our d.   SHAK 231:1
dandelions: Sheaves of drooping d.   BETJ 21:9
dandy: Candy Is d.   NASH 174:6
danger: continual fear and d.   HOBB 120:5
   everything is in d.   NIET 176:1
   Ev'n at the brink of d.   QUAR 193:8
   One would be in less d.   NASH 174:1
   Out of this nettle, d.   SHAK 212:16
   they put themselves in d.   WYATT 278:1
dangerous: Beware, I am d.   BAG 14:3
   d. to sit to Sargent   ANON 4:1
   d. to know   LAMB 147:1
   is a d. precedent   CORN 78:1
   such men are d.   SHAK 215:1
   though it were d. to meet   WHAR 269:8
dangerously: from life is to live d.   NIET 176:1
dangers: On the d. of the seas   PARK 180:11
   perils and d. of this night   PRAY 187:1
Daniel: D. come to judgment   SHAK 226:1
   second D.   SHAK 226:2
danket: Nun d. alle Gott   RINK 195:7
Danny Deever: An' they're hangin' D.   KIPL 143:17
danse: marche pas, il d.   LIG 151:15
dappled: Glory be to God for d.   HOPK 122:2
dapple-dawn-drawn: d. Falcon   HOPK 122:9
dare: Letting 'I d. not' wait   SHAK 221:4
   none d. call it treason   HAR 115:8
   You who d.   MER 165:6
dared: d. attack my Chesterton   BELL 18:25
dares: Who d. do more is none   SHAK 221:1
Darien: upon a peak in D.   KEATS 140:4
dark: blind man in a d. room   BOWEN 45:10
   children fear to go in the d.   BACON 13:5
   d., amid the blaze   MILT 170:2
   d. and true and tender   TENN 254:11
   d. as night   SHAK 237:6
   d. backward and abysm   SHAK 232:11
   d. horse   DISR 87:13
   d. night of the soul   FITZ 100:3
   d. sanctuary of incapacity   CHES 69:17
   d. Satanic mills   BLAKE 43:2
   d. womb where I began   MAS 162:18
   d. world of sin   BICK 42:4
   great leap in the d.   HOBB 120:2
   Hellish d.   SURT 248:13
   Lady is as good i' th' d.   HERR 118:20
   made a leap into the d.   BROWN 48:1
   one stride comes the d.   COL 74:11
   Out in the d. over   THOM 257:20
   That for ways that are d.   HARTE 115:12
   through the blanket of the d.   SHAK 220:11
   we are for the d.   SHAK 204:8

darken: days d. round me	TENN 252:5
darkening: sky is d. like a stain	AUDEN 11:13
darker: Save that the sky grows d.	CHES 69:19
darkest: d. day (Live till tomorrow)	COWP 79:13
darkling: are here as on a d. plain	ARN 8:13
D. I listen	KEATS 139:22
darkly: through a glass, d.	BIBLE 38:16
darkness: Aye on the shores of d.	KEATS 140:5
cast away the works of d.	PRAY 187:6
cast off the works of d.	BIBLE 38:5
cast out into outer d.	BIBLE 32:15
d. comprehended it not	BIBLE 36:13
d. falls at Thy behest	ELL 95:21
encounter d. as a bride	SHAK 224:2
in the d. and the cold	STEV 247:10
leaves the world to d.	GRAY 111:18
lie where shades of d.	DE L 82:10
Lighten our d.	PRAY 187:1
people that walked in d.	BIBLE 28:18
pestilence that walketh in d.	PRAY 189:24
prince of d. is a gentleman	SHAK 218:13
talks of d. at noon-day	COWP 79:17
to them that sit in d.	BIBLE 34:30
wind was a torrent of d.	NOYES 177:8
Dark Tower: 'Childe Roland to the D.	BROW 49:8
darling: d. buds of May	SHAK 235:9
d. of our crew	DIBD 83:9
She is the d. of my heart	CAREY 61:4
which was my lady's d.	CAT 65:4
dart: Time shall throw a d.	BROW 48:14
darter: d. es died o' the fever	TENN 255:17
Dasein: grössten Genuss vom D.	NIET 176:19
dashing: d. Swiss officer'	RUSS 198:14
dastard: d. in war	SCOTT 201:20
dastards: commands, and d. me	BROW 48:6
dat: Inopi beneficium bis d.	PUBL 192:8
data: theorize before one has d.	DOYLE 89:15
dateless: d. bargain to engrossing	SHAK 232:6
daughter: all to my elder d.	THOM 257:18
'D. am I in my mother's	KIPL 145:7
d. of the gods	TENN 251:12
Elderly ugly d.	GILB 109:9
farmer's d. hath soft brown	CALV 59:16
had taken his little d.	LONG 153:19
King's d. is all glorious	PRAY 189:2
put your d. on the stage	COW 79:6
so is her d.	BIBLE 30:3
Stern d. of the voice of God	WORD 276:1
Who married Noah's d.	AYT 12:18
yet more beautiful d.	HOR 123:15
daughters: d. of the uncircumcised	BIBLE 24:25
I am all the d. of my father's	SHAK 234:5
Words are men's d.	MADD 158:13
words are the d. of earth	JOHN 134:15
your d. shall prophesy	BIBLE 30:14
daunte: whom death could not d.	BALL 14:18
Dauntless: D. the slug-horn to my	BROW 49:8
so d. in war	SCOTT 201:19
dauphin: kingdom of daylight's d.	HOPK 122:9
David: Teste D. cum Sibylla	CEL 65:14
When D. did his dance	FRY 103:17
Davy: D. Abominated gravy	BENT 19:18
dawn: d. comes up like thunder	KIPL 145:3
dusk and d. many a head	MULL 174:6
face and a grey d. breaking	MAS 162:19
moon on my left and the d.	BELL 18:18
Rosy-fingered d.	HOMER 121:2
Day: alternate Night and D.	FITZ 98:17
arrow that flieth by d.	PRAY 189:24

breaks the blank d.	TENN 252:11
bright d. is done	SHAK 204:8
burden and heat of the d.	BIBLE 33:25
compare thee to a summer's d.	SHAK 235:9
darkest d. (Live till tomorrow)	COWP 79:13
d. in a pillar of a cloud	BIBLE 23:17
d. returns too soon	BYRON 59:1
d.'s at the morn	BROW 50:12
d. that comes betwixt	CAREY 61:5
d. Thou gavest	ELL 95:21
death of each d.'s life	SHAK 221:16
everlasting d.	DONNE 87:17
foul and fair a d.	SHAK 220:4
garden in the cool of the d.	BIBLE 22:12
Good things of d. begin	SHAK 222:15
have known a better d.	SCOTT 201:15
I have lost a d.	TITUS 259:16
lark at break of d.	SHAK 235:11
morning were the first d.	BIBLE 22.3
my arms till break of d.	AUDEN 11:3
night do penance for a d.	WORD 276:8
no proper time of d.	HOOD 121:9
Now's the d.	BURNS 54:20
one d. in thy courts	PRAY 189:19
shall not burn thee by d.	PRAY 190:16
stand at the latter d.	BIBLE 25:28
Sufficient unto the d.	BIBLE 32:1
There's night and d.	BORR 44:22
this long weary d. have end	SPEN 244:14
Until the d. break	BIBLE 28:2
Without all hope of d.	MILT 170:2
withstand in the evil d.	BIBLE 39:15
daylight: all the long and lone d.	SHEL 240:6
kingdom of d.'s dauphin	HOPK 122:9
days: all the d. of my life	PRAY 188:16
burnt-out ends of smoky d.	ELIOT 94:15
Chequer-board of Nights and D.	FITZ 99:7
d. and days	CARR 62:20
d. dividing lover and lover	SWIN 249:16
d. of our youth are	BYRON 59:2
d. of wine and roses	DOWS 89:9
d. that are no more	TENN 254:10
fall'n on evil d.	MILT 169:13
Length of d. is in her	BIBLE 26:5
man in his hasty d.	BRID 46:11
number of my d.	PRAY 188:25
of a woman is of few d.	BIBLE 25:24
seemed unto him but a few d.	BIBLE 23:1
teach us to number our d.	PRAY 189:23
these fair well-spoken d.	SHAK 231:3
We have seen better d.	SHAK 233:5
day-star: So sinks the d.	MILT 168:2
dazzle: mine eyes d.	WEBS 267:12
dazzled: shrine d. by your brilliance	SCH 201:2
dea: vera incessu patuit d.	VIRG 263:1
dead: act as if we were d.	POUND 186:12
both the quick and the d.	PRAY 187:13
Christ risen from the d.	BIBLE 38:18
conference With the d.	WEBS 267:9
d. Are but as pictures	SHAK 221:18
dead bury their d.	BIBLE 32:17
d. Did squeak and gibber	SHAK 206:7
D., for a ducat	SHAK 210:13
d. leaf thou mightest bear	SHEL 239:13
d. shall be raised incorruptible	BIBLE 38:22
d. shall live	DRYD 91:10
d. thing that smells sweet	THOM 257:17
d. we owe only truth	VOLT 265:8
d. woman bites not	GRAY 111:15

Faith without works is d. — BIBLE 40:14
gaze the strengthless d. — HOUS 125:11
God is d. — NIET 176:16
Harrow the house of the d. — AUDEN 11:5
He is d. and gone — SHAK 210:26
Here d. lie we because — HOUS 126:26
himself must be d. — AUST 12:16
I lain for a century d. — TENN 254:2
It struck him d. — BELL 19:2
I would that I were d. — TENN 253:18
kissed by the English d. — OWEN 179:7
ladies d. and lovely knights — SHAK 236:10
Lady Dalhousie are d. — MCG 157:10
lane to the land of the d. — AUDEN 10:10
maid is not d., but sleepeth — BIBLE 32:22
Mistah Kurtz—he d. — CONR 77:12
My lady's sparrow is d. — CAT 65:4
Nobody heard him, the d. man — SMITH 242:13
not d.—but gone before — ROG 195:19
out ten to see a d. Indian — SHAK 232:17
over the rich D. — BROO 47:5
sea gave up the d. which — BIBLE 41:6
Sea shall give up her d. — PRAY 191:11
she has been d. many times — PATER 181:8
Smiling the boy fell d. — BROW 49:16
That d. men rise up never — SWIN 250:1
There are no d. — MAET 158:14
they told me you were d. — CORY 78:12
This my son was d. — BIBLE 35:29
two months d. — SHAK 206:15
up with our English d. — SHAK 213:14
very d. of Winter — ANDR 2:11
'we are all d.' — KEYN 141:20
wench is d. — MARL 160:13
When I am d. — ROSS 197:7
where there was not one d. — BIBLE 23:16
wish their enemies d. — MONT 171:16
within full of d. men's bones — BIBLE 33:31
your remind me of the d. — SASS 200:9
youth stone d. — SASS 200:5
deadly: species is more d. than — KIPL 143:20
deaf: d., who will not fight — GREN 113:3
happen to be d. and dumb — HOUS 127:3
turn the d. ear — SWIFT 249:9
deal: don't d. in lies — KIPL 144:7
great d. of gold — JAMES 130:7
is a great d. to be said — BENT 19:17
new d. for the American — RONS 196:7
dealbabor: et super nivem d. — BIBLE 41:12
Dean: D. of Christ Church — SPR 245:5
deans: dowagers for d. — TENN 254:5
dear: d. Brutus — SHAK 215:16
D. heart how like you — WYATT 278:4
make thee terrible and d. — SHEL 240:6
Plato is d. to me — ARIS 8:8
that bread should be so d. — HOOD 121:13
this dear, d. land — SHAK 230:2
too d. for my possessing — SHAK 236:6
was to all the country d. — GOLD 110:8
dearer: d. still is truth — ARIS 8:8
little d. than his horse — TENN 253:8
dearest: near'st and d. enemy — SHAK 212:15
To throw away the d. thing — SHAK 220:9
Dearly: D. beloved brethren — PRAY 186:17
death: added a new terror to d. — WETH 269:6
added another terror to d. — LYND 155:17
After the first d. — THOM 257:8
All in the valley of D. — TENN 251:8
Any man's d. diminishes — DONNE 89:3

bargain to engrossing d. — SHAK 232:6
Be absolute for d. — SHAK 223:21
been studied in his d. — SHAK 220:9
Be thou faithful unto d. — BIBLE 40:29
Brought d. into the world — MILT 168:12
come away, d. — SHAK 234:3
copulation and d. — ELIOT 94:16
couragious whom d. could not daunte — BALL 14:18
danger of violent d. — HOBB 120:1
d. after life does greatly — SPEN 244:16
d., a necessary end — SHAK 216:6
d.; a thousand doors — SEN 203:6
D. be not proud — DONNE 88:3
d. brag thou wander'st — SHAK 235:9
D. closes all — TENN 255:14
D. devours all lovely things — MILL 166:8
D.! ere thou hast slain — BROW 48:14
D. goes dogging everywhere — HENL 117:8
D. has a thousand doors — MASS 164:6
d. hath no more dominion — BIBLE 37:35
D. hath so many doors — FLET 100:16
d. is most in apprehension — SHAK 224:1
d. is the cure of all diseases — BROW 48:8
d. no one so true Did share — SHAK 234:3
d. of each day's life — SHAK 221:16
d. shall have no dominion — THOM 256:22
d. that is immortal has — LUCR 155:8
d. the journey's end — DRYD 91:8
d. they were not divided — BIBLE 24:26
d., thou shalt die — DONNE 88:4
d. to find me planting — MONT 171:17
D. tramples it to fragments — SHEL 239:1
D., where is thy sting-a-ling-a-ling — ANON 4:12
d., where is thy sting — BIBLE 38:23
D., where is thy sting — ROSS 197:2
D. will be aghast and so — CEL 66:1
D. will come when thou — SHEL 240:7
Doubled the globe of d. — THOM 257:5
dread of something after d. — SHAK 208:24
dull cold ear of d. — GRAY 112:4
eloquent, just, and mighty D. — RAL 194:6
even hard at d.'s door — PRAY 190:7
except d. and taxes — FRAN 102:16
fear d. as children — BACON 13:5
Fear d.?—to feel the fog — BROW 50:17
fed on the fullness of d. — SWIN 250:3
give me d. — HENRY 117:16
have a rendezvous with D. — SEEG 202:4
heroes up the line to d. — SASS 200:4
I could not look on D. — KIPL 143:19
I could not stop for D. — DICK 86:1
I know d. hath ten thousand — WEBS 267:11
in love with easeful D. — KEATS 139:22
in that sleep of d. — SHAK 208:24
in the shadow of d. — BIBLE 34:30
Into the jaws of D. — TENN 251:10
kiss of d. — SMITH 242:7
life went through with d. — VEN 261:20
living d. — MILT 170:3
made a covenant with d. — BIBLE 29:2
make d. proud to take us — SHAK 204:7
Man has created d. — YEATS 278:17
midst of life we are in d. — PRAY 188:4
million-murdering D. — ROSS 197:2
Morning after D. — DICK 86:2
no mean of d. — SHAK 216:10
none blessed before his d. — BIBLE 30:22
Now boast thee, d. — SHAK 204:12
owe God a d. — SHAK 212:29

perchance of D.	THOM 258:14	ye are to d. it	PRAY 187:23
quiet us in a d. so noble	MILT 170:6	decline: idea of writing the d.	GIBB 106:8
report of my d.	TWAIN 261:6	decorum: Dulce et d. est pro patria	HOR 124:7
Riddles of d. Thebes	SHEL 239:5	decree: establish the d.	BIBLE 30:10
shall be destroyed is d.	BIBLE 38:19	dedication: d. of his life to me	ELIOT 93:7
should be glad of another d.	ELIOT 94:2	Dee: Across the sands of D.	KING 142:12
So shalt thou feed on D.	SHAK 237:3	Lived on the river D.	BICK 42:1
stories of the d. of kings	SHAK 230:8	deed: attempt and not the d.	SHAK 221:13
strange screams of d.	SHAK 222:5	blow the horrid d.	SHAK 221:1
Swarm over, D.	BETJ 21:11	d. is all	GOE 110:1
talks of Arthur's d.	SHAK 217:13	d. of dreadful note	SHAK 222:14
that sat on him was D.	BIBLE 40:32	d. without a name	SHAK 222.23
There is d. in the pot	BIBLE 25:10	good d. in a naughty	SHAK 226:8
there shall be no more d.	BIBLE 41:8	To do the right d.	ELIOT 94:13
This fell sergeant, d.	SHAK 211:20	whatever time the d. took place	ELIOT 94:9
thou art d.'s fool	SHAK 223:21	deeds: sager sort our d. reprove	CAT 65:5
thought d. had undone so many	ELIOT 94:20	Seeking His secret d.	ROSS 197:2
Thou wast not born for d.	KEATS 140:1	deep: commit his body to the d.	PRAY 191:11
through the d. of some	MAS 162:18	d. sense of some deathless	WEBS 267:14
till d. us do part	PRAY 187:28	d. upon her peerless eyes	KEATS 139:17
tragedies are finish'd by a d.	BYRON 58:5	his wonders in the d.	PRAY 190:8
valley of the shadow of d.	PRAY 188:16	in the cradle of the d.	WILL 272:10
vasty hall of d.	ARN 8:18	often lie too d. for tears	WORD 275:17
wages of sin is d.	BIBLE 37:36	one is of the d.	STEP 246:2
was much possessed by d.	ELIOT 95:8	Out of the d. have I called	PRAY 190:22
way to dusty d.	SHAK 223:15	'tis not so d. as a well	SHAK 231:27
we are to abolish the d.	KARR 138:12	too d. for his hearers	GOLD 110:16
When d. approached unlocked	GIBB 106:13	very d. did rot	COL 74:10
deathless: sense of some d. shame	WEBS 267:14	deeper: d. than did ever plummet	SHAK 233:1
deaths: More d. than one must die	WILDE 271:4	Her eyes were d. than	ROSS 197:8
Debate: Rupert of D.	BULW 51:10	Deep-meadow'd: D., happy	TENN 252:8
debauch: man may d. his friend's	BOSW 45:4	deer: I was a stricken d.	COWP 80:2
debellare: subiectis et d. superbos	VIRG 263:14	let the stricken d. go	SHAK 210:6
debonair: buxom, blithe, and d.	MILT 167:15	défauts: Quelle âme est sans d.	RIMB 195:8
deboshed: Thou d. fish thou	SHAK 232:19	defeat: in d., defiance	CHUR 71:17
debt: he paid the d. of nature	FABY 97:10	possibilities of d.	VICT 262:10
National D. is a very Good	SELL 203:3	defeated: Down with the d.	LIVY 152:9
pay a d. to pleasure	ROCH 195:14	defect: chief d. of Henry King	BELL 18:9
debts: forgive us our d.	BIBLE 31:21	defence: Lord is thy d. upon thy	PRAY 190:16
He that dies pays all d.	SHAK 232:21	defences: d. of peace must be constructed	
decay: Change and d. in all around	LYTE 156:2		ANON 4:18
d. Of that colossal wreck	SHEL 239:17	defend: d. to the death your right	VOLT 265:10
muddy vesture of d.	SHAK 226:5	mercy d. us from all perils	PRAY 187:1
decede: d. peritis	HOR 123:8	Quand on l'attaque il se d.	ANON 5:15
deceitful: d. and a virgin renowned	HOR 124:9	we shall d. our island	CHUR 71:5
heart is d. above all things	BIBLE 29:27	defended: these d.	HOUS 126:20
deceitfulness: Cat of such d. and suavity		defends: when attacked it d. itself	ANON 5:15
	ELIOT 94:9	defensoribus: Non tali auxilio nec d.	VIRG 263:6
Deceive: D. boys with toys	LYS 156:1	deferred: Hope d. maketh the heart	BIBLE 26:16
first we practise to d.	SCOTT 202:1	deficiant: Quod si d. vires	PROP 192:1
let not Time d. you	AUDEN 10:9	defiled: toucheth pitch shall be d.	BIBLE 30:23
we d. ourselves	BIBLE 40:24	define: To d. true madness	SHAK 208:6
deceived: is still d. with ornament	SHAK 225:13	definition: d. of a gentleman to say	NEWM 176:1
deceiver: I'm a gay d.	COLM 76:5	defrauding: Penalties as the d. of the State	
deceivers: Men were d. ever	SHAK 228:7		PENN 182:6
December: D. when they wed	SHAK 205:10	defy: d. the foul fiend	SHAK 218:12
In a drear-nighted D.	KEATS 140:11	dégoût: non pas des moments de d.	VOLT 265:5
old D.'s bareness	SHAK 236:8	degree: exalted them of low d.	BIBLE 34:29
Decembers: fifteen wild D.	BRON 47:3	Dei: Ad majorem D. gloriam	ANON 6:12
decent: d. obscurity of a learned	GIBB 106:9	vox D.	ALC 2:1
decently: be done d. and in order	BIBLE 38:17	deid: they're a' d.	ANON 3:15
decide: comes the moment to d.	LOW 154:17	y'er a lang time d.	ANON 3:7
decision: multitudes in the valley of d.	BIBLE 30:16	deject: ladies most d. and wretched	SHAK 209:6
deck: d. put on its leaves again	FLEC 100:11	delay: d. there lies no plenty	SHAK 233:22
d. your lower limbs	NASH 175:1	sell, or deny, or d.	MAGN 159:1
stood on the burning d.	HEM 117:1	delayed: d. till I am indifferent	JOHN 131:9
decks: he fell upon their d.	TENN 255:6	delaying: d. put the state to rights	ENN 97:1
declare: heavens d. the glory	PRAY 188:12	delays: strong through long d.	OVID 178:23
nothing to d.	WILDE 272:2		

Delectable: came to the D. Mountains
BUNY 51:22
Delenda: D. est Carthago CATO 65:3
Delia: While D. is away JAGO 129:19
deliciae: d. meae puellae CAT 65:4
délicieux: il n'y en a point de d. LA R 149:9
delight: All for your d. SHAK 227:20
bind another to its d. BLAKE 43:11
Commodity, Firmness, and *D.* WOTT 277:19
d. is in proper young BURNS 54:14
d. of battle with my peers TENN 255:12
D. of lust is gross PETR 183:3
Energy is Eternal D. BLAKE 43:21
give d., and hurt not SHAK 232:22
go to 't with d. SHAK 204:3
labour we d. in physics SHAK 222:4
Moon of my D. who know'st FITZ 99:14
She was a phantom of d. WORD 276:15
Spirit of D. SHEL 239:18
Studies serve for d. BACON 13:19
thing met conceives d. MILT 169:17
unrest which men miscall d. SHEL 238:26
delightest: d. not in burnt-offerings PRAY 189:7
delighteth: king d. to honour BIBLE 25:16
delightful: all that is d. to man MILT 170:18
two most d. things WALP 266:4
delights: midst of the fountain of d. LUCR 155:9
deliver: d. us from evil BIBLE 31:21
I will d. him unto you BIBLE 34:10
delivered: God hath d. him into mine BIBLE 24:23
delivereth: d. them out of their distress PRAY 190:9
dells: In leafy d. alone HOUS 126:22
déluge: Après nous le d. POMP 184:5
delusion: d., a mockery, and a snare DENM 82:18
d. that beauty is goodness TOLS 259:18
Demas: D., greet you BIBLE 39:22
demd: What's the d. total DICK 85:1
dementat: d. prius DUP 92:2
demented: d. with the mania of owning
WHIT 270:6
demeurer: d. en repos dans une chambre
PASC 180:16
demi-paradise: other Eden, d. SHAK 230:2
democracy: capacity for justice makes d.
NIEB 176:12
D. and proper drains BETJ 21:5
D. resumed her reign BELL 18:22
great arsenal of d. RONS 196:11
must be made safe for d. WILS 273:2
So Two cheers for D. FORS 102:1
that d. is the worst form CHUR 71:13
demon-lover: woman wailing for her d. COL 75:3
demonstrandum: Quod erat d. EUCL 97:4
den: made it a d. of thieves BIBLE 33:26
denk: d.' ich Heut und morgen LESS 151:9
Denmark: Prince of D. being left out SCOTT 202:9
rotten in the state of D. SHAK 207:11
sure it may be so in D. SHAK 207:17
deny: Room to d. ourselves KEBLE 141:9
sell, or d., or delay MAGN 159:1
thou shalt d. me thrice BIBLE 34:12
You must d. yourself GOE 109:22
deo: Ille mi par esse d. videtur CAT 65:9
depart: he will not d. from it BIBLE 26:25
I am ready to d. LAND 148:8
servant d. in peace BIBLE 35:4
Departed: D. never to return BURNS 55:9
glory is d. from Israel BIBLE 24:17
our dear brother here d. PRAY 188:5

departure: *so soon* to regret the d. THOM 258:9
dépeuplé: et tout est d. LAM 147:16
déplaît: chose qui ne nous d. pas LA R 149:8
depraved: ever suddenly became d. JUV 137:16
deprest: man is d. with cares GAY 105:12
deprived: d. of everlasting bliss MARL 160:3
depth: d. in philosophy bringeth BACON 12:23
far beyond my d. SHAK 215:9
depths: d. I have cried to thee BIBLE 41:16
deputy: also may be read by d. BACON 13:20
derangement: nice d. of epitaphs SHER 240:19
Derision: Uglification and D. CARR 63:8
descend: into the Dust d. FITZ 99:3
Descending: D. from the bus CARR 62:12
of God ascending and d. BIBLE 22:32
descensus: Facilis d. Averno VIRG 263:10
described: d. as a supreme capacity BUTL 56:15
description: He answered the d. FARQ 97:16
descriptions: d. of the fairest wights SHAK 236:10
desert: d. shall rejoice BIBLE 29:5
d. sighs in the bed AUDEN 10:10
every man after his d. SHAK 208:19
Stand in the d. SHEL 239:16
us all out into the d. CLOU 73:19
Deserts: D. of vast eternity MARV 161:21
In the d. of the heart AUDEN 11:1
deserve: we'll d. it ADD 1:7
would d. better of mankind SWIFT 248:18
you somehow haven't to d. FROST 103:3
deserves: everyone has the face he d. ORW 178:13
has the government it d. MAIS 159:3
deserving: that riches where is my d. SHAK 236:6
Designer: D. infinite THOM 258:4
designing: Say I am d. St Paul's BENT 19:20
desipere: Dulce est d. in loco HOR 124:18
desir'd: Suffer herself to be d. WALL 265:14
desire: Bring me my arrows of d. BLAKE 43:2
d. and longing to enter PRAY 189:17
d. other men's goods PRAY 187:21
d. should so many years SHAK 212:26
hours and times of your d. SHAK 236:3
it provokes the d. SHAK 222:3
man's d. is for the woman COL 75:14
mixing Memory and d. ELIOT 94:18
naught for your d. CHES 69:19
nearer to the Heart's D. FITZ 99:13
powers of Charm and D. CAT 65:4
that the d. is boundless SHAK 233:6
to get your heart's d. SHAW 238:9
weariness treads on d. PETR 183:3
wonder and a wild d. BROW 50:19
desired: d. by all healthy and good CIC 72:14
desires: By all d. which thereof DONNE 87:22
much the devices and d. PRAY 186:18
nurse unacted d. BLAKE 44:7
desirest: thou d. no sacrifice PRAY 189:7
desireth: hart d. the water-brooks PRAY 189:1
Desiring: D. this man's art SHAK 235:11
is to admire without d. BRAD 45:17
desist: d. To build at all SHAK 212:23
desks: Stick close to your d. and never GILB 108:29
desolated: they have d. and profaned GLAD 109:15
desolation: abomination of d. BIBLE 34:1
years of d. pass over JEFF 130:11
despair: begotten by d. Upon impossibility
MARV 161:13
depth of some divine d. TENN 254:10
Do not d. PUDN 192:10
have of comfort and d. SHAK 237:2

I d. pronouncing it — SHAK 230:2
If I should d. — BROO 47:16
If it were now to d. — SHAK 228:21
If we are mark'd to d. — SHAK 214:3
I must d. — BIBLE 24:20
I must d. — NASHE 175:2
it was sure to d. — MOORE 173:3
live or d. wi' Charlie — HOGG 120:14
love one another or d. — AUDEN 11:6
man can d. but once — SHAK 212:29
Muse forbids to d. — HOR 124:16
Must d. at last — DONNE 88:14
must weep or she will d. — TENN 254:13
myself to d. upon a kiss — SHAK 229:16
natural to d. as to be born — BACON 14:9
Not d. here in a rage — SWIFT 249:5
not to live, but to d. — BROW 48:9
Only we d. in earnest — RAL 194:3
'People can't d. — DICK 84:5
persons d. before they sing — COL 74:24
shall break it must d. — KIPL 145:2
shall not altogether d. — HOR 124:13
shall Trelawny d. — HAWK 115:17
should d. before I wake — ANON 4:11
should d. for the people — BIBLE 36:34
Sir Richard Grenville d. — TENN 255:6
Their's but to do and d. — TENN 251:9
thereof thou shalt surely d. — BIBLE 22:7
these who d. as cattle — OWEN 179:4
They must conquer or d. — GAY 105:22
time to d. — BIBLE 27:6
to d. for one's country — HOR 124:7
to d. in the last ditch — WILL 272:11
to morrow we shall d. — BIBLE 28:25
We shall d. alone — PASC 181:1
What 'tis to d. — BEAU 17:2
when they d. — APPL 7:11
Who did not wish to d. — SHAW 238:22
who would wish to d. — BORR 44:22
wisdom shall d. with you — BIBLE 25:23
wish to live and to d. — VILL 262:14
Dieb: er war ein D. — HEINE 116:13
died: been the same since God d. — MILL 166:5
children who d. for our lands — KIPL 143:14
darter es d. o' the fever — TENN 255:17
d. extremely well — WALP 265:15
d. to save their country — CHES 69:25
dog it was that d. — GOLD 110:15
He d. in a good old age — BIBLE 25:15
He that d. o' Wednesday — SHAK 212:18
should have d. hereafter — SHAK 223:15
There d. a myriad — POUND 186:10
thought it d. of grieving — KEATS 140:2
would God I had d. for thee — BIBLE 24:29
diem: carpe d. — HOR 123:14
d. perdidi — TITUS 259:16
dies: d. fighting has increase — GREN 113:3
D. irae — CEL 65:14
Every moment d. a man — BABB 12:19
Every moment d. a man — TENN 255:18
ev'ry word a reputation d. — POPE 185:26
gods love d. young — MEN 165:1
hath blown for ever d. — FITZ 99:4
He that d. pays all debts — SHAK 232:21
kingdom where nobody d. — MILL 166:4
king never d. — BLAC 42:14
One d. only once — MOL 171:8
summer d. the swan — TENN 255:9
who d. rich dies disgraced — CARN 62:1

diet: d. unparalleled — DICK 84:19
Dieu: D. est d'ordinaire pour — BUSS 56:1
D. n'est pas pour les gros — VOLT 265:7
Je parle espagnol à D. — CHAR 67:15
Le bon D. n'a que dix — CLEM 73:4
le Verbe, c'est D. — HUGO 127:15
Si D. n'existait pas — VOLT 264:20
differemus: nulli negabimus aut d. — MAGN 159:1
difference: d. to me — WORD 276:14
that has made all the d. — FROST 103:8
different: d. methods different men — CHUR 70:18
from those who have a d. — CONR 77:11
How d. from us — ANON 4:7
They are d. from you — FITZ 100:4
very d. from the home life — ANON 3:17
will show you something d. — ELIOT 94:19
differential: integral and d. calculus — GILB 109:1
differently: they do things d. there — HART 115:15
Difficile: D. est saturam non — JUV 137:13
difficult: d. to get up resentment — NEWM 175:18
It has been found d. — CHES 70:12
more alternatives, the more d. — ALL 2:6
which it is d. to speak — BURKE 53:6
difficulties: little local d. — MACM 157:19
difficulty: has had to face every d. — WILDE 272:5
Diffugere: D. nives — HOR 124:15
dig: d. him up and throw stones — SHAW 237:15
D. the grave and let me — STEV 247:16
d. till you gently perspire — KIPL 144:13
I cannot d. — BIBLE 35:30
nails he'll d. it up again — ELIOT 95:1
with his nails he'll d. — WEBS 267:16
digest: inwardly d. them — PRAY 187:7
digested: few to be chewed and d. — BACON 13:29
digestion: good d. wait on appetite — SHAK 222:17
diggeth: d. a pit shall fall — BIBLE 27:17
dignitate: cum d. otium — CIC 72:14
dignity: d. of this high calling — BURKE 52:18
equal in d. and rights — ANON 2:16
room with silent d. — GROS 113:5
Dignum: D. laude virum Musa vetat — HOR 124:16
digressions: at issue by eloquent d. — HUXL 128:14
dilectione: d. hominum et odio vitiorum — AUG 11:20
Dilige: D. et quod vis fac — AUG 11:19
dimanches: tous les d. sa poule au pot — HENR 117:11
dimensions: my d. are as well compact — SHAK 217:19
Dimidium: D. facti qui coepit — HOR 123:3
diminished: ought to be d. — DUNN 92:1
dimittis: Nunc d. servum tuum — BIBLE 41:19
Dimity: Such D. Convictions — DICK 86:6
dine: going to d. with some men — BENT 19:20
go to inns to d. — CHES 70:7
I d. at Blenheim once — ANON 4:10
soon d. with Jack Ketch — JOHN 133:1
this should stay to d. — CARR 62:12
dined: I have d. to-day — SMITH 242:21
dines: d. he sleeps — SURT 248:11
dining: while they thought of d. — GOLD 110:16
dinner: d. of herbs where love — BIBLE 26:21
doubtful of his d. — JOHN 134:27
They would ask him to d. — CARL 61:23
three hours' march to d. — HAZL 116:5
'What gat ye to your d. — BALL 14:17
dinner-knives: gravel paths with broken d. — KIPL 144:3
direct: House is pleased to d. — LENT 151:8
were all going d. to Heaven — DICK 85:29
directions: By indirections find d. — SHAK 208:4

rode madly off in all d.   LEAC 150:1
direful: something d. in the sound   AUST 11:24
dirge: d. of her certain ending   SHAK 235:7
dirt: poverty, hunger, and d.   HOOD 121:12
dirty: d. work for the rest   RUSK 198:9
Dis: dark D.'s door stands open   VIRG 263:10
    D. aliter visum   VIRG 263:5
    unsubstantial realms of D.   VIRG 263:12
disagreeable: doing things d. to myself
    SMITH 243:3
    enough to tell him d. truths   BULW 51:13
disappeared: He d. in the dead of winter
    AUDEN 10:15
disappointed: I am d. by that stroke   JOHN 134:25
Disappointment: D. all I endeavour end
    HOPK 122:8
disapprove: I d. of what you say   VOLT 265:10
Disaster: meet with Triumph and D.   KIPL 144:7
disbelief: willing suspension of d.   COL 75:10
disbelieve: believe in Belief...Lord I d.
    FORS 101:20
discharge: responsibility and to d.   EDW 92:11
    There is no d. in that war   BIBLE 27:11
    There's no d. in the war   KIPL 143:13
discharged: d. from the war   HOR 124:11
disciple: only in the name of a d.   BIBLE 32:29
discipline: d. of colleges and universities
    SMITH 242:2
    order and military d.   ANON 3:8
discontent: is the winter of our d.   SHAK 231:2
discontents: More d. I never had   HERR 118:19
discouragement: There's no d.   BUNY 52:2
discoveries: not much wish well to d.   JOHN 134:23
discretion: your own d. be your tutor   SHAK 209:8
discriminations: Makes no d.   WHIT 270:8
discunt: *Homines dum docent d.*   SEN 203:5
disdain: little d. is not amiss   CONG 76:24
    my dear Lady D.   SHAK 228:4
disdainful: grandeur hear with a d. smile
    GRAY 112:3
disdains: He d. all things above   OVER 178:18
diseas'd: minister to a mind d.   SHAK 223:13
disease: Cure the d. and kill   BACON 13:8
    desperate d. requires   FAWK 97:17
    d. has grown strong through   OVID 178:23
    d. of not listening   SHAK 212:20
    d. that afflicts amateurs   CHES 70:10
    is no cure for this d.   BELL 18:10
    remedy is worse than the d.   BACON 13:18
diseases: death is the cure of all d.   BROW 48:8
    D. desperate grown   SHAK 210:22
    subject to the same d.   SHAK 225:10
disfigured: snow d. the public statues
    AUDEN 10:15
disgrace: d. with fortune and men's   SHAK 235:11
disgraced: who dies...rich dies d.   CARN 62:1
disguise: Are blessings in d.   HERV 119:3
    D. fair nature with hard-favour'd   SHAK 213:14
disgust: not moments of d.   VOLT 265:5
dish: forth butter in a lordly d.   BIBLE 24:6
    Let's carve him as a d.   SHAK 216:4
    woman is a d. for the gods   SHAK 204:9
dishes: there's no washing of d.   ANON 3:14
dishonourable: find ourselves d. graves
    SHAK 215:16
disiecti: *d. membra poetae*   HOR 124:22
disinheriting: damned d. countenance   SHER 240:26
dislike: do not much d. the matter   SHAK 203:21
dismal: d. headache, and repose   GILB 107:20

    Professors of the D. Science   CARL 61:16
dismay'd: Was there a man d.   TENN 251:9
dismiss: d. us with Thy blessing   BUCK 51:5
disobedience: Of Man's first d.   MILT 168:12
disorder: sweet d. in the dress   HERR 118:18
dispensation: in the old d.   ELIOT 94:2
dispense: d. with its necessities   MOTL 174:5
displeasing: something which is not d. to us
    LA R 149:8
dispoged: lips to it when I am so d.   DICK 84:12
disponit: *sed Deus d.*   THOM 256:19
dispraised: d. were no small praise   MILT 169:23
disputations: Doubtful d.   BIBLE 38:6
dispute: right there is none to d.   COWP 80:5
dissaisiatur: *imprisonetur, aut d.*   MAGN 158:16
dissatisfied: Not one is d.   WHIT 270:6
dissect: d. nature along lines laid   WHORF 270:12
    We murder to d.   WORD 277:9
dissimulate: to d. their instability   HOUS 127:7
dissipation: d. without pleasure   GIBB 106:7
dissociation: century a d. of sensibility   ELIOT 95:12
dissolve: d., and quite forget   KEATS 139:19
dissonance: far off the barb'rous d.   MILT 169:14
distance: by d. made more sweet   WORD 276:2
    d. is nothing   DU D 91:16
    La d. n'y fait rien   DU D 91:16
    sixty seconds' worth of d.   KIPL 144:9
    'Tis d. lends enchantment   CAMP 60:18
distant: Music of a d. Drum   FITZ 98:16
    Ye d. spires   GRAY 112:8
distempered: That questions the d. part
    ELIOT 93:17
distinguished: d. thing   JAMES 130:6
    man is d. from all other   ADD 1:14
Distraction: D., Uglification and Derision
    CARR 63:8
    d. in 's aspect   SHAK 208:20
    Into a fine d.   HERR 118:18
distress: All pray in their d.   BLAKE 43:18
    delivereth them out of their d.   PRAY 190:9
distressed: afflicted, or d.   PRAY 187:5
dit: *la peine d'être d.*   BEAU 16:14
ditch: is to die in the last d.   WILL 272:11
    shall fall into the d.   BIBLE 33:9
Ditch-deliver'd: D. by a drab   SHAK 222:3
ditchwater: drinking bottled d.   SHAW 237:18
ditties: Pipe to the spirit d.   KEATS 139:13
diurnal: With visible motion her d.   WORD 275:1
dive: Heav'n's great lamps do d.   CAT 65:5
    search for pearls must d.   DRYD 90:20
diver: has been a d. in deep seas   PATER 181:8
diversion: 'tis a country d.   CONG 77:1
divided: common use has harshly d.   SCH 201:2
    death they were not d.   BIBLE 24:26
    If a house be d. against   BIBLE 34:21
    perceive here a d. duty   SHAK 228:19
    Thy kingdom is d.   BIBLE 30:9
    whole is d. into three parts   CAES 59:8
divideth: d. his spoils   BIBLE 35:16
dividing: by d. we fall   DICK 86:7
    days d. lover and lover   SWIN 249:16
divine: depth of some d. despair   TENN 254:10
    did the Countenance D.   BLAKE 43:2
    D. of Kings to govern wrong   POPE 184:9
    d. right of husbands   WOLL 274:1
    human form d.   BLAKE 43:19
    It is a good d. that follows   SHAK 224:14
    Makes drudgery d.   HERB 118:9
    to forgive, d.   POPE 185:11

what the form d.   LAND 148:12
You look d. as you advance   NASH 175:1
divinely: ever most d. in the wrong   YOUNG 280:7
most d. fair   TENN 251:12
divinest: two d. things this world   HUNT 128:7
divinity: d. doth hedge a king   SHAK 211:5
d. or school metaphysics   HUME 127:17
d. that shapes our ends   SHAK 211:15
is surely a piece of d.   BROW 48:10
Division: D. is as bad   ANON 4:8
divisions: Pope! How many d.   STAL 245:10
divorce: long d. of steel   SHAK 215:5
then this bill of my D.   DONNE 88:8
dixerunt: qui ante nos nostra d.   DON 87:16
dixit: 'Ipse d.   CIC 72:7
Do: D. as you would be done   CHES 69:7
d. for pretty girls   YEATS 279:6
D. lovely things   KING 142:9
d. something today which   COLL 75:18
d. were as easy as to know   SHAK 224:14
D. what you like   RAB 193:14
d. ye even so to them   BIBLE 32:7
having too little to d.   KIPL 144:12
How many things I can d.   SOCR 243:9
HOW NOT TO D. IT   DICK 84:9
I can d. no other   LUTH 155:12
I d. it again and again   CARR 62:18
I'll do, and I'll d.   SHAK 220:2
It revolts me, but I d. it   GILB 108:2
I will d. such things   SHAK 218:5
Let us d. or die   BURNS 54:21
Love and d. what you will   AUG 11:19
one that will d. the deed   SHAK 219:9
Their's but to d. and die   TENN 251:9
they know not what they d.   BIBLE 36:8
things we cannot all d.   LUC 155:3
This will never d.   JEFF 130:14
to d. nothing for ever   ANON 3:14
to d. those things which   KEYN 141:16
Whatever you d.   ANON 7:4
What must I d. to be saved   BIBLE 37:20
who can d. all things well   CHUR 70:18
Doasyouwouldbedoneby: her name is Mrs D.
                                          KING 142:12
docent: Homines dum d. discunt   SEN 203:5
docks: spudding up d.   HARDY 114:13
doctor: d. is a specially dangerous   SHAW 238:19
doctors: better have d. well off   SHAW 238:19
If you believe the d.   SAL 199:7
doctrine: about with every wind of d. BIBLE 39:11
doctrines: makes all d. plain and clear BUTL 56:10
documents: England are ready to sign d.
                                          HURST 128:9
Dodger: *sobriquet* of 'The artful D. DICK 85:6
doff't: Had d. her gawdy trim   MILT 168:7
dog: Beware of the d.   PETR 183:1
courtesy help a lame d.   CHIL 70:15
cut-throat d.   SHAK 224:21
d. bites a man   BOG 44:15
d. is turned to his own   BIBLE 40:23
d. it was that died   GOLD 110:15
d. returneth to his vomit   BIBLE 26:30
d., to gain some private   GOLD 110:14
engine of pollution, the d.   SPAR 244:4
every d. his day   KING 142:16
giving your heart to a d.   KIPL 145:9
good d., like a good candidate   BECK 17:6
'Hath a d. money   SHAK 225:1
Is thy servant a d.   BIBLE 25:11

living d. is better than   BIBLE 27:13
Lovell our d.   COLL 75:16
Mine enemy's d.   SHAK 218:24
'O keep the D. far hence   ELIOT 95:1
preaching is like a d.'s   JOHN 132:5
Something better than his d.   TENN 253:8
'The d. did nothing   DOYLE 89:19
whose d. are you   POPE 184:1
You call'd me d.   SHAK 225:1
dogfight: We were regaled by a d.   MAC 157:5
dogged: It's d. as does it   TROL 260:6
dogma: d. of the Ghost   RYLE 198:17
dogs: bang these d. of Seville   TENN 255:4
better I like d.   ROL 196:4
dancing d. and bears   HODG 120:4
d. eat of the crumbs which   BIBLE 33:10
hates d. and babies   ROST 197:12
Lame d. over stiles   KING 142:10
let slip the d. of war   SHAK 216:12
Mad d. and Englishmen   COW 79:5
Now for d. and apes   BROW 49:10
Things are but as straw d.   LAO 149:4
Throw physic to the d.   SHAK 223:13
Dog-star: D. rages   POPE 184:18
doileys: I'm soiling the d.   BETJ 20:14
doing: be up and d.   LONG 153:11
dread of d. what has been done   WHAR 269:9
see what she's d.   PUNCH 192:16
what everyone is d.   HERB 118:3
What was he d.   BROW 48:16
Doing-good: D., that is one   THOR 259:5
Doleful: Knight of the D. Countenance CERV 66:5
dolefull'st: there sung the d. ditty BARN 15:17
doll: doll in the d.'s house   DICK 85:12
once had a sweet little d.   KING 142:15
dollar: almighty d. is the only   ANON 4:21
dolore: Nessun maggior d.   DANTE 81:11
dolphin: That d.-torn   YEATS 278:12
domestic: d. as a plate   MILL 166:7
d. business is no less   MONT 172:2
domi: Res angusta d.   JUV 137:19
dominion: death hath no more d. over BIBLE 37:35
death shall have no d.   THOM 256:22
d. of the sea   COV 79:1
d. of the world   MAHAN 159:2
D. over palm and pine   KIPL 145:10
Dominus: D. custodierit civitatem   BIBLE 41:15
D. illuminatio mea   BIBLE 41:11
D. vobiscum   MASS 163:18
Don: D. different from those   BELL 19:1
Remote and ineffectual D.   BELL 18:25
turn'd my back upon D.   TENN 255:4
dona: d. nobis pacem   MASS 163:18
Requiem aeternam d. eis   MASS 163:11
timeo Danaos et d.   VIRG 263:3
done: been and gone and d.   GILB 106:19
consider it d.   CALL 59:15
doing what has been d. before   WHAR 269:9
d. the state some service   SHAK 229:15
If it were d. when 'tis   SHAK 220:13
let us have d. with you   CROM 80:18
present are not d. at all   KEYN 141:16
Something attempted, something d.   LONG 153:18
Something must be d.   EDW 92:10
surprised to find it d. at all   JOHN 132:5
that which shall be d.   BIBLE 27:3
they had d. very well out   BALD 14:13
they had not d. they do   SUCK 248:5
thou and I have d. before   SUCK 248:5

he d., and behold a ladder — BIBLE 22:32
I d. fast of mirth — WEVER 269:7
dreamer: d. of dreams — BIBLE 23:32
this d. cometh — BIBLE 23:4
dreamers: We are the d. of dreams — OSH 178:14
dreaming: City with her d. spires — ARN 9:3
I am now a butterfly d. — CHUA 70:17
dreams: are the dreamers of d. — OSH 178:14
because you tread on my d. — YEATS 279:3
beyond the d. of avarice — JOHN 133:17
d. happy as her day — BROO 47:16
I arise from d. of thee — SHEL 239:6
not make d. your master — KIPL 144:7
not that I have bad d. — SHAK 208:13
old men shall dream d. — BIBLE 30:14
rich beyond the d. of avarice — MOORE 172:11
stuff As d. are made on — SHAK 232:24
Than this world d. — TENN 252:7
Thou wovest d. of joy — SHEL 240:6
dreamt: d. of in your philosophy — SHAK 208:1
dreme: d. of joye — CHAU 68:21
drench'd: you have d. our steeples — SHAK 218:6
Drene: Delicately drowns in D. — BETJ 21:8
dress: does it signify how we d. — GASK 105:3
Peace, the human d. — BLAKE 43:19
Style is the d. of thought — WESL 268:21
sweet disorder in the d. — HERR 118:18
we d. when we're ruined — HARDY 114:13
dresses: neat-handed Phyllis d. — MILT 167:18
Drest: D. in a little brief authority — SHAK 223:18
drew: man a bow at a venture — BIBLE 25:9
Dr Fell: I do not love you, D. — BROWN 48:2
Dr Froyd: So then D. said that all — LOOS 154:3
dried: d. up, and withered — PRAY 189:21
drink: Doth ask a d. divine — JONS 136:3
D. and the devil had done — STEV 246:19
D. no longer water — BIBLE 39:29
d. thy wine with a merry — BIBLE 27:14
D. to me only with thine — JONS 136:3
d. unto one of these little — BIBLE 32:29
d. with you — SHAK 224:17
d. your ale — HOUS 126:16
eat, and to d. — BIBLE 27:12
five reasons we should d. — ALDR 2:2
Let us eat and d. — BIBLE 28:25
Man wants but little d. — HOLM 120:16
Nor any drop to d. — COL 74:10
now could I d. hot blood — SHAK 210:9
strong d. is raging — BIBLE 26:24
Then d., puppy — WHYT 270:14
they may follow strong d. — BIBLE 28:10
thirsty and ye gave me d. — BIBLE 34:8
We'll teach you to d. deep — SHAK 207:1
drinking: d. bottled ditchwater — SHAW 237:18
d. largely sobers us again — POPE 185:8
D. when we are not thirsty — BEAU 16:16
is the curse of the d. — WILDE 272:4
unhappy brains for d. — SHAK 228:22
drinks: Now for d. — HOR 123:18
drive: d. a coach and six horses — RICE 195:3
Drives: D. my green age — THOM 257:4
driving: d. briskly in a post-chaise — JOHN 133:3
driving is like the d. of Jehu — BIBLE 25:12
droghte: d. of March hath perced — CHAU 67:17
droits: *Toute loi qui viole les d.* — ROB 195:10
dromedary: Donne, whose muse on d. — COL 75:8
D. is a cheerful bird — BELL 18:4
Droops: D. on the little hands — MILNE 166:17
drop: d. of allaying Tiber — SHAK 205:14

d. of rain maketh a hole — LAT 149:1
One d. would save my soul — MARL 160:
To d. a limb on the head — KIPL 146:
Dropping: D. the pilot — TENN 251:
drops: changed into little water d. — MARL 160:
D. earliest to the ground — SHAK 225:1
d. on gate-bars hang — HARDY 115:
Dropt: D. from the zenith like — MILT 169:
drown: I'll d. my book — SHAK 233:
tears shall d. the wind — SHAK 221:
drown'd: d. my Glory in a Shallow — FITZ 99:1
d. the cocks — SHAK 218:
drowned: he were d. in the depth — BIBLE 33:1
drowning: not waving but d. — SMITH 242:1
drowns: Delicately d. in Drene — BETJ 21:8
drowsy: d. numbness pains — KEATS 139:1
Vexing the dull ear of a d. — SHAK 217:1
drudge: harmless d. — JOHN 131:1
drudgery: Makes d. divine — HERB 118:
drugs: d. cause cramp — PARK 180:
Drum: Music of a *distant* D. — FITZ 98:1
My pulse like a soft d. — KING 142:
Not a d. was heard — WOLFE 273:1
drums: beat the d. — MOR 173:
when the d. begin to roll — KIPL 146:
drunk: against a post when he was d. — SHAK 213:1
d. with sight of power — KIPL 145:1
eaten and d. enough — HOR 123:
Have a d. their Cup a Round — FITZ 99:
if it be d. moderately — BIBLE 30:2
once saw Wordsworth d. — HOUS 127:
Philip d. to Philip sober — ANON 3:
Was the hope d. — SHAK 221:
which hath made them d. — SHAK 221:1
drunkard: English d. made the rolling — CHES 70:
drunkards: MSS as d. use lamp-posts — HOUS 127:
drunken: stagger like a d. man — PRAY 190:
dry: being d. — ALDR 2:
I am so d. — ANON 3:18
I am so d. — FARM 97:1
old man in a d. month — ELIOT 93:21
Dublin: D., though a place much — JOHN 134:
Duchess: D. of Malfi still — WEBS 267:1
D. painted on the wall — BROW 50:4
D.! The Duchess — CARR 62:1
Duck: D. and the Kangaroo — LEAR 150:
ducks: country stealing d. — ARAB 7:1
Duke: D. of Plaza Toro — GILB 107:2
d.'s revenues on her back — SHAK 214:1
everybody praised the D. — SOUT 243:18
tell you I was made a D. — WELL 268:
Dulce: *D. est desipere in loco* — HOR 124:1
D. et decorum est pro patria — HOR 124:7
D. ridentem — CAT 65:9
D. ridentem Lalagen amabo — HOR 123:17
dulcimer: damsel with a d. — COL 75:6
dull: Anger makes d. men witty — ELIZ 95:15
can be d. in Fleet Street — LAMB 147:18
d. cold ear of death — GRAY 112:4
d. product of a scoffer's — WORD 274:14
D. would he be of soul — WORD 276:18
How d. it is to pause — TENN 255:13
is not only d. in himself — FOOTE 101:8
make dictionaries is d. — JOHN 134:16
Sherry is d. — JOHN 132:4
Though it's d. at whiles — KING 142:10
wasn't as d. as ditch water — DICK 85:11
dullard: d.'s envy of brilliant — BEER 17:19
duller: d. spectacle this earth — DE Q 83:1

E. stood hard as iron — ROSS 197:5
e. the broken arcs — BROW 48:18
E. the first of the gods — VIRG 263:16
e. to earth — PRAY 188:5
E. will hold us — ANON 6:17
even as if the e. had rolled — WORD 275:1
feel the e. move — HEM 117:5
girdle round about the e. — SHAK 227:4
gives all men all e. to love — KIPL 145:18
going to and fro in the e. — BIBLE 25:17
Heaven and E. are not ruthful — LAO 149:4
heroic for e. too hard — BROW 48:19
is thy e. so marred — THOM 258:5
It fell to e. — LONG 153:1
Lay her i' the e. — SHAK 211:13
Lie heavy on him, E. — EVANS 97:6
Man marks the e. with ruin — BYRON 57:15
naked e. is warm with Spring — GREN 113:3
new heaven and a new e. — BIBLE 41:7
new heaven, new e. — SHAK 203:17
new heavens and a new e. — BIBLE 29:23
on e. peace — BIBLE 35:3
replenish the e. — BIBLE 22:6
Rolled round in e.'s diurnal — WORD 276:17
round e.'s imagined corners — DONNE 88:2
Standing on e. — MILT 169:13
There were giants in the e. — BIBLE 22:19
they shall inherit the e. — BIBLE 31:11
This e. of majesty — SHAK 230:2
this e., this realm — SHAK 230:2
thou bleeding piece of e. — SHAK 216:11
though the e. be moved — PRAY 189:3
whole e. as their memorial — PER 182:15
Yours is the E. and everything — KIPL 144:9
earthquake: e. is not satisfied — WORD 276:9
earthy: man is of the earth, e. — BIBLE 38:21
ease: another gives its e. — BLAKE 43:10
E. after war — SPEN 244:16
e. in mine inn but I shall — SHAK 212:16
e. of the masters — SMITH 242:2
in another's loss of e. — BLAKE 43:11
Who have at home at e. — PARK 180:11
easier: e. for a camel to go through — BIBLE 33:22
East: E. is East — KIPL 143:9
e., nor from the west — PRAY 189:15
from the e. to Jerusalem — BIBLE 31:1
hold the gorgeous E. in fee — WORD 277:2
It is the e. — SHAK 231:16
me somewheres e. of Suez — KIPL 145:4
on the e. of Eden — BIBLE 22:18
Eastern: marvel save in E. clime — BURG 52:7
Out of the misty e. cave — SHEL 240:6
Eastertide: Wearing white for E. — HOUS 125:4
Easy: E. is the way down — VIRG 263:10
E. live and quiet die — SCOTT 202:5
If to do were as e. — SHAK 224:14
Now as I was young and e. — THOM 257:2
on the rack of a too e. — POPE 184:10
She bid me take love e. — YEATS 278:18
eat: day you'll e. a pork chop — CAMP 60:10
e., and to drink — BIBLE 27:12
e. our pot of honey — MER 165:2
e. the fat of the land — BIBLE 23:7
face shalt thou e. bread — BIBLE 22:14
have meat and cannot e. — BURNS 54:13
I will not e. with you — SHAK 224:17
I would e. a missionary — WILB 270:15
Let us e. and drink — BIBLE 28:5
neither should he e. — BIBLE 39:25

Nothing to e. but food — KING 142:5
One should e. to live — MOL 171:5
so we must e. we — THAC 256:13
Tell me what you e. — BRIL 46:18
that "I see what I e." — CARR 63:2
thou shalt not e. of it — BIBLE 22:7
thy princes e. in the morning — BIBLE 27:18
ye shall e. it in haste — BIBLE 23:15
eaten: e. and drunk enough — HOR 123:8
e. by missionaries — SPOQN 245:3
see God made and e. — BROW 49:1
They'd e. every one — CARR 64:3
eater: of the e. came forth meat — BIBLE 24:10
eateth: e. grass as an ox — BIBLE 26:1
e. your Master with publicans — BIBLE 32:18
eating: appetite grows by e. — RAB 193:12
e. *pâtés de foie gras* — SMITH 242:23
eats: Man is what he e. — FEUE 98:1
Eave: stranger! 'E. 'arf a brick — PUNCH 192:13
Ecce: E. homo — BIBLE 41:22
ecclesia: Anglicana e. libera — MAGN 158:15
ecclesiam: patrem qui e. non habet matrem — CYPR 81:6
Salus extra e. non est — AUG 11:18
Ecclesiastes: dixit E. — BIBLE 41:17
Echo: E. beyond the Mexique Bay — MARV 161:12
echoes: e., dying — TENN 254:9
stage but e. back the public — JOHN 135:7
echoing: e. straits between us thrown — ARN 8:15
Eclipse: E. first — OKEL 178:3
In a merciful e. — GILB 107:8
total e. — MILT 170:2
eclipsed: e. the gaiety of nations — JOHN 134:25
écoles: toutes les é. de théologie — DID 86:9
economic: attaining e. ends — KEYN 141:17
Economy: fear of Political E. — SELL 203:3
'Principles of Political E.' — BENT 19:19
ecstasy: Blasted with e. — SHAK 209:6
e., is success in life — PATER 181:10
In such an e. — KEATS 139:22
Eden: E.'s dread probationary — COWP 79:18
E. took their solitary — MILT 169:22
happier E. — MILT 169:9
on the east of E. — BIBLE 22:18
This other E. — SHAK 230:2
voice that breathed o'er E. — KEBLE 141:11
edge: children's teeth are set on e. — BIBLE 30:4
edideris: Quod non e. — HOR 122:21
edification: than the e. of the hearers — BURKE 52:8
edisti: e. satis atque bibisti — HOR 123:8
Edom: over E. will I cast — PRAY 189:10
this that cometh from E. — BIBLE 29:21
Educ: E.: during the holidays — SITW 241:13
Educating: E. the natives of Borrioboola-Gha — DICK 83:14
education: chief hand in their own e. — SCOTT 202:13
E. is what survives when — SKIN 241:14
E. made us what we are — HELV 116:17
is a part of e. — BACON 13:24
race between e. and catastrophe — WELLS 268:17
'Tis E. forms the common — POPE 184:23
with the e. of the heart — SCOTT 202:14
eels: e. boil'd in broo' — BALL 14:17
effort: e. nor the failure tires — EMPS 96:21
e. very nearly killed her — BELL 18:14
What is written without e. — JOHN 134:10
effraie: espaces infinis m'e. — PASC 180:18
égalité: majestueuse é. des lois — FRAN 102:5
égards: doit des é. aux vivants — VOLT 265:8

egg: afraid you've got a bad e.	PUNCH 193:2
full of quarrels as an e.	SHAK 231:26
See this e.	DID 86:9
that a hen is only an e.'s	BUTL 56:14
white and hairless as an e.	HERR 118:21
eggs: (Butter and e. and a pound	CALV 59:16
Lays e. inside a paper bag	ISH 129:16
weasel sucks e.	SHAK 204:20
eglantine: with e.	SHAK 227:5
ego: Et in Arcadia e.	ANON 6:16
Egypt: that there was corn in E.	BIBLE 23:5
There was a great cry in E.	BIBLE 23:16
Eheu: E. fugaces	HOR 124:4
eighty: dream you are never e.	SEXT 203:10
Einstein: Let E. be	SQUI 245:8
either: happy could I be with e.	GAY 105:14
Elaine: Daintily alights E.	BETJ 21:7
E., the lily maid of Astolat	TENN 251:19
elbow: e. has a fascination that	GILB 108:12
elder: e. man not at all	BACON 13:14
woman take An e.	SHAK 234:2
Eldorado: E. banal de tous les vieux	BAUD 16:13
election: e. is coming	ELIOT 93:1
elections: it's no go the e.	MACN 158:6
Electric: mend the E. Light	BELL 19:2
Runs the red e. train	BETJ 21:7
electrical: e. skin and glaring eyes	SMART 241:16
electrification: e. of the whole country	LEE 151:7
eleison: Kyrie e.	MASS 163:10
Elementary: 'E.,' said he	DOYLE 89:17
elements: e. of modern civilization	CARL 61:8
e. So mix'd in him	SHAK 217:6
elephant: Appears a monstrous e.	COTT 78:14
E., Is best to lodge	SHAK 234:8
E., The only harmless	DONNE 88:12
He thought he saw an E.	CARR 62:10
elevates: e. above the vulgar herd	GAIS 104:6
eleven: tells you he's only e.	GILB 107:22
elf: deceiving e.	KEATS 140:1
Elfland: horns of E. faintly blowing	TENN 254:9
Eli: E., lama sabachthani	BIBLE 34:18
Ellen: E. of brave Lochinvar	SCOTT 201:20
Ellum: E. she hateth mankind	KIPL 146:3
elms: Behind the e. last night	PRIOR 191:18
Beneath those rugged e.	GRAY 112:2
doves in immemorial e.	TENN 255:2
elm-tree: Round the e. bole are	BROW 49:12
eloquent: e. digressions and skilled	HUXL 128:14
e., just, and mighty Death	RAL 194:6
else: e. would I give it thee	PRAY 189:7
elsewhere: elsewhere live as they live e.	AMBR 2:8
Elysium: daughter of E.	SCH 201:2
What E. have ye known	KEATS 139:10
Elzevir: E. classic in your pocket	CHES 69:10
embarras: L'e. des richesses	ALL 2:6
embattled: e. nations sing and shout	SQUI 245:7
embers: Where glowing e. through	MILT 167:13
embody: e. the Law	GILB 107:12
embrace: depend on whether I e.	WILK 272:9
his right hand doth e. me	BIBLE 27:28
none I think do there e.	MARV 161:21
Emerald Isle: men of the E.	DREN 90:7
Emeralds: E. big as half a county	LAND 148:11
emigration: e. Has proved most useful	CART 64:19
emolument: positions of considerable e.	GAIS 104:6
emotion: e. in the form of art is	ELIOT 95:11
e. is immediately evoked	ELIOT 95:11
e. recollected in tranquillity	WORD 277:13

morality touched by e.	ARN 9:11
unhurried by e.	JAMES 130:5
emotions: gamut of the e. from	PARK 180:8
waste-paper basket of the e.	WEBB 267:4
emperor: ancient days by e. and clown	KEATS 140:1
emperor is the e. of ice-cream	STEV 246:14
had he never become e.	TAC 250:11
looking for the sacred E.	BRAM 46:4
Empire: Britain has lost an E.	ACH 1:2
called 'the metropolis of the e.	CODD 73:30
ni romain, ni e.	VOLT 264:21
wilderness into a glorious e.	BURKE 52:18
empires: Vaster than e.	MARV 161:20
employment: pleasantness of an e. does	AUST 12:14
To give e. to the artisan	BELL 19:2
employments: How various his e.	COWP 80:3
Emprison: E. her soft hand and let	KEATS 139:17
emptiness: behind it but panic and e.	FORS 101:14
empty: fold stands e. in the drowned	SHAK 227:2
He findeth it e.	BIBLE 33:3
men had ever very e. heads	BACON 12:21
rich he hath sent e. away	BIBLE 34:29
turn down an e. Glass	FITZ 100:1
En: E. Priamus	VIRG 263:2
enamoured: e. on peace that he would	CLAR 72:25
enchanter: like ghosts from an e.	SHEL 239:12
enchantment: distance lends e. to the view	CAMP 60:18
enchantments: e. of the Middle Age…Home	ARN 9:8
enchantress: tune the e. plays	HOUS 126:21
encounter: e. darkness as a bride	SHAK 224:2
encourage: right to e.	BAG 14:7
to e. the others	VOLT 264:15
encourager: amiral pour e. les autres	VOLT 264:15
end: A' made a finer e.	SHAK 213:12
as an e. withal, never as means	KANT 138:9
e. crowns all	SHAK 233:13
e. is where we start from	ELIOT 93:19
e. justifies the means	BUS 55:22
e. of the beginning	CHUR 71:11
God be at my e.	ANON 3:12
laid e. to end	PARK 180:10
let me know mine e.	PRAY 188:25
long weary day have e.	SPEN 244:14
look to the e.	ANON 7:4
man awaits his e.	YEATS 278:16
sans E.	FITZ 99:3
something ere the e.	TENN 255:14
there's ane e. of an old song	OGIL 177:12
there's an e. on't	JOHN 132:13
till you come to the e.	CARR 63:15
We shall go on to the e.	CHUR 71:5
what e. the gods have	HOR 123:13
Whoever wills the e.	KANT 138:8
end-all: be the be-all and the e.	SHAK 220:13
endearing: all those e. young charms	MOORE 172:13
endears: That all the more e.	TENN 254:6
endeavour: Disappointment all I e.	HOPK 122:8
ending: beginning and the e.	BIBLE 40:28
dirge of her certain e.	SHAK 235:7
so clean an e.	HOUS 126:8
endow: worldly goods I thee e.	PRAY 188:1
ends: divinity that shapes our e.	SHAK 211:15
make both e. meet	FULL 104:1
More are men's e. mark'd	SHAK 229:21

endure: e. an hour and see injustice | HOUS 126:9
e. Their going hence | SHAK 218:26
e. the toothache patiently | SHAK 228:13
heaviness may e. for a night | PRAY 188:21
if I continue to e. you | CONG 77:3
nature itselfe cant e. | FLEM 100:14
Youth's a stuff will not e. | SHAK 233:22
endured: which much is to be e. | JOHN 135:1
endureth: e. all things | BIBLE 38:15
mercy e. for ever | PRAY 190:23
enemies: left me naked to mine e. | SHAK 215:11
Love your e. | BIBLE 35:7
make thine e. thy footstool | PRAY 190:10
wish their e. dead | MONT 171:16
with their e. in the gate | PRAY 190:20
enemy: common e. and oppressor | BURKE 53:7
e. hath done this | BIBLE 33:5
e. in their mouths to steal | SHAK 228:25
Have no e. but time | YEATS 279:4
he is afraid of his e. | PLUT 183:18
How goes the e. | REYN 195:1
I am the e. you killed | OWEN 179:11
last e. that shall be destroyed | BIBLE 38:19
Mine e.'s dog | SHAK 218:24
my vision's greatest e. | BLAKE 42:20
near'st and dearest e. | SHAK 212:15
No e. But winter | SHAK 204:19
Energy: E. is Eternal Delight | BLAKE 43:21
enfants: e. de la patrie | ROUG 198:1
Les e. terribles | GAV 105:5
que les jeux d'e. ne sont | MONT 171:18
Enfer: l'E., c'est les Autres | SART 200:2
enflamment: feux qui s'e. au vent | FRAN 102:7
engine: e. that moves | HARE 115:7
that two-handed e. | MILT 167:21
enginer: sport to have the e. | SHAK 210:21
England: Be E. what she will | CHUR 70:19
E. and Saint George | SHAK 213:15
E. does not love coalitions | DISR 86:17
E. expects that every man | NELS 175:6
E. hath need of thee | WORD 276:22
E., home and beauty | BRAH 46:2
E. invented the phrase | BAG 14:6
E. is a garden that is | KIPL 144:2
E. is a nation of shopkeepers | NAP 174:12
E. is the paradise of women | FLOR 101:4
E. keep my bones | SHAK 217:14
E., my England | HENL 117:10
E.'s green & pleasant | BLAKE 43:2
E.'s winding sheet | BLAKE 42:19
E. was too pure an Air | ANON 4:15
E., with all thy faults | COWP 79:20
faithless E. | BOSS 45:3
fashion of the court of E. | SHAK 214:10
get me to E. once again | BROO 47:12
in E.'s song for ever | NEWB 175:16
Let not E. forget her precedence | MILT 170:19
Nor, E.! did I know | WORD 275:2
of a king of E. too | ELIZ 95:19
Old E. to adorn | KIPL 146:2
road that leads him to E. | JOHN 131:19
roast beef of E. | FIEL 98:4
should they know of E. | KIPL 143:18
Stately Homes of E. | COW 79:8
stately homes of E. | HEM 117:2
suffer E. to be the workshop | DISR 86:13
suspended in favour of E. | SHAW 237:18
That is for ever E. | BROO 47:16
The further off from E. | CARR 63:12

This E. never did | SHAK 217:16
this E. | SHAK 230:2
to be in E. | BROW 49:12
to ensure summer in E. | WALP 266:1
to the landscape of E. | AUST 12:1
Walk upon E.'s mountains | BLAKE 43:2
we are the people of E. | CHES 70:6
With E.'s own coal | KIPL 143:12
worst government that E. | TROL 260:9
youth of E. are on fire | SHAK 213:11
English: among the E. Poets | KEATS 141:5
angel is the E. child | BLAKE 43:15
E. Church shall be free | MAGN 158:15
E. county families | WAUGH 266:11
E. drunkard made the rolling | CHES 70:2
E. (it must be owned) a | HAZL 116:6
E., not the Turkish court | SHAK 213:3
E. take their pleasures | SULL 248:8
E. tongue a gallimaufry | SPEN 244:22
fine old E. gentleman | ANON 4:2
king's E. | SHAK 226:10
kissed by the E. dead | OWEN 179:7
principle of the E. constitution | BLAC 42:15
sort of E. up with which | CHUR 71:20
under an E. heaven | BROO 47:16
Englishman: Either for E. or Jew | BLAKE 43:1
E. thinks he is moral when | SHAW 238:8
E. to open his mouth | SHAW 238:14
stirred the heart of every E. | SCOTT 201:10
Englishmen: Honest E. | KING 142:10
Mad dogs and E. | COW 79:1
Englishwoman: This E. is so refined | SMITH 242:14
enigma: mystery inside an e. | CHUR 71:3
Resolving the e. | ELIOT 92:1
enjoy: have to go out and e. it | SMITH 242:10
most e. contented least | SHAK 235:11
enjoy'd: all times I have e. | TENN 255:11
enjoyed: little to be e. | JOHN 135:1
enjoyment: e. as the greatest orator | HUME 128:1
ennuyer: Le secret d'e. est...de tout | VOLT 265:9
Enormous: E. through the Sacred Town | BELL 19:1
enough: eaten and drunk e. | HOR 123:8
E. of science and of art | WORD 277:9
E. that he heard it once | BROW 48:19
had never had e. | GILB 106:18
that patriotism is not e. | CAV 65:15
'tis e., 'twill serve | SHAK 231:27
enquiries: remote e. | JOHN 134:27
enquiring: My object in e. is to know | HOUS 127:3
ense: sit calamus saevior e. | BURT 55:15
Entbehren: E. sollst Du | GOE 109:22
enter: Abandon all hope, you who e. | DANTE 81:8
e. into the kingdom of heaven | BIBLE 33:15
E. these enchanted woods | MER 165:6
than for a rich man to e. | BIBLE 33:22
enterprised: e., nor taken in hand | PRAY 187:24
enterprises: e. of great pith and moment | SHAK 208:24
impediments to great e. | BACON 13:11
entertain: forgetful to e. strangers | BIBLE 40:11
There e. him all the saints | MILT 168:3
To e. divine Zenocrate | MARL 160:17
entertained: e. angels unawares | BIBLE 40:11
entertainment: e. this week cost me above | PEPYS 182:13
not dull thy palm with e. | SHAK 207:6
some other custom of e. | SHAK 228:22
enthrall: Except you e. me | DONNE 88:7
enthroned: e. in the hearts of kings | SHAK 225:17

enthusiasts: how to deal with e.	MAC 156:18	E. selleth his birthright	BIBLE 22:27
Entia: E. non sunt multiplicanda	OCCAM 177:10	hands are the hands of E.	BIBLE 22:30
entirely: e. beautiful	AUDEN 11:3	*escadrons: gros e. contre les petits*	BUSS 56:1
entirety: who would dissipate my e.	MACN 158:9	*escalier: L'esprit de l'e.*	DID 86:8
entrance: some e. into the language	BACON 13:24	Escape: E. me? Never	BROW 49:17
entrances: their exits and their e.	SHAK 205:1	guilty persons e. than one innocent	BLAC 42:16
Entschluss: Der christliche E.	NIET 176:18	help those we love to e.	HUGEL 127:13
entsichere: e. ich meinen Browning	JOHST 135:12	escaped: e. with the skin of my	BIBLE 25:26
Entuned: E. in hir nose ful semely	CHAU 68:2	that out of battle I e.	OWEN 179:9
entwine: Would e. itself verdantly	MOORE 172:13	*Eseln: Reichtum den grossen E.*	LUTH 155:10
envious: e. siege Of watery Neptune	SHAK 230:2	*espaces: ces e. infinis m'effraie*	PASC 180:18
e. Time	MILT 168:11	*espagnol: Je parle e. à Dieu*	CHAR 67:15
envy: did in e. of great Caesar	SHAK 217:6	espousèd: Methought I saw my late e. Saint
e. of brilliant men	BEER 17:19		MILT 170:12
e. of less happier lands	SHAK 230:2	*esprit: jamais approché de mon e.*	METT 165:11
from e., hatred, and malice	PRAY 187:3	*L'e. de l'escalier*	DID 86:8
prisoners of e.	ILL 129:11	*l'e. et dans le coeur comme*	LA R 149:12
épatés: é., les bourgeois	PRIV 191:19	*esprits: favorise que les e. préparés*	PAST 181:6
ephemeral: grave Proves the child e.	AUDEN 11:3	*Esse: E. quam videri bonus malebat*	SALL 199:10
Ephesians: Great is Diana of the E.	BIBLE 37:25	Essentially: E. I integrate the current	BETJ 20:12
epicure: e. would say	SMITH 242:21	estate: has become a fourth e.	MAC 156:15
épidermes: et le contact de deux é.	CHAM 66:17	low e. of his handmaiden	BIBLE 34:28
Epigram: What is an E.	COL 74:23	mind, body, or e.	PRAY 187:5
epistula: Verbosa et grandis e. venit	JUV 138:3	order'd their e.	ALEX 2:4
epitaph: better have a bad e.	SHAK 208:18	esteemed: we e. him not	BIBLE 29:14
e. drear	KIPL 145:6	estimate: enough thou know'st thy e.	SHAK 236:6
epitaphs: nice derangement of e.	SHER 240:19	*esuriens: Graeculus e.*	JUV 137:18
of worms, and e.	SHAK 230:7	*État: L'É. c'est moi*	LOUI 154:5
epitome: all mankind's e.	DRYD 90:16	eternal: e. silence of these infinite	PASC 180:18
Eppur: E. si muove	GAL 104:10	E. summer gilds them yet	BYRON 58:6
equal: All men are e.	FORS 101:15	e. summer shall not fade	SHAK 235:9
All shall e. be	GILB 107:5	Grant them e. rest	MASS 163:11
are more e. than others	ORW 178:7	Hope springs e.	POPE 185:15
compel us to be e. upstairs	BARR 16:1	liberty to man is e. vigilance	CURR 81:5
e. in dignity and rights	ANON 2:16	to be boy e.	SHAK 234:19
e. poise of hope and fear	MILT 167:7	eternity: ages Of e.	CARN 62:2
faith shines e.	BRON 47:2	E. in an hour	BLAKE 42:17
men are created e.	JEFF 130:9	E. is in love with	BLAKE 44:3
equality: e. in fact as corollary	BAK 14:12	E.! thou pleasing	ADD 1:9
e. in the servants' hall	BARR 16:1	from here to E.	KIPL 144:1
principle of perfect e.	MILL 165:20	I saw E. the other night	VAUG 261:16
equanimity: No man can face with e.	GILB 107:18	sells e. to get a toy	SHAK 235:6
equation: e. will come out at last	MACN 158:4	time without injuring e.	THOR 259:2
equi: lente currite noctis e.	MARL 160:6	Until E.	DICK 86:2
equipment: shabby e. always deteriorating		white radiance of E.	SHEL 239:1
	ELIOT 93:18	etherized: Like a patient e. upon	ELIOT 94:3
equitem: Post e. sedet atra Cura	HOR 124:6	Ethiopian: Can the E. change his skin	BIBLE 29:26
equivocate: I will not e.	GARR 104:16	etiquette: It isn't e. to cut any	CARR 64:17
Equo: E. ne credite	VIRG 263:3	Where e. prevents me from	SMITH 243:3
ere: Oon e. it herde, at tothir	CHAU 68:24	*étoile: Ma seule é. est morte*	NERV 175:11
erect: e. and manly foe	CANN 61:2	Eton: during the holidays from E.	SITW 241:13
erecteth: Christ e. his Church	BANC 15:7	playing fields of E.	WELL 268:4
erection: rate the cost of the e.	SHAK 212:23	*Étonne: É.-moi*	DIAG 83:7
err: e. is human, not to, animal	FROST 103:11	*étrangers: Plus je vis d'é.*	BELL 19:10
To e. is human	POPE 185:11	*étranglés: é. avec les boyaux des*	MESL 165:10
Errand: in thy joyous E. reach	FITZ 100:1	eunuch: Though Argus were her e.	SHAK 219:9
errands: little e. for the Ministers	GILB 107:6	Eureka: E.! (I've got it	ARCH 7:18
erred: have e. exceedingly	BIBLE 24:24	Europe: are going out all over E.	LORD 113:4
We have e.	PRAY 186:18	Better fifty years of E.	TENN 253:14
erreur: L'e. n'a jamais approché	METT 165:11	glory of E. is extinguished	BURKE 53:9
error: All men are liable to e.	LOCKE 152:12	of the community of E.	GLAD 109:16
If this be e.	SHAK 236:12	of the community of E.	SAL 199:8
man that he is in an e.	LOCKE 152:11	Europeans: You are learned E.	MASS 164:2
stalking-horse to e.	BOL 44:16	Euston: three in E. waiting-room	CORN 78:6
Errors: E., like straws	DRYD 90:20	Evangelical: E. vicar, in want	KNOX 147:6
Erst: E. kommt das Fressen	BREC 46:8	Eve: fairest of her daughters E.	MILT 169:8
erstwhile: my e. dear	MILL 166:9	past E. and Adam's	JOYCE 136:16
es: je te dirai ce que tu e.	BRIL 46:18	thro' the land at e. we	TENN 254:6
Esau: E. my brother is a hairy	BIBLE 22:29	Even: (E. as you and I!)	KIPL 146:4

evening: bright exhalation in the e.   SHAK 215:8
e. and the morning were   BIBLE 22:3
in the e. it is cut down   PRAY 189:21
It is a beauteous e.   WORD 276:20
When the e. is spread out   ELIOT 94:3
winter e. settles down   ELIOT 94:15
worse at arriving in the e.   CONN 77:8
event: had over-prepared the e.   POUND 186:13
How much the greatest e.   FOX 102:3
hurries to the main e.   HOR 122:17
events: coming e. cast their shadows   CAMP 60:16
ever: beauty is a joy for e.   KEATS 138:15
e. thus with simple folk   GILB 109:12
e. wilt thou love   KEATS 139:14
hereafter for e. hold his peace   PRAY 187:26
mercy endureth for e.   PRAY 190:23
ever-fixed: it is an e. mark   SHAK 236:12
everlasting: believeth on me hath e. life   BIBLE 36:24
caught An e. cold   WEBS 267:18
have e. life   BIBLE 36:21
underneath are the e. arms   BIBLE 24:2
evermore: name liveth for e.   BIBLE 30:29
this time forth for e.   PRAY 190:17
every: e.—single—one—of—them   KIPL 144:10
e. thing there is a season   BIBLE 27:6
in e. way   COUE 78:15
everybody: that e. wants to have read   TWAIN 261:8
Everyman: E., I will go with thee   ANON 3:10
Everyone: E. likes flattery   DISR 87:6
Everything: E. must be like something   FORS 101:12
Greek can do e.   JUV 137:18
make myself laugh at e.   BAUD 16:15
sans e.   SHAK 205:1
smattering of e.   DICK 85:28
spirit of youth in e.   SHAK 236:9
evidence: case of clearer e.   ARAB 7:14
e. of things not seen   BIBLE 40:8
'it's not e.   DICK 85:21
Some circumstantial e.   THOR 259:8
We had e. and no doubt   ELIOT 94:2
evil: deliver us from e.   BIBLE 31:21
E. be thou my Good   MILT 169:6
E. be to him who evil thinks   ANON 5:17
E. communications corrupt   BIBLE 38:20
e. manners live in brass   SHAK 215:12
e. news rides post   MILT 170:4
e., that good may come   BIBLE 37:32
e. that men do lives after   SHAK 216:16
e. which I would not   BIBLE 37:37
fall'n on e. days   MILT 169:13
it would be an e. still   MILL 165:16
money is the root of all e.   BIBLE 40:1
must return good for e.   VANB 261:12
notorious e. liver   PRAY 187:9
on the e. and on the good   BIBLE 31:18
overcome e. with good   BIBLE 38:3
predicted e. consequences   TROL 260:10
Resist not e.   BIBLE 31:17
Sufficient unto the day is the e.   BIBLE 32:1
unto them that call e. good   BIBLE 28:11
Whenever God prepares e.   ANON 6:8
withstand in the e. day   BIBLE 39:15
evils: e. and the worst of crimes   SHAW 237:19
only one cure for the e.   MAC 156:19
they are necessary e.   JOHN 135:4
evil-speaking: my tongue from e.   PRAY 187:20
evince: always e. its propriety   AUST 12:14

ev'ning: us welcome peaceful e.   COWP 80:4
exact: writing an e. man   BACON 13:21
exactitude: L'e. est la politesse des   LOUI 154:8
exactness: with e. grinds He all   LOGAU 152:15
exaggeration: report of my death was an e.   TWAIN 261:6
exalted: Every valley shall be e.   BIBLE 29:9
e. them of low degree   BIBLE 34:29
God hath also highly e.   BIBLE 39:16
exalteth: e. himself shall be abased   BIBLE 35:22
Example: E. is always more efficacious   JOHN 135:3
save Europe by her e.   PITT 183:11
examples: History is philosophy from e.   DION 86:11
exaudi: e. vocem meam   BIBLE 41:16
exceed: reach should e. his grasp   BROW 48:21
excel: methods different men e.   CHUR 70:18
excellent: e. thing in woman   SHAK 219:3
is too wonderful and e.   PRAY 191:2
Parts of it are e.   PUNCH 193:2
excellently: e. bright   JONS 135:19
excels: She e. each mortal thing   SHAK 234:18
That it e. all other bliss   DYER 92:4
Excelsior: strange device, E.!   LONG 153:4
excelsis: Gloria in e. Deo   MASS 163:12
Except: E. the Lord build the house   PRAY 190:19
e. the present company   OKEE 178:2
excess: Give me e. of it   SHAK 233:14
road of e. leads   BLAKE 44:1
Nothing in e.   ANON 6:7
Such an e. of stupidity   JOHN 132:4
wasteful and ridiculous e.   SHAK 217:12
exchange: By just e. one   SIDN 241:4
e. of two fantasies   CHAM 66:17
excitability: mischievous e. is the most   BAG 14:5
excite: actresses e. my amorous   JOHN 131:5
excitin: too e.' to be pleasant   DICK 85:16
exciting: He found it less e.   GILB 107:1
excommunicate: nor be outlawed, nor e.   COKE 74:4
excrement: place of e.   YEATS 278:15
excrucior: sed fieri sentio et e.   CAT 65:11
excuse: I will not e.   GARR 104:16
prove an e. for the glass   SHER 240:25
execution: e. confined   SHAK 233:6
Executioner: yet I am mine own *E.*   DONNE 89:1
executors: Let's choose e.   SHAK 230:7
exemplaria: Vos e. Graeca   HOR 122:19
exemplars: pages of your Greek e.   HOR 122:19
exercise: mind what e. is to the body   STEE 245:14
exertions: saved herself by her e.   PITT 183:11
exhalation: fall Like a bright e.   SHAK 215:8
exhaled: through a pipe and e. in a pun'   LAMB 148:6
exile: bind your sons to e.   KIPL 146:7
Troy came destined an e.   VIRG 262:15
exiles: we are e. from our fathers'   GALT 104:11
exist: She may still e. in undiminished   MAC 156:17
should be presumed to e.   OCCAM 177:10
Why do you and I e.   JOHN 133:10
existence: loving longest, when e.   AUST 12:10
'Tis woman's whole e.   BYRON 58:2
Exit: E., pursued by a bear   SHAK 234:21
exits: men to take their e.   WEBS 267:11
their e. and their entrances   SHAK 205:1
exorciser: No e. harm thee   SHAK 206:4
expands: Work e. so as to fill   PARK 180:13
expectancy: e. and rose of the fair   SHAK 209:6

expects: England e. that every man NELS 175:6
expedient: all things are not e. BIBLE 38:11
It is e. for us BIBLE 36:34
expellas: Naturam e. furca HOR 123:4
expenditure: annual e. nineteen nineteen
DICK 84:1
expense: e. of spirit in a waste SHAK 236:13
e. which I am almost ashamed PEPYS 182:13
Would be at the e. of two CLOU 73:12
experience: acquist Of true e. MILT 170:7
e. find those words mis-plac'd CONG 76:20
of trying every e. once ANON 3:6
part of e. BACON 13:24
reporting device for e. WHORF 270:12
triumph of hope over e. JOHN 132:15
expers: Vis consili e. mole ruit HOR 124:8
expert: e. is one who knows more BUTL 56:2
to those who are e. at it HOR 123:8
Experto: E. credite VIRG 264:3
experts: you never should trust e. SAL 199:7
expires: wretched child e. BELL 18:11
expiring: thus e. do foretell SHAK 230:1
explain: unwilling to e. FROST 103:2
exploded: dust of e. beliefs MADAN 158:12
exploding: poets e. like bombs AUDEN 11:10
exploration: shall not cease from e. ELIOT 93:20
Explosionsstoff: als einen furchtbaren E.
NIET 176:15
explosive: terrible e. in the presence NIET 176:15
explosives: You darent handle high e.
SHAW 237:22
export: integrate the current e. BETJ 20:12
exposed: been much e. to authors WELL 268:6
express: e. train drew up there THOM 257:16
express'd: ne'er so well e. POPE 185:9
expresser: was a most gentle e. of it HEM 117:4
expression: others by their hunted e. LEWIS 151:13
exquisite: e. touch SCOTT 202:10
extension: L'e. des privilèges des FOUR 102:2
extenuate: nothing e. SHAK 229:15
extinguished: glory of Europe is e. BURKE 53:9
extinguishes: wind e. candles LA R 149:11
extracts: e. made of them by others BACON 13:20
extraordinary: most e. man in Europe STIL 247:18
extravagant: e. and irrational which SWIFT 249:1
extremes: show his judgement) in e. DRYD 90:17
exuletur: utlagetur, aut e. MAGN 158:16
exuvias: redit e. indutus Achilli VIRG 263:4
eye: beard and glittering e. COL 74:5
Cast a cold e. YEATS 280:3
E. for eye BIBLE 23:18
e. of heaven to garnish SHAK 217:12
e. of man hath not heard SHAK 227:16
e. of peninsulas and islands CAT 65:7
glass to his sightless e. NEWB 175:13
harvest of a quiet e. WORD 276:6
hot the e. of heaven SHAK 235:9
If thine e. offend thee BIBLE 33:17
I have neither e. to see LENT 151:8
immortal hand or e. BLAKE 43:7
is in thy brother's e. BIBLE 32:3
mild and magnificent e. BROW 50:1
Russian e. Is underlined ELIOT 95:9
There's language in her e. SHAK 233:11
they shall see eye to e. BIBLE 29:13
through the e. of a needle BIBLE 33:22
twinkling of an e. BIBLE 38:22
with his glittering e. COL 74:6
with its soft black e. MOORE 173:3

eyebrow: Made to his mistress' e. SHAK 205:1
Eyeless: E. in Gaza MILT 170:1
eyelids: Than tir'd e. upon tir'd TENN 253:16
With e. heavy and red HOOD 121:12
eyes: asked him with my e. JOYCE 137:9
beams from happy human e. STEV 247:17
bein' only e. DICK 85:22
brown of her—her e. MEW 165:13
Closed his e. in endless GRAY 112:13
close your e. with holy COL 75:7
deep upon her peerless e. KEATS 139:17
electrical skin and glaring e. SMART 241:16
e. are quickened so with GRAV 111:14
e. have seen the glory HOWE 127:9
e. have they PRAY 190:13
E., look your last SHAK 232:6
e. of gold and bramble-dew STEV 247:14
e. the break of day SHAK 224:7
Gasp and Stretch one's E. BELL 18:14
gaze not in my e. HOUS 125:8
God be in my e. ANON 3:12
greater cats with golden e. SACK 199:1
Hath not a Jew e. SHAK 225:10
her e. were wild KEATS 139:4
Her e. were deeper than ROSS 197:8
His e. drop out LOCK 152:13
I have a pair of e. DICK 85:22
is engender'd in the e. SHAK 225:12
Look not in my e. HOUS 125:8
Love in her sunny e. does COWL 79:10
Love looks not with the e. SHAK 226:14
Mine e. are full of tears SHAK 230:13
mine e. dazzle WEBS 267:12
Mine e. do itch SHAK 229:10
My mistress' e. are nothing SHAK 236:14
night has a thousand e. BOUR 45:8
Night hath a thousand e. LYLY 155:16
one, all e. WORD 276:5
open The king's e. SHAK 215:6
pair of sparkling e. GILB 107:8
pearls that were his e. SHAK 232:15
see nothing with my e. SAPP 199:12
shut her wild, wild e. KEATS 139:6
Soft e. look'd love BYRON 57:9
stuck in for face for e. SHAK 219:9
thou hast doves' e. within BIBLE 28:3
to me only with thine e. JONS 136:3
was it his bees-winged e. BETJ 20:5
whites of their e. PUTN 193:3
with fortune and men's e. SHAK 235:11
With magic in my e. HARDY 115:4
world to turn thine e. JOHN 135:9
fabric: baseless f. of this vision SHAK 232:24
Fabula: F. narratur HOR 124:19
fac: Dilige et quod vis f. AUG 11:19
face: can hear my Thisby's f. SHAK 227:22
Communism with a human f. DUBC 91:14
construction in the f. SHAK 220:9
Cover her f. WEBS 267:12
everyone has the f. he deserves ORW 178:13
f. every difficulty except WILDE 272:5
f. that launch'd a thousand MARL 160:5
False f. must hide what SHAK 221:8
glory shineth in this f. SHAK 230:14
God hath given you one f. SHAK 209:4
his prism and silent f. WORD 276:7
Lord make his f. shine BIBLE 23:20
mist in my f. BROW 50:17
My f. is pink ANON 4:10

Pity a human f.	BLAKE 43:19	she be f.	KEATS 139:14
shouldst never see my f. again	TENN 252:7	these f. well-spoken days	SHAK 231:3
sorrows of your changing f.	YEATS 280:5	thou art f.	BIBLE 28:3
spirituality about the f.	DOYLE 89:20	*faire: Laisser-f.*	DARG 7:19
stamping on a human f.	ORW 178:12	*loisir de la f. plus courte*	PASC 181:4
strong men stand face to f.	KIPL 143:9	**fairies:** Do you believe in f.	BARR 16:5
taking your f. in your hands	ANON 4:1	I don't believe in f.	BARR 16:3
then f. to face	BIBLE 38:16	There are f. at the bottom	FYL 104:4
There is a garden in her f.	CAMP 60:20	was the beginning of f.	BARR 16:2
turning your f. to the light	SASS 200:7	**fairy:** Come not near our f. queen	SHAK 227:6
twain he covered his f.	BIBLE 28:12	f. tales of science	TENN 253:6
Visit her f. too roughly	SHAK 206:15	Like f. gifts fading away	MOORE 172:13
wish I loved its silly f.	RAL 194:10	Lilly believes it was a f.	AUBR 10:7
you find your f. too clear	HOUS 125:8	**faith:** aught is want of f. in all	TENN 252:1
Your f., my thane	SHAK 220:12	break f. with us who die	MCCR 157:9
faces: Bid them wash their f.	SHAK 205:15	children in whom is no f.	BIBLE 24:1
gild the f. of the grooms	SHAK 221:18	f. and labour of love	BIBLE 39:23
grind the f. of the poor	BIBLE 28:8	f. hath made thee whole	BIBLE 32:21
In nice clean f.	BARH 15:11	f., hope, charity	BIBLE 38:16
old familiar f.	LAMB 148:4	F. is the substance	BIBLE 40:8
Private f. in public	AUDEN 11:7	f. shines equal	BRON 47:2
we hid as it were our f.	BIBLE 29:14	f. unfaithful kept him	TENN 251:20
Facilis: *F. descensus Averno*	VIRG 263:10	F. without works is dead	BIBLE 40:14
fact: irritable reaching after f.	KEATS 140:16	Fight the good fight of f.	BIBLE 40:2
faction: that the whisper of a f.	RUSS 198:12	finisher of our f.	BIBLE 40:9
facts: imagination for his f.	SHER 240:27	fought for Queen and F.	TENN 255:6
is free but f. are sacred	SCOTT 201:7	I have kept the f.	BIBLE 40:4
faculties: each according to his f.	BAK 14:12	just shall live by f.	BIBLE 37:31
f., Which sense may reach	DONNE 87:27	more f. in honest doubt	TENN 252:21
Hath borne his f. so meek	SHAK 221:1	more strongly have f.	LUTH 155:11
faculty: creatures by the f. of laughter	ADD 1:14	My staff of f. to walk	RAL 194:4
fade: f. away into the forest	KEATS 139:19	simple f. than Norman blood	TENN 253:2
F. far away	KEATS 139:19	this f. I wish to live	VILL 262:14
faded: It f. on the crowing	SHAK 206:9	though I have all f.	BIBLE 38:14
fades: f. the glimmering landscape	GRAY 111:18	which constitutes poetic f.	COL 75:10
faenore: *Solutus omni f.*	HOR 123:9	**faithful:** be mentally f. to himself	PAINE 179:12
faery: f.'s child	KEATS 139:4	Be thou f. unto death	BIBLE 40:29
in f. lands forlorn	KEATS 140:1	f. and just to me	SHAK 216:17
fail: heart and voice would f.	CLAR 73:1	F., below	DIBD 83:10
we'll not f.	SHAK 221:6	f. to thee, Cynara	DOWS 89:8
fail'd: flutter'd and f. for breath	ARN 8:18	good and f. servant	BIBLE 34:5
faileth: f. now even dream	THOM 258:3	O come, all ye f.	ANON 6:10
failli: *J'ai f. attendre*	LOUI 154:6	So f. in love	SCOTT 201:19
fails: when life f.	AUDEN 11:2	**faithless:** Human on my f. arm	AUDEN 11:3
failure: f. of hope	GIBB 106:10	**Falcon:** dapple-dawn-drawn F.	HOPK 122:9
Women can't forgive f.	CHEK 69:1	f. cannot hear the falconer	YEATS 279:15
failures: has no conceivable f.	WHIT 270:8	f., towering in her pride	SHAK 222:11
fain: f. wald lie down	BALL 14:17	**fall:** by dividing we f.	DICK 86:7
F. would I climb	RAL 194:5	diggeth a pit shall f.	BIBLE 27:17
that are without would f.	DAV 81:20	f. into the ocean	MARL 160:7
fainéant: f. government is not	TROL 260:9	F. into the hands of God	TENN 255:5
faint: f. cold fear thrills through	SHAK 232:3	f. in with the marriage	CLOU 73:9
f. praises one another	WYCH 278:6	f. Like a bright exhalation	SHAK 215:8
F., yet pursuing	BIBLE 24:8	F. of the Rupee you may	WILDE 271:11
fair: anything to show more f.	WORD 276:18	f. on the ground without	BIBLE 32:25
brave deserves the f.	DRYD 90:19	f. upon the thorns of life	SHEL 239:14
every f. from fair sometime	SHAK 235:9	fearful thing to f. into	BIBLE 40:7
F., fat, and forty	SCOTT 202:8	great was the f. of it	BIBLE 32:13
F. is foul	SHAK 219:16	harder they f.	FITZ 100:5
F. stood the wind for France	DRAY 90:5	haughty spirit before a f.	BIBLE 26:22
Fat, and forty	OKEE 178:1	Held we f. to rise	BROW 51:26
foul and f. a day	SHAK 220:4	I meditated on the F.	BETJ 21:2
How sweet and f. she seems	WALL 265:13	is down needs fear no f.	BUNY 51:26
I have sworn thee f.	SHAK 237:4	it had a dying f.	SHAK 233:14
Is she kind as she is f.	SHAK 234:18	presage the grasses' f.	MARV 161:19
Ludlow come in for the f.	HOUS 125:14	shall f. into the ditch	BIBLE 33:9
most divinely f.	TENN 251:12	Something is going to f.	AUDEN 11:13
Outward be f.	CHUR 70:21	Things f. apart	YEATS 279:15
possession of that f. thou ow'st	SHAK 235:9	*was der F. ist*	WITT 273:7

what a f. was there   SHAK 216:20
will f. into the hands   BIBLE 30:21
yet fear I to f.   RAL 194:5
Fallacy: characterize as the 'Pathetic F.
     RUSK 198:8
fallen: art thou f. from heaven   BIBLE 28:23
Babylon is f.   BIBLE 41:4
how are the mighty f.   BIBLE 24:25
How are the mighty f.   BIBLE 24:27
keeps their f. day about   PATER 181:8
lot is f. unto me   PRAY 188:11
falling: by oft f.   LAT 149:13
fall'n: f. on evil days   MILT 169:13
fallow: f. fawns invisible go   THOM 257:20
falls: then he f., as I do   SHAK 215:9
false: betrayed by what is f.   MER 165:3
Beware of f. prophets   BIBLE 32:10
F., ere I come   DONNE 88:17
F. face must hide what   SHAK 221:8
not then be f. to any man   SHAK 207:6
save them from f. Sextus   MAC 156:5
Falsehood: strife of Truth with F.   LOW 154:17
falseness: f. in all our impressions   RUSK 198:8
falser: f. than vows made in wine   SHAK 205:7
falter: Who hesitate and f. life   ARN 8:21
faltered: If I have f. more or less   STEV 247:17
Fame: F. is the spur that   MILT 167:20
love and f. to nothingness   KEATS 140:10
Man dreams of f.   TENN 252:3
nor yet a fool to f.   POPE 184:19
Physicians of the utmost f.   BELL 18:10
selfish hope of a season's f.   NEWB 175:15
familiar: Be thou f.   SHAK 207:6
F. in his mouth as household   SHAK 214:4
families: All happy f. resemble one   TOLS 259:17
English county f.   WAUGH 266:19
Mothers of large f.   BELL 18:8
famille: au gouvernement d'une f.   MONT 172:2
family: f. pride is something in-conceivable
     GILB 108:1
I am the f. face   HARDY 114:10
in the running of a f.   MONT 172:2
famous: 'But 'twas a f. victory   SOUT 243:18
f. by their birth   SHAK 230:2
f. men have the whole earth   PER 182:15
found myself f.   BYRON 59:6
Let us now praise f. men   BIBLE 30:27
fan: f. spread and streamers   CONG 76:23
fancy: Ever let the f. roam   KEATS 139:2
f. cannot cheat so well   KEATS 140:1
keep your f. free   HOUS 125:7
now the f. passes   HOUS 125:10
of most excellent f.   SHAK 211:11
Tell me where is f. bred   SHAK 225:12
young man's f.   TENN 253:7
fancy-free: In maiden meditation, f.   SHAK 227:3
fantaisies: f. et le contact de deux   CHAM 66:17
fantasies: exchange of two f.   CHAM 66:17
fantastic: horrible, f., incredible   CHAM 66:13
In a light f. round   MILT 167:6
On the light f. toe   MILT 167:17
Far: F. and few   LEAR 150:11
f., far better thing   DICK 85:30
f. from the land where   MOORE 173:1
F. from the madding crowd's   GRAY 112:6
He's happy who, f. away   HOR 123:9
keep f. from me   OVID 178:19
keep f. off, you uninitiated   VIRG 263:11
more felicity on the f.   SMITH 242:7

quarrel in a f.-away country   CHAM 66:13
seems so near and yet so f.   TENN 252:22
farce: la f. est jouée'   RAB 193:15
second as f.   MARX 162:8
fardels: Who would f. bear   SHAK 208:24
farewecl: Ae f.   BURNS 53:18
Farewel: F. my bok, and my devocioun
     CHAU 68:20
Farewell: F.! a long farewell   SHAK 215:9
f. content   SHAK 229:4
F., rewards and Fairies   CORB 70.3
F. the plumed troop   SHAK 229:4
must bid the company f.   RAL 194:9
with hope f. fear   MILT 169:6
far-flung: Lord of our f. battle-line   KIPL 145:10
farmers: f. excessively fortunate   VIRG 264:11
now the f. swear   KING 143:5
once the embattled f. stood   EMER 96.4
Three jolly F.   DE L 82:16
farms: pleasant villages and f.   MILT 169:17
what f. are those   HOUS 126:7
far-off: old, unhappy, f. things   WORD 275:9
farrago: discursus nostri f. libelli est   JUV 137:15
farrow: old sow that eats her f.   JOYCE 137:1
farther: f. you go from the church   WOTT 277:20
Farthest: F. Thule   VIRG 264:9
farthing: sparrows sold for a f.   BIBLE 32:25
Virtue knows to a f. what   WALP 266:7
farthings: sparrows sold for two f.   BIBLE 35:19
fascination: My right elbow has a f.   GILB 108:12
fashion: appear a little out of f.   SHAK 213:20
glass of f.   SHAK 209:6
in my f.   DOWS 89:8
marriage ever out of f.   BUTL 56:9
men in shape and f.   ASCH 9:19
very independent of f.   GASK 105:3
fashions: conscience to fit this year's f.
     HELL 116:16
fast: fun grew f. and furious   BURNS 55:1
he talks it so very f.   FARQ 97:15
Fasten: F. your seatbelts   DAVIS 82:4
faster: round a deal f. than it does   CARR 62:21
speed was far f. than light   BULL 51:8
fastest: He travels the f. who travels   KIPL 146:9
fasting: thank heaven, f.   SHAK 205:6
fat: eat the f. of the land   BIBLE 23:7
Fair, f., and forty   SCOTT 202:8
f. bulls of Basan   PRAY 188:14
F., fair and forty   OKEE 178:1
f. man a thin one is wildly   CONN 77:9
f. white woman   CORN 78:7
he nas nat right f.   CHAU 68:4
men about me that are f.   SHAK 215:17
she help'd him to f.   BARH 15:9
thin man inside every f.   ORW 178:9
Who's your f. friend   BRUM 50:25
fatal: So f. to my suit before   GARR 104:15
fate: am the master of my f.   HENL 117:7
F. cannot harm me   SMITH 242:21
F. keeps on happening   LOOS 153:23
f. of the great wen   COBB 73:20
take a bond of f.   SHAK 223:1
That Time and F. of all   FITZ 99:2
thou and I with F. conspire   FITZ 99:13
what I will is f.   MILT 169:15
would F. but mend it   PRIOR 191:17
fates: are masters of their f.   SHAK 215:16
Father: about my F.'s business   BIBLE 35:5
brood of Folly without f.   MILT 167:10

cannot have God for his f.	CYPR 81:6
did you last see your f.	YEAM 278:10
either my f. or my mother	STER 246:7
even as your F. which is	BIBLE 31:19
everlasting F.	BIBLE 28:19
F. had an accident there	POTT 186:5
f., Harry, to that thought	SHAK 213:1
F., I have sinned against	BIBLE 35:27
f. is gone wild into his	SHAK 213:4
F. is rather vulgar	DICK 84:10
F.'s house are many mansions	BIBLE 37:1
f.'s sword he has girded	MOORE 172:16
I had it from my f.	SHAK 215:4
It is a wise f. that knows	SHAK 225:3
leave his f. and his mother	BIBLE 22:11
man cometh unto the F.	BIBLE 37:2
My f. feeds his flocks	HOME 120:18
no more like my f.	SHAK 206:15
one God the F. Almighty	PRAY 187:12
Our F. which art in heaven	BIBLE 31:21
resembled My f.	SHAK 221:14
She gave her f. forty-one	ANON 4:3
son maketh a glad f.	BIBLE 26:12
fatherless: defendeth the f. and widow	PRAY 191:6
fatherly: thy f. goodness all those	PRAY 187:5
fathers: f.-forth whose beauty	HOPK 122:4
f. have eaten sour grapes	BIBLE 30:4
Father William: You are old, F.	CARR 62:18
You are old, F.	SOUT 243:21
fathom: Full f. five	SHAK 232:15
fathomless: My radiance rare and f.	HARDY 115:4
fatling: young lion and the f. together	BIBLE 28:21
fatted: Bring hither the f. calf	BIBLE 35:28
fatter: valley sheep are f.	PEAC 181:16
fatuous: what made f. sunbeams toil	OWEN 179:6
fault: f., dear Brutus	SHAK 215:16
happy f.	MISS 170:22
has no kind of f. or flaw	GILB 107:12
it was a grievous f.	SHAK 216:16
through my most grievous f.	MASS 163:9
What soul is without f.	RIMB 195:8
faultless: Faultily f.	TENN 253:19
faults: f. of the age come from	BALF 14:15
men are moulded out of f.	SHAK 224:9
to her f. a little blind	PRIOR 191:16
With all her f.	CHUR 70:19
with all thy f.	COWP 79:20
Faustus: F. must be damn'd	MARL 160:6
faut: Il f. que je vive	DARG 7:20
faute: c'est une f.	BOUL 45:6
Favete: F. linguis	HOR 124:5
favilla: Solvet saeclum in f.	CEL 65:14
favour: par in f. of the people	BURKE 52:9
favoured: thou art highly f.	BIBLE 34:27
favourites: persuading monarchs to choose f.	SWIFT 249:1
favours: that hangs on princes' f.	SHAK 215:9
fawning: like a f. publican he looks	SHAK 224:18
Fay: F. ce que vouldras	RAB 193:14
fayr: f. as is the rose in May	CHAU 68:19
fear: by means of pity and f.	ARIS 8:5
dread and f. of kings	SHAK 225:17
equal poise of hope and f.	MILT 167:7
F. God, and keep his commandments	BIBLE 27:24
F. God. Honour the king	BIBLE 40:19
f. in a handful of dust	ELIOT 94:19
F. no more the heat o'	SHAK 206:4
f. of God before them	CROM 80:14

f. of having to weep	BEAU 16:15
f. of little men	ALL 2:7
f. of the Lord is the beginning	PRAY 190:11
F., O Little Hunter	KIPL 145:16
f. those big words	JOYCE 137:5
f. usually ends in folly	COL 75:15
fourth is freedom from f.	RONS 196:12
From hope and f. set free	SWIN 250:1
have to fear is f. itself	RONS 196:8
I f. thee, ancient Mariner	COL 74:13
I have a faint cold f.	SHAK 232:3
is down needs f. no fall	BUNY 51:26
I will f. no evil	PRAY 188:16
Knight without f. and without	ANON 5:16
lavat'ry makes you f. the worst	COW 79:9
Men f. death	BACON 13:5
ocean in the eventide of f.	MORR 173:13
O, word of f.	SHAK 219:13
salvation with f. and trembling	BIBLE 39:13
so long as they f.	ACC 1:1
so whom shall I f.	BIBLE 41:11
There is no f. in love	BIBLE 40:26
feared: f. nor flattered any flesh	DOUG 89:6
nothing to be f. in death	LUCR 155:8
fearful: f. thing to fall into	BIBLE 40:7
snatch a f. joy	GRAY 112:9
fearfully: I am f. and wonderfully	PRAY 191:4
fears: f. may be liars	CLOU 73:17
have f. that I may cease	KEATS 140:9
I had no human f.	WORD 276:17
More pangs and f. than	SHAK 215:9
Our f. do make us traitors	SHAK 223:3
That f. his fellowship	SHAK 214:4
To saucy doubts and f.	SHAK 222:15
feast: f. of reason and the flow	POPE 185:20
great f. of languages	SHAK 219:10
nourisher in life's f.	SHAK 221:16
perpetual f. of nectared	MILT 167:8
sat at any good man's f.	SHAK 204:24
vigil f. his neighbours	SHAK 214:4
feather: Blade on the f.	CORY 78:10
Stuck a f. in his cap	BANGS 15:8
wit's a f.	POPE 185:20
feather'd: f. race with pinions	FRERE 103:1
Feather-footed: F. through the plashy fen	WAUGH 266:20
feathers: beautified with our f.	GREE 112:18
bracelets and bright f.	HARDY 114:13
shalt be safe under his f.	PRAY 189:24
featly: Foot it f. here and there	SHAK 232:13
feats: "Twas one of my f.	BYRON 58:18
What f. he did that day	SHAK 214:4
Featur'd: F. like him	SHAK 235:11
fed: bite the hand that f.	BURKE 53:14
f. on the fullness of death	SWIN 250:3
f. with the same food	SHAK 225:10
Federation: F. of the world	TENN 253:10
fee: gorgeous East in f.	WORD 277:2
feeble: poor f. sex	VICT 262:8
feed: f. his flock like a shepherd	BIBLE 29:10
f. me in a green pasture	PRAY 188:15
F. the brute	PUNCH 193:1
f. with the rich	JOHN 132:12
So shalt thou f. on Death	SHAK 237:3
feedeth: he f. among the lilies	BIBLE 28:2
feel: f. for the common chord	BROW 48:20
f. my breasts all perfume	JOYCE 137:9
f. not what they inspire	SHEL 240:12
f. the earth move	HEM 117:5

f. what wretches feel	SHAK	218:11
mean or more than they f.	CONN	77:5
Now f. that pulse no more	MOORE	172:14
thing that could not f.	WORD	276:17
tragedy to those that f.	WALP	266:2
feeling: man is as old as he's f.	COLL	75:20
womanly f. and propriety	VICT	262:8
feelings: overflow of powerful f.	WORD	277:13
fees: they took their f.	BELL	18:10
feet: better to die on your f.	IBAR	129:3
f. are always in the water	AMES	2:9
f. have they	PRAY	190:13
f. of him that bringeth	BIBLE	29:12
Her f. beneath her petticoat	SUCK	248:4
Her pretty f.	HERR	118:24
Its f. were tied	KEATS	140:2
more clothes on his f.	SHAK	213:13
my dreams under your f.	YEATS	279:3
off the dust of your f.	BIBLE	32:23
radical is a man with both f.	RONS	196:10
slipping underneath our F.	FITZ	99:6
those f. in ancient time	BLAKE	43:2
thy shoes from off thy f.	BIBLE	23:10
to guide our f. into	BIBLE	34:30
tremble under her f.	TENN	254:2
twain he covered his f.	BIBLE	28:12
wash their f. in soda water	ELIOT	95:3
what dread f.	BLAKE	43:8
felice: ricordarsi del tempo f.	DANTE	81:10
felicem: fuisse f.	BOET	44:13
felicity: Absent thee from f. awhile	SHAK	211:22
f. on the far side of baldness	SMITH	242:7
Their green f.	KEATS	140:11
Felix: F. qui potuit rerum cognoscere	VIRG	264:12
fell: among thieves	BIBLE	35:12
From morn To noon he f.	MILT	169:1
So I f. in love with	GILB	109:9
We f. out	TENN	254:6
fellow: touchy, testy, pleasant f.	ADD	1:11
fellow-men: one that loves his f.	HUNT	128:4
fellows: hath fram'd strange f.	SHAK	224:11
fellowship: right hands of f.	BIBLE	39:7
felt: Darkness which may be f.	BIBLE	23:14
female: atheist talks you dead	JOHN	135:5
f. mind is not capable	KNOX	147:7
f. of the species is more	KIPL	143:20
life for the British f.	CLOU	73:8
Male and f. created	BIBLE	22:5
male and the f.	BIBLE	22:20
Who has a polished f. friend	WHURR	270:13
feminine: she's of the f. gender	OKEE	177:14
femme: Cherchons la f.	DUMAS	91:18
elle est f.	RAC	193:16
femmes: des privilèges des f.	FOUR	102:2
fen: through the plashy f.	WAUGH	266:20
fences: f. make good neighbours	FROST	103:7
fennel: f. for you, and columbines	SHAK	211:7
fera: cela se f.	CALL	59:15
Ferments: F. and frets until 'tis	BUTL	56:13
fern: sparkle out among the f.	TENN	251:6
ferry: Crossing alone the nighted f.	HOUS	126:24
fers: partout il est dans les f.	ROUS	198:2
fertile: such a fix to be so f.	NASH	174:19
fester: Lilies that f. smell far	SHAK	236:7
Festina: F. lente	SUET	248:7
fetch: f. the age of gold	MILT	168:9
'We are going to f. you	KIPL	143:12
fetters: reason Milton wrote in f.	BLAKE	43:22
feu: et allume le f.	LA R	149:11

feux: f. qui s'enflamment au	FRAN	102:7
fever: darter es died o' the f.	TENN	255:17
f., and the fret	KEATS	139:19
f. call'd 'Living'	POE	184:1
life's fitful f.	SHAK	222:13
fevers: Time and f. burn away	AUDEN	11:3
fever-trees: all set about with f.	KIPL	146:16
Février: Generals Janvier and F.	NICH	176:10
few: f. are chosen	BIBLE	33:27
Gey f.	ANON	3:15
owed by so many to so f.	CHUR	71:7
we happy f.	SHAK	214:4
Ye are many—they are f.	SHEL	239:11
fiat: bound to say '*f. justitia*	MANS	159:11
F. justitia et pereat	FERD	97:19
F. justitia et ruant coeli	WATS	266:14
fickle: f., freckled	HOPK	122:4
fierce and f. is the South	TENN	254:11
fiction: in a f., in a dream	SHAK	208:20
Stranger than f.	BYRON	58:15
That is what F. means	WILDE	271:10
fiddle: first and I the second f.	SPR	245:6
'Fish f. de-dee	LEAR	150:18
tune played on an old f.	BUTL	56:21
fiddled: f. whisper music	ELIOT	95:6
fiddler: chemist, f., statesman	DRYD	90:16
fiddles: some are fond of f.	MAS	162:17
fide: sed fortius f. et gaude	LUTH	155:11
Fidele: To fair F.'s grassy tomb	COLL	76:1
fideles: Adeste, f.	ANON	6:10
fie: f., now would she cry	BARN	15:17
field: comes and tills the f.	TENN	255:9
Consider the lilies of the f.	BIBLE	31:25
corner of a foreign f.	BROO	47:16
f. is full of shades	THOM	257:22
f. of human conflict was	CHUR	71:7
possess the f.	CLOU	73:17
that it is a f. of battle	STEV	247:3
that lay field to f.	BIBLE	28:9
fields: ancestral f. with his own oxen	HOR	123:9
grass returns to the f. and leaves	HOR	124:15
fiend: defy the foul f.	SHAK	218:12
F. Walked up and down	MILT	169:5
knows, a frightful f.	COL	74:18
fiends: f. that plague thee thus	COL	74:8
foreigners are f.	MITF	171:3
fierce: bright and f. and fickle	TENN	254:11
f. blaze of riot cannot	SHAK	230:1
f. light which beats upon	TENN	251:15
grew more f. and wild	HERB	118:8
look not so f. on me	MARL	160:7
were f. and bald and short	SASS	200:4
fiere: my trusty f.	BURNS	53:23
fiery: burning f. furnace	BIBLE	30:8
f. soul	DRYD	90:12
that very f. particle	BYRON	58:12
fife: That practised on a f.	CARR	62:10
Fifteen: F. men on the dead man's	STEV	246:19
f. wild Decembers	BRON	47:3
maiden of bashful f.	SHER	240:25
fifth: f. column	MOLA	171:4
remember the F. of November	ANON	4:17
Fifty: F. springs are little room	HOUS	125:4
(F. thousand horse	KIPL	143:8
fig: sewed f. leaves	BIBLE	22:12
under his f. tree	BIBLE	30:17
fight: bade me f. had told me so	EWER	97:8
cannot f. against the future	GLAD	109:14
can we f. with fifty-three	TENN	255:3

f. for freedom and truth | IBSEN 129:5
f. for its King and country | ANON 4:20
Fight the good f. of faith | BIBLE 40:2
hath no stomach to this f. | SHAK 214:4
have not yet begun to f. | JONES 135:15
I have fought a good f. | BIBLE 40:4
'Let's f. till six | CARR 64:4
man being too proud to f. | WILS 273:1
Our cock won't f. | BEAV 17:4
thought it wrong to f. | BELL 18:24
Ulster will f. | CHUR 70:23
us must f. on to the end | HAIG 113:9
us who will fight and f. | GAIT 104:7
We don't want to f. | HUNT 128:2
we shall f. on the beaches | CHUR 71:5
yourselves like men, and f. | BIBLE 24:16
fighting: dies f. has increase | GREN 113:3
f. with your land army | MONT 172:8
f. with daggers in a hogshead | SCOTT 202:12
Football then was f. sorrow | HOUS 125:9
She's the F. Téméraire | NEWB 175:16
fights: captain that knows what he f. | CROM 80:14
figs: grew upon thorn | CHES 69:23
f. of thistles | BIBLE 32:11
Figura: Caballero de la Triste F. | CERV 66:5
figure: did come the strangest f. | BROW 50:11
This f. that thou here | JONS 136:5
Will she make a f. | SWIFT 249:3
filches: f. from me my good name | SHAK 228:27
filia: matre pulchra f. pulchrior | HOR 123:15
fill: f. our bowls once more | SHAK 204:2
f. the Cup | FITZ 99:6
f. the unforgiving minute | KIPL 144:9
filled: f. the hungry with good | BIBLE 34:29
they shall be f. | BIBLE 31:11
find: f. the mind's construction | SHAK 220:9
not f. anything pleasant | VOLT 264:14
one is sure to f. next | ROG 196:2
searching f. out God | BIBLE 25:22
see an author and we f. | PASC 180:15
to f., and not to yield | TENN 255:16
you f. it wond'rous short | GOLD 110:13
findeth: f. his life shall lose | BIBLE 32:28
finding: fear of f. something worse | BELL 18:12
finds: f. too late that men betray | GOLD 110:18
fine: f. into an horizontal line | WHEW 269:10
think is particularly f. | JOHN 132:18
Fine Arts: Considered as One of the F. | DE Q 83:2
finem: et respice f. | ANON 7:4
F. di dederint | HOR 123:13
finest: 'This was their f. hour' | CHUR 71:6
Finger: F. of birth-strangled babe | SHAK 222:23
his slow and moving f. | SHAK 229:8
Moving F. writes | FITZ 99:9
Whose F. do you want | ANON 5:12
fingers: cool stream thy f. wet | ARN 8:20
dead men's f. | SHAK 211:9
my f. wandered idly | PROC 191:20
smile upon his f.' ends | SHAK 213:12
With f. weary and worn | HOOD 121:12
finish: we will f. the job | CHUR 71:8
finished: been f. in half the time | WOD 273:13
I have f. my course | BIBLE 40:4
It is f. | BIBLE 37:8
love of f. years | ROSS 197:4
until it be thoroughly f. | DRAKE 90:1
finisher: author and f. of our faith | BIBLE 40:9
finishing: Don't keep f. your sentences | LONS 153:21

fio: puto deus f. | VESP 262:6
fire: at once a gentle f. has | SAPP 199:12
Bring me my chariot of f. | BLAKE 43:2
every time she shouted 'F. | BELL 18:16
f. and was burnt to ashes | GRAH 111:10
F. burn and cauldron bubble | SHAK 222:22
f. shall heat the deep | TENN 253:1
f. until you see the whites | PUTN 193:3
Heap coals of f. upon his | BIBLE 26:27
hearts the f.'s centre | SPEN 244:10
kindles f. | LA R 149:11
love what wind is to f. | BUSS 55:24
night in a pillar of f. | BIBLE 23:17
Now stir the f. | COWP 80:4
shall be found by the f. | BROW 49:3
thorough f. | SHAK 226:17
two irons in the f. | BEAU 16:21
wall next door catches f. | HOR 123:6
youth of England are on f. | SHAK 213:11
Fire Brigade: Of London's Noble F. | BELL 18:15
fire-folk: f. sitting in the air | HOPK 122:7
fires: Big f. flare up in a wind | FRAN 102:7
f. soon burn out themselves | SHAK 230:1
fireside: glass of wine by his own f. | SHER 241:1
To make a happy f. clime | BURNS 55:3
firing: have what to do after f. | REED 194:14
firmament: f. sheweth his handy-work | PRAY 188:12
is no fellow in the f. | SHAK 216:8
there's fury in the f. | SASS 200:15
Firmness: Commodity, F., and Delight | WOTT 277:19
first: be done for the f. time | CORN 78:8
f. and second class citizens | WILL 272:13
f. baby laughed | BARR 16:2
f. casualty when war | JOHN 131:1
f. city Cain | COWL 79:11
f. impulse was never | CORN 78:4
f. impulses as they are | MONT 172:9
f. in war | LEE 151:3
f., last, everlasting | DONNE 87:17
f. man is of the earth | BIBLE 38:21
f. sign of old age | HICKS 119:6
f. step that is difficult | DU D 91:16
f. time as tragedy | MARX 162:8
last shall be f. | BIBLE 33:24
morning were the f. day | BIBLE 22:3
shall suffer f. punishment | CRAN 80:6
Thou know'st the f. time | SHAK 218:23
used by Charles the f. | COW 79:9
firstborn: brought forth her f. son | BIBLE 35:1
firstfruits: f. of them that slept | BIBLE 38:18
fish: St Ives says the smell of f. | KILV 142:4
Thou deboshed f. thou | SHAK 232:19
fishers: Three f. went sailing away | KING 142:13
will make you f. of men | BIBLE 31:10
fishes: f. flew and forests walked | CHES 69:23
f. leap in silver stream | CLARE 72:22
fishified: flesh, how art thou f. | SHAK 231:24
fishing: angling or float f. I can | JOHN 134:11
On f. up the moon | PEAC 181:17
fish-knives: Phone for the f. | BETJ 20:13
fish-like: very ancient and f. smell | SHAK 232:16
fist: of f. most valiant | SHAK 213:19
fit: f. for the kingdom of God | BIBLE 35:10
f. to use their freedom | MAC 157:1
isn't f. for humans now | BETJ 21:11
Why then I'll f. you | KYD 147:10
fitful: life's f. fever | SHAK 222:13

fittest: survival of the f.	SPEN 244:6
five: Full fathom f.	SHAK 232:15
These f. kings did a king	THOM 257:5
five-pound: Wrapped up in a f. note	LEAR 150:13
fix: right to f. the boundary	PARN 180:14
such a f. to be so fertile	NASH 174:19
fixed: great gulf f.	BIBLE 36:1
fizz: sheer necessity of f.	BELL 19:3
flabbiness: f. born of the bitch-goddess	
	JAMES 130:8
flag: spare your country's f.	WHIT 270:9
We'll keep the red f. flying	CONN 77:4
Flag-flapper: Jelly-bellied F.	KIPL 146:25
flagons: Stay me with f.	BIBLE 27:28
flakes: Some f. have lost their	HARDY 114:14
flame: f. out like shining from	HOPK 121:18
hard, gemlike f.	PATER 181:10
Kindled a f. I still deplore	GARR 104:15
only change th'expiring f.	GAY 105:21
flames: Commit it then to the f.	HUME 127:17
F. in the forehead	MILT 168:2
flaming: thou f. minister	SHAK 229:13
flammes: met le monde entier en f.	VOLT 264:19
Flanders: F. fields the poppies blow	MCCR 157:8
flannelled: f. fools at the wicket	KIPL 144:11
flaps: May month f. its glad green	HARDY 114:8
flashes: occasional f. of silence	SMITH 242:20
Flask: F. of Wine	FITZ 98:15
flatten: His hide is sure to f.	BELL 18:6
Flatter: F. the mountain-tops with	SHAK 235:14
flattered: being them most f.	SHAK 216:5
who neither feared nor f.	DOUG 89:6
flatterers: I tell him he hates f.	SHAK 216:5
flattering: Some with a f. word	WILDE 271:3
flattery: Everyone likes f.	DISR 87:6
is paid with f.	JOHN 134:20
Flaubert: His true Penelope was F.	POUND 186:8
flaunt: syntactically in order to f.	FEAR 97:18
flavour: from its high celestial f.	BYRON 58:4
flaw: no kind of fault or f.	GILB 107:12
sans crack or f.	SHAK 219:11
flayed: Last week I saw a woman f.	SWIFT 249:7
flea: between a louse and a f.	JOHN 134:1
f. Hath smaller fleas	SWIFT 249:12
Fleas: f. know not whether they	LAND 148:15
f. that tease in the high	BELL 19:9
Fled: F. is that music	KEATS 140:1
I f. Him	THOM 258:1
Whence all but he had f.	HEM 117:1
world that I am f.	SHAK 236:4
flee: f. away, and be at rest	PRAY 189:8
f. from the wrath to come	BIBLE 31:5
Sorrow and sighing shall f.	BIBLE 29:6
They f. from me	WYATT 278:3
wicked f. when no man pursueth	BIBLE 26:32
fleece: forest f. the Wrekin	HOUS 126:4
fleet: All in the Downs the f.	GAY 105:23
F. in which we serve	PRAY 191:9
F. is all lit up	WOOD 274:7
F. the time carelessly	SHAK 204:13
fleets: interested in armies and f.	AUDEN 10:13
Fleet Street: who can be dull in F.	LAMB 147:18
flesh: All f. is as grass	BIBLE 40:17
all f. shall see it together	BIBLE 29:9
closed up the f. instead	BIBLE 22:9
delicate white human f.	FIEL 98:9
fair and unpolluted f.	SHAK 211:13
f., alas, is wearied	MALL 159:4
f. and blood so cheap	HOOD 121:13

f., how art thou fishified	SHAK 231:24
f. of my flesh	BIBLE 22:10
F. perishes, I live on	HARDY 114:10
more f. than another man	SHAK 212:17
my heart and my f. rejoice	PRAY 189:17
not against f. and blood	BIBLE 39:15
sinful lusts of the f.	PRAY 187:19
these our f. upright	DONNE 87:24
they shall be one f.	BIBLE 22:11
to me a thorn in the f.	BIBLE 39:6
too solid f. would melt	SHAK 206:15
wants to make your f. creep	DICK 83:14
willing but the f. is weak	BIBLE 34:15
Word was made f.	BIBLE 36:16
WORD WAS MADE F.	MASS 163:21
fleurs: amas de f. étrangères	MONT 172:7
flew: f. the web and floated	TENN 253:4
flies: f. to wanton boys	SHAK 218:18
murmurous haunt of f.	KEATS 139:21
flight: alarms of struggle and f.	ARN 8:13
His f. was madness	SHAK 223:3
now wing thy distant f.	HAER 113:8
Swift be thy f.	SHEL 240:6
that puts the Stars to F.	FITZ 98:14
flinch: cowards f. and traitors	CONN 77:4
fling: f. the ringleaders from	ARN 9:17
I'll have a f.	FLET 100:18
flirtation: Merely innocent f.	BYRON 58:13
floated: Out flew the web and f.	TENN 253:4
flock: feed his f. like a shepherd	BIBLE 29:10
f. to gaze the strengthless	HOUS 125:11
hair is as a f. of goats	BIBLE 28:3
keeping watch over their f.	BIBLE 35:1
tainted wether of the f.	SHAK 225:5
was the f. in woolly fold	KEATS 138:16
flocks: My father feeds his f.	HOME 120:18
shepherds watch'd their f.	TATE 250:17
flog: f. the rank and file	ARN 9:17
Flood: nearly spoiled ta F.	AYT 12:18
taken at the f.	SHAK 217:3
ten years before the F.	MARV 161:20
Thorough f.	SHAK 226:17
floods: f. came	BIBLE 32:13
heavily and fell in f.	WORD 276:10
neither can the f. drown it	BIBLE 28:5
floor: fell upon the sanded f.	PAYN 181:12
how the f. of heaven	SHAK 226:5
floors: across the f. of silent seas	ELIOT 94:6
Flores: F. in the Azores Sir Richard	TENN 255:3
floribus: aliquid quod in ipsis f. angat	LUCR 155:9
flotte: Elle f.	RAC 193:16
flourish: Princes and lords may f.	GOLD 110:6
flourishing: f. like a green bay-tree	PRAY 188:24
flout: scout 'em, and f. 'em	SHAK 232:20
Flow: F. gently	BURNS 54:7
foolish tears would f.	CLAR 73:1
reason and the f. of soul	POPE 185:20
revolving pleasures f.	GAY 105:21
rivers of blood must yet f.	JEFF 130:11
flower: art the f. of cities all	DUNB 91:23
cometh forth like a f.	BIBLE 25:24
f. is born to blush unseen	GRAY 112:5
F. that once hath blown	FITZ 99:4
f. thereof falleth away	BIBLE 40:17
From every opening f.	WATTS 266:16
glory of man as the f.	BIBLE 40:17
Heaven in a Wild F.	BLAKE 42:17
learning lightly like a f.	TENN 252:26
look like the innocent f.	SHAK 220:12

meanest f. that blows	WORD 275:17
of glory in the f.	WORD 275:16
pluck this f., safety	SHAK 212:10
this same f. that smiles	HERR 118:23
white f. of a blameless life	TENN 251:15
flower-pots: Water your damned f.	BROW 50:20
flowers: bunch of other men's f.	MONT 172:7
f. appear on the earth	BIBLE 27:29
F. in the garden	STEV 247:15
f. of the forest are a'	ELL 95:22
f. that bloom in the spring	GILB 108:15
frosts are slain and f.	SWIN 249:16
it won't be f.	AUDEN 11:13
Larded with sweet f.	SHAK 210:27
Letting a hundred f. blossom	MAO 159:13
play with f. and smile	SHAK 213:12
pretty f.	HOW 127:10
swath and all its twined f.	KEATS 140:13
flowing: All things are a f.	POUND 186:9
land f. with milk	BIBLE 23:11
flown: see all the birds are f.	CHAR 67:9
flow'rs: Insnar'd with f.	MARV 161:15
flows: Everything f. and nothing stays	HER 118:1
(methinks) how sweetly f.	HERR 119:1
Flushed: F. and confident	IBSEN 129:8
flutes: tune of f. kept stroke	SHAK 203:22
Flutter: F. and bear him up	BETJ 20:9
flutter'd: f. and fail'd for breath	ARN 8:18
fluttered: On f. folk and wild	KIPL 146:7
Fluttering: F. and dancing in the breeze	
	WORD 275:3
fly: all things f. thee	THOM 258:5
F. fishing may be a very	JOHN 134:11
make the fur F.	BUTL 56:7
said a spider to a f.	HOW 127:11
small gilded f.	SHAK 218:20
sparks f. upward	BIBLE 25:21
with twain he did f.	BIBLE 28:12
flyer: no high f.	PEPYS 182:9
flyin'-fishes: Where the f. play	KIPL 145:3
flying: asleep the snow came f.	BRID 46:12
dear little kangaroos f.	WILDE 271:16
irretrievable time is f.	VIRG 264:13
foam: opening on the f.	KEATS 140:1
was wild and dank with f.	KING 142:12
foe: erect and manly f.	CANN 61:2
f. was folly and his weapon	HOPE 121:15
met my dearest f. in heaven	SHAK 207:2
wolf far thence that's f.	WEBS 267:16
Foeda: F. est in coitu et brevis	PETR 183:3
foes: f. nor loving friends can	KIPL 144:9
f. they captive make	CHAN 67:4
fog: Fear death?—to feel the f.	BROW 50:17
f. that rubs its back upon	ELIOT 94:4
London particular…A f.	DICK 83:13
through the f. and filthy air	SHAK 219:16
foil: like shining from shook f.	HOPK 121:18
Than dumb-bell and f.	YEATS 279:17
fold: f. his legs and have out	JOHN 133:6
f. stands empty	SHAK 227:2
like the wolf on the f.	BYRON 57:16
mill and the f.	HOUS 125:14
Shall f. their tents	LONG 153:3
folded: ocean Is f. and hung	AUDEN 10:8
folding: f. of the hands to sleep	BIBLE 26:9
folds: tinklings lull the distant f.	GRAY 111:18
folk: On fluttered f. and wild	KIPL 146:7
folk-dancing: excepting incest and f.	ANON 3:6
folks: folks rail against other f.	FIEL 98:7

was leaving home and my f.	STEV 247:10
follies: f., and misfortunes	GIBB 106:11
pretty f. that themselves	SHAK 225:6
Follow: F. me	BIBLE 31:10
F. your spirit	SHAK 213:15
I f. the worse	OVID 178:22
Pay, pack, and f.	BURT 55:12
really ought to f. them	LEDR 151:2
to f. mine own teaching	SHAK 224:14
we f. the Cambridge lead	JOW 136:14
Follow up: F.! Follow up	BOWEN 45:12
folly: fear usually ends in f.	COL 75:15
foe was f. and his weapon	HOPE 121:15
fool according to his f.	BIBLE 26:29
fool returneth to his f.	BIBLE 26:30
He knew human f. like	AUDEN 10:13
lovely woman stoops to f.	ELIOT 95:4
lovely woman stoops to f.	GOLD 110:18
of F. without father bred	MILT 167:10
this mad, wicked f.	VICT 262:8
'Tis f. to be wise	GRAY 112:12
would persist in his f.	BLAKE 44:4
fond: reason to be f. of grief	SHAK 217:10
When men were f.	SHAK 223:20
fonder: makes the heart grow f.	ANON 2:12
fons: f. Bandusiae splendidior	HOR 124:10
vicinus iugis aquae f.	HOR 125:1
font: portable, second-hand f.	KNOX 147:6
fonte: Medio de f. leporum	LUCR 155:9
food: Books, and my f.	STEV 247:17
fed with the same f.	SHAK 225:10
F. enough for a week	MERR 165:9
nourishing, and wholesome f.	SWIFT 249:6
fool: Call me not f. till heaven	SHAK 204:21
Dost thou call me f.	SHAK 218:2
every f. is not a poet	POPE 184:17
f. according to his folly	BIBLE 26:29
f. all the people some	LINC 151:18
f. at forty is a fool indeed	YOUNG 280:6
f. hath said in his heart	PRAY 188:9
F. lies here who tried	KIPL 145:6
f. returneth to his folly	BIBLE 26:30
f. sees not the same tree	BLAKE 44:2
f. there was and he made	KIPL 146:4
f., this night thy soul	BIBLE 35:20
f. would persist in his	BLAKE 44:4
I have played the f.	BIBLE 24:24
is the laughter of a f.	BIBLE 27:9
nor yet a f. to fame	POPE 184:19
Remains a f. his whole	LUTH 155:13
thou art death's f.	SHAK 223:21
wisest f. in Christendom	HENR 117:14
worm at one end and a f.	JOHN 134:11
foolish: exempt from saying a f. thing	STER 246:12
f. consistency is the hobgoblin	EMER 96:15
f., fond old man	SHAK 218:25
f. son is the heaviness	BIBLE 26:12
f. tears would flow	CLAR 73:1
f. thing was but a toy	SHAK 234:14
He never said a f. thing	ROCH 195:15
is a f. thing well done	JOHN 132:16
shall be likened unto a f.	BIBLE 32:13
foolishly: don't *think* f.	JOHN 134:2
foolishness: Mix a little f. with your	HOR 124:18
fools: flannelled f. at the wicket	KIPL 144:11
f. in town on our side	TWAIN 261:5
f. rush in where angels	POPE 185:14
f., who came to scoff	GOLD 110:9
I am two f.	DONNE 88:21

most part of f. and knaves | BUCK 51:2
Poems are made by f. like | KILM 142:2
prov'd plain f. at last | POPE 185:7
shoal of f. for tenders | CONG 76:23
Silence is the virtue of f. | BACON 12:22
things people make f. | SHAW 237:10
what f. these mortals be | SHAK 227.10
yesterdays have lighted f. | SHAK 223:15
ye suffer f. gladly | BIBLE 39:5
foot: caught my f. in the mat | GROS 113:5
f. for foot | BIBLE 23:18
f. it flatly here and there | SHAK 232.13
f.—slog—slog | KIPL 143:13
her f. speaks | SHAK 233:11
her f. was light | KEATS 139:4
his f. upon the stirrup | DE L 82:15
One f. in sea | SHAK 228:7
shining F. shall pass | FITZ 100:1
squeeze a right-hand f. | CARR 64:15
suffer thy f. to be moved | PRAY 190:16
that thou hurt not thy f. | PRAY 190:1
Football: F. then was fighting sorrow | HOUS 125:9
Foot-in-the-grave: F. young man | GILB 108:23
foot-path: jog on the f. way | SHAK 234:23
foot-print: looking for a man's f. | BEER 17:18
Footprints: F. on the sands of time | LONG 153:10
footsteps: plants his f. in the sea | COWP 79:14
footstool: make thine enemies thy f. | PRAY 190:10
fops: creating a whole tribe of f. | SHAK 217:19
for: If I am not f. myself | HILL 119:10
know f. whom the *bell* tolls | DONNE 89:3
forbid: f. them not | BIBLE 34:26
He shall live a man f. | SHAK 220:3
forbidden: fruit Of that f. tree | MILT 168:12
force: f. alone is but *temporary* | BURKE 52:16
f. however great can stretch | WHEW 269:10
F., if unassisted by judgement | HOR 124:8
f. its way | IBSEN 129:9
f. that through the green | THOM 257:4
know the limitations of f. | TROT 260:17
own no argument but f. | BROW 48:15
Who overcomes By f. | MILT 168:17
Forced: F. her to do your pleasure | WEBS 267:15
forefathers: rude f. of the hamlet | GRAY 112:2
foregone: denoted a f. conclusion | SHAK 229:6
foreign: corner of a f. field | BROO 47:16
courtly f. grace | TENN 255:6
f. policy of the noble | DER 83:4
past is a f. country | HART 115:15
ships and the f. faces | SWIN 249:15
foreigners: f. are fiends | MITF 171:3
more f. I saw | BELL 19:10
foremost: f. in battle was Mary Ambree | BALL 14:18
you've spoken the f. word | BALL 14:16
forest: flowers of the f. are a' | ELL 95:22
f. fleece the Wrekin | HOUS 126:4
thee fade away into the f. | KEATS 139:19
unfathomable deep F. | THOM 257:19
forests: green days in f. | STEV 247:12
In the f. of the night | BLAKE 43:7
When fishes flew and f. | CHES 69:23
forever: f. taking leave | RILKE 195:5
Man has F. | BROW 49:10
safire bracelet lasts f. | LOOS 153:24
That is f. England | BROO 47:16
forge: f. and the mill | HOUS 125:14
f. des Dieux à douzaines | MONT 172:6
forget: conversing I f. all time | MILT 169:10

do not quite f. | CHES 70:6
do not thou f. me | ASTL 10:2
F. six counties overhung | MORR 173:14
f. thee, O Jerusalem | PRAY 191:1
if thou wilt, f. | ROSS 197:3
Lest we f. | KIPL 145:10
nor worms f. | DICK 84:18
not to f. we are gentlemen | BURKE 52:11
Old men f. | SHAK 214:4
we f. because we must | ARN 8:11
you should f. and smile | ROSS 197:6
forgetfulness. Not in entire f. | WORD 275.15
forgetting: is but a sleep and a f. | WORD 275:15
world f. | POPE 184:14
forgive: Father, f. them | BIBLE 36:8
f. us our debts | BIBLE 31:21
f. us our trespasses | PRAY 186:21
good Lord will f. me | CATH 65:2
I f. him? till seven times | BIBLE 33:19
I'll f. Thy great big one | FROST 103:6
lambs could not f. | DICK 84:18
ought to f. our friends | MED 164:12
rarely, if ever, do they f. | WILDE 271:27
woman can f. another | GAY 105:8
Women can't f. failure | CHEK 69:1
forgiven: f.; for she loved much | BIBLE 35:9
forgiveness: ask of thee f. | SHAK 218:27
forgives: which f. itself anything | SHAW 238:15
forgo: chilly stars I can f. | CORY 78:13
forgot: by the world f. | POPE 184:14
God f. me | BROW 49:2
I believe I f. to tell | WELL 268:1
I have f. much | DOWS 89:7
forgotten: been learnt has been f. | SKIN 241:14
f. nothing and learnt nothing | DUM 91:20
f. nothing | TALL 250:14
had f. to say 'When | WOD 273:18
of them is f. before God | BIBLE 35:19
Our God's f. | QUAR 193:8
ruins of f. times | BROW 48:11
forks: They pursued it with f. | CARR 62:8
forlorn: cheerless, and f. | HAER 113:8
F.! the very word is like | KEATS 140:1
Form: F. remains | WORD 276:12
mould of f. | SHAK 209:6
thy f. from off my door | POE 184:2
time to lick it into f. | BURT 55:13
'To every F. of being is | WORD 274:16
what the f. divine | LAND 148:12
former: again thy f. light restore | SHAK 229:13
f. things are passed away | BIBLE 41:8
forms: f. of things unknown | SHAK 227:18
formula: f. of that *particular* emotion | ELIOT 95:11
Fornication: F.? But that was in another | MARL 160:13
forsake: f. her Cyprian groves | DRYD 91:5
is a woman that you f. | KIPL 144:6
forsaken: f. beliefs | ARN 9:8
never the righteous f. | PRAY 188:23
why hast thou f. me | BIBLE 34:18
Forsaking: F. all other | PRAY 187:27
Forsan: F. et haec olim meminisse | VIRG 262:17
forsworn: That so sweetly were f. | SHAK 224:7
fort: Hold the f. | BLISS 44:11
La raison du plus f. est | LA F 147:14
fortes: Vixere f. ante Agamemnona | HOR 124:17
forth: Man goeth f. to his work | PRAY 190:5
fortiter: Esto peccator et pecca f. | LUTH 155:11
fortress: This f. built by Nature | SHAK 230:2

fortunatam: f. natam me consule	CIC 72:15
fortunate: he is at best but f.	SOLON 243:12
fortunatos: f. nimium	VIRG 264:11
fortune: arrows of outrageous f.	SHAK 208:24
disgrace with f. and men's eyes	SHAK 235:11
F., that favours fools	JONS 135:16
happily upon a plentiful f.	JOHN 131:22
hath given hostages to f.	BACON 13:11
heaven hath sent me f.	SHAK 204:21
he shall see F.	BACON 13:7
I am F.'s fool	SHAK 231:29
leads on to f.	SHAK 217:3
little value of f.	STEE 245:15
possession of a good f.	AUST 12:11
so many men of large f.	AUST 12:2
forty: Fair, fat, and f.	SCOTT 202:8
Fat, fair and f.	OKEE 178:1
fool at f. is a fool indeed	YOUNG 280:6
F. years on	BOWEN 45:11
man over f. is a scoundrel	SHAW 238:14
passing rich with f. pounds	GOLD 110:8
forty-three: may very well pass for f.	GILB 109:10
forward: f. let us range	TENN 253:13
marched breast f.	BROW 48:22
not look f. to posterity	BURKE 53:8
to hold from this day f.	PRAY 187:28
foster-child: f. of silence and slow	KEATS 139:12
fou: f. qui se croyait Victor	COCT 74:1
I wasna f.	BURNS 54:4
fought: courses f. against Sisera	BIBLE 24:5
f. at Arques and you were	HENR 117:12
I have f. a good fight	BIBLE 40:4
their lives f. for life	SPEN 244:10
what they f. each other	SOUT 243:17
foul: f. and fair a day	SHAK 220:4
f. is fair	SHAK 219:16
f. sluts in dairies	CORB 78:3
however f. within	CHUR 70:21
foul-mouthed: rather a f. nation	HAZL 116:6
found: f. myself famous	BYRON 59:6
f. my sheep which was lost	BIBLE 35:24
f. the Roman nation	VIRG 262:16
have it f. out by accident	LAMB 148:3
lost, and is f.	BIBLE 35:29
not yet f. a role	ACH 1:2
shall be f. by the fire	BROW 49:3
When f., make a note	DICK 84:7
foundation: number is the f. of morals	BENT 19:14
fount: fresh f.	JONS 135:18
fountain: athirst of the f. of the water	BIBLE 41:9
f. of delights rises something	LUCR 155:9
Let the healing f. start	AUDEN 11:1
mighty f. momently was	COL 75:3
founts: falling in the courts	CHES 69:26
four: f. essential human freedoms	RONS 196:12
It is f. times as big	LEAR 150:3
fourscore: strong that they come to f.	PRAY 189:22
Fourteen: F.? The good Lord has	CLEM 73:4
fourth: reporters sit has become a f. estate	MAC 156:15
foweles: smale f. maken melodye	CHAU 67:18
fowl: 'You elegant f.	LEAR 150:14
fox: ar'n't fool I loves the f.	SURT 248:12
f. knows many things	ARCH 7:17
galloping after a f.	WILDE 271:24
foxes: f. have a sincere interest	ELIOT 93:1
f. have holes	BIBLE 32:16
little f.	BIBLE 28:1
may be a portion for f.	PRAY 189:11
foy: f. je veuil vivre et mourir	VILL 262:14
frabjous: f. day	CARR 63:17
fragments: Death tramples it to f.	SHEL 239:1
f. have I shored against	ELIOT 95:7
Frailty: F., thy name is woman	SHAK 206:15
therefore more f.	SHAK 212:17
frame: f. thy fearful symmetry	BLAKE 43:7
sensuous f. Is rack'd	TENN 252:14
framed: England is to have it f.	WALP 266:1
framework: experience but a defining f.	WHORF 270:12
français: aurait toujours parlé f.	VOLT 265:3
f. aux hommes et allemand	CHAR 67:15
pas clair n'est pas f.	RIV 195:9
France: England the nearer is to F.	CARR 63:12
Fair stood the wind for F.	DRAY 90:5
Our fertile F.	SHAK 214:5
this matter better in F.	STER 246:4
vasty fields of F.	SHAK 213:8
frankincense: f., and myrrh	BIBLE 31:2
fraud: this pious f.	GAY 105:16
Wilcox family has a f.	FORS 101:14
frauds: Well stored with pious f.	BURKE 52:8
freckled: fickle, f.	HOPK 122:4
Of f. Human Nature	DICK 86:6
freckles: f., and doubt	PARK 180:4
In those f. live their	SHAK 226:17
free: appal the f.	SHAK 208:21
English Church shall be f.	MAGN 158:15
f. as nature first made	DRYD 90:22
F. speech, free passes	BETJ 21:5
f. verse is like playing	FROST 103:13
Greece might still be f.	BYRON 58:7
half slave and half f.	LINC 151:17
human beings are born f.	ANON 2:16
Man was born f.	ROUS 198:2
never shall be f.	DONNE 88:7
O'er the land of the f.	KEY 141:15
only less f. Than thou	SHEL 239:13
Teach the f. man how	AUDEN 11:1
Thou art f.	ARN 9:1
truth shall make you f.	BIBLE 36:28
We must be f. or die	WORD 276:21
Who died to make verse f.	PRES 191:15
wholly slaves or wholly f.	DRYD 91:4
Who would be f. themselves	BYRON 57:8
freed: thousands He hath f.	CHAN 67:4
freedom: are fit to use their f.	MAC 157:1
can do for the f. of man	KENN 141:13
fight for f. and truth	IBSEN 129:5
F. and Whisky gang thegither	BURNS 53:24
f. of speech	TWAIN 261:2
F. of the press in Britain	SWAF 248:16
If I have f. in my love	LOV 154:9
I gave my life for f.	EWER 97:8
Let f. ring	SMITH 242:11
newly acquired f. produces	MAC 156:19
Perfect f. is reserved	COLL 75:19
freedoms: four essential human f.	RONS 196:12
freeze: To f. the blood I have	WORD 274:18
freezings: What f. have I felt	SHAK 236:8
French: dislike the F.	WALP 266:6
how it's improved her F.	GRAH 111:7
is not clear is not F.	RIV 195:9
some are fond of F.	MAS 156:21
Speak in F. when you can't	CARR 63:19
to men F.	CHAR 67:15
would always have spoken F.	VOLT 265:3

Frenchies: Those F. seek him everywhere ORCZY 178:5
Frenssh: F. of Parys was to hire CHAU 68:2
F. she spak ful faire CHAU 68:2
frenzy: in a fine f. rolling SHAK 227:18
frequent: f. hearses shall besiege POPE 184:12
when young did eagerly f. FITZ 99:5
frère: mon semblable,—mon f.
Sois mon f. CHAM 67:3
fresh: f. revolving pleasures GAY 105:21
f. woods, and pastures MILT 168:5
freshness: glory and the f. of a dream
WORD 275:13
Fressen: Erst kommt das F. BREC 46:8
fressh: f. as is the month of May CHAU 68:1
fret: fever, and the f. KEATS 139:19
frets: struts and f. his hour SHAK 223:15
Fretted: F. the pigmy body to decay DRYD 90:12
Freude: F. schöner Götterfunken SCH 201:2
friars: while the barefoot f. were GIBB 106:8
fricassee: will equally serve in a f. SWIFT 249:6
friend: country and betraying my f. FORS 101:21
every mess I finds a f. DIBD 83:8
F. and associate of this HAER 113:8
F., go up higher BIBLE 35:21
f. in power is a friend ADAMS 1:4
f. of every country CANN 61:1
f. that sticketh closer BIBLE 26:23
f. unseen FLEC 100:13
from the candid f. CANN 61:2
guide, philosopher, and f. POPE 185:19
He was my f. SHAK 216:17
I can merely be your f. LEAR 150:8
never want a f. in need DICK 84:7
not use a f. as I use Thee HERB 118:16
to have a f. is to be one EMER 96:11
what he can find a f. sincere BULW 51:13
who lost no f. POPE 185:5
Who's your fat f. BRUM 50:25
yet f. to truth POPE 185:5
friendly: f. seas they softly run FLEC 100:10
f. swarry DICK 85:25
nor yet is it f. HOLM 120:15
friends: down his life for his f. BIBLE 37:3
F. and loves we have none MAS 163:3
F., Romans, countrymen SHAK 216:16
f. thou hast SHAK 207:6
glory was I had such f. YEATS 279:10
golden f. I had HOUS 126:11
I have lost f. WOOLF 274:9
In spite of all their f. LEAR 150:12
like him with f. possess'd SHAK 235:11
misfortune of our best f. LA R 149:8
My f. forsake me like CLARE 72:21
neither foes nor loving f. KIPL 144:9
ought to forgive our f. MED 164:12
remembering my good f. SHAK 230:3
friendship: f. from knowledge BUSS 55:23
F. should be more than ELIOT 94:12
him to cultivate your f. JOHN 133:19
let us swear eternal f. SMITH 242:17
should keep his f. in constant JOHN 133:11
frighted: f. with false fire SHAK 210:5
frighten: street and f. the horses CAMP 60:11
frightened: why should you be f. WEBB 267:2
fringe: movement has a lunatic f. RONS 196:15
Fritter-my-wig: Fry me!' or 'F. CARR 62:5
Frocks: F. and Curls DICK 86:5
From: F. each according to his BAK 14:12

f. here to Eternity KIPL 144:1
gamut of the emotions f. PARK 180:8
fromages: 265 spécialités de f. DE G 82:6
frost: Thaw not the f. which binds SHEL 238:24
third day comes a f. SHAK 215:9
frosts: f. are slain and flowers SWIN 249:16
froward: are a very f. generation BIBLE 24:1
frown: more the f. o' the great SHAK 206:4
frowst: f. with a book by the fire KIPL 144:13
frowzy: f. couch in sorrow steep BURNS 54:6
frozen: Architecture in general is f. music
SCH 201:1
milk comes f. home in pail SHAK 219:14
Fruchtbarkeit: F. und den grössten Genuss
NIET 176:19
fruit: f. Of that forbidden tree MILT 168:12
them f. for their songs ADD 1:13
weakest kind of f. SHAK 225:16
fruitful: Be f. BIBLE 22:6
f. vine: upon the walls PRAY 190:21
fruitfulness: of mists and mellow f. KEATS 140:12
fruits: By their f. ye shall know BIBLE 32:12
frustra: f. vigilat qui custodit BIBLE 41:15
Fry: F. me!' or 'Fritter-my-wig CARR 62:5
fubbed: have been f. off SHAK 212:24
fugaces: Eheu f. HOR 124:4
fugit: f. inreparabile tempus VIRG 264:13
fugitive: f. and cloistered virtue MILT 170:17
f. from th' law of averages MAUL 164:9
fuisse: f. felicem BOET 44:13
fulfil: not to destroy, but to f. BIBLE 31:15
Full: F. and fair ones HERR 118:17
F. fathom five SHAK 232:15
F. of life now WHIT 269:17
f. of human existence JOHN 132:19
Reading maketh a f. man BACON 13:21
Serenely f. SMITH 242:21
that hath his quiver f. PRAY 190:20
world is so f. of a number STEV 247:9
fulmen: Jovi f. viresque tonandi MAN 159:9
fumble: f. with the sheets SHAK 213:12
fumo: sed ex f. dare lucem HOR 122:16
Fun: F. is fun but no girl wants LOOS 154:2
f. to punt than to be punted SAY 200:16
I thought *What Jolly F.* RAL 194:10
I've taken my f. where KIPL 144:15
Were more f. to be with NASH 174:15
You have had enough f. HOR 123:8
Function: F. never dies WORD 276:12
fundamentally: woman was f. sensible JOHN 133:18
funèbre: mais toute la nuit f. PROU 192:5
funeral: f. bak'd meats SHAK 207:2
f. train which the bridegroom CLOU 73:9
speak in Caesar's f. SHAK 216:16
funny: Whatever is f. is subversive ORW 178:8
funny-ha-ha: Funny-peculiar or f. HAY 115:18
Funny-peculiar: F. or funny-ha-ha HAY 115:18
fur: make the f. Fly BUTL 56:7
my f. and whiskers CARR 62:17
furca: Naturam expellas f. HOR 123:4
furious: amazed, temperate, and f. SHAK 222:8
fun grew fast and f. BURNS 55:1
which makes the Queen so f. VICT 262:8
furiously: heathen so f. rage PRAY 188:6
he driveth f. BIBLE 25:12
ideas sleep f. CHOM 70:16
furnace: burning fiery f. BIBLE 30:8
lover, Sighing like f. SHAK 205:1
furnish: Would f. all we ought KEBLE 141:9

furrow: half-reap'd f. sound asleep KEATS 140:13
further: I was much f. out than SMITH 242:13
shalt thou go and no f. PARN 180:14
fury: full of sound and f. SHAK 223:15
f. like an ex-wife searching CONN 77:7
F. slinging flame TENN 252:14
F. with th' abhorred shears MILT 167:20
Nor Hell a f. CONG 76:19
there's f. in the firmament SASS 200:15
fuse: that through the green f. THOM 257:4
fust: who gets his blow in f. BILL 42:5
future: cannot fight against the f. GLAD 109:14
f., and it works STEF 245:16
f. contained in time past ELIOT 93:13
f. in the slightest HOR 123:14
f. sees BLAKE 43:6
I dipt into the f. TENN 253:10
manners of f. generations JOHN 134:28
want a picture of the f. ORW 178:12
Whose terrible f. may have AUDEN 10:14
fyve: god that I have wedded f. CHAU 68:16
gabardine: spet upon my Jewish g. SHAK 224:21
Gaels: great G. of Ireland CHES 69:20
gai: toujours g., archy MARQ 161:3
gaiety: which has eclipsed the g. JOHN 134:25
gain: shall g. the whole world BIBLE 33:14
gained: greatest misery is a battle g. WELL 268:5
gale: g., it plies the saplings HOUS 126:4
galère: allait-il faire dans cette g. MOL 171:9
Galilean: You have won, G. JUL 137:10
Galilee: rolls nightly on deep G. BYRON 57:16
gall: take my milk for g. SHAK 220:11
to g. a new-healed wound SHAK 212:22
wormwood and the g. BIBLE 30:1
gallant: died a very g. gentleman ATK 10:3
gallantry: What men call g. BYRON 57:18
galleon: moon was a ghostly g. tossed
NOYES 177:8
gallery: g. in which the reporters MAC 156:15
Gallia: G. est omnis divisa CAES 59:8
gallimaufry: g. or hodgepodge of all SPEN 244:22
gallop: does he gallop and g. about STEV 247:8
G. about doing good SMITH 242:12
G. apace SHAK 232:1
galloped: we g. all three BROW 49:15
galloping: Hooves with a g. sound VIRG 264:1
gallows: on the g., or of the pox WILK 272:9
statue to him under the g. SMITH 243:1
galumphing: He went g. back CARR 63:17
gambling: crew is g. in the forecastle SHAW 237:18
game: g. on these lone heaths HAZL 116:5
g.'s afoot SHAK 213:15
g., That must be lost BEAU 17:2
how you played the g. RICE 195:2
It's more than a g. HUGH 127:14
of time to win this g. DRAKE 90:2
shuttlecock's a wery good g. DICK 85:16
games: their g. should be seen MONT 171:18
gamut: g. of the emotions from PARK 180:8
Gang: G. aft a-gley BURNS 55:6
he be doing in this g. MOL 171:9
they may g. a kennin wrang BURNS 53:17
Ganges: by the Indian G.' side MARV 161:20
gaol: world's thy g. DONNE 88:10
Garde: La G. meurt CAMB 60:5
garden: at the bottom of our g. FYL 104:4
Come into the g. TENN 254:1
g. and a spring HOR 125:1
g. is a lovesome thing BROWN 48:3

g. of bright images BRAM 46:5
g., That grows to seed SHAK 206:15
g. to cut a cabbage-leaf FOOTE 101:7
Glory of the G. lies KIPL 144:2
God Almighty first planted a g. BACON 13:9
God the first g. made COWL 79:11
I value my g. more ADD 1:13
man and a woman in a g. WILDE 271:26
Mr McGregor's g. POTT 186:5
Nothing grows in our g. THOM 257:12
Our England is a g. that KIPL 144:2
That every Hyacinth the G. FITZ 99:1
There is a g. in her face CAMP 60:20
this best g. of the world SHAK 214:5
Through this same G. after me FITZ 99:14
walking in the g. in the cool BIBLE 22:12
gardener: Adam was a g. KIPL 144:4
Adam was a g. SHAK 215:1
That half a proper g.'s KIPL 144:4
gardens: closing time in the g. CONN 77:10
Down by the salley gardens YEATS 278:18
Thames bordered by its g. MORR 173:14
gare: say au-dessus de sa g. RATT 194:12
garland: g. briefer than a girl's HOUS 125:11
that immortal g. MILT 170:17
wither'd is the g. of the war SHAK 204:6
garlanded: All g. with carven imag'ries
KEATS 138:18
garlands: fantastic g. did she come SHAK 211:9
To her let us g. bring SHAK 234:18
garment: g. was white as snow BIBLE 30:11
garments: dyed g. from Bozrah BIBLE 29:21
Stuffs out his vacant g. SHAK 217:10
garnished: swept, and g. BIBLE 33:3
garret: jewels into a g. four stories BACON 13:8
Garter: I like the G. MELB 164:13
garters: thine own heir-apparent g. SHAK 212:8
gas: All is g. and gaiters DICK 85:3
G. smells awful PARK 180:6
Gasp: G. and Stretch one's Eyes BELL 18:14
When he was at the last g. BIBLE 30:30
gate: A-sitting on a g. CARR 64:14
matters not how strait the g. HENL 117:7
poor man at his g. ALEX 2:4
their enemies in the g. PRAY 190:20
Wide is the g. BIBLE 32:8
gate-bars: drops on g. hang in a row HARDY 115:2
gates: g., and be ye lift up PRAY 188:18
g. of hell shall not prevail BIBLE 33:12
Gath: Tell it not in G. BIBLE 24:25
gather: g. the lambs with his arm BIBLE 29:10
G. ye rosebuds while ye HERR 118:23
gathered: two or three are g. PRAY 186:24
where two or three are g. BIBLE 33:18
Gathering: G. her brows like gathering
BURNS 54:22
Gaudeamus: G. igitur ANON 6:17
gaudy: have one other g. night SHAK 204:2
Neat, but not g. WESL 268:21
rich, not g. SHAK 207:6
Gaul: G. as a whole is divided CAES 59:8
I've lost G. KIPL 145:13
Gaunt: seige of the city of G. BALL 14:18
gave: g. his only begotten Son BIBLE 36:21
Lord g. BIBLE 25:18
gay: g. as soft YOUNG 280:9
I'm a g. deceiver COLM 76:5
second best's a g. goodnight YEATS 279:1
Gaza: Eyeless in G. MILT 170:1

aze: g. not in my eyes	HOUS 125:8
to g. out from the land	LUCR 155:6
azelle: never nurs'd a dear g.	MOORE 173:3
ear: hate all that Persian g.	HOR 124:1
my ships are out of g.	TENN 255:3
Gedanke: 'Zwei Seelen und ein G.	HALM 114:5
Geese: G. are swans	ARN 8:16
Like g. about the sky	AUDEN 10:8
swans of others are g.	WALP 266:5
Gefahr: vor dem Alles in G. ist	NIET 176:15
gefährlich: g. leben	NIET 176:19
Gehonnai to G. or up to the Throne	KIPL 146:9
em: Full many a g. of purest	GRAY 112:5
Thinking every tear a g.	SHEL 239:10
emlike: hard, g. flame	PATER 181:10
ender: she's of the feminine g.	OKEE 177:14
General: country was good for G.	WILS 272:14
good morning!' the g.	SASS 200:12
'twas caviare to the g.	SHAK 209:17
enerals: *bite* some of my other g.	GEOR 106:3
Russia has two g. in whom	NICH 176:10
eneration: g. of vipers	BIBLE 31:5
they are a very froward g.	BIBLE 24:1
ye are a chosen g.	BIBLE 40:18
You're all a lost g.	STEIN 245:18
enerations: g. shall call me blessed	BIBLE 34:28
g. of living creatures	LUCR 155:7
No hungry g. tread thee	KEATS 140:1
enerous: impulses as they are always g.	
	MONT 172:9
My mind as g.	SHAK 217:19
they have more g. sentiments	JOHN 132:2
énie: j'ai mis mon g. dans ma vie	WILDE 272:1
Le g. n'est qu'une plus	BUFF 51:7
vous croyez un grand g.	BEAU 16:17
Geniumque: G. loci primamque deorum	
	VIRG 263:16
enius: Consult the g. of the place	POPE 185:3
G. been defined as a supreme	BUTL 56:15
G. is one per cent inspiration	EDIS 92:7
G. is only a greater aptitude	BUFF 51:7
g. of the Constitution	PITT 183:9
g. that could cut a Colossus	JOHN 134:4
'G.' (which means transcendent	CARL 61:10
Gives g. a better discerning	GOLD 110:17
have put my g. into my life	WILDE 272:1
instantly recognizes g.	DOYLE 89:28
Ramp up my g.	JONS 136:4
to declare except my g.	WILDE 272:2
When a true g. appears	SWIFT 249:8
yourself to be a great g.	BEAU 16:17
enteelly: he may cheat at cards g.	BOSW 45:4
entes: Augescunt aliae g.	LUCR 155:7
entil: parfit g. knyght	CHAU 67:19
entle: day shall g. his condition	SHAK 214:4
Do not go g. into that	THOM 256:23
G. Jesus	WESL 268:18
g. rain from heaven	SHAK 225:17
His life was g.	SHAK 217:6
I have seen them g.	WYATT 278:3
entleman: almost a definition of a g.	NEWM 176:1
Be a little g.	HOFF 120:8
died a very gallant g.	ATK 10:3
he cannot make a g.	BURKE 53:12
last g. in Europe	LEV 151:10
Like a fine old English g.	ANON 4:2
little too pedantic for a g.	CONG 76:16
mariner with the g.	DRAKE 90:4
prince of darkness is a g.	SHAK 218:13

Gentleman-rankers: G. out on the spree	
	KIPL 144:1
Gentlemen: Dust was G. and Ladies	DICK 86:5
g. in England	SHAK 214:4
Great-hearted g.	BROW 49:6
not to forget we are g.	BURKE 52:11
while the G. go	KIPL 145:15
You g. of England	PARK 180:11
gentleness: Let g. my strong enforcement	
	SHAK 204:24
Gentlewomen: Cherubic Creatures—These G.	
	DICK 86:6
Gently: G. they go	MILL 166:3
roar you as g. as any sucking	SHAK 226:16
genus: Hoc g. omne	HOR 124:20
Genuss: G. vom Dasein einzuernten	NIET 176:19
geographical: Italy is a g. expression	METT 165:12
Geography: G. is about maps	BENT 19:16
geometrical: increases in a g. ratio	MALT 159:7
George the Third: G. Ought never	BENT 19:21
geraniums: cot with a pot of pink g.	MACN 158:6
German: they just shovel in G.	TWAIN 261:7
to my horse —G.	CHAR 67:15
Germans: bomb the G.	BETJ 21:4
Gesang: Das ist der ewige G.	GOE 109:22
Weib und G.	LUTH 155:13
Gestern: G. liebt' ich	LESS 151:9
get: g. me to England once again	BROO 47:12
Getting: G. and spending	WORD 277:7
Ghastly: G. Good Taste	BETJ 21:15
g. thro' the drizzling	TENN 252:11
We were a g. crew	COL 74:17
Ghost: Come, Holy G.	PRAY 191:12
g. of Roger Casement	YEATS 279:2
G. unlaid forbear thee	SHAK 206:4
I'll make a g. of him that	SHAK 207:10
like a g. she glimmers	TENN 254:15
of the G. in the machine	RYLE 198:17
to the bowling of a g.	THOM 257:22
Vex not his g.	SHAK 219:5
with some old lover's g.	DONNE 88:11
ghosties: From ghoulies and g.	ANON 3:11
ghosts: g. from an enchanter fleeing	SHEL 239:12
newspaper and I seem to see g. gliding	
	IBSEN 129:6
ghoulies: g. and ghosties and long-leggety	
	ANON 3:11
giant: are upon the body of a g.	LAND 148:15
arrows in the hand of the g.	PRAY 190:20
g. refreshed with wine	PRAY 189:16
To have a g.'s strength	SHAK 223:17
when a g. dies	SHAK 224:1
giants: g. in the earth in those	BIBLE 22:19
on the shoulders of g.	BERN 20:2
on the shoulders of g.	NEWT 176:7
gibber: dead Did squeak and g.	SHAK 206:7
giberne: dans sa g. le baton	LOUI 154:7
gibes: Where be your g. now	SHAK 211:11
gift-horse: To look a g. in the mouth	BUTL 56:6
giftie: wad some Pow'r the g. gie	BURNS 55:4
gifts: all the good g. of nature	SHAK 233:16
even when they bring g.	VIRG 263:3
g. of God are strown	HEBER 116:10
g. wax poor when givers	SHAK 209:1
They presented unto him g.	BIBLE 31:2
gig: crew of the captain's g.	GILB 106:21
gild: g. the faces of the grooms	SHAK 221:18
To g. refined gold	SHAK 217:12
gilded: bug with g. wings	POPE 184:22

Gilding: G. pale streams with heavenly
SHAK 235:14
Gilead: Is there no balm in G.   BIBLE 29:25
that appear from mount G.   BIBLE 28:3
Gilpin: G. was a citizen Of credit   COWP 79:12
Gin: G. was mother's milk   SHAW 238:17
Gipfeln: Über allen G. Ist Ruh'   GOE 110:2
Gird: G. up now thy loins like   BIBLE 25:32
girded: With your loins g.   BIBLE 23:15
girdle: g. round about the earth   SHAK 227:4
girl: at a g. throwing a ball   WOOLF 274:8
garland briefer than a g.'s   HOUS 125:11
g. like I   LOOS 153:22
Home is the g.'s prison   SHAW 238:13
mountainous sports g.   BETJ 21:10
no g. wants to laugh all   LOOS 154:2
There was a little g.   LONG 153:20
girl-graduates: sweet g. in their golden TENN 254:5
girlish: to the brim with g. glee   GILB 108:6
girls: All very agreeable g.   GILB 107:13
At g. who wear glasses   PARK 180:5
before to virgin g. and boys   HOR 124:5
do for pretty g.   YEATS 279:6
lads for the g.   HOUS 125:14
My life with g. has ended   HOR 124:11
Of all the g. that are   CAREY 61:4
pallor of g.' brows   OWEN 179:5
girt: loins g. about with truth   BIBLE 39:15
Gitche Gumee: By the shore of G.   LONG 153:12
give: all other things g. place   GAY 105:18
blessed to g. than to receive   BIBLE 37:26
G. all thou canst   WORD 277:5
G., and it shall be given   BIBLE 35:8
'G. crowns and pounds   HOUS 125:7
G. every man thine ear   SHAK 207:6
g. me back my heart   BYRON 58:19
G. me,' quoth I   SHAK 220:2
g. me the sun   IBSEN 129:7
G. me your tired   LAZ 149:19
G. to me the life I love   STEV 247:11
g. to the poor   BIBLE 33:21
G. us the tools   CHUR 71:8
G. us this day our daily   BIBLE 31:21
G. what you command   AUG 11:17
never g. up their liberties   BURKE 53:5
such as I have g. I thee   BIBLE 37:13
What will ye g. me   BIBLE 34:10
given: he would not have g. me   WOLS 274:5
one that hath shall be g.   BIBLE 34:6
unto us a son is g.   BIBLE 28:19
giver: author and g. of all good   PRAY 187:8
loveth a cheerful g.   BIBLE 39:4
givers: poor when g. prove unkind SHAK 209:1
gives: g. to airy nothing   SHAK 227:18
much good who g. quickly   PUBL 192:8
giving: not in the g. vein to-day   SHAK 231:6
Stealing and g. odour   SHAK 233:14
glacier: g. knocks in the cupboard AUDEN 10:10
Glad: G. did I live and gladly   STEV 247:16
g. that you won   BETJ 21:13
I was g. when they said   PRAY 190:18
moments of g. grace   YEATS 280:5
shew ourselves g. in him   PRAY 190:2
son maketh a g. father   BIBLE 26:12
To g. me with its soft   MOORE 173:3
Trying to be g.   HOUS 125:9
was made to make men g.   BIBLE 30:25
gladder: My heart is g. than all   ROSS 197:3
glade: alone in the bee-loud g.   YEATS 279:7

That crown the wat'ry g.   GRAY 112:
gladness: g. of the best   HERB 118:1
serve the Lord with g.   PRAY 190:
Teach me half the g.   SHEL 240:
Glamis: G. hath murder'd sleep   SHAK 221:1
G. thou art, and Cawdor   SHAK 220:1
glance: Doth g. from heaven   SHAK 227:1
glare: There is a g. in some men's   BAG 14:
glass: baying for broken g.   WAUGH 266:1
dome of many-coloured g.   SHEL 239.
g. is falling hour by hour   MACN 158:
g. of blessings standing   HERB 118:1
g. to his sightless eye   NEWB 175:1
his own face in the g.   WILDE 271:1
prove an excuse for the g.   SHER 240:2
sound of broken g.   BELL 19:
through a g., darkly   BIBLE 38:1
turn down an empty G.   FITZ 100:
you break the bloody g.   MACN 158:
glasses: At girls who wear g.   PARK 180:
were two g. and two chairs   MACN 158:
gleamed: first she g. upon my sight WORD 276:1
glean'd: pen has g. my teeming   KEATS 140:
glee: brim with girlish g.   GILB 108:
Piping songs of pleasant g.   BLAKE 43:1
glen: Down the rushy g.   ALL 2:
Glenlivet: Only half G.   AYT 12:1
gliding: I seem to see ghosts g.   IBSEN 129:
glisters: Nor all, that g., gold   GRAY 112:
glittering: g. prizes to those who   BIRK 42:
how that g. taketh me   HERR 119:
gloat: Hear me g.   KIPL 146:2
globe: g. of death and halved   THOM 257:
great g. itself   SHAK 232:2
globule: primordial atomic g.   GILB 108:
gloire: Le jour de g. est arrivé   ROUG 198:
gloom: light to counterfeit a g.   MILT 167:1
Gloria: G. in excelsis Deo   MASS 163:1
G. Patri   MASS 163:
gloriam: Ad majorem Dei g.   ANON 6:1
sed nomini tuo da g.   BIBLE 41:1
gloried: Jamshyd g. and drank deep FITZ 98:1
glories: g. of our blood and state   SHIR 241:
glorious: all g. within   PRAY 189:
shown no g. morning face   STEV 247:1
That burns in g. Araby   DARL 81:1
'tis a g. thing   GILB 107:
glory: are the days of our g.   BYRON 59:
brittle g. shineth in this   SHAK 230:1
day of g. has arrived   ROUG 198:
drown'd my G. in a Shallow Cup   FITZ 99:1
earth is full of his g.   BIBLE 28:1
finished yields the true g.   DRAKE 90:
G. and loveliness have   KEATS 140:
g. and the freshness   WORD 275:1
g. and the dream   WORD 275:1
G. be to God for dappled   HOPK 122:
g. in the name of Briton   GEOR 106:
g. is departed from Israel   BIBLE 24:1
g. of Europe is extinguished   BURKE 53:
g. of man as the flower   BIBLE 40:1
g. of the Attic stage   ARN 9:
G. of the Garden lies   KIPL 144:
g. of the Lord shall be   BIBLE 29:
g. of the Lord shone round   BIBLE 35:
g. shone around   TATE 250:1
G. to God in the highest   BIBLE 35:
G. to Man in the highest   SWIN 250:
g. was I had such friends   YEATS 279:1

g. was not arrayed like	BIBLE 31:25
heavens declare the g.	PRAY 188:12
infirm g. of the positive	ELIOT 93:9
King of g. shall come	PRAY 188:18
left him alone with his g.	WOLFE 273:22
long hair, it is a g.	BIBLE 38:13
Mine eyes have seen the g.	HOWE 127:9
My gown of g.	RAL 194:4
not the g.	GOE 110:1
of g. in the flower	WORD 275:16
passed away a g.	WORD 275:13
passes the g. of the world	ANON 7:5
paths of g. lead	GRAY 112:3
quickly the world's g.	THOM 256:18
that will die in their g.	HOUS 126:1
'There's g. for you	CARR 64:8
To the g. that was Greece	POE 184:3
To the greater g. of God	ANON 6:12
to thy name give g.	BIBLE 41.14
trailing clouds of g.	WORD 275:15
Vain pomp and g. of this	SHAK 215:9
glove: were a g. upon that hand	SHAK 231:17
gloves: through the fields in g.	CORN 78:7
Glücklichen: Die Welt des G. ist eine	WITT 273:9
Glyn: With Elinor G.	ANON 5:13
gnashing: weeping and g. of teeth	BIBLE 32:15
gnat: which strain at a g.	BIBLE 33:30
go: g. about the country stealing	ARAB 7:16
G., and do thou likewise	BIBLE 35:14
G., and he goeth	BIBLE 32:14
g. at once	SHAK 222:19
G., for they call you	ARN 8:19
g. gentle into that good	THOM 256:23
G., litel bok	CHAU 68:27
G., lovely Rose	WALL 265:13
G. to the ant thou sluggard	BIBLE 26:8
g. to 't with delight	SHAK 204:3
g. we know not where	SHAK 224:4
G. West	GREE 112:14
G. West, young man	SOULE 243:15
I g. on for ever	TENN 251:7
I like to g. by myself	HAZL 116:4
In the name of God, g.	CROM 80:18
it's no g. the rickshaw	MACN 158:5
I will arise and g. now	YEATS 279:7
Let my people g.	BIBLE 23:13
Let us g. then	ELIOT 94:3
not g., For weariness	DONNE 88:14
thinking jest what a Rum G.	WELLS 268:15
unto Caesar shalt thou g.	BIBLE 37:28
Victoria Station and g.	BEVIN 21:18
we'll g. no more a roving	BYRON 58:22
will g. into the house	PRAY 190:18
will g. onward the same	HARDY 114:11
goal: g. stands up	HOUS 126:3
grave is not its g.	LONG 153:9
stood I to keep the g.	HOUS 125:9
Will be the final g. of ill	TENN 252:15
goat-footed: This g. bard	KEYN 141:18
goats: g. on the left	BIBLE 34:7
hair is as a flock of g.	BIBLE 28:3
separate me from the g.	CEL 66:3
gobbled: Has g. up the infant child	HOUS 127:5
goblins: have one of sprites and g.	SHAK 234:20
God: acceptable unto G.	BIBLE 38:1
apprehension how like a g.	SHAK 208:14
are like the peace of G.	JAM 130:1
atheist half believes a G.	YOUNG 280:11
been the same since G. died	MILL 166:5

by Yours faithfully, G.	ANON 3:9
called the children of G.	BIBLE 31:11
cannot serve G. and mammon	BIBLE 31:24
daughter of the voice of G.	WORD 276:1
dear G. who loveth us	COL 74:20
discussing their duty to G.	WHIT 270:6
door-keeper in the house of my G.	PRAY 189:19
Fear G., and keep his commandments	
	BIBLE 27:24
Fear G.. Honour the king	BIBLE 40:19
fit for the kingdom of G.	BIBLE 35:10
gifts of G. are strewn	HERBER 116:10
Glory to G. in the highest	BIBLE 35:3
G. all things are possible	BIBLE 33:23
G. and soldiers we alike	QUAR 193:8
G. arranges	THOM 256:19
G. be in my head	ANON 3:12
G. be merciful to me	BIBLE 36:5
'G. bless us every one	DICK 83:19
G. cannot change the past	AGAT 1:18
G. does not play dice	EINS 92:14
G. exists only for leader-writers	GREE 112:17
G. first maked man	CHAU 68:12
G. forgot me	BROW 49:2
G. for his father who has	CYPR 81:6
G. fulfils himself in many	TENN 252:6
G. has given you good abilities	ARAB 7:16
G. hath also highly exalted	BIBLE 39:16
G. hath joined together	BIBLE 33:20
G. hath joined together	PRAY 188:2
G. hath numbered thy kingdom	BIBLE 30:9
G. help the Minister that	MELB 164:16
G. is dead	NIET 176:16
G. is love	BIBLE 40:25
G. is no respecter of persons	BIBLE 37:18
G. is not mocked	BIBLE 39:9
G. is our hope and strength	PRAY 189:3
G. is thy law, thou mine	MILT 169:10
G. is usually on the side	BUSS 56:1
G. made the country	COWP 79:19
G. moves in a mysterious	COWP 79:14
G. Must think it exceedingly	KNOX 147:5
G. now accepteth thy works	BIBLE 27:14
G. of love my Shepherd	HERB 118:15
G. of our fathers	KIPL 145:10
G. save the king	BIBLE 24:18
G. saw that it was good	BIBLE 22:4
G. shall wipe away all	BIBLE 40:33
G. shall wipe away all	BIBLE 41:8
G. si Love	FORS 101:19
G.'s in his heaven	BROW 50:12
G. so loved the world	BIBLE 36:21
G.'s sons are things	MADD 158:13
G.'s thoughts we must	NIGH 177:4
G. tempers the wind	STER 246:6
G. the first garden made	COWL 79:11
G. this, God that	SQUI 245:7
G., to me, it seems	FULL 103:22
G. walking in the garden	BIBLE 22:12
G., who is our home	WORD 275:15
G. will pardon me	HEINE 116:15
G. would destroy He first	DUP 92:2
good to them that love G.	BIBLE 37:38
govern nor no G. could please	DRYD 90:11
grace of G. there goes	BRAD 45:16
granted scarce to G. above	SPEN 244:21
greater glory of G.	ANON 6:12
Had I but serv'd my G.	SHAK 215:11
Had I but served G.	WOLS 274:5

hand into the hand of G.	HASK 115:16
hands of the living G.	BIBLE 40:7
Have G. to be his guide	BUNY 51:26
He for G. only	MILT 169:7
he thinks little of G.	PLUT 183:18
honest G. is the noblest	ING 129:13
honest G.'s the noblest	BUTL 56:16
hope of the City of G.	MAS 163:3
how can he love G. whom	BIBLE 40:27
If G. did not exist	VOLT 264:20
If G. were to take one	ANON 3:19
if there be a G.	ANON 4:13
is forgotten before G.	BIBLE 35:19
It is an attribute to G.	SHAK 225:17
justify the ways of G. to Men	MILT 168:14
kills the image of G.	MILT 170:15
leaping, and praising G.	BIBLE 37:14
Like to a g. he seems	CAT 65:9
Lord G. made them all	ALEX 2:3
Lord thy G. is with thee	BIBLE 24:3
mad all are in G.'s keeping	KIPL 146:19
men as had the fear of G.	CROM 80:14
men that G. made mad	CHES 69:20
mighty G.	BIBLE 28:19
mills of G. grind slowly	LOGAU 152:15
my King and my G.	PRAY 189:17
Nearer, my G., to thee	ADAMS 1:6
nearer you are to G.	WOTT 277:20
not tempt the Lord thy G.	BIBLE 31:9
now G. alone knows	KLOP 147:2
Our G.'s forgotten	QUAR 193:8
out of the mouth of G.	BIBLE 31:8
owe G. a death	SHAK 212:29
peace of G.	BIBLE 39:19
people is the voice of G.	ALC 2:1
put G. in his statements	WHIT 269:16
reason and the will of G.	ARN 9:7
relenting G. Hath placed	ROSS 197:2
safe stronghold our G.	LUTH 155:14
searching find out G.	BIBLE 25:22
servant of the Living G.	SMART 241:15
she for G. in him	MILT 169:7
spirit shall return unto G.	BIBLE 27:22
Standeth G. within	LOW 154:18
such is the kingdom of G.	BIBLE 34:26
that be are ordained of G.	BIBLE 38:4
There is no G.	PRAY 188:9
they shall see G.	BIBLE 31:11
think I am becoming a g.	VESP 262:6
Thou shalt have one G. only	CLOU 73:12
three person'd G.	DONNE 88:6
throws himself on G.	BROW 49:11
thy God is a jealous G.	BIBLE 23:31
thy God my G.	BIBLE 24:14
To G. I speak Spanish	CHAR 67:15
To justify G.'s ways	HOUS 126:12
TO THE UNKNOWN G.	BIBLE 37:23
trust in G.	AUDEN 11:12
us from the love of G.	BIBLE 37:39
Verb is G.	HUGO 127:15
walk humbly with thy G.	BIBLE 30:19
was the holy Lamb of G.	BLAKE 43:2
What G. abandoned	HOUS 126:20
What hath G. wrought	BIBLE 23:27
Whenever G. prepares evil	ANON 6:8
When G. at first made man	HERB 118:14
whole armour of G.	BIBLE 39:14
whole armour of G.	BIBLE 39:15
who saw the face of G.	MARL 160:3

with the grandeur of G.	HOPK 121:18
Word was with G.	BIBLE 36:12
Y blessed be g. that I have wedded	CHAU 68:16
ye believe in G.	BIBLE 36:36
Yellow G. forever gazes	HAYES 116:1
yet G. has not said a word	BROW 50:16
you must believe in G.	JOW 136:15
you think the laws of G.	SHAW 237:18
God Almighty: G. first planted a garden	
	BACON 13:9
Goddamm: Lhude sing G.	POUND 186:6
Goddess: G., excellently bright	JONS 135:19
she was in truth a g.	VIRG 263:1
Godfathers: G. and Godmothers in my	
	PRAY 187:18
godly: may hereafter live a g.	PRAY 186:20
Godmothers: Godfathers and G. in my Baptism	
	PRAY 187:18
Godolphin Horne: G. was nobly born	BELL 18:8
Godot: We're waiting for G.	BECK 17:5
gods: daughter of the g.	TENN 251:12
dish fit for the g.	SHAK 216:14
fit love for G.	MILT 169:18
g. love dies young	MEN 165:1
g. thought otherwise	VIRG 263:5
he creates G. by the dozen	MONT 172:6
not recognizing the g.	PLATO 183:14
on a par with the g.	SAPP 199:12
people clutching their g.	ELIOT 94:2
Whatever g. may be	SWIN 250:1
winning cause pleased the g.	LUCAN 155:1
woman is a dish for the g.	SHAK 204:9
goes: grace of God there g.	BRAD 45:16
How g. the enemy	REYN 195:1
it g. off at night	SHER 240:23
goest: whithersoever thou g.	BIBLE 24:3
whither thou g.	BIBLE 24:14
goeth: whither it g.	BIBLE 36:20
going: endure Their g. hence	SHAK 218:26
g. down of the sun	BINY 42:6
g. one knows not where	MAS 163:4
g. to and fro in the earth	BIBLE 25:17
knowing to what he was g.	HARDY 114:12
gold: bow of burning g.	BLAKE 43:2
bringing g.	BIBLE 25:3
buttercup Had blessed with g.	OWEN 179:8
clothing is of wrought g.	PRAY 189:2
fetch the age of g.	MILT 168:9
From the red g. keep thy	SCOTT 202:5
gleaming in purple and g.	BYRON 57:16
g., and frankincense	BIBLE 31:2
g. and silver becks me	SHAK 217:9
G. is for the mistress	KIPL 143:16
great deal of g.	JAMES 130:7
hearts of g. and lungs	BELL 19:1
If g. ruste	CHAU 68:6
Ionian white and g.	ELIOT 95:5
Nor all, that glisters, g.	GRAY 112:7
streets are paved with g.	COLM 76:3
To gild refined g.	SHAK 217:12
travell'd in the realms of g.	KEATS 140:3
us rarer gifts than g.	BROO 47:5
vine and grapes in g.	FLEC 100:10
with patines of bright g.	SHAK 226:5
golden: by the g. light of morn	HOOD 121:11
g. apples of the sun	YEATS 279:18
g. bowl be broken	BIBLE 27:22
g. days of Saturn's reign	VIRG 264:6
G. lads and girls all must	SHAK 206:4

G. opinions from all sorts | SHAK 221:2
G. Road to Samarkand | FLEC 100:8
G. slumbers kiss your eyes | DEKK 82:7
g. years return | SHEL 239:4
Someone who loves the g. mean | HOR 124:3
that there are no g. rules | SHAW 238:10
they did in the g. world | SHAK 204:13
Goldengrove: Over G. unleaving | HOPK 122:5
Goldsmith: Here lies Nolly G. | GARR 104:14
To Oliver G. | JOHN 133:2
one: all are g. | LAMB 148:4
been and g. and done | GILB 100.19
g. into the world of light | VAUG 261:15
g. to-morrow | BEHN 18:1
g. to the demnition bow-wows | DICK 85:4
g. up with a merry noise | PRAY 189:4
g. with the wind | DOWS 89:7
great spirit g. | SHAK 203:18
I have g. here and there | SHAK 236:11
not dead — but g. before | ROG 195:19
not the days that are g. | SOUT 244:1
She's g. for ever | SHAK 219:2
they are g. | KEATS 139:1
welcomest when they are g. | SHAK 214:7
what haste I can to be g. | CROM 80:20
ong: that g.-tormented sea | YEATS 278:12
ongs: g. groaning as the guns | CHES 70:1
struck regularly, like g. | COW 79:4
ood: any g. thing therefore | GREL 113:2
apprehension of the g. | SHAK 229:20
author and giver of all g. | PRAY 187:8
Be g., sweet maid | KING 142:9
g. can be g. in the country | WILDE 271:22
common g. to all | SHAK 217:6
cook was a g. cook | SAKI 199:6
country for our country's g. | CART 64:19
country was g. for General | WILS 272:14
do a g. action by stealth | LAMB 148:3
evil and on the g. | BIBLE 31:18
Evil be thou my G. | MILT 169:6
evil, that g. may come | BIBLE 37:32
filches from me my g. name | SHAK 228:27
Ghastly G. Taste | BETJ 21:15
God said that it was g. | BIBLE 22:4
G. Americans | APPL 7:11
g. and faithful servant | BIBLE 34:5
g. are so harsh | WORD 274:10
g. as thou art beautiful | TENN 251:18
g. deed in a naughty | SHAK 226:8
g. divine that follows | SHAK 224:14
g. dog, like a good candidate | BECK 17:6
g. ended happily | WILDE 271:10
G. hunting | KIPL 146:10
g. Indian is a dead Indian | SHER 240:13
g. in everything | SHAK 204:16
g. is oft interred with | SHAK 216:16
g. of the people is | CIC 72:6
g. opinion of a man who | TROL 260:8
g. people were clever | WORD 274:10
g. Shall come of water | BROO 47:8
g. that I would I do not | BIBLE 37:37
G. Thing | SELL 203:1
G. things of day begin | SHAK 222:15
g. to be out on the road | MAS 163:4
g. to them which hate you | BIBLE 35:7
g. will toward men | BIBLE 35:3
have never had it so g. | MACM 157:18
He wos wery g. to me | DICK 83:16
hold fast that which is g. | BIBLE 39:24

is the enemy of the g. | VOLT 264:18
is to be a g. animal | SPEN 244:5
is what I call g. company | AUST 12:8
I will be g. | VICT 262:7
likes that little g. | BUTL 56:17
must return g. for evil | VANB 261:12
nothing either g. or bad | SHAK 208:12
only g. thing left to me | MUSS 174:7
overcome evil with g. | BIBLE 38:3
policy of the g. neighbour | RONS 196:9
rather than to seem g. | SALL 199:10
them that call evil g. | BIBLE 28:11
Then the g. minute goes | BROW 50:23
There is so much g. | ANON 5:2
There's a g. time coming | MACK 157:12
they may see your g. works | BIBLE 31:14
things are of g. report | BIBLE 39:20
those who go about doing g. | CREI 80:12
we trust that somehow g. | TENN 252:15
what g. came of it | SOUT 243:18
When she was g. | LONG 153:20
while g. news baits | MILT 170:4
work for g. to them that love | BIBLE 37:38
yet don't look too g. | KIPL 144:7
goodbye: kissed his sad Andromache g. |
| CORN 78:6
goodly: g. to look | BIBLE 24:22
I have a g. heritage | PRAY 188:11
goodness: delusion that beauty is g. | TOLS 259:18
'G. had nothing to do with | WEST 269:1
goodnight: gay g. and quickly turn | YEATS 279:1
g., sweet ladies | SHAK 211:3
G., sweet prince | SHAK 212:1
say g. till it be morrow | SHAK 231:22
goods: desire other men's g. | PRAY 187:21
precious as the G. they sell | FITZ 99:12
worldly g. I thee endow | PRAY 188:1
goose: every g. a swan | KING 142:16
gott'st thou that g. look | SHAK 223:11
gorge: my g. rises at it | SHAK 211:11
gory: never shake Thy g. locks | SHAK 222:18
Welcome to your g. bed | BURNS 54:20
Gossip: G. is a sort of smoke that | ELIOT 92:16
Got: G. 'tween asleep and wake | SHAK 217:19
I've g. a little list | GILB 108:4
Gott: G. *ist tot* | NIET 176:16
G. *würfelt nicht* | EINS 92:14
Nun danket alle G. | RINK 195:7
Gottes: Krieg ein Glied in G. Weltordnung |
| MOLT 171:15
Gottesmühlen: G. mahlen langsam | LOGAU 152:15
gout: I say give them the g. | MONT 171:16
gouverne: règne et le peuple se g. | THIE 256:17
gouvernement: g. d'une famille que d'un |
| MONT 172:2
le g. qu'elle mérite | MAIS 159:3
Gouverner: G., c'est choisir | LEVIS 151:12
govern: He that would g. others | MASS 164:1
out and g. New South Wales | BELL 18:13
people g. themselves | THIE 256:17
such should g. | FLET 100:17
To g. is to make choices | LEVIS 151:12
governed: nation is not g. | BURKE 52:16
government: All g. is evil | OSUL 178:15
best g. is that which | OSUL 178:15
consequence of cabinet g. | BAG 14:6
country has the g. it deserves | MAIS 159:3
fainéant g. is not | TROL 260:9
fit for a nation whose g. | SMITH 242:1

g. shall be upon his shoulder BIBLE 28:19
How can the G. be carried WELL 268:10
important thing for G. KEYN 141:16
indispensable duty of g. PAINE 179:14
is no art which one g. SMITH 242:3
is the worst form of G. CHUR 71:13
Is this the g. of Britain's SHAK 214:10
rule nations by your g. VIRG 263:14
'That g. is best which THOR 258:16
Under a g. which imprisons THOR 259:1
governments: g. never have learned anything
HEGEL 116:11
G. need to have both shepherds VOLT 265:6
governs: government is that which g. least
OSUL 178:15
g. the passions and resolutions HUME 128:1
gowd: man's the g. for a' that BURNS 54:8
gown: loose g. from her shoulders WYATT 278:4
My g. of glory RAL 194:4
sail in amply billowing g. BELL 19:1
grace: Angels and ministers of g. SHAK 207:9
courtly foreign g. TENN 255:6
G. me no grace SHAK 230:4
g. of God there goes BRAD 45:16
grow old with a good g. STEE 245:13
heaven such g. did lend her SHAK 234:18
inward and spiritual g. PRAY 187:22
moments of glad g. YEATS 280:5
sweet attractive g. MILT 169:7
Take heart of g. GILB 108:30
Ye are fallen from g. BIBLE 39:8
Graces: that the G. do not seem CHES 69:11
gracious: Lord, for he is g. PRAY 190:23
Remembers me of all his g. SHAK 217:10
So hallow'd and so g. is SHAK 206:9
gradual: Was the g. day SPEN 244:12
gradualness: inevitability of g. WEBB 267:3
Graeca: Vos exemplaria G. HOR 122:19
Graeculus: G. esuriens JUV 137:18
grain: to a g. of mustard seed BIBLE 33:6
without one g. of sense DRYD 91:2
World in a G. of Sand BLAKE 42:17
gramina: redeunt iam g. campis HOR 124:15
grammar: g., and nonsense, and learning
GOLD 110:17
Heedless of g. BARH 15:13
posterity talking bad g. DISR 87:14
Grammatici: G. certant et adhuc sub HOR 122:13
Grammaticus: G., rhetor JUV 137:18
granary: sitting careless on a g. floor
KEATS 140:13
grand: these hoary woods are g. GALT 104:11
grandeur: charged with the g. of God HOPK 121:18
g. that was Rome POE 184:3
grandfather: having an ape for his g. HUXL 128:14
grandsire: Church your g. cut his throat
SWIFT 249:13
grange: at the moated g. SHAK 224:5
Upon the lonely moated g. TENN 253:18
granites: g. which titanic wars had OWEN 179:9
granting: hold thee but by thy g. SHAK 236:6
grants: no go the Government g. MACN 158:6
grape: g. who will the vine destroy SHAK 235:6
grapes: fathers have eaten sour g. BIBLE 30:4
g. of wrath are stored HOWE 127:9
men gather g. of thorns BIBLE 32:11
vine and g. in gold FLEC 100:10
grapeshot: whiff of g. CARL 61:12
Grapple: G. them to thy soul with SHAK 207:6

grasp: reach should exceed his g. BROW 48:2
grass: away suddenly like the g. PRAY 189:2
child said What is the g. WHIT 270:
eateth g. as an ox BIBLE 26:
From the heaps of couch g. HARDY 114:1
g. returns to the fields HOR 124:1
g. withereth BIBLE 40:1
happy as the g. was green THOM 257:
I am the g. SAND 199:1
I become paler than g. SAPP 199:1
I fall on g. MARV 161:1
isn't g. to graze a cow BETJ 21:1
know the g. beyond the door ROSS 197:
Of splendour in the g. WORD 275:1
snake hidden in the g. VIRG 264:
Star-scattered on the G. FITZ 100:
That g. is green STEP 246:
two blades of g. to grow SWIFT 248:1
grasses: presage the g.' fall MARV 161:1
Grate: G. on their scrannel pipes MILT 167:
gratifying: g. feeling that our duty GILB 107:
Gratuity: taking of a Bribe or G. PENN 182:
grave: Dig the g. and let me lie STEV 247:1
glory lead but to the g. GRAY 112:
g. is not its goal LONG 153:
g. Proves the child ephemeral AUDEN 11:
g.'s a fine and private MARV 161:2
G., thy victoree ANON 4:1
g., where is thy victory BIBLE 38:2
hairs with sorrow to the g. BIBLE 23:
her heart in his g. is MOORE 173:
In ev'ry g. make room DAV 81:1
is a kind of healthy g. SMITH 243:
is gone wild into his g. SHAK 213:
kingdom for a little g. SHAK 230:
like Alcestis from the g. MILT 170:1
pompous in the g. BROW 48:1
pot of honey on the g. MER 165:
receive no letters in the g. JOHN 134:
renowned be thy g. SHAK 206:
see myself go into my g. PEPYS 182:1
she is in her g. WORD 276:1
Thy victory, O G. ROSS 197:
When my g. is broke up DONNE 88:1
graves: g. of little magazines PRES 191:1
g. stood tenantless SHAK 206:
into their voluntarie g. HERB 118:1
Let's talk of g. SHAK 230:
ourselves dishonourable g. SHAK 215:1
they watch from their g. BROW 50:
gravy: Davy Abominated g. BENT 19:1
disliked g. all my life SMITH 242:1
gray: g. hairs with sorrow BIBLE 23:
Graymalkin: I come, G. SHAK 219:1
great: behind the g. possessions JAMES 130:
creatures g. and small ALEX 2:
g. deal of gold JAMES 130:
g. gulf fixed BIBLE 36:
G. is Diana of the Ephesians BIBLE 37:2
g. is to be misunderstood EMER 96:1
g. is truth BROO 47:1
g. spirit gone SHAK 203:1
g. things from the valley CHES 70:
g. was the fall of it BIBLE 32:1
heights by g. men reached LONG 153:
Hence no force however g. WHEW 269:1
his weaknesses are g. KIPL 143:
Lives of g. men all remind LONG 153:1
No g. man lives in vain CARL 61:1

Rightly to be g. SHAK 210:24
those who were truly g. SPEN 244:10
thou wouldst be g. SHAK 220:10
Great Britain: seem to be natives of G. CHES 69:11
greater: g. cats with golden eyes SACK 199:1
G. love hath no man BIBLE 37:3
g. than a private citizen TAC 250:11
that we are g. than we know WORD 276:13
greatest: g. event it is that ever FOX 102:3
g. of these is charity BIBLE 38:16
g. pains to human nature BAG 14:9
g. thing in the world is MONT 172:3
happiness of the g. number BENT 19:14
Great-hearted: G. gentlemen BROW 49:6
greatness: farewell, to all my g. SHAK 215:9
having intended g. for men ELIOT 93:4
some have g. thrust upon SHAK 234:6
Greece: G. a tear BYRON 58:9
I dream'd that G. might BYRON 58:7
isles of G. BYRON 58:6
To the glory that was G. POE 184:3
greedy: not g. of filthy lucre BIBLE 39:27
Greek: G. can do everything JUV 137:18
it was G. to me SHAK 216:2
small Latin, and less G. JONS 136:6
That questioned him in G. CARR 62:11
upon the study of G. GAIS 104:6
your G. exemplars by night HOR 122:19
Greeks: G. a blush BYRON 58:9
I fear the G. even when VIRG 263:3
When G. joined Greeks LEE 151:4
green: blue or the shore-sea g. FLEC 100:10
children are heard on the g. BLAKE 43:16
Colourless g. ideas CHOM 70:16
England's g. & pleasant Land BLAKE 43:2
feed me in a g. pasture PRAY 188:15
force that through the g. fuse THOM 257:4
g. days in forests STEV 247:12
G. I love you green GARC 104:13
g. thought in a green shade MARV 161:16
In the morning it is g. PRAY 189:21
Making the g. one red SHAK 222:1
not quite so g. KIPL 146:20
Time held me g. and dying THOM 257:3
wearin' o' the G. ANON 3:20
When I was g. in judgment SHAK 203:20
when the trees were g. CLARE 72:17
greenery-yallery: g., Grosvenor Galley GILB 108:23
green-ey'd: g. monster which doth mock SHAK 229:1
greenness: Could have recovered g. HERB 118:10
greens: plain water and raw g. AUDEN 11:12
greenwood: Under the g. tree SHAK 204:19
gregarious: It is rather a g. instinct FROST 103:12
Greise: Ward mancher Kopf zum G. MULL 174:6
grene: In a harbour g. aslepe WEVER 269:7
Grenville: Azores Sir Richard G. lay TENN 255:3
grew: So we g. together SHAK 227:11
Grex: G. rather than sex FROST 103:12
grey: head grown g. in vain SHEL 238:26
lend me your g. mare BALL 15:6
wither'd cheek and tresses g. SCOTT 201:15
world has grown g. from SWIN 250:3
greyhounds: stand like g. in the slips SHAK 213:15
grief: acquainted with g. BIBLE 29:14
are quickened so with g. GRAV 111:14
Can I see another's g. BLAKE 43:20
G. fills the room up SHAK 217:10

Pitched past pitch of g. HOPK 122:1
plague of sighing and g. SHAK 212:12
Smiling at g. SHAK 234:4
son of g. at cricket HOUS 125:9
Thus g. still treads upon CONG 76:20
time remembered is g. forgotten SWIN 249:16
Was there g. once NICH 176:11
griefs: Surely he hath borne our g. BIBLE 29:14
grieve: what could it g. KEATS 140:2
grieving: are you g. HOPK 122:5
grievous: through my most g. fault MASS 163:9
grim ending with the g. CARR 63:1
grind: g. the faces of the poor BIBLE 28:8
mills of God g. slowly LOGAU 152:15
grinning: to mock your own g. SHAK 211:11
Grishkin: G. is nice ELIOT 95:9
groan: Condemn'd alike to g. GRAY 112:11
hear each other g. KEATS 139:19
Grocer: God made the wicked G. CHES 70:7
grooms: gild the faces of the g. SHAK 221:18
grooves: In predestinate g. HARE 115:7
ringing g. of change TENN 253:13
gros: g. escadrons contre les BUSS 56:1
gross: lust is g. and brief PETR 183:3
things rank and g. in nature SHAK 206:15
grossen: Volkes...einer g. Lüge HITL 119:13
Grosvenor Galley: greenery-yallery, G. GILB 108:23
grotesque: At so g. a blunder BENT 19:21
from the g. to the horrible DOYLE 89:22
ground: commit his body to the g. PRAY 188:5
fallen unto me in a fair g. PRAY 188:11
five miles of fertile g. COL 75:2
having so little g. SCOTT 202:12
In a fair g. KIPL 145:18
let us sit upon the g. SHAK 230:8
lose to-morrow the g. won ARN 8:21
stirrup and the g. CAMD 60:8
thou standest is holy g. BIBLE 23:10
groves: truth in the g. of Academe HOR 123:7
grow'd: short laugh...'I 'spect I g. STOWE 247:19
growl: sit and g. JOHN 133:21
grown: When we are g. and take KIPL 143:15
grows: Nothing g. in our garden THOM 257:12
grub: old ones, g. SHAW 237:8
grudge: feed fat the ancient g. SHAK 224:19
gruel: Make the g. thick and slab SHAK 222:23
grumble: we g. a little now GOLD 110:22
Grundy: What will Mrs G. think MORT 174:3
gruntled: he was far from being g. WOD 273:12
guard: marrying one of the g. MILNE 166:11
They're changing g. MILNE 166:11
use its g. staying awake BIBLE 41:15
guardian: constitutional g. GILB 107:13
Guards: G. die but do not surrender CAMB 60:5
Lord g. the city BIBLE 41:15
to guard the g. JUV 137:21
Up G. and at them again WELL 268:13
gudeman: When our g.'s awa' ANON 5:3
guerdon: fair g. when we hope MILT 167:20
guerre: mais ce n'est pas la g. BOSQ 45:1
guessing: 'g. what was at the other WELL 267:22
guest: receive an honoured g. AUDEN 10:17
speed the going g. POPE 185:21
guests: Unbidden g. SHAK 214:7
guide: g. our feet into the way BIBLE 34:30
g., philosopher, and friend POPE 185:19
Have God to be his g. BUNY 51:26
Who art a light to g. WORD 276:1

h. on his shoulder smote	NEWB 175:15	Your little h. were made	BELL 18:3
h. that rocks the cradle	WALL 265:11	**handsaw:** I know a hawk from a h.	SHAK 208:16
h. that signed the paper	THOM 257:5	**handsome:** my h. young man	BALL 14:17
h. will be against every	BIBLE 22:24	**handy-work:** firmament sheweth his h.	
Heaving up my either h.	HERR 119:2		PRAY 188:12
Her h. on her bosom	SHAK 229:9	**hang:** Go h. thyself in thine	SHAK 212:8
him with his skinny h.	COL 74:6	h. and brush their bosoms	BROW 50:22
His mind and h. went together	HEM 117:4	h. a pearl in every cowslip's	SHAK 226:17
I fear thy skinny h.	COL 74:13	H. it all, Robert Browning	POUND 186:7
immortal h. or eye	BLAKE 43:7	h. your hat on a pension	MACN 158:6
I put my h. into the bed	SHAK 213:13	H. your husband and be	GAY 105:10
it will go into his h.	BIBLE 25:14	H. yourself	HENR 117:12
kingdom of heaven is at h.	BIBLE 31:3	Here they h. a man first	MOL 171:12
left h. is under my head	BIBLE 27:28	man as O'Connell is to h.	SMITH 243:1
let me kiss that h.	SHAK 218:21	must indeed all h. together	FRAN 102:12
let not thy left h. know	BIBLE 31:20	shall all h. separately	FRAN 102:12
lily in your medieval h.	GILB 108:21	she would h. on him	SHAK 206:15
man's h. is not able	SHAK 227:16	**hang'd:** my poor fool is h.	SHAK 219:4
On this side my h.	SHAK 230:11	**hanged:** h. for stealing horses	HALE 114:3
onward lend thy guiding h.	MILT 169:24	h. with the Bible under	AUBR 10:4
right h. forget her cunning	PRAY 191:1	harps, we h. them up	PRAY 191:1
Sword sleep in my h.	BLAKE 43:2	If I were h. on the highest	KIPL 145:5
Then join hand in h.	DICK 86:7	to be h. in a fortnight	JOHN 133:4
there's a h.	BURNS 53:23	**hangin:** they're h.' men an' women	ANON 3:20
touch of a vanish'd h.	TENN 251:5	they're h. Danny Deever	KIPL 143:17
unto you with mine own h.	BIBLE 39:10	**Hanging:** H. is too good for him	BUNY 51:20
was the h. that wrote it	CRAN 80:6	h.-look to me	CONG 76:14
were a glove upon that h.	SHAK 231:17	H. of his cat on Monday	BRAT 46:7
Whatsoever thy h. findeth to do	BIBLE 27:15	h. prevents a bad marriage	SHAK 233:18
whose h. is ever at his	KEATS 139:17	That's cured by h. from	KING 143:4
Your h., your tongue	SHAK 220:12	**hangman:** naked to the h.'s noose	HOUS 125:6
handbook: it was a constable's h.	KING 142:17	**hangs:** that h. on princes' favours	SHAK 215:9
Handel: Compar'd to H.'s a mere	BYROM 57:1	thereby h. a tale	SHAK 204:22
handful: fear in a h. of dust	ELIOT 94:19	What h. people…is the unfortunate	STEV 247:5
handkerchief: feels like a damp h.	MACK 157:13	**hank:** rag and a bone and a h.	KIPL 146:4
handle: I polished up the h.	GILB 108:28	**Hanover:** By famous H. city	BROW 50:9
One old jug without a h.	LEAR 150:7	**happen:** h. to somebody else	MARQ 161:4
to h. honesty and truth	SHAW 237:22	poetry makes nothing h.	AUDEN 10:16
handles: hath two h.	BURT 55:16	**happens:** dependent on what h. to her	ELIOT 93:2
handmaiden: low estate of his h.	BIBLE 34:28	h. anywhere	LARK 149:5
hands: accept refreshment at any h.	GILB 108:3	**happier:** is remembering h. things	TENN 253:9
Before rude h. have touch'd	JONS 136:9	that I am h. than I know	MILT 169:16
clap your h.	BARR 16:5	That Pobbles are h. without	LEAR 150:20
crag with crooked h.	TENN 251:13	**happiest:** h. time of all the glad	TENN 254:3
folding of the h. to sleep	BIBLE 26:9	record of the best and h.	SHEL 240:11
h., and handle not	PRAY 190:13	**happily:** h. upon a plentiful fortune	JOHN 131:22
h. are the hands of Esau	BIBLE 22:30	**happiness:** away you take away his h.	IBSEN 129:10
h. from picking and stealing	PRAY 187:20	H. consists in the multiplicity	JOHN 132:9
h. I commend my spirit	BIBLE 36:11	h. for the greatest numbers	HUTC 128:11
h. of the living God	BIBLE 40:7	h. of the greatest number	BENT 19:14
h. that hold the aces which	BETJ 20:11	h. of the human race	BURKE 52:18
hath not a Jew h.	SHAK 225:10	In my great task of h.	STEV 247:17
house not made with h.	BIBLE 39:3	lifetime of h.	SHAW 237:24
house not made with h.	BROW 49:4	pursuit of h.	JEFF 130:9
into the h. of the Lord	BIBLE 30:21	recall a time of h. in misery	DANTE 81:10
I warmed both h. before	LAND 148:8	recipe for h. I ever heard	AUST 12:3
Let us hold h. and look	BETJ 21:3	result h.	DICK 84:1
Licence my roving h.	DONNE 87:25	secret of h. is to admire	BRAD 45:17
Lift not thy h. to *It*	FITZ 99:10	so great my h.	YEATS 280:4
not into the h. of Spain	TENN 255:5	so much h. is produced	JOHN 132:25
Pale h. I loved	HOPE 121:16	***happy:*** *Are you all h. now*	LAND 148:9
plunge your h. in water	AUDEN 10:10	Be h. while y'er leevin	ANON 3:7
right h. of fellowship	BIBLE 39:7	Call no man h.	SOLON 243:12
some mischief still for h.	MADAN 158:11	h. as the grass was green	THOM 257:2
their h. are blue	LEAR 150:11	h. could I be with either	GAY 105:14
these h. ne'er be clean	SHAK 223:7	h. families resemble one	TOLS 259:17
they reached out their h.	VIRG 263:14	H. he who like Ulysses	DU B 91:15
violent h. upon themselves	PRAY 188:3	h. issue out of all their	PRAY 187:5
Wash your h.	SHAK 223:9	H. is that city which	ANON 3:13

H. is the man who fears	BIBLE 41:13
H. is the man that hath	PRAY 190:20
h. is the rose distill'd	SHAK 226:12
h. low, lie down	SHAK 212:27
h. noise to hear	HOUS 125:12
H. the people whose annals	CARL 61:11
H. those early days	VAUG 261:14
He's h. who, far away	HOR 123:9
How h. is he born and taught	WOTT 277:15
make a h. fire-side clime	BURNS 55:3
making of an old woman h.	FRAN 102:10
myself in nothing else so h.	SHAK 230:3
should all be as h. as kings	STEV 247:9
This h. breed	SHAK 230:2
Thrice h. he who	MARV 162:2
'Twere now to be most h.	SHAK 228:21
who so h.	LEAR 150:9
world of the h. is quite	WITT 273:9
Happy Isles: be we shall touch the H.	TENN 255:15
harbour: h. grene aslepe whereas	WEVER 269:7
Hard: H. pounding this	WELL 268:7
'H.,' replied the Dodger	DICK 85:7
harder: h. they fall	FITZ 100:5
they would be h. to them	TROL 260:3
hard-faced: lot of h. men who look	BALD 14:13
hardly: He's h. ever sick at sea	GILB 108:26
Hardy: Kiss me, H.	NELS 175:9
hare: h. limp'd trembling through	KEATS 138:16
it look'd like h.	BARH 15:9
lion than to start a h.	SHAK 212:6
Take your h. when it is	GLAS 109:17
hares: little hunted h.	HODG 120:4
harlot: h.'s cry from street	BLAKE 42:19
prerogative of the h. throughout	KIPL 146:29
HARLOTS: MOTHER OF H. AND ABOMI-NATIONS	BIBLE 41:5
harm: I fear we'll come to h.	BALL 15:3
No people do so much h.	CREI 80:12
prevent h. to others	MILL 165:15
Shall h. Macbeth	SHAK 222:26
harmless: Elephant, The only h.	DONNE 88:12
h. as doves	BIBLE 32:24
h. necessary cat	SHAK 225:15
harmonious: Such h. madness	SHEL 240:5
harmony: from heavenly h.	DRYD 91:9
h. is in immortal souls	SHAK 226:5
touches of sweet h.	SHAK 226:5
with your ninefold h.	MILT 168:8
harness: between the joints of the h.	BIBLE 25:9
hear the h. jingle	HOUS 126:2
To wait in heavy h.	KIPL 146:7
Harp: H. not on that string	SHAK 231:7
h. that once through Tara's	MOORE 172:14
his wild h. slung behind	MOORE 172:16
harps: h., we hanged them up	PRAY 191:1
Harris: 'Bother Mrs H.	DICK 84:17
Harrow: H. the house of the dead	AUDEN 11:5
toad beneath the h. knows	KIPL 145:8
Harry: Cry 'God for H.	SHAK 213:15
H., Harry	SHAK 213:3
little touch of H.	SHAK 213:7
hart: h. desireth the water-brooks	PRAY 189:1
pants the h. for cooling	TATE 250:15
harvest: h. of a quiet eye	WORD 276:6
harvests: Deep h. bury all his pride	POPE 185:4
Harwich: about in a steamer from H.	GILB 107:21
has: 'one of the h. beens	HONE 121:3
hasard: de l'observation le h.	PAST 181:5
hässlich: Welt h. und schlecht	NIET 176:18

haste: h., persuade	WHIT 270:8
I h. me to my bed	SHAK 235:10
I said in my h.	PRAY 190:14
Make h. slowly	SUET 248:7
what h. I can to be gone	CROM 80:20
ye shall eat it in h.	BIBLE 23:15
You h. away so soon	HERR 118:22
hasty: man in his h. days	BRID 46:11
hat: Antichrist in that lewd h.	JONS 135:17
away with a h. like that	LOOS 154:1
hang your h. on a pension	MACN 158:6
himself in a shocking bad h.	SURT 248:14
looking for a black h.	BOWEN 45:10
hatch'd: new-h., unfledg'd comrade	SHAK 207:6
hatches: is continually under h.	KEATS 141:2
hatchet: did it with my little h.	WASH 266:13
hate: cherish those hearts that h.	SHAK 215:10
do good to them which h.	BIBLE 35:7
h. all Boets and Bainters	GEOR 106:1
h. and detest that animal	SWIFT 249:4
h. any one that we know	HAZL 116:7
h. him for he is a Christian	SHAK 224:18
h. the idle pleasures	SHAK 231:3
I h. and I love	CAT 65:11
I h. the unholy masses	HOR 124:5
Let them h.	ACC 1:1
Of a pure impartial h.	THOR 259:11
sprung from my only h.	SHAK 231:15
time to h.	BIBLE 27:7
hated: being h., don't give way	KIPL 144:7
hates: h. dogs and babies	ROST 197:12
hateth: h. his brother	BIBLE 40:27
rod h. his son	BIBLE 26:18
hath: one that h. shall be given	BIBLE 34:6
hating: don't give way to h.	KIPL 144:7
special reason for h. school	BEER 17:15
hatless: young man lands h.	BETJ 20:10
hatred: from envy, h., and malice	PRAY 187:3
h. for the Tory Party	BEVAN 21:16
h. or bitterness towards	CAV 65:13
like love to h. turn'd	CONG 76:19
stalled ox and h.	BIBLE 26:21
hats: so many shocking bad h.	WELL 268:2
haughty: h. spirit before a fall	BIBLE 26:22
haunt: h. of flies on summer eves	KEATS 139:21
haunts: h. of coot and hern	TENN 251:6
mothers and fathers that h. us	IBSEN 129:6
have: because other folks h.	FIEL 98:7
h. and to hold from this	PRAY 187:28
I h. thee not	SHAK 221:10
long as you h. your life	JAMES 130:2
trouble for till I h. it	SELD 202:20
have-his-carcase: h., next to the perpetual	DICK 85:26
haven: their h. under the hill	TENN 251:5
have-nots: haves and the h.	CERV 66:7
haves: h. and the have-nots	CERV 66:7
Havoc: Cry, 'H.!'	SHAK 216:12
hawk: know a h. from a handsaw	SHAK 208:16
hawks: h. favoured an air strike	BART 16:8
hay: dance an antic h.	MARL 160:9
he: 'Because it was h.	MONT 172:1
H. that hath wife and children	BACON 13:11
poorest is h. that is in England	RAIN 194:1
head: bear with a sore h.	MARR 161:5
begins a journey in my h.	SHAK 235:10
bowed his comely h.	MARV 161:18
dawn many a h. has turned white	MULL 174:6
God be in my h.	ANON 3:12

h. could carry all he knew	GOLD 110:11
h. is as full of quarrels	SHAK 231:26
H. of a traveller	HOUS 127:3
heart or in the h.	SHAK 225:12
her h. on her knee	SHAK 229:9
If you can keep your h.	KIPL 144:7
incessantly stand on your h.	CARR 62:18
Lay your sleeping h.	AUDEN 11:3
left hand is under my h.	BIBLE 27:28
My h. is bloody	HENL 117:6
never broke any man's h	SHAK 213:16
not where to lay his h.	BIBLE 32:16
Off with his h.	CIBB 72:2
out of King Charles's h.	DICK 84:3
repairs his drooping h.	MILT 168:2
shake of his poor little h.	GILB 108:18
Stamps o'er his H.	FITZ 98:18
Thou wilt show my h.	DANT 81:12
Uneasy lies the h. that	SHAK 212:27
which binds so dear a h.	SHEL 238:24
your h. are all numbered	BIBLE 32:26
headache: awake with a dismal h.	GILB 107:20
head-in-air: Johnny h.	PUDN 192:10
Headpiece: H. filled with straw	ELIOT 93:22
heads: had ever very empty h.	BACON 12:21
Lift up your h.	PRAY 188:18
Their h. are green	LEAR 150:11
head-stone: become the h. in the corner	PRAY 190:15
headstrong: She's as h. as an allegory	SHER 240:20
head-waiter: plump h. at the Cock	TENN 255:19
heal: h. me of my grievous wound	TENN 252:8
healed: with his stripes we are h.	BIBLE 29:15
healer: It is not a great h.	COMP 76:8
sharp compassion of the h.'s	ELIOT 93:17
healing: no h. has been necessary	COMP 76:8
health: h. and wealth have missed	HUNT 128:5
he that will this h. deny	DYER 92:5
in sickness and in h.	PRAY 187:28
Look to your h.	WALT 266:10
there is no h. in us	PRAY 186:19
thy saving h. among all	PRAY 189:12
heap: h. of all your winnings	KIPL 144:8
was struck all of a h.	SHER 240:17
hear: at my back I always h.	MARV 161:21
can h. my Thisby's face	SHAK 227:22
child may joy to h.	BLAKE 43:13
h. it in the deep heart's	YEATS 278:14
H., O Israel	BIBLE 23:30
He cannot choose but h.	COL 74:6
He that hath ears to h.	BIBLE 34:22
houses h. clocks ticking	BETJ 20:10
I h. you	HOUS 125:13
in such wise h. them read	PRAY 187:7
music that I care to h.	HOPK 121:19
They never would h.	SWIFT 249:9
we shall h. it	BROW 48:19
you will h. me	DISR 86:12
heard: Enough that he h. it once	BROW 48:19
H. melodies are sweet	KEATS 139:13
I will be h.	GARR 104:16
then is h. no more	SHAK 223:15
You ain't h. nothin' yet	JOLS 135:13
hearers: edification of the h.	BURKE 52:8
too deep for his h.	GOLD 110:16
heareth: thy servant h.	BIBLE 24:15
hears: She neither h. nor sees	WORD 276:17
hearse: Underneath this sable h.	BROW 48:14
hearses: frequent h. shall besiege	POPE 184:12
heart: after Heaven's own h.	DRYD 90:10
Batter my h.	DONNE 88:6
Blessed are the pure in h.	BIBLE 31:11
brains in my head and the h.	HOUS 127:1
Bury my h. at Wounded Knee	BENET 19:12
Calais' lying in my h.	MARY 162:12
calm sunshine of the h.	CONS 77:15
can no longer tear his h.	SWIFT 249:14
Dear h. how like you	WYATT 278:4
education of the h.	SCOTT 202:14
God be in my h.	ANON 3:12
hear it in the deep h.'s	YEATS 279:8
h. and my flesh rejoice	PRAY 189:17
h. and stomach of a king	ELIZ 95:19
h. and voice would fail	CLAR 73:1
h. as sound as a bell	SHAK 228:10
h. has felt the tender	GAY 105:16
h. has its reasons which	PASC 181:2
h.—how shall I say	BROW 50:5
h. in his grave is lying	MOORE 173:1
h. is deceitful above all	BIBLE 29:27
h. is Highland	GALT 104:11
h. is like a singing bird	ROSS 197:3
h. is sick	TENN 252:14
h. of a man is deprest	GAY 105:12
h. of lead	POPE 184:7
h. the keener	ANON 5:7
he tears out the h.	KNOW 147:3
humble and a contrite h.	KIPL 145:10
I am sick at h.	SHAK 206:6
I feel my h. new open'd	SHAK 215:9
If thy h. fails thee	ELIZ 95:17
I had lock'd my h.	BALL 15:5
in the h. or in the head	SHAK 225:12
I said to H.	BELL 18:19
is the darling of my h.	CAREY 61:4
look in thy h. and write	SIDN 241:3
make a stone of the h.	YEATS 278:20
Makes my h. go pit-a-pat	BROW 50:10
makes the h. grow fonder	ANON 2:12
man after his own h.	BIBLE 24:19
Mercy has a human h.	BLAKE 43:19
merry h. maketh a cheerful	BIBLE 26:20
mighty h. is lying still	WORD 276:19
moving Toyshop of their h.	POPE 185:24
My h. aches	KEATS 139:18
My h. in hiding	HOPK 122:10
My h. is heavy	GOE 109:23
My h. leaps up when I behold	WORD 275:11
My h.'s in the Highlands	BURNS 54:16
My h. would hear her	TENN 254:2
nearer to the H.'s Desire	FITZ 99:13
nor his h. to report	SHAK 227:16
not your h. be troubled	BIBLE 36:36
not your h. away	HOUS 125:7
rag-and-bone shop of the h.	YEATS 278:14
rebuke hath broken my h.	PRAY 189:14
Shakespeare unlocked his h.'	BROW 49:14
since man's h. is small	KIPL 145:18
softer pillow than my h.	BYRON 59:4
some h. did break	TENN 252:11
So the h. be right	RAL 194:8
Sweeping up the H.	DICK 86:2
Take h. of grace	GILB 108:30
Taming my wild h. to thy	SHAK 228:9
that had the lion's h.	CHUR 71:15
That the h. grows old	YEATS 279:17
then burst his mighty h.	SHAK 216:20
there will your h. be also	BIBLE 31:23

thought my shrivel'd h.	HERB 118:10
thy beak from out my h.	POE 184:2
thy h. lies open	TENN 254:15
thy wine with a merry h.	BIBLE 27:14
tiger's h. wrapp'd	SHAK 215:3
to get your h.'s desire	SHAW 238:9
twist the sinews of thy h.	BLAKE 43:8
warmth about my h. like a load	KEATS 141:4
wear him In my h.'s core	SHAK 209:9
wear my h. upon my sleeve	SHAK 228:14
With a h. for any fate	LONG 153:11
With your crooked h.	AUDEN 10:11
your h. to a dog to tear	KIPL 145:9
heart-ache: sleep to say we end The h.	
	SHAK 208:24
heart-break: h. in the heart of things	GIBS 106:15
hearth: By this still h.	TENN 255:10
Save the cricket on the h.	MILT 167:13
hearth-fire: h. and the home-acre	KIPL 144:6
heartily: h. rejoice in the strength	PRAY 190:2
hearts: first in the h. of his	LEE 151:3
h. and intellects like	MILL 166:2
h. are more than coronets	TENN 253:2
H. just as pure and fair	GILB 107:14
h. of gold and lungs	BELL 19:1
H. that have lost their	HOUS 126:22
h., that once beat high	MOORE 172:14
hidden in each other's h.	DICK 84:15
is enthroned in the h.	SHAK 225:17
keep your h. and minds	BIBLE 39:19
sleepless children's h. are glad	BETJ 20:7
stout h. and sharp swords	BIRK 42:9
thousand h. beat happily	BYRON 57:9
Two h. that beat as one	HALM 114:5
heat: burden and h. of the day	BIBLE 33:25
Fear no more the h. o'	SHAK 206:4
Lap your loneliness in h.	BETJ 20:6
not without dust and h.	MILT 170:17
white h. of this revolution	WILS 272:16
you can't stand the h.	TRUM 260:19
heated: When h. in the chase	TATE 250:15
heath: likewise a wind on the h.	BORR 44:22
Upon the h.	SHAK 219:16
Upon this blasted h. you	SHAK 220:5
heathen: Guard even h. things	CHES 69:21
h. in his blindness	HEBER 116:10
h. so furiously rage	PRAY 188:6
heaths: some game on these lone h.	HAZL 116:5
heaven: art thou fallen from h.	BIBLE 28:23
become the hoped-for h.	MILL 166:2
be hell that are not h.	MARL 160:4
betwixt H. and Charing Cross	THOM 258:7
created the h. and the earth	BIBLE 22:1
earth breaks up and h.	BROW 49:4
eye of h. to garnish	SHAK 217:12
Father which art in h.	BIBLE 31:21
Give the jolly h. above	STEV 247:11
God's in his h.	BROW 50:12
have sinned against h.	BIBLE 35:27
h. above me and the moral	KANT 138:6
H. and earth shall pass	BIBLE 34:3
H. and Earth are not ruthful	LAO 149:4
h. by sea as by land	GILB 106:17
H. in a Wild Flower	BLAKE 42:17
H. in Hell's despair	BLAKE 43:10
H. lies about us in our	WORD 275:15
h. peep through the blanket	SHAK 220:11
H.'s light forever shines	SHEL 239:1
h.'s vaults should crack	SHAK 219:2

H. take my soul	SHAK 217:14
h. will help you	LA F 147:1
hot the eye of h.	SHAK 235:9
how the floor of h.	SHAK 226:2
I cannot go to h.	NORF 177:9
kingdom of h. is at hand	BIBLE 31:6
met my dearest foe in h.	SHAK 207:2
my thirtieth year to h.	THOM 257:9
new h. and a new earth	BIBLE 41:1
new h., new earth	SHAK 203:17
open face of h.	KEATS 140:1
Parting is all we know of h.	DICK 86:3
Puts all H. in a Rage	BLAKE 42:18
shalt have treasure in h.	BIBLE 33:21
sings hymns at h.'s gate	SHAK 235:11
steep and thorny way to h.	SHAK 207:5
summons thee to h. or to hell	SHAK 221:11
theirs is the kingdom of h.	BIBLE 31:11
there was silence in h.	BIBLE 40:34
things are the sons of h.	JOHN 134:15
to be young was very h.	WORD 274:17
top of it reached to h.	BIBLE 22:32
trouble deaf h. with my	SHAK 235:11
'Twould ring the bells of H.	HODG 120:4
under an English h.	BROO 47:16
waitest for the spark from h.	ARN 8:21
We are all going to H.	GAIN 104:5
what's a h.	BROW 48:21
yourselves treasures in h.	BIBLE 31:22
heavens: create new h. and a new earth	
	BIBLE 29:23
h. declare the glory	PRAY 188:12
h. fill with commerce	TENN 253:10
promise h. free from strife	CORY 78:13
heaviness: h. may endure for a night	PRAY 188:21
I am full of h.	PRAY 189:14
is the h. of his mother	BIBLE 26:12
melody, in our h.	PRAY 191:1
Heav'n: H. has no rage	CONG 76:19
H.'s great lamps do dive	CAT 65:5
than serve in h.	MILT 168:15
heavy: not of the h. batallions	VOLT 265:7
he-bear: Himalayan peasant meets the h.	
	KIPL 143:20
Hebrides: in dreams behold the H.	GALT 104:11
Hector: ago H. took off his plume	CORN 78:6
greatly changed from that H.	VIRG 263:4
Hecuba: What's H. to him or he	SHAK 208:20
hedge: divinity doth h. a king	SHAK 211:5
hedgehog: h. one *big* one	ARCH 7:17
hedge-hogs: Thorny h.	SHAK 227:6
hedges: with filigree h.	WALP 265:16
heed: lesson you should h.	HICK 119:7
Heedless: H. of grammar	BARH 15:13
heels: upon the h. of pleasure	CONG 76:20
height: there on that sad h.	THOM 257:1
What pleasure lives in h.	TENN 255:1
heightening: June for beauty's h.	ARN 9:3
heights: h. by great men reached	LONG 153:6
heir-apparent: in thine own h. garters	SHAK 212:8
held: h. the human race in scorn	BELL 18:8
Helden: Land, das H. nötig hat	BREC 46:9
Helen: Dust hath closed H.'s eye	NASHE 175:2
H., thy beauty is to me	POE 184:3
Past ruin'd Ilion H. lives	LAND 148:10
hell: all h. broke loose	MILT 169:11
all we need of h.	DICK 86:3
be h. that are not heaven	MARL 160:4
bells of H. go ting-a-ling-a-ling	ANON 4:12

Better to reign in h.	MILT 168:15
come hot from h.	SHAK 216:12
dunnest smoke of h.	SHAK 220:11
gates of h. shall not prevail	BIBLE 33:12
Heaven in H.'s despair	BLAKE 43:10
h. for horses	BURT 55:19
H. hath no limits nor is	MARL 160:4
H. is full of musical amateurs	SHAW 238:7
H. is murky	SHAK 223:6
h. of a good universe	CUMM 81:3
h. of horses	FLOR 101:4
Into the mouth of H.	TENN 251:10
it would be h. on earth	SHAW 237:24
Nor H. a fury	CONG 76:19
printing house in H.	BLAKE 44:8
That riches grow in h.	MILT 168:18
thee to heaven or to h.	SHAK 221:11
where we are is H.	MARL 160:4
Why this is h.	MARL 160:3
with h. are we at agreement	BIBLE 29:2
Hell-fires: dreamin' H. to see	KIPL 144:15
Hellish: H. dark	SURT 248:13
help: cannot h. nor pardon	AUDEN 11:11
from whence cometh my h.	PRAY 190:16
heaven will h. you	LA F 147:11
h. a lame dog over a stile	CHIL 70:15
H. of the helpless	LYTE 156:2
h. those we love to escape	HUGEL 127:13
H. thou mine unbelief	BUTL 56:18
hour that requires such h.	VIRG 263:6
make him an h. meet for him	BIBLE 22:8
place where h. wasn't hired	ANON 3:14
present h. in time of trouble	ANON 3:3
Since there's no h.	DRAY 90:6
there is no h. in them	PRAY 191:5
very present h. in trouble	PRAY 189:3
your countrymen cannot h.	JOHN 131:16
Helping: H., when we meet them	KING 142:10
helpless: Help of the h.	LYTE 156:2
hemlock: though of h. I had drunk	KEATS 139:18
hen: h. is only an egg's way	BUTL 56:14
Hence: H., loathed Melancholy	MILT 167:14
H., vain deluding joys	MILT 167:10
Henry King: chief defect of H.	BELL 18:9
Heraclitus: Sage H. says	POUND 186:9
Heraclitus: H., they told me you were	CORY 78:12
heraldry: boast of h.	GRAY 112:3
herb: h. of grace o' Sundays	SHAK 211:7
herbe: et l'h. qui verdoye	PERR 182:16
herbs: dinner of h. where love	BIBLE 26:21
have it for a garden of h.	BIBLE 25:7
h., and other country	MILT 167:18
Hercules: Than I to H.	SHAK 206:15
herd: elevates above the vulgar h.	GAIS 104:6
lowing h. wind slowly o'er	GRAY 111:18
Herden-Instinkt: Moralität ist H. in Einzelnen	
	NIET 176:17
herd-instinct: Morality is the h.	NIET 176:17
Here: H. am I; send me	BIBLE 28:14
H., a sheer hulk	DIBD 83:9
H.'s a how-de-doo	GILB 108:10
H.'s tae us	ANON 3:15
H.'s to the widow of fifty	SHER 240:25
H. we go round the prickly	ELIOT 93:23
Lafayette, we are h.	STAN 245:12
we are h. to-day	BEHN 18:1
Why are you not h.	THOR 259:10
hereafter: h. for ever hold his peace	PRAY 187:26
She should have died h.	SHAK 223:15

world may talk of h.	COLL 75:18
hereditas: Damnosa h.	GAIUS 104:8
heresies: begin as h. and to end as superstitions	
	HUXL 128:13
heritage: I have a goodly h.	PRAY 188:11
hermit: grievous torment than a h.'s	KEATS 139:8
hermitage: gorgeous palace for a h.	SHAK 230:9
That for an h.	LOV 154:9
hern: haunts of coot and h.	TENN 251:6
hero: conquering h. comes	MOR 173:8
man is a h. to his valet	CORN 78:9
Soldiers who wish to be a h.	ROST 197:13
very valet seem'd a h.	BYRON 57:3
Herod: it out-herods H.	SHAK 209:7
heroes: Britain a fit country for h.	GEOR 105:25
frightened both the h. so	CARR 63:21
h. up the line to death	SASS 200:4
land that needs h.	BREC 46:9
heroic: finish'd A life h.	MILT 170:5
h. for earth too hard	BROW 48:19
heroine: h. goes mad she always	SHER 240:16
heron: h. Priested shore	THOM 257:6
héros: h. pour son valet de chambre	CORN 78:9
Herren-Moral: H. und Sklaven-Moral	NIET 177:2
herring: plague o' these pickle h.	SHAK 233:3
herte: tikleth me aboute myn h. roote	CHAU 68:18
Herz: Mein H. ist schwer	GOE 109:23
Herzen: Zwei H. und ein Schlag	HALM 114:5
hesitate: h. and falter life away	ARN 8:21
hésite: elle h.	RAC 193:16
Hesperus: H. entreats thy light	JONS 135:19
It was the schooner H.	LONG 153:19
heterodoxy: h. is another man's doxy	
	WARB 266:11
Heu: H., miserande puer	VIRG 263:15
heures: Trois h., c'est toujours trop tard	SART 200:3
Heureux: H. qui comme Ulysse a fait	DU B 91:15
Heut: denk' ich H. und morgen	LESS 151:9
Heute: H. leid' ich	LESS 151:9
hew: h. him as a carcass fit	SHAK 216:4
hewers: h. of wood and drawers	BIBLE 24:4
hey: Then h. for boot and horse	KING 142:16
hey-day: h. in the blood is tame	SHAK 210:16
Hi: He would answer to 'H.	CARR 62:5
Hic jacet: these two narrow words, H.	RAL 194:6
hid: assumed when he h. himself among women	
	BROW 48:12
h. as it were our faces	BIBLE 29:14
on an hill cannot be h.	BIBLE 31:13
to keep that h.	DONNE 88:22
hidden: Half h. from the eye	WORD 276:14
h. in a cloud of crimson	FRY 103:17
h. in each other's hearts	DICK 84:15
h. meaning —like Basingstoke	GILB 109:7
hide: h. is sure to flatten 'em	BELL 18:6
it a world to h. virtues	SHAK 233:17
To h. her shame from every	GOLD 110:18
wrapp'd in a woman's h.	SHAK 215:3
Hiding: H. thy bravery in their	SHAK 235:15
My heart in h.	HOPK 122:10
Hier: H. stehe ich	LUTH 155:12
Hierusalem: H., my happy home	ANON 3:16
high: Altogether upon the h. horse	BROWN 47:18
Broad and I'm the H.	SPR 245:5
h. aesthetic line	GILB 108:19
h. aesthetic band	GILB 108:21
h. road that leads him	JOHN 131:19
h. that proved too high	BROW 48:19
h. tide and the turn	CHES 69:22

no h. flyer   PEPYS 182:9
slain in thine h. places   BIBLE 24:27
This h. man   BROW 49:11
higher: find my own the h.   CORN 78:5
go up h.   BIBLE 35:21
subject unto the h. powers   BIBLE 38:4
highest: Glory to God in the h.   BIBLE 35:3
needs must love the h.   TENN 251:17
Highland: heart is H.   GALT 104:11
Highlands: chieftain to the H. bound   CAMP 60:17
My heart's in the H.   BURNS 54:16
highly: what thou wouldst h.   SHAK 220:10
highwayman: h. came riding   NOYES 177:8
highways: happy h. where I went   HOUS 126:7
hill: every mountain and h. shall   BIBLE 29:9
hunter home from the h.   STEV 247:16
laughing is heard on the h.   BLAKE 43:16
Mahomet will go to the h.   BACON 13:2
other side of the h.   WELL 267:22
set on an h. cannot be hid   BIBLE 31:13
shall rest upon thy holy h.   PRAY 188:10
their haven under the h.   TENN 251:5
hills: blue remembered h.   HOUS 126:7
forth upon our clouded h.   BLAKE 43:2
h. of the South Country   BELL 19:7
immutable as the H.   KIPL 146:20
little h. like young sheep   PRAY 190:12
old brown h.   MAS 163:5
Over the h. and far away   GAY 105:11
though he h. be carried   PRAY 189:3
up mine eyes unto the h.   PRAY 190:16
hill-side: h.'s dew-pearled   BROW 50:12
Him: H. that walked the waves   MILT 168:2
I hid from H.   THOM 258:1
'That's h.   BARH 15:13
Himalayan: H. peasant meets the he-bear
                                                     KIPL 143:20
himself: end by loving h. better   COL 75:9
'He h. said it'   CIC 72:7
when the ado is about h.   TROL 260:2
Hinc: H. illae lacrimae   TER 256:2
hinder: dog's walking on his h.   JOHN 132:5
hindrances: h. to human improvement
                                                     MILL 165:20
hinds: Soft maids and village h.   COLL 76:1
hinges: door on its h.   WATTS 266:18
hip: catch him once upon the h.   SHAK 224:19
I have thee on the h.   SHAK 226:2
smote them h. and thigh   BIBLE 24:11
Hippocrene: blushful H.   KEATS 139:19
Hippopotamus: found it was A H.   CARR 62:12
I shoot the H.   BELL 18:6
hire: labourer is worthy of his h.   BIBLE 35:11
hissed: h. along the polished ice   WORD 274:20
histoire: l'h. n'est que le tableau   VOLT 265:1
Historian: H.Imagination is not required
                                                     JOHN 131:18
Histories: H. make men wise   BACON 13:22
history: have no h.   ELIOT 93:6
H. came   SELL 203:4
H. is a nightmare from   JOYCE 137:6
H. is more or less bunk   FORD 101:10
h. is nothing more than   VOLT 265:1
H. is past politics   FREE 102:19
H. is philosophy from examples   DION 86:11
h. of all hitherto existing   MARX 162:4
h. of the world is   CARL 61:14
H. to the defeated   AUDEN 11:11
Human h. becomes more   WELLS 268:17

learned anything from h.   HEGEL 116:11
no h.; only biography   EMER 96:13
serious attention than h.   ARIS 8:6
Thames is liquid h.   BURNS 53:16
this strange eventful h.   SHAK 205:1
world's h. is the world's   SCH 201:4
history-books: annals are blank in h.   CARL 61:11
hit: two h. it off as they should   WORD 274:10
very palpable h.   SHAK 211:19
Hitch: H. your wagon to a star   EMER 96:18
hitch'd: then he h. his trousers up   BARH 15:15
hither: come h.   SHAK 204:19
H. and thither moves   FITZ 99:7
hive: h. for the honey-bee   YEATS 279:7
ho: music, h.   SHAK 204:1
hoarse: raven himself is h.   SHAK 220:11
hobgoblin: consistency is the h. of little minds
                                                     EMER 96:15
Hoc: H. erat in votis   HOR 125:1
H. opus   VIRG 263:10
hock: at a weak h. and seltzer   BETJ 20:5
hodgepodge: tongue a gallimaufry or h.
                                                     SPEN 244:8
hodmen: unconscious h. of the men   HEINE 116:14
hoe: darned long row to h.   LOW 154:15
large h. and a shovel also   KIPL 144:13
hog: all England under a h.   COLL 75:16
hogshead: fighting with daggers in a h.
                                                     SCOTT 202:12
Höhlen: jahrtausendlang H. geben   NIET 176:16
Hoist: H. with his own petar   SHAK 210:21
hold: Earth will h. us   ANON 6:17
He will h. thee   TENN 253:8
h. a candle to my shames   SHAK 225:7
H., enough!   SHAK 223:16
h. fast that which is good   BIBLE 39:24
H. Infinity in the palm   BLAKE 42:17
h. thee but by thy granting   SHAK 236:6
H. the fort   BLISS 44:11
H. them cheap   HOPK 122:2
keep a h. of Nurse   BELL 18:12
she h. the gorgeous East   WORD 277:2
To cry 'H., hold   SHAK 220:11
to have and to h. from   PRAY 187:28
holds: h. him with his skinny   COL 74:6
hole: poisoned rat in a h.   SWIFT 249:5
holes: foxes have h.   BIBLE 32:16
holiday: Being h.   SHAK 232:4
Butcher'd to make a Roman h.   BYRON 57:13
Is this a h.   SHAK 215:13
now I am in a h. humour   SHAK 205:9
holidays: during the h. from Eton   SITW 241:13
year were playing h.   SHAK 212:5
holier: I am h. than thou   BIBLE 29:22
Holiest: Praise to the H.   NEWM 176:3
holiness: h. of the heart's affections   KEATS 140:15
holloa: we'll whoop and we'll h.   WHYT 270:14
hollow: We are the h. men   ELIOT 93:22
holsters: h. and cartridge boxes   SHAW 237:8
holy: another with an h. kiss   BIBLE 38:7
h., acceptable unto   BIBLE 38:1
h. city of Byzantium   YEATS 279:14
H., fair, and wise   SHAK 234:18
h. hush of ancient sacrifice   STEV 246:15
h., is the Lord of hosts   BIBLE 28:12
h. nation   BIBLE 40:18
h. time is quiet as a nun   WORD 276:20
thou standest is h. ground   BIBLE 23:10
Holy Ghost: is the temple of the H.   BIBLE 38:8

Holy, holy, holy: H., Lord God Almighty
                      BIBLE 40:31

Holy Spirit: H., and send out from   LANG 149:3
Holze: Aus so krummem H.   KANT 138:10
home: beating begins at h.   FLET 101:2
  her princes are come h.   SHAK 217:16
  h. and beauty   BRAH 46:2
  H. art gone and ta'en thy   SHAK 206:4
  H. is home   CLAR 73:2
  H. is the girl's prison   SHAW 238:13
  'H. is the place where   FROST 103:3
  H. is the sailor   STEV 247:16
  H. of lost causes   ARN 9:8
  h. of the brave   KEY 141:15
  home, sweet, sweet h.   PAYNE 181:14
  H. they brought her warrior   TENN 254:13
  h., you idle creatures   SHAK 215:13
  I was leaving h.   STEV 247:10
  Kiss till the cow comes h.   BEAU 17:3
  man goeth to his long h.   BIBLE 27:22
  straitened circumstances at h. JUV 137:19
  there's no place like h.   PAYNE 181:13
  this day and comes safe h.   SHAK 214:4
  very different from the h.   ANON 3:17
home-acre: hearth-fire and the h. KIPL 144:6
Home-keeping: H. youth have ever homely
                    SHAK 234:16
homely: Home-keeping youth have ever h. wits
                    SHAK 234:16
  Their h. joys   GRAY 112:3
  though it be never so h.   CLAR 73:2
  very h. household savour   BYRON 58:4
Homer: sometimes even excellent H. nods
                    HOR 122:20
Homes: Stately H. of England   COW 79:8
  stately h. of England   HEM 117:2
homeward: Look h., Angel   MILT 168:1
  rooks in families h. go   HARDY 115:2
hommage: L'hypocrisie est un h. LA R 149:10
homme: et on trouve un h.   PASC 180:15
  imprescriptibles de l'h.   ROB 195:10
  le style est l'h. même   BUFF 51:6
  le vray étude de l'h.   CHAR 67:16
  L'h. est bien insensé   MONT 172:6
  L'h. n'est qu'un roseau   PASC 181:3
homo: Ecce h.   BIBLE 41:22
  Lupus est h. homini   PLAU 183:16
honest: h. God is the noblest   ING 129:13
  h. God's the noblest   BUTL 56:16
  h. madam's issue   SHAK 217:19
  h. man's the noblest   POPE 185:18
  in a general h. thought   SHAK 217:6
  Though I am not naturally h. SHAK 235:2
  whatsoever things are h.   BIBLE 39:20
honestly: If possible h.   HOR 123:2
honey: did but taste a little h. BIBLE 24:20
  flowing with milk and h.   BIBLE 23:11
  gather h. all the day   WATTS 266:16
  h. of his music vows   SHAK 209:6
  How a bear likes h.   MILNE 166:18
  is there h. still for tea   BROO 47:14
  our hives with h. and wax SWIFT 248:17
  pot of h. on the grave   MER 165:2
  They took some h.   LEAR 150:13
honey-dew: he on h. hath fed COL 75:7
Honi: H. soit qui mal y pense ANON 5:17
honour: Giving h. unto the wife BIBLE 40:20
  greater share of h.   SHAK 214:3
  His h. rooted in dishonour TENN 251:20

  H. all men   BIBLE 40:19
  h. and his quality taken   BLUN 44:12
  h. and life have been spared FRAN 102:6
  h.? A word   SHAK 212:18
  H. be yours   NEWB 175:12
  h. is the subject of my   SHAK 215:15
  I h. him   SHAK 216:14
  in h. clear   POPE 185:5
  is leisure with h.   CIC 72:14
  king delighteth to h.   BIBLE 25:16
  left hand riches and h.   BIBLE 26:5
  louder he talked of his h. EMER 96:10
  Lov'd I not h. more   LOV 154:11
  Mine h. is my life   SHAK 229:17
  peace I hope with h.   DISR 87:2
  peace with h.   CHAM 66:14
  places where their h. died POPE 185:1
  prophet is not without h. BIBLE 33:8
  Though loss of h. was   GRAH 111:7
  When h.'s at the stake   SHAK 210:24
  your quaint h. turn to dust MARV 161:21
honourable: Brutus is an h. man SHAK 216:16
  Brutus is an h. man   SHAK 216:17
  Let us make an h. retreat SHAK 205:4
honour'd: He hath h. me of late SHAK 221:2
  h. of them all   TENN 255:12
  More h. in the breach than SHAK 207:8
honouring: Not so much h. thee JONS 136:3
honours: am stripped of all my h. BURKE 53:13
  bears his blushing h. thick SHAK 215:9
hood-wink'd: h. boy I call'd in aid GARR 104:15
hoofs: When the plunging h. were DE L 82:15
hook: great h. nose like thine BLAKE 42:20
  out leviathan with an h.   BIBLE 26:2
hooting: life to shunting and h. BURR 55:11
Hop: H. forty paces through SHAK 203:23
hope: Abandon all h., you who enter DANTE 81:8
  against hope believed in h. BIBLE 37:33
  do not h. to know again   ELIOT 93:9
  equal poise of h. and fear MILT 167:7
  failure of h.   GIBB 106:10
  faith, h., charity   BIBLE 38:16
  From h. and fear set free SWIN 250:1
  God is our h. and strength PRAY 189:3
  H. deferred maketh   BIBLE 26:16
  h. for the best   SMITH 242:15
  h. of the City of God   MAS 163:3
  H. springs eternal   POPE 185:15
  h. that keeps up a wife's GAY 105:9
  in sure and certain h.   PRAY 188:5
  Never to h. again   SHAK 215:9
  Nor dread nor h. attend YEATS 278:16
  poet's h.   AUDEN 11:9
  tender leaves of h.   SHAK 215:9
  to one more rich in h.   SHAK 235:11
  triumph of h. over experience JOHN 132:15
  Was the h. drunk   SHAK 221:3
  when existence or when h. AUST 12:10
  with h. farewell fear   MILT 169:6
hoped: substance of things h. BIBLE 40:8
hoped-for: already become the h. heaven
                    MILL 166:2
hopefully: To travel h. is a better STEV 247:4
hopeless: h. than a scheme of merriment
                    JOHN 134:22
  perennially h.   DICK 83:12
hopes: great h. from Birmingham AUST 11:24
  If h. were dupes   CLOU 73:17
hopeth: h. all things   BIBLE 38:15

hoping: Dreading and h. all — YEATS 278:16
hops: h., and women — DICK 85:13
Horace: What H. says is — BARH 15:10
Horatius: Then out spake brave H. — MAC 156:4
  well H. kept the bridge — MAC 156:11
höre: Wenn ich Kultur h. — JOHST 135:12
horizon: h. recedes as we advance — PATT 181:11
horizontal: however fine into an h. — WHEW 269:10
horn: blowing loud his wreathed h. — SPEN 244:13
Hornby: my H. and my Barlow — THOM 257:22
horns: h. of Elfland faintly blowing — TENN 254:9
  sound of h. and motors — ELIOT 95:3
Horny-handed: H. sons of toil — KEAR 138:14
horrible: grotesque to the h. — DOYLE 89:22
  h., fantastic, incredible — CHAM 66:13
  O, h.! most horrible! — SHAK 207:15
horrid: 'Mongst h. shapes — MILT 167:14
  she was bad she was h. — LONG 153:20
Horror: H. so refined — DICK 86:6
horrors: have supp'd full with h. — SHAK 223:14
hors: was his h. as is a rake — CHAU 68:4
horse: Altogether upon the high h. — BROWN 47:18
  behold a pale h. — BIBLE 40:32
  dark h. — DISR 87:13
  Do not trust the h. — VIRG 263:3
  h. of that colour — SHAK 234:1
  If he were a h. — BAG 14:5
  little dearer than his h. — TENN 253:8
  my kingdom for a h. — SHAK 231:9
  nothing but talk of his h. — SHAK 224:15
  to h. — BROW 49:7
  to my h. —German — CHAR 67:15
  want of a h. the rider — FRAN 102:11
  where's the bloody h. — CAMP 60:13
  With an old h. that stumbles — HARDY 114:11
Horseman: *H., pass by* — YEATS 280:3
horses: best carriage he — TROL 260:11
  chariots, and some in h. — PRAY 188:13
  drive a coach and six h. — RICE 195:3
  entirely by the spade and no h. — MILL 165:19
  hanged for stealing h. — HALE 114:3
  hell of h. — FLOR 101:4
  street and frighten the h. — CAMP 60:11
  than the h. of instruction — BLAKE 44:5
Hortus: *H. ubi et tecto vicinus* — HOR 125:1
Hosanna: *H. in excelsis* — MASS 163:16
hospes: *deferor h.* — HOR 123:1
hospital: not an inn, but an h. — BROW 48:9
hostages: all of them h. given — LUCAN 155:2
  hath given h. to fortune — BACON 13:11
hostile: universe is not h. — HOLM 120:15
hosts: Even the Lord of h. — PRAY 188:19
hot: benison of h. water — BROO 47:7
  H. and rebellious liquors — SHAK 204:17
  h. for certainties in this — MER 165:5
  h. ice and wondrous strange — SHAK 227:19
  h. the eye of heaven — SHAK 235:9
  iron while it is h. — DRYD 91:12
hotch-potch: h. of my little book — JUV 137:15
hotel-keepers: h. continue to give them
   — TROL 260:7
Hottentot: him as a respectable H. — CHES 69:14
hound: by the faithful h. — LONG 153:5
  he'll grow into a h. — WHYT 270:14
  slepyng h. to wake — CHAU 68:23
hounds: carcass fit for h. — SHAK 216:4
  h. all join in glorious — FIEL 98:11
  h. of spring are on winter's — SWIN 249:15
hour: carefully upon your h. — SHAK 206:5

crowded h. of glorious life — MORD 173:5
glory of the positive h. — ELIOT 93:9
h. that requires such help — VIRG 263:6
I also had my h. — CHES 69:24
Improve each shining h. — WATTS 266:16
its h. come round at last — YEATS 279:16
matched us with His h. — BROO 47:15
mine h. is not yet come — BIBLE 36:19
now's the h. — BURNS 54:20
one bare h. to live — MARL 160:6
struts and frets his h. — SHAK 223:15
'This was their finest h. — CHUR 71:6
Time and the h. runs through — SHAK 220:8
hours: h. will take care of themselves — CHES 69:8
  lazy leaden-stepping h. — MILT 168:11
  To chase the glowing H. — BYRON 57:10
  two h.' traffick — SHAK 231:11
  Woman! in our h. of ease — SCOTT 202:2
housbonde: Whan myn h. is fro — CHAU 68:16
Housbondes: H. at chirche dore she — CHAU 68:7
house: built his h. upon the sand — BIBLE 32:13
  Bustle in a H. — DICK 86:2
  called the h. of prayer — BIBLE 33:26
  Carrying his own h. still — DONNE 88:10
  Except the Lord build the h. — PRAY 190:19
  Father's h. are many mansions — BIBLE 37:1
  go into the h. of the Lord — PRAY 190:18
  Harrow the h. of the dead — AUDEN 11:5
  h. be divided against itself — BIBLE 34:21
  h. is a living-machine — LE C 151:1
  H. is pleased to direct — LENT 151:8
  h. not made with hands — BIBLE 39:3
  h. not made with hands — BROW 49:4
  H. of Lords as from any — NORF 177:6
  h. of the Lord for ever — PRAY 188:16
  h. where I was born — HOOD 121:7
  h. with lawns enclosing — STEV 247:15
  Lord has built the h. — BIBLE 41:15
  see the figure of the h. — SHAK 212:23
  Set thine h. in order — BIBLE 29:7
  sparrow hath found her an h. — PRAY 189:17
  substance of his h. for love — BIBLE 28:5
  That this h. will in no — ANON 4:20
  them that join house to h. — BIBLE 28:9
  There's nae luck about the h. — ANON 5:3
  upon the walls of thine h. — PRAY 190:21
  water near the h. — HOR 125:1
  What! in our h. — SHAK 222:6
  zeal of thine h. hath even — PRAY 189:13
household: Down to a very homely h. — BYRON 58:4
  Familiar in his mouth as h. — SHAK 214:4
housemaids: damp souls of h. — ELIOT 94:10
House of Peers: H., throughout the war
   — GILB 107:19
houses: h. thick and sewers annoy — MILT 169:17
  h. thunder on your head — JOHN 135:5
  very h. seem asleep — WORD 276:19
housewife: to the h. that's thrifty — SHER 240:25
how: can't remember h. They go — CALV 59:18
  H. and Where and Who — KIPL 144:14
  H. are the mighty fallen — BIBLE 24:27
  H. can they use such names — SASS 200:13
  H. could they tell — PARK 180:9
  H. do I love thee — BROW 49:5
  H. doth the little crocodile — CARR 62:16
  H. many things I can do — SOCR 243:9
  h. much it is — BROW 49:5
  H. NOT TO DO IT — DICK 84:9
  h. you played the game — RICE 195:2

Howard: Then sware Lord Thomas H.

TENN 255:3

how-de-doo: Here's a h.   GILB 108:10

Howl: H., howl, howl, howl   SHAK 219:2

howling: Imagine h.   SHAK 224:4

Howth Castle: recirculation back to H.

JOYCE 136:16

huddled: h. masses yearning   LAZ 149:19

  with your legs ungainly h.   SASS 200:8

hues: thee all her lovely h.   DAV 82:2

***Hugo:** croyait Victor H.*   COCT 74:1

  H.—hélas   GIDE 106:16

  Victor H. madman   COCT 74:1

hulk: Here, a sheer h.   DIBD 83:9

human: Are all the h. frame requires…'   BELL 18:11

  Communism with a h. face   DUBC 91:14

  err is h., not to, animal   FROST 103:11

  happiness of the h. race   BURKE 52:18

  held the h. race in scorn   BELL 18:8

  h. beings are born free   ANON 2:16

  H. kind Cannot bear   ELIOT 93:14

  H. on my faithless arm   AUDEN 11:3

  laugh at h. actions   SPIN 245:1

  milk of h. kindness   SHAK 220:10

  nothing h. foreign to me   TER 256:3

  Peace, the h. dress   BLAKE 43:19

  proportioned to the h. constitution   BERK 20:1

  purest of h. pleasures   BACON 13:9

  think the full tide of h.   JOHN 132:19

  To err is h.   POPE 185:11

  To step aside is h.   BURNS 53:17

  wish I loved the H. Race   RAL 194:10

***humani:** h. nil a me alienum puto*   TER 256:3

humanity: crooked timber of h.   KANT 138:10

  So act as to treat h.   KANT 138:9

  still, sad music of h.   WORD 275:6

human race: h., to which so many   CHES 70:11

humans: It isn't fit for h. now   BETJ 21:11

Humber: Of H. would complain   MARV 161:20

humble: Be it ever so h.   PAYNE 181:13

  He that is h. ever shall   BUNY 51:26

  h. and a contrite heart   KIPL 145:10

  such names and not be h.   SASS 200:13

humbled: maintains that I am h. now   CORN 78:5

humbleness: whispering h.   SHAK 225:1

humbleth: he that h. himself shall   BIBLE 35:22

humbly: walk h. with thy God   BIBLE 30:19

Humiliation: valley of H.   BUNY 51:18

humility: 'Had he but the gift of h.   STIL 247:18

  modest stillness and h.   SHAK 213:14

humour: ever woman in this h. won   SHAK 231:5

humours: In all thy h.   ADD 1:11

hump: Camel's h. is an ugly lump   KIPL 144:12

  uglier yet is the H. we get   KIPL 144:12

***humus:** Nos habebit h.*   ANON 6:17

hundred: His h.'s soon hit   BROW 49:11

  would be all the same a h.   DICK 84:22

hundreds: h. to Ludlow come   HOUS 125:14

hung: ocean Is folded and h.   AUDEN 10:8

Hunger: H. allows no choice   AUDEN 11:6

  h. and thirst after righteousness   BIBLE 31:11

  H. is the best sauce   CERV 66:6

  poverty, h., and dirt   HOOD 121:12

hungred: I was an h.   BIBLE 34:8

hungry: ate when we were not h.   SWIFT 249:2

  Cassius has a lean and h.   SHAK 215:17

  He hath filled the h. with   BIBLE 34:29

  she makes h.   SHAK 203:24

hunt: We h. them for the beauty   TENN 254:12

hunted: others by their h. expression   LEWIS 151:13

hunter: h. home from the hill   STEV 247:16

  H. of the East has caught   FITZ 98:14

  Nimrod the mighty h. before   BIBLE 22:23

hunting: Good h.   KIPL 146:10

  I'm weary wi' h.   BALL 14:17

  I went h. wild   OWEN 179:10

  than to h. and shooting   BURR 55:11

huntress: Queen and h.   JONS 135:19

Huntsman: H., rest   SCOTT 201:13

  h. winds his horn   FIEL 90:11

hurly-burly: h. of the chaise-longue   CAMP 60:12

  When the h.'s done   SHAK 219:16

hurricanoes: You cataracts and h.   SHAK 218:6

hurry: old man in a h.   CHUR 70:24

hurt: h. not thy foot against   PRAY 190:1

  h. with the same weapons   SHAK 225:10

  It h. too much to laugh   STEV 246:16

  Those have most power to h.   BEAU 17:1

hurting: once it has stopped h.   BOWEN 45:13

husband: Hang your h. and be dutiful   GAY 105:10

  h. could have made me like   CONG 76:17

  h. is, the wife is   TENN 253:8

  life her h. makes for her   ELIOT 93:3

  so may my h.   SHAK 224:9

  Thy h. is thy lord   SHAK 232:10

  woman is a crown to her h.   BIBLE 26:14

husbandry: There's h. in heaven   SHAK 221:9

husbands: *divine right* of h.   WOLL 274:1

hush: holy h. of ancient sacrifice   STEV 246:15

  H., hush, Nobody cares   MORT 174:1

  H. your tongues   HOR 124:5

  old man who said, 'H.   LEAR 150:3

  There's a breathless h.   NEWB 175:15

Hushing: H. the latest traffic   BRID 46:12

husks: come is strew'd with h.   SHAK 233:12

hustle: who tried to h. the East   KIPL 146:9

hut: Love in a h.   KEATS 139:8

Hyacinth: every H. the Garden wears   FITZ 99:1

hymn-book: h. too   WILB 270:15

hymns: Chanting faint h.   SHAK 226:12

  happy h. of farmers   KING 143:5

  sings h. at heaven's gate   SHAK 235:11

Hyperion: H. to a satyr   SHAK 206:15

***hypocrisie:** L'h. est un hommage que le*   LA R 149:10

hypocrisy: h.; from envy   PRAY 187:3

  That would be h.   WILDE 271:12

***Hypocrite:** H. lecteur*   BAUD 16:11

  h. lecteur   ELIOT 95:1

  is a h. in his pleasures   JOHN 134:5

hyssop: shalt purge me with h.   PRAY 189:6

  will sprinkle me with h.   BIBLE 41:12

I: I. am fearfully and wonderfully   PRAY 191:4

  I. am the batsman   LANG 148:17

  if I. had not been there   WELL 267:21

***Iam:** I. redit et virgo*   VIRG 264:6

***ianua:** dies patet atri i. Ditis*   VIRG 263:10

***Ibant:** I. obscuri sola sub nocte*   VIRG 263:12

***ibit:** in caelum iusseris i.*   JUV 137:18

ice: hissed along the polished i.   WORD 274:20

  his urine is congealed i.   SHAK 224:6

  hot i. and wondrous strange   SHAK 227:19

  I. formed on the butler's   WOD 273:17

  In skating over thin i.   EMER 96:14

  is good to break the i.   BACON 13:4

  penny i. and cold meat   GILB 107:22

  To smooth the i.   SHAK 217:12

ice-cream: emperor is the emperor of i.

STEV 246:14

I., of course   SASS 200:15
iced: three parts i. over   ARN 9:14
Iceland: is not so bad as I.   JOHN 134:6
I-chabod: named the child I.   BIBLE 24:17
icicles: When i. hang by the wall   SHAK 219:14
icumen: Sumer is i.   ANON 4:19
idea: against invasion by an i.   HUGO 127:16
  is the pain of a new i.   BAG 14:9
  young i. how to shoot   THOM 258:13
ideas: green i. sleep   CHOM 70:16
idées: Elle a des i. au-dessus   RATT 194:12
  pas à l'invasion des i.   HUGO 127:16
identity: His i. presses upon me   KEATS 141:3
ides: Beware the i. of March   SHAK 215:14
  i. of March are come   SHAK 216:7
idiot: i. who praises   GILB 108:5
  portrait of a blinking i.   SHAK 225:8
  tale Told by an i.   SHAK 223:15
  your I. Boy   WORD 274:19
idle: be not i.   BURT 55:21
  home, you i. creatures   SHAK 215:13
  i. as a painted ship   COL 74:9
  i. chatter of a transcendental   GILB 108:20
  i. hands to do   WATTS 266:17
  idle than when wholly i.   CIC 72:9
  Most 'scruciating i.   KIPL 146:13
  not learnt how to be i.   MADAN 158:11
  solitary, be not i.   JOHN 133:13
  whom the world Calls i.   COWP 80:3
Idleness: I. is only the refuge   CHES 69:12
  round of strenuous i.   WORD 276:8
idolatry: on this side i.   JONS 136:8
Idols: I. I have loved so long   FITZ 99:11
idoneus: *Vixi puellis nuper i.*   HOR 124:11
If: I. I am not for myself   HILL 119:10
  I. you can keep your head   KIPL 144:7
Ignorance: I. of the law excuses no   SELD 202:18
  pure i.   JOHN 131:12
  there is no sin but i.   MARL 160:10
  where i. is bliss   GRAY 112:12
  women in a state of i.   KNOX 147:8
ignorant: Confound the i.   SHAK 208:21
  i. armies clash by night   ARN 8:13
  In language, the i.   DUPPA 92:3
  they should always be i.   AUST 12:6
ignotum: *omne i. pro magnifico est*   TAC 250:7
île: *î. triste et noire*   BAUD 16:13
Ilium: topless towers of I.   MARL 160:5
ill: bad epitaph than their i.   SHAK 208:18
  be the final goal of i.   TENN 252:15
  I. fares the land   GOLD 110:6
  I. met by moonlight   SHAK 227:1
  There is some i. a-brewing   SHAK 225:5
ill-bred: so illiberal and so i.   CHES 69:4
ill breeding: sign of guilt, or of i.   CONG 76:21
Ille: *I. mi par esse deo videtur*   CAT 65:9
illiberal: nothing so i. and so ill-bred   CHES 69:4
illiteracy: at the i. of scientists   SNOW 243:6
illness: i. should attend it   SHAK 220:10
ills: have they of i. to come   GRAY 112:10
  i. the scholar's life assail   JOHN 135:9
  sure one for all i.   RAL 194:7
ill-spent: was a sign of an i. youth   SPEN 244:9
ill-tempered: Some think him i. and queer   LEAR 150:4
illuminatio: *Dominus i. mea*   BIBLE 41:11
Illumine: What in me is dark I.   MILT 168:14
illumined: Chaos, i.   WILDE 272:3

ill-usage: complaints of i. contemptible   MELB 164:18
illusion: i. that it is the other   GOW 111:5
  nothing but sophistry and i.   HUME 127:17
image: Best i. of myself and dearer   MILT 169:12
  i. of his Maker   SHAK 215:10
  Scatter'd his Maker's i.   DRYD 90:10
images: garden of bright i.   BRAM 46:5
imagination: abhorred in my i. it is   SHAK 211:11
  affections and the truth of i.   KEATS 140:15
  Are of i. all compact   SHAK 227:17
  if i. amend them   SHAK 227:23
  i. resembled the wings   MAC 156:13
  i. bodies forth   SHAK 227:18
  requisite for an Historian...I.   JOHN 131:18
  scattered the proud in the i.   BIBLE 34:29
  to his i. for his facts   SHER 240:27
  to sweeten my i.   SHAK 218:21
imagine: may as well i. the scene   COMP 76:9
  people i. a vain   PRAY 188:6
imitate: i. the action of the tiger   SHAK 213:14
imitator: was a happy i. of Nature   HEM 117:4
Immanuel: shall call his name I.   BIBLE 28:16
immaturity: that common symptom of i.   WHAR 269:9
immorality: nurseries of all vice and i.   FIEL 98:6
immortal: i. hand or eye   BLAKE 43:7
  I. longings in me   SHAK 204:10
  I. youth to mortal maids   LAND 148:10
  lost the i. part of myself   SHAK 228:24
  make me i. with a kiss   MARL 160:5
  orient and i. wheat   TRAH 259:21
  when death that is i. has   LUCR 155:8
immortalis: *Mortalem vitam mors cum i.*   LUCR 155:8
immortality: heart like a load of i.   KEATS 141:4
  If I. unveil   DICK 86:3
Immortals: President of the I. (in   HARDY 115:5
immutable: She was as i. as the Hills   KIPL 146:20
imp: i. of fame   SHAK 213:19
Imparadised: I. in one another's arms   MILT 169:9
impartial: Of a pure i. hate   THOR 259:11
  security for its i. administration   PEEL 182:1
impeach: I i. him in the name   BURKE 53:7
impeachment: I own the soft i.   SHER 240:22
impediment: cause, or just i.   PRAY 187:23
impediments: i. to great enterprises   BACON 13:11
imperasset: *consensu capax imperii nisi i.*   TAC 250:11
Imperativ: *I. ist kategorisch*   KANT 138:7
imperative: i. is Categorical   KANT 138:7
imperial: Of the i. theme   SHAK 220:6
Imperialism: sane I.   ROS 196:16
imperio: *Tu regere i. populos*   VIRG 263:14
imponere: *Ter sunt conati i.*   VIRG 264:10
import: works and ones of great i.   HOR 122:12
importance: subject of almost equal i.   BRAM 46:5
important: importunate for being less i.   MONT 172:2
importantes: *occupations domestiques moins i.*   MONT 172:2
importune: I here i. death awhile   SHAK 204:5
importunes: *n'en sont pas moins i.*   MONT 172:2
impose: You i. continency upon us   AUG 11:17
impossibile: *Certum est quia i. est*   TERT 256:8
impossibilities: Probable i. are to be preferred   ARIS 8:7
impossibility: begotten by despair Upon i.   MARV 161:13

impossible: believed as many as six i.   CARR 64:6
certain because it is i.   TERT 256:8
have eliminated the i.   DOYLE 89:24
i.? cela se fera   CALL 59:15
i. loyalties   ARN 9:8
i. to be silent   BURKE 53:6
i.? that will be done   CALL 59:15
In two words: i.   GOLD 111:2
That not i. she   CRAS 80:11
With men this is i.   BIBLE 33:23
impostor: these two i. just the same   KIPL 144:7
impotently: Rolls i. on as Thou   FITZ 99:10
imprecision: general mess of i.   ELIOT 93:18
impressive: i. sights in the world   BARR 16:7
Imprisoned: I. in every fat man a thin   CONN 77:9
i. in the viewless winds   SHAK 224:4
imprisonetur: i., aut dissaisiatur   MAGN 158:16
improbable: preferred to i. possibilites   ARIS 8.7
improper: only hope it is not i.   GASK 105:4
proper or i.   FULL 103:22
impropriety: without i.   GILB 107:20
Improve: I. each shining hour   WATTS 266:16
I. his shining tail   CARR 62:16
improvement: hindrances to human i.   MILL 165:20
impudence: men starve for want of i.   DRYD 91:2
much of Cockney i. before   RUSK 198:6
impulse: first i. was never a crime   CORN 78:4
from the i. of the moment   AUST 12:12
impulses: no truck with first i.   MONT 172:9
impune: Nemo me i. lacessit   ANON 7:1
impunity: one provokes me with i.   ANON 7:1
impure: Puritan all things are i.   LAWR 149:15
impurity: we bring i. much rather   MILT 170:17
in: thy coming i.   PRAY 190:17
inactivity: wise and masterly i.   MACK 157:14
inane: along the illimitable i.   TENN 253:17
inania: Ditis vacuas et i. regna   VIRG 263:12
Inapprehensible: I., we clutch thee   THOM 258:6
inarticulate: raid on the i.   ELIOT 93:18
incapacity: dark sanctuary of i.   CHES 69:17
incarnadine: multitudinous seas i.   SHAK 222:1
incense: strong thick stupefying i.-smoke   BROW 49:1
unfabled I. Tree   DARL 81:13
incest: excepting i. and folk-dancing'   ANON 3:6
inch: every i. a king   SHAK 218:19
Inchcape: It is the I. Rock   SOUT 243:20
incident: 'That was the curious i.   DOYLE 89:19
incite: les couvre, les nourrit, les i.   MONT 172:4
inclination: ought to read just as i.   JOHN 131:20
inclin'd: tree's i.   POPE 184:23
Incline: I. our hearts to keep this   PRAY 187:10
include: You can i. me out   GOLD 111:3
income: Annual i. twenty pounds   DICK 84:1
£40,000 a year a moderate i.   LAMB 148:7
large i. is the best recipe   AUST 12:3
incompetent: cursing his staff for i. swine   SASS 200:12
incomplete: research is always i.   PATT 181:11
in-conceivable: pride is something i.   GILB 108:1
incorruptible: dead shall be raised i.   BIBLE 38:22
seagreen I.   CARL 61:13
increase: cares were to i. his store   HOME 120:18
dies fighting has i.   GREN 113:3
incredible: horrible, fantastic, i.   CHAM 66:13
increment: Unearned i.   MILL 165:14
indeed: Hubert Stanley is praise i.   MORT 174:2
indefatigable: That i. and unsavoury engine   SPAR 244:4

Index: publishes a book without an I.   CAMP 60:9
India: final message of I.   FORS 101:19
Indian: good Indian is a dead I.   SHER 240:13
Like the base I.   SHAK 229:15
out ten to see a dead I.   SHAK 232:17
Indicat: I. Motorem Bum...   GODL 109:19
indictment: i. against an whole people   BURKE 52:17
indifference: i. closely bordering   STEV 246:18
me i. and a coach and six   COLM 76:2
indifferent: been delayed till I am i.   JOHN 131:9
i. in a week   AUDEN 10:17
It is simply i.   HOLM 120:15
indignatio: facit i. versum   JUV 137:14
indignation: Where fierce i. can no   SWIFT 249:14
indirections: By i. find directions out   SHAK 208:4
indiscretion: one blazing i.   MORL 173:9
individual: liberty of the i. must   MILL 165:17
individuals: all my love is towards i.   SWIFT 249:4
worth of the i. composing it   MILL 165:18
indivisible: Peace is i.   LITV 152:8
indomitable: Still the i. Irishry   YEATS 280:4
induce: wrong could religion i.   LUCR 155:4
indulgent: comprendre rend très i.   STAEL 245:9
industries: Is solemnest of i.   DICK 86:2
industry: i. only, but his judgement   BURKE 52:14
i. without art is brutality   RUSK 198:7
indutus: Hectore qui redit exuvias i.   VIRG 263:4
inebriate: That cheer but not i.   COWP 80:4
to cheer but not i.   BERK 20:1
ineffectual: Remote and i. Don   BELL 18:25
ineptior: Nam risu inepto res i.   CAT 65:8
inevitability: i. of gradualness   WEBB 267:3
inevitable: Awaits alike th' i. hour   GRAY 112:3
inexactitude: risk of terminological i.   CHUR 71:1
inextinguishable: spark of i. thought   SHEL 240:9
infallible: We are none of us i.   THOM 258:10
infâme: écrasez l'i.   VOLT 265:2
infancy: lies about us in our i.   WORD 275:15
milkiness of i.   BURKE 52:10
infant: At first the i.   SHAK 205:1
describe the i. phenomenon   DICK 85:2
Has gobbled up the i. child   HOUS 127:5
i. crying in the night   TENN 252:16
Sooner murder an i.   BLAKE 44:7
to a little i.   BACON 13:6
infanticide: is as indefensible as i.   WEST 269:3
infant's: should be on every i. tongue   CALV 59:17
infect: out briskly to i. a city   AUDEN 10:14
infected: All seems i. that th'infected   POPE 185:12
infection: Against i. and the hand of war   SHAK 230:2
infelicity: i. Seem'd to have years   WEBS 267:12
infidel: i., I have thee   SHAK 226:2
Wine has play'd the I.   FITZ 99:12
Infidelity: I. does not consist   PAINE 179:12
infini: Malgré moi l'i. me tourmente   MUSS 174:8
infinite: dark unbottom'd i. abyss   MILT 169:3
eternal silence of these i.   PASC 180:18
idea of the i. torments   MUSS 174:8
that the will is i.   SHAK 233:6
Infinity: Hold I. in the palm   BLAKE 42:17
infirm: i. glory of the positive   ELIOT 93:9
infirmities: sake and thine often i.   BIBLE 39:29
infirmity: last i. of noble mind   MILT 167:20
inflicts: is one who never i. pain   NEWM 176:1
influence: Corrupt i.   BURKE 52:20
i. of the Crown has increased   DUNN 92:1
i. them till they ask   HUGEL 127:13

inform: How all occasions do i.   SHAK 210:23
informally: Quite i.   COW 79:9
information: I only ask for i.   DICK 84:4
Inglese: I. Italianato   ASCH 9:19
ingots: take i. with us to market   CHAM 66:16
Ingratitude: I., more strong than traitors'
   SHAK 216:20
   unkind As man's i.   SHAK 205:2
inherit: they shall i. the earth   BIBLE 31:11
   To-night it doth i.   ARN 8:18
inheritance: Ruinous i.   GAIUS 104:8
inherited: i. it brick and left it   AUG 11:22
inheritor: i. of the kingdom of heaven PRAY 187:18
inhibitions: was to cultivate a few i.   LOOS 154:3
inhumanity: Man's i. to man   BURNS 54:15
iniquities: was bruised for our i.   BIBLE 29:15
iniquity: Rejoiceth not in i.   BIBLE 38:15
iniuria: Nulla i. est   ULP 261:9
injure: feared it might i. the brain   CARR 62:18
injuries: is adding insult to i.   MOORE 172:10
   one revenge me of the i.   HENR 117:17
injustice: endure an hour and see i.   HOUS 126:9
   man's inclination to i.   NIEB 176:12
   No i. is done to someone   ULP 261:9
ink: i. in my pen ran cold   WALP 265:17
inlaid: i. with patines of bright   SHAK 226:5
inland: tract Of i. ground   WORD 274:15
inn: by a good tavern or i.   JOHN 132:25
   Do you remember an I.   BELL 19:8
   not an i., but an hospital   BROW 48:9
   room for them in the i.   BIBLE 35:1
   take mine ease in mine i.   SHAK 212:16
   world's an i.   DRYD 91:8
Innisfree: go to I.   YEATS 279:7
innocence: ceremony of i. is drowned
   YEATS 279:15
innocent: escape than one i. suffer   BLAC 42:16
   i. and the beautiful   YEATS 279:4
   i. as gay   YOUNG 280:9
   Of the brave and i.   AUDEN 10:17
inns: go to i. to dine   CHES 70:7
inopportune: be magnanimous at an i.
   TROT 260:16
inreparabile: fugit i. tempus   VIRG 264:13
insane: Only the i. take themselves   BEER 17:20
insaniae: tumultuositas vulgi semper i.   ALC 2:1
inscription: found an altar with this i. BIBLE 37:23
inscriptions: In lapidary i. a man is   JOHN 132:23
inscrutable: i. workings of Providence BIRK 42:10
inside: mortal blow right i.   AESC 1:16
   thin man i. every fat   ORW 178:9
insincerity: mark of i. of purpose   BRAM 46:4
insolence: flown with i. and wine   MILT 168:16
   i. of wealth will creep   JOHN 133:9
   that i. is not invective   DISR 86:16
   wretch who supports with i.   JOHN 134:20
inspiration: Genius is one per cent i.   EDIS 92:7
   is not drawing, but *i.*   CONS 77:14
inspire: feel not what they i.   SHEL 240:12
   our souls i.   PRAY 191:12
instability: to dissimulate their i.   HOUS 127:7
instances: wise saws and modern i.   SHAK 205:1
instancy: majestic i.   THOM 258:2
instant: Every i. grow   GRAV 111:14
instantaneous: I mean i. courage   NAP 174:10
Institute: I., Legion and Social   BETJ 20:11
institution: It's an i.   HUGH 127:14
instruction: wiser than the horses of i. BLAKE 44:5

insubstantial: like this i. pageant faded
   SHAK 232:24
insufferable: Oxford that has made me i.
   BEER 17:15
insularum: Paene i.   CAT 65:7
insult: is adding i. to injuries   MOORE 172:10
intangible: world i.   THOM 258:6
Integer: I. vitae scelerisque   HOR 123:16
integral: i. and differential calculus   GILB 109:1
integrate: Essentially I i. the current   BETJ 20:12
intellect: i. of man is forced   YEATS 278:13
   'Is it weakness of i.   GILB 108:18
   Our meddling i.   WORD 277:9
   restless and versatile i.   HUXL 128:14
intellects: few hearts and i. like   MILL 166:2
intellectual: All i. improvement arises JOHN 132:17
   I am an i. chap   GILB 107:16
   i. life of our century   ARN 9:8
   word 'I.' suggests straight   AUDEN 11:8
intelligent: i., the witty, the brave   MILL 166:6
   Want it to be i.   SU T 248:9
intelligere: sed i.   SPIN 245:1
intensity: Are full of passionate i.   YEATS 279:15
intent: His first avow'd i.   BUNY 52:2
   Our true i. is   SHAK 227:20
   prick the sides of my i.   SHAK 221:1
   When on love i.   YEATS 278:15
interchange: calm quiet i. of sentiments
   JOHN 132:22
interest: I *du* in i.   LOW 154:16
   unbound by any i. to pay   HOR 123:9
interested: subsequent proceedings i.
   HARTE 115:14
interesting: statements was i.   TWAIN 260:22
interpreted: i. the world in various   MARX 162:9
interred: good is oft i. with their   SHAK 216:16
interstices: with i. between the intersections
   JOHN 134:18
intervals: Lucid i. and happy pauses BACON 13:27
   Not in the lucid i.   WORD 274:13
intervention: No i.   LAND 148:9
interview: first strange and fatal i.   DONNE 87:22
into: i. the Dust descend   FITZ 99:3
intolerant: Time that is i.   AUDEN 10:17
Intreat: I. me not to leave thee   BIBLE 24:14
intrepid: behaviour was natural and i.
   WALP 265:15
intricated: Poor i. soul   DONNE 89:4
introduced: any one you've been i.   CARR 64:17
   when I'm i. to one   RAL 194:10
intrude: I hope I don't i.   POOLE 184:6
intruding: i. fool, farewell   SHAK 210:14
invasion: résiste pas à l'i. des idées   HUGO 127:16
invective: that insolence is not i.   DISR 86:16
invent: would be necessary to i. him   VOLT 264:20
   would i. some other custom   SHAK 228:22
invented: England i. the phrase   BAG 14:6
invention: brightest heaven of i.   SHAK 213:7
   it is a happy i.   ANON 6:9
   Knight said…'It's my own i.   CARR 64:13
inverted: i. Bowl we call The Sky   FITZ 99:10
invida: fugerit i. Aetas   HOR 123:14
invisible: all things visible and i.   PRAY 187:12
   with thy bloody and i. hand   SHAK 222:15
   world i.   THOM 258:6
   yet she is not i.   BACON 13:7
involved: because I am i. in *Mankind*   DONNE 89:3
inward: i. and spiritual grace   PRAY 187:22
   i. tranquillity which religion   FORB 101:9

jests: He j. at scars   SHAK 231:16
to his memory for his j.   SHER 240:27
Jesu: J., by a nobler deed   CHAN 67:4
J., the very thought   CASW 65:1
Jesus: Blood of J. whispers   BICK 42:4
Gentle J.   WESL 268:18
J. the author and finisher   BIBLE 40:9
J. they run into millions   ROST 197:13
J. wept   BIBLE 36:33
name of J. every knee   BIBLE 39:16
sure this J. will not do   BLAKE 43:1
sweet reasonableness of J.   ARN 9:13
Jesus Christ: If J. were to come to-day   CARL 61:23
J. the same yesterday   BIBLE 40:12
jeunesse: Si j. savoit   EST 97:3
jeux: j. d'enfants ne sont pas   MONT 171:18
Jew: Either for Englishman or J.   BLAKE 43:1
Hath not a J. eyes   SHAK 225:10
This is the J.   POPE 185:27
which am a J. of Tarsus   BIBLE 37:27
jewel: immediate j. of their souls   SHAK 228:27
Lest my j. I should tine   BURNS 53:25
Like a rich j. in an Ethiop's   SHAK 231:14
precious j. in his head   SHAK 204:16
jewels: j. into a garret four stories   BACON 12:21
Jews: born King of the J.   BIBLE 31:1
conversion of the J.   MARV 161:20
J., a headstrong   DRYD 90:11
spurn the J.   BROW 48:4
To choose The J.   EWER 97:9
Jim: gorging J. to guzzling Jacky   THAC 256:13
they called him Sunny J.   HANFF 114:6
jingle: hear the harness j.   HOUS 126:2
jingo: by j. if we do   HUNT 128:2
Joan: J. doth keel the pot   SHAK 219:14
Miss J. Hunter Dunn   BETJ 21:14
Job: heard of the patience of J.   BIBLE 40:15
I am as poor as J.   SHAK 212:21
we will finish the j.   CHUR 71:8
jocunditie: jasper of j.   DUNB 91:23
jog: j. on the foot-path way   SHAK 234:23
man *might j. on with*   LAMB 148:7
John: back to the shop Mr J.   LOCK 152:14
J. Anderson my jo   BURNS 54:12
Johnny: J. head-in-air   PUDN 192:10
Little J. Head-In-Air   HOFF 120:9
Johnson: There is no arguing with J.   GOLD 111:1
join: them that j. house to house   BIBLE 28:9
joined: persons should not be j.   PRAY 187:23
Those whom God hath j.   PRAY 188:2
What therefore God hath j.   BIBLE 33:20
joint: j. and motive of her body   SHAK 233:11
Remove the j.   CARR 64:17
time is out of j.   SHAK 208:3
joke: custard pie… A dirty j.   ORW 178:8
jokes: my little j. on Thee   FROST 103:6
jolitee: on my j.   CHAU 68:18
jollity: Jest and youthful j.   MILT 167:16
Jolly: J. boating weather   CORY 78:10
There was a j. miller once   BICK 42:1
Jonathan: Saul and J. were lovely   BIBLE 24:26
Joseph: Israel loved J.   BIBLE 23:3
jostle: Philistines may j.   GILB 108:21
jostling: done by j. in the street   BLAKE 43:5
journalism: from Christianity and j.   BALF 14:15
journalist: British j.   WOLFE 273:23
Journalists: J. say a thing that they   BENN 19:13
journey: death the j.'s end   DRYD 91:8
I have a long j. to take   RAL 194:9

On a j. North   COW 79:9
such a long j.   ELIOT 93:25
then begins a j. in my head   SHAK 235:10
to take a j.   ANDR 2:11
when the j.'s over   HOUS 125:5
world is going on a j.   HAZL 116:4
journeying: third-class seat sat the j. boy   HARDY 114:12
Journeys: J. end in lovers meeting   SHAK 233:22
Jowett: my name is J.   BEEC 17:11
joy: beauty is a j. for ever   KEATS 138:15
Brightened with j.   WORD 274:15
child may j. to hear   BLAKE 43:13
Gemme of all j.   DUNB 91:3
good tidings of great j.   BIBLE 35:2
J., beautiful radiance   SCH 201:2
j. cometh in the morning   PRAY 188:21
J., whose hand is ever   KEATS 139:17
let j. be unconfined   BYRON 57:10
My scrip of j.   RAL 194:4
purchase pain with all that j.   POPE 184:24
snatch a fearful j.   GRAY 112:9
sons of God shouted for j.   BIBLE 25:33
Surprised by j.   WORD 277:4
Variety's the source of j.   GAY 105:21
joye: dreme of j.   CHAU 68:21
joyful: be j. in the Lord   PRAY 190:4
J. and triumphant   ANON 6:10
joyous: j. Errand reach the Spot   FITZ 100:1
joys: eternal j. of heaven   MARL 160:3
J. in another's loss   BLAKE 43:20
minds me o' departed j.   BURNS 55:9
season made for j.   GAY 105:13
Thy j. when shall I see   ANON 3:16
vain deluding j.   MILT 167:10
What lasting j. the man   WHURR 270:13
judge: after a time they j. them   WILDE 271:27
Forbear to j.   SHAK 214:13
glory to j. both the quick   PRAY 187:13
J. none blessed before   BIBLE 30:22
J. not   BIBLE 32:2
J. not the play before   QUAR 193:9
now I am a J.   GILB 109:11
to make answer to the j.   CEL 66:1
judged: whereby the world will be j.   CEL 66:1
judgement: common pursuit of true j.   ELIOT 95:10
His critical j. is so exquisite   FRY 103:16
history is the world's j.   SCH 201:4
if unassisted by j.   HOR 124:8
industry only, but his j.   BURKE 52:14
judgment: on better j. making   SHAK 236:6
reserve thy j.   SHAK 207:6
waits upon the j.   SHAK 210:16
judgments: reasons of state to influence our j.   MANS 159:11
judicious: like a little j. levity   STEV 247:6
Judy O'Grady: Colonel's Lady an' J.   KIPL 145:1
jug: old j. without a handle   LEAR 150:7
juggler: perceive a j.'s sleight   BUTL 56:8
jug-jug: j., pu-we   NASHE 175:3
Julia: Whenas in silks my J. goes   HERR 119:1
Jumblies: lands where the J. live   LEAR 150:11
jump: j. the life to come   SHAK 220:13
June: needs not J. for beauty's   ARN 9:3
Jungle: this is the Law of the J.   KIPL 145:2
Juno: J.'s never-forgetting   VIRG 262:15
Jupiter: Quem J. vult perdere   DUP 92:2
just: faithful and j. to me   SHAK 216:17
j. and lasting peace   LINC 152:3

j. man is also a prison	THOR 259:1	K. du es wohl	GOE 110:3
j. shall live by faith	BIBLE 37:31	Kensal Green: to Paradise by way of K.	CHES 70:4
meanly j.	JOHN 135:9	to Paradise by way of K.	CHES 70:5
Only the actions of the j.	SHIR 241:3	Kent: everybody knows K.	DICK 85:13
over ninety and nine j.	BIBLE 35:25	talk I'm k. the better	BURNS 54:19
rain it raineth on the j.	BOWEN 45:9	Kentish: K. Sir Byng stood for his	BROW 49:6
sendeth rain on the j.	BIBLE 31:18	Kentish Town: dandelions to the courts of K.	
so what I plead is j.	HOPK 122:8		BETJ 21:9
that hath his quarrel j.	BILL 42:5	kept: I have k. the faith	BIBLE 40:4
that hath his quarrel j.	SHAK 214:12	Ketch: soon dine with Jack K.	JOHN 133:1
Thou art indeed j., Lord	HOPK 122:8	Kew: down to K. in lilac time	NOYES 177:7
whatsoever things are j.	BIBLE 39:20	his Highness' dog at K.	POPE 184:16
With j. enough of learning	BYRON 58:16	key: away the k. of knowledge	BIBLE 35:18
justice: believing in the j. of our cause	HAIG 113:9	Turn the k. deftly	KEATS 140:8
j., In fair round belly	SHAK 205:1	keys: half that's got my k.	GRAH 111:9
J. is open to all	MATH 164:7	Over the noisy k.	PROC 191:20
j. makes democracy possible	NIEB 176:12	Khatmandu: idol to the north of K.	HAYES 116:1
j. should not only be done	HEW 119:5	Khayyám: come with old K.	FITZ 99:4
'J.' was done	HARDY 115:5	kick: I'll k. you downstairs	CARR 62:19
Let j. be done	FERD 97:19	to k. against the pricks	BIBLE 37:17
Let j. be done though	WATS 266:14	kicked: any k. up stairs before	HALE 114:4
Revenge is a kind of wild j.	BACON 13:16	cursed and k. the stairs	MILL 166:7
right or j.	MAGN 159:1	kid: shall lie down with the k.	BIBLE 28:21
temper so J. with mercy.	MILT 169:20	Thou shalt not seethe a k.	BIBLE 23:20
what you think j. requires	MANS 159:12	kiddies: k. have crumpled the serviettes	BETJ 20:13
When mercy seasons j.	SHAK 225:17	kill: animals never k. for sport	FROU 103:15
you have ravish'd j.	WEBS 267:15	disease and k. the patient	BACON 13:8
justified: man can only be j.	ROS 196:17	I k. you	CHAM 67:3
justifies: end j. the means	BUS 55:22	I'll k. you if you quote it	BURG 52:6
justify: j. the ways of God to Men	MILT 168:14	k. a man as kill a good	MILT 170:15
To j. God's ways to man	HOUS 126:12	k. a wife with kindness	SHAK 232:9
justitia: are bound to say 'fiat j.	MANS 159:11	k. sick people groaning	MARL 160:12
Fiat j. et pereat	FERD 97:19	let's k. all the lawyers	SHAK 214:14
justitiam: rectum aut j.	MAGN 159:1	nor yet canst thou k. me	DONNE 88:3
justly: to do j.	BIBLE 30:19	prepared to k. one another	SHAW 237:23
Juvenes: J. dum sumus	ANON 6:17	They k. us for their sport	SHAK 218:18
juventutem: Post jucundam j.	ANON 6:17	Thou shalt not k.	CLOU 73:13
Kangaroo: Duck and the K.	LEAR 150:9	When you have to k. a man	CHUR 71:18
kangaroos: dear little k. flying about		kill'd: I kiss'd thee ere I k.	SHAK 229:16
	WILDE 271:15	killed: effort very nearly k. her	BELL 18:14
kann: Ich k. nicht anders	LUTH 155:12	I am the enemy you k.	OWEN 179:11
Wovon man nicht sprechen k.	WITT 273:10	k. a calf he would do it	AUBR 10:6
Kaspar: Old K.'s work was done	SOUT 243:16	killeth: letter k.	BIBLE 39:2
kategorisch: Dieser Imperativ ist k.	KANT 138:7	killing: k. a cat than choking	KING 143:1
Keats: K., who was kill'd off	BYRON 58:12	k. Kruger with your mouth	KIPL 143:6
What porridge had John K.	BROW 50:13	K. myself to die upon	SHAK 229:16
Who killed John K.	BYRON 58:18	K. no Murder Briefly Discourst	SEXBY 203:9
keel: Joan doth k. the pot	SHAK 219:14	k. of a mouse on Sunday	BRAT 46:7
keener: grows k. with constant use	IRV 129:15	Men talk of k. time	BOUC 45:5
with his k. eye	MARV 161:17	kills: man k. the thing he loves	WILDE 271:3
keep: Except the Lord k. the city	PRAY 190:19	my heart an air that k.	HOUS 126:7
If you can k. your head	KIPL 144:7	waste remains and k.	EMPS 96:21
k. a hold of Nurse	BELL 18:12	kin: If one's own k. and kith	NASH 174:15
k. his friendship in constant	JOHN 131:14	little more than k.	SHAK 206:11
k. on saying it long enough	BENN 19:13	makes the whole world k.	SHAK 233:9
k. the bridge with me	MAC 156:6	kind: beautiful, the tender, the k.	MILL 166:3
k. thee in all thy ways	PRAY 190:1	be cruel only to be k.	SHAK 210:20
k. the wolf far thence	WEBS 267:16	had been k.	JOHN 131:9
k. your hearts and minds	BIBLE 39:19	Is she k. as she is fair	SHAK 234:18
need k. the shutters up	DICK 84:15	just try to be k.	FOAK 101:5
'O k. the Dog far hence	ELIOT 95:1	k. of people do they think	CHUR 71:9
they should k. who can	WORD 275:10	less than k.	SHAK 206:11
keeper: Am I my brother's k.	BIBLE 22:16	people were a k. of solution	CAV 65:12
k. Stands up	HOUS 126:3	people will always be k.	SASS 200:7
Lord himself is thy k.	PRAY 190:16	to her virtues very k.	PRIOR 191:16
keepeth: he that k. thee	PRAY 190:16	kindles: k. fire	LA R 149:11
Kempenfelt: When K. went down	COWP 79:16	kindliness: cool k. of sheets	BROO 47:6
kenne: Ich k. mich auch nicht	GOE 109:21	kindness: In vain with lavish k.	HEBER 116:10
Kennst: K. du das Land	GOE 110:3	kill a wife with k.	SHAK 232:9

it is a k.	SHAK 221:11
Sea-nymphs hourly ring his k.	SHAK 232:15
strikes like a rising k.	BYRON 57:9
knew: head could carry all he k.	GOLD 110:11
I k. not where	LONG 153:1
knife: k. see not the wound it	SHAK 220:11
'War even to the k.	BYRON 57:7
War to the k.	PAL 179:17
wind's like a whetted k.	MAS 163:2
knight: gentle k. was pricking	SPEN 244:15
He is k. dubbed with unhatched	SHAK 234:12
K. at arms	KEATS 139:3
K. of the Doleful Countenance	CERV 66:5
K. without fear and without	ANON 5:16
There never was k. like	SCOTT 201:19
Knightly: ever the K. years were gone	HENL 117:9
knights: ladies dead and lovely k.	SHAK 236:10
knits: Sleep that k. up the ravell'd	SHAK 221:16
knitting: twisted braids of lilies k.	MILT 167:9
knock: k., and it shall be opened	BIBLE 32:5
K. as you please	POPE 184:15
k. me down with the butt-end	CIBB 72:1
right to k. him down for it	JOHN 133:14
stand at the door, and k.	BIBLE 40:30
Knocked: K. on my sullen heart	STEV 247:17
knocker: Tie up the k.	POPE 184:18
Knocking: K. on the moonlit door	DE L 82:13
knocks: k. you down with the butt	GOLD 111:1
knoll'd: bells have k. to church	SHAK 204:24
knot: So the k. be unknotted	ELIOT 93:11
knot-grass: bunches of k.	KEATS 138:18
knots: pokers into true-love k.	COL 75:8
know: all ye need to k.	KEATS 139:16
canvassers whom they do not k.	HURST 128:9
creditors would hardly k.	FOX 102:4
does not k. himself	LA F 147:13
go we k. not where	SHAK 224:4
hate any one that we k.	HAZL 116:7
have much ado to k. myself	SHAK 224:10
I do not k. myself	GOE 109:21
I k. myself a man	DAV 82:1
k. of England who only	KIPL 143:18
k. that my redeemer liveth	BIBLE 25:28
k. thee not, old man	SHAK 213:6
K. then thyself	POPE 185:17
k. the place for the first	ELIOT 93:20
K. thyself	ANON 6:6
'K. thyself'	CARL 61:21
k. to be useful	MORR 173:16
'K. what thou canst work	CARL 61:21
K. you the land where	GOE 110:3
let me k. mine end	PRAY 188:25
no one to k. what it is	ANON 2:13
now I k. it	GAY 105:20
they k. not what they do	BIBLE 36:8
to others that we k. not	SHAK 208:24
we k. in part	BIBLE 38:15
We k. our will is free	JOHN 132:13
What do I k.	MONT 172:5
What they are yet I k. not	SHAK 218:5
when it came to k. me well	MOORE 173:3
knowed: that there is to be k.	GRAH 111:12
knoweth: He that loveth not k. not	BIBLE 40:25
knowing: lust of k. what should	FLEC 100:8
misfortune of k. any thing	AUST 12:6
knowledge: all k. to be my province	BACON 13:28
desire more love and k.	SHAK 204:15
he would bring home k.	JOHN 133:8
increaseth k. increaseth sorrow	BIBLE 27:5

K. comes	TENN 253:11
K. itself is power	BACON 14:2
k., it shall vanish	BIBLE 38:15
k. of London was extensive	DICK 85:17
k. of nothing	DICK 85:28
k. of a lifetime	WHIS 269:13
Out-topping k.	ARN 9:1
Such k. is too wonderful	PRAY 191:2
taken away the key of k.	BIBLE 35:18
What I don't know isn't k.	BEEC 17:11
known: know even as also I am k.	BIBLE 38:16
knowing what should not be k.	FLEC 100:8
k. for his well-knownness	BOOR 44:18
k. of old	KIPL 145:10
light and safer than a k.	HASK 115:16
Soldier of the Great War K.	KIPL 146:28
That thy way may be k.	PRAY 189:12
till I am k.	JOHN 131:9
knows: HE k.—HE knows	FITZ 99:8
k. more and more about	BUTL 56:2
k. of a better 'ole	BAIR 14:10
now God alone k.	KLOP 147:2
knyf: smylere with the k. under	CHAU 68:9
knyght: parfit gentil k.	CHAU 67:19
Kopf: *Ward mancher K. zum Greise*	MULL 174:6
Kraken: K. sleepeth	TENN 252:27
Krieg: *Der K. ist nichts als eine*	CLAU 73:3
K. ein Glied in Gottes	MOLT 171:15
Kruger: you've finished killing K.	KIPL 143:6
krummem: *Aus so k. Holze*	KANT 138:10
Kubla: 'mid this tumult K. heard	COL 75:5
Kubla Khan: In Xanadu did K.	COL 75:2
Kultur: *Wenn ich K. höre*	JOHST 135:12
Kurd: say the same about the K.	BELL 18:4
Kurtz: Mistah K.—he dead	CONR 77:12
Kyrie: K. eleison	MASS 163:10
labor: *hic l. est*	VIRG 263:10
laboraverunt: *in vanum l. qui aedificant*	BIBLE 41:15
labour: faith and l. of love	BIBLE 39:23
l. against our own cure	BROW 48:8
l. we delight in physics	SHAK 222:4
Learn to l. and to wait	LONG 153:11
ruined by Chinese cheap l.	HARTE 115:13
sore l.'s bath	SHAK 221:16
strength then but l. and sorrow	PRAY 189:22
that l. are heavy laden	BIBLE 32:31
their l. is but lost that	PRAY 190:19
to his l.	PRAY 190:5
To painful l. both by sea	SHAK 232:10
true success is to l.	STEV 247:4
laboured: builders have l. in vain	BIBLE 41:15
labourer: l. is worthy of his hire	BIBLE 35:11
labouring: sleep of a l. man is sweet	BIBLE 27:8
labours: Children sweeten l.	BACON 13:15
labyrinthical: l. soul	DONNE 89:4
labyrinthine: l. ways Of my own mind	THOM 258:1
lace: l. my bodice blue	HUNT 128:8
Through the Nottingham l.	BETJ 20:5
Laces: L. for a lady	KIPL 145:15
lacessit: *Nemo me impune l.*	ANON 7:1
Lachende: *L. Löwen müssen kommen*	NIET 176:14
lack: I sigh the l. of many	SHAK 235:12
therefore can I l. nothing	PRAY 188:12
lack'd: If I l. any thing	HERB 118:11
lacrimae: *Hinc illae l.*	TER 256:2
Sunt l. rerum	VIRG 263:2
lad: was a l. I served a term	GILB 108:28
ladder: he dreamed, and behold a l.	BIBLE 22:32

Now that my l.'s gone | YEATS 278:14
laden: labour and are heavy l. | BIBLE 32:31
ladies: Come from a l.' seminary | GILB 108:7
Dust was Gentlemen and L. | DICK 86:5
l. dead and lovely knights | SHAK 236:10
l. most deject and wretched | SHAK 209:6
ribs was sport for l. | SHAK 204:14
lads: l. in their hundreds | HOUS 125:14
lady: I met a l. in the meads | KEATS 139:4
l. doth protest too much | SHAK 210:2
L. is as good i' th' dark | HERR 118:20
l. that's known as Lou | SERV 203:8
Lord and L. Dalhousie | MCG 157:10
when a l.'s in the case | GAY 105:18
Lady Bountiful: My L. | FARQ 97:13
lady-smocks: l. all silver-white | SHAK 219:13
Lafayette: L., we are here | STAN 245:12
laggard: l. in love | SCOTT 201:20
laid: l. end to end | PARK 180:10
l. him in a manger | BIBLE 35:1
not where they have l. him | BIBLE 37:9
These l. the world away | BROO 47:5
laisse: On l. un peu de soi-même | HAR 114:7
Laisser: L.-faire | DARG 7:19
laisser faire: laisser passer et de l. | QUES 193:10
laity: conspiracies against the l. | SHAW 237:14
lake: black Cyprus with a l. | FLEC 100:9
I hear l. water lapping | YEATS 279:8
into the bosom of the l. | TENN 254:16
Lalage: I've lost L. | KIPL 145:13
lama: l. sabachthani | BIBLE 34:18
Lamb: Behold the L. of God | BIBLE 36:18
Did he who made the L. | BLAKE 43:9
l. to the slaughter | BIBLE 29:16
Little L. | BLAKE 43:14
Mary had a little l. | HALE 113:12
'Pipe a song about a L. | BLAKE 43:12
save one little ewe l. | BIBLE 24:28
shall dwell with the l. | BIBLE 28:21
was the holy L. of God | BLAKE 43:2
lambs: gather the l. with his arm | BIBLE 29:10
l. could not forgive | DICK 84:18
Lame: L. dogs over stiles | KING 142:10
lament: yet you l. not the days | SOUT 244:1
Lamentings: L. heard i' the air | SHAK 222:5
lamp: smell too strong of the l. | STER 246:9
When the l. is shattered | SHEL 239:8
lampada: quasi cursores vitai l. | LUCR 155:7
lamp-posts: MSS as drunkards use l. | HOUS 127:7
lamprey: like the l. | WEBS 267:7
lamps: Heav'n's great l. do dive | CAT 65:5
l. are going out all over | LORD 113:4
old l. for new | ARAB 7:12
lancer: 'listed at home for a l. | HOUS 126:15
land: abroad throughout the l. | BRIG 46:14
afternoon they came unto a l. | TENN 253:15
Ceres re-assume the l. | POPE 185:4
eat the fat of the l. | BIBLE 23:7
England's green & pleasant L. | BLAKE 43:2
for a parcel of l. | HOR 125:1
heaven by sea as by l. | GILB 106:17
Ill fares the l. | GOLD 110:6
l. flowing with milk | BIBLE 23:11
l. is bright | CLOU 73:17
l. of lost content | HOUS 126:7
L. of our birth | KIPL 143:15
L. was ours before we were | FROST 103:5
L. where my fathers died | SMITH 242:11
l. where the Bong-tree | LEAR 150:14

O'er the l. of the free | KEY 141:15
on this windy sea of l. | MILT 169:5
sent to spy out the l. | BIBLE 23:26
She is far from the l. | MOORE 173:1
There's the l., or cherry-isle | HERR 118:17
This l. of such dear souls | SHAK 230:2
thro' the l. at eve we went | TENN 254:6
to gaze out from the l. | LUCR 155:6
landlord: had better have a rich l. | SHAW 238:19
landmark: removeth his neighbour's l. | BIBLE 23:35
lands: children who died for our l. | KIPL 143:14
envy of less happier l. | SHAK 230:2
l. were fairly portioned | MAC 156:7
l. where the Jumblies live | LEAR 150:11
young man l. hatless | BETJ 20:10
landscape: fades the glimmering l. | GRAY 111:18
l. of England in general | AUST 12:1
lane: l. was made | DICK 84:16
lang: y'er a l. time deid | ANON 3:7
langage: coeur comme dans le l. | LA R 149:12
language: bottom the l. of the unheard | KING 142:7
conceive you may use any l. | GILB 107:20
In l., the ignorant | DUPPA 92:3
l. and ways of behaving | JUV 137:17
l. convey more than they | CONN 77:5
language…L. is not simply a reporting | WHORF 270:12
l. that would make your | GILB 109:6
L. was not powerful enough | DICK 85:2
Learned his great l. | BROW 50:1
…My l. fails | BELL 18:13
my l. is plain | HARTE 115:12
no respect for their l. | SHAW 238:16
some entrance into the l. | BACON 13:24
There's l. in her eye | SHAK 233:11
with no l. but a cry | TENN 252:16
Worships l. and forgives | AUDEN 10:17
You taught me l. | SHAK 232:12
languages: at a great feast of l. | SHAK 219:14
speaks three or four l. | SHAK 233:16
langueur: une l. Monotone | VERL 262:2
languid: through the music of the l. | LANG 148:16
languors: lilies and l. of virtue | SWIN 249:18
Lap: your loneliness in heat | BETJ 20:6
lapidary: l. inscriptions a man is | JOHN 132:23
lapwing: like a l. | SHAK 228:8
lards: l. the lean earth as he | SHAK 212:9
large: It's as l. as life | CARR 64:12
l. a letter I have written | BIBLE 39:10
l. a trunk before | BELL 18:7
Mothers of l. families | BELL 18:7
sufficiently l. scale | SPEN 244:8
largely: drinking l. sobers us again | POPE 185:8
largest: l. lamp is lit | MAC 156:11
lark: l. at break of day | SHAK 235:11
l. at heaven's gate sings | SHAK 206:3
l.'s on the wing | BROW 50:12
No l. more blithe than he | BICK 42:1
We rise with the l. | BRET 46:10
Larks: Four L. and a Wren | LEAR 150:2
hear the l. so high | HOUS 125:12
larkspur: l. listens, 'I hear | TENN 254:2
Lars: L. Porsena of Clusium | MAC 156:3
LASCIATE: L. OGNI SPERANZA VOI CH'EN-TRATE | DANTE 81:8
lash: dost thou l. that whore | SHAK 218:22
rum, sodomy and the l. | CHUR 71:21
lashed: yes O at lightning and l. | HOPK 122:11
lass: every l. a queen | KING 142:16

l. unparallel'd	SHAK 204:12
Sweet l. of Richmond Hill	MACN 158:2
was a lover and his l.	SHAK 205:12
lasse: tout l.	ANON 6:5
last: It will not l. the night	MILL 166:6
l. act crowns	QUAR 193:9
l. breath he drew in	LAMB 148:6
l. enemy that shall be	BIBLE 38:19
l. gentleman in Europe	LEV 151:10
l. red leaf is whirl'd	TENN 252:12
l. rose of summer	MOORE 173:2
L. scene of all	SHAK 205:1
l. shall be first	BIBLE 33:24
l. syllable of recorded	SHAK 223:15
l. taste of sweets	SHAK 229:21
L. week in Babylon	HODG 120:6
l. words of Marmion	SCOTT 202:3
Look thy l. on all things	DE L 82:11
present were the world's l. night	DONNE 88:5
that's the l. thing I shall	PALM 180:2
Tristram Shandy did not l.	JOHN 132:24
When he was at the l. gasp	BIBLE 30:30
lasting: just and l. peace	LINC 152:3
memorial longer l. than bronze	HOR 124:12
latchet: shoe's l. I am not worthy	BIBLE 36:17
late: damned fella will be l.	MITF 171:1
Farmer Ledlow l. at plough	HARDY 114:9
l. for medicine to be prepared	OVID 178:23
l. or too early for anything	SART 200:3
So l. into the night	BYRON 58:22
that leaves him out so l.	FROST 103:9
when it comes l. in life	JERR 130:19
later: It is l. than you think	SERV 203:7
l. by George the Fourth	COW 79:9
there will be sunlight l.	MACN 158:4
Latet: L. anguis in herba	VIRG 264:2
Latin: half L. and half Greek	SCOTT 201:8
he speaks L.	SHAK 215:2
measures is L. for a whopping	ANST 7:10
small L., and less Greek	JONS 136:6
latter: stand at the l. day	BIBLE 25:28
To carry off the l.	PEAC 181:16
Laudamus: L. te	MASS 163:12
Te Deum l.	ANON 7:7
laudator: l. temporis acti	HOR 122:18
laudi: concedant lqwrea l.	CIC 72:8
laugh: behind her a meaning l.	EWART 97:7
do we not l.	SHAK 225:10
I l. at any mortal thing	BYRON 58:11
it hurt too much to l.	STEV 246:16
L. and the world laughs	WILC 271:2
l. at human actions	SPIN 245:1
l. at them in our turn	AUST 12:13
l. that spoke the vacant	GOLD 110:7
make her l. at that	SHAK 211:11
make myself l. at everything	BEAU 16:15
no girl wants to l. all	LOOS 154:2
sillier than a silly l.	CAT 65:8
Thy lovely l.	CAT 65:9
laughed: first baby l.	BARR 16:2
they l. consumedly	FARQ 97:14
When he l.	AUDEN 10:13
laughing: l. is heard on the hill	BLAKE 43:16
L. lions must come	NIET 176:14
L. Water	LONG 153:13
speaking sweetly and l. sexily	SAPP 199:12
laughs: he l. much louder than	MILL 166:5
l. so sweetly and talks	HOR 123:17
laughter: audible l.	CHES 69:4
creatures by the faculty of l.	ADD 1:14
l. and ability and Sighing	DICK 86:5
L. holding both his sides	MILT 167:17
l., learnt of friends	BROO 47:16
mirth hath present l.	SHAK 233:22
so is the l. of a fool	BIBLE 27:9
under running l.	THOM 258:1
launch'd: face that l. a thousand	MARL 160:5
laurel: burnèd is Apollo's l.	MARL 160:8
L. is green for a season	SWIN 250:3
laurels: Are worth all your l.	BYRON 59:2
l. all are cut	ANON 6:3
l. to paeans	CIC 72:8
lauriers: les l. sont coupés	ANON 6:3
lavat'ry: l. makes you fear the worst	COW 79:9
lave: Let the l. go by me	STEV 247:11
law: above me and the moral l.	KANT 138:6
Any l. which violates	ROB 195:10
ashamed the l. is such an ass	CHAP 67:8
Bumble…'the l. is a ass	DICK 85:8
dusty purlieus of the l.	TENN 252:20
egalitarianism of the l.	FRAN 102:5
fugitive from th' l. of averages	MAUL 164:9
God is thy l., thou mine	MILT 169:10
hearts to keep this l.	PRAY 187:10
Ignorance of the l. excuses	SELD 202:18
is the L. of the Jungle	KIPL 145:2
l. and the prophets	BIBLE 32:7
L. is the true embodiment	GILB 107:12
l.'s delay	SHAK 208:24
lesser breeds without the L.	KIPL 145:12
Necessity gives the l.	PUBL 192:9
Necessity hath no l.	CROM 80:19
nine-tenths of the l. of chivalry	SAY 200:16
ought l. to weed it out	BACON 14:3
people is the chief l.	CIC 72:6
perfection of our l.	ANON 2:15
there is not a single l.	PEEL 182:1
very good l. for all that	SCOTT 202:7
windward of the l.	CHUR 70:20
windy side of the l.	SHAK 234:11
lawful: All things are l. for me	BIBLE 38:11
art L. as eating	SHAK 235:3
is l. prize	GRAY 112:7
seas upon their l. occasions	PRAY 191:10
that which is l. and right	BIBLE 30:5
lawns: house with l. enclosing	STEV 247:15
Laws: L. are like spider's webs	SOLON 243:10
l. but to obey them	HORS 125:2
l. of God will be suspended	SHAW 237:18
make the l. of a nation	FLET 100:15
prescribed l. to the learned	DUPPA 92:3
sweeps a room as for Thy l.	HERB 118:9
Unequal l. unto a savage race	TENN 255:10
war has its l.	NEWM 175:19
lawyers: l.! for ye have taken	BIBLE 35:18
let's kill all the l.	SHAK 214:14
Lay: L. her i' the earth	SHAK 211:13
l. my bones amongst you	WOLS 274:4
L. on, Macduff	SHAK 223:16
L. your sleeping head	AUDEN 11:3
man l. down his wife	JOYCE 135:8
oneself is that one can l.	BUTL 56:20
prepared to l. down my life	CLOU 73:8
lays: constructing tribal l.	KIPL 144:10
She l. it on with a trowel	CONG 76:12
lead: if the blind l. the blind	BIBLE 33:9
L., kindly Light	NEWM 176:4
L. us, Heavenly Father	EDM 92:8

l. us not into temptation — BIBLE 31:21
little child shall l. them — BIBLE 28:21
shall gently l. those that — BIBLE 29:10
To l. such dire attack — MAC 156:8
to l. them the way — BIBLE 23:17
leaden: Because if I use l. ones — BELL 18:6
l. foot time creeps along — JAGO 129:19
leaden-stepping: Call on the lazy l. hours — MILT 168:11
leader: I am their l. — LEDR 151:2
Over the face of the l. — WHIT 270:9
leader-writers: God exists only for l. — GREE 112:17
leading: I owe no light or l. received — MILT 170:20
leaf: If I were a dead l. thou — SHEL 239:13
last red l. is whirl'd — TENN 252:12
league: Half a l. onward — TENN 251:8
Leaking: L. the brightness away — SPEN 244:12
lean: has a l. and hungry look — SHAK 215:17
on which if a man l. — BIBLE 25:14
She help'd him to l. — BARH 15:9
Lean'd: L. her breast up-till — BARN 15:17
Leans: L. to the sun's kiss glorying — GREN 113:3
leap: great l. in the dark — HOBB 120:2
made a l. into the dark — BROWN 48:1
leaped: God have I l. over a wall — BIBLE 24:30
thousand swords must have l. — BURKE 53:9
leaping: l., and praising God — BIBLE 37:14
Lear: pleasant to know Mr L. — LEAR 150:4
learn: An' l. about women from me — KIPL 144:15
craft so long to l. — HIPP 119:12
l., and inwardly digest — PRAY 187:7
L. to labour and to wait — LONG 153:11
men l. — SEN 203:5
We live and l. — POMF 184:4
learned: decent obscurity of a l. — GIBB 106:9
governments never have l. — HEGEL 116:11
grew within this l. man — MARL 160:8
L. his great language — BROW 50:1
loads of l. lumber — POPE 185:13
prescribed laws to the l. — DUPPA 92:3
learning: encourage a will to l. — ASCH 9:18
grammar, and nonsense, and l. — GOLD 110:17
I grow old ever l. — SOLON 243:11
just enough of l. to misquote — BYRON 58:16
l. lightly like a flower — TENN 252:26
little l. is a dang'rous — POPE 185:8
much l. doth make thee mad — BIBLE 37:29
that loyal body wanted l. — TRAPP 259:22
to be written for our l. — PRAY 187:7
Wear your l. — CHES 69:9
Whence is thy l. — GAY 105:17
learnt: been l. has been forgotten — SKIN 241:14
forgotten nothing and l. — DUM 91:20
They have l. nothing — TALL 250:14
lease: summer's l. hath all too — SHAK 235:9
least: is best which governs l.' — THOR 258:16
is that which governs l. — OSUL 178:15
l. of these my brethren — BIBLE 34:9
leather: attired in l. boots — HOUS 127:3
leave: forever taking l. — RILKE 195:5
how I l. my country — PITT 183:13
Intreat me not to l. thee — BIBLE 24:14
l. a living name behind — WEBS 267:6
L. her to heaven — SHAK 207:16
l. his father and his mother — BIBLE 22:11
l. me here a little — TENN 253:5
l. me there to die — ANON 3:18
L. not a rack behind — SHAK 232:24
L. off first for manners' — BIBLE 30:24

l. the world unseen — KEATS 139:19
under l. of Brutus — SHAK 216:16
wilt thou l. me thus — WYATT 278:2
leaves: bags full of l. — FROST 103:4
Close up these barren l. — WORD 277:9
fields and l. to the trees — HOR 124:15
l. dead Are driven — SHEL 239:12
l. grow on the tree — YEATS 278:18
l. the world to darkness — GRAY 111:18
one l. behind a part — HAR 114:7
sewed fig l. — BIBLE 22:12
tender l. of hope — SHAK 215:9
thick on Severn snow the l. — HOUS 126:4
When yellow l. — SHAK 236:5
whole deck put on its l. — FLEC 100:11
leaving: Became him like the l. it — SHAK 220:9
L. his country for his — FITZ 98:13
leben: gefährlich l. — NIET 176:19
l. wir und nehmen immer — RILKE 195:5
lecher: Does l. in my sight — SHAK 218:20
Lechery: L., sir, it provokes — SHAK 222:3
led: Carlyle has l. us all out — CLOU 73:19
l. his regiment from behind — GILB 107:1
leene: l. was his hors as is — CHAU 68:4
lees: drink Life to the l. — TENN 255:11
left: he has l. us there — CLOU 73:19
l. him alone with his glory — WOLFE 273:22
'tis better to be l. than — CONG 76:22
We l. our country for our — CART 64:19
Ye have l. your souls — KEATS 139:11
'You l. us in tatters — HARDY 114:13
leg: kiss my Julia's dainty l. — HERR 118:21
legacy: l. from a rich relative — BIRK 42:8
lege: Tolle l. — AUG 11:16
legem: Necessitas dat l. non ipsa — PUBL 192:9
Legion: My name is L. — BIBLE 34:23
legislation: foundation of morals and l. — BENT 19:14
legislator: l. of mankind — JOHN 134:28
legislators: are the unacknowledged l. — SHEL 240:12
legitimate: such a thing as l. warfare — NEWM 175:19
legs: cannon-ball took off his l. — HOOD 121:5
Four l. good — ORW 178:6
losing your l. — SASS 200:7
vast and trunkless l. — SHEL 239:16
Walk under his huge l. — SHAK 215:16
your l. ungainly huddled — SASS 200:8
leid: Heute l.' ich — LESS 151:9
leisure: improvement arises from l. — JOHN 132:17
is l. with honour — CIC 72:14
we may polish it at l. — DRYD 91:12
lemon: l. is squeezed — GEDD 105:24
lemon-trees: land where the l. bloom — GOE 110:3
lend: I'll l. you thus much moneys — SHAK 225:1
l. me your ears — SHAK 216:16
onward l. thy guiding hand — MILT 169:24
lender: borrower, nor a l. be — SHAK 207:6
lenders: thy pen from l.' books — SHAK 218:12
Length: L. of days is in her right — BIBLE 26:5
lente: Festina l. — SUET 248:7
l. currite noctis equi — MARL 160:6
Léonie: Weep not for little L. — GRAH 111:7
leopard: l. his spots — BIBLE 29:26
l. shall lie down with — BIBLE 28:21
leporum: Medio de fonte l. — LUCR 155:9
lerne: wolde he l. and gladly teche — CHAU 68:5
Lesbia: L. let us live and love — CAT 65:5
L. with her sparrow — MILL 166:8
mea L. — CAT 65:5

less: l. brilliant pen | BEER 17:13
more about less and l. | BUTL 56:2
small Latin, and l. Greek | JONS 136:6
still the l. they understand | BUTL 56:8
'Tis l. than to be born | BEAU 17:2
lessen: 'because they l. from day | CARR 63:9
lesson: still harder l. | PORT 186:4
'Tis a l. you should heed | HICK 119:7
lessons: reason they're called l. | CARR 63:9
Lest: L. we forget | KIPL 145:10
let: before you l. the sun | THOM 257:10
L. justice be done | FERD 97:19
L. my people go | ANON 5:11
L. them eat cake | MAR 160:1
L. there be light | BIBLE 22:2
l. the sounds of music | SHAK 226:5
l. who can be clever | KING 142:9
Lethe: on the wharf of L. waiting | HOUS 126:24
Lethean: have drunken of things L. | SWIN 250:3
letter: large a l. I have written | BIBLE 39:10
l. from his wife | CARR 62:10
l. killeth | BIBLE 39:2
till you write your l. | DONNE 88:17
wordy l. came from Capri | JUV 138:3
letters: l. for a spy | KIPL 145:15
l. mingle souls | DONNE 88:9
No arts; no l. | HOBB 120:1
receive no l. in the grave | JOHN 134:8
than a man of l. | STER 246:12
level: Are l. now with men | SHAK 204:6
leviathan: draw out l. with an hook | BIBLE 26:2
levity: like a little judicious l. | STEV 247:6
lewd: l. fellows of the baser | BIBLE 37:21
lex: populi suprema est l. | CIC 72:6
Lexicographer: L.: a writer of dictionaries | JOHN 131:13
l. can only hope to escape | JOHN 134:13
lexicography: am not yet so lost in l. | JOHN 134:15
liaison: l. man and partly P.R.O. | BETJ 20:12
liar: he is a l. | BIBLE 36:29
only answered 'Little L. | BELL 18:16
liars: All men are l. | PRAY 190:14
fears may be l. | CLOU 73:17
Liber: L. scriptus proferetur | CEL 66:1
Nullus l. homo capiatur | MAGN 158:16
libera: Anglicana ecclesia l. | MAGN 158:15
Liberal: Is either a little L. | GILB 107:16
Liberté: L.! Égalité | ANON 6:2
liberties: never give up their l. | BURKE 53:5
libertine: puff'd and reckless l. | SHAK 207:5
liberty: Enjoy such l. | LOV 154:9
give me l. | HENRY 117:16
insolent and L. to be saucy | HALE 114:2
it certainly destroys l. | JOHN 133:20
l. of the individual must | MILL 165:17
L.'s in every blow | BURNS 54:21
l. to man is eternal vigilance | CURR 81:5
life, and l. | JEFF 130:9
life, l. | ANON 5:9
men are to wait for l. | MAC 157:1
mountain nymph, sweet L. | MILT 167:17
O liberty! O l. | ROL 196:3
People contend for their L. | HALE 114:1
power and to lose l. | BACON 13:10
primordial condition of l. | BAK 14:12
proclaim l. to the captives | BIBLE 29:20
Sweet land of l. | SMITH 242:11
tree of l. must be refreshed | JEFF 130:10
were thy chosen music, L. | WORD 277:6

Liberty-Hall: This is L. | GOLD 110:21
library: l. of sixty-two thousand | GIBB 106:12
libre: L'homme est né l. | ROUS 198:2
licence: l. to print your own money | THOM 258:15
licentious: all l. passages are left | GIBB 106:9
rapacious and l. soldiery | BURKE 53:4
Licht: Mehr L. | GOER 110:4
lick: time to l. it into form | BURT 55:13
Liddell: this is Mrs L. | SPR 245:6
lie: big l. than to a small | HITL 119:13
Cannot come, l. follows | PROU 192:6
iain wald l. down | BALL 14.17
He makes me down to l. | SCOT 202:15
I cannot tell a l. | WASH 266:13
l. as quietly among | EDW 92:12
l. diagonally in his bed | STER 246:11
L. follows by post | BER 19:22
L. heavy on him, Earth | EVANS 97:6
l. in cold obstruction | SHAK 224:4
l. where shades of darkness | DE L 82:10
l. with your legs ungainly | SASS 200:8
long night through must l. | HOUS 125:8
My love and I would l. | HOUS 125:12
not l. easy at Winchelsea | BENET 19:12
obedient to their laws we l. | SIM 241:9
sent to l. abroad | WOTT 278:1
shall l. through centuries | BROW 49:1
When he speaketh a l. | BIBLE 36:29
Whoever would l. usefully | HERV 119:4
Who loves to l. with me | SHAK 204:19
lieb: sich beide so herzlich l. | HEINE 116:13
Liebe: Was ist denn L. | HALM 114:5
liebt: Gestern l.' ich | LESS 151:9
lied: being l. about | KIPL 144:7
lies: ever-bubbling spring of endless l. | COWP 79:18
L. are the mortar that | WELLS 268:16
L. in his bed | SHAK 217:10
Matilda told such Dreadful L. | BELL 18:14
matter which way the head l. | RAL 194:3
Rest is L. | FITZ 99:4
There are three kinds of l. | DISR 87:15
though I know she l. | SHAK 237:1
white l. to ice a cake | ASQ 10:1
life: all human l. is there | JAMES 130:4
all the days of my l. | PRAY 188:10
Anythin' for a quiet l. | DICK 85:27
bitterness of l. | CARR 62:10
Book of L. begins with | WILDE 271:26
busy scenes of crowded l. | JOHN 135:8
by brisking about the L. | SMART 241:16
careless of the single l. | TENN 252:17
changing scenes of l. | TATE 250:10
C Major of this l. | BROW 48:20
crowded hour of glorious l. | MORD 173:5
day-to-day business l. is | LAF 147:15
dedication of l. | ELIOT 93:7
devils in l. and condition | ASCH 9:19
down his l. for his friends | BIBLE 37:3
dreamed that l. was Beauty | HOOP 121:14
drink L. to the lees | TENN 255:11
fall upon the thorns of l. | SHEL 239:14
findeth his l. shall lose | BIBLE 32:28
finish'd A l. heroic | MILT 170:5
fountain of the water of l. | BIBLE 41:9
freezes up the heat of l. | SHAK 232:3
give thee a crown of l. | BIBLE 40:29
giveth his l. for the sheep | BIBLE 36:31
Give to me the l. I love | STEV 247:11
hands before the fire of l. | LAND 148:8

have everlasting l.   BIBLE 36:21
His l. was gentle   SHAK 217:6
I know my l.'s a pain   DAV 82:1
I'm in mourning for my l.   CHEK 68:30
In balance with this l.   YEATS 279:5
In his pleasure is l.   PRAY 188:21
intellectual l. of our century   ARN 9:8
in the sea of l. enisled   ARN 8:15
jump the l. to come   SHAK 220:13
lad of l.   SHAK 213:19
lay hold on eternal l.   BIBLE 40:2
L., a Fury slinging flame   TENN 252:14
l., and liberty   JEFF 130:9
l. closed twice before   DICK 86:3
L. for life   BIBLE 23:18
L. is a jest   GAY 105:20
L. is as tedious as a twice-told   SHAK 217:11
L. is but an empty dream   LONG 153:9
l. is colour and warmth   GREN 113:3
L. is just one damned   OMAL 178:4
L. is real   LONG 153:9
l., liberty   ANON 5:9
L., like a dome of many-coloured   SHEL 239:1
l.: no man cometh unto   BIBLE 37:2
l. now, compact, visible   WHIT 269:17
l. of man   HOBB 120:1
L.'s but a walking shadow   SHAK 223:15
l.'s first native source   SPEN 244:20
l. so short   HIPP 119:12
l. to lose for my country   HALE 113:11
l. went through with death   VEN 261:20
l. with girls has ended   HOR 124:11
l., without a dream   ROST 197:11
L. without industry is   RUSK 198:7
little l. Is rounded   SHAK 232:24
London all that l. can afford   JOHN 133:5
long as you have your l.   JAMES 130:2
Madam L.'s a piece in bloom   HENL 117:8
many doors to let out l.   FLET 100:16
me hath everlasting l.   BIBLE 36:24
middle of the road of our l.   DANTE 81:7
midst of l. we are in death   PRAY 188:4
most loathed worldly l.   SHAK 224:4
my l. with coffee spoons   ELIOT 94:5
No, no, no l.   SHAK 219:4
nourisher in l.'s feast   SHAK 221:16
of man's l. a thing apart   BYRON 58:2
only honour and l. have   FRAN 102:6
Perfection of the l.   YEATS 278:13
prepared to lay down my l.   CLOU 73:8
purpose to a life beyond l.   MILT 170:16
put my genius into my l.   WILDE 272:1
regardeth the l. of his beast   BIBLE 26:15
runners relay the torch of l.   LUCR 155:7
shade the evening of l.   GIBB 106:10
slits the thin-spun l.   MILT 167:20
sphere of private l.   MELB 164:14
spirit giveth l.   BIBLE 39:2
Squat on my l.   LARK 149:7
sweet is this human l.   CORY 78:13
that L. flies   FITZ 99:4
their lives fought for l.   SPEN 244:10
therefore choose l. that   BIBLE 23:36
There's the l. for ever   STEV 247:11
this gives l. to thee   SHAK 235:9
Thorough the iron gates of l.   MARV 162:1
those who live Call L.   SHEL 240:3
Thou art my l.   QUAR 193:7
thousand doors to let out l.   MASS 164:6

'Tis the sunset of l. gives   CAMP 60:16
unblemished l. and spotless record   HOR 123:16
Variety's the very spice of l.   COWP 80:1
voyage of their l.   SHAK 217:3
well-written L. is almost   CARL 61:7
What is this l.   DAV 82:3
what l. is then to a man   BIBLE 30:25
When I consider how my l.   NASH 174:17
when it comes late in l.   JERR 130:19
which leadeth unto l.   BIBLE 32:9
Who saw l. steadily   ARN 9:5
wine of l. is drawn   SHAK 222:7
life-blood: book is the precious l.   MILT 170:16
life-lie: Take the l. away from   IBSEN 129:10
life's: l. fitful fever   SHAK 222:13
lifetime: knowledge of a l.   WHIS 269:13
lift: l. me as a wave   SHEL 239:14
L. not thy hands to *It*   FITZ 99:10
l. up mine eyes   PRAY 190:16
l. up your heads   PRAY 190:16
light: against the dying of the l.   THOM 256:23
are the l. of the world   BIBLE 31:13
Be near me when my l. is   TENN 252:14
blasted with excess of l.   GRAY 112:13
can again thy former l.   SHAK 229:13
darkness have seen a great l.   BIBLE 28:18
dusk with a l. behind   GILB 109:10
give l. to them that sit   BIBLE 34:30
gone into the world of l.   VAUG 261:19
heaven the beam of your l.   LANG 149:3
if bereav'd of l.   BLAKE 43:15
if once we lose this l.   JONS 136:11
if they fear'd the l.   SUCK 248:4
In a l. fantastic round   MILT 167:6
infant crying for the l.   TENN 252:16
It gives a lovely l.   MILL 166:6
It is the l. of Terewth   DICK 83:17
Lead, kindly L.   NEWM 176:4
let perpetual l. shine   MASS 163:11
Let there be l.   BIBLE 22:2
l. emerging from the smoke   HOR 123:16
L. (God's eldest daughter)   FULL 104:2
l. in the dust lies dead   SHEL 239:8
l. of his countenance   PRAY 189:12
l. or leading received   MILT 170:20
l. shineth in darkness   BIBLE 36:13
l. such a candle by God's   LAT 149:14
l. that I may tread safely   HASK 115:16
l. that loses   SWIN 249:16
l. that never was   WORD 274:12
l. to counterfeit a gloom   MILT 167:13
mend the Electric L.   BELL 19:2
More l.   GOE 110:4
Of beauty from the l. retir'd   WALL 265:14
of pure and endless l.   VAUG 261:16
once set is our little l.   CAT 65:5
On the l. fantastic toe   MILT 167:17
outwalked the furthest city l.   FROST 103:2
pursuit of sweetness and l.   ARN 9:7
put on the armour of l.   BIBLE 38:5
Put out the l.   SHAK 229:13
source of my l. and my safety   BIBLE 41:11
That was the true L.   BIBLE 36:14
Thou art my l.   QUAR 193:7
to give them l.   BIBLE 23:17
took away the l.   MILT 168:10
turning your face to the l.   SASS 200:7
Turret in a Noose of L.   FITZ 98:14
upon us the armour of l.   PRAY 187:6

was far faster than l.   BULL 51:8
We all *know* what l. is   JOHN 132:28
what l. through yonder   SHAK 231:16
When I consider how my l.   MILT 170:10
which are sweetness and l.   SWIFT 248:17
Yet the l. of a whole life   BOUR 45:8
your l. so shine before men   BIBLE 31:14
Light Brigade: 'Forward the L.   TENN 251:9
lighted: l. rooms Inside your head   LARK 149:6
Lighten: L. our darkness   PRAY 187:1
l. with celestial fire   PRAY 191:12
lighter: Is l. than vanity   DUNY 51.19
lightfoot: many a l. lad   HOUS 126:11
lighthouse: sitivation at the l.   DICK 85:27
lightly: unadvisedly, l., or wantonly   PRAY 187:24
lightning: Fear no more the l. flash   SHAK 206:4
from Jove the l.   MAN 159:9
illumined by flashes of l.   WILDE 272:3
It is to keep the l. out   I3H 129.16
It must be done like l.   JONS 136:2
Shakespeare by flashes of l.   COL 75:12
yes O at l.   HOPK 122:11
lights: are but broken l. of thee   TENN 252:9
l. around the shore   ROSS 197:9
like: Dear heart how l. you   WYATT 278:4
husband could have made me l.   CONG 76:17
l. a little bit of butter   MILNE 166:15
L. as the hart desireth   PRAY 189:1
l. of each thing that   SHAK 219:8
shall not look upon his l.   SHAK 207:3
sort of thing they l.   LINC 152:4
so what is this l.   FORS 101:12
that l. that sort of place   SHAW 238:4
therefore do as they l.   THUR 259:15
liked: Because I l. you better   HOUS 126:25
l. whate'er She looked   BROW 50:5
likened: be l. unto a foolish man   BIBLE 32:13
likewise: do thou l.   BIBLE 35:14
liking: I have a l. old   CALV 60:4
Lilacs: L. out of the dead land   ELIOT 94:18
lilac-time: Go down to Kew in l.   NOYES 177:7
lilia: Manibus date l. plenis   VIRG 263:15
lilies: Consider the l. of the field   BIBLE 31:25
Give me l. in armfuls   VIRG 263:15
had three l. in her hand   ROSS 197:8
he feedeth among the l.   BIBLE 28:2
l. and languors of virtue   SWIN 249:18
L. that fester smell far   SHAK 236:7
pale, lost l.   DOWS 89:7
Where roses and white l.   CAMP 60:20
which feed among the l.   BIBLE 28:4
lilting: I've heard them l.   ELL 95:22
lily: I see a l. on thy brow   KEATS 139:4
l. of the valleys   BIBLE 27:26
l. whispers, 'I wait   TENN 254:2
Now folds the l. all her   TENN 254:16
poppy or a l. in your medieval   GILB 108:21
to paint the l.   SHAK 217:12
you seen but a bright l.   JONS 136:9
limbs: deck your lower l. in pants   NASH 175:1
l. of a poet   HOR 124:22
limelight: always backing into the l.   BERN 20:3
limit: act a slave to l.   SHAK 233:6
limitations: to know the l. of force   TROT 260:17
limn: wood ere Thou canst l.   THOM 256:4
limousine: want is a l. and a ticket   MACN 158:5
Limpopo: greasy L. River   KIPL 146:16
linages: Dos l. sólos hay en el   CERV 66:7
line: *active* l. on a walk moving   KLEE 147:1

are six ships of the l.   TENN 255:3
back to cancel half a L.   FITZ 99:9
heroes up the l. to death   SASS 200:4
high aesthetic l.   GILB 108:19
l. upon line   BIBLE 29:1
thin red l.   RUSS 198:15
We carved not a l.   WOLFE 273:22
will the l. stretch out   SHAK 223:2
linen: very fine l.   BRUM 50:27
lines: consisted of l. like these   CALV 59:16
l. so loves oblique may   MARV 161:14
Proso is when all the l   BENT 19:15
town-crier spoke my l.   SHAK 209:7
lingering: I alone sit l. here   VAUG 261:15
Something l.   GILB 108:13
lingots: au marché avec des l.   CHAM 66:16
lingua: l., gloriosi   THOM 256:20
l., gloriosi   VEN 261:19
linguam: Et l. et mores   HV 137:17
lion: is better than a dead l.   BIBLE 27:13
l. and the fatling together   BIBLE 28:21
L. and the Lizard keep   FITZ 98:18
Now the hungry l. roars   SHAK 228:1
righteous are bold as a l.   BIBLE 26:32
roaring l.   BIBLE 40:22
that gets the fattest l.   SAKI 199:5
that had the l.'s heart   CHUR 71:15
There is a l. in the way   BIBLE 26:31
To rouse a l. than to start   SHAK 212:6
lions: Laughing l. must come   NIET 176:14
Rise like L. after slumber   SHEL 239:11
they were stronger than l.   BIBLE 24:26
lip: 'Keep a stiff upper l.   CARY 64:21
Teach not thy l. such scorn   SHAK 231:4
lips: Be through my l. to unawakened   SHEL 239:15
Here hung those l. that   SHAK 211:11
l. are not yet unsealed   BALD 14:14
l. of dying men   ARN 9:2
l. that touch liquor must   YOUNG 280:12
l. to it when I am so dispoged   DICK 84:12
people of unclean l.   BIBLE 28:13
pretty form to the l.   DICK 84:10
Red l. are not so red   OWEN 179:7
take those l. away   SHAK 224:7
Thy l. are like a thread   BIBLE 28:3
Truth from his l. prevail'd   GOLD 110:9
very good words for the l.   DICK 84:10
When the l. have spoken   SHEL 239:8
Where my Julia's l. do smile   HERR 118:17
liquefaction: That l. of her clothes   HERR 119:1
liquid: let their l. siftings fall   ELIOT 94:17
Thames is l. history   BURNS 53:16
liquidity: purpose in l.   BROO 47:8
liquor: Good l.   GOLD 110:17
lads for the l.   HOUS 125:14
lips that touch l. must   YOUNG 280:12
l. Is quicker   NASH 174:16
lisp'd: I l. in numbers   POPE 184:19
list: I've got a little l.   GILB 108:4
listed: 'l. at home for a lancer   HOUS 126:15
listen: Darkling I l.   KEATS 139:22
Do you think I can l. all   CARR 62:19
world should l. then   SHEL 240:5
Listened: soul L. intensely   WORD 274:15
listening: is the disease of not l.   SHAK 212:20
listeth: wind bloweth where it l.   BIBLE 36:20
lit: Fleet is all l. up   WOOD 274:7
Literature: L. is news that STAYS news
   POUND 186:14

louse in the locks of l.   TENN 256:1
littérature: Et tout le reste est l.   VERL 262:3
littered: l. under Mercury   SHAK 234:22
  l. with remembered kisses   MACN 158:3
little: contemptible l. Army   WILH 272:7
  drink unto one of these l.   BIBLE 32:29
  here a l.   BIBLE 29:1
  it was a very l. one   MARR 161:6
  L. drops of water   CARN 62:2
  l. learning is a dang'rous   POPE 185:8
  l. life Is rounded   SHAK 232:24
  little l. grave   SHAK 230:9
  l. local difficulties   MACM 157:19
  l. more   BROW 49:5
  l. philosophy inclineth   BACON 12:23
  l. the mind is actually   JOHN 132:20
  L. things affect little   DISR 87:11
  Lo here a l. volume   CRAS 80:9
  'Man wants but l. here   BUTL 56:17
  Man wants but l.   GOLD 110:12
  Man wants but l.   YOUNG 280:10
  So l. done   TENN 252:19
  There was a l. girl   LONG 153:20
  this l. world   SHAK 230:2
  though she be but l.   SHAK 227:13
littlenesses: Before a thousand peering l.
   TENN 251:15
liv'd: has never l.   GAY 105:15
live: Can these bones l.   BIBLE 30:7
  certified how long I have to l.   PRAY 188:25
  Come l. with me   DONNE 87:18
  Come l. with me   MARL 160:14
  darkest day (L. till tomorrow)   COWP 79:13
  don't know how to l. right   HOR 123:8
  Flesh perishes, I l. on   HARDY 114:10
  Glad did I l. and gladly   STEV 247:16
  He shall not l.   SHAK 217:1
  I cannot l. with you   MART 161:9
  ill report while you l.   SHAK 208:18
  I must l.   DARG 7:20
  in him we l., and move   BIBLE 37:24
  I wish to l. and to die   VILL 262:14
  just shall l. by faith   BIBLE 37:31
  Lesbia let us l. and love   CAT 65:5
  lief not be as l. to be   SHAK 215:15
  life is to *l. dangerously*   NIET 176:19
  L. all you can   JAMES 130:2
  l. and shame the land from   HOUS 126:26
  l. as they live elsewhere   AMBR 2:8
  L. a thousand years   SHAK 216:10
  l. or die wi' Charlie   HOGG 120:14
  l. well on nothing a year   THAC 256:11
  long as ye both shall l.   PRAY 187:27
  nothing but a rage to l.   POPE 184:24
  not l. within thy means   AUDEN 11:12
  not to l., but to die   BROW 48:9
  one bare hour to l.   MARL 160:6
  One should eat to l.   MOL 171:5
  shall no man see me and l.   BIBLE 23:22
  shall not l. by bread alone   BIBLE 31:8
  suffer a witch to l.   BIBLE 23:19
  Teach him how to l.   PORT 186:4
  teaching nations how to l.   MILT 170:19
  Tell me whom you l. with   CHES 69:5
  than to l. on your knees   IBAR 129:3
  To l. with thee   RAL 194:2
  tri'd To l. without him   WOTT 277:17
  turn and l. with animals   WHIT 270:6
  We l. and learn   POMF 184:4

we that l. to please   JOHN 135:7
wouldn't *l.* under Niagara   CARL 61:24
You might as well l.   PARK 180:6
lived: He who has not l. during   TALL 250:13
  I have l. long enough   SHAK 223:12
  L. in his mild and magnificent   BROW 50:1
  Many brave men l. before   HOR 124:17
  Never to have l. is best   YEATS 279:1
liver: notorious evil l.   PRAY 187:9
livery: l. of the burnish'd sun   SHAK 225:2
lives: ends mark'd than their l.   SHAK 229:21
  evil that men do l. after   SHAK 216:16
  l. in hope daneeth without   HERB 118:5
  L. of great men all remind   LONG 153:10
  l. of quiet desperation   THOR 259:3
  man who l. by his own work   COLL 75:19
  pleasant in their l.   BIBLE 24:26
  sort of woman who l. for   LEWIS 151:13
  That no man l. forever   SWIN 250:1
  who lives more l. than one   WILDE 271:4
liveth: know that my redeemer l.   BIBLE 25:28
  name l. for evermore   BIBLE 30:29
living: are you yet l.   SHAK 228:4
  bodies a l. sacrifice   BIBLE 38:1
  fever call'd 'L.   POE 184:1
  From too much love of l.   SWIN 250:1
  hands of the l. God   BIBLE 40:7
  I am l. in the Midlands   BELL 19:7
  Let the l. creature lie   AUDEN 11:3
  Living and partly l.   ELIOT 94:11
  l. death   MILT 170:3
  l. dog is better than   BIBLE 27:13
  L.? The servants will   VILL 262:12
  Plain l. and high thinking   WORD 277:1
  substance with riotous l.   BIBLE 35:26
  There is no l. with thee   ADD 1:11
  truly to get mine own l.   PRAY 187:21
  unexamined life is not worth l.   SOCR 243:7
living-machine: house is a l.   LE C 151:1
Livingstone: for L., I presume   STAN 245:11
livres: et j'ai lu tous les l.   MALL 159:4
  ses *l. disposés*   PROU 192:5
Lizard: say the Lion and the L.   FITZ 98:18
Lizzie Borden: L. took an axe   ANON 4:3
load: heart like a l. of immortality   KEATS 141:4
  him how to l. and bless   KEATS 140:12
  l. every rift of your subject   KEATS 141:7
loads: l. of learned lumber   POPE 185:13
Loaf: with a L. of Bread beneath   FITZ 98:15
loan: l. oft loses both itself   SHAK 207:6
loathe: I l. the country   CONG 77:1
lobster: 'Tis the voice of the l.   CARR 63:13
local: little l. difficulties   MACM 157:19
  l., but prized elsewhere   AUDEN 11:9
  l. habitation and a name   SHAK 227:18
  not l. prejudices ought   BURKE 52:15
Lochinvar: young L. is come out   SCOTT 201:18
loci: Geniumque l. primamque   VIRG 263:16
lock'd: l. my heart in a case o'   BALL 15:5
locks: few l. which are left you   SOUT 243:21
  louse in the l. of literature   TENN 256:1
  never shake Thy gory l.   SHAK 222:18
  Your l. were like the raven   BURNS 54:12
locust: you the years that the l.   BIBLE 30:13
locuta: Roma l. est   AUG 11:21
lodge: Elephant, Is best to l.   SHAK 234:8
lodger: mere l. in my own house   GOLD 110:19
lodgest: where thou l.   BIBLE 24:14
l'offense: monde est ce qui fait l.   MOL 171:14

Rejoice in the L. alway — BIBLE 39:18
Sae let the L. be thankit — BURNS 54:13
Seek ye the L. while he — BIBLE 29:17
shall we sing the L.'s song — PRAY 191:1
sought the L. aright — BURNS 54:2
soul doth magnify the L. — BIBLE 34:28
They have taken away my L. — BIBLE 37:9
'twur the will o' the L. — TENN 255:17
we own thee L. — ANON 7:7
what hour your L. doth come — BIBLE 34:4
Lord Jesus: Even so, come, L. — BIBLE 41:10
Lord Randal: L., my Son — BALL 14:17
Lords: is only a wit among L. — JOHN 131:10
l. who lay you low — SHEL 240:1
thither from the House of L. — NORF 177:6
lore: all the l. its scholars — KEBLE 141:10
lose: day you may l. them all' — LEAR 150:18
findeth his life shall l. — BIBLE 32:28
is nothing much to l. — HOUS 126:26
l., and start again — KIPL 144:8
l. his own soul — BIBLE 33:14
l. our ventures — SHAK 217:3
l. the name of action — SHAK 208:24
l. to-morrow the ground — ARN 8:21
power and to l. liberty — BACON 13:10
to l. itself in the sky — BROW 48:19
to l. myself in a mystery — BROW 48:7
To l. one parent — WILDE 271:8
losers: all are l. — CHAM 66:12
losing: l. one pleased Cato — LUCAN 155:1
loss: black as our l. — SITW 241:12
breathe a word about your l. — KIPL 144:8
enow To do our country l. — SHAK 214:3
l. of honour was a wrench — GRAH 111:7
upon thy so sore l. — THOM 258:7
losses: l. are restor'd and sorrows — SHAK 235:13
lost: are paradises we have l. — PROU 192:7
better to have loved and l. — TENN 252:13
Britain has l. an Empire — ACH 1:2
found my sheep which was l. — BIBLE 35:24
Hearts that have l. their — HOUS 126:22
Home of l. causes — ARN 9:8
horse the rider was l. — FRAN 102:11
I have l. a day — TITUS 259:16
l., and is found — BIBLE 35:29
l. to love and truth — BURNS 54:3
l. to me — BARH 15:10
love it and be l. like — HOUS 125:8
my bosom and be l. in me — TENN 254:16
next to a battle l. — WELL 268:5
see your country is l. — WILL 272:11
than never to have l. — BUTL 56:22
Though lovers be l. love — THOM 256:22
yet so l. in lexicography — JOHN 134:15
You're all a l. generation — STEIN 245:18
lot: l. has fallen to me — KIPL 145:18
l. is fallen unto me — PRAY 188:11
Our loving l. was cast — HOOD 121:4
policeman's l. is not — GILB 109:2
Lothario: gay L. — ROWE 198:4
Lou: lady that's known as L. — SERV 203:8
loud: him upon the l. cymbals — PRAY 191:8
louder: l. he talked of his honour — EMER 96:10
louse: between a l. and a flea — JOHN 134:1
l. in the locks of literature — TENN 256:1
louts: oafish l. remember Mum — BETJ 20:7
lov'd: Had we never l. sae kindly — BURNS 53:20
l. not at first sight — SHAK 205:8
nor no man ever l. — SHAK 236:12

She who has never l. — GAY 105:15
till we l. — DONNE 88:1
love: Absence is to l. what wind — BUSS 55:24
all for l. — SPEN 244:17
all her outward parts L.'s — COWL 79:10
All l. at first — BUTL 56:13
all men all earth to l. — KIPL 145:18
are l. not a gaping pig — SHAK 225:14
Because my l. is come — ROSS 197:3
be my l. — DONNE 87:18
be my l. — MARL 160:14
bring those who l. Thee — TER 256:5
dinner of herbs where l. — BIBLE 26:21
do not fall in l. with me — SHAK 205:7
Eternity is in l. with — BLAKE 44:3
ever wilt thou l. — KEATS 139:14
faith and labour of l. — BIBLE 39:23
fathom deep I am in l. — SHAK 205:11
fit l. for Gods — MILT 169:18
fitter L. for me — DONNE 88:14
From too much l. of living — SWIN 250:1
Give to me the life I l. — STEV 247:11
God of l. my Shepherd — HERB 118:15
God si L. — FORS 101:19
good man's l. — SHAK 205:6
good to them that l. God — BIBLE 37:38
Greater l. hath no man — BIBLE 37:3
help those we l. to escape — HUGEL 127:17
His banner over me was l. — BIBLE 27:27
honeying and making l. — SHAK 210:17
How do I l. thee — BROW 48:17
how l. and murder will out — CONG 76:13
how this spring of l. resembleth — SHAK 234:17
human l. will be seen — FORS 101:17
I am sick of l. — BIBLE 27:28
I could not l. thee (Dear) — LOV 154:11
I do l. nothing — SHAK 228:12
I do not l. you — BROWN 48:2
I don't l. you — MART 161:8
if my l. were in my arms — ANON 5:10
I hae parted frae my L. — BURNS 54:11
I hate and I l. — CAT 65:11
I have been half in l. — KEATS 139:22
I have freedom in my l. — LOV 154:9
I know whose l. would follow — KIPL 145:5
I l. a lass — OKEE 177:14
I l. the lovely bully — SHAK 213:19
I'm tired of L. — BELL 18:20
In books and l. — GAY 105:21
is l.'s great artillery — CRAS 80:10
last acquainted with L. — JOHN 131:8
leave to come unto my l. — SPEN 244:14
Lesbia let us live and l. — CAT 65:5
let me l. — DONNE 87:20
let us l. our occupations — DICK 83:18
like l. to hatred turn'd — CONG 76:19
little duty and less l. — SHAK 214:8
look'd at me as she did l. — KEATS 139:5
lost to l. and truth — BURNS 54:3
l. all beauteous things — BRID 46:11
L. and a cottage — COLM 76:2
L. and do what you will — AUG 11:19
l. and fame to nothingness — KEATS 140:10
l. and knowledge of you — SHAK 204:15
l. and thanks of men — PAINE 179:15
l. and toil in the years — KIPL 143:15
l. a woman so well when — ELIOT 93:4
L. bade me welcome — HERB 118:11
L. can transpose to form — SHAK 226:14

l., cherish, and to obey	PRAY 187:28	my true l. said	PEELE 182:2
L. comes from blindness	BUSS 55:23	My vegetable l. should	MARV 161:20
L. conquers all things	VIRG 264:8	Need we say it was not l.	MILL 166:9
L., curiosity	PARK 180:4	Of kindness and of l.	WORD 275:5
L. doth to her eyes repair	SHAK 234:18	Only our l. hath no decay	DONNE 87:17
L., forgive us	KEATS 139:8	pangs of dispriz'd l.	SHAK 208:24
l. God whom he hath not	BIBLE 40:27	passing the l. of women	BIBLE 24:27
L. has pitched his mansion	YEATS 278:15	perfect l. casteth out	BIBLE 40:26
l. he had to her	BIBLE 23:1	possible to l. such a man	CHES 69:14
L. in a hut	KEATS 139:8	putting l. away	DICK 86:2
L. in a palace is perhaps	KEATS 139:8	separate us from the l. of God	BIBLE 37:39
L. in her sunny eyes does	COWL 79:10	service of my l.	SPR 243:4
L. in this part	BYRON 59:5	shackles of an old l. straiten'd	TENN 251:20
l. is a thing that can	PARK 180:3	She never told her l.	SHAK 234:4
L. is like any other luxury	TROL 260:14	should I your true l. know	SHAK 210:25
L. is like the measles	JER 130:16	sports of l.	JONS 136:10
L. is not love	SHAK 236:12	substance of his house for l.	BIBLE 28:5
l. is of man's life a thing	BYRON 58:2	swear thou think'st I l.	DONNE 88:20
L. is our Lord's meaning	JUL 137:12	That l. had been sae ill	BALL 15:5
l. is sweet.for a day	SWIN 250:3	there's no l. lost between	GOLD 110:22
l. is then our duty	GAY 105:13	They l. us for it	TENN 254:12
l. is towards individuals	SWIFT 249:4	thy sweet l. remember'd	SHAK 235:11
l. it and be lost like	HOUS 125:8	time to l.	BIBLE 27:7
l. it more than tongue	BROW 50:23	To be wise, and l.	SHAK 233:7
l., let us be true	ARN 8:12	To be wise and eke to l.	SPEN 244:21
L. looks not with the eyes	SHAK 226:14	To business that we l.	SHAK 204:3
L. me little	ANON 4:4	to l. and rapture's due	ROCH 195:14
l. me long	ANON 4:4	to see her was to l. her	BURNS 53:19
l. of finished years	ROSS 197:4	turns to thoughts of l.	TENN 253:7
l. of money is the root	BIBLE 40:1	very few to l.	WORD 276:14
L. one another or die	AUDEN 11:6	Was there l. once	NICH 176:11
L. seeketh not itself	BLAKE 43:10	Werther had a l. for Charlotte	THAC 256:15
L. seeketh only Self	BLAKE 43:11	What is commonly called l.	FIEL 98:9
L.'s like the measles	JERR 130:19	What is l.	SHAK 233:22
L.'s not Time's fool	SHAK 236:12	What l. I bore to thee	WORD 275:7
L.'s pleasure lasts	FLOR 101:3	What l. is	HALM 114:5
L. still has something	SEDL 202:16	when I l. thee not	SHAK 228:26
l.'s young dream	MOORE 172:15	when I was in l. with you	HOUS 125:10
L. that dare not speak	DOUG 89:5	when l. and duty clash	TENN 254:7
L., that had robbed us	MER 165:4	When my l. swears that	SHAK 237:1
l. the babe that milks	SHAK 221:6	which was more than l.	POE 183:19
L. the Beloved Republic	FORS 102:1	wilder shores of l.	BLAN 44:10
L. the brotherhood	BIBLE 40:19	will not l. his country	SHAK 216:15
l. the highest when we	TENN 251:17	woman wakes to l.	TENN 252:3
L., the human form divine	BLAKE 43:19	world and l. were young	RAL 194:2
l. the offender	POPE 184:13	You cannot call it l.	SHAK 210:16
l. those who love you	VOLT 265:2	your true l.'s coming	SHAK 233:22
L., thou art absolute	CRAS 80:8	**loved:** better to have l. and lost	TENN 252:13
l. thy neighbour as thyself	BIBLE 23:24	forgiven; for she l. much	BIBLE 35:9
L. thyself last	SHAK 215:10	God so l. the world	BIBLE 36:21
l. we bear one another	BETJ 21:3	he l. the time too well	CLARE 72:17
l. which consists in this	RILKE 195:6	Indeed the Idols I have l.	FITZ 99:11
l. with a cold climate	SOUT 244:2	Israel l. Joseph	BIBLE 23:3
l. you for yourself alone	YEATS 278:21	l. each other beyond belief	HEINE 116:13
l. your crooked neighbour	AUDEN 10:11	l. one all together	BROW 50:6
L. your enemies	BIBLE 35:7	l., sir—used to meet	BROW 49:9
L. you ten years before	MARV 161:20	l. Three whole days together	SUCK 248:6
l. you till the ocean Is	AUDEN 10:8	more I l. my homeland	BELL 19:10
lyric L.	BROW 50:19	Not that I l. Caesar less	SHAK 216:13
making l. all year round	BEAU 16:16	Pale hands I l.	HOPE 121:16
Marriage from l., like vinegar	BYRON 58:4	pressed to say why I l. him	MONT 172:1
mind where people make l.	CAMP 60:11	so young, I l. him so	BROW 49:2
music be the food of l.	SHAK 233:14	than never to have been l.	CONG 76:22
My l. and I would lie	HOUS 125:12	'Tis better to have l.	BUTL 56:22
My l. is of a birth	MARV 161:13	We that had l. him so	BROW 50:1
my l. is slain	DONNE 87:23	**loveliest:** l. and best	FITZ 99:2
My l. to thee is sound	SHAK 219:11	l. fairy in the world	KING 142:19
My only l. sprung from	SHAK 231:15	L. of trees	HOUS 125:4
My true l. hath my heart	SIDN 241:4	**loveliness:** Glory and l. have pass'd	KEATS 140:6

Its l. increases — KEATS 138:15
Lovell: Cat, the Rat, and L. — COLL 75:16
lovely: billboard l. as a tree — NASH 174:18
down in l. muck I've lain — HOUS 126:13
It gives a l. light — MILL 166:6
Lap from some once l. Head — FITZ 99:1
l. is the rose — WORD 275:13
l. rice pudding for dinner — MILNE 166:16
l. woman stoops to folly — ELIOT 95:4
l. woman stoops to folly — GOLD 110:18
more l. and more temperate — SHAK 235:9
thy last on all things l. — DE L 82:11
whatsoever things are l. — BIBLE 39:20
you have l. hair — CHEK 69:3
lover: days dividing lover and l. — SWIN 249:16
give repentance to her l. — GOLD 110:18
I sighed as as a l. — GIBB 106:6
It was a l. and his lass — SHAK 205:12
l., and the poet — SHAK 227:17
l., Sighing like furnace — SHAK 205:1
searching for a new l. — CONN 77:7
since I cannot prove a l. — SHAK 231:3
true a l. — SHAK 204:18
with some old l.'s ghost — DONNE 88:11
lovers: Journeys end in l. meeting — SHAK 233:22
laughs at l.' perjuries — OVID 178:20
l. be lost love shall not — THOM 256:22
l. cannot see — SHAK 225:6
l. fled away into the storm — KEATS 139:1
l. must Consign to thee — SHAK 206:4
motions l.' seasons run — DONNE 88:18
pair of star-cross'd l. — SHAK 231:10
loves: ar'n't that I l. the fox less — SURT 248:12
Friends and l. we have — MAS 163:3
lines so l. oblique may — MARV 161:14
man kills the thing he l. — WILDE 271:3
one that l. his fellow-men — HUNT 128:4
Who l. not woman — LUTH 155:13
love-sick: winds were l. with them — SHAK 203:22
lovesome: garden is a l. thing — BROWN 48:3
loveth: He made and l. all — COL 74:20
Lord l. he correcteth — BIBLE 26:4
Lord l. he chasteneth — BIBLE 40:10
l. a cheerful giver — BIBLE 39:4
that l. not knoweth not God — BIBLE 40:25
loving: heart be still as l. — BYRON 58:22
l. himself better than — COL 75:9
l. longest, when existence — AUST 12:10
l. that old arm-chair — ELIZ 78:1
night was made for l. — BYRON 59:1
so l. to my mother — SHAK 206:15
too much l. you — SHAK 229:2
loving-kindness: thy l. and mercy shall — PRAY 188:16
low: exalted them of l. degree — BIBLE 34:29
l. estate of his handmaiden — BIBLE 34:28
Sweet and l. — TENN 254:8
That l. man seeks a little — BROW 49:11
Lowells: L. talk only to Cabots — BOSS 45:2
Löwen: Lachende L. müssen kommen — NIET 176:14
lowly: in the l. air — GILB 107:14
Loyal: L. and neutral, in a moment — SHAK 222:8
loyalties: impossible l. — ARN 9:8
loyalty: learned body wanted l. — TRAPP 259:22
lqwrea: concedant l. laudi — CIC 72:8
lucem: sed ex fumo dare l. — HOR 122:16
Lucid: L. intervals and happy — BACON 13:27
l. intervals of life — WORD 274:13
Lucifer: he falls like L. — SHAK 215:9

L., son of the morning — BIBLE 28:2
luck: Has he l. — NAP 174:1
There's nae l. about the house — ANON 5:
watching his l. was his — SERV 203:
luckless: l. man — CAT 65:
Lucky: L. to touch it — KIPL 145:1
lucrative: When it's so l. to cheat — CLOU 73:1
lucre: not greedy of filthy l. — BIBLE 39:2
Lucy: When L. ceased to be — WORD 276:1
Ludlow: hundreds to L. come — HOUS 125:1
Lüge: Volkes…einer grossen L. — HITL 119:1
lugere: non l., neque detestare — SPIN 245:
Lugete: L., O Veneres Cupidinesque — CAT 65:
lugger: forcing her on board the l. — JOHN 135:1
Luke: L., the beloved physician — BIBLE 39:2
lullaby: dreamy l. — GILB 107:2
I will sing a l. — DEKK 82:
lumber: loads of learned l. — POPE 183:1
l. of the schools — SWIFT 249:1
lunatic: l., the lover — SHAK 227:1
reform movement has a l. fringe — RONS 196:1
Lunch: cleared away L. — CALV 60:
lungs: gold and l. of bronze — BELL 19:
l. of London — PITT 183:1
Lupus: L. est homo homini — PLAU 183:1
lure: l. it back to cancel half — FITZ 99:
luscious: over-canopied with l. woodbine — SHAK 227:
Lusisti: L. satis — HOR 123:
lust: Delight of l. is gross — PETR 183:
horrible that l. and rage — YEATS 279:1
into ashes all my l. — MARV 161:2
Is l. in action — SHAK 236:1
L. der Zerstörung ist — BAK 14:1
l. of knowing what should — FLEC 100:
lustily: sing praises l. unto him — PRAY 188:2
lustre: Where is thy l. now — SHAK 218:1
lusts: sinful l. of the flesh — PRAY 187:1
lust'st: hotly l. to use her — SHAK 218:2
lusty: l. stealth of nature — SHAK 217:1
lute: little rift within the l. — TENN 252:
Orpheus with his l. made trees — SHAK 215:
When the l. is broken — SHEL 239:
Luve: L.'s like a red red rose — BURNS 54:1
lux: l. perpetua luceat eis — MASS 163:1
Luxe: L., calme et volupté — BAUD 16:1
luxuries: between l. and necessaries — GALB 104:
Give us the l. of life — MOTL 174:
luxury: Love is like any other l. — TROL 260:1
l., peace — BAUD 16:1
Lycidas: So L. sunk low — MILT 168:
lying: l., and slandering — PRAY 187:2
l. awake with a dismal — GILB 107:2
One of you is l. — PARK 180:
Lyonnesse: When I set out for L. — HARDY 115:
lyre: hang my weapons and my l. — HOR 124:11
'Omer smote 'is bloomin' l. — KIPL 146:
lyve: worthy womman al hir l. — CHAU 68:
M: N or M. — PRAY 187:1
Macaroni: called it M. — BANGS 15:
Macaulay: M. is well for a while — CARL 61:2
Macavity: there's no one like M. — ELIOT 94:
Macbeth: M. does murder sleep — SHAK 221:1
M. shall sleep no more — SHAK 221:1
Shall harm M. — SHAK 222:2
There to meet with M. — SHAK 219:1
Macduff: Lay on, M. — SHAK 223:1
mace: that fool's bauble, the m. — CROM 80:1
Macedonia: Come over into M. — BIBLE 37:1

malheurs: tableau des crimes et des m.   VOLT 265:1
malice: from envy, hatred, and m.   PRAY 187:3
  Nor set down aught in m.   SHAK 229:15
  With m. toward none   LINC 152:3
malignity: with a m. truly diabolical   BURKE 52:10
malorum: religio potuit suadere m.   LUCR 155:4
Malt: M. does more than Milton   HOUS 126:12
mammon: cannot serve God and m.   BIBLE 31:24
man: all that may become a m.   SHAK 221:5
  ambition of m.   RAL 194:6
  apparel oft proclaims the m.   SHAK 207:6
  become the servant of a m.   SHAW 237:17
  better angel is a m. right   SHAK 237:2
  bold bad m.   SHAK 215:6
  Child is father of the M.   WORD 275:11
  coiner the mintage of m.   HOUS 126:1
  Cristen m. shall wedde   CHAU 68:16
  detest that animal called m.   SWIFT 249:4
  dog bites a m.   BOG 44:15
  first m. is of the earth   BIBLE 38:21
  God first maked m.   CHAU 68:12
  good almost kill a m.   MILT 170:15
  Greater love hath no m.   BIBLE 37:3
  Happy is the m. that hath   PRAY 190:20
  heart of a m. is deprest   GAY 105:12
  He was a m.   SHAK 207:3
  I know myself a m.   DAV 82:1
  I met a m. who wasn't there   MEAR 164:11
  I not a m. and a brother   WEDG 267:19
  is another m. within me   BROW 48:6
  I saw a m. this morning   SHAW 238:22
  it is the number of a m.   BIBLE 41:3
  last thing civilized by M.   MER 165:7
  like a m.'s hand   BIBLE 25:5
  looking for a m.'s foot-print   BEER 17:18
  make a m. a woman   PEMB 182:4
  m. after his own heart   BIBLE 24:19
  m. among a thousand have   BIBLE 27:10
  m. and a woman looking   WOOLF 274:8
  M. comes and tills   TENN 255:9
  m. come through a door   CHAN 67:5
  m. delights not me   SHAK 208:14
  M. dreams of fame   TENN 252:3
  m. for all seasons   WHIT 270:11
  m. goes riding   STEV 247:8
  M. goeth forth to his work   PRAY 190:5
  m. goeth to his long home   BIBLE 27:22
  M. has created death   YEATS 278:17
  M. has Forever   BROW 49:10
  M. has his will   HOLM 120:17
  M. has never been the same   MILL 166:5
  m. in his hasty days   BRID 46:11
  M. is an embodied paradox   COLT 76:7
  M. is a noble animal   BROW 48:13
  m. is as old as he's feeling   COLL 75:20
  M. is Heaven's masterpiece   QUAR 193:6
  M. is only a reed   PASC 181:3
  m. is quite insane   MONT 172:6
  m. is seldom ashamed   ELIOT 93:4
  m. *so* in the way   GASK 105:2
  M. is the hunter   TENN 254:12
  M. is the master of things   SWIN 250:2
  M. is the measure of all   PROT 192:2
  M. is the only animal that   TWAIN 261:3
  M. is the shuttle   VAUG 261:13
  m. made the town   COWP 79:19
  m. of culture rare   GILB 108:19
  m. of infinite-resource   KIPL 146:12
  m. over forty is a scoundrel   SHAW 238:14

  m. plans   THOM 256:19
  M., proud man   SHAK 223:18
  m. recover'd of the bite   GOLD 110:15
  m.'s a man for a' that   BURNS 54:9
  m.'s desire is   COL 75:14
  M.'s first disobedience   MILT 168:17
  m. shall have his mare   SHAK 227:14
  M.'s inhumanity to man   BURNS 54:15
  m.'s the gowd for a' that   BURNS 54:8
  m. that hath no music   SHAK 226:7
  M. that is born of a woman   BIBLE 25:24
  'M. wants but little here   BUTL 56:17
  M. wants but little   GOLD 110:12
  m. who said 'God Must think   KNOX 147:5
  m. who should loose me   LOW 154:14
  m. who used to notice such   HARDY 114:8
  more wonderful than m.   SOPH 243:13
  mother's life made me a m.   MAS 162:18
  noblest work of m.   BUTL 56:16
  not m. have the upper hand   PRAY 188:8
  Not mine, but m.'s   HOUS 126:23
  now thy loins like a m.   BIBLE 25:32
  old m. in a hurry   CHUR 70:24
  Only a m. harrowing clods   HARDY 114:11
  only m. is vile   HEBER 116:10
  people arose as one m.   BIBLE 24:13
  piece of work is a m.   SHAK 208:14
  right m. in the right place   JEFF 130:13
  sabbath was made for m.   BIBLE 34:20
  science and study of m.   CHAR 67:16
  single m. in possession   AUST 12:11
  sing of arms and the m.   VIRG 262:15
  So unto the m. is woman   LONG 153:14
  strain of m.'s bred   SHAK 233:4
  study of mankind is m.   POPE 185:17
  style is the m.   BUFF 51:6
  That the m. I am may cease   TENN 253:20
  that the m. should be alone   BIBLE 22:8
  that the new m. may be   PRAY 187:17
  therefore let him pass for a m.   SHAK 224:16
  This is the state of m.   SHAK 215:9
  'This was a m.   SHAK 217:6
  together let no m. put asunder   PRAY 188:2
  war as is of every m. against   HOBB 119:17
  way of a m. with a maid   BIBLE 26:33
  What bloody m. is that   SHAK 220:1
  when a m. should marry   BACON 13:14
  When God at first made m.   HERB 118:14
  when I became a m.   BIBLE 38:16
  Who's master, who's m.   SWIFT 249:10
  Whoso sheddeth m.'s blood   BIBLE 22:21
  will be against every m.   BIBLE 22:24
  wise m. so much of Sir Chr   FLET 100:15
  wise m. will make   BACON 13:3
  you'll be a M.   KIPL 144:9
Mandarin: M. style…is beloved   CONN 77:5
mandrake: Get with child a m. root   DONNE 88:15
manger: laid him in a m.   BIBLE 35:1
  m. pour vivre et non pas   MOL 171:5
manges: Dis-moi ce que tu m.   BRIL 46:18
manhood: ancient customs and its m.   ENN 97:2
manhoods: m. cheap whiles any speaks   SHAK 214:4
maniac: m. scattering dust   TENN 252:14
manifest: m. destiny to overspread   OSUL 178:16
manifestly: m. and undoubtedly be seen   HEW 119:5
manifold: our m. sins and wickedness   PRAY 186:17
man-in-the-street: To the m.   AUDEN 11:8

mankind: Ellum she hateth m.	KIPL 146:3
How beauteous m. is	SHAK 233:3
legislator of m.	JOHN 134:28
misfortunes of m.	GIBB 106:11
one giant leap for m.	ARMS 8:10
rather as a spectator of m.	ADD 1:10
ride m.	EMER 96:5
study of m. is man	POPE 185:17
mankind's: all m. epitome	DRYD 90:16
manna: Exalted m.	HERB 118:13
manner: m. of his speech	SHAK 203:21
shall be well and all m.	JUL 137:11
stolzen M. der Tat	HEINE 116:14
there is no m. of doubt	GILB 107:3
to the m. born	SHAK 207:8
very good bedside m.	PUNCH 192:19
manners: communications corrupt good m.	
	BIBLE 38:20
evil m. live in brass	SHAK 215:12
Leave off first for m.'	BIBLE 30:24
m. of a dancing master	JOHN 131:11
m. of a Marquis with	GILB 109:5
printing thereby to rectify m.	MILT 170:18
times! Oh, the m.	CIC 72:11
manque: Un seul être vous m.	LAM 147:16
mansion: Love has pitched his m.	YEATS 278:15
m. call the fleeting breath	GRAY 112:4
mansions: Father's house are many m.	BIBLE 37:1
mantle: in russet m. clad	SHAK 206:10
m. muffling up his face	SHAK 216:20
manure: It is its natural m.	JEFF 130:10
manuscript: m. put away at home	HOR 122:21
many: m. are called	BIBLE 33:20
owed by so m. to so few	CHUR 71:7
So m. worlds	TENN 252:19
There's m. a good tune played	BUTL 56:21
we are m.	BIBLE 34:23
why he makes so m. of them	LINC 152:5
Ye are m.—they are few	SHEL 239:11
many-splendoured: That miss the m. thing	
	THOM 258:7
map: Roll up that m.	PITT 183:12
maps: Geography is about m.	BENT 19:16
mar: m. all with this starting	SHAK 223:7
Marathon: M. looks on the sea	BYRON 58:7
marble: dwelt in m. halls	BUNN 51:15
Glowed on the m.	ELIOT 95:2
it brick and left it m.	AUG 11:22
m. index of a mind	WORD 276:7
m. to retain	BYRON 57:4
Not m.	SHAK 236:2
Marcellus: Tu M. eris	VIRG 263:15
March: ashbuds in the front of M.	TENN 251:14
Beware the ides of M.	SHAK 215:14
Did m. to the seige	BALL 14:18
droghte of M. hath perced	CHAU 67:17
ides of M. are come	SHAK 216:7
That highte M.	CHAU 68:2
three hours' m. to dinner	HAZL 116:5
winds of M. with beauty	SHAK 235:1
marched: m. breast forward	BROW 48:22
M. them along	BROW 49:6
marches: army m. on its stomach	NAP 174:14
marching: 'Tis the people m.	MORR 173:13
mare: lend me your grey m.	BALL 15:6
man shall have his m. again	SHAK 227:14
Margaret: It is M. you mourn	HOPK 122:6
mari: m. magno turbantibus aequora	LUCR 155:6
Maria: Ave M.	ANON 6:14

mariages: Il y a de bons m.	LA R 149:9
Mariana: resides this dejected M.	SHAK 224:5
Maries: Yestreen the Queen had four M.	
	BALL 15:1
Marie Seaton: There was M.	BALL 15:1
mariner: haul and draw with the m.	DRAKE 90:4
It is an ancient M.	COL 74:5
Marion: M.'s nose looks red	SHAK 219:14
mark: hundred m. is a long one	SHAK 212:24
Lord set a m. upon Cain	BIBLE 22:17
m., learn	PRAY 187:7
m. of insincerity of purpose	BRAM 46:4
That m. our place	MCCR 157:8
marked: All m. with mute surmise	HARDY 115:4
market: take ingots with us to m.	CHAM 66:16
marking: malady of not m.	SHAK 212:20
Marmion: Were the last words of M.	SCOTT 202:3
Marquis: combines the manners of a M.	
	GILB 109:5
marred: married is a man that's m.	SHAK 203:14
marriage: comedies are ended by a m.	BYRON 58:5
fall in with the m.-procession	CLOU 73:9
furnish forth the m. tables	SHAK 207:2
hanging prevents a bad m.	SHAK 233:18
M. from love, like vinegar	BYRON 58:4
M. has many pains	JOHN 135:2
M. is like life in this	STEV 247:3
M. is popular because it	SHAW 238:12
M. is the result	CAMP 60:12
M. is the waste-paper basket	WEBB 267:4
My definition of m.	SMITH 242:19
nor are given in m.	BIBLE 33:29
that is m., Lily thought	WOOLF 274:8
to the m. of true minds	SHAK 236:12
Was m. ever out of fashion	BUTL 56:9
marriages: There are good m.	LA R 149:9
we will have no more m.	SHAK 209:5
married: if ever we had been m.	GAY 105:7
if we were not m. at all	CONG 77:2
I m. him	BRON 47:1
imprudently m. the barber	FOOTE 101:7
let us be m.	LEAR 150:14
m. is a man that's marred	SHAK 203:14
m. life three is company	WILDE 271:7
m. past redemption	DRYD 91:6
m. with mine uncle	SHAK 206:15
M. women are kept women	SMITH 242:8
Mocks m. men	SHAK 219:13
Unpleasing to a m. ear	SHAK 219:13
woman's business to get m.	SHAW 238:5
marries: much signify whom one m.	ROG 196:2
marry: better to m. than to burn	BIBLE 38:9
Carlyle and Mrs Carlyle m.	BUTL 56:24
'Doänt thou m. for munny	TENN 254:4
Every woman should m.	DISR 87:9
persons about to m..— 'Don't	PUNCH 192:11
resurrection they neither m.	BIBLE 33:29
when a man should m.	BACON 13:14
marry'd: At leisure m.	CONG 76:20
his throat before he m.	SWIFT 249:13
M. in haste	CONG 76:20
marrying: Alice is m. one of the guard	
	MILNE 166:11
Martha: M. was cumbered about much	
	BIBLE 35:15
martial: his m. cloak around him	WOLFE 273:21
martinet: I am a perfect m.	SMITH 243:3
martyr: if thow deye a m.	CHAU 68:25
Martyrdom: M. is the test	JOHN 133:14

marvel: m. My birthday Away THOM 257:7
m. save in Eastern clime BURG 52:7
marvellous: he hath done m. things PRAY 190:3
Marxist: know is that I am not a M. MARX 162:11
Mary: Hail M. ANON 6:14
M. had a little lamb HALE 113:12
Mary Ambree: foremost in battle was M.
BALL 14:18
Mary Jane: What *is* the matter with M.
MILNE 166:16
mask: had a m. like Castlereagh SHEL 239:9
mass: blessed mutter of the m. BROW 49:1
Paris is well worth a m. HENR 117:13
Masse: breite M. eines Volkes HITL 119:13
masses: huddled m. yearning LAZ 149:19
I hate the unholy m. HOR 124:5
massive: m. paws of elder persons BELL 18:3
mast: m. burst open with a rose FLEC 100:11
master: choice and m. spirits SHAK 216:10
Cold Iron—is m. KIPL 143:16
eateth your M. with publicans BIBLE 32:18
I am M. of this college BEEC 17:11
I am the m. of my fate HENL 117:7
Man is the m. of things SWIN 250:2
m. of himself MASS 164:1
swear allegiance to any m. HOR 123:1
Thrice blessed they that m. SHAK 226:12
'which is to be m. CARR 64:9
Who's m., who's man SWIFT 249:10
masterly: wise and m. inactivity MACK 157:14
masterpiece: Man is Heaven's m. QUAR 193:6
Nature's great m. DONNE 88:12
masters: ease of the m. SMITH 242:2
noble and approv'd good m. SHAK 228:17
people are the m. BURKE 53:1
prevail on our future m. LOWE 154:12
serve two m. BIBLE 31:24
their Victory but new m. HALE 114:1
time are m. of their fates SHAK 215:16
We are the m. at the moment SHAW 238:21
mastery: achieve of, the m. of HOPK 122:10
match: Almighty made 'em to m. the men
ELIOT 92:15
bread and the big m. JUV 138:4
to make and the m. to win NEWB 175:15
matched: has m. us with His hour BROO 47:15
matches: m. of the Southron folk THOM 257:22
mate: bold m. of Henry Morgan MAS 162:17
great artificer Made my m. STEV 247:14
m. of the *Nancy* brig GILB 106:21
mated: thou art m. with a clown TENN 253:8
mater: Magna ista scientiarum m. BACON 14:1
M. saeva Cupidinum HOR 124:14
Stabat M. dolorosa JAC 129:18
Materialismus: Krieg würde die Welt in M.
MOLT 171:15
mathematics: m., subtile BACON 13:22
M., rightly viewed RUSS 198:11
Matilda: M. told such Dreadful Lies BELL 18:14
matre: m. pulchra filia pulchrior HOR 123:15
matrem: ecclesiam non habet m. CYPR 81:6
Matrimony: joined together in holy M.
PRAY 187:23
matter: beginning of any great m. DRAKE 90:1
Does it m. SASS 200:7
if it is it doesn't m. GILB 109:8
More m. with less art SHAK 208:7
not much m. which we say MELB 164:15
order, said I, this m. STER 246:4

What *is* the m. with Mary Jane MILNE 166:16
mattering: m. once it has stopped BOWEN 45:13
Matthew: M., Mark ANON 4:6
mature: have in our m. years TROL 260:12
maturing: bosom-friend of the m. sun
KEATS 140:12
Maud: Come into the garden, M. TENN 254:1
mavult: enim m. homo verum esse BACON 13:30
Maxim: got The M. Gun BELL 19:4
maxima: mea m. culpa MASS 163:9
maximum: m. of temptation SHAW 238:12
May: darling buds of M. SHAK 235:9
fayr as is the rose in M. CHAU 68:19
fressh as is the month of M. CHAU 68:1
know not what we m. be SHAK 211:1
laurel outlives not M. SWIN 250:3
least the seventh of M. TROL 260:4
maids are M. when they SHAK 205:10
matter for a M. morning SHAK 234:10
may say that M. is come CLARE 72:2
merry month of M. BALL 13:9
merry month of M. BARN 15:17
Than wish a snow in M.'s SHAK 219:8
Maypole: where's the M. in the Strand BRAM 46:6
Maytime: Now in M. to the wicket HOUS 125:9
McGregor: Mr M.'s garden POTT 186:5
me: because it was m. MONT 172:1
meadows: Do paint the m. with delight
SHAK 219:13
golden face the m. green SHAK 235:14
is set in enamelled m. WALP 265:16
meads: Fair these broad m. GALT 104:11
mean: convey more than they m. CONN 77:5
Down these m. streets CHAN 67:6
no m. of death SHAK 216:10
nothing common did or m. MARV 161:17
not m. But be MACL 157:14
should say what you m. CARR 63:2
what I choose it to m. CARR 64:8
who loves the golden m. HOR 124:3
meandering: Meeting those m. down they
HARDY 114:14
miles m. with a mazy motion COL 75:4
meaner: because only m. things ELIOT 93:2
meaning: hidden m. —like Basingstoke GILB 109:7
Love is our Lord's m. JUL 137:12
m. doesn't matter if it's GILB 108:20
m. of religion is thus ARN 9:11
meanings: there are two m. packed CARR 64:10
wrestle With words and m. ELIOT 93:16
means: as an end withal, never as m. KANT 138:9
end justifies the m. BUS 55:22
have to die beyond my m. WILDE 272:6
I don't know what it m. GILB 106:20
m. in his power which are KANT 138:8
not live within thy m. AUDEN 11:12
measles: Love is like the m. JER 130:16
Love's like the m. JERR 130:19
measure: good m., pressed down BIBLE 35:8
Man is the m. of all things PROT 192:2
narrow m. spans HOUS 126:23
measured: I've m. it from side WORD 277:10
m. out my life with coffee spoons ELIOT 94:5
meat: abhorred all manner of m. PRAY 190:7
benison to fall On our m. HERR 119:2
eater come forth m. BIBLE 24:10
egg is full of m. SHAK 231:26
m. in the hall STEV 247:15
penny ice and cold m. GILB 107:22

Some have m. and cannot eat — BURNS 54:13
ye gave me m. — BIBLE 34:8
méchant: Cet animal est très m. — ANON 5:15
meddle: 'm. and muddle' — DER 83:4
Medes: given to the M. and Persians — BIBLE 30:9
law of the M. and Persians — BIBLE 30:10
medias: eventum festinat et in m. res — HOR 122:17
medicina: sero m. paratur — OVID 178:23
medicine: it's late for m. to be — OVID 178:23
medieval: lily in your m. hand — GILB 108:21
Mediui M. tutissimus ibis — OVID 178:21
médiocres: L'absence diminue les m. passions — LA R 149:11
mediocritatem: Auream quisquis m. — HOR 124:3
Mediocrity: M. knows nothing higher — DOYLE 89:28
meditate: m. the thankless Muse — MILT 167:20
meditated: I m. on the Fall — BETJ 21:2
meditation: disposed to abstracted m. — JOHN 134:27
let us all to m. — SHAK 214:13
Mediterranean: see the shores of the M. — JOHN 132:27
medium: m. is the message — MCL 157:16
meek: believing that the m. shall — BIRK 42:7
Blessed are the m. — BIBLE 31:11
borne his faculties so m. — SHAK 221:1
meet: If we do m. again — SHAK 217:5
It is m. and right so — PRAY 187:16
loved, sir—used to m. — BROW 49:9
make both ends m. — FULL 104:1
m. my Maker brow to brow — CORN 78:5
men and mountains m. — BLAKE 43:5
Never to m. again — BURNS 54:11
shall we three m. again — SHAK 219:16
Though infinite can never m. — MARV 161:14
will make him an help m. — BIBLE 22:8
meeter: therefore deemed it m. — PEAC 181:16
meeting: if I was a public m. — VICT 262:11
Journeys end in lovers m. — SHAK 233:22
melancholy: black sun of m. — NERV 175:11
charm can soothe her m. — GOLD 110:18
had this trick of m. — SHAK 203:15
Hail divinest M. — MILT 167:11
have a rare recipe for m. — LAMB 147:18
loathed M., Of Cerberus — MILT 167:14
m. out of a song as a weasel — SHAK 204:20
moping m. — MILT 169:21
with a green and yellow m. — SHAK 234:4
meliora: Video m. — OVID 178:22
meliorist: not an optimist but a m. — ELIOT 93:8
mellows: tart temper never m. with — IRV 129:15
Mellstock: lie in M. churchyard now — BETJ 20:11
lie in M. churchyard now — HARDY 114:9
melodies: Heard m. are sweet — KEATS 139:13
Sweetest m. — WORD 276:2
melodious: Move in m. time — MILT 168:8
melody: m., in our heaviness — PRAY 191:1
melodye: smale foweles maken m. — CHAU 67:18
melons: Stumbling on m. — MARV 161:15
melt: m. with ruth — MILT 168:1
too solid flesh would m. — SHAK 206:15
melted: Are m. into air — SHAK 232:24
member: he is a m. of *parliament* — BURKE 52:15
he is not m. of Bristol — BURKE 52:15
was made a m. of Christ — PRAY 187:18
members: m. one of another — BIBLE 39:12
membra: disiecti m. poetae — HOR 124:22
Membranis: M. intus positis — HOR 122:21

meminisse: Forsan et haec olim m. iuvabit — VIRG 262:17
memorial: m. longer lasting than — HOR 124:12
which have no m. — BIBLE 30:28
whole earth as their m. — PER 182:15
Memory: Fond M. brings the light — MOORE 173:4
from the m. a rooted sorrow — SHAK 223:13
'His m. is going — JOHN 133:22
mixing M. and desire — ELIOT 94:18
to his m. for his jests — SHER 240:27
men: all m. are created equal — ANON 5:9
all things to all m. — BIBLE 30:10
created m. and women different — VICT 262:8
despised and rejected of m. — BIBLE 29:14
fear of little m. — ALL 2:7
finds too late that m. betray — GOLD 110:18
justify the ways of God to M. — MILT 168:14
lips of dying m. — ARN 9:2
make you fishers of m. — BIBLE 31:10
many m. of large fortune — AUST 12:2
m. and mountains meet — BLAKE 43:5
m. and women with our race — KIPL 143:15
M. are April when they — SHAK 205:10
m. are created equal — JEFF 130:9
m. decay — GOLD 110:6
M. don't know women — TROL 260:3
M. fear death — BACON 13:5
m. in shape and fashion — ASCH 9:19
m. may come and men may — TENN 251:7
m. must work — KING 142:14
M. seldom make passes — PARK 180:5
M. were deceivers ever — SHAK 228:7
m. who will support me — MELB 164:17
m., women, and clergymen — SMITH 242:18
Mocks married m. — SHAK 219:13
need of a world of m. — BROW 50:7
of those m. in England — SHAK 214:2
proper young m. — BURNS 54:14
purgatory of m. — FLOR 101:4
schemes o' mice an' m. — BURNS 55:6
sorts and conditions of m. — PRAY 187:4
them to have power over m. — WOLL 274:3
therefore...exceeding tall m. — BACON 12:21
to form Christian m. — ARN 9:16
tongues of m. and of angels — BIBLE 38:14
unnecessary things are m. — ROCH 195:13
When m. were all asleep — BRID 46:12
When m. were fond — SHAK 223:20
Where Destiny with M. — FITZ 99:7
Words are m.'s daughters — MADD 158:13
men-children: Bring forth m. only — SHAK 221:7
mend: m. the Electric Light — BELL 19:2
mendax: Splendide m. et in omne virgo — HOR 124:9
mended: all is m. — SHAK 228:3
mendier: de m. dans les rues et — FRAN 102:5
MENE: M.; God hath numbered — BIBLE 30:9
mens: m. sana in corpore sano — JUV 138:5
Menschen: Alle M. werden Brüder — SCH 201:2
Mental: will not cease from M. — BLAKE 43:2
merchantman: monarchy is a m. which — AMES 2:9
mercies: tender m. of the wicked — BIBLE 26:15
Thanks for m. past receive — BUCK 51:5
merciful: Blessed are the m. — BIBLE 31:11
God be m. to me a sinner — BIBLE 36:5
God be m. unto us — PRAY 189:12
In a m. eclipse — GILB 107:8
merciless: black and m. things — JAMES 130:3
Mercury: littered under M. — SHAK 234:22
words of M. are harsh after — SHAK 219:15

mercy: easy in the m. of his means THOM 257:3
God ha' m. on such as we KIPL 144:1
m. endureth for ever PRAY 190:23
M. has a human heart BLAKE 43:19
M. I asked CAMD 60:8
m. Of a rude stream SHAK 215:9
m. upon us miserable sinners PRAY 187:2
quality of m. is not strain'd SHAK 225:17
so is his m. BIBLE 30:21
temper so Justice with m.. MILT 169:20
they shall obtain m. BIBLE 31:11
to love m. BIBLE 30:19
When m. seasons justice SHAK 225:17
Meredith: M. is a prose Browning WILDE 272:3
merely: I can m. be your friend LEAR 150:8
merit: m. raise the tardy bust JOHN 135:9
talk of m. for a bishopric WEST 269:5
there is no damned m. in it MELB 164:13
mérite: gouvernement qu'elle m. MAIS 159:3
Mermaid: Choicer than the M. Tavern
KEATS 139:10
Done at the M. BEAU 16:18
mermaids: have heard the m. singing ELIOT 94:8
merrily: m. hent the stile-a SHAK 234:23
m. shall I live now SHAK 233:2
merriment: hopeless than a scheme of m.
JOHN 134:22
m. of parsons is mighty JOHN 133:16
merry: all went m. as a marriage BYRON 57:9
cheerful, m. Dr Brighton THAC 256:9
gone up with a m. noise PRAY 189:4
I am never m. when I hear SHAK 226:6
m. heart goes all the day SHAK 234:23
m. heart maketh a cheerful BIBLE 26:20
m. monarch ROCH 195:16
m. month of May BALL 15:2
m. month of May BARN 15:17
to be m. BIBLE 27:12
to have such a m. day once PEPYS 182:13
merrygoround: It's no go the m. MACN 158:5
meruit: Palmam qui m. JORT 136:13
mess: birthright for a m. of potage BIBLE 22:27
every m. I finds a friend DIBD 83:8
message: medium is the m. MCL 157:16
messe: Paris vaut bien une m. HENR 117:13
messenger: m. of Satan to buffet me BIBLE 39:6
messengers: bade his m. ride forth MAC 156:3
messes: other country m. MILT 167:18
messing: simply m. about in boats GRAH 111:11
met: Hail, fellow, well m. SWIFT 249:10
know how first he m. her THAC 256:15
m. my dearest foe in heaven SHAK 207:2
never be m. with again CARR 62:7
metal: Here's m. more attractive SHAK 210:5
metaphysic: m. wit can fly BUTL 56:4
métaphysiciens: dirais volontiers des m. CHAM 67:1
metaphysics: of divinity or school m. HUME 127:1
method: m. and secret and sweet ARN 9:13
yet there is m. in't SHAK 208:10
Methodist: with the morals of a M. GILB 109:5
methods: different m. different men excel
CHUR 70:18
You know my m. DOYLE 89:16
You know my m. DOYLE 89:25
Methought: M. I heard a voice cry SHAK 221:16
métier: c'est son m. CATH 65:2
metropolis: called…'the m. of the empire'
COBB 73:20
mettle: undaunted m. should compose SHAK 221:7

metuant: dum m. ACC 1:
me. t: On ne m. qu'une fois MOL 171:8
Mewling: M. and puking in the nurse's
SHAK 205:1
Mexique Bay: Echo beyond the M. MARV 161:12
mezzanine: to slip down to the m. WOD 273:14
mezzo: m. del cammin di nostra DANTE 81:7
mice: Like little m. SUCK 248:4
schemes o' m. an' men BURNS 55:6
Michelangelo: Talking of M. ELIOT 94:4
microscopes: magnifyin' gas m. of hextra power
DICK 85:22
middle: cannot steer A m. course MASS 164:3
companions for m. age BACON 13:13
into the m. of things HOR 122:17
m. course is the safest OVID 178:21
M. of Next Week CARR 62:11
m. of the road of our life DANTE 81:7
Middle Age: enchantments of the M. Home
ARN 9:8
last enchantment of the M. BEER 17:17
Restraining reckless m. YEATS 279:16
middle-ageing: With m. care POUND 186:13
Middle Class: M. was quite prepared BELL 18:13
Midlands: When I am living in the M. BELL 19:7
Midnight: blackest M. born MILT 167:14
books consum'd the m. oil GAY 105:17
budding morrow in m. KEATS 140:5
heard the chimes at m. SHAK 212:28
m. never come MARL 160:6
mock the m. bell SHAK 204:2
Not to be a-bed after m. SHAK 233:21
sigh'd upon a m. pillow SHAK 204:18
troubled m. and the noon's ELIOT 93:12
upon the m. with no pain KEATS 139:22
visions before m. BROW 48:5
mid-sea: Painted the m. blue FLEC 100:10
midshipmite: bo'sun tight, and a m. GILB 106:21
midst: m. of life we are in death PRAY 188:4
midsummer: this is very m. madness SHAK 234:9
mid-winter: In the bleak m. ROSS 197:5
mien: dark hair and lovesome m. TENN 251:3
mieux: je vais de mieux en m. COUE 78:15
m. est l'ennemi du bien VOLT 264:18
Tout est pour le m. dans VOLT 264:16
might: do it with thy m. BIBLE 27:15
Exceeds man's m. SHAK 233:7
'It m. have been HARTE 115:11
'It m. have been WHIT 270:10
Lord of all power and m. PRAY 187:8
majority has the m. IBSEN 129:4
our m. lessens ANON 5:7
You m. as well live PARK 180:6
mightier: pen is m. than the sword BULW 51:11
mightiest: 'Tis m. in the mightiest SHAK 225:17
mighty: how are the m. fallen BIBLE 24:25
How are the m. fallen BIBLE 24:27
m. from their seats BIBLE 34:29
mild: brought reg'lar and draw'd m. DICK 84:13
m. and magnificent eye BROW 50:1
miles: hundred m. away HARDY 115:3
m. around the wonder grew HOUS 125:10
m. to go before I sleep FROST 103:10
na on the lang Scots m. BURNS 54:22
People come m. to see it GILB 108:12
militant: state of Christ's Church m. PRAY 187:15
military: order and m. discipline ANON 3:8
thing to be left to the m. CLEM 73:5
militavi: Et m. non sine gloria HOR 124:11

miseries: bound in shallows and in m. SHAK 217:3
misery: certain amount of m. which LOWE 154:13
greatest m. is a battle gained WELL 268:5
M. acquaints a man with SHAK 232:18
pens dwell on guilt and m. AUST 12:4
result m. DICK 84:1
through the vale of m. PRAY 189:18
time of happiness in m. DANTE 81:10
misfortune: m. of our best friends LA R 149:8
sort of m. is to have been BOET 44:13
misfortunes: All the m. of men derive PASC 180:16
m. of mankind GIBB 106:11
tableau of crimes and m. VOLT 265:1
they make m. more bitter BACON 13:15
misleading: words generate m. thoughts
SPEN 244:7
Mislike: M. me not for my complexion
SHAK 225:2
misquote: enough of learning to m. BYRON 58:16
miss: catching a train is to m. CHES 70:14
missa: Ite m. est MASS 163:19
vox m. reverti HOR 122:21
missed: who never would be m. GILB 108:4
Missing: M. so much and so much CORN 78:7
missionaries: eaten by m. SPOON 245:3
missionary: I would eat a m. WILB 270:15
Mississippi: I have seen the M. BURNS 53:16
mist: grey m. on the sea's face MAS 162:19
m. in my face BROW 50:17
m. is dispell'd when GAY 105:12
mistake: it's a m. not JAMES 130:2
m. in the translation VANB 261:12
m. to theorize before one DOYLE 89:15
We will pardon Thy M. BETJ 21:4
when she made any such m. DICK 84:22
mistaken: here, unless I am m. DOYLE 89:21
possible you may be m. CROM 80:15
mistakes: man who makes no m. does PHEL 183:4
mistress: Art is a jealous m. EMER 96:9
lordship's principles or your m. WILK 272:9
m. in my own KIPL 145:7
m. mine SHAK 233:22
m. of the Earl of Craven WILS 272:18
m. should be like a little WYCH 278:5
m. some rich anger shows KEATS 139:17
mistresses: I shall have m. GEOR 106:2
Wives are young men's m. BACON 13:13
mists: Season of m. and mellow KEATS 140:12
when the m. in autumn KING 143:5
misunderstood: To be great is to be m. EMER 96:16
misused: m. words generate misleading SPEN 244:7
Mithras: M., God of the Morning KIPL 145:17
Mithridates: M., he died old HOUS 126:14
mitigation: some m. of the criminal law PEEL 182:1
Mittel: Einmischung anderer M. CLAU 73:3
niemals bloss als M. brauchest KANT 138:9
unentbehrlich notwendige M. KANT 138:8
Mix: M. a little foolishness HOR 124:18
mixture: Had the m. peen AYT 12:18
Moab: M. is my wash-pot PRAY 189:10
moan: Everything did banish m. BARN 15:17
made sweet m. KEATS 139:5
moanday: All m., tearsday, wailsday JOYCE 136:18
moaning: still he lay m. SMITH 242:13
there be no m. of the bar TENN 251:11
moated: at the m. grange SHAK 224:5
mob: occasions to do what the m. do DICK 85:15
mock: m. on, Voltaire, Rousseau BLAKE 43:3
m. the midnight bell SHAK 204:2

m. the riddled corpses SASS 200:6
They m. the air with idle GRAY 111:16
to m. your own grinning SHAK 211:11
mock'd: if he m. himself SHAK 216:1
mocked: God is not m. BIBLE 39:9
mocker: Wine is a m. BIBLE 26:24
mocking-bird: Out of the m.'s throat WHIT 270:6
Mocks: M. married men SHAK 219:13
model: m. of a modern Major-General GILB 109:1
moderate: £40,000 a year a m. income LAMB 148:7
moderately: if it be drunk m. BIBLE 30:25
moderation: astonished at my own m. CLIVE 73:7
taught to think that m. BURKE 52:19
modern: model of a m. Major-General GILB 109:1
unsettling element in m. art WHAR 269:9
modester: People ought to be m. CARL 61:22
modesty: o'erstep not the m. of nature SHAK 209:8
Modified: M. rapture GILB 108:8
Möglichen: Politik ist die Lehre von M. BISM 42:11
moi: Étonne-m. DIAG 83:7
parce que c'était m. MONT 172:1
moins: du m. des choses nouvelles VOLT 264:14
molis: Tantae m. erat Romanam VIRG 262:16
mome: m. raths outgrabe CARR 63:16
moment: Every m. dies a man BABB 12:19
Every m. dies a man TENN 255:18
from the impulse of the m. AUST 12:12
This little m. mercifully MER 165:4
moments: little m. CARN 62:2
m. of glad grace YEATS 280:5
Wagner has lovely m. ROSS 197:10
monarch: I am m. of all I survey COWP 80:5
merry m. ROCH 195:16
throned m. better than SHAK 225:17
monarchs: m. to choose favourites SWIFT 249:1
monarchy: constitutional m. such as ours
BAG 14:7
m. is a merchantman which AMES 2:9
Monday: Hanging of his cat on M. BRAT 46:7
is going to do on M. YBAR 278:9
monde: Le scandale du m. est ce MOL 171:14
money: blessing that m. cannot buy WALT 266:10
draining m. from the pockets SMITH 242:3
except for m. JOHN 132:26
'Hath a dog m. SHAK 225:1
Her voice is full of m. FITZ 100:3
licence to print your own m. THOM 258:15
love of m. is the root BIBLE 40:1
m. answereth all things BIBLE 27:19
M. gives me pleasure all BELL 18:20
M. has no smell VESP 262:5
M. is like muck BACON 13:17
M. is the most important SHAW 237:20
mustn't be romantic about m. SHAW 238:6
No m. RAC 193:18
pleasant it is to have m. CLOU 73:11
plenty of m. LEAR 150:13
Put m. in thy purse SHAK 228:20
sinews of war, unlimited m. CIC 72:13
somehow, make m. HOR 124:20
That's the way the m. goes MAND 159:8
that time is m. FRAN 102:8
We haven't the m. RUTH 198:16
with m. which they have HURST 128:9
money-bags: I did dream of m. to-night
SHAK 225:5
moneys: m. is your suit SHAK 225:1
monkey: Into baboon and m. SHAK 233:4
monkeys: m. and cats JAMES 130:4

shown no glorious m. face — STEV 247:17
started that m. from Devon — GILB 107:22
take the wings of the m. — PRAY 191:3
this morning m.'s minion — HOPK 122:9
three o'clock in the m. — FITZ 100:2
mornings: *always* had m. like this — MILNE 167:3
morris: nine men's m. is filled — SHAK 227:2
morrow: therefore no thought for the m. — BIBLE 32:1
Mors: M. stupebit et natura — CEL 66:1
mort: Je veux…que la m. me trouve — MONT 171:17
veut abolir la peine de m. — KARR 138:12
mortal: if I laugh at any m. thing — BYRON 58:11
M., guilty — AUDEN 11:3
m. millions live *alone* — ARN 8:15
shuffled off this m. coil — SHAK 208:24
struck a m. blow right inside — AESC 1:16
time of this m. life — PRAY 187:6
Mortalem: M. vitam mors cum immortalis — LUCR 155:8
mortalia: mentem m. tangunt — VIRG 263:2
mortality: it smells of m. — SHAK 218:21
m. touches the heart — VIRG 263:2
Old m. — BROW 48:11
urns and sepulchres of m. — CREWE 80:13
mortals: m. to command success — ADD 1:7
what fools these m. be — SHAK 227:10
morts: doit aux m. que la vérité — VOLT 265:8
Il n'y a pas de m. — MAET 158:14
mortuus: Passer m. est meae puellae — CAT 65:4
Moscow: If I lived in M. I don't — CHEK 69:2
One is don't march on M. — MONT 172:8
Moses: which M. sent to spy out — BIBLE 23:26
mot: Le m., c'est le Verbe — HUGO 127:15
mote: Why beholdest thou the m. — BIBLE 32:3
moth: m. and rust doth corrupt — BIBLE 31:22
mother: and…never called me m. — WOOD 274:6
Behold thy m. — BIBLE 37:7
'Daughter am I in my m.'s — KIPL 145:7
either my father or my m. — STER 246:7
gave her m. forty whacks — ANON 4:3
heaviness of his m. — BIBLE 26:12
I had No m. — BROW 49:2
is the m. — BIBLE 30:3
is the m. of Parliaments — BRIG 46:17
leave his father and his m. — BIBLE 22:11
m. bids me bind my hair — HUNT 128:8
m., do not cry — FARM 97:12
m. know that you are out — BARH 15:16
M. OF HARLOTS AND ABOMINATIONS — BIBLE 41:5
m. of months in meadow — SWIN 249:15
m. of the lovely Cupids — HOR 124:14
m. o' mine — KIPL 145:5
m.'s life made me a man — MAS 162:18
my m. cried — SHAK 228:6
not the church for his m. — CYPR 81:6
standing the sorrowing M. — JAC 129:18
That great m. of sciences — BACON 14:1
There was their Dacian m. — BYRON 57:13
Took great Care of his M. — MILNE 166:12
Upon his m.'s grave — WORD 276:5
What a beautiful m. — HOR 123:15
Mothers: M. of large families — BELL 18:7
women become like their m. — WILDE 271:9
mother-wits: jigging veins of rhyming m. — MARL 160:15
motion: God order'd m. — VAUG 261:13
his m. like an angel sings — SHAK 226:5

meandering with a mazy m. — COL 75:4
next to the perpetual m. — DICK 85:26
No m. has she now — WORD 276:17
rolled With visible m. — WORD 275:1
motions: m. of his spirit are dull — SHAK 226:7
motive: joint and m. of her body — SHAK 233:11
Motley: M.'s the only wear — SHAK 204:23
myself a m. to the view — SHAK 236:11
Motor Bus: Can it be a M. — GODL 109:19
Motoribus: Cincti Bis M. — GODL 109:19
motors: sound of horns and m. — ELIOT 95:3
mould: then broke the m. — ARIO 8:1
moulded: men are m. out of faults — SHAK 224:9
Mount: Singing of M. Abora — COL 75:6
mountain: from yonder m. height — TENN 255:1
He watches from his m. — TENN 251:13
'If the m. will not…') — BACON 13:2
m. and hill shall be made — BIBLE 29:9
m. sheep are sweeter — PEAC 181:16
sun looked over the m.'s — BROW 50:7
tiptoe on the misty m. — SHAK 232:2
Up the airy m. — ALL 2:7
mountainous: m. sports girl — BETJ 21:10
Mountains: came to the Delectable M. — BUNY 51:22
heaped-up m. with a thunderbolt — VIRG 264:10
men and m. meet — BLAKE 43:5
Molehills seem m. — COTT 78:14
m. by the winter sea — TENN 252:4
M. divide us — GALT 104:11
m. look on Marathon — BYRON 58:7
m. skipped like rams — PRAY 190:10
M. will heave in childbirth — HOR 122:15
One of the m. — WORD 277:6
that I could remove m. — BIBLE 38:14
mountain-tops: Flatter the m. with sovereign — SHAK 235:14
m. that freeze — SHAK 215:7
mourir: foy je veuil vivre et m. — VILL 262:14
Partir c'est m. un peu — HAR 114:7
mourn: Blessed are they that m. — BIBLE 31:14
countless thousands m. — BURNS 54:15
don't m. for me never — ANON 3:14
It is Margaret you m. — HOPK 122:6
M., you powers of Charm — CAT 65:4
No longer m. for me when — SHAK 236:11
now can never m. — SHEL 238:16
mourn'd: Would have m. longer — SHAK 206:15
mourning: I'm in m. for my life — CHEK 68:30
m. that either his mother — AUST 12:16
widow bird sate m. — SHEL 239:2
mourra: On m. seul — PASC 181:1
mouse: killing of a m. on Sunday — BRAT 46:7
Not a m. Shall disturb — SHAK 228:2
silly little m. will be born — HOR 122:15
Mouse-trap: *Hamlet:* The M. — SHAK 210:3
make a better m. — EMER 96:19
moustache: who didn't wax his m. was — KIPL 146:22
mouth: cleave to the roof of my m. — PRAY 191:1
Englishman to open his m. — SHAW 238:16
God be in my m. — ANON 3:12
m. of the Lord hath spoken — BIBLE 29:9
m. of very babes and sucklings — PRAY 188:7
proceedeth out of the m. of God — BIBLE 31:8
purple-stained m. — KEATS 139:19
mouths: enemy in their m. to steal — SHAK 228:25
Make m. upon me when — SHAK 227:12
m., and speak not — PRAY 190:13
m. were made for tankards — MAS 162:17

moutons: Revenons à ces m.   ANON 6:4
mouvement: Un premier m. ne fut jamais
   CORN 78:4
mouvements: Défiez-vous des premiers m.
   MONT 172:9
move: feel the earth m.   HEM 117:5
   If I could pray to m.   SHAK 216:8
   in him we live, and m.   BIBLE 37:24
   it does m.   GAL 104:10
moved: suffer thy foot to be m.   PRAY 190:16
   though the earth be m.   PRAY 189:3
moves: God m. in a mysterious   COWP 79:14
moving: m. accident is not my trade   WORD 274:18
   M. Finger writes   FITZ 99:9
   m. Toyshop of their heart   POPE 185:24
MPs: in that House M. divide   GILB 107:17
   Of dull M. in close proximity   GILB 107:18
MSS: M. as drunkards use lamp-posts
   HOUS 127:7
Much: M. have I seen and known   TENN 255:12
   so m. to do   TENN 252:19
   'There won't be m. for us   CARR 62:12
muchness: Much of a m.   VANB 261:11
muck: down in lovely m. I've   HOUS 126:13
   Money is like m.   BACON 13:17
   when to stop raking the m.   RONS 196:14
muckrake: with a m. in his hand   BUNY 51:25
muck-rakes: men with the m. are often
   RONS 196:14
mud: come of water and of m.   BROO 47:8
   Longing to be back in the m.   AUG 11:14
   Me name is M.   DENN 82:19
   morris is filled up with m.   SHAK 227:2
   M.'s sister, not himself   HOUS 127:4
   One sees the m.   LANG 149:1
muddied: m. oafs at the goals   KIPL 144:11
muddle: manage somehow to m. through
   BRIG 46:16
   'meddle and m.   DER 83:4
muddy: m. vesture of decay   SHAK 226:5
muffling: in his mantle m. up his   SHAK 216:20
mules: m. of politics   POWER 186:15
multiplicanda: Entia non sunt m. praeter
   OCCAM 177:10
Multiplication: M. is vexation   ANON 4:8
multiplicity: m. of agreeable consciousness
   JOHN 132:9
multiply: m., and replenish   BIBLE 22:6
multiplying: of our yearly m. millions   OSUL 178:16
multitude: giddy m.   MASS 164:5
multitudes: I contain m.   WHIT 270:7
   m. in the valley of decision   BIBLE 30:16
munch'd: m., and munch'd   SHAK 220:2
mundi: cito transit gloria m.   THOM 256:18
   Sic transit gloria m.   ANON 7:5
   tollis peccata m.   MASS 163:18
mundus: justitia et pereat m.   FERD 97:19
   Unde m. iudicetur   CEL 66:1
munny: 'Doänt thou marry for m.   TENN 254:4
muove: Eppur si m.   GAL 104:10
murals: with its m. on the wall   BETJ 21:2
Murder: I met M. in the way   SHEL 239:9
   Killing no M. Briefly Discourst   SEXBY 203:9
   Macbeth does m. sleep   SHAK 221:16
   m. an infant in its cradle   BLAKE 44:7
   m. cannot be hid long   SHAK 225:4
   M. Considered as One   DE Q 83:2
   M. most foul   SHAK 207:12
   See how love and m. will   CONG 76:13

Thou shalt do no m.   PRAY 187:11
   We m. to dissect   WORD 277:9
murder'd: Our royal master's m.   SHAK 222:6
murderers: taken by our friends the m.
   KARR 138:12
murex: Who fished the m. up   BROW 50:13
murmuring: m. of innumerable bees   TENN 255:2
mus: nascetur ridiculus m.   HOR 122:15
Musa: laude virum M. vetat mori   HOR 124:16
Musarum: Audita M. sacerdos   HOR 124:5
muscles: m. of his brawny arms   LONG 153:17
muse: Donne, whose m. on dromedary   COL 75:8
   M. of fire   SHAK 213:7
   praise the M. forbids to die   HOR 124:16
Muses: priest of the M.   HOR 124:5
Music: brave M. of a *distant*   FITZ 98:16
   by will make the m. mute   TENN 252:2
   Extraordinary how potent cheap m.   COW 79:3
   fiddled whisper m.   ELIOT 95:6
   Fled is that m.   KEATS 140:1
   If m. be the food of love   SHAK 233:14
   in general is frozen m.   SCH 201:1
   let the sounds of m.   SHAK 226:5
   Like softest m. to attending   SHAK 231:21
   man that hath no m.   SHAK 226:7
   M. and women I cannot   PEPYS 182:11
   m. at the close   SHAK 229:21
   m. for to lilt upon   MAS 162:17
   M. has charms to sooth   CONG 76:18
   m., ho   SHAK 204:1
   m. is the brandy   SHAW 238:7
   m. of the languid hours   LANG 148:16
   M. shall untune the sky   DRYD 91:10
   M. that gentlier   TENN 253:16
   m. that I care to hear   HOPK 121:19
   soul of m. shed   MOORE 172:14
   still, sad m. of humanity   WORD 275:6
   struck one chord of m.   PROC 191:21
   This m. crept by me upon   SHAK 232:14
   thou hast thy m. too   KEATS 140:14
   towards the condition of m.   PATER 181:9
   We are the m. makers   OSH 178:14
   when I hear sweet m.   SHAK 226:6
musical: m. as is Apollo's lute   MILT 167:8
   So m. a discord   SHAK 227:15
Music-halls: be no more jokes in M.   SASS 200:6
musician: lady is a m.   DOYLE 89:20
musick: hope danceth without m.   HERB 118:5
musicologist: m. is a man who can read   BEEC 17:9
musing: sat m. amidst the ruins   GIBB 106:8
musk-rose: coming m.   KEATS 139:21
musk-roses: With sweet m.   SHAK 227:5
muss: darüber m. man schweigen   WITT 273:10
   M. es sein   BEET 17:21
mussel: m. pooled and the heron   THOM 257:6
must: if we can we m.   HOUS 126:16
   Is m. a word   ELIZ 95:20
   It m. be   BEET 17:21
   Something m. be done   EDW 92:10
   we forget because we m.   ARN 8:11
mustard seed: is like to a grain of m.   BIBLE 33:6
mustered: m. their soldiers by two   BALL 14:18
mutabile: Varium et m. semper   VIRG 263:7
mutamur: et nos m. in illis   ANON 7:8
Mutato: M. nomine de te   HOR 124:19
mutatus: Quantum m. ab illo   VIRG 263:4
mute: m. inglorious Milton here   GRAY 112:5
   street and pavement m.   HARDY 114:14
   will make the music m.   TENN 252:2

mutter: blessed m. of the mass — BROW 49:1
Wizards that peep and that m. — BIBLE 28:17
mutton: m. with the usual trimmings — DICK 85:25
muzzle: m. the ox when he treadeth — BIBLE 23:34
my: m. Hornby and my Barlow — THOM 257:22
myriad: There died a m. — POUND 186:10
myrrh: frankincense, and m. — BIBLE 31:2
m. is my wellbeloved unto — BIBLE 27:25
myrtle: m. and ivy of sweet two-and-twenty — BYRON 59:2
m. and turkey part of it — AUST 12:3
myrtles: Which a grove of m. made — BARN 15:17
myself: Am quite m. again — HOUS 125:10
I celebrate m. — WHIT 270:4
I do not know m. — GOE 109:21
If I am not for m. — HILL 119:10
M. when young did eagerly — FITZ 99:5
of such a thing as I m. — SHAK 215:15
mysteries: understand all m. — BIBLE 38:14
mysterious: God moves in a m. — COWP 79:14
mystery: in a m. inside an enigma — CHUR 71:3
I shew you a m. — BIBLE 38:22
M., BABYLON THE GREAT — BIBLE 41:5
m. of the glorious Body — THOM 256:20
m. of the cross shines — VEN 261:20
out the heart of my m. — SHAK 210:7
to lose myself in a m. — BROW 48:7
N: N. or M — PRAY 187:18
nail: blows his n. — SHAK 219:14
...for want of a n. — FRAN 102:11
nails: 'As n. — DICK 85:7
n. he'll dig them up again — WEBS 267:16
nineteen hundred and forty n. — SITW 241:12
naître: êtes donné la peine de n. — BEAU 16:17
Naïve: It's a N. Domestic Burgundy — THUR 259:12
naked: left me n. to mine enemies — SHAK 215:11
N., and ye clothed me — BIBLE 34:8
n. ape self-named *Homo* — MORR 173:11
n. into the conference — BEVAN 21:17
n. to the hangman's noose — HOUS 125:6
outcries pluck me from my n. bed — KYD 147:9
we are ashamed of our n. — SHAW 238:1
With n. foot — WYATT 278:3
nakedness: not in utter n. — WORD 275:15
name: deed without a n. — SHAK 222:25
ev'n for his own n.'s sake — SCOT 202:15
filches from me my good n. — SHAK 228:27
forget your n. or who you are — CLARE 72:23
glory in the n. of Briton — GEOR 106:4
have forgotten your n. — SWIN 250:4
He left the n. — JOHN 135:10
in the n. of human nature — BURKE 53:7
king's n. is a tower — SHAK 231:8
leave a living n. behind — WEBS 267:6
Let me not n. it to you — SHAK 229:12
local habitation and a n. — SHAK 227:18
my n. is Jowett — BEEC 17:11
My n. is Legion — BIBLE 34:23
n. Achilles assumed — BROW 48:12
n. liveth for evermore — BIBLE 30:29
n. of Jesus every knee — BIBLE 39:16
N. of the Lord our God — PRAY 188:13
n. of the slough was Despond — BUNY 51:17
n. shall be called Wonderful — BIBLE 28:19
n. was writ in water — KEATS 141:8
number of his n. — BIBLE 41:2
refuse thy n. — SHAK 231:18
talk not to me of a n. — BYRON 59:2
that dare not speak its n. — DOUG 89:5

to thy n. give glory — BIBLE 41:14
What is your N. — PRAY 187:18
What's in a n. — SHAK 231:19
which is above every n. — BIBLE 39:16
worth an age without a n. — MORD 173:5
yet can't quite n. — LARK 149:6
named: n. the child I-chabod — BIBLE 24:17
nameless: n., unremembered, acts — WORD 275:5
NAMES: have THREE DIFFERENT N. — ELIOT 94:14
n. in many a mused rhyme — KEATS 139:22
N. that should be on every — CALV 59:17
use such n. and not be humble — SASS 200:13
Naming: N. of Cats is a difficult — ELIOT 94:14
To-day we have n. of parts — REED 194:14
Napoleon: He is the N. of crime — DOYLE 89:18
nappy: we sit bousing at the n. — BURNS 54:22
Narr: bleibt ein N. sein Leben lang — LUTH 155:13
narrative: bald and unconvincing n. — GILB 108:14
narratur: Fabula n. — HOR 124:19
narrow: Every bed is n. — MILL 166:8
n. is the way — BIBLE 32:9
n. measure spans — HOUS 126:23
nasty: n., brutish, and short — HOBB 120:1
Something n. in the woodshed — GIBB 106:14
natam: fortunatam n. me consule — CIC 72:15
nati: sunt n. — LUCAN 155:2
nation: against the voice of a n. — RUSS 198:12
dream that one day this n. — KING 142:8
England is a n. of shopkeepers — NAP 174:2
great deal of *ruin* in a n. — SMITH 242:4
holy n. — BIBLE 40:18
lift up sword against n. — BIBLE 28:7
n. is not governed — BURKE 52:16
n. of shop-keepers are — ADAMS 1:5
n. of shopkeepers — SMITH 242:1
n. shall rise against nation — BIBLE 33:33
N. shall speak peace — REND 194:18
N. spoke to a Nation — KIPL 145:7
Think of what our N. stands — BETJ 21:5
National: N. Debt is a very Good — SELL 203:3
nations: heard the embattled n. — SQUI 245:7
like the happiest n. — ELIOT 93:6
People formed Two N. — DISR 87:12
See n. slowly wise — JOHN 135:9
sets all n. by the ears — LAND 148:9
teaching n. how to live — MILT 170:19
native: found him a n. of the rocks — JOHN 131:8
my n. land — SCOTT 201:16
Warble his n. wood-notes wild — MILT 167:19
natives: Educating the n. of Borrioboola-Gha — DICK 83:14
natura: Mors stupebit et n. — CEL 66:1
N. il fece — ARIO 8:1
N. vacuum abhorret — RAB 193:13
natural: behaviour was n. and intrepid — WALP 265:15
n. to die as to be born — BACON 13:6
swear her colour is n. — SHER 240:23
term of N. Selection — DARW 81:15
that n. fear in children — BACON 13:5
twice as n. — CARR 64:12
When we see a n. style — PASC 180:15
naturaliter: testimonium animae n. Christianae — TERT 256:6
Naturam: N. expellas furca — HOR 123:4
nature: be aghast and so will n. — CEL 66:1
cruel works of n. — DARW 81:16
great n.'s second course — SHAK 221:16

than n. to have lost at all BUTL 56:22
who n. would be missed GILB 108:4
You must n. go down MILNE 166:13
Nevermore: 'N.' POE 184:2
new: Among n. men TENN 252:5
brave n. world SHAK 233:3
customary fate of n. truths HUXL 128:13
n. deal for the American RONS 196:7
n. heaven and a new earth BIBLE 41:7
n. heaven, new earth SHAK 203:17
n. man may be raised up PRAY 187:17
N. occasions teach new LOW 154:19
N. opinions are always LOCKE 152:10
n. race descends from high VIRG 264:6
n. song: sing praises lustily PRAY 188:22
N. styles of architecture AUDEN 11:5
n. wine into old bottles BIBLE 32:20
no n. thing under the sun BIBLE 27:3
old lamps for n. ARAB 7:12
shall find something n. VOLT 264:14
sing unto the Lord a n. song PRAY 190:3
yielding place to n. TENN 252:6
new-born: use of a n. child FRAN 102:17
new-comer: blithe n. WORD 277:11
newest: oldest sins the n. SHAK 213:2
news: bites a dog that is n. BOG 44:15
evil n. rides post MILT 170:4
good n. from a far country BIBLE 26:28
Literature is n. that STAYS POUND 186:14
n. that's fit to print OCHS 177:11
N. value RALPH 194:11
What n. on the Rialto SHAK 224:17
newspaper: n. and I seem to see ghosts IBSEN 129:6
Newton: Let N. be POPE 185:6
statue stood Of N. WORD 276:7
Newts: N., and blind-worms SHAK 227:6
New York: O Carthage! O N. SASS 200:15
New Yorker: Read The N. AUDEN 11:12
next: n. to a battle lost WELL 268:5
next door: wall n. catches fire HOR 123:6
nexus: sole n. of man to man CARL 61:9
nez: Le n. de Cléopâtre PASC 180:17
Niagara: wouldn't *live* under N. CARL 61:24
nice: Cusins is a very n. fellow SHAW 237:21
n. sort of place, Oxford SHAW 238:4
nicer: Are wiser and n. AUDEN 11:7
nicht-gown: down stairs in his n. MILL 166:10
Niger: left bank of the N. DICK 83:14
night: acquainted with the n. FROST 103:2
afraid for any terror by n. PRAY 189:24
are alternate N. and Day FITZ 98:17
ask of thee, beloved N. SHEL 240:7
black bat, n. TENN 254:1
by n. in a pillar of fire BIBLE 23:17
City is of N. THOM 258:14
dangers of this n. PRAY 187:1
dark n. of the soul FITZ 100:2
dusky n. rides down the sky FIEL 98:11
hangs upon the cheek of n. SHAK 231:14
heaviness may endure for a n. PRAY 188:21
ignorant armies clash by n. ARN 8:13
in endless n. GRAY 112:13
infant crying in the n. TENN 252:16
in such a n. as this SHAK 226:4
In the forests of the n. BLAKE 43:7
in the silence of the n. ROSS 197:4
in the stilly n. MOORE 173:4
I often wish the n. HOOD 121:7
Is it n. WHIT 270:3

it goes off at n. SHER 240:23
Last n. in Rome HODG 120:6
lonely n. through the shadow VIRG 263:12
meaner beauties of the n. WOTT 277:18
middle of the n. CARR 63:23
Morning in the Bowl of N. FITZ 98:14
neither the moon by n. PRAY 190:16
n. an atheist half believes YOUNG 280:11
n. cometh BIBLE 36:30
n. do penance for a day WORD 276:8
n. has a thousand eyes BOUR 45:8
N. hath a thousand eyes LYLY 155:16
N. makes no difference HERR 118:20
n.'s black agents SHAK 222:15
N.'s candles are burnt SHAK 232:2
n. she'll hae but three BALL 15:1
n. That either makes me SHAK 229:11
n. that wins SWIN 249:16
n. was made for loving BYRON 59:1
One for the long n. through HOUS 125:8
only for a n. and away WYCH 278:5
Out of the n. that covers HENL 117:6
past as a watch in the n. PRAY 189:21
Read out my words at n. FLEC 100:13
returned home the previous n. BULL 51:8
shades of n. were falling LONG 153:4
sleep one ever-during n. CAT 65:5
So late into the n. BYRON 58:22
sound lovers' tongues by n. SHAK 231:21
sound of revelry by n. BYRON 57:9
Spirit of N. SHEL 240:6
tender is the n. KEATS 139:20
that go bump in the n. ANON 7:5
There's n. and day BORR 44:22
'Tis with us perpetual n. JONS 136:11
toiling upward in the n. LONG 153:6
were the world's last n. DONNE 88:5
what of the n. BIBLE 28:24
nighted: Crossing alone the n. ferry HOUS 126:24
night-gown: put on your n. SHAK 223:9
nightingale: brown bright n. amorous SWIN 249:15
little brown n. bills his HARDY 114:15
n. in the sycamore STEV 247:15
roar you as 'twere any n. SHAK 226:16
Save the n. alone BARN 15:17
nightingales: n. are singing near ELIOT 94:17
nightmare: History is a n. from which JOYCE 137:6
Nights: Chequer-board of N. and Days FITZ 99:7
n. are wholesome SHAK 206:9
nihil: Aut Caesar, aut n. BORG 44:21
Vox et praeterea n. ANON 7:9
Nil: *N. desperandum Teucro duce* HOR 123:11
N. posse creari De nilo LUCR 155:5
Nile: on the banks of the N. SHER 240:20
pour the waters of the N. CARR 62:16
Where's my serpent of old N. SHAK 203:19
nilo: Nil posse creari De n. LUCR 155:5
Nimrod: N. the mighty hunter before BIBLE 22:23
Nimshi: son of N. BIBLE 25:12
nine: n. and sixty ways of constructing KIPL 144:10
N. bean-rows will I have YEATS 279:7
n. men's morris is filled SHAK 227:2
nine-tenths: n. of the law of chivalry SAY 200:16
ninety: n. and nine just persons BIBLE 35:25
That n. lives have been MCG 157:11
Nineveh: Is one with N. and Tyre KIPL 145:11
Quinquireme of N. from MAS 162:14
ninth: be kept till the n. year HOR 122:21
Niobe: Like N., all tears SHAK 206:15

nip: I'll n. him in the bud   ROCHE 195:12
nipping: is a n. and an eager air   SHAK 207:7
nipple: plucked my n.   SHAK 221:6
Nisi: N. Dominus aedificaverit   BIBLE 41:15
nives: Diffugere n.   HOR 124:15
No: Araminta, say 'N.   PRAED 186:16
   n. better than you should   BEAU 16:19
   N. money   RAC 193:18
   N. sun—no moon!   HOOD 121:9
   people cried, 'O N.   BARH 15:14
   There is n. God   PRAY 188:9
Noah: N. he often said to his   CHES 70:8
   Who married N.'s daughter   AYT 12:18
nobis: Non n.   BIBLE 41:14
noble: n. and nude and antique   SWIN 249:17
   n. animal, splendid   BROW 48:13
   n. mind is here o'erthrown   SHAK 209:6
   not birth that makes us n.   FLET 100:17
   quiet us in a death so n.   MILT 170:6
   Some work of n. note   TENN 255:14
   What's brave, what's n.   SHAK 204:7
   woods the n. savage ran   DRYD 90:22
nobleman: king may make a n.   BURKE 53:12
nobler: Whether 'tis n.   SHAK 208:24
nobles: their n. with links of iron   PRAY 191:7
Noblesse: N. oblige   LEVIS 151:11
noblest: art the ruins of the n.   SHAK 216:11
   honest God is the n.   ING 129:13
   honest God's the n.   BUTL 56:16
   honest man's the n.   POPE 185:18
   n. prospect which a Scotchman   JOHN 131:19
   n. Roman of them all   SHAK 217:6
Nobody: Hush, hush, N. cares   MORT 174:1
   kingdom where n. dies   MILL 166:4
   N. heard him, the dead man   SMITH 242:13
   N. speaks the truth when   BOWEN 45:15
   there's n. at home   POPE 184:15
   wants to have read and n.   TWAIN 261:8
Nocturna: N. versate manu   HOR 122:19
Nod: dwelt in the land of N.   BIBLE 22:18
   N. with your hand to signify   HOUS 127:3
nods: even excellent Homer n.   HOR 122:20
   N., and becks   MILT 167:16
noes: yeas and honest kersey n.   SHAK 219:11
noir: Porte le soleil n. de la   NERV 175:11
noire: île triste et n.   BAUD 16:13
noise: gone up with a merry n.   PRAY 189:4
   happy n. to hear   HOUS 125:12
   inexplicable dumb-shows and n.   SHAK 209:7
   n. of battle roll'd   TENN 252:4
   the n. the people   ANON 4:14
noiseless: n. tenor of their way   GRAY 112:6
noises: isle is full of n.   SHAK 232:22
Nokomis: Stood the wigwam of N.   LONG 153:12
Noli: N. me tangere   BIBLE 41:24
nominate: boldly n. a spade a spade   JONS 136:4
Nomine: In N. Patris   MASS 163:7
nomini: sed n. tuo da gloriam   BIBLE 41:14
nom'native: Is her n. case   OKEE 177:14
non: saturam n. scribere   JUV 137:13
Nonconformist: N. Conscience makes cowards   BEER 17:14
none: answer came there n.   SCOTT 201:12
   Then n. was for a party   MAC 156:7
   they n. of them know one   GRAH 111:12
nonsense: grammar, and n., and learning   GOLD 110:17
   n. which was knocked out   BEER 17:16
   That sounds like n.   SCOTT 202:7

Non-U: 'U' and 'N.   ROSS 197:1
Nonumque: N. prematur in annum   HOR 122:21
noon: amid the blaze of n.   MILT 170:2
   troubled midnight and the n.'s   ELIOT 93:12
noon-day: talks of darkness at n.   COWP 79:17
   that destroyeth in the n.   PRAY 189:24
no one: there's n. about in the Quad   KNOX 147:5
Noose: Turret in a N. of Light   FITZ 98:14
Nooses: N. give   PARK 180:6
Norfolk: bear him up the N. sky   BETJ 20:9
   Very flat, N.   COW 79:2
norint: sua si bona n.   VIRG 264:11
Norman: simple faith than N. blood   TENN 253:2
North: On a journey N.   COW 79:9
   true and tender is the N.   TENN 254:11
North-easter: wild N.   KING 142:11
northern: constant as the n. star   SHAK 216:8
Norval: My name is N.   HOME 120:18
nose: Entuned in hir n. ful semely   CHAU 68:2
   Had Cleopatra's n. been   PASC 180:17
   Marion's n. looks red   SHAK 219:14
   Mine has a snub n. like   BLAKE 42:20
   n. was as sharp as a pen   SHAK 213:12
   ring at the end of his n.   LEAR 150:14
   Thine has a great hook n.   BLAKE 42:20
nose-painting: n., sleep, and urine   SHAK 222:3
noses: flatter n. than ourselves   CONR 77:11
   n. have they   PRAY 190:13
nostalgie: La n. de la boue   AUG 11:14
nostra: qui ante nos n. dixerunt   DON 87:16
not: lov'd n. wisely but too well   SHAK 229:15
   N. bloody likely   SHAW 238:18
   n. waving but drowning   SMITH 242:13
note: living had no n.   GIBB 106:13
notes: all the compass of the n.   DRYD 91:9
   n. and our dead bodies   SCOTT 201:10
   N. are often necessary   JOHN 135:4
nothing: brought n. into this world   BIBLE 39:30
   Closes n., refuses nothing   WHIT 270:8
   cuckoo shouts all day at n.   HOUS 126:22
   gives to airy n.   SHAK 227:18
   'Goodness had n. to do   WEST 269:1
   Have n. to do with the case   GILB 108:15
   having n., yet hath all   WOTT 277:16
   How to live well on n.   THAC 256:11
   I am n.   BIBLE 38:14
   I do n. upon my self   DONNE 89:1
   I have n. to do to-day   DOYLE 89:13
   I'm going to do n.   ANON 3:14
   in this world n. can be   FRAN 102:16
   it was n. more   WORD 276:3
   I will say n.   SHAK 218:8
   knowledge of n.   DICK 85:28
   n. a-year, paid quarterly   SURT 248:15
   n. done while aught remains   ROG 195:18
   n. extenuate   SHAK 229:15
   n. for reward   SPEN 244:17
   N. in excess   ANON 6:7
   N. is ever done in this   SHAW 237:23
   N. is here for tears   MILT 170:6
   N., like something   LARK 149:5
   N. to do but work   KING 142:5
   N. will come of nothing   SHAK 217:17
   Signifying n.   SHAK 223:15
   there is n. left remarkable   SHAK 204:6
   When you have n. to say   COLT 76:6
nothingness: love and fame to n.   KEATS 140:10
   Pass into n.   KEATS 138:15
notice: n. whether it's winter   CHEK 69:2

short n. was her speciality | SAKI 199:3
was a man who used to n. | HARDY 114:8
nötig: Land, das Helden n. hat | BREC 46:9
notorious: n. evil liver | PRAY 187:9
Nottingham: N. lace of the curtains | BETJ 20:5
nought: n. shall make us rue | SHAK 217:16
noun: verb not a n. | FULL 103:22
nourisher: n. in life's feast | SHAK 221:16
nourishing: n. a youth sublime | TENN 253:6
nourrit: les couvre, les n., les incite | MONT 172:4
nouvelles: du moins des choses n. | VOLT 264:14
novel: n. tells a story | FORS 101:13
November: no birds,— N. | HOOD 121:10
remember the Fifth of N. | ANON 4:17
now: If it be n. | SHAK 211:17
If not n. when | HILL 119:10
N. for dogs and apes | BROW 49:10
N. I lay me down to sleep | ANON 4:11
nowhere: rest n. | OKEL 178:3
Nox: N. est perpetua una dormienda | CAT 65:5
noxious: Of all n. animals | KILV 142:3
nuclear: edge of the n. abyss | STEV 246:17
nude: noble and n. and antique | SWIN 249:17
nudula: Pallidula rigida n. | HAER 113:8
nuisance: himself a n. to other people | MILL 165:17
nulli: n. negabimus aut differemus | MAGN 159:1
Nullius: N. addictus iurare in verba | HOR 123:1
nullum: n. fere scribendi genus | JOHN 133:2
number: count the n. of the beast | BIBLE 41:3
full of a n. of things | STEV 247:9
greatest n. is the foundation | BENT 19:14
if I Called the Wrong N. | THUR 259:13
n. of his name | BIBLE 41:7
n. of my days | PRAY 188:25
teach us to n. our days | PRAY 189:23
numbered: God hath n. thy kingdom | BIBLE 30:9
of your head are all n. | BIBLE 32:26
numbers: happiness for the greatest n. | HUTC 128:11
n. came | POPE 184:19
numbness: drowsy n. pains | KEATS 139:18
numeros: n. veniebat ad aptos | OVID 179:1
Nun: Come, pensive N. | MILT 167:12
holy time is quiet as a n. | WORD 276:20
nunc: et n., et semper | MASS 163:8
N. dimittis servum tuum | BIBLE 41:19
N. est bibendum | HOR 123:18
nunnery: Get thee to a n. | SHAK 209:2
n. Of thy chaste breast | LOV 154:10
nurs'd: never n. a dear gazelle | MOORE 173:3
nurse: Dear n. of arts | SHAK 214:5
keep a hold of N. | BELL 18:12
my most kindly n. | SPEN 244:20
n. unacted desires | BLAKE 44:7
sucks the n. asleep | SHAK 204:11
nurseries: Public schools are the n. of all vice | FIEL 98:6
nursery: n. still leaps out in all | BYRON 57:5
nurses: old men's n. | BACON 13:13
Nursing: N. her wrath to keep it | BURNS 54:22
nuthin: Tar-baby ain't sayin' n. | HARR 115:9
nuts: Brazil—where the n. | THOM 256:21
nut-shell: could be bounded in a n. | SHAK 208:13
Nymphs: N. and as yet unknown rivers | VIRG 263:16
O: Within this wooden O. | SHAK 213:8
oafs: muddied o. at the goals | KIPL 144:11
Oak: O., and Ash, and Thorn | KIPL 146:2
o. and three-ply bronze | HOR 123:10

thee the reed is as the o. | SHAK 206:4
oaks: like one of those old o. | BURKE 53:13
O altitudo: pursue my reason to an *O.* | BROW 48:7
oars: o. were silver | SHAK 203:22
oath: Cophetua sware a royal o. | TENN 251:3
He who cheats with an o. | PLUT 183:18
inscriptions a man is not upon o. | JOHN 132:23
oaths: God pardon all o. that | SHAK 230:12
men with o. | LYS 156:1
soldier, Full of strange o. | SHAK 205:1
obedient: o. to their laws we lie | SIM 241:9
obey: if anyone is born to o. | COMP 76:10
love, cherish, and to o. | PRAY 187:28
with the laws but to o. | HORS 125:2
obeyed: I o. as a son | GIBB 106:6
obeys: she o. him | LONG 153:14
object: advertisers don't o. | SWAF 248:16
grand o. of travelling is | JOHN 132:27
My o. all sublime | GILB 108:11
o. in enquiring is to know | HOUS 127:3
objection: I see no o. to stoutness | GILB 107:10
objectionable: many ways extremely o. | KEYN 141:17
objective: art is by finding an 'o. correlative' | ELIOT 95:11
oblige: Noblesse o. | LEVIS 151:11
oblivion: rummend To cold o. | SHEL 239:3
formless ruin of o. | SHAK 233:12
mere o. | SHAK 205:1
Wherein he puts alms for o. | SHAK 233:8
oblivious: with some sweet o. antidote | SHAK 223:13
obnoxious: o. to each carping tongue | BRAD 46:1
obscure: palpable o. find out | MILT 169:3
obscuri: Ibant o. sola sub nocte | VIRG 263:12
obscurity: decent o. of a learned | GIBB 106:9
observation: Let o. with extensive view | JOHN 135:8
l'o. le hasard ne favorise | PAST 181:6
observe: you do not o. | DOYLE 89:14
observed: o. of all observers | SHAK 209:6
Since o. by Yours faithfully | ANON 3:9
observer: Is a keen o. of life | AUDEN 11:8
obsta: Principiis o. | OVID 178:23
occasions: New o. teach new duties | LOW 154:19
o. do inform against me | SHAK 210:23
seas upon their lawful o. | PRAY 191:10
occupation: Othello's o.'s gone | SHAK 229:5
pleasant o. | GILB 107:13
occupations: let us love our o. | DICK 83:18
occupy: o. their business in great | PRAY 190:8
ocean: be back on the vast o. | HOR 123:12
great o. of truth | NEWT 176:8
In th' o.'s bosom unespied | MARV 161:11
Make the mighty o. | CARN 62:2
Neptune's o. wash this blood | SHAK 222:1
o. and the sky together | SHEL 239:7
o. in the eventide of fear | MORR 173:13
o. Is folded and hung | AUDEN 10:8
thou deep and dark blue O. | BYRON 57:15
unfathom'd caves of o. | GRAY 112:5
Upon a painted o. | COL 74:9
O'Connell: such a man as O. | SMITH 243:1
odd: choose the o. | AUDEN 11:9
How o. Of God | EWER 97:9
Nothing o. will do long | JOHN 132:24
not so o. | BROW 48:4
think it exceedingly o. | KNOX 147:5
this was o. | CARR 63:23
odds: o. is gone | SHAK 204:6

Was by a mousing o. hawk'd	SHAK 222:11
white o. in the belfry	TENN 255:8
owls: companion to o.	BIBLE 25:30
There I couch when o. do	SHAK 233:2
Two O. and a Hen	LEAR 150:2
own: beam that is in thine o.	BIBLE 32:3
every country but his o.	CANN 61:1
his o. received him not	BIBLE 36:15
know how to be one's o.	MONT 172:3
owning: demented with the mania of o.	
	WHIT 270:6
ox: eateth grass as an o.	BIBLE 26:1
o. goeth to the slaughter	BIBLE 26:10
shalt not muzzle the o.	BIBLE 23:34
stalled ox and hatred	BIBLE 26:21
oxen: fields with his own o.	HOR 123:9
Many o. are come about	PRAY 188:14
Oxenford: Clerk ther was of O. also	CHAU 68:4
Oxford: At O., as you know	JOW 136:14
back at O. or Cambridge	BEER 17:16
clever men at O.	GRAH 111:12
King to O. sent a troop	BROW 48:15
nice sort of place, O.	SHAW 238:4
O. is on the whole more	BAED 14:4
O. that has made me insufferable	BEER 17:15
To O. sent a troop of horse	TRAPP 259:22
oxlips: o. and the nodding violet	SHAK 227:5
Oxtail: to the University of O.	JOYCE 137:8
oyster: then the world's mine o.	SHAK 226:11
oysters: He had often eaten o.	GILB 106:18
Ozymandias: 'My name is O.	SHEL 239:17
pace: Creeps in this petty p.	SHAK 223:15
Requiescant in p.	MASS 163:20
unperturbèd p.	THOM 258:2
pacem: dona nobis p.	MASS 163:18
Qui desiderat p.	VEG 261:18
Solitudinem faciunt p.	TAC 250:8
Paces: P. about her room again	ELIOT 95:4
three p. thro' the room	TENN 253:4
paciencia: p. y barajar	CERV 66:8
Pacific: He star'd at the P.	KEATS 140:4
pack: I will p.	BROO 47:12
Pay, p., and follow	BURT 55:12
pack-horse: rather of the p. on the down	
	MORR 173:14
pack-horses: Shall p.	SHAK 212:25
pact: p. with you, Walt Whitman	POUND 186:11
pad: I march with bat and p.	HOUS 125:9
Paddington: than at P.	CONN 77:8
Paddock: P. calls	SHAK 219:16
paddocks: Cold as p. though they	HERR 119:2
padlock: p.—on her mind	PRIOR 191:16
paeans: laurels to p.	CIC 72:8
Paene: *P. insularum*	CAT 65:7
Pagan: P. suckled in a creed outworn	WORD 277:8
page: I turn the p.	BROW 49:3
pageant: like this insubstantial p.	SHAK 232:24
pages: almost turned down the p.	POUND 186:13
paid: have p. thy utmost blessing	DE L 82:11
nothing a-year, p. quarterly	SURT 248:15
p. that is well satisfied	SHAK 226:3
pain: because it gave p. to the bear	MAC 157:3
delight in physics p.	SHAK 222:4
I feel no p. dear mother	ANON 3:18
I have no p.	FARM 97:12
intermission of p.	SELD 202:20
life's a p. and but a span	DAV 82:1
midnight with no p.	KEATS 139:22
one who never inflicts p.	NEWM 176:1

purchase p. with all that joy	POPE 184:24
quite sure she felt no p.	BROW 50:15
rues et de voler du p.	FRAN 102:5
shall there be any more p.	BIBLE 41:8
tender for another's p.	GRAY 112:11
tongueless vigil and all the p.	SWIN 249:15
well and she hasn't a p.	MILNE 166:16
When p. and anguish wring	SCOTT 202:2
painful: one is as p. as the other	BACON 13:6
pains: His present and your p.	SHAK 213:10
One of the greatest p.	BAG 14:9
possessors into p. of all kinds	BUTL 56:15
with p. that conquer trust	TENN 252:14
paint: let her p. an inch thick	SHAK 211:11
p. in the public's face	RUSK 198:6
p. my picture truly like	CROM 80:16
p. the meadows with delight	SHAK 219:13
to p. the lily	SHAK 217:12
painted: Duchess p. on the wall	BROW 50:4
idle as a p. ship	COL 74:9
P. the mid-sea blue	FLEC 100:10
p. veil which those who	SHEL 240:3
She p. her face	BIBLE 25:13
so young as they are p.	BEER 17:12
That fears a p. devil	SHAK 221:18
This p. child of dirt	POPE 184:22
was p. on the wall	PETR 183:1
painters: know of two p. in the world	WHIS 269:12
paintings: have heard of your p. too	SHAK 209:4
paint-pots: p. and his words a foot	HOR 122:14
pair: been a p. of ragged claws	ELIOT 94:6
resembles a p. of shears	SMITH 242:19
Take a p. of sparkling eyes	GILB 107:8
pal: 'E won't split on a p.	KIPL 146:27
palace: Be thine own p.	DONNE 88:10
gorgeous p. for a hermitage	SHAK 230:9
I will make a p. fit	STEV 247:12
leads to the p. of wisdom	BLAKE 44:1
Love in a p. is perhaps	KEATS 139:8
palaces: Dragons in their pleasant p.	BIBLE 28:22
gorgeous p.	SHAK 232:24
Mid pleasures and p. though	PAYNE 181:13
pale: behold a p. horse	BIBLE 40:32
bond Which keeps me p.	SHAK 222:15
look not so p.	SHAK 223:9
P. grew thy cheek and cold	BYRON 59:3
P. hands I loved	HOPE 121:16
p. prime-roses	SHAK 235:1
turn not p., beloved snail	CARR 63:12
which the world grew p.	JOHN 135:10
Why so p. and wan	SUCK 248:3
paler: I become p. than grass	SAPP 199:12
pall: brows shall be their p.	OWEN 179:5
Pallidula: P. rigida nudula	HAER 113:8
pallor: of girls' brows	OWEN 179:5
palls: everything p.	ANON 6:5
palm: condemn'd to have an itching p.	SHAK 217:2
has won it bear the p.	JORT 136:13
Hold Infinity in the p.	BLAKE 42:17
palmerworm: caterpillar, and the p.	BIBLE 30:13
palms: p. before my feet	CHES 69:24
paltry: aged man is but a p. thing	YEATS 279:13
Pam: P., you great big mountainous	BETJ 21:10
pampered: God's p. people	DRYD 90:11
Pan: great god P.	BROW 48:16
Pandoemonium: P., the high capitol	MILT 169:2
Pandora's Box: If you open that P. you	
	BEVIN 21:19
Panem: P. et circenses	JUV 138:4

panes: diamonded with p. of quaint   KEATS 138:18
pang: sufferance finds a p. as great   SHAK 224:1
Pange: P., lingua   THOM 256:20
P., lingua   VEN 261:19
pangs: p. and fears than wars   SHAK 215:9
panic: it but p. and emptiness   FORS 101:14
p.'s in thy breastie   BURNS 55:5
Panjandrum: grand P. himself   FOOTE 101:7
pansies: p., that's for thoughts   SHAK 211:6
pantaloon: lean and slipper'd p.   SHAK 205:1
pants: p. the hart for cooling   TATE 250:15
your lower limbs in p.   NASH 175:1
Papa: P., potatoes, poultry   DICK 84:10
paper: atomic bomb is a p. tiger   MAO 159:15
hand that signed the p.   THOM 257:5
just for a scrap of p.   BETH 20:4
paradis: sont les p. qu'on a perdus   PROU 192:7
Paradise: drunk the milk of P.   COL 75:7
England is a p. for women   BURT 55:19
England is the p. of women   FLOR 101:4
P. by way of Kensal Green   CHES 70:4
P. by way of Kensal Green   CHES 70:5
shalt thou be with me in p.   BIBLE 36:10
Wilderness is P. enow   FITZ 98:15
paradises: paradises are p. we have lost
   PROU 192:7
paradox: Man is an embodied p.   COLT 76:7
parallel: ours so truly p.   MARV 161:14
Parce que: 'P. c'était lui   MONT 172:1
Parcere: P. subiectis et debellare   VIRG 263:14
parchment: rotten p. bonds   SHAK 230:2
pard: p.-like Spirit   SHEL 238:25
pardon: beseech you of your p.   SHAK 229:2
cannot help nor p.   AUDEN 11:11
God may p. you   ELIZ 95:16
God will p. me   HEINE 116:15
p. all oaths that are broke   SHAK 230:12
thousand Ta's and P.'s   BETJ 21:7
We cannot beg for p.   MACN 158:10
We will p. Thy Mistake   BETJ 21:4
pardonnera: Et le bon Dieu me p.   CATH 65:2
parent: don't object to an aged p.   DICK 84:8
To lose one p.   WILDE 271:8
parents: begin by loving their p.   WILDE 271:27
Of p. good   SHAK 213:19
parfit: p. gentil knyght   CHAU 67:19
paries: Barbiton hic p. habebit   HOR 124:11
p. cum proximus ardet   HOR 123:6
pariete: in p. erat pictus superque   PETR 183:1
Paris: Americans die they go to P.   WILDE 271:23
go to P.   APPL 7:11
P. is well worth a mass   HENR 117:13
sans moi P. serait pris   ANON 5:18
should go and live in P.   ANON 3:19
parium: judicium p. suorum   MAGN 158:16
Parliament: Bidding the crop-headed P.
   BROW 49:6
In the P. of man   TENN 253:10
p. can do any thing   PEMB 182:4
p. is a *deliberative* assembly   BURKE 52:15
P. speaking through reporters   CARL 61:17
Parliaments: England is the mother of P.
   BRIG 46:17
parlour: Is it a party in a p.   WORD 276:4
'Will you walk into my p.   HOW 127:11
Parnell: Poor P.   JOYCE 136:21
parody: devil's walking p.   CHES 69:23
parson: coughing drowns the p.'s saw
   SHAK 219:14

If P. lost his senses   HODG 120:4
p. own'd his skill   GOLD 110:10
parsons: This merriment of p. is   JOHN 133:16
part: come let us kiss and p.   DRAY 90:6
now I know in p.   BIBLE 38:16
p. to tear a cat   SHAK 226:15
Shall I p. my hair behind   ELIOT 94:8
till death us do p.   PRAY 187:28
parted: a' p. even just between   SHAK 213:12
I hae p. frae my Love   BURNS 54:11
Mine never shall be p.   MILT 169:19
When we two p.   BYRON 59:3
particular: London p.   DICK 83:13
should love a bright p. star   SHAK 203:11
Parting: p. is all we know of heaven   DICK 86:3
p. is such sweet sorrow   SHAK 231:22
speed the p. guest   POPE 185:22
this p. was well made   SHAK 217:5
Partir: P. c'est mourir un peu   HAR 114:7
partly: Living and p. living   ELIOT 94:11
parts: his time plays many p.   SHAK 205:1
P. of it are excellent   PUNCH 193:2
To-day we have naming of p.   REED 194:14
Parturient: P. montes   HOR 122:15
party: again to save the p. we love   GAIT 104:7
'Collapse of Stout P.'   ANON 5:8
Is it a p. in a parlour   WORD 276:4
nature of a political p.   TROL 260:11
p. of friends   GILB 107:22
sooner every p. breaks   AUST 11:23
Stick to your p.   DISR 87:4
Then none was for a p.   MAC 156:7
Parys: Frenssh of P. was to hire   CHAU 68:2
pas: n'y a que le premier p.   DU D 91:16
pasarán: No p.   IBAR 129:2
pass: I shall not p. this way   GREL 113:2
let him p.   SHAK 219:5
let this cup p. from me   BIBLE 34:13
let us p.   BURKE 53:2
my words shall not p. away   BIBLE 34:3
p., and turn again   EMER 96:3
P. into nothingness   KEATS 138:15
p. the ammunition   FORGY 101:11
pay us, p. us   CHES 70:6
shining Foot shall p.   FITZ 100:1
therefore let him p. for a man   SHAK 224:16
They shall not p.   IBAR 129:2
They shall not p.   NIV 177:5
to p. through this world   GREL 113:2
well p. for forty-three   GILB 109:10
Will she p. in a crowd   SWIFT 249:3
passage: ever you meet with a p.   JOHN 132:18
passageways: With smell of steaks in p.
   ELIOT 94:15
passe: Tout p.   ANON 6:5
passed: I have p. by the watchman   FROST 103:2
p. by on the other side   BIBLE 35:13
Passer: P. mortuus est meae puellae   CAT 65:5
passeront: Ils ne p. pas   NIV 177:5
passes: Everything p.   ANON 6:5
Men seldom make p.   PARK 180:5
p. the glory of the world   ANON 7:5
passeth: which p. all understanding   BIBLE 39:19
passing: Deign on the p. world   JOHN 135:9
p. the love of women   BIBLE 24:27
passing-bells: What p. for these who die
   OWEN 179:4
passion: all p. spent   MILT 170:7
Bards of P. and of Mirth   KEATS 139:11

connect the prose and the p.	FORS 101:17
has felt the tender p.	GAY 105:16
he vows his p. is	PARK 180:7
in a dream of p.	SHAK 208:20
p. that left the ground	BROW 48:19
periwig-pated fellow tear a p.	SHAK 209:7
Queen was in a furious p.	CARR 63:6
ruling p. in man is not	FROST 103:12
ruling p. conquers reason	POPE 185:2
That is not p.'s slave	SHAK 209:9
when his p. shall have	TENN 253:8
passionate: Are full of p. intensity	YEATS 279:15
passions: *après les instants de p.*	VOLT 265:5
diminue les médiocres p.	LA R 149:11
governs the p. and resolutions	HUME 128:1
passive: p., recording, not thinking	ISH 129:17
passover: it is the Lord's p.	BIBLE 23:15
passport: his p. shall be made	SHAK 214:4
past: are p. our dancing days	SHAK 231:13
future contained in time p.	ELIOT 93:13
God cannot change the p.	AGAT 1:18
more than things long p.	SHAK 229:21
p., and future sees	BLAKE 43:6
p. as a watch in the night	PRAY 189:21
p. is a foreign country	HART 115:15
p. is the only dead thing	THOM 257:17
P. ruin'd Ilion Helen lives	LAND 148:10
remembrance of things p.	SHAK 235:12
shall be p. making love	PRIOR 191:17
What's p.	SHAK 233:12
pastors: some ungracious p. do	SHAK 207:5
pasture: feed me in a green p.	PRAY 188:15
pastures: fresh woods, and p.	MILT 168:5
On England's pleasant p.	BLAKE 43:2
patches: king of shreds and p.	SHAK 210:18
thing of shreds and p.	GILB 107:24
patent: so my p. back again is	SHAK 236:6
Paterna: *P. rura bubus*	HOR 123:9
path: beaten p. to his door	EMER 96:19
was a p. of gold for him	BROW 50:7
Pathetic: characterize as the 'P. Fallacy'	RUSK 198:8
Is not p.	WHIT 270:8
pathos: true p. and sublime	BURNS 55:3
paths: all her p. are peace	BIBLE 26:6
make his p. straight	BIBLE 31:4
p. of glory lead	GRAY 112:3
patience: be the pattern of all p.	SHAK 218:8
grande aptitude à la p.	BUFF 51:7
greater aptitude for p.	BUFF 51:7
have heard of the p. of Job	BIBLE 40:15
long will you abuse our p.	CIC 72:10
My p. is now at an end	HITL 119:15
old abusing of God's p.	SHAK 226:10
p., and shuffle the cards	CERV 66:8
p. possess ye your souls	BIBLE 36:6
p. under their sufferings	PRAY 187:5
sat like p. on a monument	SHAK 234:4
Though with p. He stands	LOGAU 152:15
patient: disease and kill the p.	BACON 13:8
not so p.	SHAK 212:21
p. etherized upon a table	ELIOT 94:3
p. Must minister to himself	SHAK 223:13
p., not a brawler	BIBLE 39:27
sit thou a p. looker-on	QUAR 193:9
Thou must be p.	SHAK 218:23
patines: inlaid with p. of bright gold	SHAK 226:5
patrem: *Deum p. qui ecclesiam*	CYPR 81:6
patria: *decorum est pro p. mori*	HOR 124:7

patrie: *plus j'aimai ma p.*	BELL 19:10
patriot: soldier and the sunshine p.	PAINE 179:15
steady p. of the world	CANN 61:1
patriotism: larger p.	ROS 196:16
P. is the last refuge	JOHN 132:21
realize that p. is not enough	CAV 65:13
patriots: blood of p. and tyrants	JEFF 130:10
So to be p.	BURKE 52:11
True p. we	CART 64:19
Patron: Is not a P.	JOHN 131:9
p. and the jail	JOHN 106:9
patter: unintelligible p.	GILB 109:8
pattern: be the p. of all patience	SHAK 218:8
cunning'st p. of excelling nature	SHAK 229:13
In a p. called a war	LOW 154:14
Made him our p. to live	BROW 50:1
patterns: What are p.	LOW 154:14
patuit: *Et vera incessu p. dea*	VIRG 263.1
Paul: crush Under P.'s dome	HODG 120:6
pause: How dull it is to p.	TENN 255:13
p. awhile from letters	JOHN 135:9
pauses: intervals and happy p.	BACON 13:27
pauvre: *p. paysan en mon royaume*	HENR 117:11
pauvres: *p. sont les nègres de*	CHAM 67:2
paved: streets are p. with gold	COLM 76:3
pavement: street and p. mute	HARDY 114:14
pavements: on the p. gray	YEATS 279:8
pavilion: p. cat	LANG 148:17
paws: massive p. of elder persons	BELL 18:3
my dear p.	CARR 62:17
pax: *et in terra p. hominibus*	MASS 163:12
P. Domini sit semper vobiscum	MASS 163:17
P. Vobis	BIBLE 41:20
pay: going to p. every penny	GEDD 105:24
now I must p. for my fun	KIPL 144:15
p. a debt to pleasure	ROCH 195:14
P., pack, and follow	BURT 55:12
p. us, pass us	CHES 70:6
sum of things for p.	HOUS 126:20
unbound by any interest to p.	HOR 123:9
payment: p. of half twenty shillings	BURKE 52:12
pays: p. your money and you takes	ANON 5:14
rassembler à froid un p.	DE G 82:6
peace: all her paths are p.	BIBLE 26:6
bad p.	FRAN 102:15
calls it—p.	BYRON 57:6
chastisement of our p.	BIBLE 29:15
feet into the way of p.	BIBLE 34:30
first in p.	LEE 151:3
Give p. in our time	PRAY 186:22
give thee p.	BIBLE 23:25
hereafter for ever hold his p.	PRAY 187:26
I am for 'P.	BRIG 46:15
I came not to send p.	BIBLE 32:27
in p., goodwill	CHUR 71:17
just and lasting p.	LINC 152:3
Let him who desires p.	VEG 261:18
Let war yield to p.	CIC 72:8
luxury, p.	BAUD 16:12
makes a good p.	HERB 118:4
mountain tops is p.	GOE 110:2
My p. is gone	GOE 109:23
my reign is p.	LAND 148:9
Nation shall speak p.	REND 194:18
not p. at any price	JERR 130:20
on earth p.	BIBLE 35:3
p. and propagation are	WALP 266:4
P. be unto you	BIBLE 41:20
p. for our time	CHAM 66:14

P. hath her victories	MILT 170:14
p. I hope with honour	DISR 87:2
P. is indivisible	LITV 152:8
P. its ten thousands	PORT 186:3
p. of God	BIBLE 39:19
p. of the double bed after	CAMP 60:12
P., perfect peace	BICK 42:4
P., the human dress	BLAKE 43:19
p. there's nothing so becomes	SHAK 213:14
P. to him that is far off	BIBLE 29:19
poor, and mangled P.	SHAK 214:5
Prince of P.	BIBLE 28:19
servant depart in p.	BIBLE 35:4
So enamoured on p. that	CLAR 72:25
that publisheth p.	BIBLE 29:12
that the defences of p.	ANON 4:18
There is no p.	BIBLE 29:11
time of p.	BIBLE 27:7
verses are like the p. of God	JAM 130:1
ways upon a state of p.	VIRG 263:14
when there is no p.	BIBLE 29:24
wilderness and call it p.	TAC 250:8
peacemakers: Blessed are the p.	BIBLE 31:11
peach: Do I dare to eat a p.	ELIOT 94:8
nectarine and curious p.	MARV 161:15
peacock: milk-white p. like a ghost	TENN 254:15
peacocks: apes, and p.	BIBLE 25:3
apes and p.	MAS 162:14
terraces and p. strutting	KIPL 144:2
pea-green: In a beautiful p. boat	LEAR 150:13
peak: small things from the p.	CHES 70:9
peal: wildest p. for years	HODG 120:4
pear: go round the prickly p.	ELIOT 93:23
pearl: hang a p. in every cowslip's	SHAK 226:17
One p. of great price	BIBLE 33:7
threw a p. away	SHAK 229:15
pearls: are p. that were his eyes	SHAK 232:15
Give p. away and rubies	HOUS 125:7
search for p. must dive	DRYD 90:20
ye your p. before swine	BIBLE 32:4
pears: our French withered p.	SHAK 203:12
Pearse: P. summoned Cuchulain	YEATS 279:20
peasant: what a rogue and p. slave	SHAK 208:20
peasantry: bold p.	GOLD 110:6
pebble: only p. on the beach	BRAI 46:3
peccata: tollis p. mundi	MASS 163:18
peccator: Esto p. et pecca fortiter	LUTH 155:11
Peccavi: P.—I have Sindh	WINK 273:4
P.—I've Scinde	PUNCH 192:14
Quia p. nimis cogitatione	MASS 163:9
pécher: p. que pécher en silence	MOL 171:14
peculiar: London was extensive and p.	DICK 85:17
p. people	BIBLE 40:18
Pecunia: P. non olet	VESP 262:5
pecuniam: p. infinitam	CIC 72:13
pedantic: little too p. for a gentleman	CONG 76:16
pede: nunc p. libero	HOR 123:18
peep: that would p. and botanize	WORD 276:5
Wizards that p. and that	BIBLE 28:17
peeping: Came p. in at morn	HOOD 121:7
peepshow: ticket for the p.	MACN 158:5
peignoir: Complacencies of the p.	STEV 246:15
peine: donné la p. de naître	BEAU 16:17
la p. d'être dit	BEAU 16:14
pelago: Commisit p. ratem	HOR 123:10
pelican: wonderful bird is the p.	MERR 165:9
Pelion: pile Ossa on P.	VIRG 264:10
pen: Biting my truant p.	SIDN 241:5
could use the sword and p.	LAND 148:11

His fingers held the p.	COWP 79:16
ink in my p. ran cold	WALP 265:17
less brilliant p.	BEER 17:13
nose was as sharp as a p.	SHAK 213:12
p. has glean'd my teeming	KEATS 140:9
p. is mightier than	BULW 51:11
p. is worse than the sword	BURT 55:15
product of a scoffer's p.	WORD 274:14
Waverley p.	ANON 5:4
penance: night do p. for a day	WORD 276:8
pence: Take care of the p.	LOWN 154:20
pendre: par faire p. un homme	MOL 171:12
Pends-toi: P., brave Crillon	HENR 117:12
Penelope: His true P. was Flaubert	POUND 186:8
peninsulas: eye of p. and islands	CAT 65:7
penitence: distinguish p. from love	POPE 184:13
penny: one p. the worse	BARH 15:12
pens: p. dwell on guilt and misery	AUST 12:4
pensant: mais c'est un roseau p.	PASC 181:3
pension: hang your hat on a p.	MACN 158:6
pensive: In vacant or in p. mood	WORD 277:2
pent-house: Hang upon his p. lid	SHAK 220:3
people: August for the p. and their	AUDEN 10:12
belongs to the P.	LINC 152:1
bourgeois are other p.	REN 194:17
doubt but ye are the p.	BIBLE 25:23
good of the p. is the chief	CIC 72:6
Good p. all	GOLD 110:13
indictment against an whole p.	BURKE 52:17
into a room full of p.	WEBB 267:2
Let my p. go	ANON 5:11
man should die for the p.	BIBLE 36:34
mean ye that ye beat my p.	BIBLE 28:8
p. are never in the wrong	BURKE 52:9
p. are the masters	BURKE 53:1
P. come miles to see it	GILB 108:12
p. contend for their Liberty	HALE 114:1
p. govern themselves	THIE 256:17
p. imagine a vain	PRAY 188:6
P. you know	LARK 149:6
Privileged and the P. formed	DISR 87:12
sake look after our p.	SCOTT 201:9
saying the voice of the p.	ALC 2:1
That has such p. in't	SHAK 233:3
the noise…and the p.	ANON 4:14
thy people shall be my p.	BIBLE 24:14
'Tis the p. marching	MORR 173:13
two p. with the one pulse	MACN 158:8
we are the p. of England	CHES 70:6
What kind of p. do they	CHUR 71:9
whole world is bereft of p.	LAM 147:16
You can fool all the p.	LINC 151:18
perception: doors of p. were cleansed	BLAKE 44:9
perchance: p. to dream	SHAK 208:24
perdere: Quem Jupiter vult p.	DUP 92:2
perdidi: diem p.	TITUS 259:16
Perdition: P. catch my soul	SHAK 228:26
perdus: les paradis qu'on a p.	PROU 192:7
Pereant: P., inquit	DON 87:16
pereat: justitia et p. mundus	FERD 97:19
perennius: monumentum aere p.	HOR 124:12
PERES: P.; Thy kingdom is divided	BIBLE 30:9
perfect: Be ye therefore p.	BIBLE 31:19
he was a p. cavaliero	BYRON 57:3
If thou wilt be p.	BIBLE 33:21
p. presence of mind	JAMES 130:5
p. round	BROW 48:18
perfection: Dead p.	TENN 253:19
P., of a kind	AUDEN 10:13

P. of the life	YEATS 278:13
pursuit of p.	ARN 9:7
right praise and true p.	SHAK 226:9
she did make defect p.	SHAK 203:23
very pink of p.	GOLD 110:20
perfectly: She's p. well and she hasn't	
	MILNE 166:16
perfide: La p. Albion	XIM 278:8
la p. Angleterre	BOSS 45:3
perfidious: her own waters p. Albion	XIM 278:8
perform: His wonders to p.	COWP 79:14
performance: it takes away the p.	SHAK 222:3
so many years outlive p.	SHAK 212:26
that any artistic p. requires	JAMES 130:5
perfume: feel my breasts all p.	JOYCE 137:9
p. and most melodious twang	AUBR 10:7
throw a p. on the violet	SHAK 217:12
perfumes: No p.	BRUM 50:27
p. of Arabia will not sweeten	SHAK 223:8
perhaps: seek a great p.	RAB 193:15
peril: those in p. on the sea	WHIT 269:15
perils: p. and dangers of this	PRAY 187:1
through the p. of winter	TROL 260:4
periphrastic: p. study in a worn-out	ELIOT 93:16
perish: believeth in him should not p.	BIBLE 36:21
P. the thought	CIBB 72:3
shall p. with the sword	BIBLE 34:16
though the world p.	FERD 97:19
whole nation p. not	BIBLE 36:34
you as well as I P.	HOUS 125:8
perished: Just because it p.	MILL 166:9
perishes: everything p.	ANON 6:5
peritis: decede p.	HOR 123:8
periuria: ex alto p. ridet amantum	OVID 178:20
periwig-pated: p. fellow tear a passion	SHAK 209:7
perjuries: high laughs at lovers' p.	OVID 178:20
permitted: p. to make all the ballads	FLET 100:15
pernicious: most p. woman	SHAK 207:17
p. soul Rot	SHAK 229:14
perpetua: *lux p. luceat eis*	MASS 163:11
Nox est p. una dormienda	CAT 65:5
perpetual: let p. light shine on them	MASS 163:11
make P. day	MARL 160:6
next to the p. motion	DICK 85:26
'Tis with us p. night	JONS 136:11
perpetually: which is p. to be conquered	
	BURKE 52:16
persecutest: why p. thou me	BIBLE 37:16
Persepolis: ride in triumph through P.	
	MARL 160:16
persever: Ay, do, p.	SHAK 227:12
Persian: I hate all that P. gear	HOR 124:1
Persians: given to the Medes and P.	BIBLE 30:9
law of the Medes and P.	BIBLE 30:10
Persicos: P. odi	HOR 124:1
persist: fool would p. in his folly	BLAKE 44:4
person: adornment of his p. he	THOM 258:11
Ancient p. of my heart	ROCH 195:17
I am a most superior p.	ANON 4:9
p. on business from Porlock	COL 75:1
Personal: P. relations are the important	
	FORS 101:16
persons: God is no respecter of p.	BIBLE 37:18
massive paws of elder p.	BELL 18:3
p. should not be joined	PRAY 187:23
perspiration: ninety-nine per cent p.	EDIS 92:7
perspire: dig till you gently p.	KIPL 144:13
persuade: p., threaten	WHIT 270:8
persuadest: p. me to be a Christian	BIBLE 37:30

Pert: P. as a schoolgirl well	GILB 108:6
perturbed: Rest, rest, p. spirit	SHAK 208:2
Peru: from China to P.	JOHN 135:8
pessimist: p. fears this is true	CAB 59:7
Pestilence: P.-stricken multitudes	SHEL 239:12
p. that walketh in darkness	PRAY 189:24
petal: Now sleeps the crimson p.	TENN 254:14
petar: Hoist with his own p.	SHAK 210:21
Peter: Thou art P.	BIBLE 33:12
to see Shock-headed P.	HOFF 120:12
petits: escadrons contre les p.	BUSS 56:1
petty: Creeps in this p. pace	SHAK 223:15
we p. men	SHAK 215:16
petulance: learn that p. is not sarcasm	DISR 86:16
peuple: règne et le p. se gouverne	THIE 256:17
peur: Chevalier sans p. et sans	ANON 5:16
peut-être: p. Puis il avait expiré	RAB 193:15
pews: Talk about the p. and steeples	CHES 69.18
phagocytes: Stimulate the p.	SHAW 237:13
phantasma: p., or a hideous dream	SHAK 216:3
phantom: She was a p. of delight	WORD 276:15
Pharisees: scribes and the P. brought	BIBLE 36:25
phenomenon: describe the infant p.	DICK 85:2
Philip: Appeal from P. drunk	ANON 3:4
Let me see if P. can	HOFF 120:8
Philippi: I will see thee at P.	SHAK 217:4
Philistines: P., and Populace	ARN 9:6
Though the P. may jostle	GILB 108:21
Philosophen: Wie ich den P. verstehe	NIET 176:15
philosopher: guide, p., and friend	POPE 185:19
nothing so absurd but some p.	CIC 72:5
P.!—a fingering slave	WORD 276:5
too in my time to be a p.	EDW 92:13
What I understand by 'p.'	NIET 176:15
philosophers: p. have only interpreted	MARX 162:9
philosophical: p. and more worthy of serious	
	ARIS 8:6
philosophie: la p. les éteint	VOLT 264:19
philosophy: All good moral p. is	BACON 12:20
are dreamt of in your p.	SHAK 208:1
History is p. from examples	DION 86:11
How charming is divine p.	MILT 167:8
little p. inclineth man's	BACON 12:23
natural p., deep	BACON 13:22
now-a-days professors of p.	THOR 259:4
p. quenches them	VOLT 264:19
P.! the lumber	SWIFT 249:11
P. will clip an Angel's	KEATS 139:9
Phoebus: P. 'gins arise...	SHAK 206:3
Phone: P. for the fish-knives	BETJ 20:13
Why Did You Answer the P.	THUR 259:13
phrase: England invented the p.	BAG 14:6
phrases: Certain p. stick in the throat	RUSS 198:14
Phyllis: neat-handed P. dresses	MILT 167:18
physic: Take p., pomp	SHAK 218:11
Throw p. to the dogs	SHAK 223:13
physician: beloved p.	BIBLE 39:22
into the hand of the p.	BIBLE 30:26
P. art thou	WORD 276:5
P., heal thyself	BIBLE 35:6
physicians: It is incident to p.	JOHN 131:4
P. of the utmost fame	BELL 18:10
physics: delight in p. pain	SHAK 222:4
physique: To a beautiful p.	AUDEN 10:17
pianist: Please do not shoot the p.	ANON 4:16
Piccadilly: walk down P. with a poppy	
	GILB 108:21
picked: shall have my pocket p.	SHAK 212:16
picking: hands from p. and stealing	PRAY 187:20

platinum: With bullets made of p.　BELL 18:6
Plato: Amicus P.　ARIS 8:8
　P. is dear to me　ARIS 8:8
Platz: unseren P. an der Sonne　BULOW 51:9
play: Better than a p.　CHAR 67:11
　I could p. Ercles rarely　SHAK 226:15
　Judge not the p. before　QUAR 193:9
　noted that children at p.　MONT 171:18
　our p. is done　SHAK 234:15
　P. it　BOG 44:14
　p.'s the thing　SHAK 208:23
　p. the game　NEWB 175:15
　p. the man　LAT 149:14
　p. the wantons with our　SHAK 230:10
　sheets and p. with flowers　SHAK 213:12
　They will not let my p. run　DENN 82:21
　what to say about a p.　SHAW 237:16
　You would p. upon me　SHAK 210:7
playboy: p. of the western world　SYNGE 250:6
play'd: That's sweetly p. in tune　BURNS 54:17
played: how you p. the game　RICE 195:2
　I have p. the fool　BIBLE 24:24
　p. the King as though under　FIELD 98:3
player: poor p., That struts　SHAK 223:15
　There as strikes the P.　FITZ 99:8
　wrapped in a p.'s hide　GREE 112:18
players: men and women merely p.　SHAK 205:1
　see the p. well bestowed　SHAK 208:18
playing: from the purpose of p.　SHAK 209:8
　on the p. fields of Eton　WELL 268:4
playmates: I have had p.　LAMB 148:4
plays: p. the king shall be welcome　SHAK 208:15
plaything-house: is a little p. that I got　WALP 265:16
plea: Though justice be thy p.　SHAK 225:17
pleasance: Youth is full of p.　SHAK 235:4
pleasant: do not find anything p.　VOLT 264:14
　England's p. pastures seen　BLAKE 43:2
　few think him p. enough　LEAR 150:4
　gets too excitin' to be p.　DICK 85:16
　How p. it is to have money　CLOU 73:11
　'How p. to know Mr Lear　LEAR 150:4
　so many p. things are　GASK 105:4
pleasanter: proves the p. the colder　BUTL 56:13
pleasantness: Her ways are ways of p.　BIBLE 26:6
　p. of an employment does　AUST 12:14
please: after life does greatly p.　SPEN 244:16
　coy, and hard to p.　SCOTT 202:2
　seeketh only Self to p.　BLAKE 43:11
　strive to p. you every day　SHAK 234:15
　To tax and to p.　BURKE 52:13
　we that live to p.　JOHN 135:7
pleased: are p. to call your mind　WEST 269:4
　in whom I am well p.　BIBLE 31:7
　p. not the million　SHAK 208:17
pleases: Though every prospect p.　HEBER 116:10
Pleasure: aching P. nigh　KEATS 139:17
　because it gave p.　MAC 157:3
　did p. me in his top-boots　MARL 160:2
　Forced her to do your p.　WEBS 267:15
　general read without p.　JOHN 134:10
　I have no p. in them　BIBLE 27:21
　In his p. is life　PRAY 188:21
　In youth is p.　WEVER 269:7
　It becomes a p.　WILDE 271:13
　meant by the p. of life　TALL 250:13
　Money gives me p. all　BELL 18:20
　on by their favourite p.　VIRG 264:4
　pay a debt to p.　ROCH 195:14

perfect type of a perfect p.　WILDE 271:21
　P. at the helm　GRAY 111:17
　P. is nothing else　SELD 202:20
　P. never is at home　KEATS 139:2
　p. of the fleeting year　SHAK 236:8
　public stock of harmless p.　JOHN 134:25
　Refrain from the unholy p.　BELL 18:2
　then my heart with p. fills　WORD 275:4
　There is a p. sure　DRYD 91:11
　thy most pointed p. take　STEV 247:17
　treads upon the heels of p.　CONG 76:20
　What p. lives in height　TENN 255:1
　when Youth and P. meet　BYRON 57:10
pleasure-dome: stately p. decree　COL 75:2
pleasures: After the p. of youth　ANON 6:17
　English take their p. sadly　SULL 248:8
　fresh revolving p. flow　GAY 105:21
　hate the idle p. of these　SHAK 231:3
　is a hypocrite in his p.　JOHN 134:5
　My p. are plenty　HOUS 127:1
　other knows what p. man　YEATS 279:6
　p. and palaces though we　PAYNE 181:13
　p. with youth pass away　SOUT 244:1
　purest of human p.　BACON 13:9
　suck'd on country p.　DONNE 88:1
　we will all the p. prove　MARL 160:14
　we will some new p. prove　DONNE 87:18
pledge: I will p. with mine　JONS 136:3
　we p. to thee　KIPL 143:15
Pleni: P. sunt coeli et terra　MASS 163:16
plenties: p., and joyful births　SHAK 214:5
plenty: delay there lies no p.　SHAK 233:22
　just had p.　BURNS 54:4
　that here is God's p.　DRYD 91:13
pleuré: d'avoir quelquefois p.　MUSS 174:7
pleurer: d'être obligé d'en p.　BEAU 16:15
plie: Je p. et ne romps pas　LA F 147:12
plies: it p. the saplings double　HOUS 126:4
plight: I p. thee my troth　PRAY 187:28
plods: ploughman homeward p. his　GRAY 111:18
Plot: Gunpowder Treason and P.　ANON 4:17
　Passions spin the p.　MER 165:3
　p. thickens very much upon　BRY 51:3
　This blessed p.　SHAK 230:2
　We first survey the p.　SHAK 212:23
plough: put his hand to the p.　BIBLE 35:10
　Speed his p.　CHAP 67:7
　this morning held the p.　BETJ 20:11
　wherefore p.　SHEL 240:1
ploughing: 'Is my team p.　HOUS 126:2
ploughman: p. homeward plods his weary　GRAY 111:18
　Whilst the heavy p. snores　SHAK 228:1
plowshares: beat their swords into p.　BIBLE 28:7
　Beat your p. into swords　BIBLE 30:15
pluck: p. it out　BIBLE 33:17
pluck'd: p. the ripen'd ears　TENN 254:6
plucked: p. my nipple　SHAK 221:6
　We p. them as we passed　HOOD 121:4
plume: Hector took off his p.　CORN 78:6
　saw the helmet and the p.　TENN 253:4
plumed: Farewell the p. troop　SHAK 229:4
plunder: Take your ill-got p.　NEWB 175:17
plunge: p. your hands in water　AUDEN 10:10
plunging: When the p. hoofs were gone　DE L 82:15
plures: Abiit ad p.　PETR 183:2
Plus: P. ça change　KARR 138:11
　p. royaliste que le roi　ANON 5:19
Plush: would as soon assault a P.　DICK 86:6

pneumatic: Gives promise of p. bliss	ELIOT 95:9
Pobble: P. who has no toes	LEAR 150:18
Pobbles: P. are happier without	LEAR 150:20
pocket: in your p. or purse	WILS 272:15
not scruple to pick a p.	DENN 82:20
shall have my p. picked	SHAK 212:16
pocket-money: furnished with p.	DICK 84:19
poem: p. lovely as a tree	KILM 142:1
p. should not mean	MACL 157:15
Poems: P. are made by fools like	KILM 142:2
poet: apothecary than a starved p.	LOCK 152:14
because he was a true P.	BLAKE 43:22
better p. than Porson	HOUS 127:8
consecration, and the P.'s dream	WORD 274:12
every fool is not a p.	POPE 184:17
I was a p.	FLEC 100:13
limbs of a p.	HOR 124:22
lover, and the p.	SHAK 227:17
p. can do today is to warn	OWEN 179:3
p.'s eye	SHAK 227:18
This is truth the p. sings	TENN 253:9
Thus every p.	SWIFT 249:12
what is left the p. here	BYRON 58:9
poetae: disiecti membra p.	HOR 124:22
poetic: Meet nurse for a p. child	SCOTT 201:17
which constitutes p. faith	COL 75:10
poetical: study in a worn-out p.	ELIOT 93:16
poetrie: Jonson his best piece of p.	JONS 135:21
Poetry: In whining P.	DONNE 88:21
p. he invented was easy	AUDEN 10:13
P. is in the pity	OWEN 179:2
p. is something more philosophical	ARIS 8:6
P. is the record	SHEL 240:11
P. is the spontaneous overflow	WORD 277:13
P. is what gets lost	FROST 103:14
P. is when some of them	BENT 19:15
p. makes nothing happen	AUDEN 10:16
p.; the *best* words	COL 75:13
was trying to say was p.	OVID 179:1
what is p.	JOHN 132:28
Poets: among the English P.	KEATS 141:5
Irish p.	YEATS 280:1
P. are…the trumpets which	SHEL 240:12
p. exploding like bombs	AUDEN 11:10
p., witty	BACON 13:22
Souls of p. dead and gone	KEATS 139:10
true P. must be truthful	OWEN 179:3
We p. in our youth begin	WORD 276:11
point: 'Not to put too fine a p.	DICK 83:15
n'y en a p. de délicieux	LA R 149:9
P. d'argent	RAC 193:18
p. his slow and moving	SHAK 229:8
Up to a p., Lord Copper	WAUGH 267:1
poison: if you p. us	SHAK 225:10
I go about and p. wells	MARL 160:12
p. in jest	SHAK 210:3
p. the wells	NEWM 175:19
P. while the bee-mouth	KEATS 139:17
Slowly the p. the whole	EMPS 96:21
poisoned: p. rat in a hole	SWIFT 249:5
poke: heart to p. poor Billy	GRAH 111:10
pole: Beloved from pole to p.	COL 74:16
not rapt above the P.	MILT 169:13
policeman: p.'s lot is not a happy	GILB 109:2
terrorist and the p. both	CONR 77:13
policemen: first time how young the p.	HICKS 119:6
policy: foreign p. of the noble	DER 83:4
My p. is to be able	BEVIN 21:18

p. of the good neighbour	RONS 196:9
polish: we may p. it at leisure	DRYD 91:12
polished: I p. up the handle	GILB 108:28
Who has a p. female friend	WHURR 270:13
polite: costs nothing to be p.	CHUR 71:18
politesse: L'exactitude est la p.	LOUI 154:8
political: is by nature a p. animal	ARIS 8:4
nature of a p. party	TROL 260:11
not regard p. consequences	MANS 159:11
off for fear of P. Economy	SELL 203:3
'P. power grows out	MAO 159:14
'Principles of P. Economy'	BENT 19:19
politicians: fault of our p.	TROL 260:9
race of p. put together	SWIFT 248:18
politics: From p.	AUST 12:7
History is past p.	FREE 102:19
In p.	COL 75:15
mules of p.	POWER 186:15
p. and little else beside	CAMP 60:14
P. is not a science…but	BISM 42:12
week is a long time in p.	WILS 272:17
pollution: unsavoury engine of p.	SPAR 244:4
polygamy: Before p. was made a sin	DRYD 90:9
pomegranate: of a p. within thy locks	BIBLE 28:3
Pomp: after Sultan with his P.	FITZ 98:17
all our p. of yesterday	KIPL 145:11
nor the tide of p.	SHAK 213:23
p. and glory of this world	SHAK 215:9
p. of pow'r	GRAY 112:3
Take physic, p.	SHAK 218:11
Pompey: base of P.'s statua	SHAK 216:20
pompous: p. in the grave	BROW 48:13
pomps: p. and vanity of this wicked	PRAY 187:19
ponies: Five and twenty p.	KIPL 145:15
Her p. have swallowed their	BETJ 20:15
wretched, blind, pit p.	HODG 120:4
ponts: de coucher sous les p.	FRAN 102:5
pooled: mussel p. and the heron	THOM 257:6
pools: p. are filled with water	PRAY 189:18
Where the p. are bright	HOGG 120:13
poop: p. was beaten gold	SHAK 203:22
poor: Blessed are the p. in spirit	BIBLE 31:1
Bring in hither the p.	BIBLE 35:23
destruction of the p. is	BIBLE 26:13
give to the p.	BIBLE 33:21
grind the faces of the p.	BIBLE 28:8
I have very p. and unhappy	SHAK 228:21
makes me p. indeed	SHAK 228:27
open to the p. and the rich	ANON 2:15
p. always ye have with	BIBLE 36:35
p. are Europe's blacks	CHAM 67:2
p. feeble sex	VICT 262:8
p. have become poorer	SHEL 240:10
P. little rich girl	COW 79:7
p. man at his gate	ALEX 2:4
p. man had nothing	BIBLE 24:28
p. soul sat sighing	SHAK 229:9
P. wandering one	GILB 108:30
Resolve not to be p.	JOHN 133:20
rich and p. alike to sleep	FRAN 102:5
simple annals of the p.	GRAY 112:3
so p. that he is unable	HENR 117:11
specially dangerous man when p.	SHAW 238:19
your tired, your p.	LAZ 149:19
poorer: richer for p.	PRAY 187:28
poorest: p. he that is in England	RAIN 194:1
Pop: P. goes the weasel	MAND 159:8
Pope: P.! How many divisions	STAL 245:10

Railing and p. were his — DRYD 90:17
pram: than the p. in the hall — CONN 77:6
prance: man has a mind to *p.* — JOHN 132:11
pray: All p. in their distress — BLAKE 43:18
at the senators and I p. — HALE 113:10
I am just going to p. — SMITH 243:2
If I could p. to move — SHAK 216:8
nor p. with you — SHAK 224:17
remain'd to p. — GOLD 110:9
this manner therefore p. ye — BIBLE 31:21
To whom the Romans p. — MAC 156:9
Watch and p. — BIBLE 34:15
we do p. for mercy — SHAK 225:17
prayer: called the house of p. — BIBLE 33:26
let the p. re-echo — LINL 152:7
P. the Church's banquet — HERB 118:13
things are wrought by p. — TENN 252:7
prayers: Christopher Robin is saying his p.
— MILNE 166:17
it for this I uttered p. — MILL 166:7
Knelt down with angry p. — HODG 120:4
p. in the hall and some — ASHF 9:20
This was one of my p. — HOR 125:1
prayeth: He p. best — COL 74:20
He p. well — COL 74:20
praying: Nay that's past p. — SHAK 212:11
preach: p. a better sermon — EMER 96:19
p. it long — POPE 184:9
preach'd: he practis'd what he p. — ARMS 8:9
preacher: advantage of the p. than the edification
— BURKE 52:8
preaching: woman's p. is like a dog's — JOHN 132:5
precedency: point of p. between a louse
— JOHN 134:1
precedent: is a dangerous p. — CORN 78:8
p. embalms a principle — STOW 248:2
precept: more efficacious than p. — JOHN 135:3
p. must be upon precept — BIBLE 29:1
precepts: these few p. in thy memory — SHAK 207:6
precious: p. as the Goods they sell — FITZ 99:12
p. stone set in the silver — SHAK 230:2
precipices: p. show untrodden green — KEATS 140:5
predicted: p. evil consequences — TROL 260:10
prees: Flee fro the p. — CHAU 68:29
prefer: p. not Jerusalem in my — PRAY 191:1
preferred: who coming after me is p. — BIBLE 36:17
pregnancies: p. and at least four miscarriages
— BEEC 17:10
prejudice: Conduct…to the p. of good order
— ANON 3:8
result of PRIDE AND P. — BURN 53:15
prejudices: his personal p. and cranks ELIOT 95:10
it p. a man so — SMITH 242:22
not local p. ought to guide — BURKE 52:15
of the proprietor's p. — SWAF 248:16
premier: p. mouvement ne fut jamais — CORN 78:4
que le p. pas qui coûte — DU D 91:16
premiers: p. mouvements parce qu'ils — MONT 172:9
prepare: good God p. me — PEPYS 182:14
I go to p. a place for you — BIBLE 37:1
p. to shed them now — SHAK 216:19
P. ye the way of the Lord — BIBLE 31:4
préparés: favorise que les esprits p. — PAST 181:6
preposterousest: To the p. end — BUTL 56:12
prerogative: p. of the harlot throughout
— KIPL 146:29
presage: p. the grasses' fall — MARV 161:19
presence: before his p. with a song — PRAY 190:4
his p. with thanksgiving — PRAY 190:2

his p. on the field made — WELL 268:8
perfect p. of mind — JAMES 130:5
was conspicuous by its p. — RUSS 198:13
present: All p. and correct — ANON 2:17
except the p. company — OKEE 178:2
mirth hath p. laughter — SHAK 233:22
No time like the p. — MANL 159:10
p. and your pains we thank — SHAK 213:10
p. help in time of trouble — ANON 3:3
p. were the world's last — DONNE 88:5
Such p. joys therein — DYER 92:4
un-birthday p. — CARR 64:7
very p. help in trouble — PRAY 189:3
When the P. has latched — HARDY 114:8
preserve: Lord shall p. thy going out — PRAY 190:17
P. it as your chiefest — BELL 18:2
Preserver: Creator and P. of all mankind
— PRAY 187:4
President: P. of the Immortals (in — HARDY 115:5
press: Freedom of the p. in Britain — SWAF 248:16
of our idolatry, the p. — COWP 79:18
P. was squared — BELL 18:13
racket is back in its p. — BETJ 21:13
presume: p. not God to scan — POPE 185:17
Presumption: You'll be Amused by its P.
— THUR 259:12
Pretender: who P. is — BYROM 57:2
pretending: p. to be wicked and being
— WILDE 271:12
Pretendur: James II, and the Old P. — GUED 113:6
pretty: do for p. girls — YEATS 279:6
It must be so p. with all — WILDE 271:15
post-chaise with a p. woman — JOHN 133:3
p. chickens and their dam — SHAK 223:5
p. follies that themselves — SHAK 225:6
p. women to deserve them — AUST 12:2
p. young wards in Chancery — GILB 107:13
Puts on his p. looks — SHAK 217:10
Which is p. — GILB 106:20
prevail: shall p. — BROO 47:17
prevails: it p. — BIBLE 41:25
prevent: p. harm to others — MILL 165:15
we have a right to p. it — MILN 167:4
prevention: some p. of abuse — PEEL 182:1
prey: down alone bent on his p. — MILT 169:5
to hast'ning ills a p. — GOLD 110:6
whole fastening on her p. — RAC 193:17
Priamus: En P. — VIRG 263:2
price: have bought it at any p. — CLAR 72:25
her p. is far above rubies — BIBLE 26:34
knows the p. of everything — WILDE 271:17
One pearl of great p. — BIBLE 33:7
prices: contrivance to raise p. — SMITH 241:18
dirty and charging high p. — ELIOT 94:1
prick: If you p. us — SHAK 225:10
p. the sides of my intent — SHAK 221:1
pricking: By the p. of my thumbs — SHAK 222:24
knight was p. on the plain — SPEN 244:15
Prickly: P. pear prickly pear — ELIOT 93:23
pricks: to kick against the p. — BIBLE 37:17
pride: from p. — PRAY 187:3
here have P. and Truth — YEATS 279:11
He that is low no p. — BUNY 51:26
my family p. is something — GILB 108:1
my high-blown p. — SHAK 215:9
p., cruelty, and ambition — RAL 194:6
P. goeth before destruction — BIBLE 26:22
result of P. AND PREJUDICE — BURN 53:15
So sleeps the p. of former — MOORE 172:14

priest: ghastly p. doth reign   MAC 156:12
sustained from one turbulent p.   HENR 117:17
priestcraft: ere p. did begin   DRYD 90:9
Priested: heron P. shore   THOM 257:6
priesthood: royal p.   BIBLE 40:18
priests: strangled in the guts of p.   MESL 165:10
priketh: p. hem nature in hir corages)   CHAU 67:18
Prime Minister: girl or a turned out P.
    MELB 164:18
next P. but three   BELL 18:13
prime-roses: pale p.   SHAK 235:1
primordial: p. condition of liberty   BAK 14:12
protoplasmal p. atomic   GILB 108:1
primrose: p. by a river's brim   WORD 276:3
p. path of dalliance treads   SHAK 207:5
Prince: 'God bless the P. of Wales   LINL 152:7
Good-night, sweet p.   SHAK 212:1
great P. in prison lies   DONNE 87:27
p. d'Aquitaine à la tour   NERV 175:11
p. of darkness is a gentleman   SHAK 218:13
P. of Denmark being left out   SCOTT 202:9
princerple: I *don't* believe in p.   LOW 154:16
princes: her p. are come home again   SHAK 217:16
of instructing p. to know   SWIFT 249:1
P. and lords may flourish   GOLD 110:6
put not your trust in p.   PRAY 191:5
That sweet aspect of p.   SHAK 215:9
Princesse: j'aime la P. Lointaine   ROST 197:11
principalities: against p.   BIBLE 39:15
p., nor powers   BIBLE 37:39
principe: femmes est le p. général de tous progrès
    FOUR 102:2
Principiis: P. obsta   OVID 178:23
Principle: *active* P.   WORD 274:16
precedent embalms a p.   STOW 248:2
p. of the English constitution   BLAC 42:15
rights is the basic p.   FOUR 102:2
principles: Damn your p.   DISR 87:4
lordship's p. or your mistress   WILK 272:9
'P. of Political Economy'   BENT 19:19
print: licence to p. your own money   THOM 258:15
news that's fit to p.   OCHS 177:11
printed: that they were p. in a book   BIBLE 25:27
Printing: P., and the Protestant   CARL 61:8
p. thereby to rectify manners   MILT 170:18
was in a p. house in Hell   BLAKE 44:8
prisca: Ut p. gens mortalium   HOR 123:9
prism: especially prunes and p.   DICK 84:10
with his p. and silent face   WORD 276:7
prison: Else a great Prince in p.   DONNE 87:27
girl's p. and the woman's   SHAW 238:13
In the p. of his days   AUDEN 11:1
I was in p.   BIBLE 34:8
just man is also a p.   THOR 259:1
let's away to p.   SHAK 218:27
opening of the p. to them   BIBLE 29:20
p. for the colour of his   HOUS 127:2
Stone walls do not a p.   LOV 154:9
This p. where I live unto   SHAK 230:15
prisoners: addiction and the p. of envy   ILL 129:11
prison-house: Shades of the p. begin   WORD 275:15
prisons: Madhouses, p., whore-shops
    CLARE 72:18
private: grave's a fine and p. place   MARV 161:21
invade the sphere of p. life   MELB 164:14
p. advantage of the preacher   BURKE 52:8
P. faces in public   AUDEN 11:7
privates: her p., we   SHAK 208:11
privato: Maior p. visus dum privatus   TAC 250:11

Privilege: power which stands on P.   BELL 18:22
p. and pleasure   GILB 107:6
p. I claim for my own sex   AUST 12:10
Privileged: P. and the People formed   DISR 87:12
privilèges: L'extension des p. des femmes
    FOUR 102:2
stand for your p. we know   HEM 117:3
prizes: to offer glittering p.   BIRK 42:9
prizing: past all p., best   SOPH 243:14
P.R.O.: liaison man and partly P.   BETJ 20:12
Probable: P. impossibilities are   ARIS 8:7
probationary: Eden's dread p. tree   COWP 79.10
proboque: Video meliora, p.   OVID 178:22
proceed: p. no further in this business   SHAK 221:2
proceedings: p. interested him no more
    HARTE 115:14
procession: in a p. of one   DICK 84:16
in with the marriage-p.   CLOU 73:9
proclaims: apparel oft p. the man   SHAK 207.6
Procrastination: P. is the thief of time
    YOUNG 280:8
procreation: ordained for the p. of children
    PRAY 187:25
proctors: With prudes for p.   TENN 254:5
procul: o p. este, profani   VIRG 263:11
P. hinc   OVID 178:19
qui p. negotiis   HOR 123:9
prodigality: perennial spring of all p.   BURKE 52:20
productions: love with the p. of time   BLAKE 44:3
Proelium: P. certaminis   VEN 261:19
profane: p. one   BRAT 46:7
profaned: they have desolated and p.   GLAD 109:15
profani: o procul este, p.   VIRG 263:11
profanum: Odi p. vulgus et arceo   HOR 124:5
profession: discharge of any p.   JOHN 132:20
of the most ancient p.   KIPL 146:21
ornament to her p.   BUNY 52:1
professions: p. are conspiracies against
    SHAW 237:14
professor: Zarathustra, sometime regius p.
    JOYCE 137:8
professors: conscientious p. thereof   PAINE 179:14
P. of the Dismal Science   CARL 61:16
p. of philosophy but not   THOR 259:4
profited: What is a man p.   BIBLE 33:14
profits: It little p. that an idle   TENN 255:10
profound: turbid look the most p.   LAND 148:14
profundis: De p. clamavi ad te   BIBLE 41:16
progenies: Iam nova p. caelo demittitur   VIRG 264:6
progrès: principe général de tous p.   FOUR 102:2
progress: It was no summer p.   ANDR 2:11
To swell a p.   ELIOT 94:7
proie: entière à sa p. attachée   RAC 193:17
proletarian: substitution of the p.   LEE 151:6
proletariat: dictatorship of the p.   MARX 162:10
prologues: p. to the swelling act   SHAK 220:6
prolong: Youth to p.   YEATS 279:17
prolonging: p. the lives of the poultry   ELIOT 93:1
Promethean: not where is that P. heat
    SHAK 229:13
promise: p.-crammed   SHAK 209:10
threaten, p.   WHIT 270:8
Who broke no p.   POPE 185:5
Whose p. none relies   ROCH 195:15
Why didst thou p. such   SHAK 235:15
promises: I have p. to keep   FROST 103:10
promoting: by p. the wealth   BURKE 52:18
promotion: p. cometh neither from   PRAY 189:15
pronounce: not frame to p. it right   BIBLE 24:9

proofs: p. of holy writ · SHAK 229:3
propagation: know that peace and p. · WALP 266:4
propensities: excite my amorous p. · JOHN 131:5
proper: always know our p. stations · DICK 83:18
p. or improper · FULL 103:22
p. study of mankind · POPE 185:17
p. subject of conversation · CHES 69:16
p. young men · BURNS 54:14
properly: Who never did anything p. · LEAR 150:22
property: consider himself as public p. · JEFF 130:12
give me a little snug p. · EDG 92:6
P. has its duties as well · DRUM 90:8
P. is theft · PROU 192:3
prophecies: p., they shall fail · BIBLE 38:15
verification of his own p. · TROL 260:10
prophecy: though I have the gift of p. · BIBLE 38:14
trumpet of a p.! O, Wind · SHEL 239:15
prophesy: we p. in part · BIBLE 38:15
your daughters shall p. · BIBLE 30:14
prophesying: p. with accents terrible · SHAK 222:5
voices p. war · COL 75:5
prophet: Methinks I am a p. new inspir'd · SHAK 230:1
p. is not without honour · BIBLE 33:8
prophetic: p. soul! My uncle · SHAK 207:13
With such p. greeting · SHAK 220:5
prophets: Beware of false p. · BIBLE 32:10
this is the law and the p. · BIBLE 32:7
Propinquity: 'P. does it' · WARD 266:12
proponit: Nam homo p. · THOM 256:19
proportion: some strangeness in the p. · BACON 13:1
proportioned: p. to the human constitution · BERK 20:1
propre: moins p. à la société · CHAM 66:16
propriété: La p. c'est le vol · PROU 192:3
proprietor: of the p.'s prejudices · SWAF 248:16
propriety: not always evince its p. · AUST 12:14
womanly feeling and p. · VICT 262:8
prose: connect the p. and the passion · FORS 101:17
Meredith is a p. Browning · WILDE 272:3
only p. · BROW 49:3
P. is when all the lines · BENT 19:15
p.; words in their best · COL 75:13
speaking p. without knowing · MOL 171:6
that is not p. is verse · MOL 171:7
unattempted yet in p. or rhyme · MILT 168:13
prospect: noblest p. which a Scotchman · JOHN 131:19
Though every p. pleases · HEBER 116:10
prosper: I grow, I p. · SHAK 218:1
that shall keep it may p. · KIPL 145:2
Why do sinners' ways p. · HOPK 122:8
prosperity: jest's p. lies in the ear · SHAK 219:12
protect: I'll p. it now · MORR 173:12
protest: lady doth p. too much · SHAK 210:2
Protestant: I am the P. whore · GWYN 113:7
P. counterfoot · BEEC 17:8
P. Religion · CARL 61:8
Proteus: Have sight of P. rising · WORD 277:8
protoplasmal: p. primordial atomic · GILB 108:1
proud: Death be not p. · DONNE 88:3
he hath scattered the p. · BIBLE 34:29
make death p. to take us · SHAK 204:7
man being too p. to fight · WILS 273:1
p. and angry dust · HOUS 126:16
p. and yet a wretched thing · DAV 82:1
woman can be p. and stiff · YEATS 278:15
you p. men of action · HEINE 116:14
prov'd: To have p. most royally · SHAK 212:3

prove: let us p. · JONS 136:10
P. all things · BIBLE 39:24
p. the sweetness of a shower · THOM 257:21
since I cannot p. a lover · SHAK 231:3
proved: Which was to be p. · EUCL 97:4
proverb: p. and a byword among all · BIBLE 25:1
Providence: I go the way that P. dictates · HITL 119:14
I may assert eternal P. · MILT 168:14
inscrutable workings of P. · BIRK 42:10
P. their guide · MILT 169:22
province: all knowledge to be my p. · BACON 13:28
p. they have desolated · GLAD 109:15
provoke: voice p. the silent dust · GRAY 112:4
provokes: one p. me with impunity · ANON 7:1
proximus: paries cum p. ardet · HOR 123:6
prudence: p. never to practise either · TWAIN 261:2
prudenter: p. agas · ANON 7:4
prudes: With p. for proctors · TENN 254:5
prunes: especially p. and prism · DICK 84:10
pruninghooks: their spears into p. · BIBLE 28:7
your p. into spears · BIBLE 30:15
psalms: ourselves glad in him with p. · PRAY 190:2
public: exempt from p. haunt · SHAK 204:16
if I was a p. meeting · VICT 262:11
man assumes a p. trust · JEFF 130:12
ministers to consult the p. · SWIFT 249:1
pot of paint in the p.'s · RUSK 198:6
Private faces in p. · AUDEN 11:7
servants of the p. · GOW 111:5
publican: How like a fawning p. he · SHAK 224:18
publicans: Master with p. and sinners · BIBLE 32:18
Public schools: P. are the nurseries · FIEL 98:6
Publish: P. and be damned · WELL 268:14
p. it not in the streets · BIBLE 24:25
published: whatever you haven't p. · HOR 122:21
publisher: Now Barabbas was a p. · CAMP 60:19
puellis: Vixi p. nuper idoneus · HOR 124:15
puerisque: Virginibus p. canto · HOR 124:5
puero: Se p. · HOR 122:18
puking: Mewling and p. in the nurse's · SHAK 204:5
pulchrior: matre pulchra filia p. · HOR 123:15
Pulsanda: P. tellus · HOR 123:18
pulse: My p. like a soft drum · KING 142:6
Now feel that p. no more · MOORE 172:14
people with the one p. · MACN 158:8
p. in the eternal mind · BROO 47:16
pumpkins: Where the early p. blow · LEAR 150:7
pun: could make so vile a p. · DENN 82:20
pipe and exhaled in a p. · LAMB 148:6
punch: Some sipping p. · WORD 276:4
Punctuality: P. is the politeness · LOUI 154:8
punished: should be p. with as severe · PENN 182:6
punishment: it shall suffer first p. · CRAN 80:6
To let the p. fit the crime · GILB 108:11
punishments: charged with p. the scroll · HENL 117:17
punt: admit it is more fun to p. · SAY 200:16
slow p. swings round · ARN 8:20
story get out of the p. · JOYCE 136:17
puppy: let ev'ry p. drink · WHYT 270:14
purchase: p. pain with all that joy · POPE 184:24
purchasing: I am not worth p. · REED 194:16
pure: Because my heart is p. · TENN 255:7
Blessed are the p. in heart · BIBLE 31:11
pure all things are p. · BIBLE 40:5
That England was too p. · ANON 4:15
whatsoever things are p. · BIBLE 39:20
purest: p. of human pleasures · BACON 13:9

urgatory: p. of men | FLOR 101:4
urge: shalt p. me with hyssop | PRAY 189:6
urified: every creature shall be p. | MARL 160:4
urifies: that which p. us is trial | MILT 170:17
Puritan: P. all things are impure | LAWR 149:15
P. hated bear-baiting | MAC 157:3
Puritane-one: Where I saw a P. | BRAT 46:7
urlieus: dusty p. of the law | TENN 252:20
urple: gleaming in p. and gold | BYRON 57:16
I never saw a P. Cow | BURG 52:5
some p. patch or other | HOR 122:12
urpose: any p. perverts art | CONS 77:16
are the measure of his p. | NIGH 177:4
Infirm of p. | SHAK 221:18
mark of insincerity of p. | BRAM 46:4
My p. is, indeed | SHAK 234:1
p. in liquidity | BROO 47:8
Shake my fell p. | SHAK 220:11
time to every p. under | BIBLE 27:6
Purpureus: P., late qui splendeat | HOR 122:12
urse: Costly thy habit as thy p. | SHAK 207:6
Put money in thy p. | SHAK 228:20
Who steals my p. steals | SHAK 228:27
ursue: p. my reason to an O altitudo | BROW 48:7
thing we all p. | BEAU 17:2
who p. Culture in bands | WHAR 269:8
ursued: p. it with forks and hope | CARR 62:8
ursueth: wicked flee when no man p. | BIBLE 26:32
ursuing: Still achieving, still p. | LONG 153:11
yet p. | BIBLE 24:8
ursuit: common p. of true judgement | ELIOT 95:10
full p. of the uneatable | WILDE 271:24
liberty and the p. of happiness | ANON 5:9
p. of happiness | JEFF 130:9
p. of perfection | ARN 9:7
urus: vitae scelerisque p. | HOR 123:16
Pusset: Used to call his cat P. | HARE 115:6
Pussy: What a beautiful P. you are | LEAR 150:13
Pussy-Cat: Owl and the P. went | LEAR 150:13
ut: can p. off till to-morrow | PUNCH 192:12
never be p. out | LAT 149:14
p. beneath Thy special | BETJ 21:5
p. his hand to the plough | BIBLE 35:10
P. it down a we | DICK 85:20
P. money in thy purse | SHAK 228:20
p. not your trust in princes | PRAY 191:5
P. off thy shoes from off | BIBLE 23:10
P. out the light | SHAK 229:13
p. too fine a point upon | DICK 83:15
p. upon us the armour | PRAY 187:6
p. up with bad things th | TROL 260:7
with which I will not p. | CHUR 71:20
puto: p. deus fio | VESP 262:6
Puts: P. on his pretty looks | SHAK 217:10
puzzle: Rule of three doth p. me | ANON 4:8
schoolmasters p. their brain | GOLD 110:17
Pyrenees: P. have ceased to exist | LOUI 154:4
that tease in the high P. | BELL 19:9
Pythagoras: this 'himself' was P. | CIC 72:7
Quaäker: I knaw'd a Q. feller | TENN 254:4
Quad: always about in the Q. | ANON 3:9
no one about in the Q. | KNOX 147:5
Quadripedante: Q. putrem sonitu quatit | VIRG 264:1
quadruped: hairy q. | DARW 81:14
quaff'd: jested, q., and swore | DOYLE 89:29
quailing: No q., Mrs Gaskell | BRON 47:4
qualis: Non sum q. eram bonae | HOR 124:14
qualités: Des q. trop supérieures | CHAM 66:16
Qualities: Q. too elevated often unfit | CHAM 66:16

quality: composition and fierce q. | SHAK 217:19
his honour and his q. taken | BLUN 44:12
q. of his despair | CONN 77:10
q. of mercy is not strain'd | SHAK 225:17
Quantum: Q. mutatus ab illo | VIRG 263:4
quarks: Three q. for Muster Mark | JOYCE 136:19
quarrel: arm'd that hath his q. just | SHAK 214:12
armed that hath his q. just | BILL 42:5
Beware Of entrance to a q. | SHAK 207:6
greatly to find q. in a straw | SHAK 210:24
q. in a far-away country | CHAM 66:13
They quite forgot their q. | CARR 63:21
quarrels: of q. as an egg is full | SHAK 231:26
Quarterly: 'I,' says the Q. | BYRON 58:18
quarters: Sprinkle the q. | HOUS 126:18
Quatorze: Q.? Le bon Dieu n'a que | CLEM 73:4
quean: flaunting, extravagant q. | SHER 240:25
Queen: am the Ruler of the Q.'s | GILB 108:28
beggar maid shall be my q. | TENN 251:3
life of our own dear Q. | ANON 3:17
Q. and Faith like a valiant | TENN 255:6
Q. and huntress | JONS 135:19
Q. asked The Dairymaid | MILNE 166:14
q. of Scots is this day | ELIZ 95:14
Q. so furious that she | VICT 262:8
Q. was in a furious passion | CARR 63:6
right-down regular Royal Q. | GILB 107:4
we love our Q. | GILB 109:3
Yestreen the Q. had four Maries | BALL 15:1
Queen Elizabeth: No scandal about Q. | SHER 240:15
Queen o' the May: I'm to be Q. | TENN 254:3
Queens: Q. have died young | NASHE 175:2
queer: him ill-tempered and q. | LEAR 150:4
quench: If I q. thee | SHAK 229:13
Many waters cannot q. love | BIBLE 28:5
quench'd: What hath q. them hath | SHAK 221:12
quest: to whose winding q. | VAUG 261:13
what thy q. | BRID 46:13
questing: fen passes the q. vole | WAUGH 266:20
question: man with such a silly q. | STER 246:8
Others abide our q. | ARN 9:1
what is the q. | STEIN 246:1
questioned: That q. him in Greek | CARR 62:11
questions: have answered three q. | CARR 62:19
q. the distempered part | ELIOT 93:17
Them that asks no q. isn't | KIPL 145:15
There are innumerable q. | JOHN 133:10
quia: Certum est q. impossibile est | TERT 256:8
quick: both the q. and the dead | PRAY 187:13
Touched to the q. | BROW 49:16
quickened: eyes are q. so with grief | GRAV 111:14
quicker: liquor Is q. | NASH 174:16
quickly: much good who gives q. | PUBL 192:8
Quidquid: Q. agas | ANON 7:4
Q. agunt homines | JUV 137:15
quiet: All q. along the Potomac | MCCL 157:7
Easy live and q. die | SCOTT 202:5
In q. she reposes | ARN 8:17
lives of q. desperation | THOR 259:3
my scallop-shell of q. | RAL 194:4
q. us in a death so noble | MILT 170:6
quietly: lie as q. among the graves | EDW 92:12
Q. they go | MILL 166:3
quietness: unravish'd bride of q. | KEATS 139:12
quietus: himself might his q. make | SHAK 208:24
quills: tender stops of various q. | MILT 168:4
quince: slices of q. | LEAR 150:16

Quinquireme: Q. of Nineveh from distant
    MAS 162:14
quinta: La q. columna   MOLA 171:4
Quires: Q. and Places where they PRAY 186:23
quiring: q. to the young-eyed cherubins
    SHAK 226:5
Quit: Q. you like men   BIBLE 39:1
 Q. yourselves like men BIBLE 24:16
quiver: man that hath his q. full PRAY 190:20
quivers: q. in the sunny breeze GREN 113:3
Quo: Q. vadis   BIBLE 41:21
Quot: Q. homines tot sententiae TER 256:4
quotations: man to read books of q. CHUR 71:16
quote: I'll kill you if you q. BURG 52:6
Quoth: Q. the Raven POE 184:2
quotidienne: que la vie est q. LAF 147:15
Quoting: Q., for shallow conversational
    SASS 200:13
Quousque: Q. tandem abutere CIC 72:10
race: avails the sceptred r. LAND 148:12
 feather'd r. with pinions FRERE 103:1
 happiness of the human r. BURKE 52:18
 men and women with our r. KIPL 143:15
 now a new r. descends from VIRG 264:6
 r. between education WELLS 268:17
 r. is not to the swift BIBLE 27:16
 r. that is set before us BIBLE 40:9
 till thou run out thy r. MILT 168:11
 unprotected r. CLARE 72:20
 wish I loved the Human R. RAL 194:10
races: Some r. increase LUCR 155:7
Rachel: seven years for R. BIBLE 23:1
rack: Leave not a r. behind SHAK 232:24
 r. of a too easy chair POPE 184:10
 r. of this tough world SHAK 219:5
racket: r. is back in its press BETJ 21:13
rackets: match'd our r. to these balls SHAK 213:10
radiance: beautiful r. of the gods SCH 201:2
 My r. rare and fathomless HARDY 115:4
radical: r. is a man with both feet RONS 196:10
raft: republic is a r. which AMES 2:9
rag: r. and a bone and a hank KIPL 146:4
rag-and-bone: foul r. shop of the heart
    YEATS 278:14
rage: heathen so furiously r. PRAY 188:6
 Heav'n has no r. CONG 76:19
 horrible that lust and r. YEATS 279:19
 nature with hard-favour'd r. SHAK 213:14
 Not die here in a r. SWIFT 249:5
 nothing but a r. to live POPE 184:24
 Puts all Heaven in a R. BLAKE 42:18
 r. against the dying THOM 256:23
 r. of Caliban WILDE 271:19
rages: Dog-star r. POPE 184:18
 older that the weight of r. SPOON 245:2
raging: strong drink is r. BIBLE 26:24
rag-time: Lurching to r. tunes SASS 200:6
rail: folks r. against other folks FIEL 98:7
Rails: Star-spiked R. a fiery Smite THOM 258:8
Railway: Beautiful R. Bridge MCG 157:11
railway-share: threatened its life with a r.
    CARR 62:8
rain: droppeth as the gentle r. SHAK 225:17
 Dull roots with spring r. ELIOT 94:18
 r. came heavily and fell WORD 276:10
 r. descended BIBLE 32:13
 r. is over and gone BIBLE 27:29
 r. it raineth on the just BOWEN 45:9
 r. it raineth every day SHAK 234:14

r. set early in to-night BROW 50:14
sendeth r. on the just BIBLE 31:18
small rain down can r. ANON 5:10
Still falls the R. SITW 241:12
sun and the r. Clash FRY 103:17
thro' the drizzling r. TENN 252:11
rainbow: another hue Unto the r. SHAK 217:12
 heart is like a r. shell ROSS 197:3
 r. comes and goes WORD 275:13
 r. in the sky WORD 275:11
 r.'s glory is shed SHEL 239:8
 was the R. gave thee birth DAV 82:2
Raineth: R. drop and staineth slop POUND 186:6
 rain it r. on the just BOWEN 45:9
raise: contrivance to r. prices SMITH 241:14
raised: Christ being r. from BIBLE 37:35
 dead shall be r. incorruptible BIBLE 38:22
raison: r. du plus fort est toujours LA F 147:14
raisons: Le coeur a ses r. que la PASC 181:2
rake: was his hors as is a r. CHAU 68:4
raking: when to stop r. the muck RONS 196:14
ram: r. caught in a thicket BIBLE 22:26
ramas: Verde r. GARC 104:13
rams: mountains skipped like r. PRAY 190:12
Rangoon: chunkin' from R. to Mandalay
    KIPL 145:3
rank: my offence is r. SHAK 210:17
 things r. and gross in nature SHAK 206:15
 you will r. as an apostle GILB 108:21
ranks: even the r. of Tuscany MAC 156:10
ransom: Of the world's r. SHAK 230:2
rapacious: r. and licentious soldiery BURKE 53:4
rape: r.! a rape WEBS 267:15
rapid: This particularly r. GILB 109:8
rapier: dubbed with unhatched r. SHAK 234:12
rapture: 'All this to love and r.'s
    ROCH 195:14
 first fine careless r. BROW 49:13
 Modified r. GILB 108:8
raptures: r. and roses of vice SWIN 249:18
Rara: R. avis in terris nigroque JUV 137:20
rare: man of culture r. GILB 108:19
rarely: r., comest thou SHEL 239:18
rarer: made us r. gifts than gold BROO 47:5
rassembler: r. à froid un pays qui DE G 82:16
Rat: Cat, the R., and Lovell COLL 75:16
 How now! a r. SHAK 210:13
 I smell a r. ROCHE 195:12
 like a r. without a tail SHAK 220:2
 like the sound of a r. BROW 50:10
 poisoned r. in a hole SWIFT 249:5
ratem: Commisit pelago r. HOR 123:10
rather: r. tough worm in your little GILB 108:17
rational: between them and r. converse
    WOLL 274:2
rattle: spoilt his nice new r. CARR 63:21
Rattlesnake: He thought he saw a R. CARR 62:11
rav'd: r. and grew more fierce HERB 118:8
rave: age should burn and r. THOM 256:23
 soft hand and let her r. KEATS 139:17
raven: locks were like the r. BURNS 54:12
 Quoth the R. POE 184:2
 r. himself is hoarse SHAK 220:11
ravening: inwardly they are r. wolves BIBLE 32:10
ravenous: They're a r. horde GILB 107:22
ravish: except you r. me DONNE 88:7
ravish'd: you have r. justice WEBS 267:15
ravished: least would have r. her FIEL 98:5
ray: 'the r. of rays DICK 83:17
Razors: R. pain you PARK 180:6

reach: all things above his r.   OVER 178:18
   r. should exceed his grasp   BROW 48:21
   will r. the bottom first   GRAH 111:8
reached: heights by great men r.   LONG 153:6
   top of it r. to heaven   BIBLE 22:32
reaching: r. after fact and reason   KEATS 140:16
reactionaries: All r. are paper tigers   MAO 159:15
read: be r. but not curiously   BACON 13:20
   general r. without pleasure   JOHN 134:10
   have r. and nobody wants   TWAIN 261:8
   May r. strange matters   SHAK 220:12
   r. a book before reviewing   SMITH 242:22
   r. just as inclination   JOHN 131:20
   such wise hear them r.   PRAY 187:7
   Take up and r.   AUG 11:16
   to r., and censure   HEM 117:3
   What do you r.   SHAK 208:9
readable: chief need is that it be r.   TROL 260:1
Reader: R., I married him   BRON 47:1
readers: so many of my r. belong   CHES 70:11
readiness: r. is all   SHAK 211:17
Reading: R. is to the mind what   STEE 245:14
   R. maketh a full man   BACON 13:21
ready: conference a r. man   BACON 13:21
   I am r. to depart   LAND 148:8
real: any less r. and true   SHAW 237:10
Realism: dislike of R.   WILDE 271:19
reality: Cannot bear very much r.   ELIOT 93:14
realm: this earth, this r.   SHAK 230:2
   welfare of this r. do chiefly   CHAR 67:10
realms: travell'd in the r. of gold   KEATS 140:3
reap: that shall he also r.   BIBLE 39:9
   they shall r. the whirlwind   BIBLE 30:12
   you r. a habit   READE 194:13
reaped: which never should be r.   TRAH 259:21
reaps: seed ye sow, another r.   SHEL 240:2
rear: she shall r. my dusky race   TENN 253:12
   to r. the tender thought   THOM 258:1
reason: feast of r. and the flow   POPE 185:20
   How noble in r.   SHAK 208:14
   in erring r.'s spite   POPE 185:16
   kills r. itself   MILT 170:15
   noble and most sovereign r.   SHAK 209:6
   Now tell me the r.   SOUT 244:1
   pursue my r. to an O altitudo   BROW 48:7
   r. and the will of God   ARN 9:7
   r. why gunpowder treason   ANON 4:17
   right deed for the wrong r.   ELIOT 94:13
   that wants discourse of r.   SHAK 206:15
   Their's not to r. why   TENN 251:9
reasonableness: secret and sweet r.   ARN 9:13
reasons: five r. we should drink   ALDR 2:2
   never give your r.   MANS 159:12
reasons of state: r. to influence our judgments   MANS 159:11
reave: my two troubles they r.   HOUS 127:1
rebellion: if r. was the certain consequence   MANS 159:11
   r. against the existing   SHAW 237:17
rebellious: Hot and r. liquors in my   SHAK 204:17
rebuke: r. hath broken my heart   PRAY 189:14
recall: greater sorrow than to r.   DANTE 81:6
recedes: research the horizon r.   PATT 181:11
receive: blessed to give than to r.   BIBLE 37:26
   Wax to r.   BYRON 57:4
received: his own r. him not   BIBLE 36:15
receives: heart That watches and r.   WORD 277:9
recipe: rare r. for melancholy   LAMB 147:18
reciprocal: r. civility of authors   JOHN 134:24

recirculation: commodius vicus of r. back   JOYCE 136:16
reckless: Restraining r. middle age   YEATS 279:11
reckoning: very much at your own r.   TROL 260:13
recks: r. not his own rede   SHAK 207:5
recognizing: r. the gods that the city   PLATO 183:14
recollect: does not r. where he laid   JOHN 133:22
record: puts a r. on the gramophone   ELIOT 95:4
recording: passive, r., not thinking   ISH 129:17
recte: Si possis r.   HOR 123:2
   Vivere si r. nescis   HOR 123:8
rectum: r. aut justitiam   MAGN 159:1
recurret: tamen usque r.   HOR 123:4
red: hectic r.   SHEL 239:12
   Luve's like a r. red rose   BURNS 54:17
   Making the green one r.   SHAK 222:1
   more red than her lips' r.   SHAK 236:14
   Nature, r. in tooth and claw   TENN 252:18
   pays us poor beggars in r.   KIPL 146:8
   r. flag flying here   CONN 77:4
   Red lips are not so r.   OWEN 179:7
   that never blows so r.   FITZ 99:1
   thin r. line   RUSS 198:15
rede: recks not his own r.   SHAK 207:5
redeemer: know that my r. liveth   BIBLE 25:28
   such and so mighty a R.   MISS 170:22
redemption: married past r.   DRYD 91:6
Redemptorem: tantum meruit habere R.   MISS 170:22
redeunt: r. Saturnia regna   VIRG 264:6
reed: he is a thinking r.   PASC 181:3
   r. shaken with the wind   BIBLE 32:30
   staff of this bruised r.   BIBLE 25:14
   thee the r. is as the oak   SHAK 206:4
reeds: Down in the r. by the river   BROW 48:16
reel: They r. to and fro   PRAY 190:9
references: always to verify your r.   ROUTH 198:3
refined: *never* be r. if I twitch   THOM 257:13
   This Englishwoman is so r.   SMITH 242:14
reform: r. movement has a lunatic   RONS 196:15
   r.', the watchword   BRIG 46:15
Refrain: R. from the unholy pleasure   BELL 18:2
refreshed: giant r. with wine   PRAY 189:16
refreshment: I accept r. at any hands   GILB 108:3
refuge: eternal God is thy r.   BIBLE 24:2
   thou hast been our r.   PRAY 189:20
refusal: great r.   DANTE 81:9
refused: stone which the builders r.   PRAY 190:1
refuses: Closes nothing, r. nothing   WHIT 270:8
refute: Who can r. a sneer   PALEY 179:18
regardless: r. of their doom   GRAY 112:10
regiment: He led his r. from behind   GILB 107:1
   Monstrous R. of Women   KNOX 147:4
register: than the r. of the crimes   GIBB 106:11
reg'lar: brought r. and draw'd mild   DICK 84:13
regret: I only r. that I have   HALE 113:11
   r. the departure of our   THOM 258:9
   'The one thing I r.   CARR 62:11
regrets: wild r.   WILDE 271:4
regular: icily r.   TENN 253:19
   right-down r. Royal Queen   GILB 107:4
regulate: we must r. all recreations   MILT 170:18
Reichtum: gemeiniglich R. den grossen Eseln   LUTH 155:10
reign: Better to r. in hell   MILT 168:15
   had the capacity to r.   TAC 250:11
   my r. is peace   LAND 148:9
reigneth: Thy God r.   BIBLE 29:12
reigns: king r.   THIE 256:17

Reise: *Auf dieser ganzen R.* MULL 174:6
rejected: despised and r. of men BIBLE 29:14
rejoice: desert shall r. BIBLE 29:5
  let us heartily r. PRAY 190:2
  Let us then r. ANON 6:17
  R. in the Lord alway BIBLE 39:18
rejoiced: my spirit hath r. in God BIBLE 34:28
relation: nobody like a r. THAC 256:10
relations: Bless the squire and his r. DICK 83:18
relaxes: Bless r. BLAKE 44:6
relent: Shall make him once r. BUNY 52:2
relenting: r. God Hath placed ROSS 197:2
relic: cas'd up, like a holy r. WEBS 267:8
relics: hallow'd r. should be hid MILT 168:6
relief: not seek for kind r. BLAKE 43:20
  this r. much thanks SHAK 206:6
reliev'd: desperate appliances are r. SHAK 210:22
relieve: thee to comfort and r. them PRAY 187:5
religio: *Tantum r. potuit suadere* LUCR 155:4
religion: I count r. but a childish MARL 160:10
  inward tranquillity which r. FORB 101:9
  is but an handmaid to r. BACON 12:20
  men's minds about to r. BACON 12:23
  Notre r. est faite pour MONT 172:4
  One r. is as true as another BURT 55:20
  r., I hold it to be PAINE 179:14
  r. is allowed to invade MELB 164:14
  R. is by no means a proper CHES 69:16
  R. the opium of the people MARX 162:7
  r. must still be allowed CHES 69:13
  slovenliness is no part of r. WESL 268:19
  some of r. EDG 92:6
  some other new r. PLATO 183:14
  Superstition is the r. BURKE 53:11
  true meaning of r. is thus ARN 9:11
  We must have r. for religion's COUS 78:16
  When I mention r. FIEL 98:8
religions: are sixty different r. CAR 61:3
rem: *quocumque modo r.* HOR 123:2
remains: nothing done while aught r. ROG 195:18
  One r. SHEL 239:1
  Strength in what r. behind WORD 275:16
remark: Which I wish to r. HARTE 115:12
remarkable: there is nothing left r. SHAK 204:6
remarks: said our r. before DON 87:16
remedy: r. is worse than the disease BACON 13:18
  requires a dangerous r. FAWK 97:17
  Things without all r. SHAK 222:12
  'Tis a sharp r. RAL 194:7
remember: can't r. how They go CALV 59:18
  Do you r. an Inn BELL 19:8
  glad to r. even these VIRG 262:17
  he'll r. with advantages SHAK 214:4
  If I do not r. thee PRAY 191:1
  if thou wilt, r. ROSS 197:7
  I r. Drake DRAKE 90:3
  I r., I remember HOOD 121:7
  Must I r. SHAK 206:15
  oafish louts r. Mum BETJ 20:7
  r. me when thou comest BIBLE 36:9
  R. now thy Creator BIBLE 27:21
  r. the Fifth of November ANON 4:17
  We will r. them BINY 42:6
  you should r. and be sad ROSS 197:6
remember'd: flowing cups freshly r. SHAK 214:4
  r. for a very long time MCG 157:11
remembered: blue r. hills HOUS 126:7
Remembering: R. without ceasing your BIBLE 39:23

soul r. my good friends SHAK 230:3
Remembers: R. me of all his gracious SHAK 217:10
remembrance: rosemary, that's for r. SHAK 211:6
  summon up r. of things past SHAK 235:12
  Writ in r. more than things SHAK 229:21
remembreth: Crist! whan that it r. CHAU 68:18
remind: sleep your r. me of the dead SASS 200:9
reminiscence: r. sing WHIT 270:2
remission: shedding of blood is no r. BIBLE 40:6
remnant: r. of our Spartan dead BYRON 58:10
remorse: access and passage to r. SHAK 220:11
Remote: R. and ineffectual Don BELL 18:25
  r. enquiries JOHN 134:27
remover: bends with the r. to remove SHAK 236:12
rend: *mais ne se r. pas* CAMB 60:5
render: r. back from out thy breast BYRON 58:10
  r. The deeds of mercy SHAK 225:17
  R. therefore unto Caesar BIBLE 33:28
rendezvous: I have a r. with Death SEEG 202:17
renew: Although a subtler Sphinx r. SHEL 239:5
renounce: r. the devil and all his PRAY 187:19
renown: citizen Of credit and r. COWP 79:12
rent: That has not been r. YEATS 278:15
repairs: anon r. his drooping head MILT 168:2
repay: I will r. BIBLE 38:2
  Will find a Tiger well r. BELL 18:7
repeats: r. his words SHAK 217:10
repent: I hardly ever r. NASH 174:17
  R. ye BIBLE 31:3
  they r. in haste CONG 76:20
  we may r. at leisure CONG 76:20
Repentance: R. on a Sunday YBAR 278:9
  sinners to r. BIBLE 32:19
  To give r. to her lover GOLD 110:18
repente: *Nemo r. fuit turpissimus* JUV 137:16
repented: much r. BYRON 58:1
repenteth: over one sinner that r. BIBLE 35:25
repetita: *Occidit miseros crambe r.* JUV 138:2
replenish: r. the earth BIBLE 22:6
reply: Their's not to make r. TENN 251:9
Report: R. me and my cause aright SHAK 211:21
  whatsoever things are of good r. BIBLE 39:20
reporter: I am a r. GREE 112:17
reporters: gallery in which the r. MAC 156:15
  through r. to Buncombe CARL 61:17
reporting: r. device for experience WHORF 270:12
repos: *demeurer en r. dans une chambre* PASC 180:16
repose: dear r. for limbs with SHAK 235:10
  Has earned a night's r. LONG 153:18
  Pray for the r. of His soul ROLFE 196:5
  r. is taboo'd by anxiety GILB 107:20
reposes: In quiet she r. ARN 8:17
reprehend: If I r. any thing in this SHER 240:19
representation: Taxation and r. CAMD 60:7
  Taxation without r. is OTIS 178:17
representative: expressed by himself or r. CAMD 60:7
  Your r. owes you BURKE 52:14
represents: It r. health SHAW 237:17
repress: r. the speech they know ELIOT 92:18
reproach: only hope to escape r. JOHN 134:13
reproche: *Chevalier sans peur et sans r.* ANON 5:16
reprove: sager sort our deeds r. CAT 65:5
Republic: Only Love the Beloved R. FORS 102:1
  r. is a raft which will AMES 2:9
reputability: of r. to the gentleman VEBL 261:17
reputation: At ev'ry word a r. dies POPE 185:26
  Dear for her r. through SHAK 230:2

I have lost my r.   SHAK 228:24
Seeking the bubble r.   SHAK 205:1
sold my R. for a Song   FITZ 99:11
Requiem: *R. aeternam dona eis*   MASS 163:11
thy high r. become a sod   KEATS 139:22
Requiescant: *R. in pace*   MASS 163:20
require: What doth the Lord r.   BIBLE 30:19
required: captive r. of us then a song   PRAY 191:1
night thy soul shall be r.   BIBLE 35:20
rerum: *Sunt lacrimae r.*   VIRG 263:2
res: *festinat et in medias r.*   HOR 122:17
R. angusta domi   JUV 137:19
research: r. is always incomplete   PATT 181:11
resemble: we will r. you in that   SHAK 225:10
resentment: difficult to get up r.   NEWM 175:18
reserve: r. the more weighty voice   BACON 13:4
resigned: I am not r.   MILL 166:3
resist: fascination that few can r.   GILB 108:12
I never r. temptation   SHAW 237.7
r. everything except temptation   WILDE 271:14
R. not evil   BIBLE 31:17
resolution: In war, r.   CHUR 71:17
results of thought and r.   TROL 260:12
thus the native hue of r.   SHAK 208:24
resolutions: governs the passions and r.   HUME 128:1
Resolve: R. not to be poor   JOHN 133:20
resolved: speech they have r. not   ELIOT 92:18
resonance: r. of his solitude   CONN 77:10
resource: infinite-r.-and-sagacity   KIPL 146:12
respect: How I did r. you when you   TROL 260:3
respectable: consider him as a r. Hottentot   CHES 69:14
Not one is r. or unhappy   WHIT 270:6
respecter: God is no r. of persons   BIBLE 37:18
respice: *et r. finem*   ANON 7:4
responsibility: heavy burden of r.   EDW 92:11
Power without r.   KIPL 146:29
rest: a-brewing towards my r.   SHAK 225:5
choose Their place of r.   MILT 169:22
far better r. that I go   DICK 85:30
flee away, and be at r.   PRAY 189:8
From r. and sleep   DONNE 88:3
Grant them eternal r.   MASS 163:11
I will give you r.   BIBLE 32:31
Now she's at r.   DRYD 91:3
one crept silently to R.   FITZ 99:2
ordain'd no r.   VAUG 261:13
R. in soft peace   JONS 135:21
r. is silence   SHAK 211:23
r. quiet in Montparnasse   BENET 19:12
R., rest, perturbed spirit   SHAK 208:2
shall r. upon thy holy hill   PRAY 188:10
there the weary be at r.   BIBLE 25:20
reste: *J'y suis, j'y r.*   MACM 157:17
tout le r. est littérature   VERL 262:3
resting: quiet r. from all jealousy   BEAU 17:2
restituit: *homo nobis cunctando r.*   ENN 97:1
restless: and versatile intellect   HUXL 128:14
restraint: r. with which they write   CAMP 60:13
Resurrection: certain hope of the R.   PRAY 188:5
r. they neither marry   BIBLE 33:29
r., and the life.   BIBLE 36:32
symbol of his r.   PROU 192:5
retain: marble to r.   BYRON 57:4
reticulated: Anything r. or decussated   JOHN 134:18
retire: r. at half-past eight   MILL 166:7
retirement: there must be no r.   HAIG 113:9

retrace: Thy steps r.   GILB 108:30
retreat: conquer or die who've no r.   GAY 105:22
I will not r. a single   GARR 104:16
us make an honourable r.   SHAK 205:4
retreating: Have you seen yourself r.   NASH 175:1
retrenchment: r., and reform'   BRIG 46:15
retrograde: be not r.   JONS 136:4
return: Let us r. to our sheep   ANON 6:4
spirit shall r. unto God   BIBLE 27:22
unto dust shalt thou r.   BIBLE 22:15
returned: r. home the previous night   BULL 51:8
We r. to our places   ELIOT 94:2
Returning: R. were as tedious as go   SHAK 222:21
re-unite: r. what common   SCH 201:2
rêve: *Vivre sans r., qu'est-ce*   ROST 197:11
revealed: of the Lord shall be r.   BIBLE 29:9
Revelations: It ends with R.   WILDE 271:26
revelry: sound of r. by night   BYRON 57:9
revels. Our r. now are ended   SHAK 232:24
revenge: one r. me of the injuries   HENR 117:17
ranging for r.   SHAK 216:12
R. is a kind of wild justice   BACON 13:16
shall we not r.   SHAK 225:10
spur my dull r.   SHAK 210:23
revenges: of time brings in his r.   SHAK 234:13
Revenons: *R. à ces moutons*   ANON 6:4
revenues: She bears a duke's r.   SHAK 214:11
Revere: midnight ride of Paul R.   LONG 153:8
reverence: none so poor to do him r.   SHAK 216:18
reversion: no bright r. in the sky   POPE 184:11
reverti: *vox missa r.*   HOR 122:21
reviewing: read a book before r.   SMITH 242:22
revocare: *Sed r. gradum superasque*   VIRG 263:10
revolts: It r. me, but I do it   GILB 108:2
revolution: impossible without a violent r.   LEE 151:6
is…a sort of mental r.   ORW 178:8
R., by Saturn   VERG 262:1
white heat of this r.   WILS 272:16
revolutionary: their r. right to dismember   LINC 152:1
revolutions: share in two r. is living   PAINE 179:16
reward: in no wise lose his r.   BIBLE 32:29
nothing for r.   SPEN 244:17
only r. of virtue is virtue   EMER 96:11
rewards: r. and Fairies   CORB 78:3
Rex: *R. tremendae maiestatis*   CEL 66:2
rhetoric: logic and r.   BACON 13:22
obscure them by an aimless r.   HUXL 128:14
rhetorician: sophistical r.   DISR 87:3
rheum: void your r. upon my beard   SHAK 225:1
rheumatism: to me to complain of r.   SAKI 199:4
rhyme: names in many a mused r.   KEATS 139:22
still more tired of R.   BELL 18:20
unattempted yet in prose or r.   MILT 168:13
Rialto: What news on the R.   SHAK 224:17
riband: r. to stick in his coat   BROW 49:18
ribbed: is the r. sea-sand   COL 74:13
ribbon: blue r. of the turf   DISR 87:8
road was a r. of moonlight   NOYES 177:8
ribboned: sake of a r. coat   NEWB 175:15
ribbons: Tie up my sleeves with r.   HUNT 128:8
ribs: breaking of r. was sport   SHAK 204:14
he took one of his r.   BIBLE 22:9
Ribstone Pippin: 'Right as a R.   BELL 18:19
rice: *it's lovely r. pudding*   MILNE 166:16
rich: am r. beyond the dreams   MOORE 172:11
behave as the r. behave   SMITH 242:9
better have a r. landlord   SHAW 238:19

ever by chance grow r.   THOM 257:18
ever seems it r. to die   KEATS 139:22
feed with the r.   JOHN 132:12
from the r. man's table   BIBLE 35:31
is not r. enough to do it   REED 194:16
like to one more r. in hope   SHAK 235:11
no sin, but to be r.   SHAK 217:8
passing r. with forty pounds   GOLD 110:8
Poor little r. girl   COW 79:7
r. and poor alike to sleep   FRAN 102:5
r. have become richer   SHEL 240:10
r. he hath sent empty away   BIBLE 34:29
R. in good works   BIBLE 40:3
r. man in his castle   ALEX 2:4
r. man to enter into   BIBLE 33:22
r., not gaudy   SHAK 207:6
something r. and strange   SHAK 232:15
tell you about the very r.   FITZ 100:4
to the poor and the r.   ANON 2:15
who dies…r. dies disgraced   CARN 62:1
richer: Becomes the r. still the older   BUTL 56:13
r. for poorer   PRAY 187:28
R. than all his tribe   SHAK 229:15
riches: Infinite r. in a little room   MARL 160:11
left hand r. and honour   BIBLE 26:5
r. to those gross asses   LUTH 155:10
r., which dispersed lie   HERB 118:14
That r. grow in hell   MILT 168:18
Richmond Hill: Sweet lass of R.   MACN 158:2
richness: Here's r.   DICK 84:20
rickshaw: it's no go the r.   MACN 158:5
ricordarsi: *Che r. del tempo felice*   DANTE 81:10
rid: be r. of one thorn out   HOR 123:8
riddle: r. wrapped in a mystery   CHUR 71:3
Riddles: R. of death Thebes   SHEL 239:5
ride: r. in triumph through Persepolis   MARL 160:16
we r. them down   TENN 254:12
rideau: en disant 'Tirez le r.   RAB 193:15
ridentem: Dulce r.   CAT 65:9
Dulce r. Lalagen amabo   HOR 123:17
rider: horse the r. was lost   FRAN 102:11
r.'s back sits dark Anxiety   HOR 124:6
ridere: humanas actiones non r.   SPIN 245:1
rides: r. upon the storm   COWP 79:14
ridiculous: from the sublime to the r.   NAP 174:9
Is wasteful and r. excess   SHAK 217:12
one step above the r.   PAINE 179:13
r. as the British public   MAC 157:2
ridiculus: nascetur r. mus   HOR 122:15
riding: man goes r.   STEV 247:8
Ridley: good comfort Master R.   LAT 149:14
rifiuto: Il gran r.   DANTE 81:9
rifle: r. all the breathing spring   COLL 76:1
rifles: stuttering r.' rapid rattle   OWEN 179:4
rift: little r. within the lute   TENN 252:2
riggish: Bless her when she is r.   SHAK 203:24
right: All's r. with the world   BROW 50:12
convincing myself that I am r.   AUST 12:15
defend to the death your r.   VOLT 265:10
divine r. of husbands   WOLL 274:1
I'm all r.   BONE 44:17
laid out just the r. books   POUND 186:13
minority is always r.   IBSEN 129:4
Of r. and wrong he taught   ARMS 8:9
our country, r. or wrong   DEC 82:5
'R. as a Ribstone Pippin   BELL 18:19
r. deed for the wrong reason   ELIOT 94:13
r. good captain too   GILB 108:25

r. hands of fellowship   BIBLE 39:7
r. little, tight little   DIBD 83:11
r. man in the right place   JEFF 130:13
r. or justice   MAGN 159:1
r. side of the blanket   ASHF 9:21
r. there is none to dispute   COWP 80:5
r. to a child with   SHAW 237:17
r. to be consulted   BAG 14:7
serve him r.   BELL 19:2
Sit thou on my r. hand   PRAY 190:10
So the heart be r.   RAL 194:8
that was r.   HOUS 126:8
their constitutional r.   LINC 152:1
Ulster will be r.   CHUR 70:23
When r., to be kept right   SCH 201:16
which is lawful and r.   BIBLE 30:5
with firmness in the r.   LINC 152:3
righteous: have seen the r. forsaken   BLUN 44:12
I never the r. forsaken   PRAY 188:23
not come to call the r.   BIBLE 32:19
r., and sober life   PRAY 186:20
r. are bold as a lion   BIBLE 26:32
r. man regardeth the life   BIBLE 26:15
righteousness: hunger and thirst after r.   BIBLE 31:11
on the breastplate of r.   BIBLE 39:15
what r. really is   ARN 9:13
Within the paths of r.   SCOT 202:15
right-hand: standing me on the r. side   CEL 66:3
rights: equal in dignity and r.   ANON 2:1
extension of women's r.   FOUR 102:2
folly of 'Woman's R.'   VICT 262:8
r. inherent and inalienable   JEFF 130:9
r. of man is essentially   ROB 195:10
whose r. he has trodden   BURKE 53:7
rime: making beautiful old r.   SHAK 236:10
outlive this powerful r.   SHAK 236:2
Rime Intrinsica: R., Fontmell Magna   BETJ 20:11
ring: both the shires they r.   HOUS 125:12
Bright is the r. of words   STEV 247:13
only pretty r. time   SHAK 205:12
r. at the end of his nose   LEAR 150:14
R. out, wild bells   TENN 252:23
R. out ye crystal spheres   MILT 168:8
They now r. the bells   WALP 266:8
what shall we do for a r.   LEAR 150:14
With this R. I thee wed   PRAY 188:1
Ring'd: R. with the azure world   TENN 251:13
ringleaders: fling the r. from the Tarpeian   ARN 9:17
riot: rash fierce blaze of r.   SHAK 230:1
r. is at bottom the language   KING 142:7
rioting: r., the old Roman way   ARN 9:17
riotous: Wasted his substance with r. living   BIBLE 35:26
riotousness: r. of the crowd is always   ALC 2:1
ripe: we r. and ripe   SHAK 204:22
Ripeness: R. is all   SHAK 218:26
ripening: His greatness is a-r.   SHAK 215:9
rire: me presse de r. de tout   BEAU 16:15
rise: Held we fall to r.   BROW 48:22
nation shall r. against   BIBLE 33:33
R., take up thy bed   BIBLE 36:22
r. with the lark and go   BRET 46:10
That dead men r. up never   SWIN 250:1
to r. out of obscurity   JUV 137:19
Woe unto them that r. up   BIBLE 28:10
Rise up: R., my love   BIBLE 27:29
risible: authors is one of the most r.   JOHN 134:24

rising: Moon of Heav'n is r. once · FITZ 99:14
risk: r. it on one turn of pitch-and-toss · KIPL 144:8
risu: r. inepto res ineptior · CAT 65:8
Ritz: open to all, like the R. · MATH 164:7
river: Alph, the sacred r. · COL 75:2
dale the sacred r. ran · COL 75:4
House of Parliament upon the r. · WELL 268:3
in the reeds by the r. · BROW 48:16
living r. by the door · STEV 247:15
On a tree by a r. a little · GILB 108:17
On either side the r. lie · TENN 253:3
r. jumps over the mountain · AUDEN 10:8
That even the weariest r. · SWIN 250:1
twice into the same r. · HER 118:2
riverrun: r., past Eve and Adam's · JOYCE 136:16
rivers: Nymphs and as yet unknown r. · VIRG 263:16
R. are damp · PARK 180:6
r. of blood must yet flow · JEFF 130:11
road: along the 'ard 'igh r. · PUNCH 192:15
good to be out on the r. · MAS 163:4
is the high r. that leads · JOHN 131:19
On the r. to Mandalay · KIPL 145:3
r. of excess leads · BLAKE 44:1
r. through the woods · KIPL 146:5
r. was a ribbon of moonlight · NOYES 177:8
rolling English r. · CHES 70:2
that on a lonesome r. · COL 74:18
winding r. before me · HAZL 116:5
roads: Two r. diverged in a wood · FROST 103:8
roadway: While I stand on the r. · YEATS 279:8
roaming: where are you r. · SHAK 233:22
roar: called upon to give the r. · CHUR 71:15
r. you as gently as any · SHAK 226:16
they r. their ribs out · GILB 109:12
roareth: What is this that r. thus · GODL 109:19
roaring: There was a r. in the wind · WORD 276:10
robb'd: r. me of my Robe of Honour · FITZ 99:12
'Ye have r. · NEWB 175:17
robbed: that had r. us of immortal · MER 165:4
robber: Now Barabbas was a r. · BIBLE 37:5
robbery: end in conquest and r. · JOHN 134:23
robe: Give me my r. · SHAK 204:10
intertissued r. of gold · SHAK 213:23
robes: r. ye weave, another wears · SHEL 240:2
Robespierre: R. war nichts als die Hand · HEINE 116:14
Robin: R. Redbreast in a Cage · BLAKE 42:18
robur: R. et aes triplex · HOR 123:10
rock: of a serpent upon a r. · BIBLE 26:33
r. I will build my church · BIBLE 33:12
sea-wet r. sat down and combed · HOUS 126:19
Rocked: R. in the cradle · WILL 272:10
rocks: hand that r. the cradle · WALL 265:11
him a native of the r. · JOHN 131:8
She is older than the r. · PATER 181:8
rocky: king sate on the r. brow · BYRON 58:8
rod: child and spares the r. · HOOD 121:8
r. and thy staff comfort · PRAY 188:16
r. out of the stem of Jesse · BIBLE 28:20
spareth his r. hateth · BIBLE 26:18
rode: r. madly off in all directions · LEAC 150:1
roes: breasts are like two young r. · BIBLE 28:4
rogue: Has he not a r.'s face · CONG 76:14
r. and peasant slave am · SHAK 208:20
rogues: see the r. flourish · BROW 49:6
Roland: R. to the dark tower came · SHAK 218:15
Roll: R. on, thou deep and dark · BYRON 57:15
R. up that map · PITT 183:12

us r. all our strength · MARV 162:1
rolling: drunkard made the r. English road · CHES 70:2
Rolls: R. impotently on as Thou · FITZ 99:10
Roma: R. locuta est · AUG 11:21
Romae: Si fueris R. · AMBR 2:8
romain: ni r., ni empire · VOLT 264:21
Romam: natam me consule R. · CIC 72:15
Roman: after the high R. fashion · SHAK 204:7
at Rome live in the R. · AMBR 2:8
Butcher'd to make a R. holiday · BYRON 57:13
found the R. nation · VIRG 262:16
I am a R. citizen · CIC 72:12
noblest R. of them all · SHAK 217:6
R. came to Rye or out · CHES 70:2
R. Conquest was · SELL 203:1
R.'s life, a Roman's arms · MAC 156:9
that would not be a R. · SHAK 216:13
You, R., make your task · VIRG 263:14
Romana: Moribus antiquis res stat R. virisque · ENN 97:2
Romance: R. at short notice was · SAKI 199:3
Romans: Friends, R., countrymen · SHAK 216:16
R. were like brothers · MAC 156:7
romantic: mustnt be r. about money · SHAW 238:6
Romanus: Civis R. sum · CIC 72:12
Rome: go from the church of R. · WOTT 277:20
grandeur that was R. · POE 184:3
happy R. · CIC 72:15
high and palmy state of R. · SHAK 206:7
R. has spoken · AUG 11:21
'R. is above the Nations · KIPL 145:17
R. live in the Roman style · AMBR 2:8
that I loved R. more · SHAK 216:13
when R. falls · BYRON 57:14
Romeo: wherefore art thou R. · SHAK 231:18
Ronsard: 'R. sang of me in the days · RONS 196:6
roof: cleave to the r. of my mouth · PRAY 191:1
r. of blue Italian weather · SHEL 239:7
rooks: r. are blown about · TENN 252:12
r. in families homeward · HARDY 115:2
room: In ev'ry grave make r. · DAV 81:18
Infinite riches in a little r. · MARL 160:11
into a r. full of people · WEBB 267:2
is always r. at the top · WEBS 267:5
no r. for them in the inn · BIBLE 35:1
R. to deny ourselves · KEBLE 141:9
rooms: lighted r. Inside your head · LARK 149:6
root: money is the r. of all evil · BIBLE 40:1
nips his r. · SHAK 215:9
unto the r. of the trees · BIBLE 31:6
roote: me aboute myn herte r. · CHAU 68:18
roots: shall grow out of his r. · BIBLE 28:20
stirring Dull r. · ELIOT 94:18
rope: to set his hand to a r. · DRAKE 90:4
rose: blossom as the r. · BIBLE 29:5
Christmas I no more desire a r. · SHAK 219:8
earthlier happy is the r. · SHAK 226:12
English unofficial r. · BROO 47:10
expectancy and r. · SHAK 209:6
fayr as is the r. in May · CHAU 68:19
Go, lovely R. · WALL 265:13
I am the r. of Sharon · BIBLE 27:26
I pluck the r. · BROW 50:23
last r. of summer · MOORE 173:2
lovely is the r. · WORD 275:13
Luve's like a red red r. · BURNS 54:17
mast burst open with a r. · FLEC 100:11
R. as where some buried · FITZ 99:1

r. By any other name | SHAK 231:19
R. is a rose is a rose | STEIN 245:17
R., were you not extremely | PRIOR 191:18
Roves back the r. | DE L 82:8
tiger sniffs the r. | SASS 200:14
to tell the crooked r. | THOM 257:4
white r. weeps | TENN 254:2
roseau: mais c'est un r. pensant | PASC 181:3
Rose Aylmer: R., all were thine | LAND 148:12
rosebuds: Gather ye r. while ye may | HERR 118:23
rose-lipt: many a r. maiden | HOUS 126:11
rosemary: r., that's for remembrance | SHAK 211:6
you there's r. and rue | SHAK 234:24
Rosencrantz: R. and Guildenstern are | SHAK 212:2
rose-red: r. city 'half as old | BURG 52:7
roses: days of wine and r. | DOWS 89:9
It was the time of r. | HOOD 121:4
not a bed of r. | STEV 247:3
own red r. there may blow | THOM 257:22
Plant thou no r. at my | ROSS 197:7
raptures and r. of vice | SWIN 249:18
r., all the way | BROW 50:8
r. and white lilies grow | CAMP 60:20
Strew on her r. | ARN 8:17
'Two red r. across the moon | MORR 173:15
rosy: sent thee late a r. wreath | JONS 136:3
Rosy-fingered: R. dawn | HOMER 121:2
rot: cold obstruction and to r. | SHAK 224:4
pernicious soul R. | SHAK 229:14
R. inwardly and foul contagion | MILT 167:21
very deep did r. | COL 74:10
we r. and rot | SHAK 204:22
rotten: r. in the state of Denmark | SHAK 207:11
rough: from children who were r. | SPEN 244:11
r. magic I here abjure | SHAK 233:1
r. male kiss of blankets | BROO 47:6
r. places plain | BIBLE 29:9
r. than polished diamond | CHES 69:11
R. winds do shake the darling | SHAK 235:9
Rough-hew: R. them how we will | SHAK 211:15
roughs: among his fellow r. | DOYLE 89:29
Roumania: I am Marie of R. | PARK 180:3
this might be R. | MARY 162:13
round: perfect r. | BROW 48:18
r. the world away | KING 142:16
r. unvarnish'd tale deliver | SHAK 228:18
roundabouts: What's lost upon the r. | CHAL 66:9
rounded: little life Is r. | SHAK 232:24
Roundheads: R. (Right but Repulsive) | SELL 203:2
rouse: r. a lion than to start | SHAK 212:6
Rousseau: dessen Seele R. geschaffen | HEINE 116:14
mock on, Voltaire, R. | BLAKE 43:3
Roves: R. back the rose | DE L 82:8
roving: we'll go no more a r. | BYRON 58:22
row: darned long r. to hoe | LOW 154:15
watermen, that r. one way | BURT 55:14
royal: r. priesthood | BIBLE 40:18
R. slice of bread | MILNE 166:14
This r. throne of kings | SHAK 230:2
royaliste: plus r. que le roi | ANON 5:19
royally: To have prov'd most r. | SHAK 212:3
Royalty: when you come to R. you | DISR 87:6
ruat: r. caelum' | MANS 159:11
rub: there's the r. | SHAK 208:24
What r. or what impediment | SHAK 214:5
rubies: Give pearls away and r. | HOUS 125:7
her price is far above r. | BIBLE 26:34
price of wisdom is above r. | BIBLE 25:29

rubs: yellow fog that r. its | ELIOT 94:4
ruddier: r. than the cherry | GAY 105:6
ruddy: Now he was r. | BIBLE 24:22
R. Ball has taken flight | THOM 258:8
rude: r. forefathers of the hamlet | GRAY 112:2
r. hands have touch'd it | JONS 136:9
Rudyards: R. cease from kipling | STEP 246:3
rue: nought shall make us r. | SHAK 217:16
there's rosemary and r. | SHAK 234:24
there's r. for you | SHAK 211:7
With r. my heart is laden | HOUS 126:11
ruffian: He's the r. on the stair | HENL 117:8
rug: In a r. | FRAN 102:14
rugged: Beneath those r. elms | GRAY 112:2
Ruh: Meine R.' ist hin | GOE 109:23
Über allen Gipfeln Ist R.' | GOE 110:2
Ruhm: nichts der R. | GOE 110:1
ruin: around the dear r. | MOORE 172:13
great deal of r. in a nation | SMITH 242:4
marks the earth with r. | BYRON 57:15
R. seize thee | GRAY 111:16
Spreading r. and scattering | BROW 48:16
ruined: nation was ever r. by trade | FRAN 102:9
r. by Chinese cheap labour | HARTE 115:13
r. Mr Hampden's fortune | BURKE 52:12
we dress when we're r. | HARDY 114:13
Ruining: R. along the illimitable | TENN 253:17
Ruinous: R. inheritance | GAIUS 104:8
ruins: I shored against my r. | ELIOT 95:7
r. of the noblest man | SHAK 216:11
sketch the r. of St Paul's | MAC 156:17
Ruislip: Gaily into R. Gardens | BETJ 21:7
ruit: consili expers mole r. | HOR 124:8
rule: broken the second r. of war | MONT 172:8
recognize but one r. of commerce | QUES 193:10
R., Britannia | THOM 258:12
R. of three doth puzzle | ANON 4:8
r. the waves | THOM 258:12
Rule Britannia: When you've shouted 'R.' | KIPL 143:6
Ruler: R. of the Queen's Navee | GILB 108:28
that is to be r. in Israel | BIBLE 30:18
Rulers: R. have no authority from | MAYH 164:10
rules: hand that r. the world | WALL 265:11
pretences to break known r. | CROM 80:19
there are no golden r. | SHAW 238:10
ruling: r. passion in man is not | FROST 103:12
r. passion conquers reason | POPE 185:2
rum: r., sodomy and the lash | CHUR 71:21
what a R. Go everything is | WELLS 268:15
Yo-ho-ho, and a bottle of r. | STEV 246:19
Rumble: R. thy bellyful | SHAK 218:7
Rumoresque: R. senum severiorum | CAT 65:5
rumour: sound and r. | MORR 173:13
rumours: hear of wars and r. of wars | BIBLE 33:32
run: nearest r. thing | WELL 267:21
R., run, Orlando | SHAK 205:3
r.-stealers flicker | THOM 257:22
r. with patience the race | BIBLE 40:9
significant than the long r. | KEYN 141:20
true love never did r. smooth | SHAK 226:13
yet we will make him r. | MARV 162:1
runcible: He weareth a r. hat | LEAR 150:6
R. Cat with crimson whiskers | LEAR 150:19
they ate with a r. spoon | LEAR 150:16
runnable: r. stag | DAV 81:19
running: takes all the r. *you* can do | CARR 63:20
runs: So r. the world away | SHAK 210:6
who r. may read | KEBLE 141:10

run-way: stretched beyond the r.   BETJ 20:10
Rupee: chapter on the Fall of the R.   WILDE 271:11
Rupert: R. of Debate   BULW 51:10
rura: Paterna r. bubus   HOR 123:9
rural: lovely woman in a r. spot   HUNT 128:7
Rural Dean: sly shade of a R.   BROO 47:11
Rus: R. in urbe   MART 161:10
rushed: r. past the grand stand   DISR 87:13
russet: r. yeas and honest kersey   SHAK 219:11
russet-coated: r. captain that knows what   CROM 80:14
Russian: R. has two generals   NICH 176:10
   to you the action of R.   CHUR 71:3
Russians: R. shall not have Constantinople   HUNT 128:2
rust: moth and r. doth corrupt   BIBLE 31:22
   To r. unburnish'd   TENN 255:13
   to wear out than to r.   CUMB 81:1
Ruth: Through the sad heart of R.   KEATS 140:1
ruthful: Heaven and Earth are not r.   LAO 149:4
ruthless: r. King   GRAY 111:16
Rye: Before the Roman came to R.   CHES 70:2
   fields of barley and of r.   TENN 253:3
   r. reach to the chin   PEELE 182:2
rymyng: r. is nat worth a toord   CHAU 68:15
sabachthani: lama s.   BIBLE 34:18
Sabbath: last S. day of 1879   MCG 157:11
   s. was made for man   BIBLE 34:20
Sabidi: Non amo te, S.   MART 161:8
Sabrina: S. fair   MILT 167:9
Sack: S. the lot   FISH 98:12
Sacred: Enormous through the S. Town   BELL 19:1
   is free but facts are s.   SCOTT 201:7
Sacred Heart: convent of the S.   ELIOT 94:17
sacrifice: bodies a living s.   BIBLE 38:1
   holy hush of ancient s.   STEV 246:15
   measure of his s.   ROS 196:17
   s. of God is a troubled   PRAY 189:7
   stands Thine ancient s.   KIPL 145:10
   thou desirest no s.   PRAY 189:7
   Too long a s.   YEATS 278:20
   your prayers one sweet s.   SHAK 215:5
sacrifices: he s. it to your opinion   BURKE 52:14
   he who s. an hundred thousand   WALP 266:3
sad: All my s. captains   SHAK 204:2
   know not why I am so s.   SHAK 224:10
   s. and bad and mad   BROW 49:9
   s. I am   BETJ 21:13
   s. tale's best for winter   SHAK 234:20
   should remember and be s.   ROSS 197:6
   tell s. stories   SHAK 230:8
   there on that s. height   THOM 257:1
   Your s. tires in a mile-a   SHAK 234:23
sadder: s. and a wiser man   COL 74:21
saddle: Things are in the s.   EMER 96:5
sadly: take their pleasures s.   SULL 248:8
sadness: Good day s.   ELUA 96:2
   shade of s.   WHIT 270:9
   such a want-wit s. makes   SHAK 224:10
saeclorum: integro s. nascitur ordo   VIRG 264:6
saeclum: Solvet s. in favilla   CEL 65:14
saecula: et in s. saeculorum   MASS 163:8
safe: s. I sing with mortal voice   MILT 169:13
   see me s. up   MORE 173:6
   Winds somewhere s. to sea   SWIN 250:1
safeguard: was the s. of the West   WORD 277:2
safely: I'd toddle s. home   SASS 200:5
   tread s. into the unknown'   HASK 115:16

safer: s. than a known way   HASK 115:16
safest: middle course is the s.   OVID 178:21
safety: our s. is in our speed   EMER 96:14
   pluck this flower, s.   SHAK 212:10
   source of my light and my s.   BIBLE 41:11
safety-catch: s. on my pistol   JOHST 135:12
safire: diamond and s. bracelet   LOOS 153:24
safliest: s. when with one man mann'd   DONNE 87:25
sager: s. sort our deeds reprove   CAT 65:5
said: fool hath s. in his heart   PRAY 188:9
   He s. he was against it   COOL 78:2
   is a great deal to be s.   BENT 19:17
   never s. a foolish thing   ROCH 195:15
   (S. I to myself   GILB 107:15
   s. our remarks before   DON 87:16
   S. the Piggy, 'I will.'   LEAR 150:15
   They haif s.   KEITH 141.12
sail: s. in amply billowing gown   BELL 19:1
   sieve I'll thither s.   SHAK 220:2
   white s.'s shaking   MAS 162:19
sailed: have s. the seas and come   YEATS 279:14
   S. off in a wooden shoe   FIELD 98:2
   They s. away for a year   LEAR 150:14
sailor: Home is the s.   STEV 247:16
   No man will be a s. who   JOHN 131:15
   s. frae the main   BURNS 54:11
   s.'s wife had chestnuts   SHAK 220:2
Sailor-men: It's very odd that S. should   BARH 15:15
sails: argosies of magic s.   TENN 253:10
   Purple the s.   SHAK 203:22
saint: en aucune manière ni s.   VOLT 264:21
Saint George: England and S.   SHAK 213:15
Saint Martin: Expect S.'s summer   SHAK 214:6
saints: thy slaughtered s.   MILT 170:9
saisons: Ô s., ô châteaux   RIMB 195:8
sake: country for his country's s.   FITZ 98:13
   my s. shall find it   BIBLE 32:28
   wine for thy stomach's s.   BIBLE 39:29
salad: My s. days   SHAK 203:20
Salamis: looks o'er sea-born S.   BYRON 58:8
Salisbury: S. makes a great speech   MORL 173:9
salley: Down by the s. gardens   YEATS 278:18
sallow: s. waiter brings me beans   SASS 200:15
sally: I make a sudden s.   TENN 251:6
   There's none like pretty S.   CAREY 61:4
salmon: s.-falls   YEATS 279:12
   s. sing in the street   AUDEN 10:8
salsa: s. del mundo es el hambre   CERV 66:6
salt: are the s. of the earth   BIBLE 31:12
   eating an egg without s.   KIPL 146:22
   she became a pillar of s.   BIBLE 22:25
Salus: S. extra ecclesiam non   AUG 11:18
   S. populi suprema   CIC 72:6
salutant: morituri te s.   ANON 6:13
Salute: S. one another with   BIBLE 38:7
   who are about to die s.   ANON 6:13
Salva: S. me   CEL 66:2
salvation: My bottle of s.   RAL 194:4
   no s. outside the church   AUG 11:18
   s. of our own souls   JOHN 132:10
   s. with fear and trembling   BIBLE 39:17
   Should see s.   SHAK 225:17
   strength of our s.   PRAY 190:2
   that publisheth s.   BIBLE 29:12
   things necessary to s.   PRAY 191:13
Samarkand: take the Golden Road to S.   FLEC 100:8

same: he is much the s.	ANON 3:2
Jesus Christ the s. yesterday	BIBLE 40:12
more they are the s.	KARR 138:11
s. a hundred years hence	DICK 84:22
this will go onward the s.	HARDY 114:11
we must all say *the s.*	MELB 164:15
you are the s. you	MART 161:9
samite: Clothed in white s.	TENN 251:16
Samson: S. hath quit himself	MILT 170:5
sancta: s. simplicitas	HUSS 128:10
sed s. simplicitas	JER 130:15
sanctuary: dark s. of incapacity	CHES 69:17
Sanctus: S., sanctus, sanctus	MASS 163:16
sand: built his house upon the s.	BIBLE 32:13
Little grains of s.	CARN 62:2
s. against the wind	BLAKE 43:3
Such quantities of s.	CARR 64:1
World in a Grain of S.	BLAKE 42:17
sandal: his s. shoon	SHAK 210:25
sandals: still morn went out with s.	MILT 168:4
Sandalwood: S., cedarwood	MAS 162:14
sands: Across the s. of Dee	KING 142:12
Footprints on the s. of time	LONG 153:10
lone and level s. stretch	SHEL 239:17
sang: I s. in my chains like	THOM 257:3
morning stars s.	BIBLE 25:33
s. to a small guitar	LEAR 150:13
song the Syrens s.	BROW 48:12
Thus s. the uncouth swain	MILT 168:4
sanglots: Les s. longs	VERL 262:2
sanguis: semen est s. Christianorum	TERT 256:7
Sanitas: S. sanitatum et omnia sanitas	MEN 164:20
sanitatum: Sanitas s. et omnia sanitas	MEN 164:20
sano: mens sana in corpore s.	JUV 138:5
sans: s. End	FITZ 99:3
S. teeth, sans eyes	SHAK 205:1
sapere: s. aude	HOR 123:3
sapienti: Dictum s. sat est	PLAU 183:17
saplings: it plies the s. double	HOUS 126:4
Sappho: Where burning S. loved	BYRON 58:6
sarcasm: that petulance is not s.	DISR 86:16
Sargent: dangerous to sit to S.	ANON 4:1
sat: Babylon we s. down and wept	PRAY 191:1
Dictum sapienti s. est	PLAU 183:17
You have s. too long here	CROM 80:18
Satan: capitol Of S. and his peers	MILT 169:2
Get thee behind me, S.	BIBLE 33:13
messenger of S. to buffet	BIBLE 39:6
S. finds some mischief	WATTS 266:17
Satanic: dark S. mills	BLAKE 43:2
satiable: full of 's. curtiosity	KIPL 146:15
satin: always goes into white s.	SHER 240:16
satire: It's hard not to write s.	JUV 137:13
S. or sense	POPE 184:21
satisfied: well paid that is well s.	SHAK 226:3
satisfies: Where most she s.	SHAK 203:24
satisfy: That poorly s. our eyes	WOTT 277:18
satisfying: a voracious appetite	FIEL 98:9
saturam: s. non scribere	JUV 137:13
Saturday: S. and Monday	CAREY 61:5
what he did on S.	YBAR 278:9
Saturnia: redeunt S. regna	VIRG 264:6
sauce: et une seule s.	CAR 61:3
Hunger is the best s.	CERV 66:6
only one s.	CAR 61:3
saucy: deep-search'd with s.	SHAK 219:7
Saul: S. and Jonathan were lovely	BIBLE 24:26
S., why persecutest thou	BIBLE 37:16
savage: Unequal laws unto a s.	TENN 255:10

wild in woods the noble s.	DRYD 90:22
will take some s. woman	TENN 253:12
save: God s. king Solomon	BIBLE 24:31
himself he cannot s.	BIBLE 34:17
s. my soul	ANON 4:13
shall s. his soul alive	BIBLE 30:5
saved: He s. others	BIBLE 34:17
s. herself by her exertions	PITT 183:11
they only s. the world	CHES 69:25
What must I do to be s.	BIBLE 37:20
saves: who freely s. those who	CEL 66:2
saving: s. health among all nations	PRAY 189:12
Saviour: S.'s birth is celebrated	SHAK 206:9
savoir: c'est de s. être à soi	MONT 172:3
savour: salt have lost his s.	BIBLE 31:12
Seeming and s. all the winter	SHAK 234:24
saw: drowns the parson's s.	SHAK 219:10
I s. a man this morning	SHAW 238:22
I who s. the face of God	MARL 160:3
Nor do not s. the air too	SHAK 209:7
saws: s. and modern instances	SHAK 205:1
say: Have something to s.	ARN 9:15
Lat thame s.	KEITH 141:12
Need we s. it was not love	MILL 166:9
S. I'm weary	HUNT 128:5
S. not the struggle naught	CLOU 73:17
should s. what you mean	CARR 63:2
think till I see what I s.	WALL 265:12
to s. about a play when	SHAW 237:16
we must all s. *the same*	MELB 164:15
you have nothing to s.	COLT 76:6
saying: if something is not worth s.	BEAU 16:14
that if they keep on s.	BENN 19:13
scabbard: he threw away the s.	CLAR 72:24
scabbards: have leaped from their s.	BURKE 53:9
scaffold: Truth forever on the s.	LOW 154:18
scale: sufficiently large s.	SPEN 244:8
Scalinger: S. used to say of the Basques	
	CHAM 67:1
scallop-shell: Give me my s. of quiet	RAL 194:4
scan: Then gently s. your brother	BURNS 53:17
scandal: It is public s. that constitutes	MOL 171:14
s. about Queen Elizabeth	SHER 240:15
scandale: s. du monde est ce qui	MOL 171:14
scandalous: s. and poor	ROCH 195:16
scapegoat: Let him go for a s. into	BIBLE 23:23
Scarf: S. up the tender eye	SHAK 222:15
scarlet: are like a thread of s.	BIBLE 28:3
'His sins were s.	BELL 18:21
Though your sins be as s.	BIBLE 28:6
scars: sleeve and show his s.	SHAK 214:4
scattered: s. the proud in the imagination	
	BIBLE 34:29
s. the heaped-up mountains	VIRG 264:10
scatterest: soon as thou s. them they	PRAY 189:21
scelerisque: vitae s. purus	HOR 123:16
scene: Last s. of all	SHAK 205:1
start a s. or two	ELIOT 94:7
well imagine the s.	COMP 76:9
scenes: busy s. of crowded life	JOHN 135:8
changing s. of life	TATE 250:16
no more behind your s.	JOHN 131:5
scent: methinks I s. the morning air	SHAK 207:14
scepter'd: this s. isle	SHAK 230:2
sceptic: s. to deny the possibility	HUXL 129:1
What ever s. could inquire	BUTL 56:3
sceptre: His s. shows the force	SHAK 225:17
s. and the ball	SHAK 213:23
sceptred: avails the s. race	LAND 148:12

schaffende: Zerstörung ist zugleich eine s.
| | BAK 14:11 |

Schatten: denen man seinen S. zeigt NIET 176:16
  wollen niemand in den S. BULOW 51:9
Scheme: sorry S. of Things FITZ 99:13
schemes: s. o' mice an' men BURNS 55:6
Schlag: Zwei Herzen und ein S. HALM 114:5
schlecht: Welt hässlich und s. NIET 176:18
scholar: better s. than Wordsworth HOUS 127:8
  There mark what ills the s.'s JOHN 135:9
Scholars: S. dispute HOR 122:13
school s. nonsense which was knocked
  BEER 17:16
  special reason for hating s. BEER 17:15
  Unwillingly to s. SHAK 205:1
  vixen when she went to s. SHAK 227:13
schoolboy: Every s. knows who imprisoned
  MAC 156:16
  then the whining s. SHAK 205:1
schoolboys: s. playing in the stream PEELE 182:2
schoolgirl: Pert as a s. well can be GILB 108:6
schoolmasters: s. puzzle their brain GOLD 110:17
schools: lumber of the s. SWIFT 249:11
  s. of thought contend MAO 159:13
Schosse: aus dem S. der Zeit HEINE 116:14
schweigen: darüber muss man s. WITT 273:10
Sciatica: S.: he cured it AUBR 10:5
science: La vraye s. et le vray CHAR 67:16
  only applications of s. PAST 181:7
  Professors of the Dismal S. CARL 61:16
  With the fairy tales of s. TENN 253:6
sciences: That great mother of s. BACON 14:1
scientia: et ipsa s. potestas est BACON 14:2
scientiarum: Magna ista s. mater BACON 14:1
scientific: s. names of beings animalculous
  GILB 109:1
scientists: at the illiteracy of s. SNOW 243:6
scire: s. nefas HOR 123:13
scissor-man: red-legged s. HOFF 120:10
scoff: who came to s. GOLD 110:9
scoffer: dull product of a s.'s pen WORD 274:14
scole: s. of Stratford atte Bowe CHAU 68:2
scope: that man's s. SHAK 235:11
Scorer: when the One Great S. comes RICE 195:2
scorn: deal of s. looks beautiful SHAK 234:7
  figure for the time of s. SHAK 229:8
  held the human race in s. BELL 18:8
  little s. is alluring CONG 76:24
  S. not the Sonnet WORD 277:3
  S. the sort now growing YEATS 280:1
  s. to change my state SHAK 235:11
  Teach not thy lip such s. SHAK 231:4
  We s. their bodies BAST 16:10
scorn'd: s. his spirit SHAK 216:1
scorpions: will chastise you with s. BIBLE 25:4
scotch'd: We have s. the snake SHAK 222:12
Scotchman: noblest prospect which a S.
  JOHN 131:19
Scotland: do indeed come from S. JOHN 131:16
  in S. supports the people JOHN 134:19
  Stands S. where it did SHAK 223:4
Scots: S., wha hae wi' Wallace BURNS 54:20
Scotsman: world than a S. on the make BARR 16:7
scoundrel: last refuge of a s. JOHN 132:21
  man over forty is a s. SHAW 238:14
scout: s. 'em, and flout 'em SHAK 232:20
scrap: just for a s. of paper BETH 20:4
scraps: stolen the s. SHAK 219:10
scream: Does not s. WHIT 270:8

screams: strange s. of death SHAK 222:5
screw: s. your courage SHAK 221:6
scribble: s. your courage GLOU 109:18
scribendi: Qui nullum fere s. genus JOHN 133:2
  S. cacoethes et aegro JUV 138:1
scribere: saturam non s. JUV 137:13
scribes: s. and the Pharisees brought BIBLE 36:25
scrip: My s. of joy RAL 194:4
  yet with s. and scrippage SHAK 205:4
Scripture: devil can cite S. for his SHAK 224:20
  Holy S. containeth PRAY 191:13
  S. moveth us in sundry PRAY 186:17
Scriptures: hast caused all holy S. PRAY 187:7
scroll: with punishments the s. HENL 117:7
scrotum: s.tightening sea JOYCE 137:3
sculpture: like that of s. RUSS 198:11
scum: composed of the s. of the earth WELL 268:9
Scuttling: S across the floors ELIOT 94.6
Scylla: S. and Charybdis SHEL 240:10
sea: Alone on a wide wide s. COL 74:14
  beneath in the abysmal s. TENN 252:27
  blue days at s. STEV 247:12
  cold gray stones, O S. TENN 251:4
  crown'd with summer s. TENN 252:8
  desks and never go to s. GILB 108:29
  dominion of the s. COV 79:1
  frail boat on the rough s. HOR 123:10
  full s. are we now afloat SHAK 217:3
  has something of the s. SEDL 202:16
  heaven by s. as by land GILB 106:17
  he cast into the s. BIBLE 36:2
  his footsteps in the s. COWP 79:14
  home from s. STEV 247:16
  if we gang to s. master BALL 15:3
  in my chains like the s. THOM 257:3
  in the midst of the s. BIBLE 26:33
  in the s. of life enisled ARN 8:15
  into the midst of the s. PRAY 189:3
  little cloud out of the s. BIBLE 25:5
  mirrors of the s. are strewn FLEC 100:12
  mountains by the winter s. TENN 252:4
  never sick at s. GILB 108:26
  of a sudden came the s. BROW 50:7
  one is of the s. WORD 277:6
  on this windy s. of land MILT 169:5
  paddles in a halcyon s. ROSS 197:3
  s. gave up the dead which BIBLE 41:6
  s. rises higher CHES 69:19
  S. shall give up her dead) PRAY 191:11
  s.! the sea XEN 278:7
  serpent-haunted s. FLEC 100:7
  sheet and a flowing s. CUNN 81:4
  snotgreen s. JOYCE 137:3
  stone set in the silver s. SHAK 230:2
  summers in a s. of glory SHAK 215:9
  sun was shining on the s. CARR 63:23
  that gong-tormented s. YEATS 278:12
  there was no more s. BIBLE 41:7
  they sink through the s. THOM 256:22
  this kingdom by the s. POE 183:19
  those in peril on the s. WHIT 269:15
  union with its native s. WORD 274:15
  uttermost parts of the s. PRAY 191:3
  water in the rough rude s. SHAK 230:5
  waves on the great s. LUCR 155:6
  we'll o'er the s. HOGG 120:14
  When I put out to s. TENN 251:11
  why the s. is boiling hot CARR 64:2
  wrinkled s. beneath him TENN 251:13

sea-change: doth suffer a s.   SHAK 232:15
seagreen: s. Incorruptible   CARL 61:13
seal: opened the seventh s.   BIBLE 40:34
S. then this bill of my   DONNE 88:8
S. up the mouth of outrage   SHAK 232:7
You Heard a S. Bark   THUR 259:14
sealing-wax: like sticks of s.   DICK 83:20
shoes—and ships—and s.   CARR 64:2
Seals: S. of love   SHAK 224:7
sea-maid: report a s. spawn'd him   SHAK 224:6
sear: s., the yellow leaf   SHAK 223:12
search: s. for pearls must dive   DRYD 90:20
search'd: deep-s. with saucy   SHAK 219:7
searching: s. find out God   BIBLE 25:22
seas: floors of silent s.   ELIOT 94:6
multitudinous s. incarnadine   SHAK 222:1
must down to the s. again   MAS 162:19
now through friendly s.   FLEC 100:10
On the dangers of the s.   PARK 180:11
such as pass on the s.   PRAY 191:10
sea-sand: is the ribbed s.   COL 74:13
sea-shore: boy playing on the s.   NEWT 176:8
season: each thing that in s. grows   SHAK 219:8
every thing there is a s.   BIBLE 27:6
it is but for a s.   HOUS 126:9
S. of mists and mellow   KEATS 140:12
things by s. season'd are   SHAK 226:9
Youth's the s. made   GAY 105:13
seasons: man for all s.   WHIT 270:11
O s., O castles   RIMB 195:8
seat: this s. of Mars   SHAK 230:2
seatbelts: Fasten your s.   DAVIS 82:4
Seated: S. one day at the organ   PROC 191:20
sea-wet: Spartans on the s. rock   HOUS 126:19
seaworms: Battening upon huge s.   TENN 253:1
second: All things have s. birth   WORD 276:9
first and s. class citizens   WILL 272:13
grounds for the s. time   PEAC 181:15
Is s. childishness   SHAK 205:1
s. as farce   MARX 162:8
s. best's a gay goodnight   YEATS 279:1
S. Law of Thermodynamics   SNOW 243:6
Some s. guest to entertain   DONNE 88:13
unto my wife my s. best bed   SHAK 237:6
secret: bread eaten in s. is pleasant   BIBLE 26:11
I know that's a s.   CONG 76:15
s. and sweet reasonableness   ARN 9:13
s. of happiness is to admire   BRAD 45:17
Seeking His s. deeds   ROSS 197:2
then in s. sin   CHUR 70:21
sect: attached to that great s.   SHEL 239:3
sectes: Angleterre soixante s.   CAR 61:3
secure: He is s.   SHEL 238:26
security: allowed to be a collateral s.   CHES 69:13
s. for its impartial administration   PEEL 182:1
Sedan chair: flood of tears and a S.   DICK 85:24
sedens: Qui s. adversus identidem   CAT 65:9
sedge: s. is wither'd from   KEATS 139:3
seducer: Thou strong s.   DRYD 91:1
Sedula: S. curavi   SPIN 245:1
see: Can I s. another's woe   BLAKE 43:20
come up sometime, s. me   WEST 269:2
'I'm damned if I s. it'   NEWB 175:13
into the wilderness to s.   BIBLE 32:30
I s. a voice   SHAK 227:22
I s. the better way   OVID 178:22
"Is. what I eat" is   CARR 63:2
more I s. of men   ROL 196:4
no man s. me more   SHAK 215:8

s. an author and we find   PASC 180:15
s. God made and eaten   BROW 49:1
shall no man s. me and live   BIBLE 23:22
Then I shall s. thee again   SHAK 217:4
to s. her was to love her   BURNS 53:19
To s. oursels as others   BURNS 55:4
we can s. more than they   BERN 20:2
yet I s. thee still   SHAK 221:10
you last s. your father   YEAM 278:10
seed: garden, That grows to s.   SHAK 206:15
s. ye sow, another reaps   SHEL 240:2
seeds: I find thy cunning s.   ROSS 197:2
Some s. fell by the wayside   BIBLE 33:4
seek: If you s. for a monument   ANON 7:6
not s. for kind relief   BLAKE 43:20
s., and ye shall find   BIBLE 32:5
s. power and to lose   BACON 13:10
S. ye the Lord while he   BIBLE 29:17
that sometime did me s.   WYATT 278:3
To strive, to s.   TENN 255:16
We s. him here   ORCZY 178:5
Seeking: S. His secret deeds   ROSS 197:2
S. shall find Him   BROW 49:11
Seele: dessen S. Rousseau geschaffen   HEINE 116:14
Seelen: 'Zwei S. und ein Gedanke   HALM 114:5
seem: be rather than to s. good   SALL 199:10
things are not what they s.   LONG 153:9
Seeming: S. and savour all the winter   SHAK 234:24
seems: I know not 's.'   SHAK 206:13
seen: evidence of things not s.   BIBLE 40:8
God whom he hath not s.   BIBLE 40:27
have seen what I have s.   SHAK 209:6
If I have s. further it   NEWT 176:7
I have s. the future   STEF 245:16
manifestly and undoubtedly be s.   HEW 119:5
persons whom one has never s.   NEWM 175:18
s., and yet have believed   BIBLE 37:11
s. but a bright lily grow   JONS 136:9
things which I have s.   WORD 275:13
What things have we s.   BEAU 16:18
sees: future s.   BLAKE 43:6
She neither hears nor s.   WORD 276:17
seethe: s. a kid in his mother's   BIBLE 23:20
seige: Did march to the s.   BALL 14:18
seigneur: vous êtes un grand s.   BEAU 16:17
seldom: when they s. come   SHAK 212:5
select: that each one should s.   SHEL 239:3
Selection: term of Natural S.   DARW 81:15
Self: seeketh only S. to please   BLAKE 43:11
self-consumer: I am the s. of my woes   CLARE 72:21
self-evident: hold these truths to be s.   ANON 5:9
selfish: sensible people are s.   EMER 96:7
self-slaughter: His canon 'gainst s.   SHAK 206:15
sell: go and s. that thou hast   BIBLE 33:21
must poorly s. ourselves   SHAK 233:10
no man might buy or s.   BIBLE 41:2
precious as the Goods they s.   FITZ 99:12
s., or deny, or delay   MAGN 159:1
s. with you   SHAK 224:17
sells: s. eternity to get a toy   SHAK 235:6
seltzer: sipped at a weak hock and s.   BETJ 20:5
semblable: mon s.,—mon frère   BAUD 16:11
semen: s. est sanguis Christianorum   TERT 256:7
seminary: Come from a ladies' s.   GILB 108:7
semper: et nunc, et s.   MASS 163:8
Sempronius: S.; we'll deserve it   ADD 1:7
senators: look at the s. and I pray   HALE 113:10
respectable s. burst with   AUDEN 10:13
send: Here am I; s. me   BIBLE 28:14

S. me not this | DONNE 88:20
senectutem: Post molestam s. | ANON 6:17
se'nnights: s. nine times nine | SHAK 220:3
sensation: Awaiting the s. of a short | GILB 108:9
sensational: It is somewhat too s. | WILDE 271:11
sense: deep s. of some deathless | WEBS 267:14
faculties, Which s. may reach | DONNE 87.27
I know my s. is mock'd | DAV 82:1
Satire or s. | POPE 184:21
Take care of the s. | CARR 63:7
without one grain of s. | DRYD 91:2
senses: If Parson lost his s. | HODG 120:4
power to touch our s. so) | MILT 168:8
sensibility: century a dissociation of s. | ELIOT 95:12
sensible: All s. people are selfish | EMER 96:7
be bold and be s. | HOR 123:3
which a s. person would | AUST 12:6
woman was *fundamentally* s. | JOHN 133:18
sensibly: things they behave s. about | SHAW 237:10
sensual: Not to the s. ear | KEATS 139:13
sentences: keep finishing your s. | LONS 153:21
sententiae: Quot homines tot s. | TER 256:4
sentiments: quiet interchange of s. | JOHN 132:22
sentinels: s. to warn th' immortal | MARL 160:17
senum: Rumoresque s. severiorum | CAT 65:5
separate: s. me from the goats | CEL 66:3
to s. us from the love | BIBLE 37:39
September: Thirty days hath S. | ANON 5:5
sepulchra: Per s. regionum | CEL 66:1
sepulchres: are like unto whited s. | BIBLE 33:31
urns and s. of mortality | CREWE 80:13
sequestra: Et ab haedis me s. | CEL 66:3
sequor: Deteriora s. | OVID 178:22
seram: 'Pone s. | JUV 137:21
seraphims: Above it stood the s. | BIBLE 28:12
serfs: With vassals and s. | BUNN 51:15
sergeant: This fell s., death | SHAK 211:20
series: great s. of lifetimes starts | VIRG 264:6
sérieuses: comme leurs plus s. actions | MONT 171:18
serious: War is much too s. a thing | CLEM 73:5
seriously: take themselves quite s. | BEER 17:20
sermon: preach a better s. | EMER 96:19
Sermons: S. and soda-water the day | BYRON 58:3
S. in stones | SHAK 204:16
sero: s. medicina paratur | OVID 178:23
serpent: be the s. under't | SHAK 220:12
last it biteth like a s. | BIBLE 26:26
s.-haunted sea | FLEC 100:7
sharper than a s.'s tooth | SHAK 218:3
way of a s. upon a rock | BIBLE 26:33
Where's my s. of old Nile | SHAK 203:19
serpents: ye therefore wise as s. | BIBLE 32:24
servant: good and faithful s. | BIBLE 34:5
Is thy s. a dog | BIBLE 25:11
s. depart in peace | BIBLE 35:4
s. of the Living God | SMART 241:15
s. to be bred at an University | CONG 76:16
s. with this clause | HERB 118:9
thou thy s. depart in peace | BIBLE 41:19
thy s. heareth | BIBLE 24:15
to become the s. of a man | SHAW 237:17
'Your s.'s cut in half | GRAH 111:9
servants: are the s. of the public | GOW 111:5
equality in the s.' hall | BARR 16:1
s. will do that for us | VILL 262:12
serv'd: s. my God with half | SHAK 215:11
serve: Fleet in which we s. | PRAY 191:9
once to s. our country | ADD 1:8
s. the Lord with gladness | PRAY 190:4

s. two masters | BIBLE 31:24
s. who only stand and wait | MILT 170:11
than s. in heav'n | MILT 168:15
wear weapons, and s. | PRAY 191:14
served: s. God as diligently | WOLS 274:5
Youth will be s. | BORR 44:23
serveth: That s. not another's will | WOTT 277:15
service: do more essential s. | SWIFT 248:18
done the state some s. | SHAK 229:15
no s. | RAC 193:18
s. of my love | SPR 245:4
soong the s. dyvyne | CHAU 68:2
Weary and old with s. | SHAK 215:9
serviettes: kiddies have crumpled the s. | BETJ 20:13
servile: man is freed from s. bands | WOTT 277:16
S. to all the skyey influences | SHAK 223:21
serving: cumbered about much s. | BIBLE 35:15
keep six honest s.-men | KIPL 144:11
serviteurs: les s. feront cela pour | VILL 262:12
servitude: base laws of s. began | DRYD 90:22
s. is at once the consequence | CURR 81:5
Sesame: Open S. | ARAB 7:13
sesquipedalia: Proicit ampullas et s. | HOR 122:14
sessions: s. of sweet silent thought | SHAK 235:12
set: But s. down This | ELIOT 94:2
if he will s. himself doggedly | JOHN 131:6
I have s. before you life | BIBLE 23:36
patience the race that is s. | BIBLE 40:9
play a s. | SHAK 213:10
setting: Hath had elsewhere its s. | WORD 275:15
time is s. with me | BURNS 54:18
settle: less will you s. to one | KIPL 144:15
seul: s. bien qui me rest au | MUSS 174:7
seven: acts being s. ages | SHAK 205:1
Jacob served s. years | BIBLE 23:1
of the deadly s. it is | SHAK 224:3
s. maids with seven mops | CARR 64:1
s. stars go squawking | AUDEN 10:8
stars in her hair were s. | ROSS 197:8
Until seventy times s. | BIBLE 33:19
Seven Dials: Of S. | GILB 107:14
sevene: world on six and s. | CHAU 68:25
seven-fold: dost thy s. gifts impart | PRAY 191:12
seventeenth: s. century a dissociation | ELIOT 95:12
seventh: opened the s. seal | BIBLE 40:34
seventy: Until s. times seven | BIBLE 33:19
Seventy-five: eighteenth of April in S. | LONG 153:8
sever: Nothing in life shall s. | CORY 78:11
then we s. | BURNS 53:18
To s. for years | BYRON 59:3
severae: procul este, s. | OVID 178:19
severity: set in with its usual s. | COL 75:11
Severn: came to Rye or out to S. | CHES 70:2
S. breeds worse men than | HOUS 126:6
thick on S. snow the leaves | HOUS 126:4
Seville: bang these dogs of S. | TENN 255:4
sewed: s. fig leaves | BIBLE 22:12
sewers: Where houses thick and s. | MILT 169:17
sewing: done nor sweeping nor s. | ANON 3:14
sex: Grex rather than s. | FROST 103:12
poor feeble s. | VICT 262:8
practically conceal its s. | NASH 174:19
s. that of loving longest | AUST 12:10
subordination of one s. | MILL 165:20
talk on 'S. and Civics | BETJ 21:2
sexes: there are three s. | SMITH 242:18
sexton: s. toll'd the bell | HOOD 124:5
Sextus: save them from false S. | MAC 156:5
shabby: tamed and s. tigers | HODG 120:4

shackles: s. of an old love straiten'd   TENN 251:20
shade: gentlemen of the s.   SHAK 212:4
　green thought in a green s.   MARV 161:16
　Sitting in a pleasant s.   BARN 15:17
　sitting in the s.   KIPL 144:3
　sly s. of a Rural Dean   BROO 47:11
　That anyway trusts her s.   KIPL 146:3
shades: field is full of s.   THOM 257:22
　lie where s. of darkness   DE L 82:10
　s. of night were falling   LONG 153:4
　S. of the prison-house   WORD 275:15
shadow: darkness and in the s. of death
　　BIBLE 34:30
　he fleeth also as a s.   BIBLE 25:24
　Life's but a walking s.   SHAK 223:15
　Like a vast s. mov'd   VAUG 261:16
　softly flits a s. and a sigh   KIPL 145:16
　valley of the s. of death   PRAY 188:16
　which his s. will be shown   NIET 176:16
　Your s. at morning striding   ELIOT 94:19
shadows: coming events cast their s.   CAMP 60:16
　If we s. have offended   SHAK 228:3
　in this kind are but s.   SHAK 227:23
　millions of strange s.   SHAK 236:1
　s. flee away   BIBLE 28:2
　s. now so long do grow   COTT 78:14
shake: also may be used to s.   BELL 18:3
　s. off the dust of your   BIBLE 32:23
　s. of his poor little head   GILB 108:18
　s. their wicked sides   YEATS 279:11
　Upon those boughs which s.   SHAK 236:5
shaken: tempests and is never s.   SHAK 236:12
Shake-scene: only S. in a country   GREE 112:18
Shakespeare: entirely as I despise S.   SHAW 237:15
　It was for gentle S. cut   JONS 136:5
　S. unlocked his heart'   BROW 49:14
　S. was of us   BROW 50:1
　S. by flashes of lightning   COL 75:12
　S. unlocked his heart   WORD 277:3
　stuff as great part of S.   GEOR 106:5
　sweetest S.   MILT 167:19
　That S. wanted Art   JONS 136:12
　tongue That S. spake   WORD 276:21
　What needs my S. for his   MILT 168:6
shaking: s., crazy   ROCH 195:17
shall: His absolute 's.'   SHAK 205:17
shallow: There s. draughts intoxicate   POPE 185:8
shallows: bound in s. and in miseries   SHAK 217:3
shame: blush of s.   WHIT 270:9
　I must keep from s.   HOUS 126:6
　is now bound in with s.   SHAK 230:2
　sense of some deathless s.   WEBS 267:14
　spirit in a waste of s.   SHAK 236:13
　To live and s. the land   HOUS 126:26
　wrought the deed of s.   MAC 156:5
shameful: s. conquest of itself   SHAK 230:2
shames: hold a candle to my s.   SHAK 225:7
shank: his shrunk s.   SHAK 205:1
shape: men in s. and fashion   ASCH 9:19
shaped: s., made aware   BROO 47:16
shapen: I was s. in wickedness   PRAY 189:5
share: greater s. of honour   SHAK 214:3
　no one so true Did s.   SHAK 234:3
　s. in two revolutions is   PAINE 179:16
　turned to s. the transport   WORD 277:4
Sharon: I am the rose of S.   BIBLE 27:26
sharp: 'Tis a s. remedy   RAL 194:7
sharper: s. than a serpent's tooth   DICK 85:11
　s. than a serpent's tooth   SHAK 218:3

shatter: Would not we s. it to bits   FITZ 99:13
shatterday: thumpsday, frightday, s.   JOYCE 136:18
Shattered: S. in shard on shard   THOM 258:5
　When the lamp is s.   SHEL 239:8
she: That not impossible s.   CRAS 80:11
　unexpressive s.   SHAK 205:3
shears: Fury with th' abhorred s.   MILT 167:20
　resembles a pair of s.   SMITH 242:19
she-bear: s. thus accosted rends   KIPL 143:20
shed: man shall his blood be s.   BIBLE 22:21
　prepare to s. them now   SHAK 216:19
shedding: s. of blood is no remission   BIBLE 40:6
sheep: found my s. which was lost   BIBLE 35:24
　from thy ways like lost s.   PRAY 186:18
　giveth his life for the s.   BIBLE 36:31
　hungry s. look up   MILT 167:21
　Let us return to our s.   ANON 6:4
　like s. have gone astray   BIBLE 29:15
　little hills like young s.   PRAY 190:12
　mountain s. are sweeter   PEAC 181:16
　of an old half-witted s.   STEP 246:2
　of s. that are even shorn   BIBLE 28:3
　s. in sheep's clothing   GOSSE 111:3
　s. on his right hand   BIBLE 34:7
　s. set me a place and separate   CEL 66:3
　to you in s.'s clothing   BIBLE 32:10
sheet: England's winding s.   BLAKE 42:19
　wet s. and a flowing sea   CUNN 81:4
sheets: cool kindliness of s.   BROO 47:6
　fumble with the s.   SHAK 213:12
shell: convolutions of a smooth-lipped s.
　　WORD 274:15
　heart is like a rainbow s.   ROSS 197:3
Shelley: Burns, S., were with us   BROW 50:1
　did you once see S. plain   BROW 50:3
　What S. shrilled   SASS 200:13
sheltered: In youth it s. me   MORR 173:12
Shepherd: call you, S.   ARN 8:19
　Dick the s.   SHAK 219:14
　feed his flock like a s.   BIBLE 29:10
　God of love my S.   HERB 118:15
　good s. giveth his life   BIBLE 36:31
　Lord is my s.   PRAY 188:15
　slighted, s.'s trade   MILT 167:20
　truth in every s.'s tongue   RAL 194:2
　weather the s. shuns   HARDY 115:1
shepherds: have both s. and butchers   VOLT 265:6
　s. abiding in the field   BIBLE 35:1
　s. watch'd their flocks   TATE 250:17
　That liberal s. give   SHAK 211:9
shew: man can s. any just cause   PRAY 187:26
　s. ourselves glad in him   PRAY 190:2
Shibboleth: Say now S.   BIBLE 24:9
shield: shall be thy s. and buckler   PRAY 189:24
shieling: From the lone s.   GALT 104:11
shift: down let me s. for my self   MORE 173:6
shillin: s.' a day   KIPL 145:14
shilling: willing to sell for one s.   LEAR 150:15
shillings: payment of half twenty s.   BURKE 52:12
shimmered: Jeeves s. out   WOD 273:11
shine: anxious for to s. in the high   GILB 108:19
　Let your light so s. before   BIBLE 31:14
　Lord make his face s.   BIBLE 23:25
　not to s. in use   TENN 255:13
shines: s. the moon in clouded   TENN 251:3
shineth: light s. in darkness   BIBLE 36:13
shining: Even to s. ones who dwell   BETJ 20:7
　I see it s. plain   HOUS 126:7
　s. Foot shall pass   FITZ 100:1

s. morning face	SHAK 205:1	longing for the further s.	VIRG 263:13
S. unto no higher end	MARV 161:19	Stops with the s.	BYRON 57:15
will flame out like s.	HOPK 121:18	**shored:** These fragments have I s.	ELIOT 95:7
ship: all I ask is a tall s.	MAS 162:19	**shoreless:** s. watery wild	ARN 8:15
idle as a painted s.	COL 74:9	**shores:** s. of darkness there is	KEATS 140:5
It was so old a s.	FLEC 100:11	s. of the Mediterranean	JOHN 132:27
s., an isle	FLEC 100:12	wilder s. of love	BLAN 44:10
s. has weather'd every	WHIT 270:1	**shore-sea:** blue or the s. green	FLEC 100:10
s. is being in a jail	JOHN 131:15	**shorn:** sheep that are even s.	BIBLE 28:3
S. of State	LONG 153:2	**short:** life so s.	HIPP 119:12
s, was still as she could	SOUT 243:19	nasty, brutish, and s.	HOBB 120:1
splendid s.	BRID 46:13	take s. views	AUDEN 11:12
'There was a s.	COL 74:6	Take s. views	SMITH 242:15
way of a s. in the midst	BIBLE 26:33	you find it wond'rous s.	GOLD 110:13
What is a s. but a prison	BURT 55:17	**shorter:** time to make it s.	PASC 181:4
ships: go down to the sea in s.	PRAY 190:8	**shot:** have s. mine arrow o'er	SHAK 211:18
launch'd a thousand s.	MARL 160:5	s. heard round the world	EMER 96:4
my s. are out of gear	TENN 255:3	S.? so quick	HOUS 126:8
s. and the foreign faces	SWIN 249:15	**shots:** of the best s.	VOLT 265:7
s., by thousands	BYRON 58:8	**shoulder:** Captain's hand on his s.	NEWB 175:15
s. sail like swans asleep	FLEC 100:9	government shall be upon his s.	BIBLE 28:19
S. that pass in the night	LONG 153:16	S. the sky	HOUS 126:16
S., towers, domes	WORD 276:18	**shoulder-blade:** left s. that is a miracle	GILB 108:12
shoes—and s.—and sealing wax	CARR 64:2	**shoulders:** dwarfs on the s. of giants	BERN 20:2
'Spanish s. of war	TENN 255:3	lawn about the s. thrown	HERR 118:18
stately s. go	TENN 251:5	loose gown from her s.	WYATT 278:4
storm-beaten s.	MAHAN 159:2	standing on the s. of giants	NEWT 176:7
We are six s. of the line	TENN 255:3	**shout:** s. for me	SHAW 238:23
shires: both the s. they ring them	HOUS 125:12	'S. with the largest	DICK 85:15
s. have seen it plain	HOUS 125:3	There was a s. about my ears	CHES 69:24
shirt: your s. and your socks	GILB 107:23	Who s. and bang and roar	BELL 19:1
shoal: bank and s. of time	SHAK 220:13	**shouted:** sons of God s. for joy	BIBLE 25:33
s. of fools for tenders	CONG 76:23	**shouting:** heavens fill with s.	TENN 253:10
shock: short, sharp s.	GILB 108:9	tumult and the s. dies	KIPL 145:10
we shall s. them	SHAK 217:16	**shouts:** cuckoo s. all day at nothing	HOUS 126:22
shock-headed: my s. victor	BETJ 21:13	He s. to scare the monster	KIPL 143:20
Than to see S. Peter	HOFF 120:12	**shovel:** limits they just s. in German	TWAIN 261:7
shocking: himself in a s. bad hat	SURT 248:14	take a large hoe and a s.	KIPL 144:13
shocks: thousand natural s.	SHAK 208:24	**show:** s. my head to the people	DANT 81:12
shoe: Edom will I cast out my s.	PRAY 189:10	s. you something different	ELIOT 94:19
I kiss his dirty s.	SHAK 213:19	To s. our simple skill	SHAK 227:20
Into a left-hand s.	CARR 64:15	**shower:** prove the sweetness of a s.	THOM 257:21
s.'s latchet I am not	BIBLE 36:17	**showers:** s. betumble the chestnut	HARDY 114:15
s. was lost	FRAN 102:11	Small s. last long	SHAK 230:1
shoes: adorns my s.	HOUS 127:4	With true-love s.	SHAK 210:27
ere those s. were old	SHAK 206:15	**Showery:** S., Flowery	ELLIS 96:1
his s. were far too tight	LEAR 150:10	**shows:** So may the outward s. be	SHAK 225:13
Put off thy s. from off	BIBLE 23:10	**shreds:** king of s. and patches	SHAK 210:18
s.—and ships—and sealing wax	CARR 64:2	thing of s. and patches	GILB 107:24
To boil eggs in your s.	LEAR 150:22	**Shropshire:** In London streets the S.	HOUS 126:6
without s. or socks	HARDY 114:13	**shroud:** My s. of white	SHAK 234:3
your s. on your feet	BIBLE 23:15	stiff dishonoured s.	ELIOT 94:17
shoe-string: careless s.	HERR 118:18	White his s. as the mountain	SHAK 210:27
shone: glory of the Lord s. round	BIBLE 35:1	**shrug:** borne it with a patient s.	SHAK 224:21
Shook: Ten Days that S. the World	REED 194:15	**shudder:** s. in the loins engenders	YEATS 279:9
shoon: night in her silver s.	DE L 82:17	**shun:** let me s. that	SHAK 218:10
shoot: I s. the Hippopotamus	BELL 18:6	**shuns:** weather the shepherd s.	HARDY 115:1
Please do not s. the pianist	ANON 4:16	**shunting:** to s. and hooting than	BURR 55:11
young idea how to s.	THOM 258:13	**shut:** beggar's shop is s.	SHAK 232:4
shooting: than to hunting and s.	BURR 55:11	s. her wild, wild eyes	KEATS 139:6
shop: back to the s. Mr John	LOCK 152:14	s. the door	POPE 184:18
beggar's s. is shut	SHAK 232:4	**shuts:** s. none out	WHIT 270:8
shopkeepers: England is a nation of s.	NAP 174:12	**shutter:** Borne before her on a s.	THAC 256:16
nation of s. are very seldom	ADAMS 1:5	**shutters:** close the s. fast	COWP 80:4
only for a nation of s.	SMITH 242:1	we'd need keep the s. up	DICK 84:15
shops: might shun the awful s.	CHES 70:7	**shuttle:** Man is the s.	VAUG 261:13
shore: By the s. of Gitche Gumee	LONG 153:12	musical s.	WHIT 270:2
high s. of this world	SHAK 213:23	**shuttlecock:** Battledore and s.'s	DICK 85:16
lights around the s.	ROSS 197:9	*Si:* S. possis recte	HOR 123:2

Sibylla: *Teste David cum S.*   CEL 65:14
sich: believe there's no s. a person   DICK 84:17
sick: cattle then are s.   KING 143:5
 half my men are s.   TENN 255:3
 have on our hands a s. man   NICH 176:9
 I am s.   NASHE 175:2
 I am s. of love   BIBLE 27:28
 I was s.   BIBLE 34:8
 kill s. people groaning   MARL 160:12
 never s. at sea   GILB 108:26
 person seldom falls s.   EMER 96:8
 s. that surfeit with too   SHAK 224:13
 They do not make me s.   WHIT 270:6
 were you not extremely s.   PRIOR 191:18
 when s. for home   KEATS 140:1
sicken: Will s. soon and die   MILT 168:9
sickening: monstrous head and s. cry CHES 69:23
sickle: bending s.'s compass come   SHAK 236:12
sickly: smiled a kind of s. smile   HARTE 115:14
sickness: in s. and in health   PRAY 187:28
 s. that destroyeth   PRAY 189:24
side: on the s. of the angels   DISR 86:18
 passed by on the other s.   BIBLE 35:13
 s. my hand and on that   SHAK 230:11
sides: shake their wicked s.   YEATS 279:11
siege: envious s. Of watery Neptune SHAK 230:2
Siesta: Englishmen detest a S.   COW 79:5
sieve: in a s. I'll thither sail   SHAK 220:2
 they went to sea in a S.   LEAR 150:11
siftings: let their liquid s. fall ELIOT 94:17
Sigh: S. no more   SHAK 228:7
 s. the lack of many a thing   SHAK 235:12
sigh'd: s. his soul toward   SHAK 226:4
sighed: I s. as a lover   GIBB 106:6
Sighing: laughter and ability and S. DICK 86:5
 plague of s. and grief   SHAK 212:12
 poor soul sat s. by a sycamore   SHAK 229:9
 Sorrow and s. shall flee   BIBLE 29:6
sighs: Spent in star-defeated s.   HOUS 125:8
sight: out of s. is out of mind   CLOU 73:18
 s. to dream   COL 74:22
 spread in the s. of any bird   BIBLE 26:3
 triple s. in blindness keen   KEATS 140:5
 years in thy s. are but as yesterday PRAY 189:21
sights: few more impressive s.   BARR 16:7
 Her s. and sounds   BROO 47:16
sign: first s. of old age   HICKS 119:6
 it's always a bad s.   MITF 171:2
 outward and visible s.   PRAY 187:22
 s. documents which they   HURST 128:9
signal: really do not see the s.   NELS 175:4
signals: fading s. and grey eternal BEER 17:17
signed: hand that s. the paper   THOM 257:5
signify: does it s. how we dress   GASK 105:3
 Nod with your hand to s.   HOUS 127:3
signiors: reverend s.   SHAK 228:17
signo: *In hoc s. vinces*   CONS 77:17
signs: s. of the times   BIBLE 33:11
Silence: Elected S., sing to me   HOPK 121:19
 eternal s. of these infinite   PASC 180:18
 ever widening slowly s. all   TENN 252:2
 In s. and tears   BYRON 59:3
 in s. with all subjection   BIBLE 39:26
 maintaining the 'conspiracy of s.'   COMTE 76:11
 me in the s. of the night   ROSS 197:4
 My gracious s., hail   SHAK 205:16
 occasional flashes of s.   SMITH 242:20
 pécher que pécher en s.   MOL 171:14
 rest is s.   SHAK 211:23

S. is the virtue of fools   BACON 12:22
s. surged softly backward   DE L 82:15
S. that dreadful bell   SHAK 228:23
Thou foster-child of s.   KEATS 139:12
to be in s.   BIBLE 39:26
was an easy step to s.   AUST 10:7
was s. in heaven about   BIBLE 40:34
silent: All s. and all damn'd   WORD 276:14
 approached unlocked her s. throat   GIBB 106:13
 Comes s.   CLOU 73:17
 impossible to be s.   BURKE 53:6
 S. and amazed even when   WHIT 269:16
 S., upon a peak in Darien   KEATS 140:4
silk: Delicate-filmed as new-spun s. HARDY 114:8
 s. stockings and white   JOHN 131:5
silks: Whenas in s. my Julia goes   HERR 119:1
silk-worm: Does the s. expend her   TOUR 259:20
siller: pinn'd it wi' a s. pin   BALL 15:5
sillier: nothing s. than a silly laugh CAT 65:8
silly: it's lovely to be s.   HOR 124:18
 wish I loved its s. face   RAL 194:10
 with such a s. question   STER 246:8
silvae: *Et paulum s. super his*   HOR 125:1
silvas: *s. Academi quaerere verum* HOR 123:7
silver: An' fill it in a s.   BURNS 54:10
 Between their s. bars   FLEC 100:12
 ever the s. cord be loosed   BIBLE 27:22
 handful of s. he left us   BROW 49:18
 night in her s. shoon   DE L 82:17
 S. and gold have I none   BIBLE 37:13
 s. apples of the moon   YEATS 279:18
 s. for the maid   KIPL 143:16
 s., ivory   BIBLE 25:3
 s. plate on a coffin   OCON 177:13
 take s. or small change   CHAM 66:16
 thirty pieces of s.   BIBLE 34:10
 When gold and s. becks   SHAK 217:9
silver-sweet: How s. sound lovers' tongues
                                       SHAK 231:21
Silv'ry: Bridge of the S. Tay   MCG 157:11
Simon Pure: real S.   CENT 66:4
simple: 'Tis ever thus with s.   GILB 109:12
simplicitas: *sancta s.*   HUSS 128:10
 sed sancta s.   JER 130:15
simplicity: holy s.   HUSS 128:10
 holy s.   JER 130:15
 Pity my s.   WESL 268:18
 s. of the three per cents   STOW 248:1
Simplify: frittered away by detail…S. THOR 259:6
sin: Be sure your s. will find   BIBLE 23:28
 Be ye angry and s. not   BIBLE 39:13
 dark world of s.   BICK 42:4
 He that is without s. among   BIBLE 36:26
 How shall I lose the s.   POPE 184:13
 I'll s. till I blow up   THOM 257:14
 it is no s.   SHAK 224:3
 my brother s. against me   BIBLE 33:19
 no s., but to be rich   SHAK 217:8
 say that we have no s.   BIBLE 40:24
 Shall we continue in s.   BIBLE 37:34
 S. is behovely   JUL 137:11
 s. no more   BIBLE 36:27
 s. to God above   THOR 259:11
 s. which doth so easily   BIBLE 40:9
 that s. fell the angels   SHAK 215:10
 then in secret s.   CHUR 70:21
 there is no s. but ignorance   MARL 160:10
 to s. in secret is not   MOL 171:14
 wages of s. is death   BIBLE 37:36

which taketh away the s.	BIBLE 36:18
Would you like to s.	ANON 5:13
Sindh: I have S.	WINK 273:4
sinecure: part of the world is no s.	BYRON 59:5
sinews: one of the s. of the soul	FULL 104:3
Stiffen the s.	SHAK 213:14
twist the s. of thy heart	BLAKE 43:8
sing: cannot s. the old songs now	CALV 59:18
charmingly sweet you s.	LEAR 150:14
come, let us s.	PRAY 190:2
Elected Silence, s. to me	HOPK 121:19
More safe I s. with mortal	MILT 169:13
Of thee I s.	SMITH 242:11
persons die before they s.	COL 74:24
Places where they s.	PRAY 186:23
S. all a green willow	SHAK 229:9
s. like birds i' the cage	SHAK 218:27
s. myself	WHIT 270·4
S., my tongue	VEN 261:19
S. no sad songs for me	ROSS 197:7
S. thy songs of happy cheer	BLAKE 43:12
S. unto the Lord a new	PRAY 188:22
S. unto the Lord a new	PRAY 190:3
S. us one of the songs	PRAY 191:1
S. whatever is well made	YEATS 280:1
Soul clap its hands and s.	YEATS 279:18
Still wouldst thou s.	KEATS 139:22
That can s. both high	SHAK 233:22
that they will s. to me	ELIOT 94:8
world in ev'ry corner s.	HERB 118:6
singeing: s. of the King of Spain's	DRAKE 90:3
Singer: sans S.	FITZ 99:3
s. not the song	ANON 5:6
S. of sweet Colonus	ARN 9:5
Thou the s.	GILB 107:11
When the s. sings them	STEV 247:13
singers: ago he was one of the s.	LEAR 150:5
singing: Everyone suddenly burst out s.	
	SASS 200:10
have heard the mermaids s.	ELIOT 94:8
me s. in the Wilderness	FITZ 98:15
nest of s. birds	JOHN 131:3
s. beneath the dome	VERL 262:4
s. in their glory move	MILT 168:3
S. of Mount Abora	·COL 75:6
s. will never be done	SASS 200:11
Singing-boys: six little S.	BARH 15:11
single: in s. blessedness	SHAK 226:12
s. in the field	WORD 275:8
s. man in possession	AUST 12:11
they come not s. spies	SHAK 211:4
sings: he s. each song twice over	BROW 49:13
motion like an angel s.	SHAK 226:5
one tell me what she s.	WORD 275:9
Singularity: S. is almost invariably	DOYLE 89:10
sink: raft which will never s.	AMES 2:9
S. me the ship	TENN 255:5
s. through the sea they	THOM 256:22
sinks: It s.	LAND 148:8
So s. the day-star	MILT 168:2
sinned: I have s. against heaven	BIBLE 35:27
s. against than sinning	SHAK 218:9
sinner: Be a s. and sin strongly	LUTH 155:11
be merciful to me a s.	BIBLE 36:5
over one s. that repenteth	BIBLE 35:25
sinners: Master with publicans and s.	BIBLE 32:18
mercy upon us miserable s.	PRAY 187:2
s. to repentance	BIBLE 32:19
thou be a breeder of s.	SHAK 209:2

we are s. all	SHAK 214:13
Why do s.' ways prosper	HOPK 122:8
sinning: sinned against than s.	SHAK 218:9
sins: Commit The oldest s.	SHAK 213:2
cover the multitude of s.	BIBLE 40:21
dark and weep for their s.	WHIT 270:6
Her s., which are many	BIBLE 35:9
'His s. were scarlet	BELL 18:21
s. and offences of my youth	PRAY 188:20
s., they are inclin'd	BUTL 56:5
Though your s. be as scarlet	BIBLE 28:6
Sint: S. ut sunt aut non sint	CLEM 73:6
Sion: one of the songs of S.	PRAY 191:1
we remembered thee, O S.	PRAY 191:1
Sirens: Blest pair of S.	MILT 167:5
Sirmio: S., bright eye of peninsulas	CAT 65:7
Sisera: courses fought against S.	BIBLE 24:5
sister: moon is my s.	BELL 18:18
s. Anne replied	PERR 182:16
To live a barren s. all	SHAK 226:12
sisters: Are s. under their skins	KIPL 145:1
Sphere-born harmonious s.	MILT 167:5
sit: dangerous to s. to Sargent	ANON 4:1
he can't S. still	MILL 166:5
'I shall s. here	CARR 62:20
let us s. upon the ground	SHAK 230:8
s. and look at it for hours	JER 130:18
S. on your arse for fifty	MACN 158:6
S. thou on my right hand	PRAY 190:10
S. thou still when kings	SCOTT 202:5
Teach us to s. still	ELIOT 93:10
them that s. in darkness	BIBLE 34:30
Though I s. down now	DISR 86:12
To s. still for once	HOFF 120:8
where men s. and hear each	KEATS 139:19
sittin: of it's s.' and thinkin'	KIPL 144:15
sitting: Are you s. comfortably	LANG 148:18
Lord s. upon a throne	BIBLE 28:12
s. in one place rather	ELIOT 93:5
s. in the shade	KIPL 144:3
situation: s. excellente	FOCH 101:6
s. excellent	FOCH 101:6
Six: S. hundred threescore and six	BIBLE 41:3
s. impossible things before	CARR 64:6
s. little Singing-boys	BARH 15:11
S. o'clock	ELIOT 94:15
s. of one and half-a-dozen	MARR 161:7
world on s. and sevene	CHAU 68:25
six hundred: Rode the s.	TENN 251:8
sixte: Welcome the s.	CHAU 68:16
sixth: s. age shifts	SHAK 205:1
sixty: are s. different religions	CAR 61:3
s. seconds' worth of distance	KIPL 144:9
skating: In s. over thin ice	EMER 96:14
sketch: s. the ruins of St Paul's	MAC 156:17
skies: common people of the s.	WOTT 277:18
look up at the s.	HOPK 122:7
some watcher of the s.	KEATS 140:4
skill: parson own'd his s.	GOLD 110:10
skin: Ethiopian change his s.	BIBLE 29:26
skull beneath the s.	ELIOT 95:8
throws her enamell'd s.	SHAK 227:5
with the s. of my teeth	BIBLE 25:26
skinny: holds him with his s. hand	COL 74:6
I fear thy s. hand	COL 74:13
skins: beauty of their s.	TENN 254:12
sisters under their s.	KIPL 145:1
skipped: mountains s. like rams	PRAY 190:12
skipper: s. had taken his little	LONG 153:19

Sklaven-Moral: *Herren-Moral und S.* NIET 177:2
Skugg: Here S. Lies snug FRAN 102:14
skull: s. beneath the skin ELIOT 95:8
sky: bear him up the Norfolk s. BETJ 20:9
clear blue s. over my head HAZL 116:5
inverted Bowl we call The S. FITZ 99:10
night rides down the s. FIEL 98:11
shoulders held the s. suspended HOUS 126:20
Shoulder the s. HOUS 126:16
s. changes when they are SHAK 205:10
s. grows darker yet CHES 69:19
s. is darkening like AUDEN 11:13
to lose itself in the s. BROW 48:19
watched the ocean and the s. SHEL 239:7
wide and starry s. STEV 247:16
You'll get pie in the s. HILL 119:8
slacks: girls in s. remember Dad BETJ 20:7
slain: beauty of Israel is s. BIBLE 24:25
ere thou hast s. another BROW 48:14
I am s. by a fair cruel SHAK 234:3
if the s. think he is slain EMER 96:3
jaw of an ass have I s. BIBLE 24:12
shall himself be s. MAC 156:12
s. in thine high places BIBLE 24:27
slander: Fear not s. SHAK 206:4
slandering: lying, and s. PRAY 187:20
slaughter: brought as a lamb to the s. BIBLE 29:16
out threatenings and s. BIBLE 37:15
ox goeth to the s. BIBLE 26:10
slaughter'd: 'ye have s. and made NEWB 175:17
slaughtered: thy s. saints MILT 170:9
slave: Being your s. SHAK 236:3
fingering s. WORD 276:5
half s. and half free LINC 151:17
soundly as the wretched s. SHAK 213:23
very s. of circumstance BYRON 58:20
would have made him a s. BURKE 52:12
you were a Christian S. HENL 117:9
slaverie: Chains and s. BURNS 54:20
slavery: classified as s. CHUR 71:1
state is a state of S. GILL 109:13
slaves: Britons never will be s. THOM 258:12
inevitably two kinds of s. ILL 129:11
too pure an Air for S. ANON 4:15
wholly s. or wholly free DRYD 91:4
slayer: priest who slew the s. MAC 156:12
red s. think he slays EMER 96:3
slays: red slayer think he s. EMER 96:3
s. A thousand LAND 148:9
War its thousands s. PORT 186:3
sleek: s. and shining creatures TENN 254:12
Sleek-headed: S. men and such as sleep SHAK 215:17
sleekit: s., cow'rin' BURNS 55:5
sleep: Can s. so soundly SHAK 213:23
come to the borders of s. THOM 257:19
deep s. to fall upon Adam BIBLE 22:9
Do I wake or s. KEATS 140:1
dreamless, uninvaded s. TENN 252:27
first sweet s. of night SHEL 239:6
folding of the hands to s. BIBLE 26:9
From rest and s. DONNE 88:3
gray and full of s. YEATS 280:5
ideas s. furiously CHOM 70:16
inhibitions and get some s. LOOS 154:3
In s. a king SHAK 236:6
in soot I s. BLAKE 43:17
keepeth thee will not s. PRAY 190:16
life Is rounded with a s. SHAK 232:24

Macbeth does murder s. SHAK 221:16
Macbeth shall s. no more SHAK 221:17
miles to go before I s. FROST 103:10
nose-painting, s., and urine SHAK 222:3
Now I lay me down to s. ANON 4:11
One short s. past DONNE 88:4
poor alike to s. under bridges FRAN 102:5
Sleek-headed men and such as s. SHAK 215:17
S. after toil SPEN 244:16
s. and a forgetting WORD 275:15
s. and a sweet dream when MAS 163:2
S. is sweet to the labouring BUNY 51:23
S.! it is a gentle thing COL 74:16
'S. no more SHAK 221:16
s. of a labouring man is BIBLE 27:8
s. one ever-during night CAT 65:5
S., pretty wantons DEKK 82:7
S. shall neither night SHAK 220:3
S. to wake BROW 48:22
S. will come when thou SHEL 240:7
Sword s. in my hand BLAKE 43:2
them they are even as a s. PRAY 189:21
There'll be time enough to s. HOUS 125:5
To die: to s. SHAK 208:24
to s. at a bank from ten JER 130:17
We shall not all s. BIBLE 38:22
We shall not s. MCCR 157:9
while some must s. SHAK 210:6
would not s. with the brave HOUS 126:15
Sleepers: snorted we in the Seven S. DONNE 88:1
sleepeth: maid is not dead, but s. BIBLE 32:22
sleepin': art tha s. there below NEWB 175:14
sleeping: Lay your s. head AUDEN 11:3
s. and the dead Are SHAK 221:18
wakened us from s. BROO 47:15
sleeps: dines he s. SURT 248:11
moon s. with Endymion SHAK 226:9
Now s. the crimson petal TENN 254:14
s. the pride of former MOORE 172:14
s. up in the attic there MEW 165:13
That broods and s. on his WORD 276:6
sleepwalker: with the assurance of a s. HITL 119:14
sleeve: wear my heart upon my s. SHAK 228:14
sleeves: Tie up my s. with ribbons HUNT 128:8
sleight: more th' admire his s. BUTL 56:8
slept: firstfruits of them that s. BIBLE 38:18
while their companions s. LONG 153:6
slepyng: s. hound to wake CHAU 68:23
slew: I s. him SHAK 216:14
slice: matter how thin you s. it SMITH 242:5
slime: slimier s. BROO 47:9
slimier: s. slime BROO 47:9
slimy: s. things did crawl with COL 74:10
thousand thousand s. things COL 74:15
slings: s. and arrows of outrageous SHAK 208:24
slip: caused his chest to s. WOD 273:14
Since he gave us all the s. BROW 50:24
s. Into my bosom TENN 254:16
Slit: S. your girl's KING 143:3
slits: s. the thin-spun life MILT 167:20
Sloane Square: S. and South Kensington GILB 107:22
slog: foot—s.—slog KIPL 143:13
slop: Raineth drop and staineth s. POUND 186:6
slopes: on the butler's upper s. WOD 273:14
slothful: s. man saith BIBLE 26:31
Slouches: S. towards Bethlehem YEATS 279:16
Slough: bombs, and fall on S. BETJ 21:12

name of the s. was Despond	BUNY 51:17
slovenliness: s. is no part of religion	WESL 268:19
slow: clock is always s.	SERV 203:7
sloeblack, s., black, crowblack	THOM 257:9
s., fresh fount	JONS 135:18
To point his s. and moving	SHAK 229:8
slowly: Make haste s.	SUET 248:7
sluggard: Go to the ant thou s.	BIBLE 26:8
'Tis the voice of the s.	WATTS 266:18
slug-horn: Dauntless the s. to my	BROW 49:8
sluicing: excellent browsing and s	WOD 272:16
Slumber: Ere S.'s chain has bound	MOORE 173:4
little sleep, a little s.	BIBLE 26:9
shall neither s. not sleep	PRAY 190:16
s. did my spirit seal	WORD 276:17
slumber'd: That you have but s. here	SHAK 228:3
slumbers: Golden s. kiss your eyes	DEKK 82:7
sluts: foul s. in dairies	CORB 78:3
sly: s., ensnaring art	BURNS 54:3
small: arms long and s.	WYATT 278:4
creatures great and s.	ALEX 2:3
S. is beautiful	SCH 201:5
s. Latin, and less Greek	JONS 136:6
s. things from the peak	CHES 70:9
squadrons against the s.	BUSS 56:1
still s. voice	BIBLE 25:6
smaller: flea Hath s. fleas	SWIFT 249:12
smattering: s. of everything	DICK 85:28
smell: I s. a rat	ROCHE 195:12
Money has no s.	VESP 262:5
s. and hideous hum	GODL 109:19
s. of bread and butter	BYRON 57:5
s. of fish there is sometimes	KILV 142:4
s. of the blood still	SHAK 223:8
s. the blood of a British	SHAK 218:15
s. too strong of the lamp	STER 246:9
sweet keen s.	ROSS 197:9
smelleth: he s. the battle afar off	BIBLE 25:34
smells: dead thing that s. sweet	THOM 257:17
it s. of mortality	SHAK 218:21
it s. to heaven	SHAK 210:11
smile: betwixt that s. we would	SHAK 215:9
Let me s. with the wise	JOHN 132:12
s., and be a villain	SHAK 207:17
S. at us	CHES 70:6
smiled a kind of sickly s.	HARTE 115:14
s. upon his fingers' ends	SHAK 213:12
we shall s.	SHAK 217:5
When you call me that, *s.*	WIST 273:5
Where my Julia's lips do s.	HERR 118:17
you should forget and s.	ROSS 197:6
smiles: charmed it with s. and soap	CARR 62:8
corner of the world s.	HOR 124:2
Seldom he s.	SHAK 216:1
S. awake you when you rise	DEKK 82:7
There's daggers in men's s.	SHAK 222:10
wreathed s.	MILT 167:16
smilest: Thou s. and art still	ARN 9:1
Smiling: S. at grief	SHAK 234:4
S. the boy fell dead	BROW 49:16
smite: s. thee on thy right cheek	BIBLE 31:17
Stands ready to s. once	MILT 167:21
Star-spiked Rails a fiery S.	THOM 258:8
smith: s., a mighty man is he	LONG 153:17
smoke: bravery in their rotten s.	SHAK 235:15
coaster with a salt-caked s.	MAS 162:15
counties overhung with s.	MORR 173:14
light emerging from the s.	HOR 122:16
Only thin s. without flame	HARDY 114:11

smokeless: glittering in the s. air	WORD 276:18
smooth: I am a s. man	BIBLE 22:29
neat knave with a s. tale	WEBS 267:7
To s. the ice	SHAK 217:12
true love never did run s.	SHAK 226:13
smote: s. the king of Israel between	BIBLE 25:9
s. them hip and thigh	BIBLE 24:11
smylere: s. with the knyf under	CHAU 68:9
snaffle: use the s. and the curb	CAMP 60:13
snail: creeping like s.	SHAK 205:1
in snay paced) this s.	DONNE 88:10
said a whiting to a s.	CARR 63:10
s.'s on the thorn	BROW 50:12
Worm nor s.	SHAK 227:7
snails: Like s. did creep	HERR 118:24
snake: earth doth like a s. renew	SHEL 239:4
like a wounded s.	POPE 185:10
a. hidden in the grass	VIRG 264:5
there the s. throws her	SHAK 227:5
We have scotch'd the s.	SHAK 222:12
snakes: There are no s. to be met	JOHN 133:7
You spotted s. with double	SHAK 227:6
snapper-up: s. of unconsidered trifles	SHAK 234:22
snare: delusion, a mockery, and a s.	DENM 82:18
Snark: If your S. be a Boojum	CARR 62:7
S. *was* a Boojum	CARR 62:9
snatch: s. a fearful joy	GRAY 112:9
sneaking: petty s. knave I knew	BLAKE 43:4
sneer: flinch and traitors s.	CONN 77:4
teach the rest to s.	POPE 184:20
Who can refute a s.	PALEY 179:18
sneering: I was born s.	GILB 108:1
sneezed: Not to be s.	COLM 76:4
sneezes: beat him when he s.	CARR 62:22
snicker-snack: vorpal blade went s.	CARR 63:17
sniffs: tiger s. the rose	SASS 200:14
snorted: s. we in the Seven Sleepers	DONNE 88:1
snot: s.green sea	JOYCE 137:3
snow: asleep the s. came flying	BRID 46:12
cherry hung with s.	HOUS 125:4
fall o' the s.	JONS 136:9
garment was white as s.	BIBLE 30:11
shall be as white as s.	BIBLE 28:6
shall be whiter than s.	PRAY 189:6
sit brooding in the s.	SHAK 219:14
s. disfigured the public	AUDEN 10:15
s. in May's new-fangled	SHAK 219:8
S. on snow	ROSS 197:5
wondrous strange s.	SHAK 227:19
snows: are the s. of yesteryear	VILL 262:13
s. have dispersed	HOR 124:15
Snowy: S., Flowy	ELLIS 96:1
snub: has a s. nose like to mine	BLAKE 42:20
snuff'd: be s. out by an article	BYRON 58:12
snug: Here Skugg Lies s.	FRAN 102:14
what a s. little Island	DIBD 83:11
so: s. to bed	PEPYS 182:7
soap: charmed it with smiles and s.	CARR 62:8
I used your s. two years	PUNCH 192:20
soaping: s. her breasts in the bath	EWART 97:7
soared: He has out-s. the shadow	SHEL 238:26
sobbed: He s. and cursed and kicked	MILL 166:7
sober: Be s., be vigilant	BIBLE 40:22
once saw Porson s.	HOUS 127:8
Philip drunk to Philip s.	ANON 3:4
righteous, and s. life	PRAY 186:20
Their s. wishes never learn'd	GRAY 112:6
woman s.	PEPYS 182:9
sobs: s. of the violins	VERL 262:2

social: man into the s. masonry WELLS 268:16
S. Contract is nothing WELLS 268:16
socialist: proceed to construct the s. LEE 151:5
société: homme moins propre à la s. CHAM 66:16
societies: solemn troops and sweet s. MILT 168:3
society: first duty to serve s. JOHN 132:10
In the affluent s. no useful GALB 104:9
no s. HOBB 120:1
often unfit a man for s. CHAM 66:16
Our s. distributes itself ARN 9:6
socks: your shirt and your s. GILB 107:23
Socrates: difficulty contradict S. PLATO 183:15
S. commits a crime by corrupting PLATO 183:14
sod: high requiem become a s. KEATS 139:22
soda-water: Sermons and s. the day BYRON 58:3
wash their feet in s. ELIOT 95:3
sodden: That are s. and unkind BELL 19:7
Sodium: Of having discovered S. BENT 19:18
sodomy: rum, s. and the lash CHUR 71:21
sods: s. with our bayonets turning WOLFE 273:20
sofa: wheel the s. round COWP 80:4
soft: I own the s. impeachment SHER 240:22
seson whan s. was the sonne LANG 149:2
s. answer turneth away BIBLE 26:19
s. as young YOUNG 280:9
S. morning, city JOYCE 136:20
so white! O so s. JONS 136:9
softer: s. pillow than my heart BYRON 59:4
softly: s. and suddenly vanish CARR 62:7
softness: s. of my body will be guarded LOW 154:14
s. she and sweet attractive MILT 169:7
soger: s. frae the wars returns BURNS 54:11
soi: c'est de savoir être à s. MONT 172:3
soil: Before the s. hath smutch'd JONS 136:9
soixante: s. sectes religieuses différentes CAR 61:3
sold: book which somehow s. well BOOR 44:19
s. a goodly manor SHAK 203:15
s. his birthright unto BIBLE 22:28
s. my Reputation FITZ 99:11
sparrows s. for a farthing BIBLE 32:25
sparrows s. for two farthings BIBLE 35:19
stocks were s. BELL 18:13
Then spoils were fairly s. MAC 156:7
Soldan: S. of Byzantium is smiling CHES 69:26
soldats: capitaine de vingt-quatre s. ANON 5:18
soldier: 'A s. STER 246:12
Ben Battle was a s. bold HOOD 121:5
British s. can stand up SHAW 237:12
not tell us what the s. DICK 85:21
s., and afeard SHAK 223:6
s., Full of strange oaths SHAK 205:1
s. is flat blasphemy SHAK 223:19
S. of the Great War Known KIPL 146:28
s.'s life is terrible hard MILNE 166:11
s.'s pole is fall'n SHAK 204:6
summer s. and the sunshine PAINE 179:15
tell an old s. SHAW 237:8
soldiers: God and s. we alike adore QUAR 193:8
having s. under me BIBLE 32:14
if you believe the s. SAL 199:7
Now the s. he smiled SASS 200:12
our s. slighted QUAR 193:8
S. who wish to be a hero ROST 197:13
steel my s.' hearts SHAK 214:1
They mustered their s. BALL 14:18
soldiery: rapacious and licentious s. BURKE 53:4
sole: absolute s. Lord CRAS 80:8
nothing can be s. or whole YEATS 278:15
soleil: rien que le s. qui poudroye PERR 182:16

s. *noir de la* mélancolie NERV 175:11
Soles: S. occidere et redire possunt CAT 65:5
soliciting: This supernatural s. SHAK 220:7
solitary: Be not s. BURT 55:21
s., be not idle JOHN 133:13
Through Eden took their s. MILT 169:22
till I am s. JOHN 131:9
Yon s. Highland lass WORD 275:8
solitude: He makes a s. BYRON 57:6
s. or the quality of his CONN 77:10
Which is the bliss of s. WORD 275:4
solitudes: that two s. protect RILKE 195:6
Solitudinem: S. faciunt pacem appellant TAC 250:8
Solomon: 'in the Proverbs of S. DICK 84:7
S. in all his glory was BIBLE 31:25
solum: nec minus s. quam cum solus CIC 72:9
solution: people were a kind of s. CAV 65:12
Solutus: S. omni faenore HOR 123:9
some: s. are fond of fiddles MAS 162:17
S. have meat and cannot BURNS 54:13
s. must watch SHAK 210:6
somebodee: When every one is s. GILB 107:9
somebody: happen to s. else MARQ 161:4
someone: morning that it was s. else ROG 196:2
yourself necessary to s. EMER 96:6
somer: s. seson whan soft was LANG 149:2
Somerset House: aphorism in the records of S. BIRK 42:7
something: Everything must be like s. FORS 101:12
's. for Posterity ADD 1:15
S. is going to fall like AUDEN 11:13
S. must be done EDW 92:10
S. nasty in the woodshed GIBB 106:14
Time for a little s. MILNE 167:2
sometime: that s. did me seek WYATT 278:3
sometimes: I have s. wept MUSS 174:7
somewhat: More than s. RUNY 198:5
somewhere: you want to get s. else CARR 63:20
son: bare-legg'd beggarly s. of a gun CALV 60:1
bear a s. BIBLE 28:16
behold thy s. BIBLE 37:7
day leichter of a fair s. ELIZ 95:14
Fhairshon had a s. AYT 12:18
forth her firstborn s. BIBLE 35:1
gave him only begotten S. BIBLE 36:21
rod hateth his s. BIBLE 26:18
s. of a first rate butcher ASHF 9:21
s. of a hundred Kings KIPL 143:8
S. of man hath not where BIBLE 32:16
This is my beloved S. BIBLE 31:7
This my s. was dead BIBLE 35:29
two-legged thing, a s. DRYD 90:14
unto us a s. is given BIBLE 28:19
whom if his s. ask bread BIBLE 32:6
wise s. maketh a glad BIBLE 26:12
worthy to be called thy s. BIBLE 35:27
song: Give ear unto my s. GOLD 110:13
goodly manor for a s. SHAK 203:15
have I to spur me into s. YEATS 279:19
his presence with a s. PRAY 190:4
if such holy s. MILT 168:9
Is the burden of my s. ANON 4:4
I the s. GILB 107:11
my Reputation for a S. FITZ 99:11
One grand sweet s. KING 142:9
'Pipe a s. about a Lamb BLAKE 43:12
required of us then a s. PRAY 191:1
sans S. FITZ 99:3
s. as a weasel sucks SHAK 204:20

s. the Syrens sang — BROW 48:12
s. was wordless — SASS 200:11
s. well sung — MAS 162:17
That is the s. that never — GOE 109:22
there's ane end of ane old s. — OGIL 177:12
this the burthen of his s. — BICK 42:2
unto the Lord a new s. — PRAY 188:22
unto the Lord a new s. — PRAY 190:3
songs: all their s. are sad — CHES 69:20
cannot sing the old s. — CALV 59:18
cannot sing the old s. — CLAR 73:1
Fair the fall of s. — STEV 247:13
harsh after the s. of Apollo — SHAK 219:15
I wrote my happy s. — BLAKE 43:13
Piping s. of pleasant glee — BLAKE 43:12
Sing no sad s. for me — ROSS 197:7
s. never heard before — HOR 124:5
Their lean and flashy s. — MILT 167:21
them fruit for their s. — ADD 1:13
us one of the s. of Sion — PRAY 191:1
Where are the s. of Spring — KEATS 140:14
sonitu: s. quatit ungula campum — VIRG 264:1
sonne: seson whan soft was the s. — LANG 149:2
unseren Platz an der S. — BULOW 51:9
Sonnet: Scorn not the S. — WORD 277:3
sons: God's s. are things — MADD 158:13
s. and your daughters shall — BIBLE 30:14
s. of God shouted for joy — BIBLE 25:33
Their s., they gave — BROO 47:5
things the s. of heaven — JOHN 134:15
soon: Come s., soon — SHEL 240:7
sooner: s. every party breaks up — AUST 11:23
soong: s. the service dyvyne — CHAU 68:2
soot: in s. I sleep — BLAKE 43:17
sooth: charms to s. a savage breast — CONG 76:18
sophistry: nothing but s. and illusion — HUME 127:17
Sordello: can but be the one 'S.' — POUND 186:7
sore: bear with a s. head — MARR 161:5
s. throats are always worse — AUST 12:9
sorrow: hairs with s. to the grave — BIBLE 23:6
In s. thou shalt bring — BIBLE 22:13
knowledge increaseth s. — BIBLE 27:5
Lycidas your s. is not dead — MILT 168:2
memory a rooted s. — SHAK 223:13
more in s. than in anger — SHAK 207:4
not be in s. too — BLAKE 43:20
Nought but vast s. was there — DE L 82:12
parting is such sweet s. — SHAK 231:22
S. and sighing shall flee — BIBLE 29:6
sorrow like unto my s. — BIBLE 29:28
s. than to recall a time — DANTE 81:10
That a s.'s crown of sorrow — TENN 253:9
then but labour and s. — PRAY 189:22
Write s. on the bosom — SHAK 230:7
sorrowing: was standing the s. Mother — JAC 129:18
sorrows: carried our s. — BIBLE 29:14
Half the s. of women — ELIOT 92:18
losses are restor'd and s. — SHAK 235:3
man of s. — BIBLE 29:14
shall my s. have an end — ANON 3:16
s. of your changing face — YEATS 280:5
When s. come — SHAK 211:4
sorry: s., now, I wrote it — BURG 52:6
s. Scheme of Things — FITZ 99:13
Very s. can't come — BER 19:22
sort: all the s. of person you — CARL 61:6
is a s. of treason — BURKE 52:19
see a s. of traitors here — SHAK 230:13
s. of thing they like — LINC 152:4

sorts: s. and conditions of men — PRAY 187:4
sothfastnesse: dwelle with s. — CHAU 68:29
sought: lack of many a thing I s. — SHAK 235:12
s. the Lord aright — BURNS 54:2
They s. it with thimbles — CARR 62:8
soul: am the captain of my s. — HENL 117:5
art pouring forth thy s. — KEATS 139:22
call upon my s. within — SHAK 233:20
fool, this night thy s. — BIBLE 35:20
Heaven take my s. — SHAK 217:14
he shall save his s. alive — BIBLE 30:3
hushed Casket of my S. — KEATS 140:8
if I have a s. — ANON 4:13
iron entered into his s. — PRAY 190:6
lift my s. to heaven — SHAK 215:5
lose his own s. — BIBLE 33:14
man loved the pilgrim s. — YEATS 280:5
My s. he doth restore again — SCOT 202:15
My s. in agony — COL 74:14
my s. is white — BLAKE 43:15
my unconquerable s. — HENL 117:6
night of the s. it is always three o'clock — FITZ 100:2
No coward s. is mine — BRON 47:2
of the sinews of the s. — FULL 104:3
Perdition catch my s. — SHAK 228:26
Poor intricated s. — DONNE 89:4
pray the Lord my s. to keep — ANON 4:11
pray the Lord my s. to take — ANON 4:11
reason and the flow of s. — POPE 185:20
Rest of their bones and s.'s — DONNE 88:3
sigh'd his s. toward — SHAK 226:4
so longeth my s. after — PRAY 189:1
S. clap its hands and sing — YEATS 279:13
s. doth magnify the Lord — BIBLE 34:28
s. is dead that slumbers — LONG 153:9
s. of our dear brother — PRAY 188:5
S. that rises with us — WORD 275:15
subject's s. is his own — SHAK 213:22
taught my s. to fancy aught — VAUG 261:14
They had stolen my s. away — TURN 260:20
two to bear my s. away — ANON 4:6
Was not spoken of the s. — LONG 153:9
waters to a thirsty s. — BIBLE 26:28
yet my s. drew back — HERB 118:11
souls: damp s. of housemaids — ELIOT 94:10
harmony is in immortal s. — SHAK 226:5
Have ye s. in heaven too — KEATS 139:11
letters mingle s. — DONNE 88:9
nor s. to be condemned — THUR 259:15
patience possess ye your s. — BIBLE 36:6
s. descend T'affections — DONNE 87:27
S. of poets dead and gone — KEATS 139:10
s. with but a single thought — HALM 114:5
they have no s. — COKE 74:4
times that try men's s. — PAINE 179:15
sound: full of s. and fury — SHAK 223:15
Like the s. of a great Amen — PROC 191:21
mind in a s. body — JUV 138:5
My love to thee is s. — SHAK 219:11
sighing s. — ROSS 197:9
something direful in the s. — AUST 11:24
s. and rumour — MORR 173:13
s. of broken glass — BELL 19:6
s. of revelry by night — BYRON 57:9
that s. awakes my woes — BURNS 54:6
you would s. me from my — SHAK 210:7
sounded: trumpets s. for him — BUNY 52:5
sounding: I am become as s. brass — BIBLE 38:14
soundless: tears on a s.-clapping host — THOM 257:22

sounds: Her sights and s. | BROO 47:16
let the s. of music | SHAK 226:5
S. and sweet airs | SHAK 232:22
s. will take care of themselves | CARR 63:7
with concord of sweet s. | SHAK 226:7
Soup: S. of the evening | CARR 63:14
take the nasty s. away | HOFF 120:7
sour: fathers have eaten s. grapes | BIBLE 30:4
s., sober beverage | BYRON 58:4
source: life's first native s. | SPEN 244:20
Lord is the s. of my light | BIBLE 41:11
Variety's the s. of joy | GAY 105:21
sourest: things turn s. by their deeds | SHAK 236:7
South: beaker full of the warm S. | KEATS 139:19
fierce and fickle is the S. | TENN 254:11
nor yet from the s. | PRAY 189:15
South Africa: S., renowned both far | CAMP 60:14
South Country: great hills of the S. | BELL 19:7
southern: bore me in the s. wild | BLAKE 43:15
South Kensington: at Sloane Square and S. | GILB 107:22
Southron: matches of the S. folk | THOM 257:22
south-wind: world-wide whisper of the s. | TENN 253:10
Sovereign: S. has | BAG 14:7
Soviet: Communism is S. power plus | LEE 151:7
sow: Ireland is the old s. that | JOYCE 137:1
S. an act | READE 194:13
soweth: whatsoever a man s. | BIBLE 39:9
sown: nor was ever s. | TRAH 259:21
They have s. the wind | BIBLE 30:12
space: myself a king of infinite s. | SHAK 208:13
spade: boldly nominate a s. | JONS 136:4
cultivated entirely by the s. | MILL 165:19
s. is never so merely | FRY 103:21
S.! with which Wilkinson | WORD 277:12
Spades: S. take up leaves | FROST 103:4
Spain: not into the hands of S. | TENN 255:5
spak: Frenssh she s. ful faire | CHAU 68:2
span: Contract into a s. | HERB 118:14
life's a pain and but a s. | DAV 82:1
Spaniards: to thrash the S. too | DRAKE 90:2
Spanish: some are fond of S. wine | MAS 162:16
'S. ships of war | TENN 255:3
To God I speak S. | CHAR 67:15
spans: narrow measure s. | HOUS 126:23
spare: s. bed for my friends | PEPYS 182:12
s. that tree | MORR 173:12
s. the beechen tree | CAMP 60:15
S. their women for Thy | BETJ 21:4
s. time and in his working | GILL 109:13
s. your country's flag | WHIT 270:9
to s. those who have submitted | VIRG 263:14
spared: honour and life have been s. | FRAN 102:6
spares: man that s. these stones | SHAK 237:5
spareth: s. his rod hateth | BIBLE 26:18
spark: s. of inextinguishable | SHEL 240:9
waitest for the s. from heaven | ARN 8:21
sparkle: s. out among the fern | TENN 251:6
sparks: s. fly upward | BIBLE 25:21
sparrow: Lesbia with her s. | MILL 166:8
My lady's s. is dead | CAT 65:4
providence in the fall of a s. | SHAK 211:17
s. hath found her an house | PRAY 189:17
sparrows: s. sold for a farthing | BIBLE 32:25
s. sold for two farthings | BIBLE 35:19
Spartan: remnant of our S. dead | BYRON 58:10
Spartans: praiseworthy amongst the S. | SPEN 244:8
S. on the sea-wet rock | HOUS 126:19

tell the S. | SIM 241:9
spat: you s. on me Wednesday | SHAK 225:1
spawn'd: Some report a sea-maid s. | SHAK 224:6
Spayne: make castels thanne in S. | CHAU 68:21
speak: did he stop and s. to you | BROW 50:3
duty to s. one's mind | WILDE 271:13
'Is that it cannot s. | CARR 62:11
let him now s. | PRAY 187:26
'Let us not s. | BETJ 21:3
Nation shall s. peace | REND 194:18
neither s. they through | PRAY 190:13
one that can s. so well | MASS 164:4
s. in Caesar's funeral | SHAK 216:16
S., Lord | BIBLE 24:15
S. low, if you speak love | SHAK 228:5
S. not when the people | SCOTT 202:5
S. roughly to your little | CARR 62:22
'S. softly and carry a big | RONS 196:13
S. the speech | SHAK 209:7
s. when he is spoken | STEV 247:7
'S. when you're spoken | CARR 64:16
S. ye comfortably to Jerusalem | BIBLE 29:8
that dare not s. its name | DOUG 89:5
they s. with their enemies | PRAY 190:20
Whereof one cannot s. | WITT 273:10
which it is difficult to s. | BURKE 53:6
speaketh: he s. of his own | BIBLE 36:29
speaks: her foot s. | SHAK 233:11
He s. to Me as if I was | VICT 262:1
spear: Bring me my s. | BLAKE 43:2
spears: their s. into pruninghooks | BIBLE 28:7
their s. was like stars | BYRON 57:16
your pruninghooks into s. | BIBLE 30:15
speciality: short notice was her s. | SAKI 199:3
species: female of the s. is more | KIPL 143:20
spectacles: With s. on nose and pouch | SHAK 205:1
spectare: magnum alterius s. laborem | LUCR 155:6
Spectat: S. et audit | CAT 65:9
spectator: s. of mankind than as one | ADD 1:10
spectre: s. of Communism | MARX 162:3
speech: aspersion upon my parts of s. | SHER 240:18
freedom of s. and expression | RONS 196:12
freedom of s. | TWAIN 261:2
have strange power of s. | COL 74:19
make a s. | AUBR 10:6
manner of his s. | SHAK 203:21
Speak the s. | SHAK 209:7
s. they have resolved not | ELIOT 92:18
thy s. is comely | BIBLE 28:3
speed: Deliberate s. | THOM 258:2
our safety is in our s. | EMER 96:14
S. his plough | CHAP 67:7
s. the going guest | POPE 185:21
s. the parting guest | POPE 185:22
s. was far faster than | BULL 51:8
spell: foreigners always s. better | TWAIN 261:4
Who lies beneath your s. | HOPE 121:16
with the s. of far Arabia | DE L 82:9
spend: most of what we yet may s. | FITZ 99:3
whatever you have, s. less | JOHN 133:20
spending: Getting and s. | WORD 277:7
*SPERANZA: LASCIATE OGNI S. VOI CH'EN-
TRATE* | DANTE 81:8
spet: s. upon my Jewish gabardine | SHAK 224:21
sphere: these walls thy s. | DONNE 88:19
spheres: Driv'n by the s. | VAUG 261:16
spherical: His body is perfectly s. | LEAR 150:6
Sphinx: Although a subtler S. renew | SHEL 239:5
spice: Variety's the very s. of life | COWP 80:1

spices: land of s.	HERB 118:13
spider: said a s. to a fly	HOW 127:11
spiders: Weaving s. come not here	SHAK 227:7
spin: neither do they s.	BIBLE 31:25
spinis: *iuvat s. de pluribus una*	HOR 123:8
spinners: Hence you long-legg'd s.	SHAK 227:7
spinning: candle-light at evening s.	RONS 196:6
spires: City with her dreaming s.	ARN 9:3
Ye distant s.	GRAY 112:8
spirit: Blessed are the poor in s.	BIBLE 31:11
cabin'd ample S.	ARN 8:18
great s. gone	SHAK 203:18
Hail to thee, blithe S.	SHEL 240:4
hands I commend my s.	BIBLE 36:11
haughty s. before a fall	BIBLE 26:22
motions of his s. are dull	SHAK 226:7
never approached my s.	METT 165:11
no s. can walk abroad	SHAK 206:9
of God is a troubled s.	PRAY 189:7
Pipe to the s. ditties	KEATS 139:13
slumber did my s. seal	WORD 276:17
s. giveth life	BIBLE 39:2
s. hath rejoiced in God	BIBLE 34:28
s. indeed is willing	BIBLE 34:15
S. of Delight	SHEL 239:18
s. of youth in everything	SHAK 236:9
s. shall return unto God	BIBLE 27:22
stab my s. broad awake	STEV 247:17
there is a s. in the woods	WORD 275:12
vanity and vexation of s.	BIBLE 27:4
whether a good s. or a bad	AUBR 10:7
yet a s. still	WORD 276:16
spirits: choice and master s.	SHAK 216:10
her wanton s. look out	SHAK 233:11
I can call s. from	SHAK 212:13
S. overwrought	WORD 276:8
spiritu: *Et cum s. tuo*	MASS 163:6
spiritual: inward and s. grace	PRAY 187:22
s. wickedness in high places	BIBLE 39:15
spirituality: There is a s. about the face	
	DOYLE 89:20
Spiritus: *Sancte S.*	LANG 149:3
spite: beating myself for s.	SIDN 241:5
s. of all their friends	LEAR 150:12
Spitzbübin: *S. war sie*	HEINE 116:13
splendeat: *Purpureus, late qui s.*	HOR 122:12
splendid: s. in ashes	BROW 48:13
s. ship	BRID 46:13
Splendide: *S. mendax et in omne virgo*	HOR 124:9
splendour: more-than-oriental-s.	KIPL 146:14
Of s. in the grass	WORD 275:16
s. falls on castle walls	TENN 254:9
s. of Ionian white	ELIOT 95:5
split: an' 'E won't s. on a pal	KIPL 146:27
downright inhuman to s. it up	TWAIN 261:7
s. the ears of the groundlings	SHAK 209:7
to make all s.	SHAK 226:15
spoiled: nearly s. ta Flood	AYT 12:18
spoils: divideth his s.	BIBLE 35:16
s. the child and spares	HOOD 121:8
Then s. were fairly sold	MAC 156:7
victor belong the s.	MARCY 159:16
spoken: mouth of the Lord hath s.	BIBLE 29:9
possible to the s. one	CONN 77:5
Rome has s.	AUG 11:21
speak when he is s.	STEV 247:7
'Speak when you're s.	CARR 64:16
that never have s. yet	CHES 70:6
When the lips have s.	SHEL 239:8

you've s. the foremost word	BALL 14:16
spoons: faster we counted our s.	EMER 96:10
let us count our s.	JOHN 131:21
No better than s.	FROST 103:4
sport: animals never kill for s.	FROU 103:15
had ended his s. with Tess	HARDY 115:5
it's the s. of kings	SURT 248:10
make s. for our neighbours	AUST 12:13
ribs was s. for ladies	SHAK 204:14
S. that wrinkled Care derides	MILT 167:17
They kill us for their s.	SHAK 218:18
To s. with Amaryllis	MILT 167:20
To s. would be as tedious	SHAK 212:5
sported: by him s. on the green	SOUT 243:16
sports: mountainous s. girl	BETJ 21:10
s. of love	JONS 136:10
spot: each one s. shall prove	KIPL 145:18
Out, damned s.	SHAK 223:6
Tip me the black s.	STEV 247:1
with a s. I damn him	SHAK 217:1
spotless: unblemished life and s.	HOR 123:16
spots: leopard his s.	BIBLE 29:26
spotted: s. snakes with double tongue	SHAK 227:6
spout: cataracts and hurricanoes, s.	SHAK 218:6
sprang: I s. to the stirrup	BROW 49:15
spread: I have s. my dreams under	YEATS 279:3
net is s. in the sight	BIBLE 26:3
not good except it be s.	BACON 13:17
'S. ALARM and DESPONDENCY	PEN 182:5
Spreading: S. ruin and scattering	BROW 48:16
sprechen: *Wovon man nicht s. kann*	WITT 273:10
spree: Gentleman-rankers out on the s.	KIPL 144:1
spring: Blossom by blossom the s.	SWIN 249:16
can S. be far behind	SHEL 239:15
ever-bubbling s. of endless lies	COWP 79:18
flowers that bloom in the s.	GILB 108:15
garden and a s.	HOR 125:1
heart be full of the s.	SWIN 250:5
hounds of s. are on winter's	SWIN 249:15
I been absent in the s.	SHAK 236:9
perennial s. of all prodigality	BURKE 52:20
rifle all the breathing s.	COLL 76:1
S. a young man's fancy lightly	TENN 253:7
S., nor Summer beauty	DONNE 87:21
s. of Bandusia	HOR 124:10
S., the sweet spring	NASHE 175:3
Sweet lovers love the s.	SHAK 205:12
this s. of love resembleth	SHAK 234:17
to Greece the direful s.	HOMER 120:19
Where are the songs of S.	KEATS 140:14
springs: from seventy s. a score	HOUS 125:4
Sprinkle: S. the quarters	HOUS 126:18
You will s. me with hyssop	BIBLE 41:12
sprite: fleeting, wav'ring s.	HAER 113:8
sprites: have one of s. and goblins	SHAK 234:24
Sprouting: S. despondently at area	ELIOT 94:10
spudding: s. up docks	HARDY 114:13
spumantem: *Thybrim multo s. sanguine*	VIRG 263:9
spur: Fame is the s. that	MILT 167:20
have I to s. me into song	YEATS 279:19
I have no s.	SHAK 221:1
spurn: you s. a stranger cur	SHAK 225:1
spy: sent to s. out the land	BIBLE 23:26
squad: Don't let the awkward s.	BURNS 55:10
squadrons: big s. against the small	BUSS 56:1
squared: Press was s.	BELL 18:13
squawking: seven stars go s.	AUDEN 10:8
squeak: dead Did s. and gibber	SHAK 206:7
until the pips s.	GEDD 105:24

squeeze: madly s. a right-hand foot	CARR 64:15
squeezed: they are going to be s.	GEDD 105:24
squint: gladly banish s. suspicion	MILT 167:7
squire: Bless the s. and his relations	DICK 83:18
stab: s. my spirit broad awake	STEV 247:17
Stabant: *S. orantes primi transmittere*	VIRG 263:13
Stabat: *S. Mater dolorosa*	JAC 129:18
stadium: it's no go the s.	MACN 158:6
staff: By his cockle hat and s.	SHAK 210:25
I'll break my s.	SHAK 233:1
s. of faith to walk upon	RAL 194:4
thy rod and thy s. comfort	PRAY 188:16
trustest upon the s. of this bruised	BIBLE 25:14
your s. in your hand	BIBLE 23:15
stag: runnable s.	DAV 81:19
stage: All the world's a s.	SHAK 205:1
drown the s. with tears	SHAK 208:21
glory of the Attic s.	ARN 9:5
your daughter on the s.	COW 79:6
stagger: s. like a drunken man	PRAY 190:9
stagnant: fen Of s. waters	WORD 276:22
stain: is darkening like a s.	AUDEN 11:13
of the world's slow s.	SHEL 238:26
To s. the stiff dishonoured	ELIOT 94:17
stains: of s. and splendid dyes	KEATS 138:18
S. the white radiance	SHEL 239:1
stair: He's the ruffian on the s.	HENL 117:8
I was going up the s.	MEAR 164:11
'Tis but a s.	MEW 165:13
Staircase: S. wit	DID 86:8
stairs: cursed and kicked the s.	MILL 166:7
stake: yonder like another s.	TWAIN 261:7
stalk: Half asleep as they s.	HARDY 114:11
stalked: s. through the Post Office	YEATS 279:20
stalking: s. in my chamber	WYATT 278:3
stalking-horse: truth serve as a s. to error	BOL 44:16
stall: have gone to s. and bin	FROST 103:9
stalled: s. ox and hatred	BIBLE 26:21
stalls: Tank come down the s.	SASS 200:6
stamp: is but the guinea's s.	BURNS 54:8
stampa: *e poi roppe la s.*	ARIO 8:1
stamping: boot s. on a human face	ORW 178:12
stand: By uniting we s.	DICK 86:7
Here s.	LUTH 155:12
incessantly s. on your head	CARR 62:18
I s. at the door	BIBLE 40:30
serve who only s. and wait	MILT 170:11
s. at the latter day	BIBLE 25:28
s. at the window	AUDEN 10:11
S. by thyself	BIBLE 29:22
S. in the trench, Achilles	SHAW 238:23
s. me now and ever in good	JOYCE 137:2
s. out of my sun a little	DIOG 86:10
s. up for bastards	SHAK 218:1
s. up for Jesus	DUFF 91:17
time to s. and stare	DAV 82:3
who will s. on either hand	MAC 156:6
standards: With the s. of the peoples	TENN 253:10
Stands: S. the Church clock	BROO 47:14
Stanley: how S. scorns	BULW 51:10
star: bright particular s.	SHAK 203:11
catch a falling s.	DONNE 88:15
constant as the northern s.	SHAK 216:8
Fair as a s.	WORD 276:14
Hitch your wagon to a s.	EMER 96:18
is a tall ship and a s.	MAS 162:19
our life's S.	WORD 275:15
seen his s. in the east	BIBLE 31:1

s. of stars	DICK 83:17
S.-scattered on the Grass	FITZ 100:1
s. to every wandering bark	SHAK 236:12
Sunset and evening s.	TENN 251:11
then there was a s. danced	SHAK 228:6
Twinkle, twinkle, little s.	TAYL 250:18
violate a S.	DICK 86:6
with one bright s.	COL 74:12
zenith like a falling s.	MILT 169:1
star-cross'd: s. lovers take their life	SHAK 231:10
star-defeated: Spent in s. sighs	HOUS 125:8
stare: s. in the basin	AUDEN 10:10
time to stand and s.	DAV 82:3
starlight: s. lit my lonesomeness	HARDY 115:3
stars: chilly s. I can forgo	CORY 78:13
Fast as the s. are slow	THOM 257:20
Hard and high to the s.	ANON 7:2
is not in our s.	SHAK 215:16
Look at the s.	HOPK 122:7
looked up to the S. above	LEAR 150:13
morning's. sang	BIBLE 25:33
one the s.	LANG 149:1
seven s. go squawking	AUDEN 10:8
s. are shining bright	SHEL 239:6
s. have not dealt me	HOUS 127:1
s. in her hair were seven	ROSS 197:8
s. in their courses fought	BIBLE 24:5
s. rush out	COL 74:11
that puts the S. to Flight	FITZ 98:14
that's the way to the s.	VIRG 264:2
us are looking at the s.	WILDE 271:16
with how splendid s.	FLEC 100:12
you chaste s.	SHAK 229:12
star-shine: bird-song at morning and s.	STEV 247:12
star-spangled: 'Tis the s. banner	KEY 141:15
start: s. again at your beginnings	KIPL 144:8
Stop it at the s.	OVID 178:23
started: be to arrive where we s.	ELIOT 93:20
it s. like a guilty thing	SHAK 206:8
s. out to happen to somebody	MARQ 161:4
s. that morning from Devon	GILB 107:22
starting: you mar all with this s.	SHAK 223:7
starts: Was everything by s.	DRYD 90:16
starve: s. for want of impudence	DRYD 91:2
starved: s. apothecary than a starved	LOCK 152:14
starving: you have a s. population	DISR 86:14
star-y-pointing: Under a s. pyramid	MILT 168:6
state: by delaying put the s.	ENN 97:1
defrauding of the S.	PENN 182:6
done the s. some service	SHAK 229:15
duty in that s. of life	PRAY 187:21
everwhere a s. in which much is	JOHN 135:1
I am the S.	LOUI 154:5
O Lord, to what a s.	TER 256:5
scorn to change my s.	SHAK 235:11
Ship of S.	LONG 153:2
S. in wonted manner keep	JONS 135:19
s. is a state of Slavery	GILL 109:13
S. is not 'abolished'	ENG 96:22
Then all were for the s.	MAC 156:7
worth of a S.	MILL 165:18
Stately: S. Homes of England	COW 79:8
s. homes of England	HEM 117:2
states: goodly s. and kingdoms seen	KEATS 140:3
statesman: chemist, fiddler, s.	DRYD 90:16
constitutional s. is	BAG 14:8
S., yet friend to truth	POPE 185:5
station: It isn't that sort of s.	RATT 194:12

then s. everyone from doing   HERB 118:3
to s. the church clock   KILV 142:4
when the kissing had to s.   BROW 50:21
stopped: you've said can't be s.   HOR 122:21
stoppeth: he s. one of three   COL 74:5
stops: tender s. of various quills   MILT 168:4
would seem to know my s.   SHAK 210:7
store: seen thee oft amid thy s.   KEATS 140:13
were to increase his s.   HOME 120:18
stories: jewels into a garret four s.   BACON 12:21
tell sad s.   SHAK 230:8
storm: lovers fled away into the s.   KEATS 139:1
rides upon the s.   COWP 79:14
S. and stress   KAUF 138:13
s. has gone over me   BURKE 53:13
when the s. is drawing near   MORR 173:13
storms: explanation of our gusts and s.
    ELIOT 92:17
sudden s. are short   SHAK 230:1
storm-troubled: trembler in the world's s.
    BRON 47:2
story: about you, that s.   HOR 124:19
novel tells a s.   FORS 101:13
Still is the s. told   MAC 156:11
that the s. need be long   THOR 259:9
To tell my s.   SHAK 211:22
Stout: 'Collapse of S. Party'   ANON 5:8
s. Cortez when with eagle   KEATS 140:4
s. hearts and sharp swords   BIRK 42:9
stoutness: see no objection to s.   GILB 107:10
St Patrick: Wearing, by S.'s bounty   LAND 148:11
St Paul: Say I am designing S.'s   BENT 19:20
sketch the ruins of S.'s   MAC 156:17
straight: crooked shall be made s.   BIBLE 29:9
make his paths s.   BIBLE 31:4
might have grown full s.   MARL 160:8
walked s. out of the Ark   SMITH 242:16
straightway: He goeth after her s.   BIBLE 26:10
strain: s. of man's bred   SHAK 233:4
That s. again   SHAK 233:14
which s. at a gnat   BIBLE 33:30
strains: s. of unpremeditated art   SHEL 240:4
strait: Into a desperate s.   MASS 164:3
S. is the gate   BIBLE 32:9
straitened: s. circumstances at home   JUV 137:19
straits: With echoing s. between   ARN 8:15
Strand: where's the Maypole in the S.   BRAM 46:6
strange: be very s. and well-bred   CONG 77:2
Into something rich and s.   SHAK 232:15
is not that s.   SHAK 228:12
man with s. bedfellows   SHAK 232:18
millions of s. shadows   SHAK 236:1
Nature hath fram'd s. fellows   SHAK 234:11
owe this s. intelligence   SHAK 220:5
Poverty has s. bedfellows   BULW 51:12
song: in a s. land   PRAY 191:1
s., and unnatural   SHAK 207:12
s. faces, other minds   TENN 252:5
stranger in a s. land   BIBLE 23:8
strangeness: some s. in the proportion
    BACON 13:1
stranger: From the wiles of a s.   NASH 174:15
I was a s.   BIBLE 34:8
Look, s.   AUDEN 11:4
s. and afraid   HOUS 126:17
s.! 'Eave 'arf a brick   PUNCH 192:13
s. in a strange land   BIBLE 23:8
S. than fiction   BYRON 58:15
strangers: forgetful to entertain s.   BIBLE 40:11

Lord careth for the s.   PRAY 191:6
strangest: in did come the s. figure   BROW 50:11
strangled: s. her   BROW 50:15
s. in the guts of priests   MESL 165:10
strangling: Than s. in a string   HOUS 125:6
straw: Headpiece filled with s.   ELIOT 93:22
Take a s. and throw it   SELD 202:19
Things are but as s. dogs   LAO 149:4
Strawberries: S. swimming in the cream
    PEELE 182:2
stray: with me you'd fondly s.   GAY 105:11
strayed: s. from thy ways like lost   PRAY 186:18
Though thou hast surely s.   GILB 108:30
stream: cool s. thy fingers wet   ARN 8:20
fishes leap in silver s.   CLARE 72:22
mercy Of a rude s.   SHAK 215:9
schoolboys playing in the s.   PEELE 182:2
Still glides the S.   WORD 276:12
streamers: s. waving in the wind   GAY 105:23
with her fan spread and s.   CONG 76:23
streams: Gilding pale s. with heavenly
    SHAK 235:14
hart for cooling s.   TATE 250:15
S. like the thunder-storm   BYRON 57:12
street: done by jostling in the s.   BLAKE 43:5
inability to cross the s.   WOOLF 274:9
On the bald s.   TENN 252:11
salmon sing in the s.   AUDEN 10:8
s. and pavement mute   HARDY 114:14
streets: children cried in the s.   MOTL 174:4
Down these mean s.   CHAN 67:6
lion is in the s.   BIBLE 26:31
not in the s. of Askelon   BIBLE 24:25
s. are paved with gold   COLM 76:3
when night Darkens the s.   MILT 168:16
strength: God is our hope and s.   PRAY 189:3
hath shewed s. with his arm   BIBLE 34:29
impulse of thy s.   SHEL 239:13
Let us roll all our s.   MARV 162:1
name is a tower of s.   SHAK 231:8
S. in what remains behind   WORD 275:16
strength is as the s. of ten   TENN 255:7
sucklings hast thou ordained s.   PRAY 188:7
their s. then but labour   PRAY 189:22
To have a giant's s.   SHAK 223:17
will go from s. to strength   PRAY 189:18
strengtheneth: through Christ which s.
    BIBLE 39:21
strengthless: flock to gaze the s. dead   HOUS 125:11
stress: Storm and s.   KAUF 138:13
Stretch: Gasp and S. one's Eyes   BELL 18:14
S. him out longer   SHAK 219:5
stretched: was things which he s.   TWAIN 260:21
Strew: S. on her roses   ARN 8:17
stricken: I was a s. deer   COWP 80:2
let the s. deer go weep   SHAK 210:6
stride: At one s. comes the dark   COL 74:11
strife: ancient forms of party s.   TENN 252:24
curse to party s.   WORD 274:13
madding crowd's ignoble s.   GRAY 112:6
none was worth my s.   LAND 148:8
promise heavens free from s.   CORY 78:13
strike: in the street I could s.   CLOU 73:8
s. his father's crown   SHAK 213:10
s. it out   JOHN 132:18
then no planets s.   SHAK 206:9
striker: no s.   BIBLE 39:27
strikes: There as s. the Player goes   FITZ 99:8
string: chewing little bits of s.   BELL 18:9

s. that ties them together	MONT 172:7
strings: whisper music on those s.	ELIOT 95:6
Strip: S. thine own back	SHAK 218:22
Then will he s. his sleeve	SHAK 214:4
stripes: buttons off an' cut 'is s.	KIPL 143:17
with his s. we are healed	BIBLE 29:15
strive: need'st not s.	CLOU 73:13
To s., to seek	TENN 255:16
striving: s. evermore for these	GREN 113:3
strokes: amorous of their s.	SHAK 203:22
strong: Are s. as iron bands	LONG 153:17
nor the battle to the s	BIBLE 27:16
s. and of a good courage	BIBLE 24:3
s. came forth sweetness	BIBLE 24:10
s. drink is raging	BIBLE 26:24
s. in will	TENN 255:16
s. that they come to fourscore	PRAY 189:7
wants that little s.	HOLM 120:16
when disease has grown s.	OVID 170.23
Yet still the blood is s.	GALT 104:11
stronger: they were s. than lions	BIBLE 24:26
strongest: s. is always the best	LA F 147:14
stronghold: safe s. our God is still	LUTH 155:14
strongly: Be a sinner and sin s.	LUTH 155:11
strove: I s. with none	LAND 148:8
little still she s.	BYRON 58:1
unbecoming men that s.	TENN 255:14
struck: I s. the board	HERB 118:7
I was s. all of a heap	SHER 240:17
s. a mortal blow right	AESC 1:16
s. regularly, like gongs	COW 79:4
struggle: alarms of s. and flight	ARN 8:13
class s. necessarily leads	MARX 162:10
gods themselves s. in vain	SCH 201:3
history of class s.	MARX 162:4
Say not the s. naught availeth	CLOU 73:17
strumpet: Into a s.'s fool	SHAK 203:16
She was a s.	HEINE 116:13
struts: poor player, That s.	SHAK 223:15
Stuck: Amen' S. in my throat	SHAK 221:15
Student: S. of our sweet English	FLEC 100:13
students: benefit of the s.	SMITH 242:2
Studies: S. serve for delight	BACON 13:19
studio: Sine ira et s.	TAC 250:9
study: much s. is a weariness	BIBLE 27:23
periphrastic s. in a worn-out	ELIOT 93:16
proper s. of mankind	POPE 185:17
result of previous s.	AUST 12:12
science and s. of man is man	CHAR 67:16
S. is like the heaven's	SHAK 219:7
s. of Greek literature	GAIS 104:6
studying: been s. how I may compare	SHAK 230:15
stuff: bosom of that perilous s.	SHAK 223:13
s. as great part of Shakespeare	GEOR 106:5
What s. 'tis made	SHAK 224:10
written such volumes of s.	LEAR 150:4
stuffed: We are the s. men	ELIOT 93:22
Stuffs: S. out his vacant garments	SHAK 217:10
stultitiam: Misce s. consiliis	HOR 124:18
stump: You must stir it and s.	GILB 109:4
stumps: s., and all	LANG 148:17
stupefying: strong thick s. incense-smoke	BROW 49:1
stupidity: Such an excess of s.	JOHN 132:4
With s. the gods themselves	SCH 201:3
Sturm: S. und Drang	KAUF 138:13
sty: Over the nasty s.	SHAK 210:17
Stygian: In S. cave forlorn	MILT 167:14
style: is the only secret of s.	ARN 9:15

le s. est l'homme même	BUFF 51:6
Mandarin s. beloved	CONN 77:5
S. is the dress of thought	WESL 268:21
s. is the man	BUFF 51:6
vaunting s. of a soldier	DRAKE 90:3
When we see a natural s.	PASC 180:15
would do it in a high s.	AUBR 10:6
suadere: *religio potuit s. malorum*	LUCR 155:4
Suave: *S., mari magno turbantibus*	LUCR 155:6
suavity: such deceitfulness and s.	ELIOT 94:9
subdue: power To chasten and s.	WORD 275:6
s. it	BIBLE 22:6
submitted and to s. the arrogant	VIRG 263:14
subiectis: *Parcere s. et debellare*	VIRG 263:14
subject: honour is the s. of my	SHAK 215:15
Lies the s. of all verse	BROW 48:14
s. of almost equal importance	BRAM 46:5
s.'s duty is the king's	SHAK 213:22
s. unto the higher powers	BIBLE 38:4
subjection: in silence with all s.	BIBLE 39:26
sublime: One step above the s.	PAINE 179:13
s. to the ridiculous	NAP 174:9
true pathos and s.	BURNS 55:3
We can make our lives s.	LONG 153:17
submit: Must he s.	SHAK 230:9
subordination: s. of one sex to the other	MILL 165:20
subsequence: mistake s. for consequence	JOHN 131:4
Subsistence: S. only increases	MALT 159:7
substance: s. of his house for love	BIBLE 28:5
What is your s.	SHAK 236:1
substitution: s. of the proletarian	LEE 151:6
subtilty: Thy brother came with s.	BIBLE 22:31
subtle: know not well the s. ways	EMER 96:3
suburb: At the new s. stretched	BETJ 20:10
suburbs: In the south s.	SHAK 234:8
subversive: Whatever is funny is s.	ORW 178:8
succeed: If at first you don't s.	HICK 119:7
shall s. me in my pilgrimage	BUNY 52:3
success: ecstasy, is s. in life	PATER 181:17
mortals to command s.	ADD 1:7
of the bitch-goddess S.	JAMES 130:8
requisite to s. in life	SPEN 244:5
S. is counted sweetest	DICK 86:4
These s. encourages	VIRG 263:8
true s. is to labour	STEV 247:4
very lively hope of s.	SMITH 243:2
Successful: S. crimes alone are justified	DRYD 91:7
Such: S. knowledge is too wonderful	PRAY 191:2
suck: I have given s.	SHAK 221:6
Suck-a-Thumb: To naughty little S.	HOFF 120:11
suck'd: s. on country pleasures	DONNE 88:1
sucker: s. born every minute	BARN 15:18
sucking: s. at the bung	MAS 162:17
you as gently as any s.	SHAK 229:18
sucklings: babes and s. hast thou ordained strength	PRAY 188:7
sucks: s. the nurse asleep	SHAK 204:11
weasel s. eggs	SHAK 204:20
sudden: s. storms are short	SHAK 230:1
sue: We were not born to s.	SHAK 229:18
Suez: me somewheres east of S.	KIPL 145:4
suffer: doth s. a sea-change	SHAK 232:15
escape than one innocent s.	BLAC 42:16
s. a witch to live	BIBLE 23:19
S. the little children	BIBLE 34:26
s. thy foot to be moved	PRAY 190:16
ye s. fools gladly	BIBLE 39:5

sufferance: s. is the badge of all SHAK 224:21
suffer'd: have s. greatly TENN 255:11
sufferings: myriad s. for the Achaeans
   HOMER 120:19
  patience under their s. PRAY 187:5
Sufficient: S. unto the day BIBLE 32:1
suff'rings: To each his s. GRAY 112:11
sugar: I must s. my hair CARR 63:13
suis: J'y s., j'y reste MACM 157:17
Suisse: point de S. RAC 193:18
suit: moneys is your s. SHAK 225:1
suitable: no s. material to work COMP 76:10
suitably: s. attired in leather HOUS 127:3
suits: Than s. a man to say HOUS 126:25
  trappings and the s. of woe SHAK 206:14
suivre: il fallait bien les s. LEDR 151:2
Sultan: Sultan after S. with his Pomp FITZ 98:17
sultry: where the climate's s. BYRON 57:18
sum: ergo s. DESC 83:5
  s. of things for pay HOUS 126:20
Sumer: S. is icumen ANON 4:19
summer: After s. merrily SHAK 233:2
  compare thee to a s.'s day SHAK 235:9
  Eternal s. gilds them yet BYRON 58:6
  Expect Saint Martin's s. SHAK 214:6
  hollows crown'd with s. sea TENN 252:8
  last rose of s. MOORE 173:2
  Spring, nor S. beauty DONNE 87:21
  s. dies the swan TENN 255:9
  S. has set in with its COL 75:11
  s. in England is to have WALP 266:1
  s.'s lease hath all too SHAK 235:9
  s. soldier and the sunshine PAINE 179:15
  thy eternal s. shall not SHAK 235:9
  'Tis S. Time on Bredon KING 143:5
  whether it's winter or s. CHEK 69:2
summers: s. in a sea of glory SHAK 215:9
summertime: S. and the livin' HOUS 125:12
summits: snowy s. old in story TENN 254:9
summon: To s. his array MAC 156:3
summoned: Pearse s. Cuchulain YEATS 279:20
  S. the Immediate Aid BELL 18:15
summons: That s. thee to heaven SHAK 221:11
  Upon a fearful s. SHAK 206:8
sun: all the beauty of the s. SHAK 234:17
  are nothing like the s. SHAK 236:14
  before you let the s. THOM 257:10
  black s. of melancholy NERV 175:11
  bosom-friend of the maturing s. KEATS 140:12
  Busy old fool, unruly S. DONNE 88:18
  Close to the s. in lonely TENN 251:13
  except their s. BYRON 58:6
  front the s. climbs slow CLOU 73:17
  give me the s. IBSEN 129:7
  going down of the s. BINY 42:6
  golden apples of the s. YEATS 279:18
  heaven's glorious s. SHAK 219:7
  I am too much i' the s. SHAK 206:12
  Juliet is the s. SHAK 231:16
  livery of the burnish'd s. SHAK 225:2
  make our s. Stand still MARV 162:1
  new thing under the s. BIBLE 27:3
  Now the s. is laid to sleep JONS 135:19
  now the s. is rising WORD 276:10
  our own place in the s. BULOW 51:9
  setting s. SHAK 229:21
  summer by this s. of York SHAK 231:2
  s. and the rain Clash FRY 103:17
  s. go down upon your wrath BIBLE 39:13

s. has gone SMITH 242:10
s. looked over the mountain's BROW 50:7
s. of suns DICK 83:17
s. shall not burn thee PRAY 190:16
s. shines warm WORD 275:14
S.'s rim dips COL 74:11
s. to rise on the evil BIBLE 31:18
s. was shining on the sea CARR 63:23
sweetheart of the s. HOOD 121:11
tired the s. with talking CORY 78:12
will be ere the set of s. SHAK 219:16
you stand out of my s. DIOG 86:10
sun-beams: extracting s. out of cucumbers
  SWIFT 248:19
  what made fatuous s. toil OWEN 179:6
Sunday: chicken in his pot every S. HENR 117:11
  Here of a S. morning HOUS 125:12
  killing of a mouse on S. BRAT 46:7
  Repentance on a S. YBAR 278:9
  than a rainy S. in London DE Q 83:1
sundial: I am a s. BELL 18:23
sung: ever she s. from noon MORR 173:15
  s. the dolefull'st ditty BARN 15:17
sunk: All s. beneath the wave COWP 79:15
  So Lycidas s. low MILT 168:2
sunlight: s. on the garden MACN 158:10
  there will be s. later MACN 158:4
Sunny: then they called him S. Jim HANFF 114:6
Suns: S., that set JONS 136:11
sunset: beliefs may make a fine s. MADAN 158:12
  Now the s. breezes shiver NEWB 175:16
  S. and evening star TENN 251:11
  s. of life gives me mystical CAMP 60:16
sunshine: calm s. of the heart CONS 77:15
  s. is a glorious birth WORD 275:13
sunt: Sint ut s. aut non sint CLEM 73:6
  S. lacrimae rerum VIRG 263:2
superbos: subiectis et debellare s. VIRG 263:14
superfluity: barren s. of words GARTH 105:1
superior: I am a most s. person ANON 4:9
  'S. people never make long MOORE 172:17
  s. to time and place JOHN 134:28
superiority: unfounded airs of s. WALP 266:6
superman: I teach you the s. NIET 176:13
supernatural: This s. soliciting SHAK 220:7
superstition: superstition in avoiding s.
  BACON 13:23
  S. is the religion of feeble BURKE 53:11
  S. sets the whole world VOLT 264:19
superstitions: heresies and to end as s.
  HUXL 128:13
  It is one of the s. VOLT 265:4
supp'd: have s. full with horrors SHAK 223:14
supped: 'Hobson has s. MILT 168:10
support: want is men who will s. MELB 164:17
  what is low raise and s. MILT 168:14
supports: wretch who s. with insolence
  JOHN 134:20
suprema: populi s. est lex CIC 72:6
sure: it was s. to die MOORE 173:3
  Most s. in all His ways NEWM 176:3
  What nobody is s. about BELL 18:13
surfeit: They are as sick that s. SHAK 224:13
  Where no crude s. reigns MILT 167:8
surge: s. and thunder of the Odyssey LANG 148:16
surged: how the silence s. softly DE L 82:15
surgeon: wounded s. plies the steel ELIOT 93:17
surmise: each other with a wild s. KEATS 140:4
surpassed: Man is something to be s. NIET 176:13

s. must have leaped from | BURKE 53:9
your plowshares into s. | BIBLE 30:15
swore: By the nine gods he s. | MAC 156:3
jested, quaff'd, and s. | DOYLE 89:29
My tongue s. | EUR 97:5
sworn: had I so s. as you | SHAK 221:6
sycamore: nightingale in the s. | STEV 247:15
syllable: last s. of recorded time | SHAK 223:15
Sylvia: Who is S. | SHAK 234:18
symbol: s. of his resurrection | PROU 192:5
s. of Irish art | JOYCE 137:4
symmetry: Could frame thy fearful s. | BLAKE 43:7
sympathize: her great Master so to s. | MILT 168:7
symphony: consort to th' angelic s. | MILT 168:8
symptoms: dying of a hundred good s. | POPE 186:2
Syrens: song the S. sang | BROW 48:12
Syrian: S. Orontes has now | JUV 137:17
systems: Our little s. have their | TENN 252:9
T: description the page gave to a T. | FARQ 97:16
Ta: thousand T.'s and Pardon's | BETJ 21:7
tabernacle: who shall dwell in thy t. | PRAY 188:10
table: behave mannerly at t. | STEV 247:7
from their masters' t. | BIBLE 33:10
from the rich man's t. | BIBLE 35:31
olive-branches: round about thy t. | PRAY 190:21
though you cannot make a t. | JOHN 131:17
Thou shalt prepare a t. | PRAY 188:16
tableau: *l'histoire n'est que le t. des crimes*
| VOLT 265:1
Table Bay: horse and foot going to T. | KIPL 143:8
taboo: repose is t.'d by anxiety | GILB 107:20
tail: guinea-pig up by the t. | LOCK 152:13
he's treading on my t. | CARR 63:10
Improve his shining t. | CARR 62:16
like a rat without a t. | SHAK 220:2
such a little t. behind | BELL 18:5
tails: were stings in their t. | BIBLE 41:1
tainted: t. wether of the flock | SHAK 225:16
take: got to t. under my wing | GILB 108:16
She bid me t. love easy | YEATS 278:18
T. a pair of sparkling | GILB 107:8
T. care of the pence | LOWN 154:20
T. me, Lieutenant | BETJ 21:6
t. those lips away | SHAK 224:7
T. your hare when it is | GLAS 109:17
That they should t. | WORD 275:10
They have to t. you in' | FROST 103:3
taken: Lord hath t. away | BIBLE 25:18
only *t. from the French* | SHER 240:14
They have t. away my Lord | BIBLE 37:9
takes: money and you t. your choice | ANON 5:14
t. two to speak the truth | THOR 259:7
taketh: which t. away the sin | BIBLE 36:18
taking-off: deep damnation of his t. | SHAK 221:1
tale: adorn a t. | JOHN 135:10
bodies must tell the t. | SCOTT 201:10
I should have had a t. | SCOTT 201:10
I tell the t. that I heard | HOUS 126:14
mere t. of a tub | WEBS 267:13
round unvarnish'd t. deliver | SHAK 228:18
t. Told by an idiot | SHAK 223:15
tedious as a twice-told t. | SHAK 217:11
thereby hangs a t. | SHAK 204:22
Trust the t. | LAWR 149:18
With a t. forsooth he cometh | SIDN 241:6
talent: into my works is my t. | WILDE 272:1
mon t. dans mes oeuvres | WILDE 272:1
t. instantly recognizes | DOYLE 89:28
T. which is death to hide | MILT 170:10

talents: career open to t. | NAP 174:11
ministry of all the t. | ANON 5:1
tales: children is increased with t. | BACON 13:5
tali: *t. auxilio nec defensoribus* | VIRG 263:6
talk: chance to t. a little wild | SHAK 215:4
legs and have out his t. | JOHN 133:6
mair they t. I'm kent | BURNS 54:19
nothing but t. of his horse | SHAK 224:15
No use to t. to me | HOUS 125:7
should t. so very queer | BARH 15:15
T. about the pews and steeples | CHES 69:18
t. not to me of a name | BYRON 59:2
t. of wills | SHAK 230:7
t. too much | DRYD 90:15
t. with crowds and keep | KIPL 144:9
t. with some old lover's | DONNE 88:11
t. with you | SHAK 224:17
To t. about the rest | ANON 5:2
'To t. of many things | CARR 64:2
wished him to t. on for ever | HAZL 116:3
world may t. of hereafter | COLL 75:18
talk'd: t. like poor Poll | GARR 104:14
talked: I believe they t. of me | FARQ 97:14
worse than being t. about | WILDE 271:20
talking: children, quietly t. alone | BOWEN 45:14
that you will still be t. | SHAK 228:4
tired the sun with t. | CORY 78:12
talks: t. it so very fast that | FARQ 97:15
t. of Arthur's death | SHAK 217:13
t. of darkness at noon-day | COWP 79:17
wish I liked the way it t. | RAL 194:10
tall: divinely t. | TENN 251:12
He's as t. a man as any's | SHAK 233:15
t. men had ever very empty | BACON 12:21
tame: Be not too t. neither | SHAK 209:8
hey-day in the blood is t. | SHAK 210:16
Taming: T. my wild heart to thy | SHAK 228:9
Tandy: I met wid Napper T. | ANON 3:20
tangere: *Noli me t.* | BAG 14:5
Noli me t. | BIBLE 41:24
tangled: t. web we weave | SCOTT 202:1
tangles: t. of Neaera's hair | MILT 167:20
Tank: T. come down the stalls | SASS 200:6
tankards: mouths were made for t. | MAS 162:17
Tantae: *T. molis erat Romanam condere*
| VIRG 262:16
Tantum: *T. religio potuit suadere* | LUCR 155:4
taper: with t. light | SHAK 217:12
Tara: harp that once through T.'s | MOORE 172:14
when T. rose so high | LAND 148:11
Tar-baby: T. ain't sayin' nuthin' | HARR 115:9
tar-barrel: black as a t. | CARR 63:21
tard: *Trois heures, c'est toujours trop t.* | SART 200:3
tares: t. to which we are all | ELIOT 95:10
tarnished: is neither t. nor afraid | CHAN 67:6
Tarquin: That the great house of T. | MAC 156:3
tarried: too long we have t. | LEAR 150:14
tarry: Boatman, do not t. | CAMP 60:17
Longer will t. | DRAY 90:5
tarry'd: job too long he t. | SWIFT 249:13
Tarsus: man which am a Jew of T. | BIBLE 37:27
Tart: T., cathartic virtue | EMER 96:12
task: All with weary t. fordone | SHAK 228:1
long day's t. is done | SHAK 204:4
that's the t. | VIRG 263:10
thy worldly t. hast done | SHAK 206:4
what he reads as a t. will | JOHN 131:20
What is our t. | GEOR 105:25
taste: authority on t. | TAC 250:10

tempt: not t. the Lord thy God   BIBLE 31:9
T. not a desperate man   SHAK 232:5
t. with wand'ring feet   MILT 169:3
temptabam: *quod t. dicere versus*   OVID 179:1
temptation: I never resist t.   SHAW 237:7
insist on their resisting t.   KNOX 147:8
last t.   ELIOT 94:13
lead us not into t.   BIBLE 31:21
maximum of t.   SHAW 238:12
of t. is just to yield   GRAH 111:6
out of the power of t.   TROL 260:12
resist everything except t.   WILDE 271:14
that ye enter not into t.   BIBLE 34:15
under t. to it   LOCKE 152:12
tempts: Not all that t. your wand'ring   GRAY 112:7
tempus: fugit inreparabile t.   VIRG 264:13
T. abire tibi est   HOR 123:8
ten: Church clock at t. to three   BROO 47:14
good Lord has only t.   CLEM 73:4
T. Days that Shook   REED 194:15
tenant: She's the t. of the room   HENL 117:8
tenantless: graves stood t.   SHAK 206:7
Tendebantque: T. manus ripae ulterioris   VIRG 263:13
tender: beautiful, the t., the kind   MILL 166:3
heart has felt the t. passion   GAY 105:16
t. for another's pain   GRAY 112:11
t. is the night   KEATS 139:20
t. mercies of the wicked   BIBLE 26:15
that are t. and unpleasing   BACON 13:4
true and t. is the North   TENN 254:11
ténébreux: Je suis le t.   NERV 175:11
tenement: Like to a t. or pelting   SHAK 230:2
tenir: son el tenir y el no t.   CERV 66:7
tenor: They kept the noiseless t.   GRAY 112:6
tents: in the t. of ungodliness   PRAY 189:19
Shall fold their t.   LONG 153:3
Ter: T. sunt conati imponere   VIRG 264:10
Tereu: Tereu, T.   BARN 15:17
Terewith: It is the light of T.   DICK 83:17
term: was a lad I served a t.   GILB 108:28
Termagant: whipped for o'erdoing T.   SHAK 209:7
terminate: which must t. in sensory   ELIOT 95:11
terminological: risk of t. inexactitude   CHUR 71:1
Terms: very seldom upon good T.   HALE 114:2
terra: t. pax hominibus bonae   MASS 163:12
terrarum: Ille t. mihi praeter omnis   HOR 124:2
terre: tous les temples de la t.   DID 86:9
terrible: t. beauty is born   YEATS 278:19
t. future may have just   AUDEN 10:14
Which make thee t. and dear   SHEL 240:6
territorial: last t. claim which I have   HITL 119:16
terror: added a new t. to death   WETH 269:6
added another t. to death   LYND 155:17
afraid for any t. by night   PRAY 189:24
Thy t., O Christ   HOPK 122:11
terrorist: t. and the policeman both   CONR 77:13
terrors: t. of the earth   SHAK 218:5
tetigit: scribendi genus non t.   JOHN 133:2
Teucer: T. shall lead and his star   HOR 123:11
thame: Lat t. say   KEITH 141:12
Thames: On banks of T. they must   HOUS 126:6
stripling T. at Bab-lock-hithe   ARN 8:20
Sweet T., run softly   SPEN 244:19
T. bordered by its gardens   MORR 173:14
T. is liquid history   BURNS 53:16
thank: I t. whatever gods may   HENL 117:6
Now t. you all your God   RINK 195:7
t. heaven, fasting   SHAK 205:6

We t. with brief thanksgiving   SWIN 250:1
thankit: Sae let the Lord be t.   BURNS 54:13
thankless: To have a t. child   SHAK 218:3
thanks: deserves the love and t.   PAINE 179:15
give t. unto the Lord   PRAY 190:23
I will give t. unto thee   PRAY 191:4
T. for mercies past receive   BUCK 51:5
thanksgiving: before his presence with t.   PRAY 190:2
Tharshish: years came the navy of T.   BIBLE 25:3
thatch: worn the ancient t.   TENN 253:18
thatch-eaves: vines that round the t.   KEATS 140:12
theatre: t. is irresistible   ARN 9:9
theatres: t., and temples lie   WORD 276:18
Thebes: Riddles of death T.   SHEL 239:5
theft: clever t. was praiseworthy   SPEN 244:8
Property is t.   PROU 192:3
themselves: violent hands upon t.   PRAY 188:3
theologians: if you believe the t.   SAL 199:7
théologie: toutes les écoles de t.   DID 86:9
theories: kinds of old defunct t.   IBSEN 129:6
theorize: capital mistake to t. before   DOYLE 89:15
there: Because it is t.   MALL 159:5
if I had not been t.   WELL 267:21
therein: all that t. is   PRAY 188:17
thereto: t. I give thee my troth   PRAY 187:28
Thermodynamics: describe the Second Law of T.   SNOW 243:6
Thermopylae: There was an old man of T.   LEAR 150:22
To make a new T.   BYRON 58:10
thickens: now the plot t. very much   BRY 51:3
thicker: When the loo paper gets t.   MITF 171:2
thicket: ram caught in a t.   BIBLE 22:26
thief: he was a t.   HEINE 116:13
Opportunity makes a t.   BACON 13:29
subtle t. of youth   MILT 170:8
thieves: fell among t.   BIBLE 35:12
have made it a den of t.   BIBLE 33:26
t. break through and steal   BIBLE 31:22
thigh: smote them hip and t.   BIBLE 24:11
thimbles: They sought it with t.   CARR 62:8
thin: Imprisoned in every fat man a t.   CONN 77:9
into t. air   SHAK 232:24
it's 'T. red line of 'eroes'   KIPL 146:1
t. man inside every fat   ORW 178:9
t. red line   RUSS 198:15
thine: not my will, but t.   BIBLE 36:7
t. is the kingdom   BIBLE 31:21
thing: most unattractive old t.   GILB 108:16
nearest run t.   WELL 267:21
one damned t.   OMAL 178:4
play's the t.   SHAK 208:23
t. of beauty is a joy   KEATS 138:15
things: all t. to all men   BIBLE 38:10
black and merciless t.   JAMES 130:3
full of a number of t.   STEV 247:9
God's sons are t.   MADD 158:13
love all beauteous t.   BRID 46:11
sorry Scheme of T.   FITZ 99:13
such t. to be   TENN 252:19
there are tears shed for t.   VIRG 263:2
T. are in the saddle   EMER 96:5
t. are not what they seem   LONG 153:9
t. are the sons of heaven   JOHN 134:11
T. fall apart   YEATS 279:15
t. in boards that moderns   LAMB 148:2
t. that go bump   ANON 3:11
t. through Christ which   BIBLE 39:21

times her little t. around — BROW 50:15
To cut his t. before he — SWIFT 249:13
to feel the fog in my t. — BROW 50:17
unlocked her silent t. — GIBB 106:13
throats: My sore t. are always worse — AUST 12:9
throne: everyone before the t. — CEL 66:1
Gehenna or up to the T. — KIPL 146:9
light which beats upon a t. — TENN 251:15
like a burnished t. — ELIOT 95:2
Lord sitting upon a t. — BIBLE 28:12
This royal t. of kings — SHAK 230:2
t. he sits — SHAK 213:23
T. sent word to a Throne — KIPL 145:7
Wrong forever on the t. — LOW 154:18
thronum: Coget omnes ante t. — CEL 66:1
through: who has gone t. it — VIRG 264:3
wind that blows t. me — LAWR 149:17
throw: me to dig him up and t. — SHAW 237:15
t. away the dearest thing — SHAK 220:9
Time shall t. a dart — BROW 48:14
thrown: then t. out — JOHN 134:9
throws: t. himself on God — BROW 49:11
thrush: That's the wise t. — BROW 49:13
Thule: Ultima T. — VIRG 264:9
thumb: Do you bite your t. — SHAK 231:12
thumbs: By the pricking of my t. — SHAK 222:24
Leastways if you reckon two t. — LEAR 150:5
thumping: such a t. crook — BETJ 21:3
thunder: dawn comes up like t. outer — KIPL 145:3
Here falling houses t. — JOHN 135:5
lightning shaft and power to t. — MAN 159:9
such sweet t. — SHAK 227:15
surge and t. of the Odyssey — LANG 148:16
they steal my t. — DENN 82:21
t. of the captains — BIBLE 25:34
thunderbolt: heaped-up mountains with a t. — VIRG 264:10
like a t. he falls — TENN 251:13
thunder-stone: Nor the all-dreaded t. — SHAK 206:4
thunder-storm: peoples plunging thro' the t. — TENN 253:10
Thus: T. have I had thee — SHAK 236:6
T., or words to that — JOYCE 137:8
Why dost thou t. — DONNE 88:18
Thybrim: T. multo spumantem sanguine — VIRG 263:9
thyme: bank whereon the wild t. — SHAK 227:5
sweet t. true — FLET 100:19
thyself: thou art beside t. — BIBLE 37:29
T. thou gav'st — SHAK 236:6
Tiber: drop of allaying T. — SHAK 205:14
Tiber! father T. — MAC 156:9
T. foaming with much blood — VIRG 263:9
Tiberim: Syrus in T. defluxit Orontes — JUV 137:17
Ticket: In his hat a Railway-T. — LEAR 150:10
t. at Victoria Station — BEVIN 21:18
tickle: if you t. us — SHAK 225:10
tide: call of the running t. — MAS 163:1
'except when the t.'s — DICK 84:5
going out with the t. — DICK 84:5
high t.!' King Alfred — CHES 69:22
t. in the affairs of men — SHAK 217:3
tidings: him that bringeth good t. — BIBLE 29:12
you good t. of great joy — BIBLE 35:2
Tie: T. up my sleeves with ribbons — HUNT 128:8
ties: only the string that t. — MONT 172:7
tiger: atomic bomb is a paper t. — MAO 159:15
imitate the action of the t. — SHAK 213:14
master o' the T. — SHAK 220:2

that with his t.'s heart — GREE 112:1
t.'s heart wrapp'd — SHAK 215:
t. sniffs the rose — SASS 200:1
t. that hadn't *got* a Christian — PUNCH 192:1
T. well repay the trouble — BELL 18:
tiger-moth: are the t.'s deep-damask'd — KEATS 138:1
tigers: tamed and shabby t. — HODG 120:
t. of wrath are wiser than — BLAKE 44:
tiger-skin: On a t. — ANON 5:1
tight: his shoes were far too t. — LEAR 150:1
long black hair out t. — ELIOT 95:
wearing arm-chairs t. — WOD 273:1
tikleth: t. me aboute myn herte — CHAU 68:1
tills: Man comes and t. the field — TENN 255:
timber: crooked t. of humanity — KANT 138:1
Timbuctoo: On the plains of T. — WILB 270:1
time: abbreviation of t. — GIBB 106:1
All of the olden t. — ANON 4:
backward and abysm of t. — SHAK 232:1
bank and shoal of t. — SHAK 220:1
been a t. for such a word — SHAK 223:1
be more than biting T. — ELIOT 94:1
bid t. return — SHAK 230:
but for all t. — JONS 136:
chronicle of wasted t. — SHAK 236:1
city 'half as old as T. — BURG 52:7
conversing I forget all t. — MILT 169:1
Cormorant devouring T. — SHAK 219:
drew from the womb of t. — HEINE 116:1
envious T. — MILT 168:1
first t. of asking — PRAY 187:2
Fleet the t. carelessly — SHAK 204:1
Footprints on the sands of t. — LONG 153:1
Give peace in our t. — PRAY 186:2
half as old as T. — ROG 196:
Have no enemy but t. — YEATS 279:
he loved the t. too well — CLARE 72:1
How goes the t. — TENN 255:1
How soon hath T. — MILT 170:8
How T. is slipping underneath — FITZ 99:
irretrievable t. is flying — VIRG 264:1
It was the t. of roses — HOOD 121:
let not T. deceive you — AUDEN 10:9
lines to t. thou grow'st — SHAK 235:9
long result of T. — TENN 253:6
Look like the t. — SHAK 220:1
Love's not T.'s fool — SHAK 236:1
Men talk of killing t. — BOUC 45:5
Never the t. and the place — BROW 50:6
No t. like the present — MANL 159:1
now doth t. waste me — SHAK 231:1
old common arbitrator, T. — SHAK 233:1
Old T. is still a-flying — HERR 118:2
plenty of t. to win this game — DRAKE 90:2
Procrastination is the thief of t. — YOUNG 280:
remember'd for a very long t. — MCG 157:11
spare t. and in his working — GILL 109:1
superior to t. and place — JOHN 134:2
syllable of recorded t. — SHAK 223:1
that t. is money — FRAN 102:8
That t. may cease — MARL 160:
That t. of year thou mayst — SHAK 236:
There's a good t. coming — MACK 157:1
those feet in ancient t. — BLAKE 43:2
three minutes is a long t. — HOUS 127:6
Thus the whirligig of t. — SHAK 234:13
T., a maniac scattering — TENN 252:14
T. and Fate of all their — FITZ 99:2

T. and fevers burn away	AUDEN 11:3
T. and the hour runs through	SHAK 220:8
t. and times are done	YEATS 279:18
T. for a little something	MILNE 167:2
t. has come	CARR 64:2
'T. has too much credit	COMP 76:8
T. hath, my lord, a wallet	SHAK 233:8
T. held me green and dying	THOM 257:3
T. in hours	VAUG 261:16
T. is on our side	GLAD 109:14
t. is out of joint	SHAK 208:3
t. is setting with me	DUNB 91:10
T. makes ancient good uncouth	LOW 154:19
t. of the singing of birds	BIBLE 27:29
T. present and time past	ELIOT 93:13
t. remembered is grief	SWIN 249:16
t. requireth	WHIT 270:11
T. shall throw a dart	BROW 48:14
T.'s wingèd chariot hurrying	MARV 161.21
T. that is intolerant	AUDEN 10:17
t. to audit The accounts	MACN 158:4
t. to be born	BIBLE 27:6
t. to every purpose under	BIBLE 27:6
t. to make it shorter	PASC 181:4
t. to stand and stare	DAV 82:3
T. was away and somewhere	MACN 158:8
t. will come when you will	DISR 86:12
t. will have meanly run	HOR 123:14
T. will run back	MILT 168:9
t. without injuring eternity	THOR 259:2
T., you old gypsy man	HODG 120:5
t. you were off	HOR 123:8
unconscionable t. dying	CHAR 67:14
What's not destroy'd by T.'s	BRAM 46:6
whips and scorns of t.	SHAK 208:24
With leaden foot t. creeps	JAGO 129:19
with the productions of t.	BLAKE 44:3
yet t. hath his revolution	CREWE 80:13
timebo: quem t.	BIBLE 41:11
timendum: nobis nil esse in morte t.	LUCR 155:8
timeo: t. Danaos et dona	VIRG 263:3
times: In pious t.	DRYD 90:9
It was the best of t.	DICK 85:29
my dear t.' waste	SHAK 235:12
praiser of the t. that	HOR 122:18
ruins of forgotten t.	BROW 48:11
signs of the t.	BIBLE 33:11
T. change	ANON 7:8
T. go by turns	SOUT 244:3
t.! Oh, the manners	CIC 72:11
t. that try men's souls	PAINE 179:15
Timor: T. mortis conturbat me	DUNB 91:21
tine: Lest my jewel I should t.	BURNS 53:25
tinge: t. with a browner shade	GIBB 106:10
tinkling: t. cymbal	BIBLE 38:14
tinklings: t. lull the distant folds	GRAY 111:18
tip: Within the nether t.	COL 74:12
tippled: Have ye t. drink more fine	KEATS 139:10
tiptoe: t. on the misty mountain	SHAK 232:2
Will stand a t. when this	SHAK 214:4
tired: can wait and not be t.	KIPL 144:7
He was so t.	ROLFE 196:5
I'm t. of Love	BELL 18:20
one grows t. of the world	WALP 265:18
Thou art t.	ARN 8:16
t. her head	BIBLE 25:13
t. the sun with talking	CORY 78:12
When a man is t. of London	JOHN 133:5
who can ever be t. of Bath	AUST 12:5

woman who always was t.	ANON 3:14
your t., your poor	LAZ 149:19
tirent: pour ceux qui t. le mieux	VOLT 265:7
tires: effort nor the failure t.	EMPS 96:21
He t. betimes that spurs	SHAK 230:1
tiresomeness: t. of old age	ANON 6:17
Tirez: en disant 'T. le rideau	RAB 193:15
title: farced t. running 'fore	SHAK 213:23
Who gain'd no t.	POPE 185:5
titles: All thy other t. thou hast	SHAK 218:2
Conquering kings their t.	CHAN 67:4
ti-willow: t., tiwillow	GILB 108:17
Toad: intelligent Mr T.	GRAH 111:12
should I let the t. work	LARK 149:7
t. beneath the harrow knows	KIPL 145:8
t., ugly and venomous	SHAK 204:16
toast: Let the t. pass	SHER 240:25
never had a piece of t.	PAYN 181:12
toasted: dreamed of cheese—t.	STEV 247:2
Toasted-cheese: enemies, 'T.	CARR 62:6
tobacco: cigarette t.	DOYLE 89:11
sweeter t. comes from Virginia	THAC 256:12
TO-DAY: about them if T. be sweet	FITZ 99:6
Never do t. what you can	PUNCH 192:12
pick t.'s fruits	HOR 123:14
such a day to-morrow as t.	SHAK 234:19
that he is wiser t. than	POPE 186:1
t. I suffer	LESS 151:9
T. we have naming of parts	REED 194:14
t. which the world may	COLL 75:18
we are here t.	BEHN 18:1
toe: printless t.	BROO 47:11
toes: happier without their t.	LEAR 150:20
Pobble who has no t.	LEAR 150:20
togae: Cedant arma t.	CIC 72:8
together: Are we here t. alone	WHIT 270:3
comfortably so long t.	GAY 105:7
Swing, swing t.	CORY 78:10
toil: double t. and trouble	SHAK 222:22
Horny-handed sons of t.	KEAR 138:14
Our love and t.	KIPL 143:15
Remark each anxious t.	JOHN 135:8
they t. not	BIBLE 31:25
T., envy	JOHN 135:9
t., tears and sweat'	CHUR 71:4
toiling: tears and t. breath	ROSS 197:2
Were t. upward in the night	LONG 153:6
token: t. of a covenant between	BIBLE 22:22
told: mainly he t. the truth	TWAIN 260:21
Ought to be t. to come	FROST 103:9
they t. me you were dead	CORY 78:12
what we formerly were t.	BLUN 44:12
who bade me fight had t.	EWER 97:8
Toll: T. for the brave	COWP 79:15
To t. me back from thee	KEATS 140:1
Tolle: T. lege	AUG 11:16
tollis: t. peccata mundi	MASS 163:18
tolls: It t. for thee	DONNE 89:3
Tom: Poor T.'s a-cold	SHAK 218:14
Uncle T. Cobbleigh	BALL 15:6
tomb: buried in the silent t.	WORD 277:4
dozen of Claret on my T.	KEATS 141:6
fair Fidele's grassy t.	COLL 76:1
totter towards the t.	SAY 200:17
tombs: through the t. of all regions	CEL 66:1
Tommy: it's T. this	KIPL 145:19
to-morrow: gone t.	BEHN 18:1
such a day t. as to-day	SHAK 234:19
T., and to-morrow	SHAK 223:15

T. for the young | AUDEN 11:10
t. I die | LESS 151:9
t. is another day | MITC 170:23
T. we'll be back | HOR 123:12
t. we shall die | BIBLE 28:25
Unborn T. | FITZ 99:6
you can put off till t. | PUNCH 192:12
Tom Pearse: T., lend me your grey | BALL 15:6
tom-tit: by a river a little t. | GILB 108:17
tonandi: Jovi fulmen viresque t. | MAN 159:9
tone: in that t. of voice | PUNCH 192:21
t. of the company that | CHES 69:6
tones: Sweet t. are remembered | SHEL 239:8
tongue: be on every infant's t. | CALV 59:17
God's sake hold your t. | DONNE 87:20
his t. is the clapper | SHAK 228:10
his t. to conceive | SHAK 227:16
I mean the t. | WEBS 267:7
instead my t. freezes into | SAPP 199:12
my t. from evil-speaking | PRAY 187:20
My t. swore | EUR 97:5
nor t. to speak here | LENT 151:8
obnoxious to each carping t. | BRAD 46:1
sharp t. is the only edged | IRV 129:15
Sing, my t. | VEN 261:19
t. cleave to the roof | PRAY 191:1
use of my oracular t. | SHER 240:19
vibrates her eternal t. | YOUNG 280:7
would that my t. could utter | TENN 251:4
Your hand, your t. | SHAK 220:12
tongueless: t. vigil and all the pain | SWIN 249:15
tongues: Finds t. in trees | SHAK 204:16
t. of men and of angels | BIBLE 38:14
t., they shall cease | BIBLE 38:15
Wild t. that have not Thee | KIPL 145:12
took: 'E went an' t. | KIPL 146:6
person you and I t. me | CARL 61:6
t. the trouble to be born | BEAU 16:17
ye t. me | BIBLE 34:8
tool: Man is a t.-using animal | CARL 61:20
tool-making: Man is a t. animal | FRAN 102:13
tools: Give us the t. | CHUR 71:8
toord: rymyng is nat worth a t. | CHAU 68:15
tooth: Nature, red in t. and claw | TENN 252:18
sharper than a serpent's t. | DICK 85:11
sharper than a serpent's t. | SHAK 218:3
t. for tooth | BIBLE 23:18
toothache: That could endure the t. | SHAK 228:13
tooth-point: Exactly where each t. goes | KIPL 145:8
top: is always room at the t. | WEBS 267:5
t. of it reached to heaven | BIBLE 22:32
topless: t. towers of Ilium | MARL 160:5
torch: runners relay the t. of life | LUCR 155:7
torches: she doth teach the t. | SHAK 231:14
Tories: are T. born wicked | ANON 4:5
T. own no argument | BROW 48:15
torment: t. than a hermit's fast | KEATS 139:8
tormented: Am not t. with ten thousand | MARL 160:3
torrents: t. of her myriad universe | TENN 253:17
torture: t. them, into believing | NEWM 176:2
Tory: hatred for the T. Party | BEVAN 21:16
I may be a T. | PEEL 182:1
tossing: t. about in a steamer from | GILB 107:21
tot: Gott ist t. | NIET 176:16
toujours trop tard ou trop t. | SART 200:3
total: What's the demd t. | DICK 85:1
totter: t. towards the tomb | SAY 200:17

totters: Who t. forth | SHEL 240:8
touch: Do not t. me | BIBLE 41:24
One t. of nature makes | SHAK 233:9
T. me not | BIBLE 37:10
T. not the cat but a glove | SCOTT 202:6
t. of earthly years | WORD 276:17
t. of Harry in the night | SHAK 213:17
touched: t. none that he did not | JOHN 133:2
T. to the quick | BROW 49:16
touches: t. of sweet harmony | SHAK 226:5
Who t. this touches a man | WHIT 270:3
toucheth: t. pitch shall be defiled | BIBLE 30:23
tough: was interesting, but t. | TWAIN 260:22
tour: *Comme en sa t. d'ivoire* | SAIN 199:2
d'Aquitaine à la t. abolie | NERV 175:11
tourist: loathsome is the British t. | KILV 142:3
whisper to the t. | BEER 17:17
tourmente: Malgré moi l'infini me t. | MUSS 174:8
tous: à t. points de vue | COUE 78:15
T. pour un | DUMAS 91:19
toves: slithy t. | CARR 63:16
tower: Child Roland to the dark t. | SHAK 218:15
name is a t. of strength | SHAK 231:8
within his ivory t. | SAIN 199:2
towers: branchy between t. | HOPK 121:17
cloud-capp'd t. | SHAK 232:24
topless t. of Ilium | MARL 160:5
Towery: T. city and branchy between | HOPK 121:17
town: Country in the t. | MART 161:10
country retreat near the t. | WYCH 278:5
end of the t. | MILNE 166:13
Enormous through the Sacred T. | BELL 19:1
man made the t. | COWP 79:19
spreading of the hideous t. | MORR 173:14
town-crier: lief the t. spoke my lines | SHAK 209:7
toy: foolish thing was but a t. | SHAK 234:14
sells eternity to get a t. | SHAK 235:6
toys: All is but t. | SHAK 222:7
Deceive boys with t. | LYS 156:1
make you brooches and t. | STEV 247:12
Toyshop: moving T. of their heart | POPE 185:24
trace: can t. my ancestry back | GILB 108:1
traces: spring are on winter's t. | SWIN 249:15
trade: craftsman cunning at his t. | KIPL 143:16
It is His t. | HEINE 116:15
nation was ever ruined by t. | FRAN 102:9
not your t. to make tables | JOHN 131:17
that's my t. | CATH 65:2
Trade-Unionists: There are the T. | KEYN 141:17
tradition: talk to me about naval t. | CHUR 71:21
traducción: original es infiel a la t. | BORG 44:20
traffic: Hushing the latest t. | BRID 46:1
t. of Jacob's ladder | THOM 258:7
traffick: two hours' t. | SHAK 231:11
tragedies: There are two t. in life | SHAW 238:9
t. are finish'd by a death | BYRON 58:5
tragedy: first time as t. | MARX 162:8
T. is thus a representation | ARIS 8:5
t. to those that feel | WALP 266:2
tragedye: litel myn t. | CHAU 68:7
tragic: In t. life, God wot | MER 165:3
trahison: La t. des clercs | BENDA 19:11
Trahit: T. sua quemque voluptas | VIRG 264:4
trailing: t. clouds of glory | WORD 275:15
T. in the cool stream thy | ARN 8:20
train: catching a t. is to miss | CHES 70:14
his t. filled the temple | BIBLE 28:12
Of heat the express t. | THOM 257:16
take a t. | BROO 47:12

Trojan: T. 'orses will jump out	BEVIN 21:19
Trolley-bus: T. and windy street	BETJ 20:6
troop: Farewell the plumed t.	SHAK 229:4
troops: solemn t. and sweet societies	MILT 168:3
tropics: nuisance of the t. is	BELL 19:3
troth: thereto I give thee my t.	PRAY 187:28
Trotting: T. through the dark	KIPL 145:15
trouble: double toil and t.	SHAK 222:22
full of t.	BIBLE 25:24
has t. enough of its own	WILC 271:2
Man is born unto t.	BIBLE 25:21
present help in time of t.	ANON 3:3
save t. I wed again	CLARE 72:19
Today the Roman and his t.	HOUS 126:5
took the t. to be born	BEAU 16:17
transcendent capacity of taking t.	CARL 61:10
t. deaf heaven with my	SHAK 235:11
t. out of King Charles's	DICK 84:3
troubled: Let not your heart be t.	BIBLE 36:36
t. midnight and the noon's	ELIOT 93:12
t. spirit: a broken	PRAY 189:7
troubles: arms against a sea of t.	SHAK 208:24
t. of our proud and angry	HOUS 126:16
t. they reave me of rest	HOUS 127:1
written t. of the brain	SHAK 223:13
troubling: wicked cease from t.	BIBLE 25:20
trousers: bottoms of my t. rolled	ELIOT 94:8
never have your best t.	IBSEN 129:5
shall wear white flannel t.	ELIOT 94:8
then he hitch'd his t.	BARH 15:15
trout: gray t. lies asleep	HOGG 120:13
you find a t. in the milk	THOR 259:8
trovato: è molto ben t.	ANON 6:9
trowel: She lays it on with a t.	CONG 76:12
should lay it on with a t.	DISR 87:6
Troy: ringing plains of windy T.	TENN 255:12
sacked T.'s sacred city	HOMER 121:1
T. came destined an exile	VIRG 262:15
Where's T.	BRAM 46:6
true: any less real and t.	SHAW 237:10
course of t. love never did run	SHAK 226:13
dark and t. and tender	TENN 254:11
finished yields the t. glory	DRAKE 90:1
If it is not t.	ANON 6:9
is it t.	BETJ 20:7
let us be t.	ARN 8:12
long enough it will be t.	BENN 19:13
man would like to be t.	BACON 13:30
My t. love hath my heart	SHAK 217:19
my t. love said	SIDN 241:4
tell you three times is t.	PEELE 182:2
That was the t. Light	CARR 62:4
to itself do rest but t.	BIBLE 36:14
to thine own self be t.	SHAK 217:16
t. a lover	SHAK 207:6
t. beginning of our end	SHAK 204:18
t. paradises are paradises	SHAK 227:20
t. pathos and sublime	PROU 192:7
T. patriots we	BURNS 55:3
unfaithful kept him falsely t.	CART 64:19
Whatsoever things are t.	TENN 251:20
'You are not t.	BIBLE 39:20
true-love: iron pokers into t. knots	WILB 271:1
truer: Thou heardst me t. than	COL 75:8
trump: at the last t.	HOPK 122:11
with the sound of the t.	BIBLE 38:22
trumpet: blow your own t.	PRAY 189:4
t. shall sound	GILB 109:4
	BIBLE 38:22
t. shall be heard on high	DRYD 91:10
t. will fling out a wonderful	CEL 66:1
trumpets: He saith among the t.	BIBLE 25:34
pâtés de foie gras to the sound of t.	SMITH 242:23
snarling t. 'gan to chide	KEATS 138:17
Sound the t.	MOR 173:8
t. sounded for him	BUNY 52:4
t. which sing to battle	SHEL 239:16
trunk: large a t. before	BELL 18:5
trunkless: vast and t. legs	SHEL 239:16
trust: absolute t.	SHAK 220:9
If you can t. yourself	KIPL 144:7
man assumes a public t.	JEFF 130:12
never should t. experts	SAL 199:7
put not your t. in princes	PRAY 191:5
put their t. in chariots	PRAY 188:13
t. in God	SMITH 242:15
T. one who has gone through	VIRG 264:3
T. the tale	LAWR 149:18
t. to two securities than	CHES 69:13
with pains that conquer t.	TENN 252:14
trusted: his armour wherein he t.	BIBLE 35:16
Let no such man be t.	SHAK 226:7
trustest: t. upon the staff of this	BIBLE 25:14
truth: 'Beauty is t.	KEATS 139:16
casualty when war comes is t.	JOHN 131:1
Christianity better than T.	COL 75:9
Communist must grasp the t.	MAO 159:14
dared to speak the t. to me	TROL 260:3
dead we owe only t.	VOLT 265:8
dearer still is t.	ARIS 8:8
fight for freedom and t.	IBSEN 129:5
Great is t.	BIBLE 41:25
great is t.	BROO 47:17
great ocean of t.	NEWT 176:8
have not maintained for t.	SWIFT 249:1
here have Pride and T.	YEATS 279:11
him in possession of t.	LOCKE 152:11
I am the way, the t.	BIBLE 37:2
loins girt about with t.	BIBLE 39:15
lost to love and t.	BURNS 54:3
mainly he told the t.	TWAIN 260:21
Nobody speaks the t. when	BOWEN 45:15
rejoiceth in the t.	BIBLE 38:15
she was in t. a goddess	VIRG 263:1
simple t. his utmost skill	WOTT 277:15
Strict Regard for T.	BELL 18:4
strife of T. with Falsehood	LOW 154:17
takes two to speak the t.	THOR 259:7
that she is made of t.	SHAK 237:1
to handle honesty and t.	SHAW 237:22
T. forever on the scaffold	LOW 154:18
T. from his lips prevail'd	GOLD 110:9
t. in every shepherd's	RAL 194:2
t. in the groves of Academe	HOR 123:7
t. is always strange	BYRON 58:15
t. is not in us	BIBLE 40:24
t. is rarely pure	WILDE 271:6
t. of imagination	KEATS 140:15
t. serve as a stalking-horse	BOL 44:16
t. shall make you free	BIBLE 36:28
T., Sir, is a cow	JOHN 132:1
T. sits upon the lips	ARN 9:2
t. which you cannot contradict	PLATO 183:15
T. will come to light	SHAK 225:4
utter what he thinks t.	JOHN 133:14
What is t.	BACON 13:25
What is t.	BIBLE 37:4
Which heavenly t. imparts	KEBLE 141:10

would keep abreast of T.   LOW 154:19
    yet friend to t.   POPE 185:5
truthful: true Poets must be t.   OWEN 179:3
truths: customary fate of new t.   HUXL 128:13
    Some random t. he can impart   WORD 276:6
    tell him disagreeable t.   BULW 51:13
    T. as refin'd as ever Athens   ARMS 8:9
    Two t. are told   SHAK 220:6
    We hold these t. to be   ANON 5:9
    We hold these t. to be   JEFF 130:9
try: times that t. men's souls   PAINE 179:15
    t. him afterwards   MOL 171:12
    T., try again   HICK 119:7
Trying: T. to be glad   HOUS 125:9
trysting: named a t. day   MAC 156:3
tu: Et t.   CAES 59:10
    Et t., Brute   SHAK 216:9
    T. Marcellus eris   VIRG 263:15
    T. regere imperio populos   VIRG 263:14
tua: Nam t. res agitur   HOR 123:6
tub: mere tale of a t.   WEBS 267:13
Tuba: T. mirum sparget sonum   CEL 66:1
tue: ou je te t.   CHAM 67:3
tuer: t. de temps en temps un   VOLT 264:15
tug of war: then was the t.   LEE 151:4
tulips: Here t. bloom as they are   BROO 47:10
tumult: t. and the shouting dies   KIPL 145:10
    t. Kubla heard from far   COL 75:5
tumultuositas: t. vulgi semper insaniae   ALC 2:1
tune: out of t. and harsh   SHAK 209:6
    That's sweetly play'd in t.   BURNS 54:17
    There's many a good t.   BUTL 56:21
    t. the enchantress plays   HOUS 126:21
tunes: should have all the good t.   HILL 119:9
tunnel: Down some profound dull t.   OWEN 179:9
turbid: t. look the most profound   LAND 148:14
Turbot: 'T., Sir,' said the waiter   WELBY 267:20
turbulent: sustained from one t. priest
                                                HENR 117:17
turf: blue ribbon of the t.   DISR 87:8
    green t. beneath my feet   HAZL 116:5
    his head a grass-green t.   SHAK 210:26
    Where heaves the t.   GRAY 112:2
Turk: unspeakable T. should be   CARL 61:18
turkey: It was a t.   DICK 83:20
    secure all the myrtle and t.   AUST 12:3
Turkish: English, not the T. court   SHAK 213:3
turmoil: with ceaseless t. seething   COL 75:3
turn: goodnight and quickly t.   YEATS 279:1
    high tide and the t.   CHES 69:22
    I t. the page   BROW 49:3
    t. down an empty Glass   FITZ 100:1
    t. to him the other also   BIBLE 31:17
    T. wheresoe'er I may   WORD 275:13
    you will t. it over once   WEST 269:4
turn'd: never t. my back upon Don   TENN 255:4
turned: almost t. down the pages   POUND 186:13
    'in case anything t. up   DICK 83:23
    never t. his back   BROW 48:22
    weather t. around   THOM 257:7
turning: Turning and t. in the widening
                                                YEATS 279:15
turns: Times go by t.   SOUT 244:3
    t. no more his head   COL 74:18
turpissimus: Nemo repente fuit t.   JUV 137:16
turtle: think it clever of the t.   NASH 174:19
    voice of the t. is heard   BIBLE 27:29
Tuscany: even the ranks of T.   MAC 156:10
tutissimus: Medio t. ibis   OVID 178:21

Tu-whit: T., tu-who   SHAK 219:14
twain: never the t. shall meet   KIPL 143:9
    t. he covered his face   BIBLE 28:12
twang: perfume and most melodious t.   AUBR 10:7
Tweedledum: T. and Tweedledee   CARR 63:21
    'Twixt T. and Tweedledee   BYROM 57:1
twelve: t. months in all the year   BALL 15:2
twenty: draw but t. miles a day   MARL 161:1
    payment of half t. shillings   BURKE 52:12
twenty-one: Are over the age of t.   GILB 107:13
twice: it is t. bless'd   SHAK 223:17
    My life closed t. before   DICK 86:3
    step t. into the same river   HER 118:2
    t. as often as any other   COKE 74:2
    T. a week the winter thorough   HOUS 125:9
twice-told: tedious as a t. tale   SHAK 217:11
twig: Bent every t. with it   HARDY 114:14
    Just as the t. is bent   POPE 184:23
twilight: full Surrey t.   BETJ 21:14
    Pilots of the purple t.   TENN 253:10
twinkle: t., little bat   CARR 63:4
    T., twinkle, little star   TAYL 250:18
twinkling: Innumerable t. of the waves   AESC 1:17
    in the t. of an eye   BIBLE 38:22
twins: threw the t. she nursed   GRAH 111:8
    whereof every one bear t.   BIBLE 28:3
twist: to bribe or t.   WOLFE 273:23
    t. the sinews of thy heart   BLAKE 43:8
twitch: never be refined if I t.   THOM 257:13
twitch'd: t. his mantle blue   MILT 168:5
two: be in t. places at once   ROCHE 195:11
    In t. words   GOLD 111:2
    my troubles are t.   HOUS 127:1
    serve t. masters   BIBLE 31:24
    takes t. to speak the truth   THOR 259:7
    that t. solitudes protect   RILKE 195:6
    There were in t. and two   BIBLE 22:20
    t. contradictory beliefs   ORW 178:11
    t. ears of corn   SWIFT 248:18
    t. hours' traffick   SHAK 231:11
    t. irons in the fire   BEAU 16:21
    t. legs bad   ORW 178:6
    t. meanings packed up into   CARR 64:10
    T. men look out through   LANG 149:1
    t. or three are gathered   BIBLE 33:18
    t. or three are gathered   PRAY 186:24
    t. people miserable instead   BUTL 56:24
    t. people with the one   MACN 158:8
    T. voices are there   STEP 246:2
    Wandering between t. worlds   ARN 8:14
    When t. strong men stand   KIPL 143:9
    with t. seeming bodies   SHAK 227:11
two-and-twenty: myrtle and ivy of sweet t.
                                                BYRON 59:2
two-handed: that t. engine at the door   MILT 167:21
two hundred: About t. pounds a year   BUTL 56:10
two-legged: that unfeather'd t. thing   DRYD 90:14
two-pence: I care not t.   BEAU 16:20
Tyburn: me...has a damn'd T.-face   CONG 76:14
Tyger: T.! burning bright   BLAKE 43:7
tyme: had my world as in my t.   CHAU 68:18
    t. ylost may nought recovered   CHAU 68:26
type: So careful of the t. she   TENN 252:17
typewriter: t. does not generate   DOYLE 89:20
tyrannous: t. To use it like a giant   SHAK 223:17
tyrant: art past the t.'s stroke   SHAK 206:4
    little t. of his fields   GRAY 112:5
tyrants: blood of patriots and t.   JEFF 130:10
    now the t.   KEYN 141:19

Tyre: one with Nineveh and T. KIPL 145:11
U: 'U. and 'Non-U ROSS 197:1
uffish: in u. thought he stood CARR 63:17
ugly: world u. and bad has made NIET 176:18
Ulster: U. will fight CHUR 70:23
ulterioris: Tendebantque manus ripae u.
VIRG 263:13
Ultima: U. Cumaei venit iam carminis VIRG 264:6
U. Thule VIRG 264:9
Ulysses: Happy he who like U. has DU B 91:15
umble: likewise a very 'u. person DICK 84:2
umbrella: unjust steals the just's u. BOWEN 45:9
umbrellas: who possess u. FORS 101:15
umpire: u., the pavilion cat LANG 148:17
una: iuvat spinis de pluribus u. HOR 123:8
unacceptable: u. face of capitalism HEATH 116:9
unacknowledged: inspire…Poets are the u. legislators SHEL 240:12
unadvisedly: u., lightly, or wantonly PRAY 187:24
unalienable: Creator with certain u. rights
ANON 5:9
Unarm: U., Eros SHAK 204:4
unattempted: u. yet in prose or rhyme MILT 168:13
unattractive: most u. old thing GILB 108:16
not against the u. GREE 112:15
unawares: entertained angels u. BIBLE 40:11
unbearable: in victory, u. CHUR 71:19
unbeatable: In defeat, u. CHUR 71:19
unbecoming: u. men that strove with TENN 255:14
unbelief: help thou mine u. BIBLE 34:25
Help thou mine u. BUTL 56:18
help thou my u. FORS 101:20
unbelov'd: poor u. ones BETJ 20:6
un-birthday: u. present CARR 64:7
unborn: To you yet u. these WHIT 269:17
unbowed: head is bloody, but u. HENL 117:6
unbribed: man will do u. WOLFE 273:23
uncertain: sometimes with u. steps JOW 136:14
U., coy SCOTT 202:2
uncharitableness: from all u. PRAY 187:3
uncircumcised: daughters of the u. triumph
BIBLE 24:25
uncle: married with mine u. SHAK 206:15
nor u. me no uncle SHAK 230:4
prophetic soul! My u. SHAK 207:13
U. Tom Cobbleigh BALL 15:6
unclean: midst of a people of u. lips BIBLE 28:13
unclubable: very u. man JOHN 132:8
uncomfortable: moral when he is only u.
SHAW 238:8
unconfin'd: Let all her ways be u. PRIOR 191:16
unconfined: let joy be u. BYRON 57:10
unconfused: u., unhurried by emotion
JAMES 130:5
unconscious: u. hodmen of the men HEINE 116:14
unconsidered: snapper-up of u. trifles SHAK 234:22
uncontrollable: less free Than thou, O u.
SHEL 239:13
unconvincing: bald and u. narrative GILB 108:14
Uncorseted: U., her friendly bust ELIOT 95:9
uncouth: His u. way MILT 169:3
Time makes ancient good u. LOW 154:19
under: u. an English heaven BROO 47:16
U. bare Ben Bulben's head YEATS 280:3
Undergraduates: U. owe their happiness
BEER 17:16
underground: thinking Lays lads u. HOUS 126:10
underlings: that we are u. SHAK 215:16
undersized: He's a bit u. GILB 107:22

understand: are said to u. one another CHAM 67:1
be understood or to u. GREE 112:17
invented was easy to u. AUDEN 10:13
still the less they u. BUTL 56:8
Then you u. Latin FARQ 97:15
to u. them SPIN 245:1
understanding: all thy getting get u. BIBLE 26:7
shall light a candle of u. BIBLE 30:20
they pass all u. JAM 130:1
To be totally u. makes STAEL 245:9
which passeth all u. BIBLE 39:19
understood: something u. HERB 118:13
those that u. him smiled SHAK 216:2
u. or to understand I would GREE 112:17
Underworld: way down to the U. VIRG 263:10
undiscover'd: u. country from whose bourn
SHAK 208:24
undiscovered: ocean of truth lay all u. NEWT 176:8
undo: thee does she u. herself TOUR 259:20
u. this button SHAK 219:4
undoctored: Against the u. incident KIPL 143:10
undone: I am u. BIBLE 28:13
not thought death had u. ELIOT 94:20
'save the u. years OWEN 179:10
We have left u. those things PRAY 186:19
undoubtedly: u. be seen to be done HEW 119:5
Unearned: U. increment MILL 165:14
Uneasy: U. lies the head that wears SHAK 212:27
uneatable: full pursuit of the u. WILDE 271:24
unexamined: u. life is not worth living SOCR 243:7
unexpected: Old age is the most u. TROT 260:15
unexpectedness: which I call *u.* PEAC 181:15
unfabled: u. Incense Tree DARL 81:13
Unfaith: U. in aught is want TENN 252:1
unfathomable: u. deep Forest THOM 257:19
unfeeling: Th' u. for his own GRAY 112:11
unfit: often u. a man for society CHAM 66:16
unfledg'd: new-hatch'd, u. comrade SHAK 207:6
unforgiving: fill the u. minute KIPL 144:9
unfriendly: hostile and the towns u. ELIOT 94:1
Ungeheuern: Wer mit U. kämpft NIET 177:1
ungentlemanly: knows how u. he can look
SURT 248:14
unglücklich: u. das Land BREC 46:9
Unglücklichen: eine andere als die des U.
WITT 273:9
ungodliness: dwell in the tents of u. PRAY 189:19
ungodly: seen the u. in great power PRAY 188:24
ungula: putrem sonitu quatit u. VIRG 264:1
unhappy: each u. family is unhappy TOLS 259:17
is not cannot be made u. LUCR 155:8
Not one is respectable or u. WHIT 270:6
u. the land that needs BREC 46:9
which make us so u. JOYCE 137:5
unheard: language of the u. KING 142:7
those u. Are sweeter KEATS 139:13
unholy: sights u. MILT 167:14
unhonour'd: Unwept, u., and unsung
SCOTT 201:17
unhurried: u. by emotion JAMES 130:5
uninitiated: keep far off, you u. VIRG 263:11
unintelligible: u. patter GILB 109:8
union: Mysterious u. with its native sea
WORD 274:15
U., strong and great LONG 153:2
yet an u. in partition SHAK 227:11
unit: Misses an u. BROW 49:11
unite: Workers of the world, u. MARX 162:5
uniting: By u. we stand DICK 86:7

universal: This u. frame began	DRYD 91:9
U. peace is declared	ELIOT 93:1
universe: better ordering of the u.	ALF 2:5
hell of a good u.	CUMM 81:3
I accept the u.	CARL 61:25
pretend to understand the U.	CARL 61:22
u. and give me yesterday	JONES 135:14
u. is not hostile	HOLM 120:15
u. is so vast and so ageless	ROS 196:17
will turn the u. to ashes	CEL 65:14
universities: discipline of colleges and u.	
	SMITH 242:2
University: servant to be bred at an U.	
	CONG 76:16
true U. of these days is	CARL 61:15
We are the U.	SPR 245:5
unjust: just and on the u.	BIBLE 31:18
u. steals the just's umbrella	BOWEN 45:9
unkind: me not (Sweet) I am u.	LOV 154:10
poor when givers prove u.	SHAK 209:1
That are sodden and u.	BELL 19:7
unkindest: u. cut of all	SHAK 216:20
unknowable: world u.	THOM 258:6
unknown: everything u. is held	TAC 250:7
TO THE U. GOD	BIBLE 37:23
tread safely into the u.'	HASK 115:16
unleaving: Over Goldengrove u.	HOPK 122:5
unlocked: Shakespeare u. his heart'	BROW 49:14
unloose: latchet I am not worthy to u.	BIBLE 36:17
unlucky: who is so u.	MARQ 161:4
unmapped: u. country within us which	
	ELIOT 92:17
unmarried: keep u. as long as he can	SHAW 238:5
unnatural: cruel, not u.	SHAK 210:10
unnecessary: vain, u. things	ROCH 195:13
unofficial: English u. rose	BROO 47:10
unparallel'd: lass u.	SHAK 204:12
unpleasing: that are tender and u.	BACON 13:4
U. to a married man	SHAK 219:13
unpopular: I was not u. there	BEER 17:15
u. names	ARN 9:8
unpremeditated: strains of u. art	SHEL 240:4
unprofitable: flat, and u.	SHAK 206:15
unproportion'd: Nor any u. thought his	
	SHAK 207:6
unprotected: u. race	CLARE 72:20
unravaged: u. by the fierce intellectual	ARN 9:8
unredressed: there is a wrong left u.	KING 143:2
unremembered: nameless, u., acts	WORD 275:5
unrest: u. which men miscall delight	SHEL 238:26
unruly: night has been u.	SHAK 222:5
unsatisfied: it leaves one u.	WILDE 271:21
unsealed: my lips are not yet u.	BALD 14:14
unsex: u. me here	SHAK 220:11
unspeakable: u. Turk should be immediately	
	CARL 61:18
u. in full pursuit	WILDE 271:24
unsubstantial: dwellings and u. realms of Dis	
	VIRG 263:12
unsung: Unwept, unhonour'd, and u.	
	SCOTT 201:17
untender: So young, and so u.	SHAK 217:18
unting: ain't the 'u. as 'urts 'im	PUNCH 192:15
'U. is all that's worth	SURT 248:10
untried: left u.	CHES 70:12
untrodden: dwelt among the u. ways	WORD 276:14
untrue: man who's u. to his wife	AUDEN 11:8
unutterably: Abroad is u. bloody	MITF 171:3
unvanquishable: In u. number	SHEL 239:11

unwash'd: Another lean u. artificer	SHAK 217:13
Unwept: U., unhonour'd, and unsung	
	SCOTT 201:17
unwithered: find u. on its curls	HOUS 125:11
unwritten: that u. law	DAV 81:17
up: after midnight is to be u.	SHAK 233:21
be u. and doing	LONG 153:11
sort of English u. with which	CHUR 71:20
U. Guards and at them again	WELL 268:13
U., Lord	PRAY 188:8
U., to a point, Lord Copper	WAUGH 267:1
UPHARSIN: TEKEL, U.	BIBLE 30:9
upper: let not man have the u.	PRAY 188:8
Like many of the u. class	BELL 19:6
To prove the u. classes	COW 79:8
uproar: u.'s your only music	KEATS 141:1
upside: turneth it u. down	PRAY 191:6
upside down: have turned the world u.	BIBLE 37:22
upstairs: compel us to be equal u.	BARR 16:1
never knew any kicked u.	HALE 114:4
U. and down stairs in his	MILL 166:10
urban: Being u.	BROO 47:13
urbe: Rus in u.	MART 161:10
urge: u. for destruction is also	BAK 14:11
urgent: bosom of the u. West	BRID 46:13
Uricon: Are ashes under U.	HOUS 126:5
urine: Cannot contain their u.	SHAK 225:14
his u. is congealed ice	SHAK 224:6
nose-painting, sleep, and u.	SHAK 222:3
urn: bubbling and loud-hissing u.	COWP 80:4
storied u. or animated bust	GRAY 112:4
urns: u. and sepulchres of mortality	CREWE 80:13
us: Not unto u., Lord	BIBLE 41:14
use: hotly lust'st to u. her	SHAK 218:22
How can they u. such names	SASS 200:13
U. every man after his	SHAK 208:19
u. of a new-born child	FRAN 102:17
u. rather than for ostentation	GIBB 106:12
'What is the u. of a book'	CARR 62:13
used: then I have u. no other	PUNCH 192:20
u. by Charles the First	COW 79:9
useful: ambition mock their u.	GRAY 112:3
be the way to what is u.	COUS 78:16
know to be u.	MORR 173:16
Useless: U. each without the other	LONG 153:14
uses: all the u. of this world	SHAK 206:15
usual: people is 'Business as u.	CHUR 71:2
usurp: u. authority over the man	BIBLE 39:26
utile: être la voie ni de l'u.	COUS 78:16
utlagetur: u., aut exuletur	MAGN 158:16
utter: leaps out in all they u.	BYRON 57:5
uttered: he u. with that easiness	HEM 117:4
uttermost: u. parts of the sea	PRAY 191:3
vacant: In v. or in pensive mood	WORD 275:4
laugh that spoke the v. mind	GOLD 110:7
Stuffs out his v. garments	SHAK 217:10
V. heart and hand	SCOTT 202:5
vacations: No extras, no v.	DICK 84:19
vacuum: Nature abhors a v.	RAB 193:13
vadis: Quo v.	BIBLE 41:21
Vae: V. victis	LIVY 152:9
vain: builders have laboured in v.	BIBLE 41:15
I watched in v.	FLEC 100:11
No great man lives in v.	CARL 61:14
on my sullen heart in v.	STEV 247:17
people imagine a v.	PRAY 188:6
seal'd in v.	SHAK 224:7
tricks that are v.	HARTE 115:12
v. the net is spread	BIBLE 26:3

v., unnecessary things — ROCH 195:13
watchman waketh but in v. — PRAY 190:19
vain-glory: v., and hypocrisy — PRAY 187:3
vainly: v. breaking — CLOU 73:17
vale: cool sequester'd v. of life — GRAY 112:6
v. of misery use it — PRAY 189:18
valet: his very v. seem'd a hero — BYRON 57:3
man is a hero to his v. — CORN 78:9
valet de chambre: point de héros pour son v.
— CORN 78:9
valiant: he was v. — SHAK 216:14
v. never taste of death — SHAK 216:6
valley: All in the v. of Death — TENN 251:8
Every v. shall be exalted — BIBLE 29:9
great things from the v. — CHES 70:9
multitudes in the v. of decision — BIBLE 30:16
To bicker down a v. — TENN 251:6
v. of Humiliation — BUNY 51:18
v. which was full of bones — BIBLE 30:6
walk through the v. of the shadow — PRAY 188:16
valleys: lily of the v. — BIBLE 27:26
Piping down the v. wild — BLAKE 43:12
valour: contemplation he and v. — MILT 169:7
There is much care and v. — SHAK 213:20
thou mighty man of v. — BIBLE 24:7
Who would true v. see — BUNY 52:2
value: everything and the v. of nothing
— WILDE 271:17
little v. of fortune — STEE 245:15
v. my garden more for being — ADD 1:13
Vanbrugh: Dead Sir John V.'s house — EVANS 97:6
Vandyke: V. is of the company — GAIN 104:5
vanish: softly and suddenly v. away — CARR 62:7
vanished: time it v. quite slowly — CARR 63:1
Vanitas: V. vanitatum — BIBLE 41:17
vanities: Vanity of v. — BIBLE 41:17
vanity: administering to the v. of others — AUST 12:6
pomps and v. of this wicked — PRAY 187:19
speckled V. — MILT 168:9
v. and vexation of spirit — BIBLE 27:4
V. of vanities — BIBLE 27:2
V. of vanities — BIBLE 41:17
Vanity-Fair: beareth the name of V. — BUNY 51:19
vanquish'd: e'en though v. — GOLD 110:10
Quite v. him — SHAK 216:20
vanum: v. laboraverunt qui aedificant — BIBLE 41:15
vapours: v. weep their burthen — TENN 255:9
variable: love prove likewise v. — SHAK 231:20
v. as the shade — SCOTT 202:2
variety: Her infinite v. — SHAK 203:24
one because it admits v. — FORS 102:1
V.'s the very spice — COWP 80:1
V.'s the source of joy — GAY 105:21
various: A man so v. — DRYD 90:16
How v. his employments — COWP 80:3
Varium: V. et mutabile semper — VIRG 263:7
vassals: v. and serfs at my side — BUNN 51:15
vast: v. and trunkless legs — SHEL 239:16
Vaster: V. than empires — MARV 161:20
vasty: v. hall of death — ARN 8:18
vats: parcel of boilers and v. — JOHN 133:17
Vaulting: V. ambition — SHAK 221:1
vécu: J'ai v. — SIEY 241:8
Qui n'a pas v. dans les — TALL 250:13
vegetable: in matters v. — GILB 109:1
My v. love should grow — MARV 161:20
veil: Lift not the painted v. — SHEL 240:3
wrapped in a gauzy v. — SHEL 240:8
vein: am not in the giving v. — SHAK 231:6

veins: v. of rhyming mother-wits — MARL 160:15
warmth hidden in my v. — RAC 193:17
Velasquez: 'why drag in V. — WHIS 269:12
vendemus: Nulli v. — MAGN 159:1
Veneres: V. Cupidinesque — CAT 65:4
Veneris: Et taedet V. statim peractae — PETR 183:3
vengeance: line a sudden v. waits — POPE 184:12
V. is mine — BIBLE 38:2
Veni: V., Sancte Spiritus — LANG 149:3
V., vidi — CAES 59:11
venit: Benedictus qui v. in nomine — MASS 163:16
Venite: V. adoremus — ANON 6:11
v. in Bethlehem — ANON 6:10
venomous: They are as v. as the poison — PRAY 189:9
vent: ce qu'est au feu le v. — BUSS 55:24
le v. éteint les bougies — LA R 149:11
qui s'enflamment au v. — FRAN 102:7
venture: damn her at a v. — LAMB 148:5
Each v. Is a new beginning — ELIOT 93:18
ventures: lose our v. — SHAK 217:3
Vénus: C'est V. tout entière — RAC 193:17
verb: v. has a hard time enough — TWAIN 261:7
V. is God — HUGO 127:15
v. not a noun — FULL 103:22
word is the V. — HUGO 127:15
verba: iurare in v. magistri — HOR 123:1
Verbe: Le mot, c'est le V. — HUGO 127:15
le V., c'est Dieu — HUGO 127:15
Verbosa: V. et grandis epistula — JUV 138:3
verbosity: exuberance of his own v. — DISR 87:3
revered always not crude v. — JER 130:15
Verbrennt: wo man Bücher V. — HEINE 116:12
VERBUM: V. CARO FACTUM EST
— MASS 163:21
volat irrevocabile v. — HOR 123:5
Verde: V. que te quiero verde — GARC 104:13
verification: v. of his own prophecies — TROL 260:10
verify: always to v. your references — ROUTH 198:3
verily: v., I say unto you — BIBLE 36:24
verisimilitude: intended to give artistic v.
— GILB 108:14
veritas: Magna est v. — BIBLE 41:25
(magna est v. et praevalebit) — BROO 47:17
sed magis amica v. — ARIS 8:8
vérité: doit aux morts que la v. — VOLT 265:8
vermin: they are lower than v. — BEVAN 21:16
Vermont: bishop, elect, of V. — KNOX 147:6
vero: Se non è v. — ANON 6:9
vers: chantant mes v. — RONS 196:6
n'est point prose est v. — MOL 171:7
Versailles: lady at the court of V. — VOLT 265:3
versate: Nocturna v. manu — HOR 122:19
versatile: restless and v. intellect — HUXL 128:14
Verse: Book of V. — FITZ 98:15
bumbast out a blank v. — GREE 112:18
indignation makes me write v. — JUV 137:14
Lies the subject of all v. — BROW 48:14
Ne'er a v. to thee — KING 142:11
Not v. now — BROW 49:3
that is not prose is v. — MOL 171:7
They say my v. is sad — HOUS 126:23
V. calls them forth — LAND 148:10
v. you grave for me — STEV 247:16
Voice and V. — MILT 167:5
Who died to make v. free — PRES 191:15
Writing free v. is like — FROST 103:13
verses: How many v. have I thrown — LAND 148:13
you murmur my v. — RONS 196:6
versum: facit indignatio v. — JUV 137:14

versus: quod temptabam dicere v. — OVID 179:1
vertu: virginité pouvait être une v. — VOLT 265:4
verum: Ave v. corpus — ANON 6:15
  Quod enim mavult homo v. — BACON 13:30
  silvas Academi quaerere v. — HOR 123:7
very: remember'd for a v. long time — MCG 157:11
vespers: friars were singing v. — GIBB 106:8
vessel: Let the Irish v. lie — AUDEN 10:17
  unto the weaker v. — BIBLE 40:20
vesture: muddy v. of decay — SHAK 226:5
vexation: Multiplication is v. — ANON 4:8
  vanity and v. of spirit — BIBLE 27:4
Vexilla: V. regis prodeunt — VEN 261:20
Vexing: V. the dull ear of a drowsy — SHAK 217:11
viable: basically I'm v. from ten — BETJ 20:12
vibration: That brave v. each way — HERR 119:1
vicar: Evangelical v., in want — KNOX 147:6
vice: Hypocrisy is a tribute which v. — LA R 149:10
  lost by not having been v. — WALP 266:7
  no v., but beggary — SHAK 217:8
  of all v. and immorality — FIEL 98:6
  raptures and roses of v. — SWIN 249:18
  V. itself lost half its — BURKE 53:10
vices: made so as to wipe out v. — MONT 172:4
  Most v. may be committed — BOSW 45:4
vici: vidi, v. — CAES 59:11
vicinity: this well-nightingaled v. — HOUS 127:3
Vicisti: V., Galilaee — JUL 137:10
victa: sed v. Catoni — LUCAN 155:1
victim: Any v. demands allegiance — GREE 112:16
  that a v. must be found — GILB 108:4
victims: little v. play — GRAY 112:10
victis: Vae v. — LIVY 152:9
Victor: croyait V. Hugo — COCT 74:1
  my shock-headed v. — BETJ 21:13
  v. belong the spoils — MARCY 159:16
  V. Hugo…A madman — COCT 74:1
victoree: thy v. — ANON 4:12
Victoria: ticket at V. Station and go — BEVIN 21:18
  worse at V. and Waterloo — CONN 77:8
victories: Peace hath her v. — MILT 170:14
victory: 'But 'twas a famous v. — SOUT 243:18
  grave, where is thy v. — BIBLE 38:23
  in v., magnanimity — CHUR 71:17
  One more such v. and we — PYRR 193:4
  Thy v., O Grave — ROSS 197:2
Victrix: V. causa deis placuit — LUCAN 155:1
victuals: About their v. — CALV 60:2
vicus: v. of recirculation back — JOYCE 136:16
vidders: Be wery careful o' v. all — DICK 85:18
Video: V. meliora — OVID 178:22
vie: et la v. qui est saulve — FRAN 102:6
  mis mon génie dans ma v. — WILDE 272:1
  que la v. est quotidienne — LAF 147:15
vieille: Quand vous serez bien v. — RONS 196:6
vieillesse: si v. pouvoit — EST 97:3
viento: Verde v. — GARC 104:13
vieux: Eldorado banal de tous les v. — BAUD 16:13
view: lends enchantment to the v. — CAMP 60:18
vigil: tongueless v. and all the pain — SWIN 249:15
vigilance: liberty to man is eternal v. — CURR 81:5
vigilant: Be sober, be v. — BIBLE 40:22
vigilat: frustra v. qui custodit — BIBLE 41:15
vile: In durance vile here must — BURNS 54:6
  only man is v. — HEBER 116:10
  Things base and v. — SHAK 226:14
  v. a pun would not scruple — DENN 82:20
vilest: v. things Become themselves — SHAK 203:24
village: loveliest v. of the plain — GOLD 110:5

Some v.-Hampden — GRAY 112:5
villages: pleasant v. and farms — MILT 169:17
  v. dirty and charging high — ELIOT 94:1
villain: determined to prove a v. — SHAK 231:3
  lecherous, kindless v. — SHAK 208:22
  No v. need be — MER 165:3
  smiling, damned v. — SHAK 207:17
vinces: In hoc signo v. — CONS 77:17
Vinci: They spell it V. and pronounce — TWAIN 261:4
vincit: Amor v. omnia — CHAU 68:2
  Omnia v. Amor — VIRG 264:8
vine: every man under his v. — BIBLE 30:17
  luscious clusters of the v. — MARV 161:5
  shall be as the fruitful v. — PRAY 190:21
  sweet grape who will the v. — SHAK 235:6
  v. and grapes in gold — FLEC 100:10
  With v, leaves in his hair — IBSEN 129:8
vinegar: Marriage from love, like v. — BYRON 58:4
vines: that spoil the v. — BIBLE 28:1
  v. that round the thatch-eaves — KEATS 140:12
vineyard: Give me thy v. — BIBLE 25:7
vingt-quatre: capitaine de v. soldats — ANON 5:18
Vintage: Fate of all their V. prest — FITZ 99:2
Vintners: often wonder what the V. buy — FITZ 99:12
violations: v. committed by children — BOWEN 45:14
viol-de-gamboys: He plays o' the v. — SHAK 233:16
violent: All v. feelings…produce — RUSK 198:8
  v. hands upon themselves — PRAY 188:3
violet: oxlips and the nodding v. — SHAK 227:5
  throw a perfume on the v. — SHAK 217:12
  v. by a mossy stone — WORD 276:14
  v. smells to him as it — SHAK 213:21
violets: breathes upon a bank of v. — SHAK 233:14
  v. dim — SHAK 235:1
  When daisies pied and v. — SHAK 219:13
violins: v. of autumn — VERL 262:2
violons: v. De l'automne — VERL 262:2
vipers: generation of v. — BIBLE 31:5
vir: Beatus v. qui timet Dominum — BIBLE 41:13
virgin: Gloriously deceitful and a v. — HOR 124:9
  Now too the v. goddess — VIRG 264:6
  v. shall conceive — BIBLE 28:16
Virginibus: V. puerisque canto — HOR 124:5
virginité: v. pouvait être une vertu — VOLT 265:4
virginity: No, no; for my v. — PRIOR 191:18
  That long preserved v. — MARV 161:21
  your old v. — SHAK 203:12
virgo: Iam redit et v. — VIRG 264:6
  in omne v. Nobilis — HOR 124:9
virisque: antiquis res stat Romana v. — ENN 97:2
virtue: Assume a v. — SHAK 210:19
  cathartic v. — EMER 96:12
  crowds and keep your v. — KIPL 144:9
  either of v. or mischief — BACON 13:11
  fugitive and cloistered v. — MILT 170:17
  if there be any v. — BIBLE 39:20
  is no v. like necessity — SHAK 229:19
  lilies and languors of v. — SWIN 249:18
  only reward of v. is virtue — EMER 96:11
  Silence is the v. of fools — BACON 12:22
  tribute which vice pays to v. — LA R 149:10
  v., and not birth — FLET 100:17
  V. knows to a farthing — WALP 266:7
  wisdom, capacity and v. — SWIFT 249:1
  Young men have more v. — JOHN 132:2
virtues: Be to her v. very kind — PRIOR 191:16
  his v. Will plead — SHAK 221:1

Is it a world to hide v.   SHAK 233:17
it makes some v. impracticable   JOHN 133:20
plant whose v. have not   EMER 96:17
v. We write in water   SHAK 215:12
virtuous: because thou art v.   SHAK 233:23
infancy to think all men v.   BURKE 52:10
v. woman is a crown   BIBLE 26:14
which is the most v. man   WALP 266:3
Who can find a v. woman   BIBLE 26:34
Vis: V. consili expers mole   HOR 124:8
visage: working all his v. wann'd   SHAK 208:20
visibilium: v. omnium et invisibilium   MASS 163:13
visible: life now, compact, v.   WHIT 269:17
outward and v. sign   PRAY 187:22
things v. and invisible   PRAY 187:12
vision: baseless fabric of this v.   SHAK 232:24
In a v. once I saw   COL 75:6
Saw the V. of the world   TENN 253:10
V. of Christ that thou   BLAKE 42:20
Was it a v.   KEATS 140:1
visionary: Whither is fled the v. gleam
   WORD 275:15
visions: v. before midnight   BROW 48:5
While these v. did appear   SHAK 228:3
young men shall see v.   BIBLE 30:14
visited: ye v. me   BIBLE 34:8
visitor: takes me I travel as a v.   HOR 123:1
visits: people never make long v.   MOORE 172:12
vita: del cammin di nostra v.   DANTE 81:7
vitae: Integer v. scelerisque   HOR 123:16
vitai: cursores v. lampada tradunt   LUCR 155:7
Vitality: V. in a woman is a blind   SHAW 238:2
vitiorum: dilectione hominum et odio v.   AUG 11:20
Vivamus: V., mea Lesbia   CAT 65:5
vivants: doit des égards aux v.   VOLT 265:8
vive: Il faut que je v.   DARG 7:20
vivere: Nec tecum possum v. nec   MART 161:9
vivito: v. sicut ibi   AMBR 2:8
vivre: foy je veuil v. et mourir   VILL 262:14
Il faut manger pour v.   MOL 171:5
V.? les serviteurs feront   VILL 262:12
V. sans rêve, qu'est-ce   ROST 197:11
vixen: v. when she went to school   SHAK 227:13
Vixere: V. fortes ante Agamemnona   HOR 124:17
Vixi: V. puellis nuper idoneus   HOR 124:11
Vobis: Pax V.   BIBLE 41:20
vobiscum: Dominus v.   MASS 163:6
Pax Domini sit semper v.   MASS 163:17
vocabulary: v. of 'Bradshaw' is nervous
   DOYLE 89:27
vocation: I have not felt the v.   CLOU 73:8
vocem: exaudi v. meam   BIBLE 41:16
voice: against the v. of a nation   RUSS 198:12
base barreltone v.   JOYCE 137:7
hear a v. in every wind   GRAY 112:9
hear my v.   BIBLE 41:16
hear my v.   PRAY 190:22
heart and v. would fail   CLAR 73:1
Hear the v. of the Bard   BLAKE 43:6
hear the v. of the charmer   PRAY 189:9
Her v. is full of money   FITZ 100:3
Her v. was ever soft   SHAK 219:3
his big manly v.   SHAK 205:1
I have lost my v.   WEBS 267:18
in that tone of v.   PUNCH 192:21
I see a v.   SHAK 227:22
reserve the more weighty v.   BACON 13:4
sound of a v. that is still   TENN 251:5
still small v.   BIBLE 25:6

'Tis the v. of the lobster   CARR 63:13
'Tis the v. of the sluggard   WATTS 266:18
v. and nothing more   ANON 7:9
V. and Verse   MILT 167:5
V. beat   THOM 258:2
v. I hear this passing   KEATS 140:1
v. is Jacob's voice   BIBLE 22:30
v. of one crying   BIBLE 31:4
v. of the Lord God walking   BIBLE 22:12
v. of the people is   ALC 2:1
v. of the turtle is heard   BIBLE 27:29
v. that breathed o'er Eden   KEBLE 141:11
voices: Two v. are there   STEP 246:2
Two V. are there   WORD 277:6
v. of children are heard   BLAKE 43:1
v. prophesying war   COL 75:5
void: v. your rheum upon my beard   SHAK 225:1
voix: v. d'enfants chantants   VERL 262:4
vol: propriété c'est le v.   PROU 192:3
volat: v. irrevocabile verbum   HOR 123:6
volcanoes: range of exhausted v.   DISR 87:1
vole: passes the questing v.   WAUGH 266:20
Volkes: V. grossen Lüge   HITL 119:13
Volscians: Flutter'd your V. in Corioli   SHAK 206:1
Voltaire: mock on, V., Rousseau   BLAKE 43:3
voluisse: in magnis et v. sat est   PROP 192:1
volume: Lo here a little v.   CRAS 80:9
volumes: v. attested the variety   GIBB 106:12
written such v. of stuff   LEAR 150:4
volunt: homines id quod v. credunt   CAES 59:9
voluptas: est in coitu et brevis v.   PETR 183:3
Trahit sua quemque v.   VIRG 264:4
volupté: Luxe, calme et v.   BAUD 16:12
vomit: dog returneth to his v.   BIBLE 26:30
turned to his own v. again   BIBLE 40:23
vote: One man shall have one v.   CART 64:20
v. just as their leaders   GILB 107:17
votis: Hoc erat in v.   HOR 125:1
vouldras: Fay ce que v.   RAB 193:14
voulu: Vous l'avez v.   MOL 171:10
Vovi: V.— I've Oude'   PUNCH 192:14
vow: I v. to thee, my country   SPR 245:4
vows: falser than v. made in wine   SHAK 205:7
God keep all v. unbroke   SHAK 230:12
honey of his music v.   SHAK 209:6
vox: nescit v. missa   HOR 122:21
V. et praeterea nihil   ANON 7:9
V. populi   ALC 2:1
voyage: about to take my last v.   HOBB 120:2
all the v. of their life   SHAK 217:3
first to make the v.   VIRG 263:13
Ulysse a fait un beau v.   DU B 91:15
Voyaging: V. through strange seas   WORD 276:7
vrais: v. paradis sont les paradis   PROU 192:7
vulgar: elevates above the v. herd   GAIS 104:6
Father is rather v.   DICK 84:10
it is looked upon as v.   WILDE 271:5
it's v.   PUNCH 192:18
vulgi: tumultuositas v. semper insaniae   ALC 2:1
wabe: gyre and gimble in the w.   CARR 63:16
wade: should I w. no more   SHAK 222:21
Waffen: Ein' gute Wehr und W.   LUTH 155:14
wage: give themselves for w.   YEATS 279:11
one can w. a pitiless war   GREE 112:15
wager: Have lost the w.   SHAK 206:2
wages: art gone and ta'en thy w.   SHAK 206:4
w. of sin is death   BIBLE 37:36
Wagner: W. has lovely moments   ROSS 197:10
wagon: Hitch your w. to a star   EMER 96:18

wail: mirth to w. a week	SHAK 235:6
with old woes new w.	SHAK 235:12
wailing: woman w. for her demon-lover	COL 75:3
wait: can w. and not be tired	KIPL 144:7
I almost had to w.	LOUI 154:6
Learn to labour and to w.	LONG 153:11
serve who only stand and w.	MILT 170:11
w. for liberty till they	MAC 157:1
We had better w. and see	ASQ 9:22
waiter: sallow w. brings me beans	SASS 200:15
waitest: w. for the spark from heaven	ARN 8:21
Waiting: W. for the end, boys	EMPS 96:20
We're w. for Godot	BECK 17:5
waiting-room: now we three in Euston w.	
	CORN 78:6
wak'd: 'You have w. me too soon	WATTS 266:18
wake: Do I w. or sleep	KEATS 140:1
Got 'tween asleep and w.	SHAK 217:19
should die before I w.	ANON 4:11
slepyng hound to w.	CHAU 68:23
w. and call me early	TENN 254:3
W.! for the Ruddy Ball	THOM 258:8
we w. eternally	DONNE 88:4
wakened: w. us from sleeping	BROO 47:15
waking: w., no such matter	SHAK 236:6
Wales: bless the Prince of W.	LINL 152:7
good of going to W.	AUDEN 11:2
walk: Doth w. in fear and dread	COL 74:18
In a slow silent w.	HARDY 114:11
I w. through the valley	PRAY 188:16
me to w. doth make	SCOT 202:15
take up thy bed, and w.	BIBLE 36:22
w. down Piccadilly with	GILB 108:21
w. for a walk's sake	KLEE 147:1
w. humbly with thy God	BIBLE 30:15
w. over the western wave	SHEL 240:6
W. under his huge legs	SHAK 215:16
W. upon England's mountains	BLAKE 43:2
w. with Kings	KIPL 144:9
w. with you	SHAK 224:17
w. ye in it	BIBLE 29:4
Where'er you w.	POPE 185:23
Why do you w. through	CORN 78:7
'Will you w. a little faster	CARR 63:10
'Will you w. into my parlour	HOW 127:11
walk'd: w. through the wilderness	BUNY 51:16
walked: He w. by himself	KIPL 146:17
I have w. out in rain	FROST 103:2
w. in darkness have seen	BIBLE 28:18
walking: from w. up and down	BIBLE 25:17
God w. in the garden	BIBLE 22:12
I nauseate w.	CONG 77:1
W., and leaping	BIBLE 37:14
w. by his wild lone	KIPL 146:18
walks: She w. in beauty	BYRON 58:21
W. o'er the dew of yon	SHAK 206:10
w. up and down with me	SHAK 217:10
wish I liked the way it w.	RAL 194:10
wall: close the w. up with our	SHAK 213:14
Duchess painted on the w.	BROW 50:4
have I leaped over a w.	BIBLE 24:30
w. will hang my weapons	HOR 124:11
With our backs to the w.	HAIG 113:9
Wallace: wha hae wi' W. bled	BURNS 54:20
wallet: Time hath, my lord, a w.	SHAK 233:8
walls: upon the w. of thine house	PRAY 190:21
w. Of Magnus Martyr	ELIOT 95:5
Washes its w. on the southern	BROW 50:9
wooden w. are the best	COV 79:1

Walrus: W. and the Carpenter	CARR 64:1
waly, waly: w., up the bank	BALL 15:4
wander: to w. unchecked through	BRAM 46:5
wander'd: Here about the beach I w.	TENN 253:6
wandered: I w. lonely as a cloud	WORD 275:3
who w. far and wide after	HOMER 121:1
Wanderer: W., await it too	ARN 8:21
wayworn w. bore	POE 184:3
wandering: Poor w. one	GILB 108:30
W. between two worlds	ARN 8:14
w. minstrel	GILD 107:24
w. voice	WORD 277:11
wand'ring: tempt with w. feet	MILT 169:3
want: articles which they do not w.	HURST 128:9
I'll not w.	SCOT 202:15
must be in w. of a wife	AUST 12:11
third is freedom from w.	RONS 196:12
Though much I w. which	DYER 92:4
w. of a horse the rider	FRAN 102:11
w. of a thing is perplexing	VANB 261:10
What can I w. or need	HERB 118:15
wanting: balances and art found w.	BIBLE 30:9
wanton: wightly w. with a velvet brow	SHAK 219:9
wantonly: unadvisedly, lightly, or w.	PRAY 187:24
wantonness: Kindles in clothes a w.	HERR 118:18
wantons: Shall we play the w. with	SHAK 230:10
wants: Man w. but little	GOLD 110:12
Man w. but little	HOLM 120:16
Man w. but little	YOUNG 280:10
work does what he w. to do	COLL 75:19
want-wit: w. sadness makes of me	SHAK 224:10
war: All the business of w.	WELL 267:22
Austria is going to the w.	CHES 70:1
broken the second rule of w.	MONT 172:8
can wage a pitiless w.	GREE 112:15
casualty when w. comes is truth	JOHN 131:1
condition which is called w.	HOBB 119:17
endless w. still breed	MILT 170:13
ever another w. in Europe	BISM 42:13
first in w.	LEE 151:3
image of w. without its	SURT 248:10
In a pattern called a w.	LOW 154:14
infection and the hand of w.	SHAK 230:2
In w., resolution	CHUR 71:17
In w., whichever side	CHAM 66:12
is the garland of the w.	SHAK 204:6
it is not w.	BOSQ 45:1
let slip the dogs of w.	SHAK 216:12
Let w. yield to peace	CIC 72:8
makes a good w.	HERB 118:4
midst of a cold w.	BAR 16:9
Minstrel Boy to the w.	MOORE 172:16
nature of w. consisteth	HOBB 119:17
no discharge in that w.	BIBLE 27:11
prepare for w.	VEG 261:18
shall they learn w. any more	BIBLE 28:7
sinews of w., unlimited money	CIC 72:13
'Spanish ships of w.	TENN 255:3
subject of it is W.	OWEN 179:2
that made this great w.	LINC 152:6
There never was a good w.	FRAN 102:15
time of peace thinks of w.	ANON 3:13
time of w.	BIBLE 27:7
To w. and arms I fly	LOV 154:10
used to w.'s alarms	HOOD 121:5
very well out of the w.	BALD 14:13
voices prophesying w.	COL 75:5
'W. even to the knife	BYRON 57:7
w. has its laws	NEWM 175:19

W. is a necessary part — MOLT 171:15
W. is much too serious — CLEM 73:5
w. is regarded as wicked — WILDE 271:5
W. its thousands slays — PORT 186:3
W.'s annals will cloud — HARDY 114:11
W. to the knife — PAL 179:17
when the blast of w. blows — SHAK 213:14
when the w. is done — SASS 200:5
warbling: thought w. his Doric lay — MILT 168:4
wardrobe: silken dalliance in the w. — SHAK 213:11
war-drum: Till the w. throbb'd no — TENN 253:10
wards: deftly in the oiled w. — KEATS 140:8
pretty young w. in Chancery — GILB 107:13
warfare: that her w. is accomplished — BIBLE 29:8
Waring: What's become of W. — BROW 50:24
warm: she's w. — SHAK 235:3
This is too w. work — NELS 175:7
w. the air in raw inclement — SWIFT 248:19
w. wind, the west wind — MAS 163:5
warmed: I w. both hands before — LAND 148:8
w. and cooled by the same — SHAK 225:10
warmth: His vigorous w. did — DRYD 90:10
w. about my heart like — KEATS 141:4
warn: poet can do today is to w. — OWEN 179:3
right to w. — BAG 14:7
warned: be w. by me — BELL 18:11
So be w. by my lot (which — KIPL 144:15
warning: Give w. to the world that — SHAK 236:4
War Office: anything except the British W. — SHAW 237:12
warrior: he lay like a w. taking — WOLFE 273:21
Home they brought her w. — TENN 254:13
wars: all their w. are merry — CHES 69:20
granites which titanic w. — OWEN 179:9
I see w. — VIRG 263:9
serve in the w. — PRAY 191:14
Since w. begin in the minds — ANON 4:18
wars and rumours of w. — BIBLE 33:32
warts: w., and everything — CROM 80:16
war-war: jaw-jaw is better than to w. — CHUR 71:14
wash: art can w. her guilt — GOLD 110:18
Bid them w. their faces — SHAK 205:15
Tears w. out a Word — FITZ 99:9
w. the balm from an anointed — SHAK 230:5
w. their feet in soda water — ELIOT 95:3
W. your hands — SHAK 223:9
Washes: W. its walls on the southern — BROW 50:9
washing: country w. — BRUM 50:27
only w. — THOM 257:12
w. ain't done nor sweeping — ANON 3:14
which came up from the w. — BIBLE 28:3
wash-pot: Moab is my w. — PRAY 189:10
waste: my dear times' w. — SHAK 235:12
now doth time w. me — SHAK 231:1
spirit in a w. of shame — SHAK 236:13
w. its sweetness — GRAY 112:5
w. of breath the years — YEATS 279:5
w. remains and kills — EMPS 96:21
w. the remains of life — WALP 265:18
we lay w. our powers — WORD 277:7
Wasted: W. his substance with riotous — BIBLE 35:26
wasteful: w., blundering, low — DARW 81:16
waste-paper: Marriage is the w. basket — WEBB 267:4
wastes: that w. her time and me — WALL 265:13
wasting: w. in despair — WITH 273:6
watch: could ye not w. with me — BIBLE 34:14
done far better by a w. — BELL 18:23

He can w. a grass or leaf — GRAV 111:14
keeping w. over their flock — BIBLE 35:1
keeping w. above his own — LOW 154:18
like your w. in a private — CHES 69:9
Lord w. between me — BIBLE 23:2
past as a w. in the night — PRAY 189:21
She shall w. all night — SHAK 232:9
some must w. — SHAK 210:2
W. and pray — BIBLE 34:15
W. therefore — BIBLE 34:4
W. the wall — KIPL 145:15
watchdog: w.'s voice that bay'd — GOLD 110:7
watched: I w. in vain — FLEC 100:11
watcher: like some w. of the skies — KEATS 140:4
watches: heart That w. and receives — WORD 277:9
w. from his mountain walls — TENN 251:13
watchman: w. waketh but in vain — PRAY 190:19
W., what of the night — BIBLE 28:24
water: benison of hot w. — BROO 47:7
By trinking up ta w. — AYT 12:18
don't care where the w. — CHES 70:8
Drink no longer w. — BIBLE 39:29
feet are always in the w. — AMES 2:9
fountain of the w. of life — BIBLE 41:9
good Shall come of w. — BROO 47:8
Is wetter w. — BROO 47:9
Laughing W. — LONG 153:13
Little drops of w. — CARN 62:2
name was writ in w. — KEATS 141:8
plain w. and raw greens — AUDEN 11:12
plunge your hands in w. — AUDEN 10:10
virtues We write in w. — SHAK 215:12
wasn't as dull as ditch w. — DICK 85:11
w. clears us of this deed — SHAK 222:2
w., every where — COL 74:10
w. in the rough rude sea — SHAK 230:5
W. like a stone — ROSS 197:5
W. your damned flower-pots — BROW 50:20
We'll o'er the w. to Charlie — HOGG 120:14
with w. and a crust — KEATS 139:8
with w. of affliction — BIBLE 25:8
wood and drawers of w. — BIBLE 24:4
water-brooks: hart desireth the w. — PRAY 189:1
waterfall: From the w. he named her — LONG 153:13
water-lily: She saw the w. bloom — TENN 253:4
Waterloo: high at Austerlitz and W. — SAND 199:11
man meets his W. at last — PHIL 183:5
W. was won on the playing — WELL 268:4
worse at Victoria and W. — CONN 77:8
watermen: w., that row one way — BURT 55:14
waters: beside the w. of comfort — PRAY 188:15
Cast thy bread upon the w. — BIBLE 27:20
crept by me upon the w. — SHAK 232:14
Many w. cannot quench love — BIBLE 28:5
Over the rolling w. go — TENN 254:8
pour the w. of the Nile — CARR 62:16
quiet w. — SCOT 202:15
Stolen w. are sweet — BIBLE 26:11
their business in great w. — PRAY 190:8
w. of affliction — BIBLE 29:3
w. of Babylon we sat — PRAY 191:1
W. on a starry night — WORD 275:13
w. to a thirsty soul — BIBLE 26:28
watery: shoreless w. wild — ARN 8:15
wattles: of clay and w. made — YEATS 279:7
waul: We w. and cry — SHAK 218:23
wave: All sunk beneath the w. — COWP 79:15
lift me as a w. — SHEL 239:14
translucent w. — MILT 167:9

w. to pant beneath thy	SHEL 239:13
When the blue w. rolls	BYRON 57:16
Waverley: W. pen	ANON 5:4
waves: Him that walked the w.	MILT 168:2
Innumerable twinkling of the w.	AESC 1:17
rule the w.	THOM 258:12
What are the wild w. saying	CARP 62:3
while the tired w.	CLOU 73:17
waving: not w. but drowning	SMITH 242:13
w. his wild tail	KIPL 146:18
wax: hives with honey and w.	SWIFT 249:17
W. to receive	BYRON 57:4
way: broad is the w.	BIBLE 32:8
every one to his own w.	BIBLE 29:15
I am the w., the truth	BIBLE 37:2
Prepare ye the w. of the Lord	BIBLE 31:4
That's the w. for Billy	HOGG 120:13
that's the w. to the stars	VIRG 264.2
This is the w.	BIBLE 29:4
Thou art my w.	QUAR 193:7
w. may be known upon earth	PRAY 189:12
w. of an eagle in the air	BIBLE 26:33
w. of transgressors is	BIBLE 26:17
w. that Providence dictates	HITL 119:14
w. to dusty death	SHAK 223:15
woman has her w.	HOLM 120:17
ways: all her w. be unconfin'd	PRIOR 191:16
keep then in all thy w.	PRAY 190:1
Let me count the w.	BROW 48:17
neither are your ways my w.	BIBLE 29:18
That for w. that are dark	HARTE 115:12
There are nine and sixty w.	KIPL 144:10
w. are ways of pleasantness	BIBLE 26:6
w. deep and the weather	ELIOT 93:25
whose heart are thy w.	PRAY 189:18
wayside: Some seeds fell by the w.	BIBLE 33:4
we: Put it down a w.	DICK 85:20
weak: Made w. by time and fate	TENN 255:16
willing but the flesh is w.	BIBLE 34:15
Weakening: W. the will	SPEN 244:12
weaker: unto the w. vessel	BIBLE 40:20
weakest: in addition the w. executive	DISR 86:14
w. kind of fruit	SHAK 225:16
weakness: amiable w.	FIEL 98:10
'Is it w. of intellect	GILB 108:18
weaknesses: his w. are great	KIPL 143:7
wealth: all that w. e'er gave	GRAY 112:3
insolence of w. will creep	JOHN 133:9
love remember'd such w.	SHAK 235:11
Say that health and w.	HUNT 128:5
their w. increaseth	MARL 160:11
w. ye find, another keeps	SHEL 240:2
Where w. accumulates	GOLD 110:6
wealthy: business of the w. man	BELL 19:2
wean'd: were we not w. till then	DONNE 88:1
weapon: folly and his w. wit	HOPE 121:15
weapons: wear w., and serve	PRAY 191:14
will hang my w. and my lyre	HOR 124:11
wear: Nothing to w. but clothes	KING 142:5
w. him In my heart's core	SHAK 209:9
w. out than to rust out	CUMB 81:1
w. your rue with a difference	SHAK 211:7
wearies: you say it w. you	SHAK 224:10
weariest: w. and most loathed worldly	SHAK 224:4
wearin: w.' o' the Green	ANON 3:20
weariness: much study is a w.	BIBLE 27:23
w., the fever	KEATS 139:19
w. treads on desire	PETR 183:3
wearing: w. arm-chairs tight	WOD 273:15

weary: Age shall not w. them	BINY 42:6
All with w. task fordone	SHAK 228:1
I'm w. wi' hunting	BALL 14:17
I sae w. fu' o' care	BURNS 55:8
I was w. and ill at ease	PROC 191:20
there the w. be at rest	BIBLE 25:20
w., stale, flat	SHAK 206:15
W. with toil	SHAK 235:10
weasel: Methinks it is like a w.	SHAK 210:8
Pop goes the w.	MAND 159:8
w. ouelie eggs	SHAK 204.20
weather: first talk is of the w.	JOHN 134:21
her madness and her w.	AUDEN 10:16
If it prove fair w.	SUCK 248:6
Jolly boating w.	CORY 78:10
no such thing as bad w.	RUSK 198:10
not in fine w.	CLOU 73:10
roof of blue Italian w.	SHEL 239:7
w. the cuckoo likes	HARDY 114:15
w. the shepherd shuns	HARDY 115:1
w. turned around	THOM 257:7
winter and rough w.	SHAK 204:19
you won't hold up the w.	MACN 158:7
weave: tangled web we w.	SCOTT 202:1
W. a circle round him thrice	COL 75:7
w. but nets to catch	WEBS 267:6
weaving: thread of my own hand's w.	KEATS 140:2
web: She left the w.	TENN 253:4
tangled w. we weave	SCOTT 202:1
web-foot: Every fork like a white w.	HARDY 114:14
webs: Laws are like spider's w.	SOLON 243:10
Webster: W. was much possessed	ELIOT 95:8
wed: December when they w.	SHAK 205:10
save trouble I w. again	CLARE 72:19
think to w. it	SHAK 203:11
With this Ring I thee w.	PRAY 188:1
wedde: Cristen man shall w.	CHAU 68:16
wedded: god that I have w. fyve	CHAU 68:16
Wedding-Guest: W. here beat his breast	COL 74:7
Wedlock: W., indeed, hath oft compared	DAV 81:20
yet w.'s the devil	BYRON 58:17
Wee: W., sleekit	BURNS 55:5
W. Willie Winkie rins through	MILL 166:10
weed: more ought law to w. it	BACON 13:16
What is a w.	EMER 96:17
weeds: At grubbing w. from gravel	KIPL 144:3
smell far worse than w.	SHAK 236:7
week: mirth to wail a w.	SHAK 235:6
w. is a long time in politics	WILS 272:17
weep: fear of having to w.	BEAU 16:15
I w. for Adonais	SHEL 238:24
must w. or she will die	TENN 254:13
'Tis that I may not w.	BYRON 58:11
W., and you weep alone	WILC 271:2
W. not for little Léonie	GRAH 111:7
'w.! 'weep	BLAKE 43:17
we w. to see	HERR 118:22
women must w.	KING 142:14
weeping: Doth that bode w.	SHAK 229:10
w. and gnashing of teeth	BIBLE 32:15
Wehr: *Ein' gute W. und Waffen*	LUTH 155:14
Weib: *W. und Gesang*	LUTH 155:13
weighed: art w. in the balances	BIBLE 30:9
weighs: Which w. upon the heart	SHAK 223:13
weight: let us lay aside every w.	BIBLE 40:9
w. of rages will press	SPOON 245:2
whose words are of less w.	BACON 13:4

weighty: reserve the more w. voice — BACON 13:4
Wein: Wer nicht liebt W. — LUTH 155:13
welcome: bear w. in your eye — SHAK 220:12
Love bade me w. — HERB 118:11
us w. peaceful ev'ning — COWP 80:4
W. the sixte — CHAU 68:16
W. to your gory bed — BURNS 54:20
welcomest: w. when they are gone — SHAK 214:7
welfare: w. of this realm do chiefly — CHAR 67:10
Welfare-State: are led to that of the W. — TEMP 251:1
welkin: let the w. roar — SHAK 212:25
well: as w. him — JOYCE 137:9
it is a foolish thing w. — JOHN 132:16
misery use it for a w. — PRAY 189:18
Sing whatever is w. made — YEATS 280:1
'tis not so deep as a w. — SHAK 231:27
w. and all manner of thing — JUL 137:11
W. building hath three — WOTT 277:19
when looking w. can't move — SUCK 248:3
who can do all things w. — CHUR 70:18
well-aired: to have the morning w. — BRUM 50:26
wellbeloved: bundle of myrrh is my w. — BIBLE 27:25
well-bred: be very strange and w. — CONG 77:2
well-conducted: Like a w. person — THAC 256:16
well-dressed: w. gives a feeling of inward — FORB 101:9
well-informed: To come with a w. mind — AUST 12:6
well-knownness: who is known for his w. — BOOR 44:18
well-nightingaled: To this w. vicinity — HOUS 127:3
wells: go about and poison w. — MARL 160:12
poison the w. — NEWM 175:19
well-shot: Spirits of w. woodcock — BETJ 20:9
well-spent: almost as rare as a w. one — CARL 61:7
well-tuned: him upon the w. cymbals — PRAY 191:8
well-written: w. Life is almost as rare — CARL 61:7
Welsh: devil understands W. — SHAK 212:14
Welshman: care and valour in this W. — SHAK 213:20
Welt: Die W. ist alles — WITT 273:7
W. des Glücklichen ist — WITT 273:9
W. hässlich und schlecht — NIET 176:18
W. in Materialismus versumpfen — MOLT 171:15
Weltgeschichte: Die W. ist das Weltgericht — SCH 201:4
Weltordnung: ein Glied in Gottes W. — MOLT 171:15
wen: fate of the great w. — COBB 73:20
wench: stuff fit only for a w. — MAS 162:16
w. is dead — MARL 160:13
Wenlock Edge: W. the wood's in trouble — HOUS 126:4
went: they w. to sea in a Sieve — LEAR 150:11
w. to the Bar as a very — GILB 107:15
wept: Babylon we sat down and w. — PRAY 191:1
he w. to hear — BLAKE 43:12
I have sometimes w. — MUSS 174:7
I w. as I remembered how — CORY 78:12
Jesus w. — BIBLE 36:33
Werther: W. had a love for Charlotte — THAC 256:15
Weser: river W. — BROW 50:9
West: bosom of the urgent W. — BRID 46:13
east, nor from the w. — PRAY 189:15
Go W. — GREE 112:14
Go W., young man — SOULE 243:15
in the gardens of the W. — CONN 77:10
safeguard of the W. — WORD 277:2
sailing away to the w. — KING 142:13
W. is West — KIPL 143:9

western: Swiftly walk over the w. — SHEL 240:6
westward: w., look — CLOU 73:17
you are stepping w. — WORD 275:7
wet: w. sheet and a flowing — CUNN 81:4
wether: tainted w. of the flock — SHAK 225:16
wetter: Is w. water — BROO 47:9
whacks: gave her mother forty w. — ANON 4:3
whale: gull's way and the w.'s — MAS 163:2
Very like a w. — SHAK 210:8
wharf: w. of Lethe waiting — HOUS 126:24
what: being for my own self w. am — HILL 119:10
He knew what's w. — BUTL 56:4
not tell us w. the soldier — DICK 85:21
W. and Why and When — KIPL 144:14
W. is our task — GEOR 105:25
W. *is* the matter with Mary Jane — MILNE 166:16
W., never — GILB 108:26
w. rough beast — YEATS 279:16
W. was he doing — BROW 48:16
Whatever: W. happens — BELL 19:4
what-is-it: certain w. in his voice — WOD 273:12
what-not: w. the afternoon passed — WOD 273:16
Whatsoever: W. things are true — BIBLE 39:20
wheat: orient and immortal w. — TRAH 259:21
wheel: w. broken at the cistern — BIBLE 27:22
w.'s kick and the wind's — MAS 162:19
wheels: all the w. of Being slow — TENN 252:14
When: had forgotten to say 'W. — WOD 273:18
If not now w. — HILL 119:10
What and Why and W. — KIPL 144:14
w. a man should marry — BACON 13:4
w. did you last see your — YEAM 278:10
W. I am dead — ROSS 197:7
w. she was bad she was — LONG 153:20
w. the sun set where were — BYRON 58:8
W. you are old and gray — YEATS 280:5
whence: canst not tell w. it cometh — BIBLE 36:20
from w. cometh my help — PRAY 190:16
Where: How and W. and Who — KIPL 144:14
when the sun set w. were — BYRON 58:8
W. are you now — HOPE 121:16
w. but here have Pride — YEATS 279:11
W. is Bohun — CREWE 80:13
w. is your comforting — HOPK 122:1
w. we are is Hell — MARL 160:4
wherefore: every why he had a w. — BUTL 56:3
w. art thou Romeo — SHAK 231:18
w. seeking whom Whence — HOUS 127:3
Whereof: W. one cannot speak — WITT 273:10
whether: w. I embrace your lordship's — WILK 272:9
whetstone: There is no such w. — ASCH 9:18
whiffling: w. through the tulgey wood — CARR 63:17
Whigs: Gentleman caught the W. bathing — DISR 86:15
W. admit no force but argument — BROW 48:15
while: w. my pretty one — TENN 254:8
whimper: Not with a bang but a w. — ELIOT 93:24
whine: w. about their condition — WHIT 270:6
whipp'd: w. the offending Adam out — SHAK 213:9
whipping: ought to get a *good w.* — VICT 262:8
who should 'scape w. — SHAK 208:19
whips: hath chastised you with w. — BIBLE 25:4
w. and scorns of time — SHAK 208:24
whirligig: w. of time brings in his — SHAK 234:13
whirlwind: they shall reap the w. — BIBLE 30:12
whiskers: my fur and w. — CARR 62:17
Runcible Cat with crimson w. — LEAR 150:19
whiskey: w. afterwards as he was — ASHF 9:20

Whisky: Freedom and W. gang thegither

BURNS 53:24

whisper: fiddled w. music   ELIOT 95:6
We w. in her ear   WILB 271:1
w. of a faction should   RUSS 198:12
w. of the south-wind rushing   TENN 253:10
W. who dares   MILNE 166:17

whispered: it's w. every where   CONG 76:15
whispering: ...w. from her towers   ARN 9:8
whispers: Blood of Jesus w.   BICK 42:4
whisp'ring: voice that bay'd the w. wind

GOLD 110:7

whist: whist upon w. drive   BETJ 20:11
whistle: was hir joly w. wel ywet   CHAU 68:14
w., and I'll come to you   BURNS 55:7
W. and she'll come to you   FLET 101:1
whistles: w. in his sound   SHAK 205:1
Whistling: W. to keep myself from   DRYD 90:21
white: always goes into w. satin   SHER 240:16
fat w. woman   CORN 78:7
garment was w. as snow   BIBLE 30:11
How ill w. hairs become   SHAK 213:6
Ionian w. and gold   ELIOT 95:5
it here in black and w.   JONS 136:1
many a head has turned w.   MULL 174:6
my soul is w.   BLAKE 43:15
O'er the w. Alps alone   DONNE 87:23
so w.! O so soft   JONS 136:9
Take up the W. Man's burden   KIPL 146:7
they shall be as w. as snow   BIBLE 28:6
Wearing w. for Eastertide   HOUS 125:4
w. and hairless as an egg   HERR 118:21
W. as an angel is the English   BLAKE 43:15
w. heat of this revolution   WILS 272:16
W. his shroud as the mountain   SHAK 210:27
w. lies to ice a cake   ASQ 10:1
w. races are really pinko-gray   FORS 101:18
whited: like unto w. sepulchres   BIBLE 33:31
whiter: I shall be w. than snow   PRAY 189:6
whites: w. of their eyes   PUTN 193:3
whither: one knows not w. nor why   MAS 163:4
w. it goeth   BIBLE 36:20
W., O splendid ship   BRID 46:13
whiting: said a w. to a snail   CARR 63:10
Whitman: pact with you, Walt W.   POUND 186:11
Whizzing: W. them over the net   BETJ 21:10
Who: How and Where and W.   KIPL 144:14
W. killed John Keats   BYRON 58:18
Whoever: W. it is that leaves him   FROST 103:9
whole: faith hath made thee w.   BIBLE 32:21
nothing can be sole or w.   YEATS 278:15
wholesome: nights are w.   SHAK 206:9
wholly: some few to be read w.   BACON 13:20
whoop: we'll w. and we'll holloa   WHYT 270:14
whooping: out of all w.   SHAK 205:5
whopping: measures is Latin for a w.   ANST 7:10
whore: dost thou lash that w.   SHAK 218:22
I am the Protestant w.   GWYN 113:7
teach the morals of a w.   JOHN 131:11
whores: Out ye w.   PEMB 182:3
whore-shops: Madhouses, prisons, w.

CLARE 72:18

Whose: W. Finger do you want   ANON 5:12
why: every w. he had a wherefore   BUTL 56:3
I can't tell you w.   MART 161:8
knows not whither nor w.   MAS 163:4
What and W. and When   KIPL 144:14
W. are you not here   THOR 259:10
W., Edward, tell me why   WORD 274:11

wicked: are Tories born w.   ANON 4:5
be equally w. and corrupt   BURKE 52:10
desperately w.   BIBLE 29:27
It's worse than w.   PUNCH 192:18
mercies of the w. are cruel   BIBLE 26:15
pomps and vanity of this w.   PRAY 187:19
pretending to be w.   WILDE 271:12
shake their w. sides   YEATS 279:11
Something w. this way comes   SHAK 222:24
this mad, w. folly   VICT 262:8
unto the w.   BIBLE 29:11
war is regarded as w.   WILDE 271:5
w. cease from troubling   BIBLE 25:20
w. flee when no man pursueth   BIBLE 26:32
wickedness: I was shapen in w.   PRAY 189:5
our manifold sins and w.   PRAY 186:17
spiritual w. in high places   BIBLE 39:15
w. that he hath committed   BIBLE 30:5
wicket: flannelled fools at the w.   KIPL 144:11
Now in Maytime to the w.   HOUS 125:9
slow W. of the Night   THOM 258:8
Widdicombe Fair: I want for to go to W.

BALL 15:6

wide: feet long and two feet w.   WORD 277:10
nor so w. as a church door   SHAK 231:27
w. as his command   DRYD 90:10
W. is the gate   BIBLE 32:8
widow: defendeth the fatherless and w.

PRAY 191:6

'eard o' the W. at Windsor   KIPL 146:8
Here's to the w. of fifty   SHER 240:25
w. bird sate mourning   SHEL 239:2
widowhood: comfortable estate of w.   GAY 105:9
Widow-maker: go with the old grey W.   KIPL 144:6
wife: account w. and children   BACON 13:12
Caesar's w. must be above   CAES 59:13
degrees dwindle into a w.   CONG 77:3
every port he finds a w.   BICK 42:3
Giving honour unto the w.   BIBLE 40:20
Here lies my w.   DRYD 91:3
He that hath w. and children   BACON 13:11
hope that keeps up a w.'s   GAY 105:9
husband is, the w. is   TENN 253:8
In every port a w.   DIBD 83:8
is no fury like an ex-w.   CONN 77:7
kill a w. with kindness   SHAK 232:9
Match'd with an aged w.   TENN 255:10
must be in want of a w.   AUST 12:11
often said to his w.   CHES 70:8
sailor's w. had chestnuts   SHAK 220:2
shall cleave unto his w.   BIBLE 22:11
that a man lay down his w.   JOYCE 137:8
They took me from my w.   CLARE 72:19
To weans and w.   BURNS 55:3
who's untrue to his w.   AUDEN 11:8
w. looked back   BIBLE 22:25
w. of thy bosom   BIBLE 23:33
w. shall be as the fruitful   PRAY 190:21
Your w. arranges accordingly   JUV 137:21
wight: Yonder a maid and her w.   HARDY 114:11
wights: descriptions of the fairest w.   SHAK 236:10
wigwam: Stood the w. of Nokomis   LONG 153:12
wild: are the w. waves saying   CARP 62:3
bore me in the southern w.   BLAKE 43:15
chance to talk a little w.   SHAK 215:4
grew more fierce and w.   HERB 118:8
I went hunting w.   OWEN 179:10
My father is gone w. into   SHAK 213:4
Revenge is a kind of w. justice   BACON 13:16

shoreless watery w.   ARN 8:15
Through what w. centuries   DE L 82:8
wilder: w. shores of love   BLAN 44:10
Wilderness: Beside me singing in the W.
    FITZ 98:15
given it for a w. of monkeys   SHAK 225:11
make a w. and call it peace   TAC 250:8
of one crying in the w.   BIBLE 31:4
through the w. of this world   BUNY 51:16
w. into a glorious empire   BURKE 52:18
ye out into the w. to see   BIBLE 32:30
wildest: w. beauty in the world   OWEN 179:10
wiles: From the w. of a stranger   NASH 174:15
wanton w.   MILT 167:16
Wilhelmine: His little grandchild W.   SOUT 243:16
will: complies against his w.   BUTL 56:11
even to have had the w.   PROP 192:1
Man has his w.   HOLM 120:17
not because we w.   ARN 8:11
not my w., but thine   BIBLE 36:7
reason and the w. of God   ARN 9:7
that the w. is infinite   SHAK 233:6
Thy w. be done in earth   BIBLE 31:21
'twur the w. o' the Lord   TENN 255:17
We *know* our w. is free   JOHN 132:13
W. in over-plus   SHAK 236:15
W. you, won't you   CARR 63:11
You w., Oscar   WHIS 269:14
Willie: Wee W. Winkie rins through   MILL 166:10
willing: spirit indeed is w. but the flesh   BIBLE 34:15
w. to sell for one shilling   LEAR 150:15
Willow: Sang 'W.   GILB 108:17
Sing all a green w.   SHAK 229:9
There is a w. grows aslant   SHAK 211:9
wills: talk of w.   SHAK 230:7
win: hope to w. by't   SHAK 215:10
w. the trick   HOYLE 127:12
Winchelsea: shall not lie easy at W.   BENET 19:12
wind: all aloud the w. doth blow   SHAK 219:14
bay'd the whisp'ring w.   GOLD 110:7
blow, thou winter w.   SHAK 205:2
Fair stood the w. for France   DRAY 90:5
fires flare up in a w.   FRAN 102:7
Frosty w. made moan   ROSS 197:5
God tempers the w.   STER 246:6
gone with the w.   DOWS 89:7
hear a voice in every w.   GRAY 112:9
how the w. doth ramm   POUND 186:6
impatient as the W.   WORD 277:4
likewise a w. on the heath   BORR 44:22
love what w. is to fire   BUSS 55:24
nets to catch the w.   WEBS 267:6
Nor ever w. blows loudly   TENN 252:8
of a rushing mighty w.   BIBLE 37:12
reed shaken with the w.   BIBLE 32:30
sand against the w.   BLAKE 43:3
streamers waving in the w.   GAY 105:23
swoln with w. and the rank   MILT 167:21
tears shall drown the w.   SHAK 221:1
that which way the w. is   SELD 202:19
They have sown the w.   BIBLE 30:12
thunder-storm *against* the w.   BYRON 57:12
trumpet of a prophecy! O, W.   SHEL 239:15
warm wind, the west w.   MAS 163:5
Western w.   ANON 5:10
western w. was wild   KING 142:12
wheel's kick and the w.'s   MAS 162:19
When the sweet w. did gently   SHAK 226:4
when the w. is southerly   SHAK 208:16

wild West W.   SHEL 239:12
w. and the rain   SHAK 234:14
w. bloweth where it listeth   BIBLE 36:20
w. extinguishes candles   LA R 149:11
w. of change is blowing   MACM 158:3
W. of the western sea   TENN 254:8
w. takes me I travel   HOR 123:1
w. that blows through me   LAWR 149:17
w. that follows fast   CUNN 81:4
w. was a torrent of darkness   NOYES 177:8
with every w. of doctrine   BIBLE 39:11
winder: w., a casement   DICK 84:21
winding: England's w. sheet   BLAKE 42:19
window: little w. where the sun   HOOD 121:7
stand at the w.   AUDEN 10:11
window-panes: rubs its back upon the w.
    ELIOT 94:4
windows: not by eastern w. only   CLOU 73:17
winds: beteem the w. of heaven   SHAK 206:15
imprisoned in the viewless w.   SHAK 224:4
when the w. are churning   LUCR 155:6
When the w. are breathing   SHEL 239:6
w., and crack your cheeks   SHAK 218:6
w. blew   BIBLE 32:13
W. of March with beauty   SHAK 235:1
W. of the World   KIPL 143:18
w. were love-sick with   SHAK 203:22
Windsmoor: Well-cut W. flapping lightly
    BETJ 21:8
Windsor: 'eard o' the Widow at W.   KIPL 146:8
windy: o' the w. side of the law   SHAK 234:11
wine: are fond of Spanish w.   MAS 162:16
bin of w.   STEV 247:15
cup of hot w. with not a drop   SHAK 205:14
days of w. and roses   DOWS 89:9
doesn't get into the w.   CHES 70:8
drink thy w. with a merry   BIBLE 27:14
falser than vows made in w.   SHAK 205:7
fetch to me a pint o' w.   BURNS 54:10
Flask of w.   FITZ 98:15
flown with insolence and w.   MILT 168:16
giant refreshed with w.   PRAY 189:16
I'll not look for w.   JONS 136:3
'I rather like bad w.   DISR 87:10
Let us have w. and women   BYRON 58:3
like generous w.   BUTL 56:13
Look not thou upon the w.   BIBLE 26:26
man that is without w.   BIBLE 30:25
mouth do crush their w.   MARV 161:15
new w. into old bottles   BIBLE 32:20
Not given to w.   BIBLE 39:27
Sans W.   FITZ 99:3
sweet white w.   MAS 162:14
Sweet w. of youth   BROO 47:5
take a glass of w.   SHER 241:1
Than mine host's Canary w.   KEATS 139:10
when the w. is   BECON 17:7
w. for thy stomach's sake   BIBLE 39:29
W. has play'd the Infidel   FITZ 99:12
W. is a mocker   BIBLE 26:24
W. maketh merry   BIBLE 27:19
w. of life is drawn   SHAK 222:7
wing: got to take under my w.   GILB 108:16
wings: Angel of Death spread his w.   BYRON 57:5
bug with gilded w.   POPE 184:22
defend thee under his w.   PRAY 189:24
hear the beating of his w.   BRIG 46:14
resembled the w. of an ostrich   MAC 156:13
take the w. of the morning   PRAY 191:3

that I had w. like a dove | PRAY 189:8
wink: never came a w. too soon | HOOD 121:7
winners: there are no w. | CHAM 66:12
winning: w. cause pleased the gods | LUCAN 155:1
winning-post: boats began to near the w. | COKE 74:2
winnings: one heap of all your w. | KIPL 144:8
winnowing: hair soft-lifted by the w. | KEATS 140:13
winter: English w. | BYRON 58:14
If W. comes | SHEL 239:15
It was not in the w, | HOOD 121:4
It was the w. wild | MILT 168:7
mountains by the w. sea | TENN 252:4
No enemy But w. | SHAK 204:19
out in the Middle of W. | ADD 1:12
sad tale's best for w. | SHAK 234:20
Seeming and savour all the w. | SHAK 234:24
spring are on w.'s traces | SWIN 249:15
through the perils of w. | TROL 260:4
Twice a week the w. thorough | HOUS 125:9
very dead of W. | ANDR 2:11
very dead of w. | ELIOT 93:25
w. hath my absence been | SHAK 236:8
W. is icummen | POUND 186:6
w. is past | BIBLE 27:29
w. of our discontent | SHAK 231:2
w. or summer when they're | CHEK 69:2
w.'s rains and ruins are | SWIN 249:16
wipe: God shall w. away all tears | BIBLE 40:33
God shall w. away all tears | BIBLE 41:8
Let me w. it first | SHAK 218:21
w. the tears for ever from | MILT 168:3
wire: electric w. the message came | ANON 3:2
wires: If hairs be w. | SHAK 236:14
wisdom: apply our hearts unto w. | PRAY 189:23
is the beginning of w. | PRAY 190:11
leads to the palace of w. | BLAKE 44:1
price of w. is above rubies | BIBLE 25:29
such w. as many of us have | TROL 260:12
w., capacity and virtue | SWIFT 249:1
W. is the principal thing | BIBLE 26:7
w. lingers | TENN 253:11
w. of the crocodiles | BACON 13:26
w. shall die with you | BIBLE 25:23
wise: awhile from letters to be w. | JOHN 135:9
be w. | BIBLE 26:8
be w. in his own conceit | BIBLE 26:29
came w. men from the east | BIBLE 31:1
I heard a w. man say | HOUS 125:7
In a bowl to sea went w. | PEAC 181:17
leave the W. | FITZ 99:4
Let me smile with the w. | JOHN 132:12
Nor ever did a w. one | ROCH 195:15
nor talk too w. | KIPL 144:7
same tree that a w. man | BLAKE 44:2
therefore w. as serpents | BIBLE 32:24
things w. and wonderful | ALEX 2:3
'Tis folly to be w. | GRAY 112:12
To be w., and love | SHAK 233:7
To be w. and eke to love | SPEN 244:21
Who can be w. | SHAK 222:8
w. and masterly inactivity | MACK 157:14
w. father that knows his | SHAK 225:3
w. man will make | BACON 13:3
w. son maketh a glad | BIBLE 26:12
wisedoom: what is bettre than w. | CHAU 68:10
wisely: Be w. worldly | QUAR 193:5
Of one that lov'd not w. | SHAK 229:15
wiser: Are w. and nicer | AUDEN 11:7

not the w. grow | POMF 184:4
sadder and a w. man | COL 74:21
w. to-day than he was yesterday | POPE 186:1
wisest: w. fool in Christendom | HENR 117:14
wish: Thy w. was father | SHAK 213:1
Who did not w. to die | SHAW 238:22
Whoever hath her w. | SHAK 236:15
who would w. to die | BORR 44:22
willingly believe what they w. | CAES 59:9
w. I loved the Human Race | RAL 194:10
w. their enemies dead | MONT 171:16
wishes: there is exact to my w. | ANON 3:14
wision: you see my w.'s limited | DICK 85:22
wit: accepted w. has | GILB 109:12
are at their w.'s end | PRAY 190:9
Brevity is the soul of w. | SHAK 208:5
fancy w. will come | POPE 184:15
folly and his weapon w. | HOPE 121:15
he but have drawn his w. | JONS 136:5
is only a w. among Lords | JOHN 131:10
metaphysic w. can fly | BUTL 56:4
nor all thy Piety nor W. | FITZ 99:9
spice of w. | STEV 247:15
Staircase w. | DID 86:8
to sharpen a good w. | ASCH 9:18
use my w. as a pitchfork | LARK 149:7
w. is nature to advantage | POPE 185:9
w. is out | BECON 17:7
w. its soul | COL 74:23
w.'s a feather | POPE 185:18
w. with dunces | POPE 184:8
witch: suffer a w. to live | BIBLE 23:19
witchcraft: Nor no w. charm thee | SHAK 206:4
witching: very w. time of night | SHAK 210:9
with: sort of English up w. which | CHUR 71:20
thou art w. me | PRAY 188:16
withdraw: to w. one's steps | VIRG 263:10
wither: Age cannot w. her | SHAK 203:24
wither'd: It could not w. be | JONS 136:3
w. cheek and tresses grey | SCOTT 201:15
w. is the garland | SHAK 204:6
withered: dried up, and w. | PRAY 189:21
withereth: Fast w. too | KEATS 139:4
withers: it w. away | ENG 96:22
our w. are unwrung | SHAK 210:4
within: are w. would fain go out | DAV 81:20
he never went w. | COWL 79:10
I have that w. | SHAK 206:14
kingdom of God is w. you | BIBLE 36:3
without: nor w. you | MART 161:9
that are w. would fain go | DAV 81:20
that is w. sin among you | BIBLE 36:26
w. whose never-failing | WOD 273:13
withstand: w. in the evil day | BIBLE 39:15
witness: w. against you this day | BIBLE 23:29
witnesses: so great a cloud of w. | BIBLE 40:9
wits: They have stolen his w. | DE L 82:9
warming his five w. | TENN 255:8
w. are sure to madness | DRYD 90:13
youth have ever homely w. | SHAK 234:16
wittles: We have no w. | THAC 256:13
witty: am not only w. in myself | SHAK 212:19
intelligent, the w., the brave | MILL 166:3
Pretty w. Nell | PEPYS 182:10
wives: changes when they are w. | SHAK 205:10
profane and old w.' fables | BIBLE 39:28
W. are young men's mistresses | BACON 13:13
Wizards: W. that peep and that mutter | BIBLE 28:17

woe: Can I see another's w.   BLAKE 43:20
Converting all your sounds of w.   SHAK 228:7
trappings and the suits of w.   SHAK 206:14
W. is me   BIBLE 28:13
W. to thee, O land   BIBLE 27:18
W. unto them that join   BIBLE 28:9
W. unto them that rise   BIBLE 28:10
woe, w.   POUND 186:12
woeful: New-hatch'd to the w. time   SHAK 222:5
woes: Of w. unnumbered   HOMER 120:19
self-consumer of my w.   CLARE 72:21
that sound awakes my w.   BURNS 54:6
with old w. new wail   SHAK 235:12
wolf: grim w. with privy paw   MILT 167:21
keep the w. far thence   WEBS 267:16
like the w. on the fold   BYRON 57:16
w. also shall dwell with   BIBLE 28:21
w. behowls the moon   SHAK 228:1
W. that shall keep it may   KIPL 145:2
wolves: inwardly they are ravening w.   BIBLE 32:10
woman: born of a w. is of few days   BIBLE 25:24
can find a virtuous w.   BIBLE 26:34
Come to my w.'s breasts   SHAK 220:11
dead w. bites not   GRAY 111:15
Die because a w.'s fair   WITH 273:6
dispell'd when a w. appears   GAY 105:12
Each thought on the w.   KING 142:13
excellent thing in w.   SHAK 219:3
fat white w.   CORN 78:7
folly of 'W.'s Rights'   VICT 262:8
Frailty, thy name is w.   SHAK 206:15
if a w. have long hair   BIBLE 38:13
Is w.'s happiest knowledge   MILT 169:10
Let us look for the w.   DUMAS 91:18
like a w. scorn'd   CONG 76:19
Lives a w. true and fair   DONNE 88:16
lovely w. stoops to folly   ELIOT 95:4
lovely w. stoops to folly   GOLD 110:18
lovely w. in a rural spot   HUNT 128:7
made he a w.   BIBLE 22:9
make a man a w.   PEMB 182:4
man and a w. looking   WOOLF 274:8
most pernicious w.   SHAK 207:17
never trust a w.   WILDE 271:25
of a weak and feeble w.   ELIZ 95:19
perfect w.   WORD 276:16
post-chaise with a pretty w.   JOHN 133:3
prison and the w.'s workhouse   SHAW 238:13
she's a w.   RAC 193:16
sort of bloom on a w.   BARR 16:6
sort of w. who lives for   LEWIS 151:13
So unto the man is w.   LONG 153:14
suffer not a w. to teach   BIBLE 39:26
support of the w. I love   EDW 92:11
that he cannot love a w.   ELIOT 93:4
'Tis w.'s whole existence   BYRON 58:2
very ordinary little w.   BETJ 21:3
virtuous w. is a crown   BIBLE 26:14
Vitality in a w. is a blind   SHAW 238:2
Was ever w. in this humour   SHAK 231:5
when a w. isn't beautiful   CHEK 69:3
will take some savage w.   TENN 253:12
woman always a w.   WOLL 274:2
w. among all those have   BIBLE 26:14
w. as old as she looks   COLL 75:20
W., behold thy son   BIBLE 37:7
w. can be proud and stiff   YEATS 278:15
w. can forgive another   GAY 105:8
w. can hardly ever choose…she   ELIOT 93:2

w. colour'd ill   SHAK 237:2
w. drew her long black   ELIOT 95:6
w. especially   AUST 12:6
w. has her way   HOLM 120:17
W.! in our hours of ease   SCOTT 202:2
w. is a dish for the gods   SHAK 204:9
w. is his game   TENN 254:12
w. is only a woman   KIPL 143:1
w. learn in silence with   BIBLE 39:26
w., let her be as good   ELIOT 93:3
w. sat, in unwomanly rags   HOOD 121:12
w.'s business to get married   SHAW 238:5
w.'s desire is rarely   COL 75:14
w. sober   PEPYS 182:9
w.'s preaching is like   JOHN 132:5
w. take An elder   SHAK 234:2
w. taken in adultery   BIBLE 36:25
w. that you forsake her   KIPL 144:6
w., therefore to be won   SHAK 214:9
w. wakes to love   TENN 252:3
W., what have I to do   BIBLE 36:19
w. who always was tired   ANON 3:14
w. who did not care)   KIPL 146:4
w. who wrote the book that   LINC 152:6
W. will be the last thing   MER 165:7
wrapp'd in a w.'s hide   SHAK 215:3
woman-head: graves have learnt that w.   DONNE 88:13
womanly: w. feeling and propriety   VICT 262:8
womb: dark w. where I began   MAS 162:18
this teeming w. of royal   SHAK 230:2
w. of time the body whose   HEINE 116:14
women: An' learn about w. from   KIPL 144:15
blessed art thou among w.   BIBLE 34:27
created men and w. different   VICT 262:8
denyin' the w. are foolish   ELIOT 92:15
England is the paradise of w.   FLOR 101:4
experience of w. which   DOYLE 89:23
Half the sorrows of w.   ELIOT 92:18
happiest w.   ELIOT 93:6
he hid himself among w.   BROW 48:12
hops, and w.   DICK 85:13
Let us have wine and w.   BYRON 58:3
Married w. are kept women   SMITH 242:8
men and w. with our race   KIPL 143:15
Men don't know w.   TROL 260:3
men, w., and clergymen   SMITH 242:18
Monstrous Regiment of W.   KNOX 147:4
Most w. are not so young   BEER 17:12
Music and w. I cannot   PEPYS 182:11
old w. (of both sexes)   STER 246:10
other w. cloy   SHAK 203:24
passing the love of w.   BIBLE 24:27
pretty w. to deserve them   AUST 12:2
room the w. come and go   ELIOT 94:4
Spare their w. for Thy   BETJ 21:4
stir up the zeal of w.   MILL 166:1
then God help all w.   CAMP 60:10
W. and Champagne)   BELL 18:22
w. are in furious secret   SHAW 237:17
w. become like their mothers   WILDE 271:9
W. can't forgive failure   CHEK 69:1
w. in a state of ignorance   KNOX 147:8
w. like that part which   WEBS 267:7
w. must weep   KING 142:14
w. should be struck regularly   COW 79:4
w.'s rights is the basic   FOUR 102:2
womman: is bettre than a good w.   CHAU 68:10
worthy w. al hir lyve   CHAU 68:7

won: not that you w. or lost RICE 195:2
prize we sought is w. WHIT 270:1
to-morrow the ground w. ARN 8:21
woman in this humour w. SHAK 231:5
woman, therefore to be w. SHAK 214:9
wonder: all a w. and a wild desire BROW 50:19
all the w. that would be TENN 253:10
I w. by my troth DONNE 88:1
still the w. grew GOLD 110:11
w. what you've missed AUDEN 10:10
wonderful: All things wise and w. ALEX 2:2
knowledge is too w. and excellent PRAY 191:2
most w. wonderful SHAK 205:5
name shall be called W. BIBLE 28:19
There are many w. things SOPH 243:13
wonderfully: fearfully and w. made PRAY 191:4
wonders: his w. in the deep PRAY 190:8
His w. to perform COWP 79:14
rich relative work w. BIRK 42:8
wond'rous: What w. life is this MARV 161:15
woo: are April when they w. SHAK 205:10
Come, w. me SHAK 205:9
wood: hewers of w. and drawers BIBLE 24:4
must Thou char the w. ere THOM 258:4
On Wenlock Edge the w.'s HOUS 126:4
Out of this w. do not desire SHAK 227:9
roads diverged in a w. FROST 103:8
therefore to be w. SHAK 214:9
whiffling through the tulgey w. CARR 63:17
you that broke the new w. POUND 186:11
woodbine: over-canopied with luscious w. SHAK 227:5
woodcock: Spirits of well-shot w. BETJ 20:9
wooden: Sailed off in a w. shoe FIELD 98:2
this w. O the very casques SHAK 213:8
w. walls are the best walls COV 79:1
woodland: a bit of w. HOR 125:1
stands about the w. ride HOUS 125:4
woodman: w., spare the beechen CAMP 60:15
wood-notes: Warble his native w. wild MILT 167:19
woods: enchanted w. of Celtic antiquity KEYN 141:18
Enter these enchanted w. MER 165:6
road through the w. KIPL 146:5
there is a spirit in the w. WORD 275:12
through the Wet Wild W. KIPL 146:18
We'll to the w. no more ANON 6:3
w. are lovely FROST 103:10
w. decay and fall TENN 255:9
woodshed: Something nasty in the w. GIBB 106:14
wooing: w. mind shall be express'd SHAK 219:11
wool: his head like the pure w. BIBLE 30:11
word: been a time for such a w. SHAK 223:15
beginning was the W. BIBLE 36:12
by every w. that proceedeth BIBLE 31:8
honour? A w. SHAK 212:18
meanings packed up into one w. CARR 64:10
one Peculiar w. LAND 148:13
suit the action to the w. SHAK 209:8
Tears wash out a W. FITZ 99:7
That I kept my w. DE L 82:14
what the w. did make it ELIZ 95:13
'When I use a w. CARR 64:8
w. is the Verb HUGO 127:15
w. takes wing irrevocably HOR 123:5
W. was made flesh BIBLE 36:16
W. WAS MADE FLESH MASS 163:21
w. which in wartime has BETH 20:4
yesterday the w. of Caesar might SHAK 216:18

yet God has not said a w. BROW 50:16
wordless: song was w. SASS 200:11
words: all sad w. of tongue WHIT 270:10
barren superfluity of w. GARTH 105:1
best w. in the best order COL 75:13
Bright is the ring of w. STEV 247:13
common, little, easy w. WESL 268:20
experience find those w. CONG 76:20
fear those big w. JOYCE 137:5
his paint-pots and his w. HOR 122:14
How often misused w. generate SPEN 244:7
In all his w. most wonderful NEWM 176:3
long w. Bother me MILNE 167:1
my w. are my own CHAR 67:12
my w. shall not pass away BIBLE 34:3
of all w. of tongue HARTE 115:11
repeats his w. SHAK 217:10
that my w. were now written BIBLE 25:27
that w. are the daughters JOHN 134:15
threw w. like stones SPEN 244:11
whose w. are of less weight BACON 13:4
with these two narrow w. RAL 194:6
W. are men's daughters MADD 158:13
w. of Mercury are harsh SHAK 219:15
w. That are only fit FRY 103:19
W. without thoughts never SHAK 210:12
W., words, words SHAK 208:9
wrestle With w. and meanings ELIOT 93:16
Wordsworth: better scholar than W. HOUS 127:8
W., both are thine STEP 246:2
work: be as tedious as to w. SHAK 212:5
do the hard and dirty w. RUSK 198:9
Do the w. that's nearest KING 142:10
honest man's the noblest w. POPE 185:18
If any would not w. BIBLE 39:25
I like w. JER 130:18
I'll w. on a new and original GILB 107:15
'I've got my w. cut out SQUI 245:7
'Know what thou canst w. CARL 61:21
Man goeth forth to his w. PRAY 190:5
men must w. KING 142:14
noblest w. of man BUTL 56:16
Old Kaspar's w. was done SOUT 243:16
pleasant and clean w. RUSK 198:9
should I let the toad w. LARK 149:7
That do no w. to-day SHAK 214:2
This is too warm w. NELS 175:7
To w. my mind SHAK 235:10
What a piece of w. is a man SHAK 208:14
when no man can w. BIBLE 36:30
who lives by his own w. COLL 75:19
W. expands so as to fill PARK 180:13
w. for good to them that BIBLE 37:38
W. is the curse WILDE 272:4
W. out your own salvation BIBLE 39:17
Workers: W. of the world MARX 162:5
workhouse: prison and the woman's w. SHAW 238:13
working: spare time and in his w. GILL 109:13
works: cast away the w. of darkness PRAY 187:6
cast off the w. of darkness BIBLE 38:5
cruel w. of nature DARW 81:16
devil and all his w. PRAY 187:19
Faith without w. is dead BIBLE 40:14
future, and it w. STEF 245:16
God now accepteth thy w. BIBLE 27:14
into my w. is my talent WILDE 272:1
Look on my w. SHEL 239:17
Rich in good w. BIBLE 40:3

they may see your good w. — BIBLE 31:14
workshop: suffer England to be the w. — DISR 86:13
world: All's right with the w. — BROW 50:12
All the w.'s a stage — SHAK 205:1
are the light of the w. — BIBLE 31:13
at which the w. grew pale — JOHN 135:10
aweary of this great w. — SHAK 224:12
bestride the narrow w. — SHAK 215:16
brave new w. — SHAK 233:3
brought nothing into this w. — BIBLE 39:30
contagion of the w.'s — SHEL 238:26
corners of the w. in arms — SHAK 217:16
dark w. of sin — BICK 42:4
Days that Shook the W. — REED 194:15
deed in a naughty w. — SHAK 226:8
From this vile w. — SHAK 236:4
God so loved the w. — BIBLE 36:21
great while ago the w. begun — SHAK 234:15
had my w. as in my tyme — CHAU 68:18
Had we but w. enough — MARV 161:20
In a w. I never made — HOUS 126:17
leave the w. unseen — KEATS 139:19
Let the great w. spin — TENN 253:13
Mad w. — SHAK 217:7
milk the cow of the w. — WILB 271:1
month in which the w. bigan — CHAU 68:12
nature makes the whole w. kin — SHAK 233:9
need of a w. of men — BROW 50:7
only interpreted the w. — MARX 162:9
passes the glory of the w. — ANON 7:5
rack of this tough w. — SHAK 219:5
shall gain the whole w. — BIBLE 33:14
shot heard round the w. — EMER 96:4
So runs the w. away — SHAK 210:6
subsidized to provoke the w. — FRY 103:20
then the w.'s mine oyster — SHAK 226:11
There is a w. elsewhere — SHAK 205:18
These laid the w. away — BROO 47:5
they only saved the w. — CHES 69:25
This is the way the w. ends — ELIOT 93:24
though the w. perish — FERD 97:19
to pass through this w. — GREL 113:2
triple pillar of the w. — SHAK 203:16
turned the w. upside down — BIBLE 37:22
warm kind w. is all I know — CORY 78:13
What a w. — SHAW 237:22
When all the w. is young — KING 142:16
whereby the w. will be judged — CEL 66:1
where I live unto the w. — SHAK 230:15
Why was this w. created — JOHN 133:10
wilderness of this w. — BUNY 51:16
w. And all her train — VAUG 261:16
w. forgetting — POPE 184:14
w. has grown grey from — SWIN 250:3
w., I count it not — BROW 48:9
W. in a Grain of Sand — BLAKE 42:17
w. invisible — THOM 258:6
w. is a comedy to those — WALP 266:2
w. is everything that is — WITT 273:7
w. is so full of a number — STEV 247:9
w. is still deceived with — SHAK 225:13
w. is too much with us — WORD 277:7
w. may talk of hereafter — COLL 75:18
w. of the happy is quite — WITT 273:9
w.'s an inn — DRYD 91:8
w.'s at an end — DAV 81:18
w.'s glory passes away — THOM 256:18
w.'s great age begins — SHEL 239:4
w.'s history is the world's — SCH 201:4

w.'s storm-troubled sphere — BRON 47:2
w. would go round a deal — CARR 62:21
worldly: Be wisely w. — QUAR 193:5
w. goods I thee endow — PRAY 188:1
worlds: best of all possible w. — CAB 59:7
Wandering between two w. — ARN 8:14
what w. away — BROW 49:5
worm: concealment, like a w. — SHAK 234:4
'Or a rather tough w. — GILB 108:18
w. at one end and a fool — JOHN 134:11
W. nor snail — SHAK 227:7
worms: have made w.' meat of me — SHAK 231:28
nor w. forget — DICK 84:18
then w. shall try — MARV 161:21
with vilest w. to dwell — SHAK 236:4
wormwood: w. and the gall — BIBLE 30:1
worse: altered her person for the w. — SWIFT 249:7
better for w. — PRAY 187:28
from w. to better — JOHN 134:14
greater feeling to the w. — SHAK 229:20
It is w. than a crime — BOUL 45:6
More will mean w. — AMIS 2:10
of finding something w. — BELL 18:12
one penny the w. — BARH 15:12
remedy is w. than the disease — BACON 13:16
w. when it comes late — JERR 130:19
worst are no w. — SHAK 227:23
worship: are come to w. him — BIBLE 31:1
is the only object of w. — ANON 4:21
to w. God in his own way — RONS 196:12
with my body I thee w. — PRAY 188:1
worshipped: w. stocks and stones — MILT 170:9
Worships: W. language and forgives — AUDEN 10:17
worst: best and the w. of this — SWIN 250:4
best is like the w. — KIPL 145:4
His w. is better than any — HAZL 116:2
it was the w. of times — DICK 85:29
Just the w. time — ELIOT 93:25
lavat'ry makes you fear the w. — COW 79:9
me the w. they could do — HOUS 127:1
No w., there is none — HOPK 122:1
that democracy is the w. — CHUR 71:13
'This is the w. — SHAK 218:17
w. is yet to come — JOHN 131:2
w. time of the year — ANDR 2:11
worth: Are w. all your laurels — BYRON 59:2
charter of thy w. gives — SHAK 236:6
I am not w. purchasing — REED 194:16
If a thing is w. doing — CHES 70:13
not w. going to see — JOHN 133:12
rymyng is nat w. a toord — CHAU 68:15
thy own w. then not knowing — SHAK 236:6
turned out w. anything — SCOTT 202:13
Whose w.'s unknown — SHAK 236:12
w. an age without a name — MORD 173:5
w. by poverty depress'd — JOHN 135:6
w. of a State — MILL 165:18
Worthington: Missis W. — COW 79:6
worthy: labourer is w. of his hire — BIBLE 35:11
latchet I am not w. to unloose — BIBLE 36:17
philosophical and more w. — ARIS 8:6
w. to be called thy son — BIBLE 35:27
w. womman al hir lyve — CHAU 68:7
wotthehell: w. archy wotthehell — MARQ 161:2
would: He w., wouldn't he — RIC 195:4
wouldst: what thou w. highly — SHAK 220:10
wound: first did help to w. itself — SHAK 217:16
heal me of my grievous w. — TENN 252:8
keen knife see not the w. — SHAK 220:11

long yellow string I w.	BROW 50:15
that never felt a w.	SHAK 231:16
to gall a new-healed w.	SHAK 212:22
wounded: w. for our transgressions	BIBLE 29:15
'You're w.	BROW 49:16
Wounded Knee: Bury my heart at W.	BENET 19:12
wounds: bind up the nation's w.	LINC 152:3
'These w. I had on Crispin's	SHAK 214:4
Wovon: W. man nicht sprechen kann	WITT 273:10
wrang: they may gang a kennin w.	BURNS 53:17
wrapped: w. him in swaddling clothes	BIBLE 35:1
wrapti All meanly w. in the rude	MILT 168:7
wrath: answer turneth away w.	BIBLE 26:19
day of w.	CEL 65:14
Nursing her w. to keep	BURNS 54:22
sun go down upon your w.	BIBLE 39:13
tigers of w. are wiser	BLAKE 44:5
where the grapes of w.	HOWE 127:9
you to flee from the w.	BIBLE 31:5
wreath: sent thee late a rosy w.	JONS 136:3
wreck: decay Of that colossal w.	SHEL 239:17
wrecks: w. of a dissolving dream	SHEL 239:4
Wrekin: forest fleece the W.	HOUS 126:4
Wren: Sir Christopher W.	BENT 19:20
w. goes to't	SHAK 218:20
wrestle: we w. not against flesh	BIBLE 39:15
w. With words and meanings	ELIOT 93:16
wretched: is a proud and yet a w.	DAV 82:1
ladies most deject and w.	SHAK 209:6
w. child expires	BELL 18:11
wretches: feel what w. feel	SHAK 218:11
How shall w. live like	GODL 109:19
wring: will soon w. their hands	WALP 266:8
wrist: Plunge them in up to the w.	AUDEN 10:10
writ: I never w.	SHAK 236:12
name was w. in water	KEATS 141:8
write: baseness to w. fair	SHAK 211:16
If a man w. a better book	EMER 96:19
look in thy heart and w.	SIDN 241:5
man may w. at any time	JOHN 131:6
restraint with which they w.	CAMP 60:13
virtues We w. in water	SHAK 215:12
will w. for Antiquity	LAMB 148:1
W. me as one that loves	HUNT 128:4
W. sorrow on the bosom	SHAK 230:7
writer: Every great and original w.	WORD 277:14
writers: Clear w., like fountains	LAND 148:14
writing: incurable disease of w.	JUV 138:1
rest is mere fine w.	VERL 262:3
sign the w.	BIBLE 30:10
this is the w. that was	BIBLE 30:9
w. an exact man	BACON 13:21
writing paper: thicker and the w. thinner	
	MITF 171:2
written: adversary had w. a book	BIBLE 25:31
have written I have w.	BIBLE 37:6
is w. without effort is	JOHN 134:10
large a letter I have w.	BIBLE 39:10
that my words were now w.	BIBLE 25:27
those who would make the w.	CONN 77:5
wrong: absent are always in the w.	DESC 83:6
always in the w.	DRYD 90:16
credit in this World much w.	FITZ 99:11
Divine of Kings to govern w.	POPE 184:9
if I Called the W. Number	THUR 259:13
is a w. left unredressed	KING 143:2
me when I am in the w.	MELB 164:17
most divinely in the w.	YOUNG 280:7
own he has been in the w.	POPE 186:1

people are never in the w.	BURKE 52:9
reason to fear I may be w.	AUST 12:15
Should suffer w. no more	MAC 156:3
That the king can do no w.	BLAC 42:15
when w., to be put right	SCH 201:6
w. could religion induce	LUCR 155:4
W. forever on the throne	LOW 154:18
wrote: blockhead ever w.	JOHN 132:26
I w. my happy songs	BLAKE 43:13
sorry, now, I w. it	BURG 52:6
Who w. like an angel	GARR 104:14
wrought: What hath God w.	BIBLE 23:27
würfelt: Gott w. nicht	EINS 92:14
wyndow: clapte the w.	CHAU 68:11
Wynken: W., Blynken	FIELD 98:2
Xanadu: In X. did Kubla Khan	COL 75:2
Yankee Doodle: Y. came to town	BANGS 15:8
yarn: all I ask is a merry y.	MAS 163:2
Yblessed: Y. be god that I have wedded	
	CHAU 68:16
yea: Let your y. be yea	BIBLE 40:16
Y., yea; Nay, nay	BIBLE 31:16
year: fit this y.'s fashions	HELL 116:16
pleasure of the fleeting y.	SHAK 236:8
stood at the gate of the y.	HASK 115:16
That time of y. thou mayst	SHAK 236:5
twelve months in all the y.	BALL 15:2
y.'s at the spring	BROW 50:12
yearning: huddled masses y.	LAZ 149:19
years: age are threescore y.	PRAY 189:22
down the arches of the y.	THOM 258:1
ever the Knightly y. were	HENL 117:9
infelicity Seem'd to have y.	WEBS 267:12
love of finished y.	ROSS 197:4
nor the y. condemn	BINY 42:6
'save the undone y.	OWEN 179:10
seven y. for Rachel	BIBLE 23:1
thousand y. in thy sight	PRAY 189:21
touch of earthly y.	WORD 276:17
y. are slipping by	HOR 124:4
Y. glide away	BARH 15:10
y. of desolation pass over	JEFF 130:11
y. that the locust hath	BIBLE 30:13
y. to come seemed waste	YEATS 279:5
yeas: In russet y. and honest	SHAK 219:11
Yeats: churchyard Y. is laid	YEATS 280:3
William Y. is laid to rest	AUDEN 10:17
yellow: Come unto these y. sands	SHAK 232:13
sear, the y. leaf	SHAK 223:12
When y. leaves	SHAK 236:5
Y., and black	SHEL 239:12
Y. God forever gazes down	HAYES 116:1
yeoman: It did me y.'s service	SHAK 211:16
Yes: yes I said yes I will Y.	JOYCE 137:9
y. O at lightning	HOPK 122:11
yesterday: all our pomp of y.	KIPL 145:11
call back y.	SHAK 230:6
dead Y.	FITZ 99:6
Jesus Christ the same y.	BIBLE 40:12
thy sight are but as y.	PRAY 189:21
universe and give me y.	JONES 135:14
Y. I loved	LESS 151:9
you'd think it was only y.	MILL 166:5
yesterdays: all our y. have lighted	SHAK 223:15
yesteryear: where are the snows of y.	VILL 262:13
Yestreen: Y. the Queen had four Maries	
	BALL 15:1
yet: continency—but not y.	AUG 11:15
young man not y.	BACON 13:14

yew: never a spray of y.   ARN 8:17
  stuck all with y.   SHAK 234:3
yew-tree: that y.'s shade   GRAY 112:2
yield: temptation is just to y.   GRAH 111:6
  to find, and not to y.   TENN 255:16
Yo-ho-ho: Y., and a bottle of rum   STEV 246:19
yoke: bear the y. in his youth   BIBLE 30:2
yonge: O y., fresshe folkes   CHAU 68:28
Yorick: Alas, poor Y.   SHAK 211:11
you: I cannot live with y.   MART 161:9
  Y., that way   SHAK 219:15
young: atrocious crime of being a y.   PITT 183:6
  been y., and now am old   PRAY 188:23
  crime by corrupting the y.   PLATO 183:14
  embarrassing y.   GAV 105:5
  gods love dies y.   MEN 165:1
  how y. the policemen look   HICKS 119:6
  I have been y.   BLUN 44:12
  I was y.   FLEC 100:13
  love's y. dream   MOORE 172:15
  Most women are not so y.   BEER 17:12
  No y. man believes he shall   HAZL 116:8
  proper y. men   BURNS 54:14
  she died y.   WEBS 267:12
  So y., and so untender   SHAK 217:18
  so y., I loved him so   BROW 49:2
  those that are with y.   BIBLE 29:10
  to be y. was very heaven   WORD 274:17
  Tomorrow for the y.   AUDEN 11:10
  When I was y.   MILNE 167:3
  While we are y.   ANON 6:17
  Wives are y. men's mistresses   BACON 13:13
  world and love were y.   RAL 194:2
  y. and easy under the apple   THOM 257:2
  y. as beautiful   YOUNG 280:9
  y. girl miserable may give   FRAN 102:10
  y. In one another's arms   YEATS 279:12
  y. man lands hatless   BETJ 20:10
  y. man not yet   BACON 13:14
  y. man's soul   HOUS 125:9
  Y. men have more virtue   JOHN 132:2
  y. men shall see visions   BIBLE 30:14
  y. men think it is   HOUS 126:26
  y. to fall asleep for ever   SASS 200:9
youngest: not even the y. of us   THOM 258:10
Yours: Y. are the limbs, my sweeting   NASH 175:1
  Y. is the Earth and everything   KIPL 144:9
yourself: Could love you for y. alone
           YEATS 278:21
Keep yourself *to* y.   DICK 85:19
you're not good enough y.   TROL 260:13

youth: After the pleasures of y.   ANON 6:17
  bear the yoke in his y.   BIBLE 30:2
  Crabbed age and y.   SHAK 235:4
  Creator in the days of thy y.   BIBLE 27:21
  days of our y. are   BYRON 59:2
  flower of their y.   VIRG 264:7
  If y. knew   EST 97:3
  In y. is pleasure   WEVER 269:7
  Jenny's unsuspecting y.   BURNS 54:3
  nourishing a y. sublime   TENN 253:6
  sign of an ill-spent y.   SPEN 244:9
  sins and offences of my y.   PRAY 188:20
  spirit of y. in everything   SHAK 236:9
  subtle thief of y.   MILT 170:8
  Sweet wine of y.   BROO 47:5
  when Y. and Pleasure meet   BYRON 57:10
  y. And a little beauty   WEBS 267:8
  Y. are boarded   DICK 84:19
  y., I do adore thee   SHAK 235:5
  y. is bent by the same   THOM 257:4
  y. of England are on fire   SHAK 213:11
  Y. on the prow   GRAY 111:17
  Y.'s a stuff will not   SHAK 233:22
  Y.'s the season made   GAY 105:3
  y. stone dead   SASS 200:5
  Y. to prolong   YEATS 279:17
  y. unkind   BAST 16:10
  Y., which is forgiven   SHAW 238:15
  Y. will be served   BORR 44:23
  Y. will come here and beat   IBSEN 129:9
youthful: y. passion for abstracted   JOHN 132:10
yowthe: Upon my y.   CHAU 68:18
ywet: hir joly whistle wel y.   CHAU 68:14
Zadok: Z. the priest took an horn   BIBLE 24:31
Zarathustra: Z., sometime regius professor
           JOYCE 137:8
zeal: not the slightest z.   TALL 250:12
  z. of thine house hath   PRAY 189:13
  z. of women themselves   MILL 166:1
Zeit: aus dem Schosse der Z.   HEINE 116:14
zèle: *Surtout, Messieurs, point de z.*   TALL 250:12
zephyr: Odes to every z.   KING 142:11
zero: Are practically z.   ROST 197:13
Zerstörung: Die Lust der Z. ist zugleich   BAK 14:11
Zion: Lord shall bring again Z.   BIBLE 29:13
Zitronen: wo die Z. blühn   GOE 110:3
Zoo: well you may see at the Z.   KIPL 144:12
Zuleika: Z., on a desert island   BEER 17:18
Zweck: jederzeit zugleich als Z.   KANT 138:9
  Wer den Z. will   KANT 138:8

GREEK INDEX